Information Security and Cryptography

More information about this series at http://www.springer.com/series/4752

Information Security and Cryptography

Series Editors

David Basin
Kenny Paterson

Advisory Board

Michael B. ...
Gilles Barthe
Ronald Cramer
Ivan Damgård
Joseph H. ...
Christopher Kruegel
Tatsuaki Okamoto
Adrian Perrig
Bart Preneel
Carmela Troncoso
Moti Yung

More information about this series at http://www.springer.com/series/4752

Arno Mittelbach • Marc Fischlin

The Theory of Hash Functions and Random Oracles

An Approach to Modern Cryptography

 Springer

Arno Mittelbach
AGT International
Darmstadt, Germany

Marc Fischlin
Technische Universität Darmstadt
Darmstadt, Germany

ISSN 1619-7100 ISSN 2197-845X (electronic)
Information Security and Cryptography
ISBN 978-3-030-63289-2 ISBN 978-3-030-63287-8 (eBook)
https://doi.org/10.1007/978-3-030-63287-8

This Springer imprint is published by the registered company Springer Nature Switzerland AG
The registered company address is: Gewerbestrasse 11, 6330 Cham, Switzerland

Preface

For thousands of years cryptography was considered an art: the artistry of code design and that of breaking codes, which both required creativity and personal skill from those who pursued it, in particular, since no or only very little theory was available.[1] Over the course of the 20th century the cryptographic landscape changed dramatically and, slowly, cryptography transformed from art to science. Today, cryptography is based on a solid mathematical foundation and has only little to do with what it was fifty, let alone a hundred or a thousand years ago.

With rigorous formalisms also new avenues opened up. While cryptography used to be concerned only with the question of how to transmit secret messages, cryptography today is at the core of a large number of applications. Cryptography deals with any form of computation that may come under any form of attack. As such, cryptography is ubiquitous and most users are unaware of all the cryptographic measures around them. From accessing secure websites, making calls on mobile phones, controlling the shutters of your (smart) home, driving cars, or watching movies, there is hardly any technological activity that comes without some form of cryptography.

Securing computation requires a large number of tools and techniques, many of which utilize so-called *hash functions* which are often described as the cryptographer's Swiss Army knife. Classical tasks of hash functions include the secure storage of passwords and ensuring the integrity of data. But hash functions are also at the basis of digital signature schemes, they form the backbone of blockchains, and are used to extract randomness from biased entropy sources. Hash functions can also be used to build encryption schemes or message authentication codes, and in fact, almost all cryptographic protocols make use of hash functions in some form or other.

The reason that hash functions are such a versatile cryptographic primitive is that we expect a cryptographic hash function to simultaneously possess a

---

[1] See David Kahn [3] or Simon Singh [5] for an introduction into the fascinating history of cryptography.

vast number of properties. On the outset we have structural requirements such as that hash functions should be able to process arbitrarily long messages whereas other primitives like modern block ciphers usually have a fixed input length. The classical security property one expects is that finding a collision is still hard, i.e. finding two distinct values that hash (aka evaluate) to the same result under the hash function, despite the hash function compressing inputs. But since hash functions are used in so many places nowadays, hash functions are required to satisfy many more properties. We also expect hash functions to be one-way, meaning that they can be efficiently evaluated but they should be hard to invert. Furthermore, in some applications the output of a hash function should not be distinguishable from randomly chosen bit strings. As we will see over the course of this book, these are just a handful of the properties that we may attribute to hash functions.

Hash functions have also inspired one of the most successful paradigms for the construction of practical cryptographic schemes: the *random oracle methodology*. In simple terms, the random oracle methodology states that during the design and study of a cryptographic scheme we assume that all parties involved in the computation—when modeling, for example, an encryption scheme this would be the sender, the recipient, and the adversary— have access to a *random oracle*. A random oracle is an oracle implementing a random function mapping arbitrary bit strings to bit strings of, say, 256 bits. A less intuitive but technically often more useful alternative is to think of a random oracle as a magic box that on the input of a bit string outputs a bit string in the following way: if it has already been asked for the input string, it returns the same output value as before. If it has not yet been asked for the input, it chooses a uniformly random 256-bit value as return value. The important thing to note is that all boxes are perfectly synchronized. Thus, if party A asks its box for value x and then party B asks for x, both get the same result. The queries by a party to its box remain, however, private. So party B does not see the queries by party A.

As it turns out, assuming the existence of such a random oracle is incredibly useful and facilitates many cryptographic proofs. The random oracle methodology now states that to simplify the design and analysis of a scheme we assume the existence of a random oracle during the design and when proving its security and then when implementing the scheme in practice we choose a "good cryptographic hash function that behaves like a random oracle." For this we usually choose one of the well-studied cryptographic hash functions such as SHA-2 or SHA-3. Vice versa, one can view the random oracle approach as an idealization of strong practical hash functions.

While a large number of secure and highly efficient schemes have been designed using the random oracle methodology, there is a catch. At least in theory, applying the random oracle methodology may lead to the creation of seemingly secure schemes which are utterly broken in practice. The reason lies in the mismatch between the random oracle model as an ideal hash function in a magic box whereas real hash functions are structured functions whose code is available. An important open question is thus how to properly interpret results that are based on random oracles.

Guide to This Book

Even though hash functions play an integral part in today's cryptography, existing textbooks discuss hash functions only in passing and instead often put an emphasis on other primitives like encryption schemes. In this book we take a different approach and place hash functions at the center. The result is not only an introduction to the theory of hash functions and the random oracle model but a comprehensive introduction to modern cryptography with an emphasis on hash functions. While we devote an entire chapter to introducing the concepts behind public- and private-key encryption schemes, we focus on the instantiation of such schemes from hash functions and do not go into detail on the various schemes that can be constructed, for example, down to number-theoretic assumptions. This means we do not provide a detailed discussion of RSA or discrete-logarithm-based public-key encryption schemes, although we discuss *RSA and discrete-log-based hash functions*. Similarly, we do not go into detail on various modes of operations of block ciphers for building (authenticated) encryption or message authentication codes nor discuss in detail DES (the Data Encryption Standard) nor AES (the Advanced Encryption Standard). We here only briefly discuss DES and AES as well as block cipher modes of operation for encryption schemes but instead focus our discussion of block ciphers on the *ideal cipher model* and *block-cipher-based compression functions* which are at the heart of many real-world hash functions. The compromises we made in reducing the presentation of, for example, specific public-key encryption schemes allow us to discuss a number of important results that hitherto only exist in not easily accessible research papers. These include:

- A detailed treatment of the random oracle methodology including proof techniques used with random oracles, a discussion of limitations of random oracles and the impossibility of basing key agreement on random oracles as well as a discussion of uninstantiability, the fact that schemes exist that are provably secure in the random oracle model but trivially broken in the real world.
- A discussion of generic attacks on hash functions including second-preimage attacks using fixed-points and Nostradamus-type attacks.
- An in-depth analysis of constructions of privately-keyed hash functions to build message authentication codes and pseudorandom functions. This includes a full security proof of HMAC.
- A presentation of the popular real-world hash functions MD5, SHA-1, SHA-2, and SHA-3 in one place, including a detailed discussion of underly-

ing building blocks: the iteration schemes Merkle–Damgård and Sponge, as well as block-cipher based compression functions.

- A detailed discussion of why it is difficult to construct collision-resistant hash functions from one-way functions, a core cryptographic primitive that is sufficient for the construction of symmetric encryption or digital signature schemes.

- An introduction into weaker forms of hash functions (here called non-cryptographic hash functions) that can be shown to exist unconditionally and which have various applications in cryptography. This includes a proof of the leftover hash lemma as well as a construction of universal one-way hash functions from one-way permutations.

- A discussion of indifferentiability, an important property of hash functions that we expect any modern construction to possess. In simple terms, an indifferentiable hash function can replace a random oracle assuming that the primitive the hash function is built from (e.g., a block cipher) has no weaknesses.

- An introduction to the Universal Computational Extractor framework for specifying security properties of strong hash functions as an alternative to random oracles.

Besides our focus on hash functions, also our presentation differs from other introductory textbooks as we present definitions and results closely to how they could be presented in research results published by the cryptographic community at conferences or in journals. This, of course, does not mean that the results are compact and hard to follow. On the contrary, we have put a lot of effort into the presentation of results as well as into discussing the techniques used within the proofs. We have tried not to take shortcuts where possible and hope that the result helps students of cryptography as well as interested practitioners find their way into the wealth of research that is provided by the cryptographic community every year. To this end, each chapter also comes with a notes and references section providing pointers to relevant papers and articles.

As good companions to this work we suggest the textbooks by Stinson and Paterson (*Cryptography: Theory and Practice* [6]), Katz and Lindell (*Introduction to Modern Cryptography* [4]) as well as the works of Goldreich (*Foundations of Cryptography* Volumes 1 and 2 [1, 2]).

Target audience. Our intended target audience for this book are students of computer science in general and students of cryptography in particular. Of course, our intended audience also includes lecturers and teachers of cryptography who can use the book as main textbook for both introductory courses—introductory courses should cover most of the material presented in Part I—as well as for graduate-level courses, in particular, specialized courses on the theory of hash functions. However, this book is also for practitioners with a neck for theory and who wish to better understand functions such as SHA-2, SHA-3, or HMAC and the guarantees they do (or do not) provide. The book can also serve as a reference for advanced researchers to find information about hash function properties, their relation, and construction in one place.

Required background. Cryptography is based on mathematics and computer science, and as mentioned above the goal of this book is not to hide the details from readers but instead to expose them. We thus need to assume a basic background in these fields. In particular, a basic understanding of computability theory, algorithms, and probability theory is helpful. Having said that, most math used in this book should be understandable by readers who have followed university entry-level math courses. To facilitate the learning experience, we have structured the book such as to gradually add new concepts and techniques. Of course, a certain basis is required, but we have tried to be as self-contained as possible and provide in Chapter 1 a (fast-paced) introduction to relevant concepts from computability theory, probability theory, information theory, and complexity theory.

Structure and Content

The book is split into a preliminary chapter followed by three parts. Each chapter comes with a set of exercises as well as with a notes and references section which points the reader to additional material and the origin of the presented results. Part I (Foundations of Modern Cryptography) introduces hash functions and their basic properties. This means covering the foundation of modern cryptography and introducing various cryptographic concepts and primitives as well as relevant proof techniques. Part II (The Random Oracle Methodology) introduces random oracles and discusses the random oracle methodology, and in Part III (Hash Function Constructions) we look at how to construct cryptographic hash functions and, to some extent, random oracles. In detail:

- Chapter 1 introduces basic concepts from computability theory, probability theory, information theory, and complexity theory that we need throughout the book. In addition we cover information-theoretic security and introduce the one-time pad encryption scheme.

Part I (Foundations of Modern Cryptography). Introduces the foundations of hash functions and modern cryptography. This part covers a number of schemes, concepts, and proof techniques including computational security, one-way functions, pseudorandomness and pseudorandom functions, game-based proofs, message authentication codes, encryption schemes, signature schemes, and collision-resistant (hash) functions. The part closes with a chapter on non-cryptographic hashing, that is, properties of hash functions which do not depend on any hardness assumption but which can be proven unconditionally.

- Chapter 2 introduces the concept of *computational security* that is at the heart of modern cryptography. We will look at the notion of *one-way functions* which are amongst the most basic cryptographic primitives and which are, for example, required for secure storage of passwords. The chapter also contains the first (of many) cryptographic security reductions, an important proof technique that we will encounter again and again throughout the course of this book.

- In Chapter 3 we discuss the concept of *indistinguishability* which formalizes that an adversary cannot distinguish between two distributions, for example between seeing genuine ciphertext or random garbage. We continue with presenting two important proof techniques: the *hybrid argument* and *game-based proofs*. Together with indistinguishability this allows us to introduce the concept of *pseudorandomness* as well as *pseudorandom generators*, *pseudorandom functions*, and *message authentication codes*.

- In Chapter 4 we present "classic" hash function properties such as *collision resistance*, *second-preimage resistance* and *target-collision resistance*, and investigate the relationship between the various properties. We also introduce the important birthday bound for collision-resistant functions. We close the chapter with an in-depth discussion on the impossibility of constructing collision-resistant hash functions from one-way functions (via black-box constructions).

- Chapter 5 is dedicated to the discussion of *encryption schemes*, both in the symmetric (aka private-key) and in the asymmetric (aka public-key) setting. We study security notions such as *indistinguishability under chosen plaintext/ciphertext attacks* for both settings and discuss how to build such schemes from the primitives introduced so far. In the case of *public-key encryption schemes* we additionally need *trapdoor functions* and *hardcore functions* that are introduced here.

- Chapter 6 introduces the concept of *signature schemes*. Hash functions are at the basis of almost all practical signature schemes, as usually we do not sign messages but only the hash of a message. In Chapter 6 we study the formal underpinnings of this *hash-and-sign* approach as well as the construction of one-time and many-time signatures from hash functions and hash trees.

- Chapter 7 is dedicated to the concept of *non-cryptographic hashing*. Non-cryptographic hashing refers to hash functions that are not based on computational hardness assumptions but instead can be constructed unconditionally. Here we will cover *universal* and *pairwise independent hash functions* and show how to construct message authentication codes unconditionally based on universal hashing. In addition we will look at *randomness extractors* prove the *leftover hash lemma* and show how to construct *target-collision-resistant hash functions* from one-way permutations (and universal hash functions).

Part II (The Random Oracle Methodology). Part II introduces the random oracle methodology which covers the random oracle model, proof techniques used with random oracles, random oracle constructions as well as examples of real-world random oracle schemes but also limitations of random oracles and a discussion of the random oracle controversy, the fact that *uninstantiable schemes* exist which are provably secure in the random oracle model but which become insecure with any real-world hash function.

- Chapter 8 introduces random oracles and discusses the difference between the *random oracle model* and the *standard model* of security. We close this chapter with a discussion of the *random oracle methodology*, a design methodology for the construction of highly efficient and practical cryptographic schemes based on random oracles.
- Chapter 9 is dedicated to the full power of random oracles. We will discuss various proof techniques and show what makes random oracles so powerful. With each new type of security reduction introduced, we introduce a random oracle scheme that we prove secure. We will see how to construct efficient public-key encryption and signature schemes from random oracles and introduce the notions of *correlated input secure hash functions* and *deterministic public-key encryption* and show how to build such primitives in the random oracle model.
- In Chapter 10 we discuss practical random oracle schemes, in particular, *Fiat–Shamir*, *RSA-OAEP*, *RSA-PSS*, and the *Fujisaki–Okamoto hybrid encryption scheme*. We here also give a brief introduction to number theory and, in particular, introduce the RSA and discrete logarithm problems.
- Chapter 11 discusses limitations of random oracles. For this, we will introduce the notions of *key exchange* and *Merkle puzzles* to then show that random oracles alone are not sufficient to construct secure key exchange protocols.
- Chapter 12 presents the important *uninstantiability result* for random oracles which states that there are schemes that can be proven secure in the random oracle model but which are trivially broken when implemented in the real world. Consequently, the random oracle methodology for constructing secure cryptographic schemes is not sound in the sense that it allows the construction of insecure schemes, and we discuss the implications of this result.

Part III (Hash Function Constructions). Part III focuses on constructions of hash functions. This includes a treatment of iterative hash functions and generic attacks against hash functions, constructions of hash functions based on block ciphers and number-theoretic assumptions, a discussion of privately keyed hash functions including a full security proof for HMAC, and a presentation of real-world hash functions. This part closes with an in-depth treatment of indifferentiability and universal computational extractors (UCEs). Indifferentiability is a property that, in simple terms, states that a hash function is as good as a random oracle assuming that an internal building block has optimal security. UCEs, on the other hand, try to provide an alternative to random oracles, that is a weaker definition of security which is still sufficiently strong to facilitate proofs of also complex schemes but which does not succumb to the uninstantiability results of random oracles.

- Chapter 13 studies constructions of hash functions that can process arbitrarily long messages via iteration. We introduce the *Merkle–Damgård transformation* and the *sponge construction*, iteration schemes which are at the core of many real-world hash functions such as MD5, SHA-1, SHA-2, or SHA-3. Besides discussing the security of iteration schemes, we present generic attacks on Merkle–Damgård-style hash functions.
- Chapter 14 discusses how to construct collision-resistant compression functions to be used in Merkle–Damgård-style hash functions. For this we introduce the notion of *block ciphers*, important cryptographic primitives that were originally designed for the creation of symmetric encryption schemes (aka private-key encryption schemes) but which can also form the basis for the construction of collision-resistant compression functions. Besides constructions from block ciphers we also look at constructions based on number-theoretic hardness problems. Finally, we introduce *chameleon hashes* and discuss number-theoretic constructions thereof.
- Chapter 15 is dedicated to the description of important real-world hash functions, and we discuss in detail the widely deployed hash functions MD5, SHA-1, SHA-2, and SHA-3.
- Chapter 16 looks at hash function constructions with hidden keys. This allows the creation of message authentication codes and pseudorandom functions, and we see how we can turn Merkle–Damgård-style hash functions into such privately keyed primitives. In particular, we will look in-depth at the popular *HMAC construction* and prove its security. We also introduce the notion of *key derivation* and discuss how HMAC is used in HKDF, a widely used key derivation function.
- In Chapter 17 we return to the random oracle model and discuss how iterated hash functions need to be constructed to be (almost) *as good as random oracles*. This leads to the notion of *indifferentiability*, which we introduce in detail. We then discuss existing hash function constructions and prove that, while certain versions of SHA-2 are indifferentiable, MD5 or SHA-1 are not.
- Chapter 18 introduces the framework of *Universal Computational Extractors* (UCEs). UCEs allow the design of hardness assumptions for hash functions with the express goal of providing an alternative to random oracles.

Comments and Errata

We have set out to put together a modern introduction to the theory of cryptography and hash functions, and we hope that the result is not only relevant but also accessible and enjoyable. We are curious to hear your feedback and, in particular, are looking forward to much constructive criticism. While we have tried to be thorough, it is unlikely that there are no errors or typos in this book and we would greatly appreciate it if you would let us know in case you spot anything that is not correct. We will keep an up-to-date list of known errata at `https://hash-book.info`, where you can also find our contact details.

Acknowledgements

We would like to thank our editors Kenny Paterson, David Basin, and Ronan Nugent, who not only gave us the opportunity to write this book, but who stuck with us also when it became clear that we had highly underestimated the time and effort that is required to finish such a project. Furthermore, we would like to thank Johannes Braun, Chris Brzuska, Jean Paul Degabriele, Felix Günther, Christian Janson, Pihla Karanko, Sogol Mazaheri, Daniele Venturi, and Alexander Wiesmaier, for reading and commenting on early drafts of this work. Of course, any remaining errors are entirely our own. Last but certainly not least, we would like to thank our respective wives and kids for their understanding, support, and patience during the many hours and long days that we have spent on this project.

Bibliography

1. Oded Goldreich. *Foundations of Cryptography: Basic Tools.* Cambridge University Press, New York, NY, USA, 2007.
2. Oded Goldreich. *Foundations of Cryptography: Basic Applications.* Cambridge University Press, New York, NY, USA, 2009.
3. David Kahn. *The Codebreakers: The Comprehensive History of Secret Communication from Ancient Times to the Internet.* Scribner, 1996.
4. Jonathan Katz and Yehuda Lindell. *Introduction to Modern Cryptography.* Chapman & Hall/CRC, 2014.
5. Simon Singh. *The Code Book: The Science of Secrecy from Ancient Egypt to Quantum Cryptography.* Anchor, 2011.
6. Douglas Robert Stinson and Maura Paterson. *Cryptography: Theory and Practice.* Chapman & Hall/CRC, 2018.

Contents

Chapter 1
Foundations

Hash functions are amongst the most versatile objects in cryptography. This is in large portion due to the manifold different security properties that we would like a hash function to possess. Without any further specification the term *hash function* should be understood as a mathematical function that maps elements from a usually very large, or even infinite domain to a small range; hash functions are compressing. Hash functions that we encounter in this book are usually of the form $\mathsf{H} : \{0,1\}^* \to \{0,1\}^\lambda$, that is, they map bit strings of arbitrary length to bit strings of a fixed length λ, where $\lambda \in \mathbb{N}$ is some positive integer. Take the SHA-256 hash function[1], as an example. It takes arbitrarily long inputs (to be precise, input strings may not exceed $2^{64} - 1$ bits) and produces hash values of 256 bits.

Compression alone is not sufficient for most cryptographic tasks. Instead, in order to be useful in cryptographic settings, we consider compressing functions that have one or more special security properties. For example, hash functions can be *one-way*: Loosely speaking a function is one-way if every adversary whose computational power is reasonably restricted will only be able to find a preimage when given a random hash value with minute probability.

One-wayness is only one of many security properties for hash functions that have been introduced by cryptographers over the years, and consequently, hash functions today play an important role in almost all areas of cryptography. However, before we can delve into the theory behind hash functions we need to discuss some cryptographic foundations. While a sound mathematical background and basic knowledge of theoretical computer science will certainly be helpful, we aim at providing a self-contained textbook that introduces all the necessary concepts. For this, in the following chapter we present a (fast-paced) introduction into the relevant concepts from computability theory, complexity theory, probability theory, and information theory. We refer to Arora and Barak's textbook (*Computational Complexity - A Modern*

---

[1] SHA-256 is part of the SHA-2 family of real-world hash functions standardized by the National Institute of Standards and Technology (NIST). We will discuss SHA-256 in detail in Chapter 15.

© Springer Nature Switzerland AG 2021
A. Mittelbach, M. Fischlin, *The Theory of Hash Functions and Random Oracles*,
Information Security and Cryptography, https://doi.org/10.1007/978-3-030-63287-8_1

Approach [3]), which is an excellent resource for further information on many of the topics discussed in this chapter.

1.1 Notational Conventions

We begin by defining the notational conventions that are used throughout this book. We suggest to skim this section on a first read and come back to it as needed.

Standard notation. We let $\mathbb{Z} = \{0, \pm 1, \pm 2, \pm 3, \ldots\}$ denote the set of integers and denote the set of natural numbers (non-negative integers) by $\mathbb{N}$. We let $\mathbb{R}$ denote the set of real numbers. We sometimes write $\mathbb{R}^+$ to denote the subset of positive real numbers, and $\mathbb{R}_0^+ := \mathbb{R}^+ \cup \{0\}$ for the non-negative real numbers. Similarly, we write $\mathbb{N}^+$ to denote the subset of positive integers.

We usually go by the convention that the small letters n, i, j, and ℓ as well as the greek letter λ (which will be given the special role of *security parameter*) denote natural numbers. If $n \in \mathbb{N}$ is a natural number, then we denote its unary representation (i.e., the string consisting of n many ones) by 1^n. We denote by $\langle n \rangle_\ell$ the standard binary representation of $n \in \mathbb{N}$ using ℓ bits (for $\ell \in \mathbb{N}$ and $n < 2^\ell$). If we consider an integer in a number system other than the decimal one, we use the prefix 0x to refer to the hexadecimal system (with digits from 0 to f) and also sometimes 0b for the binary system (with digits 0 and 1), e.g., the integer 29 can also be written as 0x1d and 0b11101. For $n \geq 1$ write $[n]$ to represent the set $\{1, 2, \ldots, n\}$ and we define $[n]$ for $n < 1$ to be the empty set. We let $i..j$ for $i \leq j$ denote the closed natural interval $\{i, i+1, \ldots, j\}$ and again define $i..j$ for $j < i$ to be the empty set.

If not stated otherwise, logarithms will always be to base two and denoted by $\log(x)$. If $x \in \mathbb{R}$ then $\lfloor x \rfloor$ and $\lceil x \rceil$ denote rounding functions where $\lfloor x \rfloor$ (rounding down) is defined as the largest integer $n \in \mathbb{Z}$ such that $n \leq x$. Similarly, $\lceil x \rceil$ (rounding up) denotes the smallest integer $n \in \mathbb{Z}$ such that $n \geq x$.

For integers $a, b, c \in \mathbb{Z}$ and positive integer $m \in \mathbb{N}^+$ we write $a = b = c \bmod m$ to denote that a, b, and c are congruent modulo m (they leave the same remainder when divided by m). We may also use $(a \bmod m)$ to denote the remainder of a when divided by m.

The cardinality of a set S is given by $|S|$. For a finite set this corresponds to the number of elements in the set. We denote by $\{\,\}$ the empty set, the set containing no elements and with cardinality 0. For a non-empty set S we denote by $S^\ell = S \times S \times \cdots \times S$ the ℓ-fold Cartesian product. We write $Q \subseteq S$ to denote that Q is a subset of (or identical to) S and denote by $Q \subsetneq S$ that Q is a strict subset of S. We use standard set notation for intersection $\cap$, union $\cup$, and set difference $\setminus$.

Assignments and equalities. We write $A := B$ to denote that the two statements A and B are equal *by definition*. We write $x \leftarrow 5$ to denote that x is assigned value 5 (think variable). If S is a set we write $x \leftarrow_\$ S$ to denote that x is assigned a value from set S uniformly at random (we will discuss notation for probabilities shortly). If x and y are two values, then we write $x = y$ as a test for equality which evaluates to the Boolean value false or true (which we often also refer to as 0 or 1, respectively).

Strings. If S is a finite set then we call a finite ordered tuple of elements in S a *string over the alphabet S*. We will also refer to ordered tuples as *sequences*. We will mostly work with strings over the alphabet $\{0, 1\}$ (containing the *bits* 0 and 1), which we call *bit strings* or simply *strings*. The string $1^n = 11 \ldots 1$ is the unary string given by n ones. By $|x|$ we denote the length of string x, given by the number of elements in the tuple representing x.

We denote the set of all bit strings of length ℓ by $\{0, 1\}^\ell$, the set of all bit strings of finite length by $\{0, 1\}^*$, and by $\{0, 1\}^\infty$ the set of all infinite binary strings. We denote by $\{0, 1\}^{\leq \ell}$ the set of all bit strings of length ℓ or shorter. We write ε to denote the empty string, having length 0. The concatenation of two strings $x_1, x_2 \in \{0, 1\}^*$ is given by $x_1 \| x_2$. The ith bit of a string x is specified by $x[i]$; the first bit in a string x is $x[1]$. By $x[i..j] = x[i] \| \ldots \| x[j]$ we denote the substring consisting of bit i up to, and including, bit j of x. By convention for $i > j$ we let $x[i..j] = \varepsilon$ be the empty string. A string x is a prefix of a string y if $|x| \leq |y|$ and $x = y[1..|x|]$, i.e., if y starts with the string x. It is a suffix of y if $|x| \leq |y|$ and $x = y[|y| - |x| + 1..|y|]$, i.e., if y ends with x. In particular, the empty string is always a prefix and suffix of any other string.

A vector of strings $\mathbf{x}$ is written in boldface, and $\mathbf{x}[i]$ denotes its ith entry. Again, indexes are 1-based and the first element of a vector $\mathbf{x}$ is $\mathbf{x}[1]$. The number of entries of $\mathbf{x}$ is denoted by $|\mathbf{x}|$. We can encode such vectors $\mathbf{x} = (\mathbf{x}[1], \ldots, \mathbf{x}[|\mathbf{x}|])$ of strings as a single string if we ensure that this encoding allows to recover the vector again. There are various options for doing this; one is to simply encode each bit by duplicating it, $0 \mapsto 00$ and $1 \mapsto 11$, and inserting delimiters 01 between the encoded strings of $\mathbf{x}[i]$ and $\mathbf{x}[i + 1]$. Given such a string it is easy to identify the separators 01 and to recover each entry in the vector.

A table of strings T is a set of string pairs such that for all pairs $(a, b) \in T$ and $(a', b') \in T$ it holds that $a \neq a'$. We write $T[a] \leftarrow b$ to denote the insertion of pair (a, b) into the table. If a pair is already present with first component a then this entry is removed first. By $T[a]$ we denote element b such that $(a, b) \in T$. If no such tuple is present then $T[a]$ is set to $\perp$, a special symbol to denote that the entry is not present. Deletion of an entry a is denoted by $T[a] \leftarrow \perp$. Unless stated otherwise, we assume that tables are initialized to empty, written $T \leftarrow [\,]$, such that $T[a] = \perp$ for any a upon creation. Similarly to vectors, we can encode tables as a single string.

Finite fields. We denote by $\mathbb{GF}(2)$ or $\mathbb{F}_2$ the finite field consisting of the two elements 0 and 1, and by $\mathbb{GF}(p^n)$ or $\mathbb{F}_{p^n}$ the field with p^n elements for prime $p \geq 2$ and integer $n \geq 1$. For the special case $n = 1$ we sometimes also use the common term $\mathbb{Z}_p$ to identify the field with the elements given by $0, 1, \ldots, p - 1$. For $p = 2$ we often switch between field elements from $\mathbb{GF}(2^n)$ and n-bit strings in the natural way. Recall that the characteristic of a (finite) field is the smallest natural number c such that the c-fold sum of 1 satisfies $1 + 1 + \cdots + 1 = 0$. Fields of the form $\mathbb{GF}(2^n)$ have characteristic 2. This means that adding an element to itself always yields 0 in such fields.

Bit operations and logical connectives. We write $\wedge$, $\vee$, and $\neg$ for the Boolean operations AND, OR, and NOT (negation). We use Boolean operators both on bit strings (evaluated bit-wise and assuming that both strings are of the same length)—for example, $001 \wedge 101 = 001$—as well as in the logical sense, for example in probability statements (introduced shortly). We denote the exclusive-or of two bits $a, b \in \{0, 1\}$ by $a \oplus b$ defined as $a \oplus b := (a \wedge \neg b) \vee (\neg a \wedge b)$. If $x, y \in \{0, 1\}^*$ are two bit strings of the same length then $x \oplus y$ denotes the result of performing a bit-wise exclusive-or operation on the bits of x and y. By $\langle x, y \rangle$ we denote the inner product of x and y over $\mathbb{GF}(2)$, that is, $\langle x, y \rangle := \oplus_{i=1}^{|x|} (x[i] \cdot y[i])$ where $\cdot$ is the multiplication in the field and we interpret the bits $x[i]$ and $y[i]$ as the field elements 0 and 1.

If $\mathcal{A}$ and $\mathcal{B}$ are two logical statements (which are either true or false) then we use $\mathcal{A} \implies \mathcal{B}$ to denote that $\mathcal{A}$ implies $\mathcal{B}$, that is, if $\mathcal{A}$ is true then so is $\mathcal{B}$. This is logically equivalent to $\neg \mathcal{A} \vee \mathcal{B}$. Note that if $\mathcal{A}$ is false in the implication then the whole expression is trivially true. We write $\mathcal{A} \iff \mathcal{B}$ to denote the logical biconditional "if, and only if": If $\mathcal{A}$ is true then so is $\mathcal{B}$, and if $\mathcal{B}$ is true then so is $\mathcal{A}$.

Quantifiers. We make use of the universal quantifier $\forall$ (for all), the existential quantifier $\exists$ (exists), and the uniqueness quantifier $\exists!$ (exists exactly one). More formally, if $\mathcal{P}(n)$ is a predicate (a Boolean function) with argument n, and S is a set, then $\forall n \in S : \mathcal{P}(n)$ means "$\mathcal{P}(n)$ evaluates to true for all $n \in S$", $\exists n \in S : \mathcal{P}(n)$ means "there exists one or more $n \in S$ such that $\mathcal{P}(n)$ evaluates to true", and $\exists!n \in S : \mathcal{P}(n)$ means "there exists exactly one value $n \in S$ such that $\mathcal{P}(n)$ evaluates to true".

Polynomials. We call a function $\mathsf{p} : \mathbb{N} \to \mathbb{R}$ a *polynomial* if function p can be written as

$$\mathsf{p}(\lambda) = \sum_{i=0}^{n} a_i \lambda^i$$

for some fixed $n \in \mathbb{N}$ (called the *degree*) and fixed constants $a_i \in \mathbb{R}$ for $i \in \{0, 1, \ldots, n\}$. We sometimes demand that the polynomial p only takes positive or non-negative values and write $\mathsf{p} : \mathbb{N} \to \mathbb{R}^+$ or $\mathsf{p} : \mathbb{N} \to \mathbb{R}_0^+$ then.

We occasionally write $\mathsf{poly}(\lambda)$ to denote an arbitrary, not further specified polynomial function.

Probabilities. In Section 1.5.1 we give a brief introduction into the most important concepts from probability theory that we will use in this book and here only clarify notation. We note that, unless mentioned otherwise, we work here with discrete distributions over a finite (or at most countable) number of outcomes.

If E is an event then we denote by $\Pr[E]$ its probability, and if X is a (discrete) random variable then $\Pr[X = x]$ denotes the probability that X takes on value x. We denote the complement of event E by $\overline{E}$ or $\neg E$. When not clear from context, we will specify the probability space explicitly by putting it in subscript, for example, we write $\Pr_{x \leftarrow \$[10]}[x = 5]$ to denote the probability of x being 5 when x is chosen uniformly at random from the set $\{1, 2, \ldots, 10\}$. Alternatively, we may separate the probability space by a colon from the statement and separate multiple steps by semicolons: That is, we write

$$\Pr\Big[y = 8 \, : \, x \leftarrow\!\$ \, [10]; \; y \leftarrow\!\$ \, [2x]\Big]$$

to denote the probability that y takes value 8 if x is sampled uniformly from $[10]$ and then y from $[2x]$. We denote by $\Pr[E \mid B]$ the conditional probability of event E given B, or when working with random variables denote by $\Pr[X = x \mid Y = y]$ the probability of X taking value x given that $Y = y$. The expectation of a random variable X is given by $\mathbb{E}[X]$. For binary random variables X with range $\{0, 1\}$ or the set of Boolean values $\{\mathsf{false}, \mathsf{true}\}$, we write $\Pr[X]$ to denote the probability that X takes the value 1 (or, true).

Function definitions. We will often encounter (families of) functions that are parameterized by a security parameter $\lambda \in \mathbb{N}$. (We will discuss the role of the security parameter in detail in Section 1.3.5.) In this case we often consider functions to have fixed input and output lengths defined by security parameter λ. For example, we may consider a function $\mathsf{F} : \{0,1\}^{\mathsf{il}(\lambda)} \to \{0,1\}^{\mathsf{ol}(\lambda)}$ where $\mathsf{il}, \mathsf{ol} : \mathbb{N} \to \mathbb{N}$ are polynomials describing the input length (resp. output length). Besides il and ol we also use kl and rl to denote the length of keys and the length of randomness.

Landau notation. We make use of Landau notation (aka big-O notation) to characterize the asymptotic behavior of functions for large input values. This is especially useful for characterizing the runtime of algorithms.

For two functions f and g we say that $f \in \mathcal{O}(g)$ if for all sufficiently large values, function f is upper bounded by g up to a constant factor. Similarly, if f is lower bounded by g we write $f \in \Omega(g)$. Finally, we say $f \in \omega(g)$ if f asymptotically grows faster than g.

Formally, we define the classes as: $f \in \mathcal{O}(g)$ (resp. $f \in \Omega(g)$) if there exists some λ_0 and $c \in \mathbb{N}$ such that for all $\lambda \geq \lambda_0$ we have that $f(\lambda) \leq c \cdot g(\lambda)$ (resp. $f(\lambda) \geq c \cdot g(\lambda)$). We say $f \in \omega(g)$ if for all $c \in \mathbb{N}$ there exists λ_0 such that for all $\lambda \geq \lambda_0$ we have that $f(\lambda) \geq c \cdot g(\lambda)$.[2]

---

[2] In the literature the classes are defined via the absolute terms $|f(\lambda)|$ and $|g(\lambda)|$ of function values. Since we are considering the classes in connection with positive-valued runtimes, bit lengths, or probabilities, we have omitted this here.

1.2 Formalizing Cryptography

Generally speaking, cryptographic schemes (or cryptosystems) provide means for *secure communication*. The formalization of a cryptographic scheme consists of two parts:

1. A precise definition of how a task is to be performed (a formalization of the cryptographic scheme), and
2. A precise definition of what exactly it means for a scheme to be secure (*a mathematical security definition*).

The precise formalization of *the scheme* itself allows anybody to use it correctly, while the formalization of *security* provides a clear description to users of what kind of protection to expect from a scheme. Furthermore, the formalization of scheme and security allows cryptographers and cryptanalysts to properly study schemes to either provide security proofs or counter-arguments to the fact that the scheme indeed achieves the level of security claimed.

An important approach (and also the approach taken in this book) to modern cryptography is that of *provable security*. In essence, provable security asks that cryptographic schemes should always be accompanied by a security proof of the form:

> *Given that conditions* A, B, C, ... *hold, the cryptographic scheme* S *has security property* Q.

Note that the above security proof template is a conditional statement, and indeed most theorems in cryptography are only known to hold relative to unproven assumptions. Still, the statement itself—that property Q holds under the conditions—is mathematically sound and eternal truth, this is what the security proof should guarantee. But if any of the assumptions A, B, C, ... fails then the security of scheme S *may* become void. This means that one may indeed be able to break property Q, but one may also be able to resurrect property Q under different conditions. The term "provable security" should be understood in this sense.

At the heart of the assumptions on which modern cryptography is based on is the P vs. NP question, which we briefly look at in Section 1.4. The security of almost any modern cryptographic scheme is based on the assumption that NP $\neq$ P. Consequently, modern cryptography and complexity theory are closely related. One aspect in which this becomes apparent are cryptographic proofs themselves, which are very often in the form of a *reduction*, and we will see countless examples through the course of this book. First, however, we need to introduce the necessary formalisms to study cryptographic schemes which will be the goal of this section. As a running example we will use *symmetric encryption schemes*.

Encryption Schemes

Encryption schemes are used to provide *confidentiality*, which intuitively captures the idea that a message is transmitted to a recipient in such a way that only the intended recipient can *decipher* (i.e., make sense of) the message. Confidentiality can be formalized in different ways, and we will see several security definitions that capture different forms of the concept. Similarly, there can be different means to achieve confidentiality, yet the standard cryptographic method to provide confidentiality is via an encryption scheme. The cryptographic setting here is the following: we (usually) consider two honest parties, often named Alice and Bob, who want to exchange confidential messages in the presence of an adversary, often named Eve.[3] Alice and Bob are connected via an insecure channel on which they can send any type of data, that is, any type of bit string. The channel being *insecure* means that there is no guarantee whatsoever on what happens to the data in-flight. In particular, we assume that adversary Eve cannot only read any data sent over the channel but may also be able to tamper with the data. The latter, for example, becomes relevant when we ask questions regarding the *authenticity* of data, such as "how can Bob be sure that the transmission he received was indeed sent by Alice?". For now we will focus on the basics, i.e., encryption and confidentiality of messages.

An encryption scheme provides confidentiality as follows. Before sending a message m to Bob, Alice *encrypts* (transforms) the message according to the rules of the encryption scheme to obtain a ciphertext c, which she then sends to Bob. To recover message m, Bob similarly applies the rules of the corresponding decryption scheme to ciphertext c: He *decrypts* ciphertext c to recover plaintext message m. Note that as Eve can read anything that is sent over the channel she can intercept ciphertext c. Furthermore, if she knew everything Bob knew, then she could also perform the decryption operation to recover plaintext message m from ciphertext c, simply by performing the exact same operations as Bob. Thus, in order to give Alice and Bob a fighting chance we need to assume that there is something that Alice and Bob share to encrypt, but which Eve does not know. This information is usually called the *key*.

Kerckhoffs' principle. When considering security of encryption schemes (or cryptosystems in general) the general rule to obey is *Kerckhoffs' principle*. This is one of the fundamental principles of modern cryptography and states that the security of a cryptosystem (e.g., an encryption scheme) should be based solely on the secrecy of a (short) key. That is, a cryptographic system should be parameterized by a key and it should be assumed that an adversary

---

[3] Alice, Bob, and Eve are canonical "protagonists" used widely in the cryptographic community. Alice and Bob are used as generic parties A and B, while Eve is usually an adversarial character. Many more characters with specific roles exist in the cryptographic literature, but we will mostly hang out with Alice, Bob, and Eve.

knows everything about the system except for the particular key used in an instantiation of the scheme.

Applying Kerckhoffs' principle to encryption, we could thus assume that Alice and Bob know a shared secret key k which they can use for encryption and decryption but which is unknown to adversary Eve. In other words we have made a *setup assumption* that at some point Alice and Bob have met and *securely* agreed upon a key k. Now, when they want to transmit a confidential message they first use an encryption algorithm to compute a ciphertext c from the key k and plaintext message m. They then transmit ciphertext c in the hope that only a person who knows key k can reverse the process and recover message m from ciphertext c. This form of encryption scheme in which the communicating parties are assumed to know a *shared secret* is referred to as *symmetric encryption*. This is in contrast to *asymmetric* or *public-key encryption*, which we will introduce in Chapter 5, where both parties hold distinct but correlated key parts.

Formalizing Symmetric Encryption

So far, we have informally described what a symmetric encryption scheme is, but how can we capture this mathematically? To formalize encryption schemes we first need to formalize the ingredients (i.e., messages, ciphertexts, and keys). In other words, we need to define what are valid messages (the set of all messages is called the *message space*), what are valid ciphertexts (the *ciphertext space*), and what are valid keys (the *key space*).

While it seems natural to consider that messages consist of characters from some "natural" alphabet, say the Latin characters a–z or any unicode character, we usually consider one of the simplest possible alphabets: we work on finite-length bit strings that consist of only zeros and ones. We thus define our alphabet as $\{0, 1\}$ (the set that contains the elements 0 and 1) and consider the message space $\mathcal{M}$ to be $\{0, 1\}^n$ (all bit strings of length n). We often also set $\mathcal{M} = \{0, 1\}^{\leq n}$ or $\mathcal{M} = \{0, 1\}^*$, that is, we consider any message of length less than or equal to n or any finite-length bit string to be a valid message. Similarly for ciphertexts and keys we usually restrict ourselves to bit strings. Note that this choice is without loss of generality as for any alphabet Σ we can define an encoding, i.e., a function that maps characters $c \in \Sigma$ to words $w \in \{0, 1\}^\ell$ and thus messages over Σ to bit strings. Further note that the length ℓ needed to encode characters in Σ depends on the cardinality $|\Sigma|$ of alphabet Σ (i.e., the number of elements in Σ).

Let us now present a first definition of a symmetric encryption scheme. The definition will contain some items and concepts whose formal foundation we will learn later. We discuss some aspects informally after having stated the definition.

Definition 1.1 (Symmetric Encryption Scheme). *A symmetric encryption scheme* SE *is a tuple of three efficient algorithms* SE = (SE.KGen, SE.Enc, SE.Dec) *such that*

SE.KGen: *The probabilistic* key generation algorithm *on input the security parameter* 1^λ *outputs a key* $k \in \{0,1\}^*$.

SE.Enc: *The probabilistic* encryption algorithm *takes as input the security parameter* 1^λ, *a key* k, *and a message* $m \in \{0,1\}^*$ *and outputs a ciphertext* $c \in \{0,1\}^*$.

SE.Dec: *The deterministic* decryption algorithm *takes as input the security parameter* 1^λ, *a key* k, *and a ciphertext* c *and outputs a message* m *or a special error symbol* $\perp$.

Correctness: *We say that a symmetric encryption scheme is* correct *if for all* $\lambda \in \mathbb{N}$ *and all* $m \in \{0,1\}^*$ *it holds that*

$$\Pr\left[\mathsf{SE.Dec}(\mathsf{SE.Enc}(k,m)) = m \mid k \leftarrow_\$ \mathsf{SE.KGen}(1^\lambda)\right] = 1.$$

Our above definition captures a symmetric encryption scheme as consisting of three algorithms: one for generating keys, one for encrypting a message, and one for decrypting a ciphertext. As message space $\mathcal{M}$, key space $\mathcal{K}$, and ciphertext space $\mathcal{C}$ we chose $\{0,1\}^*$, that is, bit strings of finite length. We note that not all encryption schemes can handle arbitrarily long messages (e.g., we will shortly introduce the one-time pad which requires that messages and keys are of the same length) and that in a more general definition message-, key-, and ciphertext space would be parameterized. Further note that, so far, we only require *correctness*, meaning that any message which was "properly" encrypted can be decrypted with the correct (i.e., the very same) key. There is, however, no notion yet as to what kind of security an encryption scheme should offer. In particular, the above definition could be easily met by a scheme that outputs the plaintext as ciphertext, that is, where encryption and decryption are simply the identity function.

Even though this first definition attempt is simple and does not yet capture security, it contains various concepts that have not yet been introduced. To start with, we have not yet specified what exactly we mean by an *algorithm*, let alone an *efficient algorithm*. Furthermore, the definition speaks of a *security parameter* 1^λ which is given as an additional input to all three algorithms (and which could also be used to parameterize the underlying message-, key-, and ciphertext space), appealing to some notion of complexity. We will introduce these concepts in the following sections starting with the notion of algorithms.

1.3 Algorithms, Turing Machines, and Circuits

Informally, we can think of an algorithm as a finite set of precise instructions to solve a problem or class of problems. The term itself goes back to the 9th century Persian mathematician al-Khwārizmī, but a formal study of algorithms only started in the early 20th century. Indeed, as long as we do not intend to formally prove statements such as "no algorithm exists that solves the problem" then a formalization is unnecessary as for positive results it usually suffices to simply state the algorithm. (Naturally, when wanting to prove, for example, correctness a formal model is helpful.)

The necessity of a formal algorithm model was triggered with the formulation of David Hilbert's Entscheidungsproblem (the decision problem) in 1928. Hilbert asked whether there exists a finite set of precise instructions (an algorithm) that when followed will prove or disprove a mathematical statement from a given set of axioms. In 1936 Alonzo Church and Alan Turing independently showed that such an algorithm cannot exist. Church based his result on the so-called *lambda calculus* that he developed in the early 1930s, while Turing based his result on what is nowadays known as *Turing machines*.

We say that a function is *effectively computable* if for all possible inputs the correct function value can be obtained by *rigorously following a finite set of instructions*. A similarly vague description of an *effectively computable function* is that for all inputs the function values can be obtained by some *mechanical calculation device* (e.g., a computer) if given access to unlimited time and storage space.

Both Turing and Church set out to give precise mathematical definitions of what it means for a function to be *computable* by specifying a so-called *model of computation*—the Turing machine and the lambda calculus, respectively— in order to formalize the notion of an algorithm. Turing machines are the predominant model of computation in the field of cryptography, and we will formally introduce them in the upcoming sections. As Turing machines can be captured by a precise mathematical definition this allows us to formalize what it means for a function to be *computable*.

> **Definition 1.2.** *We call a function* computable *if it can be computed by a Turing machine.*

Intriguingly, it can be shown that the expressiveness of Turing machines and the lambda calculus is identical. That is, any computation that can be modeled by a Turing machine can also be modeled within the lambda calculus, and vice versa. A computational model which has (at least) the same expressiveness as a Turing machine is also called *Turing complete*, and for many computational models that have been introduced since, it was shown that they possess this property.

An important question is whether any computational model is *complete* in the sense that it captures each and every function that is "effectively

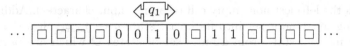

Fig. 1.1: A simple representation of a Turing machine consisting of a single tape, somewhere in its program execution. The read/write head is currently above a cell with content 1 and the Turing machine is in state q_1.

computable"? The general belief is that this is indeed the case and that Turing machines (and hence any Turing-complete computational model) capture precisely the class of functions that are also *intuitively computable*. The hypothesis that this is indeed so is usually referred to as the *Church–Turing Thesis*:

> **Church–Turing Thesis:** Any function that is *effectively computable* is also *computable*.

Remark 1.3. The Church–Turing Thesis is a hypothesis that cannot be proven since the notion of *intuitively* or *effectively computable functions* is not based on a precise mathematical statement.

In modern cryptography one of the main tasks is to prove that under reasonable assumptions no *efficient algorithm* exists that can break the security of a cryptographic scheme with good probability. Thus, a formal notion of an algorithm is essential to the theory of cryptography. As mentioned, the predominant model of computation is the Turing machine, which we will formalize next.

1.3.1 Turing Machines

In its simplest form, a Turing machine consists of a single, infinitely long tape that is divided into cells. Each cell contains a symbol from an alphabet Σ (we usually restrict ourselves to $\Sigma = \{0, 1\}$) or a special symbol $\square$ to denote that the cell is empty. In addition to the tape there is a read/write head that is able to move from cell to cell and read from or write to the cell underneath it. The program state q of the machine is taken from a finite set $\mathcal{Q}$ and may change in dependence of the tape content and, vice versa, influence the value written to the cell. The changes in state, tape content, and head position are described by a set of rules Δ. An illustration of a Turing machine is given in Figure 1.1.

When we speak of a Turing machine we usually do not only mean the imaginary mechanical device, but the device coupled with a fixed program. A Turing machine M processes an input string $x \in \Sigma^*$ in the following fashion: To begin, input x is written onto the tape and the Turing machine head is placed on the leftmost non-empty cell (the first input character). Additionally, the Turing machine is set into its initial state $q \leftarrow q_{\text{start}}$. State q_{start} is a specially marked state from a finite set of states $\mathcal{Q}$ which are part of the Turing machine program. Then, in each *step* the following operations are performed.

1. The cell below the head is read to obtain symbol $s \in \Sigma \cup \{\Box\}$.
2. A finite set of rules Δ is consulted to obtain an action a for (q, s), that is for the combination of the current state q and the read symbol s. An action a consists of a state $q_{\text{next}} \in \mathcal{Q}$, a symbol $s_{\text{next}} \in \Sigma \cup \{\Box\}$, and a direction $d \in \{\curvearrowleft, \curvearrowright\}$. Then, according to action $a = (q_{\text{next}}, s_{\text{next}}, d)$,

    a. The head writes symbol s_{next} onto the current cell,
    b. The heads moves one position to the left ($\curvearrowleft$) or right ($\curvearrowright$) according to direction d, and
    c. The Turing machine's state is updated to $q \leftarrow q_{\text{next}}$.

These steps are repeated until the Turing machine enters state $q_{\text{halt}} \in \mathcal{Q}$ that denotes the special halting state indicating that the processing has finished. In this case we say the Turing machine M halts on input x with output M(x), where output M(x) is defined as the string $x \in \Sigma^*$ consisting of the concatenation of the leftmost non-empty cells up to the first empty cell. For example, if a Turing machine M over alphabet $\Sigma = \{0, 1\}$ halts with the following tape

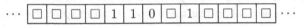

then the output M(x) is the bit string 110.

Remark 1.4. The above definition of the output is somewhat arbitrary, similarly to, for example, the definition that the head of the Turing machine has to move after every write operation. All of these definitional choices do, however, not change the expressiveness of Turing machines (i.e., the class of functions that can be implemented as a Turing machine).

Remark 1.5. A Turing machine does not necessarily need to halt but instead may run forever and never reach the halting state q_{halt}. We will usually restrict ourselves to Turing machines M that halt on every possible input such that for every $x \in \{0, 1\}^*$ (assuming the binary alphabet) the output value M(x) is properly defined. Thus, unless stated otherwise, whenever we speak of an algorithm or a Turing machine, we assume it stops/halts after a finite number of steps on every input.

We can formalize a Turing machine as a six tuple M = $(\Sigma, \Box, \mathcal{Q}, \Delta, q_{\text{start}}, q_{\text{halt}})$. That is, a Turing machine M consists of a description of the alphabet Σ, a special "blank" symbol $\Box \notin \Sigma$, a finite set of states $\mathcal{Q}$, two special states for starting $q_{\text{start}} \in \mathcal{Q}$ and halting $q_{\text{halt}} \in \mathcal{Q}$, as well as a transition table Δ (the set of rules) mapping pairs $(q, s) \in (\mathcal{Q} \times \Sigma \cup \{\Box\})$ onto actions

$a \in (\mathcal{Q} \times \Sigma \cup \{\square\} \times \{\curvearrowleft, \curvearrowright\})$. Note that we only consider transition tables that can be described by a function $\delta : (\mathcal{Q}, \Sigma \cup \{\square\}) \to (\mathcal{Q}, \Sigma \cup \{\square\}, \{\curvearrowleft, \curvearrowright\})$. In other words the entries are unambiguous and for each possible combination of state and symbol there is exactly one action in the table. (We will shortly come to *probabilistic* Turing machines, where we will review this definitional choice.)

From here onwards we will no longer explicitly state which alphabet is used but always consider the alphabet $\Sigma = \{0, 1\}$.

Remark 1.6. There are many definitional choices when it comes to Turing machines. For example, we could consider a variant which consists of three tapes, a read-only input tape, a read–write work tape and a write-only output tape. While such variants can make it easier to state algorithms as Turing machine programs, they are usually equivalent as to what sort of algorithms can be expressed. With the above definition we have opted for a simplistic definition as we will later not be working at the level of Turing machines but instead at the level of pseudocode.

Computable Functions

The notion of Turing machines together with the Church–Turing Thesis provides a formal vehicle for the study of computable functions, i.e., functions that can be computed via an algorithm. Formally, we say that a function $f : \{0, 1\}^* \to \{0, 1\}^*$ is *computable* if there exists a Turing machine M such that for all $x \in \{0, 1\}^*$ we have that $f(x) = \mathsf{M}(x)$.

Now that we have a precise notion of computable functions, an interesting question is whether functions exist that are not computable. Such *uncomputable functions* do indeed exist, and we will see an example later in this section.

Running Time of Turing Machines

We define by $\mathsf{time}_\mathsf{M}(x)$ the *runtime* of Turing machine M on input $x \in \{0, 1\}^*$ which captures the number of steps (number of head movements) the Turing machine takes to process input x until it reaches the halting state $q_{\mathtt{halt}}$. As we only consider Turing machines that halt on every possible input the runtime function time_M of Turing machine M is well-defined.

Most of the time, we are not interested in the runtime of a Turing machine M for a particular input x but in the worst-case runtime of M for any x of a particular length $|x| = \lambda$. We let $\mathsf{time}_\mathsf{M}(\lambda)$ for $\lambda \in \mathbb{N}$ denote this worst-case runtime of Turing machine M on an input of length λ, that is,

$$\mathsf{time}_\mathsf{M}(\lambda) := \max_{x \in \{0,1\}^\lambda} \mathsf{time}_\mathsf{M}(x).$$

Efficient Turing machines. Our definition of a symmetric encryption scheme (Definition 1.1 on page 9) speaks of *efficient* algorithms. We call an algorithm efficient if there exists a Turing machine that implements the algorithm and which has a "reasonably" restricted runtime. Here, cryptography follows the complexity-theoretic approach to identify "reasonably bounded runtime" with polynomial time, that is, we call a Turing machine *efficient* or *polynomial time* if its runtime is bounded by a polynomial. This means that there exists a polynomial p such that for large enough λ we have that $\text{time}_M(\lambda) \leq p(\lambda)$. Here the formulation "for large enough λ" means that there exists a value $\Lambda \in \mathbb{N}$ such that for all values $\lambda \geq \Lambda$ the statement holds.

Remark 1.7. We sometimes write $\text{time}_M(\lambda) = \text{poly}(\lambda)$ if it is polynomial for some unspecified polynomial.

Again, we can translate the notion of efficiency from Turing machines to (computable) functions. We call a function $f : \{0,1\}^* \rightarrow \{0,1\}^*$ *efficiently computable* if there exists an efficient Turing machine M such that for all $x \in \{0,1\}^*$ we have that $f(x) = M(x)$.

Using polynomials to define efficiency of computation has several advantages. In particular it provides us with a measure that is closed under combination via "subroutines" and thus allows us to combine algorithms: If Turing machine A runs Turing machine B for a polynomially number of times and Turing machine B is efficient then so is Turing machine A. This is true, because the product of two polynomials is again a polynomial (albeit usually of higher degree).

It should be noted that efficiency in the above sense and efficiency in a *practical* sense have little in common. If an (efficient) algorithm runs in time, say n^{100}, then it will be hardly practical since already for inputs of length $n = 2$ the algorithm will probably not return an answer in any reasonable amount of time. However, empirically, it seems to be the case that if a polynomial-time algorithm is found then the runtime can usually be optimized to be bounded by small-degree polynomials.

Probabilistic Turing Machines

Our basic Turing machine is *deterministic*. That is, when we run a Turing machine M on the same input x multiple times, then we will always get the same result $M(x)$.

For many cryptographic applications a deterministic algorithm is insufficient. Consider, for example, the task of key generation in an encryption scheme. Here, we will usually assume that on each invocation the key generator picks a random key from the key space. To model *probabilistic* algorithms, i.e., algorithms that can make random choices, we use *probabilistic Turing machines*. There are again many definitional choices when formalizing probabilistic Turing machines. We could, for example, consider a Turing machine

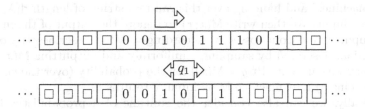

Fig. 1.2: A probabilistic Turing machine. The top tape is filled with independent random bits at the beginning of each invocation. The head for the randomness tape is read only and can only move to the right. Below, we have again the read–write tape where the head is currently above a cell with content 0. The Turing machine is in state q_1.

that has not only one transition table but two tables Δ_0 and Δ_1, and in each step one table is chosen at random with probability $\frac{1}{2}$ and independently of any previous choices.

The way we usually define probabilistic Turing machines in cryptography (and we will also take this view in this book) is the following. A probabilistic Turing machine is a deterministic Turing machine which has an extra tape called the *randomness tape*, and an extra read-only head that moves along the randomness tape. At the beginning of each invocation, the randomness tape is filled with independent random bits. The transition table is adapted such that actions are chosen depending on the current symbol on the regular tape, the bit on the randomness tape and the current state. Actions are extended to contain not only a direction for the regular head, but also a decision on whether or not the randomness head is moved one position to the right. (For simplicity one can assume that the randomness head only moves in one direction.) See Figure 1.2 for an illustration of the above formalization of a probabilistic Turing machine.

Yet another formalization is to consider that a probabilistic Turing machine is a deterministic machine that can choose to toss a coin at any point during the computation (which costs a single step) and then base the next steps also on the outcome of this coin toss. We often employ this image of coin tosses when speaking about probability spaces where we, for example, say that the probability is over *the random coins of an algorithm*.

We let $\mathsf{rl}(\lambda)$ (short for *randomness length*) denote the maximal length of the random tape (or the maximal number of coin tosses the machine requires) for its (finite) computation on inputs of length λ. Note that we may simply assume that the machine makes exactly $\mathsf{rl}(\lambda)$ coin tosses for each input x of length λ, simply by letting the machine make redundant coin tosses if necessary.

It is often convenient to consider a probabilistic Turing machine M as a deterministic one, executed with a specific random tape. For this we can consider tossing sufficiently many coins $r \leftarrow\!\!\$ \{0,1\}^{\mathsf{rl}(\lambda)}$ in advance and "outside of the machine," and handing over this random string of length $\mathsf{rl}(\lambda)$ as an additional input. We then write $\mathsf{M}(x;r)$ to denote the output of the machine M on input x and coin tosses r. Accordingly, $\mathsf{M}(x)$ describes the output distribution, described by sampling r uniformly and outputting $\mathsf{M}(x;r)$. In particular, we can write $\Pr[y = \mathsf{M}(x)]$ for the probability (over the choice of random coins r) that machine M on input x returns y.

Naturally, we can also consider the runtime of a probabilistic Turing machine. With the notion of probabilistic Turing machines and the viewpoint of a deterministic one with additional random input, we can use the definition of the runtime as before and write $\mathsf{time}_\mathsf{M}(x;r)$ as well as

$$\mathsf{time}_\mathsf{M}(\lambda) = \max_{(x,r)\in\{0,1\}^\lambda\times\{0,1\}^{\mathsf{rl}(\lambda)}} \mathsf{time}_\mathsf{M}(x;r).$$

If this runtime is polynomial then we call the machine *efficient* or speak of a probabilistic polynomial-time (PPT) Turing machine.

Note that if a probabilistic Turing machine M runs in polynomial time $\mathsf{p}(\lambda)$ in the input length $|x|$, then it can make at most $\mathsf{rl}(\lambda) \le \mathsf{p}(\lambda)$ coin tosses during the computation. The length of each pair $(x;r)$ is then at most $\mathsf{q}(\lambda) = \lambda + \mathsf{p}(\lambda)$, which is again a polynomial in λ. Hence, a polynomial runtime in $|(x;r)|$ implies a polynomial runtime in $|x|$, albeit for a different polynomial. To highlight the importance of $\mathsf{rl}(\lambda)$ being polynomially bounded, observe that if the Turing machine was able to consume, say, exponentially many random bits, $\mathsf{rl}(\lambda) = 2^\lambda$, then a polynomial runtime in $|(x;r)|$ would not necessarily imply polynomial time in $|x|$. In this sense the definition above is robust with respect to polynomial-time algorithms.

Interactive Turing Machines

In cryptography we rarely consider program executions in isolation but instead consider algorithms that can interact with one another. For example, to define security for encryption schemes we will look at adversaries that can interact with an encryption routine to generate encryptions for messages of their choice. When considering the security of signature schemes we similarly provide the adversary with a routine to generate signatures of its choice. In this case, however, the signature generation routine is not only generating signatures but also keeps track of those messages for which the adversary requested signatures in order to only consider a forgery of the adversary valid if it is different from all requested signatures.

To formally capture such interaction we extend the model of (probabilistic) Turing machines in the following way (we here briefly discuss a possible model for two machines, which can however easily be extended to capture multiple machines): The set of states $\mathcal{Q}$ is extended by an extra *waiting* state q_{wait}, and both machines get access to an extra read–write *communication tape*. The transition tables are augmented accordingly.

If Turing machine A wants to communicate with B then it writes an input onto the communication tape and goes into state q_{wait}. Once A goes into the waiting state, B is awoken and starts processing. Once B goes into the waiting state q_{wait} or halts, Turing machine A is awoken again and can continue processing. An important observation is that, during a single execution of Turing machine A, it can call B multiple times. In order for B to "build up state over multiple invocations" we allow B to keep its work tape intact in-between calls. This allows B, for example, to count the number of times it was called or the messages it was called on and the responses it provided. Note that if A is efficient then B can be called at most polynomially many times and each query can be at most of polynomial length. Thus keeping a list of all queries can be done in polynomial space, allowing an efficient B to "remember" all its interactions. Here we make use of the fact that the product of two polynomials is again a polynomial.

The runtime of an interactive Turing machine is measured by the steps the machine makes when activated but does not account for the steps of the other machines. In particular, a polynomially bounded interactive Turing machine can only read polynomially many bits from the communication tape, even if the connected Turing machine may run in exponential time and write exponentially long messages on the tape.

Oracle Turing Machines

Oracle Turing machines can be regarded as an extension to the interactive Turing machine model that focuses on the question of what an algorithm A can do when given access to some functionality O (called an *oracle*) that it can interact with but where the internals of oracle O are of no particular importance. We denote an execution of oracle Turing machine A relative to oracle O by A^O. In case the oracle can be implemented by a Turing machine the resulting machine A^O is, in fact, an interactive Turing machine. We note, however, that oracles do not necessarily need to be implementable by a Turing machine and could thus also implement, for example, an uncomputable function.

To formally capture the interaction of an oracle machine $A^{O_1, O_2, \ldots, O_\ell}$ with its oracles we extend the Turing machine model and give an oracle machine a special oracle tape, one for each of its oracles. When a question to the oracle should be posed, the machine writes the question onto the corresponding oracle tape and then enters a special oracle state. Then, in a single time step the oracle's answer will be written onto the tape.

The runtime of an oracle Turing machine is measured similarly to that of an interactive Turing machine. We count only the steps the machine makes

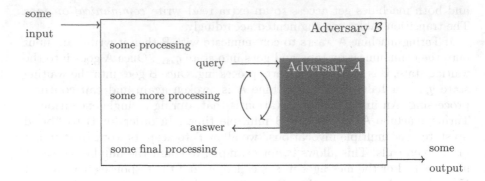

Fig. 1.3: Schematic of a reduction. Adversary $\mathcal{B}$ uses adversary $\mathcal{A}$ as a *black box* that can be communicated with via input and output messages but which completely hides the internals of its computation. In particular, this means that $\mathcal{A}$ may not be implementable by a Turing machine but still could implement any form of function.

and count each invocation of an oracle as a single step (plus the time to write the query and to read the response).

Oracles only expose *black-box* access, which means that an algorithm can interact with the oracle but cannot make any assumption about how it works internally. This is a key concept that is widely used in cryptography, for example, when proving the security of a cryptographic scheme. Most cryptographic security proofs come in the form of a *security reduction* which takes the form of a proof by contradiction (reductio ad absurdum). Assume we want to prove the security of some scheme Γ. To this end, we will show that the existence of an adversary $\mathcal{A}$ against scheme Γ induces the existence of another adversary $\mathcal{B}$ against a primitive Π that is assumed to be secure. As the existence of such an adversary $\mathcal{B}$ would imply that primitive Π cannot be secure this contradicts the assumption that Π is secure. Hence, if the assumption is correct and Π is, indeed, secure then it must follow that $\mathcal{B}$ does not exist. Consequently, adversary $\mathcal{A}$ cannot exist and thus also scheme Γ must be secure.

To formalize such reductions we will need to construct adversary $\mathcal{B}$ (or a Turing machine describing the actions of $\mathcal{B}$) from the assumed adversary $\mathcal{A}$. The simplest form of such a construction is a so-called *black-box* construction which treats adversary $\mathcal{A}$ as a black box that can only be communicated with via inputs and outputs but nothing about its internal computation is known. Formally, we will treat adversary $\mathcal{B}$ as an oracle Turing machine that has one oracle: adversary $\mathcal{A}$. We write $\mathcal{B}^{\mathcal{A}}$ to emphasize the fact that $\mathcal{B}$ uses $\mathcal{A}$ as a black box and give a sketch depicting the constructed adversary $\mathcal{B}^{\mathcal{A}}$ in Figure 1.3.

Efficient oracle machines. Let us stress that, for determining whether or not an oracle Turing machine is efficient, the internals of its oracles are meaningless. Each invocation of an oracle is counted as one step (plus the time to write the query and to read the response). The input–output behavior of an oracle, on the other hand, can have an impact on the efficiency. This means that, if an oracle is replaced by one that implements the same function, the runtime of the oracle Turing machine remains unchanged. On the other hand, if the function implemented by the oracle changes, this may change also the runtime of the oracle Turing machine.

Assuming now that our adversary $\mathcal{B}^{\mathcal{A}}$ with access to oracle $\mathcal{A}$ is efficient we can make the following argument. In case we have an efficient implementation of $\mathcal{A}$, i.e., a polynomial-time algorithm, then replacing the oracle in $\mathcal{B}$ with this algorithm as a subroutine $\mathcal{A}$ within $\mathcal{B}$ will again yield a polynomial-time algorithm. This is because $\mathcal{B}$ runs $\mathcal{A}$ at most a polynomial number of times (since the original oracle Turing machine is efficient) and $\mathcal{A}$ runs in a polynomial number of steps. As the product of two polynomials is again a polynomial, the statement follows.

The Universal Turing Machine

An important fact about Turing machines is that we can encode Turing machines as (bit-)strings and we denote by $\langle M \rangle$ the encoding of Turing machine M. If we fix the right encoding strategy we can ensure that

- Every Turing machine has an encoding,
- The encoding is injective, that is, different Turing machines (as tuples) are mapped to different encodings,
- Given a string it can be efficiently decided (by a Turing machine) whether the encoding corresponds to a Turing machine or not, and
- Given the encoding $\langle M \rangle$ of a Turing machine one can reconstruct the Turing machine M, where we actually define reconstruction below through a universal Turing machine.

This has several important consequences. For example, it means that the number of Turing machines and thus the number of possible algorithms and computable functions is *countable* since we can uniquely identify every bit string representing a Turing machine by a natural number. Furthermore, it allows us to show the existence of a so-called *universal* Turing machine UM that takes as input the description $\langle M \rangle$ of a Turing machine M and an input x. On input $(\langle M \rangle, x)$ the universal Turing machine is able to simulate the computation of M on input x and output whatever Turing machine M outputs on input x. Thus, we have that $UM(\langle M \rangle, x) = M(x)$. We sometimes say that UM is able to *reconstruct* M in the sense that it can run M on any input.

Noteworthy is that the overhead necessary for a Turing machine to simulate the computation of another Turing machine is "small," i.e., it is polynomial. In other words, if Turing machine M is a polynomial-time Turing machine, then M can be efficiently simulated given its encoding $\langle M \rangle$.

1.3.2 Uncomputable Functions

Earlier we noted that there are functions that cannot be computed by a Turing machine: so-called *uncomputable functions*. In the following we briefly discuss one such example.

As pointed out in the previous section, we can assume that if we fix the right encoding then every bit string represents a Turing machine (simply map meaningless bit strings to a canonical Turing machine). Furthermore, we can fix an encoding such that each and every Turing machine M can be identified by at least one bit string $\langle M \rangle$. By identifying each bit string $\langle M \rangle$ with a natural number $\lambda \in \mathbb{N}$—identify $\langle M \rangle$ with the binary expansion of $1 \| \langle M \rangle$—we get a bijection from the natural numbers to Turing machines.

Let M_λ denote the Turing machine identified by $\lambda \in \mathbb{N}$ according to encoding $\langle \cdot \rangle$. Value λ is also called the *Gödel number* (after the mathematician Kurt Gödel) of Turing machine M_λ. Let us now consider the following function (which, strictly speaking, depends on the concrete encoding $\langle \cdot \rangle$):

$$ f(x) = \begin{cases} 0 & \text{given that } x = 1^\lambda \text{ and the } \lambda\text{th Turing machine } M_\lambda \\ & \quad \text{outputs 1 on input } 1^\lambda \\ 1 & \text{otherwise} \end{cases} $$

Let us give an "algorithmic description" of function f. Function f takes as input some string x and first checks if x is the unary representation of a natural number $\lambda \in \mathbb{N}$.[4] If so it outputs 0 if the Turing machine M_λ on input 1^λ outputs 1. Otherwise it outputs 1. Similarly, in case x is not the unary representation of a natural number then $f(x) = 1$. In the following we will establish that function f is *not computable*, that is, there is no Turing machine M such that $M(x) = f(x)$ for every $x \in \{0,1\}^*$.

Proposition 1.8. *Function f as defined above is uncomputable, independently of the specific encoding $\langle \cdot \rangle$.*

Proof. Let us fix an encoding as described above. Let us assume that f is computable. Then there exists a Turing machine M such that for every input $x \in \{0,1\}^*$ we have that $M(x) = f(x)$. Then there exists $\lambda \in \mathbb{N}$ such that M_λ

---

[4] Note that for this example, it is not necessary to use unary representations. We will, however, come back to this function in Section 1.3.3, where the unary representation does play an important role.

is exactly our Turing machine M, that is, $\langle M \rangle = \langle M_\lambda \rangle$. Then, however, we have that

$$M(1^\lambda) = M_\lambda(1^\lambda) = f(1^\lambda).$$

However, by definition of f we have that

$$f(1^\lambda) = 0 \iff M_\lambda(1^\lambda) = 1,$$

which contradicts the assumption that $M(x) = f(x)$ for all $x \in \{0,1\}^*$. It follows that no Turing machine exists that computes function f. □

Remark 1.9. The technique used in the above proof is known as a *diagonalization argument*. Consider an infinite matrix that in the nth row contains entries corresponding to the nth Turing machine whereas each column corresponds to an input.

	1	2	...	λ	...
M_1	$M_1(1^1)$				
M_2		$M_2(1^2)$			
$\vdots$			$\ddots$		
M_λ				$M_\lambda(1^\lambda)$	
$\vdots$					$\ddots$

Function $f(x)$ is now defined as the inverse of the diagonal, and it is easy to see that no Turing machine can exist that computes the function, as this would mean that there exists some row n that is identical to the inverse of the diagonal. However, by definition on input n the value must be the inverse of what it is which, of course, cannot be. The diagonalization technique goes back to the mathematician Georg Cantor and his proof that the real numbers are uncountable.

1.3.3 Circuits: A Non-uniform Computational Model

The Turing machine model is a so-called *uniform* model of computation where *uniform* relates to the fact that Turing machines consist of a single program which is used for every input $x \in \{0,1\}^*$ independent of its size $|x|$. In contrast, a *non-uniform* model of computation defines an infinite sequence of programs $(P_1, P_2, \ldots, P_\lambda, \ldots)$ where program P_λ is used to compute values on inputs of size $|x| = \lambda$.

The most prominent non-uniform model of computation is that of *Boolean circuits*, which are also often used in cryptographic analyses as a model for adversaries (so called non-uniform adversaries). Before we get back to the discussion of uniformity vs. non-uniformity and the role circuits play in cryptography let us quickly introduce circuits. A pictorial representation of a circuit is given in Figure 1.4, and following is a formal definition.

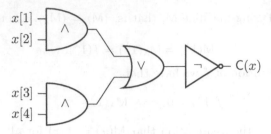

Fig. 1.4: A simple Boolean circuit for inputs of length 4 computing the function $C(x) = \neg((x[1] \wedge x[2]) \vee (x[3] \wedge x[4]))$. The diagram uses the ANSI symbols for the logical gates.

Definition 1.10. *For $\lambda \in \mathbb{N}$ we have that a λ-input deterministic Boolean circuit C is a directed acyclic graph with λ sources (vertices without any ingoing edges but possibly unbounded outgoing edges) and one or more sinks (vertices with one incoming edge but without any outgoing edges). Sources and sinks are numbered. Each vertex (or node) that is not a sink or a source is called a gate and is labeled with one operation of $\wedge$, $\vee$, or $\neg$. Each gate has exactly one outgoing edge (fan-out 1). Each gate labeled with $\wedge$ or $\vee$ has exactly two ingoing edges (fan-in 2) and each gate labeled with $\neg$ has fan-in 1.*

Let C be a λ-input circuit with $m \in \mathbb{N}$ sinks and let $x \in \{0,1\}^{\lambda}$ be a bit string. We define $C(x)$, the value of circuit C on input x, as

$$C(x) := C(x)[1]\| \ldots \|C(x)[m].$$

For this, we assign to every vertex v a value as follows. If v is the ith source (for $i \in [\lambda]$) then v is assigned the value $x[i]$. If v is a gate, then the value of v is defined recursively by applying the Boolean operation that v is labeled with to the values of the ingoing vertices. If v is a sink, then its value is that of the ingoing vertex. Finally, we set $C(x)[j]$ for $j \in [m]$ to be the value of the jth sink.

We say that circuit C has output length $m \in \mathbb{N}$ if C has m sinks. We let the size of C, denoted by $|C|$, be defined as the number of vertices of C. A circuit C has depth d if the longest path from a source to a sink passes d many vertices.

Let us stress that circuits are acyclic, which in particular means that there can be no "loops" within a circuit. Also note that we can of course present the graph-based notion of a circuit as a string such that we can talk about the (bit) description of a circuit in a straightforward way.

There are many possible variants of the above definition of circuits which yield the same computational complexity. For example, instead of allowing three different gate-types (AND, OR, and NOT gates), we could have also used only a single gate, given that it is *universal*. We say that a gate is universal if every circuit as defined above can be transformed into a circuit that consists only of the universal gates. An example of a universal gate is the so-called NAND gate defined as

$$\text{NAND}(x, y) := \neg(x \wedge y).$$

A second common variation to our circuit definition is to allow for *constant wires*, that is, to allow for two specific vertices within the circuit whose values are mapped to 0 and 1, respectively.

Probabilistic circuits. We can extend our circuit model to allow for *probabilistic* circuits by introducing a finite number of special input wires that at the beginning of an evaluation are fixed to a random value and which can be used as inputs to gates or sinks. Note that the restriction to finitely many *random wires* is without loss of generality as a circuit of size $k = |C|$ can at most make use of 2^k random input wires. If C is a probabilistic circuit then we write $C(x; r)$ to denote the value of circuit C on input x and with random wires fixed to value r. If C is probabilistic, then $C(x)$ denotes the output distribution $C(x; r)$ when sampling r uniformly at random.

Interactive and oracle circuits. Similarly to Turing machines we can consider *interactive* and *oracle* circuits. For this we add special gates (with a finite number of input wires) that implement the other circuit or oracle, respectively.

Circuit families. The value of a circuit C on input x is only defined for values $x \in \{0, 1\}^\lambda$ if C has exactly λ input wires (or sources). We thus cannot capture an algorithm in its entirety by a single circuit since usually an algorithm is independent of the problem (or input) size. Instead of a single circuit with a fixed input size we thus consider a *circuit family* $C = (C_\lambda)_{\lambda \in \mathbb{N}}$. A circuit family is a sequence of circuits $C_\lambda : \{0, 1\}^{\lambda + rl(\lambda)} \to \{0, 1\}^{ol(\lambda)}$ where $rl : \mathbb{N} \to \mathbb{N}$ and $ol : \mathbb{N} \to \mathbb{N}$ describe the number of random coins and the output length, respectively. In case the circuit family is deterministic then $rl(\lambda) = 0$ for all $\lambda \in \mathbb{N}$.

A circuit family now allows us to capture an algorithm in its entirety. For a bit string $x \in \{0, 1\}^\lambda$ we let $C(x) := C_\lambda(x)$ be the value of the circuit family on input x.

Efficient circuits. We have defined efficiency for Turing machines by restricting their runtime to be bounded by a polynomial in the input size. For circuits we instead consider their size. That is, we call a family of circuits $C = (C_\lambda)_{\lambda \in \mathbb{N}}$ *efficient* if there exists a polynomial p and an integer $\Lambda \in \mathbb{N}$ such that for all $\lambda \geq \Lambda$ we have that $|C_\lambda| \leq p(\lambda)$. For a family of circuits C we also write

$$\text{size}_C(\lambda) := |C_\lambda|$$

to denote the size of circuit C_λ.

1.3.3.1 Circuits vs. Turing Machines

Both Turing machines and circuits are models of computation. While a Turing machine consists only of a single program which is used for all inputs, a family of circuits defines a different circuit for inputs of different lengths. Turing machines are thus also referred to as *uniform* whereas circuits as *non-uniform*. The attributes uniform and non-uniform should however not be understood to be tied to either Turing machines or circuits but to whether or not different input lengths are handled by the same program or by different programs. In particular we can extend the Turing machine model to capture non-uniformity and restrict circuits to become uniform.

> **Definition 1.11.** *We call a family of circuits* $C = (C_\lambda)_{\lambda \in \mathbb{N}}$ *uniform if there exists a Turing machine* M *that on input* λ *outputs a description of circuit* C_λ.

In other words, if the circuit family can be generated by a Turing machine then we call the circuit family uniform. This means that, although the circuit family itself is a sequence of more or less independent circuits, the circuits share some common (uniform) method to describe them. Similarly, we can also extend the Turing machine model to capture non-uniformity. Here, the idea is to consider Turing machines that "take advice." That is, we consider Turing machines that take an extra input $a = a(|x|)$ which only depends on the length of input x.

By definition of a circuit we have that for any circuit C with λ input sources the value $C(x)$ is well-defined for all $x \in \{0,1\}^\lambda$. In other words the computation of a circuit halts on any input since "loops" are not allowed. For Turing machines that is not the case, and it is easy to define a Turing machine that never stops running. For example, consider the Turing machine that simply ignores what is on the tape and instead moves the head one position to the right. While for this simple Turing machine it is easy to spot that it will not halt on any input, in general it is not possible to "algorithmically" decide whether a given Turing machine will stop on a given input or not. In other words, function $f(\langle M \rangle, x)$ that takes as input the description of a Turing machine and a bit string and outputs 1 if M halts on input x and 0 otherwise is *uncomputable*. This problem is also know as the HALTING problem which is one of the classical problems of computability theory. Proving that $f(\langle M \rangle, x)$ is uncomputable can be done via a diagonalization argument similarly to our proof of existence of uncomputable functions (see Section 1.3.2). Since in cryptography we usually demand that a Turing machine halts on any input we do not further pursue this discussion.

When we restrict Turing machines to only those machines that halt on every input, then the resulting computational models of Turing machines and circuits are very similar as the following theorem shows.

Theorem 1.12 (Turing Machines and Circuits). *The following statements hold for Turing machines that halt within a finite number of steps on any input.*

1. *For every deterministic (resp. probabilistic) Turing machine* M *there exists a deterministic (resp. probabilistic) circuit family* C := $(C_\lambda)_{\lambda \in \mathbb{N}}$ *that implements Turing machine* M. *That is, for all* $\lambda \in \mathbb{N}$ *and all* $x \in \{0,1\}^\lambda$ *we have that* M(x) = C(x) *or in case the Turing machine and circuit family is probabilistic we have that the distributions* M(x) *and* C(x) *are identical.*

2. *For every uniform circuit family* C := $(C_\lambda)_{\lambda \in \mathbb{N}}$ *there exists a Turing machine* M *that implements* C.

3. *For every circuit family* C := $(C_\lambda)_{\lambda \in \mathbb{N}}$ *there exists a Turing machine* M *with advice* a = a(|x|) *that implements* C.

4. *The above relationships remain valid if we replace Turing machine and circuit family by* efficient *Turing machine and* efficient *circuit family. That is, every efficient Turing machine can be implemented by an efficient circuit family, every efficient and uniform circuit family can be implemented by an efficient Turing machine, and every efficient but possibly non-uniform circuit family can be implemented by an efficient Turing machine that takes advice. For the last part we have the additional restriction that the advice function* a = a(|x|) *is bounded by a polynomial, that is,* $|a(\lambda)| = \mathsf{poly}(\lambda)$.

5. *There exist functions that can be computed by a family of circuits but not by a Turing machine.*

We will not formally prove these claims here but will provide some intuition. In essence, statements 1 to 4 show that the difference between circuits and Turing machines is exactly the difference between uniformity (one program for all inputs) and non-uniformity (a different program for each input length). The last statement finally establishes that, as might be expected, non-uniform models are "more powerful" than uniform models. That is, there are so-called *uncomputable functions* that cannot be implemented by a (uniform) Turing machine but by a (non-uniform) circuit family.

Let us provide some intuition for the proof of Theorem 1.12. The first statement says that any Turing machine can be implemented by a circuit family. In order to construct a circuit for a Turing machine the idea is to consider a circuit that consists of "levels" where each level corresponds to one computational step of the Turing machine. As we restrict Turing machines to run in finitely many steps, we thus get a circuit consisting of finitely many levels. In the nth level the circuit encodes the *configuration* of the Turing machine on its nth step which corresponds to the current tape, the position of the head, and its current state. The circuit levels are then "connected" by computations that "simulate" the possible actions of the Turing machine.

While for Turing machines it is quite common that the runtime of the machine may differ on two inputs x_1 and x_2 of the same length (i.e., $|x_1| = |x_2|$), we have that the size of a circuit—the circuit equivalence to the runtime of Turing machines—is, of course, fixed for all inputs. This is also reflected in the above recipe to construct a circuit for a Turing machine: here the circuit for inputs of size λ contains one level for every possible step of the Turing machine and thus $\mathsf{time}(\lambda)$ many levels.

For item 2 note that this follows from the definition of a *uniform circuit family*. It is easy to see that a Turing machine can simulate the execution of a fixed circuit C_λ (not a circuit family). By definition of a uniform circuit we know that there exists a Turing machine T that on input λ generates the description of circuit C_λ. Thus, our Turing machine first checks the length of its input x, then runs T on $|x|$ to get the description of C_λ, and finally simulates the execution of C_λ on input x.

For item 3 we encode the description of circuit C_λ as advice on inputs of length λ and can then use the previous strategy to simulate the circuit computation.

Point 4 states that the above remain valid even if we restrict ourselves to the class of *efficient* Turing machines and circuit families. Let us provide some intuition as to why a circuit constructed from a Turing machine by the above blueprint is of polynomial size in case the Turing machine is efficient. We must show that there is some polynomial that bounds size_C for the constructed circuit family C. We have already stated that the circuit C_λ consists of $\mathsf{time}(\lambda)$ many levels where $\mathsf{time}(\lambda)$ is bounded by a polynomial by definition of the efficiency of the Turing machine. Each of the levels encodes a possible Turing machine configuration which consists of the Turing machine's tape, its state, and its head position. Since the Turing machine is efficient, the number of cells it can access is bounded by a polynomial. Furthermore, the number of possible states the Turing machine can be in is constant. We can encode such a configuration by a bit string, and a bit string within a circuit can be simply thought of as a number of wires whose values together make up the bit string. It follows that each level consists of a polynomially bounded number of wires. What remains is the logic necessary to transform one configuration to the next, i.e., the logic of how the circuit goes from one level to the next. Again, the size of this logic can be bounded by a polynomial. For this consider, for example, a wire corresponding to the contents of a cell of the Turing machine's working tape. The logic would now check whether the head position corresponds to that cell and if so capture the outcome of the writing operation of the Turing machine given the cell's content (the value of the wire) and the state of the Turing machine. This building block is of constant size. The same is true for the building blocks for wires encoding the state and head position. All in all, we end up with a huge circuit which however is polynomially bounded: we have a polynomially bounded number of levels p_1, each consisting of a polynomially bounded number of wires p_2, and each wire is connected to a constant size "transformation subcircuit" to transform the wire's value from one level to the next. Thus, if c is the maximum size of a transformation subcircuit then the overall number of gates is upper bounded by $c \cdot \mathsf{p}_1(\lambda) \cdot \mathsf{p}_2(\lambda)$.

Finally, point 5 states that the non-uniformity property of circuit families allows to capture certain uncomputable functions. Indeed, we have already seen an uncomputable function for which this is the case. Let us recall the uncomputable function from Section 1.3.2.

$$f(x) = \begin{cases} 0 & \text{given that } x = 1^\lambda \text{ and the } \lambda\text{th Turing machine } \mathsf{M}_\lambda \\ & \text{outputs 1 on input } 1^\lambda \\ 1 & \text{otherwise} \end{cases}$$

Function f outputs 0 if x is the unary representation of $\lambda \in \mathbb{N}$ (i.e., $x = 1^\lambda$) and the λth Turing machine M_λ (for some fixed encoding) outputs 1 on input 1^λ. In Section 1.3.2 we showed that this function is uncomputable. However, there exists an efficient (non-uniform) circuit family that computes f: Circuit C_λ simply has value $f(1^\lambda)$ hardcoded and outputs $f(1^\lambda)$ in case the input matches 1^λ and 1 otherwise.

Church–Turing and circuits. Recall the Church–Turing Thesis, which states that any effectively computable function can be computed by a Turing machine. What we have just seen is that there are functions that can be implemented by a circuit family but not by a Turing machine. So, does that contradict the Church–Turing Thesis?

The answer is no, it does not contradict the Church–Turing Thesis because function f is not *effectively computable*. For this also note how we implemented the function as a circuit family. The circuits do not have a "mechanism" that somehow "computes" function f but instead simply have the function value for each input length hardcoded. Furthermore, the function was especially designed to allow for this as by definition of f there is exactly one "interesting function value" per input length.

1.3.3.2 Non-uniformity in Cryptography

You may well ask: why this lengthy discussion on circuits given that we have said that we will model algorithms as Turing machines anyway. The reason is that we may want to model adversaries as circuits from time to time given that circuit adversaries are "stronger" than Turing machine adversaries. And, showing that a very strong adversary cannot break a cryptographic scheme is, naturally, a more reassuring result than showing that a more restricted adversary cannot break some scheme.

As seen in the previous discussion, non-uniformity can provide an edge in that it allows to use some "precomputed" values within the computation.

Since the precomputed values may only depend on the input size (and not on the actual input) this advantage is often small, but as we have seen it may allow to compute otherwise uncomputable functions. Indeed, for certain properties non-uniformity poses a difficulty. Consider the property of collision resistance. We will study collision resistance in detail in Chapter 4 and here only provide some intuition. Intuitively, we call a function H collision resistant if it is difficult to find two distinct inputs $m \neq m'$ such that $H(m) = H(m')$. Now consider that function H is compressing, that is, its output length is shorter than its input length. Then collisions must necessarily exist, simply because there are more inputs than outputs. While we may be able to show that such collisions are "hard to find" for a uniform adversary, a non-uniform adversary can rely on precomputation and simply have collisions hardcoded for each security parameter as part of its advice. Thus, such a non-uniform adversary can easily "find" collisions. Of course, as in the discussion above, "finding" is not really the right word since the non-uniform adversary does not actually do anything clever, but just outputs a precomputed value.

In order to strengthen adversaries and to provide the strongest possible security guarantees, cryptographers often model the adversary as a family of circuits rather than as a Turing machine. This means that when considering the security of a cryptographic scheme we not only ask "can we find an adversary" but instead "is there an adversary assuming we have infinite preprocessing power at our disposal." The way this is usually done and which is also the style we follow in this book is to give *security reductions*. In order to show that a scheme Π is secure we show that there exists a reduction R such that for any (possibly non-uniform) adversary $\mathcal{A}$ against scheme Π reduction $R^{\mathcal{A}}$ which can make use of adversary $\mathcal{A}$ (usually in a black-box manner) can break a well-studied problem that is assumed to be hard. Thus, if we believe the problem to be hard then $\mathcal{A}$ cannot exist, as reduction R in combination with adversary $\mathcal{A}$ would solve the problem.

Such a reductionist argument is usually indifferent to the specific workings of adversary $\mathcal{A}$ as we usually consider black-box reductions that only call the adversary on its specified interface and which are independent of the inner workings of the adversary. Thus, whether or not the adversary is uniform or non-uniform is not important to the reduction.

For reductions, on the other hand, we usually aim to give them in the uniform rather than the non-uniform model. While on the theoretical side, non-uniform reductions make a similar claim "if there exists an adversary then there exists a solution to solve some hard problem," the conclusion may, however, be only theoretical since we cannot construct it: the precomputation needed may simply be too much. Even worse, it could be the case that the precomputation needed for the adversary against the scheme in question is much less than the precomputation needed to construct the reduction even with access to the adversary, thus questioning the interpretation of the conclusion of the result. But, non-uniform reductions even have one additional subtlety to consider, especially when arguing actual security bounds for practical schemes.

If we consider the reduction in the non-uniform model we cannot argue with bounds on the underlying security target in the uniform model but instead must consider also non-uniform bounds there. These may, however, be a lot lower than the best known bounds against uniform adversaries, which can cause the resulting bounds of the reduction to be of little value in practice.

As an example, let us consider pseudorandom functions, which we will study in detail in Chapter 3. Intuitively, a pseudorandom function F is a keyed function that has the property that no adversary can distinguish getting oracle access to the function with a randomly chosen (and hidden) key or whether to get access to a completely random function. If we consider keys to be bit strings of length kl then there are 2^{kl} different keys and we expect a uniform adversary to take roughly 2^{kl} operations in order to distinguish a random function from the pseudorandom function with decent probability. However, with the right precomputation it can be shown that a non-uniform adversary may, indeed, be a lot faster and get reasonable distinguishing advantage with only $2^{kl/2}$ steps. Consequently, the assumed security bound for a uniform adversary of 2^{kl} shrinks to only $2^{kl/2}$ for non-uniform adversaries. Thus, just by choosing a non-uniform reduction we introduce a loss of $2^{kl/2}$, which may defeat the practical implications of the result.

Remark 1.13. All reductions presented in this book are in the uniform model of computation.

1.3.4 Writing Algorithms

If you have never written a Turing machine algorithm, then now is a good time to consider Exercise 1.3.

While writing algorithms in Turing machine notation may be a good exercise, extracting the essence of a Turing machine algorithm is cumbersome and difficult since the notation is too detailed. Instead of Turing machine notation we write algorithms in the form of pseudocode, and following is a pseudocode representation of a palindrome checker:

isPalindrome(w)
_____

1 :   **for** $i = 1 .. \lfloor |w|/2 \rfloor$ **do**

2 :   **if** $w[i] \neq w[|w| + 1 - i]$ **then**

3 :   **return** false

4 :   **return** true

Pseudocode that we encounter will usually not be much more complicated than the above example, that is, we restrict ourselves to simple control structures such as **for**-loops and **if**-conditions and basic mathematical notation. Blocks are identified by indention, that is, the block corresponding to the **for**-loop in the above example comprises lines 2 and 3, while the block corresponding to the **if**-expression in line 2 consists of only line 3.

In the example we consecutively check for the characters in the given word whether they match the corresponding character when reading the word backwards. Here **for** $i = 1..\lfloor|w|/2\rfloor$ **do** is to be understood as: assign to i each element of the right-hand side expression in turn and execute the corresponding block. That is, we assign $i \leftarrow 1$ and check whether $w[1] = w[|w|]$, i.e., whether the first character matches the last character. If so we continue with the **for**-loop, assign $i \leftarrow 2$ and check the second against the second last character. We repeat this for the first half of the characters. If one of the checks fails, we stop the execution of the loop and return false as result (line 3). If all checks succeed the algorithm returns true (line 4) indicating that the word is indeed a palindrome. Note that for the palindrome "BOB" the **for**-loop in the above algorithm is only executed for $i = 1$ since $\lfloor\frac{3}{2}\rfloor = 1$.

1.3.5 The Security Parameter

Now that we have a formalization of algorithms we can return to our definition of a symmetric encryption scheme (Definition 1.1 on page 9). Since the definition was quite some pages ago, best go back and reread it.

Definition 1.1 captures that a symmetric encryption scheme consists of three efficient algorithms (polynomial-time Turing machines) for key generation, encryption, and decryption. The key generation algorithm and encryption algorithm are probabilistic, that is, they may make use of random choices during the computation. The decryption algorithm, on the other hand, is deterministic and does not have any random coins.

All algorithms take as an additional parameter a so-called *security parameter* 1^λ that we have not yet explained. Its role is best understood with an example. For this let us formalize a very weak security property. Note that Definition 1.1 does not speak of security. The only property that it defines is *correctness*, meaning that decryption should always be able to recover the correct plaintext given the correct key.

The weak security property that we want to formalize next should give the following guarantee:

> *An adversary that intercepts a ciphertext that was generated with a random key and for a random plaintext should not be able to retrieve the plaintext.*

The way we are going to formalize this is via a *security experiment* which creates an environment for an adversary to test whether the adversary can *break the security of the scheme.* The experiment consists of the following steps:

1. A random key k is generated.
2. A random message m is generated.
3. Message m is encrypted with key k to get ciphertext c.
4. The adversary is given ciphertext c and outputs a guess m' for message m.
5. If the adversary's guess is correct, then we say that the adversary *wins*.

We often refer to such experiments in which an adversary "plays" against a cryptosystem as a *game*. The party *running* the steps outside of the adversary is then called the *challenger*, that is, in the above example the challenger generates key k, message m, and ciphertext c and decides whether or not the adversary wins by checking whether the adversary's guess m' matches the correct plaintext message m.

Can we construct an encryption scheme such that no adversary exists that can win the above game? The answer is no. As the winning condition (outputting a message m' that matches the random message m) can be guessed there is always a trivial adversary that does nothing clever but simply outputs a guess for message m. The probability that this trivial adversary wins the game can be easily computed if we know the length of message m. Consider the case that we have single-bit messages. Then the adversary that outputs a random bit as its guess for message m will win with probability $\frac{1}{2}$. If, however, we consider 10-bit messages the winning probability of the trivial adversary is already down to $1/2^{10}$.

Similarly, the length of the key plays a crucial role in the analysis of adversaries. Consider the case that the key is only a single bit long. Then there exists the slightly more advanced adversary that does the following. It guesses a random key k' $\leftarrow\!\!\!\$ \{0, 1\}$ of length one bit. Then it attempts to decrypt the ciphertext that it got as input with its key k' and returns the result as its guess for m. With probability $\frac{1}{2}$ its guess for the key was correct and thus due to the correctness property of the encryption scheme its guess for m is also correct with probability $\frac{1}{2}$. Again if we do not consider single-bit keys but, say, 10-bit keys, then the success probability of this second adversary also goes down to $1/2^{10}$.

What the discussion of these two adversaries shows is that the lengths of the key and message are strongly tied to the success probability of an adversary. To capture this, we do not consider a single fixed input length but instead state our experiments relative to the so-called *security parameter* $\lambda \in \mathbb{N}$. Let us formalize the above experiment as an algorithm (i.e., we formalize the challenger) that is parameterized by the symmetric encryption scheme SE and the adversary $\mathcal{A}$. Furthermore, we state the lengths of the key and message relative to security parameter λ, which thus becomes an input parameter to the experiment. The result will be $\mathsf{Exp}_{\mathsf{SE},\mathcal{A}}(\lambda)$ defined as follows:

Experiment $\mathsf{Exp}_{\mathsf{SE},\mathcal{A}}(\lambda)$

---

1 : $k \leftarrow\!\!\$ \ \mathsf{SE.KGen}(1^{\lambda})$

2 : $m \leftarrow\!\!\$ \ \{0,1\}^{\lambda}$

3 : $c \leftarrow\!\!\$ \ \mathsf{SE.Enc}(1^{\lambda}, k, m)$

4 : $m' \leftarrow\!\!\$ \ \mathcal{A}(1^{\lambda}, c)$

5 :   **return** $m = m'$

By providing security parameter λ as an input to the experiment we indirectly specify the key length: The key generation algorithm $\mathsf{SE.KGen}$ is given the security parameter λ as input and can thus generate a key based on λ. (Note that the security parameter is passed in unary notation; we will shortly discuss the reason behind this choice.) The security parameter also directly specifies the choice of message length: we choose messages of length λ. This choice indeed is somewhat restricting, and we could have chosen the more liberal approach of specifying the message length as a function $\mathsf{ml} : \mathbb{N} \to \mathbb{N}$ of λ. In this case line 2 would change to

$$m \leftarrow\!\!\$ \ \{0,1\}^{\mathsf{ml}(\lambda)}.$$

Of course, we could have also chosen a maximum length and considered $\{0,1\}^{\leq \mathsf{ml}(\lambda)}$.

For a particular choice of λ we can regard the experiment $\mathsf{Exp}_{\mathsf{SE},\mathcal{A}}(\lambda)$ as a binary random variable which outputs either true or false. (We will often use 1 and 0 instead of true and false to indicate Boolean values.) The success probability of an adversary in our experiment can thus be described by

$$\Pr\left[\mathsf{Exp}_{\mathsf{SE},\mathcal{A}}(\lambda) = 1\right].$$

Note that we will usually simplify notation and write $\Pr\left[\mathsf{Exp}_{\mathsf{SE},\mathcal{A}}(\lambda)\right]$ to express the probability that the experiment outputs 1.

Remark 1.14. While we usually formalize security games or experiments in pseudocode (such as experiment $\mathsf{Exp}_{\mathsf{SE},\mathcal{A}}(\lambda)$ above), this setup can also be captured pictorially as in Figure 1.5.

Notation for Security-Parameter-Dependent Functions

As described above, in many cases the parameters of a scheme are given relative to the security parameter 1^{λ}, for example, we might restrict inputs to an encryption scheme to a specific length per security parameter, in which case this configuration might be captured by some function $\mathsf{il} : \mathbb{N} \to \mathbb{N}$. If we consider *efficient* adversaries then not only are the parameters of the cryptosystem depending on the security parameter but also the runtime of the

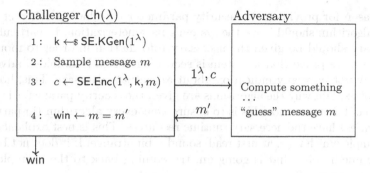

Fig. 1.5: A pictorial representation of the security experiment $\mathsf{Exp}_{\mathsf{SE},\mathcal{A}}(\lambda)$ for our weak security property of a symmetric encryption scheme.

adversary, which for a PPT adversary must be polynomially bounded in the security parameter. If p is a polynomial bound—we usually write polynomials such as $\mathsf{p} : \mathbb{N} \to \mathbb{N}$ in bold face without serifs to emphasize that these are functions and not scalars—for the runtime of an adversary $\mathcal{A}$, we might show that the adversary's success probability in breaking a cryptosystem is bounded from above by, say,

$$\frac{\mathsf{p}(\lambda)}{2^\lambda}.$$

At times such bounds as well as the steps to establish such bounds can be quite involved, in which case explicitly stating the dependency on the security parameter may complicate notation and perception of equations. We may thus drop the explicit dependence on the security parameter and might write

   "*Let* $\mathsf{q} := \mathsf{q}(\lambda)$ *be a polynomial* ..."

and subsequently simply refer to q instead of $\mathsf{q}(\lambda)$, in which case the above bound would be written as $\frac{\mathsf{q}}{2^\lambda}$. In this case any appearance of q should, however, still be understood as being dependent on the security parameter. Simply consider this as having fixed λ to a not further specified value or, alternatively, simply replace any occurrence of q with $\mathsf{q}(\lambda)$ in your mind.

1.3.6 Running Time of Adversaries

Our above experiment still holds one oddity: All algorithms that are called as part of the experiment (key generation in line 1, encryption in line 3, and the adversary in line 4) are given as an additional input the security parameter λ in unary notation. That is, they are given the security parameter as

$$1^\lambda = \underbrace{1111111 \ \dots \ 1111111}_{\lambda \text{ times}}.$$

The reason for providing the security parameter is to have a coherent setup: every algorithm should know the system's parameterization. In particular the adversary should be given the necessary information in order to mount an attack—if we prove that a system is secure against a blindfolded adversary this may not have any indication about an actual adversary. This, however, does not explain why the algorithms are given the security parameter in unary notation. The reason for this is to ensure that every algorithm (in particular adversaries) have the necessary runtime resources. This is best explained with an example which may, at first read, sound a bit strange. If it does not become clear immediately what is going on, try coming back to the example after finishing Chapter 2.

A fundamental building block of cryptography are one-way functions, which we formally introduce in Section 2.3. Informally, a function is called one-way if no *efficient* adversary can invert a random image. That is, for function F we consider the following setting: a random preimage x is chosen, image $y \leftarrow \mathsf{F}(x)$ is computed and given to the adversary whose task is to find a preimage x' such that $\mathsf{F}(x') = \mathsf{F}(x)$. Function F is called one-way if no *efficient* adversary can do so with "good probability."[5] As with encryption schemes, the success probability of the adversary (i.e., the inverter) is measured relative to the security parameter $\lambda \in \mathbb{N}$, which in the case of one-way functions defines the preimage space. In Figure 1.6 we present the one-wayness experiment once with the adversary being given the security parameter in binary and once in unary.

Remember that the efficiency of an algorithm is defined relative to the input length: An algorithm is called *efficient* if its runtime is bound by a polynomial in the input size. Let us consider the length function as a (flawed) candidate for a one-way function. The length function

$$\mathsf{F}(x) := \langle |x| \rangle_{\lceil \log |x| \rceil}$$

takes as input a bit string $x \in \{0,1\}^*$ and outputs length $|x|$ in binary notation. To write down length $|x| \in \mathbb{N}$ in binary notation we need $\lceil \log |x| \rceil$ many bits, where log denotes the logarithm to base 2 and $\lceil s \rceil$ denotes the round-up function, that is,

$$\lceil s \rceil := \min_{n \in \mathbb{N}} n \geq s.$$

In order for the length function not to be one-way there needs to be an efficient algorithm that can find preimages for random images. That is, on input $y \leftarrow \mathsf{F}(x)$ for a random x the algorithm must find a value x' such that $\mathsf{F}(x) = \mathsf{F}(x')$. However, for an image y under the length function we have that every preimage x' is of length y bits and thus of length $2^{|y|}$. This then means that an algorithm must run in time $2^{|y|}$ just to write down a preimage of y. If now image y would be the sole input to our inverter this would imply that it

---

[5] We will discuss in detail what we mean by "good probability" in Section 2.1

Experiment $\mathsf{Exp}_{\mathsf{F},\mathcal{A}}^{\mathrm{owf}}(\lambda)$

1 : $x \leftarrow\!\!\$ \{0,1\}^{\lambda}$

2 : $y \leftarrow \mathsf{F}(x)$

3 : $x^* \leftarrow\!\!\$ \mathcal{A}(\lambda, y)$ // instead of $\mathcal{A}(1^{\lambda}, y)$

4 : **return** $\mathsf{F}(x^*) = y$

Fig. 1.6: One-wayness experiment. In line 3 we are presenting two alternatives. The correct definition would give the security parameter λ in unary notation to adversary $\mathcal{A}$. The flawed definition, instead runs $x^* \leftarrow\!\!\$ \mathcal{A}(\lambda, y)$ and provides the security parameter in binary. In this case, we find that functions that are strongly compressing (such as the length function) would be one-way.

runs in exponential rather than in polynomial time (measured relative to its input) and thus would not qualify as an efficient algorithm.

In order to avoid definitions of security that put the scheme and adversary on an unequal footing—the one-way function in the above example was able to run in time polynomial in $|x| \gg |y|$ whereas the adversary was only given a runtime polynomial in $|y|$—the security parameter is given to all participating algorithms in unary notation. We stress again that if the security parameter is not explicitly given as input (for example, above we wrote $\mathsf{F}(x)$ instead of $\mathsf{F}(1^{\lambda}, x)$) that this is solely a simplification of notation and one should always imagine that it is implicitly part of the input.

With the introduction of the security parameter 1^{λ} we have covered the last undefined entity of Definition 1.1 and our definition of a symmetric encryption scheme should now, hopefully, be clear. As noted before, Definition 1.1 does not specify security properties but instead defines the overall semantics of what an encryption scheme should be: there should be a key, given this key one can encrypt messages, and if the resulting ciphertext is decrypted with the same key then the original message should be recovered. We are thus, so far, missing a discussion of actual security properties.

In Section 1.5 we will consider a branch of security properties referred to as *unconditionally secure* or *information-theoretically secure*. Such properties cover the strongest possible form of security as they are required to hold for any adversary: even unbounded adversaries that have no limit on their runtime or amount of memory used. From Chapter 2 onward and in particular in Chapter 5 we will discuss security properties referred to as *computationally secure*, which are weaker than the properties we discuss next, but in many cases much more practical. But now for something completely different.

1.4 Complexity Theory

Modern cryptography ultimately requires hard problems. For instance, for
a good encryption scheme it should be infeasible to recover the encrypted
message. The structure and relationship of (easy and hard) problems is the
topic of complexity theory. It is thus handy to consider some basic notions
from this area.

The central notion in complexity theory are languages. Such languages
identify elements x with similar properties, for example, the language may
contain exactly the palindromes. We work here over the binary alphabet $\{0,1\}$
such that elements are encoded as bit strings, and in general a language thus
defines a subset of all strings:

Definition 1.15 (Language). *A language $\mathscr{L}$ is a subset of $\{0,1\}^*$.*

Strings $x \in \mathscr{L}$ are called *yes-instances*, and strings $x \notin \mathscr{L}$ are called
no-instances. Trivial examples of languages are the empty language $\mathscr{L} = \{\}$
having no element, and the language $\mathscr{L} = \{0,1\}^*$ containing all strings from
$\{0,1\}^*$. A non-trivial language is $\mathscr{L}_w = \{x \in \{0,1\}^* \mid \mathrm{w}(x) \text{ is even}\}$ for $\mathrm{w}(x)$
counting the number of 1-bits in the string x. This language contains the
strings ε, 0, 00, 11, 000, 011, 101, 110, etc., but 111 with weight 3 is not in
the language.

1.4.1 Easy-to-Decide Languages

Languages immediately give rise to easy and hard problems: Given a string x,
decide if x is in the language or not. For the language $\mathscr{L}_w$ of strings with
even weight this is easy. One can simply parse the individual bits of x and
check if the number of 1's is even. More generally, one defines the class of
easy languages with respect to deterministic Turing machines as:

Definition 1.16 (Class P). *The class P contains exactly the languages $\mathscr{L}$
such that there exists a deterministic polynomial-time Turing machine M
such that for all $x \in \{0,1\}^*$ we have*

$$x \in \mathscr{L} \iff \mathsf{M}(x) = 1.$$

Note that the Turing machine M can, and in general will, depend on
the language $\mathscr{L}$. This Turing machine thus gives an efficient way to decide
membership in $\mathscr{L}$. Run M on input x, and only if M outputs 1 then x lies
in $\mathscr{L}$. Note that such an efficient Turing machine operates in the worst-case
scenario with respect to two dimensions: It decides correctly for all strings
$x \in \{0,1\}^*$, and its runtime is polynomial in $|x|$ for any $x \in \{0,1\}^*$.

If we expand our algorithm universe to also cover probabilistic Turing machines and allow the machine to err with some small probability (over its internal randomness) then we obtain the probabilistic analog to P:

Definition 1.17 (Class BPP). *The class* BPP *contains exactly the languages* $\mathscr{L}$ *such that there exists a probabilistic polynomial-time Turing machine* M *such that*

$$\Pr[M(x) = 1] \geq \tfrac{2}{3} \ \textit{for all } x \in \mathscr{L}.$$
$$\Pr[M(x) = 1] \leq \tfrac{1}{3} \ \textit{for all } x \notin \mathscr{L}.$$

The condition says that M errs with probability at most $\frac{1}{3}$ for any $x \in \{0,1\}^*$. Here the error constant $\frac{1}{3}$ can be replaced by almost any other value without changing the class BPP. For example, given a machine with error $\frac{1}{3}$ one can decrease the error by making majority decisions over polynomial repetitions to get an error of at most $2^{-\mathsf{poly}(|x|)}$. This means that the machine *almost* always decides correctly. The amplification technique by majority vote also works if we start with a machine which only decides correctly with probability at least $\frac{1}{2} + \frac{1}{\mathsf{poly}(|x|)}$, i.e., slightly better than guessing. Indeed, in the literature one also finds BPP defined with this looser requirement. This is equivalent to our definition.

While BPP appears to display some average-case behavior—after all, the machine may give a wrong answer occasionally—the requirement is still a worst-case definition. Namely, the machine also needs to run in polynomial time in $|x|$ for all x, and it must decide correctly for all x with some small error. The only average-case property refers to the fact that the machine decides correctly on the majority of uniformly chosen randomness.

Finally, instead of relating to (deterministic or probabilistic) Turing machines with polynomial runtime as the "efficient" class of algorithms, one can also use polynomial-size circuit families. This yields the class P/poly:

Definition 1.18 (Class P/poly). *The class* P/poly *contains exactly the languages* $\mathscr{L}$ *such that there exists a polynomial-size circuit family* $C = (C_\lambda)_{\lambda \in \mathbb{N}}$ *with* $C_\lambda : \{0,1\}^\lambda \to \{0,1\}$ *such that for all* $x \in \{0,1\}^*$ *we have*

$$x \in \mathscr{L} \iff C(x) = C_{|x|}(x) = 1.$$

The name P/poly of the class stems from the alternative view of circuits as Turing machines which take a short, polynomial advice as additional input (cf. Theorem 1.12). We note that one could also define the class BPP/poly of languages recognized by probabilistic polynomial-size circuit families. But it turns out that this class is identical to P/poly.

We give the following relationship of the classes without a proof:

Theorem 1.19. *We have* P $\subseteq$ BPP $\subsetneq$ P/poly, *where the latter inclusion is strict.*

The inclusion P $\subseteq$ BPP is trivial when viewing a probabilistic Turing machine which forgoes using randomness as a deterministic one. Whether or not this inclusion is strict is currently unknown. In Section 9.5.1 we will discuss that in the presence of a random oracle the two classes are identical. The inclusion BPP $\subsetneq$ P/poly is shown by fixing a suitable random string as uniform advice. Theorem 1.12 presented a function f which is not computable by a (probabilistic) Turing machine but easy for circuit families. The family is of polynomial size such that the proper inclusion of BPP in P/poly follows from the fact that there are uncomputable functions in P/poly.

1.4.2 Easy-to-Verify Languages

No matter which machine model one uses to define easy languages, deterministic or probabilistic Turing machines or circuit families, any reasonably secure cryptographic primitive cannot be linked to such easy-to-decide languages, because then breaking the primitive would be easy. Interestingly, while cryptography must therefore lie outside of classes like P, very often they are also bounded in terms of complexity from above. Namely, whereas recovering encrypted messages should be hard for outsiders, this task is very easy if one has the secret key and can simply decrypt. Put differently, the problem becomes easy when having some useful extra information. Similar properties hold for other cryptographic primitives besides encryption. In terms of complexity theory these are easy-to-verify problems.

Complexity theory now specifies the class of languages which are easy with some extra help, usually called the *witness*, as the class NP:

Definition 1.20 (Class NP). *The class* NP *contains exactly the languages* $\mathscr{L}$ *such that there exists a deterministic polynomial-time Turing machine* M *and a polynomial* p $: \mathbb{N} \to \mathbb{N}$ *such that for all* $x \in \{0,1\}^*$ *we have*

$$x \in \mathscr{L} \iff \exists w \in \{0,1\}^{\leq \mathsf{p}(|x|)} : \mathsf{M}(x,w) = 1.$$

The name NP comes from the equivalent definition of the class via the notion of non-deterministic polynomial-time Turing machines which decide in polynomial time given only x. Here, non-deterministic polynomial time refers to another model of Turing machine execution which non-deterministically performs several computations simultaneously. The witness-based approach is usually more convenient in the cryptographic setting. It is sometimes also helpful to think in terms of an NP-relation $\mathscr{R}$ to a language $\mathscr{L} \in$ NP and the underlying machine M and polynomial p, capturing the pairs of elements and witnesses:

$$\mathscr{R} = \left\{ (x, w) \,\middle|\, w \in \{0, 1\}^{\leq \mathsf{p}(|x|)} \land \mathsf{M}(x, w) = 1 \right\}.$$

Note that the relation depends on the specific Turing machine M and the polynomial p. A different machine usually yields a different relation. This is why one usually pursues the opposite direction and defines the language $\mathscr{L} = \{x \in \{0, 1\}^* \mid \exists w \in \{0, 1\}^* : (x, w) \in \mathscr{R}\}$ from such an NP-relation $\mathscr{R}$. But since the machine in question is often irrelevant, we use either approach when appropriate.

As an example of an NP-language consider a deterministic symmetric encryption algorithm SE.Enc allowing to encrypt messages $m \in \{0, 1\}^\lambda$ under keys $k \in \{0, 1\}^\lambda$. Define

$$\mathscr{L}_{\mathsf{SE.Enc}} = \left\{ (1^\lambda, C) \in \{0, 1\}^* \,\middle|\, \right.$$
$$\left. \exists m, k \in \{0, 1\}^\lambda : C = \mathsf{SE.Enc}(k, m) \land \mathsf{w}(m) \text{ even} \right\}$$

to consist of the ciphertexts which encapsulate a message of even weight. Then this language is not known to be in any of the easy classes P, BPP, or P/poly, because a good encryption scheme should hide any information about the encrypted message. But the language is in NP because the data m, k serves as a (polynomial-size) witness: Given m, k in addition to $(1^\lambda, C)$ one can check efficiently that $k, m \in \{0, 1\}^\lambda$, that they encrypt to C, and that the weight of m is even. This example also shows that witnesses may change with the relation, although the relations describe the same language: If decryption is errorless then the key k suffices as a witness, because one can use it to first recover the message m and then perform the above check.

Obviously, P $\subseteq$ NP. The converse is not known to be true, and it is in general believed that P $\neq$ NP. In fact, if P = NP was true then this would mean that deciding languages like $\mathscr{L}_{\mathsf{SE.Enc}}$ is easy, even without having knowledge about the secret key k. This would mean that the encryption scheme—and almost all other cryptographic primitives—cannot be secure. We show that in case P = NP we can not only decide the language easily, but also compute the witness efficiently. In terms of our language $\mathscr{L}_{\mathsf{SE.Enc}}$ this means that P = NP allows to recover a key and message which encrypt to C. This is shown in the following theorem:

Theorem 1.21. *Assume that* P = NP. *Then for any* NP-*relation* $\mathscr{R}$ *there exists a deterministic polynomial-time Turing machine* W *such that for all* $x \in \mathscr{L}$ *we have*

$$(x, \mathsf{W}(x)) \in \mathscr{R}.$$

In other words, for inputs in the language, machine W always finds a witness with respect to the relation $\mathscr{R}$ based on M and p.

Proof. Consider the prefix language $\mathscr{L}_{\mathrm{pre}}$ to $\mathscr{R}$, defined as

$$\mathscr{L}_{\mathrm{pre}} = \{(x, z) \mid \exists w \in \{0,1\}^* : (x, w) \in \mathscr{R} \wedge z \text{ is prefix of } w\},$$

where we efficiently encode pairs (x, z) as strings. This language contains strings $x \in \mathscr{L}$ for which a partial witness z has been found. It is clearly in NP because for any $x \in \mathscr{L}$ we can take a witness $w \in \{0,1\}^{\leq \mathsf{p}(|x|)}$ for x, which contains z as prefix. This witness serves also as a witness for $(x, z) \in \mathscr{L}_{\mathrm{pre}}$. Verifying the conditions of the language can be done in polynomial time because checking membership in $\mathscr{R}$ is easy and comparing z against w is easy, too.

Since we assume P = NP there exists a polynomial-time algorithm A such that $\mathsf{A}(x, z) = 1$ iff $(x, z) \in \mathscr{L}_{\mathrm{pre}}$, for any $x, z \in \{0,1\}^*$. We use this algorithm to find a witness w for any $x \in \mathscr{L}$. The algorithm W receives x as input and searches, bit by bit and starting with $z \leftarrow \varepsilon$, the next bit of a witness. This is done by checking if extending the current value z by 0 is in $\mathscr{L}_{\mathrm{pre}}$, and if not verifying the same for $z\|1$. These checks can be performed in polynomial time with the help of algorithm A for $\mathscr{L}_{\mathrm{pre}}$:

W(x)

---

1 : $z \leftarrow \varepsilon, \mathsf{cont} \leftarrow \mathsf{true}$

2 :   **while** cont **do**

3 :   **if** $\mathsf{A}(x, z\|0) = 1$ **then** $z \leftarrow z\|0$

4 :   **elseif** $\mathsf{A}(x, z\|1) = 1$ **then** $z \leftarrow z\|1$

5 :   **else** $\mathsf{cont} \leftarrow \mathsf{false}$

6 :   **return** z

Note that the algorithm first tries to expand the current value z with 0 and thus favors witnesses with leading 0-bits. In fact, it can be easily modified to always find the lexicographically smallest witness by stopping the search if z is already a witness. It runs in polynomial time because for $x \in \mathscr{L}$ witnesses have size at most $\mathsf{p}(|x|)$, such that the algorithm terminates after at most $\mathsf{p}(|x|)$ iterations. In each iteration it needs to make at most two calls to A, which itself runs in polynomial time (in the size of the encoding of (x, z), but which in turn is polynomial in $|x|$). For $x \notin \mathscr{L}$ there does not exist a witness at all, such that in the first iteration both calls to A return 0. Algorithm W hence immediately stops with output ε in this case.   □

Concerning the other easy-to-decide complexity classes, it is not known if BPP $\subseteq$ NP, neither is it currently known if NP $\subseteq$ BPP (although the latter is conjectured to be not the case). Certainly P/poly $\not\subseteq$ NP because the class P/poly contains undecidable languages. It is conjectured that NP $\not\subseteq$ P/poly.

$$\text{message } m: \quad \dots, 0, 0, 0, 1, 1, \boxed{1}, 0, 0, 1, 1, 0, 1, 1, \dots$$

$$\oplus$$

$$\text{key } \mathsf{k}: \quad \dots, 0, 1, 1, 1, 1, \boxed{0}, 0, 1, 0, 0, 0, 1, 0, \dots$$

$$\text{ciphertext } c: \quad \dots, 0, 1, 1, 0, 0, \boxed{1}, 0, 1, 1, 1, 0, 0, 1, \dots$$

Fig. 1.7: A stream cipher in action. A possibly endless stream of key bits is used to encrypt a possibly endless stream of message bits. Note that encryption and decryption are identical operations: the key stream is XORed with the message (resp. ciphertext) stream.

1.5 Information-Theoretic Security

In 1917 Gilbert Vernam invented the stream cipher, a form of encryption that produces a ciphertext by bitwise computation: each bit of the plaintext message is combined with a bit from the key to produce a ciphertext bit. Usually, the ciphertext is computed as the exclusive or (XOR) of the two bits, and thus we can write the encryption operation as

$$\mathsf{Enc}(\mathsf{k}, m) = \mathsf{k} \oplus m,$$

assuming that the key k and message m have the same length. We can decrypt a ciphertext by once more performing the XOR operation, now on the ciphertext and key

$$\mathsf{Dec}(\mathsf{k}, c) = \mathsf{k} \oplus c.$$

The term *stream cipher* stems from the idea that both message and key are assumed to be a long and possibly endless stream of characters (or bits) which are processed character by character (or bit by bit) as they come in. Figure 1.7 presents a schematic of the idea.

Vernam patented his invention in 1919. In his patent he describes a machine that produces a ciphertext by combining a pre-chosen random key with a message via the XOR operation. Once every character—Vernam's machine used the Baudot code[6] to encode characters—of the key was used up, the key was simply reused. Shortly after Vernam had demonstrated his machine to the navy, it was Joseph Mauborgne, back then a captain in the US Army Signal Corps, who realized that only if the key was chosen randomly and such that it never repeats would the resulting code be unbreakable. When operated in this fashion, that is, when a key is chosen at random and used only once, the encryption scheme is also referred to as a *one-time pad*.

---

[6] The Baudot code is an encoding for characters for use in telegraphy. Think ancestor to ASCII.

While it was suspected that the one-time pad was indeed unbreakable it took until 1949 for a sound mathematical proof to be published (this is not too surprising as there was no formal definition of what *unbreakable* should mean). With his ground-breaking paper *Communication Theory of Secrecy Systems* Claude Shannon provided a rigorous definition of what it means for an encryption scheme to be *unbreakable* and showed not only that the one-time pad is indeed unbreakable but also that it is optimal. In this section we are going to study the one-time pad and introduce some of Shannon's ideas. In particular, we will see several (equivalent) security definitions for the one-time pad showing that a message that was encrypted with a random one-time key is unconditionally secure. Here *secure* means that the ciphertext leaks no information except for the length of the message and *unconditionally* means that this holds for every adversary independent of its resources. The framework in which we are going to formulate these concepts will be probability theory, and in the next section we will define the basic concepts that we will use.

1.5.1 Basic Probability Theory

To study the security of an encryption scheme such as the one-time pad in the information-theoretic setting we treat message, key, and the resulting ciphertext as random variables. In order to define a random variable we first need the concept of a *probability distribution* (or simply *distribution*). We note that we only define the concepts necessary to understand the later chapters and thus aim at simplicity rather than full generality. In particular, we only consider finite settings here but emphasize that all statements transfer to the (infinite but) countable cases.

Definition 1.22 (Probability Distribution). *Let $S = \{s_1, \ldots, s_i, \ldots, s_n\}$ be a finite set. We call $\mathbb{P}_S = \{p_1, \ldots, p_i, \ldots, p_n\}$ a* probability distribution *on S if $|S| = |\mathbb{P}_S|$, $p_i \geq 0$ for all $i \in [n]$ and $\sum_{i=1}^{n} p_i = 1$.*

We associate with each element $s_i \in S$ the probability p_i denoted by $\Pr[s_i]$. We call a subset $E \subseteq S$ an event *and denote by $\Pr[E]$ its probability defined by*

$$\Pr[E] = \sum_{s \in E} \Pr[s].$$

As an example of a distribution consider the *uniform distribution* over some set S which assigns to each element in S the same probability:

$$\forall s \in S : \Pr[s] := \frac{1}{|S|}.$$

With probability distributions we can now define random variables.

Definition 1.23 (Random Variable). *A random variable X consists of a finite set $\mathcal{X} = \{x_1, \ldots, x_i, \ldots, x_n\}$ together with an associated probability distribution $\mathbb{P}_X = \{p_1, \ldots, p_i, \ldots, p_n\}$. The probability that random variable X takes on value x_i is p_i and is denoted by $\Pr[X = x_i]$.*

Remark 1.24. We will often use the term *distribution* to mean both the distribution and a random variable with the associated distribution. For example, we may consider the uniform distribution U_n over bit strings in $\{0, 1\}^n$ where we refer to U_n both as the distribution as well as a random variable that is uniformly distributed over strings $\{0, 1\}^n$.

Remark 1.25. A more general definition of a random variable is to define it as a measurable function from a set of outcomes of some random experiment to some measurable space. For our purposes the simpler definition above suffices, and hence we do not distinguish between the outcome of a random experiment and the subsequent value the random variable takes on. We also refer to set $\mathcal{X}$ that underlies our random variables as *possible outcomes* of the random variable.

We sometimes abbreviate notation and write $\Pr[x_i]$ to denote the probability that X takes on value x_i, that is, $\Pr[X = x_i]$. We simply write $\Pr[X]$ to denote $\Pr[X = x]$ for an arbitrary but fixed value x. The exception to this rule is when random variable X is a binary random variable, that is, its image is $\{0, 1\}$. In this case we write $\Pr[X]$ to denote the probability that random variable X takes on value 1, that is, in this case $\Pr[X] := \Pr[X = 1]$. This, for example, is often the case if we consider a security game such as the one-wayness game (see Figure 1.6). Here we can treat $\mathsf{Exp}_{\mathsf{F},\mathcal{A}}^{\mathsf{owf}}(\lambda)$ as a binary random variable and write

$$\Pr\left[\mathsf{Exp}_{\mathsf{F},\mathcal{A}}^{\mathsf{owf}}(\lambda)\right]$$

to denote the success probability of the adversary, i.e., the probability that the game returns 1.

Expectation. An important characterization of a random variable is its *expected value*, the value it takes "on average" over an arbitrarily large number of realizations.

Definition 1.26 (Expectation). *Let X be a random variable with outcomes $\mathcal{X} = \{x_1, \ldots, x_i, \ldots, x_n\}$ and associated probability distribution $\mathbb{P}_X = \{p_1, \ldots, p_i, \ldots, p_n\}$. Then we define the expectation (or expected value) of X as*

$$\mathbb{E}[X] := \sum_{i=1}^{n} x_i p_i.$$

Joint probability. Given two or more random variables we can consider their *joint probability*.

> **Definition 1.27** (Joint Probability). *Let X and Y be two random variables. Then the joint probability $\Pr[X = x, Y = y]$ denotes the probability that X takes on value x and Y takes on value y.*

Instead of using commas we may also use Boolean notation and write $\Pr[X = x \wedge Y = y]$ to denote a joint probability. When considering two events A and B then the probability $\Pr[A \cap B]$ is also called the *joint probability* of events A and B.

The union bound. The probability that $X = x$ **or** $Y = y$ is given by

$$\Pr[X \vee Y] = \Pr[X] + \Pr[Y] - \Pr[X, Y].$$

Similarly for two events E_1 and E_2 we have that

$$\begin{aligned} \Pr[E_1 \cup E_2] &= \Pr[E_1] + \Pr[E_2] - \Pr[E_1 \cap E_2] \\ &\leq \Pr[E_1] + \Pr[E_2]. \end{aligned} \tag{1.1}$$

The above inequality (1.1) is called the *union bound*, which we will regularly make use of. Note that the union bound generalizes to n events, that is,

$$\Pr\left[\bigcup_{i=1}^{n} E_i\right] \leq \sum_{i=1}^{n} \Pr[E_i].$$

Marginal probability. Via summation we can obtain the *marginal probability* $\Pr[X = x]$ from joint probabilities $\Pr[X, Y]$:

$$\Pr[X = x] = \sum_{y \in \mathcal{Y}} \Pr[X = x, Y = y].$$

Conditional probabilities. Given two or more random variables we may also consider the *conditional probability* of one given the outcome of the other.

> **Definition 1.28** (Conditional Probability). *Let X and Y be two random variables. Then the conditional probability $\Pr[X = x \mid Y = y]$ denotes the probability that X takes on value x given that Y takes on value y.*

The conditional probability of two random variables is related to their joint probability via the so-called *product rule*

$$\Pr[X = x, Y = y] = \Pr[X = x \mid Y = y] \cdot \Pr[Y = y].$$

Similarly by exchanging the roles of X and Y (and in briefer notation)

$$\Pr[x, y] = \Pr[y \mid x] \cdot \Pr[x].$$

Note that the conditional probability $\Pr[x \mid y]$ is undefined in case $\Pr[y] = 0$.

Law of total probability. By combining marginalization and conditional probabilities we derive the *law of total probability*

$$\Pr[X] = \sum_{y \in \mathcal{Y}} \Pr[X \mid Y = y] \cdot \Pr[Y = y].$$

Bayes' Theorem. From the product rule we can directly derive *Bayes' Theorem*, which relates the conditional probabilities $\Pr[x \mid y]$ and $\Pr[y \mid x]$.

Theorem 1.29. *Let X and Y be two random variables. Assuming that $\Pr[y] > 0$ then*

$$\Pr[x \mid y] = \frac{\Pr[y \mid x] \cdot \Pr[x]}{\Pr[y]}.$$

Independence. Finally, we need to consider the concept of independence of events and random variables.

Definition 1.30. *Two events A and B are called* independent *if, and only if,*

$$\Pr[A \cap B] = \Pr[A] \cdot \Pr[B].$$

Two random variables X and Y are called independent *if for all pairs of events $A \subseteq \mathcal{X}$ and $B \subseteq \mathcal{Y}$, A and B are independent.*

Equivalently we can define independence via conditional probabilities: Two random variables X and Y are independent if and only if

$$\Pr[x \mid y] = \Pr[x]$$

for all $x \in \mathcal{X}$ and $y \in \mathcal{Y}$. Similarly, the two variables are independent if and only if

$$\Pr[x, y] = \Pr[x] \cdot \Pr[y]$$

for all $x \in \mathcal{X}$ and $y \in \mathcal{Y}$.

1.5.2 Perfect Secrecy

We now have the necessary concepts to properly study the one-time pad. The one-time pad is said to be *unbreakable* or to have the *perfect secrecy* property. With the help of conditional probabilities we can formalize what this means. Let M denote a random variable describing the choice of message to be encrypted. Let K be the random variable describing the distribution $\mathbb{K}$ of the key, which is determined by the key generation algorithm SE.KGen of the encryption scheme. Let C be a random variable describing the ciphertext. Note that the ciphertext is determined by the distributions for M and K and possibly further randomness if encryption is probabilistic. The reader may for now think of encryption being deterministic, such that $C := \mathsf{SE.Enc}(K, M)$ for the symmetric encryption scheme.

Now, what we want from a perfect system is that the ciphertext does not provide any information as to the content of the message, unless one has the key of course, in which case one can decrypt the ciphertext to the message. In other words, whether or not an adversary knows the ciphertext c should make no difference, assuming that it lacks knowledge of the key. This we can formalize via conditional probabilities and thus say that, if for an encryption scheme we have that

$$\Pr[M] = \Pr[M \mid C = c],$$

then this encryption scheme enjoys *perfect secrecy*. This should hold no matter how the message is chosen such that we quantify over all message distributions in the formal definition:

Definition 1.31 (Perfect Secrecy). *Let* $\mathsf{SE} = (\mathsf{SE.KGen}, \mathsf{SE.Enc}, \mathsf{SE.Dec})$ *be a symmetric encryption scheme and* $\mathsf{il} : \mathbb{N} \to \mathbb{N}$ *be a function describing the message length for security parameter* λ. *If for every security parameter* $\lambda \in \mathbb{N}$, *every probability distribution* $\mathbb{M}$ *over* $\{0,1\}^{\mathsf{il}(\lambda)}$, *every message* $m \in \{0,1\}^{\mathsf{il}(\lambda)}$, *and every ciphertext* $c \in \{0,1\}^*$ *with* $\Pr[c] > 0$ *we have that*

$$\Pr[M = m] = \Pr[M = m \mid C = c],$$

then we say that SE *is* perfectly secret.

By applying the definition of independence we get the following useful characterization of perfect secrecy:

Lemma 1.32. *An encryption scheme is* perfectly secret *if random variables* M *and* C *describing the choice of message and corresponding ciphertext are independent.*

Note that in the above definition we needed to fix the input length with respect to the security parameter. This is because the ciphertext will necessarily leak the (maximum) length of the encrypted message. Furthermore, as we will see shortly, the key length needs to be chosen in accordance to the message length if one wants to obtain a perfectly secret symmetric encryption scheme.

Remark 1.33. The definition of perfect secrecy only considers a single encryption. We note that this is crucial. That is, if we considered a generalized version where several messages are encrypted with the same key, then it can be shown that no encryption scheme can meet the definition.

1.5.2.1 The One-Time Pad Is Perfectly Secret

Let us move on to show that the one-time pad indeed enjoys the property of being perfectly secret. For completeness let us first give a proper definition of the one-time pad encryption scheme.

Construction 1.34 (One-Time Pad). *The* one-time pad *encryption scheme* OTP *is a symmetric encryption scheme with algorithms for key generation, encryption, and decryption defined as follows:*

OTP.KGen(1^λ)	OTP.Enc(k, m)	OTP.Dec(k, c)
$k \leftarrow\!\!\$\ \{0,1\}^\lambda$	$c \leftarrow m \oplus k$	$m \leftarrow c \oplus k$
return k	**return** c	**return** m

For security parameter $\lambda \in \mathbb{N}$ it holds that key space, message space, and ciphertext space are
$$\mathcal{K} = \mathcal{M} = \mathcal{C} = \{0,1\}^\lambda.$$

We next show that the one-time pad is perfectly secure.

Theorem 1.35. *The one-time pad is* perfectly secret.

Proof. Fix a security parameter $\lambda \in \mathbb{N}$ and a ciphertext $c \in \{0,1\}^\lambda$. Then for each possible choice of message $m \in \{0,1\}^\lambda$ there exists exactly one key $k \in \{0,1\}^\lambda$ such that
$$c = m \oplus k.$$
We thus have that

$$\Pr[C = c \mid M = m] = \Pr[K = m \oplus c] = \frac{1}{2^\lambda}. \tag{1.2}$$

By using marginalization and the product rule we get that

$$\Pr[C = c] = \sum_{m \in \{0,1\}^\lambda} \Pr[C = c, M = m]$$
$$= \sum_{m \in \{0,1\}^\lambda} \Pr[C = c \mid M = m] \cdot \Pr[M = m].$$

Now noting that Equation (1.2) holds for all choices of m we can move $\Pr[C = c \mid M = m]$ as a factor out of the summation to obtain

$$= \frac{1}{2^\lambda} \sum_{m \in \{0,1\}^\lambda} \Pr[M = m] = \frac{1}{2^\lambda}.$$

It follows that

$$\Pr[C = c \mid M = m] = \Pr[C = c]$$

for all c and all m and thus that M and C are independent. The proof follows with Lemma 1.32.   □

1.5.3 Shannon's Theorem

Shannon not only showed that the one-time pad achieves perfect secrecy but also proved it to be optimal. That is, he showed that an encryption scheme can only achieve perfect secrecy if the key space is at least as large as the message space. In other words the (one-time) keys must be at least as long as the message in order to achieve a truly unbreakable system. The following theorem also holds for probabilistic encryption processes:

> **Theorem 1.36.** *If a (probabilistic) encryption scheme is perfectly secret then we have that* $|\mathcal{K}| \geq |\mathcal{M}|$.

One can further show that if for an encryption scheme we have that $|\mathcal{M}| = |\mathcal{K}| = |\mathcal{C}|$ then the scheme is perfectly secure if and only if the scheme picks a key uniformly at random and if for every pair of message m and ciphertext c there exists exactly one key k such that $c = \mathsf{Enc}(\mathsf{k}, m)$. Note that this is exactly the situation we have with the one-time pad. We leave the proof as Exercise 1.10 and go on to prove Theorem 1.36.

Theorem 1.36. Assume that $|\mathcal{K}| < |\mathcal{M}|$. Fix a ciphertext $c \in \mathcal{C}$ which is hit by encryption with non-zero probability (i.e., $\Pr[C = c] > 0$) and let M_c denote the set of messages that c can be decrypted to, that is,

$$M_c := \{m \in \mathcal{M} : \exists \mathsf{k} \in \mathcal{K} \text{ such that } m = \mathsf{Dec}(\mathsf{k}, c)\}.$$

As the decryption operation is deterministic—recall that decryption is also deterministic in case we consider a probabilistic encryption scheme—we have that $|M_c| \leq |\mathcal{K}| < |\mathcal{M}|$. But then there must exist a message $m' \in \mathcal{M}$ such that $m' \notin M_c$. This means that this message for sure cannot be encrypted in c because otherwise, by correctness, c would also have to decrypt to m'. Hence, given $C = c$ we can be sure that $M \neq m'$ and thus $\Pr[M = m' \mid C = c] = 0$. If we now pick an arbitrary distribution $\mathbb{M}$ over the messages such that $\Pr[M = m'] > 0$ then we get

$$\Pr[M = m'] \neq \Pr[M = m' \mid C = c],$$

which concludes the proof.   □

1.5.4 Measuring Information—Entropy

In the previous sections we have established that the one-time pad provides perfect secrecy only if the key is chosen uniformly at random and used only once. This was not the case for Vernam's original encryption machine, which used a key tape to encrypt a message and in case the key was shorter than the message the key was simply reused. Our previous analysis tells us that in this case the resulting cipher cannot possibly provide perfect secrecy: If the key is reused we have that $|\mathcal{K}| < |\mathcal{M}|$, which is a violation of Shannon's Theorem. What Shannon's Theorem does not tell us is how bad it is exactly to reuse a key in the one-time-pad encryption scheme. The short answer is: "It's bad. Don't do it." For a more elaborate answer we need a few concepts from the field of *information theory* which also goes back to Shannon.

1.5.4.1 Measuring Information

Assume that you toss a fair coin. How much information do you get when you learn the outcome of the random experiment? As we can encode the outcome of a coin by a single bit (use 0 for heads and 1 for tails, or vice versa) we could say that learning the outcome of a coin toss provides one bit of information. Let us now assume that the coin is skewed to the extreme and that it will always come up heads. Now how much information would you get in this case if you learned the outcome of a coin toss? As the coin always comes up heads there would be no surprise learning that the coin toss came up heads again. Thus, the outcome for a coin that always comes up heads effectively conveys no information whatsoever.

Shannon formalized the concept of "information in random experiments" and defined the *information content in an outcome x*:

Definition 1.37. *Let X be a random variable. The information content of value x with $\Pr[X = x] > 0$ is*

$$h(x) = \log \frac{1}{\Pr[X = x]}.$$

The information is measured in bits.

Applying Shannon's measure of information to our example of a coin toss we get that the information content of a coin that comes up heads given that the coin is fair (in which case $\Pr[\text{heads}] = \frac{1}{2}$) is one bit. In case we have a skewed coin with, say, heads coming up with probability 0.75 and we learn that the outcome is heads, then this conveys $\log(\frac{4}{3}) \approx 0.4$ bits of information. On the other hand, if our skewed coin comes up tails (which is the less likely of the two possible outcomes) then the information conveyed is $\log(4) = 2$ bits.

If we average over all the information contents possible for a random variable X we obtain the *entropy* of X.

Definition 1.38. *Let X be a random variable with $\mathcal{X} = \{x_1, \ldots, x_n\}$ being the set of possible outcomes for X (i.e., $\Pr[X = x_i] > 0$ for all $i \in [n]$). Then the* entropy *of X denoted by $\mathrm{H}(X)$ is defined as*

$$\mathrm{H}(X) := \sum_{x \in \mathcal{X}} \Pr[X = x] \cdot h(x)$$

$$= \sum_{x \in \mathcal{X}} \Pr[X = x] \cdot \log \frac{1}{\Pr[X = x]}.$$

Remark 1.39. Shannon chose the term *entropy* as an analogy to the notion of entropy in thermodynamics where entropy can be thought of as a measure of the disorder or randomness in a system. The higher the entropy, the more randomness in the system. In information theory, entropy relates to the randomness in (or obliviousness about) the source of the information, and the higher the entropy the less is known about the source. Indeed, it is often convenient in cryptography to take the attacker's viewpoint, and think about the entropy of a random variable as the amount of information which the adversary lacks, e.g., about a cryptographic key.

For our extreme coin that comes up heads every time, there is only a single outcome (i.e., heads) with positive probability: $\Pr[\text{heads}] = 1$. In this case the entropy of the coin reduces to 0 as the last factor becomes $\log(1) = 0$. For a more meaningful example, consider a random variable X defined as

$$\Pr[X = 1] = \frac{1}{2} \qquad \Pr[X = 2] = \frac{1}{4} \qquad \Pr[X = 3] = \frac{1}{4},$$

then the entropy of X (or the average amount of information in X) can be computed as

$$\mathrm{H}(X) = \frac{1}{2} \log 2 + \frac{1}{4} \log 4 + \frac{1}{4} \log 4 = 1.5.$$

In other words, an outcome of X on average contains 1.5 bits of information.

We can consider the joint entropy of two random variables X and Y as well as the conditional entropy of X given Y, similarly to joint probabilities and conditional probabilities.

Definition 1.40. *Let X and Y be two random variables. The* joint entropy *of X and Y is defined as*

$$\mathrm{H}(X, Y) = \sum_{x \in \mathcal{X}, y \in \mathcal{Y}} \Pr[X = x, Y = y] \cdot \log \frac{1}{\Pr[X = x, Y = y]}.$$

Here the sum is only over pairs $x \in \mathcal{X}, y \in \mathcal{Y}$ for which $\Pr[x, y] > 0$.

The conditional entropy of X given Y denoted by $\mathrm{H}(X \mid Y)$ is defined as the weighted sum of $\mathrm{H}(X \mid Y = y)$. That is,

$$
\begin{aligned}
\mathrm{H}(X \mid Y) &:= \sum_{y \in \mathcal{Y}} \Pr[Y = y] \cdot \mathrm{H}(X \mid Y = y) \\
&= \sum_{y \in \mathcal{Y}} \Pr[Y = y] \cdot \sum_{x \in \mathcal{X}} \Pr[X = x \mid Y = y] \cdot \log \frac{1}{\Pr[X = x \mid Y = y]} \\
&= \sum_{x \in \mathcal{X}, y \in \mathcal{Y}} \Pr[X = x, Y = y] \cdot \log \frac{\Pr[Y = y]}{\Pr[X = x, Y = y]}.
\end{aligned}
$$

Again the sum is only over pairs $x \in \mathcal{X}, y \in \mathcal{Y}$ for which $\Pr[x, y] > 0$.

Remark 1.41. In order to not have to explicitly remove entries from sums for which probabilities are zero, it is a common convention to set

$$
0 \cdot \log \frac{1}{0} := 0.
$$

Let us establish a few properties of entropy that are helpful when estimating the entropy of random variables. We will not prove these statements here but leave the proof as Exercise 1.11.

Theorem 1.42. *Let X and Y be two random variables. The following properties hold:*

1. *A lower bound for entropy is 0. That is*

$$
\mathrm{H}(X) \geq 0
$$

   with $\mathrm{H}(X) = 0$ if and only if $\Pr[X = x] = 1$ for some x.
2. *An upper bound for entropy is*

$$
\mathrm{H}(X) \leq \log |\mathcal{X}|
$$

   with equality if and only if $\forall x \in \mathcal{X} : \Pr[X = x] = \frac{1}{|\mathcal{X}|}$.
3. *The joint entropy is additive if and only if random variables X and Y are independent. That is,*

$$
\mathrm{H}(X, Y) = \mathrm{H}(X) + \mathrm{H}(Y) \iff \Pr[X, Y] = \Pr[X] \cdot \Pr[Y].
$$

4. *We can decompose the joint entropy as*

$$
\mathrm{H}(X, Y) = \mathrm{H}(X \mid Y) + \mathrm{H}(Y) = \mathrm{H}(Y \mid X) + \mathrm{H}(X).
$$

5. *An upper bound for the conditional entropy of random variable X given Y is given by*

$$H(X \mid Y) \leq H(X)$$

with equality if and only if X and Y are independent.

These properties reflect our intuitive understanding of entropy. The information measure cannot go below 0 (item 1), one needs at most logarithmic bits to encode elements in a set (item 2), and if random variables are independent then one needs to describe the information about both outcomes, whereas one can save fractions of a bit if the variables tend to yield correlated outcomes (item 3). Item 4 says that we can first determine the information of the outcome of one of the variables and then determine the "remaining part" of information about the other variable. The last point 5 says that having additional knowledge about a random variable X in the form of Y can only decrease the remaining information about X and such information does not help if the variables are independent.

1.5.4.2 Entropy and Perfect Secrecy

Entropy allows us to provide a different formalization of the concept of perfect secrecy. Let M and C again be random variables describing the plaintext and corresponding ciphertext for an encryption process. Then $H(M)$ captures the amount of information present in M, that is, the amount of information obtained when learning that $M = m$. A different way to look at this is to consider $H(M)$ as the amount of *uncertainty* present in M. That is, if an adversary had to guess which message was encrypted then the higher $H(M)$ the less the adversary knows about message m. (This is, in fact, not quite true, as we will see in a moment, but good enough for now.) What we would want from a perfect system is that learning ciphertext C does not change the information known about message m (or the uncertainty about message m). This allows us to provide the following characterization of perfect secrecy:

Lemma 1.43. *An encryption scheme is* perfectly secret *if for random variables M and C describing the choice of message and corresponding ciphertext it holds that*

$$H(M) = H(M \mid C).$$

In other words, knowing ciphertext c should not provide any additional information about the unknown message m.

1.5.5 A Worst-Case Treatment of Entropy—Min-Entropy

The entropy measure as we have defined it so far is an *average-case* measure of information. What this means is best explained with an example. Consider a λ-bit random variable X that is sampled according to the following procedure:

$$
\begin{aligned}
&1: \quad r \xleftarrow{\$} \{0,1\} \\
&2: \quad \textbf{if } r = 0 \textbf{ then} \\
&3: \quad \quad \textbf{return } 0^\lambda \\
&4: \quad \textbf{else} \\
&5: \quad \quad y \xleftarrow{\$} \{0,1\}^{\lambda-1} \\
&6: \quad \quad \textbf{return } 1\|y
\end{aligned}
$$

That is, with probability $\frac{1}{2}$ random variable X takes on value 0^λ and otherwise it takes a value uniformly at random in $\{0,1\}^{\lambda-1}$ which is prefixed with a 1-bit for the output.[7]

Let us compute the entropy of variable X. If we go the direct route, we need the probabilities of the possible outcomes. For this, we can distinguish between the cases that $X = 0^\lambda$ and that $X \neq 0^\lambda$. For the first case (line 3) we have that

$$
\Pr[X = 0^\lambda] = \frac{1}{2}.
$$

For the case of a value chosen in line 5 ($X \neq 0^\lambda$), we have that every possible value is equiprobable. That is, for all $y \in \{0,1\}^{\lambda-1}$ it holds that

$$
\Pr[X = 1\|y] = \frac{1}{2} \cdot \frac{1}{2^{\lambda-1}} = \frac{1}{2^\lambda}.
$$

With this we can go on to compute the entropy of X as

$$
\begin{aligned}
\mathrm{H}(X) &= \sum_{x \in \{0,1\}^\lambda} \Pr[X = x] \cdot \log \frac{1}{\Pr[X = x]} \\
&= \Pr[X = 0^\lambda] \cdot \log \frac{1}{\Pr[X = 0^\lambda]} + \sum_{y \in \{0,1\}^{\lambda-1}} \Pr[X = 1\|y] \cdot \log \frac{1}{\Pr[X = 1\|y]} \\
&= \frac{1}{2} \log 2 + 2^{\lambda-1} \cdot \frac{1}{2^\lambda} \cdot \log 2^\lambda = \frac{1}{2} + \frac{1}{2}\lambda.
\end{aligned}
$$

Consider now that you were asked to guess the value of X. A natural guess would be 0^λ, and you would be right in half of the cases. That is, you would guess the right answer with the same probability as predicting the outcome of a fair coin toss. On the other hand, the entropy in X is much larger than

---

[7] The sampling from $\{0,1\}^{\lambda-1}$ and prefixing the result with a 1-bit rather than sampling from $\{0,1\}^\lambda$ in line 5 is purely for simplification of the entropy computation.

the entropy in a random coin toss (which is 1). The reason why this is the case is that entropy is an *average-case* measure. That is, entropy measures the amount of information revealed *on average* by learning the outcome of a random experiment.

Example 1.44. *Let us now translate this example into the cryptographic world to understand the significance. Consider an adaptation of the one-time pad where the key used to encrypt is one bit longer than the message and the first bit of the key denotes whether or not to encrypt. That is, if the first bit of the key is 0 then the encryption scheme simply returns the message in clear text. Otherwise it uses the remaining λ bits of the key to encrypt according to the rules of the one-time pad. Formally, this yields the following encryption scheme SE:*

SE.KGen(1^λ)	SE.Enc(k, m)	SE.Dec(k, c)
1 : $k \leftarrow\!\!\$ \{0, 1\}^{\lambda+1}$	*1 :* **if** $k[1] = 0$ **then**	*1 :* **if** $k[1] = 0$ **then**
2 : **return** k	*2 :* $c \leftarrow m$	*2 :* $m \leftarrow c$
	3 : **else**	*3 :* **else**
	4 : $c \leftarrow m \oplus k[2..\lambda + 1]$	*4 :* $m \leftarrow c \oplus k[2..\lambda + 1]$
	5 : **return** c	*5 :* **return** m

This scheme should obviously not be considered secure. In half the cases, the ciphertext is simply the plaintext message. So how does this relate to Lemma 1.43? We said at the end of the previous section that entropy is sometimes also used as a measure of *uncertainty* and that the higher the entropy the less an adversary knows about a message. However, being an average-case measure, entropy describes the average amount of uncertainty and says nothing about a single instance.

For cryptographic purposes average-case analyses of entropy are usually not good enough. If, on average, it is difficult to break a cryptographic scheme this can also mean that there are many instances of the scheme that are trivially broken. In the above example the scheme was perfectly secure in half of the cases, but completely insecure in the other half of the cases. To be on the safe side we usually thus consider a worst-case variant of the entropy measure called *min-entropy*.

Min-Entropy

Min-entropy can be thought of as measuring uncertainty in the best case for an adversary. To understand what this means, consider an adversary that has to guess the outcome of a random variable (e.g., guess the content of a message, given the ciphertext). If the adversary has all the time in the world to analyze the underlying probability distribution then its guess would be the message that has the highest probability of matching the ciphertext. Min-entropy measures the success probability of this unrestricted adversary, that is, it tells us how many bits an adversary would need to guess correctly in order to correctly identify the outcome of the random variable given that the adversary has no computational restrictions. In other words, it tells us how *unpredictable* the outcome of a random variable truly is.

In the above example of the adapted one-time pad, an adversary could *predict* the message in half of the cases. In other words, guessing the message is as difficult as predicting the outcome of a fair coin toss or as guessing a single bit. This is captured by min-entropy, which considers the information content of the most likely outcome.

Definition 1.45. *Let X be a random variable with $\mathcal{X} = \{x_1, \ldots, x_n\}$ being the set of possible outcomes for X (i.e., $\Pr[X = x_i] > 0$ for all $i \in [n]$). Then the* min-entropy *of X denoted by $\mathrm{H}_\infty(X)$ is defined as*

$$\mathrm{H}_\infty(X) := \min_{x \in \mathcal{X}} h(x)$$
$$= -\log \max_{x \in \mathcal{X}} \Pr[X = x].$$

In other words, a random variable X has min-entropy $\mathrm{H}_\infty(X) \geq k$ if for all x the probability that X takes on value x is at most 2^{-k}. For an adversary this means that it cannot guess the value of X with probability better than 2^{-k} even if it has unbounded computing resources.

The following theorem, which we do not prove here, relates Shannon entropy and min-entropy:

Theorem 1.46. *Let X be a random variable with possible outcomes $\mathcal{X} = \{x_1, \ldots, x_n\}$. Then*

$$\mathrm{H}(X) \geq \mathrm{H}_\infty(X),$$

with equality if and only if X is uniformly distributed over $\mathcal{X}$.

Similar to Shannon entropy we can consider a conditional variant of min-entropy where some information about the random variable is known.

Definition 1.47. *Let X and Y be two random variables with possible outcomes $\mathcal{X}$ and $\mathcal{Y}$. The* min-entropy *of X conditioned on Y denoted by $\mathrm{H}_\infty(X \mid Y)$ is defined as*

$$\mathrm{H}_\infty(X \mid Y) := -\log \max_{x \in \mathcal{X}, y \in \mathcal{Y}} \Pr[X = x \mid Y = y]$$
$$= \min_{y \in \mathcal{Y}} \mathrm{H}_\infty(X \mid Y = y)$$

with $\mathrm{H}_\infty(X \mid Y = y) = -\log \max_{x \in \mathcal{X}} \Pr[X = x \mid Y = y]$.

Note the fine-grained distinction between $H_\infty(X \mid Y)$—which describes the entropy in the worst case over both random variables X and Y—and $H_\infty(X \mid Y = y)$—which describes the worst-case value over X given that Y has taken the value y.

The above definition of conditional min-entropy is sometimes too conservative in cryptographic settings. Consider for example the conditional min-entropy of a message M given the ciphertext C. With $H_\infty(M \mid C)$ we would correctly measure the best guess of the adversary for the encapsulated message, but over the worst ciphertext one can have. Assume for example that a (contrived) encryption algorithm would output the message in the clear with probability $2^{-\lambda}$ and otherwise uses the secure one-time pad encryption. To distinguish the two cases the encryption algorithm prepends ciphertexts with 0 in the first case and 1 in the second case. Then this unlikely event of a trivial ciphertext (starting with 0) intuitively does not harm security significantly. Yet, the conditional min-entropy $H_\infty(M \mid C)$ would be 0, because the trivial ciphertext leaves no uncertainty about the message.

In the example above it would be more appropriate to average over all ciphertexts such that the unlikely trivial ciphertext does not contribute excessively to the measurement of the best guess for the message. This is why one often considers an average version of min-entropy where one computes the min-entropy of X over an average Y:

Definition 1.48. *Let X and Y be two random variables with possible outcomes $\mathcal{X}$ and $\mathcal{Y}$. The average min-entropy of X conditioned on Y denoted by $\tilde{H}_\infty(X \mid Y)$ is defined as*

$$\tilde{H}_\infty(X \mid Y) = -\log \left(\sum_{y \in \mathcal{Y}} \Pr[Y = y] \cdot \max_{x \in \mathcal{X}} \Pr[X = x \mid Y = y] \right).$$

An easy computation shows that $\tilde{H}_\infty(X \mid Y) \geq H_\infty(X \mid Y)$.

Algorithmic treatment of min-entropy. A more algorithmic way of capturing min-entropy is to consider the best possible (unbounded) algorithm to predict the outcome of random variable X. That is, we quantify over all possible algorithms and define the min-entropy of X to be the negative logarithm of the probability that the best algorithm correctly predicts the outcome of random variable X:

$$H_\infty(X) := -\log \max_{\mathcal{A}} \Pr[X = \mathcal{A}()].$$

Similarly, we can capture the averaged version of conditional min-entropy by considering the best possible algorithm to predict random variable X when given the outcome of random variable Y:

$$\tilde{H}_\infty(X \mid Y) := -\log \max_{\mathcal{A}} \Pr[X = \mathcal{A}(Y)].$$

Note that here the probability is over the coins of the adversary and the outcome of Y.

Example 1.44 continued. Let us now use min-entropy to characterize the strength of the adapted one-time pad from our previous example (page 54). Let M denote a random variable describing the choice of message and C a random variable denoting the choice of ciphertext. Then, the conditional min-entropy $\mathrm{H}_\infty(M \mid C)$ gives us an upper bound on the probability that an algorithm recovers the plaintext from the ciphertext. For the standard one-time pad we have that for all possible ciphertext values $c \in \mathcal{C}$ it holds that:

$$\mathrm{H}_\infty(M \mid C = c) = -\log \max_{m \in \mathcal{M}} \Pr[M = m \mid C = c]$$
$$= -\log \max_{m \in \mathcal{M}} \Pr[M = m]$$
$$= \mathrm{H}_\infty(M)$$

and thus

$$\mathrm{H}_\infty(M \mid C) = \min_{c \in \mathcal{C}} \mathrm{H}_\infty(M \mid C = c) = \mathrm{H}_\infty(M),$$

showing perfect security of the regular one-time pad encryption, even when considering the worst-case ciphertext.

For our adapted one-time pad scheme on the other hand, we have that with probability $\frac{1}{2}$ plaintext and ciphertext are identical. Hence, we have that the predictor P that simply outputs the ciphertext as its guess for the plaintext will be right with probability at least $\frac{1}{2}$. It follows that

$$\mathrm{H}_\infty(M \mid C) \le \tilde{\mathrm{H}}_\infty(M \mid C)$$
$$= -\log \max_{\mathcal{A}} \Pr[M = \mathcal{A}(C)]$$
$$\le -\log \Pr[M = \mathsf{P}(C)]$$
$$\le -\log \frac{1}{2} = 1.$$

Min-entropy thus provides us with an accurate measure of uncertainty. If a plaintext has conditional min-entropy 1 given the ciphertext this tells us that an adversary (with unbounded resources) can guess the correct plaintext with probability $\frac{1}{2}$.

1.5.6 Key Reuse in One-Time Pads

We can now attempt to analyze what happens if a one-time pad key is reused. One thing to note is that we need to make at least some assumption about the message. Consider that we encrypt only uniformly random messages but

#	Word	Freq.	#	Word	Freq.	#	Letter	Freq.	#	Letter	Freq.
1	the	7.14%	14	be	0.65%	1	E	12.49%	14	M	2.51%
2	of	4.16%	15	by	0.63%	2	T	9.28%	15	F	2.40%
3	and	3.04%	16	on	0.62%	3	A	8.04%	16	P	2.14%
4	to	2.60%	17	not	0.61%	4	O	7.64%	17	G	1.87%
5	in	2.27%	18	he	0.55%	5	I	7.57%	18	W	1.68%
6	a	2.06%	19	i	0.52%	6	N	7.23%	19	Y	1.66%
7	is	1.13%	20	this	0.51%	7	S	6.51%	20	B	1.48%
8	that	1.08%	21	are	0.50%	8	R	6.28%	21	V	1.05%
9	for	0.88%	22	or	0.49%	9	H	5.05%	22	K	0.54%
10	it	0.77%	23	his	0.49%	10	L	4.07%	23	X	0.23%
11	as	0.77%	24	from	0.47%	11	D	3.82%	24	J	0.16%
12	was	0.74%	25	at	0.46%	12	C	3.34%	25	Q	0.12%
13	with	0.70%	26	which	0.42%	13	U	2.73%	26	Z	0.09%

Table 1.1: An estimate of the 26 most frequently used words on the left and estimated frequencies of individual letters on the right.

always with the same key. In this case, we can simply reverse the role of key and message and thus the adversary is none the wiser. Yet, usually making a few assumptions about the underlying message is feasible. In the following we make the assumption that the plaintext was valid English text and for simplicity we restrict the English alphabet to its 26 uppercase letters.

Now, valid English text is quite different from uniformly random data. For example, the letter "e" is much more common than, say, the letter "q". On the other hand, in case you know that the first letter of a word is "q" then with very high probability the next letter is "u". An analysis can reveal that the most frequent word used in the English language is the word "the" with a frequency of about 7.14% followed by "of" with a frequency of 4.16%. Similarly, we can count the frequencies of individual letters; the counts for all letters and the top 26 words are given in Table 1.1.

The bottom line from this discussion is that the average information of a word or letter in an English (or any natural) plaintext is not uniformly distributed. Knowing that a text contains the word "the" yields much less information than knowing that it contains "cryptanalysis".

Redundancy in Languages

In the following we want to put the above observation on more formal grounds. If we want a bit-wise representation of the English language then we need to encode each letter via a bit sequence. In an alphabet of 26 characters the average information per character would be $\log(26) \approx 4.7$ if the probability of each character was identical. The value $\log(|\Sigma|)$ is called the *rate* of alphabet Σ.

The difference between the rate and the actual information contained in a realization of a random variable is called the *redundancy*.

Definition 1.49. *We define the* redundancy *of a random variable X with possible outcomes $\mathcal{X}$ as*

$$R(X) = \log(|\mathcal{X}|) - H(X).$$

From the frequency counts in Table 1.1 we can estimate the entropy per letter of the English language as

$$\sum_{x=A}^{Z} \text{frequency}(x) \cdot \log\left(\frac{1}{\text{frequency}(x)}\right) \approx 4.14.$$

This is, however, only the case if we consider each letter individually. If we take into account the frequency of words and letter combinations, a more accurate estimation can be derived. For example, if we consider the statistical distribution of letter pairs we can derive an entropy per letter of roughly 3.6. Shannon used yet another technique and estimated the entropy per word and the average number of letters per word to arrive at

$$\frac{\text{entropy per word}}{\text{average number of letters}} = \frac{11.82}{4.5} \approx 2.6.$$

While the actual value may even be less, this means that the redundancy of the English language should be no lower than 2. In other words, on average we can remove every second character from an English text without losing information.

Redundancy and Key Reuse

Shannon observed that the redundancy of a source or language is related not only to how well it can be compressed but also to the security of a cryptosystem in case keys are reused. Consider a ciphertext of length 5. While there are 26^5 possible ciphertexts (over the English alphabet) there are only roughly 10,000 English words of length 5. Given a ciphertext c we can define the set of *plausible keys* $K(c)$ for an encryption scheme $(\mathsf{KGen}, \mathsf{Enc}, \mathsf{Dec})$ as the set of keys that when used to decrypt ciphertext c yield a plausible plaintext (i.e., a plaintext m with $\Pr[M = m] > 0$):

$$K(c) := \{\mathsf{k} \in \mathcal{K} : \exists m \in \mathcal{M} \text{ such that } \Pr[M = m] > 0 \wedge m = \mathsf{Dec}(\mathsf{k}, c)\}.$$

Those keys that do not decrypt to a plausible plaintext are also referred to as *spurious keys*. We denote the average number of plausible keys over all ciphertexts by

$$\mathbb{E}[|K(C)|] = \sum_{c \in \mathcal{C}} \Pr[C = c] \cdot K(c). \qquad (1.3)$$

We can consider plausible keys also for multiple ciphertexts $c_1, \dots, c_n$ in which case we define the set of plausible keys as the set of keys that decrypt to a plausible plaintext for each of the ciphertexts:

$K(c_1, \dots, c_n) := \{ \mathsf{k} \in \mathcal{K} : \forall i \in [n] \; \exists m_i \in \mathcal{M} \text{ such that}$
$$\Pr[M = m_i] > 0 \wedge m_i = \mathsf{Dec}(\mathsf{k}, c_i) \}$$
$= K(c_1) \cap \dots \cap K(c_n).$

Given that the amount of plausible keys may be much smaller than the amount of possible keys, we can consider the average uncertainty of a key given a ciphertext: $\mathrm{H}(K \mid C)$. The uncertainty of the key after observing some ciphertext is also known as the *key equivocation*.

We can give a trivial upper bound on the key equivocation using Theorem 1.42 (item 2) and the number of plausible keys for the given ciphertext:

$$\mathrm{H}(K \mid C) \leq \log |K(C)|.$$

Now consider that the same key is reused to encrypt two different plaintexts yielding ciphertexts c_1 and c_2. In this case, an adversary with unlimited resources could first find all plausible keys for both ciphertexts and then discard any key in $K(c_1)$ that does not yield a plausible plaintext when used to decrypt c_2. The key equivocation is thus reduced to

$$\mathrm{H}(K \mid C_1, C_2) \leq \log(|K(C_1, C_2)|) = \log |K(C_1) \cap K(C_2)|. \qquad (1.4)$$

It is clear that given sufficiently many ciphertexts, the uncertainty about the actual key quickly approaches zero if the number of plausible keys is on average a lot less than the number of possible keys.

We will shortly make this more tangible and consider what the above means for the case of one-time pads. For the analysis we do, however, need one final ingredient which yields a second characterization of the key equivocation, which is given by the following theorem.

> **Theorem 1.50.** *Let K, M, C be random variables denoting the choice of key, plaintext, and corresponding ciphertext in a symmetric encryption scheme that is correct and that has deterministic encryption (e.g., the one-time pad). Then the key equivocation fulfills the following property:*
> $$\mathrm{H}(K \mid C) = \mathrm{H}(K) + \mathrm{H}(M) - \mathrm{H}(C).$$

Proof of Theorem 1.50. Theorem 1.42 allows us to decompose the joint entropy $\mathrm{H}(K, M, C)$ as

$$\mathrm{H}(K, M, C) = \mathrm{H}(C \mid K, M) + \mathrm{H}(K, M).$$

Since key and message are chosen independently, we have that $H(K, M) = H(K) + H(M)$. Furthermore, since we consider an encryption scheme with deterministic encryption operation, plaintext and key uniquely identify the ciphertext and thus $H(C \mid K, M) = 0$. It follows that

$$H(K, M, C) = H(K) + H(M).$$

Similarly, since we assume that the encryption scheme is correct we have that $H(M \mid K, C) = 0$, and we thus have that

$$H(K, M, C) = H(M \mid K, C) + H(K, C) = H(K, C).$$

Putting it all together we obtain

$$\begin{aligned} H(K \mid C) &= H(K, C) - H(C) \\ &= H(K, M, C) - H(C) \\ &= H(K) + H(M) - H(C). \end{aligned}$$

Here, the first equality is also due to Theorem 1.42.   □

Key Reuse in One-Time Pads

Let us apply the above discussion to a "Vernam"-like cipher with a key length λ. The scheme is identical to the one-time pad from Definition 1.34 except that we will reuse the same key for encrypting multiple messages. For this, let us consider n plaintexts (each also of length λ) that were encrypted with the same key of length λ. Since each ciphertext is of length λ bits we have that

$$H(C_1, \ldots, C_n) \leq n \log |\mathcal{C}| = n \cdot \lambda,$$

where we used Theorem 1.42 (item 2) to obtain the upper bound. Definition 1.49 gives us a characterization of the entropy of plaintext messages in relation to the redundancy of the underlying (assumed) language. From this we get for each plaintext M_i for $i \in [n]$ that

$$H(M_i) = \log |\mathcal{M}_i| - R(M_i) = \log |\mathcal{M}| - R(M).$$

The second equality is due to our assumption that all plaintexts were independently sampled from the same distribution. Thus, $\mathcal{M}$ denotes our plaintext space (English texts of length λ) and $R(M)$ the corresponding redundancy.

In the following we relate the number of plausible keys remaining after having seen n ciphertexts to the redundancy of the underlying plaintexts. For this we will upper and lower bound the key equivocation. The lower bound is given by Theorem 1.50 as

$$\mathrm{H}(K \mid C_1, \ldots, C_n) = \mathrm{H}(K) + \mathrm{H}(M_1, \ldots, M_n) - \mathrm{H}(C_1, \ldots, C_n)$$
$$\geq \mathrm{H}(K) + n \cdot (\log |\mathcal{M}| - R(M)) - n \cdot \log |\mathcal{C}|.$$

Note that plaintext space and ciphertext space are the same (bit strings of length λ) and thus $\log |\mathcal{M}| = \log |\mathcal{C}|$. This yields our lower bound on the key equivocation as

$$\mathrm{H}(K \mid C_1, \ldots, C_n) \geq \mathrm{H}(K) - n \cdot R(M). \qquad (1.5)$$

Next we upper bound the key equivocation and, for this, start from the definition of conditional entropy as follows:

$$\mathrm{H}(K \mid C_1, \ldots, C_n) =$$
$$\sum_{(c_1, \ldots, c_n) \in \mathcal{C} \times \ldots \times \mathcal{C}} \Pr[C_1 = c_1, \ldots, C_n = c_n] \cdot \mathrm{H}(K \mid C_1 = c_1, \ldots, C_n = c_n).$$

Using Equation 1.4 we can rewrite the right-hand side as

$$\leq \sum_{(c_1, \ldots, c_n) \in \mathcal{C} \times \ldots \times \mathcal{C}} \Pr[C_1 = c_1, \ldots, C_n = c_n] \cdot \log |K(c_1) \cap \ldots \cap K(c_n)|$$

and using Jensen's inequality[8] we can pull out the logarithm to obtain

$$\leq \log \sum_{(c_1, \ldots, c_n) \in \mathcal{C} \times \ldots \times \mathcal{C}} \Pr[C_1 = c_1, \ldots, C_n = c_n] \cdot |K(c_1) \cap \ldots \cap K(c_n)|.$$

Note that the right-hand side within the logarithm is exactly the expected number of plausible keys (Equation 1.3). We can thus simplify the above to obtain our upper bound on the key equivocation as

$$\mathrm{H}(K \mid C_1, \ldots, C_n) \leq \log \mathbb{E}[K(C_1, \ldots, C_n)]. \qquad (1.6)$$

Combining Equations 1.5 and 1.6 we get a characterization of the expected number of plausible keys in relation to the number of ciphertexts, the entropy of keys, and the redundancy in the underlying plaintexts:

$$\log \mathbb{E}[K(C_1, \ldots, C_n)] \geq \mathrm{H}(K) - n \cdot R(M).$$

Taking the exponential of both sides, it follows that the expected number of plausible keys in the one-time pad scenario with an n time key reuse satisfies

$$\mathbb{E}[K(C_1, \ldots, C_n)] \geq \frac{2^{\mathrm{H}(K)}}{2^{n \cdot R(M)}}.$$

---

[8] Jensen's inequality says that if f is a continuous and concave function and $p_1, \ldots, p_n \in \mathbb{R}^+$ with $\sum_{i=1}^{n} p_i = 1$ then $f(\sum_{i=1}^{n} p_i x_i) \geq \sum_{i=1}^{n} p_i f(x_i)$. In case f is convex, the inequality is flipped.

Setting the expected number of plausible keys to 1 and solving for n we get our sought-after result:

$$n \geq \frac{H(K)}{R(M)}.$$

The above yields a bound on the number of ciphertexts (or amount of ciphertext) that an adversary needs to see on average in order to be able to uniquely extract the used key and thus break the cipher. The amount of ciphertexts at which the key becomes uniquely defined is also called the *unicity distance*.

> **Definition 1.51.** *Let K and M be random variables denoting the choice of key and message, respectively. Let $R(M)$ be the redundancy of a plaintext source and K the keyspace of a cryptosystem. We define the* unicity distance *of the cryptosystem as*
>
> $$n_0 := \frac{H(K)}{R(M)}.$$

Remark 1.52. Note that the unicity distance is a theoretical value that denotes how much ciphertext on average we would need such that a brute-force search can find the correct key. It does not say anything about how difficult that brute-force search actually is.

For our example of key reuse in one-time pads we considered a single λ-bit key and, thus, had a keyspace of $|\mathcal{K}| = 2^\lambda$ many distinct keys. Assuming that the redundancy in the English language is 2 and keys are all equiprobable we obtain a unicity distance of

$$n_0 = \frac{H(K)}{R(M)} = \frac{\log |\mathcal{K}|}{R(M)} = \frac{\lambda}{2}.$$

In other words, after seeing roughly $\frac{\lambda}{2}$ ciphertexts generated with the same key, the used key can be uniquely identified, given unbounded amount of computational resources.

In case of the one-time pad without key reuse the analysis stays the same, except that the keyspace grows with the message length. Hence an adversary will never see enough ciphertext for a single key to reach the unicity distance, and thus the correct key remains information-theoretically hidden.

Remark 1.53. At the beginning of Section 1.5.6 we argued that we need some assumption on the plaintext distribution as otherwise we can simply reverse the role of plaintext and key. The unicity distance yields a formal foundation for this statement. If the redundancy of a plaintext space tends towards $R(M) = 0$, plaintexts are chosen uniformly at random. And, in this case, the unicity distance tends towards infinity.

Key Reuse in Practice

As mentioned before, the unicity distance is a theoretical measure. However, our derivation of the unicity distance provides ideas for practical attacks on Vernam ciphers, i.e., "one-time pads" with reused keys. Let us assume an attacker obtains two ciphertexts c_1 and c_2 that have been generated with the same key. Let us further assume that the underlying plaintext is English. In this case, an attacker could attempt a decryption as follows. As a first step the adversary takes the exclusive or of both ciphertexts:

$$\tau := c_1 \oplus c_2 = (m_1 \oplus \mathsf{k}) \oplus (m_2 \oplus \mathsf{k}) = m_1 \oplus m_2.$$

If we would know that one of the two messages starts with the word "crypto", we could obtain the first 6 letters of message m_2 by simply encoding the word into binary and computing

$$\tau[1..6] \oplus \langle \text{crypto} \rangle.$$

Since we do not know, it is a process of trial and error executed as follows:

1. Take a common word (e.g., "the") or a word the attacker suspects to be part of one of the messages.
2. Encode the word, place it at every possible location, and XOR it onto τ.
3. Check the resulting string. If it looks and reads like English we guess the word and expand the search. Otherwise we move on to the next position.

This process of *dragging likely words across the ciphertext* is also referred to as *crib dragging*. Using sophisticated analysis of languages this process can, of course, be further optimized and automated.

This concludes our discussion of key reuse, the information-theoretic setting, and this chapter. In the upcoming chapter we will focus on the computational setting, that is, efficient algorithms and adversaries, and discuss security in this context.

Chapter Notes and References

An excellent reference for many of the fundamental concepts presented in this chapter can be found in *Computational Complexity - A Modern Approach* by Arora and Barak [3]. For further information on computability theory we can recommend the *Introduction to Automata Theory, Languages, and Computation* by Hopcroft et al. [12]. A good introduction to information theory is MacKay's *Information Theory, Inference and Learning Algorithms* [17].

Alonzo Church presented the lambda calculus in 1936 [5] a few months before Alan Turing (independently from Church) formalized his notion of Turing machines [26]. While the two models are identical in their expressiveness, Turing machines are the predominant model of computation in theoretical computer science today. Lambda calculus, on the other hand, had a large influence on the design of programming languages and, in particular, inspired LISP. Both Turing and Church showed that functions exist that cannot be computed in their respective models. The idea of a universal Turing machine goes back to Turing.

The study of efficiency and complexity of computation was initiated in the early 1960s, and a fascinating overview of the early history of computational complexity is given by Cook in his 1983 Turing award lecture [8]. A vast reference of all kinds of complexity classes is given in the Complexity Zoo [1].

The notion of polynomial time and the description of complexity class P go back to Rabin [19], Cobham [6], and Edmonds [9]. The notion of NP goes back to Cook [7] and Levin [16] who showed, in the early 1970s and independently of each other, that the Boolean satisfiability problem (also known as SAT) is NP-complete. The formulation of P and NP as we use it today is due to Karp [13]. For the study of NP problems, Cook, Levin, and Karp also introduced notions of reductions. The *Cook reduction* also known as *Turing reduction* first presented in Cook's seminal 1971 paper [7] is essentially a black-box (security) reduction. Probabilistic complexity classes and, in particular, BPP were first introduced by Gill [10]. Adleman [2] showed how to derandomize probabilistic algorithms with the help of non-uniformity, implying BPP $\subseteq$ P/poly.

The canonical characters Alice and Bob were introduced by Rivest, Shamir, and Adleman, who used them in their seminal 1978 paper on the RSA cryptosystem [20].

Many ideas and concepts presented in this chapter can be traced back to Claude Elwood Shannon, who established the field of information theory with his 1948 paper "A Mathematical Theory of Communication" [25]. Shannon used his concepts as a basis to study cryptography and was the first to formally prove the security of the one-time pad [21]. While Shannon published his two seminal papers in 1948 and 1949, the concepts were already developed in 1945 when they were published in a classified report [24]. Shannon also studied the English language, in particular, with regards to entropy and redundancy [23]. He estimated the entropy per letter in the English language to be approximately 2.6.

The frequency counts of words and letters used in Section 1.5.6 and presented in Table 1.1 are due to Peter Norvig's analysis [18] of the Google *n*-gram corpus [11].

Non-uniformity and the study of circuits have a long tradition in cryptography which can also be traced back to Shannon [22]. A discussion on non-uniformity and the difficulties that arise from using non-uniform reductions in cryptography are given by Koblitz and Menezes [14, 15] and Bernstein and Lange [4].

Exercices

Exercise 1.1. Argue that the following alternative encoding of a vector $\mathbf{x}$ of strings into a single string allows to recover the vector again:

$$(\mathbf{x}[1], \ldots, \mathbf{x}[\ell]) \mapsto 1^{|\mathbf{x}[1]|}0||\mathbf{x}[1]||1^{|\mathbf{x}[2]|}0||\mathbf{x}[2]|| \cdots ||1^{|\mathbf{x}[\ell]|}0||\mathbf{x}[\ell].$$

Exercise 1.2. In Remark 1.6 (page 13) we claimed that there are many definitional choices when it comes to Turing machines. Show that our simple definition with a single read–write tape is as expressive as a variant which consists of three tapes: a read-only input tape, a read–write work tape, and a write-only output tape.

Exercise 1.3. Write a Turing machine algorithm that outputs 1 in case its input is a *palindrome*[9] and 0 otherwise. Can you also give a circuit for 5- and 6-bit inputs that computes the same function?

Exercise 1.4. We call a Turing machine *oblivious* if its head movement does not depend on the exact input string but only on the length of the input. That is, for each input string $x \in \{0,1\}^*$ the head position in step $i \in \mathbb{N}$ is only a function of $|x|$ and i. Show that for any efficient Turing machine there exists an efficient oblivious Turing machine.

Exercise 1.5. In Section 1.3.1 we discussed *universal Turing machines* and claimed that we can find an encoding of Turing machines as bit strings such that every Turing machine M has an injective encoding $\langle M \rangle$ in such a way that a Turing machine can efficiently decide if an encoding corresponds to a Turing machine and, furthermore, that the functionality of M can be recovered from $\langle M \rangle$ by a universal Turing machine. Give an example of such an encoding scheme and encode the Turing machine created in Exercise 1.3.

Exercise 1.6. Show that NAND gates are universal.

Exercise 1.7. Show that any circuit that makes use of *constant wires* (wires that are fixed to 0 or 1) can be transformed into a circuit that does not have constant wires.

Exercise 1.8. Let SHORTESTPATH denote the language that contains all tuples $(\mathcal{G}, s, t, n)$ where $\mathcal{G}$ is an encoding of a graph (as an adjacency matrix), s and t are two vertices in $\mathcal{G}$, and $n \in \mathbb{N}$ is an integer denoting the length of the

---

[9] A palindrome is a word or phrase that reads forwards the same as backwards. The names *BOB*, *ANNA*, and *OTTO* are examples of simple word palindromes.

shortest path between s and t. Show that SHORTESTPATH is in complexity class P.

Exercise 1.9. A famous problem known to be in complexity class NP is the decision problem of the *traveling salesman*. Given as input the distances between n cities the problem is to verify whether a route exists that visits all cities with a total distance less than d. Let SALESMAN denote the language that contains all tuples $(\mathcal{G}, d)$ where $\mathcal{G}$ is an encoding of a fully connected graph representing the cities and their pairwise distance (e.g., as an adjacency matrix) and $d \in \mathbb{N}$ is such that there exists a route through all cities with total distance less than d. Show that SALESMAN is in NP.

Exercise 1.10. Prove the following statement about symmetric encryption schemes with $|\mathcal{M}| = |\mathcal{K}| = |\mathcal{C}|$. If message space, key space, and ciphertext space are of the same size then the scheme is perfectly secure if and only if the scheme picks a key uniformly at random and if for every pair of message m and ciphertext c there exists exactly one key k such that $c = \mathsf{Enc}(\mathsf{k}, m)$.

Exercise 1.11. Prove Theorem 1.42 (page 51), which contains various helpful properties when working with entropy.

Exercise 1.12. Show $\tilde{\mathrm{H}}_\infty(X \mid Y) \geq \mathrm{H}_\infty(X \mid Y)$, as stated after Definition 1.48 on page 56.

Chapter Bibliography

1. Scott Aaronson, Greg Kuperberg, Christopher Granade, and Vincent Russo. Complexity zoo. https://complexityzoo.uwaterloo.ca/Complexity_Zoo.
2. Leonard Adleman. Two theorems on random polynomial time. In *19th Annual Symposium on Foundations of Computer Science (SFCS 1978)*, pages 75–83. IEEE, 1978.
3. Sanjeev Arora and Boaz Barak. *Computational Complexity: A Modern Approach*. Cambridge University Press, New York, NY, USA, 1st edition, 2009.
4. Daniel J. Bernstein and Tanja Lange. Non-uniform cracks in the concrete: The power of free precomputation. In Kazue Sako and Palash Sarkar, editors, *Advances in Cryptology – ASIACRYPT 2013, Part II*, volume 8270 of *Lecture Notes in Computer Science*, pages 321–340, Bengalore, India, December 1–5, 2013. Springer, Heidelberg, Germany.
5. Alonzo Church. An unsolvable problem of elementary number theory. *American journal of mathematics*, 58(2):345–363, 1936.
6. Alan Cobham. The intrinsic computational difficulty of functions. *Proceedings of the 1964 Congress on Logic, Mathematics and the Methodology of Science*, pages 24–30, 1964.
7. Stephen A Cook. The complexity of theorem-proving procedures. In *Proceedings of the Third Annual ACM Symposium on Theory of Computing*, pages 151–158. ACM, 1971.
8. Stephen A Cook. An overview of computational complexity. *Communications of the ACM*, 26(6):400–408, 1983.
9. Jack Edmonds. Paths, trees, and flowers. *Canadian Journal of mathematics*, 17:449–467, 1965.

10. John Gill. Computational complexity of probabilistic Turing machines. *SIAM Journal on Computing*, 6(4):675–695, 1977.
11. Google Books ngram viewer. `http://storage.googleapis.com/books/ngrams/books/datasetsv2.html`.
12. John E. Hopcroft, Rajeev Motwani, and Jeffrey D. Ullman. *Introduction to Automata Theory, Languages, and Computation*. Addison-Wesley Longman Publishing Co., Inc., Boston, MA, USA, 2006.
13. Richard M Karp et al. Complexity of computer computations. *Reducibility among combinatorial problems*, 23(1):85–103, 1972.
14. Neal Koblitz and Alfred Menezes. Another look at non-uniformity. Cryptology ePrint Archive, Report 2012/359, 2012. `http://eprint.iacr.org/2012/359`.
15. Neal Koblitz and Alfred Menezes. Another look at non-uniformity. *Groups Complexity Cryptology*, 5(2):117–139, 2013.
16. Leonid Anatolevich Levin. Universal sequential search problems. *Problemy peredachi informatsii*, 9(3):115–116, 1973.
17. David J. C. MacKay. *Information Theory, Inference, and Learning Algorithms*. Cambridge University Press, 2003.
18. Peter Norvig. English letter frequency counts. `http://norvig.com/mayzner.html`.
19. Michael Oser Rabin. Degree of difficulty of computing a function and a partial ordering of recursive sets. *Technical Report 2*, 1960.
20. Ronald L. Rivest, Adi Shamir, and Leonard M. Adleman. A method for obtaining digital signatures and public-key cryptosystems. *Communications of the Association for Computing Machinery*, 21(2):120–126, 1978.
21. Claude E Shannon. Communication theory of secrecy systems. *Bell System Technical Journal*, 28(4):656–715, 1949.
22. Claude E Shannon. The synthesis of two-terminal switching circuits. *The Bell System Technical Journal*, 28(1):59–98, 1949.
23. Claude E Shannon. Prediction and entropy of printed English. *Bell System Technical Journal*, 30(1):50–64, 1951.
24. Claude Elwood Shannon. A mathematical theory of cryptography. *Bell System Technical Memo MM 45-110-02*, 9 1945.
25. Claude Elwood Shannon. A mathematical theory of communication. *Bell System Technical Journal*, 27(3):379–423, 1948.
26. Alan Mathison Turing. On computable numbers, with an application to the Entscheidungsproblem. *Proceedings of the London Mathematical Society*, 2(1):230–265, 1937.

Part I
Foundations of Modern Cryptography

Chapter 2
Computational Security

In the first part of this book we will look at the foundations of modern cryptography in general and the foundations of hash functions in particular. The goal of this part is to introduce the basic primitives such as one-way functions, pseudorandom functions, and collision-resistant hash functions, but also important applications such as encryption or digital signature schemes. We will build up the basics gradually, proving in detail most of the presented results. Our focus for this part is thus also on the presentation of important proof techniques that are used over and over in the field of cryptography, in particular within the field of provable security.

We will begin our journey into the theory of hash functions and modern cryptography with a discussion of *computational security*, which complements Shannon's *information-theoretic security* that we have discussed in the previous chapter and which allows to go beyond the impossibility results presented there. We will introduce computational security with the example of a one-way function F, which is a function that is easy to compute but hard to invert: Given a value $y \leftarrow \mathsf{F}(x)$ for a random input x it should be difficult to find some x' such that $\mathsf{F}(x') = \mathsf{F}(x)$. Note that such a notion cannot exist in an information-theoretic setting as an unbounded adversary can easily invert any function, simply by brute-force search for a preimage. We will also encounter our first *security reduction*: the bread-and-butter proof technique of modern cryptography which provides us with a means to make conditional statements of the form: if scheme $\mathcal{A}$ is secure, then so is scheme $\mathcal{B}$. Or, more tangible, if secure one-way functions exist then secure symmetric encryption schemes exist that have short keys.

2.1 The Indispensability of Computational Security

Recall our discussion of key reuse in one-time pads. Here we showed that the key must be at least as long as the message in order for the scheme to

© Springer Nature Switzerland AG 2021
A. Mittelbach, M. Fischlin, *The Theory of Hash Functions and Random Oracles*,
Information Security and Cryptography, https://doi.org/10.1007/978-3-030-63287-8_2

be perfectly secure. Furthermore, the key may not be reused as otherwise the information-theoretic guarantees quickly become void. Not being able to reuse keys is impractical, to say the least. Especially if keys are required to be as long as the message they are supposed to encrypt. Fortunately, there are ways around Shannon's lower bound, but these come at a cost: we will trade efficiency for information-theoretic security and instead settle with *computational* security guarantees. The difference is roughly that security only holds against bounded adversaries. While computational security can give us more efficient and practical solutions than the information-theoretic setting, the computational setting is not only about efficiency. The computational setting also provides us with additional capabilities that are simply impossible to achieve in the information-theoretic setting.

Let us consider a simple password-based access control to underline the necessity of the notion of computational security. In this example a client stores a randomly chosen password x on a server, protected under some cryptographic function F as $y = \mathsf{F}(x)$. The function should be such that recovering the password x from y is hard: In case the server is compromised and y is revealed, the stolen data should not allow to recover the client's password. The client can log in by providing x to the server, which recomputes $y' \leftarrow \mathsf{F}(x)$ and verifies that y' matches the previously stored value y. We note that this abstractly models how most real-world systems actually manage passwords.[1]

Neglecting the obvious security risk of unprotected transmission of the password from the client to the server and the commonly limited entropy of passwords (people tend not to choose random or very long passwords), an adversary who learns y can impersonate as the client only if it is able to find a matching password to y. Since the server would accept any x^* which maps to $y = \mathsf{F}(x^*)$, the adversary does not even need to find the exact password: any alternative password with the same image would work.

Can we achieve information-theoretic security in such a setting? Information-theoretic security asks that no adversary (even one that has unbounded resources) can break the system. In this case this translates to that it needs to be impossible to find a valid x^* given only y such that $\mathsf{F}(x^*) = y$. Following Kerckhoffs' principle that the security of the system should only depend on the cryptographic secret but not on *keeping the algorithm hidden*, we can assume that the adversary knows the function F. But since in the information-theoretic setting the adversary has unlimited resources it can thus simply check, in a brute-force attack, for each possible string $0, 1, 00, 01, 10, 11, 000, \ldots$ whether

---

[1] Do not take this abstract model as a blueprint for a real-world scheme. In real-world systems usually a *salted* password scheme should be used. Here for each user the server generates a random string s (the salt) and then stores $(s, \mathsf{F}(s, x))$, that is, the server stores the salt as well as the function value of the salt combined with the user's password. Using a salted password scheme protects against a variety of attacks such as lookup or rainbow tables (see also page 74).

or not it maps to y under F. Eventually, the adversary will find a preimage, possibly even the original password x itself.

Note that the above attack is generic and, in particular, independent from the specifics of function F and we have thus shown that no such authentication scheme can exist that is secure in the information-theoretic setting. On the other hand, real-world adversaries are never equipped with unlimited resources and information-theoretic security guarantees may be stronger than necessary for most practical applications. This is where computational security comes into play.

Information-theoretic security aims at constructing schemes that simply cannot be broken down to the laws of nature. With these strong guarantees come strict requirements that need to be fulfilled, and as we saw in the above example, certain scenarios cannot be captured in this setting. Computational security, on the other hand, is based on the assumption that certain problems exist that are hard to solve (yet solvable with sufficient time and resources). Here, "hard to solve" means that no algorithm exists that can solve the problem in *reasonable time* except with *negligible probability*. If reasonable time means "spending decades or even millenia using the combined computing resources currently available" and negligible probability means "guessing the right atom in the known universe" then a scheme that is thus computationally secure is for most practical purposes secure.

The existence of such hard problems is inherently tied to the notion of easy and hard problems in complexity theory, where the question of whether hard problems exist at all culminates in the question of whether the complexity classes P and NP are identical. Similar to the setting there, where it is usually believed that hard problems exist and that $\mathsf{P} \neq \mathsf{NP}$, in cryptography we have promising candidate constructions for all the abstract primitives considered in this book.

In the following we will formalize the notion of computational security, which requires us to define what we mean by *reasonably secure* and by *negligible probability*. This will be the topic of the upcoming section.

2.2 Bounding Adversarial Resources

The above example of the password-based login system and the brute-force attack shows that we somehow need to restrict the number of trials an adversary can make. Whereas for the login system one option may be to restrict the number of admissible attempts before canceling access completely, this approach may not be viable in all situations. For instance, in case y is revealed because of a server breach how can we restrict the number of attempts given to an adversary? A more abstract solution is to consider natural limitations of adversaries, i.e., consider that the adversary's runtime is limited and hence the number of verification trials. That is, instead of trying to achieve

---

Rainbow Tables

Rainbow tables are space-optimized lookup tables for inverting one-way (hash) functions that are based on the idea of *lookup chains*[a]. Assume that you want to be able to efficiently invert a (hard-to-invert) function F on a subset of its image, say, images of length 8 that consist only of lowercase letters (think cracking passwords). A naïve approach is to precompute all values $y \leftarrow \mathsf{F}(x)$ for relevant preimages x and store pairs (x, y) in a lookup table. The resulting table would be of size linear in the number of relevant inputs. Lookup chains allow to make a trade-off and trade storage space for lookup time. A lookup chain requires a mapping function M (sometimes also called a reduction function) that maps images of F back to relevant inputs in the domain of F. To construct a lookup chain data structure, we compute m chains of length ℓ such as

$$x_1^1 = \text{``aapasswd''} \xrightarrow{\mathsf{F}} y_1^1 = \mathsf{F}(x_1^1) \xrightarrow{\mathsf{M}} x_1^2 = \mathsf{M}(y_1^1) \xrightarrow{\mathsf{F}} \cdots \xrightarrow{\mathsf{F}} y_1^\ell \xrightarrow{\mathsf{M}} x_1^{\ell+1}$$
$$\vdots$$
$$x_m^1 = \text{``zsecretpw''} \xrightarrow{\mathsf{F}} y_m^1 = \mathsf{F}(x_m^1) \xrightarrow{\mathsf{M}} x_m^2 = \mathsf{M}(y_m^1) \xrightarrow{\mathsf{F}} \cdots \xrightarrow{\mathsf{F}} y_m^\ell \xrightarrow{\mathsf{M}} x_m^{\ell+1}.$$

For each chain the first and the last entry is stored. Note that in case of collisions (e.g., $\mathsf{M}(y_j^s) = \mathsf{M}(y_k^t)$ for some $j, k \in [m]$ and $s, t \in [\ell]$) chains may "merge" and the resulting data structure thus, in the best case, allows to invert up to $m \cdot \ell$ distinct entries.

Continued on next page $\hookrightarrow$

---

[a] Lookup chains have originally been called hash chains. The term *hash chain* today, however, usually refers to the successive application of a hash function, such as, $\mathsf{H}(\mathsf{H}(\mathsf{H}(x)))$.

---

security against *any* adversary we settle for security against *any efficient* adversary. As explained in Section 1.3.1 cryptography follows the complexity-theoretic approach to identify "reasonably bounded runtime" with polynomial time, a quite conservative notion of efficiency. Computational security can thus be translated into *security against any polynomial-time adversary*.

Can we now simply demand that no polynomial-time algorithm can find some preimage x^* for a given $y = \mathsf{F}(x)$ and with $|x| = \lambda$, where the complexity is given by the security parameter 1^λ (which here defines the length of x)? This would most likely exclude the brute-force attack since there are 2^λ strings of length λ and, consequently, the trial verification requires exponential time, thus exceeding any polynomial runtime bound. Unfortunately, the adversary, instead of successively trying all strings, may now apply a guessing strategy and simple check for (a polynomial number of) random values x^* such that the runtime remains polynomial. Though most of the time this will not be successful, by pure chance the adversary may hit the right value x^*. In the

---

Rainbow Tables (continued)

To check whether the data structure contains some value y^* we compute $x^* \leftarrow \mathsf{M}(y^*)$ and then compute a lookup chain of length at most $\ell - 1$ starting from x^*. After each intermediate mapping step M we test whether the result matches one of the stored chain ends $x_i^{\ell+1}$ (for some $i \in [m]$). If after $\ell - 1$ steps we did not find a matching chain, then value y^* is not in the data structure. If, on the other hand, we find a matching chain, we can recover a preimage for y^* by recomputing the corresponding chain until we find value x^* such that $y^* = \mathsf{F}(x^*)$.

Rainbow tables build upon the idea of lookup chains, but instead of using a single mapping function, a rainbow table uses up to ℓ mapping functions, one for each step. This greatly reduces the risk of collisions and the merging of chains, as a collision needs to occur at the same step for two chains to merge. Consequently, when trying to invert a value y^* one now needs to compute chains starting from each possible mapping function/step.

To protect against rainbow tables (or lookup tables in general) when storing passwords, passwords should be stored salted: Passwords should be stored as $(s, \mathsf{F}(s, x))$, where s is a random string (the salt). The huge amount of different possible salt values makes the use of rainbow tables impractical as now rainbow tables would need to be created per salt.

---

following section we show how to deal with such a guessing strategy in a formal way.

2.2.1 Bounding the Success Probability

What form of security can we hope for in the login example? Demanding that no PPT adversary exists that can find a preimage given only y leads to a security definition that cannot be met by any cryptographic scheme, since even outputting a single random guess $x^* \leftarrow\!\!{}_\$ \{0,1\}^\lambda$ has a success probability of at least $2^{-\lambda}$. The probability may actually be larger if F is, say, many-to-one, because then the adversary wins if it hits any of the multiple preimages.

To capture small probabilities which are larger than 0 but still "too small to matter" we use the notion of *negligible functions* in cryptography. The definition of negligible functions follows the complexity-theoretic concept of identifying reasonable runtime via polynomial time, by stating that any polynomial fraction $\frac{1}{\mathsf{p}(\lambda)}$ should be considered a *noticeable probability*. Negligible functions now demand that the function is asymptotically smaller than any polynomial fraction. This is analogous to declaring algorithms as inefficient if their runtime is not polynomial. For both notions of efficiency and negligible functions we take the precautious approach and try to err on the safe side. We call an algorithm inefficient if it exceeds the polynomial bound for infinitely many input lengths λ. As an example consider an algorithm that exceeds the runtime bound only on input lengths λ that are even, or to give a more extreme example, consider an algorithm that exceeds the bound only on input lengths that are powers of 2. Both algorithms would be inefficient according to our definition. Similarly for negligible functions we want to ensure that there do not exist loopholes and we thus conservatively require that the function value lies beneath any polynomial fraction *for all sufficiently large parameters* λ.

Definition 2.1 (Negligible Function). *A function* $\epsilon : \mathbb{N} \to \mathbb{R}$ *is negligible if for any polynomial* $\mathsf{p} : \mathbb{N} \to \mathbb{R}^+$ *there exists an integer* Λ *such that for all* $\lambda \geq \Lambda$ *we have*

$$\epsilon(\lambda) \leq \frac{1}{\mathsf{p}(\lambda)}.$$

An example of a negligible function is $\epsilon(\lambda) = 2^{-\lambda}$ since, in the inverse case, exponential growth exceeds polynomial growth. Another example is the function $\epsilon(\lambda) = \lambda^{-\log \lambda}$, although this function tends much slower to 0 than the previous one. Also, any function which becomes less than or equal to 0 for all large values λ is negligible. In particular, functions which become negative at some point and stay negative are negligible. Examples of functions which are not negligible are polynomial fractions, $\frac{1}{\mathsf{q}(\lambda)}$ for some positive polynomial q, or constants $\epsilon(\lambda) = c > 0$.

Remark 2.2. Note that a function which is *not* negligible must not be larger than a polynomial fraction for all sufficiently large λ's. It suffices that the function is *infinitely often* larger than $\frac{1}{\mathsf{p}(\lambda)}$ for some (positive) polynomial. For instance, the function

$$\delta(\lambda) = \begin{cases} 0 & \text{for odd } \lambda \\ \lambda^{-5} & \text{for even } \lambda \end{cases}$$

is non-negligible.

For a not further specified negligible function we write $\epsilon(\lambda) = \mathsf{negl}(\lambda)$. Similarly, we write $\epsilon(\lambda) = \frac{1}{2} + \mathsf{negl}(\lambda)$ if the function ϵ exceeds $\frac{1}{2}$ only by a negligible amount. Since we allow negligible functions to be negative, the latter example also includes cases where $\epsilon(\lambda) < \frac{1}{2}$. For a non-negligible function δ we write $\delta(\lambda) \neq \mathsf{negl}(\lambda)$.

Let us return to our login system example. We can now more formally state what we expect from our authentication scheme:

For any PPT *algorithm* $\mathcal{A}$ *the probability of finding some preimage should be negligible.*

This is clearly true for an injective function F and the simple attacker which merely outputs a random guess and succeeds with probability $2^{-\lambda}$. The requirement, however, allows for arbitrary polynomial-time adversaries which can try several random guesses. For any such adversary making $p(\lambda)$ many guesses for some polynomial p, the success probability of finding a preimage (for an injective function F) is at most $p(\lambda) \cdot 2^{-\lambda}$ by the union bound (see Section 1.5.1). This value is still negligible for arbitrary polynomials p, as the next proposition about the robustness of the notion shows:

Theorem 2.3 (Basic Properties of Negligible Functions). *Let* ϵ, ϵ' : $\mathbb{N} \to \mathbb{R}$ *be negligible functions,* $\delta : \mathbb{N} \to \mathbb{R}$ *be a non-negligible function, and* $q : \mathbb{N} \to \mathbb{R}^+$ *be a polynomial. Then the following holds:*

1. *The sum of two negligible functions is negligible:*

$$\epsilon(\lambda) + \epsilon'(\lambda) = \mathsf{negl}(\lambda).$$

2. *A polynomial factor still leaves the function negligible:*

$$q(\lambda) \cdot \epsilon(\lambda) = \mathsf{negl}(\lambda).$$

3. *Subtracting only a negligible function from a non-negligible one yields a non-negligible function:*

$$\delta(\lambda) - \epsilon(\lambda) \neq \mathsf{negl}(\lambda).$$

4. *A function which is bounded by a negligible function is negligible itself: Let* $\gamma : \mathbb{N} \to \mathbb{R}$ *be a function such that there exists* Λ *with* $\gamma(\lambda) \leq \epsilon(\lambda)$ *for all* $\lambda \geq \Lambda$. *Then* γ *is negligible.*

Proof. To show 1 fix some arbitrary positive polynomial p. Note that $2p(\lambda)$ is still a polynomial and, since ϵ and ϵ' are negligible by assumption, there exists Λ and Λ' such that

$$\epsilon(\lambda) \leq \frac{1}{2p(\lambda)} \text{ for } \lambda \geq \Lambda, \quad \text{and} \quad \epsilon'(\lambda) \leq \frac{1}{2p(\lambda)} \text{ for } \lambda \geq \Lambda'.$$

This in particular means that for all $\lambda \geq \max\{\Lambda, \Lambda'\}$ we have

$$\epsilon(\lambda) + \epsilon'(\lambda) \leq \frac{1}{2p(\lambda)} + \frac{1}{2p(\lambda)} = \frac{1}{p(\lambda)}.$$

Together with the fact that the polynomial p was arbitrary and that the sum is eventually smaller than any polynomial inverse, this proves that the sum is negligible, too.

For claim 2 fix again an arbitrary positive polynomial p. By assumption, the product $q(\lambda) \cdot p(\lambda)$ is again a positive polynomial and we have a bound Λ such that for all $\lambda \geq \Lambda$ we have for the negligible function ϵ:

$$\epsilon(\lambda) \le \frac{1}{q(\lambda) \cdot p(\lambda)}.$$

This immediately implies for all $\lambda \ge \Lambda$ that

$$q(\lambda) \cdot \epsilon(\lambda) \le \frac{q(\lambda)}{q(\lambda) \cdot p(\lambda)} = \frac{1}{p(\lambda)},$$

showing 2.

Statement 3 easily follows from 1: If $\delta(\lambda) - \epsilon(\lambda)$ was negligible, then so would be the sum

$$\big(\delta(\lambda) - \epsilon(\lambda)\big) + \epsilon(\lambda) = \delta(\lambda),$$

in contradiction to the assumption about δ being non-negligible.

Finally, the fourth property follows easily from the previous ones. If we assume that $\gamma(\lambda)$ was non-negligible then so would be $\gamma(\lambda) - \epsilon(\lambda)$ by the previous claim. But this difference is eventually 0, or even less than 0, and thus negligible.   □

It can be shown that the first property can be extended to not only hold for the sum of two negligible functions but also for the sum of constantly many negligible functions. This is formalized in the following proposition. We leave the proof as Exercise 2.3.

> **Proposition 2.4.** *Let ϵ_i for $i \in \mathbb{N}$ be a sequence of negligible functions and let $q_i : \mathbb{N} \to \mathbb{R}^+$ be polynomials. Then for any constant $c \in \mathbb{N}$ the sum is negligible:*
>
> $$\sum_{i=1}^{c} q_i(\lambda)\epsilon_i(\lambda) = \mathsf{negl}(\lambda).$$

It is important to note that if the number of functions to be summed up depends on the security parameter (and is thus not constant), then the result may no longer be negligible:

Example 2.5. *Consider the following sequence of negligible functions:*

$$\epsilon_i(\lambda) = \begin{cases} 1 & \text{if } i \ge \lambda \\ 0 & \text{otherwise} \end{cases}$$

Individually each of the functions is negligible as for large enough λ the functions become 0. However, the function that sums up the first λ many ϵ_i's defined as

$$\epsilon(\lambda) = \sum_{i=1}^{\lambda} \epsilon_i(\lambda)$$

is not negligible. In fact, we have that $\epsilon(\lambda) = 1$ for all $\lambda \in \mathbb{N}$.

2.2.2 Asymptotic vs. Concrete Security

With the notion of negligible functions we have the necessary ingredients to provide a formal security definition for our login system example. The security property needed for the login example—here ignoring the fact that people tend to choose weak passwords that are far from random—is that of *one-wayness*:

Definition 2.6 (One-Way Function). *An efficiently computable function* $\mathsf{F} : \{0,1\}^* \to \{0,1\}^*$ *is one-way if for any* PPT *algorithm* $\mathcal{A}$ *the following probability is negligible:*

$$\Pr_{x \leftarrow_\$ \{0,1\}^\lambda} \left[\mathcal{A}(1^\lambda, \mathsf{F}(x)) \in \mathsf{F}^{-1}(\mathsf{F}(x)) \right] = \mathsf{negl}(\lambda).$$

Here, the probability is over the choice of $x \leftarrow_\$ \{0,1\}^\lambda$ *and the random coins of adversary* $\mathcal{A}$.

We will discuss one-way functions in greater detail in later sections but here want to point out a characteristic of the above definition that is important to understand. The above definition is *asymptotic* in the sense that it considers the properties for sufficiently large values of λ. A negligible function, for instance, *eventually* vanishes faster then any polynomial fraction. For small choices of λ the function values, often representing adversarial success probabilities, may still be quite large. The asymptotic approach hence gives little intuition on how to choose a concrete security parameter λ in practice to thwart attacks.

When studying security properties, asymptotic definitions and analyses are a good starting point as they are often easier to follow and allow for easier presentation. In this book we will also mostly work with asymptotic definitions as is the custom in large parts of the (theoretic) cryptographic literature. Indeed, for many fundamental questions working in the asymptotic settings is sufficient. Consider, for example, feasibility (or infeasibility) results such as the question of whether it is possible to construct a *secure encryption scheme* from a *one-way function*. However, when looking at schemes to be implemented in real-world systems one needs to go beyond the asymptotic analysis and look at *concrete security*. Here instead of asking that no PPT adversary can find a preimage with non-negligible probability, we demand that no adversary running in time t can find a preimage with probability better than ϵ. If t is chosen to be sufficiently large such that it is infeasible to construct any adversary that exceeds a runtime of t, this then gives us a concrete bound on the success probability for any real-world attack.

In the concrete security approach we also speak of (t, ϵ)-security. Following is the definition of a one-way function adapted to the concrete setting.

Definition 2.7 (One-Way Function). *Let* $t : \mathbb{N} \to \mathbb{N}$ *and* $\epsilon : \mathbb{N} \to \mathbb{R}$ *be two functions. An efficiently computable function* $\mathsf{F} : \{0,1\}^* \to \{0,1\}^*$ *is* (t, ϵ)*-one-way if for all* $\lambda \in \mathbb{N}$ *and any algorithm* $\mathcal{A}$ *running in time* $t(\lambda)$ *it holds that*

$$\Pr_{x \leftarrow \$\{0,1\}^\lambda} \left[\mathcal{A}(1^\lambda, \mathsf{F}(x)) \in \mathsf{F}^{-1}(\mathsf{F}(x)) \right] \leq \epsilon(\lambda).$$

Here, the probability is over the choice of $x \leftarrow \$ \{0,1\}^\lambda$ *and the random coins of adversary* $\mathcal{A}$.

If we have a (t, ϵ)-secure one-way function F we can get a concrete security bound $\epsilon(\lambda)$ by fixing a security parameter $\lambda \in \mathbb{N}$. Bound $\epsilon(\lambda)$ then upper bounds the success probability of all adversaries restricted to a runtime of $t(\lambda)$.

Remark 2.8. One should be careful with interpreting concrete security bounds.[2] One question that needs to be answered is how exactly does t measure the runtime. Is it the number of steps of a Turing machine or the number of, say, CPU cycles and, if so, of which CPU? Furthermore, even if a bound is rather conservative with respect to the fastest supercomputer known today, attacks might be feasible if it is, for example, possible to parallelize an attack. An attacker could use a cloud infrastructure or bot-net to carry out the attack, thereby drastically increasing the overall runtime. Also note that when using the concrete security approach we must always speak of (t, ϵ)-security rather than simply saying that a scheme is secure as it is not at all clear what choices of t and ϵ should be deemed secure.

2.3 One-Way Functions

In the above discussion of computational security and the password-based authentication scheme we have seen a first definition of a one-way function. In the following we want to discuss the notion of one-wayness in more detail.

A cryptographic one-way function provides one of the most simple forms of hard problems, as required to thwart adversaries from deriving unauthorized information. Intuitively, a function $\mathsf{F} : \{0,1\}^* \to \{0,1\}^*$ is one-way if no efficient adversary $\mathcal{A}$ can, given $\mathsf{F}(x)$ for random input x, find a preimage with non-negligible probability. At the same time, computing the function F "in the forward direction" can be done efficiently:

---

[2] Of course, one should be even more careful interpreting asymptotic security bounds.

While this picture looks like what we would expect from an encryption scheme let us stress that one-way functions are *not* encryption schemes. In fact, a one-way function can reveal quite a lot of information about its preimages as long as some significant part remains hidden. We will see examples of such "leaking" one-way functions in Section 2.4. Similarly, it may also be that recovering exactly the preimage x from $\mathsf{F}(x)$ may be impossible, i.e., if F is not one-to-one.

2.3.1 A Game-Based Definition

Formally, as seen in Definition 2.6 we define a one-way function by demanding that no efficient algorithm can invert $\mathsf{F}(x)$ for a random value $x \in \{0,1\}^\lambda$ with non-negligible probability. Definition 2.6 represents a mathematical description of the property in terms of probabilities. An equivalent, but more algorithmic approach is to capture the exact steps of the adversary's task and measure its success in a game-based notion as follows:

Definition 2.9 (One-Way Function, alternative definition). *An efficiently computable function* $\mathsf{F} : \{0,1\}^* \to \{0,1\}^*$ *is* one-way *if for all* PPT *adversaries* $\mathcal{A}$ *the advantage* $\mathsf{Adv}^{\mathrm{owf}}_{\mathsf{F},\mathcal{A}}(\lambda)$ *defined as*

$$\mathsf{Adv}^{\mathrm{owf}}_{\mathsf{F},\mathcal{A}}(\lambda) := \Pr\left[\mathsf{Exp}^{\mathrm{owf}}_{\mathsf{F},\mathcal{A}}(\lambda)\right]$$

is negligible and where experiment $\mathsf{Exp}^{\mathrm{owf}}_{\mathsf{F},\mathcal{A}}(\lambda)$ *is defined as*

$$\underline{\text{Experiment } \mathsf{Exp}^{\mathrm{owf}}_{\mathsf{F},\mathcal{A}}(\lambda)}$$

1 : $\quad x \leftarrow\!\!\$\ \{0,1\}^\lambda$

2 : $\quad y \leftarrow \mathsf{F}(x)$

3 : $\quad x^* \leftarrow\!\!\$\ \mathcal{A}(1^\lambda, y)$

4 : $\quad \textbf{return } \mathsf{F}(x^*) = y$

Remark 2.10. Recall that we will often abbreviate experiments (or binary random variables in general) outputting 1 and simply write $\Pr[\mathsf{Exp}(\lambda)]$ to denote $\Pr[\mathsf{Exp}(\lambda) = 1]$.

In such game-based definitions the security is modeled as an experiment (or game) in which the adversary "plays" against a challenger. In the above case the challenger chooses a random value $x \in \{0,1\}^\lambda$, computes $y \leftarrow \mathsf{F}(x)$, and then runs the adversary on input the security parameter 1^λ and value y. The adversary eventually outputs a value x^* and wins if $\mathsf{F}(x^*) = y$. A pictorial representation of the experiment is given in Figure 2.1.

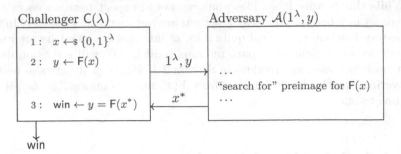

Fig. 2.1: A pictorial representation of the *one-way experiment*. The challenger chooses a random value $x \in \{0,1\}^*$, computes $y \leftarrow F(x)$, and then passes y to the adversary together with the security parameter 1^λ. The adversary eventually returns a value x^* and wins if $F(x^*) = y$.

The experiment itself defines a random variable which in our case directly describes the adversary's success probability of "winning" and thus the quantity that we want to upper bound. In many cases, the experiment will, however, not ask an adversary to find a specific value (in the above case find a preimage for y) but to distinguish between two different values (e.g., to guess whether a ciphertext c is an encryption of message m or m'). In such cases the adversary can win the experiment with probability $\frac{1}{2}$ simply by guessing. It is thus helpful to introduce a helper function which describes the *advantage* an adversary has over the trivial adversary that simply guesses. We call this function $\mathsf{Adv}(\lambda)$ and write $\mathsf{Adv}_{F,\mathcal{A}}^{\mathrm{owf}}(\lambda)$ to denote the advantage of adversary $\mathcal{A}$ against function F with regard to security property *owf* (where *owf* is short for one-way function).

It is not too difficult to see that Definitions 2.6 and 2.9 are, in fact, equivalent: Experiment $\mathsf{Exp}_{F,\mathcal{A}}^{\mathrm{owf}}(\lambda)$ is simply an algorithmic and more explicit representation of the same random variable and we have

$$\Pr\left[\mathsf{Exp}_{F,\mathcal{A}}^{\mathrm{owf}}(\lambda)\right] = \Pr\left[\mathcal{A}(1^\lambda, F(x)) \in F^{-1}(F(x))\right].$$

Furthermore, in both definitions we require the above quantity to be negligible and call function F one-way if this is the case. As we feel that the algorithmic write-up often helps the understanding of the definition, from here on we will mostly work with game-based definitions. As we will see there are also various variations of the definition which are often easier to represent in the explicit game-based approach. In the following we will discuss two such variations: generalized input distributions and *keyed* one-way functions (or families of one-way functions).

Remark 2.11. One-wayness as a property for hash functions is often referred to as *preimage resistance*.

Remark 2.12. In the one-way experiment the adversary is only required to find *some* preimage, but not necessarily the original x. Although subtle, this has an important consequence. Assume that instead we asked the adversary actually to recover x. If so, then there would be examples of alleged one-way functions which are, intuitively, easy to invert. Suppose for example that $\mathsf{F}(x) = 1^{|x|}$ outputs the input length of x in unary. Then finding a preimage of some image 1^λ under F is easy (e.g., outputting 0^λ already suffices). Yet, finding the original input x beyond the negligible guessing probability of $2^{-\lambda}$ is impossible.

Remark 2.13. Further note that giving the adversary the security parameter (in unary) as input 1^λ in addition to the image $\mathsf{F}(x)$ again excludes contrived cases. As an example of such a contrived case see Section 1.3.6 (page 33).

2.3.2 Generalized Input Distributions

In our above definition we assumed that input x is chosen uniformly at random in the set $\{0,1\}^\lambda$. It is sometimes convenient to allow for arbitrary (PPT) input distributions instead. Technically, we need to consider a sequence of distributions $\mathsf{D} = (\mathsf{D}_\lambda)_{\lambda \in \mathbb{N}}$, one distribution for each security parameter λ. We say that D is *sampleable* if there exists a (possibly non-uniform) probabilistic algorithm Sam such that for all $\lambda \in \mathbb{N}$ we have that $\mathsf{Sam}(1^\lambda; r)$ is a random variable (over the choice of r) with associated probability distribution D_λ. In other words, for all x we have that $\Pr[\mathsf{Sam}(1^\lambda) = x]$ matches the probability assigned to x by D_λ. We call a distribution efficiently sampleable if Sam is efficient.

Remark 2.14. We also sometimes speak of PPT random variables. We call a random variable with associated probability distribution PPT if the distribution is efficiently sampleable.

We can now consider functions that are one-way for specific (sampleable) distributions by generating the preimage as $x \leftarrow_\$ \mathsf{D}(1^\lambda)$ (where $\mathsf{D}(1^\lambda)$ is short for running the corresponding sample algorithm). The probability space then also spans over the random coins of the input sampler Sam. We then say that F is one-way with respect to distribution D. In this sense this notion generalizes the definition before (for the uniform distribution).

Can we hope to find a function that is one-way for all input distributions? It is easy to see that this cannot be the case since "all distributions" also include highly predictable distributions such as the constant distribution which always chooses the same value $x \in \{0,1\}^\lambda$. We thus, at the very least, require that the distribution is *unpredictable*. We can capture unpredictable distributions by requiring that their corresponding sample algorithm Sam has super-logarithmic min-entropy

$$H_\infty(\mathsf{Sam}(1^\lambda)) \in \omega(\log(\lambda)),$$

which is the same as saying that all (possibly unbounded) algorithms P can predict the outcome of $\mathsf{Sam}(1^\lambda)$ only with negligible probability.

2.3.3 Keyed One-Way Functions

Another common variation is to consider *keyed one-way functions*, possibly in combination with the generalized input distributions. Roughly speaking, keyed one-way functions include a choice of a function from a set of functions for some public key (also sometimes called index or parameter) fk. This can be viewed by considering function F to take two inputs, a message x, and in addition a key fk. It is now convenient to write F as a pair of algorithms, $\mathsf{F} = (\mathsf{F.KGen}, \mathsf{F.Eval})$, one for generating the key fk and the other one for evaluating the function.

Formally, for keyed one-way functions we first efficiently pick a key of a specific function from a family of functions as $\mathsf{fk} \leftarrow\!\!{\scriptstyle\$}\ \mathsf{F.KGen}(1^\lambda)$. In the case of generalized distributions we then sample $x \leftarrow\!\!{\scriptstyle\$}\ \mathsf{D}(1^\lambda, \mathsf{fk})$ (note that we allow the sampler to depend on function key fk), efficiently compute the image $y \leftarrow \mathsf{F.Eval}(\mathsf{fk}, x)$, and let the adversary run on input $(1^\lambda, \mathsf{fk}, y)$. The goal of the adversary is again to find a preimage.

Following is the full definition for keyed one-way functions with general input distributions:

Definition 2.15 (Keyed One-Way Function). *We call a pair of efficient algorithms* $\mathsf{F} = (\mathsf{F.KGen}, \mathsf{F.Eval})$ *one-way for sampleable distribution* D *if for all* PPT *adversaries* $\mathcal{A}$ *the advantage* $\mathsf{Adv}^{\mathrm{owf}}_{\mathsf{F},\mathsf{D},\mathcal{A}}(\lambda)$ *defined as*

$$\mathsf{Adv}^{\mathrm{owf}}_{\mathsf{F},\mathsf{D},\mathcal{A}}(\lambda) := \Pr\left[\mathit{Exp}^{\mathrm{owf}}_{\mathsf{F},\mathsf{D},\mathcal{A}}(\lambda)\right]$$

is negligible and where experiment $\mathit{Exp}^{\mathrm{owf}}_{\mathsf{F},\mathsf{D},\mathcal{A}}(\lambda)$ *is defined as*

Experiment $\mathit{Exp}^{\mathrm{owf}}_{\mathsf{F},\mathsf{D},\mathcal{A}}(\lambda)$
1: $\quad \mathsf{fk} \leftarrow\!\!{\scriptstyle\$}\ \mathsf{F.KGen}(1^\lambda)$
2: $\quad x \leftarrow\!\!{\scriptstyle\$}\ \mathsf{D}(1^\lambda, \mathsf{fk})$
3: $\quad y \leftarrow \mathsf{F.Eval}(\mathsf{fk}, x)$
4: $\quad x^* \leftarrow\!\!{\scriptstyle\$}\ \mathcal{A}(1^\lambda, \mathsf{fk}, y)$
5: $\quad$ **return** $\mathsf{F.Eval}(\mathsf{fk}, x^*) = y$

If the key-sampling algorithm F.KGen always returns a constant, say 1^λ, and we consider the uniform distribution then we capture our basic setting above with this notion.

Candidate One-Way Functions

A natural candidate for a keyed one-way function is discrete exponentiaton (with the underlying hard inversion problem being the discrete logarithm problem). For the case of working over residue class rings, the key generation algorithm picks a prime p of size proportional to λ as well as a generator g of a subgroup $\langle g \rangle = \left\{ g^i \mid i \in \{0, 1, \ldots, q-1\} \right\} \subseteq \mathbb{Z}_p^*$ of order q, with q usually being prime. It outputs p, q, and g. The function itself is given by the evaluation algorithm which maps $x \in \mathbb{Z}_q$ to $y = g^x \bmod p$. This can be done in polynomial time in λ. Finding the (unique) preimage x to such a y is considered to be hard for appropriate choices of p, q, and g; the exact requirements for these parameters are beyond our scope here. We give a more detailed introduction into the discrete logarithm problem in Chapter 10.

Remark 2.16. A (keyed) one-way function is called *one-to-one* or *injective* if F (resp. $\mathsf{F.Eval}(fk, \cdot)$ for any $fk \xleftarrow{\$} \mathsf{F.KGen}(1^\lambda)$) describes a one-to-one function. It is called a *one-way permutation* if in addition $\mathsf{F}(\{0,1\}^\lambda) = \{0,1\}^\lambda$ (resp. $\mathsf{F.Eval}(fk, \cdot)$) is a permutation.

Remark 2.17. In Definition 2.6 we considered functions of the form $\mathsf{F} : \{0,1\}^* \to \{0,1\}^*$ while in Definition 2.15 above we have not further specified the input and output of function family F. It is often convenient to consider fixed input and output lengths that are parameterized with the security parameter and consider functions of the form $\{0,1\}^{\mathsf{F.il}(\lambda)} \to \{0,1\}^{\mathsf{F.ol}(\lambda)}$. In this case il and ol are polynomials and an (implicit) part of the function definition. We may also use kl to explicitly model the length of keys as output by a key generation function $\mathsf{KGen}(1^\lambda)$.

2.4 Security Reductions and Leaky One-Way Functions

In the following we give a first example of a cryptographic security reduction and study the security of one-way functions when the adversary is able to learn individual bits of the input. To be more specific and to simplify the presentation, we show that if the first bit $x[1]$ of the input is "leaked" a one-way function remains secure.

Our approach to show that one-way functions may leak the first input bit is as follows. We assume from the outset that there exists a one-way function $\mathsf{F} = (\mathsf{F.KGen}, \mathsf{F.Eval})$, otherwise the claim is trivial. However, we do not make any assumption about this function beyond the fact that it is one-way, i.e., the function F may be arbitrary as long as it is hard to invert. Given F we build another one-way function $G = (G.KGen, G, Eval)$ by using the same key generation algorithm, $G.KGen = F.KGen$, and letting $G.Eval(gk, x)$ evaluate $F.Eval(gk, x)$. But instead of simply outputting the value, G in addition outputs the first input bit $x[1]$ together with the value under F. The following pseudocode captures function G:

$G.KGen(1^\lambda)$	$G.Eval(gk, x)$
1 : gk ←$ F.KGen(1^λ)	1 : y ←$ F.Eval(gk, x)
2 : return gk	2 : return $x[1]\|y$

   In order to show that leaking the first bit of the input for a computation of F only slightly increases the success probability of an adversary we need to show that our derived function G inherits the one-wayness property from F. Intuitively, the extra output bit should not facilitate the search for a preimage significantly. For example, the brute-force adversary, which simply tries all possible preimages, may be able to find a preimage slightly faster since it only needs to search among all input values with the matching first bit. On the other hand, the speed-up should be minimal compared with the search time for the remainder. Our goal here is to turn this intuition into a rigorous proof via a security reduction. A security reduction helps us to rule out all attacks and not just specific attacks such as the before-mentioned brute-force attack. It even lets us quantify exactly in terms of concrete security how the security level is affected by outputting the first input bit in the clear. Formally, we will prove the following statement:

Proposition 2.18. *Let* $F = (F.KGen, F.Eval)$ *be a keyed function family and define* G *as above. Then for each efficient adversary* $\mathcal{B}$ *(against the one-wayness of* G*) there exists an efficient adversary* $\mathcal{A}$ *(against the one-wayness of* F*) such that*

$$\mathsf{Adv}^{owf}_{G,\mathcal{B}}(\lambda) \leq 2 \cdot \mathsf{Adv}^{owf}_{F,\mathcal{A}}(\lambda).$$

   Let us discuss how Proposition 2.18 states that function G is one-way given that F is one-way. Proposition 2.18 relates the security of function G to F by giving an upper bound on the success probability (the advantage) of an adversary: for each adversary $\mathcal{B}$ against G there exists an adversary $\mathcal{A}$ against F which is at least half as successful as $\mathcal{B}$. In other words, the best possible adversary against F gives us an upper bound for the success probability of any adversary against G. A G-adversary can at most be twice as good as the best adversary against F. Now, if we assume that F is a one-way function we know that for any efficient $\mathcal{A}$ (and thus also for the best possible) it holds that

$$\mathsf{Adv}^{owf}_{F,\mathcal{A}}(\lambda) = \mathsf{negl}(\lambda)$$

and thus also

$$\mathsf{Adv}^{owf}_{G,\mathcal{B}}(\lambda) = \mathsf{negl}(\lambda).$$

It follows that G is one-way if F is one-way since the advantage gain of a factor 2 does not change the fact that the advantage remains negligible.

Formally, we will prove the above statement via a security reduction which will relate the success probability of an arbitrary PPT algorithm $\mathcal{B}$ trying to invert G to the success probability of some PPT algorithm $\mathcal{A}$ which we derive from $\mathcal{B}$ and which plays against the original one-way function F. The reduction itself describes the algorithm $\mathcal{A}$. An important accompanying step is a thorough analysis of $\mathcal{A}$'s success probability in terms of $\mathcal{B}$'s success rate. If we can show that $\mathcal{B}$'s probability does not exceed $\mathcal{A}$'s probability significantly, then we can conclude from the security of F that $\mathcal{A}$'s success rate and hence also $\mathcal{B}$'s success rate must be sufficiently small.

The idea for constructing our algorithm $\mathcal{A}$ is to use algorithm $\mathcal{B}$ as a subroutine. For this $\mathcal{A}$ takes its input, a key fk of the one-way function F, and an image y and turns it into a valid input for algorithm $\mathcal{B}$. This is necessary since $\mathcal{B}$ expects a key of the function G (but which coincides with a key for F) and an image which has an extra bit; by Kerckhoffs' principle we must once more assume that adversary $\mathcal{B}$ knows the underlying primitives F and G and how G is built from F. This in particular means that $\mathcal{A}$ needs to augment the value y by an extra bit to make it a valid image y' under G, before it can use it together with the coinciding key fk to execute algorithm $\mathcal{B}$ on fk and y'. The idea is now to let $\mathcal{A}$ simply guess the missing bit $c \leftarrow\!\!\!\$\ \{0,1\}$. It then sets $y' \leftarrow c\|y$ to be the concatenation of this bit and the original image.

Before analyzing $\mathcal{A}$'s success probability we describe our adversary $\mathcal{A}$ more formally. There are (at least) two equivalent ways to describe such reductions. We will usually use code-based descriptions similar to the ones we have used to define experiments before.

$$\underline{\mathcal{A}(1^\lambda, \mathsf{fk}, y)}$$

1 : $\quad c \leftarrow\!\!\!\$\ \{0,1\}$

2 : $\quad x^* \leftarrow\!\!\!\$\ \mathcal{B}(1^\lambda, \mathsf{fk}, c\|y)$

3 : $\quad$ **return** x^*

An alternative, more graphical representation of adversary $\mathcal{A}$ which highlights the fact that adversary $\mathcal{B}$ is used as a black-box subroutine could look as given in Figure 2.2. Note that the construction of $\mathcal{A}$ is independent of the specifics of $\mathcal{B}$, that is, $\mathcal{A}$ uses only $\mathcal{B}$'s specified input–output behavior.

It remains to analyze $\mathcal{A}$'s success probability. We will first argue that, if $\mathcal{A}$'s guess for c equals the actual input bit $x[1]$, then the input given to $\mathcal{B}$ in the subroutine call of $\mathcal{A}$ has the same distribution as in $\mathcal{B}$'s original one-wayness experiment $\mathsf{Exp}_{\mathsf{G},\mathcal{B}}^{\mathrm{owf}}(\lambda)$ (see Definition 2.15). Therefore, the probability that $\mathcal{B}$ returns a preimage in the subroutine case is the same as in the original attack. We will then argue that the success probability of $\mathcal{A}$ of finding a preimage is therefore only by a factor $\frac{1}{2}$ smaller than $\mathcal{B}$'s probability.

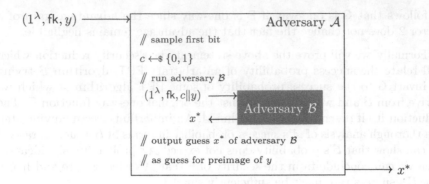

Fig. 2.2: A graphical representation of adversary $\mathcal{A}$ in the proof of Proposition 2.18. Note that adversary $\mathcal{A}$ is using adversary $\mathcal{B}$ as a black box, that is, adversary $\mathcal{A}$ does not depend on the exact implementation of $\mathcal{B}$ but only on its input–output behavior.

To see that the input distributions for $\mathcal{B}$ in the subroutine call and in the original experiment coincide, given that $c = x[1]$, consider how the values are generated. Adversary $\mathcal{A}$ receives a random key fk $\leftarrow\!\!{\scriptstyle\$}$ F.KGen(1^λ) and a value $y = $ F.Eval(fk, x) for random $x \leftarrow\!\!{\scriptstyle\$} \{0,1\}^\lambda$ as input. It then forwards key fk and $y' = c\|y$ to adversary $\mathcal{B}$. Since the key generation algorithms of F and G are identical by construction, the forwarded key has the same distribution as in $\mathcal{B}$'s original experiment. Secondly, since we assume that $c = x[1]$ the value y' is distributed identically to computing it as G.Eval(fk, x) for random $x \leftarrow\!\!{\scriptstyle\$} \{0,1\}^\lambda$.

We conclude that for a correct guess of bit $c = x[1]$ by $\mathcal{A}$, adversary $\mathcal{B}$ finds a preimage x^* in the subroutine with the same probability as in the one-wayness experiment. Here we use the fact that any preimage x^* under an image $y' = c\|y$ for G is also a preimage for y under F. Next note that the random bit $c \leftarrow\!\!{\scriptstyle\$} \{0,1\}$ chosen by $\mathcal{A}$ equals the correct bit $x[1]$ of $\mathcal{A}$'s input value y with probability $\frac{1}{2}$. Furthermore, the bit is chosen independently of the other steps such that conditioning on $c = x[1]$ does not affect the probability of $\mathcal{B}$ returning a preimage.

Formally, we can combine the above observations as follows:

$$\mathsf{Adv}^{\mathrm{owf}}_{\mathsf{F},\mathcal{A}}(\lambda) = \Pr\!\left[\mathsf{Exp}^{\mathrm{owf}}_{\mathsf{F},\mathcal{A}}(\lambda)\right] \geq \Pr\!\left[\mathsf{Exp}^{\mathrm{owf}}_{\mathsf{F},\mathcal{A}}(\lambda) \wedge c = x[1]\right]$$

$$= \Pr[c = x[1]] \cdot \Pr\!\left[\mathsf{Exp}^{\mathrm{owf}}_{\mathsf{F},\mathcal{A}}(\lambda) \,\middle|\, c = x[1]\right]$$

$$= \frac{1}{2} \cdot \Pr\!\left[\mathsf{Exp}^{\mathrm{owf}}_{\mathsf{G},\mathcal{B}}(\lambda)\right] = \frac{1}{2} \cdot \mathsf{Adv}^{\mathrm{owf}}_{\mathsf{G},\mathcal{B}}(\lambda).$$

Multiplying by 2 yields the desired result

$$\mathsf{Adv}^{\mathrm{owf}}_{\mathsf{G},\mathcal{B}}(\lambda) \leq 2 \cdot \mathsf{Adv}^{\mathrm{owf}}_{\mathsf{F},\mathcal{A}}(\lambda).$$

The final step in the analysis is to note that adversary $\mathcal{A}$ is a PPT algorithm if $\mathcal{B}$ is. The runtime of adversary $\mathcal{A}$ is dominated by the single execution of algorithm $\mathcal{B}$ (which runs in polynomial time) plus the extra steps to sample the random bit c and to prepend it to the input value y. The latter steps add only a polynomial overhead to the execution time of $\mathcal{B}$.

In conclusion, the reduction gives a PPT algorithm $\mathcal{A}$ against F whose success probability bounds the one of $\mathcal{B}$ against G (times a factor of 2). Since $\mathcal{A}$'s advantage must be negligible, so must be $\mathcal{B}$'s advantage. Furthermore, since $\mathcal{B}$ is arbitrary, and we can thus derive an adversary $\mathcal{A}$ as above for every adversary $\mathcal{B}$, we obtain that the success probability of any PPT adversary $\mathcal{B}$ is negligible. This wraps up the security reduction and the proof of Proposition 2.18.

Black-box reduction. The reduction above is a so-called *black-box* reduction. The adversary $\mathcal{A}$ does not rely on the internal structure of adversary $\mathcal{B}$; it only uses $\mathcal{B}$ in a black-box way by choosing the input and observing the output. One sometimes writes $\mathcal{A}^{\mathcal{B}}$ instead of $\mathcal{A}$ for such constructions, to emphasize that the reduction (adversary $\mathcal{A}$) uses $\mathcal{B}$ as a black box. The notion usually also comprises the fact that the subroutine uses its internal and unbiased randomness for executions, although technically the full reduction is a single Turing machine and has one random tape which both algorithms must share accordingly.

Time–probability trade-off. An alternative (black-box) reduction to the one above is to have $\mathcal{A}$ run $\mathcal{B}$ twice, one time for input $(\mathsf{fk}, 0\|y)$ and the other time for input $(\mathsf{fk}, 1\|y)$, and to check if one of the returned values x_0^* (in the first execution) or x_1^* (in the second execution) gives a preimage. Adversary $\mathcal{A}$ would then output the corresponding value as its solution. This adversary is given in Figure 2.3.

An argument as above shows that one of the two executions yields a preimage for y under F with the same probability as $\mathcal{B}$ inverts G. This is independent of the question of whether both executions use the same internal randomness or not. It follows that $\mathcal{A}$'s success probability is at least as large as $\mathcal{B}$'s probability, now saving the loss factor 2 in the reduction. In return, the runtime of $\mathcal{A}$ increases roughly by a factor 2, since it now executes algorithm $\mathcal{B}$ twice (and also needs to check in polynomial time by running F.Eval which of the two returned values x_0^* and x_1^* may be the right one). Such trade-offs between runtime and success probabilities occur often in cryptographic reductions.

2.5 Computational Security—Summary

As the concept of computational security provides the basis for modern cryptography, let us briefly summarize a few important points. Computational

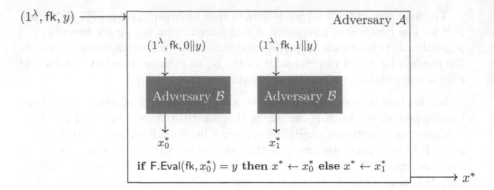

Fig. 2.3: Time–probability trade-off: alternative construction of adversary $\mathcal{A}$ against F from adversary $\mathcal{B}$ against G.

security introduces two important relaxations compared with information-theoretic security. We consider adversaries to have bounded resources where bounded means that we consider PPT adversaries: probabilistic adversaries that run in polynomial time. Furthermore, we allow the success probability of an adversary to be greater than zero given that it is negligible in the security parameter. We have seen that both relaxations are necessary to bypass the restrictions of information-theoretic security.

Security proofs are given either in the *asymptotic setting* or in the *concrete setting*. In the asymptotic setting, security is specified relative to the security parameter 1^λ and it needs to hold for all sufficiently large $\lambda \in \mathbb{N}$ that no PPT adversary can break the security of the scheme with better than negligible probability. In contrast, in the concrete setting we consider (t, ϵ)-security meaning that a scheme cannot be broken by any adversary running in time $t(\lambda)$ with probability better than $\epsilon(\lambda)$, which needs to hold for all $\lambda \in \mathbb{N}$.

Computational security is fundamentally based on the assumption that hard problems exist and thus $P \neq NP$. As such, proving any security statement unconditionally needs to contain a proof that $P \neq NP$. Because of today such a proof seems out of reach, security statements in the computational security setting are usually given in relation to some hard task or in relation to some other security property. For example, we can show that some function G is one-way given that some other function F is. We can furthermore quantify the loss in security in such a relation and, for example, show that an adversary against G cannot have a better advantage than twice the advantage of the best adversary against F. Such proofs are usually given in the form of a *security reduction* where we show that the existence of an adversary $\mathcal{B}$ against the scheme in question (for example a symmetric encryption scheme) induces the existence of an adversary $\mathcal{A}$ against some underlying scheme (say a one-way function).

Chapter Notes and References

While notions of computational security and reductions were discussed already earlier (see, for example, [2, 9]) they were first formally defined by Goldwasser and Micali in 1982 [4, 5]. In their highly influential paper, Goldwasser and Micali presented two computational security models for public-key encryption schemes, namely the notion of *semantic security* and that of *indistinguishability* (see Chapter 5), and related the notions. With this they laid the complexity-theoretic foundations for modern cryptography, which was honored in 2012 with the ACM A.M. Turing Award [1].

Notions of one-way functions go back at least to the early 1970s, and authentication schemes based on one-way functions were presented by Purdy [8] as well as Evans *et al.* [3]. A general discussion of one-way functions was given by Diffie and Hellman [2] in their seminal 1976 paper on public-key cryptography. A first formal definition of one-way functions was given by Yao in 1982 [10].

The idea of using lookup chains as a method to speed up online attack time at the cost of offline precomputation and storage space was suggested by Hellman in 1980 [6]. Rainbow tables, presented by Oechslin in 2003, improve upon the original ideas [7]. While Hellman suggested the lookup structure as a means of attacking block ciphers such as the Data Encryption Standard (DES) by speeding up exhaustive key searches, rainbow tables today are mostly associated with inverting hash functions on low-entropy inputs (such as passwords).

Exercices

Exercise 2.1. Let $c \in \mathbb{N}$ be a constant, let $\epsilon_1, \epsilon_2 : \mathbb{N} \to \mathbb{R}$ be negligible functions, and let $\delta : \mathbb{N} \to \mathbb{R}$ be a non-negligible function. Which of the following functions is negligible:

a) $f_1(\lambda) := \log(\lambda)^{-\log(\lambda)}$

b) $f_2(\lambda) := \binom{\lambda}{c}^{-1}$

c) $f_3(\lambda) := \lambda^{-42}$

d) $f_4(\lambda) := \frac{\lambda^7}{2^\lambda}$

e) $f_5(\lambda) := \epsilon_1\left(\lceil \epsilon_2(\lambda) \rceil\right)$

f) $f_6(\lambda) := \epsilon_1\left(\lceil \epsilon_2^{-1}(\lambda) \rceil\right)$

g) $f_7(\lambda) := \epsilon_1\left(\lceil \delta(\lambda) \rceil\right)$

h) $f_8(\lambda) := \delta\left(\lceil \epsilon_1(\lambda) \rceil\right)$

i) $f_9(\lambda) := \delta\left(\lceil \epsilon_1^{-1}(\lambda) \rceil\right)$

Exercise 2.2. A function f grows *super-logarithmically* in its input, denoted by $f(\lambda) \in \omega(\log(\lambda))$, if for every constant $c \in \mathbb{N}$ there exists $\Lambda \in \mathbb{N}$ such that for all $\lambda \geq \Lambda$ we have that

$$f(\lambda) > c \cdot \log(\lambda).$$

Let f be such a function and define $\epsilon(\lambda) := 2^{-f(\lambda)}$. Show that ϵ is negligible.

Exercise 2.3. Prove that the sum of constantly many negligible functions is negligible. That is, prove Proposition 2.4 (page 78).

Exercise 2.4. Consider once more our login system example where the client deposits the image $y \leftarrow \mathsf{F.Eval}(\mathsf{fk}, x)$ of password x under the one-way function F, and the server can check the validity of a login attempt by comparing the image of the entered password with the deposited value y. Suppose that the server would like to save on storage and instead of keeping the full image y it truncates the value by cutting off the final B bits. To check, the server would recompute the image of the entered password, as before, and compare the prefix of the result with the stored truncated value.

For what values of B is the above secure, that is, for what values of B is function $\mathsf{G} = (\mathsf{G.KGen}, \mathsf{G.Eval})$ a one-way function where G is derived from one-way function F by keeping the key generation and evaluation algorithms but truncating the output of the evaluation by B bits:

$$\mathsf{G.Eval}(1^\lambda, x, \mathsf{fk}) := \mathsf{F.Eval}(1^\lambda, x, \mathsf{fk})[1 \ldots \mathsf{F.ol}(\lambda) - B].$$

Exercise 2.5. Show that no function can be one-way for a predictable distribution.

Exercise 2.6. Let F and G be length-preserving unkeyed one-way functions (i.e., $|\mathsf{F}(x)| = |x|$). Which of the following functions are one-way?

a) $\mathsf{F}_1(x) = 1$

b) $\mathsf{F}_2(x) = \begin{cases} 0^{|x|} & \text{if } x = 0^{|x|} \\ \mathsf{F}(x) & \text{otherwise} \end{cases}$

c) $\mathsf{F}_3(x) = \mathsf{F}(x)[1..\mathsf{F.ol}(\lambda)/2]$

d) $\mathsf{F}_4(x) = \mathsf{F}(\mathsf{F}(x))$

e) $\mathsf{F}_5(x) = \mathsf{F}(x\|0)\|\mathsf{F}(x\|1)$

f) $\mathsf{F}_6(x) = \mathsf{F}(x)\|\mathsf{G}(x)$

g) $\mathsf{F}_7(x) = \mathsf{F}(x) \oplus \mathsf{G}(x)$

h) $\mathsf{F}_8(x) = \begin{cases} \mathsf{F}(x) & \text{if } x[0] = 1 \\ \mathsf{G}(x) & \text{otherwise} \end{cases}$

Exercise 2.7. Consider once more functions $\mathsf{F}_6(x) := \mathsf{F}(x)\|\mathsf{G}(x)$ and $\mathsf{F}_7(x) = \mathsf{F}(x) \oplus \mathsf{G}(x)$ from the previous exercise. Show that these can be one-way even if both F and G are not one-way. That is, show that there exist length-preserving functions F and G that are not one-way but such that F_6 (resp. F_7) is one-way.

Exercise 2.8. The previous two exercises considered length-preserving one-way functions, that is, functions F for which $|\mathsf{F}(x)| = |x|$. Show that if one-way functions exist at all, then also length-preserving one-way functions exist.

Exercise 2.9. Show that there can be no one-way function of the form $\{0,1\}^\lambda \to \{0,1\}^{\lfloor \log(\lambda) \rfloor}$. Furthermore, show that the same holds for functions of the form $\{0,1\}^{\lfloor \log(\lambda) \rfloor} \to \{0,1\}^\lambda$.

Exercise 2.10. Recall the complexity classes P and NP from Section 1.4 (page 36). Show that the existence of one-way functions implies that $\mathsf{P} \neq \mathsf{NP}$.

Exercise 2.11. We have seen two variants of one-way functions: unkeyed one-way functions (Definition 2.9; page 81) and keyed one-way functions (Definition 2.15; page 84). Show the following statement: Unkeyed one-way functions exist if, and only if, keyed one-way functions exist.

Chapter Bibliography

1. Association for Computing Machinery. Press release: Goldwasser and Micali receive ACM Turing Award for advances that revolutionized the science of cryptography. https://www.acm.org/binaries/content/assets/press_releases/turing_award_2012.pdf, 3 2013.
2. Whitfield Diffie and Martin E. Hellman. New directions in cryptography. *IEEE Transactions on Information Theory*, 22(6):644–654, 1976.
3. Arthur Evans, Jr., William Kantrowitz, and Edwin Weiss. A user authentication scheme not requiring secrecy in the computer. *Communications of the ACM*, 17(8):437–442, August 1974.
4. Shafi Goldwasser and Silvio Micali. Probabilistic encryption and how to play mental poker keeping secret all partial information. In *14th Annual ACM Symposium on Theory of Computing*, pages 365–377, San Francisco, CA, USA, May 5–7, 1982. ACM Press.
5. Shafi Goldwasser and Silvio Micali. Probabilistic encryption. *Journal of Computer and System Sciences*, 28(2):270–299, 1984.
6. Martin Hellman. A cryptanalytic time-memory trade-off. *IEEE Transactions on Information Theory*, 26(4):401–406, 1980.
7. Philippe Oechslin. Making a faster cryptanalytic time-memory trade-off. In Dan Boneh, editor, *Advances in Cryptology – CRYPTO 2003*, volume 2729 of *Lecture Notes in Computer Science*, pages 617–630, Santa Barbara, CA, USA, August 17–21, 2003. Springer, Heidelberg, Germany.
8. George B. Purdy. A high security log-in procedure. *Commun. ACM*, 17(8):442–445, August 1974.
9. Michael O Rabin. Digitalized signatures and public-key functions as intractable as factorization, 1979. MIT Laboratory for Computer Science, Technical Report 212.
10. Andrew Chi-Chih Yao. Theory and applications of trapdoor functions (extended abstract). In *23rd Annual Symposium on Foundations of Computer Science*, pages 80–91, Chicago, Illinois, November 3–5, 1982. IEEE Computer Society Press.

Chapter 3
Pseudorandomness and Computational Indistinguishability

In the previous chapter we began our study of hash function properties with the introduction of *computational security* and *one-wayness*. While one-way functions are at the core of computational security and modern cryptography, the security guarantees given by a function that is merely one-way are relatively few. One-way functions may be sufficient to provide a secure authentication scheme but only under the additional assumption that passwords chosen by users are uniformly random; an assumption that rarely holds in practice.

Also, as a substitute for encryption schemes one-way functions are by no means sufficient. While the one-way function experiment reads somewhat similar to an encryption operation—an adversary is given $F(x)$ and cannot invert the operation—there is a major functional difference: encryption schemes come with a decryption procedure which allows the intended recipient to recover the encrypted data. In addition, there are also important differences in terms of security. We have seen that one-way functions can leak quite a bit of information of the preimage. In particular, one-way functions are also defined only over distributions of super-logarithmic min-entropy, that is, distributions that cannot be predicted. Indeed the standard definition assumes the uniform distribution. When two parties want to communicate they, however, rarely want to send uniformly random messages across but instead they want to fully control the messages they send.

We thus require stronger security properties in order to build, for example, computationally secure encryption schemes. In this chapter we will lay a lot of the groundwork for exactly this task. We will begin by introducing the concept of *computational indistinguishability*. The idea is that if an efficient adversary cannot distinguish between two distributions, for example, a uniformly random distribution and one which is not really random but just seems so to adversaries with limited computational resources, then for the sake of analysis we can exchange the two distributions. Thus, we may analyze parts of a scheme in the information-theoretic setting, arguing that an efficient adversary cannot understand the difference.

© Springer Nature Switzerland AG 2021

A. Mittelbach, M. Fischlin, *The Theory of Hash Functions and Random Oracles*,
Information Security and Cryptography, https://doi.org/10.1007/978-3-030-63287-8_3

This will lead to the definition of *pseudorandomness*. We say that a source is pseudorandom if it is not identical to a uniformly random source, but the difference cannot be understood by efficient adversaries. Pseudorandomness is at the heart of various additional security properties we often attribute to hash functions. For example, we may want to use a hash function as a so-called *pseudorandom function*. That is, a keyed function that, when used with a hidden key, produces values that an adversary cannot distinguish from uniformly random values. Another important flavor of pseudorandomness are *pseudorandom generators*. A pseudorandom generator takes as input a short uniformly random string and outputs a string that is longer than its input. The crux is that, if the pseudorandom generator is *secure*, then no efficient adversary can distinguish the output of the generator from a string of the same length chosen uniformly at random. Pseudorandom generators and pseudorandom functions are key ingredients when it comes to designing computationally secure encryption schemes.

While pseudorandomness is all about an adversary not being able to distinguish a value from a truly random value, for some applications this guarantee is more than is needed. An important application of hash functions is not only in the authentication of users as in the login example of the previous chapter but also in the authentication of messages. Consider Alice and Bob who are interchanging messages between them. How can Alice be sure when she receives a message that it indeed originated from Bob? In case Bob added a *tag* to the message that he computed from the message and a hidden key that only Bob and Alice know then Alice could simply recompute the tag and compare it with the one Bob sent. For this we usually use *message authentication codes* (short MAC) which produce *tags* which are not necessarily pseudorandom but which should be *unpredictable* without access to the hidden key. Indeed, *unpredictability* is a property that we often attribute to hash functions and many practical MACs are, in fact, based on hash functions.

3.1 Indistinguishability

What does it mean for a value or bit string to "look random"? A simple, yet of course insufficient requirement is that the number of ones and zeros are roughly the same. Defining the essence of randomness via rules is, however, a very difficult endeavor. Thus, instead of focusing on what a random value "looks like" we instead focus on the restrictions of efficient algorithms. Suppose R_λ^{fake} is a distribution that supposedly generates *random-looking values* of length λ and let U_λ^{random} be the uniform distribution on $\{0,1\}^\lambda$. Then we can call R_λ^{fake} *random looking* or *pseudorandom* if no efficient algorithm can distinguish between seeing values from either R_λ^{fake} or from U_λ^{random}. In order to formalize this idea, we need to introduce the concept of *(computational) indistinguishability*, which will be the topic of this section.

3.1.1 Probability Ensembles

In the above example we considered distributions $U_\lambda^{\mathsf{random}}$ and $R_\lambda^{\mathsf{fake}}$ that are indexed by security parameter λ. Recall that we are using the term *distribution* synonymously to refer to both the distribution and the random variable associated with that distribution. We thus considered the random variables $U_\lambda^{\mathsf{random}}$ and $R_\lambda^{\mathsf{fake}}$ and asked whether or not they are indistinguishable. The important point being that we did not consider the indistinguishability of two single random variables but the indistinguishability of two random variables indexed by the security parameter. As we will see, indistinguishability will be an asymptotic definition and we will thus always consider sequences of random variables. This leads to the definition of *probability ensembles*.

> **Definition 3.1** (Probability Ensemble). *Let $\mathbb{I}$ be a countable index set. We call a collection of random variables $\{X_i\}_{i\in\mathbb{I}}$ indexed by set $\mathbb{I}$ a* probability ensemble.

For us, index set $\mathbb{I}$ is usually the set of natural numbers $\mathbb{N}$ and we thus consider probability ensembles that are *sequences of random variables*; one random variable per security parameter $\lambda \in \mathbb{N}$. We thus also usually use sequence notation and write $(X_\lambda)_{\lambda\in\mathbb{N}}$ rather than $\{X_\lambda\}_{\lambda\in\mathbb{N}}$ and speak of a sequence of random variables rather than a probability ensemble.

Note that this concept also translates to security experiments which can be regarded as sequences of random variables. Recall the advantage definition (page 81) of an adversary $\mathcal{A}$ in the one-way function experiment for some function F

$$\mathsf{Adv}_{\mathsf{F},\mathcal{A}}^{\mathsf{owf}}(\lambda) := \Pr\Big[\mathsf{Exp}_{\mathsf{F},\mathcal{A}}^{\mathsf{owf}}(\lambda) = 1\Big].$$

Here we can regard experiment $\mathsf{Exp}_{\mathsf{F},\mathcal{A}}^{\mathsf{owf}}(\cdot)$ as a sequence of random variables $(E_\lambda)_{\lambda\in\mathbb{N}}$ with

$$E_\lambda := \mathsf{Exp}_{\mathsf{F},\mathcal{A}}^{\mathsf{owf}}(\lambda).$$

As we will see, we will, in fact, often consider the indistinguishability of random variables described by experiments or games.

Let $X = (X_\lambda)_{\lambda\in\mathbb{N}}$ be a sequence of random variables. Then we write $x \leftarrow_\$ X(1^\lambda)$ to denote sampling a value from distribution X_λ. Giving the security parameter λ as input to X, possibly in unary, takes on a more algorithmic standpoint such that we can easily switch back and forth between (efficient) algorithms and distributions. When clear from context we also often simply speak of a random variable X meaning a sequence of random variables

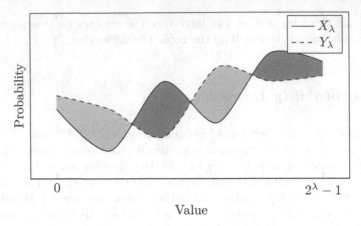

Fig. 3.1: Statistical distance between two distributions X_λ and Y_λ on values in $\{0,1\}^\lambda$. The plot displays the density functions of X_λ and Y_λ, i.e., the weight they put on each value. The statistical distance is the area between the curves scaled to a value between 0 and 1.

$X = (X_\lambda)_{\lambda \in \mathbb{N}}$ indexed by the security parameter. In particular in this chapter we consider X, Y, and Z to always be sequences of random variables.

3.1.2 Statistical Distance

The *statistical distance* is an information-theoretic distance that measures how alike two distributions are by summing up the difference of probabilities they assign to each value. In Figure 3.1 we plot the density functions of two exemplary distributions: the statistical distance corresponds to the area between the curves scaled to a value between 0 and 1. The statistical distance maximizes if the distributions put their weight on disjoint sets of values. In case the distributions are identical the statistical distance is 0. In Figure 3.2 we plot examples of distributions with a statistical distance of 0 and 1, respectively. Formally, we define statistical distance for two random variables (or distributions) as follows:

Definition 3.2 (Statistical Distance). *The* statistical distance *of two sequences of random variables* $X = (X_\lambda)_{\lambda \in \mathbb{N}}$ *and* $Y = (Y_\lambda)_{\lambda \in \mathbb{N}}$ *is defined as*

$$\mathsf{SD}_{X,Y}(\lambda) := \frac{1}{2} \cdot \sum_{z \in \{0,1\}^*} \left| \Pr\left[X(1^\lambda) = z\right] - \Pr\left[Y(1^\lambda) = z\right] \right|.$$

The factor $\frac{1}{2}$ normalizes the statistical distance to a value between 0 and 1. Loosely speaking the factor ensures that distances are not counted twice: a

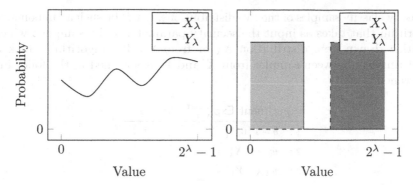

Fig. 3.2: Two extreme examples of statistical distances. In the first case (on the left) the distributions are identical and hence the statistical distance is 0. On the right, the distributions are disjoint, that is the distributions put their weight on disjoint sets of values. Hence their statistical distance is 1.

larger density at some points must be compensated for by a smaller density at other points. This is best seen when considering the extreme case where the distributions are disjoint (Figure 3.2 on the right). Without normalization, summing up the differences here would lead to a value of 2.

3.1.3 Information-Theoretic Indistinguishability

The statistical distance allows us to define an information-theoretic notion of *indistinguishability*.

> **Definition 3.3.** Let $X = (X_\lambda)_{\lambda \in \mathbb{N}}$ and $Y = (Y_\lambda)_{\lambda \in \mathbb{N}}$ be two sequences of random variables.
>
> **Perfectly indistinguishable.** *We say that the two random variables are* perfectly indistinguishable, *denoted by* $X \overset{p}{=} Y$, *if for all* $\lambda \in \mathbb{N}$ *their statistical distance is* 0.
>
> **Statistically indistinguishable.** *We say that the two random variables are* statistically indistinguishable, *denoted by* $X \overset{s}{\approx} Y$, *if their statistical distance* $\mathsf{SD}_{X,Y}(\lambda)$ *is negligible.*

In other words two random variables are *perfectly indistinguishable* if their underlying distributions are identical and their statistical distance is 0. In case their statistical distance is not 0 but a negligible function in the security parameter, then we say that the random variables are *statistically indistinguishable*.

We can characterize statistical indistinguishability also algorithmically. For this we consider the success probability of an unbounded algorithm to correctly classify samples of the two distributions. Let $\mathcal{D}$ be such an unbounded algorithm that takes as input the security parameter and a sample z which is either drawn from distribution X_λ or from Y_λ. The algorithm's task is to distinguish between samples from X and Y as specified in the following experiment:

$$\underline{\text{Experiment } \mathsf{Exp}^{\text{indist}}_{X,Y,\mathcal{D}}(\lambda)}$$

1 : $b \leftarrow\!\!\$ \{0,1\}$

2 : $w_0 \leftarrow\!\!\$ X(\lambda)$

3 : $w_1 \leftarrow\!\!\$ Y(\lambda)$

4 : $b' \leftarrow\!\!\$ \mathcal{D}(1^\lambda, w_b)$ $/\!\!/ \; b' \in \{0,1\}$

5 : **return** $b = b'$

Random variables X and Y are statistically indistinguishable if no (possibly unbounded) algorithm $\mathcal{D}$ can succeed significantly better than by guessing the bit b. That is, if and only if, for all algorithms $\mathcal{D}$ the advantage

$$\mathsf{Adv}^{\text{indist}}_{X,Y,\mathcal{D}}(\lambda) := 2 \cdot \left| \Pr\left[\mathsf{Exp}^{\text{indist}}_{X,Y,\mathcal{D}}(\lambda) = 1 \right] - \frac{1}{2} \right| \qquad (3.1)$$

is negligible. Note that for experiment $\mathsf{Exp}^{\text{indist}}_{X,Y,\mathcal{D}}(\lambda)$ it is trivial to win with probability $1/2$ since the task is to guess a random bit. We thus define the advantage to measure in how far an adversary is better than guessing. The factor 2 again normalizes the advantage to a value between 1 and 0.

An equivalent way of writing the advantage $\mathsf{Adv}^{\text{indist}}_{X,Y,\mathcal{D}}(\lambda)$ often found in cryptographic literature is

$$\mathsf{Adv}^{\text{indist}}_{X,Y,\mathcal{D}}(\lambda) := \left| \Pr\left[\mathcal{D}(1^\lambda, X(1^\lambda)) = 1 \right] - \Pr\left[\mathcal{D}(1^\lambda, Y(1^\lambda)) = 1 \right] \right|, \qquad (3.2)$$

and it is instructive to convince yourself that the two formulations are, indeed, equivalent (Exercise 3.2). Yet another useful characterization of the advantage of an adversary to distinguish between two distributions is given in the following proposition:

Proposition 3.4. *Let* $X = (X_\lambda)_{\lambda \in \mathbb{N}}$ *and* $Y = (Y_\lambda)_{\lambda \in \mathbb{N}}$ *be two sequences of random variables. Then for all (possibly unbounded) algorithms* $\mathcal{D}$ *outputting bits, it holds that*

$$\mathsf{Adv}^{\text{indist}}_{X,Y,\mathcal{D}}(\lambda) = \mathsf{SD}_{\mathcal{D}(X),\mathcal{D}(Y)}(\lambda).$$

Here $\mathcal{D}(Z) := (\mathcal{D}(Z))(1^\lambda)$ *denotes the random variable that first chooses* $z \leftarrow\!\!\$ Z(1^\lambda)$ *for random variable* Z *and subsequently outputs a bit* $b \leftarrow\!\!\$ \mathcal{D}(1^\lambda, z)$.

The proof follows by a straightforward calculation. For the intuition, apply the "graphical" interpretation of statistical distance being the area between the density functions as in Figure 3.1. We can view the output of $\mathcal{D}$ as a distribution on bits and thus write the advantage $\mathsf{Adv}^{\text{indist}}_{X,Y,\mathcal{D}}(\lambda)$ as the statistical distance between the probabilities that $\mathcal{D}$ on input X resp. Y outputs 1 (as in Equation (3.2)). This already measures the statistical distance between the random variables $\mathcal{D}(X)$ and $\mathcal{D}(Y)$ at point $b' = 1$. By symmetry the difference is furthermore identical to the one for the output $b' = 0$ of $\mathcal{D}$, such that the normalization factor of $\frac{1}{2}$ in the notion of statistical distance takes care of this doubling. The proof formalizes the above intuition.

Proof. We note that

$$\left| \Pr\left[\mathcal{D}(1^\lambda, X(1^\lambda)) = 1\right] - \Pr\left[\mathcal{D}(1^\lambda, Y(1^\lambda)) = 1\right] \right|$$
$$= \left| (1 - \Pr\left[\mathcal{D}(1^\lambda, X(1^\lambda)) = 0\right]) - (1 - \Pr\left[\mathcal{D}(1^\lambda, Y(1^\lambda)) = 0\right]) \right|$$
$$= \left| \Pr\left[\mathcal{D}(1^\lambda, X(1^\lambda)) = 0\right] - \Pr\left[\mathcal{D}(1^\lambda, Y(1^\lambda)) = 0\right] \right|.$$

This allows us to rewrite the advantage as follows. By definition we have that

$$\mathsf{Adv}^{\text{indist}}_{X,Y,\mathcal{D}}(\lambda) = \left| \Pr\left[\mathcal{D}(1^\lambda, X(1^\lambda)) = 1\right] - \Pr\left[\mathcal{D}(1^\lambda, Y(1^\lambda)) = 1\right] \right|.$$

Inserting the above observation and rearranging the equation yields

$$= \frac{1}{2} \cdot \left(\left| \Pr\left[\mathcal{D}(1^\lambda, X(1^\lambda)) = 1\right] - \Pr\left[\mathcal{D}(1^\lambda, Y(1^\lambda)) = 1\right] \right| \right.$$
$$\left. + \left| \Pr\left[\mathcal{D}(1^\lambda, X(1^\lambda)) = 0\right] - \Pr\left[\mathcal{D}(1^\lambda, Y(1^\lambda)) = 0\right] \right| \right)$$
$$= \frac{1}{2} \cdot \left(\sum_{b'=1} \left| \Pr\left[\mathcal{D}(1^\lambda, X(1^\lambda)) = b'\right] - \Pr\left[\mathcal{D}(1^\lambda, Y(1^\lambda)) = b'\right] \right| \right.$$
$$\left. + \sum_{b'=0} \left| \Pr\left[\mathcal{D}(1^\lambda, X(1^\lambda)) = b'\right] - \Pr\left[\mathcal{D}(1^\lambda, Y(1^\lambda)) = b'\right] \right| \right)$$
$$= \frac{1}{2} \cdot \sum_{b' \in \{0,1\}} \left| \Pr\left[\mathcal{D}(1^\lambda, X(1^\lambda)) = b'\right] - \Pr\left[\mathcal{D}(1^\lambda, Y(1^\lambda)) = b'\right] \right|$$
$$= \mathsf{SD}_{\mathcal{D}(X),\mathcal{D}(Y)}(\lambda),$$

where we used in the last step that it suffices to sum over all possible outputs of $\mathcal{D}$ (instead of over all strings). This concludes the proof. □

3.1.4 Computational Indistinguishability

Statistical indistinguishability is a very strong notion as it requires distributions to be indistinguishable even by algorithms which have unbounded resources. A natural weakening of the definition is to restrict adversaries to

be computationally bounded, that is, adversaries that are efficient. This leads
to the definition of *computational indistinguishability*.

Definition 3.5. *Let $X = (X_\lambda)_{\lambda \in \mathbb{N}}$ and $Y = (Y_\lambda)_{\lambda \in \mathbb{N}}$ be two sequences
of random variables. We call X and Y computationally indistinguishable,
denoted by $X \overset{c}{\approx} Y$, if for all efficient algorithms $\mathcal{D}$ the advantage*

$$\mathsf{Adv}^{\mathrm{indist}}_{X,Y,\mathcal{D}}(\lambda) := \left| \Pr\left[\mathcal{D}(1^\lambda, X(1^\lambda)) = 1\right] - \Pr\left[\mathcal{D}(1^\lambda, Y(1^\lambda)) = 1\right] \right|$$

is negligible.

Note that the definition of advantage $\mathsf{Adv}^{\mathrm{indist}}_{X,Y,\mathcal{D}}(\lambda)$ is identical to before
and thus also identical to the experiment-based definition from before. The
difference is merely that we now only consider *efficient* (i.e., PPT) distinguishers.

3.1.5 Properties of Indistinguishability

In the following we highlight various properties of the above indistinguishability
definitions. All indistinguishability notions form an equivalence relation. Yet,
some care must be taken with applying the transitivity rule multiple times in
dependence of the security parameter.

Proposition 3.6. *Let $X = (X_\lambda)_{\lambda \in \mathbb{N}}, Y = (Y_\lambda)_{\lambda \in \mathbb{N}}$, and $Z = (Z_\lambda)_{\lambda \in \mathbb{N}}$
be sequences of random variables. Then for all above indistinguishability
notions $\approx \in \{\overset{p}{\equiv}, \overset{s}{\approx}, \overset{c}{\approx}\}$ it holds that:*

Reflexivity: $X \approx X.$
Symmetry: $X \approx Y \implies Y \approx X.$
Transitivity: $X \approx Y, Y \approx Z \implies X \approx Z.$

Before we prove Proposition 3.6 let us stress that the transitivity rule, in
general, can only be applied a constant number of times. We will revisit the
transitivity rule when discussing hybrid arguments in Section 3.2.2.

Proof of Proposition 3.6. The first claim (reflexivity) is clearly correct. We
prove the second and third claim for statistical and perfect indistinguishability.
Since we have that

$$\mathsf{Adv}^{\mathrm{indist}}_{X,Y,\mathcal{D}}(\lambda) = \mathsf{SD}_{\mathcal{D}(X),\mathcal{D}(Y)}(\lambda)$$

for all algorithms $\mathcal{D}$ that output a single bit, the claims also follow for
computational indistinguishability.

Symmetry can be established by noting that $|a| = |-a|$ for all $a \in \mathbb{R}$. This
allows us to exchange the roles of random variables within the definition of
statistical distance:

$$\mathsf{SD}_{X,Y}(\lambda) = \frac{1}{2} \cdot \sum_{z \in \{0,1\}^*} \left| \Pr\left[X(1^\lambda) = z \right] - \Pr\left[Y(1^\lambda) = z \right] \right|$$

$$= \frac{1}{2} \cdot \sum_{z \in \{0,1\}^*} \left| - \Pr\left[X(1^\lambda) = z \right] + \Pr\left[Y(1^\lambda) = z \right] \right|$$

$$= \mathsf{SD}_{Y,X}(\lambda).$$

Hence, if $\mathsf{SD}_{X,Y}(\lambda)$ is negligible then so is $\mathsf{SD}_{Y,X}(\lambda)$, establishing symmetry. To show transitivity we will use the triangle inequality: $|a + b| \leq |a| + |b|$.

$$\mathsf{SD}_{X,Z}(\lambda) = \frac{1}{2} \cdot \sum_{z \in \{0,1\}^*} \left| \Pr\left[X(1^\lambda) = z \right] - \Pr\left[Z(1^\lambda) = z \right] \right|$$

$$= \frac{1}{2} \cdot \sum_{z \in \{0,1\}^*} \left| \Pr\left[X(1^\lambda) = z \right] - \Pr\left[Y(1^\lambda) = z \right] \right.$$

$$\left. + \Pr\left[Y(1^\lambda) = z \right] - \Pr\left[Z(1^\lambda) = z \right] \right|$$

$$\leq \frac{1}{2} \cdot \sum_{z \in \{0,1\}^*} \left| \Pr\left[X(1^\lambda) = z \right] - \Pr\left[Y(1^\lambda) = z \right] \right|$$

$$+ \frac{1}{2} \cdot \sum_{z \in \{0,1\}^*} \left| \Pr\left[Y(1^\lambda) = z \right] - \Pr\left[Z(1^\lambda) = z \right] \right|$$

$$= \mathsf{SD}_{X,Y}(\lambda) + \mathsf{SD}_{Y,Z}(\lambda).$$

Since the sum of two negligible functions is still negligible (Theorem 2.3; page 77), this shows the claim. $\qquad\square$

We next show that the indistinguishability notions can be arranged to form a hierarchy.

Proposition 3.7. *Let $X = (X_\lambda)_{\lambda \in \mathbb{N}}$ and $Y = (Y_\lambda)_{\lambda \in \mathbb{N}}$ be two sequences of random variables. Then it holds that*

- $X \overset{p}{\equiv} Y \implies X \overset{s}{\approx} Y$, *and*
- $X \overset{s}{\approx} Y \implies X \overset{c}{\approx} Y$.

Furthermore, it holds for any (possibly unbounded) algorithm $\mathcal{D}$ that

$$\mathsf{Adv}^{\mathrm{indist}}_{X,Y,\mathcal{D}}(\lambda) \leq \mathsf{SD}_{X,Y}(\lambda).$$

Proof. The first two statements follow directly from the definitions. Perfect indistinguishability means that the statistical distance is 0 and hence negligible. The difference between computational and statistical indistinguishability is whether or not the considered algorithms are efficient, and clearly it is the case that an inefficient algorithm can do whatever an efficient algorithm can do. It remains to show the third claim, that

$$\mathsf{Adv}^{\mathrm{indist}}_{X,Y,\mathcal{D}}(\lambda) \leq \mathsf{SD}_{X,Y}(\lambda).$$

To see this, fix algorithm $\mathcal{D}$ and note that since $\mathcal{D}$ is a distinguisher in the indistinguishability game it outputs bits. Now from Proposition 3.4 we know

$$\mathsf{Adv}_{X,Y,\mathcal{D}}^{\text{indist}}(\lambda) = \mathsf{SD}_{\mathcal{D}(X),\mathcal{D}(Y)}(\lambda)$$

$$= \frac{1}{2} \cdot \sum_{z \in \{0,1\}^*} \left| \Pr\big[\mathcal{D}(1^\lambda, X(1^\lambda)) = z\big] - \Pr\big[\mathcal{D}(1^\lambda, Y(1^\lambda)) = z\big] \right|.$$

Applying the law of total probability we can reformulate the above as

$$= \frac{1}{2} \cdot \sum_{z \in \{0,1\}^*} \left| \sum_{z' \in \{0,1\}^*} \left(\Pr\big[\mathcal{D}(1^\lambda, z') = z \mid X(1^\lambda) = z'\big] \cdot \Pr\big[X(1^\lambda) = z'\big] \right. \right.$$
$$\left. \left. - \Pr\big[\mathcal{D}(1^\lambda, z') = z \mid Y(1^\lambda) = z'\big] \cdot \Pr\big[Y(1^\lambda) = z'\big] \right) \right|.$$

Note that for given value z' algorithm $\mathcal{D}$ is oblivious to whether z' was generated by X or by Y and we thus have $\Pr\big[\mathcal{D}(1^\lambda, z') = z \mid X(1^\lambda) = z'\big] = \Pr\big[\mathcal{D}(1^\lambda, z') = z \mid Y(1^\lambda) = z'\big]$. If we additionally apply the triangle inequality we have that

$$\leq \frac{1}{2} \cdot \sum_{\substack{z \in \{0,1\}^*, \\ z' \in \{0,1\}^*}} \left| \Pr\big[\mathcal{D}(1^\lambda, z') = z \mid X(1^\lambda) = z'\big] \cdot \right.$$
$$\left. (\Pr\big[X(1^\lambda) = z'\big] - \Pr\big[Y(1^\lambda) = z'\big]) \right|$$

$$= \frac{1}{2} \cdot \sum_{z' \in \{0,1\}^*} \left(\left| \Pr\big[X(1^\lambda) = z'\big] - \Pr\big[Y(1^\lambda) = z'\big] \right| \cdot \right.$$
$$\left. \sum_{z \in \{0,1\}^*} \Pr\big[\mathcal{D}(1^\lambda, z') = z \mid X(1^\lambda) = z'\big] \right)$$

$$\leq \frac{1}{2} \cdot \sum_{z' \in \{0,1\}^*} \left| \Pr\big[X(1^\lambda) = z'\big] - \Pr\big[Y(1^\lambda) = z'\big] \right|$$

$$= \mathsf{SD}_{X,Y}(\lambda).$$

For the last inequality note that for any fixed value $z' \in \{0,1\}^*$ it holds that $\sum_{z \in \{0,1\}^*} \Pr\big[\mathcal{D}(1^\lambda, z') = z \mid X(1^\lambda) = z'\big]$ is at most 1. The claim follows. $\quad\square$

What we have exploited in the previous proof is that the statistical distance cannot be increased by a transformation, even if the algorithm implementing the transformation is probabilistic and has unbounded resources. More formally, we have shown:

Lemma 3.8. *Let $X = (X_\lambda)_{\lambda \in \mathbb{N}}$ and $Y = (Y_\lambda)_{\lambda \in \mathbb{N}}$ be two sequences of random variables and let T be a (possibly unbounded) probabilistic algorithm. Then it holds that*

$$\mathsf{SD}_{T(X),T(Y)}(\lambda) \leq \mathsf{SD}_{X,Y}(\lambda).$$

This has immediate consequences for indistinguishability under transformations: Two random variables remain indistinguishable even after transformation.

> **Theorem 3.9.** *Let $X = (X_\lambda)_{\lambda \in \mathbb{N}}$ and $Y = (Y_\lambda)_{\lambda \in \mathbb{N}}$ be two sequences of random variables and let T be a probabilistic algorithm. Then the following statements hold:*
>
> **Perfect Indistinguishability:**
>
> $$X \overset{p}{=} Y \implies T(X) \overset{p}{=} T(Y)$$
>
> **Statistical Indistinguishability:**
>
> $$X \overset{s}{\approx} Y \implies T(X) \overset{s}{\approx} T(Y)$$
>
> **Computational Indistinguishability:** *If transformation T is efficient, then it holds that*
>
> $$X \overset{c}{\approx} Y \implies T(X) \overset{c}{\approx} T(Y).$$
>
> *In particular, for any efficient distinguisher $\mathcal{D}_T$ against $T(X)$ and $T(Y)$, there exists an efficient distinguisher $\mathcal{D}$ against X and Y with*
>
> $$\mathsf{Adv}^{\mathrm{indist}}_{T(X),T(Y),\mathcal{D}_T}(\lambda) \leq \mathsf{Adv}^{\mathrm{indist}}_{X,Y,\mathcal{D}}(\lambda).$$

For the last case, distinguisher $\mathcal{D}$ can be easily constructed from $\mathcal{D}_T$ via the composition of T and $\mathcal{D}_T$, namely $\mathcal{D}(1^\lambda, z) := \mathcal{D}_T(1^\lambda, T(1^\lambda, z))$. This distinguisher first transforms the input according to T and then runs $\mathcal{D}_T$ on the result. It is clear that $\mathcal{D}$ has the same distinguishing advantage as distinguisher $\mathcal{D}_T$. Furthermore, since transformation T is efficient, algorithm $\mathcal{D}$ can be implemented efficiently.

Note that the requirement of efficiency of T is indeed necessary for the last claim. If X and Y are computationally indistinguishable but not statistically indistinguishable this means that there exists an unbounded algorithm that can distinguish the two with better than negligible probability. If we now consider this distinguisher as our transformation outputting the distinguishing bit 0 or 1, then the resulting random variables $T(X)$ and $T(Y)$ would be distinguishable also by an efficient distinguisher.

3.2 Proof Techniques

Indistinguishability is at the core of many cryptographic concepts and, in particular, used in many cryptographic proofs. In the following we introduce two important proof techniques that we will use again and again over the course of this book. The first technique is referred to as *game hopping* and is a technique to transform cryptographic experiments in such a way that adversaries do not take notice but that in the resulting adapted experiment it becomes possible to argue security. We will see examples shortly which should make this idea much more accessible. The second technique that we will discuss is the so-called *hybrid argument*, which is used to argue that distributions are indistinguishable from one another.

3.2.1 Game Hopping

We usually formalize security notions via security games or security experiments. In a security experiment, a challenger provides an environment for an adversary that has to perform a given task. For this the challenger interacts with the adversary and finally decides whether or not the adversary "wins." A sketch how this could look like is given in Figure 2.1 (page 82), which contains a pictorial representation of the security game used to define the notion of one-way functions. In the following we capture this setting of a challenger "playing against an adversary" more formally. The following may sound quite abstract at first, but once we proceed and discuss more and more examples of security games and the game hopping technique the reader will get accustomed to the approach.

Security Games

Games or experiments[1] consist of procedures which, in turn, consist of a sequence of statements together with some input arguments and zero or more outputs. Think functions in a program where the game is the entirety of the program. Procedures can call other procedures. If a procedure P gets (blackbox) access to procedure F we denote this by adding it in superscript P^F. All variables used by procedures are assumed to be of local scope. An exception are variables of the distinguished MAIN procedure, which may be globally scoped. After the execution of a procedure the variable values are left as they were after the execution of the last statement. If procedures are called multiple times, this allows them to keep track of their state.

A Game consists of a distinguished procedure, which we here refer to as MAIN and which takes the security parameter as input. Think of the MAIN procedure as the starting point for the security experiment. A game can make use of one or more functionalities F (a collection of procedures, for example a one-way function or a message authentication code) and one or

---

[1] We will use the two terms interchangeably but try to refer to experiments within definitions and games within proofs. Hence, also the name *game hopping* as a proof technique.

	Assmpt # 1	Assmpt # 2	Assmpt # 3	

$\mathsf{Game}_1(\lambda)$	$\mathsf{Game}_2(\lambda)$	$\mathsf{Game}_3(\lambda)$	$\mathsf{Game}_4(\lambda)$
// original game	// some changes	// more changes	// easy-to-analyze game
1: Step 1	Step 1	Step 1	Modified step 1
2: Step 2	Modified step 2	Modified step 2	Modified step 2
3: Step 3	Step 3	Modified step 3	Modified step 3

Fig. 3.3: Game hopping technique: example with four games and three hops. The changes from game to game are highlighted. The arrows going from game to game indicate the reason why the modification does only affect the adversary's success probability by a negligible amount.

more adversarial procedures $\mathcal{A}$ (together called "the adversary"). We restrict access to adversarial procedures to the game's MAIN procedure, i.e., only it can call adversarial procedures and, in particular, adversarial procedures cannot call one another directly.

By $\mathsf{Game}_\mathsf{F}^{\mathcal{A}}$ we denote a game using the functionality F and adversary $\mathcal{A}$. We denote by $\mathsf{Game}_\mathsf{F}^{\mathcal{A}}(\lambda) = y$ the event that Game produces output y, that is, procedure MAIN returns value y.[2] If Game uses any probabilistic procedure then $\mathsf{Game}_\mathsf{F}^{\mathcal{A}}$ is a random variable and by $\Pr[\mathsf{Game}_\mathsf{F}^{\mathcal{A}}(\lambda) = y]$ we denote the probability (over the combined randomness space of the game) that it takes on value y. We usually encounter binary games (i.e., games that output a binary value; 0 or 1). In this case we write $\Pr[\mathsf{Game}_\mathsf{F}^{\mathcal{A}}(\lambda) = 1]$ (or short $\Pr[\mathsf{Game}_\mathsf{F}^{\mathcal{A}}(\lambda)]$) to denote the probability that the game outputs 1. As examples for games consider all the experiment-based security definitions that we had so far. Here the *experiment* denotes the main procedure.

Game Hopping

An often deployed proof strategy in security proofs is *game hopping*. We will next abstract out this approach by investigating the general game hopping technique before giving an example.

The idea of game hopping is to view the adversary's attack on the construction as a security experiment and to gradually change the game. In each hop one usually takes away some of the attack surfaces, thus limiting the adversary's strategies, till one finally reaches a game in which the adversary's success probability is easy to compute. See Figure 3.3.

Usually each game hop affects the adversary's success probability and we need to account for this. Limiting the adversary's success options in a game

---

[2] The fact that games are not necessarily efficient is hinted at by not supplying the security parameter in unary notation, that is, we write $\mathsf{Game}(\lambda)$ rather than $\mathsf{Game}(1^\lambda)$.

means that the success probability decreases and we need to quantify this loss. Letting $\Pr[\mathsf{Game}_i(\lambda)]$ denote the probability that the adversary wins in game $\mathsf{Game}_i(\lambda)$, e.g., finds a valid forgery, we are thus interested in (a tight bound on) the loss $\epsilon_i(\lambda)$ when performing a game hop:

$$\Pr[\mathsf{Game}_i(\lambda)] \leq \Pr[\mathsf{Game}_{i+1}(\lambda)] + \epsilon_i(\lambda).$$

Note that the "loss" $\epsilon_i(\lambda)$ appears on the right-hand side of the inequality to balance out the smaller probability in game Game_{i+1}.

The compensation probability $\epsilon_i(\lambda)$ is typically bounded by giving a reduction to some underlying cryptographic assumption. Occasionally, the quantification may not even require a cryptographic reduction but be based on a purely probabilistic argument, for example, if the hop is based on a large random value not being equal to 0.

If we can present bounds for all game hops we can bound the success probability of the original as

$$\Pr[\mathsf{Game}_1(\lambda)] \leq \Pr[\mathsf{Game}_2(\lambda)] + \epsilon_1(\lambda)$$
$$\leq \Pr[\mathsf{Game}_3(\lambda)] + \epsilon_1(\lambda) + \epsilon_2(\lambda)$$
$$\vdots$$
$$\leq \Pr[\mathsf{Game}_m(\lambda)] + \sum_{i=1}^{m-1} \epsilon_i(\lambda).$$

In the final and easy-to-analyze game, one is then usually able to determine the (remaining) success probability straightforwardly. In general, given a bound $\epsilon_m(\lambda)$ on the final game, we can then give a bound on the success probability of some adversary $\mathcal{B}$ against the scheme (running security experiment $\mathsf{Game}_1(\lambda)$) as

$$\Pr[\mathsf{Game}_1(\lambda)] \leq \sum_{i=1}^{m} \epsilon_i(\lambda).$$

If, say, all functions $\epsilon_i(\lambda)$ are negligible and m is constant, the attack probability of $\mathcal{B}$ must then also be negligible.

Next, we make the above discussion formal for a simple example. You will find many more examples of the game hopping technique throughout this book.

Example of the Game-Hopping Technique

Consider the one-way function definition for distributions (Definition 2.15 on page 84). Let X^1 and X^2 be two efficiently sampleable distributions that are computationally indistinguishable, that is, $X^1 \stackrel{c}{\approx} X^2$. Let F be a one-way function for distribution X^1. For simplicity of presentation we here consider

F to be an unkeyed one-way function. We now show that F necessarily is also one-way for X^2, that is, we show that no efficient adversary $\mathcal{A}$ can win the following game with more than negligible probability:

$$\text{Experiment } \mathsf{Exp}^{\mathrm{owf}}_{\mathsf{F},\mathcal{A}}(\lambda)$$

1 : $x \leftarrow\!\!\$\ X^2(1^\lambda)$

2 : $y \leftarrow \mathsf{F}(x)$

3 : $x^* \leftarrow\!\!\$\ \mathcal{A}(1^\lambda, y)$

4 : **return** $\mathsf{F}(x^*) = y$

The intuition for why it should be hard for $\mathcal{A}$ to find a preimage is that, since $X^1 \overset{c}{\approx} X^2$, it should not matter much to $\mathcal{A}$ if it needs to invert for a sample from X^1 or from X^2. In order to formally show that F is one-way also for X^2 we will use game hopping to change the above game to a variant for which we know that adversary $\mathcal{A}$ cannot win. We will often provide both a text-based and a pseudocode-based description when using game hopping. Both in the text description and the pseudocode description we highlight the main argument used. Let us prove the above claim formally to show how this could look like. The pseudocode description of how the game is changed is given in Figure 3.4. Following is a text description:

$\left.\begin{array}{c}\\ \end{array}\right\} X^1 \overset{c}{\approx} X^2$ Game$_1(\lambda)$: The game is identical to the $\mathsf{Exp}^{\mathrm{owf}}_{\mathsf{F},\mathcal{A}}(\lambda)$ experiment where the preimage is drawn from distribution X^2.

Game$_2(\lambda)$: The game is as before except that the random preimage is drawn from distribution X^1 instead of X^2.

How does that help us in proving the claim? Since function F is one-way for X^1 we have that for Game$_2$ no efficient adversary exists that has more than negligible probability of winning. That is, for all efficient algorithms $\mathcal{A}$ it holds that

$$\Pr\left[\mathsf{Game}^{\mathcal{A}}_2(\lambda) = 1\right] = \mathsf{negl}(\lambda)$$

is negligible. But what we were interested in instead is showing the same for Game$_1$. However, we are one step closer, since now that we have shown that the success probability is negligible in Game$_2$ all that remains is to show that games Game$_1$ and Game$_2$ are "negligibly close." That is, we need to show that for all efficient adversaries the distributions induced by Game$_1$ and Game$_2$ are computationally indistinguishable:

$$\left|\Pr\left[\mathsf{Game}^{\mathcal{A}}_2(\lambda) = 1\right] - \Pr\left[\mathsf{Game}^{\mathcal{A}}_1(\lambda) = 1\right]\right| = \mathsf{negl}(\lambda).$$

Because then we can deduce that

$$\Pr\left[\mathsf{Game}^{\mathcal{A}}_1(\lambda) = 1\right] \leq \Pr\left[\mathsf{Game}^{\mathcal{A}}_2(\lambda) = 1\right] + \mathsf{negl}(\lambda)$$
$$= \mathsf{negl}(\lambda) + \mathsf{negl}(\lambda) = \mathsf{negl}(\lambda),$$

$$\text{Game}_1^{\mathcal{A}}(\lambda) \xrightarrow{\quad X^1 \overset{c}{\approx} X^2 \quad} \text{Game}_2^{\mathcal{A}}(\lambda)$$

1 : $\quad x \leftarrow\!\!\$\ X^2(1^\lambda)$	$x \leftarrow\!\!\$\ X^1(1^\lambda)$
2 : $\quad y \leftarrow \mathsf{F}(x)$	$y \leftarrow \mathsf{F}(x)$
3 : $\quad x^* \leftarrow\!\!\$\ \mathcal{A}(1^\lambda, y)$	$x^* \leftarrow\!\!\$\ \mathcal{A}(1^\lambda, y)$
4 : $\quad$**return** $\mathsf{F}(x^*) = y$	**return** $\mathsf{F}(x^*) = y$

Fig. 3.4: Exemplifying a game hop. The changes from game to game are highlighted. In the example in Game_2 the preimage is now obtained by sampling from distribution X^1. Since $X^1 \overset{c}{\approx} X^2$ the two games define distributions that are computationally indistinguishable and thus any efficient adversary that has non-negligible advantage in the setting provided by Game_2 also has non-negligible advantage in the setting provided by Game_1.

which is the result we were looking for.

Game_1 to Game_2. To complete the proof it remains to show that games Game_1 and Game_2 are negligibly close. Both in the text description and in the pseudocode description (Figure 3.4) of the single game hop we have hinted at the reason for why the two games are close: the computational indistinguishability of X^1 and X^2. We can view the attempt of $\mathcal{A}$ to find a preimage and the verification of success as a transformation T of the input:

$$\text{Experiment } T(1^\lambda, x)$$

1 : $\quad y \leftarrow \mathsf{F}(x)$
2 : $\quad x^* \leftarrow\!\!\$\ \mathcal{A}(1^\lambda, y)$
3 : $\quad$**return** $\mathsf{F}(x^*) = y$

With this we clearly have that $T(X^1)$ corresponds exactly to $\text{Game}_2^{\mathcal{A}}$, and $T(X^2)$ perfectly mimics the game $\text{Game}_1^{\mathcal{A}}$. Furthermore, T is efficient, since evaluation of the one-way function can be done in polynomial time and the adversary runs in probabilistic polynomial time, too. From Theorem 3.9, which states that computational indistinguishability is preserved under efficient transformations, it follows that $T(X^1) \overset{c}{\approx} T(X^2)$ and thus that the two games are close: $\text{Game}_1^{\mathcal{A}} \overset{c}{\approx} \text{Game}_2^{\mathcal{A}}$. This completes the game-hopping argument.

We will see many more examples of the game-hopping technique over the course of this book. Although the games and the proofs that games are negligibly close can be much more complex than in the above example, the basic structure, however, is always the same: gradually transform a game such that in the final game it can be easily shown that the adversary can no longer win. As for n many games we can bound the probability of Game_1 by

$$\Pr[\mathsf{Game}_1(\lambda) = 1] \leq \tag{3.3}$$

$$\sum_{i=1}^{n-1} |\Pr[\mathsf{Game}_{i+1}(\lambda) = 1] - \Pr[\mathsf{Game}_i(\lambda) = 1]| + \Pr[\mathsf{Game}_n(\lambda) = 1],$$

it remains to show that each of the intermediary steps are negligibly close.

Game-Playing Hybrids

The game-playing technique can be regarded as a special case of the *hybrid argument*, which is the topic of the next section. Jumping ahead, the hybrid argument is a technique to show that two distributions are indistinguishable. If you reconsider Equation (3.3) then this is exactly what we are doing there. We are upper bounding the difference between distributions $\Pr[\mathsf{Game}_1(\lambda) = 1]$ and $\Pr[\mathsf{Game}_n(\lambda) = 1]$. As we will see, the hybrid argument provides another way to derive the above bound. There we start with the distance (for simpler notation we drop the "$= 1$" in the probability statements)

$$\Pr[\mathsf{Game}_1(\lambda)] - \Pr[\mathsf{Game}_n(\lambda)],$$

which we "enlarge" by adding zeros as follows:

$$\Pr[\mathsf{Game}_1(\lambda)] - \Pr[\mathsf{Game}_n(\lambda)] = \Pr[\mathsf{Game}_1(\lambda)] - \Pr[\mathsf{Game}_2(\lambda)] +$$
$$\Pr[\mathsf{Game}_2(\lambda)] - \Pr[\mathsf{Game}_3(\lambda)] +$$
$$\dots +$$
$$\Pr[\mathsf{Game}_{n-1}(\lambda)] - \Pr[\mathsf{Game}_n(\lambda)].$$

Reshuffeling and applying the triangle inequality we can rewrite the above as

$$\Pr[\mathsf{Game}_1(\lambda)] - \Pr[\mathsf{Game}_n(\lambda)] \leq \sum_{i}^{n-1} |\Pr[\mathsf{Game}_{i+1}(\lambda)] - \Pr[\mathsf{Game}_i](\lambda)|.$$

Adding $\Pr[\mathsf{Game}_n(\lambda)]$ on both sides finally yields bound (3.3).

3.2.2 The Hybrid Argument

The hybrid argument is a general technique to show that two distributions of a certain form are (computationally) indistinguishable and is thus often used in game hopping to show that two adjacent games are negligibly close. To motivate the technique we revert to random variables. Since games can be viewed as special cases of random variables our discussion applies to games as well. Assume that we have two random variables X and Y which are computationally indistinguishable. Now consider the t-fold repetition $X_{\times t}$ of X which is the random variable which on input 1^λ outputs the vector $(x_1, \ldots, x_t)$ of t independent samples $x_i \leftarrow\!\!\$\ X(1^\lambda)$ of X. It is convenient to write $X_{\times t} = (X, X, X, \ldots, X)$ with the understanding that each entry corresponds to an independent copy of the random variable X. Define $Y_{\times t}$ analogously. Are these t-fold repetitions also computationally indistinguishable if X and Y are?

The *hybrid method* (or hybrid argument) provides an answer to such questions. The idea is to consider a sequence of hybrid random variables $H^0, \ldots H^t$, such that H^0 corresponds to $X_{\times t}$ and H^t to $Y_{\times t}$, and each transition from H^i to H^{i+1} only corresponds to an indistinguishable change.[3] In other words, the sequence H^0 to H^t causes a gradual shift from $X_{\times t}$ to $Y_{\times t}$ but such that the intermediate steps are not harmful, implying that the two extreme hybrids must be indistinguishable. In the case of the t-fold repetitions the hybrids could, starting from the vector $(X, X, X, \ldots, X)$ of X-samples, step-wise replace one copy of X with Y until all occurrences have been replaced:

$$
\begin{aligned}
H^0 \ \ &= (\ X,\ X,\ X,\ \ldots X,\ X\ ) \\
H^1 \ \ &= (\ Y,\ X,\ X,\ \ldots X,\ X\ ) \\
H^2 \ \ &= (\ Y,\ Y,\ X,\ \ldots X,\ X\ ) \\
&\ \ \vdots \\
H^{t-1} &= (\ Y,\ Y,\ Y,\ \ldots Y,\ X\ ) \\
H^t \ \ &= (\ Y,\ Y,\ Y,\ \ldots Y,\ Y\ )
\end{aligned}
$$

Intuitively, since each pair H^i and H^{i+1} only differs in the $(i+1)$st entry, namely, X or Y, and X and Y are computationally indistinguishable, all hybrids should be close. Our goal is to provide a formal proof for this intuition. To this end, let us first formalize the statement that we want to prove in this section via the hybrid argument.

Lemma 3.10. *Let $X = (X_\lambda)_{\lambda \in \mathbb{N}}$ and $Y = (Y_\lambda)_{\lambda \in \mathbb{N}}$ be two sequences of random variables that are computationally indistinguishable, that is, $X \stackrel{c}{\approx} Y$. Then for any polynomial $\mathsf{t} : \mathbb{N} \to \mathbb{N}$ also the t-fold repetitions*

$$
X_{\times \mathsf{t}} := (X_\lambda^1, X_\lambda^2, \ldots, X_\lambda^{\mathsf{t}(\lambda)})_{\lambda \in \mathbb{N}} \quad and \quad Y_{\times \mathsf{t}} := (Y_\lambda^1, Y_\lambda^2, \ldots, Y_\lambda^{\mathsf{t}(\lambda)})_{\lambda \in \mathbb{N}}
$$

are computationally indistinguishable. Here all X_λ^i (resp. Y_λ^i) are independent copies of random variable X_λ (resp. Y_λ).

Note that in Proposition 3.6 we have shown that our indistinguishability notions satisfy the properties of an equivalence relation. While we have shown that transitivity holds, that is, if $X \approx Y$ and $Y \approx Z$, then also $X \approx Z$, we have also mentioned that transitivity only holds for a constant number of steps.

---

[3] While we usually consider indexes to start at 1 it is here convenient to have 0-based indices for hybrids as this simplifies the writing of sums in later analyses.

This implies that the desired result easily follows for a constant number t of intermediate hybrids. But for cryptographic applications we often make a polynomially number of hops, such that we need to make some additional stipulation on the random variables.

In the following we formalize the *hybrid argument* which extends the constant transitivity of indistinguishability notions to polynomially many steps under certain assumptions. The different requirements for the hybrid argument to work can be subtle, and indeed they are often glossed over in the cryptographic literature. We will here present four versions of the hybrid argument that can be used in different situations. Each version comes with different assumptions and conclusions and there is no strict hierarchy between the various versions.

Remark 3.11. We will present the following sections for computational indistinguishability as this is usually the setup in which the hybrid argument is used. However, all the results can also be shown for statistical indistinguishability. The proofs will be almost identical except that we consider unbounded algorithms. Furthermore, note that for perfect indistinguishability the transitivity rule can trivially be applied an arbitrary number of times.

3.2.2.1 Constant Number of Hybrids

We begin with the simplest form of the hybrid argument for a constant number of hybrids. That is, for a constant $t \in \mathbb{N}$ we consider sequences of random variables (or hybrids) $H^0, H^1, \ldots, H^t$ and show that if any two neighboring hybrids are indistinguishable, then so are hybrids H^0 and H^t. A common example are game-hopping-based proofs where one often has a constant number of game hops in the proof. This result for a constant number of hybrids immediately follows from Proposition 3.6, but it helps to formalize the proof for the upcoming discussions.

Theorem 3.12 (Hybrid Argument for Constant Number of Hybrids).

Let $t \in \mathbb{N}$ be a fixed integer and let $H^0, H^1, \ldots, H^t$ be sequences of random variables (i.e., $H^i = (H^i_\lambda)_{\lambda \in \mathbb{N}}$). Then it holds that

$$\forall i \in [t-1] : H^i \overset{c}{\approx} H^{i+1} \implies H^0 \overset{c}{\approx} H^t.$$

Proof. Let us fix an arbitrary algorithm $\mathcal{A}$ that can distinguish distributions H^0 and H^t with advantage $\mathsf{Adv}^{\mathrm{indist}}_{H^0, H^t, \mathcal{A}}(\lambda)$:

$$\mathsf{Adv}^{\mathrm{indist}}_{H^0, H^t, \mathcal{A}}(\lambda) = \left| \Pr\left[\mathcal{A}(1^\lambda, H^0(1^\lambda)) = 1\right] - \Pr\left[\mathcal{A}(1^\lambda, H^t(1^\lambda)) = 1\right] \right|.$$

By "adding the overall term of 0" this can be rewritten in a telescoping sum as follows:

$$= \left| \Pr\left[\mathcal{A}(1^\lambda, H^0(1^\lambda)) = 1\right] - \Pr\left[\mathcal{A}(1^\lambda, H^1(1^\lambda)) = 1\right] \right.$$
$$+ \Pr\left[\mathcal{A}(1^\lambda, H^1(1^\lambda)) = 1\right] - \Pr\left[\mathcal{A}(1^\lambda, H^2(1^\lambda)) = 1\right]$$
$$+ \Pr\left[\mathcal{A}(1^\lambda, X^2(1^\lambda)) = 1\right] - \Pr\left[\mathcal{A}(1^\lambda, H^3(1^\lambda)) = 1\right]$$
$$+ \ldots$$
$$\left. + \Pr\left[\mathcal{A}(1^\lambda, H^{t-1}(1^\lambda)) = 1\right] - \Pr\left[\mathcal{A}(1^\lambda, H^t(1^\lambda)) = 1\right] \right|.$$

More compactly:

$$= \left| \sum_{i=0}^{t-1} \Pr\left[\mathcal{A}(1^\lambda, H^i(1^\lambda)) = 1\right] - \Pr\left[\mathcal{A}(1^\lambda, H^{i+1}(1^\lambda)) = 1\right] \right|.$$

Finally, applying the triangle inequality $|a + b| \le |a| + |b|$ we derive

$$\le \sum_{i=0}^{t-1} \left| \Pr\left[\mathcal{A}(1^\lambda, H^i(1^\lambda)) = 1\right] - \Pr\left[\mathcal{A}(1^\lambda, H^{i+1}(1^\lambda)) = 1\right] \right|$$
$$= \sum_{i=0}^{t-1} \mathsf{Adv}_{H^i, H^{i+1}, \mathcal{A}}^{\mathsf{indist}}(\lambda). \tag{3.4}$$

By assumption $H^i \stackrel{c}{\approx} H^{i+1}$, and thus the advantages in Equation (3.4) are negligible for any PPT adversary $\mathcal{A}$. As a constant sum of negligible functions is negligible (see Lemma 2.3; page 92) it follows that also Equation (3.4) denotes a negligible function, which concludes the proof. $\qquad\square$

3.2.2.2 Polynomial Number of Hybrids with a Universal Distinguishing Bound

As discussed earlier, a constant number of hybrids is often not sufficient for cryptographic applications. Instead, we usually require a polynomial number of hybrids $H^0, H^1, \ldots, H^{\mathsf{p}(\lambda)}$ for some polynomial p. Note that in this case we consider random variables where both the number of hybrids as well as the hybrids themselves depend on the security parameter. To capture the dependency of the index of the hybrid from the security parameter we usually consider a function $I : \mathbb{N} \to \mathbb{N}$ which maps every parameter λ to the index $i = I(\lambda) \in \{0, 1, \ldots, \mathsf{p}(\lambda)\}$ in question. With this we denote by H^I the hybrid given by $H^I(1^\lambda) := H^{I(\lambda)}(1^\lambda)$ which samples according to the ith hybrid for parameter 1^λ, where $i = I(\lambda)$. We call the function I p-*indexing* if $I(\lambda) \in \{0, 1, \ldots, \mathsf{p}(\lambda) - 1\}$ for all λ. It is sometimes also convenient to write H^{I+1} for the distribution $H^{I(\lambda)+1}(1^\lambda)$ and H^{p} for $H^{\mathsf{p}(\lambda)}(1^\lambda)$.

When attempting to show that $H^i \stackrel{c}{\approx} H^{i+1}$ for all $i \in \{0, 1, \ldots, \mathsf{p}(\lambda) - 1\}$ implies that also $H^0 \stackrel{c}{\approx} H^{\mathsf{p}}$ via the proof for the constant number of hybrids we run into difficulties in the very last step of the proof. Before, in Equation (3.4), we argued that the sum of a constant number of negligible functions is negligible. But as we have seen in Example 2.5 (page 78) the sum of a polynomial number of negligible functions does not have to be negligible and, consequently, assuming only $H^i \stackrel{c}{\approx} H^{i+1}$ is insufficient for the polynomial case of the hybrid argument.

We can even show that the hybrid argument of Theorem 3.12 in general fails for a polynomial number $\mathsf{p}(\lambda)$ of hybrids. To this end let $\mathsf{p}(\lambda) = \lambda$ be linear and for any $i \in \{0, 1, \ldots, \mathsf{p}(\lambda)\}$ set

$$H^i(1^\lambda) = \begin{cases} 1 & \text{if } i \geq \lambda \\ 0 & \text{else} \end{cases}$$

Then for any given i we have $H^i \stackrel{c}{\approx} H^{i+1}$ and even $H^i \stackrel{s}{\approx} H^{i+1}$ since both random variables eventually become 0, i.e., $H^i(1^\lambda) = H^{i+1}(1^\lambda) = 0$ for all $\lambda \geq i+2$. But we now have a linear number of hybrids, too, such that we can still find a non-vanishing hybrid for any given security parameter λ. In fact, if one compares $H^0(1^\lambda) = 0$ and $H^\lambda(1^\lambda) = 1$ then it follows that the hybrids H^0 and H^p for the growing $\mathsf{p}(\lambda) = \lambda$ are clearly not indistinguishable, even though any two neighboring hybrids H^i, H^{i+1} are individually close.

In the following we will see three variants of how we can work around the issue. The easiest is to assume that for each adversary $\mathcal{A}$ there exists a single negligible function ϵ that upper bounds the distinguishing advantage for any pair of neighboring hybrids. In this case we can upper bound Equation (3.4) (translated to polynomially many hybrids) as

$$\mathsf{Adv}^{\text{indist}}_{H^0,H^{\mathsf{p}(\lambda)},\mathcal{A}}(\lambda) \leq \sum_{i=0}^{\mathsf{p}(\lambda)-1} \mathsf{Adv}^{\text{indist}}_{H^i,H^{i+1},\mathcal{A}}(\lambda) \leq \sum_{i=0}^{\mathsf{p}(\lambda)-1} \epsilon(\lambda) = \mathsf{p}(\lambda) \cdot \epsilon(\lambda).$$

Since a negligible function times a polynomial remains negligible (see Lemma 2.3; page 92) we thus obtain a negligible upper bound for advantage $\mathsf{Adv}^{\text{indist}}_{H^0,H^{\mathsf{p}(\lambda)},\mathcal{A}}(\lambda)$. This is formalized in the following theorem:

Theorem 3.13 (Hybrid Argument for Universal Distinguishing Bound). *Let $\mathsf{p} : \mathbb{N} \to \mathbb{N}$ be a polynomial and let $H^0, H^1, H^2, \ldots$ be sequences of random variables (i.e., $H^i = (H^i_\lambda)_{\lambda \in \mathbb{N}}$). If for adversary $\mathcal{A}$ there exists a function ϵ such that there exists an integer $\Lambda \in \mathbb{N}$ such that for all $\lambda \geq \Lambda$ and all p-indexing functions I we have*

$$\mathsf{Adv}^{\text{indist}}_{H^I,H^{I+1},\mathcal{A}}(\lambda) \leq \epsilon(\lambda),$$

then it holds that

$$\mathsf{Adv}^{\text{indist}}_{H^0,H^{\mathsf{p}(\lambda)},\mathcal{A}}(\lambda) \leq \mathsf{p}(\lambda) \cdot \epsilon(\lambda)$$

for all $\lambda \geq \Lambda$. If ϵ is negligible then it follows that H^0 and H^p are computationally indistinguishable.

Finding a fixed upper bound for all neighboring hybrids is usually not easy, and Theorem 3.13 gives no indication of how to go about finding such an ϵ. Next, we will discuss sufficient conditions for the hybrid distributions such that we can immediately bound the distinguishing advantage $\mathsf{Adv}^{\mathrm{indist}}_{H^0,H^{\mathsf{p}(\lambda)},\mathcal{A}}(\lambda)$. These will yield the final two variants of the hybrid argument.

3.2.2.3 Polynomial Number of Hybrids: Non-uniform Variant

The following variant is based on the non-uniform model of computation (Section 1.3.3; page 21) in which an algorithm for each input length (and thus for each different security parameter) can have hardwired advice of polynomial length. The idea will be to exploit such advice to find a non-uniform upper bound on the distinguishing advantage of distributions H^0 and H^{p}.

Let us go back to the proof for the case of constantly many hybrids and there to the last step: Equation (3.4). Translated to polynomially many hybrids here we have that

$$\mathsf{Adv}^{\mathrm{indist}}_{H^0,H^{\mathsf{p}(\lambda)},\mathcal{A}}(\lambda) \leq \sum_{i=0}^{\mathsf{p}(\lambda)-1} \mathsf{Adv}^{\mathrm{indist}}_{H^i,H^{i+1},\mathcal{A}}(\lambda).$$

Now, for each $\lambda \in \mathbb{N}$ there must exist an $i_{\max} \in \{0,1,\ldots,\mathsf{p}(\lambda)-1\}$ that maximizes the distinguishing advantage. This we can capture as a p-indexing function of the security parameter as

$$I_{\max}(\lambda) := \operatorname*{arg\,max}_{i \in \{0,1,\ldots,\mathsf{p}(\lambda)-1\}} \mathsf{Adv}^{\mathrm{indist}}_{H^i,H^{i+1},\mathcal{A}}(\lambda)$$

and with this, we can rewrite the above as

$$\mathsf{Adv}^{\mathrm{indist}}_{H^0,H^{\mathsf{p}(\lambda)},\mathcal{A}}(\lambda) \leq \sum_{i=0}^{\mathsf{p}(\lambda)-1} \mathsf{Adv}^{\mathrm{indist}}_{H^i,H^{i+1},\mathcal{A}}(\lambda)$$

$$\leq \sum_{i=0}^{\mathsf{p}(\lambda)-1} \mathsf{Adv}^{\mathrm{indist}}_{H^{I_{\max}},H^{I_{\max}+1},\mathcal{A}}(\lambda)$$

$$= \mathsf{p}(\lambda) \cdot \mathsf{Adv}^{\mathrm{indist}}_{H^{I_{\max}},H^{I_{\max}+1},\mathcal{A}}(\lambda). \tag{3.5}$$

Note that $H^{I_{\max}}$ is a single distribution which, for each security parameter, "picks" a hybrid from the set of hybrids $H^0, H^1, \ldots, H^{\mathsf{p}(\lambda)-1}$. If we could now show that $H^{I_{\max}} \stackrel{\mathrm{c}}{\approx} H^{I_{\max}+1}$, then we have once more found an upper bound on the distinguishing advantage between distributions H^0 and H^{p}. Showing that $H^{I_{\max}} \stackrel{\mathrm{c}}{\approx} H^{I_{\max}+1}$ is, however, not straightforward since the helper function $I_{\max}$ may not be efficiently computable—it may even be uncomputable. As we have seen when discussing circuits and the non-uniform model of computation

(Section 1.3.3) non-uniform algorithms with polynomial advice may allow for "computing" uncomputable functions. It is that property that we will exploit shortly by hardwiring the function values $I_{max}(\lambda)$ into a non-uniform distinguisher.

The above discussion tells us where to look for the designated breaking point (via I_{max}), but does not yet give any hint on how to exploit this point. The idea for using the breaking point will be to take a "reductionist" approach. Usually when one aims to apply the hybrid method the indistinguishability of the extreme hybrids is related to the indistinguishability of two simpler random variables X and Y. A concrete example is our introductory question about the indistinguishability of the t-fold repetitions $X_{\times t}$ and $Y_{\times t}$ of X and Y. The indistinguishability of the hybrids $H^0 = (X, X, \dots, X)$ and $H^t = (Y, Y, \dots, Y)$ should somehow follow from $X \overset{c}{\approx} Y$ in the sense that any successful distinguisher against H^0 and H^t should allow us to build a successful distinguisher against X and Y. In our common terminology this is a reduction, or viewed vice versa in light of constructions of random variables, we transform X and Y into the hybrids.

More formally, we start with two random variables X and Y for which we can show that $X \overset{c}{\approx} Y$. In addition we require the existence of an efficient (possibly non-uniform) transformation T such that $T(i, X) \overset{D}{=} H^i$ and $T(i, Y) \overset{D}{=} H^{i+1}$. That is, if T receives the index $i = I(\lambda)$ and is given a sample from $X(1^\lambda)$ it implements the ith hybrid, and if given a sample from $Y(1^\lambda)$ it implements the $(i+1)$st hybrid. Below we use the shorthand $T(I, X)(1^\lambda) := T(1^\lambda, I(\lambda), X(1^\lambda))$.

Note that we require the transformation T to be identically distributed to the hybrids. If we required only statistically indistinguishability, then the theorem would not hold anymore. Namely, consider once more the efficient hybrids $H^i(1^\lambda)$, which are 1 if $i \geq \lambda$ and 0 else. Each hybrid itself is statistically close to the constant 0 function, and any neighboring hybrids are statistically close to each other. For these hybrids the constant transformation $T(i, z) = 0$ would be statistically close to any hybrid (for arbitrary random variables X, Y), and yet the extreme hybrids $H^0(1^\lambda) = 0$ and $H^\lambda(1^\lambda) = 1$ would be easy to distinguish.

Example 3.14. *As an example transformation consider once again our opening example of a t-fold repetition of variables X and Y (page 112) for efficiently sampleable X and Y. Here, the ith hybrid was defined as $(Y_{\times i}, X_{\times t-i})$ and we can thus define the transformation T as*

$$T(i, z) := (Y_1, Y_2, \dots, Y_i, z, X_1, X_2, \dots, X_{t-i-1}),$$

where values Y_j (for $j \in [i]$) and X_k (for $k \in [t-i-1]$) are independent samples of random variables Y and X, respectively. Note that for this we need to assume that distributions X and Y are efficiently sampleable. Now if value z is sampled from $X(1^\lambda)$ then $T(i, z) \overset{D}{=} H^i$ and, similarly, if z is drawn according to $Y(1^\lambda)$ then $T(i, z) \overset{D}{=} H^{i+1}$.

For each $\lambda \in \mathbb{N}$ the value of the p-indexing function $I_{max}(\lambda)$ is an integer from the set $\{0, 1, \ldots p(\lambda) - 1\}$ and thus clearly polynomially bounded in its size. If we consider a non-uniform algorithm we can thus embed the function value $I_{max}(1^\lambda)$ in its advice for security parameter λ. With this, we can now construct a *non-uniform* adversary $\mathcal{B}$ as follows. Non-uniform adversary $\mathcal{B}$ will have the index function value $I_{max}(\lambda)$ hardwired in its advice for parameter λ, and we write $\mathcal{B}[I_{max}]$ to make this explicit. In addition the algorithm $\mathcal{B}$ will use the efficient transformation T and the (efficient) adversary $\mathcal{A}$ (from Equation (3.5)) in a black-box way such that

$$\mathsf{Adv}^{indist}_{H^{I_{max}}, H^{I_{max}+1}, \mathcal{A}}(\lambda) = \mathsf{Adv}^{indist}_{X, Y, \mathcal{B}^{\mathcal{A}, T}[I_{max}]}(\lambda). \qquad (3.6)$$

Since, by assumption, distributions X and Y are computationally indistinguishable we have that the right-hand side is negligible, which yields the desired bound on distributions H^0 and $H^{p(\lambda)}$:

$$\mathsf{Adv}^{indist}_{H^0, H^{p(\lambda)}, \mathcal{A}}(\lambda) \leq p(\lambda) \cdot \mathsf{Adv}^{indist}_{H^{I_{max}(\lambda)}, H^{I_{max}(\lambda)+1}, \mathcal{A}}(\lambda)$$
$$= p(\lambda) \cdot \mathsf{Adv}^{indist}_{X, Y, \mathcal{B}^{\mathcal{A}, T}[I_{max}]}(\lambda)$$
$$= p(\lambda) \cdot \mathsf{negl}(\lambda).$$

It remains to construct efficient non-uniform adversary $\mathcal{B}^{\mathcal{A}, T}[I_{max}]$ which plays to distinguish distributions X and Y internally using transformation T and adversary $\mathcal{A}$ and which has function value $I_{max}(1^\lambda)$ hardcoded as part of its non-uniform advice. Adversary $\mathcal{B}^{\mathcal{A}, T}[I_{max}]$ gets as input a value z which is either drawn from X or from Y for parameter 1^λ. It proceeds as follows:

$\underline{\mathcal{B}^{\mathcal{A}, T}[I_{max}](1^\lambda, z)}$

1:   $i \leftarrow I_{max}(\lambda)$ // Read out value from advice

2:   $z^* \leftarrow\!\!{\scriptstyle\$}\, T(1^\lambda, i, z)$

3:   $b' \leftarrow\!\!{\scriptstyle\$}\, \mathcal{A}(1^\lambda, z^*)$

4:   **return** b'

If value z was sampled from distribution $X(1^\lambda)$, then by the definition of transformation T we have that z^* is sampled according to hybrid $H^{I_{max}(\lambda)}(1^\lambda)$. If instead z came from $Y(1^\lambda)$, then z^* is sampled according to hybrid $H^{I_{max}(\lambda)+1}(1^\lambda)$. Adversary $\mathcal{B}$ thus perfectly simulates the distinguishing experiment for adversary $\mathcal{A}$, thereby establishing the equality in Equation (3.6).

Remark 3.15. Using the above variant of the hybrid argument yields a non-uniform reduction, and as discussed in Section 1.3.3.2 (page 27), it is not always clear how to interpret such reductions. We thus here do not formulate a theorem statement for the non-uniform case, but instead discuss how we can obtain a uniform version of the above.

Remark 3.16. Above we asked from transformation T that it is such that $T(I, X) \stackrel{\text{D}}{=} H^I$ and $T(I, Y) \stackrel{\text{D}}{=} H^{I+1}$ for two distributions X and Y. In fact, it is sufficient that

$$\mathsf{Adv}^{\text{indist}}_{H^{I_{\max}(\lambda)}, H^{I_{\max}(\lambda)+1}, \mathcal{A}}(\lambda) \leq \mathsf{Adv}^{\text{indist}}_{T(I_{\max}(\lambda), X), T(I_{\max}(\lambda), Y), \mathcal{A}}(\lambda)$$

which is necessarily the case if $T(I, X) \stackrel{\text{D}}{=} H^I$ and $T(I, Y) \stackrel{\text{D}}{=} H^{I+1}$. However, exploiting the non-uniformity of $\mathcal{B}$ and thus T we can also derandomize the transformation and fix the best possible coins as part of the advice such as to maximize the distinguishing probability. This technique is also known as *coin fixing*: Instead of using random choices we use a (precomputed) sequence of choices that maximizes the advantage and which is embedded in the non-uniform advice. With this, the non-uniform version of the hybrid argument can be used to, for example, show that the t-fold repetition of random variables X and Y is computationally indistinguishable given that $X \stackrel{\text{c}}{\approx} Y$ even if X and Y are not efficiently sampleable. Here note that in Example 3.14 above we required X and Y to be efficiently sampleable. With coin fixing we could instead define transformation T as

$$T(i, z) := (y_1, y_2, \ldots, y_i, z, x_1, x_2, \ldots, x_{t-i-1}),$$

where y_i and x_i are part of the advice and chosen such that the distinguishing advantage is maximized. However, as mentioned above it is not clear how to interpret such a result in practice, which is why we do not pursue the matter of coin fixing and non-uniform hybrid arguments further.

3.2.2.4 Polynomial Number of Hybrids: Uniform Variant

In order to adapt the above non-uniform argument to the uniform case we need slightly stronger requirements, namely that transformation T is *uniform* and efficient (i.e., a PPT algorithm). As before, we will use transformation T together with adversary $\mathcal{A}$ to construct an adversary $\mathcal{B}$ that distinguishes distributions X and Y. Of course, now $\mathcal{B}$ needs to be uniform and we thus can no longer hardcode the index function value $I_{\max}(\lambda)$. Instead of trying to find the two hybrids that maximize the distinguishing advantage of adversary $\mathcal{A}$ for each security parameter, the idea now will be to simply guess the right hybrids. Why and how this works is best seen in the proof of the statement which we will describe comprehensively next.

While specifying a transformation T can in certain cases make proofs simpler, in other cases it is not quite clear how to choose the underlying distributions X and Y. For these cases we show that it also suffices to prove that

$$H^U \stackrel{\text{c}}{\approx} H^{U+1}, \tag{3.7}$$

where $U(\lambda)$ is a random variable distributed uniformly in $\{0, 1, \ldots, \mathsf{p}(\lambda) - 1\}$. Choosing the hybrids uniformly at random might look strange at first. Note however, that Equation (3.7) simply translates to advantage

$$\mathsf{Adv}^{\mathrm{indist}}_{H^{U(\lambda)}, H^{U(\lambda)+1}, \mathcal{A}}(\lambda) := \Big| \Pr\Big[\mathcal{A}(1^\lambda, H^{U(\lambda)}(1^\lambda)) = 1\Big]$$
$$- \Pr\Big[\mathcal{A}(1^\lambda, H^{U(\lambda)+1}(1^\lambda)) = 1\Big]\Big|,$$

being negligible for all efficient adversaries $\mathcal{A}$, where $U + 1$ describes the (dependent) random variable which outputs the same as U, incremented by 1. Here, adversary $\mathcal{A}$ gets as input a sample chosen as follows: First we choose $i \leftarrow\!\!{}_\$ \{0, 1, \ldots, \mathsf{p}(\lambda) - 1\}$ to then sample a value from hybrid $H^i(1^\lambda)$ on the left or a value $H^{i+1}(1^\lambda)$ on the right. If we can show that the advantage is negligible for any efficient adversary $\mathcal{A}$ then we can also argue that distributions H^0 and H^p are computationally indistinguishable. This is formalized as item 2 of the following theorem. For item 1 recall that a function $I : \mathbb{N} \mapsto \mathbb{N}$ is p-indexing if $I(\lambda) \in \{0, 1, \ldots, \mathsf{p}(\lambda) - 1\}$ for all λ.

> **Theorem 3.17** (The Hybrid Argument (uniform case)).
> Let $\mathsf{p} : \mathbb{N} \to \mathbb{N}$ be a polynomial and let $H^0, H^1, H^2, \ldots$ be sequences of random variables (i.e., $H^i = (H^i_\lambda)_{\lambda \in \mathbb{N}}$).
>
> 1. Assume that there exist random variables X and Y with $X \stackrel{c}{\approx} Y$. Assume further that for any PPT algorithm $\mathcal{A}$ there exists a PPT algorithm T such that $T(I, X) \stackrel{\mathsf{p}}{=} H^I$ and $T(I, Y) \stackrel{\mathsf{p}}{=} H^{I+1}$ for all p-indexing functions I. Then H^0 and H^p are computationally indistinguishable. In particular, for any PPT distinguisher $\mathcal{A}$ there exists a PPT distinguisher $\mathcal{B}$ with
>
> $$\mathsf{Adv}^{\mathrm{indist}}_{H^0, H^{\mathsf{p}(\lambda)}, \mathcal{A}}(\lambda) \leq \mathsf{p}(\lambda) \cdot \mathsf{Adv}^{\mathrm{indist}}_{X, Y, \mathcal{B}}(\lambda).$$
>
> 2. Let $U(\lambda)$ denote the random variable distributed uniformly in $\{0, 1, \ldots, \mathsf{p}(\lambda) - 1\}$. Then, for any PPT distinguisher $\mathcal{A}$ it holds that
> $$\mathsf{Adv}^{\mathrm{indist}}_{H^0, H^{\mathsf{p}(\lambda)}, \mathcal{A}}(\lambda) \leq \mathsf{p}(\lambda) \cdot \mathsf{Adv}^{\mathrm{indist}}_{H^{U(\lambda)}, H^{U(\lambda)+1}, \mathcal{A}}(\lambda).$$

Remark 3.18. Note that the transformation T in the first item may depend on algorithm $\mathcal{A}$. We will indeed take advantage of this dependency in the proof of Theorem 3.38 on page 144 showing how to build pseudorandom functions from pseudorandom generators.

Remark 3.19. The statement in the second point provides the hybrid samples as input to the adversary. In Section 16.2.3 we use this claim in Lemma 16.14 (page 638) in a more general version where the hybrids are given as oracles and the adversary may interact with the corresponding hybrids. Inspecting the proof below one sees that this version follows the same line of argument.

Proof of Theorem 3.17. We will first prove item 1, the hybrid argument with a transformation T. The first part of the proof is identical to the proof for constantly many hybrids (Theorem 3.12), and we here thus only provide the abbreviated version. Let us fix an arbitrary algorithm $\mathcal{A}$ that can distinguish distributions H^0 and H^{p} with advantage $\mathsf{Adv}^{\mathrm{indist}}_{H^0,H^{\mathsf{p}(\lambda)},\mathcal{A}}(\lambda)$:

$$\mathsf{Adv}^{\mathrm{indist}}_{H^0,H^{\mathsf{p}(\lambda)},\mathcal{A}}(\lambda) = \left| \Pr\left[\mathcal{A}(1^\lambda, H^0(1^\lambda)) = 1\right] - \Pr\left[\mathcal{A}(1^\lambda, H^{\mathsf{p}(\lambda)}(1^\lambda)) = 1\right] \right|.$$

By again "adding the overall term of 0" this can be rewritten as

$$= \left| \sum_{i=0}^{\mathsf{p}(\lambda)-1} \Pr\left[\mathcal{A}(1^\lambda, H^i(1^\lambda)) = 1\right] - \Pr\left[\mathcal{A}(1^\lambda, H^{i+1}(1^\lambda)) = 1\right] \right|. \qquad (3.8)$$

We next build our algorithm $\mathcal{B}^{\mathcal{A},T}$ which tries to distinguish inputs z produced either from random variable X or from random variable Y. Algorithm $\mathcal{B}^{\mathcal{A},T}$ internally uses adversary $\mathcal{A}$ and transformation T (which in turn may depend on $\mathcal{A}$) as follows:

$\mathcal{B}(1^\lambda, z)$

---

1 : $\quad i \leftarrow\!\!\$\ \{0, 1, \ldots, \mathsf{p}(\lambda) - 1\}$

2 : $\quad z' \leftarrow\!\!\$\ T(1^\lambda, i, z)$

3 : $\quad b' \leftarrow\!\!\$\ \mathcal{A}(1^\lambda, z')$

4 : **return** b'

Assume for the moment that i has been chosen already in line 1 and is fixed. If value z is a sample from $X(1^\lambda)$ then $z' \leftarrow\!\!\$\ T(1^\lambda, i, z)$ corresponds to a random sample from $T(i, X)$ for parameter 1^λ and is thus distributed as $H^i(1^\lambda)$ by assumption about T. It follows that $\mathcal{B}$'s output in this case has the same distribution as $\mathcal{A}(1^\lambda, H^i(1^\lambda))$. If, on the other hand, for the same i the input z stems from $Y(1^\lambda)$, then $T(i, z)$ is a random sample according to $T(i, Y)$ and thus distributed as a sample from $H^{i+1}(1^\lambda)$. In this case $\mathcal{B}$'s output has the same distribution as $\mathcal{A}(1^\lambda, H^{i+1}(1^\lambda))$. Hence we have

$$\left| \Pr\left[\mathcal{B}(1^\lambda, X(1^\lambda)) = 1\right] - \Pr\left[\mathcal{B}(1^\lambda, Y(1^\lambda)) = 1\right] \right|$$

$$= \left| \sum_{j=0}^{\mathsf{p}(\lambda)-1} \left(\Pr\left[\mathcal{B}(1^\lambda, X(1^\lambda)) = 1 \wedge i = j\right] - \Pr\left[\mathcal{B}(1^\lambda, Y(1^\lambda)) = 1 \wedge i = j\right]\right) \right|$$

$$= \left| \sum_{j=0}^{\mathsf{p}(\lambda)-1} \Pr[i = j] \cdot \left(\Pr\left[\mathcal{B}(1^\lambda, X(1^\lambda)) = 1 \,\middle|\, i = j\right] \right.\right.$$
$$\left.\left. - \Pr\left[\mathcal{B}(1^\lambda, Y(1^\lambda)) = 1 \,\middle|\, i = j\right]\right) \right|.$$

Here the first equality is due to marginalizing over all possible choices of index $i \in \{0, 1, \dots, p(\lambda) - 1\}$ and the second is due to rewriting the probabilities as conditional probabilities. By noting that $\Pr[i = j] = \frac{1}{p(\lambda)}$ for all values of $j \in \{0, 1, \dots, p(\lambda) - 1\}$ and that, furthermore, by definition of algorithm $\mathcal{B}$ we have that $\Pr[\mathcal{B}(1^\lambda, X(1^\lambda)) = 1 \mid i = j] = \Pr[\mathcal{A}(1^\lambda, H^j(1^\lambda)) = 1]$, we can rewrite the above as

$$= \frac{1}{p(\lambda)} \cdot \left| \sum_{j=0}^{p(\lambda)-1} \Pr[\mathcal{A}(1^\lambda, H^j(1^\lambda)) = 1] - \Pr[\mathcal{A}(1^\lambda, H^{j+1}(1^\lambda)) = 1] \right|.$$

And, finally, using the presentation as a telescoping sum, we get

$$= \frac{1}{p(\lambda)} \cdot \left| \Pr[\mathcal{A}(1^\lambda, H^0(1^\lambda)) = 1] - \Pr\left[\mathcal{A}(1^\lambda, H^{p(\lambda)}(1^\lambda)) = 1 \right] \right|.$$

Note that in case $\mathcal{A}$ is efficient then $\mathcal{B}$ only performs efficient steps, because transformation T is PPT by assumption and can be incorporated into the code of $\mathcal{B}$. Hence, we derive that the advantage of $\mathcal{A}$ against H^0 and $H^{p(\lambda)}$ is at most $p(\lambda)$ times the advantage of $\mathcal{B}$ against X and Y. Since this advantage is negligible by assumption so must be the advantage of $\mathcal{A}$. This concludes the proof for item 1.

Proof of item 2. For item 2 (the hybrid argument without a transformation T) we start once more with an arbitrary algorithm $\mathcal{A}$ and rewrite its distinguishing advantage for hybrids H^0 and $H^{p(\lambda)}$ as in Equation (3.8) above:

$$\mathsf{Adv}^{\mathrm{indist}}_{H^0, H^{p(\lambda)}, \mathcal{A}}(\lambda) = \left| \Pr[\mathcal{A}(1^\lambda, H^0(1^\lambda)) = 1] - \Pr\left[\mathcal{A}(1^\lambda, H^{p(\lambda)}(1^\lambda)) = 1 \right] \right|,$$

which can be rewritten in a telescoping sum as

$$= \left| \sum_{i=0}^{p(\lambda)-1} \Pr[\mathcal{A}(1^\lambda, H^i(1^\lambda)) = 1] - \Pr[\mathcal{A}(1^\lambda, H^{i+1}(1^\lambda)) = 1] \right|.$$

Noting that we can replace index i with random variable $U(\lambda)$ and conditioning on $U(\lambda) = i$, we get

$$= \left| \sum_{i=0}^{p(\lambda)-1} \Pr\left[\mathcal{A}(1^\lambda, H^{U(\lambda)}(1^\lambda)) = 1 \,\middle|\, U(\lambda) = i \right] \right.$$
$$\left. - \Pr\left[\mathcal{A}(1^\lambda, H^{U(\lambda)+1}(1^\lambda)) = 1 \,\middle|\, U(\lambda) = i \right] \right|.$$

Finally, with the definition of conditional probabilities ($\Pr[A \mid B] = \frac{\Pr[A \wedge B]}{\Pr[B]}$) and noting that, furthermore, for any $i \in \{0, 1, \dots, p(\lambda) - 1\}$ we have that $\Pr[U(\lambda) = i] = \frac{1}{p(\lambda)}$, the above can be rewritten to yield the desired result:

$$=\mathsf{p}(\lambda) \cdot \left| \sum_{i=0}^{\mathsf{p}(\lambda)-1} \Pr\left[\mathcal{A}(1^\lambda, H^{U(\lambda)}(1^\lambda)) = 1 \wedge U(\lambda) = i\right]\right.$$

$$\left. - \Pr\left[\mathcal{A}(1^\lambda, H^{U(\lambda)+1}(1^\lambda)) = 1 \wedge U(\lambda) = i\right]\right|$$

$$=\mathsf{p}(\lambda) \cdot \left| \Pr\left[\mathcal{A}(1^\lambda, H^{U(\lambda)}(1^\lambda)) = 1\right] - \Pr\left[\mathcal{A}(1^\lambda, H^{U(\lambda)+1}(1^\lambda)) = 1\right]\right|$$

$$=\mathsf{p}(\lambda) \cdot \mathsf{Adv}^{\text{indist}}_{H^{U(\lambda)}, H^{U(\lambda)+1}, \mathcal{A}}(\lambda).$$

Here the second equality is a simple "demarginalization" (see the definition of marginal probabilities on page 44). This concludes the proof of item 2 of the theorem. $\qquad\square$

Remark 3.20. It is instructive to think about where the above proof fails when we consider super-polynomially many hybrids. Let $\mathsf{e} : \mathbb{N} \to \mathbb{N}$ be super-polynomial, that is, a function such that for all $c \in \mathbb{N}$

$$\mathsf{e}(\lambda) \in \omega(\lambda^c).$$

Function e could for example be an exponential function such as 2^λ. Now, if e is a super-polynomial then

$$\frac{1}{\mathsf{e}(\lambda)} \cdot \mathsf{Adv}^{\text{indist}}_{H^0, H^{\mathsf{e}(\lambda)}, \mathcal{A}}(\lambda)$$

may be negligible even if $\mathsf{Adv}^{\text{indist}}_{H^0, H^{\mathsf{e}(\lambda)}, \mathcal{A}}(\lambda)$ is non-negligible. Thus the argument no longer works.

Applying the Hybrid Argument

This concludes our discussion of hybrid arguments. To summarize we recall the steps required in order to show that two distributions A and B are computationally indistinguishable using Theorem 3.17. In a first step we need to come up with a path $H^0, H^1, \dots, H^{\mathsf{p}(\lambda)}$ of at most polynomially many hybrids (intermediate distributions) that form a path from A to B. These should be such that the first hybrid matches distribution A and the last hybrid matches distribution B, i.e., $H^0 \stackrel{\mathsf{p}}{=} A$ and $H^{\mathsf{p}} \stackrel{\mathsf{p}}{=} B$. For the second step we now have two possibilities. Either we can show that hybrids H^i and H^{i+1} are computationally indistinguishable for uniformly random i (this corresponds to item 2 of the theorem), or alternatively, we can relate the hybrids to two computationally indistinguishable distributions X and Y via some transformation T such that $T(i, X) \stackrel{\mathsf{p}}{=} H^i$ and $T(i, Y) \stackrel{\mathsf{p}}{=} H^{i+1}$.

An example of how Theorem 3.17 can be applied was already given as Example 3.14 above where we considered the t-fold repetition $X_{\times t}$ and $Y_{\times t}$. Here $X_{\times t}$ and $Y_{\times t}$ are the two distributions A and B and the computationally indistinguishable distributions that form the basis of transformation T are the singular versions X and Y. We will see further examples of the hybrid argument through the course of this book and, indeed, in this chapter (Proposition 3.28 and Theorem 3.38).

3.3 Pseudorandomness

Computational indistinguishability is at the core of many cryptographic proofs and primitives. For example, if we can prove that ciphertexts generated by some encryption scheme are computationally indistinguishable from uniformly random strings of the same length then we have essentially proven that a ciphertext does not leak any information about the underlying plaintext towards efficient adversaries. Generating strings (e.g., ciphertexts) that are computational indistinguishability from uniformly random strings is, in fact, so useful that multiple cryptographic primitives exist whose sole purpose is the generation of such *pseudorandom* strings.

In the following we introduce two such important cryptographic primitives: *pseudorandom functions* and *pseudorandom generators*. Pseudorandom functions (PRFs for short) are keyed (hash) functions that require the function key to remain hidden. The security of pseudorandom functions is based on the following idea: assume that you are given a box that implements a PRF with a random key. You can interact with the box by sending inputs and receiving outputs. Then, the outputs should be pseudorandom, that is, no efficient adversary should be able to distinguish the outputs from the PRF-box from a box that returns truly random (but consistent[4]) values. Pseudorandom generators, on the other hand, are unkeyed objects that take a short string and output a longer string, the idea being that if the (short) input was chosen uniformly at random then the (longer) output is pseudorandom.

3.3.1 Pseudorandom Functions

Pseudorandom functions (short PRFs) are keyed function families PRF := (PRF.KGen, PRF.Eval) that *deterministically* generate outputs that are pseudorandom, that is, the outputs look random to any efficient adversary as long as the (random but fixed) key remains hidden from the adversary. Formally, the security of pseudorandom functions is based on a variant of our computational indistinguishability definition. Instead of giving the distinguisher a sample from a distribution the distinguisher is given oracle access to a functionality that either implements the PRF with a key chosen uniformly at random or it implements a function chosen uniformly at random from the space of all

---

[4] On the same input the box returns the same value.

functions that have the same input and output lengths as the PRF. The latter is an interesting concept that is worth dwelling on a bit: how can we provide an adversary with access to a "truly random function"?

Random functions. Mathematically, there is no problem with choosing a function with finite input and output size uniformly at random. Consider the case that our PRF is length-preserving and that $\mathsf{PRF.il}(\lambda) = \mathsf{PRF.ol}(\lambda) = \lambda$. That is, input length and output length are the same and map to λ for security parameter λ. How many possible functions are there of the form $\{0,1\}^\lambda \to \{0,1\}^\lambda$? One way to define a function is to simply write down the output for every input in a (huge) table. Each function gives a table, and vice versa, each table defines a function. There are 2^λ many bit strings of length λ so we have that each function table has 2^λ many entries. Each entry can take on any value in $\{0,1\}^\lambda$ of which there are $\left|\{0,1\}^\lambda\right| = 2^\lambda$ many. We thus have a total of

$$(2^\lambda)^{(2^\lambda)} = 2^{\lambda \cdot 2^\lambda}$$

many different combinations and thus $2^{\lambda \cdot 2^\lambda}$ different functions that map from $\{0,1\}^\lambda$ to $\{0,1\}^\lambda$. Picking a random function now means to choose one of those $2^{\lambda \cdot 2^\lambda}$ uniformly at random, each function with the same probability.

Random functions are not efficiently computable. The function table of a function that maps λ-bit strings to λ-bit strings is of size $\lambda \cdot 2^\lambda$, and it can be shown that this is more or less optimal, that is, on average the function table cannot be compressed significantly. Thus, even for small values of λ, descriptions of randomly chosen functions exceed the estimated number of atoms in the universe (which is often quoted to be around $10^{80} \approx 2^{265}$, which we would already reach for $\lambda > 256$). We will discuss the topic of choosing random functions in more detail when describing random oracles in Chapter 8.

Pseudorandom functions. In our informal description of a pseudorandom function we gave an adversary (i.e., an efficient algorithm) black-box access to either the PRF (which has a short description and is efficiently computable) or to a random function (which has no short description and is not efficiently computable). In order to work in this scenario we must thus consider *oracle Turing machines* (see Section 1.3.1 on page 17) to implement the functionality as this allows our efficient algorithm to interact with the possibly inefficient functionality (i.e., the random function).

In the following we give a formal definition of a pseudorandom function and present two equivalent formulations. To simplify notation we consider only function families $\mathsf{PRF} := (\mathsf{PRF.KGen}, \mathsf{PRF.Eval})$ that have a fixed input and output length, that is, for security parameter 1^λ they accept only inputs of length $\mathsf{PRF.il}(\lambda)$ and produce outputs of $\mathsf{PRF.ol}(\lambda)$. This allows us to more easily define the set of all functions that have an identical "input–output length behavior". In our alternative definition of pseudorandom functions which will again be more algorithmically we will drop this constraint.

Definition 3.21 (Pseudorandom Function). *Let* PRF := (PRF.KGen, PRF.Eval) *be an efficiently computable keyed function family, i.e., a pair of efficient algorithms where* PRF.KGen *is a* PPT *key generation algorithm and* PRF.Eval *is a deterministic polynomial-time evaluation algorithm. Let* $\mathsf{Func}(\lambda) := \{ f \mid f : \{0,1\}^{\mathsf{PRF.il}(\lambda)} \to \{0,1\}^{\mathsf{PRF.ol}(\lambda)} \}$ *be the set of all functions mapping strings of length* $\mathsf{PRF.il}(\lambda)$ *to* $\mathsf{PRF.ol}(\lambda)$. *We say that* PRF *is a* pseudorandom function *if for any* PPT *algorithm* $\mathcal{D}$ *the advantage* $\mathsf{Adv}^{\mathrm{prf}}_{\mathsf{PRF},\mathcal{D}}(\lambda)$ *defined as*

$$\left| \mathrm{Pr}_{\mathsf{k} \leftarrow \$\mathsf{PRF.KGen}(1^\lambda)} \left[\mathcal{D}^{\mathsf{PRF.Eval}(\mathsf{k},\cdot)}(1^\lambda) = 1 \right] - \mathrm{Pr}_{\mathsf{R} \leftarrow \$\mathsf{Func}(\lambda)} \left[\mathcal{D}^{\mathsf{R}(\cdot)}(1^\lambda) = 1 \right] \right|$$

is negligible. Here the probability is over the random coins of distinguisher $\mathcal{D}$, *and in the first probability over the random choice of key* k *and over the choice of random function* R *for the second probability.*

The definition is very similar to our definition of computational indistinguishability (Definition 3.5), and as before we can also capture pseudorandom functions via an experiment-based and more algorithmic definition. Here we will also drop the above length restrictions. In our algorithmic definition we give the distinguisher access to a single *real-or-random* oracle RoR that, depending on a hidden bit b, implements either the PRF or a random function. It is worth noting that our RoR-oracle will be efficient. This is possible as it simulates a random function via a technique called *lazy sampling* that allows to efficiently mimic the behavior of a random function for a polynomial number of inputs. The idea is to implement a lookup table T that is empty at the beginning. For each new query x, oracle RoR checks whether the lookup table contains an entry for x. If so it returns $T[x]$. Otherwise it will generate a fresh random value, store it in $T[x]$, and return it. Note that an efficient distinguisher will make at most polynomially many queries to oracle RoR and thus the lookup table will never contain more than polynomially many values. We again refer to Chapter 8 about random oracles for further details.

Definition 3.22 (Pseudorandom Function, alternative definition). *An efficiently computable function family* PRF := (PRF.KGen, PRF.Eval), *i.e., a pair of efficient algorithms where* PRF.KGen *is a* PPT *key generation algorithm and* PRF.Eval *is a deterministic polynomial-time evaluation algorithm, is called a* pseudorandom function *if advantage* $\mathsf{Adv}^{\mathrm{prf}}_{\mathsf{PRF},\mathcal{D}}(\lambda)$ *defined as*

$$\mathsf{Adv}^{\mathrm{prf}}_{\mathsf{PRF},\mathcal{D}}(\lambda) := 2 \cdot \left| \mathrm{Pr}\left[\mathsf{Exp}^{\mathrm{prf}}_{\mathsf{PRF},\mathcal{D}}(\lambda) \right] - \frac{1}{2} \right|$$

is negligible for any PPT *algorithm* $\mathcal{D}$. *Here experiment* $\mathsf{Exp}^{\mathrm{prf}}_{prf,\mathcal{D}}(\lambda)$ *is defined as*

Experiment $\mathit{Exp}^{\mathrm{prf}}_{\mathsf{PRF},\mathcal{D}}(\lambda)$	$\mathrm{RoR}[\mathsf{k},b](x)$
1: $b \leftarrow_\$ \{0,1\}$	*1:* **if** $b = 0 \wedge T[x] = \bot$ **then**
2: $\mathsf{k} \leftarrow_\$ \mathsf{PRF.KGen}(1^\lambda)$	*2:* $\quad T[x] \leftarrow \mathsf{PRF.Eval}(\mathsf{k},x)$
3: $b' \leftarrow_\$ \mathcal{D}^{\mathrm{RoR}[\mathsf{k},b]}(1^\lambda)$	*3:* **elseif** $T[x] = \bot$
4: **return** $b = b'$	*4:* $\quad \ell \leftarrow |\mathsf{PRF.Eval}(\mathsf{k},x)|$ $\quad$ // *get correct length*
	5: $\quad T[x] \leftarrow_\$ \{0,1\}^\ell$
	6: **return** $T[x]$

3.3.2 Pseudorandom Permutations

As with most cryptographic primitives pseudorandom functions can come in various flavors. A particularly important one are so-called *pseudorandom permutations* (PRP). Let $\mathsf{PRP} := (\mathsf{PRP.KGen}, \mathsf{PRP.Eval}, \mathsf{PRP.Inv})$ be a family of permutations where $\mathsf{PRP.KGen}$ is a PPT key generation algorithm, $\mathsf{PRP.Eval}$ is a deterministic polynomial-time evaluation algorithm, and $\mathsf{PRP.Inv}$ is a deterministic polynomial-time inversion algorithm such that for all $\lambda \in \mathbb{N}$, all $m \in \{0,1\}^{\mathsf{PRP.il}(\lambda)}$ and all $\mathsf{k} \leftarrow_\$ \mathsf{PRP.KGen}(\lambda)$ we have that $\mathsf{PRP.Inv}(\mathsf{k}, \mathsf{PRP.Eval}(\mathsf{k},m)) = m$.[5] We call PRP a pseudorandom permutation if it satisfies Definition 3.21 with the sole difference that it must be indistinguishable from a randomly chosen permutation rather than a random function. Note that this means that the function may not be compressing as otherwise $\mathsf{Perm} := \{\pi \mid \pi : \{0,1\}^{\mathsf{PRP.il}(\lambda)} \to \{0,1\}^{\mathsf{PRP.ol}(\lambda)}\}$, the set of all permutations mapping strings from $\{0,1\}^{\mathsf{PRP.il}(\lambda)}$ to $\{0,1\}^{\mathsf{PRP.ol}(\lambda)}$, would be empty. Usually, when considering pseudorandom permutations it makes sense to restrict permutations to be *length-preserving*, that is, to consider functions for which $\mathsf{PRP.il}(\lambda) = \mathsf{PRP.ol}(\lambda)$ for all $\lambda \in \mathbb{N}$.

It is noteworthy that the discussed exchange of Func for Perm in Definition 3.21 is actually not necessary for the definition of security of pseudorandom permutations. The reason is that efficient algorithms cannot distinguish between getting black-box access to a uniformly random function or black-box access to a uniformly random permutation in the first place. In other words:

> **Lemma 3.23.** *Any pseudorandom permutation is also a pseudorandom function.*

Lemma 3.23 is also known as the *PRF/PRP switching lemma*, and Exercise 3.4 asks the reader to prove the statement formally. This indistinguishability also allows us to define security for pseudorandom permutations via Definition 3.22

---

[5] For shorter notation we may write $\mathsf{PRP}(m)$ and $\mathsf{PRP}^{-1}(m)$ to denote evaluation and inversion.

without any additional change to the real-or-random oracle RoR. Oracle RoR chooses function values uniformly at random when simulating a random permutation which is a perfect simulation as long as the same value is not chosen a second time. Since the distinguisher is efficient and can thus only call the oracle a polynomial number of times the probability of RoR choosing a duplicate value is negligible.

Strong Pseudorandom Permutations

Our above definition of a pseudorandom permutation does not consider an important aspect of security. An adversary might be able to see inverses of function values which may allow to compromise the security of a scheme. Definitions 3.21 and 3.22 provide the distinguisher only with "forward" access to the permutation. An adversary that was able to invert the function would hence be outside the definition, and any security proof would be void for said adversary. It is thus important to also consider stronger forms of security for pseudorandom permutations that capture such adversaries. If a pseudorandom permutation remains pseudorandom even against adversaries that can invert the function, we call it a *strong pseudorandom permutation*.

Definition 3.24. *Let* PRP $:=$ (PRP.KGen, PRP.Eval, PRP.Inv) *be an efficiently computable family of keyed permutations. Let furthermore* Perm $:= \left\{ \pi \mid \pi : \{0,1\}^{\mathsf{PRP.il}(\lambda)} \to \{0,1\}^{\mathsf{PRP.ol}(\lambda)} \right\}$ *be the set of all permutations mapping strings of length* PRP.il(λ) *to* PRP.ol(λ). *We say that* PRP *is a* strong pseudorandom function *if for any* PPT *algorithm* $\mathcal{D}$ *the advantage* $\mathsf{Adv}^{\mathsf{s\text{-}prp}}_{\mathsf{PRP},\mathcal{D}}(\lambda)$ *defined as*

$$
\left| \Pr_{\mathsf{k} \leftarrow \$ \mathsf{PRP.KGen}(1^\lambda)} \left[\mathcal{D}^{\mathsf{PRF.Eval}(\mathsf{k},\cdot),\mathsf{PRF.Inv}(\mathsf{k},\cdot)}(1^\lambda) = 1 \right] - \right.
$$

$$
\left. \Pr_{P \leftarrow \$ \mathsf{Perm}} \left[\mathcal{D}^{P(\cdot),P^{-1}(\cdot)}(1^\lambda) = 1 \right] \right|
$$

is negligible. Here the probability is over the random coins of distinguisher $\mathcal{D}$, *and in the first probability over the random choice of key* k *and over the choice of random permutation* P *for the second probability.*

Length-preserving, strong pseudorandom permutations are also called *block ciphers* and are an important foundation for many encryption schemes. In fact they are also an important primitive in the design of hash functions, and we will see them again in later chapters when discussing efficient constructions of hash functions (in particular in Chapter 14).

3.3.3 Constructing PRPs: The Feistel Construction

While any pseudorandom permutation is a pseudorandom function, the other direction is, of course, not true. We can, however, construct provably secure pseudorandom permutations (or even strong pseudorandom permutations) from pseudorandom functions via the so-called *Feistel construction*.[6]

Let PRF be a length-preserving pseudorandom function (i.e., $\mathsf{PRF.il}(\lambda) = \mathsf{PRF.ol}(\lambda)$) then a Feistel construction will yield a permutation PRP of length $2 \cdot \mathsf{PRF.il}(\lambda)$. The construction is computed over the course of multiple rounds where in each round one call to the underlying function PRF is made. For this, the input of length $2 \cdot \mathsf{PRF.il}(\lambda)$ is split into a left and right half $L_1 \| R_1 = x$ and processed as

$$L_2 \| R_2 = R_1 \, \| \, (L_1 \oplus \mathsf{PRF}(\mathsf{k}_1, R_1)).$$

That is, the right half of the input directly yields the left half of the output while the right half of the output is computed as $L_1 \oplus \mathsf{PRF}(\mathsf{k}_1, R_1)$. The output of one round then becomes the input to the next round. Furthermore, for each round a separate round key is used. A schematic of a 4-round Feistel network and the pseudocode of an n-round Feistel network is given in Figure 3.5.

Already a single Feistel round yields a permutation. For this note that we can invert a Feistel round by simply reversing the roles of left and right inputs. That is, given that we know the round key we can invert round i of the Feistel construction as

$$L_{i-1} \| R_{i-1} = (R_i \oplus \mathsf{PRF}(\mathsf{k}_{i-1}, L_i)) \, \| \, L_i.$$

It is easily seen that a single round of the Feistel construction cannot yield a secure pseudorandom permutation as the left half of the output is simply the right half of the input. With slightly more effort this can also be shown for two rounds. However, it can be shown that already three rounds are sufficient to turn a pseudorandom function into a pseudorandom permutation and that four rounds or more yield a strong pseudorandom permutation.

Theorem 3.25. *If pseudorandom functions exist, then pseudorandom permutations exist. In particular, a three-round Feistel construction from a secure length-preserving pseudorandom function yields a secure pseudorandom permutation and four rounds yield a strong pseudorandom permutation.*

We here omit the (rather technical) proof of Theorem 3.25 and instead provide references in the chapter notes. On the other hand, showing that 2- and 3-round Feistel networks are insufficient for the construction of pseudorandom permutations (resp. strong pseudorandom functions) is a nice riddle which we leave to the reader as Exercise 3.5.

---

[6] Feistel constructions are also known as *Feistel ciphers* or *Feistel networks*.

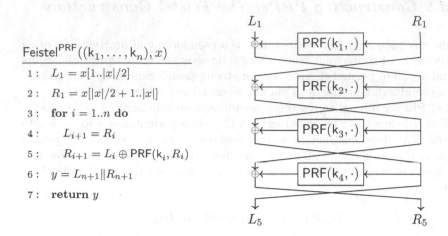

$$\text{Feistel}^{\text{PRF}}((k_1, \ldots, k_n), x)$$

1 : $L_1 = x[1..|x|/2]$

2 : $R_1 = x[|x|/2 + 1..|x|]$

3 :   **for** $i = 1..n$ **do**

4 : $L_{i+1} = R_i$

5 : $R_{i+1} = L_i \oplus \text{PRF}(k_i, R_i)$

6 : $y = L_{n+1} \| R_{n+1}$

7 :   **return** y

Fig. 3.5: Pseudocode of an n-round Feistel construction on the left and four rounds of a Feistel construction on the right. A Feistel network from at least four rounds builds a strong pseudorandom permutation from a length-preserving pseudorandom function.

3.3.4 Pseudorandom Generators

Pseudorandom functions use as the source of their *pseudorandomness* a key that needs to remain hidden in order for values from a PRF to look random. In contrast, pseudorandom generators (PRGs) do not require a hidden key but similarly to one-way functions are either unkeyed or have a publicly accessible key. The source of *pseudorandomness* of a pseudorandom generator directly comes from its input values. The idea being that on input a small truly uniformly random seed (a bit string chosen uniformly at random) a pseudorandom generator outputs a longer *pseudorandom* string.

A pseudorandom generator that can "expand" randomness has many applications. Consider, for example, encryption in the information-theoretic setting. There we have seen that in order to securely encrypt a message m we require a key k that is at least as long as the message. With a pseudorandom generator we can overcome this bound as follows, if we revert to computational security: Assume we have a short secret key k which is known to both parties. Now, in order to encrypt we use a pseudorandom generator PRG which turns the short key into an expanded key $K \leftarrow \text{PRG}(k)$, which is then used to encrypt a long message. As long as the output of the pseudorandom generator is not distinguishable from a truly random string, then intuitively the above method should be secure. In other words, if the expanded key is pseudorandom, then no PPT adversary should be able to break the encryption.

Of course, pseudorandom generators are not only used to expand keys, but to expand random values in general. We usually refer to the (small) input value as the seed s. In the formal description of the security experiment we pick a random challenge bit $b \leftarrow_\$ \{0, 1\}$, hidden from distinguisher $\mathcal{D}$, and if $b = 0$ we hand $\mathcal{D}$ a value $r_0 \leftarrow \mathsf{PRG}(s)$ (for a randomly chosen seed s), and if $b = 1$ then $\mathcal{D}$ receives a uniformly random value $r_1 \leftarrow_\$ \{0, 1\}^{\mathsf{PRG.ol}(\lambda)}$ instead. The task of the distinguisher is now to reliably predict which kind of input it received. This is measured in terms of the advantage over the pure guessing probability of $\frac{1}{2}$ such that a successful distinguisher should have a prediction probability for b which is non-negligibly larger than $\frac{1}{2}$.

We next formalize pseudorandom generators. Similarly to the case of one-way functions we also here consider families of generators (or, keyed generators). To avoid trivial cases we assume that the evaluation algorithm deterministically stretches a short random input of size $\mathsf{il}(\lambda)$ into a larger string of size $\mathsf{ol}(\lambda) > \mathsf{il}(\lambda)$.

Definition 3.26 (Pseudorandom Generator). *An efficiently computable function family* $\mathsf{PRG} = (\mathsf{PRG.KGen}, \mathsf{PRG.Eval})$, *i.e., a pair of efficient algorithms where* $\mathsf{PRG.KGen}$ *is a* PPT *key generation algorithm and* $\mathsf{PRG.Eval}$ *is a deterministic polynomial-time evaluation algorithm, is a secure* pseudorandom generator *if it satisfies the following properties:*

Stretching: *The evaluation function stretches its input, that is, for all* $\lambda \in \mathbb{N}$ *it holds that* $\mathsf{PRG.ol}(\lambda) > \mathsf{PRG.il}(\lambda)$. *We call* $\mathsf{PRG.ol}(\lambda) - \mathsf{PRG.il}(\lambda)$ *the* stretch *and the fraction* $\frac{\mathsf{PRG.ol}(\lambda)}{\mathsf{PRG.il}(\lambda)}$ *the* stretch factor *of the pseudorandom generator.*

Pseudorandom: *For every* PPT *algorithm* $\mathcal{D}$ *we have that the advantage* $\mathsf{Adv}^{\mathrm{prg}}_{\mathsf{PRG}, \mathcal{D}}(\lambda)$ *is negligible. Here, the advantage is defined as*

$$\mathsf{Adv}^{\mathrm{prg}}_{\mathsf{PRG}, \mathcal{D}}(\lambda) := 2 \cdot \left| \Pr\left[\mathsf{Exp}^{\mathrm{prg}}_{\mathsf{PRG}, \mathcal{D}}(\lambda) \right] - \frac{1}{2} \right|$$

relative to experiment $\mathsf{Exp}^{\mathrm{prg}}_{\mathsf{PRG}, \mathcal{D}}(\lambda)$:

Experiment $\mathsf{Exp}^{\mathrm{prg}}_{\mathsf{PRG}, \mathcal{D}}(\lambda)$
$1:\quad b \leftarrow_\$ \{0, 1\}$
$2:\quad \mathsf{gk} \leftarrow_\$ \mathsf{PRG.KGen}(1^\lambda)$
$3:\quad s \leftarrow_\$ \{0, 1\}^{\mathsf{PRG.il}(\lambda)}$
$4:\quad r_0 \leftarrow \mathsf{PRG.Eval}(\mathsf{gk}, s)$
$5:\quad r_1 \leftarrow_\$ \{0, 1\}^{\mathsf{PRG.ol}(\lambda)}$
$6:\quad b' \leftarrow_\$ \mathcal{D}(1^\lambda, \mathsf{gk}, r_b)$
$7:\quad \textbf{return } b = b'$

Remark 3.27. Pseudorandom generators are often used in an unkeyed setting. You can think of this as the special case where $\mathsf{PRG.KGen}$ outputs a single value for every security parameter. In this case we would simply write $\mathsf{PRG}(s)$ (or $\mathsf{PRG}(1^\lambda, s)$) to denote $\mathsf{PRG}.\mathsf{Eval}(1^\lambda, \mathsf{gk}, s)$ for the constant key gk. In the following we will also often switch to the unkeyed setting as this allows for simpler notation. Note that in these cases it should be straightforward to adapt the presented results to keyed pseudorandom generators.

PRGs with Polynomial Stretch

The definition of a pseudorandom generator requires that it stretches its input, that is the output of the generator is larger than the input. If we dropped this requirement then we could implement a trivial deterministic evaluation algorithm which either echoes or prunes the input s, such that we would have gained nothing in terms of the problem of encrypting messages which are longer than the keys. For the encryption example, the larger the stretch of the pseudorandom generator the better, since that allows us to encrypt large messages with only a short key. In the following we show that given the minimal pseudorandom generator (a PRG that stretches its input by a single bit) we can construct a pseudorandom generator with an arbitrarily long stretch.

Proposition 3.28. *Let* PRG *be a pseudorandom generator with a 1-bit stretch, i.e.,* $\mathsf{PRG}.\mathsf{ol}(\lambda) = \mathsf{PRG}.\mathsf{il}(\lambda) + 1$. *Let* $\mathsf{p} : \mathbb{N} \to \mathbb{N}$ *be an arbitrary polynomial. Then* PRG_p *defined as*

$\mathsf{PRG}_\mathsf{p}.\mathsf{Eval}(1^\lambda, s)$

$1:\quad r \leftarrow \varepsilon$

$2:\quad$ **repeat** $\mathsf{p}(\lambda)$ **times**

$3:\qquad v \leftarrow \mathsf{PRG}.\mathsf{Eval}(1^\lambda, s)$

$4:\qquad r \leftarrow r\|v[1]$ // *append first result bit to output* r

$5:\qquad s \leftarrow v[2..|v|]$ // *take remainder as new seed*

$6:\quad$ **return** r

---

is a secure pseudorandom generator with $\mathsf{PRG}_\mathsf{p}.\mathsf{ol}(\lambda) = \mathsf{p}(\lambda)$. *Furthermore, for every efficient distinguisher* $\mathcal{D}_\mathsf{p}$ *against* PRG_p *there exists an efficient distinguisher* $\mathcal{D}$ *aginst* PRG *such that*

$$\mathsf{Adv}^{\mathrm{prg}}_{\mathsf{PRG}_\mathsf{p}, \mathcal{D}_\mathsf{p}}(\lambda) \leq \mathsf{p}(\lambda) \cdot \mathsf{Adv}^{\mathrm{prg}}_{\mathsf{PRG}, \mathcal{D}}(\lambda).$$

The idea in the above construction is to iterate the pseudorandom generator and in each iteration take one result bit as an output bit and the remainder as the new seed for the next iteration. Intuitively, since in each iteration we obtain a pseudorandom string of length $|s| + 1$ we should be able to safely output a single random bit while keeping the remainder hidden such that it can be used as the seed for the next iteration. If instead a distinguisher can distinguish the result from a truly random string then this distinguisher should also be able to distinguish the underlying 1-bit stretch PRG. To prove the statement formally, we will use a hybrid argument.

Proof of Proposition 3.28. We will prove the statement using a (uniform) hybrid argument (Theorem 3.17). For this we define the following hybrid random variables $H^i(1^\lambda)$ for $0 \leq i \leq \mathsf{p}(\lambda)$ as

---

$H^i(1^\lambda)$

---
1 : $\quad s \leftarrow\!\!\$ \ \{0,1\}^{\mathsf{PRG.il}(\lambda)}$

2 : $\quad r_{\mathsf{fake}} \leftarrow\!\!\$ \ \{0,1\}^i \quad /\!\!/ \text{ if } i = 0, r_{\mathsf{fake}} \text{ is the empty string } \varepsilon$

3 : $\quad r_{\mathsf{real}} \leftarrow \varepsilon$

4 : $\quad$ **repeat** $\mathsf{p}(\lambda) - i$ **times**

5 : $\quad\quad v \leftarrow \mathsf{PRG.Eval}(1^\lambda, s)$

6 : $\quad\quad r_{\mathsf{real}} \leftarrow r_{\mathsf{real}} \| v[1]$

7 : $\quad\quad s \leftarrow v[2..|v|]$

8 : $\quad r \leftarrow r_{\mathsf{fake}} \| r_{\mathsf{real}}$

9 : $\quad$ **return** r

Hybrid variable H^i chooses the first i bits of its output at random and for the remainder iterates PRG with a random starting seed similarly to $\mathsf{PRG_p}$. The first hybrid H^0 is identically distributed to $\mathsf{PRG_p}$ on uniformly random seeds. The last hybrid $H^{\mathsf{p}(\lambda)}$, on the other hand, is distributed identically to the uniform distribution: it chooses its entire output uniformly at random.

To complete the setup for the hybrid argument we need to provide two computationally indistinguishable distributions X and Y and an efficient transformation T mapping samples from X and Y into hybrids, more precisely, it must hold that $T(i, X) \stackrel{\mathrm{D}}{=} H^i$ and $T(i, Y) \stackrel{\mathrm{D}}{=} H^{i+1}$. Note that, intuitively, two neighboring hybrids should be indistinguishable down to the security of the pseudorandom generator. In hybrid H^i the leading i bits of the output are chosen uniformly at random while in hybrid H^{i+1} the first $i + 1$ bits are chosen uniformly at random. For distributions X and Y we will thus use distributions induced by the 1-bit stretch PRG and the security notion of pseudorandom generators as follows:

$X(1^\lambda)$ $\qquad\qquad\qquad$ $Y(1^\lambda)$

---
1 : $\ s \leftarrow\!\!\$ \ \{0,1\}^{\mathsf{PRG.il}(\lambda)}$ $\qquad$ 1 :

2 : $\ r \leftarrow \mathsf{PRG.Eval}(1^\lambda, s)$ $\qquad$ 2 : $\ r \leftarrow \{0,1\}^{\mathsf{PRG.ol}(\lambda)}$

3 : **return** r $\qquad\qquad\qquad\quad$ 3 : **return** r

Random variable X chooses a random string r by sampling a uniformly random seed and setting $r \leftarrow \mathsf{PRG}(s)$. Random variable Y, on the other hand, simply chooses a uniformly random string r of length $\mathsf{PRG.ol}(\lambda)$. As by assumption PRG is a secure pseudorandom generator we have that X and Y are computationally indistinguishable. For this note that for any adversary $\mathcal{A}$ we have that

$$\begin{aligned}
\mathsf{Adv}^{\mathrm{indist}}_{X,Y,\mathcal{A}}(\lambda) &= \left|\Pr\left[\mathcal{A}(1^\lambda, X(1^\lambda)) = 1\right] - \Pr\left[\mathcal{A}(1^\lambda, Y(1^\lambda)) = 1\right]\right| \\
&= \left|\left(1 - \Pr\left[\mathsf{Exp}^{\mathrm{prg}}_{\mathsf{PRG},\mathcal{A}}(\lambda)\ \middle|\ b = 0\right]\right) - \Pr\left[\mathsf{Exp}^{\mathrm{prg}}_{\mathsf{PRG},\mathcal{A}}(\lambda)\ \middle|\ b = 1\right]\right| \\
&= \mathsf{Adv}^{\mathrm{prg}}_{\mathsf{PRG},\mathcal{A}}(\lambda).
\end{aligned}$$

Here, the second equality is due to the fact that when adversary $\mathcal{A}$ outputs 1 in case $b = 0$ that it loses the experiment and thus

$$\begin{aligned}
\Pr\left[\mathcal{A}(1^\lambda, X(1^\lambda)) = 1\right] &= \Pr\left[\mathsf{Exp}^{\mathrm{prg}}_{\mathsf{PRG},\mathcal{A}}(\lambda) = 0\ \middle|\ b = 0\right] \\
&= 1 - \Pr\left[\mathsf{Exp}^{\mathrm{prg}}_{\mathsf{PRG},\mathcal{A}}(\lambda)\ \middle|\ b = 0\right].
\end{aligned}$$

It thus remains to specify transformation T, which is almost identical to the description of hybrid H^i with the exception that it uses the first bit of its input (of length $\mathsf{PRG.ol}(\lambda) = \mathsf{PRG.il}(\lambda) + 1$) as the first "real" bit of its output and the remainder of its input as the first seed for running the pseudorandom generator:

$T(i, z)$

---

1 : $s \leftarrow\!\!\$\ z[2..|z|]$

2 : $r_{\mathsf{fake}} \leftarrow\!\!\$\ \{0,1\}^i$ // if $i = 0$, r_{fake} is the empty string ε

3 : $r_{\mathsf{real}} \leftarrow z[1]$

4 : **repeat** $\mathsf{p}(\lambda) - i - 1$ **times**

5 : $v \leftarrow \mathsf{PRG.Eval}(1^\lambda, s)$

6 : $r_{\mathsf{real}} \leftarrow r_{\mathsf{real}} \| v[1]$

7 : $s \leftarrow v[2..|v|]$

8 : $r \leftarrow r_{\mathsf{fake}} \| r_{\mathsf{real}}$

9 : **return** r

The highlighted lines changed from the description of hybrid H^i. On input a sample from X, transformation $T(i, X)$ sets the first bit of r_{real} to a pseudorandom bit and additionally initializes seed s with a pseudorandom string. This is thus exactly implementing hybrid H^i. Note that the repeat-loop is only executed $\mathsf{p}(\lambda) - i - 1$ many times as the "first execution" is taken from the input. Similarly, on input a sample from Y we have that $T(i, Y)$ sets the first bit of r_{real} to a truly random bit and initializes seed s with a uniformly random string thus implementing hybrid H^{i+1}. The proof now follows with Theorem 3.17 (page 120), which allows us to argue that for any PPT adversary $\mathcal{D}_{\mathsf{p}}$ against the extreme hybrids H^0 and H^{p}—recall that H^0 is identically distributed to PRG_p on uniformly random seeds and hybrid $H^\mathsf{p}(\lambda)$ is distributed identically to the uniform distribution—there exists a PPT adversary $\mathcal{D}$ such that

$$\mathsf{Adv}^{\mathsf{indist}}_{H^0, H^\mathsf{p}(\lambda), \mathcal{D}_\mathsf{p}}(\lambda) = \mathsf{Adv}^{\mathsf{prg}}_{\mathsf{PRG}_\mathsf{p}, \mathcal{D}_\mathsf{p}}(\lambda)$$
$$\leq \mathsf{p}(\lambda) \cdot \mathsf{Adv}^{\mathsf{indist}}_{X, Y, \mathcal{D}}(\lambda)$$
$$= \mathsf{p}(\lambda) \cdot \mathsf{Adv}^{\mathsf{prg}}_{\mathsf{PRG}, \mathcal{D}}(\lambda). \qquad \square$$

3.3.5 Pseudorandom Generators vs. One-Way Functions

A function is one-way if no efficient adversary can find a preimage to a randomly chosen image. Pseudorandom generators, on the other hand, on input a random seed output values that are computationally indistinguishable from random. Intuitively if an adversary cannot decide whether it sees a random value or a true image then it should also not be able to find a preimage. Or conversely, in case an adversary can invert the function, we should be able to also decide whether or not values are random. In the following we formalize this relationship between PRGs and one-way functions:[7]

> **Theorem 3.29.** Let $\mathsf{PRG} = (\mathsf{PRG.KGen}, \mathsf{PRG.Eval})$ be a keyed function family. If PRG is a secure pseudorandom generator then PRG is also one-way.

We will prove the statement for the simpler case where the pseudorandom generator has a stretch factor of 2 and thus doubles its input length as in this setting the proof allows for a nice application of the game-hopping technique. More concretely, we will show that in this case for every efficient adversary $\mathcal{A}$ (against the one-wayness of PRG) there exists a distinguisher $\mathcal{D}$ (against the pseudorandom generator property of PRG) such that

$$\mathsf{Adv}^{\mathsf{owf}}_{\mathsf{PRG}, \mathcal{A}}(\lambda) \leq \mathsf{Adv}^{\mathsf{prg}}_{\mathsf{PRG}, \mathcal{D}}(\lambda) + \frac{1}{2^{\mathsf{PRG.il}(\lambda)}}. \qquad (3.9)$$

For the general case it is simpler to give a proof by contradiction, that is, to give a standard reduction: Given an adversary $\mathcal{A}$ that finds preimages construct a distinguisher $\mathcal{D}$ that breaks the PRG security of the function. We leave this as Exercise 3.7.

Remark 3.30. Before we prove Theorem 3.29 let us briefly discuss the bound given in Equation (3.9) above and argue why, in particular, the bound is negligible. Since, by assumption, pseudorandom generator PRG is secure we

---

[7] Note that we here consider one-wayness for the uniform distribution (see Definition 2.15). That is, if we only speak of one-wayness without specifying a distribution we mean one-wayness for the uniform distribution.

have that advantage $\mathsf{Adv}^{\mathrm{prg}}_{\mathsf{PRG},\mathcal{D}}(\lambda)$ is negligible in the security parameter. But why should the second summand $2^{-\mathsf{PRG.il}(\lambda)}$ also be negligible? The reason is that—as we will argue in a moment—for any secure pseudorandom generator it must necessarily hold that its input length grows super-logarithmically in the security parameter, that is, $\mathsf{PRG.il}(\lambda) \in \omega(\log(\lambda))$. We can capture such super-logarithmic growth formally as follows: for every constant $c \in \mathbb{N}$ there exists $\Lambda \in \mathbb{N}$ such that for all $\lambda \geq \Lambda$ we have that

$$\mathsf{PRG.il}(\lambda) > c \cdot \log(\lambda).$$

But then function $2^{-\mathsf{PRG.il}(\lambda)}$ must be negligible as, eventually, $2^{\mathsf{PRG.il}(\lambda)}$ will outgrow any polynomial. To see this, note that $2^{c \cdot \log(\lambda)} = \lambda^c$. It remains to argue that $\mathsf{PRG.il}$ is, indeed, super-logarithmic in the security parameter. For this note that if it was not then an adversary against function PRG could compute $\mathsf{PRG}(x)$ for all possible inputs $x \in \{0,1\}^{\mathsf{PRG.il}(\lambda)}$ and remain efficient, that is, its runtime is still polynomial in the security parameter. As, by definition, $\mathsf{PRG.ol}(\lambda) > \mathsf{PRG.il}(\lambda)$ we have that there are at least twice as many outputs as inputs. Thus with probability at least $\frac{1}{2}$ a value y chosen uniformly in $\{0,1\}^{\mathsf{PRG.ol}(\lambda)}$ is such that no input $x \in \{0,1\}^{\mathsf{PRG.il}(\lambda)}$ exists such that $\mathsf{PRG}(x) = y$. Hence, an adversary $\mathcal{D}$ on input challenge value r could simply check whether there exists a preimage for r under PRG in which case it outputs 0 and otherwise it outputs 1.[8] In case r was chosen as $\mathsf{PRG}(s)$ for some seed s adversary $\mathcal{D}$ thus always outputs 0 and in case r is chosen uniformly at random in $\{0,1\}^{\mathsf{PRG.ol}(\lambda)}$ it outputs 1 with probability $\frac{1}{2}$. It follows that $\mathsf{Adv}^{\mathrm{prg}}_{\mathsf{PRG},\mathcal{D}}(\lambda) = 0.5$ and consequently function PRG would not be a secure pseudorandom generator. The assumption must thus be wrong and PRG must have an input length that grows super-logarithmically in the security parameter. With this we are now ready to prove Theorem 3.29.

Proof of Theorem 3.29. We prove Theorem 3.29 for the case that the pseudorandom generator has a stretch factor of at least 2, that is, we assume $\mathsf{PRG.ol}(\lambda) \geq 2 \cdot \mathsf{PRG.il}(\lambda)$. We will formalize the proof via an application of the game-hopping technique.

Assume there exists an adversary $\mathcal{A}$ against the one-wayness of PRG. The first game will be identical to the one-way experiment $\mathsf{Exp}^{\mathrm{owf}}_{\mathsf{PRG},\mathcal{A}}(\lambda)$, that is,

$$\Pr\left[\mathsf{Game}^{\mathcal{A}}_1(\lambda) = 1\right] = \Pr\left[\mathsf{Exp}^{\mathrm{owf}}_{\mathsf{PRG},\mathcal{A}}(\lambda) = 1\right] = \mathsf{Adv}^{\mathrm{owf}}_{\mathsf{PRG},\mathcal{A}}(\lambda).$$

We will make a single game hop exploiting the properties of the pseudorandom generator, that is, the two games will be negligibly close down to the security of the pseudorandom generator. In Game_2 we will see that it is easy for us to upper bound the advantage of adversary $\mathcal{A}$, which then allows us to prove the theorem.

---

[8] Note that since the adversary can enumerate all inputs it can efficiently check whether a preimage exists.

$$\text{Game}_1^{\mathcal{A}}(\lambda) \xrightarrow{\hspace{1.5cm}\text{PRG}\hspace{1.5cm}} \text{Game}_2^{\mathcal{A}}(\lambda)$$

1 : $\text{gk} \leftarrow\!\!{}_\$ \text{PRG.KGen}(1^\lambda)$	$\text{gk} \leftarrow\!\!{}_\$ \text{PRG.KGen}(1^\lambda)$
2 : $x \leftarrow\!\!{}_\$ \{0,1\}^{\text{PRG.il}(\lambda)}$	
3 : $y \leftarrow \text{PRG.Eval}(\text{gk}, x)$	$y \leftarrow\!\!{}_\$ \{0,1\}^{\text{PRG.ol}(\lambda)}$
4 : $x^* \leftarrow\!\!{}_\$ \mathcal{A}(1^\lambda, \text{gk}, y)$	$x^* \leftarrow\!\!{}_\$ \mathcal{A}(1^\lambda, \text{gk}, y)$
5 : **return** $\text{PRG.Eval}(\text{gk}, x^*) = y$	**return** $\text{PRG.Eval}(\text{gk}, x^*) = y$

Fig. 3.6: Game_1 is the one-wayness experiment $\text{Exp}_{\text{PRG},\mathcal{A}}^{\text{owf}}(\lambda)$ for adversary $\mathcal{A}$ against generator PRG. From Game_1 to Game_2 we change the way the "image" y is generated. In Game_1 this is done by choosing a random preimage x and computing $y \leftarrow \text{PRG.Eval}(\text{gk}, x)$. In Game_2 value y is simply chosen uniformly at random in $\{0,1\}^{\text{PRG.ol}(\lambda)}$. Intuitively the two games are indistinguishable since no efficient adversary should be able to distinguish between pseudorandom and truly random values generated by a pseudorandom generator, and this is exactly the difference between the two games.

The pseudocode of the two games is given in Figure 3.6. Following is a textual description:

$\text{Game}_1^{\mathcal{A}}(\lambda)$: The game is identical to the $\text{Exp}_{\text{PRG},\mathcal{A}}^{\text{owf}}(\lambda)$ experiment with adversary $\mathcal{A}$ playing against pseudorandom generator PRG.

$\text{Game}_2^{\mathcal{A}}(\lambda)$: The game is as before except that now "image value" y is chosen uniformly at random as $y \leftarrow\!\!{}_\$ \{0,1\}^{\text{PRG.ol}(\lambda)}$.

From our discussion of the game-hopping technique (see Section 3.2.1) we know that

$$\text{Adv}_{\text{PRG},\mathcal{A}}^{\text{owf}}(\lambda) = \Pr\left[\text{Game}_1^{\mathcal{A}}(\lambda) = 1\right]$$

$$\leq \left|\Pr\left[\text{Game}_2^{\mathcal{A}}(\lambda) = 1\right] - \Pr\left[\text{Game}_1^{\mathcal{A}}(\lambda) = 1\right]\right| + \Pr\left[\text{Game}_2^{\mathcal{A}}(\lambda) = 1\right].$$

In order to finish the proof, we must thus upper bound the right-hand side. We start with the final game Game_2.

$\text{Game}_2^{\mathcal{A}}(\lambda)$. Let us bound the success probability of adversary $\mathcal{A}$ in Game_2. In order for $\mathcal{A}$ to be successful it must find a preimage x^* such that

$$\text{PRG.Eval}(\text{gk}, x^*) = y$$

for a random key gk and for a random value $y \in \{0,1\}^{\text{PRG.ol}(\lambda)}$. However, by assumption the pseudorandom generator has a stretch of 2 and we can thus bound the probability of a preimage existing in the first place. For this note that there are $2^{\text{PRG.ol}(\lambda)}$ many choices for y but only $2^{\text{PRG.il}(\lambda)}$ possible inputs for PRG. Thus a random y has a preimage with probability at most

$$\Pr\left[\mathsf{Game}_2^{\mathcal{A}}(\lambda) = 1\right] \leq \Pr[\text{preimage exists}]$$

$$\leq \frac{2^{\mathsf{PRG.il}(\lambda)}}{2^{\mathsf{PRG.ol}(\lambda)}} \leq \frac{2^{\mathsf{PRG.il}(\lambda)}}{2^{2 \cdot \mathsf{PRG.il}(\lambda)}} = \frac{1}{2^{\mathsf{PRG.il}(\lambda)}}.$$

$\mathsf{Game}_1^{\mathcal{A}}(\lambda) \stackrel{c}{\approx} \mathsf{Game}_2^{\mathcal{A}}(\lambda)$. It remains to show that games Game_1 and Game_2 are computationally indistinguishable. We will prove this down to the security of the pseudorandom generator PRG via a reduction. Assume there exists an algorithm $\mathcal{A}$ that distinguishes games Game_1 and Game_2. From this we construct an adversary $\mathcal{D}^{\mathcal{A}}$ against the pseudorandom generator PRG as follows. Adversary $\mathcal{D}^{\mathcal{A}}$ gets as input the PRG key gk and a value r which is either a uniformly random value or a pseudorandom value generated by running a random seed through pseudorandom generator PRG. To distinguish, $\mathcal{D}^{\mathcal{A}}$ simply forwards its input to $\mathcal{A}$ to receive a potential preimage x^*. Distinguisher $\mathcal{D}^{\mathcal{A}}$ then outputs 1 if $\mathsf{PRG.Eval}(\mathsf{gk}, x^*) = r$ and 0 otherwise.

Distinguisher $\mathcal{D}^{\mathcal{A}}$ perfectly simulates the expected environments for adversary $\mathcal{A}$: if r is uniformly random it simulates Game_1, and otherwise it simulates Game_2. We thus have that

$$\left|\Pr\left[\mathsf{Game}_2^{\mathcal{A}}(\lambda) = 1\right] - \Pr\left[\mathsf{Game}_1^{\mathcal{A}}(\lambda) = 1\right]\right| = \mathsf{Adv}_{\mathsf{PRG}, \mathcal{D}^{\mathcal{A}}}^{\mathrm{prg}}(\lambda), \qquad (3.10)$$

which is negligible by the security of the pseudorandom generator.

While this concludes the proof, let us briefly discuss Equation 3.10, which may not be immediately clear. Recall the advantage definition of the pseudorandom generator security game (Definition 3.26):

$$\mathsf{Adv}_{\mathsf{PRG}, \mathcal{D}^{\mathcal{A}}}^{\mathrm{prg}}(\lambda) := 2 \cdot \left|\Pr\left[\mathsf{Exp}_{\mathsf{PRG}, \mathcal{D}^{\mathcal{A}}}^{\mathrm{prg}}(\lambda)\right] - \frac{1}{2}\right|.$$

We can rewrite $\Pr\left[\mathsf{Exp}_{\mathsf{PRG}, \mathcal{D}^{\mathcal{A}}}^{\mathrm{prg}}(\lambda)\right]$ with conditional probabilities as

$$\Pr\left[\mathsf{Exp}_{\mathsf{PRG}, \mathcal{D}^{\mathcal{A}}}^{\mathrm{prg}}(\lambda)\right] = \frac{1}{2} \cdot \Pr\left[\mathsf{Exp}_{\mathsf{PRG}, \mathcal{D}^{\mathcal{A}}}^{\mathrm{prg}}(\lambda) \mid b = 0\right]$$
$$+ \frac{1}{2} \cdot \Pr\left[\mathsf{Exp}_{\mathsf{PRG}, \mathcal{D}^{\mathcal{A}}}^{\mathrm{prg}}(\lambda) \mid b = 1\right],$$

where b denotes the hidden bit in the experiment. In case $b = 0$ the pseudorandom generator is used and in case $b = 1$ a random image is sampled. Plugging this into the advantage definition gives us

$$\mathsf{Adv}_{\mathsf{PRG}, \mathcal{D}^{\mathcal{A}}}^{\mathrm{prg}}(\lambda)$$
$$= 2 \cdot \left|\Pr\left[\mathsf{Exp}_{\mathsf{PRG}, \mathcal{D}^{\mathcal{A}}}^{\mathrm{prg}}(\lambda)\right] - \frac{1}{2}\right|$$
$$= \left|\Pr\left[\mathsf{Exp}_{\mathsf{PRG}, \mathcal{D}^{\mathcal{A}}}^{\mathrm{prg}}(\lambda) = 1 \mid b = 0\right] + \Pr\left[\mathsf{Exp}_{\mathsf{PRG}, \mathcal{D}^{\mathcal{A}}}^{\mathrm{prg}}(\lambda) = 1 \mid b = 1\right] - 1\right|.$$

In order for the first experiment to return 1 it must be the case that adversary $\mathcal{D}^{\mathcal{A}}$ outputs 0 (it guesses $b = 0$). For the other case, the experiment outputs 1 if the adversary outputs 1. It follows that

$$
\begin{aligned}
&= \left| \Pr\!\left[\mathcal{D}^{\mathcal{A}}(\mathrm{gk}, r) = 0 \mid b = 0\right] + \Pr\!\left[\mathcal{D}^{\mathcal{A}}(\mathrm{gk}, r) = 1 \mid b = 1\right] - 1 \right| \\
&= \left| (1 - \Pr\!\left[\mathcal{D}^{\mathcal{A}}(\mathrm{gk}, r) = 1 \mid b = 0\right]) + \Pr\!\left[\mathcal{D}^{\mathcal{A}}(\mathrm{gk}, r) = 1 \mid b = 1\right] - 1 \right| \\
&= \left| \Pr\!\left[\mathcal{D}^{\mathcal{A}}(\mathrm{gk}, r) = 1 \mid b = 1\right] - \Pr\!\left[\mathcal{D}^{\mathcal{A}}(\mathrm{gk}, r) = 1 \mid b = 0\right] \right| \\
&= \left| \Pr\!\left[\mathsf{Game}_2^{\mathcal{A}}(\lambda) = 1\right] - \Pr\!\left[\mathsf{Game}_1^{\mathcal{A}}(\lambda) = 1\right] \right|,
\end{aligned}
$$

which establishes Equation 3.10 and concludes the proof. □

While we have shown that any secure pseudorandom generator must necessarily be also one-way, the reverse direction does not hold. For this note that a one-way function remains one-way even if we extend all output values by appending a '1' bit. This, of course, makes it easy to distinguish values coming from this function from truly random values which, after all, end with 0 half of the time. We leave a formal proof of this statement as Exercise 3.9.

Proposition 3.31. *If there exists a secure one-way function at all, then there exists a secure one-way function that is not a secure pseudorandom generator.*

Pseudorandom Generators from One-way Functions

While there exist one-way functions that are not also pseudorandom generators, an important question is whether we can construct pseudorandom generators from one-way functions. As it turns out, the answer is yes although all known general constructions are complicated and not very efficient: the resulting pseudorandom generators require very long seeds in order to obtain a decent level of security. The result is, nevertheless, one of the classic results of modern cryptography as it shows that a large number of cryptographic applications can be built solely assuming the existence of one-way functions.

Theorem 3.32. *If there exists a secure one-way function at all, then there exist secure pseudorandom generators.*

Proving Theorem 3.32 is rather involved and very technical, and we thus here omit a formal proof of the statement. However, if we are willing to start from one-way functions that have a certain structure, such as one-way permutations (i.e., one-way functions that are permutations, that is, one-to-one), then very efficient constructions are known and we will see an example in Section 5.3.4.

3.4 Pseudorandom Functions vs. Generators

With pseudorandom functions and pseudorandom generators we have introduced two important cryptographic primitives that are based on the idea of computational indistinguishability. However, already syntactically the two are very different. The security of pseudorandom functions requires the use of a private key which necessarily needs to remain hidden. In contrast, pseudorandom generators are publicly keyed and we assume that all parties, including the adversary, know the function key. While syntactically different, we can construct one from the other. That is, we can construct pseudorandom generators from pseudorandom functions, and vice versa, we can construct pseudorandom functions from pseudorandom generators. Together with the fact that pseudorandom generators can be built from one-way functions this establishes the following important theorem:

> **Theorem 3.33.** *If there exists a secure one-way function at all, then there exist secure pseudorandom functions.*

3.4.1 PRGs from PRFs

We start with the simpler construction, a construction of a pseudorandom generator from a pseudorandom function. Here the challenge is to somehow turn a *privately keyed* primitive into a *publicly keyed* primitive. What we can make use of is the fact that in the pseudorandom generator security game input seeds are chosen uniformly at random. The idea is thus to use the seed as key and evaluate the pseudorandom function on known points. The following construction formalizes the idea. We here, for simplicity, start from a length-preserving pseudorandom function, but note that the construction can be generalized to work with arbitrary pseudorandom functions, as long as the length of the concatenation of all outputs exceeds the key length. For this we simply evaluate the pseudorandom function on more than just two points to obtain the desired output length.

Construction 3.34. *Let* $\mathsf{PRF} : \{0,1\}^\lambda \times \{0,1\}^\lambda \to \{0,1\}^\lambda$ *be a pseudorandom function with* $\mathsf{PRF.KGen}(1^\lambda) \stackrel{\text{\tiny D}}{=} U_\lambda$, *where* U_λ *is the uniform distribution over* $\{0,1\}^\lambda$. *That is, keys for* PRF *are chosen uniformly at random in* $\{0,1\}^\lambda$. *We define (unkeyed) function* $\mathsf{PRG} : \{0,1\}^\lambda \to \{0,1\}^{2\lambda}$ *with a stretch factor of* 2 *as given below:*

$\underline{\mathsf{PRG.Eval}(s)}$

1 : $r_0 \leftarrow\!\!{\scriptstyle\$}\ \mathsf{PRF.Eval}(s, 0^\lambda)$

2 : $r_1 \leftarrow\!\!{\scriptstyle\$}\ \mathsf{PRF.Eval}(s, 1^\lambda)$

3 :   **return** $r_0 \| r_1$

Proposition 3.35. *Construction 3.34 yields a secure pseudorandom generator given that the underlying function is a secure pseudorandom function.*

Proof. We can prove the statement with a standard security reduction. To this end let $\mathcal{A}$ be an adversary against the pseudorandom generator property of PRG. From this we construct a distinguisher $\mathcal{D}$ against pseudorandom function PRF as follows. Distinguisher $\mathcal{D}$ gets oracle access to some oracle O which either implements function PRF for a uniformly random key or a uniformly random function R. It queries its oracle on points 0^λ and 1^λ to obtain results r_0 and r_1. The distinguisher then calls adversary $\mathcal{A}$ on input the security parameter and value $r_0\|r_1$. Once adversary $\mathcal{A}$ returns a bit b' distinguisher $\mathcal{D}$ simply echoes the bit. Following is a pseudocode description of the distinguisher:

$$\underline{\mathcal{D}^{\mathsf{O},\mathcal{A}}(1^\lambda)}$$

$$1: \quad r_0 \leftarrow\!\!{\scriptstyle\$}\; \mathsf{O}(0^\lambda)$$

$$2: \quad r_1 \leftarrow\!\!{\scriptstyle\$}\; \mathsf{O}(1^\lambda)$$

$$3: \quad b' \leftarrow\!\!{\scriptstyle\$}\; \mathcal{A}(1^\lambda, r_0\|r_1)$$

$$4: \quad \textbf{return } b'$$

It remains to analyze the success probability of distinguisher $\mathcal{D}$. When oracle O implements a uniformly random function R then the two queries will be answered with uniformly random values and consequently $r_0\|r_1$ as given to adversary is distributed uniformly in $\{0,1\}^{2\lambda}$. This is exactly the setting of the pseudorandom generator experiment $\mathsf{Exp}^{\mathrm{prg}}_{\mathsf{PRG},\mathcal{A}}(\lambda)$ with hidden bit $b = 1$. Similarly, if oracle O implements function PRF then values r_0 and r_1 are distributed as in Construction 3.34. For this note that PRF as implemented by oracle O is instantiated with a uniformly random key and thus $\mathsf{O}_s(0^\lambda)\|\mathsf{O}_s(1^\lambda)$ (where s denotes the key that was chosen) is the same as $\mathsf{PRG}(s)$. Consequently, we have that

$$\mathsf{Adv}^{\mathrm{prg}}_{\mathsf{PRG},\mathcal{A}}(\lambda) = \mathsf{Adv}^{\mathrm{prf}}_{\mathsf{PRF},\mathcal{D}}(\lambda),$$

which concludes the proof. $\qquad\qquad\qquad\qquad\qquad\qquad\qquad\qquad\qquad\quad\square$

3.4.2 PRFs from PRGs—The GGM Construction

When constructing a pseudorandom function from a pseudorandom generator we can make use of the fact that pseudorandom functions are privately keyed and we can thus use a value that remains secret from the adversary in our construction. As pseudorandom generators are only secure if the seed remains hidden it is a natural approach to thus use the private key as input to the pseudorandom generator. This yields the following base template for our construction:

$$\mathsf{PRF}(\mathsf{k}, x) := \mathsf{PRG}(\mathsf{k}).$$

So far, we have not yet used the input x in the construction. Let us start with the simplest of inputs, that is, inputs of length $|x| = 1$. In this case we need to be able to handle two distinct inputs 0 and 1, and on each need to return a pseudorandom result. If the pseudorandom generator produces sufficiently long outputs, we can simply use distinct parts of $\mathsf{PRG}(\mathsf{k})$ as output for our pseudorandom function, for example, we can use the left half as output for $x = 0$. For this let us assume that pseudorandom generator PRG has a stretch factor of 2 and is of the form $\mathsf{PRG} : \{0,1\}^\lambda \to \{0,1\}^{2\lambda}$. We then define

$$\mathsf{PRG}_0(s) \| \mathsf{PRG}_1(s) := \mathsf{PRG}(s)$$

to denote the left and right half of the output, that is, $\mathsf{PRG}_0(s) := \mathsf{PRG}(s)[1..\lambda]$ and $\mathsf{PRG}_1(s) := \mathsf{PRG}(s)[\lambda + 1..2\lambda]$. With this we can define a PRF with a single bit b input as

$$\mathsf{PRF}(\mathsf{k}, b) := \mathsf{PRG}_b(\mathsf{k}).$$

Can we extend the above construction to also larger inputs? If we simply continued in the same fashion and for each possible input chose a fraction of the PRG's output then clearly we require an exponentially long output of the PRG to support even moderately long inputs for our PRF. Even if we restrict the output length of the resulting PRF to just a single bit, when considering inputs of length λ the PRG would be required to have an output length of $\mathsf{PRG.ol}(\lambda) = 2^\lambda$.

With Proposition 3.28 we showed that we can construct a pseudorandom generator with arbitrarily long stretch from a generator that only stretches its input by a single bit. Here, the idea was to repeatedly evaluate the underlying pseudorandom generator, in each step producing the seed for the next evaluation as well as one or more bits for the output. In the following we take a similar approach but instead of sequentially chaining calls to the pseudorandom generator, we will put them in a tree structure.

Let PRG be as before a pseudorandom generator that doubles its input. We then define a pseudorandom function recursively as follows:

$$\mathsf{PRF}(\mathsf{k}, x) := \mathsf{PRG}_x(\mathsf{k})$$

with

$$\mathsf{PRG}_{b\|x}(\mathsf{k}) = \mathsf{PRG}_x(\mathsf{PRG}_b(\mathsf{k}))$$

for $b \subset \{0,1\}$ and $|x| > 0$. The base case $\mathsf{PRG}_b(\mathsf{k})$ is given as before and denotes the left half of $\mathsf{PRG}(\mathsf{k})$ if $b = 0$ and the right half otherwise.

Example 3.36. *Let us consider an evaluation of the above* PRF *for some key* k *and for input* $x = 100$. *This unrolls to*

$$\mathsf{PRF}(\mathsf{k}, 100) = \mathsf{PRG}_{100}(\mathsf{k}) = \mathsf{PRG}_0(\mathsf{PRG}_0(\mathsf{PRG}_1(\mathsf{k}))),$$

and we thus have three executions of the underlying pseudorandom generator. The first uses as seed private key k *from which we use the right half (since* $x[1] = 1$*) as the seed for the second evaluation of* PRG. *From this, we take the left half (since* $x[2] = 0$*) as the seed for the final* PRG *evaluation. The left half of the result (since* $x[3] = 0$*) yields the overall result of the computation. A schematic of the evaluation is given in Figure 3.7.*

This tree-based construction of a pseudorandom function from a length-doubling pseudorandom generator is also known as the *GGM construction*; named after its inventors Oded Goldreich, Shafi Goldwasser, and Silvio Micali. Following we formalize the GGM construction once more in pseudocode:

Construction 3.37 (GGM construction). *Let* PRG *be a pseudorandom generator with stretch factor 2, that is,* $\mathsf{PRG.ol}(\lambda) = 2 \cdot \mathsf{PRG.il}(\lambda)$. *Then we define function* $\mathsf{PRF} : \{0,1\}^{\mathsf{PRG.il}(\lambda)} \times \{0,1\}^{\mathsf{PRG.il}(\lambda)} \to \{0,1\}^{\mathsf{PRG.il}(\lambda)}$ *as follows:*

PRF.KGen(1^λ)

1: $\mathsf{k} \leftarrow_\$ \{0,1\}^{\mathsf{PRG.il}(\lambda)}$

2. return k

PRF.Eval(k, x)

1: $s \leftarrow \mathsf{k}$

2: **for** $i = 1..|x|$ **do**

3: // *Here* t_0 *(*t_1*) denotes the left (right) half*

4: $t_0 \| t_1 \leftarrow \mathsf{PRG}(s)$

5: $s \leftarrow t_{x[i]}$

6: **return** s

While the output length of the GGM pseudorandom function is given by the underlying pseudorandom generator as $\mathsf{PRF.ol}(\lambda) = \mathsf{PRG.il}(\lambda)$, the input length is not specified by the pseudorandom generator. For this note that inputs to function PRF define a path in the computation tree and the longer the input the larger the tree. However, in order to obtain a secure pseudorandom function the input length must be fixed, that is, we must set $\mathsf{PRF.il}(\lambda) \in \mathbb{N}$ for all $\lambda \in \mathbb{N}$. Consider that this was not the case and we allowed inputs of different lengths. In this case we have that $\mathsf{PRF}(\mathsf{k}, x)$ is an intermediate value in the computation for any value $x \| x'$ that has x as prefix. Exercise 3.8 asks to discuss how this can be used to break the security of the construction.

It remains to argue that the GGM construction of a pseudorandom function does, indeed, yield a secure pseudorandom function given that the underly-

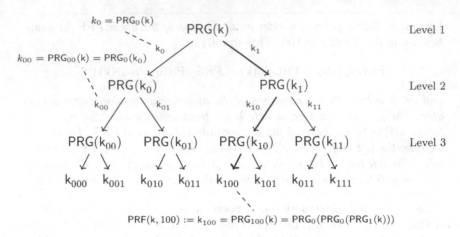

$$PRF(k, 100) := k_{100} = PRG_{100}(k) = PRG_0(PRG_0(PRG_1(k)))$$

Fig. 3.7: The GGM construction of a pseudorandom function from a length-doubling pseudorandom generator, here for inputs of length 3. Each edge transports a value of length λ. An inner node corresponds to an evaluation of pseudorandom generator PRG which takes as input the value coming on the single ingoing edge and where the left half of the output travels on the bottom left outgoing edge and the right half of the output travels on the bottom right outgoing edge. The root node at level 1 evaluates $PRG(k)$ where key k is the private key of the pseudorandom function. The output values are given as the outgoing edges of the final computation layer. Values k_x for $x \in \{0,1\}^{\leq 3}$ denote intermediate (or output) values. Highlighted value k_{100} is the result of the computation of $PRF(k, 100)$ which is computed via the highlighted path.

ing pseudorandom generator is secure. This is formalized in the following statement:

> **Theorem 3.38.** *If* PRG *is a secure and length-doubling pseudorandom generator then the GGM construction based on* PRG *is a secure pseudorandom function.*

The proof of security for the GGM construction is a classic example of the hybrid method, but with a twist. As in the proof of Proposition 3.28 (the PRG stretching construction) we will slowly replace calls to the underlying pseudorandom generator with uniformly random values. However, as we have a tree structure (cf. Figure 3.7) we have in total an exponential number of possible PRG evaluations. The hybrid method, on the other hand, only allows for a polynomial number of hybrids. One option would thus be to go level by level and define H^i to be the hybrid in which values of level i are chosen uniformly at random and only from the $(i+1)$st level we follow the path of the construction. This, however, is also problematic since at level λ we have 2^λ many values and would thus need exponentially sized storage space. And this is where the twist comes in.

Order of quantifiers in reductions. Consider again the idea of a security reduction. In order to show the security of some scheme, say a pseudorandom function PRF, we show that there exists a reduction R that, when given black-box access to an adversary $\mathcal{A}$ that breaks the security of PRF, then $R^{\mathcal{A}}$ breaks the security of some underlying functionality (e.g., that of some pseudorandom generator). All reductions we have seen so far were stated in this form: There exists a reduction R such that for all adversaries $\mathcal{A}$ the combination $R^{\mathcal{A}}$ solves some hard problem. Written with quantifiers, we considered

$$\exists R \ \forall \mathcal{A}.$$

In order to prove the security of a scheme we can, however, also reverse the order of quantifiers and consider

$$\forall \mathcal{A} \ \exists R.$$

This is, in fact, the form in which we usually phrase our proofs: Let $\mathcal{A}$ be an adversary against X, then there exists an adversary $\mathcal{B}$ (i.e., reduction R) such that $\mathcal{B}^{\mathcal{A}}$ ... The difference is that we construct a reduction for each adversary and, consequently, the specifics of the reduction can depend on the particular adversary. If, on the other hand, we consider proofs of the form $\exists R \ \forall \mathcal{A}$ then the reduction is *universal* and needs to work with just any adversary without any change.

While constructing a universal reduction yields a "stronger" result, it is usually not necessary to argue security. After all, in both cases we end up with an algorithm $R^{\mathcal{A}}$ that breaks a presumably hard problem from which we can follow that adversary $\mathcal{A}$ cannot exist.

Depending on the adversary's runtime. The idea underlying the proof of the GGM construction is to give a reduction that depends on the adversary, more precisely, that depends on the running time of the adversary. Since we only show security against efficient adversaries we know that the runtime of any adversary is bounded by some polynomial $p(\lambda)$. But this means that the adversary can also make at most $q(\lambda) \leq p(\lambda)$ many queries to its oracle and thus $q(\lambda)$ is a polynomial bound on the number of queries the reduction needs to handle. Instead of having our hybrids replace entire levels of the GGM tree we can thus go query by query and replace only those evaluations that are actually hit by the adversary's queries.

Proof of Theorem 3.38. For simpler presentation we consider a pseudorandom generator of the form $PRG : \{0,1\}^{\lambda} \to \{0,1\}^{2\lambda}$ and a resulting pseudorandom function (created via Construction 3.37) of the form $PRF : \{0,1\}^{\lambda} \times \{0,1\}^{\lambda} \to \{0,1\}^{\lambda}$.

Assume there exists a PPT adversary $\mathcal{A}$ against the pseudorandomness of the GGM construction PRF and let $q : \mathbb{N} \to \mathbb{N}$ be a polynomial that upper bounds the number of oracle queries by adversary $\mathcal{A}$. Since, by assumption, adversary $\mathcal{A}$ is efficient, such a polynomial q must exist. The idea is now to argue via a hybrid argument that $\mathcal{A}$ must have negligible advantage. For this we are going to create hybrids $H^0, H^1, \ldots, H^{\lambda}$ such that H^0 will correspond to the PRF security experiment where adversary $\mathcal{A}$ gets oracle access to the actual construction and hybrid H^λ will correspond to the case where the oracle is implementing a function R chosen uniformly at random. We will base the hybrids on the following two base distributions:

$$\text{Rand} := (U_{2\lambda}, U_{2\lambda}, \dots, U_{2\lambda}) \qquad\qquad // \text{ (random)}$$
$$\text{Prand} := (\text{PRG}(U_\lambda), \text{PRG}(U_\lambda), \dots, \text{PRG}(U_\lambda)) \qquad // \text{ (pseudorandom)}$$

where U_n denotes the uniform distribution over $\{0,1\}^n$ and each distribution consists of $q(\lambda)$ independent copies. That is, distribution Rand consists of $q(\lambda)$ many uniformly random values of size 2λ which we will use to simulate the random function R for adversary $\mathcal{A}$. Distribution Prand, on the other hand, consists of $q(\lambda)$ many pseudorandom values generated by pseudorandom generator PRG and a seed chosen uniformly at random. This will be used to simulate the genuine GGM construction for adversary $\mathcal{A}$.

In Lemma 3.10 (page 112) we showed that the t-fold repetition of two random variables is computationally indistinguishable if the two random variables are indistinguishable, from which it follows that

$$\text{Rand} \stackrel{c}{\approx} \text{Prand}.$$

Hybrids and transformation. Recall that for an application of the hybrid argument (Theorem 3.17) it is sufficient to give an efficient transformation T such that for all $i \in \{0, 1, \dots, \lambda - 1\}$ it holds that $T(i, X) \stackrel{\text{p}}{\equiv} H^i$ and $T(i, Y) \stackrel{\text{p}}{\equiv} H^{i+1}$ for two computationally indistinguishable distributions X and Y. Note that the transformation T may depend on $\mathcal{A}$, see Remark 3.18 after Theorem 3.17. We here consider the base distributions Prand and Rand and define transformation T such that

$$T(i, \mathbf{r})(1^\lambda) := \text{Sim}_i^{\mathcal{A}}(1^\lambda, \mathbf{r}),$$

where $\mathbf{r}$ is a sample of either Prand or Rand and $\text{Sim}_i^{\mathcal{A}}$ is an efficient (i.e., PPT) algorithm that simulates the PRF security game for adversary $\mathcal{A}$. Simulator $\text{Sim}_i^{\mathcal{A}}(1^\lambda, \mathbf{r})$ will be such that to answer queries by adversary $\mathcal{A}$ it chooses values from its input vector $\mathbf{r}$ for the $(i+1)$st level to then compute the genuine GGM tree from there on downwards. Thus, by construction we have that $\text{Sim}_0^{\mathcal{A}}$ will simulate the genuine GGM construction when receiving a sample from distribution Prand. It will choose a single pseudorandom value from $\mathbf{r}$ as the result of the single level 1 node (see Figure 3.7) to then follow the GGM computation. This is exactly as in the standard GGM construction where level 1 is computed as $\text{PRG}(k)$ (i.e., a pseudorandom value).

At the other end, we have that $\text{Sim}_{\lambda-1}^{\mathcal{A}}$ on receiving as input a sample from Rand will simulate a uniformly random function for adversary $\mathcal{A}$. It will replace values at level λ (the final level; level 3 in Figure 3.7) with uniformly random values from input vector $\mathbf{r}$ and then, to answer a query, choose either the left or right half of such a value. This thus perfectly simulates a uniformly random function.

Let $i \in \{0, 1, \ldots, \lambda - 1\}$, then we define hybrid H^i as $\mathsf{Sim}_i^{\mathcal{A}}$ with pseudorandom values as input and as the final hybrid H^λ we use $\mathsf{Sim}_{\lambda-1}^{\mathcal{A}}$ with uniformly random values as input. That is, we set

$$H^i(1^\lambda) := \mathsf{Sim}_i^{\mathcal{A}}(1^\lambda, \mathsf{Prand}(1^\lambda)) \quad \text{and} \quad H^\lambda(1^\lambda) := \mathsf{Sim}_{\lambda-1}^{\mathcal{A}}(1^\lambda, \mathsf{Rand}(1^\lambda)),$$

and it remains to argue that for all $i \in \{0, 1, \ldots, \lambda - 1\}$ we have that

$$T(i, \mathsf{Prand}) \stackrel{\mathrm{p}}{=} H^i \qquad \text{and} \qquad T(i, \mathsf{Rand}) \stackrel{\mathrm{p}}{=} H^{i+1}.$$

For this let us formally define the simulators $\mathsf{Sim}_i^{\mathcal{A}}$.

The simulators. Simulator Sim_i (for $i \in \{0, 1, \ldots, \lambda - 1\}$) gets as input a vector $\mathbf{r}$ of $\mathsf{q}(\lambda)$ many values which are either chosen uniformly at random or are chosen as results of evaluating the pseudorandom generator PRG on a uniformly random seed. Simulator Sim_i initializes an empty table S and a counter $j \leftarrow 1$ to then run adversary $\mathcal{A}$. To answer a query x by adversary $\mathcal{A}$, simulator Sim_i computes prefix $s \leftarrow x[1..i]$—note that the prefix is the empty string for $i = 0$—and then checks if table S contains s. If not, it sets $S[s] \leftarrow j$ and increments counter j. It then computes a key k as follows. If $x[i+1] = 0$ (that is the first bit after prefix s) then it chooses the left half of $\mathbf{r}[S[s]]$ and otherwise the right half. Here note that $S[s] \in [\mathsf{q}(\lambda)]$ contains an index and was previously set to some value j. Finally, simulator Sim_i computes $y \leftarrow \mathsf{PRG}_{x[i+2..\lambda]}(S[s])$, which it returns. Here, value $x[i+2..\lambda]$ is the remainder of query x and PRG_z is the nested evaluation of the pseudorandom generator as defined before. That is, we set

$$\mathsf{PRG}_{b\|x}(\mathsf{k}) = \mathsf{PRG}_x(\mathsf{PRG}_b(\mathsf{k}))$$

for $b \in \{0, 1\}$ and where $\mathsf{PRG}_0(\mathsf{k})$ denotes the left half of the output of $\mathsf{PRG}(\mathsf{k})$ and $\mathsf{PRG}_1(\mathsf{k})$ the right half (also see Figure 3.7). Note that in case $i = \lambda - 1$ we thus have that $x[\lambda + 1..\lambda]$ is the empty string ε for which we set

$$\mathsf{PRG}_\varepsilon(x) := x.$$

Once adversary $\mathcal{A}$ returns with a guess b', simulator Sim_i simply echoes the bit. We provide a pseudocode definition of the simulator in Figure 3.8.

Since adversary $\mathcal{A}$ asks at most $\mathsf{q}(\lambda)$ queries we have that simulator Sim_i can answer all of $\mathcal{A}$'s queries. Furthermore, note that if input vector $\mathbf{r}$ consists of *pseudorandom values* then simulator Sim_0 perfectly simulates the original pseudorandom function security game for $\mathcal{A}$ with its oracle being the GGM construction. For this note that prefix s in this case is always the empty string, and thus for any query x starting key k is chosen as either the left side or the right side of $\mathbf{r}[1]$. But since $\mathbf{r}[1]$ was generated as $\mathbf{r}[1] \leftarrow \mathsf{PRG}(\sigma)$ for some

$\mathsf{Sim}_i^{\mathcal{A}}(1^\lambda, \mathbf{r})$ // $i \in \{0, 1, \ldots, \lambda - 1\}$	$\mathsf{RoR}(x)$
1: $S \leftarrow [\,]$	1: $s \leftarrow x[1..i]$ // The empty string ε if $i = 0$
2: $j \leftarrow 1$	2: if $S[s] \neq \bot$ then
3: $b' \leftarrow\!\!\$\ \mathcal{A}^{\mathrm{RoR}}(1^\lambda)$	3: $\quad S[s] \leftarrow j$
4: return b'	4: $\quad j \leftarrow j + 1$
	5: $t_0 \| t_1 \leftarrow \mathbf{r}[S[s]]$ // split in left and right half
	6: $\mathsf{k} \leftarrow t_{x[i+1]}$
	7: $y \leftarrow \mathsf{PRG}_{x[i+2..\lambda]}(\mathsf{k})$ // $x[\lambda + 1..\lambda] := \varepsilon$
	8: return y

Fig. 3.8: Simulators $\mathsf{Sim}_i^{\mathcal{A}}$ (for $0 \leq i < \lambda$) that simulate the PRF security game for adversary $\mathcal{A}$ in the proof of Theorem 3.38.

uniformly random σ this matches exactly the situation after the 1st level in the GGM construction. We can think of σ taking the role of key k and that the first level is "computed" by the challenger and given to the simulator as input as $\mathbf{r}[1]$. The simulator Sim_0 then computes the remainder of the construction to answer queries by adversary $\mathcal{A}$.

Simulator $\mathsf{Sim}_{\lambda-1}$, on the other hand, simulates the PRF experiment with the oracle implementing a random function, in case $\mathbf{r}$ consists of *truly random values*. For this note that value y in line 7 is chosen as

$$y = \mathsf{PRG}_{x[\lambda+1..\lambda]}(\mathsf{k}) = \mathsf{PRG}_\varepsilon(\mathsf{k}) = \mathsf{k}.$$

And for each query x key k is chosen either as the left or the right half of a value in $\mathbf{r}$. Since values $\mathbf{r}$ are uniformly random we have that the oracle distribution simulated for $\mathcal{A}$ by simulator $\mathsf{Sim}_{\lambda-1}$ is identical to that of a uniformly random function.

Finally, note that

$$\mathsf{Sim}_{i+1}(1^\lambda, \mathsf{Prand}(1^\lambda)) \stackrel{\mathrm{p}}{\equiv} \mathsf{Sim}_i(1^\lambda, \mathsf{Rand}(1^\lambda)).$$

Since pseudorandom values of vector $\mathbf{r}$ are generated as an application of pseudorandom generator PRG with uniformly random seeds it is the same whether we replace the values at level $i + 1$ with uniformly random values and then compute the GGM construction or replace the values at level $i + 2$ with pseudorandom values to then compute the GGM construction.

We can thus conclude that since transformation T was defined as

$$T(i, \mathbf{r})(1^\lambda) := \mathsf{Sim}_i^{\mathcal{A}}(1^\lambda, \mathbf{r})$$

we have that

$$T(i, \mathsf{Rand})(1^\lambda) \stackrel{\mathrm{p}}{\equiv} T(i + 1, \mathsf{Prand})(1^\lambda)$$

and consequently

$$T(i, \mathsf{Prand}) \stackrel{\mathrm{D}}{=} H^i \qquad \text{and} \qquad T(i, \mathsf{Rand}) \stackrel{\mathrm{D}}{=} H^{i+1}.$$

Applying the hybrid argument. By our earlier discussion we know that

$$H^0(1^\lambda) := \mathsf{Sim}_0^{\mathcal{A}}(1^\lambda, \mathsf{Prand}(1^\lambda)) \stackrel{\mathrm{D}}{=} \mathcal{A}^{\mathsf{PRF.Eval}(k,\cdot)}(1^\lambda)$$

as well as

$$H^\lambda(1^\lambda) := \mathsf{Sim}_{\lambda-1}^{\mathcal{A}}(1^\lambda, \mathsf{Rand}(1^\lambda)) \stackrel{\mathrm{D}}{=} \mathcal{A}^{\mathsf{R}(\cdot)}(1^\lambda).$$

That is, hybrid H^0 is distributed identically to an execution of adversary $\mathcal{A}$ in the PRF security game with the oracle implementing the genuine GGM construction. Similarly, hybrid H^λ is distributed identically to an execution of adversary $\mathcal{A}$ in the PRF security game with the oracle implementing a function R chosen uniformly at random.

Noting that $\mathsf{Prand} \stackrel{\mathrm{c}}{\approx} \mathsf{Rand}$ we can apply the hybrid argument (Theorem 3.17) to conclude that $H^0 \stackrel{\mathrm{c}}{\approx} H^\lambda$ and thus that

$$H^0 \stackrel{\mathrm{D}}{=} \mathcal{A}^{\mathsf{PRF.Eval}(k,\cdot)}(1^\lambda) \stackrel{\mathrm{c}}{\approx} \mathcal{A}^{\mathsf{R}}(1^\lambda) \stackrel{\mathrm{D}}{=} H^\lambda.$$

From this it follows that also advantage $\mathsf{Adv}_{\mathsf{PRF},\mathcal{A}}^{\mathrm{prf}}(\lambda)$ is negligible, which is what we set out to show. However, to make this final step rigorously we need to relate the computational indistinguishability of H^0 and H^λ resp. $\mathcal{A}^{\mathsf{PRF.Eval}(k,\cdot)}(1^\lambda)$ and $\mathcal{A}^{\mathsf{R}}(1^\lambda)$ to the advantage against the pseudorandom function. The former says that any distinguisher does not change its behavior significantly; the latter says that the probabilities are close. Specifically, computational indistinguishability of $\mathcal{A}^{\mathsf{PRF.Eval}(k,\cdot)}(1^\lambda)$ and $\mathcal{A}^{\mathsf{R}}(1^\lambda)$ means that no PPT distinguisher $\mathcal{D}$ can distinguish between seeing samples either from the first or from the second distribution, that is,

$$\mathsf{Adv}_{\mathcal{A}^{\mathsf{PRF.Eval}(k,\cdot)},\mathcal{A}^{\mathsf{R}},\mathcal{D}}^{\mathrm{indist}}(\lambda)$$
$$= \left| \Pr\left[\mathcal{D}(1^\lambda, \mathcal{A}^{\mathsf{PRF.Eval}(k,\cdot)}(1^\lambda)) = 1\right] - \Pr\left[\mathcal{D}(1^\lambda, \mathcal{A}^{\mathsf{R}}(1^\lambda)) = 1\right] \right|$$
$$\leq \mathsf{negl}(\lambda).$$

As this is the case for any PPT distinguisher this is, in particular, the case for the concrete "identity distinguisher" $\mathcal{I}$ which simply echoes its input bit. But then

$$\mathsf{Adv}_{\mathsf{PRF},\mathcal{A}}^{\mathrm{prf}}(\lambda) = \left| \Pr\left[\mathcal{A}^{\mathsf{PRF.Eval}(k,\cdot)}(1^\lambda) = 1\right] - \Pr\left[\mathcal{A}^{\mathsf{R}}(1^\lambda) = 1\right] \right|$$
$$= \left| \Pr\left[\mathcal{I}(1^\lambda, \mathcal{A}^{\mathsf{PRF.Eval}(k,\cdot)}(1^\lambda)) = 1\right] - \Pr\left[\mathcal{I}(1^\lambda, \mathcal{A}^{\mathsf{R}}(1^\lambda)) = 1\right] \right|$$
$$= \left| \Pr\left[\mathcal{I}(1^\lambda, H^0(1^\lambda)) = 1\right] - \Pr\left[\mathcal{I}(1^\lambda, H^\lambda(1^\lambda)) = 1\right] \right|$$
$$= \mathsf{Adv}_{H^0, H^\lambda, \mathcal{I}}^{\mathrm{indist}}(\lambda) \leq \mathsf{negl}(\lambda). \qquad \square$$

3.5 Message Authentication Codes

For the final part of this chapter we will shift our discussion from the topic of pseudorandomness to *unpredictability*. If a string is pseudorandom it is essentially indistinguishable from a truly random string, at least for efficient adversaries. This is a strong security requirement, and for some use cases it is unnecessarily strong. Consider the case that two parties Alice and Bob who have met at some point to exchange a shared secret key want to exchange messages in such a way that the recipient, say Alice, can be certain that the message came from Bob and that it was not tampered with.

Pseudorandom functions provide all we need for this *authentication* scenario. When Bob wants to send a message m to Alice, he computes a tag $\tau \leftarrow$ PRF.Eval(k, m) using a pseudorandom function PRF and the shared secret key k. He then sends the pair (m, τ) to Alice. (Note that we are sending the message in the clear here.) On reception, Alice recomputes the tag as $\tau' \leftarrow$ PRF.Eval(k, m) and checks whether $\tau = \tau'$. If so Alice assumes that the message truly came from Bob and was not changed on the way. If not, she discards the message.

While we have not formalized yet what we expect from a *message authentication scheme* the above is intuitively secure as by the security of the pseudorandom function, tag τ is indistinguishable from a uniformly random string. In particular, if an adversary was to change the message the tag would indicate that something is wrong and the probability of an adversary guessing the right tag for the adapted message is negligible. In the following section we make this analysis formal to lift *message authentication codes* onto a solid theoretical foundation.

Before we discuss a formal definition, let us get back to the security of the pseudorandom function and the "necessary" property required for the message authentication scheme. What we would like to achieve, informally, is that an adversary that changes a message cannot find the corresponding tag. In other words, we want the used function to be *unpredictable* given that the key is unknown. While pseudorandom functions are unpredictable and thus a good candidate they are in fact more: they are pseudorandom which, as we will see, is the stronger of the two properties.

Formalizing Message Authentication Codes

Formally, a message authentication code MAC := (MAC.KGen, MAC.Eval) is a pair of efficient algorithms where MAC.KGen is an efficient probabilistic key generation algorithm and MAC.Eval a deterministic tagging algorithm that takes as input a key and a message and outputs a (short) tag which we usually denote by τ. Here we use a simplified approach to such authentication codes where verification is done by deterministically recomputing the tag and comparing it with the given one, as in the Alice and Bob example above. This matches the common way to build such codes from pseudorandom functions or hash functions.

While there are many variants of security notions for message authentication codes,[9] the strongest and most common is *unforgeability under adaptive chosen-message attacks*, which we define next. The security definition will have a similar structure to the security definitions seen so far. We define the advantage $\mathsf{Adv}_{\mathsf{MAC},\mathcal{A}}^{\text{uf-cma}}(\lambda)$ (where *uf-cma* is short for unforgeability under adaptive chosen-message attacks) of an adversary $\mathcal{A}$ against a message authentication scheme MAC via a security experiment $\mathsf{Exp}_{\mathsf{MAC},\mathcal{A}}^{\text{uf-cma}}(\lambda)$. Similarly to our algorithmic definition of pseudorandom functions (Definition 3.21) in which the adversary was given a real-or-random oracle RoR we will here provide adversary $\mathcal{A}$ with access to a *tagging oracle* Tag. The role of the tagging oracle is to provide the adversary with the ability to generate valid tags, under secret MAC key mk, for messages of its choice but without providing the adversary with direct access to the key. While this may be providing the adversary with more power than it might have in concrete real-world scenarios it will make security proofs according to this strong definition more robust: if even such a strong adversary cannot break the scheme, then for sure no weaker adversary can break the scheme.

Since the adversary's task is to forge a valid tag we must exclude the trivial attack in which the adversary simply forwards a tag generated by its oracle for a message as its own forgery. For this, the experiment contains a book-keeping set $\mathcal{Q}$ that stores all the oracle queries of the adversary. In the above example of Alice and Bob, this means that the parties are, for example, not able to detect replayed messages; after all, the message has already been tagged and sent by the valid partner and is therefore authentic. If one seeks to prevent such attacks then further tools need to be deployed, for example a counter which is tagged along with the message and increased with each generation.

Definition 3.39 (Unforgeability under Chosen-Message Attacks). *An efficient pair of algorithms* MAC := (MAC.KGen, MAC.Eval), *where* MAC.KGen *is a* PPT *key generation algorithm and* MAC.Eval *is a deterministic evaluation algorithm, is called a* message authentication code *that is* unforgeable under adaptively chosen-message attacks *(UF-CMA)* *if advantage* $\mathsf{Adv}_{\mathsf{MAC},\mathcal{A}}^{\text{uf-cma}}(\lambda)$ *is negligible for any* PPT *algorithm* $\mathcal{A}$. *Here, the advantage is defined as*

$$\mathsf{Adv}_{\mathsf{MAC},\mathcal{A}}^{\text{uf-cma}}(\lambda) := \Pr\left[\mathsf{Exp}_{\mathsf{MAC},\mathcal{A}}^{\text{uf-cma}}(\lambda)\right]$$

relative to experiment $\mathsf{Exp}_{\mathsf{MAC},\mathcal{A}}^{\text{uf-cma}}(\lambda)$:

---

[9] For example, we can distinguish between whether the adversary may choose the message to authenticate or whether that message is generated by the challenger.

Experiment $Exp_{MAC,\mathcal{A}}^{uf\text{-}cma}(\lambda)$	$Tag(mk, m)$
1 : $\quad Q \leftarrow \{\}$ // *record queried messages*	1 : $\quad Q \leftarrow Q \cup \{m\}$
2 : $\quad mk \leftarrow_\$ MAC.KGen(1^\lambda)$	2 : $\quad \tau \leftarrow MAC.Eval(mk, m)$
3 : $\quad (m^*, \tau^*) \leftarrow_\$ \mathcal{A}^{Tag(mk,\cdot)}(1^\lambda)$	3 : $\quad$ **return** τ
4 : $\quad$ **return** $MAC.Eval(mk, m^*) = \tau^* \wedge m^* \notin Q$	

Remark 3.40. The above security notion for message authentication codes is also often referred to as "*existential* unforgeability under adaptively chosen-message attacks" (EUF-CMA) to stress that an adversary can forge a tag for any message of its choosing (there *exists* a message) in order to win in the security game.

Our definition of MACs only considers deterministic tagging algorithms MAC.Eval. While this is a common restriction, one could also consider randomized message authentication codes where MAC.Eval is a probabilistic algorithm. In this setting, one would need an additional verification algorithm MAC.Vf that takes as input the MAC key mk, a message m, and tag τ and outputs true or false indicating whether or not the tag is valid. This becomes necessary since a simple recomputation and comparison approach (see line 4 of $Exp_{MAC,\mathcal{A}}^{uf\text{-}cma}(\lambda)$) would not suffice as in this case MAC.Eval(mk, m) is a random variable that may not be easily recovered by another evaluation.

In fact, if we consider probabilistic MACs then this also affects the security experiment. In our simpler approach we allow the adversary only a single forgery attempt, because it is known that multiple attempts cannot increase the success probability significantly. For probabilistic MACs, however, the number of available verification attempts makes a crucial difference. Some schemes are correctly marked as insecure under many verification queries even though they are secure against single-forgery attempts. For probabilistic MAC one thus better starts with a security model which allows for multiple verification queries right away.

Strongly unforgeable MACs. A stronger security notion for message authentication codes is SUF-CMA, which is short for *strong unforgeability under chosen-message attacks*. Here an adversary wins already if it can create a fresh valid tag for a previously seen message–tag pair. Formally, this notion is defined by adapting set Q to hold not only messages but message–tag pairs. Consequently, line 4 in experiment $Exp_{MAC,\mathcal{A}}^{uf\text{-}cma}(\lambda)$ would then be changed to check for $(m^*, \tau^*) \notin Q$.

Let us note that this stronger notion is guaranteed to hold for any UF-CMA secure MAC that is *deterministic* and which verifies validity by recalculating the presumably correct tag and comparing it with the given tag. Also note that this is exactly the way we defined MACs in Definition 3.39. To see that such MACs are, indeed, SUF-CMA secure note that for such message authentication codes there is exactly one single correct tag per message. When, instead, considering MACs with a dedicated tag verification algorithm as discussed above then SUF-CMA security is not necessarily implied by UF-CMA security. SUF-CMA security, on the other hand, always implies also UF-CMA security.

MACs and Pseudorandom Functions

In our introduction to message authentication codes we gave a simple scheme using a pseudorandom function to implement message authentication. In the following we show that this scheme is indeed a secure message authentication code. This is captured by the following proposition:

> **Proposition 3.41.** *Let* PRF $:=$ (PRF.KGen, PRF.Eval) *be a secure pseudorandom function with an output length that is at least super-logarithmic in the security parameter, that is, for which* PRF.ol$(\lambda) \in \omega(\log(\lambda))$. *Then* PRF *is also a secure message authentication code. That is,* PRF *is unforgeable under adaptively chosen-message attacks.*

Note the restriction in the proposition, that only such PRFs are MACs that are sufficiently long. For this, consider the extreme, a pseudorandom function with a single output bit. As the output of this PRF would be easy to guess (any guess succeeds with probability at least 50%) this PRF cannot possibly be a good message authentication code. But, in case the output length is sufficiently long, any PRF is also a secure message authentication code.

Proof of Proposition 3.41. Let us assume that PRF is not a secure MAC. Then there exists an adversary $\mathcal{A}$ which wins with non-negligible advantage $\mathsf{Adv}_{\mathsf{PRF},\mathcal{A}}^{\mathsf{uf\text{-}cma}}(\lambda)$ in the security experiment specified in Definition 3.39. We give a security reduction and show how to construct a distinguisher $\mathcal{D}$ from $\mathcal{A}$ that can distinguish outputs from PRF from random values, thus breaking the pseudorandomness property of PRF. As we assume that PRF is a secure pseudorandom function it follows that $\mathcal{D}$ and thus $\mathcal{A}$ cannot exist and that, hence, PRF must be a secure message authentication code.

Distinguisher $\mathcal{D}$ has access to an oracle O which either implements the PRF for a random key or a uniformly random function. On input the security parameter 1^λ it calls $\mathcal{A}(1^\lambda)$. Adversary $\mathcal{A}$ expects access to a tagging oracle which distinguisher $\mathcal{D}$ will simulate with the help of its own oracle O. That is, if $\mathcal{A}$ queries the tagging oracle on message m, distinguisher $\mathcal{D}$ records m in set $\mathcal{Q}$, then forwards m to O and returns the result to $\mathcal{A}$. Once adversary $\mathcal{A}$ stops and outputs a pair (m^*, τ^*) distinguisher $\mathcal{D}$ checks whether $O(m^*) = \tau^*$ and $m^* \notin \mathcal{Q}$ and if so it outputs 0. Otherwise it outputs 1.

Analysis. It remains to analyze the success probability of distinguisher $\mathcal{D}$. In case oracle O implements the PRF (hidden bit $b = 0$ in Definition 3.22) then distinguisher $\mathcal{D}$ perfectly simulates the MAC environment for adversary

$\mathcal{A}$. Thus, we have that

$$\Pr\left[\mathcal{D}^{\mathsf{O}(\cdot)}(1^\lambda) = 0 \;\middle|\; b = 0\right] = \mathsf{Adv}^{\text{uf-cma}}_{\mathsf{PRF},\mathcal{A}}(\lambda).$$

If on the other hand O implements a random function then the probability of $\mathcal{A}$ correctly predicting the result on an hitherto unseen value is $2^{-\mathsf{PRF.ol}(\lambda)}$ and thus

$$\Pr\left[\mathcal{D}^{\mathsf{O}(\cdot)}(1^\lambda) = 0 \;\middle|\; b = 1\right] \leq \frac{1}{2^{\mathsf{PRF.ol}(\lambda)}}.$$

Combining the two equations and noting that $|a| \geq a$ yields the sought-after result:

$$\mathsf{Adv}^{\text{prf}}_{\mathsf{PRF},\mathcal{D}}(\lambda) = \left|\Pr\left[\mathcal{D}^{\mathsf{O}(\cdot)}(1^\lambda) = 0 \;\middle|\; b = 0\right] - \Pr\left[\mathcal{D}^{\mathsf{O}(\cdot)}(1^\lambda) = 0 \;\middle|\; b = 1\right]\right|$$
$$\geq \mathsf{Adv}^{\text{uf-cma}}_{\mathsf{PRF},\mathcal{A}}(\lambda) - \mathsf{negl}(\lambda).$$

Here we used that $\mathsf{PRF.ol}(\lambda)$ is super-logarithmic such that $2^{-\mathsf{PRF.ol}(\lambda)}$ is negligible (also see Remark 3.30 on page 135). If $\mathcal{A}$'s advantage is now non-negligible, then so is the difference.　　　　　　　　　　　　　　　　　$\square$

While any pseudorandom function with a sufficiently long output length is also a secure MAC, the inverse direction does not hold. To see this, consider a secure pseudorandom function PRF and now adapt it such that $\mathsf{PRF}'.\mathsf{Eval}(\mathsf{k}, m) = 1\|\mathsf{PRF}.\mathsf{Eval}(\mathsf{k}, m)$. That is, function PRF behaves exactly as PRF except that it prepends any result with a single '1' bit. While this change makes function PRF' easily distinguishable from a truly random function— consider an adversary that chooses a random message m, calls its oracle on m, and outputs the first bit as its guess—the resulting function is still a secure message authentication code. This relationship is captured by the following proposition, and Exercise 3.10 asks to formalize the proof.

> **Proposition 3.42.** *If secure message authentication codes exist, then there exists a message authentication scheme that is unforgeable under adaptively chosen-message attacks, but not a secure pseudorandom function.*

Chapter Notes and References

The concept of pseudorandomness was developed in the early 1980s by Andrew Yao, who introduced the notion of computational indistinguishability, pseudorandomness, and pseudorandom generators [19]. Yao also showed how to build a pseudorandom generator based on one-way permutations, and we will see his construction in Section 5.3.4. In 2000 Yao received the ACM

A.M. Turing Award, amongst others, for his fundamental contributions to the theory of pseudorandom number generation [1].

First constructions of pseudorandom generators were given by Blum and Micali [6, 7]. Pseudorandom functions were introduced by Goldreich, Goldwasser, and Micali [9, 10], who also showed that Construction 3.37—a construction of a pseudorandom function from a pseudorandom generator—yields a secure pseudorandom function if the underlying pseudorandom generator is secure. Today the construction is known as the GGM construction. Theorem 3.32, which establishes the existence of pseudorandom generators if one-way functions exist, was proven by Håstad *et al.* [14].

The construction of permutations from functions via Feistel networks goes back to Horst Feistel [8] and his work at IBM in the 1970s. The notion of (strong) pseudorandom permutations is due to Luby and Rackoff, who also showed Theorem 3.25: A three-round Feistel network yields a pseudorandom permutation and a four-round network yields a strong pseudorandom permutation when starting from a secure pseudorandom function [17].

With their seminal paper on probabilistic encryption, Goldwasser and Micali not only laid the foundation for computational security, but also introduced the hybrid argument [11, 12]. The idea of formalizing cryptographic schemes via security experiments (or games) goes back to Yao [19] and Goldwasser and Micali [11, 12]. Over the last decades, game-playing and game-based proofs have become more and more popular in the cryptographic community. Formalizations of the technique were given by Shoup [18] as well as by Bellare and Rogaway [5]. The modeling of security games and the game-hopping technique as used in this book is based on the code-based style of Bellare and Rogaway.

Message authentication codes have a long tradition in practical cryptography and were standardized already in the 1980s [16, 15]. The security formalization usually used today and presented in Section 3.5 is due to Bellare, Kilian, and Rogaway [3, 4], who based their definition for MACs on security notions for digital signature schemes [13] (see Chapter 6). The characterization of deterministic and re-computing MACs as strongly unforgeable can be found in [2].

Exercices

Exercise 3.1. Which of the following pairs of random variables are computationally, statistically, or perfectly indistinguishable? Either prove indistinguishability or present a distinguisher.

a)

$X(1^\lambda)$	$Y(1^\lambda)$
$x \leftarrow\!\!\$\ \{0,1\}^\lambda$	$y \leftarrow\!\!\$\ \{0,1\}^\lambda$
return x	**return** $y[1..\lambda-1]\|0$

b)

$X(1^\lambda)$	$Y(1^\lambda)$
$x \leftarrow\!\!\$\ \{0,1\}^\lambda$	$y \leftarrow\!\!\$\ \{0,1\}^\lambda$
return x	**return** $y[2..\lambda]\|y[1]$

c)

$X(1^\lambda)$	$Y(1^\lambda)$
$k \leftarrow\!\!\$\ \mathsf{PRF.KGen}(1^\lambda)$	$r \leftarrow\!\!\$\ \{0,1\}^\lambda$
$x \leftarrow \mathsf{PRF}(k,0^{2\lambda})$	$y \leftarrow \mathsf{PRG}(r)$
return x	**return** y

d)

$X(1^\lambda)$	$Y(1^\lambda)$
$m \leftarrow\!\!\$\ \{0,1\}^{2\lambda}$	$m \leftarrow\!\!\$\ \{0,1\}^{2\lambda}$
$R \leftarrow\!\!\$\ \{0,1\}^{2\lambda}$	$r \leftarrow\!\!\$\ \{0,1\}^\lambda$
$c \leftarrow m \oplus R$	$c \leftarrow m \oplus \mathsf{PRG}(r)$
return (m,c)	**return** (m,c)

Here PRF is a length-preserving pseudorandom function with $\mathsf{PRF.il}(\lambda) = \mathsf{PRF.ol}(\lambda) = 2\lambda$ and PRG is a secure (unkeyed) pseudorandom generator with stretch 2.

Exercise 3.2. Show that both formulations of indistinguishability given by Equations (3.1) and (3.2) (page 100) are identical. That is, show that the following holds:

$$2 \cdot \left| \Pr\left[\mathsf{Exp}^{\mathrm{indist}}_{X,Y,\mathcal{D}}(\lambda) \right] - \frac{1}{2} \right|$$
$$= \left| \Pr\left[\mathcal{D}(1^\lambda, X(1^\lambda)) = 1 \right] - \Pr\left[\mathcal{D}(1^\lambda, Y(1^\lambda)) = 1 \right] \right|.$$

Exercise 3.3. Show that Definitions 3.21 and 3.22 (pages 126f.) for pseudorandom functions are equivalent if we restrict Definition 3.22 to also only consider functions with a fixed input and output length per security parameter.

Exercise 3.4. Let $\mathsf{Func} := \left\{ f \mid f : \{0,1\}^\lambda \to \{0,1\}^\lambda \right\}$ be the set of all length-preserving functions and let $\mathsf{Perm} := \left\{ \pi \mid \pi : \{0,1\}^\lambda \to \{0,1\}^\lambda \right\}$ be the set of all length-preserving permutations. Show that for any PPT algorithm $\mathcal{D}$ it holds that

$$\left| \Pr_{R \leftarrow\!\!\$\,\mathsf{Func}}\left[\mathcal{D}^R(1^\lambda) = 1 \right] - \Pr_{P \leftarrow\!\!\$\,\mathsf{Perm}}\left[\mathcal{D}^P(1^\lambda) = 1 \right] \right| = \mathsf{negl}(\lambda).$$

In other words, no efficient algorithm can distinguish between getting blackbox access to a uniformly random function or a uniformly random permutation. Argue why this proves Lemma 3.23.

Exercise 3.5. Let PRF be a length-preserving pseudorandom function. Show that a 2-round Feistel construction from PRF does not yield a secure pseudorandom function. Furthermore, show that a 3-round Feistel construction does not yield a strong pseudorandom permutation.

Exercise 3.6. Show that, unconditionally, there are pseudorandom functions if the sequence of all possible outputs is smaller than the key length, concretely, if $\mathsf{PRF.ol}(\lambda) \cdot 2^{\mathsf{PRF.il}(\lambda)} \leq |k|$.

Exercise 3.7. Prove Proposition 3.29 (page 135) for arbitrary pseudorandom generators, that is, for pseudorandom generators that stretch their input by at least one bit.

Exercise 3.8. Let PRG be a secure and length-doubling pseudorandom generator and let PRF be the GGM construction (Construction 3.37; page 143) from PRG. Show that, if PRF does not have a fixed input length, then PRF cannot be a secure pseudorandom function.

Exercise 3.9. Formalize a proof for Proposition 3.31 (page 139).

Exercise 3.10. Formalize a proof for Proposition 3.42 (page 154).

Exercise 3.11. Let PRF be a pseudorandom function with key length $\mathsf{PRF.kl}(\lambda) = \lambda$, that maps inputs of length λ to 1-bit outputs (that is, $\mathsf{PRF.il}(\lambda) = \lambda$ and $\mathsf{PRF.ol}(\lambda) = 1$). Show that then there exists a length-preserving pseudorandom function PRF' that maps inputs of length λ bits to outputs of length λ bits (that is, $\mathsf{PRF}'.\mathsf{il}(\lambda) = \lambda$ and $\mathsf{PRF}'.\mathsf{ol}(\lambda) = \lambda$).
Hint: Choose keys for PRF' that are bigger than keys of PRF.

Exercise 3.12. In Section 3.3.3 we saw the Feistel construction and claimed that 3-round Feistel networks yield pseudorandom permutations and 4-round Feistel networks yield strong pseudorandom permutations (see also Figure 3.5 on page 130). Show that a 3-round Feistel network that uses only a single round key, that is, function $\mathsf{Feistel}^{\mathsf{PRF}}((k, k, k), x)$, is not necessarily a pseudorandom function even if the underlying function PRF is a pseudorandom function. What about 4-round Feistel networks which use only a single round key?

Exercise 3.13. Let PRG_1 and PRG_2 be (unkeyed) pseudorandom generators and π be a permutation (of the right input/output length). Are the following functions also pseudorandom generators?

a) $\mathsf{PRG}_a(x) := \pi(\mathsf{PRG}_1(x))$
b) $\mathsf{PRG}_b(x) := \mathsf{PRG}_1(\pi(x))$
c) $\mathsf{PRG}_c(x) := \mathsf{PRG}_1(x) \| \mathsf{PRG}_2(x)$
d) $\mathsf{PRG}_d(x) := \mathsf{PRG}_1(x) \oplus \mathsf{PRG}_2(x)$

Would it change anything if the functions were keyed?

Exercise 3.14. Let $\mathsf{G}_1 := (\mathsf{G}_1.\mathsf{KGen}, \mathsf{G}_2.\mathsf{Eval})$ and $\mathsf{G}_2 := (\mathsf{G}_2.\mathsf{KGen}, \mathsf{G}_2.\mathsf{Eval})$ be two function families with identical key, input, and output lengths. Give a construction of a pseudorandom generator out of G_1 and G_2 that is secure as long as either G_1 or G_2 is secure.

Exercise 3.15. Let $\mathsf{F}_1 := (\mathsf{F}_1.\mathsf{KGen}, \mathsf{F}_2.\mathsf{Eval})$ and $\mathsf{F}_2 := (\mathsf{F}_2.\mathsf{KGen}, \mathsf{F}_2.\mathsf{Eval})$ be two function families with identical key, input, and output lengths. Give a construction of a pseudorandom function out of F_1 and F_2 that is secure as long as either F_1 or F_2 is secure.

Chapter Bibliography

1. Association for Computing Machinery. A.M. Turing award: Andrew Chi-Chih Yao. https://amturing.acm.org/award_winners/yao_1611524.cfm, 2000.
2. Mihir Bellare, Oded Goldreich, and Anton Mityagin. The power of verification queries in message authentication and authenticated encryption. Cryptology ePrint Archive, Report 2004/309, 2004. http://eprint.iacr.org/2004/309.
3. Mihir Bellare, Joe Kilian, and Phillip Rogaway. The security of cipher block chaining. In Yvo Desmedt, editor, *Advances in Cryptology – CRYPTO'94*, volume 839 of *Lecture Notes in Computer Science*, pages 341–358, Santa Barbara, CA, USA, August 21–25, 1994. Springer, Heidelberg, Germany.
4. Mihir Bellare, Joe Kilian, and Phillip Rogaway. The security of the cipher block chaining message authentication code. *Journal of Computer and System Sciences*, 61(3):362–399, 2000.
5. Mihir Bellare and Phillip Rogaway. The security of triple encryption and a framework for code-based game-playing proofs. In Serge Vaudenay, editor, *Advances in Cryptology – EUROCRYPT 2006*, volume 4004 of *Lecture Notes in Computer Science*, pages 409–426, St. Petersburg, Russia, May 28 – June 1, 2006. Springer, Heidelberg, Germany.
6. Manuel Blum and Silvio Micali. How to generate cryptographically strong sequences of pseudo random bits. In *23rd Annual Symposium on Foundations of Computer Science*, pages 112–117, Chicago, Illinois, November 3–5, 1982. IEEE Computer Society Press.
7. Manuel Blum and Silvio Micali. How to generate cryptographically strong sequences of pseudorandom bits. *SIAM Journal on Computing*, 13(4):850–864, 1984.
8. Horst Feistel. Cryptography and computer privacy. *Scientific American*, 228(5):15–23, 1973.
9. Oded Goldreich, Shafi Goldwasser, and Silvio Micali. How to construct random functions (extended abstract). In *25th Annual Symposium on Foundations of Computer Science*, pages 464–479, Singer Island, Florida, October 24–26, 1984. IEEE Computer Society Press.
10. Oded Goldreich, Shafi Goldwasser, and Silvio Micali. How to construct random functions. *Journal of the ACM*, 33(4):792–807, October 1986.
11. Shafi Goldwasser and Silvio Micali. Probabilistic encryption and how to play mental poker keeping secret all partial information. In *14th Annual ACM Symposium on Theory of Computing*, pages 365–377, San Francisco, CA, USA, May 5–7, 1982. ACM Press.
12. Shafi Goldwasser and Silvio Micali. Probabilistic encryption. *Journal of Computer and System Sciences*, 28(2):270–299, 1984.
13. Shafi Goldwasser, Silvio Micali, and Ronald L. Rivest. A digital signature scheme secure against adaptive chosen-message attacks. *SIAM Journal on Computing*, 17(2):281–308, April 1988.
14. Johan Håstad, Russell Impagliazzo, Leonid A. Levin, and Michael Luby. A pseudorandom generator from any one-way function. *SIAM Journal on Computing*, 28(4):1364–1396, 1999.
15. American National Standards Institute. ANSI - X9.9: Financial Institution Message Authentication (Wholesale), 1 1986.
16. ISO/IEC. 9797:1989: Data cryptographic techniques — Data integrity mechanism using a cryptographic check function employing a block cipher algorithm, 11 1989. Last revised 2011.
17. Michael Luby and Charles Rackoff. How to construct pseudorandom permutations from pseudorandom functions. *SIAM Journal on Computing*, 17(2), 1988.
18. Victor Shoup. Sequences of games: a tool for taming complexity in security proofs. Cryptology ePrint Archive, Report 2004/332, 2004. http://eprint.iacr.org/2004/332.

19. Andrew Chi-Chih Yao. Theory and applications of trapdoor functions (extended abstract). In *23rd Annual Symposium on Foundations of Computer Science*, pages 80–91, Chicago, Illinois, November 3–5, 1982. IEEE Computer Society Press.

Chapter 4
Collision Resistance

Consider the problem of storing a very large file whose integrity you would like to verify from time to time. Think backup. The file is too large to be stored on a flash drive, preventing you from keeping a local copy with which to verify that the file is still intact. But even in case you could keep a local copy, in order to ensure that the file is identical it would need to be brought back to the same machine for comparison—which might be infeasible. An alternative to storing a complete copy is to store only a short "fingerprint" of the file. Then, in order to check the integrity of the file, the fingerprint is recomputed and compared against the stored fingerprint. *Collision-resistant hash functions* provide us with a technique to securely produce such fingerprints.

Typically, collision-resistant hash functions map large inputs to much smaller outputs, throwing even gigabytes of input data to only a few bits, say, 256 bits of output. For the above integrity example such a fingerprint of a file, often called a *hash value*, should be quasi-unique, in the sense that finding a different file with the same hash value should be hard. This would guarantee that any modification of the file is noticeable. Compare this with the notion of message authentication codes discussed in the previous Chapter in Section 3.5. While in both cases we are trying to detect modifications of a message (or file) the underlying primitive is very different. In the case of collision resistance we consider an unkeyed or a publicly keyed function, while message authentication codes require a *secret* key.

Abstractly, collision resistance asks that given a hash function H it should be difficult to find distinct inputs x_1 and x_2 that have the same hash value, that is, for which it holds that $H(x_1) = H(x_2)$. Note that if we drop the requirement on the function to produce shorter outputs, then constructing a collision-resistant function is trivial. For instance, the identity function $F(x) := x$ is collision resistant, since colliding inputs do not exist. At the same time, in the file integrity example, we would not have gained anything from such a function since we would still need to keep a complete copy of the file. Although we do not stipulate the compression property in the following

© Springer Nature Switzerland AG 2021
A. Mittelbach, M. Fischlin, *The Theory of Hash Functions and Random Oracles,*
Information Security and Cryptography, https://doi.org/10.1007/978-3-030-63287-8_4

definition explicitly, for all practical purposes we usually only consider hash functions that compress.

Remark 4.1. Hash functions have a long tradition in computer science and have been used outside of cryptographic contexts since the 1960s, for example, as the basis for data structures, fingerprinting, or modification detection. Collision resistance is thus often regarded as the prototypical property of a cryptographic hash function, and even though we usually require from a cryptographic hash function that it is also one-way and pseudorandom we speak of one-way *functions* and pseudorandom *functions* but of collision-resistant *hash functions*.

4.1 Formalizing Collision Resistance

In the following we formalize what it means for a function to be collision resistant. Interestingly, a formalization becomes tricky when considering *unkeyed* hash functions, which we will discuss in detail in Section 4.1.1. We will thus only define the notion for keyed hash functions H = (H.KGen, H.Eval), which as before we formalize as two efficient algorithms H.KGen and H.Eval for key generation and evaluation, respectively.

Definition 4.2 (Collision-Resistant Hash Function). *An efficient keyed hash function* H = (H.KGen, H.Eval) *is called* collision resistant *(CR) if advantage* $\mathsf{Adv}^{cr}_{H,\mathcal{A}}(\lambda)$ *is negligible for all* PPT *algorithms* $\mathcal{A}$*. Here, the advantage is defined as*

$$\mathsf{Adv}^{cr}_{H,\mathcal{A}}(\lambda) := \Pr\left[\mathit{Exp}^{cr}_{H,\mathcal{A}}(\lambda)\right]$$

relative to experiment $\mathit{Exp}^{cr}_{H,\mathcal{A}}(\lambda)$:

Experiment $\mathit{Exp}^{cr}_{H,\mathcal{A}}(\lambda)$
1 : hk ←$ H.KGen(1^λ)
2 : (x_1, x_2) ←$ $\mathcal{A}(1^\lambda, hk)$
3 : **return** H.Eval(hk, x_1) = H.Eval(hk, x_2) $\wedge$ $x_1 \neq x_2$

Hash functions in practice usually have an output length of 128 to 512 bits, although 128 is nowadays considered to be too short for security reasons. For example, the SHA-3 standard for secure hash functions comes in multiple modes that allows to select output lengths between 224 to 512 bits, while the input size is not restricted.[1] For the theoretical treatment of hash functions we again consider an asymptotic setting where we require the function to be collision resistant only for sufficiently large security parameters. Due to the

---

[1] We discuss real-world hash functions including SHA-3 in detail in Chapter 15.

common coupling between security parameter and output length this usually also translates to larger output. To capture the input and output length of hash functions formally we again implicitly augment the key and evaluation algorithm by additional functions H.il and H.ol from $\mathbb{N}$ to $\mathbb{N}$, denoting the input and output size of the hash function for a given security parameter. Usually, we will allow arbitrary long messages as input for all security parameters, which makes H.il void.

4.1.1 Collision Resistance vs. Non-uniform Adversaries

Let us consider a variant of Definition 4.2 that defines collision resistance not for keyed but for unkeyed hash functions. In this case the adversary has to output different inputs which collide under the hash function. Indeed, this scenario would be much closer to practice where hash functions are usually unkeyed (consider MD5 or the SHA family). Consider now the following *non-uniform* adversary given as a sequence of circuits $\mathcal{A} := (C_1, C_2, \dots)$ where C_λ denotes the circuit used to attack the hash function on security parameter 1^λ. Note that in contrast to a Turing machine the circuit model of computation is non-uniform, meaning that we can have a different circuit for each security parameter with the only requirement being that the size of the circuits is polynomially bounded (see Section 1.3.3 for an introduction to the non-uniform model of computation). Such non-uniform adversaries are often used in the analysis of cryptographic schemes in order to show that a scheme cannot be attacked even by adversaries that hold some precoded knowledge. For *unkeyed* collision-resistant hash functions we do, however, run into a problem when we allow non-uniform adversaries as we explain next.

Let us assume that hash function H for security parameter λ produces hash values of length H.ol(λ) and that it allows for inputs of arbitrary length and thus, in particular, for inputs of length H.ol$(\lambda) + 1$. Thus, by the pigeon hole principle[2] we have that there must be distinct messages $x_{\lambda,1}$ and $x_{\lambda,2}$ of length H.ol$(\lambda) + 1$ such that $H(1^\lambda, x_{\lambda,1}) = H(1^\lambda, x_{\lambda,2})$. This is simply because there are at least twice as many inputs of length H.ol$(\lambda) + 1$ as hash values of length H.ol(λ), and hence collisions must exist. For each security parameter 1^λ fix such a pair $(x_{\lambda,1}, x_{\lambda,2})$. We now consider an adversary that uses the following circuit (written as an algorithm) to attack the hash function with security parameter λ:

$$\underline{C_\lambda[x_{\lambda,1}, x_{\lambda,2}](1^\lambda)}$$

return $(x_{\lambda,1}, x_{\lambda,2})$

---

[2] The *pigeon hole principle* states that if you have n pigeon holes and $m > n$ pigeons that all fly into the pigeon holes then there is at least one pigeon hole with two or more pigeons.

In other words, the circuit for security parameter λ has collision $(x_{\lambda,1}, x_{\lambda,2})$ hardcoded as part of its program, which we emphasize by adding the hardcoded inputs in square brackets.

We note that the adversary is a valid non-uniform adversary since the size of each circuit is bounded: since circuit C_λ simply outputs two hardcoded hash values it is of size

$$|C_\lambda[x_{\lambda,1}, x_{\lambda,2}]| = 2 \cdot (\mathsf{H.ol}(\lambda) + 1).$$

And, since hash function H is efficient, output length $\mathsf{H.ol}$ must be bounded by some polynomial and hence the above circuit size is polynomially bounded.

Note that even though the above adversary has an artificial touch to it, it is formally sound. And because it is in general difficult to exclude non-uniform adversaries from theoretical analyses, asymptotic treatments of collision resistance are therefore usually restricted to the keyed setting.

The Human Ignorance Approach

One approach to mitigate the discrepancy between real-world hash functions (which are usually unkeyed) and hash function theory (in the keyed setting) is the so-called *human ignorance approach*. For this, we must slightly reinterpret our security results which are usually given in the *existential form*:

If there exists an efficient adversary $\mathcal{A}$ against X then there exists an efficient adversary $\mathcal{B}$ against Y.

Applied to the setting of (unkeyed) hash functions, this would read:

If there exists an efficient adversary $\mathcal{A}$ against X then there exists an efficient adversary $\mathcal{B}$ that finds collisions in H.

This notion, however, does not have any meaning since we already know that there *exists* an adversary: since collisions exist there exists the adversary that has a collision hardwired in its code. However, this does not mean that us humans are able to find such a collision, let alone find one quickly. MD5 was published in 1992, but a first collision was found only in 2004. For SHA-1, which was published first in 1995, it took even longer and a first collision was published more than 20 years later in 2017. In other words, the proof of existence of an algorithm that performs a certain task does not necessarily make it easier to actually find and use that algorithm.

Coming back to hash functions, if we state our results slightly differently we can indeed show security properties also for unkeyed hash functions. For this, instead of stating an existential claim (if $\mathcal{A}$ exists then $\mathcal{B}$ exists) we consider a *constructive* claim:

If you know an efficient algorithm $\mathcal{A}$ for X then you can construct an efficient algorithm $\mathcal{B}$ that finds collisions in H as follows.

The focus in the claim shifts from assuming and showing existence to assuming access of an actual instance and constructing an actual adversary. If you look back at most of the reductions we have seen so far, most of these actually follow this constructive approach. The proofs consist of a recipe that contains every little detail to build an actual adversary against the target scheme lacking only access to an actual instance of some adversary against an underlying building block. For example, we showed how to construct a message authentication code from a pseudorandom function by giving a concrete attack against the pseudorandomness property of the function given a concrete instance of an adversary against the message authentication code.

While in this book we follow the common practice and will also mostly consider the keyed setting, the human ignorance approach yields a sound justification of constructional results as security claims for unkeyed hash functions used in practice.

4.1.2 A Generic Lower Bound for Collision Resistance

While the human ignorance approach argues that the existence of collisions does not imply that it is easy to find collisions, finding collisions via a brute-force search attack can be simpler than is generally assumed. In particular, this is why hash functions need to have sufficiently large outputs and 128 bits, today, should no longer be considered secure.

The Birthday Bound

Given any (compressing) hash function with $n = \mathsf{H.ol}(\lambda)$ bits output, one can always find collisions in roughly $2^{n/2}$ many hash evaluations, with constant probability. This is known as the *birthday bound*, as it resembles the seeming paradox that among only 23 people there is a high chance that two of them will have the same day and month of birth among the 365 possibilities. In our scenario we can envision the hash values of random inputs as their "birthdays" in a set of 2^n possibilities. Finding a collision now requires to find a birthday match among distinct inputs. Let $\mathsf{q} : \mathbb{N} \to \mathbb{N}$ be a polynomial and set $\mathsf{q} := \mathsf{q}(\lambda)$. A collision-finding algorithm $\mathcal{A}$, which evaluates the hash function q times, could now be given as follows: Adversary $\mathcal{A}$ repeatedly samples random inputs $x_i \leftarrow\!\!\$\ \{0,1\}^{\mathsf{H.il}(\lambda)}$ and computes $y_i \leftarrow \mathsf{H.Eval}(\mathsf{hk}, x_i)$ to then check whether the latest value y_i collides with any of the previously generated values y_j, in which case it outputs the collision (x_i, x_j). If after q trials it did not find a collision it stops and outputs $\bot$. Following is the collision-finding algorithm given as pseudocode:

$$\underline{\mathcal{A}(1^\lambda, \mathsf{hk})}$$

1: **for** $i = 1..q$ **do**

2:      $x_i \leftarrow\!\!\!\$\ \{0,1\}^{\mathsf{H.il}(\lambda)}$

3:      $y_i \leftarrow \mathsf{H.Eval}(\mathsf{hk}, x_i)$

4:      // check for collision

5:      **for** $j = 1..(i-1)$ **do**

6:          **if** $y_i = y_j$ **then**

7:              **return** (x_i, x_j)

8: **return** $\perp$

Assume that for any hash key hk the function $\mathsf{H.Eval}(\mathsf{hk}, \cdot)$ distributes random inputs uniformly over the output strings $\{0,1\}^n = \{0,1\}^{\mathsf{H.ol}(\lambda)}$, i.e., $\mathsf{H.Eval}(\mathsf{hk}, X)$ is uniform over $\{0,1\}^n$ for $X \leftarrow\!\!\!\$\ \{0,1\}^{\mathsf{H.il}(\lambda)}$ sampled uniformly at random. One can show that this is the worst-case scenario for finding collisions, and we will discuss this at the end of this section. We are interested in an upper bound on the probability that *no* collision $y_i = y_j$ occurs in the attack of our adversary $\mathcal{A}$, from which we can derive a lower bound for the complementary event that a collision has been found. More formally, let noColl_i denote the event that no collision occurs up to, and including, the ith sample x_i. Then we are interested in the probability of noColl_q. It is convenient to rewrite this probability in terms of conditional probabilities

$$\Pr[\mathsf{noColl}_q] = \Pr[\mathsf{noColl}_q \wedge \mathsf{noColl}_{q-1}]$$
$$= \Pr[\mathsf{noColl}_q \mid \mathsf{noColl}_{q-1}] \cdot \Pr[\mathsf{noColl}_{q-1}],$$

where the conditional probability represents the likelihood that we do not get a collision in the qth attempt, if we have not encountered a collision in the first $q - 1$ samples yet. Iterating this process we get

$$\Pr[\mathsf{noColl}_q] = \prod_{i=1}^{q} \Pr[\mathsf{noColl}_i \mid \mathsf{noColl}_{i-1}] \cdot \Pr[\mathsf{noColl}_{i-1}],$$

with $\Pr[\mathsf{noColl}_0] := 1$ by definition.

We next bound the conditional probability from above for each index i. Suppose that our algorithm is at the ith attempt and that no collision has been found so far, implying that all $i - 1$ previous hash values $y_1, \ldots, y_{i-1}$ are distinct. Then we can bound the probability that the ith hash evaluation does *not* hit any of the other $i - 1$ previous values $y_1, \ldots, y_{i-1}$ by

$$\Pr[\mathsf{noColl}_i \mid \mathsf{noColl}_{i-1}] \leq \left(1 - \frac{i-1}{2^n}\right).$$

The reason is that $i - 1$ slots have already been taken by the $i - 1$ values $y_1, \ldots, y_{i-1}$ and now the ith value $\mathsf{H}(x_i)$ is independently and uniformly distributed over the 2^n output strings.

From this we can derive an overall bound, where the second inequality is due to the fact $1 - x \leq e^{-x}$ for any real value x:

$$\Pr[\mathsf{noColl_q}] \leq \prod_{i=1}^{q} \left(1 - \frac{i-1}{2^n} \right).$$

$$\leq \prod_{i=1}^{q} e^{-\frac{i-1}{2^n}} = e^{-\frac{1}{2^n} \sum_{i=1}^{q}(i-1)} = e^{-\frac{1}{2^n} \cdot \binom{q}{2}}.$$

Conversely, this means that our algorithm $\mathcal{A}$ finds colliding images with probability at least

$$1 - e^{-\frac{1}{2^n} \cdot \binom{q}{2}}.$$

Since $\binom{q}{2} = \frac{q(q-1)}{2}$ is on the order of q^2, after roughly $q \approx \sqrt{2^n}$ attempts we find a collision with constant probability. Specifically, for $q = \lceil 2^{n/2} + 1 \rceil$ the probability is at least

$$1 - e^{-\frac{1}{2}} \geq 1 - 0.61 \geq 0.39.$$

Accounting for Trivial Collisions

Note that we are not done yet, because we still have to deal with the case that algorithm $\mathcal{A}$ chooses $x_i = x_j$ in line 2, that is, it chooses an input value twice. In case of the birthday paradox, where all "persons" x_i are distinct by definition this can of course not happen and we can thus already apply our intermediate result there. The derived bound applies there to $N = 365$, such that one already encounters a collision among roughly $\sqrt{N} \approx 19$ people with high probability. The reason for often finding the value 23 in the literature is that for this value the collision probability exceeds 0.5 (instead of 0.39 as in our bound).

To formally deal with the case of algorithm $\mathcal{A}$ finding a trivial "collision" $y_i = y_j$ with $x_i = x_j$ we have two options. We might consider adapting the algorithm to deterministically iterate over all inputs in which case, however, functions exist that have their collisions "hidden away" towards the end of the iteration. Instead, we next bound the probability of such trivial collisions.

In order to bound the probability of $\mathcal{A}$ finding a trivial "collision" $y_i = y_j$ with $x_i = x_j$ first note that if the input length was actually smaller than the output length n then there would not be much hope. That is, $\mathcal{A}$ would then almost certainly find such a trivial collision first. However, for a compressing function we have $\mathsf{H.il}(\lambda) \geq n + 1$. With this, we can bound the probability that any distinct random samples x_i, x_j accidentally collide. Since there are at most $\binom{q}{2} = \frac{q \cdot (q-1)}{2}$ such pairs, and each pair collides with probability $2^{-\mathsf{H.il}(\lambda)}$, we get that for $q := \sqrt{2^n}$ the probability of having any colliding inputs can be upper bound as[3]

$$\binom{q}{2} \cdot \frac{1}{2^{H.il(\lambda)}} \le \frac{(2^{n/2} + 2)^2}{2 \cdot 2^{H.il(\lambda)}} \le \frac{2^n + 4 \cdot 2^{n/2} + 4}{2 \cdot 2^{n+1}} \le \frac{1}{4} + \frac{1}{2^{n/2}} + \frac{1}{2^n}.$$

For $n \ge 8$ this gets smaller than 0.32. But then

$$
\begin{aligned}
0.39 \le \Pr[\exists i \ne j : y_i = y_j] \\
= \Pr[\exists i \ne j : y_i = y_j \wedge x_i = x_j] + \Pr[\exists i \ne j : y_i = y_j \wedge x_i \ne x_j] \\
\le \Pr[\exists i \ne j : x_i = x_j] + \Pr[\exists i \ne j : y_i = y_j \wedge x_i \ne x_j] \\
\le 0.32 + \Pr[\exists i \ne j : y_i = y_j \wedge x_i \ne x_j]. \quad (4.1)
\end{aligned}
$$

We conclude that we find a non-trivial collision with constant probability of at least 0.07. When considering larger input lengths the bound quickly improves. For example, for $H.il(\lambda) = 2n$ we get that

$$\binom{q}{2} \cdot \frac{1}{2^{H.il(\lambda)}} \le \frac{q^2}{2^{H.il(\lambda)}} = \frac{2^n}{2^{2n}} \le \frac{1}{2^n},$$

which is negligible, thus making $\Pr[\exists i \ne j : y_i = y_j \wedge x_i \ne x_j]$ the dominant term in Equation (4.1).

Worst-Case Behavior of the Uniform Distribution

In the above discussion we assumed that the hash function distributes its inputs uniformly over the output space, and in the following we argue that this, actually, represents the worst-case scenario for collision finders. For this, we still assume that the hash values are distributed independently. More formally, for the ith value, $i \in [q]$, we consider the random variable Y_i which is given by $Y_i \leftarrow H.Eval(hk, x_i)$ over the random choice of the input x_i for fixed key hk. We assume that the Y_i's are mutually independent, but we do not stipulate that they are uniform over the range $\{0,1\}^n$. (Recall that we assume hash values of length $H.ol(\lambda) = n$.) Independence of the hash values is, for example, given for our collision-finding algorithm $\mathcal{A}$ since each input x_i is chosen afresh.

We next argue that any non-uniform distribution of the Y_i's only allows to find collisions easier. To see this, consider the complementary probability $P(q)$ that q hash values Y_i are actually pairwise distinct, i.e., no collision occurs. Assume now that each possible hash value $j \in \{0,1\}^n$ has a probability p_j of being hit. Then the probability of obtaining a fixed sequence $i_1 < i_2 < \cdots < i_q$

---

[3] Note that the simpler, but less accurate $\binom{q}{2} \cdot \frac{1}{2^{H.il(\lambda)}} \le \frac{q^2}{2^{H.il(\lambda)}} = \frac{2^n}{2^{n+1}} = \frac{1}{2}$ yields a bound independent of n and in particular bigger than our reference value of 0.39, which is why we must resort to the more complex bound given.

of values in $0, \ldots, 2^n - 1$ for the q samples, that is, $Y_1 = i_1, Y_2 = i_2, \ldots, Y_q = i_q$, is given by the product of the individual probabilities by mutual independence. To account for all possible permutations of outcomes yielding this sequence of indexes we need to multiply this by the number q! of permutations of the Y_i's. Hence we obtain

$$P(q) = q! \cdot \sum_{i_1 < i_2 < \cdots < i_q} p_{i_1} \cdot p_{i_2} \cdots p_{i_q},$$

where the sum is over all (distinct) indexes from $0, \ldots, 2^n - 1$.

The following reasoning assumes $q \geq 2$ and that at least q of the probabilities p_j are non-zero, otherwise the setting is trivial. Consider two unequal probabilities which, for non-uniform distributions, must exist. For sake of concreteness assume these are p_0 and p_1; the argument works analogously with any other pair of probabilities. Rewrite the above probability $P(q)$ according to terms which include both p_0 and p_1, or just one of the values, or none:

$$P(q) = q! \cdot \left(\begin{array}{l} p_0 p_1 \cdot \sum_{1 < i_1 < i_2 < \cdots < i_{q-2}} p_{i_1} \cdots p_{i_{q-2}} \\ + (p_0 + p_1) \cdot \sum_{1 < i_1 < i_2 < \cdots < i_{q-1}} p_{i_1} \cdots p_{i_{q-1}} \\ + \sum_{1 < i_1 < i_2 < \cdots < i_q} p_{i_1} \cdots p_{i_q} \end{array} \right).$$

Let us next replace both probabilities p_0 and p_1 with their arithmetic mean $\frac{1}{2}(p_0 + p_1)$ such that the probabilities p_j still add up to 1. Then only the first term in the above sum changes, because $p_0 + p_1$ in the second term remains the same for the substitution and neither probability appears in the last term. For the first term observe that the arithmetic mean $\frac{1}{2}(p_0 + p_1)$ strictly exceeds the geometric mean $\sqrt{p_0 p_1}$ for unequal, non-negative values p_0, p_1. Hence, the new $P(q)$ grows strictly if we level out the distinct values p_0 and p_1. It follows that the probability $P(q)$ must be maximal if all p_j's are identical and, consequently, that the uniform distribution gives the highest probability of having no collision.

4.1.3 Collision Resistance vs. One-Wayness

How does collision resistance relate to one-wayness, the other "public-key" property defined so far which allows for compressing functions?[4] Although in both cases the adversary is given similar access to the function, we will see that the two properties are in some sense orthogonal to each other. That is, there can be one-way functions that are not collision resistant, and vice versa

---

[4] Note that pseudorandom generators which are also publicly keyed are required to expand their inputs and are thus syntactically very different from collision-resistant hash functions that compress. One-way functions, on the other hand, may be compressing.

there are collision-resistant functions that are not one-way, at least if we do not stipulate compression of the hash function. If, on the other hand, we do require the hash function to produce shorter outputs, then collision resistance implies one-wayness, as we show below.

Remark 4.3. In the context of hash functions the one-wayness property of a function is often referred to as *preimage resistance.*

In order to show that one-wayness does not imply collision resistance, let us assume that F is an arbitrary one-way function. Then we can create a tweaked version F' which is still one-way but which is not collision resistant. For this, we hardcode a trivial collision into the function as follows:

$$F'(1^\lambda, x) = \begin{cases} 0^{|x|} & \text{in case } x = 0^\lambda \\ 0^{|x|} & \text{in case } x = 1^\lambda \\ F(1^\lambda, x) & \text{otherwise} \end{cases}$$

It is easy to see that F' is not collision resistant, since for all security parameters $\lambda \in \mathbb{N}$ the inputs 0^λ and 1^λ form a collision and the trivial (uniform) adversary $\mathcal{A}$ returning $(0^\lambda, 1^\lambda)$ wins game $\mathsf{Exp}^{\mathrm{cr}}_{\mathsf{H},\mathcal{A}}(\lambda)$ of Definition 4.2 with probability 1. Also note that this modification of the one-way function F can be done in both the keyed and unkeyed setting. What remains to show is that the adapted function F' is, indeed, still one-way, which we leave as Exercise 4.1. We have thus established:

Proposition 4.4. *If one-way functions exist, then there exist one-way functions that are not collision resistant.*

For the inverse direction, that is, a collision-resistant hash function which is not one-way, recall that if we do not require the function to compress then the identity function is collision resistant but clearly not one-way. For all practical purposes, however, collision resistance is the "stronger" property. That is, collision resistance plus a compression requirement implies one-wayness as we will show next. While we usually consider hash functions that can process inputs of arbitrary length we will restrict the input length in the following proposition to get a stronger result. A compression of already a single bit suffices to show the proposition.

Proposition 4.5. *Let* $\mathsf{H} = (\mathsf{H.KGen}, \mathsf{H.Eval}, \mathsf{H.il}, \mathsf{H.ol})$ *be a keyed hash function which for security parameter* λ *processes messages of length* $\mathsf{H.il}(\lambda)$ *and produces hash values of length* $\mathsf{H.ol}(\lambda)$. *If* H *is collision resistant and for all sufficiently large* λ *it holds that* $\mathsf{H.ol}(\lambda) < \mathsf{H.il}(\lambda)$ *then we have that* H *is one-way. More concretely, then for every efficient adversary* $\mathcal{B}$ *(against the one-wayness of* H*) there exists an adversary* $\mathcal{A}$ *(against the collision resistance of* H*) such that*

$$\mathsf{Adv}^{\mathrm{owf}}_{\mathsf{H},\mathcal{B}}(\lambda) \le 4 \cdot \mathsf{Adv}^{\mathrm{cr}}_{\mathsf{H},\mathcal{A}}(\lambda).$$

The proof will once again be in the form of a reduction. For this we will assume the existence of an adversary $\mathcal{B}$ against the one-way property of function H and show how to use this adversary to find a collision. The idea for constructing adversary $\mathcal{A}$ from $\mathcal{B}$ to find collisions is to choose a random preimage x_0 and compute $y \leftarrow H(hk, x_0)$ (here hk is the hash function's key). Then adversary $\mathcal{B}$ is run on input $(1^\lambda, hk, y)$ to compute a preimage for y. Now, if $\mathcal{B}$ is successful and if y has multiple preimages, which is the case for sufficiently many y due to the requirement on the output length, then with a certain probability the preimage x_1 output by $\mathcal{B}$ is different from x_0. Since in this case both x_0 and x_1 are preimages for y and $x_0 \neq x_1$ we have found a collision and $\mathcal{A}$ is successful. It remains to formalize the idea.

Proof of Proposition 4.5. Let $\mathcal{B}$ be an efficient adversary against the one-wayness property of H. We construct an adversary $\mathcal{A}$ that utilizes $\mathcal{B}$ to find collisions for H as follows:

$$\underline{\mathcal{A}^{\mathcal{B}}(1^\lambda, hk)}$$

$1:\quad x_0 \leftarrow\!\!{}_\$ \{0,1\}^{H.\mathsf{il}(1^\lambda)}$

$2:\quad y \leftarrow H.\mathsf{Eval}(hk, x_0)$

$3:\quad x_1 \leftarrow\!\!{}_\$ \mathcal{B}(1^\lambda, hk, y)$

$4:\quad \textbf{return } (x_0, x_1)$

Let us analyze the success probability of adversary $\mathcal{A}$ of finding collisions. For now let us assume that hash function H is *regular*, which means that for every security parameter $\lambda \in \mathbb{N}$ and key $hk \leftarrow\!\!{}_\$ H.\mathsf{KGen}(1^\lambda)$ every image in $H.\mathsf{Eval}(hk, \cdot)$ has the same number of preimages. As H is compressing by at least one bit we know that there exist at least twice as many input values as hash values. Thus, each possible hash value has at least two preimages. We will later see how to drop this regularity requirement.

Adversary $\mathcal{A}$ finds a collision in case $\mathcal{B}$ is successful and if furthermore the preimage x_1 output by $\mathcal{B}$ is different from x_0. That is, we are looking for the quantity

$$\mathsf{Adv}^{\mathsf{cr}}_{H,\mathcal{A}}(\lambda) = \Pr\left[\mathsf{Exp}^{\mathsf{owf}}_{H,\mathcal{B}}(\lambda) \wedge x_0 \neq x_1\right].$$

By our above assumption that H is regular we know that for each y chosen by $\mathcal{A}$ there exist at least two preimages. The actual preimage x_0 chosen by $\mathcal{A}$ to compute y remains hidden from $\mathcal{B}$ among all possible preimages for y. Hence, from $\mathcal{B}$'s perspective each of the two (or more) preimages under y is equally likely. Therefore, the probability for $\mathcal{B}$ to be successful and to output a preimage different from x_0 is at least half the probability of being successful. That is,

$$\Pr\left[\mathsf{Exp}^{\mathsf{owf}}_{H,\mathcal{B}}(\lambda) \wedge x_0 \neq x_1\right] \geq \frac{1}{2} \cdot \Pr\left[\mathsf{Exp}^{\mathsf{owf}}_{H,\mathcal{B}}(\lambda)\right],$$

which already proves Proposition 4.5 in the case that H is regular.

The general case. It remains to analyze adversary $\mathcal{A}$ in the case where H is not necessarily regular. Here, we can revert to the above analysis only in case $\mathcal{A}$ samples a preimage y (by sampling $x_0 \leftarrow_\$ \{0,1\}^{\mathsf{H.il}(1^\lambda)}$ and computing $y \leftarrow \mathsf{H.Eval}(\mathsf{hk}, x_0)$) that has at least two preimages. Let us call this event ManyPreimages. Then we are now interested in quantifying

$$\mathsf{Adv}^{\mathsf{cr}}_{\mathsf{H},\mathcal{A}}(\lambda) = \Pr\left[\mathsf{Exp}^{\mathsf{owf}}_{\mathsf{H},\mathcal{B}}(\lambda) \wedge \mathsf{ManyPreimages} \wedge x_0 \neq x_1\right]$$

$$= \Pr\left[\mathsf{Exp}^{\mathsf{owf}}_{\mathsf{H},\mathcal{B}}(\lambda) \wedge x_0 \neq x_1 \;\middle|\; \mathsf{ManyPreimages}\right] \cdot \Pr[\mathsf{ManyPreimages}].$$

We have already analyzed the conditional probability in the regular case where ManyPreimages is always satisfied. This argument applies analogously in the non-regular case, as long as it is given that y has at least two preimages. It therefore remains to analyze $\Pr[\mathsf{ManyPreimages}]$.

Note that we can have at most $2^{\mathsf{H.ol}(\lambda)} - 1$ "bad" images y with only a single preimage. This in particular means that the probability of picking a preimage that corresponds to such a "bad" image when sampling uniformly among the input strings is at most

$$\frac{2^{\mathsf{H.ol}(\lambda)} - 1}{2^{\mathsf{H.il}(\lambda)}} < \frac{1}{2}.$$

Here we used that the hash function compresses to derive the upper bound. In the complementary event we pick some x such that the resulting image $y = \mathsf{H}(\mathsf{hk}, x)$ has at least one other preimage. In other words,

$$\Pr[\mathsf{ManyPreimages}] \geq \frac{1}{2}.$$

Putting it all together concludes the proof:

$$\mathsf{Adv}^{\mathsf{cr}}_{\mathsf{H},\mathcal{A}}(\lambda) = \Pr\left[\mathsf{Exp}^{\mathsf{owf}}_{\mathsf{H},\mathcal{B}}(\lambda) \wedge \mathsf{ManyPreimages} \wedge x_0 \neq x_1\right]$$

$$= \Pr\left[\mathsf{Exp}^{\mathsf{owf}}_{\mathsf{H},\mathcal{B}}(\lambda) \wedge x_0 \neq x_1 \;\middle|\; \mathsf{ManyPreimages}\right] \cdot \Pr[\mathsf{ManyPreimages}]$$

$$\geq \frac{1}{2} \cdot \Pr\left[\mathsf{Exp}^{\mathsf{owf}}_{\mathsf{H},\mathcal{B}}(\lambda)\right] \cdot \frac{1}{2}. \qquad\qquad\qquad \square$$

4.2 Second-Preimage and Target-Collision Resistance

Two properties that are closely related to collision resistance are *second-preimage resistance* and *target-collision resistance*. Recall that one-wayness is often referred to as *preimage resistance* in the context of hash functions, which yields a group of four related properties that, as we will see, form a strict hierarchy (given that the hash function compresses). In order to break the collision resistance property of a hash function H an adversary needs only to find an arbitrary collision, i.e., distinct messages $x \neq x'$ that have the same hash value. Both second-preimage and target-collision resistance somewhat relax the security requirement by putting further restrictions on the collision that an adversary needs to find.

4.2.1 Second-Preimage Resistance

Second-preimage resistance (SPR) relaxes the security requirement of collision resistance and instead of tasking an adversary with finding an arbitrary collision an adversary must find a colliding message x' for a randomly chosen message $x \leftarrow_\$ \{0,1\}^{\text{H.il}(\lambda)}$. Note that the task for the adversary is significantly more difficult and we will formally prove in Section 4.3 that, indeed, collision resistance implies second-preimage resistance. Formally, we define second-preimage resistance as:

Definition 4.6 (Second-Preimage-Resistant Hash Function). *An efficient keyed hash function* H = (H.KGen, H.Eval) *is called* second-preimage resistant *(SPR) if the advantage* $\text{Adv}^{\text{spr}}_{\text{H},\mathcal{A}}(\lambda)$ *is negligible for all* PPT *algorithms* $\mathcal{A}$. *Here, the advantage is defined as*

$$\text{Adv}^{\text{spr}}_{\text{H},\mathcal{A}}(\lambda) := \Pr\left[\text{Exp}^{\text{spr}}_{\text{H},\mathcal{A}}(\lambda)\right]$$

relative to experiment $\text{Exp}^{\text{spr}}_{\text{H},\mathcal{A}}(\lambda)$:

Experiment $\text{Exp}^{\text{spr}}_{\text{H},\mathcal{A}}(\lambda)$
1 : hk $\leftarrow_\$$ H.KGen(1^λ)
2 : $x \leftarrow_\$ \{0,1\}^{\text{H.il}(\lambda)}$
3 : $x' \leftarrow_\$ \mathcal{A}(1^\lambda, \text{hk}, x)$
4 : **return** H.Eval(hk, x) = H.Eval(hk, x') $\wedge$ $x \neq x'$

Remark 4.7. As with one-way functions (see Definition 2.15 on page 84) we can generalize the choice of input distribution. That is, instead of as above fixing the distribution in line 2 to be the uniform distribution we can consider an arbitrary choice of distribution D from which preimage x is sampled. In this case we would say that hash function H is second-preimage resistant on distribution D.

Second-preimage resistance is a property which pops up for example in the following application. In the GPG public-key encryption system each user generates a public key pk which other parties can use to send messages securely. The details about the encryption process are irrelevant for us here.

We are rather interested in the question of how a sender of a message can be sure that a given public key pk, say, obtained from a web site, is actually the key of the intended recipient. If the sender misidentified the receiver then the confidential information could be accessible by the wrong party. The reliable binding of public keys to users is known as certification, and there are various means to achieve this. GPG offers one possibility via so-called fingerprints: The sender checks with the intended receiver if the (obtained and genuine) public keys match by some reliable communication line, e.g., by comparing the two values in person or via telephone. But since public keys may be large it is more convenient to simply compare the shorter hash value H.Eval(hk, pk), also referred to as the public key's fingerprint.

Assume that an adversary tries to foist its own public key $pk' \neq pk$ on the sender, in order to learn the confidential message. If we assume that the adversary cannot tamper with the additional communication for checking validity of obtained keys, then the adversary must find a public key pk' whose hash value coincides with the one of the genuine key pk. This attack corresponds exactly to the setting of second-preimage resistance above. The user chooses its public key pk first, according to some key generation algorithm, such that pk plays the role of x sampled according to some distribution D. The adversary then tries to find another public key $x' = pk'$ such that this key collides under the hash function. Hence, for this application scenario second-preimage resistance of the hash function suffices, because the original key pk is chosen honestly.

4.2.2 Target-Collision Resistance

Target-collision resistance (TCR), similarly to second-preimage resistance, considers a setting in which an adversary needs to find a specific collision instead of an arbitrary collision. In contrast to second-preimage resistance here the adversary may specify one message (the target) of the collision before seeing the key. It is not difficult to show that this strengthens the definition compared with second-preimage resistance: Any target-collision resistant hash function is also second-preimage resistant. We will establish the relationships between the properties shortly.

The setup of the experiment requires the adversary $\mathcal{A}$ to work in two stages. In the first stage the adversary picks the target, then the hash key is sampled, and afterwards the adversary tries to find a collision under the key. This is usually formalized by letting $\mathcal{A} = (\mathcal{A}_1, \mathcal{A}_2)$ consist of two formally independent algorithms $\mathcal{A}_1$ and $\mathcal{A}_2$, but letting the first adversary output some state information state which is then passed to the second stage as input. Intuitively state should contain sufficient information to enable $\mathcal{A}_2$ to find the collision. Formally, we define target-collision resistance as follows:

Definition 4.8 (Target-Collision-Resistant Hash Function). *An efficient keyed hash function* $H = (H.KGen, H.Eval)$ *is called* target-collision resistant *(TCR) if advantage* $Adv^{tcr}_{H,\mathcal{A}_1,\mathcal{A}_2}(\lambda)$ *is negligible for all* PPT *algorithms* $\mathcal{A} := (\mathcal{A}_1, \mathcal{A}_2)$. *Here, the advantage is defined as*

$$Adv^{tcr}_{H,\mathcal{A}_1,\mathcal{A}_2}(\lambda) := \Pr\left[Exp^{tcr}_{H,\mathcal{A}_1,\mathcal{A}_2}(\lambda)\right]$$

relative to experiment $Exp^{tcr}_{H,\mathcal{A}_1,\mathcal{A}_2}(\lambda)$:

Experiment $Exp^{tcr}_{H,\mathcal{A}_1,\mathcal{A}_2}(\lambda)$

1: $(x_1, \text{state}) \leftarrow\!\!\$\ \mathcal{A}_1(1^\lambda)$

2: $hk \leftarrow\!\!\$\ H.KGen(1^\lambda)$

3: $x_2 \leftarrow\!\!\$\ \mathcal{A}_2(1^\lambda, hk, x_1, \text{state})$

4: **return** $H.Eval(hk, x_1) = H.Eval(hk, x_2) \wedge x_1 \neq x_2$

Remark 4.9. Target-collision-resistant hash functions are also known as *universal one-way hash functions (UOWHFs)*.

In Chapter 6 about signature schemes we will see applications of the notion of target-collision resistance.

4.3 Relating the Collision Resistance Flavors

In Section 4.1.3 we have already established that collision resistance (plus compression) implies one-wayness, while the converse does not necessarily hold. The following theorem completes the picture relating all three newly defined security properties among each other, as well as with one-wayness (aka preimage resistance in the context of hash functions). As we will see, the introduced properties form a strict hierarchy given that the hash function compresses. If this is not the case, then one-wayness is not necessarily implied by any of the other properties.

Theorem 4.10. *Let* $H = (H.KGen, H.Eval, H.il, H.ol)$ *be a keyed hash function which for security parameter* λ *processes messages of length* $H.il(\lambda)$ *and produces hash values of length* $H.ol(\lambda)$.

CR $\implies$ TCR. *If* H *is collision resistant then we have that* H *is also target-collision resistant. More concretely, then for every efficient adversary* $\mathcal{B}$ *there exists an efficient adversary* $\mathcal{A}$ *such that*

$$Adv^{tcr}_{H,\mathcal{B}}(\lambda) \leq Adv^{cr}_{H,\mathcal{A}}(\lambda).$$

TCR $\implies$ SPR. *If H is target-collision resistant then we have that H is also second-preimage resistant. More concretely, then for every efficient adversary $\mathcal{B}$ there exists an efficient adversary $\mathcal{A}$ such that*

$$\mathsf{Adv}_{\mathsf{H},\mathcal{B}}^{\mathrm{spr}}(\lambda) \leq \mathsf{Adv}_{\mathsf{H},\mathcal{A}}^{\mathrm{tcr}}(\lambda).$$

SPR plus Compression $\implies$ OWF. *If H is second-preimage resistant and for all sufficiently large λ it holds that $\mathsf{H.ol}(\lambda) < \mathsf{H.il}(\lambda)$ then we have that H is one-way. More concretely, then for every efficient adversary $\mathcal{B}$ there exists an efficient adversary $\mathcal{A}$ such that*

$$\mathsf{Adv}_{\mathsf{H},\mathcal{B}}^{\mathrm{owf}}(\lambda) \leq 4 \cdot \mathsf{Adv}_{\mathsf{H},\mathcal{A}}^{\mathrm{spr}}(\lambda).$$

Furthermore, the reverse directions do not hold, that is

OWF $\notimplies$ SPR. *If there exists a one-way function at all, then there exists a one-way function which is not second-preimage resistant.*

SPR $\notimplies$ TCR. *If there exists a second-preimage-resistant hash function at all, then there exists a second-preimage-resistant hash function which is not target-collision resistant.*

TCR $\notimplies$ CR. *If there exists a target-collision-resistant hash function at all, then there exists a target-collision-resistant hash function which is not collision resistant.*

In the following we will prove the implications via security reductions. In contrast, separations (i.e., a result of the form, property A does not imply property B) are usually proved by simply providing an example of a function that has one property but not the other. We will here separate second-preimage resistance and target-collision resistance by giving an example of a second-preimage resistant-function that is not target-collision resistant. We will leave the other separation results as exercises.

Proof: CR $\implies$ TCR. Let H be a collision-resistant hash function as in Theorem 4.10 and assume there exists an adversary $\mathcal{B}$ against the target-collision resistance property of hash function H. From $\mathcal{B}$ we will construct an adversary $\mathcal{A}$ against the collision resistance of H. As, by assumption, H is collision resistant such an adversary $\mathcal{A}$ cannot exist, and hence $\mathcal{B}$ cannot exist.

Note that the target-collision resistance adversary $\mathcal{B} = (\mathcal{B}_1, \mathcal{B}_2)$ consists of two independent stages. The first stage $\mathcal{B}_1$ creates a target message (and some state) which is then later given to the second-stage adversary $\mathcal{B}_2$ to find the target collision. We construct adversary $\mathcal{A}$ from $\mathcal{B}$ as follows. Adversary $\mathcal{A}$ gets as input security parameter 1^λ and hash key hk. It will first run stage one $\mathcal{B}_1$ on input just the security parameter 1^λ to obtain (x_1, state), which it will pass on together with key hk to the second stage $\mathcal{B}_2$. When $\mathcal{B}_2$ returns with value x_2, adversary $\mathcal{A}$ will stop and output (x_1, x_2). Following is a pseudocode description of the adversary:

$$\underline{\mathcal{A}(1^\lambda, \mathsf{hk})}$$

$1:\quad (x_1, \mathsf{state}) \leftarrow\!\!\$\; \mathcal{B}_1(1^\lambda)$

$2:\quad x_2 \leftarrow\!\!\$\; \mathcal{B}_2(1^\lambda, \mathsf{hk}, x_1, \mathsf{state})$

$3:\quad \textbf{return } (x_1, x_2)$

We note that adversary $\mathcal{A}$ perfectly simulates experiment $\mathsf{Exp}^{\mathrm{tcr}}_{\mathsf{H}, \mathcal{B}}(\lambda)$ for adversary $\mathcal{B}$. It follows that $\mathcal{A}$ outputs a collision if, and only if, $\mathcal{B}$ is successful and hence

$$\mathsf{Adv}^{\mathrm{cr}}_{\mathsf{H}, \mathcal{A}}(\lambda) = \mathsf{Adv}^{\mathrm{tcr}}_{\mathsf{H}, \mathcal{B}}(\lambda).$$

As furthermore adversary $\mathcal{A}$ is efficient if $\mathcal{B}$ is efficient this concludes the proof. □

Proof: TCR $\implies$ SPR. As before we will give a proof by reduction. A small difference to the reductions we have seen so far is that an adversary against target-collision resistance consists of two stages, and hence our reduction must also specify two adversarial stages.

Let $\mathcal{B}$ be an adversary against the second-preimage resistance of hash function H. We construct an adversary $\mathcal{A} = (\mathcal{A}_1, \mathcal{A}_2)$ from $\mathcal{B}$ against the target-collision resistance of H as follows: In the first stage $\mathcal{A}_1$ samples a random target message x uniformly at random in $\{0,1\}^{\mathsf{H}.\mathsf{il}(\lambda)}$, which it returns together with an empty state. The second stage $\mathcal{A}_2$ gets as input the random target point x together with hash key hk and executes the SPR adversary $\mathcal{B}$ to receive collision x', which it returns. Once more in pseudocode:

$$\underline{\mathcal{A}_1(1^\lambda)} \qquad\qquad \underline{\mathcal{A}_2(1^\lambda, \mathsf{hk}, x, \mathsf{state})}$$

$1:\quad x \leftarrow\!\!\$\; \{0,1\}^{\mathsf{H}.\mathsf{il}(\lambda)} \qquad 1:\quad x' \leftarrow\!\!\$\; \mathcal{B}(1^\lambda, \mathsf{hk}, x)$

$2:\quad \textbf{return } (x, \varepsilon) \qquad\qquad 2:\quad \textbf{return } x'$

Note that we set the adversary's state to $\mathsf{state} \leftarrow \varepsilon$, that is, to the empty string as we do not require any state.

First note that adversary $\mathcal{A}_1$ is always efficient as all it does is sampling a message uniformly at random in $\{0,1\}^{\mathsf{H}.\mathsf{il}(\lambda)}$. Furthermore, the second-stage adversary $\mathcal{A}_2$ is efficient if $\mathcal{B}$ is efficient as its runtime is dominated by the call to $\mathcal{B}$. It follows that, together, adversary $\mathcal{A} = (\mathcal{A}_1, \mathcal{A}_2)$ perfectly simulates the second-preimage resistance experiment $\mathsf{Exp}^{\mathrm{spr}}_{\mathsf{H}, \mathcal{B}}(\lambda)$ for adversary $\mathcal{B}$. Finally, we can conclude that $\mathcal{A}$ is successful if, and only if, $\mathcal{B}$ manages to find a collision for x and thus

$$\mathsf{Adv}^{\mathrm{tcr}}_{\mathsf{H}, \mathcal{A}}(\lambda) = \mathsf{Adv}^{\mathrm{spr}}_{\mathsf{H}, \mathcal{B}}(\lambda). \qquad\qquad \square$$

We have already seen that collision resistance implies one-wayness given that the function compresses. The proof for second-preimage resistance works analogously. Exercise 4.6 asks you to formalize the reduction.

Proving the separations. It remains to show the separation results. As an example we will show that second-preimage resistance does not imply target-collision resistance. We leave the remaining two separations as Exercise 4.7.

Proof: SPR $\not\Rightarrow$ TCR. In order to show that second-preimage resistance does not imply target-collision resistance we construct a counterexample, that is, a second-preimage-resistant hash function that is not target-collision resistance. For this, let us assume that H is a second-preimage-resistant hash function; the prerequisites of the theorem stipulate the existence of such a function. From H we construct an adapted hash function H' as follows: The key generation algorithm will be identical and the evaluation will be changed on a single point to have a known, "built-in" collision. Following is the pseudocode for hash function H':

$H'.KGen(1^\lambda)$	$H'.Eval(1^\lambda, hk, x)$
1 : hk $\leftarrow\!\!\$\ $ H.KGen(1^λ)	1 : **if** $x = 1^\lambda$ **then**
2 : **return** hk	2 : **return** H.Eval$(1^\lambda, hk, 0^\lambda)$
	3 : **return** H.Eval$(1^\lambda, hk, x)$

To complete the proof we must show two things: (i) hash function H' retains the second-preimage resistance from function H and (ii) function H' is not target-collision resistant. If properties i and ii hold then we have shown that if a second-preimage-resistant hash function exists, then from it we can construct a function as above that keeps the second-preimage resistance property but which is not target-collision resistant. Hence, second-preimage resistance cannot imply target-collision resistance.

Let us tackle the two properties in turn. The easier property to show is property ii. In order to show that function H' is not target-collision resistance it remains to give a successful attacker $\mathcal{A} = (\mathcal{A}_1, \mathcal{A}_2)$. Our adversary can simply output the built-in collision, that is, stage one outputs 0^λ and stage two outputs 1^λ:

$\mathcal{A}_1(1^\lambda)$	$\mathcal{A}_2(1^\lambda, hk, x, \text{state})$
1 : **return** 0^λ	1 : **return** 1^λ

Adversary $\mathcal{A}$ is clearly efficient and, furthermore, it is successful with probability 1 if message pair $(0^\lambda, 1^\lambda)$ is a collision. As this is the case by design of H' we have that hash function H' cannot be target-collision resistant.

It remains to show property i, that is, that hash function H' is second-preimage resistant if the underlying hash function H is. For this we will argue that any adversary $\mathcal{B}$ against the second-preimage resistance of H' induces a successful adversary against the second-preimage resistance property of H.

In the second-preimage resistance experiment $\mathsf{Exp}_{\mathsf{H},\mathcal{B}}^{\mathsf{spr}}(\lambda)$, target message x is sampled uniformly at random. Note that the only difference between H and H' lies in the output value on input 1^λ. With overwhelming probability the target message x will be different from both 1^λ and 0^λ (the hardcoded collision): A uniformly random string in $\{0,1\}^\lambda$ hits a fixed λ-bit string with probability $2^{-\lambda}$ and hence the probability to hit either 0^λ or 1^λ is at most $2 \cdot 2^{-\lambda}$. But if target message x is different from the built-in collision then if $\mathcal{B}$ is successful and finds a second preimage x' such that $\mathsf{H}'.\mathsf{Eval}(1^\lambda, \mathsf{hk}, x) = \mathsf{H}'.\mathsf{Eval}(1^\lambda, \mathsf{hk}, x')$, then this induces also a collision for the underlying hash function H: Either (x, x') or $(x, 0^\lambda)$ must be a collision for H under key hk. For this note that if $x' = 1^\lambda$ then

$$\mathsf{H}'.\mathsf{Eval}(1^\lambda, \mathsf{hk}, x') = \mathsf{H}.\mathsf{Eval}(1^\lambda, \mathsf{hk}, 0^\lambda),$$

and if $x' \neq 1^\lambda$ then

$$\mathsf{H}'.\mathsf{Eval}(1^\lambda, \mathsf{hk}, x') = \mathsf{H}.\mathsf{Eval}(1^\lambda, \mathsf{hk}, x').$$

The induced adversary $\mathcal{A}$ against the second-preimage resistance of H can thus be given as follows:

$\underline{\mathcal{A}(1^\lambda, \mathsf{hk}, x)}$

1 :   if $x = 0^\lambda \vee x = 1^\lambda$ then

2 :   fail

3 : $x' \leftarrow\!\!{\$}\; \mathcal{B}(1^\lambda, \mathsf{hk}, x)$

4 :   if $x' = 1^\lambda$ then

5 :   return 0^λ

6 :   return x'

Adversary $\mathcal{A}$ implements the above idea. If the input is 0^λ or 1^λ (line 1) then it fails (line 2).[5] Otherwise $\mathcal{A}$ runs adversary $\mathcal{B}$ against H' and returns either whatever $\mathcal{B}$ returns, or 0^λ in case $\mathcal{B}$ outputs $x' = 1^\lambda$. By the above analysis we have that in case $x \notin \{0^\lambda, 1^\lambda\}$ and furthermore $\mathcal{B}$ is successful, then so is $\mathcal{A}$ as in this case either (x, x') or $(x, 0^\lambda)$ must be a collision. Because the loss in the success probability for $\mathcal{A}$, compared with the one of $\mathcal{B}$, is at most $2 \cdot 2^{-\lambda}$, this concludes the proof. $\qquad\square$

---

[5] Alternatively, instead of failing, we could have simply guessed a second preimage.

4.4 Collision Resistance from One-Way Functions

We have seen above that any collision-resistant function, and in fact any second-preimage-resistant function, is also one-way given that the function compresses (Theorem 4.10). The reverse was easily seen not to be true. We had seen a similar constellation with pseudorandom generators. In Section 3.3.5 we saw that any function that is a secure pseudorandom generator is necessarily also one-way but, similarly here, the inverse does not hold. While both results say that a one-way function does not immediately yield a pseudorandom generator (resp. a collision-resistant hash function) they do not exclude the possibility that there exists some PPT construction P^F that with black-box access to a one-way function F yields a secure pseudorandom generator (resp. collision-resistant hash function). Indeed, Theorem 3.32 stipulates that such a black-box construction exists for pseudorandom generators and that we can construct pseudorandom generators from any one-way function. While constructions from arbitrary one-way functions are complex and inefficient, efficient and simple constructions are known that start from one-way permutations. We will see an example of such a construction in Section 5.3.4. In the following we discuss whether or not the existence of one-way functions also implies the existence of collision-resistant hash functions.

4.4.1 Target-Collision Resistance from One-Wayness

Similarly to the case of pseudorandom generators, it can be shown that a one-way function is all that is needed in order to construct a *target-collision-resistant* hash function. Also similarly to the case of showing that we can construct pseudorandom generators from one-way functions, showing the general feasibility is complex and technical. But, if we start from one-way functions with a certain structure, such as a one-to-one one-way function or a one-way permutation, then efficient and simple constructions are known. In Section 7.5 we will present one such construction based on one-way permutations. The reason we postpone the presentation of the construction and its security proof is that we require one additional ingredient: a *pairwise independent hash function*, which we will introduce in Chapter 7. As it turns out, we can construct such pairwise independent hash functions unconditionally, that is, without any security assumptions, and thus our construction immediately yields that the existence of one-way permutations implies the existence of target-collision-resistant hash functions. As discussed above, the result can be strengthened to yield:

Theorem 4.11. *If there exists a secure one-way function at all, then there exists a secure target-collision-resistant hash function.*

The result has an important implication. In Chapter 6 we introduce the concept of *cryptographic signature schemes*, and as we will see, we can construct such signature schemes based on target-collision-resistant hash functions. Applying Theorem 4.11 then immediately yields that secure signature schemes exist if one-way functions exist.

4.4.2 Impossibility of Collision Resistance from One-Wayness

Above we discussed that the existence of one-way functions implies the existence of target-collision-resistant hash functions. Maybe surprisingly, the same is not known to hold for *collision-resistant* hash functions and, indeed, it is unlikely that we can construct collision-resistant hash functions from one-way functions. We say *unlikely*, as it can be shown that no *black-box construction* from a one-way function (or even one-way permutation) can exist that yields a secure collision-resistant hash function. While this leaves open the loophole of finding a non-black-box construction—e.g., a construction of a collision-resistant hash function that somehow makes use of the *code* of the one-way function—only very few non-black-box techniques are known today, none of which has gotten us significantly closer to constructing collision-resistant hash functions from one-way functions.

Remark 4.12. In the following we discuss oracle separations, which will be easier to understand after having worked through Part II of this book where we discuss oracles and, in particular, the random oracle in great detail. Unless the reader is already familiar with random oracles and black-box reductions we suggest to only skim the section on a first read and come back to it later. The important take-away message is Theorem 4.16, which states that we cannot construct collision-resistant hash functions from one-way permutations via standard (black-box) techniques.

Black-Box Separations

When we construct a cryptographic primitive P, say a pseudorandom generator, from some other cryptographic primitive Q, such as a one-way permutation, then we usually give a construction P^Q in which primitive Q is used as a *black box*. That is, the construction uses primitive Q as a subroutine but only depends on its input and output interfaces; other than that it is oblivious to the specific implementation of Q. To argue security we then (usually) give a recipe which constructs an adversary $\mathcal{A}_Q^{\mathcal{A}_P}$ against Q from any adversary $\mathcal{A}_P$ against P. Here again, the constructed adversary uses adversary $\mathcal{A}_P$ only as a subroutine (i.e., in a black-box manner). We call such a recipe a *black-box reduction from* P *to* Q, and indeed most security arguments in this book are of this form.

To show that no construction of primitive P out of primitive Q can exist is often out of our reach, given the current understanding and techniques that we have at our disposal. In contrast, it may be feasible to show the "next best thing," that is, to show that no *black-box reduction* from P to Q can exist. As most cryptographic feasibility results are due to black-box reductions such a result, at the very least, gives a strong indication that finding a construction of P from Q will be hard. Furthermore, it tells us that we do not need to bother trying to prove the security of a candidate construction via a black-box reduction.

In order to rule out the existence of a black-box reduction from collision-resistant hash functions to one-way permutations let us first formally define the concept. Note that we here distinguish between the primitive and its implementation. An implementation is an instance of the primitive, like a concrete hash function algorithm of the abstract primitive hash function.

Definition 4.13 (Fully Black-Box Reduction.). *A fully black-box reduction from a primitive* P *to primitive* Q *consists of two* PPT *oracle Turing machines* M *and* $\mathcal{A}_Q$ *such that the following conditions hold:*

P **can be constructed from** Q: *For all (possibly inefficient) Turing machines* N *implementing* Q, *we have that* M^N *implements* P.

Breaking P **implies breaking** Q: *For all implementations* N *of* Q *and all (possibly inefficient) adversaries* $\mathcal{A}_P$ *breaking* M^N *(as an implementation of* P*), we have that* $\mathcal{A}_Q^{\mathcal{A}_P, N}$ *breaks* N *(as an implementation of* Q*).*

Remark 4.14. When we speak of implementation of a primitive in the above definition then this only considers the syntactical requirements of the primitive and not any form of security. Security is considered by the existence of an adversary that breaks the underlying primitive Q when given access to an adversary breaking primitive P (or rather their implementations). Here "break" is to be understood as violating the security definition of the primitive in question. For example, for a one-way function "break" means being able to find a preimage x' for an image $F(x)$ with non-negligible probability when x was chosen uniformly at random.

Furthermore, for simpler presentation we defined implementations of primitives and the adversary to consist of only a single Turing machine. Primitives may, however, be defined as a tuple of algorithms (consider, for example, keyed one-way functions, which consist of a key generation algorithm and an evaluation algorithm). Similarly, adversaries may consist of multiple parts. We note that the above definition can easily be extended to cover also these cases. Alternatively, one can combine the multiple interfaces into a single "dispatcher" oracle which relays the communication to the right subalgorithm.

Semi black-box reductions. When you dig deeper into the cryptographic literature you will find that many notions of security reductions exist. The weakest, but by far the most common form of reduction is the fully black-box reduction defined above. Here the reduction needs to work for any adversary and any implementation of the primitive. In other words, the reduction cannot depend on implementation details of either the primitive or the adversary. By weakening the restrictions we obtain stronger forms of reductions. For example, when we allow the reduction to depend on the adversary we obtain the so-called *semi black-box reductions*, which show results of the form: for every adversary $\mathcal{A}_P^N$ breaking construction M^N (as an implementation of primitive P) there exists an adversary $\mathcal{A}_Q^N$ that breaks N (as an implementation Q). Note the difference in the order of quantifiers. A fully black-box reduction is a single reduction valid for all adversaries, while a semi black-box reduction can be different for each adversary.

Remark 4.15. Recall the security proof of the GGM construction of a pseudorandom function from a pseudorandom generator (Theorem 3.38; page 144). Here we gave a reduction that depended on the runtime of the adversary, and thus the reduction could be classified as a semi black-box reduction. Depending on the runtime of an adversary is, however, one of the mildest form of "non black-boxness": If we choose a large enough parameter $p(\lambda)$, then a reduction based on this runtime would be successful for all adversaries with runtime less than $p(\lambda)$. In that sense the GGM reduction is very close to a fully black-box reduction.

Relativizing reductions. An important observation about fully black-box reductions, as well as semi black-box reductions, is that they are *relativizing*, which means that they remain valid *relative to any oracle*. Assume that we have a fully black-box reduction from primitive P to Q and consider a world which contains some oracle O—think of oracle O as a possibly inefficient Turing machine that every party has access to and which can be evaluated in a single step.[6] If we now have a secure implementation N^O of primitive Q then the reduction guarantees that $M^{N,O}$ yields a secure implementation of P. We say that the construction M, as well as the reduction, *relativizes*.

Impossibility of Collision Resistance from One-Way Functions

How does the discussion of relativizing reductions help? Since both fully black-box and semi black-box reductions relativize we can use this observation in order to obtain an approach on how to show negative results. If we can provide an oracle relative to which one-way permutations exist but relative

---

[6] We have already seen oracles in the definition of pseudorandom functions where the distinguisher gets oracle access to either the actual function, or a random function (Definition 3.21; page 126). Also see the discussion of oracle Turing machines on page 17.

to which no collision-resistant hash function can exist we have effectively shown that no relativizing reduction from collision-resistant hash functions to one-way permutations can exist. In fact, it can be shown that such an oracle exists, which yields the following result:

Theorem 4.16. *There exists an oracle relative to which there exist one-way permutations but no collision-resistant hash functions.*

By the above discussion we immediately obtain a corollary ruling out the possibility of basing collision-resistant hash functions via a black-box construction on one-way permutations (and thus one-way functions).

Corollary 4.17. *Collision-resistant hash functions cannot be constructed from one-way permutations via black-box constructions.*

The two-oracle technique. We will here not prove Theorem 4.16—references to the full proof are given below in the chapter notes—but instead discuss a slightly weaker result based on the so-called *two-oracle technique*, which allows to show that no *fully* black-box reduction can exist. The idea is to construct two oracles Break and SP, where SP allows to implement the *source primitive* Q (in our case a one-way permutation) and where Break allows an adversary to break all target constructions of primitive P (in our case collision-resistant hash functions). That the construction of two such oracles suffices is shown in the following proposition. We here consider two generic primitives P and Q which in our concrete case translate to collision-resistant hash functions and one-way permutations.

Proposition 4.18. *Let* P *and* Q *be two cryptographic primitives. Let* SP *and* Break *be two oracles such that:*

1. *There exists a* PPT *oracle Turing machine* N *such that* N^{SP} *implements primitive* Q;
2. *For all* PPT *oracle Turing machines* M *it holds that if* M^{SP} *implements primitive* P *then there exists a* PPT *adversary* $\mathcal{A}$ *such that* $\mathcal{A}^{Break}$ *breaks the security of* M^{SP} *(as an implementation of* P*);*
3. *There is no* PPT *adversary* $\mathcal{B}$ *such that* $\mathcal{B}^{SP,Break}$ *breaks the security of* N^{SP} *(as an implementation of* Q*).*

If the above conditions hold, then there is no fully black-box construction from P *to* Q.

Remark 4.19. Note that in the above proposition when we speak of implementation we, again, only mean the syntactical restrictions. In our concrete case, item 1 for example, requires the existence of a PPT oracle Turing machine N such that N^{SP} implements the syntactical requirements of a one-way permutation. Or, in case we consider a keyed variant, we need to consider a tuple of oracle algorithms N^{SP}.KGen and N^{SP}.Eval. As before in Definition 4.13

note that also in Proposition 4.18 we specified only the case that an implementation consists of a single Turing machine to simplify the presentation of the statement. This, however, can be easily extended.

Remark 4.20. Although we do not mention this explicitly let us stress that the oracles Break and SP may in principle depend on each other. The gist of the two-oracle technique—and this prevents us from combining the two oracles into one—is that SP is usually independent of Break. This means that the construction N^{SP} has no reference to the Break oracle such that, vice versa, Break only needs to break constructions with calls to SP (and without adversarially placed, recursive calls to Break itself). This usually simplifies the proofs significantly, but in return provides a weaker separation than relativizing results. In our separation for collision resistance and one-wayness we assume, for example, that the collision-finding oracle Break calls the one-way oracle SP but only needs to break hash function constructions which are based on SP and not on Break.

Proof of Proposition 4.18. In order to show that no fully black-box reduction exists from P to Q we need to show that the requirements of Proposition 4.18 allow to negate Definition 4.13. That is, we need to show that

1. P can be constructed from Q, but that
2. Breaking P *does not* imply breaking Q.

As discussed, "implement" is only a syntactical requirement and thus item 1 of Proposition 4.18 implies that P can be implemented as it guarantees the existence of N^{SP} as an implementation of Q. Formally, the black-box condition says that there is an efficient Turing machine M which implements P via $M^{N^{SP}}$. If we now view M^N as a single PPT machine which implements P with oracle SP, then item 2 of Proposition 4.18 states that for such an implementation of primitive P there exists an adversary $\mathcal{A}_P^{Break}$ that breaks it. A fully black-box reduction, which must work for any given adversary, primitive, and construction, would now need to ensure that there exists an adversary that breaks N^{SP} as an implementation of Q, when given oracle access to $\mathcal{A}_P^{Break}$. That is, there must be a successful adversary $\mathcal{A}_Q^{\mathcal{A}_P^{Break},N^{SP}}$ which can be recast as an algorithm $\mathcal{B}^{SP,Break}$ by incorporating the efficient algorithms $\mathcal{A}_Q$, $\mathcal{A}_P$, and N into $\mathcal{B}$. However, item 3 of Proposition 4.18 stipulates that no successful adversary against N^{SP} (as an implementation of Q) exists, from which it follows that no such fully black-box reduction can exist. □

Impossibility of collision resistance. We now apply the two-oracle technique to show a slightly weaker version of Theorem 4.16. We consider the result for fixed-input-length hash functions and one-way permutations, where fixed input length means that the hash function has a predetermined input length for a given security parameter λ but this length may vary with λ. Note that as the result is a negative result, these restrictions, indeed, strengthen the conclusion: If no fixed-input-length hash function can be constructed from a one-way permutation then, necessarily, also no variable-input-length hash function can be constructed. Furthermore, since one-way permutations are one-way functions, the result also excludes constructions of hash functions based on (arbitrary) one-way functions.

> **Proposition 4.21.** *No fully black-box reduction exists from (fixed-input-length and compressing) collision-resistant hash functions to one-way permutations.*

The following proof belongs to the more complex proofs presented in this book, and it helps to have worked through the remainder of Part I and, in particular, Part II where we discuss random oracles in detail. We also note that the proof itself is no prerequisite for understanding later parts of this work and can thus be skipped safely.

To prove Proposition 4.21 we will make use of the two-oracle technique and Proposition 4.18 and, consequently, need to construct two oracles. The first oracle should allow to implement a one-way permutation. For this we consider a sequence of oracles $(\pi_\lambda)_{\lambda \in \mathbb{N}}$ such that oracle π_λ implements a random permutation from the set of all permutations from $\{0,1\}^\lambda$ to $\{0,1\}^\lambda$. We have seen a similar concept in the definition of pseudorandom functions (Definition 3.21; page 126) where a distinguisher either gets oracle access to the real function or to a function chosen uniformly at random from the space of all functions with the same input and output behavior. We now define oracle π on inputs of arbitrary length as

$$\pi(x) := \pi_{|x|}(x).$$

The second oracle should ensure that no collision-resistant hash function can exist. That is, it must aid an adversary $\mathcal{A}$ in finding collisions for any (fixed-input-length) hash function construction H^π that may make use of oracle π. For this, we define oracle CF (short for collision finder), which operates as follows:

$\mathsf{CF}(\mathsf{C})$
***

1 : **unless** Circuit C is well formed and compresses
2 :   **return** $\perp$
3 : $a \leftarrow\!\!\$ \, \{0,1\}^{\mathsf{C}.\mathsf{il}}$
4 : $b \leftarrow\!\!\$ \, \left\{ z \in \{0,1\}^{\mathsf{C}.\mathsf{il}} \mid \mathsf{C}(z) = \mathsf{C}(a) \right\}$
5 : **return** (a,b)

Oracle CF takes as input a description of an oracle circuit C which besides standard Boolean gates may contain special π-gates denoting the computation of oracle π (see also page 23). Collision finder CF first checks whether the description of circuit C is well-formed (for this we assume a fixed and suitable encoding) and whether the circuit is compressing, i.e., C.il > C.ol. Here, C.il denotes the number of input wires (the circuit's input length) and C.ol the number of output wires. In case the circuit is not well-formed or does not compress, CF returns $\perp$. Otherwise, it samples a uniformly random value a from the circuit's domain $\{0,1\}^{\text{C.il}}$. Next, it samples a value b uniformly at random from the preimage of $C(a)$. It returns the pair (a,b). Note that since the preimage of $C(a)$ includes also value a, the collision finder CF might return pseudo-collisions of the form (a,a).

Given the two oracles as defined above, Proposition 4.21 now follows in two steps. First we will show that for a random choice of oracle π together with the corresponding collision finder CF (which also makes random choices) the requirements of Proposition 4.18 are met. We capture this formally by the following proposition which very much resembles Proposition 4.18 (the two-oracle technique) but for our specific choice of oracles and where the probability is over the random choice of oracles π and CF. Subsequently, we discuss how we can fix a single oracle pair in order to show Proposition 4.21

Proposition 4.22. *Let π and* CF *be as above. Then the following statements hold over the choice of a random permutation π with corresponding random collision finder* CF *and the random coins of the respective algorithms:*

1. *There exists a PPT oracle Turing machine* N *such that* N^π *implements a one-way function.*
2. *There exists a PPT adversary* $\mathcal{A}^{\text{CF}}$ *that breaks the collision resistance of any PPT hash function construction* H^π.
3. *Let* $q : \mathbb{N} \to \mathbb{N}$ *be a polynomial and let* $\mathcal{B}^{\pi,\text{CF}}$ *be a (possibly unbounded) adversary making at most $q(\lambda)$ oracle queries and which queries collision finder* CF *only on circuits that contain at most $q(\lambda)$ many π-gates. Then advantage* $\text{Adv}_{N^\pi, \mathcal{B}^\pi, \text{CF}}^{\text{owf}}(\lambda)$ *against the one-wayness of construction* N^π *is negligible.*

Proof of Proposition 4.22. We need to show that the two oracles defined above fulfill the requirements of Proposition 4.22. We tackle these in turn.

Item 1, existence of one-way permutations. As a first step we need to show that there exists an oracle Turing machine N^π relative to oracle π that implements a one-way permutation. Note that here we are not yet concerned about the security of the resulting construction but just about syntactical requirements. As construction we define N^π with $N.\text{il}(\lambda) = N.\text{ol}(\lambda) = \lambda$ as

$$\underline{\mathsf{N}^\pi.\mathsf{Eval}(1^\lambda, x)}$$

1 :   **if** $|x| \neq \lambda$ **then**

2 :   **return** $\bot$

3 : $y \leftarrow \pi(x)$

4 :   **return** y

That is, our construction checks that input x is of length λ and if so it forwards x to oracle π. Clearly N^π is efficient and for each security parameter $\lambda \subset \mathbb{N}$ it implements an (unkeyed) permutation. This concludes the first syntactical requirement of Proposition 4.18. We will show one-wayness of N^π soon, even in presence of the breaking oracle.[7]

Item 2, non-existence of collision resistance. Next, we need to show that relative to oracle CF no collision-resistant hash function can exist. Let H^π be a candidate construction which may make use of oracle π. Note that we can represent this function as a circuit $\mathsf{C_H}$ with π-oracle gates. We consider adversary $\mathcal{A}^{\mathsf{CF}}$ which on input the security parameter 1^λ prepares this circuit $\mathsf{C_H}$ that computes H^π for inputs of size $\mathsf{H.il}(\lambda)$. It then queries oracle CF on input $\mathsf{C_H}$ and returns the result.

First let us note that adversary $\mathcal{A}^{\mathsf{CF}}$ is efficient if construction H^π is. For this recall that for every efficient Turing machine there exists an efficient family of circuits implementing the Turing machine (see Theorem 1.12 on page 25). Further note that adversary $\mathcal{A}^{\mathsf{CF}}$ will output a collision with constant probability. The analysis is essentially identical to the analysis given in Proposition 4.5 in which we showed that (compressing) collision-resistant hash functions are also one-way. Since we can have at most $2^{\mathsf{H.ol}(\lambda)} - 1$ "bad" images y with only a single preimage the probability of hitting such a "bad image" when choosing a uniformly random point in the domain (line 3 of collision finder CF) is at most

$$\frac{2^{\mathsf{H.ol}(\lambda)} - 1}{2^{\mathsf{H.il}(\lambda)}} < \frac{1}{2}.$$

But then the probability that CF outputs a genuine collision is at least $\frac{1}{4}$—note that it might output a pseudo-collision (x, x') with $x = x'$, which induces the additional loss factor of $\frac{1}{2}$.

Item 3, collision finder CF does not help in breaking N^π. The final and most challenging step is to argue that the collision finding oracle CF does not help in breaking the security of N^π as a one-way permutation. For this, let us recall the security game of one-way functions (Definition 2.15; page 84). Here for security parameter 1^λ a preimage ρ is sampled uniformly at random from the domain of the one-way function (in our case from $\{0,1\}^\lambda$) and the

---

[7] Working with an unkeyed one-way permutation is easier for this proof. A key could, however, easily be introduced.

adversary is given the corresponding image $\tau \leftarrow \mathsf{N}^\pi.\mathsf{Eval}(1^\lambda, \rho)$. The adversary's task is to find some value ρ' such that $\mathsf{N}^\pi.\mathsf{Eval}(1^\lambda, \rho') = \mathsf{N}^\pi.\mathsf{Eval}(1^\lambda, \rho)$. But since N^π implements a permutation there exists exactly one such preimage for τ, namely the originally sampled preimage ρ.

Let $\mathcal{B}^{\pi,\mathsf{CF}}$ be an adversary against the one-wayness of N^π. Adversary $\mathcal{B}^{\pi,\mathsf{CF}}$ receives as input target value τ and needs to find the unique preimage ρ such that $\mathsf{N}^\pi.\mathsf{Eval}(1^\lambda, \rho) = \pi(\rho) = \tau$. Let $\mathsf{q} := \mathsf{q}(\lambda)$ denote an upper bound on the number of oracle queries by $\mathcal{B}$ as well as an upper bound on the number of π-oracle gates in an input circuit C of CF queries. That is, $\mathcal{B}$ makes at most q queries to oracle π and at most q queries to collision finder CF, and each circuit C sent to collision finder CF has at most q many oracle gates. Without loss of generality we assume that adversary $\mathcal{B}$ on receiving a result (a, b) by a collision finder query C immediately evaluates $\mathsf{C}^\pi(a)$ and $\mathsf{C}^\pi(b)$, retracing all π-queries in the computations.

Over the following pages we bound the success probability of adversary $\mathcal{B}$ inverting oracle π. For this we allow $\mathcal{B}$ to have an unbounded runtime but restrict the number of oracle queries q to be polynomial.[8] The idea to bound the success probability of adversary $\mathcal{B}$ is to apply the game-hopping technique from Section 3.2.1 (page 106), and we provide a brief reference of the individual game hops in Table 4.1. Our starting point in Game_1 is the original one-wayness experiment, which we will adapt over the course of six game hops such that in the final Game_7 the adversary gets a target value τ^* that is independent of the preimage ρ. In this case, it is clear that the adversary's success probability is reduced to the pure guessing probability as the sole input τ^* no longer contains any information about the actual preimage ρ. The adversary's success probability in Game_7 is thus exactly $2^{-\lambda}$.

The transition of the game hops, detailed in Table 4.1, consists of two basic ideas. One is to prevent the adversary from abusing the collision finder CF to compute the sought-for preimage ρ. We do so by removing "dangerous" π-queries in CF entirely, called puncturing CF on ρ. This is done in the step to Game_3, but before the hop to Game_2 makes sure that certain π-queries in CF, including the one for ρ, cannot occur too often ("smoothing" the adversary's queries to CF). This is accomplished by moving these queries out of CF, into the adversary itself.

The second idea of the game hops is to shift to an independent target value $\tau^* = \pi(\rho^*)$ instead of $\tau = \pi(\rho)$, but where the adversary still has to find ρ. This is done by first adding ρ^* as another image to τ, perturbing π to $\pi_{\rho^* \mapsto \tau}$, and puncturing CF also on ρ^* (Game_4). Then we change to τ^* by perturbing $\pi_{\rho \mapsto \tau^*}$ instead (Game_5). Now that we have shifted to τ^* the hop to Game_6 undoes the perturbing of π, letting ρ point to τ again, and also "unpunctures" CF on ρ. Finally, we remove the puncturing of CF for ρ^*

---

[8] The proof is actually stronger and allows an adversary even to make exponentially many queries as long as there is still a sufficient gap to exhaustively querying oracle π.

Game	Description	Adversary	Challenge
1	The original one-wayness experiment.	$\mathcal{B}^{\pi,\mathsf{CF}}(\tau)$	$\tau \leftarrow \pi(\rho)$
2	The adversary $\mathcal{B}$ is replaced by a "smoothed" version $\mathcal{B}_*$ that makes additional π-queries to ensure that all collision-finder queries C do not make "heavy" queries (queries that occur with high probability on a random input).	$\mathcal{B}_*^{\pi,\mathsf{CF}}(\tau)$	$\tau \leftarrow \pi(\rho)$
3	The collision finder is adapted and "punctured" on preimage ρ such that sampled collisions do not contain information about preimage ρ.	$\mathcal{B}_*^{\pi,\mathsf{pCF}\{\rho\}}(\tau)$	$\tau \leftarrow \pi(\rho)$
4	We adapt permutation oracle π by choosing a random second preimage $\rho^* \leftarrow\!\!{\scriptstyle\$}\ \{0,1\}^\lambda$ for which we set $\pi_{\rho^* \mapsto \tau}(\rho^*) := \tau$. In addition we puncture the collision finder also on value ρ^*.	$\mathcal{B}_*^{\pi_{\rho^* \mapsto \tau},\mathsf{pCF}\{\rho,\rho^*\}}(\tau)$	$\tau \leftarrow \pi(\rho)$
5	Target value τ is replaced by a value τ^* sampled uniformly at random and we set $\rho^* \leftarrow \pi^{-1}(\tau^*)$. Oracle π is perturbed such that preimage ρ maps to τ^*.	$\mathcal{B}_*^{\pi_{\rho \mapsto \tau^*},\mathsf{pCF}\{\rho,\rho^*\}}(\tau^*)$	$\tau^* \leftarrow\!\!{\scriptstyle\$}\ \{0,1\}^\lambda$
6	The first step of reverting the changes to oracle and collision finder. We consider again the unperturbed oracle π together with punctured collision finder $\mathsf{pCF}_{\{\rho^*\}}$ where ρ^* as before is computed as $\pi^{-1}(\tau^*)$ for uniformly random $\tau^* \leftarrow\!\!{\scriptstyle\$}\ \{0,1\}^\lambda$.	$\mathcal{B}_*^{\pi,\mathsf{pCF}\{\rho^*\}}(\tau^*)$	$\tau^* \leftarrow\!\!{\scriptstyle\$}\ \{0,1\}^\lambda$
7	The final game is again identical to the one-wayness experiment but now adversary $\mathcal{B}_*$ does not receive as input $\tau \leftarrow \pi(\rho)$ but instead a uniformly random and independently sampled value $\tau^* \leftarrow\!\!{\scriptstyle\$}\ \{0,1\}^*$ which contains no information about target preimage ρ.	$\mathcal{B}_*^{\pi,\mathsf{CF}}(\tau^*)$	$\tau^* \leftarrow\!\!{\scriptstyle\$}\ \{0,1\}^\lambda$

Table 4.1: Reference of game hops in proof of Proposition 4.21. In all games the adversary's task is to find the unique preimage $\rho \leftarrow\!\!{\scriptstyle\$}\ \{0,1\}^\lambda$.

(Game$_7$), such that the adversary now receives a challenge $\tau^* = \pi(\rho^*)$ but needs to find the unrelated preimage ρ.

We next discuss the individual games as well as the loss incurred with each game hop.

Game$_1$ The first game is the original one-wayness experiment for adversary $\mathcal{B}^{\pi,\mathsf{CF}}$ relative to random permutation π and collision finder CF. Adversary $\mathcal{B}$ gets as input a target value τ and needs to find the unique preimage ρ such that $\pi(\rho) = \tau$.

Game$_2$ In Game$_2$ we consider an adapted adversary $\mathcal{B}_*^{\pi,\mathsf{CF}}$ which internally executes $\mathcal{B}^{\pi,\mathsf{CF}}$, forwarding any queries to π but slightly changing queries to collision finder CF. The idea is that we want to ensure that with high probability queries to collision finder CF are such that circuits do not contain *heavy* π-queries. For a given oracle π we call a π-query z by some circuit C (π, ϵ)-*heavy* if the probability that z is queried when circuit C^π is evaluated on a random input is at least ϵ. We will later fix ϵ to be negligible, in which case we can translate "no heavy query" to "no query that occurs with more than negligible probability."

In order to formalize our notion of (π, ϵ)-heaviness let C^π-queries(x) denote the set of induced π-queries during the evaluation of $C^\pi(x)$:

$$C^\pi\text{-queries}(x) := \{z \mid \pi \text{ is queried on } z \text{ during evaluation of } C^\pi(x)\}.$$

We call a query z (π, ϵ)-*heavy* for circuit C relative to oracle π if

$$\Pr_{x \twoheadleftarrow \$\{0,1\}^{C.\mathrm{il}}}[z \in C^\pi\text{-queries}(x)] > \epsilon,$$

where the probability is over the choice of input x. We note that the number of (π, ϵ)-heavy queries for a circuit C can be at most q/ϵ. For this note that any ϵ-heavy query must occur at least on an ϵ-fraction of all inputs $\{0,1\}^{C.\mathrm{il}}$. In other words, it must occur on every $1/\epsilon$-th input, e.g., for $\epsilon = 1/10$ every (π, c)-heavy query must occur at least on every 10th input to circuit C. Since each circuit C makes at most q many π-oracle queries, it follows that there can be at most q/ϵ many (π, ϵ)-heavy queries.

Now, in order not to make heavy π-queries (with high probability), adapted adversary $\mathcal{B}_*^{\pi,\mathsf{CF}}$ does the following. On receiving a circuit C for collision finder CF it first samples t many random inputs to circuit C—we will fix t shortly. It then evaluates C on each of these inputs, recording all occurring π-queries and responses in a table T (where the table is freshly initialized for each call to CF). It then constructs an adapted circuit $C[T]$ which has table T hardcoded and which emulates C but only queries π on values not in table T. That is, whenever circuit C makes a π-query, circuit $C[T]$ checks whether this query is in table T in which case it uses the recorded response. Only if the query is not in T will circuit $C[T]$ make an oracle query to oracle π. As adversary $\mathcal{B}_*$ on every collision-finder query makes t many additional queries to oracle π, we have that $\mathcal{B}_*$ makes in total $q + t \cdot q$ many π-oracle queries. Once more in pseudocode:

$\mathcal{B}_*^{\pi,\mathsf{CF}}(\tau)$	$\mathsf{CF}_*(C)$	$\pi_*(x)$
1: $\rho' \twoheadleftarrow \$\, \mathcal{B}^{\pi,\mathsf{CF}_*}(\tau)$	1: $T \leftarrow []$	1: $y \leftarrow \pi(x)$
2: **return** ρ'	2: **for** $i = 1..t$ **do**	2: $T[x] = y$
	3: $\quad x \twoheadleftarrow \$\, \{0,1\}^{C.\mathrm{il}}$	3: **return** y
	4: $\quad C^{\pi_*}(x)$	
	5: construct circuit $C[T]$	
	6: $(a,b) \leftarrow \mathsf{CF}(C[T])$	
	7: **return** (a,b)	

First note that adapted adversary $\mathcal{B}_*$ always perfectly simulates adversary $\mathcal{B}$, and we thus have that

$$\Pr[\mathsf{Game}_1(\lambda) = 1] = \Pr[\mathsf{Game}_2(\lambda) = 1].$$

But, we can now bound the probability that during an execution of $\mathcal{B}_*$ a collision-finder query CF(C) occurs that results in an (π, ϵ)-heavy query. For this, let us call a query circuit C to collision finder CF (π, ϵ)-*smooth* if for all $z \in \{0, 1\}^\lambda$ we have that

$$\Pr_{x \leftarrow \$\{0,1\}^{C.\text{il}}}[z \in C^\pi\text{-queries}(x)] \leq \epsilon.$$

Let, furthermore, smooth$(\mathcal{B}_*, \pi, \epsilon)$ denote the event that all collision-finder queries by adversary $\mathcal{B}_*$ are (π, ϵ)-smooth.

Consider now a single collision-finder query $C[T]$ by $\mathcal{B}_*$ and fix any (π, ϵ)-heavy query z. By construction we have that z will be in table T except with probability $(1 - \epsilon)^t$. Using the fact that $(1 - x)^r \leq e^{-xr} \leq 2^{-xr}$ for any positive values x and r, we can bound the probability (over the coins of adversary $\mathcal{B}_*$) of z not being in table T by

$$\Pr[T[z] = \bot] \leq 2^{-t\epsilon}.$$

As adversary $\mathcal{B}_*$ makes at most q many collision-finder queries and each query circuit C has at most q/ϵ many (π, ϵ)-heavy queries, we can bound the probability of adversary $\mathcal{B}_*$ making only smooth queries by a union bound as

$$\Pr[\text{smooth}(\mathcal{B}_*, \pi, \epsilon)] = 1 - \Pr[\exists i \in [q] : i\text{th query to CF is not } (\pi, \epsilon)\text{-smooth}]$$

$$\geq 1 - \sum_{i=1}^{q} \Pr[i\text{th query to CF is not } (\pi, \epsilon)\text{-smooth}]$$

$$\geq 1 - \sum_{i=1}^{q} \frac{q}{\epsilon} \cdot 2^{-t\epsilon}$$

$$= 1 - \frac{q^2}{\epsilon} \cdot 2^{-t\epsilon}. \tag{4.2}$$

It remains to fix the number of queries t and the smoothness factor ϵ. As we want to ensure that no query circuit C contains a π-query that occurs with non-negligible probability, we set

$$\epsilon(\lambda) := \frac{1}{2^{\frac{\lambda}{2}}}.$$

(We note that the fraction $\frac{\lambda}{2}$ is chosen somewhat arbitrarily and, indeed, any fraction suffices.) Consequently, in order to ensure that event smooth$(\mathcal{B}_*, \pi, \epsilon)$ occurs with overwhelming probability we set

$$t(\lambda) := \lambda \cdot 2^{\frac{\lambda}{2}}.$$

If we identify event smooth with smooth$(\mathcal{B}_*, \pi, 2^{-\frac{\lambda}{2}})$ then we have that adversary $\mathcal{B}_*$ makes an unsmooth query with probability at most

$$\Pr\left[\overline{\text{smooth}}\right] \overset{(4.2)}{\leq} \frac{\mathsf{q}^2}{\epsilon} \cdot 2^{-t\epsilon} = \mathsf{q}^2 \cdot 2^{\frac{\lambda}{2}} \cdot 2^{-\lambda} = \mathsf{q}^2 \cdot 2^{-\frac{\lambda}{2}}. \tag{4.3}$$

Remark 4.23. By design, smooth adversary $\mathcal{B}_*$ makes

$$\mathsf{q} + t\mathsf{q} = \mathsf{q} + \mathsf{q} \cdot \lambda \cdot 2^{\frac{\lambda}{2}} \tag{4.4}$$

many queries to oracle π. Even though we restricted the original adversary $\mathcal{B}$ to only make polynomially many queries, our smoothed adversary $\mathcal{B}_*$ now makes exponentially many oracle queries. Note, however, that we are not giving a standard security reduction but directly bound the success probability of $\mathcal{B}$. As argued above, we have that

$$\Pr[\mathsf{Game}_1(\lambda) = 1] = \Pr[\mathsf{Game}_2(\lambda) = 1]$$

and thus that the success probability of adversary $\mathcal{B}$ (making polynomially many queries) is exactly the same as that of adversary $\mathcal{B}_*$. If we can now show that the success probability of the latter is negligible then we have also bounded the success probability of $\mathcal{B}$. In particular, for this argument, it is irrelevant whether or not $\mathcal{B}_*$ is efficient or makes polynomially many queries.

Game₃ In Game₃ we adapt the collision finder CF such that returned collisions $(a, b) \leftarrow\!\!\$\ \mathsf{CF}(\mathsf{C})$ will be such that preimage ρ will not be queried when evaluating $\mathsf{C}(a)$ or $\mathsf{C}(b)$. For this, let us first specify the exact steps that collision finder CF makes to sample a colliding value b after having sampled $a \leftarrow\!\!\$\ \{0,1\}^{C.\mathsf{il}}$. One option for CF is to sample a random permutation ind (short for index) over $\{0,1\}^{C.\mathsf{il}}$. Then, after having sampled $a \leftarrow\!\!\$\ \{0,1\}^{C.\mathsf{il}}$ collision finder CF loops over values $i = 0..2^{C.\mathsf{il}} - 1$ and for each i tests whether $\mathsf{C}(\mathsf{ind}(i)) = \mathsf{C}(a)$. The first collision it yields $b \leftarrow \mathsf{ind}(i)$. Once more as pseudocode where $\mathsf{Perm}(\ell)$ denotes the set of all permutations of the form $\{0,1\}^\ell \to \{0,1\}^\ell$:

CF(C)

---

1 : **unless** Circuit C is well formed and compresses

2 :   **return** $\perp$

3 : $a \leftarrow\!\!\$\ \{0,1\}^{C.\mathsf{il}}$

4 : $\mathsf{ind} \leftarrow\!\!\$\ \mathsf{Perm}(C.\mathsf{il})$ // sample random permutation over $C.\mathsf{il}$-bit strings

5 :   **for** $i = 0..2^{C.\mathsf{il}} - 1$ **do**

6 : $b \leftarrow \mathsf{ind}(i)$

7 :   **if** $\mathsf{C}(a) = \mathsf{C}(b)$ **then**

8 :   **return** (a,b) // Note that a (pseudo-)collision exists and CF always returns

We now adapt collision finder CF and consider instead a "punctured" version pCF_S that is parameterized by a set of punctured inputs $S \subseteq \{0,1\}^\lambda$. The idea is that pCF_S works exactly as CF with two exceptions. When sampled value a is such that during evaluation $C^\pi(a)$ a query to oracle π is made which is in set S (i.e., if $S \cap C^\pi\text{-queries}(a) \neq \{\,\})$ then pCF_S returns $\bot$. If this is not the case, then it samples a (pseudo-)collision b such that $C^\pi(a) = C^\pi(b)$ but such that also $S \cap C^\pi\text{-queries}(b) = \{\,\}$. Once more as pseudocode where the changes to CF are highlighted:

$\underline{\mathsf{pCF}_S(\mathsf{C})}$

1 : **unless** Circuit C is well formed and compresses

2 :   **return** $\bot$

3 : $a \leftarrow\!\!\$ \{0,1\}^{C.\mathrm{il}}$

4 : **if** $S \cap C^\pi\text{-queries}(a) \neq \{\,\}$ **then return** $\bot$

5 : $\mathrm{ind} \leftarrow\!\!\$ \mathrm{Perm}(C.\mathrm{il})$

6 : **for** $i = 0..2^{C.\mathrm{il}} - 1$ **do**

7 : $b \leftarrow \mathrm{ind}(i)$

8 :   **if** $C(a) = C(b) \wedge S \cap C^\pi\text{-queries}(b) = \{\,\}$ **then**

9 :   **return** (a, b)

In Game_3 we now consider a punctured collision finder that is punctured on target preimage ρ, that is, we consider $\mathsf{pCF}_{\{\rho\}}$. In order to bound the loss incurred by this change, we will show that relative to a punctured collision finder pCF_S an algorithm $\mathcal{A}$ works identically as if it was running relative to an unpunctured collision finder CF unless a collision-finder query induces a π-oracle query on a value in set S. This is formalized by the following claim, where we argue that this is true no matter how the randomness of π (to implement the random permutation) and CF (to search for collisions) are chosen:

Claim 4.24. *Let* $\pi : \{0,1\}^* \to \{0,1\}^*$ *be an oracle, let* $S \subseteq \{0,1\}^\lambda$ *be a set of punctured inputs, and let* $\mathcal{A}$ *be a (possibly unbounded) algorithm. Let* CF *and* pCF_S *be as above and relative to oracle* π. *Let* $\mathsf{collHit}(S)$ *denote the event that during the execution of* $\mathcal{A}^{\pi,\mathsf{CF}}(1^\lambda)$ *a query* C *to* CF *occurs with response* (a, b) *such that*

$$C^\pi\text{-queries}(a) \cap S \neq \{\,\} \qquad or \qquad C^\pi\text{-queries}(b) \cap S \neq \{\,\}.$$

Then for any security parameter $\lambda \in \mathbb{N}$ *and any* $y \in \{0,1\}^*$ *it holds that*

$$\left| \Pr\!\left[\mathcal{A}^{\pi,\mathsf{CF}}(1^\lambda) = y\right] - \Pr\!\left[\mathcal{A}^{\pi,\mathsf{pCF}_S}(1^\lambda) = y\right] \right| \leq \Pr[\mathsf{collHit}(S)].$$

Proof. Let us assume for the moment that the following identity holds (we will shortly argue that this is indeed the case):

$$\Pr\!\left[\mathcal{A}^{\pi,\mathsf{CF}}(1^\lambda) = y \,\middle|\, \overline{\mathsf{collHit}(S)}\right] = \Pr\!\left[\mathcal{A}^{\pi,\mathsf{pCF}_S}(1^\lambda) = y \,\middle|\, \overline{\mathsf{collHit}(S)}\right]. \quad (4.5)$$

Then we can upper bound the probability of algorithm $\mathcal{A}$ outputting some value y when being executed relative to oracles π and CF as

$$\Pr\left[\mathcal{A}^{\pi,\mathsf{CF}}(1^\lambda) = y\right]$$

$$= \Pr\left[\mathcal{A}^{\pi,\mathsf{CF}}(1^\lambda) = y \,\middle|\, \overline{\mathsf{collHit}(S)}\right] \cdot \Pr\left[\overline{\mathsf{collHit}(S)}\right]$$

$$+ \Pr\left[\mathcal{A}^{\pi,\mathsf{CF}}(1^\lambda) = y \,\middle|\, \mathsf{collHit}(S)\right] \cdot \Pr[\mathsf{collHit}(S)]$$

$$\leq \Pr\left[\mathcal{A}^{\pi,\mathsf{CF}}(1^\lambda) = y \,\middle|\, \overline{\mathsf{collHit}(S)}\right] \cdot \Pr\left[\overline{\mathsf{collHit}(S)}\right] + \Pr[\mathsf{collHit}(S)].$$

$$\overset{(4.5)}{=} \Pr\left[\mathcal{A}^{\pi,\mathsf{pCF}_S}(1^\lambda) = y \,\middle|\, \overline{\mathsf{collHit}(S)}\right] \cdot \Pr\left[\overline{\mathsf{collHit}(S)}\right] + \Pr[\mathsf{collHit}(S)].$$

Note the change in oracles in the last equality, where we used Equation (4.5). Applying the product rule for conditional probabilities ($\Pr[A \mid B] \cdot \Pr[B] = \Pr[A \wedge B] \leq \Pr[A]$), this can be further rewritten as

$$\leq \Pr\left[\mathcal{A}^{\pi,\mathsf{pCF}_S}(1^\lambda) = y\right] + \Pr[\mathsf{collHit}(S)]. \tag{4.6}$$

When starting with $\Pr\left[\mathcal{A}^{\pi,\mathsf{pCF}_S}(1^\lambda) = y\right]$ and again assuming that Equation (4.5) holds we can make the analogous claim that

$$\Pr\left[\mathcal{A}^{\pi,\mathsf{pCF}_S}(1^\lambda) = y\right] \leq \Pr\left[\mathcal{A}^{\pi,\mathsf{CF}}(1^\lambda) = y\right] + \Pr[\mathsf{collHit}(S)]. \tag{4.7}$$

The statement now immediately follows from Equations (4.6) and (4.7) by noting that $|a - b| \leq c$ follows from $a \leq b + c$ and $b \leq a + c$.

It thus remains to argue that Equation 4.5 holds. For this, we consider arbitrary but fixed random coins $r_\mathcal{A}$ for algorithm $\mathcal{A}$, r_π for oracle π, and r_CF for collision finder CF such that

$$\mathcal{A}^{\pi(\cdot;r_\pi),\mathsf{CF}(\cdot;r_\mathsf{CF})}(1^\lambda; r_\mathcal{A}) = y \qquad \text{and} \qquad \overline{\mathsf{collHit}(S)},$$

that is, $\mathcal{A}^{\pi(\cdot;r_\pi),\mathsf{CF}(\cdot;r_\mathsf{CF})}(1^\lambda; r_\mathcal{A})$ yields value y, and event $\mathsf{collHit}(S)$ does not materialize during the evaluation. Consider now a query C to collision finder CF during a run of algorithm $\mathcal{A}^{\pi,\mathsf{CF}}$. If event $\mathsf{collHit}(S)$ does not occur then both collision components (a, b) sampled by CF are such that

$$\mathsf{C}^\pi\text{-queries}(a) \cap S = \{\,\} \qquad \text{and} \qquad \mathsf{C}^\pi\text{-queries}(b) \cap S = \{\,\}.$$

But then punctured collision finder pCF_S on the same random coins r_CF and same query circuit C would also sample value a as the first part of the collision, and the subsequent check in line 4 would be false (and pCF_S thus continues as CF). Similarly, since b is the first colliding element found when iterating over index permutation ind in line 7 of CF, the value b will also be found by pCF_S (which also cannot find another value earlier than CF does). Since for b it holds that $\mathsf{C}^\pi\text{-queries}(b) \cap S = \{\,\}$ the additional check in line 8 of pCF_S returns true such that pCF_S also outputs (pseudo-)collision (a, b). But then, for these random coins it must also hold that also

$$\mathcal{A}^{\pi(\cdot;r_\pi),\,\mathrm{pCF}_S(\cdot;r_{\mathrm{CF}})}(1^\lambda; r_{\mathcal{A}}) = y,$$

which concludes the proof.   ∎

We can now bound the loss introduced by puncturing the collision finder on preimage ρ in Game_3. By Claim 4.24 we have that the two games are identical unless in Game_2 event $\mathsf{collHit}(\rho) := \mathsf{collHit}(\{\rho\})$ occurs, that is, a query C to collision finder CF returns a collision (a, b) such that preimage ρ is queried when evaluating $\mathsf{C}^\pi(a)$ or $\mathsf{C}^\pi(b)$, in which case

$$\rho \in \mathsf{C}^\pi\text{-queries}(a) \cup \mathsf{C}^\pi\text{-queries}(b).$$

We can upper bound the probability of event $\mathsf{collHit}(\rho)$ using the smoothness of adversary $\mathcal{B}_*$ as

$$
\begin{aligned}
\Pr[\mathsf{collHit}(\rho)] &= \Pr[\mathsf{collHit}(\rho) \wedge \mathsf{smooth}] \cdot \Pr[\mathsf{smooth}] \\
&\quad + \Pr\big[\mathsf{collHit}(\rho) \wedge \overline{\mathsf{smooth}}\big] \cdot \Pr\big[\overline{\mathsf{smooth}}\big] \\
&\leq \Pr[\mathsf{collHit}(\rho) \wedge \mathsf{smooth}] + \Pr\big[\overline{\mathsf{smooth}}\big] \\
&\overset{(4.3)}{\leq} \Pr[\mathsf{collHit}(\rho) \wedge \mathsf{smooth}] + \mathsf{q}^2 \cdot 2^{-\frac{\lambda}{2}}.
\end{aligned}
\tag{4.8}
$$

Here the last inequality follows from our bound on the smoothness of adversary $\mathcal{B}_*$ given as Equation (4.3). If, on the other hand, adversary $\mathcal{B}_*$ only makes (π, ϵ)-smooth queries to collision finder CF then we have that for any query circuit C

$$\Pr_{x \in \{0,1\}^{\mathsf{C.il}}}[\rho \in \mathsf{C}^\pi\text{-queries}(x)] \leq \epsilon.$$

Since adversary $\mathcal{B}_*$ makes at most q many queries to CF and the two components of a collision (a, b) are sampled uniformly (although not independently) we have that

$$\Pr[\mathsf{collHit}(\rho) \wedge \mathsf{smooth}] \leq 2\mathsf{q}\epsilon.
\tag{4.9}$$

For this note that for every choice of $a, b \in \{0,1\}^{\mathsf{C.il}}$ such that $\mathsf{C}(a) = \mathsf{C}(b)$ it holds that

$$
\begin{aligned}
\Pr[(a, b) = \mathsf{CF}(\mathsf{C})] &= \frac{1}{2^{\mathsf{C.il}}} \cdot \frac{1}{|\mathsf{C}^{-1}(\mathsf{C}(a))|} \\
&= \frac{1}{2^{\mathsf{C.il}}} \cdot \frac{1}{|\mathsf{C}^{-1}(\mathsf{C}(b))|} = \Pr[(b, a) = \mathsf{CF}(\mathsf{C})].
\end{aligned}
$$

Value a is sampled uniformly at random, and b is sampled uniformly from the preimage of $\mathsf{C}(a) = \mathsf{C}(b)$. It follows that the marginal distribution of each component of sampled collisions is the uniform distribution over $\{0, 1\}^{\mathsf{C.il}}$.

Combining Equations (4.8) and (4.9) and noting that we set $\epsilon(\lambda) := 2^{-\frac{\lambda}{2}}$, we can thus bound the loss introduced in Game_3 as

$$\left| \Pr[\mathsf{Game}_3(\lambda) = 1] - \Pr[\mathsf{Game}_2(\lambda) = 1] \right|$$
$$\leq \Pr[\mathsf{collHit}(\rho)]$$
$$\leq \Pr[\mathsf{collHit}(\rho) \wedge \mathsf{smooth}] + \Pr\left[\overline{\mathsf{smooth}}\right]$$
$$\leq 2\mathsf{q} \cdot 2^{-\frac{\lambda}{2}} + \mathsf{q}^2 \cdot 2^{-\frac{\lambda}{2}}$$
$$\leq 3\mathsf{q}^2 \cdot 2^{-\frac{\lambda}{2}}.$$

Game$_4$ In Game$_4$ we adapt both permutation oracle and punctured collision finder. We perturb permutation oracle π by choosing a random second preimage $\rho^* \leftarrow\!\!\!\$\ \{0,1\}^\lambda$ which we also set to τ (recall that $\tau = \pi(\rho)$). We denote the resulting oracle (which technically is no longer a permutation) by

$$\pi_{\rho^* \mapsto \tau}(x) := \begin{cases} \pi(x) & \text{if } x \neq \rho^* \\ \tau & \text{if } x = \rho^* \end{cases}.$$

In addition we puncture collision finder pCF also on second preimage ρ^* and thus consider the setting where adversary $\mathcal{B}_*^{\pi_{\rho^* \mapsto \tau}, \mathsf{pCF}_{\{\rho, \rho^*\}}}$ is relative to oracles $\pi_{\rho^* \mapsto \tau}$ and $\mathsf{pCF}_{\{\rho, \rho^*\}}$.

To argue that the loss introduced by these changes is negligible, we will make use of a variant of Claim 4.24. For this note that Claim 4.24 considers only a change in the punctured points but not a change in oracle π and is thus not directly applicable. We formalize this variant as a separate claim.

Claim 4.25. *Let $\pi : \{0,1\}^* \to \{0,1\}^*$ be an oracle, let $S \subseteq \{0,1\}^\lambda$ be a set of punctured inputs, and let $\mathcal{A}$ be a (possibly unbounded) algorithm. Let $h, z \in \{0,1\}^*$ and define oracle $\pi_{h \mapsto z}$ as*

$$\pi_{h \mapsto z}(x) := \begin{cases} \pi(x) & \text{if } x \neq h \\ z & \text{if } x = h \end{cases}.$$

Let pCF_S be a punctured collision finder as above and let $\pi\text{-hit}(h)$ denote the event that during the execution of $\mathcal{A}^{\pi, \mathsf{pCF}_S}(1^\lambda)$ a query h to oracle π occurs. Note that, as before, we assume that $\mathcal{A}$ evaluates $\mathsf{C}^\pi(a)$ and $\mathsf{C}^\pi(b)$ for any response (a,b) to a collision-finder query $\mathsf{pCF}_S(\mathsf{C})$. Then for any security parameter $\lambda \in \mathbb{N}$ and any $y \in \{0,1\}^*$ it holds that

$$\left| \Pr\left[\mathcal{A}^{\pi, \mathsf{pCF}_S}(1^\lambda) = y\right] - \Pr\left[\mathcal{A}^{\pi_{h \mapsto z}, \mathsf{pCF}_{S \cup \{h\}}}(1^\lambda) = y\right] \right| \leq \Pr[\pi\text{-hit}(h)].$$

Note that we here consider punctured collision finders in both settings. When setting set S to the empty set then we recover also the case when starting from plain collision finder CF and moving to $\mathsf{pCF}_{\{h\}}$ for some value h. Further note that the main difference from Claim 4.24 is that we here consider a joint change of oracle π and collision finder on some value h. In order to show the stronger claim we also require a stronger assumption, namely that no π-query h occurs, instead of no $\mathsf{collHit}(h)$.

Proof of Claim 4.25. The proof strategy is analogous to the proof of Claim 4.24. Here we need to show that

$$\Pr\left[\mathcal{A}^{\pi,\mathsf{pCF}_S}(1^\lambda) = y \mid \overline{\pi\text{-hit}(h)}\right] =$$

$$\Pr\left[\mathcal{A}^{\pi_{h\mapsto z},\mathsf{pCF}_{S\cup\{h\}}}(1^\lambda) = y \mid \overline{\pi\text{-hit}(h)}\right], \qquad (4.10)$$

which allows us to argue that

$$\Pr\left[\mathcal{A}^{\pi,\mathsf{pCF}_S}(1^\lambda) = y\right] \le \Pr\left[\mathcal{A}^{\pi_{h\mapsto z},\mathsf{pCF}_{S\cup\{h\}}}(1^\lambda) = y\right] + \Pr[\pi\text{-hit}(h)]$$

as well as

$$\Pr\left[\mathcal{A}^{\pi_{h\mapsto z},\mathsf{pCF}_{S\cup\{h\}}}(1^\lambda) = y\right] \le \Pr\left[\mathcal{A}^{\pi,\mathsf{pCF}_S}(1^\lambda) = y\right] + \Pr[\pi\text{-hit}(h)]$$

from which the statement follows.

In order to show Equation 4.10, fix random coins $r_{\mathcal{A}}$ for algorithm $\mathcal{A}$, r_π for oracle π, and r_{CF} for collision finder CF such that

$$\mathcal{A}^{\pi(\cdot;r_\pi),\mathsf{pCF}_S(\cdot;r_{\mathsf{CF}})}(1^\lambda;r_{\mathcal{A}}) = y \qquad \text{and} \qquad \overline{\pi\text{-hit}(h)},$$

that is, during the evaluation of $\mathcal{A}^{\pi(\cdot;r_\pi),\mathsf{pCF}_S(\cdot;r_{\mathsf{CF}})}(1^\lambda;r_{\mathcal{A}})$, event $\pi\text{-hit}(h)$ does not materialize. Since now $\mathcal{A}$ does not query oracle π on value h we have that also for all (pseudo-)collisions (a, b) as output by punctured collision finder pCF_S it holds that

$$h \notin \mathsf{C}^\pi\text{-queries}(a) \cup \mathsf{C}^\pi\text{-queries}(b).$$

In other words, as event $\mathsf{collHit}(h)$ implies $\pi\text{-hit}(h)$ because $\mathcal{A}$ evaluates the circuits $\mathsf{C}^\pi(a)$ and $\mathsf{C}^\pi(b)$ after each call to the collision finder, it follows that if $\pi\text{-hit}(h)$ does not occur then also $\mathsf{collHit}(h)$ does not occur. Consequently, if oracle $\mathsf{pCF}_{S\cup\{h\}}$ on random coins r_{CF} returns the same collisions as pCF_S then it must be that also

$$\mathcal{A}^{\pi_{h\mapsto z}(\cdot;r_\pi),\mathsf{pCF}_{S\cup\{h\}}(\cdot;r_{\mathsf{CF}})}(1^\lambda;r_{\mathcal{A}}) = y.$$

For this note that if $\mathcal{A}$ does not query $\pi_{h\mapsto z}$ on h then $\pi_{h\mapsto z}$ presents the same view towards $\mathcal{A}$ as unperturbed oracle π.

It remains to argue that oracles pCF_S and $\mathsf{pCF}_{S\cup\{h\}}$ running on the same set of coins r_{CF} answer all queries identically. Recall that, by assumption, on coins r_{CF} events $\pi\text{-hit}(h)$ and $\mathsf{collHit}(h)$ do not occur and we can thus reuse the argument from Claim 4.5 with one exception: Collision finder $\mathsf{pCF}_{S\cup\{h\}}$ operates relative to perturbed oracle $\pi_{h\mapsto z}$ while collision finder pCF_S operates relative to unperturbed oracle π. Thus, there might be a value b' such that for a query circuit C we have that

$$\mathsf{C}^\pi(b') \ne \mathsf{C}^{\pi_{h\mapsto z}}(b') = \mathsf{C}^{\pi_{h\mapsto z}}(a) = \mathsf{C}^\pi(a).$$

That is, b' collides with a under circuit C relative to $\pi_{h \mapsto z}$ but not relative to oracle π. This can, however, only be the case if $\mathsf{C}^\pi(b')$ induces a query h to oracle π and thus $h \in \mathsf{C}^\pi\text{-queries}(b')$. But then, by definition of punctured collision finder $\mathsf{pCF}_{S \cup \{h\}}$ value b' would not be considered for a collision as the check in line 8 returns false. We conclude that, assuming event $\pi\text{-hit}(h)$ does not occur, then for any circuit C, collision finders pCF_S and $\mathsf{pCF}_{S \cup \{h\}}$ running on the same coins will return the same (pseudo-)collision (a, b). The statement follows. ∎

In order to use Claim 4.25 to bound the loss incurred by the changes introduced in Game_4 we need to argue that in Game_3 value ρ^* is not queried by adversary $\mathcal{B}_*$ to oracle π, either directly or as a result of a collision-finder query: we need to show that event $\pi\text{-hit}(\rho^*)$ does not occur. Since ρ^* is picked uniformly at random and, in particular, independently from anything else in Game_3 we have that the probability of $\mathcal{B}_*$ querying π on input ρ^* in Game_3 can be upper bound by a union bound (noting that adversary $\mathcal{B}_*$ makes at most $(\mathsf{q} + \mathsf{q} \cdot \lambda \cdot 2^{\frac{\lambda}{2}})$ many π-queries) as

$$|\Pr[\mathsf{Game}_4(\lambda) = 1] - \Pr[\mathsf{Game}_3(\lambda) = 1]| \leq \Pr[\pi\text{-hit}(\rho^*)]$$

$$= \Pr[\exists i : i\text{th query to } \pi \text{ is } \rho^*]$$

$$\leq |\text{total number of } \pi\text{-queries}| \cdot \frac{1}{2^\lambda}$$

$$\overset{(4.4)}{=} (\mathsf{q} + \mathsf{q} \cdot \lambda \cdot 2^{\frac{\lambda}{2}}) \cdot \frac{1}{2^\lambda}.$$

Game_5 Up to now, adversary $\mathcal{B}_*$ (resp. adversary $\mathcal{B}$) got as input, target value τ computed as $\tau \leftarrow \pi(\rho)$. In Game_5 we change the target value given to the adversary and provide instead value $\tau^* \leftarrow\!\!\$ \{0, 1\}^\lambda$ sampled uniformly at random (and independently of target preimage ρ). In addition we adjust both oracles to reflect this change. That is, we perturb π such that preimage ρ is mapped to target value τ^*. Furthermore, instead of puncturing on value ρ^* sampled uniformly at random, we now puncture on value $\rho^* \leftarrow \pi^{-1}(\tau^*)$, that is, the (unique) preimage of τ^* under π. We thus consider oracle $\pi_{\rho \mapsto \tau^*}$ and collision finder $\mathsf{pCF}_{\{\rho, \rho^*\}}$. All changes can be regarded as syntactical relabelings as given in the table below:

	Values			Oracles	
Game_4	ρ	$\tau = \pi(\rho)$	ρ^*	$\pi_{\rho^* \mapsto \tau}$	$\mathsf{pCF}_{\{\rho, \rho^*\}}$
Game_5	$\rho^* = \pi^{-1}(\tau^*)$	τ^*	ρ	$\pi_{\rho \mapsto \tau^*}$	$\mathsf{pCF}_{\{\rho, \rho^*\}}$

For this note that values ρ and ρ^* are both sampled uniformly at random from $\{0, 1\}^\lambda$ in Game_4 while τ is computed as $\tau \leftarrow \pi(\rho)$. In Game_5 we still choose preimage $\rho \leftarrow\!\!\$ \{0, 1\}^\lambda$ uniformly at random but instead of also choosing second preimage ρ^* uniformly at random we instead choose target value $\tau^* \leftarrow\!\!\$\ \{0,1\}^\lambda$ uniformly at random and compute $\rho^* \leftarrow \pi^{-1}(\tau^*)$. As π is a permutation, the values' distribution is identical. Finally, in order to make the view identical to that in Game_4 we perturb oracle π such that preimage ρ also maps to τ^* and thus consider oracle $\pi_{\rho\mapsto\tau^*}$. We conclude that

$$\Pr[\mathsf{Game}_4(\lambda) = 1] = \Pr[\mathsf{Game}_5(\lambda) = 1].$$

Game_6 In Game_6 we start undoing our changes to the perturbed permutation oracle and collision finder and again consider the unperturbed oracle π. At the same time we remove one value from the list of punctured points and consider punctured collision finder $\mathsf{pCF}_{\{\rho^*\}}$, where as before $\rho^* \leftarrow \pi^{-1}(\tau^*)$ for a uniformly random $\tau^* \leftarrow\!\!\$\ \{0,1\}^\lambda$.

Note that the situation is symmetrical to that in Game_4. The oracles in Game_5 and Game_6 differ only in point ρ, which in Game_5 is mapped to τ^* (via perturbed oracle $\pi_{\rho\mapsto\tau^*}$) and which is, furthermore, part of the list of punctured points. Thus if ρ is not queried by adversary $\mathcal{B}_*$ in Game_6 then Game_6 is identical to Game_5. Finally note that ρ is chosen independently of all other values in Game_6. Once more applying Claim 4.25 and reusing the analysis from the hop to Game_4 thus yields

$$|\Pr[\mathsf{Game}_5(\lambda) = 1] - \Pr[\mathsf{Game}_6(\lambda) = 1]| \leq |\text{total number of }\pi\text{-queries}| \cdot \frac{1}{2^\lambda}$$

$$\overset{(4.4)}{=} (\mathsf{q} + \mathsf{q} \cdot \lambda \cdot 2^{\frac{\lambda}{2}}) \cdot \frac{1}{2^\lambda}.$$

Game_7 In the final game we again consider original collision finder CF instead of the punctured collision finder. The only difference between Game_6 and Game_7 is thus that Game_6 uses punctured collision finder $\mathsf{pCF}_{\{\rho^*\}}$. The situation is thus symmetrical to that in Game_3 and we can bound the incurred loss with the smoothness of adversary $\mathcal{B}_*$ and Claim 4.24:

$$|\Pr[\mathsf{Game}_7(\lambda) = 1] - \Pr[\mathsf{Game}_6(\lambda) = 1]|$$
$$\leq \Pr[\mathsf{collHit}(\rho^*)]$$
$$\leq \Pr[\mathsf{collHit}(\rho^*) \wedge \mathsf{smooth}] + \Pr[\overline{\mathsf{smooth}}]$$
$$\leq 2\mathsf{q} \cdot 2^{-\frac{\lambda}{2}} + \mathsf{q}^2 \cdot 2^{-\frac{\lambda}{2}}$$
$$\leq 3\mathsf{q}^2 \cdot 2^{-\frac{\lambda}{2}}.$$

Wrapping up. The final step in the analysis is to note that in Game_7 the adversary's success probability is exactly $2^{-\lambda}$. For this note that preimage ρ is chosen independently from target value τ^* that is given to the adversary as input. As the adversary has no information whatsoever about ρ it can only guess, which yields the correct value with claimed probability $2^{-\lambda}$.

It remains to sum up the individual steps. From our discussion of the game-playing method (Section 3.2.1; page 106) we know that we can bound the success probability of original adversary $\mathcal{B}$ in inverting random permutation π by

$$
\begin{aligned}
&\mathsf{Adv}^{\mathrm{owf}}_{\pi,\mathcal{B}^\pi,\mathsf{CF}}(\lambda)\\
&\quad= \Pr[\mathsf{Game}_1(\lambda)=1]\\
&\quad\le \sum_{i=1}^{6}|\Pr[\mathsf{Game}_{i+1}(\lambda)=1]-\Pr[\mathsf{Game}_i(\lambda)=1]|+\Pr[\mathsf{Game}_7(\lambda)=1]\\
&\quad\le 6\mathsf{q}(\lambda)^2\cdot 2^{-\frac{\lambda}{2}}+2\cdot(\mathsf{q}(\lambda)+\mathsf{q}(\lambda)\cdot\lambda\cdot 2^{\frac{\lambda}{2}})\cdot\frac{1}{2^\lambda}+2^{-\lambda}.
\end{aligned}
$$

As, by assumption $\mathsf{q}(\lambda)$ is polynomial in the security parameter, the above is negligible, which concludes the proof.[9]   □

Remark 4.26. In the above proof we gave a particular collision finding oracle CF. Note that the proof does not work with any such oracle. For example, a collision finder that simply samples from the set of all collisions allows an adversary to cleverly construct circuits that manipulate the collision space and ultimately allow the adversary to invert the one-way permutation. With such a collision finder the above proof breaks down in Game_3 where we argue that the two values sampled by the collision finder are sampled uniformly at random (though not independently).

Remark 4.27. While we used a random permutation in the above separation, this does not mean that a random compressing function is not collision resistant or that you cannot construct a collision-resistant (and compressing) function from a random permutation. In fact, in Chapter 8 we will see that so-called random oracles (random functions with an unbounded domain and fixed output length) are collision resistant. However, in order to construct a collision-resistant hash function from a one-way function, the construction needs to be collision resistant when starting from *any* one-way function. A *random* function, on the other hand, can be regarded as the strongest possible one-way function.

Fixing oracles π and CF. The final part in showing that Proposition 4.21 holds and that, indeed, we cannot prove the security of a collision-resistant hash function down to the security of a one-way permutation via a fully black-box reduction is to show that we can fix oracle π such that still no adversary can invert construction N^π (resp. invert oracle π). For this recall that in our above proof of Proposition 4.22 (item 3) we showed that adversary $\mathcal{B}^{\pi,\mathsf{CF}}$ cannot invert N^π with better than negligible probability over the coins of adversary $\mathcal{B}$ and *the random choice of oracle* π. Consequently, the order of quantifiers in item 3 is reversed from what we need: We have shown that if we first fix adversary $\mathcal{B}$ and then select a random permutation oracle π,

---

[9] Note that the bound even allows for an exponential number of queries.

then $\mathcal{B}$ cannot invert N^π. But this, in particular, means that we do not allow the adversary to depend on oracle π. An actual one-way function, however, is a fixed construction. Think, for example, RSA where demanding that an adversary cannot depend on the specifics of the RSA function is, of course, unrealistic. Thus, in order to show Proposition 4.21 we need to show that we can invert the order of quantifiers. In other words, we need to show that if we pick a random oracle π and fix it, then still no adversary (which now may depend on π) can break construction N^π with better than negligible probability. Since Proposition 4.21 requires both oracles $\mathsf{SP} = \pi$ and $\mathsf{Break} = \mathsf{CF}$ to be fixed, we rather show that the order of quantifiers can be exchanged for the pair (π, CF).

In order to finish the proof of Proposition 4.21 we will make use of two classic results from probability theory, which we here state without proof.[10] The first of these is *Markov's inequality*, which provides an upper bound on the probability that a non-negative random variable assumes a value greater than or equal to some positive constant. The Markov inequality for non-negative random variable X and constant $a > 0$ is given by

$$\Pr[X \geq a] \leq \frac{\mathbb{E}[X]}{a}.$$

When setting $a := \hat{a} \cdot \mathbb{E}[X]$ (for $\hat{a} > 0$) we obtain

$$\Pr[X \geq \hat{a} \cdot \mathbb{E}[X]] \leq \frac{1}{\hat{a}}, \qquad (4.11)$$

which is the form that we will use in the proof below.

The second result that we will make use of is the (first) Borel–Cantelli lemma, which states that if the sum of the probabilities of an infinite sequence of events converges, then only finitely many of the events happen. In other words, given a sequence of events $(E_\lambda)_{\lambda \in \mathbb{N}}$ such that $\sum_{\lambda=1}^{\infty} \Pr[E_\lambda] < \infty$ then there exists a value $\Lambda \in \mathbb{N}$ such that for all $\lambda \geq \Lambda$ event E_λ does not occur. In the lemma below we capture the existence of such a bound Λ by quantifying over all $k \in \mathbb{N}$ via a logical AND, encoding the statement "for each k," and describe the existence of an event "behind" such a value k by forming the logical OR over all E_λ for $\lambda \geq k$:

Lemma 4.28 (Borel–Cantelli Lemma). *Let $E_1, E_2, \ldots$ be a sequence of events on the same probability space. Then, if the sum of probabilities of events E_λ converges, then the probability that infinitely many of the events occur is 0:*

$$\sum_{\lambda=1}^{\infty} \Pr[E_\lambda] < \infty \implies \Pr\left[\bigwedge_{k=1}^{\infty} \bigvee_{\lambda \geq k} E_\lambda \right] = 0.$$

---

[10] Proofs of both statements can be found in any good introduction to probability theory.

Using Borel–Cantelli and Markov we will next show that we can, indeed, reverse the order of quantifiers to show that there is an oracle pair (π, CF) that is good for all adversaries. Proposition 4.21 then follows.

Proof of Proposition 4.21. Fix an adversary $\mathcal{B}$. Then Proposition 4.22 tells us that there exists a negligible function ϵ such that

$$\mathsf{Adv}^{\mathrm{owf}}_{\mathsf{N}^{\pi}, \mathcal{B}^{\pi}, \mathsf{CF}}(\lambda) := \Pr\left[\mathsf{Exp}^{\mathrm{owf}}_{\mathsf{N}^{\pi}, \mathcal{B}^{\pi}, \mathsf{CF}}(\lambda)\right] \leq \epsilon(\lambda),$$

where the probability is over the choice of oracles π and CF and the coins of adversary $\mathcal{B}$ and the preimage τ. Let

$$p_{\pi, \mathsf{CF}} := \Pr_{r_{\mathcal{B}}, \tau}\left[\mathsf{Exp}^{\mathrm{owf}}_{\mathsf{N}^{\pi}, \mathcal{B}^{\pi}, \mathsf{CF}}(\lambda)\right]$$

be the probability of $\mathcal{B}$ succeeding for a fixed choice of (π, CF), such that the probability is now only over $\mathcal{B}$'s random coins $r_{\mathcal{B}}$ and the choice of τ. Then we can rewrite the advantage as the average of the values $p_{\pi, \mathsf{CF}}$ over all possible choices of the oracles:

$$\mathsf{Adv}^{\mathrm{owf}}_{\mathsf{N}^{\pi}, \mathcal{B}^{\pi}, \mathsf{CF}}(\lambda) = \mathbb{E}_{\pi, \mathsf{CF}}\left[p_{\pi, \mathsf{CF}}\right].$$

Applying Markov's inequality in the form of Equation (4.11) we can give an upper bound on the probability that over the choice of oracles π and CF adversary $\mathcal{B}$ is more than λ^2 times more successful than $\epsilon(\lambda) \geq \mathbb{E}_{\pi, \mathsf{CF}}\left[p_{\pi, \mathsf{CF}}\right]$:

$$\Pr_{\pi, \mathsf{CF}}\left[p_{\pi, \mathsf{CF}} \geq \lambda^2 \cdot \epsilon(\lambda)\right] \leq \frac{1}{\lambda^2}. \tag{4.12}$$

For a fixed pair (π, CF) let E_{λ} now be the event that adversary $\mathcal{B}$ succeeds in $\mathsf{Exp}^{\mathrm{owf}}_{\mathsf{N}^{\pi}, \mathcal{B}^{\pi}, \mathsf{CF}}(\lambda)$ for security parameter λ with probability at least $\lambda^2 \cdot \epsilon(\lambda)$, over its coin tosses and the choice of preimage τ. By Equation (4.12) we have $\Pr[\mathsf{E}_{\lambda}] \leq 1/\lambda^2$ over the choice of oracles π and CF.

Since $\sum_{\lambda=1}^{\infty} \frac{1}{\lambda^2}$ converges to 2, we can now apply the Borel–Cantelli lemma, which yields that only with probability 0 can there be infinitely many security parameters λ for which $\mathcal{B}$'s success probability (over its coins and τ) in inverting N^{π} is bigger than $\lambda^2 \cdot \epsilon(\lambda)$. Note that since $\lambda^2 \cdot \epsilon(\lambda)$ is negligible—a polynomial times a negligible function is negligible (see also Theorem 2.3 on page 77)—it follows that with probability 1 adversary $\mathcal{B}$ can invert construction N^{π} only with negligible probability for all large enough λ. Put differently, no fixed $\mathcal{B}$ can win the experiment with non-negligible probability for infinitely many parameters λ.

The final step is to note that there are only countably many adversaries $\mathcal{B}$. This follows from the fact that the number of Turing machines is countable (see also our discussion on universal Turing machines on page 19). This allows us to move from a fixed adversary $\mathcal{B}$, as above, to quantify against all adversaries and use the union bound:

$$\Pr_{\pi,\mathsf{CF}}\Big[\exists\ \mathsf{PPT\ TM}\ \mathcal{B} : \Pr\Big[\mathsf{Exp}^{\mathsf{owf}}_{\mathsf{N}^\pi,\mathcal{B}^\pi,\mathsf{CF}}(\lambda)\Big]\ \text{non-negligible}\Big]$$

$$\leq \sum_{\mathsf{PPT\ TM}\ \mathcal{B}} \Pr_{\pi,\mathsf{CF}}\Big[\Pr\Big[\mathsf{Exp}^{\mathsf{owf}}_{\mathsf{N}^\pi,\mathcal{B}^\pi,\mathsf{CF}}(\lambda)\Big]\ \text{non-negligible}\Big]$$

$$= \sum_{\mathsf{PPT\ TM}\ \mathcal{B}} 0$$

$$= 0.$$

In other words, a randomly chosen oracle pair (π, CF) will work against all adversaries $\mathcal{B}$ with probability 1. This in particular means that there exists a suitable pair of oracles (π, CF); in fact, almost any pair works.[11]   □

Chapter Notes and References

The verb "to hash" either means to chop (usually food) into small pieces or to muddle or mess something up. Hashing and hash functions, i.e., functions that map data of usually arbitrary size to a fixed-size (hash) value, have a long tradition in computer science and outside of cryptography where they have been used for a variety of tasks since the 1960s. They have their roots in the construction of data structures for efficient lookup and storage of data but have since found various applications. An overview on hash functions outside of cryptographic contexts is given by Donald Knuth in [16]. Knuth also traces the origins of the birthday problem, which has been discussed by mathematicians since the 1930s and appears in the literature since the 1950s (see, for example, [7] Section 2.3).

Hash functions in the context of cryptography were first introduced by Ralph Merkle in his 1979 Ph.D. thesis [17], where he coined the term *one-way hash function* to describe functions that are one-way and compressing. A formalization of collision-resistant hash functions as well as first constructions were given by Ivan Damgård almost ten years later in 1987 [6]. Universal one-way hash functions (i.e., target-collision-resistant hash functions) were introduced by Naor and Yung in 1989 [19]. Both Damgård as well as Naor and Yung considered as applications for their new cryptographic primitives the implementation of efficient digital signature schemes (see Chapter 6). A thorough study of various hash function properties and their relationships was conducted by Rogaway and Shrimpton in 2004 [22]. The human ignorance approach of interpreting the discrepancy between keyless real-world hash functions and keyed hash functions in cryptographic theory was suggested by Rogaway in [21].

---

[11] Note that the set of possible oracles is uncountable, such that the probability can be 1 despite the fact that there may be still some "weak" oracles.

While Naor and Yung gave a construction of target-collision-resistant hash functions starting from one-way permutations [19], Rompel showed in 1990 that target-collision-resistant hash functions can, in fact, be constructed based on any one-way function [23]. A detailed write-up of this seminal result is given by Katz and Koo [15].

The birthday bound for non-uniform distributions has been discussed in various settings, starting with works by Bloom [5]. Our proof here, arguing that the uniform distribution for hash functions is the worst one for collision finders, follows the presentation of Berresford [3] and is attributed to Munford [18].

The seminal result showing that collision-resistant hash functions cannot be based on one-way functions (via black-box reductions) was given by Simon in 1998 [24], who gave an oracle relative to which one-way permutations (and thus, for example, target-collision-resistant hash functions) exist, but relative to which no collision-resistant hash function can exist. A detailed discussion of the importance of choosing the right collision finding circuit (also see Remark 4.26 following the proof of Proposition 4.18) is given by Baecher [1]. Alternative proofs have been presented by Haitner *et al.* [10, 11] and Bitansky and Degwekar [4]. Our presentation above (Proposition 4.21) follows the work by Bitansky and Degwekar.

Oracle separations in cryptography were introduced by Impagliazzo and Rudich [13, 14], who showed in 1988 that key exchange protocols cannot be constructed from random oracles (and thus from one-way functions). We will present their result in Chapter 11. In fact, the part about switching the order of quantifiers via the Borel–Cantelli lemma appears in their work. An overview over black-box separations is given by Fischlin in [8]. The two oracle technique was introduced by Hsiao and Reyzin [12].

Fully black-box constructions were first formalized in 2000 by Gertner *et al.* [9]. The version defined here is due to Hsiao and Reyzin [12]. A first systematic study of various types of reductions in cryptography was given by Reingold, Trevisan, and, Vadhan [20]. Their framework was later extended by Baecher, Brzuska, and Fischlin [2].

Exercices

Exercise 4.1. In Proposition 4.4 we saw that one-way functions do not need to be collision resistant. For this we adapted a one-way function F and defined

$$
\mathsf{F}'(1^\lambda, x) = \begin{cases} 0^{|x|} & \text{in case } x = 0^\lambda \\ 0^{|x|} & \text{in case } x = 1^\lambda \\ \mathsf{F}(1^\lambda, x) & \text{otherwise} \end{cases}
$$

Show that F' is one-way, given that F is one-way.

Exercise 4.2. If one-way functions exist, then there exists a one-way function F that ignores the first input bit. If collision-resistant hash functions exist, can there be a hash function that ignores the first input bit? How about second-preimage-resistant hash functions?

Exercise 4.3. Which of the following functions is collision resistant if H is a collision-resistant hash function?

  i) $G_1(\mathsf{hk}, x) := H(\mathsf{hk}, x)[1..H.\mathsf{ol}(\lambda) - 1]$
  ii) $G_2(\mathsf{hk}, x) := H(\mathsf{hk}, x)[1..\lfloor H.\mathsf{ol}(\lambda)/2 \rfloor]$
  iii) $G_3(\mathsf{hk}, x) := H(\mathsf{hk}, x\|0) \oplus H(\mathsf{hk}, x\|1)$
  iv) $G_4(\mathsf{hk}, x) := H(\mathsf{hk}, 0\|x)\|H(\mathsf{hk}, 1\|x)$
  v) $G_5(\mathsf{hk}, x) := H(\mathsf{hk}, H(\mathsf{hk}, x))$

For all functions G_i key generation is as in H.

Exercise 4.4. Let H be a collision-resistant hash function with λ-bit hash values and define G as

$$G(k, x) = \begin{cases} x & \text{if } |x| = \lambda \\ H(k, x) \end{cases}$$

with key generation as in H. Prove or disprove: G is collision resistant.

Exercise 4.5. Let H be a second-preimage (resp. target-collision) resistant hash function and define G as

$$G(\mathsf{hk}, x) := \begin{cases} 0^{|x|} & \text{in case } x = 0^\lambda \\ 0^{|x|} & \text{in case } x = 1^\lambda \\ H(\mathsf{hk}, x) & \text{otherwise} \end{cases}$$

with key generation identical to H. Prove or refute the following claims:

- G is second-preimage resistant if H is second-preimage resistant.
- G is target-collision resistant if H is target-collision resistant.

Exercise 4.6. Show that second-preimage resistance implies one-wayness given that the function compresses.

Exercise 4.7. Prove the remaining separation results from Theorem 4.10. That is, show that one-wayness does not imply second-preimage resistance and that target-collision resistance does not imply collision resistance.

Exercise 4.8. A hash combiner takes two hash functions H_0, H_1 and builds another hash function H out of these two functions, such that H has a security property even if only one of the two functions H_0, H_1 has this property. In other words, H is robust with respect to failure of one of the two underlying functions. Build a hash combiner for collision resistance.

Exercise 4.9. Assume pseudorandom functions exist. Give a construction of a pseudorandom function that is not collision resistant.

Chapter Bibliography

1. Paul Baecher. Simon's circuit. Cryptology ePrint Archive, Report 2014/476, 2014. http://eprint.iacr.org/2014/476.
2. Paul Baecher, Christina Brzuska, and Marc Fischlin. Notions of black-box reductions, revisited. In Kazue Sako and Palash Sarkar, editors, *Advances in Cryptology – ASIACRYPT 2013, Part I*, volume 8269 of *Lecture Notes in Computer Science*, pages 296–315, Bengalore, India, December 1–5, 2013. Springer, Heidelberg, Germany.
3. Geoffrey C Berresford. The uniformity assumption in the birthday problem. *Mathematics Magazine*, 53(5):286–288, 1980.
4. Nir Bitansky and Akshay Degwekar. On the complexity of collision resistant hash functions: New and old black-box separations. In Dennis Hofheinz and Alon Rosen, editors, *TCC 2019: 17th Theory of Cryptography Conference, Part I*, volume 11891 of *Lecture Notes in Computer Science*, pages 422–450, Nuremberg, Germany, December 1–5, 2019. Springer, Heidelberg, Germany.
5. David M Bloom. Birthday problem. *American Mathematical Monthly*, 80(10):1141–1142, 1973.
6. Ivan Damgård. Collision free hash functions and public key signature schemes. In David Chaum and Wyn L. Price, editors, *Advances in Cryptology – EUROCRYPT'87*, volume 304 of *Lecture Notes in Computer Science*, pages 203–216, Amsterdam, The Netherlands, April 13–15, 1988. Springer, Heidelberg, Germany.
7. William Feller. *An Introduction to Probability Theory and Its Applications*. Wiley, 1950.
8. Marc Fischlin. Black-box reductions and separations in cryptography (invited talk). In Aikaterini Mitrokotsa and Serge Vaudenay, editors, *AFRICACRYPT 12: 5th International Conference on Cryptology in Africa*, volume 7374 of *Lecture Notes in Computer Science*, pages 413–422, Ifrance, Morocco, July 10–12, 2012. Springer, Heidelberg, Germany.
9. Yael Gertner, Sampath Kannan, Tal Malkin, Omer Reingold, and Mahesh Viswanathan. The relationship between public key encryption and oblivious transfer. In *41st Annual Symposium on Foundations of Computer Science*, pages 325–335, Redondo Beach, CA, USA, November 12–14, 2000. IEEE Computer Society Press.
10. Iftach Haitner, Jonathan J. Hoch, Omer Reingold, and Gil Segev. Finding collisions in interactive protocols - a tight lower bound on the round complexity of statistically-hiding commitments. In *48th Annual Symposium on Foundations of Computer Science*, pages 669–679, Providence, RI, USA, October 20–23, 2007. IEEE Computer Society Press.
11. Iftach Haitner, Jonathan J Hoch, Omer Reingold, and Gil Segev. Finding collisions in interactive protocols—tight lower bounds on the round and communication complexities of statistically hiding commitments. *SIAM Journal on Computing*, 44(1):193–242, 2015.
12. Chun-Yuan Hsiao and Leonid Reyzin. Finding collisions on a public road, or do secure hash functions need secret coins? In Matthew Franklin, editor, *Advances in Cryptology – CRYPTO 2004*, volume 3152 of *Lecture Notes in Computer Science*, pages 92–105, Santa Barbara, CA, USA, August 15–19, 2004. Springer, Heidelberg, Germany.
13. Russell Impagliazzo and Steven Rudich. Limits on the provable consequences of one-way permutations. In *21st Annual ACM Symposium on Theory of Computing*, pages 44–61, Seattle, WA, USA, May 15–17, 1989. ACM Press.

14. Russell Impagliazzo and Steven Rudich. Limits on the provable consequences of one-way permutations. In Shafi Goldwasser, editor, *Advances in Cryptology – CRYPTO'88*, volume 403 of *Lecture Notes in Computer Science*, pages 8–26, Santa Barbara, CA, USA, August 21–25, 1990. Springer, Heidelberg, Germany.

15. Jonathan Katz and Chiu-Yuen Koo. On constructing universal one-way hash functions from arbitrary one-way functions. Cryptology ePrint Archive, Report 2005/328, 2005. http://eprint.iacr.org/2005/328.

16. Donald E. Knuth. *The Art of Computer Programming, Volume 3: (2nd Ed.) Sorting and Searching*. Addison Wesley Longman Publishing Co., Inc., USA, 1998.

17. Ralph Merkle. Secrecy, authentication, and public key systems. *Ph. D. Thesis, Stanford University*, 1979.

18. AG Munford. A note on the uniformity assumption in the birthday problem. *The American Statistician*, 31(3):119–119, 1977.

19. Moni Naor and Moti Yung. Universal one-way hash functions and their cryptographic applications. In *21st Annual ACM Symposium on Theory of Computing*, pages 33–43, Seattle, WA, USA, May 15–17, 1989. ACM Press.

20. Omer Reingold, Luca Trevisan, and Salil P. Vadhan. Notions of reducibility between cryptographic primitives. In Moni Naor, editor, *TCC 2004: 1st Theory of Cryptography Conference*, volume 2951 of *Lecture Notes in Computer Science*, pages 1–20, Cambridge, MA, USA, February 19–21, 2004. Springer, Heidelberg, Germany.

21. Phillip Rogaway. Formalizing human ignorance. In Phong Q. Nguyen, editor, *Progress in Cryptology - Vietcrypt 2006*, pages 211–228, Berlin, Heidelberg, 2006. Springer Berlin Heidelberg.

22. Phillip Rogaway and Thomas Shrimpton. Cryptographic hash-function basics: Definitions, implications, and separations for preimage resistance, second-preimage resistance, and collision resistance. In Bimal K. Roy and Willi Meier, editors, *Fast Software Encryption – FSE 2004*, volume 3017 of *Lecture Notes in Computer Science*, pages 371–388, New Delhi, India, February 5–7, 2004. Springer, Heidelberg, Germany.

23. John Rompel. One-way functions are necessary and sufficient for secure signatures. In *22nd Annual ACM Symposium on Theory of Computing*, pages 387–394, Baltimore, MD, USA, May 14–16, 1990. ACM Press.

24. Daniel R. Simon. Finding collisions on a one-way street: Can secure hash functions be based on general assumptions? In Kaisa Nyberg, editor, *Advances in Cryptology – EUROCRYPT'98*, volume 1403 of *Lecture Notes in Computer Science*, pages 334–345, Espoo, Finland, May 31 – June 4, 1998. Springer, Heidelberg, Germany.

Chapter 5
Encryption Schemes

An introduction to cryptographic primitives would not be complete without a chapter on encryption schemes. While encryption capabilities are not amongst the many properties that we often ascribe to hash functions,[1] hash functions can be used in the design of encryption schemes and play a vital part in larger cryptographic protocols that deploy encryption as one component.

Encryption schemes are typically categorized into two categories: *symmetric* (or *private-key*) encryption schemes and *public-key* encryption schemes. We have already come across symmetric encryption in Chapter 1 (Section 1.5; page 41) when discussing *perfectly secure encryption* and the *one-time pad*. In the symmetric scenario we consider two parties Alice and Bob who share a common secret key k which is used for both encryption and decryption. This means, Alice uses key k to encrypt a message m to obtain a ciphertext c which, if the encryption scheme is *secure*, does not reveal anything about m (except for the message's length). Alice can then send c over an insecure channel to Bob who can retrieve m by using his copy of key k. The one-time pad offers a perfectly secure solution to this problem as there we can prove without having to rely on any assumptions that no adversary (however powerful) can extract message m from ciphertext c. The *perfect security*, regrettably, comes at a price: keys cannot be reused and, furthermore, keys must be at least as long as the message.

In this chapter we introduce security models for *computationally secure* encryption schemes, that is, encryption schemes that are secure only against computationally bounded adversaries. Weakening the security requirements and only demanding security against efficient adversaries allows us to overcome Shannon's bound and the restrictions of the one-time pad. In Section 3.3.4 we have already seen that pseudorandom generators can be used to overcome the length restriction of keys. Here the idea was to use a pseudorandom generator

---

[1] For starters, hash functions usually compress their input, in which case the precise preimage can no longer be recovered reliably. In other words "decryption" would no longer work.

© Springer Nature Switzerland AG 2021

A. Mittelbach, M. Fischlin, *The Theory of Hash Functions and Random Oracles*,
Information Security and Cryptography, https://doi.org/10.1007/978-3-030-63287-8_5

PRG to extend a small key k in order to obtain a large key K ← PRG(k) which is then used for encryption within the one-time pad. However, when we want to prove that the resulting "extended one-time pad encryption scheme" is secure we run into the problem that we do not have a proper definition of what security means in the computational setting. Clearly the resulting scheme is no longer secure with regard to the definition of *perfect security* (Definition 1.31; page 46). Our first task here is thus to define what *computational security* means for symmetric encryption schemes to then discuss how we can build such schemes with the help of weaker primitives, in particular, with the help of pseudorandom functions.

When deploying symmetric encryption in larger setups one quickly runs into a *key management problem*. Consider a setup with n users that all want to talk to one another confidentially. For this each pair of users must share a common secret key and with n distinct users we have $\binom{n}{2} = \frac{n(n-1)}{2}$ many user pairs. This means that in a (relatively small) system with just 1,000 users we would need to manage almost 500,000 distinct keys. It is obvious that this does not scale well. An additional problem of symmetric encryption schemes is that keys must be shared securely between communicating parties beforehand. In many scenarios this is simply not a viable option. Just consider the internet and a user who wants to securely connect to a website. It is impractical, to say the least, for the website host to manage shared secret keys with all its users.

Public-key encryption schemes mitigate these problems by splitting up a single secret key k into a pair of keys (pk, sk) called the *public key* pk and the *private key* (or secret key) sk. The idea is that the public key which is used for encryption can be public knowledge and thus, for example, can be shared in a public register (think telephone book). The secret key, on the other hand, must remain hidden from all other parties and is used by the owner for decryption. In other words, anybody knowing a person's public key can send encrypted messages to that person but only the holder of the secret key can decrypt these messages. Because of this asymmetry of algorithms (encryption uses the public key pk while decryption uses the secret key sk) public-key encryption is often also referred to as *asymmetric encryption*.

Again we will first need to define what precisely computational security means for public-key encryption schemes. While we know that perfectly secure (but somewhat restricted) symmetric encryption schemes exist we can show that public-key encryption cannot be achieved in an information-theoretic setting. Thus, while considering computational security allows us to make symmetric encryption more practical, computational security guarantees are really the best we can hope for in the public-key setting.

5.1 Symmetric Encryption

Recall the one-time pad encryption scheme, which is a symmetric encryption scheme that achieves perfect security (see Section 1.5; page 41). Here two parties share a common secret key k which they can use to encrypt a single message m (which must be of the same length as or shorter than key k) as

$$c \leftarrow m \oplus k.$$

We defined security for the one-time pad using probability theory, demanding that given c the probability (over key k) that c decrypts to a message m is the same for all messages $m \in \{0,1\}^{|k|}$ (see Definition 1.31 on page 46). While this definition provides perfect security in the sense that a ciphertext c does not contain any information about the actual plaintext message (except for the message's length) this strong requirement comes at a cost. We have seen that to achieve perfect secrecy we must have keys that are at least as long as the messages that we want to encrypt and, furthermore, keys may not be reused. At the upside the security guarantees are unconditional and hold against any adversary, even adversaries with unbounded computational resources.

How could a definition of secure encryption look like if we required that the scheme must only be secure against efficient adversaries? In this setting we can no longer base security on a purely information-theoretic or probability-theoretic statement as these do not allow us to factor in the computational restrictions of efficient adversaries. Instead, we are again looking at a security game which formalizes what it means for an adversary to *break* a symmetric encryption scheme and then demand that no efficient adversary can win the security game with better than negligible advantage.

There are many plausible formalizations of such a definition of *breaking encryption*, many of which may, however, lead to insecure schemes. Consider, for example, the requirement:

No efficient adversary should be able to retrieve the key from a ciphertext.

While this is certainly a necessary requirement as access to the key allows decryption, it is not sufficient. Consider an encryption scheme $\mathsf{SE} = (\mathsf{SE.KGen}, \mathsf{SE.Enc}, \mathsf{SE.Dec})$ (here $\mathsf{SE.Enc}$ and $\mathsf{SE.Dec}$ denote the efficient algorithms for encryption and decryption) where encryption is defined as

$$\mathsf{SE.Enc}(k, m)$$

1 : $c \leftarrow m$

2 :   **return** c

In other words, encryption ignores the key and sets ciphertext c to be the message m. Clearly, it is infeasible to learn the key from such ciphertexts but, of course, in this scheme keys are not required to recover the plaintext from ciphertexts in the first place. Evidently, we need a stronger requirement. One idea might be to demand that

> *no efficient adversary should be able to learn any single bit of a plaintext given only the corresponding ciphertext.*

Again, this is certainly a necessary requirement for a secure encryption scheme. However, it does not prevent, for example, an adversary from learning, say, the binary weight of the underlying plaintext (i.e., the number of ones in message m).

The generally established definitions of security for symmetric encryption are based on indistinguishability (IND) of encryptions and come in various forms, the strongest of which is *indistinguishability against chosen-ciphertext attacks* (IND-CCA). In the following we are going to discuss different variants of indistinguishability-based definitions. What they all share is the underlying syntax, i.e., a common definition of the algorithms involved in a symmetric encryption scheme and the *correctness requirement* which states that ciphertexts must be decryptable to the original plaintext message.

Definition 5.1 (Symmetric Encryption Scheme). *A symmetric encryption scheme* SE *is a tuple of three efficient algorithms* SE = (SE.KGen, SE.Enc, SE.Dec) *such that*

SE.KGen: *The probabilistic* key generation algorithm *on input the security parameter* 1^λ *outputs a key* $k \in \{0,1\}^*$.

SE.Enc: *The probabilistic* encryption algorithm *takes as input the key* k *and a message* $m \in \{0,1\}^*$ *and outputs a ciphertext* $c \in \{0,1\}^*$.

SE.Dec: *The deterministic* decryption algorithm *takes as input the key* k *and a ciphertext* c *and outputs a message* m *or a special error symbol* $\perp$.

Correctness: *We say that a symmetric encryption scheme is* correct *or meets the* correctness condition *if we can always recover the correct plaintext from a ciphertext. That is, we require that for all* $\lambda \in \mathbb{N}$ *and all* $m \in \{0,1\}^*$ *the following probability is equal to 1:*

$$\Pr\left[\mathsf{SE.Dec}(k, \mathsf{SE.Enc}(k, m)) = m \mid k \leftarrow\!\!{\scriptstyle\$}\, \mathsf{SE.KGen}(1^\lambda)\right].$$

We defined the space of messages that can be encrypted to be $\{0,1\}^*$. In some cases we may instead restrict the message space to some (finite or infinite) subset $\mathcal{M} \subseteq \{0,1\}^*$, possibly making $\mathcal{M}_\lambda$ depend on the security parameter λ.

5.1.1 Indistinguishability of Ciphertexts

The first and weakest security notion for symmetric encryption schemes is *indistinguishability of ciphertexts*, usually abbreviated simply as IND. The idea behind IND is that an adversary who sees a ciphertext and knows that it decrypts to one of two possible plaintext messages cannot guess the correct plaintext message with probability better than $\frac{1}{2}$. We capture this as a security game in which the adversary is split in two, that is, we consider an adversary $\mathcal{A} := (\mathcal{A}_1, \mathcal{A}_2)$. The task of the first part of the adversary $\mathcal{A}_1$ is to output two messages (m_0, m_1) and some state state (that may contain the messages). Then according to a hidden bit b one of the messages is encrypted with a randomly generated key k to obtain ciphertext $c \leftarrow\!\!{\$}\ \mathsf{SE.Enc}(k, m_b)$. The ciphertext together with state is given to the second part of the adversary, which has to guess whether it received an encryption of m_0 or of m_1. Note that a purely guessing strategy allows to win the security game with probability $\frac{1}{2}$. Thus, the advantage of an adversary is defined as its success probability bounded away from $\frac{1}{2}$. Following is the formal definition:

Definition 5.2 (IND Security for Symmetric Encryption). *A symmetric encryption scheme* $\mathsf{SE} := (\mathsf{SE.KGen}, \mathsf{SE.Enc}, \mathsf{SE.Dec})$ *is called* IND *secure if for all efficient adversaries* $\mathcal{A} = (\mathcal{A}_1, \mathcal{A}_2)$ *advantage* $\mathsf{Adv}^{\mathrm{ind}}_{\mathsf{SE}, \mathcal{A}_1, \mathcal{A}_2}(\lambda)$ *is negligible. Here, the advantage is defined as*

$$\mathsf{Adv}^{\mathrm{ind}}_{\mathsf{SE}, \mathcal{A}_1, \mathcal{A}_2}(\lambda) := 2 \cdot \Pr\left[\mathsf{Exp}^{\mathrm{ind}}_{\mathsf{SE}, \mathcal{A}_1, \mathcal{A}_2}(\lambda)\right] - 1$$

relative to experiment $\mathsf{Exp}^{\mathrm{ind}}_{\mathsf{SE}, \mathcal{A}_1, \mathcal{A}_2}(\lambda)$ *defined as*

$$\underline{\text{Experiment } \mathsf{Exp}^{\mathrm{ind}}_{\mathsf{SE}, \mathcal{A}_1, \mathcal{A}_2}(\lambda)}$$

$1:\quad b \leftarrow\!\!{\$}\ \{0, 1\}$

$2:\quad k \leftarrow\!\!{\$}\ \mathsf{SE.KGen}(1^\lambda)$

$3:\quad (m_0, m_1, \mathsf{state}) \leftarrow\!\!{\$}\ \mathcal{A}_1(1^\lambda)$

$4:\quad \textbf{if } |m_0| \neq |m_1| \textbf{ then return } \mathsf{false}$

$5:\quad c \leftarrow\!\!{\$}\ \mathsf{SE.Enc}(k, m_b)$

$6:\quad b' \leftarrow\!\!{\$}\ \mathcal{A}_2(1^\lambda, c, \mathsf{state})$

$7:\quad \textbf{return } (b = b')$

Remark 5.3. In line 4 of the IND experiment the challenger checks whether or not the two messages output by the adversary are of the same length. An interesting question is whether this is a necessary requirement or whether it is possible for an encryption scheme to hide the length of the underlying plaintexts.

Since a long message can contain more information than a shorter message (in terms of information theory) the ciphertext for the longer message must account for that. In other words, the minimum length of a ciphertext is determined by the amount of information in the plaintext as otherwise a unique decryption would not be possible. Simply put, an encryption scheme cannot achieve better compression rates than the best possible compression algorithm. Now, if we allow plaintexts of different lengths then the encryption of the message 1 must be indistinguishable from the encryption of a message of length 1,000 bits. This is, however, only possible if the encryption scheme hides the amount of information present in the underlying plaintext, i.e., if it hides the length of the underlying plaintext. This in turn means that the encryption scheme must have an upper bound ℓ on the length of plaintexts that it can encrypt and that the encryptions of a 1-bit message and an ℓ-bit message are of the same size, as otherwise distinguishing in the IND game would be trivial. Having either a huge blow-up, or being able to only encrypt very short messages are both very impractical restrictions, which is why, in general, definitions of encryption schemes do not require the encryption scheme to hide the length of the underlying messages.

As usual with definitions that specify a "guessing game" we can provide an alternative formulation of the advantage that measures the difference of distributions $\mathsf{Exp}^{\mathsf{ind}}_{\mathsf{SE},\mathcal{A}_1,\mathcal{A}_2}(\lambda)$ with hidden bit b fixed to 0 or 1 (see for example Definitions 3.21 and 3.22; pages 126f.). That is, if we define $\mathsf{Exp}^{\mathsf{ind}\text{-}b}_{\mathsf{SE},\mathcal{A}_1,\mathcal{A}_2}(\lambda)$ (note the "-b" in IND-b) as

$$\begin{array}{l}
\hline
\text{Experiment } \mathsf{Exp}^{\mathsf{ind}\text{-}b}_{\mathsf{SE},\mathcal{A}_1,\mathcal{A}_2}(\lambda) \\
\hline
1: \quad \mathsf{k} \twoheadleftarrow\!\!{\$}\ \mathsf{SE.KGen}(1^\lambda) \\
2: \quad (m_0, m_1, \mathsf{state}) \twoheadleftarrow\!\!{\$}\ \mathcal{A}_1(1^\lambda) \\
3: \quad \textbf{if } |m_0| \neq |m_1| \textbf{ then return } \mathsf{false} \\
4: \quad c \twoheadleftarrow\!\!{\$}\ \mathsf{SE.Enc}(\mathsf{k}, m_b) \\
5: \quad b' \twoheadleftarrow\!\!{\$}\ \mathcal{A}_2(1^\lambda, c, \mathsf{state}) \\
6: \quad \textbf{return } (b = b') \\
\hline
\end{array}$$

then we can capture advantage $\mathsf{Adv}^{\mathsf{ind}}_{\mathsf{SE},\mathcal{D}}(\lambda)$ as

$$\mathsf{Adv}^{\mathsf{ind}}_{\mathsf{SE},\mathcal{D}}(\lambda) := \left| \Pr\left[\mathsf{Exp}^{\mathsf{ind}\text{-}0}_{\mathsf{SE},\mathcal{A}_1,\mathcal{A}_2}(\lambda) \right] - \Pr\left[\mathsf{Exp}^{\mathsf{ind}\text{-}1}_{\mathsf{SE},\mathcal{A}_1,\mathcal{A}_2}(\lambda) \right] \right|.$$

We leave showing the equivalence as Exercise 5.1.

Semantic security. What type of security does IND capture? It is easily seen that an IND-secure encryption scheme encompasses the two simple security definitions from the beginning of this section. That is, it hides the encryption key (as otherwise an adversary could decrypt and successfully distinguish the messages) and it also hides every individual bit of a plaintext message. To see the latter consider messages 0^λ and $0^{i-1}10^{\lambda-i}$ for some integer $i \leq \lambda$. If the encryption scheme would leak the ith bit of the plaintext message then an adversary using these two messages could distinguish successfully. However, the definition achieves a much stronger form of security as it hides not only every individual bit but also any function of the plaintexts except for the message length. Here note that hiding an individual bit is a special case as we can consider function $f_i(x) := x[i]$ that outputs the ith bit of an input. Thus, if our encryption scheme hides every function of the plaintext it must, necessarily, also hide f_i.

The idea of formalizing security of encryption schemes by demanding that a ciphertext should not leak any function of the plaintext is also known as *semantic security*, and it can be shown that a direct formalization of this idea is identical to our IND notion of security (see Exercise 5.3). The game-based IND notion is, however, easier to handle and, as we will see, forms the basis for stronger forms of security.

We have motivated the need for a computational security definition for encryption schemes with the impracticality of the one-time pad. In particular we identified two problems: (i) messages must be short as keys must be at least as long as the message they encrypt and (ii) keys cannot be reused, that is, for each encryption operation we need a fresh key. While it is not too difficult to see that the one-time pad meets the IND security notion, the IND notion also allows us to formally handle the first of the two issues as we will see next.

Encrypting Long Messages

We have informally argued that the one-time pad encryption scheme which is extended by a pseudorandom generator PRG to first expand the key and then use the expanded key to encrypt should result in a secure encryption scheme. Let us formalize this PRG-expanded one-time pad $\mathsf{OTP}^{\mathsf{PRG}}$ as:

$\mathsf{OTP}^{\mathsf{PRG}}.\mathsf{KGen}(1^\lambda)$	$\mathsf{OTP}^{\mathsf{PRG}}.\mathsf{Enc}(\mathsf{k}, m)$	$\mathsf{OTP}^{\mathsf{PRG}}.\mathsf{Dec}(\mathsf{k}, c)$
1 : $\mathsf{k} \leftarrow_\$ \{0,1\}^\lambda$	1 : $\mathsf{K} \leftarrow \mathsf{PRG}(\mathsf{k})$	1 : $\mathsf{K} \leftarrow \mathsf{PRG}(\mathsf{k})$
2 : **return** k	2 : $c \leftarrow m \oplus \mathsf{K}$	2 : $m \leftarrow c \oplus \mathsf{K}$
	3 : **return** c	3 : **return** m

The $\mathsf{OTP}^{\mathsf{PRG}}$ scheme uses keys of length λ but expands these to length $\mathsf{PRG.ol}(\lambda)$ before using them in the one-time pad construction. As the scheme thus supports messages of length $\mathsf{PRG.ol}(\lambda) > \lambda$ it cannot be perfectly secure. However, we can show that it is IND-secure.

Proposition 5.4. *The PRG-expanded one-time pad* $\mathsf{OTP}^{\mathsf{PRG}}$ *is IND-secure given that* PRG *is a secure pseudorandom generator.*

We can prove Proposition 5.4 using the game-hopping technique (Section 3.2.1). Here the first game will be the original attack game. In the second (and last) game we replace the enlarged key K with a uniformly random value which we can do down to the security of the pseudorandom generator. This game will then be identical to the original one-time pad scheme as we now have a uniformly random key which is as long as the message and which is used only once. To finish the argument, we can thus use the result that the one-time pad is perfectly secure and that in this setting an adversary has a success probability of exactly $\frac{1}{2}$.

Proof. We need to show that for any PPT adversary $\mathcal{A} = (\mathcal{A}_1, \mathcal{A}_2)$ its advantage $\mathsf{Adv}^{\mathrm{ind}}_{\mathsf{OTP}^{\mathsf{PRG}}, \mathcal{A}_1, \mathcal{A}_2}(\lambda)$ against scheme $\mathsf{OTP}^{\mathsf{PRG}}$ is negligible. For this we consider the following games which are also given in pseudocode in Figure 5.1:

$\mathsf{Game}^{\mathcal{A}}_1(\lambda)$: The setting of the first game is equivalent to the original IND security experiment $\mathsf{Exp}^{\mathrm{ind}}_{\mathsf{OTP}^{\mathsf{PRG}}, \mathcal{A}_1, \mathcal{A}_2}(\lambda)$. We thus have

$$\Pr\left[\mathsf{Game}_1(1^\lambda)\right] = \Pr\left[\mathsf{Exp}^{\mathrm{ind}}_{\mathsf{OTP}^{\mathsf{PRG}}, \mathcal{A}_1, \mathcal{A}_2}(\lambda)\right].$$

$\mathsf{Game}^{\mathcal{A}}_2(\lambda)$: In the second and final Game_2 we modify the creation of one-time pad key K (line 3). While in Game_1 the key is chosen by applying the pseudorandom generator, we choose the key uniformly at random in Game_2.

Analysis of Game_2. With the change in how key K is chosen we have that Game_2 implements the one-time pad: Key K is chosen uniformly at random and is used to encrypt a message which is as long as the key. As the one-time pad is perfectly secure (Theorem 1.35; page 47) we thus have that

$$\Pr\left[\mathsf{Game}^{\mathcal{A}}_2(\lambda)\right] = \frac{1}{2}.$$

From the discussion of the game-hopping technique (Section 3.2.1; page 106) we know that we can upper bound the probability of Game_1 outputting 1 (and thus of experiment $\mathsf{Exp}^{\mathrm{ind}}_{\mathsf{OTP}^{\mathsf{PRG}}, \mathcal{A}_1, \mathcal{A}_2}(\lambda)$) by the sum of the distances of neighboring games plus the probability of the final game outputting 1. This yields the following bound:

$$
\begin{aligned}
\mathsf{Exp}&^{\mathrm{ind}}_{\mathsf{OTP}^{\mathsf{PRG}}, \mathcal{A}_1, \mathcal{A}_2}(\lambda) \\
&= \Pr\left[\mathsf{Game}^{\mathcal{A}}_1(\lambda)\right] \\
&\leq \left|\Pr\left[\mathsf{Game}^{\mathcal{A}}_2(\lambda)\right] - \Pr\left[\mathsf{Game}^{\mathcal{A}}_1(\lambda)\right]\right| + \Pr\left[\mathsf{Game}^{\mathcal{A}}_2(\lambda)\right] \\
&= \left|\Pr\left[\mathsf{Game}^{\mathcal{A}}_2(\lambda)\right] - \Pr\left[\mathsf{Game}^{\mathcal{A}}_1(\lambda)\right]\right| + \frac{1}{2}.
\end{aligned}
\tag{5.1}
$$

$$\text{Game}_1^{\mathcal{A}}(\lambda) \xrightarrow{\hspace{2em}\text{PRG}\hspace{2em}} \text{Game}_2^{\mathcal{A}}(\lambda)$$

1 : $b \leftarrow\!\!\text{\textdollar} \{0,1\}$	$b \leftarrow\!\!\text{\textdollar} \{0,1\}$
2 : $k \leftarrow\!\!\text{\textdollar} \{0,1\}^{\lambda}$	
3 : $K \leftarrow \text{PRG.Eval}(k)$	$K \leftarrow\!\!\text{\textdollar} \{0,1\}^{\text{PRG.ol}(\lambda)}$
4 : $(m_0, m_1, \text{state}) \leftarrow\!\!\text{\textdollar} \mathcal{A}_1(1^{\lambda})$	$(m_0, m_1, \text{state}) \leftarrow\!\!\text{\textdollar} \mathcal{A}_1(1^{\lambda})$
5 : $\textbf{assert } |m_0| = |m_1| = \text{PRG.ol}(\lambda)$	$\textbf{assert } |m_0| = |m_1| = \text{PRG.ol}(\lambda)$
6 : $c \leftarrow\!\!\text{\textdollar} m_b \oplus K$	$c \leftarrow\!\!\text{\textdollar} m_b \oplus K$
7 : $b' \leftarrow\!\!\text{\textdollar} \mathcal{A}_2(1^{\lambda}, c, \text{state})$	$b' \leftarrow\!\!\text{\textdollar} \mathcal{A}_2(1^{\lambda}, c, \text{state})$
8 : $\textbf{return } (b = b')$	$\textbf{return } (b = b')$

Fig. 5.1: Game hops used in the proof of Proposition 5.4. We consider two games where the first one is the original IND game. In the second game we exchange the enlarged key K by a uniformly random value. Note that in line 5 we assert that the messages as output by the adversary are of the correct length. This is shorthand for: fail in case the assertion check returns false.

It thus remains to show that games Game_1 and Game_2 are negligibly close, that is, that they are computationally indistinguishable. Should this be the case then the first summand in Equation 5.1 is negligible, which translates to the adversary's success probability being at most negligibly better than $\frac{1}{2}$. The statement then follows with the advantage definition of the adversary (Definition 5.2).

$\textbf{Game}_1^{\mathcal{A}}(\lambda)$ **to** $\textbf{Game}_2^{\mathcal{A}}(\lambda)$. We will bound the difference between the two games down to the security of the pseudorandom generator PRG. For this let us fix an arbitrary but efficient IND adversary $\mathcal{A} = (\mathcal{A}_1, \mathcal{A}_2)$. From adversary $\mathcal{A}$ we construct a distinguishing adversary $\mathcal{D}^{\mathcal{A}_1, \mathcal{A}_2}$ against the pseudorandom generator as follows. Distinguisher $\mathcal{D}^{\mathcal{A}_1, \mathcal{A}_2}$ gets as input the security parameter 1^{λ} and a value r which is either a pseudorandom value or a value chosen uniformly at random (cf. Definition 3.26 on page 131). Distinguisher $\mathcal{D}^{\mathcal{A}_1, \mathcal{A}_2}$ calls adversary $\mathcal{A}_1$ on input the security parameter to obtain tuple (m_0, m_1, state). It then flips a bit b, computes $c \leftarrow m_b \oplus r$, to then call adversary $\mathcal{A}_2$ on input $(1^{\lambda}, c, \text{state})$ to retrieve value b'. Finally, distinguisher $\mathcal{D}^{\mathcal{A}_1, \mathcal{A}_2}$ outputs 1 if $b = b'$ and 0 otherwise. Following is a pseudocode description of distinguisher $\mathcal{D}^{\mathcal{A}_1, \mathcal{A}_2}$:

$$\mathcal{D}^{\mathcal{A}_1, \mathcal{A}_2}(1^{\lambda}, r)$$

1 :	$(m_0, m_1, \text{state}) \leftarrow\!\!\text{\textdollar} \mathcal{A}_1(1^{\lambda})$
2 :	$b \leftarrow\!\!\text{\textdollar} \{0,1\}$
3 :	$c \leftarrow m_b \oplus r$
4 :	$b' \leftarrow\!\!\text{\textdollar} \mathcal{A}_2(1^{\lambda}, c, \text{state})$
5 :	$\textbf{return } (b = b')$

In case r was chosen uniformly at random in $\{0,1\}^{\mathsf{PRG.ol}(\lambda)}$ distinguisher $\mathcal{D}^{\mathcal{A}_1,\mathcal{A}_2}(1^\lambda, r)$ perfectly simulates Game_2. If, on the other hand, value r was chosen as a pseudorandom value by applying pseudorandom generator PRG to a uniformly random seed in $\{0,1\}^\lambda$, then the distinguisher perfectly simulates Game_1. We thus have that

$$\mathsf{Adv}^{\mathsf{prg}}_{\mathsf{PRG},\mathcal{D}^{\mathcal{A}_1,\mathcal{A}_2}}(\lambda) = \left| \Pr\left[\mathsf{Game}_1^{\mathcal{A}}(\lambda)\right] - \Pr\left[\mathsf{Game}_2^{\mathcal{A}}(\lambda)\right]\right|.$$

Together with Equation (5.1) it follows that

$$\mathsf{Exp}^{\mathsf{ind}}_{\mathsf{OTP}^{\mathsf{PRG}},\mathcal{A}_1,\mathcal{A}_2}(\lambda) \leq \mathsf{Adv}^{\mathsf{prg}}_{\mathsf{PRG},\mathcal{D}^{\mathcal{A}_1,\mathcal{A}_2}}(\lambda) + \frac{1}{2}. \tag{5.2}$$

All that is left is to plug the above Equation (5.2) into the advantage definition of an IND adversary $\mathcal{A}$ against symmetric encryption scheme $\mathsf{OTP}^{\mathsf{PRG}}$ to obtain the desired result:

$$\begin{aligned}
\mathsf{Adv}^{\mathsf{ind}}_{\mathsf{SE},\mathcal{A}_1,\mathcal{A}_2}(\lambda) &= 2 \cdot \Pr\left[\mathsf{Exp}^{\mathsf{ind}}_{\mathsf{SE},\mathcal{A}_1,\mathcal{A}_2}(\lambda)\right] - 1 \\
&\leq 2 \cdot (\mathsf{Adv}^{\mathsf{prg}}_{\mathsf{PRG},\mathcal{D}^{\mathcal{A}_1,\mathcal{A}_2}}(\lambda) + \frac{1}{2}) - 1 \\
&= 2 \cdot \mathsf{Adv}^{\mathsf{prg}}_{\mathsf{PRG},\mathcal{D}^{\mathcal{A}_1,\mathcal{A}_2}}(\lambda). \qquad \square
\end{aligned}$$

5.1.2 Multiple Encryptions with IND-CPA Security

We have seen that the we can use pseudorandom generators to work around the key length restrictions of the one-time pad. However, being restricted to only encrypting a single message per key is still rather impractical and insufficient for many interesting applications. In order to bypass also this restriction we must, however, first introduce a stronger computational security notion as IND-security considers only a single message that is encrypted and thus does not require that a scheme allows for keys to be used multiple times. In other words, as an adversary in the IND-security game sees only a single encryption it could not exploit a weakness of a scheme that emerges in case multiple messages are encrypted with the same key. The one-time pad as well as the extended one-time pad $\mathsf{OTP}^{\mathsf{PRG}}$ that we have just shown to be IND-secure are good examples as both schemes become insecure once a key is reused. In order to capture attacks that require multiple encryptions we need to adapt the security game to allow an adversary not only to specify two messages (out of which one is encrypted) but multiple messages. This will lead to the so-called IND-CPA security notion which is short for *indistinguishability under chosen-plaintext attack* and which strengthens the IND notion by allowing the adversary to see multiple encryptions.

IND-CPA

Indistinguishability against chosen-plaintext attacks extends the IND security notion by providing the adversary with the means to ask for multiple encryptions. It can thus be regarded as a "multi-instance version" of IND.

There are multiple versions of the IND-CPA security experiment which can be shown to be equivalent up to a polynomial factor in the reduction. In the following we will present two such versions. The first version is *left-or-right IND-CPA* in which the adversary gets an oracle which takes as input two messages and, according to a hidden bit, encrypts either the left or the right message. The second variant we discuss is known as *find-then-guess IND-CPA*. Its definition is closer to that of the IND security notion. Let us discuss the definitions in turn.

Left-or-right IND-CPA. In the left-or-right IND-CPA security experiment for a symmetric encryption scheme SE and an adversary $\mathcal{A}$ the adversary is given access to an oracle LoR (short for left-or-right) that is initialized with a hidden bit b and a randomly chosen encryption key k. Oracle LoR takes as input two messages m_0 and m_1. In case the messages have the same length the oracle creates a fresh encryption of message m_b as

$$c \leftarrow_\$ \mathsf{SE.Enc}(\mathsf{k}, m_b),$$

which it returns. In case the messages are not of the same size the oracle returns $\bot$. To win, the adversary needs to guess the hidden bit b. Following is the formal definition of the left-or-right IND-CPA security for symmetric encryption schemes, which we here simply refer to as IND-CPA:

Definition 5.5 (IND-CPA Security for Symmetric Encryption). *A symmetric encryption scheme* SE $:=$ (SE.KGen, SE.Enc, SE.Dec) *is called* IND-CPA secure *if for all efficient adversaries* $\mathcal{A}$ *advantage* $\mathsf{Adv}^{\text{ind-cpa}}_{\mathsf{SE},\mathcal{A}}(\lambda)$ *is negligible. Here, the advantage is defined as*

$$\mathsf{Adv}^{\text{ind-cpa}}_{\mathsf{SE},\mathcal{A}}(\lambda) := 2 \cdot \Pr\left[\mathit{Exp}^{\text{ind-cpa}}_{\mathsf{SE},\mathcal{A}}(\lambda)\right] - 1,$$

where experiment $\mathit{Exp}^{\text{ind-cpa}}_{\mathsf{SE},\mathcal{A}}(\lambda)$ *is defined as*

Experiment $\mathit{Exp}^{\text{ind-cpa}}_{\mathsf{SE},\mathcal{A}}(\lambda)$	$\mathrm{LoR}(b, \mathsf{k}, m_0, m_1)$
$1:\quad b \leftarrow_\$ \{0,1\}$	$1:\quad$ **if** $\|m_0\| \neq \|m_1\|$ **then**
$2:\quad \mathsf{k} \leftarrow_\$ \mathsf{SE.KGen}(1^\lambda)$	$2:\quad$ **return** $\bot$
$3:\quad b' \leftarrow_\$ \mathcal{A}^{\mathrm{LoR}(b,\mathsf{k},\cdot,\cdot)}(1^\lambda)$	$3:\quad c \leftarrow_\$ \mathsf{SE.Enc}(\mathsf{k}, m_b)$
$4:\quad$ **return** $(b = b')$	$4:\quad$ **return** c

It is not too difficult to see that IND-CPA security is strictly stronger than IND security, as stated by the following proposition:

Proposition 5.6. *Let* SE *be a symmetric encryption scheme. If* SE *is IND-CPA secure then* SE *is also IND secure. Furthermore, there exists an IND-secure symmetric encryption scheme that is not IND-CPA secure.*

Note that the latter claim is without any assumption as the one-time pad is IND secure (but not IND-CPA secure). We leave a formal proof and separation as Exercise 5.4.

Find-then-guess IND-CPA. The find-then-guess IND-CPA definition is closer to the IND security notion where the adversary is split into two phases $\mathcal{A} = (\mathcal{A}_1, \mathcal{A}_2)$. The difference from the IND notion is that in this formalization of IND-CPA the adversary additionally gets access to an additional encryption oracle which it can use to encrypt arbitrary messages (including challenge messages m_0 and m_1):

Definition 5.7 (Find-Then-Guess IND-CPA for Symmetric Encryption). *A symmetric encryption scheme* SE $:=$ (SE.KGen, SE.Enc, SE.Dec) *is called FTG-IND-CPA secure if for all efficient adversaries* $\mathcal{A} = (\mathcal{A}_1, \mathcal{A}_2)$ *advantage* $\mathsf{Adv}^{\text{ftg-ind-cpa}}_{\text{SE},\mathcal{A}_1,\mathcal{A}_2}(\lambda)$ *is negligible. Here, the advantage is defined as*

$$\mathsf{Adv}^{\text{ftg-ind-cpa}}_{\text{SE},\mathcal{A}_1,\mathcal{A}_2}(\lambda) := 2 \cdot \Pr\left[\mathsf{Exp}^{\text{ftg-ind-cpa}}_{\text{SE},\mathcal{A}_1,\mathcal{A}_2}(\lambda)\right] - 1,$$

where experiment $\mathsf{Exp}^{\text{ftg-ind-cpa}}_{\text{SE},\mathcal{A}_1,\mathcal{A}_2}(\lambda)$ *is defined as*

Experiment $\mathsf{Exp}^{\text{ftg-ind-cpa}}_{\text{SE},\mathcal{A}_1,\mathcal{A}_2}(\lambda)$	$\mathsf{Enc}(k, m)$
1: $b \leftarrow\!\!\text{\$} \{0,1\}$	1: $c \leftarrow\!\!\text{\$} \text{SE.Enc}(k, m)$
2: $k \leftarrow\!\!\text{\$} \text{SE.KGen}(1^\lambda)$	2: **return** c
3: $(m_0, m_1, \text{state}) \leftarrow\!\!\text{\$} \mathcal{A}_1^{\text{Enc}(k,\cdot)}(1^\lambda)$	
4: **if** $|m_0| \neq |m_1|$ **then return** false	
5: $c \leftarrow\!\!\text{\$} \text{SE.Enc}(k, m_b)$	
6: $b' \leftarrow\!\!\text{\$} \mathcal{A}_2^{\text{Enc}(k,\cdot)}(1^\lambda, c, \text{state})$	
7: **return** $(b = b')$	

It can be shown that the two notions of IND-CPA and FTG-IND-CPA are identical up to a polynomial factor in the reduction, as shown in the following proposition:

Proposition 5.8. *Let* SE $:-$ (SE.KGen, SE.Enc, SE.Dec) *be a symmetric encryption scheme. Scheme* SE *is IND-CPA secure if, and only if,* SE *is also FTG-IND-CPA secure.*

More concretely, we have that for every efficient adversary $\mathcal{B}$ *against the FTG-IND-CPA security of* SE *there exists an efficient adversary* $\mathcal{A}$

such that

$$\mathsf{Adv}^{\text{ftg-ind-cpa}}_{\mathsf{SE},\mathcal{B}_1,\mathcal{B}_2}(\lambda) = \mathsf{Adv}^{\text{ind-cpa}}_{\mathsf{SE},\mathcal{A}}(\lambda).$$

Furthermore, for every efficient adversary $\mathcal{B}$ against the IND-CPA security that makes at most $\mathsf{q}(\lambda)$ calls to its LoR oracle, there exists an efficient adversary $\mathcal{A}$ such that

$$\mathsf{Adv}^{\text{ind-cpa}}_{\mathsf{SE},\mathcal{B}}(\lambda) \le \mathsf{q}(\lambda) \cdot \mathsf{Adv}^{\text{ftg-ind-cpa}}_{\mathsf{SE},\mathcal{A}_1,\mathcal{A}_2}(\lambda).$$

We leave the formal proof of Proposition 5.8 as Exercise 5.5 and here discuss only the intuition: When showing that any scheme SE that is IND-CPA secure is also FTG-IND-CPA secure we provide a reduction that uses the LoR oracle to simulate the (simpler) Enc oracle. This can be easily achieved by calling the LoR oracle with the same message as left and right message. That is, we construct from an adversary $\mathcal{B}$ against the find-then-guess IND-CPA notion an adversary $\mathcal{A}$ against the (left-or-right) IND-CPA notion as follows. Adversary $\mathcal{B}$ runs the first stage $\mathcal{A}_1$ simulating the Enc oracle with its LoR oracle as described above. When the "find phase" finishes, $\mathcal{A}_1$ outputs two messages (m_0, m_1) and some state. Adversary $\mathcal{B}$ can obtain the challenge ciphertext by calling its LoR oracle on the message pair (m_0, m_1), and it remains to finish the simulation by running $\mathcal{A}_2$.

The other direction is the more tricky one. Here, if we wanted to give a reduction we would start with an adversary $\mathcal{B}$ against the left-or-right IND-CPA security and from $\mathcal{B}$ construct an adversary $\mathcal{A}$ against the find-then-guess flavor. The challenge is that $\mathcal{B}$ consists only of a single stage, but our reduction (adversary $\mathcal{A}$) consists of two stages that jointly need to make use of adversary $\mathcal{B}$. The idea is now to use a hybrid argument. Assuming that the adversary makes at most $\mathsf{q}(\lambda)$ queries to its oracle we can simulate the LoR oracle as follows. In the ith hybrid we consider an adversary $\mathcal{A}^i$ that during its "find" stage answers the first i queries by encrypting the left message with its Enc oracle. Instead of answering the $(i+1)$st query it outputs it as its challenge. The second stage $\mathcal{A}_2^i$ receives as input an encryption c which it uses to answer $\mathcal{B}$'s earlier query. Any additional query it answers by encrypting the right message with its Enc oracle. We thus have that $\mathcal{A}^0$ when hidden bit $b = 1$ perfectly simulates the left-or-right IND-CPA game by always encrypting the right message and $\mathcal{A}^{\mathsf{q}}$ when hidden bit $b = 0$ always encrypts the left message. The proof can then be finalized with an application of the hybrid argument (Theorem 3.17).

5.1.3 IND-CPA Symmetric Encryption from PRFs

In the following we want to construct an IND-CPA-secure symmetric encryption scheme from the primitives that we have already introduced. As we will see, we already have all the necessary ingredients.

Theorem 5.9. *If one-way functions exist, then there exists a symmetric encryption scheme* SE *that is IND-CPA secure.*

An important observation when attempting to construct an IND-CPA-secure encryption scheme is that the resulting scheme must necessarily be probabilistic. To see this, consider an adversary that chooses three distinct messages m_1, m_2, m_3 and queries its LoR oracle on (m_1, m_2) and then on (m_1, m_3). Now, in case the encryption operation is deterministic and hidden bit $b = 0$ then the adversary will receive an identical ciphertext on both queries as result. On the other hand, in case the hidden bit $b = 1$ then it will receive different ciphertexts as in this case messages m_2 and m_3 get encrypted. This, of course, allows the adversary to determine the bit b easily.

The underlying idea for our construction will thus be to define a "randomized" version of the one-time pad encryption scheme. Recall that a one-time pad encrypts a message m by choosing a random key k of length $|\mathsf{k}| = |m|$ to then use the key as a bitwise mask:

$$c = m \oplus \mathsf{k}.$$

In our scheme we will use key k not directly as the *mask* but instead use it to generate a pseudorandom string that we will use instead for the encryption operation. The cryptographic primitive that perfectly lends itself to this setting is a pseudorandom function. The construction is as follows:

Construction 5.10. *Let* PRF *be a pseudorandom function. We construct a symmetric encryption scheme* SE *that encrypts messages of a fixed length* $\mathsf{SE.il}(\lambda) = \mathsf{PRF.ol}(\lambda)$ *as follows:*

$\mathsf{SE.KGen}(1^\lambda)$	$\mathsf{SE.Enc}(\mathsf{k}, m)$	$\mathsf{SE.Dec}(\mathsf{k}, (c, r))$
$1: \quad \mathsf{k} \leftarrow\!\!\$\ \mathsf{PRF.KGen}(1^\lambda)$	$1: \quad r \leftarrow\!\!\$\ \{0,1\}^{\mathsf{PRF.il}(\lambda)}$	$1: \quad \tau \leftarrow \mathsf{PRF}(\mathsf{k}, r)$
$2: \quad \textbf{return } \mathsf{k}$	$2: \quad \tau \leftarrow \mathsf{PRF}(\mathsf{k}, r)$	$2: \quad m \leftarrow c \oplus \tau$
	$3: \quad c \leftarrow m \oplus \tau$	$3: \quad \textbf{return } m$
	$4: \quad \textbf{return } (c, r)$	

The key generation of the encryption scheme is simply the key generation of the pseudorandom function. For encryption of a message m we use the exclusive-or operation to mask the plaintext as in the one-time pad. However, the mask itself is computed as $\tau \leftarrow \mathsf{PRF}(\mathsf{k}, r)$ for a random value r, and the ciphertext is then set to include this random value r. That is, the ciphertext is set to (c, r) where $c \leftarrow \tau \oplus m$. For decryption, mask τ is recomputed from value r, which then allows to recover message m from c. In the following we want to show that this simple scheme achieves IND-CPA security.

Proposition 5.11. *Let* PRF *be a secure pseudorandom function and let* SE *be the encryption scheme defined in Construction 5.10. If* PRF.il$(\lambda) \in \omega(\log(\lambda))$, *that is, the input length of the pseudorandom function grows super-logarithmically in the security parameter, then the encryption scheme* SE *is IND-CPA secure.*

Remark 5.12. To prove our construction secure, we require that the input length to the chosen pseudorandom function grows with the security parameter. As this is not necessary for pseudorandom functions in general we need to add it to the list of requirements in the proposition. However, note that Proposition 5.11 still immediately implies Theorem 5.9 since one-way functions imply the existence of such pseudorandom functions.

We will prove the statement by applying the game-hopping technique (see Section 3.2.1; page 106). For this, we will start with the original IND-CPA security experiment and gradually transform it into a setting where we can show that the adversary has no advantage down to the security of a one-time pad encryption. The pseudocode for the individual games is given in Figure 5.2 (page 233). In order to complete the proof we must first, however, come back to the game-playing technique and discuss an important result that we will use in our proof of Proposition 5.11: the so-called *Fundamental Lemma of Game Playing.*

5.1.4 The Fundamental Lemma of Game Playing

For showing that the first two games in the proof of Proposition 5.11 are negligibly close we will deploy an argument that is so common that it was termed the *Fundamental Lemma of Game Playing*. It can be applied when two games describe almost identical probabilistic programs, that is, they can be described by an identical pseudocode description which differs only on a single **if**-branch. The following two programs are an example of games that are almost identical except for an **if**-branch:

	Game$_1(\lambda)$	Game$_2(\lambda)$
1 :	Stmt A	Stmt A
2 :	Stmt B	Stmt B
3 :	Stmt C	Stmt C
4 :		**if** someEvent **do**
5 :		Stmt X
6 :	Stmt D	Stmt D

Here the two games are identical except for lines 4 and 5. However, line 4 contains an **if**-branch which by itself does not do any computation but only contains branching logic. Thus, the only difference between the computational flow is whatever happens in line 5 and this computation is only triggered in the event that the condition in the **if**-branch in line 4 evaluates to true, that is, only in the case someEvent occurs. The Fundamental Lemma of Game Playing allows us to quantify the difference between the two games by showing that the difference between the two games is upper bounded by the probability that the condition stated in the **if**-branch evaluates to true. To jump ahead, we will often make simple syntactical changes that introduce events to facilitate a game-hopping proof. If such an event is introduced in an **if**-branch that only has negligible probability of being traversed, the Fundamental Lemma of Game Playing tells us that the introduced change has only negligible impact on the outcome of the game. We will see an example of the technique shortly, when we prove Proposition 5.11.

In order to formally capture the requirements for the Fundamental Lemma of Game Playing let us introduce some terminology. An **if**-*branch* consists of a *Boolean expression* and a *block of statements* where a Boolean expression is a side-effect free expression[2] that evaluates to either true or false, and a block of statements consists of a fixed number of arbitrary statements possibly with side-effects. An **if**-branch is evaluated by first evaluating the Boolean expression of the branch. If it evaluates to true, then the statements in the if block are evaluated in their natural order. Otherwise the program evaluation continues with the evaluation of the first statement following the **if**-branch. With these simple forms of **if**-branches—our **if**-branches as defined here do not contain any additional **else**- or **elseif**-branches—we can now formalize the Fundamental Lemma of Game Playing.

> **Lemma 5.13** (The Fundamental Lemma of Game Playing). *Let* Game$_1$ *and* Game$_2$ *be two (probabilistic) security games that are identical except for a single* **if**-*branch that is present in* Game$_2$ *but not in* Game$_1$. *Let* E *denote the event that the corresponding Boolean expression of the* **if**-*branch evaluates to* true. *Then for all* $\lambda \in \mathbb{N}$ *and all* $y \in \{0,1\}^*$ *it holds that*
>
> $$|\Pr[\mathsf{Game}_1(\lambda) = y] - \Pr[\mathsf{Game}_2(\lambda) = y]| \leq \Pr[\mathsf{E}].$$
>
> *Furthermore, it holds that*
>
> $$\Pr[\mathsf{Game}_1(\lambda) = y] \leq \Pr[\mathsf{Game}_2(\lambda) = y \mid \overline{\mathsf{E}}] + \Pr[\mathsf{E}].$$

Before we prove the Fundamental Lemma of Game Playing, first note that we stated the lemma for games with arbitrary output values $y \subset \{0,1\}^*$ although we usually consider only binary games (i.e., games that return either 0 or 1; or true or false). A second thing to note is that the Fundamental

---

[2] An expression is side-effect free if it does not change the state of the program nor perform any kind of action like assignments to variables.

Lemma of Game Playing talks about *games* and not general programs. The difference being that games take only the security parameter as input but no additional inputs.[3]

Proof. We will prove the Fundamental Lemma of Game Playing using a counting argument. For this, fix a security parameter $\lambda \in \mathbb{N}$ and let $r|$ denote a common upper bound on the number of random coins used by both $\mathsf{Game}_1(\lambda)$ and by $\mathsf{Game}_2(\lambda)$. As security games do not take any input beside the security parameter it follows that we can split the set of all possible random coins $\{0,1\}^{r|}$ into two sets r_{true} denoting those in which the **if**-expression in Game_2 evaluates to true and r_{false} those in which the **if**-expression evaluates to false.

Recall that we can write $\mathsf{Game}_2(\lambda; r)$ to denote the (now deterministic) evaluation of Game_2 on input λ and with random coins r. In case the **if**-expression evaluates to false both games are identical by definition, because the evaluation of the if-condition is side-effect free. We thus have that for all y:

$$\Pr[\mathsf{Game}_1(\lambda; r) = y \mid r \in r_{\mathsf{false}}] = \Pr[\mathsf{Game}_2(\lambda; r) = y \mid r \in r_{\mathsf{false}}]. \quad (5.3)$$

It follows that for all y and all λ we can rewrite the probability that $\mathsf{Game}_1(\lambda) = y$ as

$$\Pr[\mathsf{Game}_1(\lambda) = y]$$
$$= \Pr[\mathsf{Game}_1(\lambda; r) = y \mid r \in r_{\mathsf{false}}] \cdot \Pr[r \in r_{\mathsf{false}}]$$
$$+ \Pr[\mathsf{Game}_1(\lambda; r) = y \mid r \in r_{\mathsf{true}}] \cdot \Pr[r \in r_{\mathsf{true}}]$$
$$\leq \Pr[\mathsf{Game}_1(\lambda; r) = y \mid r \in r_{\mathsf{false}}] \cdot \Pr[r \in r_{\mathsf{false}}] + \Pr[r \in r_{\mathsf{true}}].$$

Here the first equality is an application of the law of total probability (see page 45), and the following inequality is due to the fact that probability $\Pr[\mathsf{Game}_1(\lambda; r) = y \mid r \in r_{\mathsf{true}}]$ is at most 1. With Equation (5.3) we can next make the switch to Game_2:

$$= \Pr[\mathsf{Game}_2(\lambda; r) = y \mid r \in r_{\mathsf{false}}] \cdot \Pr[r \in r_{\mathsf{false}}] + \Pr[r \in r_{\mathsf{true}}]. \quad (5.4)$$

From this point on we can give two bounds. On the one hand, with the product rule for conditional probabilities ($\Pr[X \wedge Y] = \Pr[X \mid Y] \cdot \Pr[Y]$) and by noting that $\Pr[\mathsf{E}] = \Pr[r \in r_{\mathsf{true}}]$ we can give an upper bound as

$$= \Pr[\mathsf{Game}_2(\lambda; r) = y \wedge r \in r_{\mathsf{false}}] + \Pr[r \in r_{\mathsf{true}}]$$
$$\leq \Pr[\mathsf{Game}_2(\lambda; r) = y] + \Pr[r \in r_{\mathsf{true}}]$$
$$= \Pr[\mathsf{Game}_2(\lambda; r) = y] + \Pr[\mathsf{E}].$$

---

[3] While the lemma can be further generalized, using arbitrary programs makes the presentation more complicated as the additional inputs need to be dealt with. Furthermore, the additional generality is not needed for the game-hopping technique as there we are dealing with standard security games that are parameterized only by the security parameter.

This yields the first bound of Lemma 5.13 (we argue below why we can rewrite the bound as given in the lemma). And, once more starting from Equation (5.4) we can also derive the second bound as

$$\Pr[\mathsf{Game}_1(\lambda) = y]$$
$$\leq \Pr[\mathsf{Game}_2(\lambda; r) = y \mid r \in r_{\mathsf{false}}] \cdot \Pr[r \in r_{\mathsf{false}}] + \Pr[r \in r_{\mathsf{true}}]$$
$$\leq \Pr[\mathsf{Game}_2(\lambda; r) = y \mid r \in r_{\mathsf{false}}] + \Pr[r \in r_{\mathsf{true}}]$$
$$= \Pr[\mathsf{Game}_2(\lambda; r) = y \mid \overline{\mathsf{E}}] + \Pr[\mathsf{E}].$$

It remains to show that the the first bound can be rewritten as

$$|\Pr[\mathsf{Game}_1(\lambda) = y] - \Pr[\mathsf{Game}_2(\lambda; r) = y]| \leq \Pr[\mathsf{E}].$$

For this note that event E occurs with the same probability in both Game_1 and Game_2: any random coins that trigger event E in Game_2 will trigger event E in Game_1.[4] But then the derivation of the bound is symmetrical in the sense that we could start also from Game_2 to arrive at

$$\Pr[\mathsf{Game}_2(\lambda) = y] \leq \Pr[\mathsf{Game}_1(\lambda; r) = y] + \Pr[\mathsf{E}].$$

The statement follows by noting that $a \leq b + c$ and $b \leq a + c$ implies $|a - b| \leq c$. This concludes the proof.   □

Handled Events in Game-Hopping Proofs

Game-hopping proofs usually consist of more than one game hop. A nice consequence of the Fundamental Lemma of Game Playing is how we can deal with events that have been handled in an earlier game hop. Consider the following setup:

	$\mathsf{Game}_1(\lambda)$	$\mathsf{Game}_2(\lambda)$	$\mathsf{Game}_3(\lambda)$
1 :	Stmt A	Stmt A	Stmt A
2 :	Stmt B	Stmt B	Stmt B
3 :	Stmt C	Stmt C	Stmt C
4 :		**if** someEvent **do**	**if** someEvent **do**
5 :		Stmt X	Stmt X
6 :	Stmt D	Stmt D	Modified Stmt D

Here, we have added an extra game after the introduction of someEvent where we have modified the last statement. In game-hopping proofs we usually

---

[4] Note that, formally, the probability of E refers to the event that the **if**-expression evaluates to true in Game_2. We could, of course, copy the **if**-statement into Game_1 and add a no-operation code if the expression evaluates to true. We can thus regard the probability of E also with respect to Game_1.

analyze the difference between each two neighboring games (in this case games Game_1 and Game_2, as well as games Game_2 and Game_3) in addition to the last game, in this case Game_3. The Fundamental Lemma of Game Playing tells us that

$$\Pr[\mathsf{Game}_1(\lambda)] \leq \Pr[\mathsf{Game}_2(\lambda)] + \Pr[\mathsf{someEvent}]$$

but it also tells us that

$$\Pr[\mathsf{Game}_1(\lambda)] \leq \Pr\left[\mathsf{Game}_2(\lambda) \mid \overline{\mathsf{someEvent}}\right] + \Pr[\mathsf{someEvent}].$$

An important observation is that from the point onwards that we have dealt with $\mathsf{someEvent}$ we can assume that it does not occur. This is because in our analysis we have already accounted for the possibility of it occurring as part of the distinguishing advantage when moving from Game_1 to Game_2. In particular, this means that when we analyze the distance between games Game_2 and Game_3 we only need to analyze the distance on random coins that do not make $\mathsf{someEvent}$ true.

We will often call such events *bad*. For example, we may have a game hop that analyzes the probability of a collision occurring between certain values. Once we have encountered this *bad event*, e.g., collisions occurring, we can henceforth assume that the event does not occur, i.e., that there are no collisions. Of course, there is a condition as to when we can assume this: we need to ensure that in all subsequent games the probability of the bad event either stays the same or decreases. If it increases then all bets are off. However, if it is as in the above example where subsequent changes are only made to code *after* the event or in case you can otherwise prove that introduced changes do not affect the probability of the handled event you can, as described above, henceforth assume that the event does not occur.

Let us give one more example, as this is an important observation which is often used but only rarely spelled out. With the game-playing technique we aim at bounding the probability of some Game_1 by transforming it into a game that is easy to analyze and showing that each transformation changes the success probability at most by a negligible distance. That is, we transform Game_1 into Game_n and analyze each individual step as well as Game_n to obtain the following bound:

$$\Pr[\mathsf{Game}_1(\lambda)] \leq \sum_{i=1}^{n-1} |\Pr[\mathsf{Game}_{i+1}(\lambda)] - \Pr[\mathsf{Game}_i(\lambda)]| + \Pr[\mathsf{Game}_n(\lambda)].$$

If we now introduce an event $\mathsf{badEvent}$ in Game_j then we can use the Fundamental Lemma of Game Playing to argue that

$$\Pr[\mathsf{Game}_{j-1}(\lambda)] \leq \Pr\left[\mathsf{Game}_j(\lambda) \mid \overline{\mathsf{badEvent}}\right] + \Pr[\mathsf{badEvent}].$$

But then we can rewrite the above bound as

$$\Pr[\mathsf{Game}_1(\lambda)]$$

$$\leq \sum_{i=1}^{j-2} |\Pr[\mathsf{Game}_{i+1}(\lambda)] - \Pr[\mathsf{Game}_i(\lambda)]| + \Pr[\mathsf{Game}_{j-1}],$$

where by now we have moved up to Game_{j-1}. Introducing the badEvent this can be rewritten as

$$\leq \sum_{i=1}^{j-2} |\Pr[\mathsf{Game}_{i+1}(\lambda)] - \Pr[\mathsf{Game}_i(\lambda)]|$$

$$+ \Pr[\mathsf{Game}_j(\lambda) \mid \overline{\mathsf{badEvent}}] + \Pr[\mathsf{badEvent}].$$

And from here on onwards, we can now continue adapting Game_j but now assuming that event badEvent does not occur. This yields

$$\leq \sum_{i=1}^{j-2} |\Pr[\mathsf{Game}_{i+1}(\lambda)] - \Pr[\mathsf{Game}_i(\lambda)]| +$$

$$+ \sum_{i=j}^{n-1} |\Pr[\mathsf{Game}_{i+1}(\lambda) \mid \overline{\mathsf{badEvent}}] - \Pr[\mathsf{Game}_i(\lambda) \mid \overline{\mathsf{badEvent}}]|$$

$$+ \Pr[\mathsf{Game}_n(\lambda) \mid \overline{\mathsf{badEvent}}] + \Pr[\mathsf{badEvent}]$$

$$= \Pr[\mathsf{Game}_n(\lambda) \mid \overline{\mathsf{badEvent}}] + \Pr[\mathsf{badEvent}] + \sum_{i=1}^{j-2} \epsilon_i(\lambda) + \sum_{i=j}^{n-1} \epsilon_i(\lambda).$$

Here the $\epsilon_i(\lambda)$ in the last step denotes the compensation probability (aka the loss) introduced when moving from Game_i to Game_{i+1}. Note that the loss incurred on the $(j-1)$st game hop is exactly $\Pr[\mathsf{badEvent}]$ such that when we set $\epsilon_{j-1}(\lambda) := \Pr[\mathsf{badEvent}]$—note that the probability of badEvent depends on the security parameter—we can simplify the above as

$$\Pr[\mathsf{Game}_1(\lambda)] \leq \Pr[\mathsf{Game}_n(\lambda) \mid \overline{\mathsf{badEvent}}] + \sum_{i=1}^{n-1} \epsilon_i(\lambda).$$

To summarize, once we have dealt with the introduction of the bad event we can simply condition all further game hops on $\overline{\mathsf{badEvent}}$ and assume for the analysis that the bad event is not happening.

Customary shorthand notation. In the cryptographic literature, bad events in game-hopping proofs are usually not explicitly stated in subsequent games but it is implicitly assumed that once an event has been dealt with that all subsequent games are conditioned on that event not occurring. Thus it is common to write

$$\Pr[\mathsf{Game}_i] \leq \Pr[\mathsf{someEvent}] + \Pr[\mathsf{Game}_{i+1}]$$

instead of (the more correct)

$$\Pr[\mathsf{Game}_i] \leq \Pr[\mathsf{someEvent}] + \Pr[\mathsf{Game}_{i+1} \mid \overline{\mathsf{someEvent}}]$$

even though it may be assumed that someEvent does not occur from Game_{i+1} onwards. In the following we will adhere to this practice and not explicitly condition on "bad" events throughout game-hopping proofs but may implicitly assume that this is the case. It should, however, always be clear from the description if an event is assumed not to occur in a later game hop.

Visualization of handled events. In order to highlight the fact that certain events have already been handled in earlier games we set the corresponding if-branches in light-gray color as in the following example:

$\mathsf{Game}_1(\lambda)$	$\mathsf{Game}_2(\lambda)$	$\mathsf{Game}_3(\lambda)$
1 : Stmt A	Stmt A	Stmt A
2 : Stmt B	Stmt B	Stmt B
3 : Stmt C	Stmt C	Stmt C
4 :	if someEvent do	if someEvent do
5 :	Stmt X	Stmt X
6 : Stmt D	Stmt D	Modified Stmt D

5.1.5 Showing IND-CPA Security

We now have the necessary ingredients to prove Proposition 5.11 and show that our simple construction (Construction 5.10; page 222) of an encryption scheme from a pseudorandom function achieves IND-CPA security.

Proof of Proposition 5.11. We will show the proposition by applying the game-hopping technique. The individual game hops are defined in Figure 5.2 (page 233), and a textual description of each of the games is following shortly. First, let us discuss the overall idea behind the proof. Our goal is to show that the encryption scheme is IND-CPA secure. The scheme itself is closely related to the one-time pad, the difference being that instead of using a truly random value as in the one-time pad we use a pseudorandom value to mask the plaintext. The underlying idea for the security proof is now to gradually transform the original IND-CPA security game with our construction into one where we replaced the construction with the one-time pad. Once there, the security claim is easy to prove, as we already know that the one-time pad is secure. The challenge is thus to show that the individual steps up to the final game only provide negligible gain to the adversary. For this we will need only two hops:

$\mathsf{Game}_1^{\mathcal{A}}(\lambda)$:   The first game is equivalent to the IND-CPA security experiment for the encryption scheme SE. The pseudocode in the LoR procedure in Figure 5.2 contains the inlined encryption operation where a random value r is generated to be then used as input to the pseudorandom function to generate mask τ, which is finally used to encrypt message m_b. It follows that

$$\Pr\Big[\mathsf{Game}_1^{\mathcal{A}}(\lambda)\Big] = \Pr\Big[\mathsf{Exp}_{\mathsf{SE},\mathcal{A}}^{\mathsf{ind\text{-}cpa}}(\lambda)\Big].$$

$\mathsf{Game}_2^{\mathcal{A}}(\lambda)$:   In Game_2 we introduce a *bad event* which, if triggered, causes the game to abort. By convention aborting a game is counted as a win for the adversary. The difference between Game_1 and Game_2 is that in Game_2 we keep track of the random values r that are generated for encryptions. In line 3 in the LoR procedure a random r is generated which is then used as the input to the pseudorandom function. In Game_2 we keep a table T of all r-values which is updated in line 5. The introduction of table T does not yet change the outcome of the game in any way. However, in line 4 we test whether a randomly chosen value r has already occurred in a previous encryption operation. If so, we abort the game.

The difference between games Game_1 and Game_2 can be upper bounded by the Fundamental Lemma of Game Playing and thus by the probability of a value r being sampled twice within one execution of Game_2. By the requirement for the input length of pseudorandom function PRF we have that $\mathsf{PRF.il}(\lambda)$ grows super-logarithmically in the security parameter. It follows that a collision of a value r occurs only with negligible probability. To make this claim formal, let $\mathsf{q} := \mathsf{q}(\lambda)$ denote a (polynomial) upper bound on the number of LoR queries of (efficient) adversary $\mathcal{A}$. As we have seen in earlier proofs, the probability that a collision occurs when choosing q random values in $\{0,1\}^{\mathsf{PRF.il}(\lambda)}$ can be upper bounded as

$$\Pr[\mathsf{collision}] = \binom{\mathsf{q}(\lambda)}{2} \cdot \frac{1}{2^{\mathsf{PRF.il}(\lambda)}} = \frac{\mathsf{q}(\lambda)\cdot(\mathsf{q}(\lambda)-1)}{2}\cdot\frac{1}{2^{\mathsf{PRF.il}(\lambda)}} \leq \frac{\mathsf{q}(\lambda)^2}{2^{\mathsf{PRF.il}(\lambda)-1}}.$$

With the Fundamental Lemma of Game Playing we can thus upper bound the distance between games Game_1 and Game_2 as

$$\left|\Pr\Big[\mathsf{Game}_2^{\mathcal{A}}(\lambda)\Big] - \Pr\Big[\mathsf{Game}_1^{\mathcal{A}}(\lambda)\Big]\right| \leq \Pr[\mathsf{collision}]$$

$$\leq \frac{\mathsf{q}(\lambda)^2}{2^{\mathsf{PRF.il}(\lambda)-1}}.$$

Note that we technically consider the bound

$$\left|\Pr\Big[\mathsf{Game}_2^{\mathcal{A}}(\lambda)\ \big|\ \overline{\mathsf{collision}}\Big] - \Pr\Big[\mathsf{Game}_1^{\mathcal{A}}(\lambda)\Big]\right| \leq \frac{\mathsf{q}(\lambda)^2}{2^{\mathsf{PRF.il}(\lambda)-1}}$$

r-collision

and from now on condition on event collision not occurring. For simpler and more compact notation we omit the conditional probability and simply write $\Pr[\mathsf{Game}_i]$ instead of $\Pr[\mathsf{Game}_i \mid \overline{\mathsf{collision}}]$ for $i \geq 2$. This complies with the notation usually found in the cryptographic literature.

$\mathsf{Game}_3^{\mathcal{A}}(\lambda)$: For our final game we make one slight change in line 6 of the LoR oracle which effectively changes our encryption scheme into a one-time pad. Namely, instead of generating mask τ via a call to pseudorandom function PRF we instead sample τ uniformly at random from $\{0,1\}^{\mathsf{PRF.ol}(\lambda)}$.

In order to continue the game-hopping proof, we need to argue that

$$\left| \Pr\left[\mathsf{Game}_3^{\mathcal{A}}(\lambda)\right] - \Pr\left[\mathsf{Game}_2^{\mathcal{A}}(\lambda)\right] \right|$$

is negligible. For this, we will give a reduction-based argument which at its core uses the security of the pseudorandom function. Note that the difference between games Game_2 and Game_3 is exactly whether or not value τ is generated as a pseudorandom value or as a truly random value. As it turns out, this is exactly the setting in the security definition of pseudorandom functions (see Definition 3.22 on page 126) where a distinguisher must distinguish between an oracle that generates random values or pseudorandom values.

Let $\mathcal{A}$ be an adversary. We will construct a distinguisher $\mathcal{D}$ against the pseudorandom function PRF which internally uses adversary $\mathcal{A}$ as follows. As specified in Definition 3.22 distinguisher $\mathcal{D}$ gets access to an oracle RoR which either evaluates the pseudorandom function PRF using a randomly chosen key, or it chooses uniformly random values to answer oracle queries. Distinguisher $\mathcal{D}$ now does the following: it flips a coin to generate bit $b \leftarrow_\$ \{0,1\}$ to then call adversary $\mathcal{A}$ on security parameter 1^λ. To answer a query (m_0, m_1) of $\mathcal{A}$ to its LoR oracle, distinguisher $\mathcal{D}$ simulates the LoR oracle of Game_2 except that it generates τ as $\tau \leftarrow \mathrm{RoR}(r)$. In other words, it follows the program below to answer LoR queries:

$\underline{\mathrm{LoR}(m_0, m_1)}$ // as simulated by $\mathcal{D}$ for $\mathcal{A}$

1 : **if** $|m_0| \neq |m_1|$ **then**
2 :   **return** $\perp$
3 : $r \leftarrow_\$ \{0,1\}^{\mathsf{PRF.il}(\lambda)}$
4 : $\tau \leftarrow \mathrm{RoR}(r)$
5 : $c \leftarrow m_b \oplus \tau$
6 :   **return** (c, r)

Note that we have already accounted for the possibility of collisions of r values in the previous game hop and we can thus here assume that collisions do not occur (we implicitly condition on event collision not occurring; also see the discussion after Lemma 5.13).

Finally, when $\mathcal{A}$ outputs a guess b', distinguisher $\mathcal{D}$ stops and outputs $b = b'$. Now, in case the RoR oracle computes pseudorandom function PRF, distinguisher $\mathcal{D}$ perfectly simulates $\mathsf{Game}_2^{\mathcal{A}}$. If, on the other hand, oracle RoR returns uniformly random values then it perfectly simulates $\mathsf{Game}_3^{\mathcal{A}}$.

Remark 5.14. It is for the latter claim that we require that no collisions occur on r values. For this recall that a pseudorandom function is deterministic and thus on the same input will produce the same output. In the PRF definition (Definition 3.22 on page 126) we deal with this by keeping a table of the inputs and chosen outputs in order to choose the same output on the same input. In $\mathsf{Game}_3^{\mathcal{A}}$, however, we always choose a fresh value τ uniformly at random regardless of the choice of r. Thus, in case of an r-collision we would most likely choose a different τ in $\mathsf{Game}_3^{\mathcal{A}}$ while the simulation by $\mathcal{D}$ would not, as its oracle RoR would always choose the same τ for the same r.

We can now upper bound the distance between games $\mathsf{Game}_2^{\mathcal{A}}$ and $\mathsf{Game}_3^{\mathcal{A}}$ which, by the above argument, is exactly the PRF-advantage of $\mathcal{D}$ against pseudorandom function PRF:

$$\left| \Pr\left[\mathsf{Game}_3^{\mathcal{A}}(\lambda) \right] - \Pr\left[\mathsf{Game}_2^{\mathcal{A}}(\lambda) \right] \right| = \mathsf{Adv}_{\mathsf{PRF},\mathcal{D}}^{\mathrm{prf}}(\lambda).$$

To see this, call the hidden bit in Definition 3.22 here d and note that

$$\Pr\left[\mathsf{Game}_2^{\mathcal{A}}(\lambda) \right] = \Pr\left[\mathsf{Exp}_{\mathsf{PRF},\mathcal{D}}^{\mathrm{prf}}(\lambda) \,\middle|\, d = 0 \right]$$

and

$$\Pr\left[\mathsf{Game}_3^{\mathcal{A}}(\lambda) \right] = \Pr\left[\mathsf{Exp}_{\mathsf{PRF},\mathcal{D}}^{\mathrm{prf}}(\lambda) \,\middle|\, d = 1 \right].$$

As by assumption pseudorandom function PRF is secure we thus have that the difference between games $\mathsf{Game}_2^{\mathcal{A}}$ and $\mathsf{Game}_3^{\mathcal{A}}$ must be negligible.

From the game-hopping proof technique we know that we can upper bound the success probability of an adversary $\mathcal{A}$ in $\mathsf{Game}_1^{\mathcal{A}}$ by

$$\Pr\left[\mathsf{Game}_1^{\mathcal{A}}(\lambda) \right] = \left| \Pr\left[\mathsf{Game}_2^{\mathcal{A}}(\lambda) \right] - \Pr\left[\mathsf{Game}_1^{\mathcal{A}}(\lambda) \right] \right|$$
$$+ \left| \Pr\left[\mathsf{Game}_3^{\mathcal{A}}(\lambda) \right] - \Pr\left[\mathsf{Game}_2^{\mathcal{A}}(\lambda) \right] \right|$$
$$+ \Pr\left[\mathsf{Game}_3^{\mathcal{A}}(\lambda) = 1 \right],$$

which according to our previous analysis is upper bounded by

$$\leq \frac{q(\lambda)^2}{2^{\mathsf{PRF.il}(\lambda)-1}} + \mathsf{Adv}_{\mathsf{PRF},\mathcal{D}}^{\mathrm{prf}}(\lambda) + \Pr\left[\mathsf{Game}_3^{\mathcal{A}}(\lambda) = 1 \right].$$

Here q is an upper bound on the number of LoR queries by adversary $\mathcal{A}$ and $\mathcal{D}$ is the constructed PRF-distinguisher from the last game hop.

$$\text{Game}_1^{\mathcal{A}}(\lambda) \xrightarrow{\ r\text{-collision}\ } \text{Game}_2^{\mathcal{A}}(\lambda) \xrightarrow{\ \text{PRF}\ } \text{Game}_3^{\mathcal{A}}(\lambda)$$

1 : $b \leftarrow\!\!\$ \{0,1\}$	$b \leftarrow\!\!\$ \{0,1\}$	$b \leftarrow\!\!\$ \{0,1\}$
2 : $k \leftarrow\!\!\$ \text{SE.KGen}(1^{\lambda})$	$k \leftarrow\!\!\$ \text{SE.KGen}(1^{\lambda})$	$k \leftarrow\!\!\$ \text{SE.KGen}(1^{\lambda})$
3 : $b' \leftarrow\!\!\$ \mathcal{A}^{\text{LoR}(b,k,\cdot,\cdot)}(1^{\lambda})$	$b' \leftarrow\!\!\$ \mathcal{A}^{\text{LoR}(b,k,\cdot,\cdot)}(1^{\lambda})$	$b' \leftarrow\!\!\$ \mathcal{A}^{\text{LoR}(b,k,\cdot,\cdot)}(1^{\lambda})$
4 : **return** $(b = b')$	**return** $(b = b')$	**return** $(b = b')$

$\text{LoR}(b,k,m_0,m_1)$	$\text{LoR}(b,k,m_0,m_1)$	$\text{LoR}(b,k,m_0,m_1)$
1 : **if** $|m_0| \neq |m_1|$ **then**	**if** $|m_0| \neq |m_1|$ **then**	**if** $|m_0| \neq |m_1|$ **then**
2 : **return** $\perp$	**return** $\perp$	**return** $\perp$
3 : $r \leftarrow\!\!\$ \{0,1\}^{\text{PRF.il}(\lambda)}$	$r \leftarrow\!\!\$ \{0,1\}^{\text{PRF.il}(\lambda)}$	$r \leftarrow\!\!\$ \{0,1\}^{\text{PRF.il}(\lambda)}$
4 :	**if** $T[r] = \top$ **then abort**	if $T[r] = \top$ then abort
5 :	$T[r] \leftarrow \top$	$T[r] \leftarrow \top$
6 : $\tau \leftarrow \text{PRF}(k,r)$	$\tau \leftarrow \text{PRF}(k,r)$	$\tau \leftarrow\!\!\$ \{0,1\}^{\text{PRF.ol}(\lambda)}$
7 : $c \leftarrow m_b \oplus \tau$	$c \leftarrow m_b \oplus \tau$	$c \leftarrow m_b \oplus \tau$
8 : **return** (c,r)	**return** (c,r)	**return** (c,r)

Fig. 5.2: The three game hops for proving Proposition 5.11. The first game is the original IND-CPA experiment for the PRF-based symmetric encryption. The games are adjusted such that in the final game the LoR procedure, in fact, implements a one-time pad where a fresh key τ is chosen for every encryption. Note that in Game_2 we handle the "bad event" from line 4 in the LoR oracle and thus no longer need to consider it in Game_3.

To complete the proof, it remains to analyze the success probability of an adversary $\mathcal{A}$ in $\text{Game}_3^{\mathcal{A}}$. In $\text{Game}_3^{\mathcal{A}}$ the encryption operation is a one-time pad with a fresh random mask τ chosen for every encryption. The additional value r which is part of each encryption is chosen independent of mask τ. We can thus directly argue with the security of the one-time pad (Theorem 1.35) that

$$\Pr\left[\text{Game}_3^{\mathcal{A}}(\lambda)\right] = \frac{1}{2}.$$

Putting it all together we have shown that

$$\Pr\left[\text{Exp}_{\text{SE},\mathcal{A}}^{\text{ind-cpa}}(\lambda)\right] = \Pr\left[\text{Game}_1^{\mathcal{A}}(\lambda)\right] \leq \frac{q(\lambda)^2}{2^{\text{PRF.il}(\lambda)-1}} + \text{Adv}_{\text{PRF},\mathcal{D}}^{\text{prf}}(\lambda) + \frac{1}{2},$$

where $\text{Adv}_{\text{PRF},\mathcal{D}}^{\text{prf}}(\lambda)$ is negligible if PRF is a secure pseudorandom function and the first summand is negligible if the input length of PRF grows at least super-logarithmically with the security parameter (i.e., if $\text{PRF.il}(\lambda) \in \omega(\log(\lambda))$). We can thus conclude that

$$\Pr\left[\text{Exp}_{\text{SE},\mathcal{A}}^{\text{ind-cpa}}(\lambda)\right] \leq \frac{1}{2} + \text{negl}(\lambda). \qquad \square$$

On Arbitrary Message Lengths

Over the previous sections we have shown that our simple Construction 5.10 of a symmetric encryption scheme from a pseudorandom function yields an IND-CPA-secure encryption scheme for messages of a fixed size given that the underlying pseudorandom function is secure. For this recall that Construction 5.10 uses the output τ of the pseudorandom function to encrypt the message by computing a bitwise XOR which only works if the lengths of message m and mask τ match, that is, if $|m| = |\tau|$. Consequently, we have to restrict the plaintext length to match the output length of the pseudorandom function. So how can we deal with messages that are longer (or shorter) than the output of the PRF?

One option we want to discuss here is to simply put the responsibility of dealing with too large or too small messages onto the application which should properly preprocess the messages. For too short messages, one option is to pad message m with an injective padding. For example, before sending the message to the encryption scheme we could append a 1 and then as many 0s as needed in order get the message to the required length. In order to make this operation reversible we must, however, ensure that we always pad as otherwise we cannot distinguish a message m of the correct length that ends on 10 from a prefix of m which was padded with 10.

For messages that are larger than supported by the encryption scheme the simplest option is to split the message into multiple messages and encrypt each one separately. This is essentially the idea that is used when creating symmetric encryption schemes from block ciphers such as AES, a primitive that we will encounter in Chapter 14 when we discuss how to construct hash functions.[5]

Tweaking Construction 5.10. Of course, the above ideas could also be implemented directly within the encryption scheme. However, note that changing the scheme requires to also update the security proof as the proof may no longer apply to the adapted scheme. Thus, it is generally advisable to think twice about changing a cryptographic construction as even small and seemingly insignificant changes may render a scheme insecure.

---

[5] We note that block-ciphers (and thus, in particular, AES) are deterministic and thus special care needs to be taken when encrypting long messages with a single short key. We discuss various approaches for block-cipher-based encryption schemes in Section 14.1.1.

5.1.6 Indistinguishability under Chosen-Ciphertext Attacks

While IND-CPA-secure encryption schemes allow us to reuse the secret key for encrypting multiple messages, in practice you should usually choose an encryption scheme that is even stronger.

Recall our simple Construction 5.10. Here the plaintext was encrypted by XORing a pseudorandom mask on top of it. While this guarantees confidentiality of the plaintext (i.e., no adversary can learn anything but the length from the ciphertext) the scheme is vulnerable to active adversaries that can change the ciphertext. Consider an online auction where the participants send their orders in a confidential form by using our IND-CPA encryption scheme with a message length of 32 bits. If we wanted to place an order of 1,000, then we first transform 1,000 into binary, which yields the plaintext

$$m = 0000\ 0000\ 0000\ 0000\ 0000\ 0011\ 1110\ 1000.$$

If we encrypt m then we receive a ciphertext (c, r) where $c = m \oplus \mathsf{PRF}(\mathsf{k}, r)$ and where k is the secret encryption key.

A malicious party that observes our transaction could now easily change our order by flipping one or more bits in c. Consider, for example, that an adversary blocks the sending of message (c, r) and instead inserts message (c', r) where c' is the same as c except that the highest order bit (i.e., the leftmost bit in the above encoding) is flipped. Once the auction house receives the message it decrypts it to get $m' \leftarrow c' \oplus \mathsf{PRF}(\mathsf{k}, r)$, but now m' is

$$m = 1000\ 0000\ 0000\ 0000\ 0000\ 0011\ 1110\ 1000$$

in binary or 2,147,484,648 in decimal. From the auctioneer's viewpoint, however, this looks like a legit bid from us.

While IND-CPA-secure encryption schemes protect against eavesdroppers and guarantee confidentiality of messages they do not protect against tampering of ciphertexts. In other words they do not provide *authenticity* of messages. There are several stronger forms of the IND-CPA security definition that model such active adversaries. The general idea is that an adversary not only gets access to an encryption oracle, but also to a decryption oracle. Thus, the adversary can not only choose plaintexts but also ciphertexts. This is also what gives these notions their name: *indistinguishability under chosen-ciphertext attack*, or *IND-CCA* for short.

In the following definition of IND-CCA security we provide the adversary with an extra decryption oracle. However, we cannot allow the adversary to decrypt just any ciphertext as otherwise it could simply call its LoR oracle and pass the output to its decryption oracle to trivially win. Instead we need to keep track of the produced ciphertexts and disallow the adversary to decrypt any ciphertext that was previously generated by the LoR oracle.

Definition 5.15 (IND-CCA Security for Symmetric Encryption).
A symmetric encryption scheme $\mathsf{SE} := (\mathsf{SE.KGen}, \mathsf{SE.Enc}, \mathsf{SE.Dec})$ *is called* IND-CCA *secure if for all efficient adversaries* $\mathcal{A}$ *advantage* $\mathsf{Adv}_{\mathsf{SE},\mathcal{A}}^{\text{ind-cca}}(\lambda)$ *is negligible. Here, the advantage is defined as*

$$\mathsf{Adv}_{\mathsf{SE},\mathcal{A}}^{\text{ind-cca}}(\lambda) := 2 \cdot \Pr\left[\mathsf{Exp}_{\mathsf{SE},\mathcal{A}}^{\text{ind-cca}}(\lambda)\right] - 1$$

relative to experiment $\mathsf{Exp}_{\mathsf{SE},\mathcal{A}}^{\text{ind-cca}}(\lambda)$ *defined as*

$$\underline{\text{Experiment } \mathsf{Exp}_{\mathsf{SE},\mathcal{A}}^{\text{ind-cca}}(\lambda)}$$

1:   $C \leftarrow \{\}$ // *to keep track of ciphertexts*

2:   $b \leftarrow\!\!\$ \; \{0,1\}$

3:   $k \leftarrow\!\!\$ \; \mathsf{SE.KGen}(1^\lambda)$

4:   $b' \leftarrow\!\!\$ \; \mathcal{A}^{\mathrm{LoR}(b,k,\cdot,\cdot),\mathsf{Dec}(k,\cdot)}(1^\lambda)$

5:   **return** $(b = b')$

with oracles LoR *and* Dec *defined as*

$\mathrm{LoR}(b, k, m_0, m_1)$	$\mathsf{Dec}(k, c)$
1: **if** $\|m_0\| \neq \|m_1\|$ **then**	1: **if** $c \in C$ **then**
2: **return** $\bot$	2: **return** $\bot$
3: $c \leftarrow\!\!\$ \; \mathsf{SE.Enc}(k, m_b)$	3: $m \leftarrow\!\!\$ \; \mathsf{SE.Dec}(k, c)$
4: $C \leftarrow C \cup \{c\}$	4: **return** m
5: **return** c	

It is easily seen that our scheme from Construction 5.10 is not IND-CCA secure. For this consider the above auction adversary. Let the adversary call its LoR oracle on messages 0000 and 0001 (where we assume a message length of 4 bits). When the adversary gets ciphertext (c, r) it flips the highest order bit of c to obtain c' and then sends (c', r) to its decryption oracle. As this is a fresh ciphertext the oracle decrypts it to either 1000 or 1001, which can be trivially distinguished.

While the IND-CCA notion provides an adversary with a decryption oracle it does not necessarily state that an adversary should not be able to find valid ciphertexts. That is, a scheme can be IND-CCA secure even in case an adversary can find valid ciphertexts as long as the decryption of these ciphertexts do not yield any information about the encrypted challenge plaintexts. An even stronger form of security disallows even that. The *authenticated IND-CCA* security definition has a similar setup as before but declares the adversary to win already if it is able to construct a single valid ciphertext. This notion is often also referred to as *authenticated encryption*. For this security definition to make sense, the encryption scheme itself must have a notion of what it means for a ciphertext to be a *valid ciphertext*. While our Construction 5.10 simply decrypts any ciphertext of the correct format and length here we would need a decryption scheme that outputs $\perp$ (or some other failure message) on *invalid ciphertexts*. Authenticated IND-CCA security now requires that no efficient adversary can find a valid ciphertext on their own.

Definition 5.16 (Authenticated IND-CCA for Symmetric Encryption).

A symmetric encryption scheme $\mathsf{SE} := (\mathsf{SE.KGen}, \mathsf{SE.Enc}, \mathsf{SE.Dec})$ *is called authenticated IND-CCA secure if for all efficient adversaries* $\mathcal{A}$ *advantage* $\mathsf{Adv}_{\mathsf{SE},\mathcal{A}}^{\text{a-ind-cca}}(\lambda)$ *is negligible. Here, the advantage is defined as*

$$\mathsf{Adv}_{\mathsf{SE},\mathcal{A}}^{\text{a-ind-cca}}(\lambda) := 2 \cdot \Pr\left[\mathit{Exp}_{\mathsf{SE},\mathcal{A}}^{\text{a-ind-cca}}(\lambda)\right] - 1,$$

where experiment $\mathit{Exp}_{\mathsf{SE},\mathcal{A}}^{\text{a-ind-cca}}(\lambda)$ *is defined as*

Experiment $\mathit{Exp}_{\mathsf{SE},\mathcal{A}}^{\text{a-ind-cca}}(\lambda)$
1: $\quad C \leftarrow \{\}$
2: $\quad \mathsf{win} \leftarrow \mathsf{false}$
3: $\quad b \leftarrow\!\!\$\ \{0,1\}$
4: $\quad \mathsf{k} \leftarrow\!\!\$\ \mathsf{SE.KGen}(1^\lambda)$
5: $\quad b' \leftarrow\!\!\$\ \mathcal{A}^{\mathrm{LoR}(b,\mathsf{k},\cdot,\cdot),\mathsf{Dec}(\mathsf{k},\cdot)}(1^\lambda)$
6: $\quad \mathbf{return}\ (b = b' \vee \mathsf{win})$

with oracles LoR *and* Dec *defined as*

$\mathrm{LoR}(b, \mathsf{k}, m_0, m_1)$	$\mathsf{Dec}(\mathsf{k}, c)$
1: $\quad \mathbf{if}\ |m_0| \neq |m_1|\ \mathbf{then}$	1: $\quad \mathbf{if}\ c \in C\ \mathbf{then}$
2: $\quad\quad \mathbf{return}\ \perp$	2: $\quad\quad \mathbf{return}\ \perp$
3: $\quad c \leftarrow\!\!\$\ \mathsf{SE.Enc}(\mathsf{k}, m_b)$	3: $\quad m \leftarrow\!\!\$\ \mathsf{SE.Dec}(\mathsf{k}, c)$
4: $\quad C \leftarrow C \cup \{c\}$	4: $\quad \mathbf{if}\ m \neq \perp\ \mathbf{then}$
5: $\quad \mathbf{return}\ c$	5: $\quad\quad \mathsf{win} \leftarrow \mathsf{true}$
	6: $\quad \mathbf{return}\ m$

It is instructive to study the relationships between the various security notions. We have already seen that IND-CPA does not imply IND-CCA (recall the above counterexample). However, the other direction holds. Similarly, the two IND-CCA notions can be separated, which leads to the following proposition.

> **Proposition 5.17.** *Let* SE *be a symmetric encryption scheme. Then the following relationships hold: If* SE *is authenticated IND-CCA secure, then it is also IND-CCA. If* SE *is IND-CCA secure then it is also IND-CPA secure. The inverse directions do not hold.*

To prove Proposition 5.17 compare the different security definitions. The implications follow as the adversary is given more and more power to win the security game while the general structure remains the same. For the separations, we have already seen a separation between IND-CPA and IND-CCA. We leave the formalization and the separation between IND-CCA and authenticated IND-CCA as Exercise 5.8.

Achieving IND-CCA Security

A natural approach to construct IND-CCA-secure encryption schemes is to combine an IND-CPA-secure encryption scheme with a message authentication code. While there are many plausible approaches, most of them do not yield secure schemes in general. We will here discuss three such popular approaches out of which, however, only a single one is secure in general, that is, it *always* yields an IND-CCA-secure scheme when instantiated with *any* IND-CPA-secure encryption scheme and *any* UF-CMA-secure message authentication code. While this does not mean that the other two constructions can be easily broken, it means that for each new instantiation with a different encryption scheme or message authentication code the security would need to be reevaluated. As this process is error prone and tedious it is thus very much advisable to stick to a generally secure transformation to begin with.

For the following discussion let SE^* denote an IND-CPA-secure symmetric encryption scheme and let MAC^* be a SUF-CMA-secure message authentication code. Recall that strong unforgeability of a MAC says that one can neither forge valid tags for fresh messages nor find another valid tag for a previously seen message–tag pair. As noted earlier, this stronger notion is guaranteed for MACs as we have defined them in Definition 3.39: deterministic UF-CMA-secure MACs which verify validity by recalculating the presumably correct tag and comparing it with the given tag.

The constructed encryption scheme combining a MAC with an IND-CPA-secure scheme will be denoted by SE. All schemes share the same key generation algorithm which simply generates two keys, one for each primitive and which is given as

$$\underline{SE.KGen(1^\lambda)}$$

1 : $k_{se} \leftarrow_\$ SE^*.KGen(1^\lambda)$

2 : $k_m \leftarrow_\$ MAC^*.KGen(1^\lambda)$

3 : **return** (k_{se}, k_m)

It is an important point to make that even in case both encryption scheme and message authentication scheme are based on the same primitive—say we use an encryption scheme as in Construction 5.10 based on a pseudorandom function PRF and use pseudorandom function PRF in addition as message authentication code—then still we should always use two independent keys: *As a rule of thumb, each different security goal should always get its own independently sampled key.*

Encrypt-and-MAC. The *encrypt-and-mac* transformation independently computes an authentication tag τ and encryption c.

Construction 5.18 (Encrypt-and-MAC).

$\mathsf{SE.Enc}((k_{se}, k_m), m)$	$\mathsf{SE.Dec}((k_{se}, k_m), (c, \tau))$
1: $\quad c \leftarrow \mathsf{SE}^*.\mathsf{Enc}(k_{se}, m)$	*1*: $\quad m \leftarrow \mathsf{SE}^*.\mathsf{Dec}(k_{se}, c)$
2: $\quad \tau \leftarrow \mathsf{MAC}^*.\mathsf{Eval}(k_m, m)$	*2*: $\quad \tau' \leftarrow \mathsf{MAC}^*.\mathsf{Eval}(k_m, m)$
3: $\quad$ **return** (c, τ)	*3*: $\quad$ **if** $\tau \neq \tau'$ **then return** $\bot$
	4: $\quad$ **return** m

Although the encrypt-and-mac scheme might look secure at first glance it may, in fact, not even provide confidentiality as the resulting scheme may not even be IND secure. For this note that message authentication codes do not need to hide the message. Let MAC be a secure message authentication code and construct MAC′ as

$$\mathsf{MAC'.Eval}(k, m) := m[1] \| \mathsf{MAC.Eval}(k, m).$$

That is, MAC′ in addition to the original tag also outputs the first bit of the message. Naturally, if MAC is secure then so is MAC′ since in order to forge a tag for MAC′ we must also forge a tag for MAC. However, an adversary in the IND game against the encrypt-and-mac scheme with any encryption scheme and MAC′ can easily win by outputting messages 0 and 1 and then looking at the first bit of tag τ.

Remark 5.19. As with many counterexamples found in the cryptographic literature also this one feels somewhat artificial. Why should a message authentication code leak a bit of the message. The simple answer is: why should it not? Fact is, it is not possible to prove the encrypt-and-mac scheme secure which means that we cannot be sure that besides seemingly artificial attacks there are not also real attacks.

MAC-then-Encrypt. The *mac-then-encrypt* scheme first computes an authentication tag τ to then encrypt the concatenation of message m and tag τ. Note that in order to recover tag τ from the decryption we must assume that tags are of a fixed length.

Construction 5.20 (MAC-then-Encrypt).

$\mathsf{SE.Enc}((k_{se}, k_m), m)$	$\mathsf{SE.Dec}((k_{se}, k_m), c)$
1 : $\tau \leftarrow \mathsf{MAC}^*.\mathsf{Eval}(k_m, m)$	1 : $m\|\tau \leftarrow \mathsf{SE}^*.\mathsf{Dec}(k_{se}, c)$
2 : $c \leftarrow \mathsf{SE}^*.\mathsf{Enc}(k_{se}, m\|\tau)$	2 : $\tau' \leftarrow \mathsf{MAC}^*.\mathsf{Eval}(k_m, m)$
3 : **return** c	3 : **if** $\tau \neq \tau'$ **then return** $\bot$
	4 : **return** m

Similarly to the encrypt-and-mac scheme we can give a counterexample
to the general security of the mac-then-encrypt scheme. However, while the
security of the encrypt-and-mac scheme in the worst case degraded to even
below IND security, we can show that the mac-then-encrypt scheme always
yields an IND-CPA-secure encryption scheme. However, depending on the
choice of underlying encryption scheme the result may not be IND-CCA secure.
The idea for constructing a counterexample is to consider an encryption scheme
that performs an injective encoding to the message that introduces redundancy.
For example, consider a slightly adapted Construction 5.10 which we change
such that it accepts messages of length one bit shorter than the key and we
change the encryption algorithm to encrypt a message by first prepending a
random bit b which is stripped again later on decryption:

$\mathsf{SE}_{bad}.\mathsf{KGen}(1^\lambda)$	$\mathsf{SE}_{bad}.\mathsf{Enc}(k, m)$	$\mathsf{SE}_{bad}.\mathsf{Dec}(k, (c, r))$
1 : $k \leftarrow_\$ \mathsf{PRF.KGen}(1^\lambda)$	1 : $r \leftarrow_\$ \{0,1\}^{\mathsf{PRF.il}(\lambda)}$	1 : $\tau \leftarrow \mathsf{PRF}(k, r)$
2 : **return** k	2 : $b \leftarrow_\$ \{0,1\}$	2 : $b\|m \leftarrow c \oplus \tau$
	3 : $\tau \leftarrow \mathsf{PRF}(k, r)$	3 : **return** m
	4 : $c \leftarrow b\|m \oplus \tau$	
	5 : **return** (c, r)	

First note that the above change does not affect the IND-CPA security
of the scheme. But, when instantiating mac-then-encrypt with encryption
scheme SE_{bad} an adversary can now easily win in the IND-CCA security game.
For this note that a ciphertext (c, r) for a message m remains valid even if we
flip the first bit of c. The MAC is only computed over the original message
and is thus still valid. Exercise 5.9 asks to formalize the counterexample.

Encrypt-then-MAC. Our final example is the *encrypt-then-mac* scheme,
which first encrypts message m to obtain ciphertext c, which is then authenticated.

Construction 5.21 (Encrypt-then-MAC).

$\mathsf{SE.Enc}((k_{se}, k_m), m)$	$\mathsf{SE.Dec}((k_{se}, k_m), (c, \tau))$
1: $c \leftarrow \mathsf{SE^*.Enc}(k_{se}, m)$	1: $\tau' \leftarrow \mathsf{MAC^*.Eval}(k_m, c)$
2: $\tau \leftarrow \mathsf{MAC^*.Eval}(k_m, c)$	2: **if** $\tau \neq \tau'$ **then return** $\bot$
3: **return** (c, τ)	3: $m \leftarrow \mathsf{SE^*.Dec}(k_{se}, c)$
	4: **return** m

While both encrypt-and-mac as well as mac-then-encrypt can be shown to not yield IND-CCA-secure encryption schemes in general—encrypt-and-mac may even fail to achieve IND security—the *encrypt-then-mac* transformation can be shown to always result in an authenticated IND-CCA-secure encryption scheme when starting from an IND-CPA-secure scheme and a secure MAC.

> **Theorem 5.22.** *Let* SE *be an IND-CPA-secure symmetric encryption scheme and* MAC *an SUF-CMA-secure message authentication code. Then the encrypt-then-mac transformation instantiated with* SE *and* MAC *yields an authenticated IND-CCA-secure symmetric encryption scheme.*

We leave a formal proof of Theorem 5.22 to the reader as Exercise 5.7. Similarly to Proposition 5.11 which establishes the IND-CPA security of Construction 5.10, also Theorem 5.22 can be shown via an application of the game-hopping technique. Here, as first game hop we can replace the adversary's decryption oracle by an oracle that always returns $\bot$. This hop will be down to the security of the message authentication code. The remainder of the proof then follows with the IND-CPA security of the encryption scheme.

Remark 5.23. Note that the above Theorem 5.22 requires a MAC that is SUF-CMA secure. In case it is only UF-CMA secure an adversary that receives a ciphertext (c, τ) could potentially create an adapted (but still valid) tag τ' which would allow decryption of the adapted ciphertext (c, τ') via the decryption oracle.

Finally, we observe that since we can construct both IND-CPA-secure symmetric encryption schemes as well as secure message authentication codes from pseudorandom functions, which in turn can be constructed from one-way functions, we can conclude that:

> **Theorem 5.24.** *If one-way functions exist, then there exists a symmetric encryption scheme* SE *that is IND-CCA secure.*

5.2 Public-Key Encryption

Symmetric encryption schemes are widely used in practice but become impractical in case there are either too many parties involved (in which case key management becomes an issue) or in case parties want to communicate that have not met before (in which case the question arises how to securely exchange the secret key). Public-key encryption (PKE) resolves these issues by using two separate but correlated keys pk for encryption and sk for decryption instead of using only a single secret key k for both encryption *and* decryption. Due to this separation of keys for encryption and decryption public-key encryption is often also referred to as *asymmetric encryption.*

If keys pk (short for public key) and sk (short for secret key and often also called private key) are independent then it would be no problem if the public key is, as its name suggests, public knowledge and, for example, listed in a public registry or is exchanged over an insecure channel prior to the communication. For example, if Alice wants to send a confidential message to Bob she could first look up Bob's public key pk, then encrypt her message $c \leftarrow\!\$ \ \mathsf{Enc}(\mathsf{pk}, m)$ with Bob's public key and finally send ciphertext c to Bob via an insecure channel. On reception, Bob can recover the original message by applying the decryption operation using his secret key sk.

Of course, public key pk and secret key sk cannot be completely independent as somehow key sk should be sufficient to decrypt messages that were encrypted with pk. This raises the question of whether or not such schemes exist in the first place, and if so, as to what exactly the requirements are for a public-key encryption scheme.

Over the course of this book we will see that under reasonable assumptions public-key encryption schemes do exist and that hash functions play a vital role in today's constructions. However, while we can build symmetric encryption schemes from the primitives introduced so far and have seen that, in fact, pseudorandom functions (and thus one-way functions) are sufficient for the existence of such schemes we do not yet have the necessary tooling for public-key encryption schemes. Whether or not this is simply because we are missing the right proof techniques or whether public-key encryption simply cannot be based solely on the security of one-way functions is an important open question in cryptography. The odds are, however, highly stacked against the possibility as we will see in Chapter 11, and thus we require an additional assumption (i.e., a different computational primitive) to base the security of public-key encryption schemes on.

This leads to so-called *trapdoor functions* which can be regarded as an asymmetric analog to one-way functions. Recall that if F is a one-way function then it should be easy to compute $\mathsf{F}(x)$ for any input x but the reverse direction should be difficult, that is, computing any preimage $x' \in \mathsf{F}^{-1}(x)$ for a randomly chosen x should be hard for computationally bounded algorithms. Trapdoor functions have the very same requirement that computing images is easy but inversion is hard in general. However, trapdoor functions come with a special key generation algorithm that produces not only a "normal" function key but in addition a *trapdoor key* which allows efficient inversion of any image. As we will see, this property alone, while seemingly closely related to public-key encryption, is not yet sufficient to create a secure public-key encryption scheme. Instead we need to first study the so-called *hard core* of one-way functions. Combined, a trapdoor function with associated hardcore function can then be used to construct a secure public-key encryption scheme. Of course, finding such a combination is not an easy task. Luckily, hash functions will come to the rescue (but not for a few chapters).

5.2.1 Defining Public-Key Encryption

Public-key encryption is very similar to symmetric encryption from a definitional standpoint. A public-key encryption scheme is similarly defined by three efficient algorithms: key generation, encryption, and decryption. The difference is that the key generation algorithm outputs a pair of keys $(\mathsf{pk}, \mathsf{sk})$ which are short for *public key* and *secret key* (or private key). The encryption algorithm takes as input a message and the public key to produce a ciphertext, and the decryption algorithm takes the secret key and a ciphertext to recover the plaintext. Also similarly to symmetric encryption schemes we call a scheme correct if an honestly generated ciphertext for some plaintext m can always be decrypted to m. Following is the formal definition:

Definition 5.25 (Public-Key Encryption Scheme). *A public-key encryption scheme* PKE *is a tuple of three efficient algorithms* PKE = (PKE.KGen, PKE.Enc, PKE.Dec) *such that*

PKE.KGen: *The probabilistic* key generation algorithm *on input the security parameter* 1^λ *outputs a key pair* $(\mathsf{pk}, \mathsf{sk})$.

PKE.Enc: *The probabilistic* encryption algorithm *takes as input the public key* pk *and a message* $m \in \{0,1\}^*$ *and outputs a ciphertext* $c \in \{0,1\}^*$.

PKE.Dec: *The deterministic* decryption algorithm *takes as input the secret key* sk *and a ciphertext* c *and outputs a message* m *or a special error symbol* $\bot$.

Correctness: *We say that a public-key encryption scheme is* correct *or meets the* correctness condition *if for all* $\lambda \in \mathbb{N}$ *and all* $m \in \{0,1\}^*$ *it holds that the following probability is 1:*

$$\Pr\big[\mathsf{PKE.Dec}(\mathsf{sk}, \mathsf{PKE.Enc}(\mathsf{pk}, m)) = m \mid (\mathsf{pk}, \mathsf{sk}) \leftarrow_\$ \mathsf{PKE.KGen}(1^\lambda)\big].$$

As with symmetric encryption schemes we separate the syntax of the encryption scheme from security definitions. Thus, defining just any scheme that meets the above criterion is straightforward. For example, take any symmetric encryption scheme and adapt the key generation algorithm to set pk $\leftarrow$ k and sk $\leftarrow$ k. Of course, such a scheme would not be secure in the sense that we would like a public-key encryption scheme to be secure in. To formally talk about what it means that a scheme is secure in case "the public key is published" we need to provide a formal security definition. Not surprisingly, we consider similar security notions for public-key encryption schemes as for symmetric encryption schemes: definitions of the IND-CPA and IND-CCA flavor. But before doing so, we first argue that perfect security is not achievable with public-key schemes.

5.2.2 Impossibility of Perfectly Secure PKE Schemes

While the one-time pad is a perfectly secure symmetric encryption scheme it lacks both practicality and efficiency: keys can only be used once and the shared secret key needs to be as long as the plaintext. Moving from an information-theoretic definition of security to computational security definitions allowed us to improve on the one-time pad while still providing very practical security guarantees.

In the public-key setting, on the other hand, computational security guarantees are the best we can hope for as formalized by the following theorem:

> **Theorem 5.26.** *No public-key encryption scheme can be correct and perfectly secure.*

A scheme is perfectly secure if a ciphertext does not yield any information as to the encrypted message even against unbounded adversaries. In the min-entropy setting this if formalized by requiring

$$H_\infty(M \mid C = c) = H_\infty(M).$$

Knowing that a ciphertext is c should not decrease in any way the uncertainty about message m. For the one-time pad we can show that this is true by showing that for each possible plaintext there exists a key such that the ciphertext decrypts to that plaintext (see also Theorem 1.35 and Lemma 1.32 on pages 47 and 46). In the public-key setting, however, we can no longer make this argument as part of the key is known to the adversary. Let us make this argument formal.

Proof of Theorem 5.26. Fix a public-key encryption scheme PKE, let pk be a public key, and let c be a ciphertext generated for some plaintext m under public key pk. In the following we show that if the used scheme is correct then an unbounded adversary can always recover m from pk and c.

First, let us show that any valid secret key for public key pk must decrypt c to m. Assume otherwise. Then there exist two sets of random coins r_1 and

r_2 such that $(\mathsf{pk}, \mathsf{sk}_1) \leftarrow \mathsf{PKE.KGen}(1^\lambda; r_1)$ and $(\mathsf{pk}, \mathsf{sk}_2) \leftarrow \mathsf{PKE.KGen}(1^\lambda; r_2)$ and furthermore

$$\mathsf{PKE.Dec}(\mathsf{sk}_1, c) \neq \mathsf{PKE.Dec}(\mathsf{sk}_2, c).$$

This, however, violates the correctness property of the scheme and we can thus conclude that if multiple secret keys exist for a single public key that they always decrypt the same ciphertext to the same plaintext.

But then an unbounded adversary can recover message m from public key pk and ciphertext c by running key generation algorithm $\mathsf{PKE.KGen}$ on all possible random coins until a pair $(\mathsf{pk}', \mathsf{sk}')$ with $\mathsf{pk} = \mathsf{pk}'$ is found to then use secret key sk' to decrypt c.   □

In the public-key setting we have thus no other choice than to turn to computational notions of security, which we will do next.

5.2.3 IND-CPA Security for PKE Schemes

Recall the weakest notion of security that we defined for symmetric encryption schemes: IND security (Definition 5.2; page 213). Here we asked that an adversary $\mathcal{A} = (\mathcal{A}_1, \mathcal{A}_2)$ that is separated into two phases first outputs two target messages m_0 and m_1. Then, one of the two messages is selected at random and encrypted to obtain ciphertext c, which is given to the second phase of the adversary. The adversary's task now is to decide which of the two messages was encrypted.

For the case of symmetric encryption the IND notion and the stronger IND-CPA notion (Definition 5.5; page 219) which captures multiple encryptions under a single key are two separate notions, that is, schemes exist that are IND secure but which are not IND-CPA secure. One example of such a scheme is the one-time pad, which is not just IND secure but even perfectly secure. However, only if a key is used at most once, and thus the one-time pad is not IND-CPA secure. For public-key encryption things are a bit different.

Consider the *find-then-guess* IND-CPA notion for symmetric encryption schemes (Definition 5.7; page 220). The difference from IND security is that here the adversary is given an encryption oracle which allows it to encrypt arbitrarily chosen plaintexts. In the public-key case the public key is as the name states public knowledge and thus we should always assume that the adversary has knowledge of the public key. But given the public key, an adversary can create encryptions of arbitrary messages already on its own. In other words, an additional encryption oracle is not necessary. While we could formalize the left-or-right version of IND-CPA also for public-key encryption it is more common to formalize the find-then-guess version as in this case no additional oracle is needed:

Definition 5.27 (IND-CPA Security for Public-Key Encryption).
A public-key encryption scheme PKE := (PKE.KGen, PKE.Enc, PKE.Dec)
is called IND-CPA secure *if for all efficient adversaries* $\mathcal{A} = (\mathcal{A}_1, \mathcal{A}_2)$
advantage $\mathsf{Adv}_{\mathsf{PKE},\mathcal{A}}^{\mathrm{ind\text{-}cpa}}(\lambda)$ *is negligible. Here, the advantage is defined as*

$$\mathsf{Adv}_{\mathsf{PKE},\mathcal{A}}^{\mathrm{ind\text{-}cpa}}(\lambda) := 2 \cdot \Pr\left[\mathsf{Exp}_{\mathsf{PKE},\mathcal{A}}^{\mathrm{ind\text{-}cpa}}(\lambda)\right] - 1,$$

where experiment $\mathsf{Exp}_{\mathsf{PKE},\mathcal{A}}^{\mathrm{ind\text{-}cpa}}(\lambda)$ *is defined as*

Experiment $\mathsf{Exp}_{\mathsf{PKE},\mathcal{A}}^{\mathrm{ind\text{-}cpa}}(\lambda)$
1 : $(\mathsf{pk}, \mathsf{sk}) \leftarrow\!\!{\scriptstyle\$}\ \mathsf{PKE.KGen}(1^\lambda)$
2 : $(m_0, m_1, \mathsf{state}) \leftarrow\!\!{\scriptstyle\$}\ \mathcal{A}_1(1^\lambda, \mathsf{pk})$
3 : **if** $|m_0| \neq |m_1|$ **then return** false
4 : $b \leftarrow\!\!{\scriptstyle\$}\ \{0,1\}$
5 : $c \leftarrow\!\!{\scriptstyle\$}\ \mathsf{PKE.Enc}(\mathsf{pk}, m_b)$
6 : $b' \leftarrow\!\!{\scriptstyle\$}\ \mathcal{A}_2(1^\lambda, c, \mathsf{state})$
7 : **return** $(b = b')$

The main difference between the IND-CPA notions for symmetric encryption and public-key encryption is that in the public-key setting we can assume
that the adversary knows the public key and, consequently, no additional
encryption oracle is needed thus collapsing the security notions IND and
IND-CPA in the public-key setting. Nevertheless, multiple formalizations
of the IND-CPA notion are common and Exercise 5.11 asks to formalize a
left-or-right variant for the PKE setting. Here, the adversary gets access to a
left-or-right LoR oracle that is initialized with the public key and a hidden bit
b and takes as input two messages. As in the symmetric case (Definition 5.5;
page 219) the LoR oracle returns $\bot$ in case the messages are not of the same
length and otherwise encrypts the left message in case the hidden bit $b = 0$
and the right message if $b = 1$. As usual it is the task of the adversary to guess
hidden bit b. As is the case with symmetric encryption, also for public-key
encryption the two IND-CPA variants are equivalent (up to polynomial factors
in the advantages).

5.2.4 IND-CCA for Public-Key Encryption

Similarly to the symmetric setting we can again define stronger variants of
security by providing the adversary with an additional decryption oracle.
Following is a formalization of *authenticated IND-CCA* security for public-key
schemes:

Definition 5.28 (Authenticated IND-CCA Security for PKE).
A public-key encryption scheme PKE := (PKE.KGen, PKE.Enc, PKE.Dec)
is called (authenticated) IND-CCA secure *if for all efficient adversaries*
$\mathcal{A} = (\mathcal{A}_1, \mathcal{A}_2)$ *advantage* $\mathsf{Adv}_{\mathsf{PKE},\mathcal{A}}^{\mathsf{a\text{-}ind\text{-}cca}}(\lambda)$ *is negligible. Here, the advantage
is defined as*

$$\mathsf{Adv}_{\mathsf{PKE},\mathcal{A}}^{\mathsf{a\text{-}ind\text{-}cca}}(\lambda) := 2 \cdot \Pr\left[\mathsf{Exp}_{\mathsf{PKE},\mathcal{A}}^{\mathsf{a\text{-}ind\text{-}cca}}(\lambda)\right] - 1,$$

where experiment $\mathsf{Exp}_{\mathsf{PKE},\mathcal{A}}^{\mathsf{a\text{-}ind\text{-}cca}}(\lambda)$ *is defined as*

Experiment $\mathsf{Exp}_{\mathsf{PKE},\mathcal{A}}^{\mathsf{a\text{-}ind\text{-}cca}}(\lambda)$	Dec(sk, c)
1: $C \leftarrow \bot$; win $\leftarrow$ false	1: **if** $c = C$ **then**
2: $(\mathsf{pk}, \mathsf{sk}) \leftarrow\!\!\$\ \mathsf{PKE.KGen}(1^\lambda)$	2: **return** $\bot$
3: $(m_0, m_1, \mathsf{state}) \leftarrow\!\!\$\ \mathcal{A}_1^{\mathsf{Dec}(\mathsf{sk},\cdot)}(1^\lambda, \mathsf{pk})$	3: $m \leftarrow \mathsf{PKE.Dec}(\mathsf{sk}, c)$
4: **if** $|m_0| \neq |m_1|$ **then return** false	4: **if** $m \neq \bot$ **then**
5: $b \leftarrow\!\!\$\ \{0, 1\}$	5: win $\leftarrow$ true
6: $C \leftarrow\!\!\$\ \mathsf{PKE.Enc}(\mathsf{pk}, m_b)$	6: **return** m
7: $b' \leftarrow\!\!\$\ \mathcal{A}_2^{\mathsf{Dec}(\mathsf{sk},\cdot)}(1^\lambda, C, \mathsf{state})$	
8: **return** $(b = b' \lor \mathsf{win})$	

As before, we formalized the IND-CCA experiment in the find-then-guess style and leave it as Exercise 5.12 to define the left-or-right variant of the definition.

5.3 Constructing Public-Key Encryption Schemes

In the final part of this chapter we turn to the question of how to construct public-key encryption schemes from standard cryptographic primitives in order to understand the minimal assumptions necessary.

We have seen that pseudorandom functions (and thus one-way functions) are sufficient for the construction of symmetric encryption schemes. For the public-key case we require additional primitives. The first is an asymmetric variant of a one-way function called a *one-way trapdoor function* or for short a *trapdoor function*. Recall that a function F is called one-way if it is difficult to invert $\mathsf{F}(x)$ for a randomly chosen x. A trapdoor function shares this property, that is, any trapdoor function is also a one-way function. The crux is, and this is also where the function takes its name from, that there exists the possibility of generating a so-called *trapdoor key*. Given this special key, inverting the function should be easy.

As we will see, trapdoor functions are sufficient for the construction of secure public-key encryption schemes. That is, we will show that:

Theorem 5.29. *If trapdoor one-way functions exist, then there exists a public-key encryption scheme* PKE *that is IND-CPA secure.*

For the construction itself we need, however, one additional primitive called a *hardcore function*. Hardcore functions are closely tied to the notion of one-way functions. Intuitively, a one-way function needs to hide some part of its input as otherwise given $y \leftarrow F(x)$ it should be easy to recover x. But what exactly the function hides is hard to tell as, for example, we can easily construct one-way functions that leak, say, the first half or the second half of their inputs. Hardcore functions will allow us to better pinpoint what the *hard core* of a one-way function is, which in turn we can use in a construction of a public-key encryption scheme.

You might wonder why hardcore functions are not a prerequisite in Theorem 5.29. The reason is simple: we can construct hardcore functions without any additional assumption from one-way functions and thus the existence of trapdoor functions is sufficient for public-key encryption. But more on that later.

5.3.1 Trapdoor One-Way Functions

One-way functions do not support a means to invert images efficiently. If you forget your (highly entropic) password x then there is no straightforward way to recover it from $y \leftarrow F(x)$. Public-key encryption, on the other hand, follows the paradigm that someone else can create a ciphertext—which can be seen as a randomized image of the plaintext—and the holder of the secret key is able to derive the plaintext again. Albeit not immediately allowing to encrypt, trapdoor one-way functions (or for short, trapdoor functions) take a step towards public-key encryption schemes. They augment one-way functions by some trapdoor information tk which allows to invert efficiently, but such that without this information the function still constitutes a keyed one-way function. Following is a generalized definition of trapdoor functions for a sampleable distribution D. Similarly to one-way functions we need to define on which distribution the function is one-way, and as with one-way functions, we go by the convention that if no specific distribution is named then we assume the uniform distribution.

Definition 5.30 (Trapdoor One-Way Function).
Let T := (T.KGen, T.Eval, T.Inv) *be a tuple of efficient algorithms such that* T.KGen *is a probabilistic key generation algorithm that on input the security parameter outputs a pair of keys* (pk, tk) *where* pk *is an*

evaluation key and tk *is the secret trapdoor information. We call* T *a one-way trapdoor function for sampleable distribution* D *if the following two properties hold:*

One-Wayness: *Without the trapdoor information, function* T *is one-way for* D*. That is, for any* PPT *algorithm* $\mathcal{A}$ *we have that*

$$\mathsf{Adv}^{\mathsf{owf}}_{\mathsf{T,D},\mathcal{A}}(\lambda) := \Pr\left[\mathit{Exp}^{\mathsf{owf}}_{\mathsf{T,D},\mathcal{A}}(\lambda)\right]$$

is negligible, where experiment $\mathit{Exp}^{\mathsf{one-way}}_{\mathsf{T,D},\mathcal{A}}(\lambda)$ *is defined as*

Experiment $\mathit{Exp}^{\mathsf{owf}}_{\mathsf{T,D},\mathcal{A}}(\lambda)$

1: $(\mathsf{pk},\mathsf{tk}) \leftarrow_\$ \mathsf{T.KGen}(1^\lambda)$

2: $x \leftarrow_\$ \mathsf{D}(1^\lambda,\mathsf{pk})$

3: $y \leftarrow \mathsf{T.Eval}(\mathsf{pk},x)$

4: $x^* \leftarrow_\$ \mathcal{A}(1^\lambda,\mathsf{pk},y)$

5: **return** $\mathsf{T.Eval}(\mathsf{pk},x^*) = y$

Invertibility: *Given the trapdoor information, the function is efficiently invertible. That is, for any security parameter* $\lambda \in \mathbb{N}$*, any key pair* $(\mathsf{pk},\mathsf{tk}) \leftarrow_\$ \mathsf{T.KGen}(1^\lambda)$*, any* $x \leftarrow_\$ \mathsf{T.D}(1^\lambda,\mathsf{pk})$*, and* $y \leftarrow \mathsf{T.Eval}(\mathsf{pk},x)$*, we have*

$$\mathsf{T.Inv}(\mathsf{tk},y) = x.$$

Remark 5.31. Note that the one-wayness definition above is identical to our definition of a keyed one-way function (Definition 2.15 on page 84).

Remark 5.32. The invertibility property implies that the function $\mathsf{T.Eval}(\mathsf{pk},\cdot)$ for a fixed key pk must be one-to-one (injective). Often, the function is a permutation over the input domain, but this is not necessarily always the case. A trapdoor one-way function for which $\mathsf{T.Eval}(\mathsf{pk},\cdot)$ has identical domain and range for every pk potentially output by T.KGen is called a *trapdoor one-way permutation* or, for short, trapdoor permutation.

The RSA Trapdoor Function

The classical example of a trapdoor one-way permutation is the RSA function. To understand the RSA trapdoor function we need a bit of algebra and number theory, and we will formally introduce the necessary concepts in Chapter 10 where we will also take a closer look at the RSA function. In the following two paragraphs we give a brief description of the RSA function but suggest to only skim them on a first read as an understanding of the RSA function is not required for the remainder of this chapter.

For the RSA function, key generator KGen picks distinct primes p, q of bit size roughly $\lambda/2$ and sets $N = p \cdot q$. It then picks an integer $e \geq 3$ which must be co-prime to the group order $\varphi(N) = (p-1)(q-1)$ of $\mathbb{Z}_N^*$, such that there exists an efficiently computable integer d which is the multiplicative inverse of e modulo $\varphi(N)$, i.e., $d \cdot e = 1 + k \cdot \varphi(N)$ for some integer k. The algorithm outputs $\mathsf{tk} = (N, d)$ as well as $\mathsf{pk} = (N, e)$. A careful choice of the parameters—which we do not discuss here—ensures that the function below is assumed to be one-way.

The domain and range of the evaluation function for public key $\mathsf{pk} = (N, e)$ is then $\mathbb{Z}_N^*$. More precisely, we have $\mathsf{Eval}((N, e), x) = x^e \bmod N$ for any $x \in \mathbb{Z}_N^*$. The inverse function Inv on input $\mathsf{tk} = (N, d)$ and $y \in \mathbb{Z}_N^*$ then returns $\mathsf{Inv}((N, d), y) = y^d \bmod N$. By the Euler–Fermat theorem $(a^{\varphi(N)} = 1 \bmod N$ for any $a \in \mathbb{Z}_N^*)$ we have

$$\mathsf{Inv}((N, d), \mathsf{Eval}((N, e), x)) =$$
$$(x^e)^d = x^{de} = x^{1 + k \cdot \varphi(N)} = x^1 \cdot (x^{\varphi(N)})^k = x \bmod N$$

for any $(N, e), (N, d)$ generated by KGen and any x from $\mathbb{Z}_N^*$.

Trapdoor vs. One-Way Functions

Trapdoor functions are, by definition, one-way and thus the statement "if trapdoor functions exist then one-way functions exist" is trivial to show. The other direction is still an open question. While it is generally suspected that we cannot construct trapdoor one-way functions solely from one-way functions (and we will see some evidence why that might be difficult in Chapter 11) we currently also cannot unconditionally prove that it is impossible.

As for our task of constructing a public-key encryption scheme, trapdoor functions get us a good step closer. However, in the same way as one-way functions are not secure symmetric encryption schemes, trapdoor functions are not secure public-key encryption schemes. We thus need some additional tooling to make things work.

5.3.2 The Hard Core of OWFs: Hardcore Functions

A one-way function only guarantees that recovering a full preimage is hard. Yet, parts of the preimage can potentially be read off the image, e.g., a one-way function F may output the first bit of the input in the clear as part of the output. The concept of hardcore functions now allows to identify the core of the input which still looks random, even if one sees the image. Note that there must be some part which cannot be recovered as otherwise the function would not be one-way. Furthermore, it is clear that this *hard part* of the input cannot be recovered from the function value as, again, that would violate the one-wayness property.

Definition 5.33 (Hardcore Function). *Let* $F = (F.KGen, F.Eval)$ *and* $HC = (HC.KGen, HC.Eval)$ *be function families. Then* HC *is a hardcore function for* F *on sampleable distribution* D, *if* $HC.Eval$ *is deterministic and advantage* $\mathsf{Adv}^{hc}_{F,HC,\mathcal{A}}(\lambda)$ *is negligible for all* PPT *algorithms* $\mathcal{A}$. *Here, the advantage is defined as*

$$\mathsf{Adv}^{hc}_{F,HC,\mathcal{A}}(\lambda) := 2 \cdot \Pr\left[\mathsf{Exp}^{hardcore}_{F,HC,\mathcal{A}}(\lambda)\right] - 1,$$

where experiment $\mathsf{Exp}^{hardcore}_{F,HC,\mathcal{A}}(\lambda)$ *is defined as*

$$\underline{\text{Experiment } \mathsf{Exp}^{hardcore}_{F,HC,D,\mathcal{A}}(\lambda)}$$

$1:\quad b \leftarrow\!\!\$\ \{0,1\}$

$2:\quad fk \leftarrow\!\!\$\ F.KGen(1^\lambda)$

$3:\quad x \leftarrow\!\!\$\ D(1^\lambda, fk)$

$4:\quad y \leftarrow F.Eval(fk, x)$

$5:\quad hck \leftarrow\!\!\$\ HC.KGen(1^\lambda)$

$6:\quad z_0 \leftarrow HC.Eval(1^\lambda, hck, x)$

$7:\quad z_1 \leftarrow\!\!\$\ \{0,1\}^{HC.ol(\lambda)}$

$8:\quad b' \leftarrow\!\!\$\ \mathcal{A}(1^\lambda, fk, hck, y, z_b)$

$9:\quad \textbf{return } b = b'$

In the hardcore function experiment we first pick a random preimage x. The adversary then either sees the output of the hardcore function $z_0 \leftarrow HC.Eval(1^\lambda, hck, x)$ or a random value of the same length $z_1 \leftarrow\!\!\$\ \{0,1\}^{HC.ol(\lambda)}$ together with image $y \leftarrow F.Eval(fk, x)$. We call function HC hardcore for F on distribution D if no efficient adversary can tell the two settings apart on inputs x sampled according to distribution D. As usual, if no distribution is specified then we assume the uniform distribution. Also note that in the hardcore function experiment key $hck \leftarrow\!\!\$\ HC.KGen(1^\lambda)$ is generated only after function key $fk \leftarrow\!\!\$\ F.KGen(1^\lambda)$. Thus, more generally, we might even let the key of the hardcore function depend on the key fk of the function family.

Remark 5.34. In contrast to the definition of one-way functions we now demand from the adversary $\mathcal{A}$ to predict the value $HC.Eval(hck, x)$ for the actual preimage x. This enables us to define a function family F which straightforwardly supports to output the entire preimage as the hardcore function. This function F includes the constant evaluation algorithm $F.Eval(fk, x) = 0^{|x|}$ where the key fk is arbitrary. For the uniform distribution $D(1^\lambda)$ over $\{0,1\}^\lambda$ the image 0^λ does not reveal any information about the input such that no (even an unbounded) adversary can do better in distinguishing the output of the hardcore function from random than by guessing. We are, nonetheless, interested in general hardcore functions for arbitrary cryptographic functions, and in particular for (invertible) trapdoor permutations. In these cases the trivial construction above does not apply.

No hardcore functions for invertible functions. Intuitively, if the hardcore function value $\mathsf{HC.Eval}(\mathsf{hck}, x)$ is perfectly predictable from the function value $y = \mathsf{F.Eval}(\mathsf{fk}, x)$, e.g., if $\mathsf{F.Eval}(\mathsf{fk}, x) = x$ is the identity function, then no function HC can serve as a secure hardcore function. The reason is that an adversary $\mathcal{A}$ can then read off the value x from the value $y = \mathsf{HC.Eval}(\mathsf{hck}, x)$, recompute $\mathsf{HC.Eval}(\mathsf{hck}, x)$, and output $b' = 0$ if and only if this value equals the input part z (and $b' = 1$ otherwise). In this case, if $\mathcal{A}$ received the hardcore function value as z, i.e., $b = 0$, then $\mathcal{A}$ will always correctly output 0. If, on the other hand, z is random, i.e., $b = 1$, then this random value will not match the actual hardcore function value with probability at least $1 - 2^{-\mathsf{HC.ol}(\lambda)}$. Using conditional probabilities we can formalize the above argument as

$$
\Pr\left[\mathsf{Exp}_{\mathsf{F,HC},\mathcal{A}}^{\mathrm{hardcore}}(\lambda)\right]
$$
$$
= \Pr[b' = b \wedge b = 0] + \Pr[b' = b \wedge b = 1]
$$
$$
= \Pr[b = 0] \cdot \Pr[b' = b \mid b = 0] + \Pr[b = 1] \cdot \Pr[b' = b \mid b = 1]
$$
$$
\geq \frac{1}{2} \cdot 1 + \frac{1}{2} \cdot (1 - 2^{-\mathsf{HC.ol}(\lambda)}) \geq 1 - 2^{-\mathsf{HC.ol}(\lambda)-1}.
$$

We can conclude that for $\mathsf{HC.ol}(\lambda) \geq 1$ adversary $\mathcal{A}$ can distinguish successfully with non-negligible probability of at least $\frac{3}{4}$ the hardcore function value from random.

5.3.3 Goldreich–Levin Hardcore Bits

We speak of hardcore functions *for* a one-way function, which indicates that in many cases a function is hardcore for one particular one-way function but not necessarily for others. A general construction of a hardcore function is due to Goldreich and Levin, who show how to construct hardcore function GL for a one-way function F. The Goldreich–Levin hardcore function outputs only a single bit (or at most logarithmically many bits in the security parameter) and is thus usually referred to as the *Goldreich–Levin hardcore bit* or the *Goldreich–Levin predicate*.

For a single hardcore bit the function key of GL is a random string $\mathsf{hck} \leftarrow\!\!\$ $\{0, 1\}^\lambda$ and the function $\mathsf{GL.Eval}(\mathsf{hck}, x)$ returns the inner product of the key with the input x, modulo 2:

$$
\mathsf{GL.Eval}(\mathsf{hck}, x) = \langle \mathsf{hck}, x \rangle = \sum_{i=1}^{\lambda} \mathsf{hck}[i] \cdot x[i] \bmod 2.
$$

Theorem 5.35. *Let* $\mathsf{F} = (\mathsf{F.KGen}, \mathsf{F.Eval})$ *be a one-way function. The Goldreich–Levin function* $\mathsf{GL} = (\mathsf{GL.KGen}, \mathsf{GL.Eval})$ *with key length* $\mathsf{GL.kl}(\lambda) = \mathsf{F.il}(\lambda)$ *as defined above is hardcore for function* F.

Remark 5.36. We defined the Goldreich–Levin hardcore bit as a keyed hardcore function. In the literature it is often defined as an unkeyed function in which case the hardcore function is not hardcore for the original one-way function but for an adapted one-way function. Let $\mathsf{F} = (\mathsf{F.KGen}, \mathsf{F.Eval})$ be a one-way function and construct function $\mathsf{G} = (\mathsf{G.KGen}, \mathsf{G.Eval})$ as $\mathsf{G.KGen}(1^\lambda) = \mathsf{F.KGen}(1^\lambda)$ and $\mathsf{G.Eval}(k, x, r) = (\mathsf{F.Eval}(k, x), r)$ where $|x| = |r|$. We can now define an unkeyed Goldreich–Levin hardcore bit for function G as

$$\mathsf{GL}(x, r) = \langle x, r \rangle.$$

The proof of Theorem 5.35 is rather technical, and we thus here provide only the general intuition.

Proof sketch. The idea behind the proof of Theorem 5.35 is that in case GL is not a hardcore bit for one-way function F then there exists a predictor that with some probability better than guessing correctly predicts the hardcore bit given one-way image $y \leftarrow \mathsf{F}(k, x)$ and a key for the hardcore function. If we can distinguish a random bit from the hardcore bit we can also predict the hardcore bit. Note that this observation does not hold for general hardcore functions with long outputs but only for hardcore bits.

Assume now that GL is not a hardcore bit for one-way function F and let $\mathcal{P}$ be a predictor as described above. To simplify the argument we assume that predictor $\mathcal{P}$ always predicts the hardcore bit correctly. That is, on input an image $y \leftarrow \mathsf{F}(k, x)$ and a key hck it outputs $\mathsf{GL.Eval}(\mathsf{hck}, x)$ with probability 1. In the following we will use predictor $\mathcal{P}$ to construct an inverter for one-way function F.

By running $\mathcal{P}$ on a random key hck and then on the key $\overline{\mathsf{hck}} = \mathsf{hck} \oplus 10^{\lambda-1}$ we can recover the first bit $x[1]$ of the input x: If and only if the (correct) predictions differ then the first bit of x must be 1. To see this note that if the hardcore bit is identical for both hck and $\overline{\mathsf{hck}}$ then

$$\mathcal{P}(\mathsf{hck}, y) = \mathsf{GL.Eval}(\mathsf{hck}, x) = \sum_{i=1}^{\lambda} \mathsf{hck}[i] \cdot x[i] \bmod 2$$

$$= (\mathsf{hck}[1] \cdot x[1] + \sum_{i=2}^{\lambda} \mathsf{hck}[i] \cdot x[i]) \bmod 2$$

$$= (\overline{\mathsf{hck}}[1] \cdot x[1] + \sum_{i=2}^{\lambda} \overline{\mathsf{hck}}[i] \cdot x[i]) \bmod 2$$

$$= \mathsf{GL.Eval}(\overline{\mathsf{hck}}, x) = \mathcal{P}(\overline{\mathsf{hck}}, y).$$

But since hck and $\overline{\text{hck}}$ are identical on all but the first bits it must be that $x[1] = 0$. Similarly, if the bits do not match we can conclude that $x[1] = 1$. Repeating this argument analogously for the other $\lambda - 1$ bits eventually yields the entire preimage x. The runtime of this inverter would be dominated by the 2λ executions of the (efficient) predictor $\mathcal{P}$ such that the overall runtime to recover x would be polynomial. We thus derive a contradiction to the one-wayness property of F, excluding efficient inverters.

For the general case we can, of course, not assume that the predictor is always correct but only that it is correct with a probability that is noticeably better than guessing, i.e., with probability $\frac{1}{2} + \frac{1}{\text{poly}(\lambda)}$ for some polynomial $\text{poly}(\lambda)$. To deal with this case the idea is to increase the predictor's success rate by running it multiple times and taking a majority vote. The remainder of the proof is then to estimate how many times the predictor needs to run and how to cleverly lower bound the success probability of the predictor and thus of the inverter. $\qquad\qquad\qquad\qquad\qquad\qquad\qquad\qquad\qquad\qquad\qquad\qquad\square$

5.3.4 PRGs from One-Way Functions Revisited

To get a better feeling of how powerful hardcore functions and even hardcore bits can be, let us briefly show how we can use them to construct a pseudorandom generator from a one-way permutation. Note that with the RSA trapdoor function, we have already seen a number-theoretic construction of a one-way permutation; simply drop the secret trapdoor key.

Construction 5.37. *Let* P *be a one-way permutation with* $\text{P.il}(\lambda) = \text{P.ol}(\lambda) = \lambda$ *and let* HC *be a hardcore function for* P. *We define pseudorandom generator* PRG *as follows:*

PRG.KGen(1^λ)	PRG.Eval$((\text{fk}, \text{hck}), s)$
1: fk $\leftarrow_\$$ P.KGen(1^λ)	*1:* $y \leftarrow$ P.Eval(fk, s)
2: hck $\leftarrow_\$$ HC.KGen(1^λ)	*2:* $z \leftarrow$ HC.Eval(hck, s)
3: **return** (fk, hck)	*3:* **return** $y\|z$

Construction 5.37 is obviously deterministic and, furthermore, it stretches its input. For the construction to be a secure pseudorandom generator we must thus argue that no adversary can distinguish uniformly random outputs from outputs generated via the construction on uniformly random inputs. For this note that the distribution of the y-part in the output is uniformly random since P is a permutation and input s is chosen uniformly random. For the z-part note that it should be indistinguishable from random even by adversaries seeing y down to the security of the hardcore function HC. We leave a formal proof to the reader as Exercise 5.13.

5.3.5 PKE from Trapdoor and Hardcore Functions

By now we have the necessary ingredients to construct secure public-key encryption schemes, at least in theory. Let T be a trapdoor function and let HC be a hardcore function for T. We define a public-key encryption scheme as follows:

Construction 5.38. *Let* T *be a trapdoor one-way function and let* HC *be a hardcore function for* T. *Define public-key encryption scheme* PKE = (PKE.KGen, PKE.Enc, PKE.Dec) *with message length* PKE.il(λ) = HC.ol(λ) *as follows. Key generation creates keys for the underlying primitives and is given by*

$$\underline{\mathsf{PKE.KGen}(1^\lambda)}$$

$1:$ $(\mathsf{pk},\mathsf{tk}) \leftarrow\!\!{\$}\ \mathsf{T.KGen}(1^\lambda)$

$2:$ $\mathsf{hk} \leftarrow\!\!{\$}\ \mathsf{HC.KGen}(1^\lambda)$

$3:$ **return** $((\mathsf{pk},\mathsf{hk}),(\mathsf{tk},\mathsf{hk}))$

Encryption and decryption are then defined as

$\underline{\mathsf{PKE.Enc}((\mathsf{pk},\mathsf{hk}),m)}$	$\underline{\mathsf{PKE.Dec}((\mathsf{tk},\mathsf{hk}),(s,c))}$
$1:$ $r \leftarrow\!\!{\$}\ \{0,1\}^{\mathsf{T.il}(\lambda)}$	$1:$ $r \leftarrow \mathsf{T.Inv}(\mathsf{sk},s)$
$2:$ $s \leftarrow \mathsf{T.Eval}(\mathsf{pk},r)$	$2:$ $m \leftarrow c \oplus \mathsf{HC}(\mathsf{hk},r)$
$3:$ $c \leftarrow m \oplus \mathsf{HC}(\mathsf{hk},r)$	$3:$ **return** m
$4:$ **return** (s,c)	

Key generation runs the key generation algorithms of the trapdoor function and the hardcore function. The secret key is then composed of the inversion key tk for the trapdoor function and the evaluation key hk for the hardcore function. The public key consists of the evaluation keys of both the trapdoor function pk and the hardcore function hk. To encrypt, we choose a uniformly random string r from which we create a pseudorandom string $\mathsf{HC}(\mathsf{hk},r)$ via the hardcore function. The result is used to encrypt message m by XORing it onto the message, i.e., we compute $c \leftarrow m \oplus \mathsf{HC}(\mathsf{hk},r)$. The ciphertext then consists of the encrypted message c together with a blinded form of random value r computed as $s \leftarrow \mathsf{T.Eval}(\mathsf{pk},r)$. For decryption, first the randomness is recovered using the inversion key for the trapdoor function, which then allows decryption by recomputing $\mathsf{HC}(\mathsf{hk},r)$ and XORing the result to c. Observe that the scheme is correct.

Security of Construction 5.38. Let U_n denote the uniform distribution over strings in $\{0,1\}^n$. Since HC is hardcore for T, the distributions

$$(\mathsf{T.Eval}(\mathsf{pk},U_{\mathsf{T.il}(\lambda)}),\mathsf{HC}(\mathsf{hk},U_{\mathsf{T.il}(\lambda)})) \quad\text{and}\quad (\mathsf{T.Eval}(\mathsf{pk},U_{\mathsf{T.il}(\lambda)}),U_{\mathsf{HC.ol}(\lambda)})$$

are computationally indistinguishable, given evaluation keys pk and hk (but not inversion key tk). Hence, HC(fk, r) (for $r \leftarrow\!\!\$\ U_{\mathsf{T}.\mathsf{il}(\lambda)}(1^\lambda)$) is pseudorandom and the security of the scheme reduces to the security of the one-time pad. A formal proof follows a similar technique as our proof of Proposition 5.4 for the symmetric case. We leave the formalization as Exercise 5.14.

Proposition 5.39. *Let* T *be a secure trapdoor function and let* HC *be a secure hardcore function for* T*. Then, it holds that the public-key encryption scheme of Construction 5.38 is IND-CPA secure.*

Remark 5.40. Note that for Proposition 5.39 it is sufficient if trapdoor function T and hardcore function HC are secure on the uniform distribution.

Efficient Public-Key Encryption

While the above scheme is elegant and simple, its efficiency depends on the number of output bits of the hardcore function. For example, instantiated with the Goldreich–Levin hardcore predicate, we obtain a public-key encryption scheme that encrypts 1-bit messages. This is hardly practical. Regrettably, we do not know of any universal hardcore functions that could be used in the construction that have long outputs.[6] This holds, at least in non-idealized settings. In the ideal random oracle setting which we will discuss in detail in Part II we will see how to construct efficient public-key encryption schemes following the above approach. Our key ingredient for this will be *hash functions*, which take over the role of (universal) hardcore function.

Chapter Notes and References

Modern notions of security for encryption schemes go back to the landmark paper "Probabilistic Encryption" by Goldwasser and Micali published in 1982 [10, 11]. Goldwasser and Micali considered the public-key setting, for which they introduced the idea of ciphertext indistinguishability. They defined the notion of IND security (which they call *polynomial security*) and semantic security and showed that IND implies semantic security. Yao introduced a third notion of security for public-key encryption schemes inspired by information theory [16]. All three notions have been proven equivalent by Micali, Rackoff, and Sloan [13] and Goldreich [7], who considered the equivalence in the uniform setting (cfs. Section 1.3.3.2). The stronger notions of chosen ciphertext security

---

[6] We note that universal hardcore functions have been presented recently under novel and very strong assumptions about program obfuscation. Nevertheless, resulting schemes would be rather impractical, not because of output length but because of the inefficiency of existing obfuscation schemes. Also note that there are candidate constructions of hardcore functions with larger outputs for specific one-way functions.

were first considered by Naor and Yung [14] and formalized by Rackoff and Simon [15] and Dolev, Dwork, and Naor [6]. Relations between various notions of public-key encryption schemes are studied by Bellare *et al.* [2].

The first adaptations of the IND-CPA security notions for the private-key (aka symmetric) setting were given by Luby in 1996 (Chapters 11 and 12 in [12]). A rigorous study of various formulations was given by Bellare *et al.* [1], who one year later introduced the left-or-right and the find-then-guess variants presented in Section 5.1.2 for both the CPA and the CCA setting. Bellare *et al.* also gave a third variant called real-or-random in which an adversary must distinguish between either seeing an encryption for a chosen message or an encryption of a random message of the same length. They show that all three variants are equivalent up to a polynomial factor in the reduction.

Constructions of authenticated symmetric encryption schemes (i.e., authenticated IND-CCA) from IND-CPA schemes and message authentication codes were studied by Bellare and Namprempre [3]. They, in particular, considered the encrypt-and-mac, the mac-then-encrypt and the encrypt-then-mac transformations presented in Section 5.1.6 and showed that the only generally secure scheme is the encrypt-then-mac scheme.

The concept of a one-way function's hard core was introduced by Blum and Micali in 1982 [5]. The construction of a hardcore bit for every one-way function (Section 5.3.3) is due to Goldreich and Levin [9]. For an in-depth introduction to the theory of one-way functions and hardcore functions we recommend Goldreich's *Foundations of Cryptography* [8].

The construction of a pseudorandom generator from a one-way permutation and a hardcore function (Section 5.3.4) as well as the construction of an IND-CPA public-key encryption scheme from a trapdoor function and a hardcore function (Section 5.3.5) is due to Yao [16].

The Fundamental Lemma of Game Playing is due to Bellare and Rogaway [4].

Exercices

Exercise 5.1. Show that the two formulations of advantage for IND security of symmetric encryption schemes (see page 214) are equivalent.

Exercise 5.2. Show that the one-time pad meets the IND security notion for symmetric encryption schemes.

Exercise 5.3. Following is the definition of *semantic security* for symmetric encryption schemes. Show that a symmetric encryption scheme is semantically secure if, and only if, it is IND secure.

Definition 5.41 (Semantic Security). *A symmetric encryption scheme* SE := (SE.KGen, SE.Enc, SE.Dec) *is called* semantically secure *if for all efficient adversaries* (Sam, $\mathcal{A}$) *there exists a* PPT *algorithm* Sim *such that for all efficiently computable functions* hint *and* f *there exists a negligible function* negl(λ) *such that*

$$\left| \Pr\left[\mathrm{Real}_{\mathsf{SE}}^{\mathsf{Sam},\mathcal{A},\mathrm{hint},f}(1^\lambda) = 1 \right] - \Pr\left[\mathrm{Fake}_{\mathsf{SE}}^{\mathsf{Sam},\mathsf{Sim},\mathrm{hint},f}(1^\lambda) = 1 \right] \right| \leq \mathsf{negl}(\lambda).$$

Here, random variables $\mathrm{Real}_{\mathsf{SE}}^{\mathsf{Sam},\mathcal{A},\mathrm{hint},f}(1^\lambda)$ *and* $\mathrm{Fake}_{\mathsf{SE}}^{\mathsf{Sam},\mathsf{Sim},\mathrm{hint},f}(1^\lambda)$ *are defined as*

$\mathrm{Real}_{\mathsf{SE}}^{\mathsf{Sam},\mathcal{A},\mathrm{hint},f}(1^\lambda)$	$\mathrm{Fake}_{\mathsf{SE}}^{\mathsf{Sam},\mathsf{Sim},\mathrm{hint},f}(1^\lambda)$
$1:$ $\quad k \leftarrow_\$ \mathsf{SE.KGen}(1^\lambda)$	$1:$
$2:$ $\quad m \leftarrow_\$ \mathsf{Sam}(1^\lambda)$	$2:$ $\quad m \leftarrow_\$ \mathsf{Sam}(1^\lambda)$
$3:$ $\quad h \leftarrow \mathsf{hint}(m)$	$3:$ $\quad h \leftarrow \mathsf{hint}(m)$
$4:$ $\quad c \leftarrow \mathsf{SE.Enc}(k,m)$	$4:$
$5:$ $\quad \tau \leftarrow_\$ \mathcal{A}(1^\lambda, c, h)$	$5:$ $\quad \tau \leftarrow_\$ \mathsf{Sim}(1^\lambda, h)$
$6:$ **return** $(\tau = f(m))$	$6:$ **return** $(\tau = f(m))$

Exercise 5.4. Prove Proposition 5.6 (page 220). That is, show that IND-CPA implies IND security for symmetric encryption schemes but not vice versa.

Exercise 5.5. Prove Proposition 5.8 (page 220). That is, show that the two notions of IND-CPA (Definition 5.5) and FTG-IND-CPA (Definition 5.7) for symmetric encryption schemes are identical up to a polynomial factor in the reduction.

Exercise 5.6. Let SE_1 and SE_2 be two symmetric encryption schemes. Construct a new encryption scheme SE := (SE.KGen, SE.Enc, SE.Dec) that is IND-CPA secure as long as either SE_1 or SE_2 is IND-CPA secure.

Exercise 5.7. Prove Theorem 5.7 (page 258), establishing the security of the encrypt-then-mac transformation for symmetric encryption schemes.

Exercise 5.8. Prove Proposition 5.17 (page 238). That is, show that authenticated IND-CCA implies IND-CCA and IND-CCA implies IND-CPA for symmetric encryption. Furthermore, provide separations for the inverse directions.

Exercise 5.9. Show that the mac-then-encrypt transformation for symmetric encryption schemes (page 239) does not necessarily yield an IND-CCA-secure encryption scheme even if instantiated with an IND-CPA-secure encryption scheme and an UF-CMA-secure message authentication code.

Exercise 5.10. Show that the mac-then-encrypt transformation for symmetric encryption schemes (page 239) always yields an IND-CPA-secure encryption scheme even if instantiated with an IND-CPA-secure encryption scheme and an UF-CMA-secure message authentication code.

Exercise 5.11. Formalize a left-or-right (LoR) version of the IND-CPA security notion for public-key encryption schemes and show that it is identical (up to a polynomial factor in the reduction) to the notion provided as Definition 5.27 (page 246).

Exercise 5.12. Formalize a left-or-right (LoR) version of the IND-CCA security notion for public-key encryption schemes and show that it is identical (up to a polynomial factor in the reduction) to the formalization provided in Definition 5.28 (page 247).

Exercise 5.13. Prove that Construction 5.37 of a pseudorandom generator given in Section 5.3.4 (page 254) is secure given that the underlying permutation P is one-way and function HC is a secure hardcore function for P.

Exercise 5.14. Formally prove Proposition 5.39 (page 256).

Chapter Bibliography

1. Mihir Bellare, Anand Desai, Eric Jokipii, and Phillip Rogaway. A concrete security treatment of symmetric encryption. In *38th Annual Symposium on Foundations of Computer Science*, pages 394–403, Miami Beach, Florida, October 19–22, 1997. IEEE Computer Society Press.
2. Mihir Bellare, Anand Desai, David Pointcheval, and Phillip Rogaway. Relations among notions of security for public-key encryption schemes. In Hugo Krawczyk, editor, *Advances in Cryptology – CRYPTO'98*, volume 1462 of *Lecture Notes in Computer Science*, pages 26–45, Santa Barbara, CA, USA, August 23–27, 1998. Springer, Heidelberg, Germany.
3. Mihir Bellare and Chanathip Namprempre. Authenticated encryption: Relations among notions and analysis of the generic composition paradigm. In Tatsuaki Okamoto, editor, *Advances in Cryptology – ASIACRYPT 2000*, volume 1976 of *Lecture Notes in Computer Science*, pages 531–545, Kyoto, Japan, December 3–7, 2000. Springer, Heidelberg, Germany.
4. Mihir Bellare and Phillip Rogaway. The security of triple encryption and a framework for code-based game-playing proofs. In Serge Vaudenay, editor, *Advances in Cryptology – EUROCRYPT 2006*, volume 4004 of *Lecture Notes in Computer Science*, pages 409–426, St. Petersburg, Russia, May 28 – June 1, 2006. Springer, Heidelberg, Germany.
5. Manuel Blum and Silvio Micali. How to generate cryptographically strong sequences of pseudo random bits. In *23rd Annual Symposium on Foundations of Computer Science*, pages 112–117, Chicago, Illinois, November 3–5, 1982. IEEE Computer Society Press.
6. Danny Dolev, Cynthia Dwork, and Moni Naor. Non-malleable cryptography (extended abstract). In *23rd Annual ACM Symposium on Theory of Computing*, pages 542–552, New Orleans, LA, USA, May 6–8, 1991. ACM Press.
7. Oded Goldreich. A uniform-complexity treatment of encryption and zero-knowledge. *Journal of Cryptology*, 6(1):21–53, March 1993.
8. Oded Goldreich. *Foundations of Cryptography: Basic Tools*. Cambridge University Press, New York, NY, USA, 2007.

9. Oded Goldreich and Leonid A. Levin. A hard-core predicate for all one-way functions. In *21st Annual ACM Symposium on Theory of Computing*, pages 25–32, Seattle, WA, USA, May 15–17, 1989. ACM Press.

10. Shafi Goldwasser and Silvio Micali. Probabilistic encryption and how to play mental poker keeping secret all partial information. In *14th Annual ACM Symposium on Theory of Computing*, pages 365–377, San Francisco, CA, USA, May 5–7, 1982. ACM Press.

11. Shafi Goldwasser and Silvio Micali. Probabilistic encryption. *Journal of Computer and System Sciences*, 28(2):270–299, 1984.

12. Michael Luby. *Pseudorandomness and Cryptographic Applications*. Princeton Computer Science Notes. Princeton University Press, Princeton, NJ, USA, 1996.

13. Silvio Micali, Charles Rackoff, and Bob Sloan. The notion of security for probabilistic cryptosystems. In Andrew M. Odlyzko, editor, *Advances in Cryptology – CRYPTO'86*, volume 263 of *Lecture Notes in Computer Science*, pages 381–392, Santa Barbara, CA, USA, August 1987. Springer, Heidelberg, Germany.

14. Moni Naor and Moti Yung. Public-key cryptosystems provably secure against chosen ciphertext attacks. In *22nd Annual ACM Symposium on Theory of Computing*, pages 427–437, Baltimore, MD, USA, May 14–16, 1990. ACM Press.

15. Charles Rackoff and Daniel R. Simon. Non-interactive zero-knowledge proof of knowledge and chosen ciphertext attack. In Joan Feigenbaum, editor, *Advances in Cryptology – CRYPTO'91*, volume 576 of *Lecture Notes in Computer Science*, pages 433–444, Santa Barbara, CA, USA, August 11–15, 1992. Springer, Heidelberg, Germany.

16. Andrew Chi-Chih Yao. Theory and applications of trapdoor functions (extended abstract). In *23rd Annual Symposium on Foundations of Computer Science*, pages 80–91, Chicago, Illinois, November 3–5, 1982. IEEE Computer Society Press.

Chapter 6
Signature Schemes

By now we have introduced most "standard" cryptographic primitives with the exception of one: digital signature schemes. Signature schemes can be regarded as the public-key analog to message authentication codes. There we had that two parties, Alice and Bob, who share a common secret key can authenticate messages such that when Bob receives a message and corresponding tag from Alice, he can be sure that if the tag is valid the message was not tampered with and that the tag must have been generated with the shared secret key. As with symmetric encryption, authentication based on message authentication codes requires a secure exchange of keys between any two involved parties, and key management quickly becomes a limiting factor. And even in case we consider only two parties we require that the parties must have, at some point, securely exchanged keys.

Digital signature schemes (or simply signature schemes) solve both problems. Similarly to public-key encryption schemes, the key generation algorithm of a signature scheme outputs not a single secret key but a key pair $(\mathsf{pk}, \mathsf{sk})$. Here pk is the public verification key, and it is safe to publish this key in a public registry. The corresponding secret signing key sk needs to remain hidden. Assuming Alice wants to sign a message m she uses her secret signing key sk to produce a signature $\sigma \leftarrow_\$ \mathsf{Sig.Sign}(\mathsf{sk}, m)$. A signature–message pair (m, σ) can then be verified by anyone with access to Alice's public verification key by computing $\mathsf{Sig.Vf}(\mathsf{pk}, m, \sigma)$, which will return either true (signature is valid) or false (signature is invalid).

A valid signature assures the recipient that a message did indeed come from the alleged sender (authenticity) and that it was not tampered with (integrity). In contrast to message authentication codes, which also provide authenticity and integrity guarantees, signature schemes provide a third property: *non-repudiation*. While in a symmetric message authentication scheme all parties that have access to the shared secret key can authenticate messages such that the origin of a message cannot be determined exactly, in signature schemes, on the other hand, every participant has their own key pair and thus in particular

© Springer Nature Switzerland AG 2021   261
A. Mittelbach, M. Fischlin, *The Theory of Hash Functions and Random Oracles*,
Information Security and Cryptography, https://doi.org/10.1007/978-3-030-63287-8_6

their very own secret signing key. Thus given a valid signature–message pair the sender cannot easily repudiate having generated the signature.

As with many cryptographic schemes, hash functions also play an important role in the construction of practical and efficient signature schemes. A common application of signature schemes in practice are online software updates. Here signatures are used to ensure that only updates from the right vendors that have not been tampered with can be installed. As such updates can easily be several gigabytes in size we need to have very efficient schemes in place that can deal with large amounts of data. Hash functions provide an easy way out: Instead of signing the original message m we sign hash value $\mathsf{H}(m)$ under some collision-resistant hash function H. To verify the signature σ of m we first recompute $\mathsf{H}(m)$ and then verify that σ is a valid signature for $\mathsf{H}(m)$. Intuitively, this should be secure as it is hard to find any adapted message m' such that $\mathsf{H}(m) = \mathsf{H}(m')$. We will cover this *hash-and-sign* scheme in detail in Section 6.3. In addition to speeding up the signing and verification process this also has the nice effect that signatures are much shorter.

Besides for efficiency, hash functions can also be used in the construction of signature schemes. Indeed, there is a whole field called *hash-based signatures* studying constructions of signature schemes based on hash functions. In particular over the last years hash-based signatures have been shifted again into the focus of research. The most common signature schemes used in practice today are variants of the *Digital Signature Algorithm* (DSA), which are based on the discrete logarithm problem, as well as schemes based on RSA such as RSA-PSS, which are based on factoring and which we will study in greater detail in Chapter 10. Both underlying problems, discrete logarithm and factoring, are however vulnerable to attacks using quantum computers and could become insecure with a breakthrough in that field. In contrast it is suspected that hash-function-based schemes can be secure even in the presence of quantum computers.

6.1 Formalizing Secure Signature Schemes

As usual we separate the definition of syntax and correctness from definitions of security. Let us begin with a formal definition of a signature scheme.

Definition 6.1 (Signature Scheme). *A signature scheme* Sig *is a tuple of three efficient algorithms* Sig = (Sig.KGen, Sig.Sign, Sig.Vf) *such that*

Sig.KGen: *The probabilistic* key generation algorithm *on input the security parameter* 1^λ *outputs a key pair* (pk, sk).

Sig.Sign: *The (possibly probabilistic) signature algorithm on input the secret key* sk *and a message* $m \in \{0,1\}^*$ *outputs a signature* $\sigma \in \{0,1\}^*$.

Sig.Vf: *The deterministic verification algorithm on input the public key* pk, *a message* m, *and a signature* σ *outputs a bit (or Boolean value) where* 1 *(or* true*) indicates that the signature is valid.*

Correctness: *We say that a signature scheme is* correct *or meets the* correctness condition *if a valid signature can always be verified. That is, we require that for all security parameters* $\lambda \in \mathbb{N}$ *and all messages* $m \in \{0,1\}^*$ *the following probability is equal to 1:*

$$\Pr\left[\mathsf{Sig.Vf}(\mathsf{pk}, m, \mathsf{Sig.Sign}(\mathsf{sk}, m)) = \mathsf{true} \mid (\mathsf{pk}, \mathsf{sk}) \leftarrow\!\!{\scriptstyle\$}\ \mathsf{Sig.KGen}(1^\lambda)\right].$$

As usual we will consider restricted versions in which the message space is restricted to, for example, messages of a fixed length Sig.il(λ).

Similarly to encryption schemes we can consider various flavors of security definitions and types of attacks for signature schemes:

- In a *total break* the adversary not only should be able to forge signatures, but needs to recover a secret key to the given public key.
- In a *universal-forgery attack* the adversary needs to be able to forge a signature for any message.
- In a *selective-forgery attack* the adversary needs to be able to forge a signature for a self-determined message.
- In an *existential-forgery attack* the adversary only needs to generate a forgery for an arbitrary message of its choice.

For each of these, we can consider adversaries with different capabilities:

- In a *key-only attack* the adversary only receives the public key pk.
- In a *known-message attack* the adversary also receives a set of message–signature pairs, where the choice of messages is out of the adversary's control.
- In a *chosen-message attack* the adversary can ask for signatures for messages of its choice before attempting a forgery. We could further distinguish between adaptive (the choice of message can depend on earlier signatures) or non-adaptive choice of messages.

The strongest combination of the above variants is *existential unforgeability under adaptive chosen-message attacks*, which is considered the paramount requirement for modern signature schemes and the notion we will use in this book. Formally, we consider:

Definition 6.2 (Existential Unforgeability under Chosen-Message Attacks). *A signature scheme* $\mathsf{Sig} = (\mathsf{Sig.KGen}, \mathsf{Sig.Sign}, \mathsf{Sig.Vf})$ *is existentially unforgeable under chosen-message attacks if for all* PPT *algorithms* $\mathcal{A}$ *we have that advantage* $\mathsf{Adv}^{\mathsf{euf\text{-}cma}}_{\mathsf{Sig},\mathcal{A}}(\lambda)$ *is negligible. Here, the advantage is defined as*

$$\mathsf{Adv}^{\mathsf{euf\text{-}cma}}_{\mathsf{Sig},\mathcal{A}}(\lambda) := \Pr\left[\mathit{Exp}^{\mathsf{euf\text{-}cma}}_{\mathsf{Sig},\mathcal{A}}(\lambda)\right],$$

with experiment $\mathit{Exp}^{\mathsf{euf\text{-}cma}}_{\mathsf{Sig},\mathcal{A}}(\lambda)$ *defined as*

Experiment $\mathit{Exp}^{\mathsf{euf\text{-}cma}}_{\mathsf{Sig},\mathcal{A}}(\lambda)$	$\mathsf{Sign}(\mathsf{sk}, m)$
1: $\mathcal{Q} \leftarrow \{\}$ // *bookkeeping of signed messages*	1: $\mathcal{Q} \leftarrow \mathcal{Q} \cup \{m\}$
2: $(\mathsf{pk}, \mathsf{sk}) \leftarrow\!\!{\scriptstyle\$}\; \mathsf{Sig.KGen}(1^\lambda)$	2: $\sigma \leftarrow\!\!{\scriptstyle\$}\; \mathsf{Sig.Sign}(\mathsf{sk}, m)$
3: $(m^*, \sigma^*) \leftarrow\!\!{\scriptstyle\$}\; \mathcal{A}^{\mathsf{Sign}(\mathsf{sk},\cdot)}(1^\lambda, \mathsf{pk})$	3: **return** σ
4: **return** $(\mathsf{Sig.Vf}(\mathsf{pk}, m^*, \sigma^*) = \mathsf{true} \wedge m^* \notin \mathcal{Q})$	

The security definition is essentially identical to the security definition of an existentially unforgeable message authentication scheme (see Definition 3.39 on page 151). Here, instead of a tagging oracle the adversary gets access to a signing oracle to generate valid signatures. One major difference is, of course, that in the signature case the adversary has access to the public verification key and can validate any signature obtained by its signature oracle.

Remark 6.3. The above definition requires the adversary to output a valid signature for a fresh message. One sometimes considers *strongly* unforgeable schemes (SUF-CMA) where the adversary would also win if it manages to create a new signature for a previously signed message. Note that this is similar to the notion of strongly unforgeable message authentication codes (see Section 3.5 on page 152) where an adversary wins already in case it can create a fresh valid tag for a previously seen message–tag pair.

6.2 One-Time Signatures

We begin our investigation of signature schemes with, arguably, the simplest signature scheme: *One-time signature schemes*, similarly to the one-time pad, have the restriction that, in order for security to hold, keys cannot be used more than once. We will later see how we can use one-time signatures to construct many-time signatures (schemes that can be used a bounded number of times) as well as full EUF-CMA signature schemes. The security of one-time and many-time signature schemes is defined similarly to Definition 6.2 with the exception that the adversary may use its oracle only a restricted number of times. If we consider a q-time secure scheme then the adversary may ask for at most $q(\lambda)$ many signatures. Thus, for a one-time signature scheme the adversary may ask for the signature of only a single message before it needs to provide a forgery of a fresh message. As we will see, we can construct such a scheme solely based on one-way functions.

Lamport's One-Time Signatures

In the following we will present a one-time signature scheme that is usually referred to as the *Lamport one-time signature scheme*, named after its inventor Leslie Lamport. All that is needed for the scheme to be secure are one-way functions. Let F be a one-way function and let us assume that we want to sign a message consisting of n bits. As a public key, we publish $2n$ function values for randomly chosen preimages. That is, for each bit i of the message to be signed we choose two random values $x_{0,i}$ and $x_{1,i}$ and compute $\mathsf{pk}_{b,i} \leftarrow F(x_{b,i})$ for $b \in \{0,1\}$ and $i \in [n]$. This yields a total of $2n$ values which will be our public key.

$$
\begin{array}{ccccc}
\mathsf{pk}_{0,1} & \mathsf{pk}_{0,2} & \mathsf{pk}_{0,3} & \cdots & \mathsf{pk}_{0,n} \\[2mm]
\mathsf{pk}_{1,1} & \mathsf{pk}_{1,2} & \mathsf{pk}_{1,3} & \cdots & \mathsf{pk}_{1,n}
\end{array}
$$

The random preimages $x_{b,i}$ for $i \in [n]$ and $b \in \{0,1\}$ will make up our secret key sk. Now, in order to sign a message m of length at most n bits we simply publish the corresponding parts of our secret key. That is, for the ith bit of message m we publish value $x_{m[i],i}$. For example, if we want to sign message 10^{n-1} we would thus publish the preimages to the boxed values of the public key

$$
\begin{array}{ccccc}
\mathsf{pk}_{0,1} & \boxed{\mathsf{pk}_{0,2}} & \boxed{\mathsf{pk}_{0,3}} & \cdots & \boxed{\mathsf{pk}_{0,n}} \\[2mm]
\boxed{\mathsf{pk}_{1,1}} & \mathsf{pk}_{1,2} & \mathsf{pk}_{1,3} & \cdots & \mathsf{pk}_{1,n}
\end{array}
$$

Intuitively, the scheme is secure since forging a signature for another message requires to publish a preimage of one of the entries which has not been opened yet. This means inverting one or more parts of the public key which are images under a one-way function for randomly chosen inputs.

Above we have argued that if the underlying function is one-way then the resulting scheme achieves one-time EUF-CMA security. If instead of using a one-way function as the underlying primitive we consider a hash function H that is second-preimage resistant then we can even achieve the stronger security guarantee of (one-time) *strong unforgeability*. In the following we want to formalize these claims. We provide a formal definition of Lamport's scheme as Construction 6.4 below. Note that there we define the scheme for messages of length exactly $|m| = \lambda$. While signature and verification algorithms could be adapted to work for messages that are shorter, such a change also allows to easily break the security of the resulting scheme. Given a valid message signature pair (m, σ) an adversary could generate a forgery for any prefix of m by simply removing the respective values from the signature vector σ. For this note that the signature is verified bit by bit and for each bit of the message, signature σ contains a value from the secret key.

Construction 6.4 (Lamport Signature Scheme).

Let $H := (H.KGen, H.Eval)$ *be a hash function. We define the* Lamport Signature Scheme $Sig_{LL} := (Sig_{LL}.KGen, Sig_{LL}.Sign, Sig_{LL}.Vf)$ *for signing a single message of length* $Sig_{LL}.il(\lambda) := \lambda$ *as*

$Sig_{LL}.KGen(1^\lambda)$	$Sig_{LL}.Sign(sk, m)$	$Sig_{LL}.Vf((hk, pk), m, \sigma)$
$hk \leftarrow_\$ H.KGen(1^\lambda)$	if $|m| \neq \lambda$ then	if $|m| \neq \lambda$ then return false
for $i = 1..\lambda, b = 0..1$ do	return $\perp$	for $i = 1..\lambda$ do
$\quad sk_{b,i} \leftarrow_\$ \{0,1\}^{H.il(\lambda)}$	$\sigma \leftarrow (sk_{m[i],i}) : i \in [\lambda]$	$\quad h \leftarrow H.Eval(hk, \sigma[i])$
$\quad pk_{b,i} \leftarrow H.Eval(hk, sk_{b,i})$	return σ	$\quad$ if $h \neq pk_{m[i],i}$ then
$sk \leftarrow (sk_{0,i}, sk_{1,i}) : i \in [\lambda]$		$\quad\quad$ return false
$pk \leftarrow (pk_{0,i}, pk_{1,i}) : i \in [\lambda]$		return true
return $((hk, pk), sk)$		

Here $(x_i) : i \in [\lambda]$ *denotes the ordered list of* x_i *values for all* $i \in [\lambda]$.

Theorem 6.5. *If* H *is a one-way function then Construction 6.4 is a secure one-time EUF-CMA signature scheme. If* H, *in addition, is second-preimage resistant then the scheme is also one-time SUF-CMA secure.*

Recall that the strong unforgeability notion SUF-CMA says that the adversary cannot even find a new signature to a previously signed message. We also remark that a *compressing* second-preimage resistance hash function is also one-way (see Theorem 4.10 on page 175).

Proof. We first prove ordinary unforgeability based on one-wayness of the hash function and then extend the argument to strong unforgeability using second-preimage resistance on top.

Unforgeability from one-wayness. We prove the security of Lamport signatures via a reduction based on the one-wayness of H. For this let adversary $\mathcal{B}$ be an adversary that after seeing at most one signature is able to forge a signature for a new message. We construct an adversary $\mathcal{A}_{owf}$ from $\mathcal{B}$ against the one-wayness of function H. Adversary $\mathcal{A}_{owf}$ gets as input the security parameter, the evaluation key hk for H, and a challenge image y. Its task is to find a preimage for y. For this it generates $2\lambda - 1$ random preimages in

$(1^\lambda, \mathsf{hk}, y)$

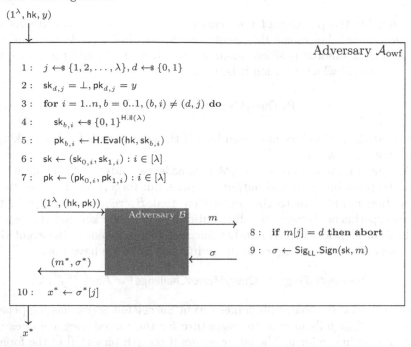

Adversary $\mathcal{A}_{\mathrm{owf}}$

1 : $j \leftarrow\!\!\!\$ \{1, 2, \ldots, \lambda\}, d \leftarrow\!\!\!\$ \{0, 1\}$

2 : $\mathsf{sk}_{d,j} = \bot, \mathsf{pk}_{d,j} = y$

3 : **for** $i = 1..n, b = 0..1, (b, i) \neq (d, j)$ **do**

4 : $\mathsf{sk}_{b,i} \leftarrow\!\!\!\$ \{0, 1\}^{\mathsf{H.il}(\lambda)}$

5 : $\mathsf{pk}_{b,i} \leftarrow \mathsf{H.Eval}(\mathsf{hk}, \mathsf{sk}_{b,i})$

6 : $\mathsf{sk} \leftarrow (\mathsf{sk}_{0,i}, \mathsf{sk}_{1,i}) : i \in [\lambda]$

7 : $\mathsf{pk} \leftarrow (\mathsf{pk}_{0,i}, \mathsf{pk}_{1,i}) : i \in [\lambda]$

$(1^\lambda, (\mathsf{hk}, \mathsf{pk}))$

Adversary $\mathcal{B}$ m

8 : **if** $m[j] = d$ **then abort**

9 : $\sigma \leftarrow \mathsf{Sig}_{\mathsf{LL}}.\mathsf{Sign}(\mathsf{sk}, m)$

σ

(m^*, σ^*)

10 : $x^* \leftarrow \sigma^*[j]$

x^*

Fig. 6.1: Reduction $\mathcal{A}_{\mathrm{owf}}$ against one-wayness from adversary $\mathcal{B}$ against one-time unforgeability of the Lamport one-time signature scheme.

$\{0, 1\}^{\mathsf{H.il}(\lambda)}$ and computes the corresponding images under H. It shuffles all images, including y, to produce public key pk, where it places its challenge at position (d, j) for a random $d \in \{0, 1\}$ and $j \in [\lambda]$. It goes on to call adversary $\mathcal{B}$ on input $(1^\lambda, (\mathsf{hk}, \mathsf{pk}))$, hoping to recover a preimage of y from the forgery. Adversary $\mathcal{A}_{\mathrm{owf}}$ is displayed in Figure 6.1.

Adversary $\mathcal{B}$ makes at most a single signature query m which adversary $\mathcal{A}_{\mathrm{owf}}$ answers as follows. In case $m[j] = d$, that is, if the jth bit of message m matches the randomly generated bit d, then it aborts. In this case it cannot continue as it would need to provide a preimage for value y as part of the signature for m to $\mathcal{B}$. If on the other hand $m[j] \neq d$ then it returns the valid signature σ for m under pk from the preimages that it chose for the construction of pk. This is possible because it knows all required preimages in this case.

Finally, at some point adversary $\mathcal{B}$ finishes and outputs a forgery for a new message $m^* \neq m$. In case the jth bit of message m^* differs, that is, if $m^*[j] = d$ then adversary $\mathcal{A}_{\mathrm{owf}}$ extracts the jth component from the forged signature which, in case the signature is valid, is a preimage for challenge value y.

Analysis. It remains to analyze the success probability of $\mathcal{A}_{\mathrm{owf}}$. Adversary $\mathcal{A}_{\mathrm{owf}}$ fails to successfully invert challenge y in case the single signature query does not hit the position of the generated public key which contains the challenge image. Let us call this event QueryMissesChallenge. As the challenge is placed at a random position, unknown to adversary $\mathcal{B}$, and the public key does not reveal which position it is, we have that

$$\Pr[\mathsf{QueryMissesChallenge}] \geq \frac{1}{2}.$$

Note that the probability may even be 1 if the adversary $\mathcal{B}$ forgoes making a signature query at all.

Assume from now on that QueryMissesChallenge holds. In this case we have that the probability that $\mathcal{B}$ outputs a successful forgery in the reduction's simulation is identical to the probability that $\mathcal{B}$ creates a forgery in the actual experiment (because the distribution of the public key and the signer's reply show identical behaviors). Let SuccessfulForgery denote the event that adversary $\mathcal{B}$ creates a forgery in the reduction. Then we have that

$$\Pr[\mathsf{SuccessfulForgery} \mid \mathsf{QueryMissesChallenge}] = \mathsf{Adv}_{\mathsf{Sig}_{\mathsf{LL}},\mathcal{B}}^{\mathsf{euf\text{-}cma}}(\lambda).$$

Even in case $\mathcal{B}$ successfully forges (event SuccessfulForgery has happened), adversary $\mathcal{A}_{\mathrm{owf}}$ fails in case the signature for the forged message does not contain a preimage for y. The latter occurs if the jth bit $m^*[j]$ of the forgery attempt is different from the reduction's choice d. Once more, since adversary $\mathcal{B}$ remains oblivious about the position of the given image, and the λ-bit message m^* must differ from the λ-bit query m in at least one position, we have that a successful forgery must contain a preimage for the challenge value y with probability at least $\frac{1}{\lambda}$. Let us call this event ForgeryHitsChallenge. Note again that the probability of this event may be larger than $\frac{1}{\lambda}$ if m^* differs from m at multiple positions.

Putting it all together we get that

$$\mathsf{Adv}_{\mathsf{H},\mathcal{A}_{\mathrm{owf}}}^{\mathrm{owf}}(\lambda)$$
$$= \Pr[\mathsf{SuccessfulForgery} \wedge \mathsf{QueryMissesChallenge} \wedge \mathsf{ForgeryHitsChallenge}]$$
$$= \Pr[\mathsf{QueryMissesChallenge}] \cdot \Pr[\mathsf{SuccessfulForgery} \mid \mathsf{QueryMissesChallenge}]$$
$$\quad \cdot \Pr[\mathsf{ForgeryHitsChallenge} \mid \mathsf{SuccessfulForgery} \wedge \mathsf{QueryMissesChallenge}]$$
$$\geq \frac{1}{2\lambda} \cdot \mathsf{Adv}_{\mathsf{Sig}_{\mathsf{LL}},\mathcal{B}}^{\mathsf{euf\text{-}cma}}(\lambda). \tag{6.1}$$

This concludes the reduction to one-wayness, because if the forgery probability is non-negligible, then so must be the inversion probability.

Strong unforgeability. We next argue that the scheme is strongly unforgeable if the hash function is second-preimage resistant. Note that we can rewrite $\mathcal{B}$'s success probability by distinguishing the cases where message m^* in the forgery is different from query m (or there is no query m), and where $m^* = m$ but in which case signature σ^* is new:

$$\text{Game}_1(\lambda) \xrightarrow{\hspace{1cm} \text{OWF} \hspace{1cm}} \text{Game}_2(\lambda)$$

	Game_1	Game_2
1 :	$\mathcal{OT} \leftarrow \bot$	$\mathcal{OT} \leftarrow \bot$
2 :	$(\text{pk}, \text{sk}) \leftarrow\!\!\$ \text{ Sig}_{\text{LL}}.\text{KGen}(1^\lambda)$	$(\text{pk}, \text{sk}) \leftarrow\!\!\$ \text{ Sig}_{\text{LL}}.\text{KGen}(1^\lambda)$
3 :	$(m^*, \sigma^*) \leftarrow\!\!\$ \mathcal{B}^{\text{Sign}(\text{sk}, \cdot)}(1^\lambda, \text{pk})$	$(m^*, \sigma^*) \leftarrow\!\!\$ \mathcal{B}^{\text{Sign}(\text{sk}, \cdot)}(1^\lambda, \text{pk})$
4 :		**if** $m^* \neq m$ **then return** false
5 :	**return**	**return**
	$\quad\text{Sig}_{\text{LL}}.\text{Vf}(\text{pk}, m^*, \sigma^*) = \text{true}$	$\quad\text{Sig}_{\text{LL}}.\text{Vf}(\text{pk}, m^*, \sigma^*) = \text{true}$
	$\quad \wedge\, (m^*, \sigma^*) \neq \mathcal{OT}$	$\quad \wedge\, (m^*, \sigma^*) \neq \mathcal{OT}$

	$\text{Sign}(\text{sk}, m)$	$\text{Sign}(\text{sk}, m)$
1 :	**if** $\mathcal{OT} \neq \bot$ **then**	**if** $\mathcal{OT} \neq \bot$ **then**
2 :	$\quad$ **return** $\bot$	$\quad$ **return** $\bot$
3 :	$\sigma \leftarrow\!\!\$ \text{ Sig}_{\text{LL}}.\text{Sign}(\text{sk}, m)$	$\sigma \leftarrow\!\!\$ \text{ Sig}_{\text{LL}}.\text{Sign}(\text{sk}, m)$
4 :	$\mathcal{OT} \leftarrow (m, \sigma)$	$\mathcal{OT} \leftarrow (m, \sigma)$
5 :	**return** σ	**return** σ

Fig. 6.2: Security games in proof of strong unforgeability of Lamport's one-time signature scheme.

$$\Pr\left[\text{Exp}_{\text{Sig}_{\text{LL}}, \mathcal{B}}^{\text{suf-cma}}(\lambda)\right] = \Pr\left[\text{Exp}_{\text{Sig}_{\text{LL}}, \mathcal{B}}^{\text{euf-cma}}(\lambda) \wedge m^* \neq m\right]$$
$$+ \Pr\left[\text{Exp}_{\text{Sig}_{\text{LL}}, \mathcal{B}}^{\text{euf-cma}}(\lambda) \wedge m^* = m \wedge \sigma^* \neq \sigma\right].$$

Formally, we can wrap this into our game-hopping technique. Let Game_1 be $\mathcal{B}$'s original attack and Game_2 be the game where we declare the adversary to lose if $m^* \neq m$. The games are depicted in Figure 6.2.

We have already bounded the difference in terms of $\mathcal{A}$'s advantage between Game_1 and Game_2 by the one-wayness property above:

$$\Pr[\text{Game}_1] \leq \Pr[\text{Game}_2] + 2\lambda \cdot \text{Adv}_{\text{H}, \mathcal{A}_{\text{owf}}}^{\text{owf}}(\lambda)$$

for adversary $\mathcal{A}_{\text{owf}}$ constructed as above. For this note that the difference in Game_1 is that the adversary may produce a forgery for a message $m^* \neq m$ but as we have seen in Equation (6.1) here its advantage is bounded by $2\lambda \cdot \text{Adv}_{\text{H}, \mathcal{A}_{\text{owf}}}^{\text{owf}}(\lambda)$.

It remains to bound the probability that Game_2 evaluates to true. Note that this can only happen if the adversary creates a forgery for the queried message for which it provides a new signature. In this case we will give a reduction $\mathcal{A}_{\text{spr}}$ to the second-preimage resistance.

We omit a formal description of adversary $\mathcal{A}_{\text{spr}}$ since it is very similar to the adversary against one-wayness. The only difference is that $\mathcal{A}_{\text{spr}}$ receives as input a hash key hk as well as a random $x \leftarrow_\$ \{0,1\}^{\mathsf{H}.\mathsf{il}(\lambda)}$. It is supposed to find an $x' \neq x$ which hashes to the same image. Other than that it proceeds as the one-wayness adversary $\mathcal{A}_{\mathrm{owf}}$, placing the input x as $\mathsf{sk}_{d,j}$ at a random position and computing the parts of the key as $\mathcal{A}_{\mathrm{owf}}$. Since adversary $\mathcal{A}_{\mathrm{spr}}$ knows the entire secret key it is able to answer the single signature request. If $\mathcal{B}$ creates a forgery (m^*, σ^*) then $\mathcal{A}_{\mathrm{spr}}$ outputs $\sigma^*[j]$.

The analysis of our adversary, too, is close to the one in the one-wayness case, only that this time we want the adversary to query about position (d, j). For this note that $\mathcal{B}$ asks for the "right" position $m[j] = d$ with probability $\frac{1}{2}$, because it is oblivious about the insertion. Since the simulation is always correct, we have that $\mathcal{B}$ creates a valid forgery (m^*, σ^*) with $m^* = m$ but $\sigma^* \neq \sigma$ with the same probability when run by $\mathcal{A}_{\mathrm{spr}}$ as in Game_2. In this case, since $\sigma^* \neq \sigma$ there must exist at least one index where the two signatures refer to the same image in the public key, but the signatures contain different preimages. With probability at least $\frac{1}{\lambda}$ this will be $\mathcal{A}_{\mathrm{spr}}$'s choice j, such that $\sigma^*[j]$ yields a colliding (and distinct) preimage to x.

Altogether, we can conclude as before that

$$\Pr[\mathsf{Game}_2] \leq 2\lambda \cdot \mathsf{Adv}^{\mathrm{spr}}_{\mathsf{H}, \mathcal{A}_{\mathrm{spr}}}(\lambda).$$

We thus have for $\mathcal{B}$'s advantage against strong unforgeability:

$$\mathsf{Adv}^{\mathrm{suf\text{-}cma}}_{\mathsf{Sig}_{\mathsf{LL}}, \mathcal{B}}(\lambda) \leq 2\lambda \cdot \left(\mathsf{Adv}^{\mathrm{owf}}_{\mathsf{H}, \mathcal{A}_{\mathrm{owf}}}(\lambda) + \mathsf{Adv}^{\mathrm{spr}}_{\mathsf{H}, \mathcal{A}_{\mathrm{spr}}}(\lambda) \right),$$

where $\mathcal{A}_{\mathrm{owf}}$ and $\mathcal{A}_{\mathrm{spr}}$ are efficient algorithms derived from $\mathcal{B}$ as described above. $\qquad\square$

Remark 6.6. Consider in Lamport's signature scheme the use of a function H that is one-way but not second-preimage resistant. In this case it may be easy for an adversary given a signature σ for message m to find a different signature $\sigma' \neq \sigma$ which is also valid for m. For this the adversary does not necessarily need to invert the function but it suffices to replace any of the preimages in σ by a second preimage. It follows that when starting from a one-way function the resulting scheme is in general only EUF-CMA secure but not strongly secure, that is, the scheme is not SUF-CMA secure (see Remark 6.3 after Definition 6.2). To achieve SUF-CMA one-time security we must instead require function H to be also second-preimage resistant. Note that, since a one-to-one one-way function is trivially second-preimage resistant with perfect security (albeit not compressing), it follows that Lamport's scheme is strongly unforgeable if instantiated with such a one-way function.

One-Time Signatures with Short Secret Keys

Both the public key as well as the secret key in Lamport's scheme are rather large. If we consider messages of length 256 bits and choose as input to our hash function also 256-bit random preimages we get a public key and secret key of length of $2 \cdot 256 \cdot 256 = 2^{17}$ bits or 16.38 kB. With a simple trick we can drastically reduce the size of the secret key. For this, instead of choosing 2λ random values (2 for each bit of the message size) we choose only a single random seed and then use a pseudorandom generator (or a pseudorandom function) to expand the seed into a large enough pseudorandom string that is then used as basis for the preimages. In this case all we need to store as part of the secret key is the seed as we can regenerate the "actual secret key" when necessary. The following shows the adapted key generation and signing algorithms using a pseudorandom function PRF.[1] Signature verification stays unchanged.

$\mathrm{Sig}_{\mathsf{LL}}.\mathsf{KGen}(1^\lambda)$	$\mathrm{Sig}_{\mathsf{LL}}.\mathsf{Sign}(\mathsf{sk}, m)$
1 : $\mathsf{hk} \leftarrow_\$ \mathsf{H.KGen}(1^\lambda)$	1 : if $|m| \neq \lambda$ then
2 : $\mathsf{k} \leftarrow_\$ \mathsf{PRF.KGen}(1^\lambda)$	2 : return $\perp$
3 : for $i = 1..\lambda, b = 0..1$ do	3 : $\mathsf{k} \leftarrow \mathsf{sk}$
4 : $\mathsf{sk}_{b,i} \leftarrow \mathsf{PRF}(\mathsf{k}, b\|\langle i\rangle_{\mathsf{PRF.il}(\lambda)-1})$	4 : for $i = 1..\lambda$ do
5 : $\mathsf{pk}_{b,i} \leftarrow \mathsf{H.Eval}(\mathsf{hk}, \mathsf{sk}_{b,i})$	5 : $\sigma[i] \leftarrow \mathsf{PRF}(\mathsf{k}, m[i]\|\langle i\rangle_{\mathsf{PRF.il}(\lambda)-1})$
6 : $\mathsf{sk} \leftarrow \mathsf{k}$	6 : return σ
7 : $\mathsf{pk} \leftarrow (\mathsf{pk}_{0,i}, \mathsf{pk}_{1,i}) : i \in [\lambda]$	
8 : return $((\mathsf{hk}, \mathsf{pk}), \mathsf{sk})$	

Once the PRF key is generated we can deterministically generate the actual secret key values by evaluating the PRF on an input that encodes bit b and index i. In the above example we chose to simply concatenate bit b with a binary representation of index i filled up with zeros to match the input size of the PRF.

Besides the above optimization to shorten the secret key, other optimizations are known that allow to also obtain shorter public keys. We provide references for the interested reader in the notes and references section of this chapter.

---

[1] Using a pseudorandom function allows for simpler pseudocode. The idea is analogous to using a pseudorandom generator except that for the PRG we generate a seed while the PRF takes a key.

6.3 Hash-and-Sign: Signing Long Messages

Lamport's signature scheme provides a simple construction of a one-time signature scheme from base primitives. Besides the restriction that we can sign only a single message the scheme also restricts the message length of the message to be signed. In the following we show how we can generally use collision-resistant hash functions and target-collision-resistant hash functions in order to create signature schemes that can process arbitrarily long messages via the so-called *hash-and-sign* approach. Here, we first hash a longer message and then sign the hash value with the input-length-restricted signature scheme.[2]

6.3.1 From Collision Resistance

The first construction based on collision resistance works with arbitrary hash functions and signature schemes as long as they are "compatible" in terms of input and output size and individually satisfy certain security properties. Since the security of the derived hash-and-sign scheme relies on the security of both primitives—the collision resistance of the underlying hash function and the unforgeability of the signature scheme—a full security argument involves two convoluted reductions. As proof technique we once again use the game-hopping technique.

The hash-and-sign construction consists of a collision-resistant hash function H and a signature scheme Sig which allows to process any message in the range of the hash function. The key generation algorithm remains unchanged, while the signing algorithm now operates on the hashed message instead, that is, we sign message m as $\sigma \leftarrow\!\!\$\ \mathsf{Sig.Sign}(\mathsf{sk}, \mathsf{H.Eval}(\mathsf{hk}, m))$. Naturally, verification also uses the hashed message $d \leftarrow\!\!\$\ \mathsf{Sig.Vf}(\mathsf{pk}, \mathsf{H.Eval}(\mathsf{hk}, m), \sigma)$.

Construction 6.7. *Let* $\mathsf{Sig} := (\mathsf{Sig.KGen}, \mathsf{Sig.Sign}, \mathsf{Sig.Vf})$ *be a signature scheme and* $\mathsf{H} := (\mathsf{H.KGen}, \mathsf{H.Eval})$ *be a collision-resistant hash function such that* $\mathsf{Sig.il}(\lambda) = \mathsf{H.ol}(\lambda)$, *that is, such that the signature scheme can process messages of the length of hash values. Then the* hash-and-sign *scheme* $\mathsf{HSig} := (\mathsf{HSig.KGen}, \mathsf{HSig.Sign}, \mathsf{HSig.Vf})$ *is constructed as*

$\mathsf{HSig.KGen}(1^\lambda)$	$\mathsf{HSig.Sign}(\mathsf{hsk}, m)$	$\mathsf{HSig.Vf}(\mathsf{hpk}, m, \sigma_\mathsf{h})$
$(\mathsf{pk}, \mathsf{sk}) \leftarrow\!\!\$\ \mathsf{Sig.KGen}(1^\lambda)$	$(\mathsf{hk}, \mathsf{sk}) \leftarrow \mathsf{hsk}$	$(\mathsf{hk}, \mathsf{pk}) \leftarrow \mathsf{hpk}$
$\mathsf{hk} \leftarrow\!\!\$\ \mathsf{H.KGen}(1^\lambda)$	$y \leftarrow \mathsf{H.Eval}(\mathsf{hk}, m)$	$y \leftarrow \mathsf{H.Eval}(\mathsf{hk}, m)$
$\mathsf{hsk} \leftarrow (\mathsf{hk}, \mathsf{sk}),\ \mathsf{hpk} \leftarrow (\mathsf{hk}, \mathsf{pk})$	$\sigma_\mathsf{h} \leftarrow\!\!\$\ \mathsf{Sig.Sign}(\mathsf{sk}, y)$	**return** $\mathsf{Sig.Vf}(\mathsf{pk}, y, \sigma_\mathsf{h})$
return $(\mathsf{hpk}, \mathsf{hsk})$	**return** σ_h	

---

[2] A more precise name would be "hash-*then*-sign" but we use the common terminology here.

Intuitively, if the hash function is collision resistant and the signature scheme is unforgeable then also the derived scheme should be unforgeable (but now allow to sign arbitrarily long messages). The informal argument is as follows. By the collision resistance of hash function H we can assume that any adversary $\mathcal{B}$ against the hash-and-sign scheme cannot produce collisions for the hashed messages. In particular, the hash value H.Eval(hk, m^*) for a forgery attempt (m^*, σ^*) against the derived scheme must be distinct from all the hash values H.Eval(hk, m_i) for messages m_i for which $\mathcal{B}$ requested to see a signature before.

The next "hop" in this argument is to note that, if adversary $\mathcal{B}$ does not find a collision in H, then the hash value H.Eval(hk, m^*) in the forgery attempt must be new and has never been signed with the underlying signature scheme Sig.Sign($sk, \cdot$) as one of the hash values H.Eval(hk, m_i). But finding such a forgery on the hash values for the original signature scheme is infeasible by our assumption that the signature scheme is unforgeable. Hence, adversary $\mathcal{B}$ cannot have a significant success probability when playing against the hash-and-sign scheme. Let us next make the claim and argument more formal.

> **Theorem 6.8.** Let Sig := (Sig.KGen, Sig.Sign, Sig.Vf) be a signature scheme which is existentially unforgeable under chosen-message attacks and let H := (H.KGen, H.Eval) be a collision-resistant hash function. Then the hash-and-sign scheme HSig := (HSig.KGen, HSig.Sign, HSig.Vf) from Construction 6.7 is existentially unforgeable under chosen-message attacks.
>
> More concretely, for any PPT algorithm $\mathcal{B}$ against HSig there exist adversaries $\mathcal{A}_H, \mathcal{A}_{Sig}$ against the security of hash function H and underlying signature scheme Sig such that
>
> $$\mathsf{Adv}_{\mathsf{HSig},\mathcal{B}}^{\mathsf{euf\text{-}cma}}(\lambda) \leq \mathsf{Adv}_{\mathsf{H},\mathcal{A}_H}^{\mathsf{cr}}(\lambda) + \mathsf{Adv}_{\mathsf{Sig},\mathcal{A}_{Sig}}^{\mathsf{euf\text{-}cma}}(\lambda).$$

Proof. The proof follows the game-hopping style using the hops as outlined above. The games are given as pseudocode in Figure 6.3. The first game Game$_1$ is the original attack of $\mathcal{B}$ on the hash-and-sign scheme. In the second game we declare adversary $\mathcal{B}$ to also lose in case the hash value of message m^* in the forgery attempt collides with one of the hash values of the signed messages in the set $\mathcal{Q}$ (lines 4 to 6).

For the analysis we will compensate for the extra stipulation in Game$_2$ by the advantage of finding collisions. We omit another game hop to a trivial game where $\mathcal{B}$ always loses and compensate for this step via the unforgeability of the signature scheme. Instead, we bound the advantage of $\mathcal{B}$ in Game$_2$ directly by this property. It follows as outlined above that $\mathcal{B}$'s success probability in the original attack is therefore bounded by the two probabilities for the first game hop and for the advantage in the last game.

We can bound the loss for the transition from Game$_1$ to Game$_2$ via the Fundamental Lemma of Game Playing (see Lemma 5.13 on page 224). Let

$\mathsf{Game}_1(\lambda)$ $\xrightarrow{\quad\text{Collision Resistance}\quad}$ $\mathsf{Game}_2(\lambda)$

1 : $\quad \mathcal{Q} \leftarrow \{\}$	$\mathcal{Q} \leftarrow \{\}$
2 : $\quad (\mathsf{hpk}, \mathsf{hsk}) \leftarrow\!\!{}_\$ \, \mathsf{HSig.KGen}(1^\lambda)$	$(\mathsf{hpk}, \mathsf{hsk}) \leftarrow\!\!{}_\$ \, \mathsf{HSig.KGen}(1^\lambda)$
3 : $\quad (m^*, \sigma_h^*) \leftarrow\!\!{}_\$ \, \mathcal{B}^{\mathsf{Sign}(\mathsf{hsk}, \cdot)}(1^\lambda, \mathsf{hpk})$	$(m^*, \sigma_h^*) \leftarrow\!\!{}_\$ \, \mathcal{B}^{\mathsf{Sign}(\mathsf{hsk}, \cdot)}(1^\lambda, \mathsf{hpk})$
4 :	**for** $m \in \mathcal{Q}$ **do**
5 :	$\quad$ **if** $m \neq m^* \wedge \mathsf{H}(\mathsf{hk}, m) = \mathsf{H}(\mathsf{hk}, m^*)$ **then**
6 :	$\quad\quad$ **return** false
7 : $\quad$ **return**	**return**
$\quad\quad \mathsf{HSig.Vf}(\mathsf{hpk}, m^*, \sigma_h^*) = \mathsf{true}$	$\mathsf{HSig.Vf}(\mathsf{hpk}, m^*, \sigma_h^*) = \mathsf{true}$
$\quad\quad \wedge\, m^* \notin \mathcal{Q}$	$\wedge\, m^* \notin \mathcal{Q}$

$\mathsf{Sign}(\mathsf{hsk}, m)$	$\mathsf{Sign}(\mathsf{hsk}, m)$
1 : $\quad \mathcal{Q} \leftarrow \mathcal{Q} \cup \{m\}$	$\mathcal{Q} \leftarrow \mathcal{Q} \cup \{m\}$
2 : $\quad \sigma_h \leftarrow\!\!{}_\$ \, \mathsf{HSig.Sign}(\mathsf{hsk}, m)$	$\sigma_h \leftarrow\!\!{}_\$ \, \mathsf{HSig.Sign}(\mathsf{hsk}, m)$
3 : $\quad$ **return** σ_h	**return** σ_h

Fig. 6.3: Security games in proof of hash-and-sign scheme. Note that for brevity we write $\mathsf{H}(\mathsf{hk}, m)$ to denote $\mathsf{H.Eval}(\mathsf{hk}, m)$ in line 4 of Game_2.

$\mathsf{HashColl}$ denote the event that adversary $\mathcal{B}$ outputs a collision, that is, it outputs a message m^* such that there exists $m \neq m^*$ in the set of recorded oracle calls $\mathcal{Q}$ such that the pair (m, m^*) collides under hash function H (lines 4 to 6 in Game_2). By the Fundamental Lemma of Game Playing[3] we have that

$$\Pr[\mathsf{Game}_1(\lambda)] \leq \Pr[\mathsf{HashColl}] + \Pr[\mathsf{Game}_2(\lambda)].$$

For upper bounding the probability of event $\mathsf{HashColl}$ we give a reduction $\mathcal{A}_\mathsf{H}$ against the collision resistance of the deployed hash function. Our adversary $\mathcal{A}_\mathsf{H}$, now playing against the hash function H, receives as input the security parameter 1^λ and a key hk of the hash function, and is supposed to find distinct inputs $x \neq x^*$ such that $\mathsf{H.Eval}(\mathsf{hk}, x) = \mathsf{H.Eval}(\mathsf{hk}, x^*)$. It does so by running algorithm $\mathcal{B}$ against the hash-and-sign scheme. For this it uses the given hash key hk, generates the signature key pair itself, and simulates the signing oracle for $\mathcal{B}$ internally. Our reduction $\mathcal{A}_\mathsf{H}$ eventually checks if $\mathcal{B}$ wins by producing a collision under $\mathsf{H.Eval}(\mathsf{hk}, \cdot)$. If so $\mathcal{A}_\mathsf{H}$ can simply output this collision. A pictorial representation of the reduction is given in Figure 6.4.

---

[3] We stated the lemma in terms of a difference of games in a single **if**-statement. Game_2 here formally differs by a **for**-statement in line 4 from Game_1, with the **if**-term appearing inside the loop. One way to think of this is that we can rewrite the **for**-statement as a single **if**-statement by quantifying over the messages in set $\mathcal{Q}$ as **if** $\exists m \in \mathcal{Q} : m \neq m^* \wedge \mathsf{H}(\mathsf{hk}, m) = \mathsf{H}(\mathsf{hk}, m^*)$.

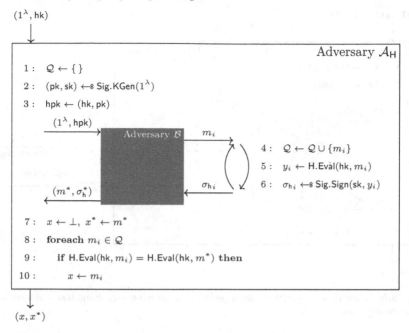

Fig. 6.4: Reduction $\mathcal{A}_{\mathsf{H}}$ against collision resistance from adversary $\mathcal{B}$ against unforgeability of hash-and-sign scheme.

For the analysis of the first game hop note that $\mathcal{A}_{\mathsf{H}}$ perfectly simulates the original attack environment for adversary $\mathcal{B}$ for the unforgeability experiment. That is, all the keys given to $\mathcal{B}$ and all oracle replies of $\mathcal{A}_{\mathsf{H}}$ have the same distribution as in the actual attack since $\mathcal{A}_{\mathsf{H}}$ perfectly simulates the signing oracle and it thus follows that

$$\Pr[\mathsf{HashColl}] = \mathsf{Adv}^{\mathrm{cr}}_{\mathsf{H},\mathcal{A}_{\mathsf{H}}}(\lambda).$$

The final step is now to analyze the winning probability of adversary $\mathcal{B}$ in the now modified game Game_2. For this we build another reduction $\mathcal{A}_{\mathsf{Sig}}$ against the unforgeability of the signature scheme Sig. Our adversary $\mathcal{A}_{\mathsf{Sig}}$ receives security parameter 1^{λ} and a verification key pk of the signature scheme as input. This time it picks the hash key hk itself to then run adversary $\mathcal{B}$ on the pair of keys. For each signature request m_i of $\mathcal{B}$, our adversary $\mathcal{A}_{\mathsf{Sig}}$ first computes the hash value y_i of the message and then forwards the hash value to its own signing oracle. Adversary $\mathcal{A}_{\mathsf{Sig}}$ passes the oracle's reply, a signature $\sigma_{\mathsf{h}i}$ on y_i, unmodified back to $\mathcal{B}$. When $\mathcal{B}$ eventually stops with a forgery attempt $(m^*, \sigma_{\mathsf{h}}^*)$ then $\mathcal{A}_{\mathsf{Sig}}$ hashes the message m^* to derive its hash value $y^* = \mathsf{H.Eval}(\mathsf{hk}, m^*)$. It outputs this hash value together with $\mathcal{B}$'s signature σ_{h}^* as its own forgery attempt. The full reduction is shown in Figure 6.5.

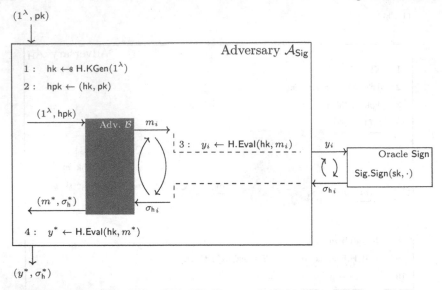

Fig. 6.5: Reduction $\mathcal{A}_{\mathsf{Sig}}$ against unforgeability from adversary $\mathcal{B}$ against unforgeability of hash-and-sign scheme.

For the analysis first note that reduction $\mathcal{A}_{\mathsf{Sig}}$ perfectly simulates the attack of $\mathcal{B}$ in Game_2 up to the point when $\mathcal{B}$ outputs the potential forgery. This holds because all inputs and simulated oracle replies in the reduction have the same distribution as in the game. Next note that adversary $\mathcal{B}$ in Game_2 can only win if the hash value of message m^* is distinct from the hash values of all queried messages m_i. This we can assume since we have already dealt with the possibility of a collision during the transition from Game_1 to Game_2 (also see our discussion on handled events within game hopping in Section 5.1.4 starting on page 226). Note that this is vital for the success of our adversary $\mathcal{A}_{\mathsf{Sig}}$ since if m^* would be part of a collision then $\mathsf{H}(\mathsf{hk}, m^*)$ would be part of the list of oracle queries by $\mathcal{A}_{\mathsf{Sig}}$ and thus the forgery by $\mathcal{A}_{\mathsf{Sig}}$ would not be valid.

It follows that $\mathcal{A}_{\mathsf{Sig}}$ wins against the signature scheme with at least the same probability with which $\mathcal{B}$ wins in Game_2:

$$\Pr[\mathsf{Game}_2(\lambda)] \leq \Pr\left[\mathsf{Exp}^{\mathsf{euf\text{-}cma}}_{\mathsf{Sig},\mathcal{A}_{\mathsf{Sig}}}(\lambda)\right].$$

Putting it all together completes the proof:

$$\Pr\left[\mathsf{Exp}^{\mathsf{euf\text{-}cma}}_{\mathsf{HSig},\mathcal{B}}(\lambda)\right] = \Pr[\mathsf{Game}_1(\lambda)]$$
$$\leq \Pr[\mathsf{HashColl}] + \Pr[\mathsf{Game}_2(\lambda)]$$
$$= \Pr\left[\mathsf{Exp}^{\mathsf{cr}}_{\mathsf{H},\mathcal{A}_{\mathsf{H}}}(\lambda)\right] + \Pr\left[\mathsf{Exp}^{\mathsf{euf\text{-}cma}}_{\mathsf{Sig},\mathcal{A}_{\mathsf{Sig}}}(\lambda)\right]. \qquad \square$$

6.3.2 From Target-Collision Resistance

We next discuss that the weaker property of target-collision resistance also suffices to securely sign longer messages. In contrast to the construction with a (full-fledged) collision-resistant hash function, the solution here however requires to generate a fresh hash key hk for each new signature. The signer then signs both the ephemeral hash key hk and the hashed message $y \leftarrow$ H.Eval(hk, m) under this key. This presumes that the signing algorithm is able to sign messages of length equal to the key length plus the hash value length. The signature also includes the hash key to enable verification.

Construction 6.9. *Let* Sig $:=$ (Sig.KGen, Sig.Sign, Sig.Vf) *be a signature scheme and* H $:=$ (H.KGen, H.Eval) *be a target-collision-resistant hash function (with hash keys of length* H.kl(λ)*) such that* Sig.il(λ) = H.kl(λ) + H.ol(λ)*, that is, such that the signature scheme can process messages of the length of hash keys and values. The* hash-and-sign construction HSig $:=$ (HSig.KGen, HSig.Sign, HSig.Vf) *is then given as*

HSig.KGen(1^λ)	HSig.Sign(sk, m)	HSig.Vf(pk, m, (hk, σ_h))
(pk, sk) $\leftarrow$s Sig.KGen(1^λ)	hk $\leftarrow$s H.KGen(1^λ)	$y \leftarrow$ H.Eval(hk, m)
return (pk, sk)	$y \leftarrow$ H.Eval(hk, m)	**return** Sig.Vf(pk, hk$\|\|y$, σ_h)
	$\sigma_h \leftarrow$s Sig.Sign(pk, hk$\|\|y$)	
	return (hk, σ_h)	

Note that since we sign the concatenation of hash key hk and hash value y it is important that keys are of a fixed length. Otherwise one would need an appropriate encoding of the pair (hk, y) into strings.

To argue security of the above signature scheme it is instructive to consider different attack strategies. First assume that the adversary tries to reuse a signature (hk, σ_h) received in response to a query m for the forgery message m^*. This would indeed succeed if $m^* \neq m$ collided under the hash key hk. But this is unlikely assuming target-collision resistance: This property demands that it is infeasible to first pick an input x and to find a colliding x' to x after having learned the hash key. This corresponds precisely to the attack strategy here. The adversary against our signature scheme first determines m, then the hash key is chosen during signature generation, and afterwards the adversary tries to find a matching m^*.

The next strategy of the adversary could be to reuse only the hash key hk of a signature query even for a non-colliding message m^*. But then the hash value y^* for m^* is different from the hash value used to create the signature in the query, such that the adversary would have to forge a signature for a fresh input under the signing key. Analogously, if the adversary uses a fresh hash key hk* in the forgery then the same argument applies, because the signer authenticates both values.

We next put the above informal idea into a rigorous proof. The proof strategy is very similar to the one with a collision-resistant hash function but differs in one important aspect. Namely, we cannot tell upfront which of the hash keys the adversary may reuse if it follows the first attack strategy above. Indeed, the adversary may decide upon this only at the very end of the attack. If we try to give a reduction against target-collision resistance then our adversary in the reduction needs to first provide the hash input m_i to receive the hash key, and only afterwards outputs a collision m^*. This means that our reduction would need to know the correct index i immediately when the signature request is made, although the adversary itself may still be oblivious about it. We overcome this dilemma by simply trying to guess the correct value i, picking a random number between 1 and the number $q(\lambda)$ of signature queries at the very beginning and succeeding with probability $\frac{1}{q(\lambda)}$. In the security bound this shows up as a factor $q(\lambda)$ in relation to the advantage against target-collision resistance.

Theorem 6.10. *Let* Sig $:=$ (Sig.KGen, Sig.Sign, Sig.Vf) *be a signature scheme which is existentially unforgeable under chosen-message attacks and let* H $:=$ (H.KGen, H.Eval) *be a target-collision-resistant hash function. Then the scheme* HSig $:=$ (HSig.KGen, HSig.Sign, HSig.Vf) *from Construction 6.9 is existentially unforgeable under chosen-message attacks.*

More concretely, for any PPT *algorithm* $\mathcal{B}$ *against* HSig *there exist adversaries* $\mathcal{A}_H, \mathcal{A}_{Sig}$ *against the security of hash function* H *and underlying signature scheme* Sig *such that*

$$\mathsf{Adv}^{\text{euf-cma}}_{\mathsf{HSig},\mathcal{B}}(\lambda) \leq \mathsf{q}(\lambda) \cdot \mathsf{Adv}^{\text{tcr}}_{\mathsf{H},\mathcal{A}_H}(\lambda) + \mathsf{Adv}^{\text{euf-cma}}_{\mathsf{Sig},\mathcal{A}_{Sig}}(\lambda).$$

Here $\mathsf{q}(\lambda)$ *is the number of signature queries* $\mathcal{B}$ *makes in experiment* $\mathsf{Exp}^{\text{euf-cma}}_{\mathsf{HSig},\mathcal{B}}(\lambda)$.

Proof. We once more use the game-hopping technique with the games being displayed in Figure 6.6. Game$_1$ is the original attack of $\mathcal{B}$ on the scheme. In Game$_2$ we declare adversary $\mathcal{B}$ to lose if it uses the hash keys hk$_i$ generated in one of the $q(\lambda)$ signature requests also as key hk* in the forgery attempt, such that the message m^* collides with the corresponding message m_i from the signing query under this hash key (lines 4 to 7). Note that if the adversary reuses the hash key but the hash values are nonetheless distinct then we do not deem the adversary to lose the game.

For the analysis we bound the loss for the transition from Game$_1$ to Game$_2$ in terms of target-collision resistance. Let THashColl denote the event that adversary $\mathcal{B}$ outputs a collision in the specified sense, such that there is a signature query for message $m \neq m^*$ with generated hash key hk $=$ hk* (lines 4 to 7 in Game$_2$). Applying once more the Fundamental Game-Playing Lemma we obtain:

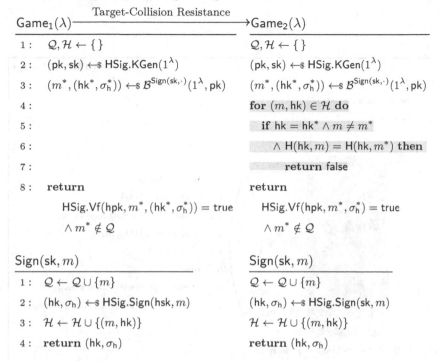

Fig. 6.6: Security games in the proof of the hash-and-sign scheme with a target-collision-resistant hash function. Note that for brevity we write $\mathsf{H}(\mathsf{hk}, m)$ to denote $\mathsf{H.Eval}(\mathsf{hk}, m)$ in line 6 of $\mathsf{Game_2}$.

$$\Pr[\mathsf{Game_1}(\lambda)] \le \Pr[\mathsf{THashColl}] + \Pr[\mathsf{Game_2}(\lambda)].$$

We next bound the probability of event $\mathsf{THashColl}$ from above, by giving a reduction $\mathcal{A}_{\mathsf{H}} = (\mathcal{A}_{\mathsf{H},1}, \mathcal{A}_{\mathsf{H},2})$ against the target-collision resistance of hash function H. This two-stage adversary $\mathcal{A}_{\mathsf{H}}$ is first required to output a value x and some state information, then receives the hash key and picks up the computation in the second stage with this hash key and the state information, producing another output $x' \ne x$.

Adversary $\mathcal{A}_{\mathsf{H},1}$ in the first stage receives the security parameter 1^λ as input. It initiates the setting for $\mathcal{B}$'s attack by generating a signature key pair $(\mathsf{pk}, \mathsf{sk}) \leftarrow\!\!\$ \; \mathsf{HSig.KGen}(1^\lambda)$ and initializing the sets $\mathcal{Q}$ and $\mathcal{H}$ to the empty set $\{\,\}$. It also picks an index j randomly between 1 and $\mathsf{q}(\lambda)$, the (maximum) number of signature queries $\mathcal{B}$ will make. In order to be able to capture the jth query, it additionally initializes a query counter i to 1. It then starts $\mathcal{B}$'s attack for public key pk.

Each time $\mathcal{B}$ makes a signature query for message m_i, we let $\mathcal{A}_{\mathsf{H},1}$ check if i has already reached j. If not (i.e., if $i < j$) then we let $\mathcal{A}_{\mathsf{H},1}$ run the genuine signing algorithm internally to get a fresh hash key hk_i and a signature over the hash key and the message, $(\mathsf{hk}_i, \sigma_{\mathsf{h}i}) \leftarrow\!\!\$ \; \mathsf{HSig.Sign}(\mathsf{sk}, \mathsf{hk}_i \| m_i)$. Adversary

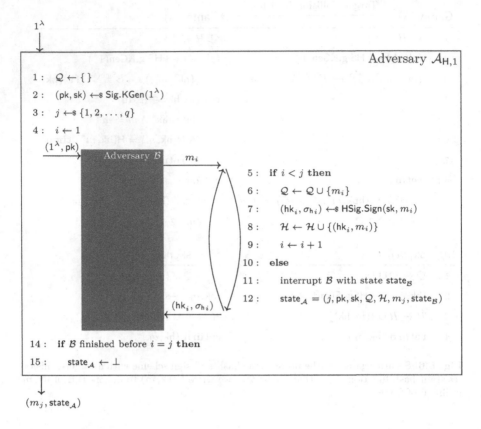

Fig. 6.7: Reduction $\mathcal{A}_H$ against collision resistance from adversary $\mathcal{B}$ against unforgeability of hash-and-sign scheme.

$\mathcal{A}_{H,1}$ returns this pair to $\mathcal{B}$ and updates the sets $\mathcal{Q}$ and $\mathcal{H}$ accordingly. Finally, it increments i to $i \leftarrow i + 1$.

The interesting case happens if $\mathcal{B}$ submits the jth signature request m_j. Then our reduction takes a snapshot of $\mathcal{B}$'s state $\text{state}_{\mathcal{B}}$. This state information contains the full information necessary to continue $\mathcal{B}$'s execution, e.g., for a Turing machine $\mathcal{B}$ the state information would contain the content of the tape(s), the position of the head(s), and the current program state. This state can be described in polynomial size since (the efficient) $\mathcal{B}$ could have used at most polynomial many cells. Adversary $\mathcal{A}_{H,1}$ sets its own state for picking up the second stage as $\text{state}_{\mathcal{A}} = (j, \text{pk}, \text{sk}, \mathcal{Q}, \mathcal{H}, m_j, \text{state}_{\mathcal{B}})$. It ends its first phase with the output m_j and $\text{state}_{\mathcal{A}}$. A pictorial representation of this first phase of the reduction is given in Figure 6.7. Note that it may happen that $\mathcal{B}$ finishes before the jth query, in which case we let $\mathcal{A}_{H,1}$ output an error state symbol $\text{state}_{\mathcal{A}} = \bot$.

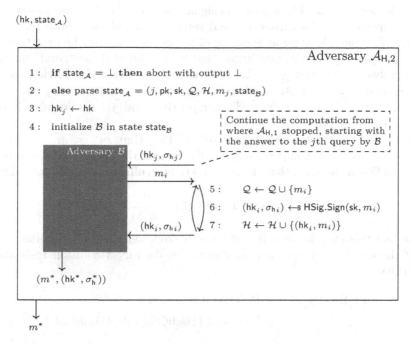

$(\mathsf{hk},\mathsf{state}_{\mathcal{A}})$

Adversary $\mathcal{A}_{\mathsf{H},2}$

1 : **if** $\mathsf{state}_{\mathcal{A}} = \perp$ **then** abort with output $\perp$

2 : **else** parse $\mathsf{state}_{\mathcal{A}} = (j, \mathsf{pk}, \mathsf{sk}, \mathcal{Q}, \mathcal{H}, m_j, \mathsf{state}_{\mathcal{B}})$

3 : $\mathsf{hk}_j \leftarrow \mathsf{hk}$

4 : initialize $\mathcal{B}$ in state $\mathsf{state}_{\mathcal{B}}$

Continue the computation from where $\mathcal{A}_{\mathsf{H},1}$ stopped, starting with the answer to the jth query by $\mathcal{B}$

Adversary $\mathcal{B}$

$(\mathsf{hk}_j, \sigma_{\mathsf{h}j})$

m_i

5 : $\mathcal{Q} \leftarrow \mathcal{Q} \cup \{m_i\}$

6 : $(\mathsf{hk}_i, \sigma_{\mathsf{h}i}) \leftarrow\!\!\$ \; \mathsf{HSig.Sign}(\mathsf{sk}, m_i)$

$(\mathsf{hk}_i, \sigma_{\mathsf{h}i})$ 7 : $\mathcal{H} \leftarrow \mathcal{H} \cup \{(\mathsf{hk}_i, m_i)\}$

$(m^*, (\mathsf{hk}^*, \sigma_{\mathsf{h}}^*))$

m^*

Fig. 6.8: Second stage $\mathcal{A}_{\mathsf{H},2}$ of reduction $\mathcal{A}_{\mathsf{H}}$ against collision resistance from adversary $\mathcal{B}$ against unforgeability of hash-and-sign scheme.

In the second phase, adversary $\mathcal{A}_{\mathsf{H},2}$ now receives a freshly sampled hash key hk as input and its state $\mathsf{state}_{\mathcal{A}}$ from the first phase. If $\mathsf{state}_{\mathcal{A}} = \perp$ we let $\mathcal{A}_{\mathsf{H},2}$ immediately abort with output $\perp$. Else, it parses the state as $(j, \mathsf{pk}, \mathsf{sk}, \mathcal{Q}, \mathcal{H}, m_j, \mathsf{state}_{\mathcal{B}})$ and prepares a response to $\mathcal{B}$'s query m_j. For this it sets $\mathsf{hk}_j \leftarrow \mathsf{hk}$ for the given key and computes a signature $\sigma_{\mathsf{h}j} \leftarrow\!\!\$$ $\mathsf{Sig.Sign}(\mathsf{sk}, \mathsf{hk}_j \| y_j)$ for $y_j \leftarrow \mathsf{H.Eval}(\mathsf{hk}, m_j)$. It continues $\mathcal{B}$'s execution on state $\mathsf{state}_{\mathcal{B}}$ and the signature $(\mathsf{hk}, \sigma_{\mathsf{h}j})$.

Algorithm $\mathcal{A}_{\mathsf{H},2}$ answers all subsequent signature queries of $\mathcal{B}$ as the signing algorithm of the scheme would, i.e., it uses the same steps as $\mathcal{A}_{\mathsf{H},1}$ on the first $j-1$ queries. Eventually $\mathcal{B}$ stops and outputs $(m^*, (\mathsf{hk}^*, \sigma_{\mathsf{h}}^*))$ as a forgery attempt. We let $\mathcal{A}_{\mathsf{H},2}$ output m^*. The algorithm is shown in Figure 6.8.

For the analysis of the first game hop note that $\mathcal{A}_{\mathsf{H}}$ precisely simulates the attack environment for adversary $\mathcal{B}$ in the unforgeability experiment, up to the step where $\mathcal{B}$ outputs its forgery (either in the first phase or in the second phase). This holds also for the jth signature response where $\mathcal{A}_{\mathsf{H},2}$ uses the externally generated but genuine hash key hk in the response, instead of generating it internally. In particular, the output distribution of $\mathcal{B}$ is independent of $\mathcal{A}_{\mathsf{H}}$'s random choice of j.

Note that for the event THashColl to occur (in Game_2) the adversary $\mathcal{B}$ must output a message m^* and hash key hk^* such that the key coincides with the key produced in a previous signature query hk, but the message m in that query is distinct from m^*, and yet the hash values of both messages collide. This must hold for at least one of the queries but may be even true for multiple queries. We can now argue that j hits one of these "good" queries with probability at least $\frac{1}{\mathsf{q}(\lambda)}$. This holds since $\mathcal{B}$ is completely oblivious about the internal choice j of $\mathcal{A}_\mathsf{H}$ of where to place the external hash key $\mathsf{hk}_j = \mathsf{hk}$; the simulation is perfect from $\mathcal{B}$'s perspective, and j is uniformly chosen between 1 and $\mathsf{q}(\lambda)$.

Let Coll_j denote the event that $\mathsf{hk}^* = \mathsf{hk}_j$, that $m^* \neq m_j$, and that $\mathsf{H.Eval}(\mathsf{hk}^*, m^*) = \mathsf{H.Eval}(\mathsf{hk}_j, m_j)$. It follows from the above that, conditioning on collisions to exist, that the probability of a collision occuring for index j is

$$\Pr[\mathsf{Coll}_j \mid \mathsf{THashColl}] \geq \frac{1}{\mathsf{q}(\lambda)}.$$

Note that this even holds if $\mathcal{B}$ decides to make fewer than $\mathsf{q}(\lambda)$ queries.

If the above happens then $\mathcal{A}_\mathsf{H}$ clearly breaks target-collision resistance, such that

$$\begin{aligned}
\Pr\left[\mathsf{Exp}_{\mathsf{H},\mathcal{A}_\mathsf{H}}^{\mathsf{tcr}}(\lambda)\right] &\geq \Pr[\mathsf{THashColl} \wedge \mathsf{Coll}_j] \\
&\geq \Pr[\mathsf{Coll}_j \mid \mathsf{THashColl}] \cdot \Pr[\mathsf{THashColl}] \\
&\geq \frac{1}{\mathsf{q}(\lambda)} \cdot \Pr[\mathsf{THashColl}].
\end{aligned}$$

Rearranging the equation yields the claimed bound.

The final game hop is now to argue that $\mathcal{B}$ must break unforgeability of the involved signature scheme. This follows as in the proof of Theorem 6.8 for collision resistance, noting that in Game_2 now we must have $\mathsf{hk}^*||y^* \neq \mathsf{hk}_i||y_i$ for all queries i. This holds because if hash key hk^* in the forgery equals one of the keys hk_i in the queries for message m_i, then the hash values y^* and y_i must be distinct for Game_2 to output true. Since all keys are of equal bit size we hence have that $\mathsf{hk}^*||y^* \neq \mathsf{hk}_i||y_i$ for all queries i. As in the previous proof this implies that we can turn $\mathcal{B}$ in Game_2 into an adversary $\mathcal{A}_\mathsf{Sig}$ against the signature scheme such that

$$\Pr[\mathsf{Game}_2(\lambda)] \leq \Pr\left[\mathsf{Exp}_{\mathsf{Sig},\mathcal{A}_\mathsf{Sig}}^{\mathsf{euf\text{-}cma}}(\lambda)\right].$$

It remains to put the above pieces together in order to complete the proof:

$$\begin{aligned}
\Pr\left[\mathsf{Exp}_{\mathsf{HSig},\mathcal{B}}^{\mathsf{euf\text{-}cma}}(\lambda)\right] &= \Pr[\mathsf{Game}_1(\lambda)] \\
&\leq \Pr[\mathsf{THashColl}] + \Pr[\mathsf{Game}_2(\lambda)] \\
&\leq \mathsf{q}(\lambda) \cdot \Pr\left[\mathsf{Exp}_{\mathsf{H},\mathcal{A}_\mathsf{H}}^{\mathsf{tcr}}(\lambda)\right] + \Pr\left[\mathsf{Exp}_{\mathsf{Sig},\mathcal{A}_\mathsf{Sig}}^{\mathsf{euf\text{-}cma}}(\lambda)\right]. \qquad \square
\end{aligned}$$

On the black-boxness of the reduction. One might argue whether or not the reduction to target-collision resistance is really a black-box reduction. First, our algorithm $\mathcal{A}$ needs to know (an upper bound of) the number $q(\lambda)$ of signature queries $\mathcal{B}$ makes. Note that this number is clearly bounded by the runtime $p(\lambda)$ of $\mathcal{B}$ since each query takes at least one step. In this sense, $q(\lambda)$ only depends on general characteristics of $\mathcal{B}$ but not an actual internal state. Also see our discussion on the order of quantifiers for the proof of Theorem 3.38 which establishes the security of the GGM construction of a pseudorandom function from a pseudorandom generator (see page 144).

Another point where our reduction $\mathcal{A}$ interferes with $\mathcal{B}$'s execution is when it interrupts $\mathcal{B}$ in the first phase and forwards $\mathcal{B}$'s internal state $\mathsf{state}_\mathcal{B}$ to the second stage, in order to run $\mathcal{B}$ from this point on again. One could also question whether this is indeed a "clean" black-box reduction. Note, however, that $\mathcal{A}$ does not modify the state nor does it use any information from within this state beyond. It uses the state solely for splitting up $\mathcal{B}$'s execution as is required by $\mathcal{A}$'s two-stage implementation. This, too, can thus be viewed as a black-box behavior.

6.4 Many-Time Signature Schemes

So far, we have introduced signature schemes that can sign a single message only. With the hash-and-sign paradigm presented in the previous section we still could not lift this restriction but at least we are now able to sign messages of arbitrary length. Indeed, the hash-and-sign paradigm is also the predominant paradigm used in practice to lift signature schemes for fixed message lengths to signature schemes that support arbitrary messages. For example, DSA—a standardized signature algorithm that has been standardized by the National Institute of Standards and Technology (NIST)—is specified to be used together with either cryptographic hash function SHA-1 or SHA-2. But hash functions cannot only be used to lift length-restricted signature schemes to signature schemes that can process messages of arbitrary length but hash functions can also be used to construct *many-time signatures* out of one-time signatures.

While many-time signatures still require a polynomial upper bound q on the number of messages that can be signed before the scheme becomes insecure they provide a significant improvement in practicality over one-time signatures. Consider the naïve construction of a q-time signature scheme based on a one-time scheme. We generate q-many key pairs of the one-time scheme and keep all the secret keys as our secret key and publish all the public keys as the public key. To sign the ith message we then simply use the ith key pair. While the Lamport scheme already creates rather large keys (and signatures) this naïve approach of course generates even larger keys: q-times larger to be precise. Luckily, this can be improved upon with the help of collision-resistant hash functions and so-called *hash trees*.

6.4.1 Hash Trees

Hash trees have a wide scope of applications. Consider, for example, that you have a database of files and want to keep one or more replicas of that database. In this scenario, we need to allow replicas to understand when they have diverged from the main database in order to start a synchronization process. A naïve approach would be to simply compare each and every file from time to time, but this is usually too expensive. A simple optimization would be to keep a list of hash values, one value for each file. If the hash function is sufficiently secure (e.g., collision resistant) we can substitute the equality check of files by an equality check of hash values. Yet, if we have thousands or millions of files this requires checking thousands or millions of hash values, which can easily become a performance bottleneck.

Hash trees provide a data structure on top of our list of hash values that allows for simpler comparison. The idea is to construct a binary tree on top of the individual hash values in such a way that each node is labeled with a hash value. The leaves of the tree are labeled with the hash values of the original data files, say, $h_1, \ldots, h_q$, where for simplicity we assume that q is a power of 2. Each inner node of the hash tree is also labeled with a hash value, namely with the value H(left child∥right child). That is, the hash values of the left child and right child are concatenated to form the input for the hash value that is used to label the parent node. This process is performed recursively until the entire tree is labeled. An example of such a tree is given in Figure 6.9.

Terminology. Let us provide some terminology for hash trees. We only consider hash trees built with a single hash function H. A hash tree is a tree where each node is labeled with a hash value. In the following let t be a hash tree. We call the *root* of the tree the single top node of the tree and denote its label by rootlabel(t). We call a node a *child node* of a *parent node* if it is directly connected to the *parent node* when moving away on a path from the root node. All nodes on the direct path between a node and the root node (including the root node) are called *ancestors* of the node. The *leaves* of the tree are those nodes without any child nodes. The leaves are labeled with the hash values of their corresponding *data block* ($d_1, \ldots, d_8$ in Figure 6.9). We say that a tree is constructed over data blocks $d_1, \ldots, d_q$ and denote the resulting hash tree by $t \leftarrow$ tree(hk, $d_1, \ldots, d_q$) where hk denotes the evaluation key for hash function H. Usually, the actual structure of the derived tree is irrelevant, but since we assume q to be a power of 2, we suppose in the following that we have a complete binary tree (as in Figure 6.9).

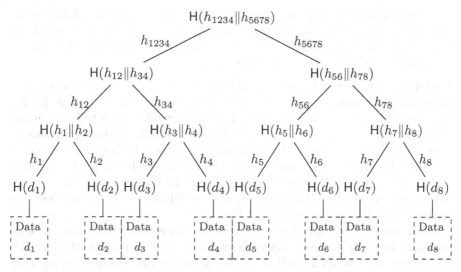

Fig. 6.9: A hash tree constructed over 8 data nodes d_1 to d_8. The tree consists of 8 leaves and 4 levels with level 1 being the root of the tree and level 4 being leaves of the tree. The tree has a height of 3 and hence $2^3 = 8$ leaves. Overall the tree has $\sum_{i=0}^{3} 2^i = 2^4 - 1$ nodes. The labels on the edges denote the value of the lower node which is then used in the hash computation of the parent. For example, h_3 denotes the value $H(d_3)$. We identify a single node by the indexes that went into the computation. Thus h_{1234} identifies the left node in the first level with value $H(h_{12}\|h_{34})$.

If t is a hash tree then we let the *height* of the tree denote the number of edges on the longest path from the root to a leaf. As mentioned before, in our case we consider only *balanced* or *complete* trees where the height is the same independent of which leaf is chosen for the computation.[4] The *depth* of a node is defined as the number of edges from the node to the tree's root node. Thus the root has depth 0 while each leaf has a depth that is equal to the tree's height. We can structure a tree into levels and assign to each node a level which is defined as depth plus 1. Thus, the root node is at level 1 while the leaf nodes are at level 1 plus the height of the tree. A *path* is a sequence of nodes and connecting edges.

Certification paths. A *certification path* is a path from a single leaf to the root which includes for each of the non-leaf nodes on the path the hash labels of both child nodes, as well as the hash label of the root, and the data block. Figure 6.10 shows an example certification path for leaf node $h_3 = H(d_3)$ corresponding to data block d_3. We denote a certification path for data block d at the ith node in tree t by $cp(t, i, d)$. For a certification path c we let $cp.data(c)$ denote the data value d in the path, $cp.pos(c)$ be the position of

---

[4] This, in particular, means that $tree(hk, d_1, \ldots, d_q)$ is defined only for q being a power of 2.

the certified data block in the tree, and cp.rootlabel(c) the hash label in the root of the path. Note that a certification path contains at most two hash values times the height of the tree, and thus the number of hash values is logarithmic in the number q of data blocks.

Verifying integrity. Let us go back to our example of a replicated file database and consider that the main database as well as all replicas have a hash tree built upon their stored files. How can a replica check that its version of the database is exactly the same as that of the main database? For this all it needs to do is to compare the root node of its own hash tree with that of the main database. In case they match, the two sets of files must be identical (as otherwise we could extract a collision for the hash function used in the tree's construction from the set of both files). Thus we have a very fast way to detect equality of the two sets of files.

Hash trees are not only fast when checking for equality. Consider the case that data block d_3 in the example tree of Figure 6.9 was updated. In this case this affects the leaf h_3 as well as all the nodes on the certification path for h_3: the nodes h_{34} and h_{1234} as well as the root node. When trying to find the changed files we can now compare two hash trees from the root downwards. When comparing the root of the original tree with the one where h_3 was changed we find that the root node changed. We go on to compare both children of the root node to find that h_{1234} was also updated while h_{5678} was not. We thus have already established that the changed data block must be on the left half of the tree, that is, it must have an index in the set $\{1, 2, 3, 4\}$. Next we check the children of h_{1234} to find that h_{34} was updated and finally, we move down to the data nodes to find that it was h_3 (and correspondingly data block d_3) that was changed. Note that in order to find the changed block we needed to check exactly those nodes in the *certification path* of the changed data block (see Figure 6.10). Consequently, the number of nodes to be checked is logarithmic in the size of the tree.

Certifying integrity. The fact that all nodes in the path of a leaf to the root change if the corresponding data block changes allows us to use hash trees to "certify the integrity" of data. Consider that you publish the root hash of a hash tree and at a later point publish a data block and claim that it was used in the computation of the hash tree. How much of the tree do you need to publish in order to have a convincing argument that this is indeed the case?

The answer is again the certification path of the node. Given the certification path and data block d_3, in order to verify we would first recompute $h_3 = \mathsf{H}(d_3)$. We would then recompute all hash values for all nodes and finally compare the resulting root hash with the original root hash. In case the two root hashes are identical we can assume down to the security of the hash function that d_3 was indeed used in the creation of the original hash tree even though we have not seen the entire tree. (All we have seen is the root hash and now the

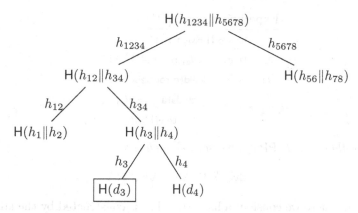

Fig. 6.10: An example certification path for the tree given in Figure 6.9. The certification path is for leaf node $h_3 = H(d_3)$ corresponding to data input d_3. Note that the same path is also valid for leaf node h_4.

certification path for node h_3.) This property will be crucial when going from one-time signatures to many-time signatures in the next section.

In the following we formalize the above property of trees. For this we first need a notion of a *valid certification path* as well as of a *forgery*.

Definition 6.11. *Fix a hash function* H *and let* t *be a hash tree using* H *over data blocks* $d_1, \ldots, d_q$. *Let* c *be a certification path.*

Validity: *We call* c valid *if the label of each non-leaf node is equivalent to the hash of the concatenated labels of its child nodes, i.e.,* $H(\text{left child} \| \text{right child})$. *We call* c *valid for tree* t *if* c *is valid and has the same root node label as* t, $\mathsf{cp.rootlabel}(c) = \mathsf{rootlabel}(t)$. *We let predicate* $\mathsf{valid}(c, \mathsf{rootlabel}(t), \mathsf{hk})$ *be true if* c *is valid for* t.

Forgery: *We call certification path* c *a forgery for tree* t *if it is valid for* t *and if* $\mathsf{cp.data}(c) \neq d_{\mathsf{cp.pos}(c)}$ *for the certified data block* d *which is not equal to the expected data value in* t.

With this we can now formalize our above result for hash trees.

Lemma 6.12. *Let* H *be a collision-resistant hash function and let* $\mathcal{A}$ *be a* PPT *adversary with advantage* $\mathsf{Adv}_{H,\mathcal{A}}^{\mathsf{cp\text{-}forge}}(\lambda)$ *defined as*

$$\mathsf{Adv}_{H,\mathcal{A}}^{\mathsf{cp\text{-}forge}}(\lambda) = \Pr\left[\mathsf{Exp}_{H,\mathcal{A}}^{\mathsf{cp\text{-}forge}}(\lambda)\right].$$

Here experiment $\mathsf{Exp}_{H,\mathcal{A}}^{\mathsf{cp\text{-}forge}}(\lambda)$ *is given as*

$$\text{Experiment } Exp_{H,\mathcal{A}}^{\text{cp-forge}}(\lambda)$$

$1:$ $\mathsf{hk} \leftarrow\!\!\$ \ \mathsf{H.KGen}(1^\lambda)$

$2:$ $(t, d_1, \ldots, d_q, c) \leftarrow\!\!\$ \ \mathcal{A}(1^\lambda, \mathsf{hk})$

$3:$ $\mathbf{return} \ \mathsf{valid}(c, \mathsf{rootlabel}(t), \mathsf{hk}) \ \wedge$

$\mathsf{cp.data}(c) \neq d_{\mathsf{cp.pos}(c)} \ \wedge$

$t = \mathsf{tree}(\mathsf{hk}, d_1, \ldots, d_q)$

Then there exists PPT *adversary* $\mathcal{B}$ *such that*

$$\mathsf{Adv}_{H,\mathcal{A}}^{\text{cp-forge}}(\lambda) = \mathsf{Adv}_{H,\mathcal{B}}^{\text{cr}}(\lambda).$$

Note that here we consider a hash tree that is constructed by the adversary which, naturally, yields a stronger result as the result also holds for any adversary seeing only (parts of) a given tree. The task of the adversary is to generate a tree t for data $d_1, \ldots, d_q$ together with a certification path forgery for tree t. As a forgery requires the root of the certificate path to be identical to that of tree t it must contain a collision with one of the nodes in t. We can thus prove Lemma 6.12 by a standard reduction. For this we create an adversary $\mathcal{B}$ against the collision resistance of the hash function from adversary $\mathcal{A}$ against the hash tree. Adversary $\mathcal{B}$ simply calls adversary $\mathcal{A}$ and if adversary $\mathcal{A}$ succeeds then adversary $\mathcal{B}$ extracts and outputs the collision from tree t and the forged certification path cp. We leave a formal proof as Exercise 6.4.

6.4.2 Merkle Signatures

Hash trees were first proposed by Ralph Merkle in the late 1970s and are today often referred to as *Merkle trees*. Merkle constructed hash trees in order to build many-time signatures from one-time signatures. In order to generate a q-time signature we construct q-many signature key pairs $(\mathsf{pk}_1, \mathsf{sk}_1), \ldots, (\mathsf{pk}_q, \mathsf{sk}_q)$ for the one-time scheme. But instead of publishing all the public keys, we generate a hash tree t using the public keys as data blocks. We then publish the root of the tree as public key, that is, $\mathsf{pk} \leftarrow \mathsf{rootlabel}(t)$. To sign a message we use a fresh secret key sk_i to produce the signature according to the one-time scheme and in addition publish the corresponding certification path $\mathsf{cp}(t, \mathsf{pk}_i)$. To verify the signature we need to verify both the one-time signature as well as the certification path.

Before we discuss the security of Merkle signatures, let us give a formal description of the scheme.

Construction 6.13 (Merkle Signatures). *Let* Sig := (Sig.KGen, Sig.Sign, Sig.Vf) *be a one-time signature scheme and let* H := (H.KGen, H.Eval) *be a collision-resistant hash function. Then the* Merkle signature scheme *for* q *many signatures (we expect* q *to be a power of 2) is constructed as follows: Key generation is given as*

$\underline{\text{MSig.KGen}(1^\lambda, q)}$

$1:$ $\text{hk} \leftarrow\!\!\text{s } \text{H.KGen}(1^\lambda)$

$2:$ **for** $i = 1..q$ **do**

$3:$ $(\text{pk}_i, \text{sk}_i) \leftarrow\!\!\text{s } \text{Sig.KGen}(1^\lambda)$

$4:$ $t \leftarrow \text{tree}(\text{hk}, \text{pk}_1, \dots, \text{pk}_q)$

$5:$ $\text{mpk} \leftarrow (\text{hk}, \text{rootlabel}(t))$

$6:$ $\text{msk} \leftarrow (t, \{(\text{pk}_i, \text{sk}_i) \mid i \in [q]\})$

$7:$ **return** (mpk, msk)

Signing of messages and verification of signature–message pairs is then performed as

---
$\underline{\text{MSig.Sign}(i, \text{msk}, m)}$	$\underline{\text{MSig.Vf}(\text{mpk}, m, \sigma_m)}$
$1:$ $\sigma \leftarrow\!\!\text{s } \text{Sig.Sign}(\text{sk}_i, m)$	$1:$ $(\text{hk}, \text{rootlabel}(t)) \leftarrow \text{mpk}$
$2:$ $c \leftarrow \text{cp}(t, \text{pk}_i)$	$2:$ $(\sigma, \text{pk}, c) \leftarrow \sigma_m$
$3:$ $\sigma_m \leftarrow (\sigma, \text{pk}_i, c)$	$3:$ **return** Sig.Vf$(\text{pk}, m, \sigma) \wedge$
$4:$ **return** σ_m	$\quad$ valid$(c, \text{rootlabel}(t), \text{hk})$

Note that we fixed q *in the above construction. We similarly could consider a function* q : $\mathbb{N} \to \mathbb{N}$ *which for each security parameter specifies the number of possible signatures.*

The Merkle signature scheme is a stateful scheme in that we need to remember which secret keys have already been used to generate signatures. In the construction we have thus extended the signing algorithm Sign to take an additional index i to denote which underlying secret key to use for the signature generation. With each signature generation this value i is incremented by 1.

Security. The security of Merkle signatures is based on the security of the underlying one-time signature scheme as well as the security of the hash tree. Intuitively, the verification of the certification path ensures that the public key of the one-time scheme was part of the original set of public keys generated. If so, then the verification of the signature reduces to the verification of the signature according to the one-time scheme. The following proposition captures the security of Merkle signatures formally. We leave a formal proof as Exercise 6.5.

Proposition 6.14. *Let* Sig *be a one-time signature scheme and* H *be a collision-resistant hash function. Then the Merkle signature scheme (Construction 6.13) yields a* q-*time secure EUF-CMA signature scheme if for each signature a different index is used.*

How Much Is Many?

Hash trees allow us to go from a one-time signature scheme to a many-time signature scheme. But in case you want to be able to really sign many messages, say a million (2^{20}) or a billion (2^{30}) the resulting trees, and therewith the storage and upfront computation cost, quickly become huge. One way to optimize the size of the resulting hash tree (at the cost of slightly larger signatures) is to consider a tree of trees. Say we have a Merkle scheme set up for 1,024 messages and call this tree t_0. Our public key remains the root node of t_0. But, now instead of using t_0 to sign actual messages, we use it to sign the root node of other Merkle trees. That is, when we want to sign our first message m, we generate a second Merkle tree t_1 and use our first signature of t_0 (the first tree) to sign the root of our newly created tree t_1. We then use the first key in t_1 to sign the actual message m and publish as the signature for message m, the signature obtained via t_1 for m as well as the signature of rootlabel(t_1) using t_0. We can then go on to use t_1 to sign messages. Once we have used up all key pairs in t_1 we can generate a new tree t_2 and again use t_0 to sign its root.

With two levels of trees and each one of a capacity of $2^{10} = 1,024$ key pairs we can thus sign a total of 2^{20} messages. Of course we can use different tree sizes or use more than two levels in order to allow signing even more messages. Further note that we do not need to store all trees but only all active trees. That is, once we have used up all signatures in a tree we can discard it. Furthermore we need not create all trees upfront but can generate a new tree as needed.

Yet even with this tree of trees scheme we need to fix an upper bound on the number of messages that we can sign. And, we are still stateful in the sense that we need to remember which key pairs have already been used. In the next section we will see how we can overcome also these restrictions.

6.5 Constructing EUF-CMA Signatures

In the following paragraphs we want to present a signature scheme that overcomes the two restrictions we still have in Merkle signatures: an apriori upper bound q on the number of signatures we can make, and the need to keep book of how many signatures we have already created in order to not accidentally reuse a one-time signature key pair. Note that especially the statefulness of schemes is a significant constraint. For example, how can you create signatures from multiple, not necessarily always connected devices? Even a single mistake, that is, even a single reuse of a one-time key pair, may compromise the entire scheme.

The idea in the following is still to base the signature scheme on the security of a one-time signature scheme, somewhat similarly to how we generated Merkle signature schemes for large number of signatures. Here a signature of a message did not only contain a single one-time signature (and a certification path) but rather multiple one-time signatures (and certification paths) certifying the way from the root of the first tree to the leaf of a different tree (possibly a few levels down) that is used to sign the actual message. In order to become stateless we use a technique similar to the trick presented at the end of Section 6.2 to create short secret keys for Lamport signatures. We will base all one-time signature key pairs on pseudorandomness rather than actual randomness and will use a single PRF key to generate those values. Thus, our secret key, as in the extended Lamport scheme, will consist only of the PRF key.

Tree Signatures

Our scheme will be based on binary trees, yet not on hash trees. Instead we will identify each node of the tree with a one-time signature key pair. The scheme will be able to sign messages of a fixed length λ. In order to lift this restriction and allow for arbitrary message lengths we can then use the hash-and-sign construction from Section 6.3.

Key generation for the tree signature scheme will consist of a key generation for a pseudorandom function yielding key k as well as the generation of a single one-time signature key pair $(\mathsf{pk}_\varepsilon, \mathsf{sk}_\varepsilon)$. The public key pk will be the public key of the one-time signature $\mathsf{pk} \leftarrow \mathsf{pk}_\varepsilon$, and the secret key will be the PRF key as well as the secret key part of the one-time signature key pair $\mathsf{sk} \leftarrow (k, \mathsf{sk}_\varepsilon)$.

For signing messages of length λ we consider a binary tree of height λ which will thus have 2^λ many leaf nodes. If we want to later use the hash-and-sign scheme we thus need to consider a value of λ matching the output size of common hash functions, for example, 256 bits for SHA-2. This means, in particular, that the tree we consider has $2^{257} - 1$ many nodes in total; way too many to construct or store. Luckily we will not need to ever construct the tree in its entirety but instead for each signature construct only a single certification path[5] from the root to a single leaf. For this we will identify with each message m of size $|m| = \lambda$ a unique path from root to a leaf. As there are exactly 2^λ leaves, each one with a single unique path to the root node, we

---

[5] Although our tree is not a hash tree, the required path matches exactly that of a certification path for a hash tree of the same size.

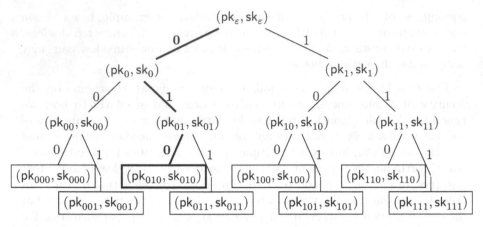

Fig. 6.11: A full tree of a tree signature scheme for messages of size $\lambda = 3$. Each node is associated with a one-time signature key pair. Each left edge is labeled with 0 and each right edge with 1. Paths from root to leaf correspond to 3-bit messages by concatenating the labels of the passed edges. The path corresponding to message $m = 010$ is highlighted.

can construct a unique mapping from message to path (and vice versa) as follows.

Each node (except for leaf nodes) has two outgoing edges: one going to the left child and one going to the right child. We label the left edge with 0 and the right edge with 1. On a binary tree of height λ we will pass over exactly λ many edges on the way from the root to a leaf and we will use the message m to guide the way.[6] Given a message m of size $|m| = \lambda$ we will construct a path as follows. The path starts from the root node. Here we take the left outgoing edge if $m[1] = 0$ and the right edge if $m[1] = 1$. In this way we work ourselves downwards towards the leaf node. At the ith node, we take the left edge if $m[i] = 0$ and the right edge otherwise. Figure 6.11 shows a tree of height $\lambda = 3$ and highlights the path for message $m = 010$.

With the above mapping not only can we map messages to paths, but with each node in the tree we can identify a bit string: the concatenation of the edge labels from the root node to that particular node. The root node will correspond to the empty string ε, nodes on level 1 correspond to bit strings of length 1, and nodes on level λ to bit strings of length λ. With each bit string w we identify a one-time signature key pair $(\mathsf{pk}_w, \mathsf{sk}_w)$ generated deterministically using the pseudorandom function as follows:

$$\underline{\mathsf{SigPair}(\mathsf{k}, w)}$$

1 : $r \leftarrow \mathsf{PRF}(\mathsf{k}, w)$

2 : $(\mathsf{pk}_w, \mathsf{sk}_w) \leftarrow \mathsf{Sig.KGen}(1^\lambda; r)$

3 : **return** $(\mathsf{pk}_w, \mathsf{sk}_w)$

---

[6] Note that this is similar to the GGM construction of a pseudorandom function where the message defines a path in a binary tree (see Section 3.4.2; page 141).

That is, we generate randomness r to be used in the creation of key pair $(\mathsf{pk}_w, \mathsf{sk}_w)$ by evaluating the PRF on input w and assuming that the PRF is defined on at least the input lengths 1 up to λ.[7] For simplicity we here also assume that the output length of the PRF produces sufficiently many pseudorandom bits to be used in the key generation of the one-time signature. Should this not be the case we could use it as the seed for a pseudorandom generator to stretch the pseudorandom string to the required length. It follows that $\mathsf{SigPair}(\mathsf{k}, w)$ is deterministic and will always generate the same key pair on the same prefix w.

The above description yields a key pair for each node within the tree except for the single root. We identify the original key pair $(\mathsf{pk}_\varepsilon, \mathsf{sk}_\varepsilon)$ generated as part of the key generation for the tree signature scheme with the root node.

We now have everything needed in order to sign a message m. For this we will work our way from the root node to leaf m on the path specified by message m. At each node w that we pass we will use the corresponding key pair $(\mathsf{pk}_w, \mathsf{sk}_w)$ to sign the public keys for both child nodes: we sign a message corresponding to $(\mathsf{pk}_{w0}, \mathsf{pk}_{w1})$, that is, we generate signature $\sigma_w \leftarrow\!\!\$\ \mathsf{Sig.Sign}(\mathsf{sk}_w, (\mathsf{pk}_{w0}, \mathsf{pk}_{w1}))$.[8] Finally when we reach the leaf with corresponding key pair $(\mathsf{pk}_m, \mathsf{sk}_m)$ we use sk_m to sign message m as $\sigma_m \leftarrow\!\!\$\ \mathsf{Sig.Sign}(\mathsf{sk}_m, m)$. The final signature then consists of all the public keys on the path identified by m and all generated signatures and corresponding messages (public key pairs), that is,

$$\sigma \leftarrow \big((\sigma_\varepsilon, (\mathsf{pk}_0, \mathsf{pk}_1)),$$
$$\{(\sigma_w, \mathsf{pk}_w, (\mathsf{pk}_{w0}, \mathsf{pk}_{w1})) \mid w \text{ is prefix of } m\},$$
$$(\sigma_m, \mathsf{pk}_m)\big).$$

For verification we check each individual signature and furthermore check that the chain of public keys is unbroken. Given message $m = 010$ we would thus check that:

- σ_ε is a valid signature for $(\mathsf{pk}_0, \mathsf{pk}_1)$ under public key $\mathsf{pk} = \mathsf{pk}_\varepsilon$,
- σ_0 is a valid signature for $(\mathsf{pk}_{00}, \mathsf{pk}_{01})$ under key pk_0,
- σ_{01} is a valid signature for $(\mathsf{pk}_{010}, \mathsf{pk}_{011})$ key pk_{01},
- σ_{010} is a valid signature for message m under key pk_{010}.

Formalizing tree signatures. Before we discuss security and properties of the scheme, let us formalize the tree signature construction.

---

[7] Alternatively we could specify an encoding such that each possible value w is mapped to a different input, possibly of the same length $\mathsf{PRF.il}$. One such encoding could be $w \| 10 \dots 0$.

[8] We here skip the details and assume a proper encoding of $(\mathsf{pk}_{w0}, \mathsf{pk}_{w1})$ as a bit string that can be signed by the one-time signature scheme.

[9] For simplicity of presentation we do not specify a detailed encoding. Further note that one-time signature schemes exist that allow to sign sufficiently long messages, for example, via the hash-and-sign paradigm (see Section 6.3).

Construction 6.15. *Let* Sig *be a one-time signature scheme and* PRF *be a pseudorandom function. We construct* TSig := (TSig.KGen, TSig.Sign, TSig.Vf) *for signing messages of length* λ *as stated below. We assume that pseudorandom function* PRF *allows evaluating messages on lengths 1 up to* λ *and that the one-time signature scheme* Sig *can sign messages of length* λ *and the size of two of its own public keys.*[9]

Key generation: *Key generation generates a key* k *for the pseudorandom function and a key pair* $(\mathsf{pk}_\varepsilon, \mathsf{sk}_\varepsilon)$ *for the one-time signature scheme. Key* pk_ε *forms the public key, keys* $(\mathsf{k}, \mathsf{sk}_\varepsilon)$ *the secret key. Following is a detailed pseudocode description:*

$$\underline{\mathsf{TSig.KGen}(1^\lambda)}$$

1 : $\mathsf{k} \leftarrow_\$ \mathsf{PRF.KGen}(1^\lambda)$

2 : $(\mathsf{pk}_\varepsilon, \mathsf{sk}_\varepsilon) \leftarrow_\$ \mathsf{Sig.KGen}(1^\lambda)$

3 : $\mathsf{tpk} \leftarrow \mathsf{pk}_\varepsilon$

4 : $\mathsf{tsk} \leftarrow (\mathsf{k}, \mathsf{sk}_\varepsilon)$

5 : **return** $(\mathsf{tpk}, \mathsf{tsk})$

Signing: *Signing a message* m *consists of signing all public keys on the path from the tree's root to the leaf corresponding to* m *(see Figure 6.11). This entails generating the necessary key pairs deterministically using pseudorandom function* PRF. *Previously generated key pair* $(\mathsf{pk}_\varepsilon, \mathsf{sk}_\varepsilon)$ *is used at the root of the tree. Following is a detailed pseudocode description:*

$\underline{\mathsf{TSig.Sign}(\mathsf{tsk}, m)}$	$\underline{\mathsf{SigPair}(\mathsf{k}, w)}$
1 : $(\mathsf{pk}_0, \mathsf{sk}_0) \leftarrow \mathsf{SigPair}(\mathsf{k}, 0)$	1 : $r \leftarrow \mathsf{PRF.Eval}(\mathsf{k}, w)$
2 : $(\mathsf{pk}_1, \mathsf{sk}_1) \leftarrow \mathsf{SigPair}(\mathsf{k}, 1)$	2 : $(\mathsf{pk}_w, \mathsf{sk}_w) \leftarrow \mathsf{Sig.KGen}(1^\lambda; r)$
3 : $\sigma_\varepsilon \leftarrow \mathsf{Sig.Sign}(\mathsf{sk}_\varepsilon, (\mathsf{pk}_0, \mathsf{pk}_1))$	3 : **return** $(\mathsf{pk}_w, \mathsf{sk}_w)$
4 : **for** $i = 1..(\lambda - 1)$ **do**	
5 : $w \leftarrow m[1..i]$	
6 : $(\mathsf{pk}_w, \mathsf{sk}_w) \leftarrow \mathsf{SigPair}(\mathsf{k}, w)$	
7 : $(\mathsf{pk}_{w0}, \mathsf{sk}_{w0}) \leftarrow \mathsf{SigPair}(\mathsf{k}, w\|0)$	
8 : $(\mathsf{pk}_{w1}, \mathsf{sk}_{w1}) \leftarrow \mathsf{SigPair}(\mathsf{k}, w\|1)$	
9 : $\sigma_w \leftarrow_\$ \mathsf{Sig.Sign}(\mathsf{sk}_w, (\mathsf{pk}_{w0}, \mathsf{pk}_{w1}))$	
10 : $(\mathsf{pk}_m, \mathsf{sk}_m) \leftarrow \mathsf{SigPair}(\mathsf{k}, m)$	
11 : $\sigma_m \leftarrow_\$ \mathsf{Sig.Sign}(\mathsf{sk}_m, m)$	
12 : $\sigma_t \leftarrow \big((\sigma_\varepsilon, (\mathsf{pk}_0, \mathsf{pk}_1)),$	
$\{(\sigma_w, \mathsf{pk}_w, (\mathsf{pk}_{w0}, \mathsf{pk}_{w1})) \mid w \text{ is prefix of } m\},$	
$(\sigma_m, \mathsf{pk}_m)\big)$	
13 : **return** σ_t	

Verification: *Verification of a signature requires verifying the chain of public keys, starting with the "root signature" σ_ε (which is to be verified with public key tpk) down to the signature for the actual message σ_m which is verified with included key pk_m. Following is a detailed pseudocode description:*

$\mathsf{TSig.Vf}(\mathsf{tpk}, m, \sigma_t)$

$1:$ $\big((\sigma_\varepsilon, (\mathsf{pk}_0, \mathsf{pk}_1)),$

$\{(\sigma_w, \mathsf{pk}_w, (\mathsf{pk}_{w0}, \mathsf{pk}_{w1})) \mid w \text{ is prefix of } m\},$

$(\sigma_m, \mathsf{pk}_m)\big) \leftarrow \sigma_t$

$2:$ **unless** $\mathsf{Sig.Vf}(\mathsf{tpk}, (\mathsf{pk}_0, \mathsf{pk}_1), \sigma_\varepsilon)$ **return** false

$3:$ **for** $i = 1..(\lambda - 1)$ **do**

$4:$ $\quad w \leftarrow m[1..i]$

$5:$ $\quad$ **unless** $\mathsf{Sig.Vf}(\mathsf{pk}_w, (\mathsf{pk}_{w0}, \mathsf{pk}_{w1}), \sigma_w)$ **return** false

$6:$ **return** $\mathsf{Sig.Vf}(\mathsf{pk}_m, m, \sigma_m)$

Construction 6.15 yields a *stateless* signature scheme. The same message corresponds to the same path in the binary tree and with the deterministic generation of the one-time signature key pairs at each node, each time the same key pairs are generated and thus the intermediate signatures are always for the same message $(\mathsf{pk}_{w0}, \mathsf{pk}_{w1})$. In particular this means that each one-time signature key pair is used to sign exactly one message. In order to forge a signature for a fresh message an adversary thus needs to either break the PRF and guess the randomness for the key generation, or break the security of the one-time signature scheme. We get the following security claim:

Proposition 6.16. *Let* Sig *be signature scheme and* PRF *be a pseudorandom function. If* Sig *is one-time EUF-CMA secure and* PRF *is a secure pseudorandom function then the tree signature construction* TSig *defined as in Construction 6.15 is EUF-CMA secure.*

A full security proof of Proposition 6.16 is rather technical and here omitted. It can be proven, for example, with the game-hopping technique, where in a first game hop the PRF is replaced by a random function to generate true randomness and in further game hops the security of the one-time signature scheme is established by showing that the adversary cannot break the first-level signature in the tree and then showing by induction that if the adversary cannot break signatures up to level i that it cannot break the signatures at level $i + 1$. We leave a formal proof as Exercise 6.6.

Efficiency. Let us consider that we use the tree signature scheme in conjunction with hash-and-sign and a popular hash function currently used in practice such as SHA-2. Here we have 256 bits of output and thus the underlying binary of the tree signature has a height of 256. A resulting signature then contains 256 one-time signatures including 2 times 256 public keys for the one-time signature. While we can optimize on the public key size (for example, a public key in the Merkle signature scheme consists of only a single hash value) as well as the signature size of one-time signature schemes the resulting signatures will still be very large due to the sheer number of signatures. With the number of one-time signatures to be created also the generation time of a signature goes up. Concluding, the tree signature scheme in this form should be regarded more as a proof of concept rather than a practical scheme.

For practical schemes it often helps to assume a bit more strength in the underlying primitives. While here we started only with one-wayness and collision resistance (or target-collision resistance) we will see in later chapters (in particular in Chapter 9 and Chapter 10) how we can use idealized hash functions to construct very efficient signature schemes.

6.6 Signature Schemes and One-Way Functions

Let us make an important and remarkable observation. Theorem 3.33 (page 140) states that pseudorandom functions can be constructed from one-way functions. Furthermore, Theorem 4.11 on page 180 states that target-collision-resistant hash functions can be constructed solely from one-way functions. Together with the fact that one-time signatures can be constructed from one-way functions (Theorem 6.5), that the hash-and-sign transformation can be based on target-collision-resistant hash functions (Theorem 6.10), and the security of the tree signature scheme (Proposition 6.16), it follows that EUF-CMA-secure signature schemes exist if one-way functions exist.

> **Theorem 6.17.** *If one-way functions exist, then EUF-CMA-secure signature schemes exist.*

6.7 Certificates and Public-Key Infrastructures

We close this chapter with a brief discussion of *public-key infrastructures*. Recall that we argued that public-key encryption allows two parties to communicate confidentially without the need to have ever met or exchanged a set of secret keys. This is only half true. For this consider Alice who wants to send a confidential message to Bob. In order to encrypt the message she looks up Bob's public key in a registry. But how can she be sure that the key given in the registry is indeed Bob's public key and not, say, Eve's who managed to infiltrate the register? Thus also in the public-key setting we require that public keys are distributed "securely."

Signature schemes provide us with the means to solve this key distribution problem. For this consider a message such as

$$m_{\text{Bob}} := \text{``pk}_{\text{Bob}} \text{ is the public key of Bob''}.$$

When combined with a signature $\sigma_{\text{Bob}} \leftarrow_\$ \text{Sig.Sign}(\text{sk}_{\text{CA}}, m_{\text{Bob}})$ we call the result a certificate

$$\text{cert}_{\text{Bob}} := (m_{\text{Bob}}, \sigma_{\text{Bob}})$$

certifying Bob's public key. If Bob now sends Alice a certificate cert_{Bob} which is signed by a party that Alice considers trustworthy—a party issuing certificates is called a *certificate authority* (CA for short)—then Alice is assured that Bob's public key is indeed pk_{Bob}. It is, of course, up to Alice to decide which CAs she trusts, a decision which she might even change on a per use-case basis. For important messages she might require multiple certificates from different CAs for her to consider a public key as trustworthy and for less important messages she might be content with just a single certificate.

Remark 6.18. Note that the currency CAs deal in is *trust*: trust that the CA properly verifies the identity of individuals for whom they issue certificates and trust in that the CA properly protects their signing key. As such, certificate authorities can be anything from companies over (governmental) organizations to individuals. CAs can also be organized in a hierarchy with a root CA that issues certificates for subsidiaries that then issue certificates for further parties.

Public-Key Infrastructures

A complete specification of how to manage certificates and public keys is referred to as a *public-key infrastructure*. This includes a specification of the available CAs, the process to apply for and grant certificates—this includes, for example, who can apply for certificates in the first place and how the identity of applicants is verified—as well as a definition of which certificates to trust and for which tasks.

Besides defining a process of how certificates can be obtained, it is equally important to define how certificates can be revoked. For this consider the case that Bob's private key got lost or stolen. While in this case he can let the CA know that he is no longer in control of his private key, if there is no process of certificate revocation in place any participant in the PKI would continue to trust previously issued certificates for Bob's public key. While there are many conceivable processes to deal with certificate revocation we here only mention two simple schemes: The insertion of an expiration date into the certificate and the regular publishing of revocation lists (lists of revoked certificates). In the first case a certificate holds not only the identity of the holder and the public key but also an expiration date until when the certificate is valid. If received after the expiration date, the certificate should not be trusted. Using certificates with expiration dates is, for example, a common practice to distribute the public keys of websites on the internet. The second option gives more control to the participants but also makes the verification process more cumbersome. Here, the certificate authority regularly issues a list of revoked certificates that clients need to update in a timely manner. For this, the usual practice is to embed a serial number inside the certificate such that the revocation list does not need to contain the entire revoked certificate but only the serial number.

It should be clear that the secure setup and operation of a PKI is a complex endeavor and a discussion of all the aspects involved goes far beyond the scope of this book. We provide references to further reading material below in the notes and references section.

Chapter Notes and References

We here considered signatures mostly from the perspective of hash functions. For a more extensive introduction into the subject we refer the interested reader to Jonathan Katz's textbook "Digital Signatures" [13]. The groundwork for public-key infrastructures was laid by Kohnfelder [15], and we refer to Buchmann *et al.* [2] for an in-depth introduction.

Signature schemes are one of the oldest primitives of modern cryptography. Early work includes the works of Diffie and Hellman [5], the work by Rivest, Shamir, and Adleman on RSA [26], Lamport's work on one-time signatures [16] (Section 6.2), the works of Rabin [24, 25] and the works by Goldwasser and Micali together with Tong and Yao [10, 11].

The notion of *existential unforgeability under adaptive chosen-message attacks* (EUF-CMA) was defined by Goldwasser, Micali, and Rivest in 1984 [8, 9]. Goldwasser *et al.* also gave the first construction of a stateful EUF-CMA-secure signature scheme, which is often referred to as the GMR signature scheme. Goldreich showed how to transform the GMR construction into a stateless construction with the help of pseudorandom generators [7]. The tree-based signature scheme from Section 6.5 is essentially a generalized version of the GMR construction following the ideas of Goldreich. The presentation is based on Katz and Lindell [14] (Chapter 12).

The hash-and-sign paradigm was introduced by Damgård in 1987 [4] in his seminal paper on collision-resistant hash functions. Two years later, Naor and Yung introduced target-collision-resistant hash functions (which they called universal one-way hash functions) and showed that the hash-and-sign transformation can also be based on this simpler notion. A generic construction of target-collision-resistant hash functions from one-way functions was given by Rompel [27], thus establishing that EUF-CMA signature schemes can indeed be constructed solely on the assumption of one-way functions.

The study of *hash-based* signatures was initiated by Lamport in 1979 with his work on one-time signatures [16], although the scheme had been already described in [5]. It is also sometimes referred to as the Lamport–Diffie one-time signature scheme. One-time signatures were later refined by Merkle, who in the late 1980s introduced hash trees and showed how these can be used to obtain stateful q-time signatures on top of one-time signature schemes [18, 19].

There is a large body of work considering hash-based signature schemes; for an early overview see Dods *et al.* [6]. Practical schemes that emerged from this line of research include the Leighton–Micali signature scheme [17] and the *extended Merkle signature scheme* (XMSS) [1, 12], both of which are currently undergoing standardization by the National Institute of Standards and Technology (NIST) as NIST SP 800-208 [23]. SP 800-208 targets to supplement FIPS 186, which was first published in 1994 [20] (last revised in 2013 [21]) and which describes the widely used *Digital Signature Algorithm* (DSA) based on the discrete logarithm problem, its elliptic curve variant ECDSA, and the *RSA signature algorithm* based on factoring.

With the emergence of quantum computers, hash-based signatures have gained renewed interest in the past decade as it is suspected that hash-based schemes are less vulnerable to quantum attacks and that it is possible to construct schemes that are not only secure in the classical setting but also secure in a quantum setting [3]. As all standardized signature schemes in FIPS 186 can be broken with quantum attacks, NIST recently initiated a process (in the form of a competition) to find and ultimately standardize one or more quantum-resistant public-key cryptographic algorithms [22].

Exercices

Exercise 6.1. Lamport's one-time signature scheme in Section 6.2 (pages 264ff.) allows to sign messages of exactly λ bits. Show that it would be insecure if verification accepted any message with length λ or less. Provide a version of the scheme which allows to sign (and verify) messages with length at most λ.

Exercise 6.2. We have seen in Theorem 6.5 (page 266) that one-way functions are sufficient to construct one-time signature schemes. Prove that the inverse is also correct, that is, the existence of one-time signature schemes implies the existence of one-way functions. This holds even in case the signature scheme is for 1-bit messages only.

Exercise 6.3. Theorem 6.10 (page 278) shows that we can hash longer messages with a target-collision-resistant hash function if we sign both the hash key and the hashed message, $hk\|y$, and add hk to the signature. Show that this is not true if we only sign y and merely put hk into the signature.

Exercise 6.4. Prove Lemma 6.12 (page 287).

Exercise 6.5. Prove Proposition 6.14 (page 290). That is, show that the Merkle signature scheme is secure, assuming the security of the hash function and the one-time signature scheme.

Exercise 6.6. Show that the tree signature scheme yields a EUF-CMA-secure signature scheme (Proposition 6.16; page 295).

Chapter Bibliography

1. Johannes A. Buchmann, Erik Dahmen, and Andreas Hülsing. XMSS - A practical forward secure signature scheme based on minimal security assumptions. In Bo-Yin Yang, editor, *Post-Quantum Cryptography - 4th International Workshop, PQCrypto 2011*, pages 117–129, Tapei, Taiwan, November 29 – December 2 2011. Springer, Heidelberg, Germany.
2. Johannes A. Buchmann, Evangelos Karatsiolis, and Alexander Wiesmaier. *Introduction to Public Key Infrastructures*. Springer Publishing Company, Incorporated, 2013.
3. Lily Chen, Stephen Jordan, Yi-Kai Liu, Dustin Moody, Rene Peralta, Ray Perlner, and Smith-Tone Daniel. NISTIR 8105: Report on post-quantum cryptography. https://csrc.nist.gov/publications/detail/nistir/8105/final, 4 2016.
4. Ivan Damgård. Collision free hash functions and public key signature schemes. In David Chaum and Wyn L. Price, editors, *Advances in Cryptology – EUROCRYPT'87*, volume 304 of *Lecture Notes in Computer Science*, pages 203–216, Amsterdam, The Netherlands, April 13–15, 1988. Springer, Heidelberg, Germany.
5. Whitfield Diffie and Martin E. Hellman. New directions in cryptography. *IEEE Transactions on Information Theory*, 22(6):644–654, 1976.
6. C. Dods, Nigel P. Smart, and Martijn Stam. Hash based digital signature schemes. In Nigel P. Smart, editor, *10th IMA International Conference on Cryptography and Coding*, volume 3796 of *Lecture Notes in Computer Science*, pages 96–115, Cirencester, UK, December 19–21, 2005. Springer, Heidelberg, Germany.
7. Oded Goldreich. Two remarks concerning the Goldwasser-Micali-Rivest signature scheme. In Andrew M. Odlyzko, editor, *Advances in Cryptology – CRYPTO'86*, volume 263 of *Lecture Notes in Computer Science*, pages 104–110, Santa Barbara, CA, USA, August 1987. Springer, Heidelberg, Germany.
8. Shafi Goldwasser, Silvio Micali, and Ronald L. Rivest. A "paradoxical" solution to the signature problem (extended abstract). In *25th Annual Symposium on Foundations of Computer Science*, pages 441–448, Singer Island, Florida, October 24–26, 1984. IEEE Computer Society Press.
9. Shafi Goldwasser, Silvio Micali, and Ronald L. Rivest. A digital signature scheme secure against adaptive chosen-message attacks. *SIAM Journal on Computing*, 17(2):281–308, April 1988.
10. Shafi Goldwasser, Silvio Micali, and Po Tong. Why and how to establish a private code on a public network (extended abstract). In *23rd Annual Symposium on Foundations of Computer Science*, pages 134–144, Chicago, Illinois, November 3–5, 1982. IEEE Computer Society Press.
11. Shafi Goldwasser, Silvio Micali, and Andrew Chi-Chih Yao. Strong signature schemes. In *15th Annual ACM Symposium on Theory of Computing*, pages 431–439, Boston, MA, USA, April 25–27, 1983. ACM Press.
12. A. Huelsing, D. Butin, S. Gazdag, J. Rijneveld, and A. Mohaisen. XMSS: extended Merkle signature scheme. RFC 8391, RFC Editor, May 2018.
13. Jonathan Katz. *Digital signatures*. Springer Science & Business Media, 2010.

14. Jonathan Katz and Yehuda Lindell. *Introduction to Modern Cryptography*. Chapman & Hall/CRC, 2014.

15. Loren M. Kohnfelder. *Towards a practical public-key cryptosystem*. PhD thesis, Massachusetts Institute of Technology, 1978.

16. Leslie Lamport. Constructing digital signatures from a one-way function. Technical Report SRI-CSL-98, SRI International Computer Science Laboratory, October 1979.

17. D. McGrew, M. Curcio, and S. Fluhrer. Leighton–Micali hash-based signatures. RFC 8554, RFC Editor, April 2019.

18. Ralph C. Merkle. A digital signature based on a conventional encryption function. In Carl Pomerance, editor, *Advances in Cryptology – CRYPTO'87*, volume 293 of *Lecture Notes in Computer Science*, pages 369–378, Santa Barbara, CA, USA, August 16–20, 1988. Springer, Heidelberg, Germany.

19. Ralph C. Merkle. A certified digital signature. In Gilles Brassard, editor, *Advances in Cryptology – CRYPTO'89*, volume 435 of *Lecture Notes in Computer Science*, pages 218–238, Santa Barbara, CA, USA, August 20–24, 1990. Springer, Heidelberg, Germany.

20. National Institute of Standards and Technology (NIST). FIPS PUB 186: Digital Signature Standard (DSS). `https://csrc.nist.gov/publications/detail/fips/186/archive/1996-12-30`, 5 1994.

21. National Institute of Standards and Technology (NIST). FIPS PUB 186-4: Digital Signature Standard (DSS). `https://csrc.nist.gov/publications/detail/fips/186/4/final`, 7 2013.

22. National Institute of Standards and Technology (NIST). Post-quantum cryptography. `https://csrc.nist.gov/Projects/post-quantum-cryptography/Post-Quantum-Cryptography-Standardization`, 2016.

23. National Institute of Standards and Technology (NIST). SP 800-208 (Draft): Recommendation for stateful hash-based signature schemes. `https://csrc.nist.gov/publications/detail/sp/800-208/draft`, 12 2019.

24. Michael O Rabin. Digitalized signatures. *Foundations of Secure Computation*, pages 155–168, 1978.

25. Michael O. Rabin. Digital signatures and public key functions as intractable as factorization. Technical Report MIT/LCS/TR-212, Massachusetts Institute of Technology, January 1979.

26. Ronald L. Rivest, Adi Shamir, and Leonard M. Adleman. A method for obtaining digital signatures and public-key cryptosystems. *Communications of the Association for Computing Machinery*, 21(2):120–126, 1978.

27. John Rompel. One-way functions are necessary and sufficient for secure signatures. In *22nd Annual ACM Symposium on Theory of Computing*, pages 387–394, Baltimore, MD, USA, May 14–16, 1990. ACM Press.

Chapter 7
Non-cryptographic Hashing

There are notions of hash functions originating from the area of fast storage and retrieval in data structures which have also found many applications in cryptography and other areas of computer science. These functions are often subsumed under the term *universal hash functions*, although we will see in this chapter that a more fine-grained view on such functions is recommended, especially in light of cryptographic applications. We call them here *non-cryptographic hash functions* because they display a significant advantage over cryptographic hash functions: A non-cryptographic hash function does not rely on any problem which is believed to be hard but where the hardness proof is currently missing. Instead, non-cryptographic hash functions can be constructed *unconditionally*. As an example of their usefulness, we will construct unconditionally secure one-time (or k-time) message authentication codes from pairwise independent hash functions, a variant of universal hash functions. In many cases, however, universal hash functions alone are insufficient for modern cryptographic purposes. Still, they are useful tools in combination with other cryptographic primitives. We will see, for example, how we can construct a target-collision-resistant hash function from a one-to-one one-way function (e.g., a one-way permutation) and a universal hash function. As the latter primitive exists unconditionally, this immediately yields that target-collision-resistant functions can be constructed from one-way permutations (see also our discussion in Section 4.4.1).

Remark 7.1. As you will see, the math behind universal hash functions is somewhat different from the math that we have used until now. The reason is that universal hash functions can be constructed unconditionally and thus results need not be framed via security reductions but can be stated directly using probability theory and results from analysis, linear algebra, and algebra. A basic understanding of these fields is thus a prerequisite for fully understanding the proofs and constructions in this chapter. We note that the concrete constructions are not required for understanding the remainder of this book and it is thus safe to skim over the details.

© Springer Nature Switzerland AG 2021
A. Mittelbach, M. Fischlin, *The Theory of Hash Functions and Random Oracles*,
Information Security and Cryptography, https://doi.org/10.1007/978-3-030-63287-8_7

7.1 Universal Hash Functions

Universal hash functions can be regarded as an information-theoretic variant of collision-resistant hash functions. There we considered a PPT adversary that given a key hk can find collisions for some hash function H, that is, two messages x and x' such that $\mathsf{H.Eval}(x) = \mathsf{H.Eval}(x')$. In the information-theoretic setting collision resistance as we have defined it in Chapter 4 cannot exist. Recall that in the information-theoretic setting (the setting of the one-time pad) an adversary has no computational restrictions. But an adversary that is unbounded can find collisions for any hash function that has collisions simply by brute force. Thus, in order to get a meaningful notion in this statistical setting we must consequently weaken the security guarantee we aim for.

The main idea underlying *universal hash functions* is to consider the *probability of collisions over the random choice of key*. This means that the adversary has to output two messages without seeing a key and wins if the two messages collide under a randomly chosen key. As the adversary in the information-theoretic setting has no computational restrictions its best strategy is to choose the two messages x and x' that maximize the probability that they collide over a randomly chosen key:

$$\arg\max_{x,x'} \Pr_{\mathsf{hk}\leftarrow_{\$}\mathsf{H.KGen}(1^\lambda)}\left[\mathsf{H.Eval}(\mathsf{hk}, x) = \mathsf{H.Eval}(\mathsf{hk}, x')\right].$$

In order to formulate security properties we can, thus, quantify over all pairs of messages instead of quantifying over all possible adversaries. As in this case the notion of an adversary helps neither the formulation nor a lot the understanding of notions, it is customary to not define universal hash functions relative to unbounded adversaries but directly via statistical properties.

We start by presenting (basic versions) of universal hash functions and their constructions.

7.1.1 ε-Almost Universal Hash Functions

A universal hash function guarantees that distinct inputs only collide under the hash function with some small probability. As discussed above, this is akin to collision-resistant hashing but here formulated as a pure statistical property:

Definition 7.2 (ϵ-Almost-Universal Hash Function). *A hash function* $H = (H.KGen, H.Eval)$ *is ϵ-almost universal (ϵ-AU) if for all $x \neq x'$ in the domain it holds that*

$$\Pr[H.Eval(hk, x) = H.Eval(hk, x')] \leq \epsilon(\lambda),$$

where the probability is over the random choice of key $hk \leftarrow\!\!\$\, H.KGen(1^\lambda)$. *The hash function is called* universal *if* $\epsilon(\lambda) = 2^{-H.ol(\lambda)}$.

Ideally, the "collision probability" ϵ should be small. (Perfect) universal hash functions map distinct inputs to the same output with the minimal probability that two uniformly distributed strings collide. Strictly speaking, this may still not be optimal. There may even be ϵ-AU hash functions with $\epsilon = 0$, e.g., the identity function has this property where the input length matches the output length. But for most applications we are interested in universal hash functions which compress and which distribute the input well.

There are two important differences between collision-resistant and universal hash functions. One difference is that universal hash functions give a different form of collision resistance in the sense that the inputs $x \neq x'$ are first fixed and only then is a random hash function key chosen. The classical notion of collision resistance says that it is hard to find collisions even after learning the hash key. Even in second-preimage resistance or target-collision resistance for cryptographic hash functions the adversary has the option to chose some input after the hash function (resp. the function's key) has been specified. Yet, for a universal hash function it suffices that a collision with high probability exists, whereas the adversary in collision-resistant hashing needs to specify such a collision.

The other difference between universal hash functions and collision-resistant hash functions lies in the hardness of building the corresponding primitive. While collision-resistant hash functions must rely on cryptographic assumptions, we show that universal hash functions can be constructed unconditionally. This is possible since they aim at a different security guarantee.

7.1.2 XOR-Universal Hash Function

An important generalization of almost-universal hash functions is the notion of almost-XOR-universal hash functions. These functions demand that the exclusive-or of two hash values maps to a predetermined value with small probability only. Since the actual constructions of XOR-universal functions and of universal functions are very similar, it is convenient to define the variant at this point:

Definition 7.3 (ϵ-Almost-XOR-Universal Hash Function). *A hash function* H = (H.KGen, H.Eval) *is* ϵ-almost XOR-universal *(ϵ-AXU) if for all* $x \neq x'$ *in the domain and all* Δ *it holds that*

$$\Pr[\mathsf{H.Eval}(hk, x) \oplus \mathsf{H.Eval}(hk, x') = \Delta] \leq \epsilon(\lambda),$$

where the probability is over the random choice of hk $\leftarrow\!\!\$$ H.KGen(1^λ).

It is easy to see that any ϵ-AXU hash function is also ϵ-AU. The converse does not hold. We summarize this in the following proposition:

Proposition 7.4 (ϵ-AXU $\Rightarrow$ ϵ-AU, ϵ-AU $\not\Rightarrow$ ϵ-AXU). *Any* ϵ-AXU *hash function* H *is also an* ϵ-AU *hash function. For any* $\epsilon(\lambda) < 1$ *there are* ϵ-AU *hash functions which are not* ϵ-AXU.

Proof. Assume that we have an ϵ-AXU hash function H. By definition, for any $x \neq x'$ and any Δ the probability that H.Eval$(hk, x) \oplus$ H.Eval$(hk, x') = \Delta$ is at most $\epsilon(\lambda)$, over the choice of hk. If we now take $\Delta = 0^{\mathsf{H.ol}(\lambda)}$ to be the all-zero string, then the exclusive-or of the hash values only equals Δ if they are equal. Hence, we can conclude that the probability that H.Eval$(hk, x) =$ H.Eval(hk, x') is at most $\epsilon(\lambda)$, as required for the ϵ-AU property.

Vice versa, take any ϵ-AU hash function H. We will show in Section 7.1.3 that such functions exist unconditionally. Modify this function to a function H' which takes an extra input bit and has an additional output bit. It removes the first bit of the input, evaluates the original hash function H on the remaining part, and prepends the original first bit to the output again:

H'.KGen(1^λ)	H'.Eval$(hk, b\|\|x)$
1 : hk $\leftarrow\!\!\$$ H.KGen(λ)	1 : $y \leftarrow$ H.Eval(hk, x)
2 : **return** hk	2 : $y' \leftarrow b\|\|y$
	3 : **return** y'

The modified hash function H' is still ϵ-AU. To collide for distinct inputs $b\|\|x$, $b'\|\|x'$ we must have $b = b'$. But then the hash values would in particular need to collide under the original hash function H.Eval$(hk, \cdot)$ for $x \neq x'$. This happens with probability at most $\epsilon(\lambda)$. But H' is *not* ϵ-AXU. For $\Delta = 1\|\|0^{\mathsf{H.ol}(\lambda)}$ the exclusive-or of the hash values for inputs $0\|\|x, 1\|\|x$ for any x would yield Δ:

$$\mathsf{H'.Eval}(hk, 0\|\|x) \oplus \mathsf{H'.Eval}(hk, 1\|\|x)$$
$$= [0\|\|\mathsf{H.Eval}(hk, x)] \oplus [1\|\|\mathsf{H.Eval}(hk, x)] = 1\|\|0^{\mathsf{H.ol}(\lambda)} = \Delta.$$

Hence, the function is not ϵ-AXU for any $\epsilon(\lambda) < 1$. $\square$

The above separation example shows that in principle ϵ-AXU hash functions are strictly stronger than ϵ-AU hash functions. In practice, however, building

ϵ-AXU hash functions is not significantly more challenging than constructing ϵ-AU functions.

7.1.3 Constructions

We next present the two most prominent approaches to build (XOR-)universal hash functions. The first is based on matrix multiplication, the second one on polynomial evaluation. It turns out that both approaches not only yield secure instantiations without requiring cryptographic assumptions, but that the solutions are also very efficient.

Hash Functions Based on Matrices

For the hash functions using matrix–vector multiplication we work over fields and for the moment we look at the field $\mathbb{Z}_2$ specifically. In this field the exclusive-or $\oplus$ is the addition $+$ with $1 + 1 = 0$. We define the hash key hk simply to be a random matrix A and hashing a value x corresponds to a matrix–vector multiplication $A \cdot x$. The input and output size are determined by the matrix dimension. It is convenient to denote by $\mathbb{Z}_2^{m \times n}$ the set of all $m \times n$ matrices A of m rows and n columns with entries in $\mathbb{Z}_2$. We identify $\mathbb{Z}_2$ with $\{0, 1\}$ in the standard way, such that we can also interpret the input value $x \in \{0, 1\}^n$ as an n-dimensional vector over $\mathbb{Z}_2$ and, vice versa, Ax as a bit string in $\{0, 1\}^m$.

Construction 7.5. *Define hash function* H *with input and output length given by* H.il(λ) *and* H.ol(λ) *as*

H.KGen(1^λ)	H.Eval(hk, x)
1 : hk $\leftarrow\!\!\$\ \mathbb{Z}_2^{\text{H.ol}(\lambda) \times \text{H.il}(\lambda)}$	1 : **return** hk $\cdot x$
2 : **return** hk	

We show that the hash function H is ϵ-AXU for $\epsilon(\lambda) = 2^{-\text{H.ol}(\lambda)}$. It follows immediately that the function is also ϵ-AU for the same function ϵ.

Fix some $x \neq x'$ and some Δ. We can view x, x', and Δ as column vectors over $\mathbb{Z}_2$ such that we need to show for the random matrix $A := hk$ that

$$Ax \oplus Ax' = A(x \oplus x') = \Delta$$

with probability at most ϵ. Note that the difference $\delta := x \oplus x'$ of the distinct inputs $x \neq x'$ is a non-zero vector. If we denote by a_i the ith row vector of matrix A and by Δ_i the ith entry of Δ, then we need to show that

$$a_i \delta = \Delta_i \quad \text{for all } i \in \{1, 2, \ldots, \mathsf{H.ol}(\lambda)\}$$

holds simultaneously with probability at most ϵ.

Since each bit entry in the matrix A is chosen independently, each vector a_i is a random vector in $\{0,1\}^{\mathsf{H.il}(\lambda)}$ and independent of the other row vectors. We claim that for any fixed non-zero vector δ we have

$$\Pr[a_i \cdot \delta = 0] = \Pr[a_i \cdot \delta = 1] = \frac{1}{2}.$$

To show this denote the jth entry in the vectors a_i and δ as $a_{i,j}$ resp. δ_j. Since $\delta \neq 0$ there exists an index k such that $\delta_k \neq 0$. We can thus rewrite the product $a_i \cdot \delta$ as

$$a_i \cdot \delta = \sum_{j=1}^{\mathsf{H.ol}(\lambda)} a_{i,j} \cdot \delta_j = a_{i,k} \cdot \delta_k + \sum_{j=1, j\neq k}^{\mathsf{H.ol}(\lambda)} a_{i,j} \cdot \delta_j.$$

Since $\delta_k \neq 0$ then the first term $a_{i,k} \cdot \delta_k$ is uniformly distributed in $\mathbb{Z}_2$. It is furthermore independent of the remaining sum because $a_{i,k}$ is independent of the other entries $a_{i,j}$. The independence of the vectors a_i ensures now that

$$\Pr[a_i \delta = \Delta_i \text{ for all } i \in \{1, 2, \ldots, \mathsf{H.ol}(\lambda)\}] = \prod_{i=1}^{\mathsf{H.ol}(\lambda)} \Pr[a_i \cdot \delta = \Delta_i] = 2^{-\mathsf{H.ol}(\lambda)}.$$

Remark 7.6. Note that for universal hash functions the above argument can be carried out over any finite field $\mathbb{F}$ in place of $\mathbb{Z}_2$: For this we interpret the inputs and outputs as vectors over $\mathbb{F}$. For XOR-universal hash functions one can use any field with characteristic 2 such as $\mathbb{F} = \mathbb{GF}(2^n)$.[1] If we use a suitable field $\mathbb{F}$ we get the bound $\epsilon(\lambda) = |\mathbb{F}|^{-\mathsf{H.ol}(\lambda)}$. For example, for $\mathbb{Z}_p$, the residue field module prime p, one immediately gets a universal hash function by letting hk be a random element $a \leftarrow\!\!\!{\scriptstyle\$}\ \mathbb{Z}_p$ and setting $\mathsf{H.Eval}(\mathsf{hk}, x) := a \cdot x \bmod p$. This function is (perfectly) universal over $\mathbb{Z}_p$. Interested readers may read more about the residue field $\mathbb{Z}_p$ in the upcoming Section 10.1.1 on page 408.

The matrix-based ϵ-AXU hash functions have two drawbacks. First, the hash key is quite large: for equal input and output length it is quadratic. Second, it only allows to process messages of fixed length. The first problem can be resolved with so-called Toeplitz matrices, which have linear size. We will address the second problem soon when considering hash functions based on polynomials.

A Toeplitz matrix $A = (a_{i,j})_{i,j}$ is fully determined by the entries $a_{1,j}$ and $a_{i,1}$ in the first row resp. the first column. All other entries in the matrix are equal to the corresponding edge element on the diagonal: $a_{i,j} = a_{k,\ell}$ iff $i - j = k - \ell$. Hence, such a Topelitz matrix has the following form:

---

[1] A field has characteristic 2 if $a + a = 0$ for all field elements.

$$A = \begin{pmatrix} a_{1,1} & a_{1,2} & a_{1,3} & \cdots & a_{1,n} \\ a_{2,1} & a_{1,1} & a_{1,2} & \cdots & a_{1,n-1} \\ a_{3,1} & a_{2,1} & a_{1,1} & \ddots & a_{1,n-2} \\ \vdots & \ddots & \ddots & \ddots & \vdots \\ a_{n,1} & a_{n-1,1} & a_{n-2,1} & \ddots & a_{n-m+1,1} \end{pmatrix} = \begin{pmatrix} a_{1,1} & a_{1,2} & a_{1,3} & \cdots & a_{1,n} \\ a_{2,1} & \searrow & \searrow & & \searrow \\ a_{3,1} & \searrow & \searrow & & \searrow \\ \vdots & \ddots & \ddots & & \vdots \\ a_{n,1} & \searrow & \searrow & & \searrow \end{pmatrix}$$

The advantage is that we can represent the matrix through the $m + n - 1$ field elements in the first row and column. In particular, letting $\mathcal{T}_2^{m \times n}$ denote all $m \times n$ Toeplitz matrices over $\mathbb{Z}_2$, we can sample a matrix uniformly at random from the set by picking $m + n - 1$ random bits $a_1, a_2, \ldots, a_{m+n-1}$ and interpreting them as the defining matrix elements: $a_{1,j} = a_j$ for $j = 1, 2, \ldots, n$ and $a_{i,1} = a_{n+i-1}$ for $i = 2, 3, \ldots, m$. The description size is $n + m - 1$ bits.

It remains to argue that Toeplitz matrices yield ϵ-AXU (and thus ϵ-AU) hash functions. As in the case of random matrices we need to look at the equation system $A\delta = \Delta$ for $\delta = x \oplus x' \neq 0$, only that the special form of Toeplitz matrices means that the individual equations are

$$\begin{aligned} a_1\delta_1 &+& a_2\delta_2 &+& a_3\delta_3 &+ \ldots +& a_n\delta_n &= \Delta_1 \\ a_{n+1}\delta_1 &+& a_1\delta_2 &+& a_2\delta_3 &+ \ldots +& a_{n-1}\delta_n &= \Delta_2 \\ a_{n+2}\delta_1 &+& a_{n+1}\delta_2 &+& a_1\delta_3 &+ \ldots +& a_{n-2}\delta_n &= \Delta_3 \\ \vdots & & \vdots & & \vdots & & \vdots & \vdots \\ a_{m+n-1}\delta_1 &+& a_{m+n-2}\delta_2 &+& a_{m+n-3}\delta_3 &+ \ldots +& a_{n-m+1}\delta_n &= \Delta_m \end{aligned}$$

Let k be the smallest index such that $\delta_k \neq 0$. By assumption about $\delta \neq 0$, such an index must exist. Since $\delta_1, \ldots, \delta_{k-1} = 0$ we obtain the following simplified system:

$$\begin{aligned} a_k\delta_k &+ \ldots +& a_n\delta_n &= \Delta_1 \\ a_{k-1}\delta_k &+ \ldots +& a_{n-1}\delta_n &= \Delta_2 \\ a_{k-2}\delta_k &+ \ldots +& a_{n-2}\delta_n &= \Delta_3 \\ \vdots & & \vdots & \vdots \\ a_{m+n-k}\delta_k &+ \ldots +& a_{n-m+1}\delta_n &= \Delta_m \end{aligned}$$

In the first row, equality with Δ_1 holds with probability $\frac{1}{2}$ over the choice of the relevant matrix elements $a_k, a_{k+1}, \ldots, a_n$, since the leading element a_k is multiplied with $\delta_k \neq 0$, making the sum a uniformly distributed element. The important observation here is that this is also true for the second row with the leading element a_{k-1}, and since this element does not appear in the first row, this is independent of equality in the first row. This is where we take advantage of the special form of the Toeplitz matrices. The argument can be set forth accordingly, because in each row one of the m elements $a_1, \ldots, a_k, a_{n+1}, \ldots, a_{m+n-k}$ appears in the kth column. Hence, we get once more that equality for the entire hash function holds with probability at most $\epsilon(\lambda) = 2^{-\text{H.ol}(\lambda)}$.

Clearly, we can also use Toeplitz matrices over other fields $\mathbb{F}$ to derive universal hash functions with bound $\epsilon(\lambda) = |\mathbb{F}|^{-\text{H.ol}(\lambda)}$. For XOR-universal hash functions we can once more use fields with characteristic 2.

Hash Functions Based on Polynomials

The second example for universal hash functions is based on polynomial evaluation. We assume that we work over an arbitrary field $\mathbb{F}$ and that each input string x can be encoded as a sequence $(x_1, x_2, \ldots, x_t)$ of elements $x_i \in \mathbb{F}$. For example, for $\mathbb{F} = \mathbb{Z}_2$ we may use the canonical bit encoding. To avoid hassles with extensions we assume that x_t is never equal to the neutral element 0. This can be accomplished, for instance, by appending a non-zero element in x_t or by encoding the length of x in the last entry. The key hk consists of a random element $a \leftarrow_\$ \mathbb{F}$ from the field. The universal hash is now given by the sum $\sum_{i=1}^{t} x_i a^i$.

Construction 7.7. *Let $\mathbb{F}$ be a field and define hash function H over $\mathbb{F}$ as*

$\text{H.KGen}(1^\lambda)$	$\text{H.Eval}(\text{hk}, x)$
1: hk $\leftarrow_\$ \mathbb{F}$	*1:* parse x as $x = (x_1, x_2, \ldots, x_t)$ for $x_i \in \mathbb{F}$ and $x_t \neq 0$
2: **return** hk	*2:* **return** $\displaystyle\sum_{i=1}^{t} x_i \cdot \text{hk}^i$

For an XOR-universal hash function one works again over field of characteristic 2.

We claim that the hash function is (XOR-)universal. Fix two inputs $x \neq x'$ with encodings $(x_1, \ldots, x_t) \neq (x'_1, \ldots, x'_{t'})$. It is convenient for the analysis to assume that the vectors are of equal length $t = t'$. This can always be achieved by appending 0-entries to the shorter vector. Since the final entries x_t and $x'_{t'}$ are different from 0 by assumption, the expanded vector is still distinct from the other vector. At the same time the polynomial evaluation still yields the same output for both vectors, since the extra 0-entries do not change the sum.

Assume now that the two inputs collide for a random hash key $a \leftarrow_\$ \mathbb{F}$. This means that the two polynomials yield the same value

$$\sum_{i=1}^{t} x_i \cdot a^i = \sum_{i=1}^{t} x'_i \cdot a^i$$

resp. that their difference vanishes:

$$\sum_{i=1}^{t}(x_i - x_i') \cdot a^i = 0.$$

Note that the formal polynomial $p(\xi) = \sum_{i=1}^{t}(x_i - x_i') \cdot \xi^i$ over the ring of polynomials $\mathbb{F}[\xi]$ in variable ξ is not the zero-polynomial because $x_k \neq x_k'$ for some index k. Hence, evaluating the hash function means to evaluate the formal, non-zero polynomial $p(\xi)$ at a random point $a \leftarrow_\$ \mathbb{F}$. We can therefore apply the Schwartz–Zippel lemma, saying that a non-zero polynomial of $\mathbb{F}[\xi]$ of degree t vanishes at a random point with probability at most $\frac{t}{|\mathbb{F}|}$. This holds because a non-zero polynomial of degree t has at most t roots over a field $\mathbb{F}$. It follows that our function is a universal hash function for $\epsilon(\lambda) = \frac{t}{|\mathbb{F}|}$ for inputs which can be encoded with at most t field elements.

For XOR-universal hash functions the argument holds correspondingly when considering the non-zero polynomial $p(\xi) = \Delta + \sum_{i=1}^{t}(x_i - x_i') \cdot \xi^i$. For a field with characteristic 2 the addition corresponds to the bit-wise exclusive-or such that the result follows.

We note that the polynomial evaluation can be carried out iteratively, such that in each iteration step one only performs a multiplication and an addition. The idea is based on the observation that

$$\sum_{i=1}^{t} x_i \cdot \mathsf{hk}^i = \mathsf{hk} \cdot (\mathsf{hk} \ldots \mathsf{hk} \cdot (\mathsf{hk} \cdot x_t + x_{t-1}) \ldots).$$

Starting with the innermost value $\mathsf{hk} \cdot x_t$ one can compute the next layer as $\mathsf{hk} \cdot (\mathsf{hk} \cdot x_t + x_{t-1})$ and continue until reaching the final layer. This is described more formally in the following algorithm:

H.Eval(hk, x)

---

1 :   parse x as $x = (x_1, x_2, \ldots, x_t)$ for $x_i \in \mathbb{F}$ and $x_t \neq 0$

2 : $y \leftarrow \mathsf{hk} \cdot x_t$

3 :   **for** $i = t - 1$ **downto** 1 **do**

4 : $y \leftarrow \mathsf{hk} \cdot (y + x_i)$

5 :   **return** y

In terms of efficiency the evaluation thus requires t field multiplications and $t - 1$ additions.

7.2 Extractors and the Leftover Hash Lemma

We next discuss a well-known application of universal hash functions, namely to smoothen the entropy of raw data. One may for example think of a Diffie–Hellman value g^{xy} generated jointly in a key exchange protocol (cf. Section 11.2). Then this value presumably carries sufficient entropy to make it infeasible to guess it. However, the value g^{xy} belongs to the group generated by g and thus has a certain structure, e.g., individual bits in the string representation may be biased. It may therefore not be applicable immediately as, say, a key for the AES block cipher (cf. Section 14.1.1), which instead requires uniformly distributed bit strings.

The notion of extractors and the main technical tool, the leftover hash lemma, allow to turn random data with sufficient min-entropy into slightly shorter, but almost uniform bit strings. The leftover hash lemma tells us that universal hash functions provide such a mechanism. We note that modern key exchange protocols often do not use the universal hash function constructions we have described in Section 7.1.3, but solutions based on cryptographic hash functions.[2] Still, this is done in light of the assumption that these cryptographic hash functions are good extractors.

7.2.1 Randomness Extractors

Intuitively, we seek a deterministic function Ext, called *extractor*, which takes as input (a sample of) an arbitrary random variable $X \in \{0,1\}^m$ with high entropy, and outputs a value $y \in \{0,1\}^n$ which is *statistically* close to uniform. Of course, the entropy of X must be at least in the range of n and we must have $m \geq n$. We first argue that deterministic functions Ext, taking only the sample X as input, cannot succeed for all high-entropy distributions, even when trying to extract only a single bit. The reason is that some specific random variable X may be bad for the extractor. We discuss this in more detail next.

Assume that we have a deterministic extractor Ext : $\{0,1\}^m \rightarrow \{0,1\}$. Fix bit b such that under the extractor at least half of the possible preimages map to b, i.e., $|\text{Ext}^{-1}(b)| \geq 2^{m-1}$. For at least one of two possibilities $b \in \{0,1\}$ this must be case, because each of the 2^m inputs must be mapped to either 0 or 1. Now consider the random variable X which is uniform on this preimage set $\text{Ext}^{-1}(b)$, such that it has high entropy of at least $m - 1$. The extractor, on the other hand, constantly outputs b for samples of X and thus cannot be close to a random bit for the variable X.

---

[2] Constructions of cryptographic hash functions are presented in Part III. We discuss key exchange protocols in Section 11.1 and key derivation functions based on cryptographic hash functions in Section 16.6.

As a general extractor in the above sense cannot exist, we proceed to *seeded extractors* which take an additional uniformly distributed seed S from some domain $\{0,1\}^s$ and which use this seed together with X to generate an almost uniformly random string. We note that the extractor does not use any randomness beyond the inputs S and X and can thus still be considered deterministic. To avoid trivial constructions, e.g., if the extractor would simply output the seed S, one needs to ensure that the extractor outputs more bits than S. With the notion of *strong* extractors this trivially holds because for such extractors the output for S and X looks uniform, even if given (the sample of) S. Put differently, for strong extractors the seed is only used to pick a specific extraction procedure from a large set and appears as part of the output.

In the definition below we follow the common approach to define extractors for fixed parameters, such as fixed seed length s, input length m, and output length n. The reason for this is that asymptotic behavior, especially negligible success probabilities of efficient adversaries, is irrelevant for these statistical properties. In the construction and analysis below one can think of the security parameter λ for the underlying universal hash function and the statistical distance as being fixed to some specific value.

Definition 7.8 (Randomness Extractor). *Fix $n, s \in \mathbb{N}$ and let U_n denote the uniform variable over $\{0,1\}^n$ (n-bit strings). Let, furthermore, S denote a uniform random variable over $\{0,1\}^s$ modeling seeds.*

A deterministic function $\mathsf{Ext} : \{0,1\}^s \times \{0,1\}^m \to \{0,1\}^n$ *is called a* (k, ϵ)-*randomness extractor if for any random variable X over $\{0,1\}^m$ with min-entropy $H_\infty(X) \geq k$ the statistical distance of $\mathsf{Ext}(S, X)$ from the uniform random variable U_n over $\{0,1\}^n$ is at most ϵ:*

$$\mathsf{SD}_{\mathsf{Ext}(S,X),U_n}(\lambda) \leq \epsilon.$$

It is called a strong (k, ϵ)-*extractor if for any random variable X over $\{0,1\}^m$ with min-entropy $H_\infty(X) \geq k$ the statistical distance of $(S, \mathsf{Ext}(S, X))$ from the uniform random variable U_{s+n} over $\{0,1\}^s \times \{0,1\}^n$ is at most ϵ:*

$$\mathsf{SD}_{(S,\mathsf{Ext}(S,X)),U_{s+n}}(\lambda) \leq \epsilon,$$

where S denotes the same sample in both occurrences in $(S, \mathsf{Ext}(S, X))$.

Remark 7.9. Definition 7.8 defines a randomness extractor that extracts true randomness in the sense that the output is *statistically close* to uniform. We can relax this requirement and demand that the output is only *computationally close* to uniform, thereby obtaining a computational variant of randomness extractors. We will need such *computational extractors* when discussing key derivation in Section 16.6.1 and define the notion as Definition 16.35 (page 675).

7.2.2 Leftover Hash Lemma

We next show that we can build strong extractors from universal hash functions. For our construction, seed S is used to pick the hash key hk for describing a function mapping from m bits to n bits. In fact, to simplify the exposition we assume that the key *is* the string S. All the previous constructions of universal hash functions have this property for appropriate fields.

Construction 7.10. *Let* H *be a hash function with* $\mathsf{H.KGen}(1^\lambda) \overset{\text{D}}{=} U_{\mathsf{H.kl}(\lambda)}$ *where* $\mathsf{H.kl}(\lambda)$ *denotes the key length for security parameter* λ *and* U_n *denotes the uniform random variable over* $\{0,1\}^n$. *In other words, key generation of function* H *picks a uniformly random string of length* $\mathsf{H.kl}(\lambda)$. *We define randomness extractor* Ext *as:*

$\underline{\mathsf{Ext}(S, X)}$

    // *Note that* $S = $ hk *by assumption on key generation*

   1:   hk $\leftarrow\!\!\$\ \mathsf{H.KGen}(1^\lambda; S)$

   2:   **return** $(S, \mathsf{H.Eval}(\mathsf{hk}, X))$

> **Theorem 7.11** (Leftover Hash Lemma). *Let* H *be a universal hash function with* $\mathsf{H.ol}(\lambda) = n$ *for* $n \leq k - 2\log\frac{1}{\epsilon}$. *Then Construction 7.10 yields a strong* $(k, \epsilon/2)$*-extractor.*

The theorem states that as long as the hash function's output length stays slightly below the expected min-entropy of the random variable, then applying the hash function yields an almost uniform bit string, even when learning the seed. Note that the loss in the output length (with the extractor consuming $2\log\frac{1}{\epsilon}$ bits) depends only logarithmically on the closeness to the uniform distribution.

Proof. We first bound the probability that the extractor's output (together with the seed) collides in two executions. There are two possibilities for this: either the samples $x \leftarrow\!\!\$\ X$ land too often on the same value, or they do not, but the hash values nonetheless collide. The former probability can be bounded in terms of the min-entropy of X, and the latter via the universality of the hash function. Then, despite being interested in the statistical distance (corresponding to the $L1$-norm $||x||_1 = \sum |x_i|$) we first consider the (squared value of the) $L2$-norm $||x||_2 = (\sum x_i^2)^{1/2}$ of the seed and the extractor's output and uniform strings of the same length. Since the $L1$-norm is at most the $L2$-norm times the square root of the dimension, we get the desired result.

We first bound the collision probability for the extractor's output. For a random variable Z let $\mathsf{Coll}(Z)$ be defined as the collision probability that two independent samples Z, Z' end up on the same value:

$$\mathsf{Coll}(Z) = \Pr[Z = Z'].$$

Using the independence of the identically distributed random variables Z, Z', we can use the multiplicativity of the probabilities and rewrite this probability as

$$\mathsf{Coll}(Z) = \Pr[Z = Z'] = \sum_z \Pr[Z = z \wedge Z' = z]$$

$$= \sum_z \Pr[Z = z] \cdot \Pr[Z' = z] = \sum_z (\Pr[Z = z])^2. \qquad (7.1)$$

Recall that the min-entropy of variable X upper bounds the maximal probability $p_{\max} := \max_x \Pr[X = x]$ the distribution assumes on the support, in the sense that $p_{\max} \leq 2^{-H_\infty(X)}$. It follows that

$$\mathsf{Coll}(X) = \sum_x (\Pr[X = x])^2 \leq p_{\max} \cdot \sum_x \Pr[X = x] \leq p_{\max} \leq 2^{-k}.$$

For the last inequality note that we are considering a $(k, \epsilon/2)$ extractor and can thus assume that the min-entropy of X is at least k.

For the extractor's output we have for independent but identically distributed pairs S, S' as well as X, X':

$$\mathsf{Coll}(S, \mathsf{Ext}(S, X))$$
$$= \Pr[(S, \mathsf{Ext}(S, X)) = (S', \mathsf{Ext}(S', X'))]$$
$$= \Pr[S = S' \wedge \mathsf{Ext}(S, X) = \mathsf{Ext}(S', X')]$$

and by applying $\Pr[A \wedge B] = \Pr[B] \cdot \Pr[A \mid B]$ for any two events A, B,

$$= \Pr[S = S'] \cdot \Pr[\mathsf{Ext}(S, X) = \mathsf{Ext}(S', X') \mid S = S'].$$

Note that the condition on equal seeds $S = S'$ can be viewed as picking S randomly and then setting $S' = S$. Hence, we can rewrite the equation as

$$= \Pr[S = S'] \cdot \Pr[\mathsf{Ext}(S, X) = \mathsf{Ext}(S, X')].$$

In the next step we replace $\Pr[S = S']$ by 2^{-s}, because both are uniformly generated strings of length s. Furthermore, we divide the collision probability on the extractor's output according to the case of collisions of X and X':

$$= 2^{-s} \cdot \big(\Pr[\mathsf{Ext}(S, X) = \mathsf{Ext}(S, X') \wedge X = X']$$
$$+ \Pr[\mathsf{Ext}(S, X) = \mathsf{Ext}(S, X') \wedge X \neq X'] \big).$$

Using once more the product rule $\Pr[A \wedge B] = \Pr[B] \cdot \Pr[A \mid B]$ and noting that probabilities are at most 1 we can upper bound the above by

$$\leq 2^{-s} \cdot \big(\Pr[X = X']$$
$$+ \Pr[\mathsf{Ext}(S, X) = \mathsf{Ext}(S, X') \wedge X \neq X'] \big)$$
$$= 2^{-s} \cdot \big(\Pr[X = X']$$
$$+ \Pr[X \neq X'] \cdot \Pr[\mathsf{Ext}(S, X) = \mathsf{Ext}(S, X') \mid X \neq X'] \big)$$
$$\leq 2^{-s} \cdot \big(\Pr[X = X']$$
$$+ \Pr[\mathsf{Ext}(S, X) = \mathsf{Ext}(S, X') \mid X \neq X'] \big).$$

Using that $\mathsf{Coll}(X) = \Pr[X = X'] \leq 2^{-k}$ (Equation (7.1)), we obtain

$$\leq 2^{-s} \cdot \big(2^{-k} + \Pr[\mathsf{Ext}(S, X) = \mathsf{Ext}(S, X') \mid X \neq X'] \big).$$

Next we note that the extractor implements a universal hash function. Hence, for any $x \neq x'$, if we pick the seed S randomly we have output collisions with probability at most $\epsilon = 2^{-n}$ (where $n = \mathsf{H.ol}(\lambda)$ denotes the output length of hash function H). Then this also holds for the random and independently chosen X, X' conditioned on $X \neq X'$. Hence, the collision probability of the extractor can be bounded by

$$= 2^{-(s+k)} + 2^{-(s+n)}$$
$$= 2^{-(s+n)} \cdot \big(1 + 2^{n-k} \big).$$

The final step is to note that $n \leq k - 2 \log \frac{1}{\epsilon}$ such that we get

$$\leq 2^{-(s+n)} \cdot \big(1 + 2^{-2 \log \frac{1}{\epsilon}} \big)$$
$$= 2^{-(s+n)} \cdot \big(1 + \epsilon^2 \big). \tag{7.2}$$

To bound the statistical distance of $(S, \mathsf{Ext}(S, X))$ and uniform strings (U_s, U_n) consider the squared $L2$-norm:

$$\|(S, \mathsf{Ext}(S, X)), (U_s, U_n)\|_2^2$$
$$= \sum_{(h,y)} \big(\Pr[(S, \mathsf{Ext}(S, X)) = (h, y)] - \Pr[(U_s, U_n) = (h, y)] \big)^2.$$

With the binomial expansion we get

$$= \sum_{(h,y)} \Pr[(S, \mathsf{Ext}(S, X)) = (h, y)]^2 + \sum_{(h,y)} \Pr[(U_s, U_n) = (h, y)]^2$$
$$- 2 \cdot \sum_{(h,y)} \Pr[(S, \mathsf{Ext}(S, X)) = (h, y)] \cdot \Pr[(U_s, U_n) = (h, y)].$$

Note that by Equation (7.1) the first summand is exactly $\mathsf{Coll}(S, \mathsf{Ext}(S, X))$. Since the pair (U_s, U_n) is uniformly distributed, it follows that

$$= \mathsf{Coll}(S, \mathsf{Ext}(S, X)) + \sum_{(h,y)} 2^{-2(s+n)}$$

$$- 2 \cdot 2^{-(s+n)} \cdot \sum_{(h,y)} \Pr[(S, \mathsf{Ext}(S, X)) = (h, y)]$$

$$= \mathsf{Coll}(S, \mathsf{Ext}(S, X)) + 2^{(s+n)} \cdot 2^{-2(s+n)} - 2 \cdot 2^{-(s+n)}$$

$$\leq \mathsf{Coll}(S, \mathsf{Ext}(S, X)) - 2^{-(s+n)}.$$

Together with the bound for the collision probability for the extractor above (Equation (7.2)), we obtain the bound

$$\leq 2^{-(s+n)} \cdot \epsilon^2. \tag{7.3}$$

The Cauchy–Schwarz inequality says that $\sum_{z \in Z} |z| \leq \sqrt{|Z|} \cdot \sqrt{\sum_{z \in Z} z^2}$ for any finite set $Z \subseteq \mathbb{R}$. Applying this bound we finally get for the statistical distance:

$$\mathsf{SD}_{(S, \mathsf{Ext}(S, X)), (U_s, U_n)}(\lambda)$$

$$= \frac{1}{2} \cdot \sum_{(h,y)} |\Pr[(S, \mathsf{Ext}(S, X)) = (h, y)] - \Pr[(U_s, U_n) = (h, y)]|$$

$$\leq \frac{1}{2} \cdot \sqrt{2^{s+n}} \cdot \sqrt{\sum_{(h,y)} (\Pr[(S, \mathsf{Ext}(S, X)) = (h, y)] - \Pr[(U_s, U_n) = (h, y)])^2}.$$

Noting that the sum in the root is exactly the squared $L2$-norm, allowing us to plug in our bound in Equation (7.3), we get

$$\leq \frac{1}{2} \cdot \sqrt{2^{s+n}} \cdot \sqrt{2^{-(s+n)} \cdot \epsilon^2}$$

$$= \epsilon/2.$$

This shows that universal hashing is a $(k, \epsilon/2)$ extractor. $\qquad\square$

7.3 Message Authentication Based on Universal Hashing

Universal hash functions, especially XOR-universal functions, can be used to build secure message authentication codes. Recall from Section 3.5 that MACs are the symmetric counterpart to signature schemes, where the tagging algorithm MAC.Eval uses a secret key to compute the authentication code, and verification is performed by recomputing the tag with the same key. The common security notion of existential unforgeability for MACs (see Definition 3.39 on page 151) says that an adversary cannot produce a valid tag τ^* for a message m^*, even after having seen MACs for other, adversarially chosen, messages.

The straightforward idea of building MACs from universal hash functions is to use the good distributional property and simply hash a message under the now secret hash key hk. The intuition should be that forging a MAC for message m^* would require to predict the hash value under an unknown key. Unfortunately, this intuition is false. The reason is that a hash value may reveal information about the hash key. Consider for instance the universal hash function $\mathsf{H}.\mathsf{Eval}(\mathsf{hk}, x) = \mathsf{hk} \cdot x \bmod p$ over $\mathbb{Z}_p$. If the adversary sees two hash values h, h' for distinct input messages m, m', then it can compute the key hk as $\mathsf{hk} = (h - h') \cdot (m - m')^{-1} \bmod p$, where $(m - m')^{-1}$ is the easy-to-compute multiplicative inverse to $m - m'$ over $\mathbb{Z}_p$. Once the adversary got hold of the key, it can easily compute hash values for arbitrary messages m^*.

The solution, instead, is to mask the hash value. We first discuss a method which uses only a universal hash function in combination with a pseudorandom function (see Section 3.3.1), where we apply the pseudorandom function to the hash value:

Construction 7.12. *Let* PRF *be a pseudorandom function and* H *be an* ϵ*-AU hash function with* $\mathsf{PRF}.\mathsf{il}(\lambda) = \mathsf{H}.\mathsf{ol}(\lambda)$*. Define message authentication code* MAC *as*

$\mathsf{MAC}.\mathsf{KGen}(1^\lambda)$	$\mathsf{MAC}.\mathsf{Eval}((\mathsf{k}, \mathsf{hk}), m)$
1 : $\mathsf{k} \leftarrow\!\!\$ \ \mathsf{PRF}.\mathsf{KGen}(1^\lambda)$	1 : $h \leftarrow \mathsf{H}.\mathsf{Eval}(\mathsf{hk}, m)$
2 : $\mathsf{hk} \leftarrow\!\!\$ \ \mathsf{H}.\mathsf{KGen}(1^\lambda)$	2 : $\tau \leftarrow \mathsf{PRF}.\mathsf{Eval}(\mathsf{k}, h)$
3 : **return** $(\mathsf{k}, \mathsf{hk})$	3 : **return** τ

Note that we assume that the input length $\mathsf{PRF}.\mathsf{il}(\lambda)$ of the PRF perfectly matches the output length $\mathsf{H}.\mathsf{ol}(\lambda)$ of the hash function. For the security we also need that the output length $\mathsf{PRF}.\mathsf{ol}(\lambda)$ of the PRF is super-logarithmic in λ, and that $\epsilon(\lambda)$ is negligible in λ.

Note that we could already derive a MAC from a pseudorandom function alone. There are two reasons why one would like to use the composition of a universal hash function with a pseudorandom function. First, the pseudorandom function may have a fixed input length such that the hash function serves as an upstream compression method, akin to the idea of the hash-and-sign approach in Section 6.3. The other reason is that, even if the pseudorandom function allowed for unbounded inputs, applying the universal hash function first may be faster.

Proposition 7.13. *Let* H *be an* ϵ*-AU hash function for negligible* $\epsilon(\lambda)$*, and* PRF *be a pseudorandom function with super-logarithmic output length* $\mathsf{PRF}.\mathsf{ol}(\lambda) = \omega(\lambda)$*. Then the above Construction 7.12 of*

> a message authentication code MAC is existentially unforgeable under
> chosen-message attacks.

Proof. The proof idea is to note that the pseudorandom function hides the hash
values (and thus the hash key) in all generated MACs. The only information
available to the adversary may be the fact that two hash values collide for
different messages, in which case the MACs, too, would be identical. But since
the hash function is ϵ-AU the probability of such collisions should be small.
It follows that the adversary, in its forgery (m^*, τ^*) must be able to predict
the (pseudo)random value at a fresh input—which is infeasible.

Formally, we proceed again in game hops and we provide the pseudocode of
the used games in Figure 7.1. To describe the hops it is convenient to denote
the $q := q(\lambda)$ tagging requests of the adversary $\mathcal{A}$ as $m_1, m_2, \ldots, m_q$, the
replies as $\tau_1, \tau_2, \ldots, \tau_q$, and the adversary's final forgery attempt as (m^*, τ^*).
To check if the adversary has won we compute the actual answer τ the tagging
oracle would have given if it had been queried on m^*, and check if $\tau = \tau^*$.
The adversary only wins if this equality holds and m^* has not been queried
before.

In the first hop we replace the outputs τ_i of the PRF in MAC computations
by random values (but in a consistent way, i.e., repeating a previous random
answer if we encounter the same hash values). We also do this with τ when
verifying the adversary's forgery attempt for m^*. It is now quite easy to
build a reduction to the definition of PRFs, Definition 3.22 on page 126.
This reduction receives security parameter 1^λ as input and gets access to
a real-or-random oracle, implementing either a pseudorandom function (for
unknown key k) or an oracle providing random but consistent answers. Our
reduction invokes the key sampling algorithm of the hash function to derive
hk $\leftarrow\!\!\$$ H.KGen(λ), and then runs the MAC adversary. For each query m_i
to the tagging oracle the reduction first computes $h_i \leftarrow$ H.Eval(hk, m_i) and
forwards this value h_i to its oracle. It hands back the answer τ_i to the MAC
adversary as the tagging oracle's reply. Eventually, our reduction also checks
if its oracle answers with τ^* for H.Eval(hk, m^*) and outputs 0 if and only if
this is the case.

For the analysis note that the original attack, Game$_1$, corresponds to
the case that the oracle implements a pseudorandom function, whereas the
other game, Game$_2$ is identical to the setting where the reduction gets random
answers. Hence, according to the security of the PRF the adversary's advantage
can only change negligibly by this change from Game$_1$ to Game$_2$.

In the next game hop we stop immediately if two distinct messages $m_i \neq m_j$
in the queries to the tagging oracle yield the same hash value, or if the
adversary's forgery m^* hashes to the same value as one of the queries m_i.
We first compute the probability that we stop with the jth query m_j to the
tagging oracle. In particular, there had been no collisions before, or else we
would have aborted already. For each of the previous (distinct) queries the
adversary only received distinct random answers, independently of the hash

$\mathsf{Game}_1(\lambda)$ $\xrightarrow{\text{PRF}}$	$\mathsf{Game}_2(\lambda)$ $\xrightarrow{\epsilon\text{-AU}}$	$\mathsf{Game}_3(\lambda)$
1 : $\quad \mathcal{Q} \leftarrow \{\}$	$\mathcal{Q} \leftarrow \{\}; T \leftarrow [\,]$	$\mathcal{Q} \leftarrow \{\}; T \leftarrow [\,]$
2 : $\quad k \leftarrow\!\!\$\ \mathsf{PRF.KGen}(1^\lambda)$	$k \leftarrow\!\!\$\ \mathsf{PRF.KGen}(1^\lambda)$	$k \leftarrow\!\!\$\ \mathsf{PRF.KGen}(1^\lambda)$
3 : $\quad hk \leftarrow\!\!\$\ \mathsf{H.KGen}(1^\lambda)$	$hk \leftarrow\!\!\$\ \mathsf{H.KGen}(1^\lambda)$	$hk \leftarrow\!\!\$\ \mathsf{H.KGen}(1^\lambda)$
4 : $\quad (m^*,\tau^*) \leftarrow\!\!\$\ \mathcal{A}^{\mathsf{Tag}(\cdot)}(1^\lambda)$	$(m^*,\tau^*) \leftarrow\!\!\$\ \mathcal{A}^{\mathsf{Tag}(\cdot)}(1^\lambda)$	$(m^*,\tau^*) \leftarrow\!\!\$\ \mathcal{A}^{\mathsf{Tag}(\cdot)}(1^\lambda)$
5 :		**if Collision then abort**
6 : $\quad$ **return**	**return**	**return**
$\quad\quad \mathsf{MAC.Eval}(mk, m^*) = \tau^*$	$\mathsf{MAC.Eval}(mk, m^*) = \tau^*$	$\mathsf{MAC.Eval}(mk, m^*) = \tau^*$
$\quad\quad \wedge\, m^* \notin \mathcal{Q}$	$\wedge\, m^* \notin \mathcal{Q}$	$\wedge\, m^* \notin \mathcal{Q}$

$\mathsf{Tag}(m)$	$\mathsf{Tag}(m)$	$\mathsf{Tag}(m)$
1 : $\quad \mathcal{Q} \leftarrow \mathcal{Q} \cup \{m\}$	$\mathcal{Q} \leftarrow \mathcal{Q} \cup \{m\}$	$\mathcal{Q} \leftarrow \mathcal{Q} \cup \{m\}$
2 : $\quad h \leftarrow \mathsf{H.Eval}(hk, m)$	$h \leftarrow \mathsf{H.Eval}(hk, m)$	$h \leftarrow \mathsf{H.Eval}(hk, m)$
3 : $\quad \tau \leftarrow \mathsf{PRF.Eval}(k, h)$	**if** $T[h] = \bot$ **then**	**if** $T[h] = \bot$ **then**
4 :	$\quad T[h] \leftarrow\!\!\$\ \{0,1\}^{\mathsf{PRF.ol}(\lambda)}$	$\quad T[h] \leftarrow\!\!\$\ \{0,1\}^{\mathsf{PRF.ol}(\lambda)}$
5 :	$\tau \leftarrow T[h]$	$\tau \leftarrow T[h]$
6 : $\quad$ **return** τ	**return** τ	**return** τ

Fig. 7.1: Games used in the proof of Proposition 7.13. The event Collision in Game_3 denotes the event that any two queries in $\mathcal{Q} \cup \{m^*\}$ (where m^* denotes the adversary's forgery) collide under hash function H, that is, there exist $m \neq m' \in \mathcal{Q} \cup \{m^*\}$ with $\mathsf{H.Eval}(hk, m) = \mathsf{H.Eval}(hk, m')$. Note that in the textual description the event is checked on every fresh query to the tagging oracle.

key. We can thus think of the hash key being chosen only at the point in time when the MAC adversary forwards m_j to the tagging oracle. At this point, however, the hash function's input m_j as well as any previous query m_i for $i < j$ have been fixed already. Therefore, the probability that m_i collides with m_j under the hash function is at most $\epsilon(\lambda)$. The probability that there exists such an index i is by the union bound thus at most $(j-1) \cdot \epsilon(\lambda)$.

We can now sum over all $\mathsf{q} + 1$ queries, including the adversary's forgery attempt m^*, such that the probability of aborting in Game_3 is at most

$$\sum_{j=2}^{\mathsf{q}+1} (j-1) \cdot \epsilon(\lambda) \leq \binom{\mathsf{q}+1}{2} \cdot \epsilon(\lambda).$$

Since the MAC adversary is polynomial, q is bounded by a polynomial, such that this probability is negligible (by the choice of ϵ).

We can now analyze the probability that the MAC adversary succeeds in Game_3, where it only receives random answers and needs to predict the random answer for a hash value distinct from all the hash values appearing in the query phase. The probability of succeeding is at most $2^{-\mathsf{PRF.ol}(\lambda)}$ and thus negligible. □

The above construction is rarely used in practice. The reason is that the security bound is quite loose. The loss is proportional to the squared number of tagging queries, $\mathsf{q}(\lambda)^2 \cdot \epsilon(\lambda)$. Using ϵ-AXU hash functions one achieves a better bound of roughly $\epsilon(\lambda) + \mathsf{q}(\lambda)^2 \cdot 2^{-\mathsf{PRF.il}(\lambda)}$ via a different masking technique. The idea is to apply the PRF to a fresh random value r and then mask the hash value with the exclusive-or of this pseudorandom value:

Construction 7.14. *Let* PRF *be a pseudorandom function and* H *be an* ϵ-*AXU hash function with* $\mathsf{PRF.ol}(\lambda) = \mathsf{H.ol}(\lambda)$. *Define message authentication code* MAC *as*

$\mathsf{MAC.KGen}(1^\lambda)$	$\mathsf{MAC.Eval}((k, hk), m)$
1: $k \leftarrow\!\!{\scriptstyle\$}\ \mathsf{PRF.KGen}(1^\lambda)$	1: $r \leftarrow\!\!{\scriptstyle\$}\ \{0,1\}^{\mathsf{PRF.il}(\lambda)}$
2: $hk \leftarrow\!\!{\scriptstyle\$}\ \mathsf{H.KGen}(1^\lambda)$	2: $h \leftarrow \mathsf{H.Eval}(hk, m)$
3: **return** (k, hk)	3: $p \leftarrow \mathsf{PRF.Eval}(k, r)$
	4: $\tau = p \oplus h$
	5: **return** (r, τ)

We do not show the security of the MAC scheme formally. Instead we explain where the ϵ-AXU property comes into effect. For this assume that the adversary in its forgery attempt (r^*, τ^*) for message m^* reuses one of the random values $r_1, \ldots, r_\mathsf{q}$ generated in the q tagging queries, i.e., assume $r^* = r_i$ and let m_i be the queried message and τ_i be the oracle's reply. Then, for a successful attempt we must have that

$$\tau^* \oplus \tau_i = \Big(\mathsf{PRF.Eval}(k, r^*) \oplus \mathsf{H.Eval}(hk, m^*)\Big)$$
$$\oplus \Big(\mathsf{PRF.Eval}(k, r_i) \oplus \mathsf{H.Eval}(hk, m_i)\Big)$$
$$= \mathsf{H.Eval}(hk, m^*) \oplus \mathsf{H.Eval}(hk, m_i).$$

In other words, the adversary must have found values m^*, m_i, and $\Delta = \tau^* \oplus \tau_i$ such that the exclusive-or of the hash values of m^* and m_i yield Δ. The probability for this is at most $\epsilon(\lambda)$. The formal proof, including an argument that the r_i's are most likely unique and that the adversary cannot predict the MAC for a fresh r^*, is left to the reader as Exercise 7.3.

7.4 Pairwise Independent Hash Functions

7.4.1 Definition

We now turn to a slightly stronger notion than universal hashing, called *pairwise independent hashing*. This property states that if we apply the randomly chosen hash function (or hash function with randomly chosen key) to different inputs, then the outputs are independently and uniformly distributed:

> **Definition 7.15** (Pairwise Independent Hash Function). *A hash function* $\mathsf{H} = (\mathsf{H.KGen}, \mathsf{H.Eval})$ *is pairwise independent if for all* $x \neq x'$ *in the domain and all* y, y' *in the range it holds that*
>
> $$\Pr[\mathsf{H.Eval}(\mathsf{hk}, x) = y \wedge \mathsf{H.Eval}(\mathsf{hk}, x') = y'] = 2^{-2 \cdot \mathsf{H.ol}(\lambda)},$$
>
> *where the probability is over the random choice of* $\mathsf{hk} \leftarrow_\$ \mathsf{H.KGen}(1^\lambda)$.

Remark 7.16. We note that one can generalize the above definition to k-wise independence where for k distinct inputs $x_1, \dots, x_k$ the probability of hitting k values $y_1, \dots, y_k$ is $2^{-k \cdot \mathsf{H.ol}(\lambda)}$. One can also work over arbitrary fields $\mathbb{F}$ in which case the bound would be $|\mathbb{F}|^{-k}$.

Remark 7.17. Note that we demand a precise bound $2^{-2 \cdot \mathsf{H.ol}(\lambda)}$ in our definition instead of an upper bound. The reason is that requiring

$$\Pr_{\mathsf{hk} \leftarrow_\$ \mathsf{H.KGen}(1^\lambda)}[\mathsf{H.Eval}(\mathsf{hk}, x) = y \wedge \mathsf{H.Eval}(\mathsf{hk}, x') = y'] \leq 2^{-2 \cdot \mathsf{H.ol}(\lambda)}$$

already implies equality. Otherwise there would be a pair (y_0, y_0') such that the probability of hitting this pair is strictly less than $2^{-2 \cdot \mathsf{H.ol}(\lambda)}$, and hence the cumulated probabilities over all $2^{2 \cdot \mathsf{H.ol}(\lambda)}$ output pairs (y, y'),

$$\sum_{(y,y')} \Pr[\mathsf{H.Eval}(\mathsf{hk}, x) = y \wedge \mathsf{H.Eval}(\mathsf{hk}, x') = y'],$$

would not add up to 1.

Remark 7.18. Another useful property of pairwise independent hash functions is that they are uniform in the following sense: For any x, y it holds, over the choice of key $\mathsf{hk} \leftarrow_\$ \mathsf{H.KGen}(1^\lambda)$, that

$$\Pr[\mathsf{H.Eval}(\mathsf{hk}, x) = y] \leq 2^{-\mathsf{H.ol}(\lambda)}.$$

To see this fix an arbitrary $x' \neq x$ and note that

$$\Pr[\mathsf{H.Eval}(\mathsf{hk}, x) = y]$$

$$= \sum_{y' \in \{0,1\}^{\mathsf{H.ol}(\lambda)}} \Pr[\mathsf{H.Eval}(\mathsf{hk}, x) = y \wedge \mathsf{H.Eval}(\mathsf{hk}, x') = y']$$

$$\leq \sum_{y' \in \{0,1\}^{\mathsf{H.ol}(\lambda)}} 2^{-2 \cdot \mathsf{H.ol}(\lambda)}$$

$$= 2^{-\mathsf{H.ol}(\lambda)}.$$

Note that in general neither ϵ-AU nor ϵ-AXU hash functions have this property. For instance, if one modifies a given hash function such that the evaluation duplicates the output, then the function inherits the ϵ-AU or ϵ-AXU property. Yet, only a small fraction of the possible images are hit.

Pairwise independent hash functions are also called *strongly universal hash functions*. This is justified by the fact that pairwise independence is a strictly stronger requirement than universality of hash functions. This holds even for (perfectly) universal hash functions.

> **Proposition 7.19.** *Any pairwise independent hash function* H *is also an (XOR-)universal hash function. But, there are (XOR-)universal hash functions which are not pairwise independent.*

Proof. Take any pairwise independent hash function H. We have to show that the function is also universal, meaning that for any $x \neq x'$,

$$\Pr[\mathsf{H.Eval}(\mathsf{hk}, x) = \mathsf{H.Eval}(\mathsf{hk}, x')] \leq \frac{1}{2^{\mathsf{H.ol}(\lambda)}},$$

where the choice is over the random key $\mathsf{hk} \leftarrow_\$ \mathsf{H.KGen}(1^\lambda)$. Fix an arbitrary pair $x \neq x'$. The pairwise independence tells us that for any $y = y'$ in the range we have

$$\Pr[\mathsf{H.Eval}(\mathsf{hk}, x) = y = y' = \mathsf{H.Eval}(\mathsf{hk}, x')] \leq \frac{1}{2^{2 \cdot \mathsf{H.ol}(\lambda)}}.$$

Since there are at most $2^{\mathsf{H.ol}(\lambda)}$ many values $y = y'$, we derive

$$\Pr[\mathsf{H.Eval}(\mathsf{hk}, x) = \mathsf{H.Eval}(\mathsf{hk}, x')]$$

$$\leq \Pr\left[\exists y \in \{0,1\}^{\mathsf{H.ol}(\lambda)} : \mathsf{H.Eval}(\mathsf{hk}, x) = y = \mathsf{H.Eval}(\mathsf{hk}, x')\right]$$

and by the union bound,

$$\leq \sum_{y \in \{0,1\}^{\mathsf{H.ol}(\lambda)}} \Pr[\mathsf{H.Eval}(\mathsf{hk}, x) = y = \mathsf{H.Eval}(\mathsf{hk}, x')]$$

$$\leq 2^{\mathsf{H.ol}(\lambda)} \cdot \frac{1}{2^{2 \cdot \mathsf{H.ol}(\lambda)}} = \frac{1}{2^{\mathsf{H.ol}(\lambda)}}.$$

This shows that the hash function is also universal. The argument can be easily transferred to the XOR-universal setting, noting that for any given Δ there are also $2^{\mathsf{H.ol}(\lambda)}$ pairs (y, y') with $y \oplus y' = \Delta$, such that we can again apply the union bound.

For the converse direction take our universal hash function based on matrices:

$$\mathsf{H.Eval}(\mathsf{hk}, x) = \mathsf{hk} \cdot x$$

for random matrix hk. This function is (XOR-)universal but not pairwise independent. The reason is that $\mathsf{H.Eval}(\mathsf{hk}, 0) = 0$ such that for $x = 0$, $y = 0$, and arbitrary $x' \neq 0, y'$ we have

$$\Pr[\mathsf{H.Eval}(\mathsf{hk}, x) = y \wedge \mathsf{H.Eval}(\mathsf{hk}, x') = y'] = \frac{1}{2^{\mathsf{H.ol}(\lambda)}} > \frac{1}{2^{2 \cdot \mathsf{H.ol}(\lambda)}}. \qquad \square$$

7.4.2 Constructions

The separating example in the previous proof, that $A \cdot x$ cannot be pairwise independent because $A \cdot 0 = 0$, could be considered to be contrived. It may therefore not be surprising that it is also easy to fix the issue by considering instead the function $Ax + b$ for random matrix A and random vector b.

Hash Functions Based on Matrices

The hash key hk is given by the random matrix A and a random vector b. Hashing x is performed by computing $A \cdot x + b$. We give the construction below for sake of simplicity for the field $\mathbb{Z}_2$ but note that it works for any other field $\mathbb{F}$ as well.

$\mathsf{H.KGen}(1^\lambda)$	$\mathsf{H.Eval}(\mathsf{hk}, x)$
1: $A \leftarrow\!\!\$\ \mathbb{Z}_2^{\mathsf{H.ol}(\lambda) \times \mathsf{H.il}(\lambda)}$	1: $(A, b) \leftarrow \mathsf{hk}$
2: $b \leftarrow\!\!\$\ \mathbb{Z}_2^{\mathsf{H.ol}(\lambda)}$	2: **return** $A \cdot x + b$
3: $\mathsf{hk} \leftarrow (A, b)$	
4: **return** hk	

Our goal is to show that for distinct $x \neq x'$ a random hash function (A, b) hits values y, y' with probability at most $2^{-2 \cdot \mathsf{H.ol}(\lambda)}$. We show that the output bits are independently distributed and that for each output bit we have equality with probability $\frac{1}{4}$. The claim then follows.

Fix an index i between 1 and $\mathsf{H.ol}(\lambda)$. For any of the strings x, x', y, y', b let $x_i, x'_i, y_i, y'_i, b_i$ denote the ith entry in the string. Also, a_i denotes the ith row vector of the matrix A, and $a_{i,j}$ its jth entry. We use a similar proof strategy as in the construction of universal hash functions but cast it in the terminology of equation systems. For the ith output bit in the computation of $Ax + b$ we are thus interested in the probabilities that

$$\sum_{j=1}^{\mathsf{H.il}(\lambda)} a_{i,j} x_j + b_i = y_i \qquad \text{and} \qquad \sum_{j=1}^{\mathsf{H.il}(\lambda)} a_{i,j} x'_j + b_i = y'_i.$$

Since $x \neq x'$ there exists an index k such that $x_k \neq x'_k$. The equations can be rewritten as

$$a_{i,k} x_k + b_i = y_i - \sum_{j=1, j \neq k}^{\mathsf{H.il}(\lambda)} \qquad \text{and} \qquad a_{i,k} x'_k + b_i = y'_i - \sum_{j=1, j \neq k}^{\mathsf{H.il}(\lambda)} a_{i,j} x'_j,$$

or, in matrix form,

$$\begin{pmatrix} x_{i,k} & 1 \\ x'_{i,k} & 1 \end{pmatrix} \cdot \begin{pmatrix} a_{i,k} \\ b_i \end{pmatrix} = \begin{pmatrix} y_i - \sum_{j=1, j \neq k}^{\mathsf{H.il}(\lambda)} a_{i,j} x_j \\ y'_i - \sum_{j=1, j \neq k}^{\mathsf{H.il}(\lambda)} a_{i,j} x'_j \end{pmatrix}.$$

If we fix the values $a_{i,j}$ for $j \neq k$ then we have a system of two equations in the variables $a_{i,k}$ and b_i. For the determinant underlying the equations we have

$$\det \begin{pmatrix} x_k & 1 \\ x'_k & 1 \end{pmatrix} = x_k \cdot 1 - x'_k \cdot 1 = x_k - x'_k \neq 0$$

such that the system has a unique solution $a_{i,k}, b_i$. Since we pick both values uniformly at random, we hit this unique solution with probability $\frac{1}{4}$. The argument holds for each row, independently of the other rows, because we pick all entries $a_{i,k}, b_i$ for $i = 1, 2, \ldots, \mathsf{H.ol}(\lambda)$ independently. The probability of satisfying the equation is thus the product over the probabilities of $\frac{1}{4}$ for each row.

Hash Functions Based on Polynomials

Similarly to the case of universal hash functions we can also use polynomials to build pairwise independent hash functions. This time, however, we cannot easily allow arbitrary input sizes but instead consider fixed inputs x from some field $\mathbb{F}$. The construction idea is similar to the matrix setting. The hash key hk consists of two random field elements a and b, and hashing a value x is given by $a \cdot x + b$.

$\mathsf{H.KGen}(1^\lambda)$	$\mathsf{H.Eval}(\mathsf{hk}, x)$
1: $a, b \leftarrow_\$ \mathbb{F}$	1: $(a, b) \leftarrow \mathsf{hk}$
2: $\mathsf{hk} \leftarrow (a, b)$	2: **return** $a \cdot x + b$
3: **return** hk	

To see that the construction is pairwise independent note that we can write the equations

$$ax + b = y \text{ and } ax' + b = y'$$

analogously to the matrix-based hashing as

$$\begin{pmatrix} x & 1 \\ x' & 1 \end{pmatrix} \cdot \begin{pmatrix} a \\ b \end{pmatrix} = \begin{pmatrix} y \\ y' \end{pmatrix}.$$

Since $x \neq x'$ the determinant of the left matrix is different from 0, such that we again have a unique solution for the system and our random choice of a, b hits this solution with probability $\frac{1}{|\mathbb{F}|^2}$.

To process longer inputs a common method is to split the input x into field elements $(x_1, \ldots, x_t)$ and to compute the hash as $b + \sum_{i=1}^{t} a_i x_i$ for random key elements b and $a_1, a_2, \ldots$ In practice, the elements $a_1, a_2, \ldots$ are often derived by stretching a seed pseudorandomly. It follows almost as before that for distinct inputs x, x' and images y, y' there is a unique key $b, a_1, a_2, \ldots$ which fits.

To get a k-wise independent hash function (for inputs x of fixed size) one can take any random polynomial $x \mapsto \sum_{i=0}^{k-1} a_i x^i$ of degree $k - 1$ over a field $\mathbb{F}$, where the coefficients $a_0, \ldots, a_{k-1}$ are chosen at random. For every k pairs $(x^{(i)}, y^{(i)})$ there is exactly one polynomial of degree $k - 1$ which maps all $x^{(i)}$'s to the $y^{(i)}$'s. This follows from the extrapolation property of polynomials. The probability of picking those k coefficients is exactly $|\mathbb{F}|^k$.

7.4.3 One-Time Message Authentication

As a cryptographic application of pairwise independent hashing we show that such functions can be used to build unconditionally secure one-time MACs. In such a MAC scheme $\mathsf{MAC} := (\mathsf{MAC.KGen}, \mathsf{MAC.Eval})$ the unbounded adversary picks a message m, then a MAC key $\mathsf{mk} \leftarrow\!\!{\scriptstyle\$}\; \mathsf{MAC.KGen}(1^\lambda)$ is chosen, and the adversary gets to see $\tau \leftarrow \mathsf{MAC.Eval}(\mathsf{mk}, m)$, and eventually the adversary needs to output a new message $m^* \neq m$ with a valid tag τ^*.

The idea for constructing secure one-time MACs based on pairwise independent hashing is to use the hash key as the secret MAC key, and to tag a message by outputting the hash value under the key:

$\mathsf{MAC.KGen}(1^\lambda)$	$\mathsf{MAC.Eval}(\mathsf{hk}, m)$
1: $\mathsf{hk} \leftarrow \mathsf{H.KGen}(1^\lambda)$	1: **return** $\mathsf{H.Eval}(\mathsf{hk}, m)$
2: **return** hk	

The intuition of the security proof is that the hash value on m^*, which the adversary tries to predict, is independent of the hash value for the previously tagged message m by the property of the hash function. The argument is not immediate though, because in the attack on the MAC the adversary first gets to see the hash value for m before choosing m^*. In the experiment for pairwise independence both messages are fixed first. We can, however, show that a pairwise independent hash function has the required property. Namely, for a pairwise independent hash function for all $x \neq x'$ and y, y' it holds that

$$\Pr[\mathsf{H.Eval}(\mathsf{hk}, x) = y \mid \mathsf{H.Eval}(\mathsf{hk}, x') = y'] = 2^{-\mathsf{H.ol}(\lambda)}$$

over the choice of the key $\mathsf{hk} \leftarrow_{\$} \mathsf{H.KGen}(1^\lambda)$. This can be seen via conditional probabilities:

$$\Pr[\mathsf{H.Eval}(\mathsf{hk}, x) = y \mid \mathsf{H.Eval}(\mathsf{hk}, x') = y']$$
$$= \frac{\Pr[\mathsf{H.Eval}(\mathsf{hk}, x) = y \wedge \mathsf{H.Eval}(\mathsf{hk}, x') = y']}{\Pr[\mathsf{H.Eval}(\mathsf{hk}, x') = y']}$$

and using the property $\Pr[\mathsf{H.Eval}(\mathsf{hk}, x) = y] = 2^{-\mathsf{H.ol}(\lambda)}$ of pairwise independent hash functions,

$$= \frac{2^{\mathsf{H.ol}(\lambda)}}{2^{2 \cdot \mathsf{H.ol}(\lambda)}} = 2^{-\mathsf{H.ol}(\lambda)}.$$

Now the security of the MAC scheme follows easily: The adversary, after having seen the hash value τ for m, has only a success probability of $2^{-\mathsf{H.ol}(\lambda)}$ of finding the right hash value for a new message m^*.

Remark 7.20. We note that the construction, as defined above, can be used with k-wise independent hash functions, too. In this case one gets a $(k-1)$-time secure MAC.

7.5 Target-Collision Resistance from One-Way Permutations

We show another application of pairwise independent hash functions, namely that one can build target-collision-resistant hash functions from such functions and one-way permutations. As remarked in Section 4.4.1 one-way functions already suffice, but the proof is much more involved. We thus discuss here the simpler case using one-way permutations.

Recall that target-collision resistance (Definition 4.8 on page 175) demands that the adversary first outputs some hash input x_1, then learns the hash key hk, and afterwards tries to find a colliding input $x_2 \neq x_1$. Our goal is now to construct such a target-collision-resistant hash function H from a pairwise independent hash function, denoted here as G, and a one-way permutation P. The idea is as follows: We will assume that the pairwise independent hash function G shrinks λ-bit inputs to $(\lambda - 1)$-bit outputs but such that each image has exactly two preimages. Then we define our target-collision-resistant hash function H as

$$H(x) = G(P(x)),$$

where we omitted the Eval algorithms and keys for simplicity. Note that the one-way permutation P preserves its input length and the pairwise independent hash function G then reduces the input by one bit, such that the derived function is indeed compressing.

Remarkably, for the formal security argument of the construction above we will only indirectly rely on the pairwise independence of the function G. Independence says that any two inputs $x \neq x'$ are mapped to independent y, y' outputs, and that a random hash key distributes the inputs well. We will take advantage of this in the reverse direction: Given any input and output pairs (x, x') and (y, y') we should be able to find a hash key which coincides with these pairs. We will in particular be interested in collisions $y = y'$. Moreover, if we pick x and y randomly, then the backwards computed key of the hash function has the same distribution as if generating it via the regular key generation algorithm:

Definition 7.21 (Reverse Key Generation). *A reverse key generation algorithm* G.RKGen *for a pairwise independent hash function* G = (G.KGen, G.Eval) *is a probabilistic polynomial-time algorithm such that for any* $\lambda \in \mathbb{N}$, *any* $x, x \in \{0, 1\}^{G.il(\lambda)}$, *any* $y \in \{0, 1\}^{G.ol(\lambda)}$, *and any* gk $\leftarrow\$ $ RKGen$(1^\lambda, x, x', y)$ *we have*

$$G.Eval(gk, x) = y = G.Eval(gk, x').$$

Furthermore, for any λ *and for any* $x' \in \{0, 1\}^{G.il(\lambda)}$ *the following distribution* RKG$(1^\lambda, x')$ *is identical to the one of algorithm* G.KGen(1^λ):

RKG$(1^\lambda, x')$
1: $x \leftarrow\$ \{0, 1\}^{G.il(\lambda)}$
2: $y \leftarrow\$ \{0, 1\}^{G.ol(\lambda)}$
3: gk $\leftarrow\$ $ G.RKGen$(1^\lambda, x, x', y)$
4: **return** gk

We need to argue that there are pairwise independent hash functions with reverse key generators. Our candidate is the hash function $ax + b$ for a, b over the field $\mathbb{GF}(2^\lambda)$, but where we truncate the last bit of the output to derive a compressing function. More formally, consider the hash function

$$G.Eval((a, b), x) := \mathsf{truncate}(a \cdot x + b)$$

over $\mathbb{GF}(2^\lambda)$ for uniformly chosen key gk $= (a, b) \leftarrow\$ $ G.KGen(1^λ), where the function truncate drops the last bit of the λ-bit string. We claim that this function has a reverse key generation algorithm according to the definition above:

$$\underline{G.RKGen(1^\lambda, x, x', y)}$$

1 : $c \leftarrow\!\!\$\; \{0, 1\}$

2 : $y_c \leftarrow y||c, \; y_{c\oplus 1} \leftarrow y||(c \oplus 1)$

3 :   **if** $x = x'$ **then**

4 : $a \leftarrow 0, b \leftarrow y_c$

5 :   **else**

6 :   solve for $a, b \in \mathrm{GF}(2^\lambda)$ in $\begin{pmatrix} x & 1 \\ x' & 1 \end{pmatrix} \cdot \begin{pmatrix} a \\ b \end{pmatrix} = \begin{pmatrix} y_c \\ y_{c\oplus 1} \end{pmatrix}$

7 :   **return gk** $\leftarrow (a, b)$

First note that the output (a, b) of the algorithm $\mathsf{RKGen}(1^\lambda, x, x', y)$ for all x, x', y satisfies

$$\mathsf{G.Eval}(\mathsf{gk}, x) = y = \mathsf{G.Eval}(\mathsf{gk}, x'),$$

because in case $x = x'$ the algorithm returns the key $(a, b) = (0, y||c)$ such that the hash value in both cases equals $\mathsf{truncate}(y||c) = y$. For $x \neq x'$ the **else**-branch in line 6 returns a key (a, b) such that x is mapped to y_c and x' is mapped to $y_{c\oplus 1}$. The $\mathsf{truncate}$ function then maps both values to y.

It remains to argue the identical output distribution as the key generation algorithm, if x and y are chosen randomly. Fix x' in the following and consider the uniformly chosen pair (x, y_c) where y is already augmented with the random bit c according to the algorithm. We first look at the **else**-case in line 6 with $x \neq x'$. In this case the system of equations

$$\begin{pmatrix} x & 1 \\ x' & 1 \end{pmatrix} \cdot \begin{pmatrix} a \\ b \end{pmatrix} = \begin{pmatrix} y_c \\ y_{c\oplus 1} \end{pmatrix}$$

has exactly one solution (a, b). Furthermore, this solution (a, b) cannot satisfy the corresponding system for any other pair $(\overline{x}, \overline{y}_{\overline{c}})$, because the second equation

$$y_{c\oplus 1} = ax' + b = \overline{y}_{\overline{c}\oplus 1}$$

necessitates $y_{c\oplus 1} = \overline{y}_{\overline{c}\oplus 1}$ and thus also $y_c = \overline{y}_{\overline{c}}$. But then the first equation for $\overline{x} \neq x$ cannot satisfy

$$ax + b = y_c = \overline{y}_{\overline{c}} = a\overline{x} + b.$$

Hence, for each of the $2^\lambda \cdot (2^\lambda - 1)$ pairs (x, y_c) with $x \neq x'$ there is a one-to-one correspondence with keys (a, b). Moreover, for $x \neq x'$ we know that the "missing" 2^λ pairs (a, b) are exactly those where $a = 0$; the reason is that $a = 0$ in case $x \neq x'$ cannot simultaneously map x to y_c and x' to the different value $y_{c\oplus 1}$:

$$\begin{pmatrix} x & 1 \\ x' & 1 \end{pmatrix} \cdot \begin{pmatrix} 0 \\ b \end{pmatrix} = \begin{pmatrix} b \\ b \end{pmatrix} \neq \begin{pmatrix} y_c \\ y_{c\oplus 1} \end{pmatrix}.$$

On the other hand, our algorithm chooses precisely the keys $(0, y_c)$ for (x', y_c) in the **if**-branch in line 4. It follows that, generally, there is a bijection between pairs (x, y_c) and keys (a, b). For uniformly random (x, y) and random c our algorithm thus outputs a uniformly distributed pair (a, b), just as the original key generation algorithm.

> **Theorem 7.22.** *Let* $P = (P.KGen, P.Eval)$ *be a one-way permutation with* $P.il(\lambda) = P.ol(\lambda) = \lambda$, *and* $G = (G.KGen, G.Eval)$ *be a pairwise independent hash function with reverse key generation algorithm* $G.RKGen$, *such that* $G.il(\lambda) = \lambda$ *and* $G.ol(\lambda) = \lambda - 1$ *and each image has exactly two preimages. Then the hash function* $H = (H.KGen, H.Eval)$ *as defined below is target-collision resistant:*
>
> | $H.KGen(1^\lambda)$ | $H.Eval((fk, gk), x)$ |
> |---|---|
> | *1*: $fk \leftarrow_\$ P.KGen(1^\lambda)$ | *1*: $z \leftarrow P.Eval(fk, x)$ |
> | *2*: $gk \leftarrow_\$ G.KGen(1^\lambda)$ | *2*: $h \leftarrow G.Eval(gk, z)$ |
> | *3*:   **return** (fk, gk) | *3*:   **return** h |

The proof idea is as follows. An adversary against target-collision resistance first outputs a value x_1 before learning the hash key. We can think of x_1 being our x' above. Then we pick a random y and use a given image $w = P.Eval(fk, v)$ under the one-way permutation as x, to create a key gk for x, x', y via reverse key generation. Now the two preimages of y are exactly $P.Eval(fk, x_1)$ and w. If the adversary against target-collision resistance now finds a colliding input x_2 to x_1 then, since P is a permutation, we must have $P.Eval(fk, x_2) = w$. This adversary has thus successfully inverted the one-way permutation for a random image w. This of course contradicts the one-wayness of P.

Proof of Theorem 7.22. Consider an adversary $\mathcal{A} = (\mathcal{A}_1, \mathcal{A}_2)$ against the target-collision resistance and assume that $\mathcal{A}$ has a non-negligible success probability. From $\mathcal{A}$ we build, via a black-box construction, an adversary $\mathcal{B}$ against the one-wayness of P. The graphical description is given in Figure 7.2. Algorithm $\mathcal{B}$ receives as input a key fk of the one-way permutation and a value $w \in \{0, 1\}^\lambda$. Its task is to find $v \in \{0, 1\}^\lambda$ such that $w = P.Eval(fk, v)$. To do so it first runs the first-stage part $\mathcal{A}_1$ of $\mathcal{A}$ on the security parameter to receive x_1. It now uses this value to compute $x' \leftarrow P.Eval(fk, x_1)$, sets $x \leftarrow w$, and chooses a random image $y \in \{0, 1\}^{\lambda - 1}$. It next generates a key gk for the universal hash function by running key generation in the reverse direction for x, x', y. It then invokes the second-stage $\mathcal{A}_2$ on (fk, gk) to receive x_2. This value serves as $\mathcal{B}$'s output v^*.

For the analysis note that the reversely computed key gk generated in $\mathcal{B}$'s simulation has the same distribution as a key generated by $G.KGen$ in an attack. This follows from the requirement for $RKGen$ and the fact that $x \leftarrow w = P.Eval(fk, v)$ is uniformly distributed over $\{0, 1\}^\lambda$ for the one-way

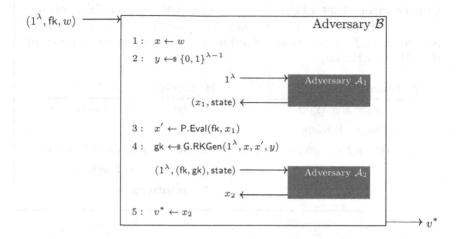

Fig. 7.2: Black-box reduction of one-wayness adversary $\mathcal{B}$ from target-collision resistance adversary $\mathcal{A} = (\mathcal{A}_1, \mathcal{A}_2)$.

permutation P, and so is y over $\{0,1\}^{\lambda-1}$. It follows that $\mathcal{A}$ creates a collision $x_1 \neq x_2$ in the simulation with the same (non-negligible) probability as in an actual attack. If this happens in the simulation, then by construction of RKGen we have

$$G.\mathsf{Eval}(\mathsf{gk}, x) = y = G.\mathsf{Eval}(\mathsf{gk}, x'),$$

where $x = w$ and $x' = \mathsf{P.Eval}(\mathsf{fk}, x_1)$. As $x_1 \neq x_2$ for a successful attack, and P is injective, we must also have

$$\mathsf{P.Eval}(\mathsf{fk}, x_1) \neq \mathsf{P.Eval}(\mathsf{fk}, x_2).$$

But then these two function values can only collide under the universal hash function G if they correspond to the two preimages x and x'. It follows that x_2 must be the preimage of w under P, such that $\mathcal{B}$ succeeds in inverting P with the same probability as $\mathcal{A}$ succeeds against target-collision resistance of hash function H. $\qquad\square$

The construction in Theorem 7.22 provides a target-collision-resistant hash function which compresses inputs by one bit only. If one now wants to build a hash function H^p with higher compression rates, mapping inputs of $\mathsf{p}(\lambda)$ bits to $\lambda-1$ bits for some fixed polynomial p, then one can iterate this construction for security parameters $\lambda, \lambda+1, \ldots, \mathsf{p}(\lambda)$ as in Construction 7.23 below which, clearly, compresses inputs of $\mathsf{p}(\lambda)$ bits to $\lambda-1$ bits. The fact that this iterative construction inherits target-collision resistance is left as Exercise 7.4.

Construction 7.23 (TCR hash function with polynomial compression). *Let* P *be a one-way permutation and* G *be a pairwise independent hash function as in Theorem 7.22. We define hash function* $\mathsf{H} = (\mathsf{H.KGen}, \mathsf{H.Eval})$ *as*

$\mathsf{H^P.KGen}(1^\lambda)$	$\mathsf{H^P.Eval}(\mathsf{hk}, x)$
1: **for** $i = \lambda .. \mathsf{p}(\lambda)$ **do**	1: $(\mathsf{hk}_\lambda, \ldots, \mathsf{hk}_{\mathsf{p}(\lambda)}) \leftarrow \mathsf{hk}$
2: $\quad \mathsf{hk}_i \leftarrow_{\$} \mathsf{H.KGen}(1^i)$	2: $x_{\mathsf{p}(\lambda)} \leftarrow x$
3: **return** $\mathsf{hk} \leftarrow (\mathsf{hk}_\lambda, \ldots, \mathsf{hk}_{\mathsf{p}(\lambda)})$	3: **for** $i = \mathsf{p}(\lambda)$ **downto** λ **do**
	4: $\quad x_{i-1} \leftarrow \mathsf{H.Eval}(\mathsf{hk}_i, x_i)$
	5: **return** $x_{\lambda-1}$

Chapter Notes and References

Carter and Wegman introduced the notion of universal hash functions and gave constructions based on matrices and linear polynomials [3, 4]. In a follow-up work they also presented the notion of k-wise independent hash functions, under the name strongly universal hashing, and discussed how to build message authentication codes [14]. In particular, they already outlined how to reuse the key of the hash function by masking the hash value with a random string.

Krawczyk introduced the notion of XOR-universal hash functions, albeit under a different name [8]. Rogaway then used the term XOR-universal, which is more common today [12]. Krawczyk subsequently also gave the construction of (XOR-)universal hash functions based on Toeplitz matrices [9].

The notion of universal one-way hash functions has been introduced by Naor and Yung [10]. They also presented the construction in Section 7.5 based on any one-way permutation. The term "target-collision resistance" for these functions was coined by Bellare and Rogaway [1]. Rompel extended the result by Naor and Yung to general one-way functions [13]. Katz and Koo later gave a comprehensive and thorough description of Rompel's construction [7].

Extractors based on universal hash functions and the leftover hash lemma were introduced by Zuckerman [15], although the name "extractor" appeared only later [11]. The leftover hash lemma appeared in the work by Imapgliazzo et al. about building pseudorandom generators from one-way functions [6]; see also the journal version of Håstad et al. [5].

The construction of a message authentication code from an ϵ-AXU hash function with masking, defined via $\mathsf{PRF.Eval}(\mathsf{k}, r) \oplus \mathsf{H.Eval}(\mathsf{hk}, m)$ as presented in Section 7.3 was formally analyzed by Rogaway [12] (for a counter value instead of a random nonce). This approach is, for example, used in Bernstein's `Poly1305-AES` message authentication code [2]. The ϵ-AXU hash function in Bernstein's scheme is based on polynomial evaluation, and AES acts as the pseudorandom function. This MAC scheme is used extensively in practice because of its efficiency and strong security bounds.

Exercices

Exercise 7.1. Show that universal hash functions in general do not constitute an unconditionally secure one-time MAC. Does this also hold if the forgery needs to be for a message $m^* \neq 0$?

Exercise 7.2. Let H_i be an ϵ_i-almost universal hash function for $i \in \{1, 2\}$. Show the following claims:

(a) Consider function G_1 that generates keys $hk_1 \leftarrow^\$ H_1(1^\lambda)$, $hk_2 \leftarrow^\$ H_2(1^\lambda)$ to then evaluate messages as $G_1((hk_1, hk_2), m) := H_1(hk_1, H(hk_2, m))$. Then function G_1 is $(\varepsilon_1 + \varepsilon_2)$-AU.
(b) Consider function G_2 which generates keys as G_1 but which generates hash values as $G_2((hk_1, hk_2), m) := H_1(hk_1, m) \| H_2(hk, m)$. Then function G_2 is $\varepsilon_1 \varepsilon_2$-AU.

Exercise 7.3. Show that Construction 7.14 (page 321) yields a message authentication code that is existentially unforgeable under chosen-message attacks given that PRF is a secure pseudorandom function and H is an ϵ-AXU hash function.

Exercise 7.4. Show that the iterative construction H^p from a target-collision-resistant hash function H (Construction 7.23; page 332) is also target-collision resistant.

Chapter Bibliography

1. Mihir Bellare and Phillip Rogaway. Collision-resistant hashing: Towards making UOWHFs practical. In Burton S. Kaliski Jr., editor, *Advances in Cryptology – CRYPTO'97*, volume 1294 of *Lecture Notes in Computer Science*, pages 470–484, Santa Barbara, CA, USA, August 17–21, 1997. Springer, Heidelberg, Germany.
2. Daniel J. Bernstein. The poly1305-AES message-authentication code. In Henri Gilbert and Helena Handschuh, editors, *Fast Software Encryption – FSE 2005*, volume 3557 of *Lecture Notes in Computer Science*, pages 32–49, Paris, France, February 21–23, 2005. Springer, Heidelberg, Germany.
3. J. Lawrence Carter and Mark N. Wegman. Universal classes of hash functions (extended abstract). In *Proceedings of the Ninth Annual ACM Symposium on Theory of Computing*, STOC '77, pages 106–112, New York, NY, USA, 1977. Association for Computing Machinery.

4. Larry Carter and Mark N. Wegman. Universal classes of hash functions. *J. Comput. Syst. Sci.*, 18(2):143–154, 1979.
5. Johan Håstad, Russell Impagliazzo, Leonid A. Levin, and Michael Luby. A pseudorandom generator from any one-way function. *SIAM Journal on Computing*, 28(4):1364–1396, 1999.
6. Russell Impagliazzo, Leonid A. Levin, and Michael Luby. Pseudo-random generation from one-way functions (extended abstracts). In *21st Annual ACM Symposium on Theory of Computing*, pages 12–24, Seattle, WA, USA, May 15–17, 1989. ACM Press.
7. Jonathan Katz and Chiu-Yuen Koo. On constructing universal one-way hash functions from arbitrary one-way functions. Cryptology ePrint Archive, Report 2005/328, 2005. http://eprint.iacr.org/2005/328.
8. Hugo Krawczyk. LFSR-based hashing and authentication. In Yvo Desmedt, editor, *Advances in Cryptology – CRYPTO'94*, volume 839 of *Lecture Notes in Computer Science*, pages 129–139, Santa Barbara, CA, USA, August 21–25, 1994. Springer, Heidelberg, Germany.
9. Hugo Krawczyk. New hash functions for message authentication. In Louis C. Guillou and Jean-Jacques Quisquater, editors, *Advances in Cryptology – EUROCRYPT'95*, volume 921 of *Lecture Notes in Computer Science*, pages 301–310, Saint-Malo, France, May 21–25, 1995. Springer, Heidelberg, Germany.
10. Moni Naor and Moti Yung. Universal one-way hash functions and their cryptographic applications. In *21st Annual ACM Symposium on Theory of Computing*, pages 33–43, Seattle, WA, USA, May 15–17, 1989. ACM Press.
11. Noam Nisan and David Zuckerman. More deterministic simulation in logspace. In *25th Annual ACM Symposium on Theory of Computing*, pages 235–244, San Diego, CA, USA, May 16–18, 1993. ACM Press.
12. Phillip Rogaway. Bucket hashing and its application to fast message authentication. In Don Coppersmith, editor, *Advances in Cryptology – CRYPTO'95*, volume 963 of *Lecture Notes in Computer Science*, pages 29–42, Santa Barbara, CA, USA, August 27–31, 1995. Springer, Heidelberg, Germany.
13. John Rompel. One-way functions are necessary and sufficient for secure signatures. In *22nd Annual ACM Symposium on Theory of Computing*, pages 387–394, Baltimore, MD, USA, May 14–16, 1990. ACM Press.
14. Mark N. Wegman and Larry Carter. New hash functions and their use in authentication and set equality. *J. Comput. Syst. Sci.*, 22(3):265–279, 1981.
15. David Zuckerman. General weak random sources. In *31st Annual Symposium on Foundations of Computer Science*, pages 534–543, St. Louis, MO, USA, October 22–24, 1990. IEEE Computer Society Press.

Part II
The Random Oracle Methodology

Chapter 8
The Random Oracle Model

In the previous chapter we looked at dedicated forms of hash functions that we categorized as non-cryptographic hash functions. Their common denominator is that we can prove the existence of constructions that fulfill the properties (e.g., pairwise independence) without having to rely on unproven assumptions. This stands in stark contrast to security properties such as pseudorandom functions which are based on assumptions that we currently do not know how to prove, although they appear to be reasonable. The possibly simplest of such cryptographic assumptions, which lies at the base of almost any cryptographic scheme, is that one-way functions exist. The difficulty of proving the existence of one-way functions is that the existence of one-way functions would imply a separation of the complexity classes P and NP. While it is a common belief in the scientific community that indeed $P \neq NP$, proving this statement has eluded researches for decades. The P vs. NP problem is one of the seven *Millennium Problems* of the Clay Mathematical Institute and generally regarded as one of the most important open problems in computer science.

In this chapter we turn to an abstraction of hash functions that is commonly used when arguing about the security of cryptographic schemes, especially cryptographic schemes deployed in practice. We look at *idealized hash functions*, that is, hash functions that simultaneously fulfill all the security notions that we have discussed so far, among others, one-wayness, pseudorandomness, and collision resistance. When we talk about *ideal* hash functions, we do, however, require more from the function than simply achieving all the security properties simultaneously. We require that the function has no single point of weakness and, in particular, achieves the best possible level of security.

The model of idealized hash functions that we introduce here is the so-called *random oracle model*. In short, random oracles can be thought of as truly random functions that every party in a cryptographic scheme (including the adversary) gets access to. As we will see, random oracles—similarly to non-cryptographic hash functions—are fundamentally different from the *provable security approach* that we have used so far where security properties

© Springer Nature Switzerland AG 2021
A. Mittelbach, M. Fischlin, *The Theory of Hash Functions and Random Oracles*,
Information Security and Cryptography, https://doi.org/10.1007/978-3-030-63287-8_8

are based on well-defined assumptions such as the existence of a one-way function. While for non-cryptographic hash functions we simply do not need any unproven assumptions the case with random oracles is that the "random oracle assumption" as such is simply too strong and it can be shown that it cannot hold. Nevertheless, the so-called *random oracle methodology* is a generally accepted—yet also controversial—*heuristic* to build cryptographic schemes and, in particular, many real-world cryptographic schemes that are used in practice are only proven secure in the *random oracle model*.

8.1 The Random Oracle Model

In Section 1.3.1 we introduced oracle Turing machines that are connected to one or more *oracles*, with which the machine can interact via special oracle tapes. In order to query an oracle, the machine writes a query on to the oracle tape and goes into a special state. Then, within a single step the oracle's answer is written onto the oracle tape. An oracle can thus simply be regarded as a *black box* with a specified functionality that the Turing machine can make use of.

So far we have used oracles mostly in two places: (black-box) reductions and security definitions. In a (black-box) reduction we consider an algorithm (the reduction) relative to a hypothetical adversary (the oracle). Here, the goal is to show that the reduction with the help of the adversary can solve a problem which is assumed "infeasible to solve," thereby showing that an adversary cannot exist as otherwise the consequence would be that the assumed infeasible problem is solvable after all: the reduction together with the adversary solves it. As for oracles as part of security definitions consider, for example, the security definition for signature schemes (Definition 6.2; page 264) where an adversary is given a signing oracle, or the definition of pseudorandom functions (Definition 3.21; page 126) where a distinguisher is given oracle access to either the real function or to a random function with identical input and output length as the alleged pseudorandom function.[1] In the random oracle model, we will use oracles not only in reductions and security definitions but, first and foremost, in constructions of primitives.

8.1.1 Random Functions

A *random oracle* RO is an oracle that implements a *random function* of the form $\{0,1\}^{\leq \mathsf{RO.il}(\lambda)} \to \{0,1\}^{\mathsf{RO.ol}(\lambda)}$ or, having an infinite domain, of the form

---

[1] We note that the random function is, indeed, what we will call here a fixed-input-length random oracle.

$\{0,1\}^* \to \{0,1\}^{\mathsf{RO.ol}(\lambda)}$. In other words a random oracle RO takes (possibly arbitrarily) long inputs and maps them to strings of length $\mathsf{RO.ol}(\lambda)$.

We have said that a random oracle implements a random function. But what exactly does this mean? We start by considering random oracles with bounded input length of at most $\mathsf{RO.il}(\lambda)$ first. This corresponds to hash functions like SHA-256 which can process inputs of less than 2^{64} bits only. We stress that for practical matters this restriction is irrelevant, though. In contrast, the SHA-3 standard does not put any restriction on the input length, such that we can view it as a candidate for a random oracle with input space $\{0,1\}^*$. The infinite domain introduces some mathematical peculiarities for random functions which we discuss at the end of the section.

Random Functions with Bounded Domains

There are several ways to think about a random oracle with bounded domains. One way is to imagine that during construction of the random oracle a function $f : \{0,1\}^{\leq \mathsf{RO.il}(\lambda)} \to \{0,1\}^{\mathsf{RO.ol}(\lambda)}$ is chosen uniformly at random from the space of all possible functions of the form $\{0,1\}^{\leq \mathsf{RO.il}(\lambda)} \to \{0,1\}^{\mathsf{RO.ol}(\lambda)}$. Since the input and output lengths are finite (for fixed security parameter λ), there are only finitely many such functions, each function having some non-vanishing probability of being chosen. We compute the exact probability below. Then on input $x \in \{0,1\}^{\leq \mathsf{RO.il}(\lambda)}$ the random oracle RO outputs the function value of x under the randomly chosen function f, that is,

$$\mathsf{RO}(x) := f(x).$$

A more algorithmic way to think about random functions is to consider a (finite) function table that lists for each possible input value $x \in \{0,1\}^{\leq \mathsf{RO.il}(\lambda)}$ the corresponding result $f(x)$, where we order the input strings x arbitrarily:

x	$f(x)$
ϵ	$f(\epsilon)$
0	$f(0)$
1	$f(1)$
00	$f(00)$
$\vdots$	$\vdots$

We now argue that selecting a random function f from the set of all functions is equivalent to choosing each entry $f(x)$ in the table randomly and independently from all other entries.

We first note that we have $|Y|^{|X|}$ many functions $f : X \to Y$ (or, tables) for any finite sets X, Y, because we can choose $|Y|$ possible values for each of the $|X|$ input values, and each complete choice for all input values determines exactly one function. Hence, picking a function f randomly from the set of

all functions means to choose one of these functions with probability $|Y|^{-|X|}$.
In our case we have $X = \{0,1\}^{\leq \text{RO.il}(\lambda)}$ and $Y = \{0,1\}^{\text{RO.ol}(\lambda)}$.

Assume now that we have chosen a random function f from the set of all
functions $\{0,1\}^{\leq \text{RO.il}(\lambda)} \to \{0,1\}^{\text{RO.ol}(\lambda)}$. Consider an arbitrary entry x in the
table and some value $y \in \{0,1\}^{\text{RO.ol}(\lambda)}$. We need to show that $f(x) = y$ with
probability $2^{-\text{RO.ol}(\lambda)}$ over the choice of the random function f, and that this
holds independently of the other entries. To show this we partition the set of
all functions according to the values at other inputs x' distinct from x. That
is, for an arbitrary subset $X' \subseteq \{0,1\}^{\leq \text{RO.il}(\lambda)} \setminus \{x\}$ of values x' distinct from
x, assume that we have already preselected function values $y_{x'} \in \{0,1\}^{\text{RO.ol}(\lambda)}$.
One can think of these pairs $(x', y_{x'})$ to be the entries in the table we have
already fixed.

We are first interested in the probability that a uniformly chosen function
$f : X \to Y$ maps exactly the selected inputs from X' to the fixed values.
If we have a subset X' of X for which we have determined the function
values already, then there are only $|Y|^{|X|-|X'|}$ many functions $f : X \to Y$
coinciding on these inputs from X', because we can only choose the images
for the remaining $|X| - |X'|$ input values. It follows that the probability that
a random function matches all fixed values from X' is given by the ratio of
good choices divided by all possible choices for the function f:

$$\Pr\left[\bigwedge_{x' \in X'} f(x') = y_{x'}\right] = \frac{|Y|^{|X|-|X'|}}{|Y|^{|X|}} = |Y|^{-|X'|}.$$

Then we can compute the conditional probability that a random function
which coincides on all values from X' with the given values takes a certain
value at input $x \notin X'$ as

$$\Pr\left[f(x) = y \;\middle|\; \bigwedge_{x' \in X'} f(x') = y_{x'}\right] = \frac{\Pr\left[f(x) = y \wedge \bigwedge_{x' \in X'} f(x') = y_{x'}\right]}{\Pr\left[\bigwedge_{x' \in X'} f(x') = y_{x'}\right]}$$

$$= \frac{\left(2^{\text{RO.ol}(\lambda)}\right)^{-(|X'|+1)}}{\left(2^{\text{RO.ol}(\lambda)}\right)^{-|X'|}}$$

$$= 2^{-\text{RO.ol}(\lambda)}.$$

This shows that choosing a random function can be represented by picking a
fresh random image in each row of the table.

Vice versa, assume that we fill a function table as above by putting random
and independent values from Y in each of the $|X|$ rows. Then the probability
of obtaining a specific table is given by $(\frac{1}{|Y|})^{|X|} = |Y|^{-|X|}$. By the one-to-
one correspondence between tables and functions it follows that we create a
function $f : X \to Y$ by this method with the same probability with which
we uniformly pick a function from the set of all functions $f : X \to Y$. We

conclude that the two views on choosing random functions yield identical results.

Lazy sampling. The above algorithmic view on random functions gives rise to a different method to represent a random oracle. The idea is to generate the entries in the table only in the moment when they are required. This technique is called *lazy sampling*, and its equivalence to selecting a function randomly has been argued above. The following probabilistic Turing machine—with unbounded runtime, unbounded storage capacity and an infinitely long tape of randomness—implements a random oracle via this technique:

$\mathsf{RO}(x)$

// initially $T[x] = \perp$ for all x

1 : **if** $T[x] = \perp$ **then**

2 : $T[x] \leftarrow_\$ \{0,1\}^{\mathsf{RO.ol}(\lambda)}$

3 : **return** $T[x]$

The idea is to consider a probabilistic and stateful Turing machine that has a table T as its state. Initially, all entries $T[x]$ in this table are undefined ($\forall x : T[x] = \perp$). On input a value x it checks whether table T already contains a value for x. If this is not the case it samples a fresh output value and stores it in table T as $T[x]$. Finally, it returns $T[x]$.

Random functions are huge. Random functions with unbounded domain, as defined above, have on average an infinite description. Even if we restricted the input domain from $\{0,1\}^*$ to only consider strings of a fixed length, e.g., to $\{0,1\}^n$, and the output length to a single bit, then the resulting function would still have a huge description. The reason for this is that uniformly random values, on average, cannot be compressed significantly below the size needed to store a table that simply lists all values. This is a direct consequence of Shannon's *source coding theorem*, a fundamental result of information theory.

Let us stress how quickly random functions exceed reasonable size bounds. If we were to compactly encode all functions from the very small domain and range $\{0,1\}^n \to \{0,1\}$ via prefix encodings then the length of the names of most functions must be exponential. The empty string encodes at most one function, with 1 bit we can encode 2^1 other functions, with 2 bits we can encode 2^2 other functions, and so forth, until all $|Y|^{|X|} = 2^{2^n}$ functions are encoded. With at most m bits we can thus encode at most

$$\sum_{i=0}^{m} 2^i = 2^{m+1} - 1$$

many functions. In particular, for $m = 2^n - 1$ we can only encode $2^{2^n} - 1$ functions, which means that at least one function requires 2^n bits for encoding it. Even worse, with $m = 2^n - 2$ bits we can represent at most $\frac{1}{2} \cdot 2^{2^n}$ functions and thus at most half of all functions. In other words, the other half of the functions requires at least $2^n - 1$ bits.

To visualize this tremendous number consider $n = 512$ (i.e., functions mapping from $\{0,1\}^{512}$ to one bit). This means that the size of most of the function descriptions is greater than 2^{510} bits (or roughly $4.19 \cdot 10^{140}$ TB). The estimated number of atoms in the universe is 10^{80}. This means that even if we were able to store a terabyte of data on each atom in the universe we would be nowhere near the number of bits required to encode a single random function that maps 512-bit strings to 1-bit strings.

Random Functions with Infinite Domain

If we now approach random oracles with unbounded input space $\{0,1\}^*$ as random functions, then we are faced with the question of whether such random functions exist at all. This question is far from moot, since we cannot define a uniform distribution on *countably* infinite values. Such a distribution U on an infinite set X would either assign the same fixed probability $p = 0$ or $p > 0$ to each element x in the entire space X. For the countable number of elements we would then have

$$\Pr[U \in X] = \Pr\left[\bigvee_{x \in X} U = x\right] = \sum_{x \in X} \Pr[U = x] = \sum_{x \in X} p,$$

such that the sum would be either 0 or diverge, although we require it to be 1.

The argument above breaks down if one considers uncountable infinite domains. In particular, we cannot reason anymore that the disjunction of the individual events $U = x$ is given by the sum over the probabilities. Fortunately, in that regard the infinite set of functions $\{0,1\}^* \to \{0,1\}^{\text{RO.ol}(\lambda)}$ is not countable. We next outline how a uniform distribution on these functions looks, and that it is unique. For this it is convenient to represent functions via their function table, only that we write down the images in a sequence $f(\epsilon), f(0), f(1), f(00), f(01), \ldots$ for all inputs in, say, lexicographic order. Since each image is from $\{0,1\}^{\text{RO.ol}(\lambda)}$ we get an infinite sequence of 0's and 1's, where each sequence describes exactly one function with infinite domain, and vice versa. If we are now able to sample uniformly over such infinite sequences of bits, we immediately get a uniform distribution over the functions $\{0,1\}^* \to \{0,1\}^{\text{RO.ol}(\lambda)}$.

Sampling infinite sequences. Sampling infinite sequences of random coin tosses $\omega = (\omega_i)_{i \in \mathbb{N}}$ is a well-known task in probability and measure theory. One starts by considering so-called cylinder sets $C_{i_1, \ldots, i_k, b_1, \ldots, b_k}$,

$$C_{i_1, \ldots, i_k, b_1, \ldots, b_k} = \left\{ \omega \mid \omega_{i_j} = b_j \text{ for } j = 1, 2, \ldots, k \right\},$$

for any distinct indices $i_1, \ldots, i_k \in \mathbb{N}$ and arbitrary bits $b_1, \ldots, b_k$. These cylinder sets determine finite subsequences of the infinite sequences. Then one defines a measure—the reader may for now think of this as the probability—Λ over these cylinder sets via

$$\Lambda(C_{i_1,\ldots,i_k,b_1,\ldots,b_k}) = 2^{-k}.$$

In terms of coin tosses one assigns the probability of 2^{-k} to each such subsequence of length k, matching our intuition that the k coin tosses should be uniform and independent.

The hard part is now to extend the function Λ to also cover arbitrary infinite sequences. A powerful tool of measure theory, namely Carathéodory's Extension Theorem, tells us that this is indeed possible, and that the derived measure coincides with the original measure Λ on the cylinder sets. Furthermore, Dynkin's π-λ-Theorem says that this is the only measure on the infinite coin toss sequences with the given "uniform behavior" on the cylinder sets. Hence, we can think of "the" uniform distribution on infinite coin toss sequences (and thus over random functions with infinite domain).

In summary, for infinite domains the uniformly distributed functions match our idea of tables with random entries closely. This follows from the profound modeling of such functions in measure theory. It also tells us that any lazy sampling of a finite subset of inputs corresponds to a cylinder set, such that each entry in the table is uniform and independently distributed.

8.1.2 Random Oracles

Given that even "small" random functions have huge descriptions, it is impossible for a computer (or a bounded Turing machine) to have a local copy of a given random function ready that it can use in computations. We can, however, study the power of algorithms that have access to a random function in a theoretical model: the *random oracle model*.

The usage of oracles stems from the field of complexity theory where oracles are used in the study of relations of complexity classes. For example we know that the complexity class P (the class of algorithms computable by deterministic polynomial-time Turing machines) is contained in the class of BPP (the class of algorithms computable by probabilistic polynomial-time Turing machines with a small error probability). Showing that P $\subseteq$ BPP is straightforward since a probabilistic polynomial-time Turing machine can of course act as a deterministic Turing machine by simply ignoring its random tape. The other direction, that is, whether or not BPP $\subseteq$ P, is however still open. (See Section 1.4 on page 36 for more details about these complexity classes.)

We can similarly study the question of whether $\mathsf{P} = \mathsf{BPP}$ in the random oracle model, where the question is now whether $\mathsf{P}^{\mathsf{RO}} = \mathsf{BPP}^{\mathsf{RO}}$ or not. Translated this asks whether a deterministic polynomial-time Turing machine with oracle access to a random oracle is as powerful as a probabilistic polynomial-time Turing machine with access to a random oracle. It has been shown that, relative to a random oracle, probabilistic and deterministic polynomial-time Turing machines are indeed coequal; a deterministic Turing machine can use a random oracle as its source of randomness and, vice versa, we can derandomize a probabilistic Turing machine with the help of a random oracle. We will later show this formally in Theorem 9.16 (page 395) when discussing derandomization more extensively in the context of cryptography.

Random Oracles in Cryptography

While the study of complexity classes is a fascinating topic, it is not the topic of this book, so let us turn our attention back to cryptography. Here we can study cryptographic schemes relative to random oracles, i.e., study them *in the random oracle model*. Studying a cryptographic scheme in the random oracle model means that all parties (including the adversary) get oracle access to a (single instance of) a random oracle. This is best explained with an example.

Consider a standard encryption setup where two parties, Alice and Bob, want to communicate in a confidential way over an insecure channel, say, the internet. Given the nature of an insecure channel it is possible for anybody to eavesdrop (or even tamper with) the messages sent between Alice and Bob. It is the goal of a cryptographic encryption scheme to ensure, for example, confidentiality even in the presence of adversaries. Given such an encryption scheme we can analyze it *in the random oracle model* in which case we assume the existence of a single random oracle RO to which every party, that is, Alice, Bob, as well as the adversary has access. If we consider Alice, Bob, and the adversary to be Turing machines Alice, Bob, and $\mathcal{A}$, then these become oracle machines $\mathsf{Alice}^{\mathsf{RO}}$, $\mathsf{Bob}^{\mathsf{RO}}$, and $\mathcal{A}^{\mathsf{RO}}$. It is important to note that the random oracle is the same oracle for all parties, but that the communication between a party and the random oracle is always private. That is, Alice does not see the random oracle calls by Bob or the adversary, and vice versa.

Besides granting a scheme's algorithms access to the random oracle, the security notions also need to be adapted accordingly. For instance, IND-security of a symmetric encryption scheme in the random oracle model then says that for all efficient adversaries $\mathcal{A} = (\mathcal{A}_1, \mathcal{A}_2)$ advantage $\mathsf{Adv}^{\mathrm{ind}}_{\mathsf{RO},\mathsf{SE},\mathcal{A}_1,\mathcal{A}_2}(\lambda)$ defined as

$$\mathsf{Adv}^{\mathrm{ind}}_{\mathsf{RO},\mathsf{SE},\mathcal{A}_1,\mathcal{A}_2}(\lambda) := 2 \cdot \mathrm{Pr}\left[\mathsf{Exp}^{\mathrm{ind}}_{\mathsf{RO},\mathsf{SE},\mathcal{A}_1,\mathcal{A}_2}(\lambda)\right] - 1,$$

$$\text{Experiment } \mathsf{Exp}^{\text{ind}}_{\mathsf{RO},\mathsf{SE},\mathcal{A}_1,\mathcal{A}_2}(\lambda)$$

1 : $b \leftarrow_\$ \{0,1\}$

2 : $\mathsf{k} \leftarrow_\$ \mathsf{SE}^{\mathsf{RO}}.\mathsf{KGen}(1^\lambda)$

3 : $(m_0, m_1, \mathsf{state}) \leftarrow_\$ \mathcal{A}_1^{\mathsf{RO}}(1^\lambda)$

4 : **if** $|m_0| \neq |m_1|$ **then return** false

5 : $c \leftarrow_\$ \mathsf{SE}^{\mathsf{RO}}.\mathsf{Enc}(\mathsf{k}, m_b)$

6 : $b' \leftarrow_\$ \mathcal{A}_2^{\mathsf{RO}}(1^\lambda, c, \mathsf{state})$

7 : **return** $(b = b')$

Fig. 8.1: The IND-security experiment of a symmetric encryption scheme in the random oracle model.

must be negligible, where experiment $\mathsf{Exp}^{\text{ind}}_{\mathsf{RO},\mathsf{SE},\mathcal{A}_1,\mathcal{A}_2}(\lambda)$ is given in Figure 8.1. Note that we do not explicitly describe in the experiment that RO is initialized as a random function (for appropriate input and output length). This is understood from stating that the security is treated in the presence of a random oracle.

Remark 8.1. Note that we wrote $\mathsf{SE}^{\mathsf{RO}}.\mathsf{KGen}$ and $\mathsf{SE}^{\mathsf{RO}}.\mathsf{Enc}$ instead of $\mathsf{SE}.\mathsf{KGen}^{\mathsf{RO}}$ and $\mathsf{SE}.\mathsf{Enc}^{\mathsf{RO}}$ to emphasize the fact that the encryption scheme as a whole is defined in the random oracle model and thus all its algorithms could potentially make use of the random oracle.

Random Oracle Model vs. Standard Model

We can informally define the random oracle model as:

Informal Definition 8.2 (Random Oracle Model). *A cryptographic scheme is said to be* in the random oracle model *if all relevant algorithms have oracle access to a single random function.*

In contrast, if a scheme does not make use of random oracles, we speak of standard model security:

Informal Definition 8.3 (Standard Model). *A cryptographic scheme is said to be* in the standard model *if no algorithm gets oracle access to a random function (or a similar idealized object).*

Note that the standard model demands the absence of all comparable oracles and not just random oracles. This is due to the fact that random oracles are by no means the only idealized object used by cryptographers to facilitate analyses. For example, the *ideal cipher model* analyzes cryptographic schemes relative to an oracle that implements a random permutation rather than a random function. Thus, analyzing a scheme in the standard model stresses the fact that there was no idealized object used in the analysis.

The idea of using idealized objects such as random oracles and what this buys us will become clearer once we start seeing more examples and when discussing the *random oracle methodology*, a heuristic for constructing cryptographic schemes which is based on the random oracle model. For now, let us study what it means for a scheme to be analyzed in the random oracle model and better understand the power random oracles provide.

8.2 Random Oracles Are Ideal Hash Functions

Random oracles, or rather random functions, are *ideal* instantiations of hash functions. In the following we will provide formal justification for this claim by showing that random functions simultaneously fulfill all the security properties that we have introduced so far for hash functions. However, before we can do so, we need to discuss a curious mismatch of a random function and a *keyed* hash function.

8.2.1 To Key or Not To Key

As we discussed in Section 4.1.1, hash functions in cryptographic theory are usually treated as keyed objects, and indeed all our security definitions require keys to be meaningful. In contrast, hash functions used in practice (for example, any function in the SHA or MD family) are inherently unkeyed. There is exactly one MD5 and exactly one SHA-1 hash function. They each take as input a message and produce a hash value. They do not allow keys as input.

A random oracle is in many senses a very good match, as similarly to the functions we use in practice it is unkeyed. It evaluates a function of the form $\{0,1\}^* \to \{0,1\}^{\mathsf{RO.ol}(\lambda)}$ and thus maps an input message to a hash value without needing an additional key. This is, however, only half the story. But this is best explained with an example. Let us consider the following question:

Example 8.4. *Can an adversary efficiently find a preimage for the all-zero hash value? That is, can an adversary efficiently find a value $x \in \{0,1\}^*$ such that $\mathsf{RO}(x) = 0^{\mathsf{RO.ol}(\lambda)}$?*

First we will need to argue that such a value x exists. Since random oracle RO implements a random function, could it be that for some reason every value $x \in \{0,1\}^*$ maps to $\mathsf{RO}(x) \neq 0^{\mathsf{RO.ol}(\lambda)}$? In short, the answer is no. That is, it can be shown that with probability 1 there exists such an x since we assume that the input space is unbounded, that is, the random oracle allows as input any value in $\{0,1\}^*$. Indeed, it can be shown that there exists not only one but infinitely many $x \in \{0,1\}^*$ such that $RO(x) = 0^{RO.ol(\lambda)}$.[2]

Now that we know that such an x exists, what about the following adversary $\mathcal{A}_x$ that has x hardcoded and simply outputs x? Maybe, somewhat counter-intuitively the adversary will most probably not win the game. In fact, it will only win with probability $2^{-RO.ol(\lambda)}$. The reason is that, while the random oracle is fixed within a single experiment (or game), it is "reinitialized" at the beginning of each new experiment. This is also what provides the probability space for the above experiment where the adversary $\mathcal{A}_x$ will be successful with probability $2^{-RO.ol(\lambda)}$ over the random coins of random oracle RO (or equivalently, over the random choice of the function implemented in the random oracle).

In some sense, the random oracle behaves as if it was keyed: If we consider the key to be the actual function that the random oracle implements within a game, then we can think of the random oracle as a keyed object, where the key is chosen uniformly at random at the beginning of the experiment and then hardcoded into the oracle. Again, this has a striking similarity to hash functions in practice. At some point, Ronald Rivest (the creator of MD5) fixed the many constants within his algorithm and called the result MD5. Similarly, NIST (the National Institute of Standards and Technology) and NSA (the National Security Agency) fixed the constants in their hash algorithm and named the result SHA-1. If we consider these constants to be the respective key, then a key was chosen at some point and hardcoded into the function. The difference is, of course, that a random oracle is set up afresh with each new experiment, while MD5 and SHA-1 will stay fixed for all users for eternity.

The take-away message from this discussion is that, while the random oracle is an unkeyed object, in some sense it behaves as if it was keyed such that any analysis in the random oracle model is always a probabilistic analysis over the random choice of the function implemented by the random oracle.

8.2.2 One-Wayness

Let us consider the question of whether random oracles are *one-way*. Recall that a function F is one-way if no probabilistic polynomial-time adversary $\mathcal{A}$ can find a preimage x' for value $F(x)$ when x was chosen uniformly at

---

[2] If you are interested in how this can be proven, have a look at the *second Borel–Cantelli Lemma*. It states that if we have an infinite sequence of events $(E_i)_{i \in \mathbb{N}}$ with $\sum_{i=1}^{\infty} (\Pr[E_i]) = \infty$ and the events are pairwise independent then $\Pr[\limsup_{i \to \infty} E_i]$ is equal to 1. Now set E_i to $\exists x \in \{0,1\}^i : RO(x) = 0^{RO.ol(\lambda)}$. We leave it to the reader to show that the sum diverges and that they are pairwise independent.

random with better than negligible probability (see Definition 2.15 on page 84). When considering random oracles, we have essentially the same setup, except that the adversary can no longer locally compute the function but must use its oracle access to make a random oracle call. Following are the security experiments, once as in Definition 2.15 for (an unkeyed) function F (on the left) and once for a random oracle RO on the right:

Experiment $\mathsf{Exp}^{\mathsf{owf}}_{\mathsf{F},\mathcal{A}}(\lambda)$	Experiment $\mathsf{Exp}^{\mathsf{owf}}_{\mathsf{RO},\mathcal{A}}(\lambda)$
1 : $x \leftarrow\!\!\$\ \{0,1\}^{\lambda}$	1 : $x \leftarrow\!\!\$\ \{0,1\}^{\lambda}$
2 : $y \leftarrow \mathsf{F}(x)$	2 : $y \leftarrow \mathsf{RO}(x)$
3 : $x^{*} \leftarrow\!\!\$\ \mathcal{A}(1^{\lambda}, y)$	3 : $x^{*} \leftarrow\!\!\$\ \mathcal{A}^{\mathsf{RO}}(1^{\lambda}, y)$
4 : return $\mathsf{F}(x^{*}) = y$	4 : return $\mathsf{RO}(x^{*}) = y$

Remark 8.5. Note that the difference here is subtle. The adversary in line 3 is given oracle access in the random oracle model version, where the random oracle is chosen at the beginning of the experiment. More explicitly, we could sample the random oracle version as a first step in the pseudocode (similarly to sampling a key for a keyed primitive) which would yield

Experiment $\mathsf{Exp}^{\mathsf{owf}}_{\mathsf{RO},\mathcal{A}}(\lambda)$
1 : $\mathsf{RO} \leftarrow\!\!\$\ \left\{ f \mid f : \{0,1\}^{\mathsf{RO.il}(\lambda)} \rightarrow \{0,1\}^{\mathsf{RO.ol}(\lambda)} \right\}$
2 : $x \leftarrow\!\!\$\ \{0,1\}^{\lambda}$
3 : $y \leftarrow \mathsf{RO}(x)$
4 : $x^{*} \leftarrow\!\!\$\ \mathcal{A}^{\mathsf{RO}}(1^{\lambda}, y)$
5 : return $\mathsf{RO}(x^{*}) = y$

To simplify notation we omit this explicit sampling and always assume implicitly that the random oracle is freshly sampled at the beginning of each experiment. In contrast, for the standard model version we assume that the adversary knows function F and can compute it locally. "Knowing a random oracle" is, however, infeasible given its tremendous size.

Let us now formally show that random oracles are one way.

Proposition 8.6. *The random oracle with output length* $\mathsf{RO.ol}(\lambda) = \lambda$ *is* one-way.

The proposition actually shows that the success probability for any (even unbounded) adversary $\mathcal{A}$ making at most $\mathsf{q}(\lambda)$ queries to the random oracle is at most $2(\mathsf{q}(\lambda) + 1) \cdot 2^{-\lambda}$. Note that if the preimage x is not chosen from $\{0,1\}^{\lambda}$ but instead from $\{0,1\}^{\mathsf{i}(\lambda)}$ for some polynomial i and we consider a not further specified output length of $\mathsf{RO.ol}(\lambda)$ then the bound becomes

$$\mathsf{Adv}^{\mathrm{owf}}_{\mathsf{RO},\mathcal{A}}(\lambda) \leq (\mathsf{q}(\lambda) + 1) \cdot \left(2^{-\mathsf{RO.ol}(\lambda)} + 2^{-\mathsf{i}(\lambda)}\right).$$

Thus both the output length of the random oracle as well as the length of the preimage play an important role in bounding the success probability of the adversary. The reader is advised to consult the proof because we will use the technique that finding a preimage with some min-entropy in queries is unlikely throughout the chapters about solutions using random oracles.

Proof. We give the proof for preimages and outputs of length λ, as stated in the proposition. The general cases of inputs of size $\mathsf{i}(\lambda)$ and outputs of length $\mathsf{RO.ol}(\lambda)$, mentioned after the proposition's statement, follow easily from this.

We need to show that no PPT adversary $\mathcal{A}$ can win in the above security experiment with better than negligible probability. To this end, let p be a polynomial that upper bounds the runtime of adversary $\mathcal{A}$. Since $\mathcal{A}$ is efficient such a polynomial exists. As $\mathcal{A}$ can make at most one query per execution step, the polynomial p also provides an upper bound on the number of random oracle queries that adversary $\mathcal{A}$ can make. Let $\mathsf{q} := \mathsf{q}(\lambda)$ denote a polynomial that bounds the actual number of queries which $\mathcal{A}$ makes in the experiment and note that $\mathsf{q}(\lambda) \leq \mathsf{p}(\lambda)$ for all $\lambda \in \mathbb{N}$.

It is convenient to denote the ith query by x_i, and to count $\mathcal{A}$'s final output x^* as the $(\mathsf{q}+1)$st query, $x_{\mathsf{q}+1} = x^*$, since the experiment evaluates RO on x^* in the final step (line 4), too. We also assume that, except for possibly the last output query $x_{\mathsf{q}+1}$, there are no repetitions among the x_i's. If the adversary does not obey this we can always construct an adversary $\mathcal{A}'$ that runs $\mathcal{A}$ and only forwards "fresh" queries to the random oracle while maintaining a table to answer duplicate queries. The success probability of both adversaries is identical, $\mathcal{A}'$ is efficient if $\mathcal{A}$ is, and the number of queries is still q (resp. $\mathsf{q}+1$ if counting the final output) or even less.

We do a first game hop in which we declare the adversary to lose if $\mathsf{RO}(x^*) = \mathsf{RO}(x)$ but $x^* \neq x$. Rearranging this condition together with the requirement that $\mathsf{RO}(x^*) = y$, we thus change line 4 of the one-way function experiment to

$$4: \quad \textbf{if } x^* \neq x \textbf{ return } 0 \textbf{ else return } \mathsf{RO}(x^*) = y.$$

We can upper bound the probability of $\mathcal{A}$ ever making any query (where we count the output x^* as the $(\mathsf{q}+1)$st query) with $x_i \neq x$ and $\mathsf{RO}(x_i) = \mathsf{RO}(x)$ by $\frac{\mathsf{q}+1}{2^{\lambda}}$. The reason is that for any fixed i the probability that x_i, being distinct from x, is thrown to the same image under the random function RO is exactly $2^{-\mathsf{RO.ol}(\lambda)} = 2^{-\lambda}$. The union bound over all $\mathsf{q}+1$ queries yields the desired bound.

The modified line 4 now asks the adversary to find *exactly* the preimage $x \in \{0,1\}^{\lambda}$. In particular, it suffices now to assume that all of $\mathcal{A}$'s queries x_i are of bit length λ; any other query will not match x for sure and does not reveal any information about x either. We can rewrite the probability of having a matching query by looking at the events where the ith query is precisely the first one where this happens:

$$\Pr[\exists i \in \{1, 2, \ldots, \mathsf{q}+1\} : x_i = x]$$
$$= \Pr[\exists i \in \{1, 2, \ldots, \mathsf{q}+1\} : x_i = x \wedge x_1, \ldots, x_{i-1} \neq x]$$
$$\leq \sum_{i=1}^{\mathsf{q}+1} \Pr[x_i = x \wedge x_1, \ldots, x_{i-1} \neq x].$$

We can rewrite the terms $\Pr[x_i = x \wedge x_1, \ldots, x_{i-1} \neq x]$ through the product rule as

$$\Pr[x_i = x \wedge x_1, \ldots, x_{i-1} \neq x] \tag{8.1}$$
$$= \Pr[x_i = x \mid x_1, \ldots, x_{i-1} \neq x] \cdot \prod_{j=1}^{i-1} \Pr[x_j \neq x \mid x_1, \ldots, x_{j-1} \neq x],$$

where the statement $x_1, \ldots, x_{j-1} \neq x$ is trivially true for $j = 1$ and the conditional probability therefore equals the probability $\Pr[x_1 \neq x]$ in this case.

We first bound the probability that $x_j \neq x$ given $x_1, \ldots, x_{j-1} \neq x$ by

$$\Pr[x_j \neq x \mid x_1, \ldots, x_{j-1} \neq x] \leq \left(1 - \frac{1}{2^\lambda - j + 1}\right) = \frac{2^\lambda - j}{2^\lambda - j + 1}$$

for $1 \leq j \leq \mathsf{q}$. Note that for $j = 1$ this is true since the first query x_1 has a probability of $1 - \frac{1}{2^\lambda}$ of being distinct from x, because when this query is made, the adversary does not yet have any information about x (beyond the value y) and $x_i \in \{0,1\}^\lambda$ may "accidentally" hit x. An analogous argument as for the first query x_1 holds for the second query x_2. Since we assume that x_2 is distinct from x_1 we now have a conditional probability of at most $1 - \frac{1}{2^\lambda - 1}$ to miss x when choosing x_2 among the remaining $2^\lambda - 1$ preimages from $\{0,1\}^\lambda$. This holds since the only information about the random x is that it does not match x_1 at this point, such that x is still uniformly distributed among the remaining preimages. Setting the argument forth to the other queries we obtain the claimed bound.

Using the established bound, we now obtain for the product in (8.1),

$$\prod_{j=1}^{i-1} \Pr[x_j \neq x \mid x_1, \ldots, x_{j-1} \neq x] \leq \prod_{j=1}^{i-1} \frac{2^\lambda - j}{2^\lambda - j + 1} = \frac{2^\lambda - i + 1}{2^\lambda}.$$

The final step is to note that

$$\Pr[x_i = x \mid x_1, \ldots, x_{i-1} \neq x] \leq \frac{1}{2^\lambda - i + 1},$$

because the best chance of the adversary finding $x_i = x$ with the ith query, given that all previous queries missed, is to pick correctly among the remaining

$2^\lambda - i + 1$ possible preimages. This is again true because the other random oracle values for $x_1, \ldots, x_{i-1}$ do not reveal any information about x, except that x is distinct.

Plugging the results into (8.1) yields

$$\Pr[x_i = x \wedge x_1, \ldots, x_{i-1} \neq x] \leq \frac{1}{2^\lambda - i + 1} \cdot \frac{2^\lambda - i + 1}{2^\lambda} = \frac{1}{2^\lambda}.$$

The claim now follows since the union bound gives

$$\Pr[\exists i \in \{1, 2, \ldots, q+1\} : x_i = x] \leq \sum_{i=1}^{q+1} \frac{1}{2^\lambda} = \frac{q+1}{2^\lambda}.$$

Hence, with this probability the adversary is able to find the original preimage x. Together with the probability $\frac{q+1}{2^\lambda}$ for finding another preimage with the same value y the proposition follows. $\square$

Let us take a step back and appreciate what we have just done. We have shown that a random oracle is one-way. The proof that we gave is, however, very different from most of the previous proofs we have seen so far in that it is not based on a security reduction. The reason is that assuming the existence of a random oracle we do not need any further assumptions to show that one-way functions exist since the random oracle itself is one-way. We could thus give a direct proof of the statement which only used probability theory. We made use of the fact that if an adversary (or any other party, for that matter) has not yet queried the random oracle on a point x then the probability of $\mathsf{RO}(x)$ being any specific target value is exactly $\frac{1}{2^{\mathsf{RO}.\mathsf{ol}(\lambda)}}$. In other words, value $\mathsf{RO}(x)$ is a random variable that is distributed according to the uniform distribution. Let us emphasize this: we can treat $\mathsf{RO}(x)$ for a value x that has never been queried as a random variable with uniform distribution. This means, for example, that we can use that

$$\Pr\left[\mathsf{RO}(x) = 1^{\mathsf{RO}.\mathsf{ol}(\lambda)}\right] = \frac{1}{2^{\mathsf{RO}.\mathsf{ol}(\lambda)}}$$

or that the min-entropy (see Section 1.5.5; page 54) of $\mathsf{RO}(x)$ is $\mathsf{RO}.\mathsf{ol}(\lambda)$, that is,

$$H_\infty(\mathsf{RO}(x)) = \mathsf{RO}.\mathsf{ol}(\lambda).$$

It is important to note that the probability space is over the choice of random function for the random oracle and not over the choice of value x. This means that, if we fix x to, say, the all-zero string, then the above relationships still hold:

$$\Pr\left[\mathsf{RO}(0^\lambda) = 1^{\mathsf{RO}.\mathsf{ol}(\lambda)}\right] = \frac{1}{2^{\mathsf{RO}.\mathsf{ol}(\lambda)}} \quad \text{and} \quad H_\infty(\mathsf{RO}(0^\lambda)) = \mathsf{RO}.\mathsf{ol}(\lambda).$$

For these statements to hold it is only important that the value was not yet queried to the random oracle, in which case it has *full entropy*: its hash value under the random oracle can be any in the oracle's output space.

Almost all proofs in the random oracle model make use of this probability at one point or another, and it is what gives the random oracle a lot of its power. In our proof that random oracles are one-way it allowed us to argue that the best thing an adversary can do is to guess. This is because, although the adversary is given the value $\mathsf{RO}(x)$ as input, this value does not contain any information whatsoever on the value x itself. Expressed in terms of entropy, over the choice of x and the random oracle, we can say that

$$H_\infty(x) = H_\infty(x \mid \mathsf{RO}(x)).$$

The min-entropy of value x—the uncertainty about value x—does not change whether or not one is given value $\mathsf{RO}(x)$. However, we note that the entropy may actually decrease if one sees further pairs $(x', \mathsf{RO}(x'))$ since $\mathsf{RO}(x') \neq \mathsf{RO}(x)$ would reveal that x is not equal to x'. For instance, if $x \leftarrow\!\!\$ \{0,1\}$ is a random bit with entropy 1, then the two values $\mathsf{RO}(x)$ and $\mathsf{RO}(0)$ together most likely (unless $\mathsf{RO}(0) = \mathsf{RO}(1)$) allow to determine x, such that the conditional entropy drops to almost 0.

We will see many more examples of how to work with the intrinsic randomness inside a random oracle to show that it possesses various cryptographic properties throughout the course of this chapter. However, as we will see, the random oracle's *randomness* is not the only power that the random has to offer. But more on that in Chapter 9.

8.2.3 Collision Resistance

In the following we show that random oracles are collision resistant and thus also meet all the related properties such as target-collision resistance or second-preimage resistance. Similarly to the one-way case, the proofs use only the randomness property of the random oracle. That is, there is no additional assumption and consequently no reduction involved.

Recall that a function is collision resistant if it is difficult to find two distinct messages x_1 and x_2 that have the same function value. Following is the security experiment for the collision-resistance property of a hash function H taken from Definition 4.2 (see page 162):

Experiment $\mathsf{Exp}^{\mathrm{cr}}_{\mathsf{H},\mathcal{A}}(\lambda)$
_____

1 : $\mathsf{hk} \leftarrow\!\!\$ \mathsf{H.KGen}(1^\lambda)$

2 : $(x_1, x_2) \leftarrow\!\!\$ \mathcal{A}(1^\lambda, \mathsf{hk})$

3 : **return** $\mathsf{H}(\mathsf{hk}, x_1) = \mathsf{H}(\mathsf{hk}, x_2) \wedge x_1 \neq x_2$

We defined collision resistance only for keyed hash functions, as for unkeyed functions there is always the trivial non-uniform adversary that has a pair of collisions hardcoded for every security parameter and which thus wins the security experiment with probability 1. As discussed in Section 8.2.1 random oracles are not keyed but their random nature makes them behave as if they were. Thus, we can adapt the collision-resistance security experiment to random oracles by simply removing the key. In other words, we say that the random oracle is collision resistant if no efficient adversary $\mathcal{A}$ can win in the following security experiment with better than negligible probability:

$$\text{Experiment } \text{Exp}^{\text{cr}}_{\text{RO},\mathcal{A}}(\lambda)$$

$$1: \quad (x_1, x_2) \leftarrow_\$ \mathcal{A}^{\text{RO}}(1^\lambda)$$

$$2: \quad \textbf{return } \text{RO}(x_1) = \text{RO}(x_2) \wedge x_1 \neq x_2$$

We can now formally state that random oracles are collision resistant, and with Theorem 4.10 (see page 175) we directly get that they are also second-preimage and target-collision resistant. We stress, however, that one needs to check that these implications are also true in the random oracle model.

> **Proposition 8.7.** *A random oracle* RO *is* collision resistant, second-preimage resistant, *and* target-collision resistant, *given that its output length is super-logarithmic in the security parameter, i.e.,* $\text{RO.ol}(\lambda) \in \omega(\log(\lambda))$.

Proof. Let $\mathcal{A}$ be a PPT adversary. Without loss of generality we assume that adversary $\mathcal{A}$ queries the random oracle on its guess for a collision (x_1, x_2) and that all queries to the oracle are distinct. Else we can again modify the adversary into another adversary $\mathcal{A}'$ that runs $\mathcal{A}$ and only forwards new queries to the random oracle, keeping track of identical queries via book keeping. Furthermore, $\mathcal{A}'$ can also send guess (x_1, x_2) to the random oracle before outputting (x_1, x_2) as its own guess. The success probability of both adversaries is identical, and $\mathcal{A}'$ is efficient if $\mathcal{A}$ is.

In the following we consider a single run of the security experiment. Here, let $\mathcal{Q}$ denote the list of queries to the random oracle by adversary $\mathcal{A}$. Formally, $\mathcal{Q}$ is a function that depends on the input of the security experiment, that is, the security parameter as well as the random coins of the experiment (i.e., the random coins of adversary $\mathcal{A}$ and the choice of random oracle RO).

As $\mathcal{A}$ is efficient, there is a polynomial q that upper bounds $\mathcal{A}$'s runtime as well as the maximum number of queries that $\mathcal{A}$ can send to random oracle RO. It follows that $|\mathcal{Q}| \leq q(\lambda)$. Adversary $\mathcal{A}$ can win the security experiment only if there are two distinct queries (x_1, x_2) in $\mathcal{Q}$ such that $\text{RO}(x_1) = \text{RO}(x_2)$.

Let now $\mathcal{R}$ denote the list of random oracle answers, that is,

$$\mathcal{R}[i] = \text{RO}(\mathcal{Q}[i]) \quad \text{for } i = 1, \ldots, |\mathcal{Q}|.$$

Since the random oracle implements a random function, list $\mathcal{R}$ is distributed identically to a list of $|\mathcal{Q}|$ independently chosen uniformly random values in $\{0,1\}^{\mathsf{RO}(\lambda)}$. In other words, the following two distributions are identical:[3]

$$
\begin{array}{ll}
\textbf{for } i = 1,\dots,|\mathcal{Q}| \textbf{ do} & \textbf{for } i = 1,\dots,|\mathcal{Q}| \textbf{ do} \\
\quad \mathcal{R}[i] \leftarrow \mathsf{RO}(\mathcal{Q}[i]) \quad\overset{\text{p}}{=}\quad & \quad \mathcal{R}[i] \leftarrow\!\!\$\ \{0,1\}^{\mathsf{RO.ol}(\lambda)} \\
\textbf{return } \mathcal{R} & \textbf{return } \mathcal{R}
\end{array}
$$

We can now estimate the success probability of adversary $\mathcal{A}$ by estimating the probability that there is a collision in $\mathcal{R}$ which can be upper bounded using a birthday bound (see also Section 4.1.2; page 165). For this, let us first compute the probability that a single pair $r_1, r_2 \in \mathcal{R}$ collides. As r_1 and r_2 are two independently drawn random values in $\{0,1\}^{\mathsf{RO}(\lambda)}$ we have that

$$
\Pr[r_1 = r_2] = \frac{1}{2^{\mathsf{RO.ol}(\lambda)}}.
$$

In total there are $\binom{|\mathcal{R}|}{2}$ many possible value pairs in list $\mathcal{R}$. The probability of any of the pairs colliding can thus be upper bounded by a union bound as follows:

$$
\begin{aligned}
\Pr[\exists i,j \in [|\mathcal{R}|] : i \neq j \wedge \mathcal{R}[i] = \mathcal{R}[j]] &\leq \binom{|\mathcal{R}|}{2} \cdot \frac{1}{2^{\mathsf{RO.ol}(\lambda)}} \\
&= \frac{|\mathcal{R}| \cdot |\mathcal{R}| - 1}{2} \cdot \frac{1}{2^{\mathsf{RO.ol}(\lambda)}} \\
&\leq \frac{q(\lambda)^2}{2^{\mathsf{RO.ol}(\lambda)-1}}.
\end{aligned}
$$

Noting that, by assumption, the output length of random oracle RO grows super-logarithmically in the security parameter we have that the above bound is negligible.

The remainder follows with Theorem 4.10 (see page 175), which states that collision resistance implies both target-collision resistance and second-preimage resistance. The reader is advised to check that these statements still hold when we work in the random oracle model. $\qquad\square$

8.2.4 Pseudorandomness

Random oracles provide a source of actual randomness, and hence it would be surprising if we could not show that random oracles meet the requirements of a pseudorandom function. Again the difficulty is a mismatch between the syntax

---

[3] Note that for the distributions to be identical we required that adversary $\mathcal{A}$ only makes distinct queries. Otherwise we would here need to take care of the duplicates.

of the random oracle, which is unkeyed, and the syntax of pseudorandom functions, which are inherently keyed. While the notion of unkeyed one-way functions or collision-resistant functions is meaningful, the notion of an unkeyed pseudorandom function is not. To understand this we need to look at the definition of a pseudorandom function (Definition 3.21 on page 126). We say a function family PRF is a pseudorandom function family if for all efficient distinguishers $\mathcal{D}$ the following distinguishing advantage is negligible:

$$\left| \Pr_{k \leftarrow \$ \mathsf{PRF.KGen}(1^\lambda)} \left[\mathcal{D}^{\mathsf{PRF.Eval}(k,\cdot)}(1^\lambda) = 1 \right] - \Pr_{R \leftarrow \$ \mathsf{Func}} \left[\mathcal{D}^R(1^\lambda) = 1 \right] \right|.$$

Here, Func denotes the set of all functions that have the same input and output restrictions as function PRF.

The distinguisher $\mathcal{D}$ either gets oracle access to function PRF, which is initialized with a randomly chosen key k, or it gets access to a truly random function. Now, if we take away the key then identifying function PRF is easy. All the distinguisher needs to do is to choose a random input x, call its oracle on x to receive y, and compare y with value $\mathsf{PRF}(x)$, which the adversary can locally compute. If the values match, then with overwhelming probability the oracle implements function PRF and not a random function.

Now where does that leave the random oracle? Even though the notion of unkeyed pseudorandom functions does not make much sense, (unkeyed) random oracles are, of course, indistinguishable from random functions. This is not surprising as they themselves are random functions. Thus, if we replace function PRF in the pseudorandom function definition with an unkeyed random oracle we get the requirement that no efficient adversary has a better than negligible distinguishing advantage in distinguishing one random function from a different and independently chosen random function. That is, we require that for all efficient distinguishers $\mathcal{D}$ it holds that

$$\left| \Pr_{\mathsf{RO} \leftarrow \$ \mathsf{Func}} \left[\mathcal{D}^{\mathsf{RO}(\cdot)}(1^\lambda) = 1 \right] - \Pr_{R \leftarrow \$ \mathsf{Func}} \left[\mathcal{D}^R(1^\lambda) = 1 \right] \right| \leq \mathsf{negl}(\lambda). \quad (8.2)$$

In fact, the above difference is not only negligible, but zero as the distributions exposed by the oracles in both settings are not only indistinguishable, but identical. Note that this also means that Equation (8.2) holds not only for efficient distinguishers but for any distinguisher even unbounded ones.

Despite being perfectly indistinguishable from random functions in the formalism above, unkeyed random oracles cannot simply be used as very secure pseudorandom functions. For example, consider the symmetric encryption scheme $(\mathsf{PRF}(k,r) \oplus m, r)$ in Construction 5.10 on page 222. If the unkeyed random oracle replaces the pseudorandom function, $(c,r) = (\mathsf{RO}(r) \oplus m, r)$, then the scheme is clearly insecure: an adversary can decrypt by evaluating RO on r. This attack exposes the difference to pseudorandom functions. In the random oracle model every party has access to RO, whereas in the pseudorandom function setting the adversary cannot evaluate the function on the unknown key k.

Pseudorandom Functions from Random Oracles

While an unkeyed random oracle does not meet the requirements of a pseudorandom function, we can easily construct a pseudorandom function from a random oracle.

Construction 8.8. *Let* RO *be a random oracle. We construct pseudorandom function* $\mathsf{PRF}^{\mathsf{RO}}$ *as follows:*

$\mathsf{PRF}^{\mathsf{RO}}.\mathsf{KGen}(1^\lambda)$	$\mathsf{PRF}^{\mathsf{RO}}.\mathsf{Eval}(\mathsf{k}, x)$
$1: \quad \mathsf{k} \leftarrow\!\!\$\ \{0,1\}^\lambda$	$1: \quad y \leftarrow \mathsf{RO}(\mathsf{k}\|x)$
$2: \quad$ **return** k	$2: \quad$ **return** y

The idea in the above construction is to generate a random key that is prepended to random oracle calls. As we will see shortly the prepending of the key separates the domain of the random oracle (Section 8.3.2), which can be thought of as an independent random oracle that remains secret to anyone not knowing key k. We leave the security proof of the above construction as Exercise 8.2. Before attempting the proof please read on through the next section, which contains a discussion of domain separation of random oracles that will help in proving the statement.

8.3 Properties of Random Oracles

In the previous section we have seen that random oracles are powerful abstractions of hash functions that simultaneously achieve all the security properties that we have introduced so far. Before we go on to show just how powerful random oracles are, we will first take a short detour and discuss various properties of random oracles which are often used in proofs involving random oracles.

8.3.1 Random Oracles against Inefficient Adversaries

If you look back at the proofs presented in Section 8.2 you will notice that in all the proofs we used the runtime restriction of adversaries only to argue that the number of queries the adversary can post to the random oracle is also restricted. The latter restriction is, in fact, the only restriction necessary in most proofs that involve random oracles. This means that in many cases—in particular, in all the cases from Section 8.2—statements hold not only for efficient adversaries but also for inefficient adversaries given that the number of oracle queries is restricted to be polynomial.

The reason for allowing us to weaken the restrictions on adversaries is that any value an adversary learns about a random oracle is independent from any other value. Formally, we have that for distinct inputs x and y we have that the min-entropy about the value of $\mathsf{RO}(y)$ is not affected by learning the values x, y, or $\mathsf{RO}(x)$:

$$H_\infty(\mathsf{RO}(y)) = H_\infty(\mathsf{RO}(y) \mid y, x, \mathsf{RO}(x)). \tag{8.3}$$

Thus, even an adversary with unbounded runtime cannot reason about any values of the random oracle that it has not seen. In contrast, when we consider a pseudorandom function, then seeing only a few values allows to uniquely identify the used key, given enough computational power (also see Exercise 8.3).

8.3.2 Domain Separation

So far, we always considered only a single random oracle that every party gets access to. But how about settings where we provide all parties with not just a single oracle, but two or even more? Would that allow us to build even more efficient schemes?

It is not too difficult to see that this is not the case. The reason is that we can always simulate multiple random oracles with just a single one. To see this consider an algorithm $\mathcal{A}^{\mathsf{RO}_1,\ldots,\mathsf{RO}_\ell}$ which has access to $\ell \geq 2$ random oracles. From this algorithm, we can construct a new algorithm $\mathcal{A}_*^{\mathsf{RO}}$ which only has access to a single random oracle but which implements an identical distribution on any input as algorithm $\mathcal{A}$. The idea is that algorithm $\mathcal{A}_*$ simply executes $\mathcal{A}$ and answers any query q to the ith oracle as

$$\mathsf{RO}(\mathsf{prefix}_i \| q),$$

where prefix_i is a unique prefix corresponding to index i, for example, $\mathsf{prefix}_i := \langle i \rangle_{\lceil \log(\ell) \rceil}$. That is, here the prefix is a binary encoding of i using $\lceil \log(\ell) \rceil$ many bits. Now, since RO is a random function, so is the projection $\mathsf{RO}(\mathsf{prefix}_i \| \cdot)$. Furthermore, each "sub-oracle" provides an independent random function. Thus the simulation of $\mathcal{A}_*$ is perfect, meaning the distributions observed by algorithm $\mathcal{A}$ are identical whether it runs relative to ℓ true random oracles or whether it runs relative to only a single random oracle that is used to simulate the ℓ random oracles.

What we have done in order to simulate ℓ random oracles is usually referred to as *domain separation*. We separated the (infinite) domain of the single random oracle into ℓ infinite but separate domains and used one each to simulate a complete random oracle.

8.3.3 Output Size Extension

We have seen that with a single random oracle we can simulate multiple
random oracles. In the following we show that given a random oracle that
produces output values of length n we can simulate a random oracle which
produces values with lengths $m > n$, that is, we can simulate a random oracle
with a longer output length. Let RO denote the original random oracle with
output length n. From this we now construct a random oracle $\mathsf{RO}_{|m|}$ that has
output length m. Let us assume for simplicity that $m = \ell \cdot n$ for $\ell \geq 2$, that
is, the output is ℓ times as long as the output of the original random oracle.
If we had ℓ independent random oracles $\mathsf{RO}_1, \ldots, \mathsf{RO}_\ell$ we could define our
single random oracle $\mathsf{RO}_{|m|}$ with long output simply as

$$\mathsf{RO}_{|m|}(x) := \mathsf{RO}_1(x)\|\mathsf{RO}_2(x)\| \ldots \|\mathsf{RO}_\ell(x).$$

Now, we only have a single random oracle RO to work with. Luckily, we can
use the technique of domain separation discussed in the previous section to
split the single random oracle into ℓ simulated random oracles. As discussed,
one way of splitting the domain is to generate ℓ different prefixes of the same
length that are prepended to the individual queries. Applied to our case here
we could thus, for example, define $\mathsf{RO}_{|m|}$ as

$$\mathsf{RO}_{|m|}(x) := \mathsf{RO}(\langle 1\rangle_{\lceil\log(\ell)\rceil}\|x) \;\|\; \mathsf{RO}(\langle 2\rangle_{\lceil\log(\ell)\rceil}\|x) \;\|\; \cdots \;\|\; \mathsf{RO}(\langle \ell\rangle_{\lceil\log(\ell)\rceil}\|x).$$

This technique of embedding a "counter" is also sometimes referred to as
running in counter mode and originally stems from a mode of operation for
block ciphers which we will meet in later parts of this book.

8.3.4 Domain Extension

We have seen how we can simulate a random oracle with long outputs from
a random oracle with short outputs. In other words, we are able to extend
the image of a random oracle. A natural follow-up question is now if we can
similarly extend the domain of a random oracle.

Consider a fixed-input-length random oracle (sometimes referred to as
FIL-RO) which takes inputs of length RO.il rather than any input in $\{0,1\}^*$.
Can we extend the domain, for example, to simulate a random oracle which
takes inputs of length $n \cdot$ RO.il, for any $n \in \mathbb{N}$ or even simulate a random
oracle without any input size restriction?

Interestingly, the answer to this question is much more complicated and
we will need to postpone this investigation until Chapter 17, where we will
introduce a generalization of the indistinguishability property called *indifferentiability*. To jump ahead, the answer to whether we can extend the domain

of a random oracle is not clear cut and depends on the situation in which the random oracle is used. We will see that with indifferentiability we will be able to show that domain extension is possible for a large number of cases. But we will also see that there are some cases in which domain extension cannot work.

8.3.5 Keyed Random Oracles

For some of the presented properties we have seen a mismatch between the random oracle and the security property due to the fact that random oracles as we have defined them are unkeyed. One way to deal with that is to construct a keyed version of a random oracle, for example, by defining

$$RO_{keyed}(k, x) := RO(k\|x), \tag{8.4}$$

that is, by prepending a key to the message.[4] The same we have already done in Construction 8.8 (page 356) in order to construct a pseudorandom function from a random oracle. A second possibility is to extend the random oracle model and to introduce keys as first-class citizens. This yields the so-called *keyed random oracle model*, where we consider functions of the form

$$RO(\cdot, \cdot) : \{0, 1\}^{RO.kl(\lambda)} \times \{0, 1\}^* \to \{0, 1\}^{RO.ol(\lambda)}$$

and where $RO.kl(\lambda)$ and $RO.ol(\lambda)$ are polynomials describing the key length and output length of the function in dependence of the security parameter. What we require from a keyed random oracle is that for each fixed key $k \in \{0, 1\}^{RO.kl(\lambda)}$ the resulting function $RO(k, \cdot) : \{0, 1\}^* \to \{0, 1\}^{RO.ol(\lambda)}$ is chosen uniformly at random and independently, that is, for each key the resulting function is an independent random oracle.

Note that the keyed random oracle model only facilitates easier presentation but does not provide any extra power over standard (unkeyed) random oracles as we can simulate one with the other. A keyed random oracle with $kl(\lambda) = 0$ is nothing but a standard random oracle, and via the above construction (Equation (8.4)) where a key is prepended we can simulate a keyed random oracle using an unkeyed random oracle.

---

[4] Note that we here need to consider fixed-length keys as otherwise for keys k_1, k_2 and values x_1, x_2 which are such that $k_1\|x_1 = k_2\|x_2$ we have that $RO(k_1, x_1) = RO(k_2, x_2)$.

8.4 The Random Oracle Methodology

We have seen that random oracles are powerful creatures that simultaneously achieve all that we would like a good hash function to achieve. However, we have also discussed that we cannot possibly implement a truly random function due to its sheer size. Even a moderately sized function that is chosen uniformly at random has a description that exceeds any storage medium in the known universe. If that is the case, then one question is:

Can we construct (hash) functions that sufficiently behave like a random oracle?

What if we were able to construct an efficient hash function that in its observed behavior cannot be distinguished from a truly random function. If so we could construct cryptographic schemes with random oracles and analyze them in the random oracle model, but then in practice replace the random oracle by said efficient hash function. As long as the chosen hash function indeed behaves sufficiently like a random function the resulting scheme would be secure.

The *random oracle methodology* proposes to do exactly that: In order to devise cryptographic schemes that are not only secure but also practical and efficient we attempt the construction in two steps:

1. Build a cryptographic scheme and prove its security in the random oracle model.
2. *Instantiate* the random oracle with a good hash function H that behaves like a random oracle in order to obtain a construction that can be implemented and used in practice.

We will see over the course of the next sections and in particular over the course of Chapters 9 and 10 that applying the random oracle methodology allows us to construct elegant, efficient, and practical cryptographic schemes for various different purposes. While for many of the schemes there exist counterparts in the *standard model* that do not use random oracles it is often the case that these schemes lack efficiency or practicality when comparing them with the random oracle schemes. Indeed, many schemes that we employ on a regular basis in everyday life, for example, various standardized public-key encryption and signature schemes, have been devised via the random oracle methodology.

8.4.1 Efficient Commitment Schemes in the ROM

Let us give a first example of a practical cryptographic scheme devised via the random oracle methodology. We will construct a so-called *non-interactive commitment scheme* which can, for example, be used in an auctioning system. In a commitment scheme we consider two parties. Alice wants to commit to some value towards Bob in such a way that the value remains hidden from Bob until Alice chooses to open it. At the same time Bob, having received the commitment, wants to be assured that Alice cannot cheat by later claiming that she, in fact, committed to a different value. We call the first property *hiding* (Bob does not learn the value) and the second property *binding* (Alice cannot change the value of the commitment).

In the following we construct such a commitment scheme in the random oracle model. For this, let us first give a precise security definition. We present the definition in the standard model. To obtain the random oracle variant, we provide access to the random oracle to the construction (i.e., the commitment scheme) and the adversary and extend the probability space of the experiment to be also over the choice of random function for the random oracle.

Definition 8.9 (Non-interactive Commitment Scheme). *We call a triple of efficient algorithms* Cmt = (Cmt.setup, Cmt.commit, Cmt.Vf) *a commitment scheme where*

Cmt.setup   *is a* PPT *algorithm that on input the security parameter* 1^λ *outputs public parameters* pp;

Cmt.commit   *is a* PPT *algorithm that on input the public parameters and a message* $m \in \{0,1\}^*$ *outputs a commitment* c *and opening value* d;

Cmt.Vf   *is deterministic and on input the public parameters* pp, *commitment* c, *message* m, *and opening value* d *outputs* true *if the verification succeeds or* false *otherwise.*

We consider the following properties for a commitment scheme:

Correctness.   *We call a commitment scheme correct if for all security parameters* $\lambda \in \mathbb{N}$, *any public parameters* pp $\leftarrow$$ Cmt.setup(1^λ), *and any message* m *in* $\{0,1\}^*$ *it holds that*

$$\Pr[\mathsf{Cmt.Vf}(\mathsf{pp}, c, m, d) = 1 : (c,d) \leftarrow\!\!\$ \mathsf{Cmt.commit}(\mathsf{pp}, m)] = 1.$$

Hiding.   *We call a commitment scheme computationally hiding if for all efficient adversaries* $\mathcal{A} = (\mathcal{A}_1, \mathcal{A}_2)$ *the advantage*

$$\mathsf{Adv}^{\mathsf{cmt\text{-}hide}}_{\mathsf{Cmt},\mathcal{A}}(\lambda) := 2 \cdot \Pr\left[\mathit{Exp}^{\mathsf{cmt\text{-}hide}}_{\mathsf{Cmt},\mathcal{A}}(\lambda)\right] - 1$$

is negligible and where experiment $\mathit{Exp}^{\mathsf{cmt\text{-}hide}}_{\mathsf{Cmt},\mathcal{A}}(\lambda)$ *is defined as*

Experiment $\mathit{Exp}^{\mathsf{cmt\text{-}hide}}_{\mathsf{Cmt},\mathcal{A}}(\lambda)$
---

1 : $b \leftarrow\!\!\$ \{0,1\}$

2 :   pp $\leftarrow\!\!\$ Cmt.setup(1^λ)

3 : $(m_0, m_1, \mathsf{state}) \leftarrow\!\!\$ \mathcal{A}_1(1^\lambda, \mathsf{pp})$

4 : $(c,d) \leftarrow\!\!\$ \mathsf{Cmt.commit}(\mathsf{pp}, m_b)$

5 : $b' \leftarrow\!\!\$ \mathcal{A}_2(1^\lambda, \mathsf{state}, \mathsf{pp}, c)$

6 :   **return** $(b = b')$

Binding.   *We call a commitment scheme* computationally binding *if for all efficient adversaries $\mathcal{A}$ the advantage*

$$\mathsf{Adv}_{\mathsf{Cmt},\mathcal{A}}^{\mathsf{cmt\text{-}bind}}(\lambda) := 2 \cdot \Pr\left[\mathsf{Exp}_{\mathsf{Cmt},\mathcal{A}}^{\mathsf{cmt\text{-}bind}}(\lambda)\right] - 1$$

is negligible and where experiment $\mathsf{Exp}_{\mathsf{Cmt},\mathcal{A}}^{\mathsf{cmt\text{-}bind}}(\lambda)$ is defined as

---

Experiment $\mathsf{Exp}_{\mathsf{Cmt},\mathcal{A}}^{\mathsf{cmt\text{-}bind}}(\lambda)$

---

1 : $\mathsf{pp} \leftarrow\!\!{\scriptstyle\$}\ \mathsf{Cmt.setup}(1^\lambda)$

2 : $(c, d, d', m, m') \leftarrow\!\!{\scriptstyle\$}\ \mathcal{A}(1^\lambda, \mathsf{pp})$

3 :   **return** $(\mathsf{Cmt.Vf}(\mathsf{pp}, c, m, d) = 1 \wedge \mathsf{Cmt.Vf}(\mathsf{pp}, c, m', d') = 1 \wedge m \neq m')$

Remark 8.10. Note that the above definition of a commitment scheme is given in the standard model. To obtain the random oracle variant simply provide access to a random oracle to all algorithms of the commitment scheme as well as to the adversary.

While it is possible to construct commitment schemes from standard primitives, for example, from pseudorandom generators, there exists a straightforward, very practical, and very efficient construction in the random oracle model.

At first glance it seems as if $\mathsf{RO}(m)$ should be a perfectly good commitment to message m, because recovering m from the image should be hard. This would yield the following scheme that does not even need any setup algorithm nor an additional opening value d:

$\mathsf{Cmt}^{\mathsf{RO}}.\mathsf{commit}(m)$ $\mathsf{Cmt}^{\mathsf{RO}}.\mathsf{Vf}(c, m)$

---

1 : $c \leftarrow \mathsf{RO}(m)$ *1 :* $c' \leftarrow \mathsf{RO}(m)$

2 :   **return** c *2 :*   **return** $(c = c')$

It is easily verified that the scheme is correct. Intuitively, the scheme is also binding because random oracles are collision resistant. Unfortunately, the above scheme is not computationally hiding as the following counterexample shows: Adversary $\mathcal{A}_1$ outputs messages $m_0 = 0$ and $m_1 = 1$. The second-stage adversary gets as input commitment c and tests whether $\mathsf{RO}(1) = c$. If so, it outputs 1 and otherwise it outputs 0. It is not difficult to see that this adversary wins with almost probability 1 in Experiment $\mathsf{Exp}_{\mathsf{Cmt},\mathcal{A}}^{\mathsf{cmt\text{-}bind}}(\lambda)$.

What we exploited was the fact that given a random oracle value $\mathsf{RO}(m)$ *and* access to the random oracle one can start testing guesses for preimage m by querying the random oracle on those guesses. If the adversary has a good idea about what the preimage could be, say, because it is short, then its access to the random oracle allows to verify its guess. For our scheme this means that we need to add some uncertainty into the commitment such that the second-phase adversary can no longer succeed by recomputing the commitment. The best way for this is to switch to the keyed random oracle model.[5] This yields our final scheme as formalized below in Construction 8.11.

Construction 8.11. *Following is a construction of a commitment scheme in the (keyed) random oracle model with keyed random oracle* RO:

$\mathsf{Cmt^{RO}.setup}(1^\lambda)$	$\mathsf{Cmt^{RO}.commit}(1^\lambda, m)$	$\mathsf{Cmt^{RO}.Vf}(1^\lambda, c, m, k)$
1: **return** 1^λ	*1:* $k \leftarrow\!\!\$\; \{0,1\}^\lambda$	*1:* $c' \leftarrow \mathsf{RO}(k, m)$
	2: $c \leftarrow \mathsf{RO}(k, m)$	*2:* **return** $(c = c')$
	3: **return** (c, k)	

Cmt.setup *outputs the security parameter as public parameters. The opening value d is set to be key* k, *which is chosen at random during commitment.*

As with the scheme before it is easy to verify that Construction 8.11 is correct. It remains to show that it is hiding and binding.

> **Proposition 8.12.** *The commitment scheme given in Construction 8.11 is computationally binding and computationally hiding in the random oracle model.*

We will show that the scheme is computationally hiding and leave the proof for computational binding as Exercise 8.4.

Proof of Proposition 8.12. To show that Construction 8.11 is computationally hiding we need to argue that no efficient adversary $\mathcal{A} = (\mathcal{A}_1, \mathcal{A}_2)$ can do considerably better than guessing in experiment $\mathsf{Exp}_{\mathsf{Cmt},\mathcal{A}}^{\mathsf{cmt\text{-}hide}}(\lambda)$. Following is once more the experiment (this time stated in the random oracle model) where we have already inlined the commitment computation from Construction 8.11:

Experiment $\mathsf{Exp}_{\mathsf{Cmt},\mathcal{A}}^{\mathsf{cmt\text{-}hide}}(\lambda)$

1: $b \leftarrow\!\!\$\; \{0,1\}$

2: $(m_0, m_1, \mathsf{state}) \leftarrow\!\!\$\; \mathcal{A}_1^{\mathsf{RO}}(1^\lambda)$

3: $k \leftarrow\!\!\$\; \{0,1\}^\lambda$

4: $c \leftarrow \mathsf{RO}(k, m_b)$

5: $d \leftarrow k$

6: $b' \leftarrow\!\!\$\; \mathcal{A}_2^{\mathsf{RO}}(1^\lambda, \mathsf{state}, c)$

7: **return** $(b = b')$

---

[5] Alternatively, a key could, of course, be introduced, for example, by prepending it to messages as in Construction 8.8 from page 356.

The important observation is that the adversary cannot guess key k with better than negligible probability. But, as long as the adversary never makes a query for key k to the random oracle, both possible preimages (k, m_0) and (k, m_1) are equally likely from $\mathcal{A}$'s perspective. Hence, it follows that, unless $\mathcal{A}$ makes a query about k, the secret bit b is perfectly hidden. So it suffices to bound the probability of $\mathcal{A}$ making a random oracle query for key k.

Let q be an upper bound for the total number of random oracle queries of adversary $\mathcal{A}$ across both stages. Similarly to the proof of Proposition 8.6 on page 348 about random oracles being one-way, one can argue that for a uniform key k the probability of hitting this key in at most $q(\lambda)$ queries is at most $\frac{q(\lambda)}{2^\lambda}$. Letting Guess denote the event that $\mathcal{A}$ in some stage makes a query of the form (k, x) to the random oracle, we can rewrite the probability that $\mathcal{A}$ succeeds in the hiding experiment as

$$\begin{aligned} \Pr[b = b'] &= \Pr[b = b' \wedge \neg\mathsf{Guess}] + \Pr[b = b' \wedge \mathsf{Guess}] \\ &\leq \Pr[b = b' \mid \neg\mathsf{Guess}] + \Pr[\mathsf{Guess}] \\ &\leq \frac{1}{2} + \frac{q(\lambda)}{2^\lambda}. \end{aligned}$$

Finally note that, as $\mathcal{A}$ is efficient, q is bounded by a polynomial and, hence, the success probability of $\mathcal{A}$ is at most $\frac{1}{2} + \frac{q(\lambda)}{2^\lambda} = \frac{1}{2} + \mathsf{negl}(\lambda)$, from which the statement follows.   □

Remark 8.13. As discussed in Section 8.3.1 many random oracle proofs are also valid for computationally unbounded adversaries given that the number of random oracle queries is bounded by a polynomial. The same holds for the previous proof, and we thus have that the commitment is even *statistically hiding* (secure against computationally unbounded adversaries) given that adversaries are restricted to making at most polynomially many queries.

8.4.2 Instantiating Random Oracles

In the previous section we constructed a commitment scheme in the random oracle model that for creating a commitment requires only a single invocation of the random oracle. We went on to show that it is secure in the random oracle model. In order to obtain a scheme that we can implement also in practice, the random oracle methodology now tells us to *instantiate* the random oracle with a *good hash function*. So which function should we choose? As it turns out, this is not easily answered. In Part III of this book we will examine practical constructions of cryptographic hash functions and, in particular in Chapters 17 and 18, discuss how to construct functions that are good candidates for replacing random oracles. However, as we will see in Chapter 12, the random oracle methodology is not without controversy as we can construct (artificial) schemes that are provably secure in the random oracle model but which fail to be secure when instantiated with *any* standard model hash function. This, maybe surprising result is at the root of the controversy. At the other extreme is the large amount of strong heuristic evidence that the random oracle methodology allows us to construct practical *and* secure cryptographic schemes. In fact, as of today, there is not a single practical scheme that has been broken due to the use of random oracles. As it stands, the question of how to interpret random oracle schemes is still an open research question, and we will return to it at various points over the remainder of this book. But for now, let us continue our study of random oracles and the power they provide.

Chapter Notes and References

Random oracles have a long tradition in the study of cryptographic schemes. They were first notably used by Fiat and Shamir in 1986 [6], who showed how to build efficient signature schemes when modeling a hash function as a random oracle. The formal treatment of random oracles is due to Bellare and Rogaway [1], who presented a design methodology for (practical) cryptographic schemes based on random oracles and who coined the term *random oracle methodology*.

The equivalence of $P^{RO} = BPP^{RO}$ relative to a random oracle has been shown by Bennett and Gill [2]. This holds even with probability 1 over the choice of the random oracle. The possibility to derandomize BPP, showing that $P = BPP$ without reference to relativization, has been discussed in a series of works: Starting with Yao's approach to use the hardness assumption of pseudorandom generators to replace the randomness [11], and culminating in the work by Impagliazzo and Wigderson saying that $P = BPP$ unless one has sub-exponential circuits for all Boolean functions in the complexity class E of exponential deterministic time [7].

Random oracles are by no means the only idealized model that finds applications in cryptography. In fact, idealized models were already used in the 1940s by Shannon in his seminal study of secrecy systems [9] where he considered idealized block ciphers, thereby introducing the so-called *ideal cipher model* which we will encounter in Chapter 14. Shannon also extensively studied *data compression*, and the fact that random functions cannot be compressed significantly below the size needed to store a table that simply lists all values is a direct consequence of his *source coding theorem*, which was first published in 1948 [10].

The idea of commitment schemes was discussed in the context of coin-flipping over telephone by Blum [3], albeit not explicitly called a commitment. The first more formal treatment of commitments as a primitive was given by Brassard *et al.* [4]. The construction of a commitment scheme based on random oracles in Section 8.4.1 seems to be folklore.

For background on probability theory behind infinite sequences of coin tosses we refer the reader to the works by Rick Durret [5] and Tom Lindstrom [8].

Exercices

Exercise 8.1. Is $\mathsf{F}^{\mathsf{RO}}(x) := \mathsf{RO}(0\|x)\|\mathsf{RO}(1\|x)$ for random oracle RO also one-way?

Exercise 8.2. Show that Construction 8.8 (page 356) of a pseudorandom function from a random oracle yields a secure pseudorandom function.

Exercise 8.3. For each security parameter $\lambda \in \mathbb{N}$ choose 2^λ random functions of the form $\{0,1\}^\lambda \to \{0,1\}$. Let PRF be the pseudorandom function family that for key $\mathsf{k} \in \{0,1\}^\lambda$ evaluates the kth function. Compute the probability with which an unbounded algorithm can guess the used key k when being given $\log(\lambda)$ many input–output pairs for $\mathsf{PRF}(\mathsf{k},\cdot)$.

Exercise 8.4. Show that the scheme given in Construction 8.11 (page 363) is computationally binding in the random oracle model.

Chapter Bibliography

1. Mihir Bellare and Phillip Rogaway. Random oracles are practical: A paradigm for designing efficient protocols. In Dorothy E. Denning, Raymond Pyle, Ravi Ganesan, Ravi S. Sandhu, and Victoria Ashby, editors, *ACM CCS 93: 1st Conference on Computer and Communications Security*, pages 62–73, Fairfax, Virginia, USA, November 3–5, 1993. ACM Press.
2. Charles H Bennett and John Gill. Relative to a random oracle a, $\mathbf{p}^a \neq \mathbf{np}^a \neq \mathrm{co}\text{-}\mathbf{np}^a$ with probability 1. *SIAM Journal on Computing*, 10(1):96–113, 1981.
3. Manuel Blum. Coin flipping by telephone. In Allen Gersho, editor, *Advances in Cryptology – CRYPTO'81*, volume ECE Report 82-04, pages 11–15, Santa Barbara, CA, USA, 1981. U.C. Santa Barbara, Dept. of Elec. and Computer Eng.
4. Gilles Brassard, David Chaum, and Claude Crépeau. Minimum disclosure proofs of knowledge. *J. Comput. Syst. Sci.*, 37(2):156–189, 1988.
5. Rick Durrett. *Probability: theory and examples*, volume 49. Cambridge University Press, 2019.
6. Amos Fiat and Adi Shamir. How to prove yourself: Practical solutions to identification and signature problems. In Andrew M. Odlyzko, editor, *Advances in Cryptology – CRYPTO'86*, volume 263 of *Lecture Notes in Computer Science*, pages 186–194, Santa Barbara, CA, USA, August 1987. Springer, Heidelberg, Germany.
7. Russell Impagliazzo and Avi Wigderson. P = BPP if E requires exponential circuits: Derandomizing the XOR lemma. In *29th Annual ACM Symposium on Theory of Computing*, pages 220–229, El Paso, TX, USA, May 4–6, 1997. ACM Press.

8. Tom L Lindstrøm. *Spaces: An Introduction to Real Analysis*, volume 29. American Mathematical Soc., 2017.

9. Claude E. Shannon. Communication theory of secrecy systems. *Bell System Technical Journal*, 28(4):656–715, 1949.

10. Claude Elwood Shannon. A mathematical theory of communication. *Bell System Technical Journal*, 27(3):379–423, 1948.

11. Andrew Chi-Chih Yao. Theory and applications of trapdoor functions (extended abstract). In *23rd Annual Symposium on Foundations of Computer Science*, pages 80–91, Chicago, Illinois, November 3–5, 1982. IEEE Computer Society Press.

Chapter 9
The Full Power of Random Oracles

We have already seen a first glimpse of how random oracles simplify cryptographic proofs when we showed how to use random oracles to construct commitment schemes. Over the course of this book we will see many additional examples of how we can prove the security of cryptographic schemes with the help of random oracles, and this chapter, in particular, is dedicated to the study of how random oracles facilitate such security proofs.

9.1 Unpredictability: Blockchains and Proofs of Work

In the first part of this chapter we will look at one of the most basic properties of random oracles: the generation of completely random and thus unpredictable values. Since random oracles can only be evaluated via an oracle call, guessing the outcome of a random oracle query for a chosen message m is as difficult as guessing the outcome of a random variable that is uniformly distributed over the range of the random oracle (see also Equation (8.3) and the corresponding discussion in Section 8.3 on page 357). This property allows us to work with random oracles purely in the information-theoretic setting, which in many cases makes analyses much simpler. In the following we look at the cryptocurrency *Bitcoin* and some of its underlying building blocks, namely, *blockchains* and *proofs of work*, both of which are built from hash functions and which can be nicely analyzed in the random oracle model by exploiting the *unpredictability property* of random oracles.

© Springer Nature Switzerland AG 2021
A. Mittelbach, M. Fischlin, *The Theory of Hash Functions and Random Oracles*,
Information Security and Cryptography, https://doi.org/10.1007/978-3-030-63287-8_9

Bitcoin

In 2009 Satoshi Nakamoto[1] published a groundbreaking paper on how to set up and operate a decentralized digital currency called *Bitcoin*, which over the last decade has become immensely popular, not only in the cryptographic community. The key innovation of Bitcoin is that it does not require a trusted central authority (e.g., a federal bank) to operate the currency, but that instead it is operated via peer-to-peer technology. In order to work without a central authority, Nakamoto had to solve, amongst others, a key problem of digital currencies which is known as the *double spending problem*. If money is only a sequence of bits, what prevents the owner from copying it and spending it not only once but multiple times? In the classic centralized scenario a trusted authority could keep records of all transactions and could thus detect if someone is trying to spend more money than he or she has. In Bitcoin this problem is solved using cryptographic tools, all of which can be constructed from hash functions. The legitimacy of transactions is ensured with the help of digital signatures (see Chapter 6). In order to transfer an amount of money from one account to another the spender signs a document saying that the amount should be taken out of his or her account and put into the account of the payee. In Bitcoin, accounts are simply public keys of a signature key pair. And, whoever knows the corresponding secret key to a bitcoin address can "spend bitcoins" from that address by signing a transaction.[2] Besides using digital signatures to authenticate transactions, Bitcoin makes use of *blockchains* and *proofs of work* in order to avoid the necessity for a central authority. We next take a closer look at these last two primitives as their predominant constructions are based on hash functions; in the case of Bitcoin they are based on SHA-256.

9.1.1 Blockchain

A key challenge for a decentralized currency system is the double spending problem as explained above. In Bitcoin this is solved by having a publicly available ledger that contains all transactions ever made. Given that such a ledger is available, any party that tries to double spend would be easily detectable by simply going over all transactions and checking whether or not the party has sufficient funds. Of course, this is only true if the public ledger

---

[1] The origins of Bitcoin are somewhat mysterious given that the name Satoshi Nakamoto is a pseudonym and until today it remains unclear which person (or persons) hide behind it.

[2] As Bitcoin addresses are not directly tied to legal entities, Bitcoin achieves some level of pseudonymity. Yet, transactions may be linkable and may allow to recover the person behind the digital address by relating the data to other information.

can be trusted to be correct and that, in particular, it is infeasible for any party to tamper with it (for example, erase some of their old transactions).

The public ledger for the Bitcoin network is implemented as a blockchain which, essentially, consists of a number of *blocks* (digital documents containing multiple transaction documents) that are *chained* together via a hash function. Consider the following Figure 9.1 of three blocks each containing three transactions (the little lock indicates that the transactions are signed documents).

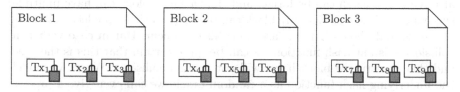

Fig. 9.1: Three blocks (i.e., digital documents) each containing three transactions.

So far each block is isolated. In order to chain the blocks together and to create a blockchain, we embed in each block the hash value of the previous block. Thus, Block 2 additionally contains hash value H(Block 1) and Block 3 contains hash value H(Block 2). Note that hash value H(Block 2) implicitly contains the hash value for the first block since this was part of the input to Block 2. The following Figure 9.2 exemplifies the construction.

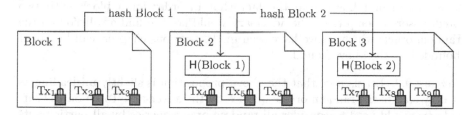

Fig. 9.2: A blockchain of length 3.

A blockchain is thus a set of ordered documents (called blocks within a block chain) where block number n contains the hash value of the previous block number $n-1$. The only block not containing a hash of a previous block is the very first block in the chain, which is often also called the *genesis block*.

Changing a block after the fact. The idea of a blockchain is that blocks that come later in the chain protect the integrity of earlier blocks. This is achieved through the above explained chaining, as changing a block also changes the block's hash value (with overwhelming probability). Thus, in order to change a block after the fact, an adversary would either need to manipulate the block's content such that the block's hash value does not change, or it would need to change all subsequent blocks. Changing a block's content while keeping the hash value intact would constitute a successful second-preimage attack: the block and its hash value are given, and it is the task of the adversary to find a second block which hashes to the same hash value. Hence, if the hash function that underlies the blockchain is second-preimage resistant we can be assured that such an attack has only negligible chances of success. As for changing all subsequent blocks we will shortly see how this can be prevented with the help of so-called *proofs of work*.

Of chains and trees. The term blockchain focuses on the idea that from any given block there exists exactly one chain back to the genesis block. While at any point a chain can be forked and thus a single block can have multiple successors, this means that any block can only have a single predecessor. This, of course, only holds true in case no collisions occur. But in case we use a collision-resistant hash function we can be quite certain that this is the case and that constructed blockchains will not contain collisions. When we model the underlying hash function as a random oracle we can even give a precise bound.

> **Proposition 9.1.** *Let* RO *be a random oracle. Let* $\mathcal{A}$ *be an adversary that makes at most* $q(\lambda)$ *many calls to random oracle* RO. *Then the probability that adversary* $\mathcal{A}$ *can output a valid blockchain over* RO *that contains a block with two possible predecessors is at most*
>
> $$\frac{q(\lambda)^2}{2^{\mathsf{RO.ol}(\lambda)-1}}.$$

The statement follows from the fact that in order for a block with two predecessors to be present the adversary would need to find a collision on the random oracle which, as we have seen in the previous chapter, can be upper bounded by the above bound.

Remark 9.2. Let us note that the above proposition is slightly misleading as it only counts the random oracle queries by the adversary. To be on the safe side we would need to consider all random oracle queries by all participants in the network. In this case, the bound remains the same but now q measures the total number of queries by all participants. Let us try to put this into perspective. As of 2019 the Bitcoin hash rate, which measures the estimated number of hash computations in the Bitcoin network, is around 100 million tera hashes (or 100 million trillion hashes) per second. This is, indeed, an enormous number, and roughly 2^{67} when expressed as a power of 2. The hash function used in Bitcoin is SHA-256, which produces 256-bit outputs. If we model SHA-256 as a random oracle and if we continued at the current rate we could thus expect to find a collision with good probability after 2^{59} seconds or roughly 18 billion years.

While blocks only have a single predecessor, blocks can, of course, have multiple successors. That is, a blockchain can fork and thus become a tree rather than a single chain as outlined in Figure 9.3. In a blockchain that

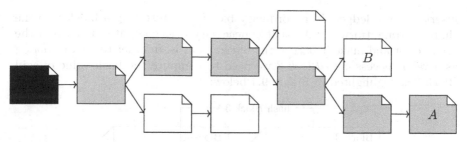

Fig. 9.3: A blockchain with forks where the main chain consists of seven blocks (highlighted in light grey). The genesis block is given in black.

contains forks we consider the longest chain to be the *main chain* which brings us back to the Bitcoin ledger. The ledger is formalized as a blockchain where each block holds a number of transactions. The ledger's main chain (i.e., the longest chain within the ledger) is regarded as the correct transaction history. This has immediate consequences. If an attacker can insert blocks into the ledger at a faster pace than the honest users then an adversary could create an alternative transaction history by creating a branch and making it part of the longest path in the chain. In Figure 9.3 we highlighted two blocks named A and B. Assume that block A contains a transaction of the adversary. If the adversary could next insert sufficiently many blocks, starting from block B, and overtake the longest path, then the transaction that was recorded previously as part of block A would no longer be part of the official transaction history and hence the adversary would be able to spend the same coins once more. In order to protect against such attacks, Bitcoin deploys so-called *proofs of work*.

9.1.2 Proofs of Work

In the Bitcoin network, security is based on the assumption that an honest majority of the participants controls a majority of the computational power. In other words, as long as an adversary does not have more computational resources than the honest parties an adversary should not be able to take control over the blockchain and *rewrite history*. To understand how Bitcoin protects its ledger we first need to discuss how new blocks become part of the ledger. This is easily explained yet harder to implement in practice: any party can become part of the Bitcoin network at any time and contribute to the network. When a user wants to make a transaction he or she announces the transaction publicly. In order to become part of the ledger the transaction must become part of a valid block in the main chain of Bitcoin's blockchain. For this, so called *miners* (any party can become a miner) group together recently announced transactions into a new block, which they then try to insert into the ledger. In an ordinary blockchain inserting a block into the chain is straightforward. All that is necessary is to compute the hash of the predecessor and make it part of the block. That is, in order to create *Block 4* as a valid successor to *Block 3* we need to compute the hash value of said Block 3 as highlighted in Figure 9.4 below:

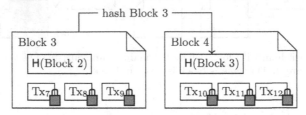

Fig. 9.4: Inserting a block into an existing blockchain.

In Bitcoin, inserting a block is not quite as easy since, if anybody could insert arbitrarily many blocks into the ledger, then anybody could rewrite the transaction history at will, which would make the whole network unsuitable for its purpose. Thus, Nakamoto introduced a *proof-of-work* puzzle to be part of the blockchain. In order to include a new block into the chain a miner must solve a cryptographic puzzle and only if the puzzle is solved correctly is the block allowed to become part of the official ledger. Nakamoto's idea was that if inserting new blocks into the ledger takes a certain amount of CPU cycles then an honest majority is always faster in recording the *correct* history than an adversary is in producing a fake transaction log.

Nakamoto's choice for a proof-of-work was to use the hash function that is already part of the blockchain. In order for a block to be valid its hash value must be less than or equal to a given target value. This, of course, requires a degree of freedom in the choice of the message block. After all, if the message block would be fixed then there was exactly one hash value. Instead, Bitcoin blocks contain a special field which can contain a number chosen by the miner, i.e., the party creating the block. This special field is usually called a *nonce* even though in Bitcoin it is not used as a nonce in the cryptographic sense.[3] Thus, Block 4 would look as follows:

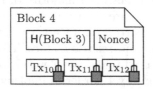

---

[3] The term *nonce* comes from the middle English phrase "then anes" which translates to "the one purpose". In cryptography a nonce usually identifies a number that is supposed to be used once (nonce $\approx$ number to be used once) and only once. When a cryptographic scheme uses nonces then reusing nonces can often have disastrous consequences to the scheme's security. In Bitcoin the nonce can, however, be chosen freely by the miner to create a valid block and nothing prevents miners from reusing nonces.

A Bitcoin miner that tries to insert Block 4 into the official ledger can now try multiple values for the Nonce until it finds one such that the hash value of Block 4 is of the correct form.

In the following we discuss the difficulty of a slightly adapted but simpler to analyze version of the proof-of-work used in Bitcoin. Instead of searching for a hash value which is less than or equal to some target value we expect it to start with a consecutive number of zero bits.

> **Proposition 9.3.** *Let* RO *be a random oracle and let* $\ell \in \mathbb{N}$ *be a positive integer such that* $\ell \leq$ RO.ol(λ). *Then a miner, on average, has to try out* 2^ℓ *many distinct values for the nonce until a valid block is found which has a hash value with* ℓ *leading 0-bits.*

Proof. The probability that a single choice for the nonce yields a valid block is $2^{-\ell}$, independent of the choice of nonce. This is due to the properties of the random oracle returning fresh random outputs for each input. Thus, the probability that a miner is successful in exactly n tries can be modeled as a geometric distribution with expected value 2^ℓ. It follows that on average a miner needs $n = 2^\ell$ many tries to find a valid block. $\square$

By choosing value ℓ we can fine-tune the difficulty of our proof-of-work. As discussed, in Bitcoin's proof-of-work a target value is fixed, and only hash values (interpreted as integers) which are less than the target value are considered valid. While in our simpler proof-of-work increasing ℓ by 1 makes the proof twice as hard, choosing the target value in Bitcoin allows to exactly control the average number of steps needed to find a valid block (see also Exercise 9.2). This fine-granular control is used to regularly adjust the difficulty level to account for an increase in computational resources (both because chips are getting better and because new users may join to contribute). For Bitcoin, the desired rate for finding a valid block is ten minutes and the target value is adjusted accordingly every 2016 blocks.

Proofs of work without random oracles. We analyzed the proof-of-work scheme in the random oracle model, which provided us with a straightforward analysis that exploited the unpredictability of random oracle responses: Unless an adversary has already queried the random oracle on a value, the result is entirely unpredictable. Without modeling the hash function as a random oracle things would look very different. Consider our standard model security properties that we have introduced so far. None of them can be used to argue that finding a value below a certain target value is difficult. Furthermore, when considering a hash function not as an oracle it becomes very difficult to argue about the *number of tries*. While we can easily count calls to the random oracle we cannot count the local evaluations of a hash function by an adversary. We treat adversaries as a black box that we cannot look into. We do not specify the technology they use and, in particular, do not assume that an adversary does not have any insights into how to evaluate a function.

For example, it could be perfectly feasible that an adversary found a way to dramatically speed up the way it evaluates a hash function.

The random oracle model gives us a way out of this dilemma by letting us look into some aspects of an adversary's computation. Namely, we can look at the random oracle queries of an adversary and argue, for example, about the average number of such queries. In the following section we will see that this *introspection* into the adversary's computation not only allows us to argue as to the number of queries an adversary needs to make but also allows us to conceive nifty reductions that exploit the fact that they see what an adversary asks.

Concluding Bitcoin. We have used Bitcoin as the running example of this section but have not given a full account on how it works but instead concentrated on the parts that use hash functions. A full specification of Bitcoin is beyond the scope of this book, but Bitcoin itself and, in particular, its use of hash functions is definitely a target worthwhile for study. We provide the necessary references as part of this chapter's notes on page 403 and here continue with our study of random oracles. In the upcoming section we discuss how reductions can make use of observing random oracle queries by an adversary and how this helps in the construction of efficient public-key encryption (PKE) schemes.

9.2 Observing Reductions: PKE from Random Oracles

In the previous section we have seen how to use the unpredictability property of random oracles to analyze blockchains and hash-function-based proof-of-work schemes. In particular in the analysis of the proof-of-work scheme we used the fact that an adversary needs to query the random oracle in order to learn a hash value for a given message. So far, our analyses were purely probabilistic arguments. In the following, we show how we can exploit the nature of random oracles within reductions which, as we will see, can simulate a random oracle for an adversary. As our running example for this section we will go back to public-key encryption schemes and show how we can use random oracles to construct very efficient schemes that are IND-CPA secure.

9.2.1 Random Oracles Are Hardcore for Any OWF

Recall our generic construction of a public-key encryption scheme from a trapdoor function T and a function HC that is hardcore for T (Section 5.3.5, page 255). In this scheme we encrypt a message m by generating an image $s \leftarrow \mathsf{T.Eval}(\mathsf{pk}, r)$ for a random value r, and masking m as $c \leftarrow m \oplus \mathsf{HC}(\mathsf{hk}, r)$

with the value of the hardcore function. The hardcore function itself guarantees that $\mathsf{HC}(\mathsf{hk}, r)$ looks random, even if given the image s of r under the trapdoor function.

One of the difficulties with the scheme above was that it is very hard to construct a trapdoor function together with a suitable hardcore function. While the Goldreich–Levin hardcore bit provides us with a general construction of hardcore bits the problem here is that the output length of the hardcore function is directly tied to the efficiency of the resulting public-key encryption scheme. A hardcore bit (rather than a hardcore function with long output) provides us with the worst possible efficiency. Random oracles, on the other hand, can be shown to yield *universal hardcore functions*. This means that a random oracle is hardcore for any one-way function. Combined with the fact that random oracles have potentially long outputs we can thus simply plug a random oracle into our Construction 5.38 to obtain a very efficient IND-CPA-secure public-key encryption scheme. In the following we make this intuition formal:

Proposition 9.4. *Let* F *be a one-way function and let* RO *be a random oracle. If function* F *does not make any calls to* RO *then random oracle* RO *is hardcore for* F.

Remark 9.5. In Proposition 9.4 we state that a random oracle is hardcore for any F that does not make any random oracle calls. The latter restriction is indeed necessary. To see this, let F be a one-way function and construct G^{RO} relative to random oracle RO as

$$\mathsf{G}^{\mathsf{RO}}(x) := \mathsf{F}(x) \| \mathsf{RO}(x).$$

It is apparent that RO cannot possibly be hardcore for G^{RO}, as $\mathsf{RO}(x)$ is embedded in the output of G. This counterexample is valid not only for random oracles but, in fact, for any unkeyed hardcore function. In other words, starting from any unkeyed function HC and a one-way function F, we can always construct a one-way function G^{HC} that depends on HC and for which HC cannot be hardcore. The simplest way to circumvent such artificial counterexamples is to use keyed hardcore functions, or in our case, a keyed random oracle.

Proof of Proposition 9.4. We prove Proposition 9.4 by giving a security reduction that exploits the fact that an adversary needs to query the random oracle which allows the reduction to observe the adversary's queries. The high-level description of the reduction is given in Figure 9.5.

Let $\mathcal{A}$ be an adversary against the hardcore property of random oracle RO. Without loss of generality, let us assume that $\mathcal{A}$ never repeats a query to its random oracle. As before, we note that if this property is not given we can always construct an adversary $\mathcal{A}'$ that runs $\mathcal{A}$, forwarding fresh queries to the random oracle while keeping a table of oracle queries to answer repeated

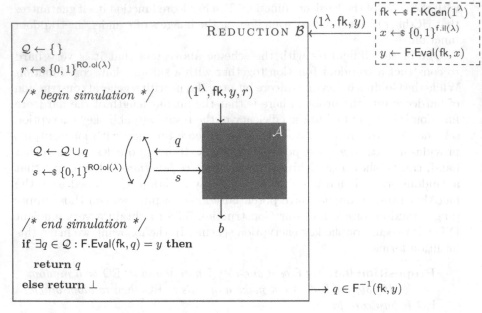

Fig. 9.5: A security reduction showing that a random oracle is a universal hardcore function. Without loss of generality we assume that adversary $\mathcal{A}$ never repeats a query to its oracle. The reduction takes as input a key fk for function f and an image y for a uniformly random preimage x. It chooses a random value r and runs adversary $\mathcal{A}$ on (fk, y, r). It simulates the random oracle for adversary $\mathcal{A}$ and answers any oracle query with a random value while keeping a list of all the queries. Finally, it checks if any of the queries are a valid preimage for $\mathsf{F.Eval}(\mathsf{fk}, x)$.

queries. From this we construct an adversary $\mathcal{B}$ against the assumed one-wayness of function F. Adversary $\mathcal{B}$ takes as input a function key fk and a value y. Its goal is to find a preimage x such that $\mathsf{F.Eval}(\mathsf{fk}, x) = y$, and it will do so by running adversary $\mathcal{A}$.

So far, the reduction follows our standard pattern. But where usually we have simply had our reductions run the adversary and use the result, we are now in a new situation. Since adversary $\mathcal{A}$ expects oracle access to a random oracle, adversary $\mathcal{B}$ needs to *simulate the random oracle* for $\mathcal{A}$.

Adversary $\mathcal{B}$ performs the following steps: It generates a random value $r \in \{0,1\}^{\mathsf{RO.ol}(\lambda)}$ and calls adversary $\mathcal{A}$ on input (fk, y, r). The idea here is that r is a placeholder for $\mathsf{RO}(x)$ or for a random value. It then simulates the random oracle for $\mathcal{A}$ as follows. Whenever $\mathcal{A}$ sends a query q to the (simulated) random oracle, then adversary $\mathcal{B}$ samples a random value $s \in \{0,1\}^{\mathsf{RO.ol}(\lambda)}$, adds q to a set $\mathcal{Q}$, and returns s to adversary $\mathcal{A}$.[4] At some point adversary $\mathcal{A}$ will finish its computation and output a bit b. At this point adversary $\mathcal{B}$ will check whether the set $\mathcal{Q}$ contains any query q such that

$$\mathsf{F.Eval}(\mathsf{fk}, q) = y.$$

If so, it will return q. In the case that there is no such q it will abort and return $\bot$.

Analysis. It remains to discuss the success probability of our adversary $\mathcal{B}$. Adversary $\mathcal{A}$ expects as value r either a uniformly random value or the hardcore value $\mathsf{RO}(x)$. By the unpredictability property of the random oracle, value $\mathsf{RO}(x)$ can be regarded as a random variable that is uniformly distributed. Thus, unless $\mathcal{A}$ queries the random oracle on value x there is no way of telling apart a uniformly random value from the actual value $\mathsf{RO}(x)$. It follows that, in case $\mathcal{A}$ has an advantage $\mathsf{Adv}_{\mathsf{HC},\mathcal{A}}^{\mathsf{hc}}(\lambda)$ that is non-negligible, then there exists a non-negligible probability that $\mathcal{A}$ queries the random oracle on value x. In fact, one can show that the probability that $\mathcal{A}$ calls random oracle RO on x is at least $\mathsf{Adv}_{\mathsf{HC},\mathcal{A}}^{\mathsf{hc}}(\lambda)$. This follows a similar line of reasoning to the proof that random oracles are one-way (see page 348). We leave the formal analysis of the last claim as an exercise.

In its simulation adversary $\mathcal{B}$ provides r as a uniformly random value to $\mathcal{A}$ and afterwards simulates the random oracle via lazy sampling. It thus perfectly imitates a random oracle, and hence adversary $\mathcal{A}$ must behave as if it was connected to an actual random oracle and must, consequently, make a query for target value x with probability at least $\mathsf{Adv}_{\mathsf{HC},\mathcal{A}}^{\mathsf{hc}}(\lambda)$. In this case, however, we have that $\mathcal{B}$ can extract value x with probability 1 and can thus invert the one-way function as $\mathsf{F}(\mathsf{fk}, x) = y$. It follows that

$$\mathsf{Adv}_{\mathsf{HC},\mathcal{A}}^{\mathsf{hc}}(\lambda) \le \mathsf{Adv}_{\mathsf{F},\mathcal{B}}^{\mathsf{owf}}(\lambda),$$

which concludes the proof. □

Observing Reductions

In the above proof we have exploited an interesting (and controversial) property of a random oracle. Our reduction, i.e., adversary $\mathcal{B}$, simulated the random oracle for adversary $\mathcal{A}$ via lazy sampling and was able to observe all of the adversary's queries to the random oracle. We call such reductions *observing reductions*. By arguing that in order to win adversary $\mathcal{A}$ must query the random oracle on a preimage x for y we could then show that $\mathcal{B}$ can simply

---

[4] Note that $\mathcal{B}$ is essentially simulating the random oracle via lazy sampling (see page 341). Furthermore, recall that we assume that adversary $\mathcal{A}$ never repeats a query. Instead, we could have also let adversary $\mathcal{B}$ keep a table of query–result pairs to answer repeated queries consistently.

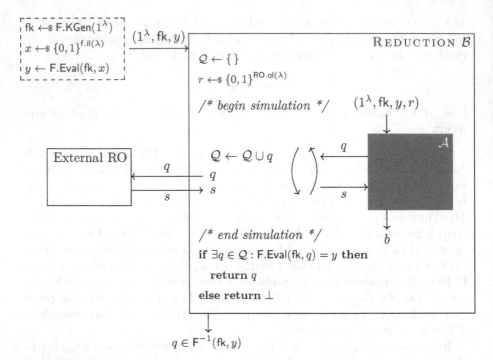

Fig. 9.6: Non-programming view on the reduction in the proof of Proposition 9.4. In contrast to before, we here assume an "external" random oracle that the reduction uses. While it sees the queries q coming from the adversary $\mathcal{A}$ as well as the answers s by the random oracle, it otherwise simply acts as an intermediary and forwards queries and responses.

extract the preimage from $\mathcal{A}$'s queries in order to win with (at least) the same probability. Sometimes such reductions are also called *non-programming*. The reason will become apparent when discussing programming reductions in the next section. For now we only note that $\mathcal{B}$ could basically work with a given random oracle RO and use that oracle to answer all of $\mathcal{A}$'s queries; see Figure 9.6.

Considering observing reductions within the random oracle model makes perfect sense. As long as the reduction simulates the random oracle in such a way that the simulation cannot be detected then from the perspective of the adversary all is fine. In fact, everything is very much the same as, for example, in a reduction from a signature scheme where a reduction simulates parts of the signature scheme to an adversary and, thus, of course sees the adversary's queries to the signature scheme.

However, when we consider the random oracle methodology this is only half the story. In the random oracle methodology we first prove the security of a scheme in the random oracle model. Then, to implement the scheme in practice we instantiate the random oracle with a cryptographic hash function.

Now, once we consider the instantiated scheme, observing reductions become problematic. As discussed before, we typically consider adversaries as black boxes that we cannot look inside. In case the random oracle is implemented with, say, SHA-256, then the adversary can compute function values locally and there is not necessarily a way to extract its "queries": There might not even be a plausible notion of "queries" as we do not know how the adversary actually computes hash values.

We will have more to say on this in Chapter 12, where we discuss in detail the controversy around random oracles. For now let us continue our exploration of random oracle schemes and show how to use the above notion of random oracles as hardcore functions to build efficient public-key encryption schemes.

9.2.2 The BR93 Public-Key Encryption Scheme

Equipped with Proposition 9.4 we can proceed to construct an efficient public-key encryption scheme from a trapdoor function and a random oracle. The scheme was first proposed by Bellare and Rogaway in 1993 as an example of how to use the random oracle methodology and is thus also often referred to as the BR93 scheme. It is a direct application of Construction 5.38 with a random oracle as hardcore function.

Construction 9.6 (BR93 Public-Key Encryption Scheme).
Let T *be a trapdoor one-way function. Define public-key encryption scheme*
$\mathsf{PKE}^{\mathsf{RO}} = (\mathsf{PKE.KGen}, \mathsf{PKE}^{\mathsf{RO}}.\mathsf{Enc}, \mathsf{PKE}^{\mathsf{RO}}.\mathsf{Dec})$ *relative to random oracle*
RO *and with message length* $\mathsf{PKE.il}(\lambda) = \mathsf{RO.ol}(\lambda)$ *as*

$\mathsf{PKE.KGen}(1^\lambda)$	$\mathsf{PKE}^{\mathsf{RO}}.\mathsf{Enc}(\mathsf{pk}, m)$	$\mathsf{PKE}^{\mathsf{RO}}.\mathsf{Dec}(\mathsf{sk}, (s, c))$
$(\mathsf{pk}, \mathsf{tk}) \leftarrow\!\!{\scriptstyle\$}\ \mathsf{T.KGen}(1^\lambda)$	$r \leftarrow\!\!{\scriptstyle\$}\ \{0,1\}^{\mathsf{T.il}(\lambda)}$	$r \leftarrow \mathsf{T.Inv}(\mathsf{tk}, s)$ $\ /\!\!/\ \mathsf{sk} = \mathsf{tk}$
return $(\mathsf{pk}, \mathsf{sk}) \leftarrow (\mathsf{pk}, \mathsf{tk})$	$s \leftarrow \mathsf{T.Eval}(\mathsf{pk}, r)$	$m \leftarrow c \oplus \mathsf{RO}(r)$
	$c \leftarrow m \oplus \mathsf{RO}(r)$	**return** m
	return (s, c)	

It remains to formally state the scheme's security properties, which follow from Proposition 9.4 above and Proposition 5.39 (page 256).

Proposition 9.7. *Construction 9.6 is an IND-CPA-secure public-key encryption scheme in the random oracle model.*

9.3 Programming Reductions: Full Domain Hash

In the previous section we have seen how to construct public-key encryption schemes from random oracles and trapdoor functions. For the construction we used an *observing reduction* (aka non-programming reduction) which exploits seeing an adversary's random oracle queries to break an underlying assumption, in our case, to invert a one-way function. In the following, we will see that reductions in the random oracle model can do even more: they can not only observe random oracle queries but can also *program* the random oracle responses. Resulting reductions are usually called *programming reductions*, which we will use to prove the security of an efficient signature scheme from a random oracle and a trapdoor function.

9.3.1 Full Domain Hash Signatures

The *full domain hash (FDH) signature scheme* is modeled after the hash-and-sign approach (see Section 6.3) in which a signature scheme is combined with a collision-resistant hash function to obtain an efficient signature scheme for arbitrarily long messages. The idea is to use a hash function H to first compute the hash value of a document m and then to sign hash value $H(m)$ instead of the document itself. It is easy to see that validation still works as any party can compute hash value $H(m)$ given document m. For the general security of the approach see the proof of Theorem 6.8 on page 273.

In the hash-and-sign construction we start with a signature scheme that is already secure: in essence the hash-and-sign construction yields a domain extension for a signature scheme. If we, however, model the hash function as a random oracle, then it is sufficient to start from any trapdoor permutation instead of from an already secure signature scheme. Furthermore, full domain hash yields a *deterministic* signature scheme. The construction is as follows:

Construction 9.8 (Full Domain Hash (FDH)).

Let RO *be a random oracle and let* T *be a trapdoor one-way permutation with* $\mathsf{T.il}(\lambda) = \mathsf{T.ol}(\lambda) = \mathsf{RO.ol}(\lambda)$ *and such that* T.Inv *is defined on* $\{0,1\}^{\mathsf{RO.ol}(\lambda)}$. *Define the deterministic signature scheme* $\mathsf{Sig}^{\mathsf{RO}} = (\mathsf{Sig.KGen}, \mathsf{Sig}^{\mathsf{RO}}.\mathsf{Sign}, \mathsf{Sig}^{\mathsf{RO}}.\mathsf{Vf})$ *relative to random oracle* RO *as follows:*

$\mathsf{Sig.KGen}(1^\lambda)$	$\mathsf{Sig}^{\mathsf{RO}}.\mathsf{Sign}(\mathsf{tk}, m)$	$\mathsf{Sig}^{\mathsf{RO}}.\mathsf{Vf}(\mathsf{pk}, m, \sigma)$
$(\mathsf{pk}, \mathsf{tk}) \leftarrow\!\!{\scriptstyle\$}\, \mathsf{T.KGen}(1^\lambda)$	$y \leftarrow \mathsf{RO}(m)$	$y \leftarrow \mathsf{RO}(m)$
return $(\mathsf{pk}, \mathsf{tk})$	$\sigma \leftarrow \mathsf{T.Inv}(\mathsf{tk}, y)$	$y' \leftarrow \mathsf{T.Eval}(\mathsf{pk}, \sigma)$
	return σ	**return** $(y = y')$

The public key of a full domain hash signature scheme is simply the evaluation key of the trapdoor function. The corresponding inversion key yields the signature key for FDH. To sign a message m, we first compute hash value $y \leftarrow \mathsf{RO}(m)$, which we then "sign" by computing the inversion under the trapdoor function, that is, by computing $\sigma \leftarrow \mathsf{T.Inv}(\mathsf{tk}, y)$. Verification is done in the natural way by recomputing hash value $y \leftarrow \mathsf{RO}(m)$ and comparing it with $y' \leftarrow \mathsf{T.Eval}(\mathsf{pk}, \sigma)$ where σ is the message's signature.

Before we formally analyze the scheme's security, let us informally argue why the scheme should be secure. The security of a trapdoor function, when the inversion key is hidden, is identical to that of a one-way function: given an image y for a randomly chosen value x it should be computationally infeasible to come up with the chosen value x or any other preimage x' that has image y. Now consider the signature operation in FDH. We can think of value y computed as $y \leftarrow \mathsf{RO}(m)$ as our image. Using the trapdoor function's secret inversion key we next compute a preimage of y, which we output as signature σ. In order to forge a signature for some message m an adversary would thus need to be able to find preimages under trapdoor function T for image $\mathsf{RO}(m)$, which is, as we have argued before, identically distributed to a uniformly random variable. Let us make this intuition formal.

Proposition 9.9. *Let* RO *be a random oracle and* T *be a trapdoor permutation with the restrictions stated in Construction 9.8. If* T *is a secure trapdoor permutation, then Construction 9.8 yields a signature scheme which is existentially unforgeable under chosen-message attacks.*

Outline. As mentioned above, we will prove Proposition 9.9 via a so-called *programming reduction* in which the reduction will carefully choose random oracle responses such that they are still uniformly distributed but in such a way that allows the reduction to generate valid signatures for all but one of the messages sent by the adversary to the random oracle. The hope is then that the adversary attempts a forgery for that particular message, in which case the reduction can extract a preimage for its own challenge. As the adversary is efficient and makes at most $\mathsf{q}(\lambda)$ queries to its random oracle, the probability of the reduction to be successful is $\frac{1}{\mathsf{q}(\lambda)}$: it needs to guess the right index into which to insert the challenge. A high-level pictorial description of the reduction is given as Figure 9.7.

Proof of Proposition 9.9. Let $\mathcal{A}$ be an adversary against the full domain hash signature scheme. From this we construct adversary $\mathcal{B}$ against the one-way property of trapdoor function T. Adversary $\mathcal{B}$ gets as input the trapdoor function's evaluation key pk as well as a target value y for which it needs to find a preimage. The idea is for $\mathcal{B}$ to internally run $\mathcal{A}$ on input pk and to let it search for a signature forgery. Since $\mathcal{A}$ expects both a signature oracle and a random oracle, these must be simulated by $\mathcal{B}$. Let us discuss in turn how $\mathcal{B}$ simulates the oracles for adversary $\mathcal{A}$.

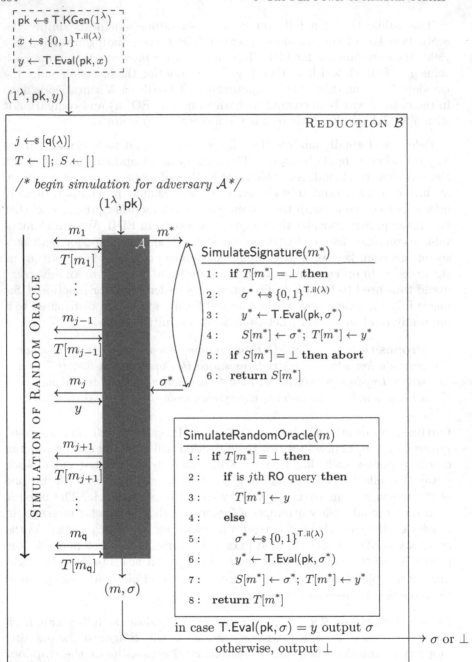

Fig. 9.7: Sketch of the security proof for the full domain hash signature scheme given as Construction 9.8. Adversary $\mathcal{B}$ simulates both signature and random oracle for adversary $\mathcal{A}$ against the existential unforgeability of signature scheme Sig. Adversary $\mathcal{B}$ injects its target value y as one of the random oracle answers in the simulation and "hopes" that the forgery of $\mathcal{A}$ is for the corresponding message m_j, in which case it is able to simulate all signature queries and, furthermore, the output signature σ is a preimage of $\mathsf{RO}(m_j) = y$, which allows $\mathcal{B}$ to successfully invert its own challenge (which is y).

Simulation of the signature oracle—Take 1. When $\mathcal{A}$ makes a query for message m^* to its signature oracle it expects back a valid signature σ^*. This means that in the simulation we need to ensure that $\mathcal{A}$ can successfully validate the generated signature, as otherwise it would immediately detect the simulation. Recall that a signature σ^* for a message m^* is validated by performing the following three steps:

$$
\begin{array}{l}
\hline
\mathsf{Sig}^{\mathsf{RO}}.\mathsf{Vf}(\mathsf{pk}, m^*, \sigma^*) \\
\hline
1: \quad y^* \leftarrow \mathsf{RO}(m^*) \\
2: \quad y' \leftarrow \mathsf{T}.\mathsf{Eval}(\mathsf{pk}, \sigma^*) \\
3: \quad \mathbf{return}\ (y^* = y') \\
\hline
\end{array}
$$

For the simulated signature to be correct we thus need to come up with a preimage of $\mathsf{RO}(m^*)$ under trapdoor function T, which requires breaking the trapdoor function as $\mathcal{B}$ does not have the secret trapdoor key tk. Instead, we take a different approach. As $\mathcal{B}$ simulates not only the signature oracle but also the random oracle we can effectively choose the "random" values that we provide to $\mathcal{A}$ on random oracle queries. As long as they are uniformly distributed, $\mathcal{A}$ cannot detect the simulation. But then instead of first choosing a random oracle value for message m^* to then try to come up with a preimage for $\mathsf{RO}(m^*)$ we can first choose a uniformly random preimage σ^*, compute $y^* \leftarrow \mathsf{T}.\mathsf{Eval}(\mathsf{pk}, \sigma^*)$, and then "program" the random oracle to return y^* for message m^*. By construction we now have that σ^* is a preimage for y^* and thus for $\mathsf{RO}(m^*)$.

In order to record the choices of random preimage and random oracle value, adversary $\mathcal{B}$ keeps two tables: T for random oracle values and S for signature values (i.e., preimages). Following is a first attempt for the simulation of signature queries given as pseudocode:

$$
\begin{array}{l}
\hline
\mathsf{SimulateSignature}(m^*) \\
\hline
1: \quad \sigma^* \leftarrow_\$ \{0, 1\}^{\mathsf{T}.\mathsf{il}(\lambda)} \\
2: \quad y^* \leftarrow \mathsf{T}.\mathsf{Eval}(\mathsf{pk}, \sigma^*) \\
3: \quad S[m^*] \leftarrow \sigma^*;\ T[m^*] \leftarrow y^* \\
4: \quad \mathbf{return}\ \sigma^* \\
\hline
\end{array}
$$

In order for the simulation to be undetectable, adversary $\mathcal{B}$ must now ensure that the choices made during signature queries are reflected in the simulation of the random oracle. In particular, after a signature query for message m^*, a random oracle query for m^* should return the corresponding value y^* which was recorded in table T as $T[m^*]$.

Simulation of the random oracle—Take 1. In contrast to the observing reduction of Proposition 9.4 our reduction here, i.e., adversary $\mathcal{B}$, cannot simply use lazy sampling for its simulation of the random oracle for adversary $\mathcal{A}$. We have already seen from the simulation of the signature oracle that some values of the random oracle have been fixed, and this needs to be handled in the simulation of the random oracle. Similarly, since adversary $\mathcal{A}$ might first query its random oracle to then query its signature oracle on the same message, the simulation of the random oracle needs to ensure that the subsequent signature oracle can be answered with a valid signature. Adversary $\mathcal{B}$ thus acts as follows: On a query m^* to the random oracle, $\mathcal{B}$ first checks whether table T contains an entry for m^*. If so, it returns $T[m^*]$, thus ensuring that any simulated signature can be correctly validated. In case $T[m^*] = \bot$, that is T does not have an entry for m^*, then adversary $\mathcal{B}$ chooses a random value $\sigma^* \in \{0,1\}^{\mathsf{T.il}(\lambda)}$ (note that $\mathsf{RO.ol}(\lambda) = \mathsf{T.il}(\lambda) = \mathsf{T.ol}(\lambda)$), computes $y^* \leftarrow \mathsf{T.Eval}(\mathsf{pk}, \sigma^*)$, registers both values in tables S and T, respectively, and finally returns y^* to adversary $\mathcal{A}$. Once more as pseudocode:

$\mathsf{SimulateRO}(m^*)$

---
1 : **if** $T[m^*] = \bot$ **then**

2 : $\sigma^* \leftarrow\!\!\$ \{0,1\}^{\mathsf{T.il}(\lambda)}$

3 : $y^* \leftarrow \mathsf{T.Eval}(\mathsf{pk}, \sigma^*)$

4 : $S[m^*] \leftarrow \sigma^*;\ T[m^*] \leftarrow y^*$

5 : **return** $T[m^*]$

Note that the generation of random oracle values (lines 2 to 4) is identical to the generation previously in $\mathsf{SimulateSignature}$.

Simulation of the signature oracle—Take 2. While we have ensured that now the simulation of the random oracle takes into account the simulation of the signature oracle, we have a problem with our simulation of the signature oracle. On the one hand, we there do not yet handle repeated queries. But, more problematic, assume the case that adversary $\mathcal{A}$ chooses a message m^* which it first sends to the random oracle to only then send it to the signature oracle. Our first attempt at the signature simulation would choose a fresh value y^* which, of course, would be detectable by adversary $\mathcal{A}$, as the verification of the generated signature would fail with overwhelming probability. Thus, we also need to take account for the random oracle simulation in the signature simulation and only generate fresh values in case message m^* was not yet registered. Note that in the simulation for random oracle RO we have already taken care of recording also the corresponding signature σ^* for a message m^* in table S. We thus need to adapt the signature simulation as follows:

$\mathsf{SimulateSignature}(m^*)$

---
1 : **if** $T[m^*] = \bot$ **then**

2 : $\sigma^* \leftarrow\!\!\$ \{0,1\}^{\mathsf{T.il}(\lambda)}$

3 : $y^* \leftarrow \mathsf{T.Eval}(\mathsf{pk}, \sigma^*)$

4 : $S[m^*] \leftarrow \sigma^*;\ T[m^*] \leftarrow y^*$

5 : **return** $S[m^*]$

Note that simulations SimulateRO and SimulateSignature are now identical except for the return value. On signature queries value $S[m^*]$ is returned (which by construction is a preimage of $T[m^*]$ under trapdoor function T), and on random oracle queries $T[m^*]$ is returned.

Simulation of the random oracle—Take 2. We now have a simulation strategy that is undetectable by adversary $\mathcal{A}$ (we still need to argue that this is actually the case), but we have not yet described how our reduction $\mathcal{B}$ can find a preimage for the provided target value y. For this, we need to slightly adapt the simulation of the random oracle queries in order to "inject" value y as a challenge into one of the responses. The idea is that a successful forgery of $\mathcal{A}$ essentially requires adversary $\mathcal{A}$ to invert the result of a random oracle query. To see this, have a look at how signatures are generated in FDH. For a message m a signature is generated as

$$\underline{\mathsf{Sig}^{\mathsf{RO}}.\mathsf{Sign}(\mathsf{tk}, m)}$$

1 : $y \leftarrow \mathsf{RO}(m)$

2 : $\sigma \leftarrow \mathsf{T}.\mathsf{Inv}(\mathsf{tk}, y)$

3 : **return** σ

Thus, in order to forge a signature for a message m, adversary $\mathcal{A}$ would need to invert value $\mathsf{RO}(m)$, which is controlled by reduction $\mathcal{B}$. The idea now is for $\mathcal{B}$ to inject target value y as one of the random oracle answers. For this, let $\mathsf{q} : \mathbb{N} \to \mathbb{N}$ denote an upper bound on the number of random oracle queries by $\mathcal{A}$ for security parameter 1^λ. On startup, $\mathcal{B}$ chooses an index $j \in [\mathsf{q}(\lambda)]$ uniformly at random, and on the jth random oracle query of $\mathcal{A}$ it returns y. Following is the full simulation of the random oracle once more as pseudocode:

$$\underline{\mathsf{SimulateRO}(m^*)}$$

1 : **if** $T[m^*] = \bot$ **then**

2 : **if** is random oracle query number j **then**

3 : $T[m^*] \leftarrow y$

4 : **else**

5 : $\sigma^* \leftarrow\!\!\$ \{0,1\}^{\mathsf{T}.\mathsf{il}(\lambda)}$

6 : $y^* \leftarrow \mathsf{T}.\mathsf{Eval}(\mathsf{pk}, \sigma^*)$

7 : $S[m^*] \leftarrow \sigma^*; \; T[m^*] \leftarrow y^*$

8 : **return** $T[m^*]$

Simulation of the signature oracle—Take 3. Note that with our final change of the simulation of random oracle RO we have introduced one query for which adversary $\mathcal{B}$ cannot simulate a signature. To account for this we simply let $\mathcal{B}$ abort in case adversary $\mathcal{A}$ asks for a signature for the jth message m_j, for which we injected the challenge. Note that for message m_j table S does not contain a value (also see line 3):

SimulateSignature(m^*)

1 : **if** $T[m^*] = \bot$ **then**

2 : $\sigma^* \leftarrow\!\!\$ \, \{0,1\}^{\text{T.il}(\lambda)}$

3 : $y^* \leftarrow \text{T.Eval}(\text{pk}, \sigma^*)$

4 : $S[m^*] \leftarrow \sigma^*$; $T[m^*] \leftarrow y^*$

5 : **if** $S[m^*] = \bot$ **then abort**

6 : **return** $S[m^*]$

Analysis. This concludes the description of adversary $\mathcal{B}$, and it remains to analyze its success probability. We will conduct this analysis in two steps. First, we argue that the simulation of the two oracles for $\mathcal{A}$ is such that the simulation cannot be detected by $\mathcal{A}$ unless adversary $\mathcal{B}$ explicitly aborts in line 5 of SimulateSignature. This then allows us to argue about the success probability of $\mathcal{B}$.

Let us first consider the simulation of the random oracle. Adversary $\mathcal{A}$ expects responses to be uniformly distributed. In the simulation, adversary $\mathcal{B}$ chooses responses for random oracle queries in one of three ways. In each case, the value is recorded in table T.

- In case the query is fresh and it is not the jth query, then the response is generated by choosing a uniformly random value $\sigma^* \leftarrow\!\!\$ \, \{0,1\}^{\text{T.il}(\lambda)}$ and computing $y^* \leftarrow \text{T.Eval}(\text{pk}, \sigma^*)$, which is returned as the result (see lines 5 to 8 of SimulateRO). Since the trapdoor function T is, by definition, a permutation and σ^* was chosen uniformly at random, it follows that also y^* is uniformly distributed.
- In case the query is fresh and it is the jth query, then the response is target value y (see line 3 of the SimulateRO algorithm). The argument is as before: Since trapdoor function T is a permutation and y was chosen by choosing a uniformly random x and computing $y \leftarrow \text{T.Eval}(\text{pk}, x)$, it follows that y is also uniformly distributed.
- Finally, in case the adversary first queried the signature oracle on message m^*, then y^* is chosen identically to case 1. For this note that lines 2 to 4 of SimulateSignature are identical to lines 5 to 7 of SimulateRO.

It follows that the simulation of the random oracle is undetectable by adversary $\mathcal{A}$.

For the simulation of the signature oracle, adversary $\mathcal{B}$ needs to ensure that the simulated signatures can be verified, which is the case if for signature σ^* for a given document m^* it holds that

$$\text{RO}(m^*) = \text{T.Eval}(\text{pk}, \sigma^*).$$

By construction, this is always the case (see lines 2 to 4 of SimulateSignature and lines 5 to 7 of SimulateRO) except for the injected challenge which is injected as the response for the jth random oracle query m_j. If adversary $\mathcal{A}$ asks for a signature for m_j then adversary $\mathcal{B}$ aborts (line 5 of SimulateSignature) as it cannot simulate a signature—after all, it is the hope of $\mathcal{B}$ that adversary $\mathcal{A}$ will forge a signature for m_j. If, on the other hand, adversary $\mathcal{A}$ does not ask for a signature for m_j then, by design, all signature queries can be answered with a valid signature and thus the simulation of also the signature oracle is perfect.

We have seen that the simulation of both oracles are undetectable for adversary $\mathcal{A}$, given that $\mathcal{A}$ does not ask for a signature for message m_j for which adversary $\mathcal{B}$ injected its challenge, that is, for which $\mathsf{RO}(m_j) = y$. If so, we can assume that if adversary $\mathcal{A}$ has advantage $\mathsf{Adv}_{\mathsf{Sig},\mathcal{A}}^{\mathsf{euf\text{-}cma}}(\lambda)$ then also in the simulation it succeeds with the same success probability in forging a signature σ for a fresh message m.

Assume now that the pair (m, σ) is a valid message–signature pair as output by adversary $\mathcal{A}$. Without loss of generality, we can assume that adversary $\mathcal{A}$ always queries the random oracle on message m in case it outputs m as a forgery. Else, we simply modify $\mathcal{A}$ to make this query before stopping, thus increasing the number $\mathsf{q}(\lambda)$ of random oracle queries by at most 1. But then it follows that with probability $\frac{1}{\mathsf{q}(\lambda)+1}$ forgery (m, σ) is for challenge message m_j (i.e., $m = m_j$). In this case, however, we have that if adversary $\mathcal{A}$'s forgery is valid then it did not ask for a signature for m_j and thus the simulation of both oracles by adversary $\mathcal{B}$ was perfect. Furthermore, since $\mathcal{A}$'s forgery is for message m_j, we have that $\mathsf{RO}(m_j) = y$ and thus it must hold that

$$\mathsf{T.Eval}(\mathsf{pk}, \sigma) = \mathsf{RO}(m_j) = y,$$

in which case σ is a preimage of y.

Summing up, we have that adversary $\mathcal{B}$ is successful in inverting y with probability $\frac{1}{\mathsf{q}(\lambda)+1}$ times the success probability of adversary $\mathcal{A}$ and hence

$$\mathsf{Adv}_{\mathsf{T},\mathcal{B}}^{\mathsf{owf}}(\lambda) = \frac{1}{\mathsf{q}(\lambda) + 1} \cdot \mathsf{Adv}_{\mathsf{Sig},\mathcal{A}}^{\mathsf{euf\text{-}cma}}(\lambda).$$

This concludes the proof. $\qquad\qquad\qquad\qquad\qquad\qquad\qquad\qquad\qquad\qquad\qquad$ □

9.3.2 The Programmable Random Oracle Model

In the above security proof for the full domain hash construction our reduction was not only observing random oracle queries but was, in fact, *programming* the responses to contain specifically chosen values. This form of reduction that actively inserts values into random oracle responses is usually called a *programming reduction.* It can be easily seen that programming reductions make a stronger assumption than observing reductions. That is, anything that can be shown with an observing reduction can be shown with a programming reduction. It can even be shown that this relationship is strict, meaning that there are scenarios that can be proven secure with a programming reduction but not with an observing reduction.

As in case of observing reductions, such a proof technique is perfectly valid within the random oracle model and the programming is not very different, for example, from the way our reduction simulated the signature oracle. Once we instantiate the random oracle and replace it with a standard model hash function things are, however, again rather unclear. As with an observable reduction, our FDH reduction would no longer work against an adversary that computes the hash function internally. In particular, in some sense, our reduction is "worse" since it not only requires observing the queries to the hash function but also needs to be able to inject values into the computation. Hence, it is not clear how far the random oracle security proof applies to the instantiated scheme: Is it a mere technicality that can be safely ignored or is it, in fact, a problem that, potentially results in the creation of insecure schemes. We postpone a detailed discussion of this discrepancy to Chapter 12.

9.4 Removing Correlation: Correlated-Input Security

In the previous two sections we have seen how reductions can exploit the fact that random oracles cannot be evaluated locally. In the following we again look at the functional properties a random oracle inherits from being a random function. Many of the standard model security properties that we have introduced require that an input is drawn from a specific distribution, where we usually assume the uniform distribution. In many cases—though not always—it can be shown that if an adversary sees not only a single value but multiple values that security still holds. As an example, consider one-way functions which remain secure also in the setting where an adversary sees polynomially many images $F(x_1), \ldots, F(x_q)$ while having only to invert a single one of them.[5] This, however, only holds in case the preimages x_i are drawn uniformly at random and *independently* of one another. If, on the other hand, an adversary is to see images $F(x), F(x + 1), F(x + 2), \ldots$ then one-wayness in general does *not* provide any security guarantees. In fact, "fraudulent" one-way functions which break down completely if an adversary sees $F(x)$ and $F(x + 1)$ can easily be constructed as shown in the following example:

---

[5] To see that this is the case, note that an adversary can easily just generate additional preimage–image pairs on its own, as all information about the one-way function is known and preimages are sampled independently.

Example 9.10. *Let* $F : \{0,1\}^\lambda \to \{0,1\}^\lambda$ *be a one-way function taking* λ*-bit inputs. We construct a one-way function* $G : \{0,1\}^{2\lambda} \to \{0,1\}^{2\lambda}$ *as*

$$G(x_\ell \| x_r) := \begin{cases} x_\ell \| F(x_r) & \text{if } x_r \text{ is even, i.e., } \mathsf{lsb}(x) = 0 \\ F(x_\ell) \| x_r & \text{otherwise} \end{cases}$$

where x_ℓ *denotes the first* λ *input bits and* x_r *denotes the second* λ *input bits. It is easily seen that* G *is one-way if* F *is, because inverting* G *requires inverting* F *(and the additional information about the least significant bit of* x_r *does not facilitate this task significantly). However, for an even* $x \in \{0,1\}^{2\lambda}$ *we have that the left and right output halves allow to reconstruct* $x + 1$:

$$(x + 1) = G(x)[1..\lambda] \| G(x+1)[\lambda + 1..2\lambda].$$

Thus, an adversary seeing $G(x)$ *and* $G(x+1)$ *can easily reconstruct* x *for any choice of* $x \in \{0,1\}^{2\lambda}$.

In the following we study a security notion that covers also the case when input values are potentially highly correlated.

9.4.1 Correlated-Input Secure Hash Functions

Correlated-input secure hash functions (CIHs) can be regarded as a strengthening of the one-wayness notion and come in various flavors. We here consider the strongest form of correlated-input secure hash functions, which is also sometimes referred to as *pseudorandomness under correlated inputs*.

In order to obtain a security definition which is as general and as strong as possible, we let the adversary choose the inputs and, thus, consider an adversary $\mathcal{A} = (\mathcal{A}_1, \mathcal{A}_2)$ which is split into two stages, similarly, to the case of an IND-CPA adversary (see Definition 5.7 on page 220). We let the first-stage adversary $\mathcal{A}_1$ choose the inputs $x_1, \ldots, x_q$ while the second-stage adversary $\mathcal{A}_2$ then has to distinguish between either seeing the corresponding images $(F(x_1), \ldots, F(x_q))$ or uniformly random values $(r_1, \ldots, r_q)$.[6]

Assume that any of the outputs of $\mathcal{A}_1$ are *predictable*. Then an adversary could trivially win by simply guessing an output x_i of $\mathcal{A}_1$, recomputing $F(x_i)$, and comparing it with the given values. Similarly, if $x_i = x_j$ for $i \neq j$ then the function values would be identical, whereas random and independent r_i, r_j would most likely not coincide. To exclude such pathological adversaries we only consider *admissible* adversaries $\mathcal{A} = (\mathcal{A}_1, \mathcal{A}_2)$. We call an adversary

---

[6] We mentioned that CIH comes in different flavors, this being the strongest form. A definition more closely related to that of a one-way function would ask the second adversary to invert one of the images.

admissible if adversary $\mathcal{A}_1$ on input the security parameter 1^λ outputs a vector $\mathbf{x}$ of distinct values. Furthermore, we require that the guessing probability of each entry is negligible, that is, the min-entropy of $\mathbf{x}[i]$ for all $i \in \{1, \ldots, |\mathbf{x}|\}$ must be at least super-logarithmic in the security parameter. This yields the following formal definition:

Definition 9.11 (Correlated-Input Secure Hashing (CIH)). *We say that a function* H *is CIH secure if the advantage of any CIH-admissible* PPT *adversary* $\mathcal{A} = (\mathcal{A}_1, \mathcal{A}_2)$ *defined as*

$$\mathsf{Adv}^{\mathrm{cih}}_{\mathsf{H},\mathcal{A}}(\lambda) := 2 \cdot \Pr\left[\mathsf{Exp}^{\mathrm{cih}}_{\mathsf{H},\mathcal{A}}(\lambda)\right] - 1$$

is negligible and where experiment $\mathsf{Exp}^{\mathrm{cih}}_{\mathsf{H},\mathcal{A}}(\lambda)$ *is defined as*

Experiment $\mathsf{Exp}^{\mathrm{cih}}_{\mathsf{H},\mathcal{A}}(\lambda)$
1: $\quad b \leftarrow_\$ \{0,1\}$
2: $\quad \mathsf{hk} \leftarrow_\$ \mathsf{H.KGen}(1^\lambda)$
3: $\quad \mathbf{x} \leftarrow_\$ \mathcal{A}_1(1^\lambda)$
4: $\quad \textbf{for } i = 1..|\mathbf{x}| \textbf{ do}$
5: $\qquad \mathbf{h}_0[i] \leftarrow_\$ \{0,1\}^{\mathsf{H.ol}(\lambda)}$
6: $\qquad \mathbf{h}_1[i] \leftarrow \mathsf{H.Eval}(\mathsf{hk}, \mathbf{x}[i])$
7: $\quad b' \leftarrow_\$ \mathcal{A}_2(1^\lambda, \mathsf{hk}, \mathbf{h}_b)$
8: $\quad \textbf{return } (b = b')$

An adversary $\mathcal{A} := (\mathcal{A}_1, \mathcal{A}_2)$ *is called* CIH admissible *if* $\mathcal{A}_1$ *implements a statistically unpredictable distribution, that is, on input the security parameter adversary* $\mathcal{A}_1$ *outputs a vector* $\mathbf{x}$ *of distinct values and where for all* $i \in \{1, \ldots, |\mathbf{x}|\}$ *and all* $x \in \{0,1\}^{\mathsf{H.il}(\lambda)}$ *it holds that*

$$\Pr\left[x = \mathbf{x}[i] : \mathbf{x} \leftarrow_\$ \mathcal{A}_1(1^\lambda)\right] \leq \mathsf{negl}(\lambda).$$

Remark 9.12. An equivalent way of formalizing the unpredictability is via min-entropy. That is, we require that for all $i \in \{1, \ldots, |\mathbf{x}|\}$

$$\mathrm{H}_\infty(\mathbf{x}[i]) \in \omega(\log(\lambda)),$$

where $\mathbf{x}[i]$ denotes the random variable that runs $\mathcal{A}_1(\lambda)$ and outputs the ith message component. This notion of unpredictability is also sometimes referred to as *statistical* unpredictability.

Remark 9.13. Another equivalent, and more algorithmic way of defining unpredictability is to ask that no unbounded algorithm P, called predictor, can predict any of the outputs of $\mathcal{A}_1$ with noticeable probability. That is, for any (potentially unbounded) predictor P there exists a negligible function $negl(\lambda)$ such that

$$\Pr\left[\left(\begin{array}{l} \mathbf{x} \leftarrow_\$ \mathcal{A}_1(1^\lambda) \\ \tau \leftarrow P(1^\lambda) \\ \text{if } \exists i : \mathbf{x}[i] = \tau \text{ then} \\ \quad \text{return } 1 \\ \text{return } 0 \end{array}\right) = 1\right] \leq negl(\lambda).$$

Here the pseudocode represents a binary random variable and the randomness is over the random coins of $\mathcal{A}_1$ (note that we can assume the predictor to be deterministic as it is unbounded and can thus compute the best coins).

Remark 9.14. You may wonder why the first-stage adversary $\mathcal{A}_1$ is not given the function key hk. The reason is that in this case it would suffice for the adversary to output even a single message to win with high probability: Consider the adversary that chooses a random message x such that the first bit of H.Eval(hk, x) is 1. Value x is clearly highly unpredictable such that $\mathcal{A}_1$ is admissible. But now, together with adversary $\mathcal{A}_2$ which simply outputs the first bit of its input, adversary $(\mathcal{A}_1, \mathcal{A}_2)$ will win with advantage $\approx \frac{1}{2}$ as the first bit of a random value will be 0 half of the time.

Correlated-Input Security in the Random Oracle Model

In the random oracle model the adversary (i.e., $\mathcal{A}_1$ and $\mathcal{A}_2$) as well as the construction can access the random oracle. Consider an adversary $\mathcal{A}_1$ that simply outputs a single message $x = \mathsf{RO}(0)$. Now, even though $\mathsf{RO}(0)$ is a uniformly random value, it is trivial for $\mathcal{A}_2$ to distinguish $H(\mathsf{RO}(0))$ from a uniformly random value. Thus, in order to get a meaningful security notion we need to strengthen the restrictions on the first adversarial stage to hold independent of the random oracle. When viewing $\mathbf{x}[i]$ as the random variable which evaluates $\mathcal{A}_1^{\mathsf{RO}}(1^\lambda)$ then the min-entropy requirement now becomes

$$H_\infty(\mathbf{x}[i] \mid \langle \mathsf{RO} \rangle) \in \omega(\log(\lambda)).$$

In other words we require that for all $i \in \{1, \ldots, |\mathbf{x}|\}$, all $x \in \{0,1\}^{\mathsf{H.il}(\lambda)}$, and each choice of random oracle RO that the probability of $\mathcal{A}_1^{\mathsf{RO}}(1^\lambda)$ choosing x is negligible:

$$\Pr\left[x = \mathbf{x}[i] : \mathbf{x} \leftarrow_\$ \mathcal{A}_1^{\mathsf{RO}}(1^\lambda)\right] \leq negl(\lambda).$$

That is, the probability is *not* over the choice of random oracle but only over the random coins of $\mathcal{A}_1$.

9.4.2 Random Oracles Are Correlated-Input Secure

Correlated-input-secure hash functions trivially exist in the random oracle model: the random oracle itself yields an unkeyed correlated-input-secure function. Furthermore, we can construct a keyed correlation-secure hash function by, for example, reusing our construction of a pseudorandom function from the previous chapter:

$$
\begin{array}{ll}
\underline{\mathsf{H^{RO}.KGen}(1^\lambda)} & \underline{\mathsf{H^{RO}.Eval}(\mathsf{fk}, m)} \\[4pt]
1: \quad \mathsf{fk} \leftarrow\!\!{}^\$ \{0,1\}^\lambda & 1: \quad y \leftarrow \mathsf{RO}(\mathsf{fk}\|m) \\[4pt]
2: \quad \mathbf{return}\ \mathsf{fk} & 2: \quad \mathbf{return}\ y
\end{array}
$$

An alternative is to consider a keyed random oracle as discussed in Section 8.3.5 (page 359). Let us state the result formally.

> **Proposition 9.15.** *Let* RO *be a random oracle. Then* RO *is CIH secure.*

To see that this is the case, note that value $\mathsf{RO}(x)$ is a uniformly random value over the choice of the random oracle. Hence the only way for the second-stage adversary $\mathcal{A}_2$ to distinguish $\mathsf{RO}(x)$ from a uniformly chosen value r would be to query the random oracle on x. But since, by assumption, x is unpredictable this should be difficult.

Proof. Consider vector $\mathbf{h}_b$ that is given to the second-stage adversary $\mathcal{A}_2$. In case $b = 0$ all entries in $\mathbf{h}_b$ are generated by choosing a uniformly random value in $\{0,1\}^{\mathsf{RO.ol}(\lambda)}$. In case $b = 1$ the ith entry (for all $i \in [|\mathbf{x}|]$) is generated as $\mathsf{RO}(\mathbf{x}[i])$. As RO is a random oracle we can think of querying RO on a value $\mathbf{x}[i]$ as generating a random response which is also fixed in a function table for future reference (see the discussion on lazy sampling on page 341). Also note that all entries $\mathbf{x}[i]$ are distinct for an admissible adversary. Thus, in both cases all entries in $\mathbf{h}$ are uniformly random values, the only difference being that in case $b = 1$ they have a correspondence in the random oracle's function table.

By definition, we have that for values $\mathbf{x}$ as chosen by the first-stage adversary it holds for every choice of random oracle that

$$
\Pr\big[x = \mathbf{x}[i] : \mathbf{x} \leftarrow\!\!{}^\$ \mathcal{A}_1^{\mathsf{RO}}(1^\lambda)\big] \leq \mathsf{negl}(\lambda). \tag{9.1}
$$

In other words the probability in Equation (9.1) is only over the random coins of the adversary and not over the choice of random oracle.

Let q be an upper bound on the number of random oracle queries by $\mathcal{A}_2$. Unless $\mathcal{A}_2$ queries the random oracle on any of the values in $\mathbf{x}$ we have that the vectors $\mathbf{h}_0$ and $\mathbf{h}_1$ are identically distributed and thus perfectly indistinguishable, even by an adversary with unbounded resources. Let $\Pr[\mathsf{Guess}]$ denote the probability of guessing a value $x \in \mathbf{x}$ in Equation (9.1). Following the same line of reasoning as in the one-wayness proof of random oracles (Proposition 8.6 on page 348), we conclude that with q queries the probability of guessing one of the values in $\mathbf{x}$ is at most $q(\lambda) \cdot |\mathbf{x}| \cdot \Pr[\mathsf{Guess}]$. Since q and $|\mathbf{x}|$ are polynomial and, by assumption, $\mathcal{A}_1$ is admissible and thus $\Pr[\mathsf{Guess}]$ is negligible, we have that also $q(\lambda) \cdot |\mathbf{x}| \cdot \Pr[\mathsf{Guess}]$ is negligible. $\qquad\square$

9.4.3 Correlated-Input Security in the Standard Model

While efficient and practical correlated-input-secure hash functions trivially exist in the random oracle model—after all, a random oracle is CIH secure—we do not have *any* standard model constructions that achieve the security notion specified in Definition 9.11.[7] Indeed, it can be shown that standard model correlated-input-secure hash functions cannot be based on many standard cryptographic assumptions, and it thus might be the case that CIH-secure standard model functions simply do not exist.

9.5 Derandomization: Deterministic PKE

It is generally assumed that randomized decision algorithms are not (much) more powerful than deterministic decision algorithms. That is, anything that can be decided in polynomial time by a probabilistic Turing machine can be decided in polynomial time by a deterministic Turing machine. In the language of complexity theory this would mean that the complexity classes P and BPP are identical. While many researchers believe that P = BPP, we are not yet able to prove that this is indeed the case. When we consider random oracles, then this suddenly changes. Relative to a random oracle it can be shown that probabilistic and deterministic polynomial-time Turing machines have the same expressiveness. Formally, this result can be captured as

Theorem 9.16. *Let* RO *be a random oracle. Then* $\mathsf{P}^{\mathsf{RO}} = \mathsf{BPP}^{\mathsf{RO}}$.

We do not give the full proof here but instead discuss the intuition behind it. The statement $\mathsf{P}^{\mathsf{RO}} = \mathsf{BPP}^{\mathsf{RO}}$ can be translated to: for any probabilistic polynomial-time Turing machine M^{RO} which has access to a random oracle (via an oracle tape) we can construct a deterministic polynomial-time Turing machine $\mathsf{M}^{\mathsf{RO}}_{\mathsf{det}}$ such that on all inputs $x \in \{0,1\}^*$ the distributions induced by the Turing machines on input x are identical, that is,

$$\mathsf{M}^{\mathsf{RO}}(x) = \mathsf{M}^{\mathsf{RO}}_{\mathsf{det}}(x).$$

---

[7] Let us note that weaker notions of correlated-input security that further restrict the form of allowed correlation or that put (very) strong entropy requirements on the first-stage adversary (thus significantly reducing the number of considered *admissible* adversaries) exist also in the standard model.

In the first case the probability is over the coins of probabilistic Turing machine M and the choice of random oracle, while in the second case the probability is only over the choice of random oracle. After all, M_{det}^{RO} is deterministic.

The challenge is thus to construct Turing machine M_{det}^{RO} from the probabilistic Turing machine M^{RO}. The key idea is that M_{det}^{RO} can simulate M^{RO} by obtaining the necessary random coins from the random oracle. However, it must do so in such a way that the simulation is not detectable by M^{RO}. Furthermore, note that M_{det}^{RO} cannot simply simulate the random oracle for M^{RO} via lazy sampling, as it is deterministic. Hence it needs to forward any random oracle query by M^{RO} to its own random oracle. Now suppose M_{det}^{RO} is generating the random coins for the execution of M^{RO} by making random oracle calls $RO(0), RO(1), RO(2), \dots$ until sufficiently many random coins were generated. Then the "fake" random coins would be uniformly distributed and, furthermore, undetectable by M^{RO} unless M^{RO} makes a random oracle call for any of the messages used in the generation of the random coins. If that happens, it can immediately tell that its random coins are not uniformly generated and could, potentially, deviate from its normal behavior.

To fix the problem above we need to ensure that the random coins used in the simulation are generated by random oracle queries that cannot possibly be made by M^{RO}. The idea for this is simple. By assumption M^{RO} is efficient and thus there exists a polynomial p that upper bounds the runtime of M^{RO}. If M_{det}^{RO} now generates the random coins by choosing random oracle queries of length $p(\lambda) + 1$ then it can be assured that M^{RO} will never make a matching query. The runtime of M^{RO} is shorter than it would take to write down the query. On the other hand, we have that M_{det}^{RO} is still efficient (although it is slightly less efficient than M^{RO}).

What this shows is that random oracles can be used to generate entropy, that is, to generate random values that appear uniformly distributed as long as the consumer does not query the random oracle on the value that was used to generate the random coins. We have exploited that fact already in the proof of Proposition 9.15, where we could argue that random oracle values generated from unpredictable queries are indistinguishable from truly random values.

In the following we look at an application of derandomization and discuss a deterministic variant of a cryptographic primitive which is usually only considered in the probabilistic setting.

9.5.1 Deterministic Public-Key Encryption

Encryption schemes are usually randomized as otherwise security notions such as IND-CPA cannot be met (see Section 5.2.3; page 245). One consequence of having randomized public-key encryption schemes is that ciphertexts are necessarily longer than the corresponding plaintext message (Exercise 9.1

asks you to prove that this is, indeed, the case). Besides longer ciphertexts, randomization has also other drawbacks, depending on the use case. Consider, for example, that you want to encrypt data in a database, but still want to allow efficient lookups. If encryption was deterministic, the standard database index structures would allow for this. In case of probabilistic encryption, the same message would be most likely mapped to different ciphertexts, such that the entire database would need to be decrypted or additional helper structures would need to be put in place.

While the examples so far were efficiency related, there is also a potential security issue with randomized encryption schemes. As shown only recently, any randomized encryption scheme is susceptible to so-called *algorithm-substitution attacks*, which consider scenarios where encryption algorithms are replaced by subverted algorithms. These subverted algorithms produce ciphertexts which are indistinguishable from the actual encryption algorithm while allowing an adversarial party—the party that generated the subverted algorithm—to compromise the encryption scheme. For example, information about the encrypted message could be leaked, or in the case of symmetric schemes even the entire secret key. One way around such algorithm-substitution attacks are *deterministic* schemes, and in the following we consider the notion of *deterministic public-key encryption*.

Defining Security for Deterministic Public-Key Encryption

The syntax of a deterministic public-key encryption scheme DPKE is defined similarly to a randomized PKE scheme with the only difference that the encryption routine is deterministic. That is, a deterministic public-key encryption scheme DPKE := (DPKE.KGen, DPKE.Enc, DPKE.Dec) consists of a PPT algorithm DPKE.KGen and two *deterministic* polynomial-time algorithms DPKE.Enc and DPKE.Dec as follows. On input the security parameter, the randomized key generation algorithm DPKE.KGen(1^λ) generates a key pair (pk, sk). The deterministic encryption algorithm DPKE.Enc(pk, m) takes public key pk and message m as input and outputs a ciphertext c. The deterministic decryption algorithm DPKE.Dec(sk, c) is given the secret key sk as well as ciphertext c and outputs a plaintext or a special error symbol $\perp$. As usual, we denote the supported message length by DPKE.il(λ). Correctness of a deterministic public-key encryption scheme is defined analogously to correctness of randomized schemes.

Strong security notions such as IND-CPA security (see Definition 5.27 on page 246) can be easily attacked once the public-key encryption scheme is deterministic. For this, consider an adversary that outputs two distinct messages m_0 and m_1 to obtain a ciphertext c. In order to distinguish whether c is an encryption of m_0 or m_1 the adversary can simply recompute the encryptions of m_0 and m_1 as it has access to the public key. Since the encryption operation is deterministic and ciphertexts should be correctly decryptable, it must be the case that either $c = \mathsf{DPKE.Enc}(\mathsf{pk}, m_0)$ or $c = \mathsf{DPKE.Enc}(\mathsf{pk}, m_1)$.

This example pinpoints the weak spot of deterministic encryption. If there is little uncertainty about the message, an adversary can decrypt ciphertexts simply by trial and error. This, of course, has consequences as to what type of security we can expect from a deterministic public-key encryption scheme, and a minimum prerequisite is that plaintexts are unpredictable.

IND security. The standard security notion for DPKE schemes is IND security (short for indistinguishability of encryptions), which considers two adversarial stages $\mathcal{A} := (\mathcal{A}_1, \mathcal{A}_2)$ that do not share any state, similarly to the security notion for correlated-input security. On input the security parameter, adversary $\mathcal{A}_1$ outputs a pair of message vectors $(\mathbf{m}_0, \mathbf{m}_1)$ that are of the same length, which both have distinct elements, and such that each cross-vector component pair has the same length, that is, $|\mathbf{m}_0[i]| = |\mathbf{m}_1[i]|$ for all i. Furthermore, we require that $\mathcal{A}_1$ is *statistically unpredictable* for each component, that is each component has super-logarithmic min-entropy.[8] Then, a key pair $(\mathsf{pk}, \mathsf{sk}) \leftarrow\!\!\$\ \mathsf{DPKE.KGen}(1^\lambda)$ is chosen and according to a secret bit b one of the two message vectors is encrypted (component-wise). The second adversary $\mathcal{A}_2$ is run on the resulting vector of ciphertexts and the public key to output a guess b'. As usual, the adversary wins the game if it correctly guesses the hidden bit b, i.e., if $b = b'$. Following is the formal definition:

Definition 9.17 (IND security for DPKE). *We say that a deterministic public-key encryption scheme* $\mathsf{DPKE} := (\mathsf{DPKE.KGen}, \mathsf{DPKE.Enc}, \mathsf{DPKE.Dec})$ *is IND secure if the advantage of any IND-admissible PPT adversary* $\mathcal{A} = (\mathcal{A}_1, \mathcal{A}_2)$ *defined as*

$$\mathsf{Adv}^{\mathrm{ind}}_{\mathsf{DPKE},\mathcal{A}}(\lambda) := 2 \cdot \Pr\left[\mathsf{Exp}^{\mathrm{ind}}_{\mathsf{DPKE},\mathcal{A}}(\lambda)\right] - 1$$

is negligible and where experiment $\mathsf{Exp}^{\mathrm{ind}}_{\mathsf{DPKE},\mathcal{A}}(\lambda)$ *is defined as*

Experiment $\mathsf{Exp}^{\mathrm{ind}}_{\mathsf{DPKE},\mathcal{A}}(\lambda)$
1: $b \leftarrow\!\!\$\ \{0, 1\}$
2: $(\mathbf{m}_0, \mathbf{m}_1) \leftarrow\!\!\$\ \mathcal{A}_1(1^\lambda)$
3: $(\mathsf{pk}, \mathsf{sk}) \leftarrow\!\!\$\ \mathsf{DPKE.KGen}(1^\lambda)$
4: **for** $i = 1 .. |\mathbf{m}_0|$ **do**
5:      $\mathbf{c}[i] \leftarrow \mathsf{DPKE.Enc}(\mathsf{pk}, \mathbf{m}_b[i])$
6: $b' \leftarrow\!\!\$\ \mathcal{A}_2(\mathsf{pk}, \mathbf{c})$
7: **return** $(b = b')$

---

[8] Note that the requirements for adversarial stage $\mathcal{A}_1$ are identical to the CIH security setup, except that the adversary now outputs two vectors.

An adversary $\mathcal{A} := (\mathcal{A}_1, \mathcal{A}_2)$ is called IND admissible *if on input the security parameter adversary $\mathcal{A}_1$ outputs a pair of message vectors $(\mathbf{m}_0, \mathbf{m}_1)$ that are of the same length (i.e., $|\mathbf{m}_0| = |\mathbf{m}_1|$) and that are such that each cross-vector component pair has the same length, that is, $|\mathbf{m}_0[i]| = |\mathbf{m}_1[i]|$ for all $i \in [|\mathbf{m}_0|]$. Each vector must contain only distinct elements, that is, for $b \in \{0,1\}$ and for all $0 \leq i < j \leq |\mathbf{m}_0|$ we have that $\mathbf{m}_b[i] \neq \mathbf{m}_b[j]$. Finally, we require that $\mathcal{A}_1$ is statistically unpredictable, that is, for any $x \in \{0,1\}^{\mathsf{DPKE.il}(\lambda)}$, any $b \in \{0,1\}$, and any $i \in \mathbb{N}$ the probability*

$$\Pr\left[x = \mathbf{m}_b[i] : (\mathbf{m}_0, \mathbf{m}_1) \leftarrow\!\!{\$}\, \mathcal{A}_1(1^\lambda)\right]$$

is negligible.

Remark 9.18. The definition of IND admissible is admittedly rather cumbersome. However, each individual exclusion (e.g., same length vectors, distinct values, unpredictability, and cross-vector length) is necessary to exclude trivial adversaries. For example, if the vectors do not have the same length, for example, if $|\mathbf{m}_0| = n$ and $|\mathbf{m}_0| = n'$ with $n \neq n'$, then adversary $\mathcal{A}_2$ could simply check whether the provided ciphertext vector is of length n or of length n'. Similar simple adversaries exist in case we drop any of the other requirements.

Remark 9.19. Note that the first-stage adversary $\mathcal{A}_1$ samples the message vectors independently of the scheme's public key pk. Unlike probabilistic schemes, deterministic schemes therefore do not necessarily allow to securely encrypt messages depending on the public key. The reason for giving $\mathcal{A}_1$ only security parameter 1^λ as input is that otherwise no scheme can be secure in the sense of the definition. In case $\mathcal{A}_1$ had access to public key pk it could choose two distinct, equal-length messages m_0, m_1, deterministically encrypt them to c_0, c_1 with knowledge of the public key, and then put in $\mathbf{m}_0 = (m_a, m_{1-a})$ the two messages in the order such that $c_a < c_{1-a}$. The other vector is given by the reverse order $\mathbf{m}_1 = (m_{1-a}, m_a)$. The second-stage adversary $\mathcal{A}_2$ now simply outputs $b' = 0$ iff $\mathbf{c}[1] < \mathbf{c}[2]$.

DPKE Security in the Random Oracle Model

As is the case for CIH-secure hash functions, in the random oracle model both adversarial stages $\mathcal{A}_1$ and $\mathcal{A}_2$ (as well as the construction) are given access to the random oracle. Furthermore, we need to strengthen the unpredictability requirement on the message distributions to hold also relative to the random oracle. In other words we require that for all $x \in \{0,1\}^{\mathsf{DPKE.il}(\lambda)}$, all $b \in \{0,1\}$ and $i \in \mathbb{N}$, and each choice of RO the probability

$$\Pr\left[x = \mathbf{m}_b[i] : (\mathbf{m}_0, \mathbf{m}_1) \leftarrow\!\!{\$}\, \mathcal{A}_1^{\mathsf{RO}}(1^\lambda)\right]$$

is negligible; that is, the probability is *not* over the choice of random oracle but only over the random coins of $\mathcal{A}_1$.

9.5.2 The Encrypt-with-Hash Transformation

In the random oracle model deterministic public-key encryption schemes achieving IND security can be constructed from any IND-CPA-secure encryption scheme via the so-called *encrypt-with-hash* transformation. As we already saw, in the random oracle model we can construct IND-CPA-secure encryption schemes from a trapdoor function and, thus, we get that trapdoor functions imply the existence of IND-secure deterministic public-key encryption schemes in the random oracle model.

> **Theorem 9.20.** *If trapdoor one-way functions exist, then IND-secure deterministic public-key encryption schemes exist in the random oracle model.*

The encrypt-with-hash (EwH) transform constructs a deterministic public-key encryption scheme EwH[PKE] from a (randomized) public-key encryption scheme PKE in the random oracle model. The idea is to use the randomized encryption scheme as is, but to derandomize the encryption operation by generating the random coins via the random oracle directly from the input message and the public key. In other words, the random coins necessary to run the (randomized) encryption operation are generated as $r \leftarrow \mathsf{RO}(\mathsf{pk}\|m)$. To simplify the presentation we will assume in the following that the random oracle always produces values that are long enough, that is, $\mathsf{RO.ol}(\lambda) \geq \mathsf{PKE.rl}(\lambda)$, where PKE.rl denotes the number of random bits required by PKE.Eval. Following is a formal definition of the EwH scheme. Here we write $\mathsf{EwH[PKE]}^{\mathsf{RO}}$ to denote that the scheme uses public-key scheme PKE.

Construction 9.21 (Encrypt-with-Hash). *Let PKE be a randomized public-key encryption scheme. We define the deterministic public-key encryption scheme EwH[PKE] as*

$$\mathsf{EwH[PKE]}^{\mathsf{RO}}.\mathsf{KGen}(1^\lambda)$$

1 : $(\mathsf{pk}, \mathsf{sk}) \leftarrow_\$ \mathsf{PKE.KGen}(1^\lambda)$

2 : **return** $(\mathsf{pk}, \mathsf{sk})$

$\mathsf{EwH[PKE]}^{\mathsf{RO}}.\mathsf{Enc}(\mathsf{pk}, m)$	$\mathsf{EwH[PKE]}^{\mathsf{RO}}.\mathsf{Dec}(\mathsf{sk}, c)$
1 : $r \leftarrow \mathsf{RO}(\mathsf{pk}\|m)$	1 : $m \leftarrow \mathsf{PKE.Dec}(\mathsf{sk}, c)$
2 : $c \leftarrow \mathsf{PKE.Enc}(\mathsf{pk}, m; r)$	2 : **return** m
3 : **return** c	

For proving IND security of the encrypt-with-hash transformation we require that the underlying scheme is IND-CPA secure as well as that it is hard to predict the public key. The latter is required as otherwise an adversary can mount the attack outlined in Remark 9.19 above. The condition is, however, easily met as we can simply add redundant (randomly chosen) bits to the public key, $\mathsf{pk}' = \mathsf{pk}\|s$.

> **Proposition 9.22.** *If* PKE *is IND-CPA secure and the probability of guessing a public key as generated by* PKE.KGen *is negligible, then* EwH[PKE]^{RO} *is IND secure in the random oracle model.*

We will here not provide a formal proof of the statement as this takes some particular care when attempting a direct proof. We will, however, see a proof of the statement in a later part of this book (Section 18.3.3) via an abstraction called *universal computational extractor*.

For an outline of a direct proof we provide in Figure 9.8 the essential game hop. Starting from the IND game (i.e., the IND experiment $\mathsf{Exp}_{\mathsf{DPKE},\mathcal{A}}^{\mathsf{ind}}(\lambda)$) with the EwH construction we replace the generation of the coins r in line 5 by uniformly random coins. The idea is to argue that adversary $\mathcal{A}_1$ never queries the random oracle on a message containing the public key. This is also where the curious extra condition "and the probability of guessing a public key as generated by PKE.KGen is negligible" stems from. In case the public key can only be guessed with negligible probability it is safe to argue that $\mathcal{A}_1$ never queries the random oracle on a string that starts with pk. If that is the case then coins generated as $\mathsf{RO}(\mathsf{pk}\|\mathbf{m}_b[i])$ are uniformly distributed. This, of course, only holds in case $\mathcal{A}_2$ also never queries the random oracle on a message of the form $\mathsf{pk}\|\mathbf{m}_b[i]$. But this can be argued down to the security of the encryption scheme PKE and the entropy restrictions on message vector $\mathbf{m}_b$. Once we have reached Game$_2$ we are done as this game cannot be won by the adversary unless it breaks the IND-CPA security of the randomized encryption scheme PKE. In fact, Game$_2$ is identical to the IND-CPA game except for that the first-stage adversary does not get to see the public key and the two stages cannot share any state: two restrictions that only make it harder for the adversary to win.

9.5.3 DPKE in the Standard Model

The case of deterministic public-key encryption is very similar to that of correlated-input security. While simple constructions exist in the random oracle model that achieve IND security, deterministic public-key encryption without the use of random oracles has so far eluded cryptographers. All constructions that exist in the standard model achieve only weaker security definitions and need to, for example, place additional restrictions on the first-stage adversary $\mathcal{A}_1$. The one notable exception is a construction from

$$\mathsf{Game}_1^{\mathcal{A}}(\lambda)\xrightarrow{\text{RO + IND-Admissible } \mathcal{A}_1}\mathsf{Game}_2^{\mathcal{A}}(\lambda)\xrightarrow{\text{IND-CPA}}$$

1 : $b \leftarrow\!\!\$ \{0,1\}$	$b \leftarrow\!\!\$ \{0,1\}$
2 : $(\mathbf{m}_0,\mathbf{m}_1) \leftarrow\!\!\$ \mathcal{A}_1^{\mathsf{RO}}(1^\lambda)$	$(\mathbf{m}_0,\mathbf{m}_1) \leftarrow\!\!\$ \mathcal{A}_1^{\mathsf{RO}}(1^\lambda)$
3 : $(\mathsf{pk},\mathsf{sk}) \leftarrow\!\!\$ \mathsf{PKE.KGen}(1^\lambda)$	$(\mathsf{pk},\mathsf{sk}) \leftarrow\!\!\$ \mathsf{PKE.KGen}(1^\lambda)$
4 : **for** $i = 1..|\mathbf{m}_0|$ **do**	**for** $i = 1..|\mathbf{m}_0|$ **do**
5 : $\quad r \leftarrow \mathsf{RO}(\mathsf{pk}\|\mathbf{m}_b[i])$	$\quad r \leftarrow\!\!\$ \{0,1\}^{\mathsf{PKE.rl}(\lambda)}$
6 : $\quad \mathbf{c}[i] \leftarrow \mathsf{PKE.Enc}(\mathsf{pk},\mathbf{m}_b[i];r)$	$\quad \mathbf{c}[i] \leftarrow \mathsf{PKE.Enc}(\mathsf{pk},\mathbf{m}_b[i];r)$
7 : $b' \leftarrow\!\!\$ \mathcal{A}_2^{\mathsf{RO}}(\mathsf{pk},\mathbf{c})$	$b' \leftarrow\!\!\$ \mathcal{A}_2^{\mathsf{RO}}(\mathsf{pk},\mathbf{c})$
8 : **return** $(b = b')$	**return** $(b = b')$

Fig. 9.8: The critical game hop for proving the security of the encrypt-with-hash transformation (Proposition 9.22).

universal computational extractors, but as we will see in Chapter 18 practical UCEs have themselves only been constructed in the random oracle model.

9.6 Conclusion

In this chapter we have exemplified the commonly used properties of random oracles by discussing selected schemes and their security guarantees. On the functional side the properties are unpredictability, correlation intractability, and the ability for derandomization. These properties follow from the mathematical modeling of random oracles as random functions where each output is independently and uniformly distributed. Regarding reductions we have discussed the properties of observability and programmability. These properties are concerned with how the adversary interacts with the random oracle and how the reduction can interfere in this interaction.

We do not claim that the five properties we have investigated are exclusive. There may be many other useful features of random oracles which can be exploited in the design of schemes and their security proofs. Yet, it seems that the properties in this chapter are the ones which appear frequently in the literature, with the properties of unpredictability, observability, and programmability arguably mentioned explicitly most often.

We, also, have not tried to formalize the five properties, as our goal was to give an overview over the techniques which can be used in connection with random oracles. Any formalizations—and there are approaches to do so, see the Chapter Notes below—are inherently tied to the context in which the random oracle is deployed. Very often there are also many subtleties and choices for the notions themselves, especially when it comes to the reductionist's properties (e.g., how we ensure that a non-programming reduction does not ignore the external random oracle and instead simulates such an oracle internally, or if an observing reduction also sees the oracle's replies). Unlike, for example, in the cases of security of encryption or signature schemes, there does not seem to be a general agreement about the right notions—a topic which we will get back to in Chapter 12. Conclusively, the inevitable lack of rigor does not allow to compare different random oracle properties, even within the mathematical domain (unpredictability, correlation intractability, and derandomization) or within the reductionist setting (observability and programmability).

The properties we have discussed here may also need to be reconsidered when switching to different attacker models, especially if the adversary has quantum power. Recall that the idea of the random oracle model is to eventually instantiate the random oracle by a real-world hash function. This hash function is publicly computable, i.e., it does not involve any secret key, such that a quantum adversary may execute the hash function on its quantum computer. This allows the adversary to evaluate the hash function in superposition, basically computing many hash values in parallel but such that the results are "combined" into a single quantum state. To capture such possibilities one can extend the random oracle model to the quantum case, allowing superposition queries to the random oracle. This model is usually called the QROM. The QROM extension, however, infringes some of the properties above, especially observability and programmability, because one may not be able to detect specific values in the superposition "cloud of queries" or to alter the answers easily.

Chapter Notes and References

Already in 1985, David Chaum introduced the idea of a digital currency [11], and proofs of work were introduced by Dwork and Naor in 1992 [12]. Nevertheless, it took another 20 years before the first fully operational cryptocurrency Bitcoin was established. On October 31st 2008 a person (or multiple people) under the pseudonym Satoshi Nakamoto published a paper introducing the Bitcoin cryptocurrency [19], which went operational in January 2009. For a detailed description of Bitcoin see [7, 1]. Further information about Satoshi Nakamoto and the history of Bitcoin can be found in [10]. A cryptographic analysis of the core of Bitcoin is given by Garay, Kiayias, and Leonardos [15, 16, 17].

The programmability of random oracles was first formally studied by Nielsen [20]. Formal definitions of (non-)programming random oracles are given by Fischlin *et al.* [13]. The BR93 public-key encryption scheme (Section 9.2.2) as well as the full domain hash construction of digital signature schemes (Section 9.3.1) is due to Bellare and Rogaway [5].

Correlated-input security for hash functions was first discussed by Goyal, O'Neill, and Rao in 2011 [18], who introduced three different flavors forming a hierarchy: *one-wayness* under correlated inputs, *unpredictability* under correlated inputs, and *pseudorandomness* under correlated inputs, which yields the strongest of the notions and which we discussed in Section 9.4.1. Standard model constructions achieving restricted forms of CIH security were given by Goyal *et al.* [18], Freeman *et al.* [14], as well as Rosen and Segev [21]. The difficulty of constructing CIH-secure functions in the standard model was explained by Wichs in 2013 [22], who showed that there exists an inefficient attack that can be efficiently simulated which means, in essence, that we cannot hope to find a security reduction for a CIH construction down to any standard (single-stage) cryptographic assumption, which includes, for example, factoring and the discrete logarithm problem.

Derandomization properties of random oracles were studied by Bennet and Gill in 1981 [6], who also showed that relative to random oracles the complexity classes BPP and P are identical. In the same work they also demonstrate that $\mathsf{P}^{\mathsf{RO}} \neq \mathsf{NP}^{\mathsf{RO}}$ relative to a random oracle.

Deterministic public-key encryption and the encrypt-with-hash transformation were introduced by Bellare, Boldyreva, and O'Neill in 2007 [2]. The IND security notion discussed in Section 9.5.1 is discussed in [3, 8]. Algorithm-substitution attacks and the vulnerability of any randomized public-key encryption scheme were first presented by Bellare, Paterson, and Rogaway in 2014 [4].

The quantum version of the ROM was introduced in the work by Boneh *et al.* [9], hinting, in particular, at the problems one may encounter in the QROM with "common random oracle techniques." Meanwhile, there have been several positive results showing that some of the techniques can still be applied (to some extent) in this setting, e.g., [23, 24].

Exercices

Exercise 9.1. Show that, in randomized public-key encryption schemes, ciphertexts are longer than the corresponding plaintext message.

Exercise 9.2. Let $0 \leq \tau < 2^\lambda$ be a target value and let RO be a random oracle with output length $\mathsf{RO.ol}(\lambda) = \lambda$. How many random oracle calls does it take on average to find a value x such that $\mathsf{RO}(x) < \tau$?

Exercise 9.3. Definition 9.17 (page 398) of a deterministic public-key encryption scheme requires adversaries to be *admissible*. Show that in case any of the listed requirements is dropped that then a trivial adversary exists that breaks IND security for any scheme DPKE.

Chapter Bibliography

1. Andreas M Antonopoulos. *Mastering bitcoin: Programming the open blockchain.* O'Reilly Media, Inc., 2017.
2. Mihir Bellare, Alexandra Boldyreva, and Adam O'Neill. Deterministic and efficiently searchable encryption. In Alfred Menezes, editor, *Advances in Cryptology – CRYPTO 2007*, volume 4622 of *Lecture Notes in Computer Science*, pages 535–552, Santa Barbara, CA, USA, August 19–23, 2007. Springer, Heidelberg, Germany.
3. Mihir Bellare, Marc Fischlin, Adam O'Neill, and Thomas Ristenpart. Deterministic encryption: Definitional equivalences and constructions without random oracles. In David Wagner, editor, *Advances in Cryptology – CRYPTO 2008*, volume 5157 of *Lecture Notes in Computer Science*, pages 360–378, Santa Barbara, CA, USA, August 17–21, 2008. Springer, Heidelberg, Germany.
4. Mihir Bellare, Kenneth G. Paterson, and Phillip Rogaway. Security of symmetric encryption against mass surveillance. In Juan A. Garay and Rosario Gennaro, editors, *Advances in Cryptology – CRYPTO 2014, Part I*, volume 8616 of *Lecture Notes in Computer Science*, pages 1–19, Santa Barbara, CA, USA, August 17–21, 2014. Springer, Heidelberg, Germany.
5. Mihir Bellare and Phillip Rogaway. Random oracles are practical: A paradigm for designing efficient protocols. In Dorothy E. Denning, Raymond Pyle, Ravi Ganesan, Ravi S. Sandhu, and Victoria Ashby, editors, *ACM CCS 93: 1st Conference on Computer and Communications Security*, pages 62–73, Fairfax, Virginia, USA, November 3–5, 1993. ACM Press.
6. Charles H Bennett and John Gill. Relative to a random oracle a, $\mathbf{p}^a \neq \mathbf{np}^a \neq \text{co-}\mathbf{np}^a$ with probability 1. *SIAM Journal on Computing*, 10(1):96–113, 1981.
7. Bitcoin Project. Bitcoin developer guide. `https://bitcoin.org/en/developer-guide`.
8. Alexandra Boldyreva, Serge Fehr, and Adam O'Neill. On notions of security for deterministic encryption, and efficient constructions without random oracles. In David Wagner, editor, *Advances in Cryptology – CRYPTO 2008*, volume 5157 of *Lecture Notes in Computer Science*, pages 335–359, Santa Barbara, CA, USA, August 17–21, 2008. Springer, Heidelberg, Germany.
9. Dan Boneh, Özgür Dagdelen, Marc Fischlin, Anja Lehmann, Christian Schaffner, and Mark Zhandry. Random oracles in a quantum world. In Dong Hoon Lee and Xiaoyun Wang, editors, *Advances in Cryptology – ASIACRYPT 2011*, volume 7073 of *Lecture Notes in Computer Science*, pages 41–69, Seoul, South Korea, December 4–8, 2011. Springer, Heidelberg, Germany.
10. Phil Champagne. The book of Satoshi. *Lexington, KY: e53 Publishing*, 2014.
11. David Chaum. Security without identification: Transaction systems to make big brother obsolete. *Communications of the ACM*, 28(10):1030–1044, 1985.
12. Cynthia Dwork and Moni Naor. Pricing via processing or combatting junk mail. In Ernest F. Brickell, editor, *Advances in Cryptology – CRYPTO'92*, volume 740 of *Lecture Notes in Computer Science*, pages 139–147, Santa Barbara, CA, USA, August 16–20, 1993. Springer, Heidelberg, Germany.
13. Marc Fischlin, Anja Lehmann, Thomas Ristenpart, Thomas Shrimpton, Martijn Stam, and Stefano Tessaro. Random oracles with(out) programmability. In Masayuki Abe, editor, *Advances in Cryptology – ASIACRYPT 2010*, volume 6477 of *Lecture Notes in Computer Science*, pages 303–320, Singapore, December 5–9, 2010. Springer, Heidelberg, Germany.
14. David Mandell Freeman, Oded Goldreich, Eike Kiltz, Alon Rosen, and Gil Segev. More constructions of lossy and correlation-secure trapdoor functions. *Journal of Cryptology*, 26(1):39–74, January 2013.
15. Juan Garay, Aggelos Kiayias, and Nikos Leonardos. The bitcoin backbone protocol: Analysis and applications. Cryptology ePrint Archive, Report 2014/765, 2014. `http://eprint.iacr.org/2014/765`.

16. Juan A. Garay, Aggelos Kiayias, and Nikos Leonardos. The bitcoin backbone protocol: Analysis and applications. In Elisabeth Oswald and Marc Fischlin, editors, *Advances in Cryptology – EUROCRYPT 2015, Part II*, volume 9057 of *Lecture Notes in Computer Science*, pages 281–310, Sofia, Bulgaria, April 26–30, 2015. Springer, Heidelberg, Germany.

17. Juan A. Garay, Aggelos Kiayias, and Nikos Leonardos. The bitcoin backbone protocol with chains of variable difficulty. In Jonathan Katz and Hovav Shacham, editors, *Advances in Cryptology – CRYPTO 2017, Part I*, volume 10401 of *Lecture Notes in Computer Science*, pages 291–323, Santa Barbara, CA, USA, August 20–24, 2017. Springer, Heidelberg, Germany.

18. Vipul Goyal, Adam O'Neill, and Vanishree Rao. Correlated-input secure hash functions. In Yuval Ishai, editor, *TCC 2011: 8th Theory of Cryptography Conference*, volume 6597 of *Lecture Notes in Computer Science*, pages 182–200, Providence, RI, USA, March 28–30, 2011. Springer, Heidelberg, Germany.

19. Satoshi Nakamoto. Bitcoin: A peer-to-peer electronic cash system. `https://bitcoin.org/bitcoin.pdf`, 10 2008.

20. Jesper Buus Nielsen. Separating random oracle proofs from complexity theoretic proofs: The non-committing encryption case. In Moti Yung, editor, *Advances in Cryptology – CRYPTO 2002*, volume 2442 of *Lecture Notes in Computer Science*, pages 111–126, Santa Barbara, CA, USA, August 18–22, 2002. Springer, Heidelberg, Germany.

21. Alon Rosen and Gil Segev. Chosen-ciphertext security via correlated products. *SIAM Journal on Computing*, 39(7):3058–3088, 2010.

22. Daniel Wichs. Barriers in cryptography with weak, correlated and leaky sources. In Robert D. Kleinberg, editor, *ITCS 2013: 4th Innovations in Theoretical Computer Science*, pages 111–126, Berkeley, CA, USA, January 9–12, 2013. Association for Computing Machinery.

23. Mark Zhandry. Secure identity-based encryption in the quantum random oracle model. In Reihaneh Safavi-Naini and Ran Canetti, editors, *Advances in Cryptology – CRYPTO 2012*, volume 7417 of *Lecture Notes in Computer Science*, pages 758–775, Santa Barbara, CA, USA, August 19–23, 2012. Springer, Heidelberg, Germany.

24. Mark Zhandry. How to record quantum queries, and applications to quantum indifferentiability. In Alexandra Boldyreva and Daniele Micciancio, editors, *Advances in Cryptology – CRYPTO 2019, Part II*, volume 11693 of *Lecture Notes in Computer Science*, pages 239–268, Santa Barbara, CA, USA, August 18–22, 2019. Springer, Heidelberg, Germany.

Chapter 10
Random Oracle Schemes in Practice

In the following we give an overview about cryptographic schemes in practice and standards which rely on the random oracle methodology. In all cases the power of random oracles facilitates the design of very efficient solutions, usually combined with suitable number-theoretic primitives such as the discrete-logarithm-based one-way function or the RSA trapdoor function. Since the math needed for these primitives is quite different from what we have encountered so far, we start with a brief introduction into the relevant concepts from algebra and number theory. Readers familiar with modular arithmetic and the assumptions may skip Section 10.1 and directly proceed to Section 10.2 about the Fiat–Shamir signature schemes.

The *Fiat–Shamir approach* is our first example of how random oracles emerge in modern schemes. It is a general construction method for building fast signature schemes and, historically, can be seen as the origin of the random oracle methodology. Because of this, we present the security argument for this proof in the random oracle model in detail, focusing on the discrete-logarithm case for sake of concreteness. This version of the Fiat–Shamir approach is also known as the Schnorr signature scheme and appears, for example, in the ISO 14888-3 standard and in the EdDSA standard RFC 8032 of the Internet Engineering Task Force (IETF). The latter is one of the supported signature algorithms in the Transport Layer Security protocol TLS in version 1.3 to protect Internet communication.

The other examples of real-world random oracle schemes we present in this chapter are the *optimal asymmetric encryption padding (OAEP)*, the *probabilistic signature scheme (PSS)*, and the *Fujisaki–Okamato hybrid encryption transform*. OAEP enables IND-CCA-secure encryption based on trapdoor permutations like RSA, with a small expansion factor. The scheme is, for instance, described in the RFC 8017 standard of the IETF. This standard also defines the probabilistic signature scheme (PSS), which is also based on the RSA trapdoor function. The PSS scheme is another supported signature scheme in TLS 1.3. In between, we present the Fujisaki–Okamato hybrid

© Springer Nature Switzerland AG 2021
A. Mittelbach, M. Fischlin, *The Theory of Hash Functions and Random Oracles*,
Information Security and Cryptography, https://doi.org/10.1007/978-3-030-63287-8_10

encryption transform, a widely applicable method to lift the security of a public-key encryption scheme from IND-CPA to IND-CCA.

10.1 Number-Theoretic Assumptions

In the following we introduce two well-known problems in cryptography: the *discrete-logarithm problem* yielding a candidate for a one-way function and the *RSA problem* as a candidate for a trapdoor permutation. Note that we here speak of candidates because, given our current knowledge, we are unable to prove that the problems are, indeed, cryptographically hard. However, after having withstood several decades of attacks they are believed to be hard. Below we begin with the discrete-logarithm problem and then discuss RSA, but before introduce some number-theoretic basics for both problems.

10.1.1 Number-Theoretic Background

Groups

The discrete-logarithm problem was originally introduced for the residue class $\mathbb{Z}_p^*$ over the integers, but nowadays one often uses so-called elliptic curves. Both mathematical structures can be subsumed abstractly under so-called *groups*.

Definition 10.1 (Group). *A group $\mathcal{G}$ is a set of elements with an operation $\diamond : \mathcal{G} \times \mathcal{G} \to \mathcal{G}$ on the group elements such that the following hold:*

Associativity: $(a \diamond b) \diamond c = a \diamond (b \diamond c)$ *for all $a, b, c \in \mathcal{G}$.*
Identity Element: *There exists an identity element $e \in \mathcal{G}$ such that $a \diamond e = e \diamond a = a$ for all $a \in \mathcal{G}$.*
Inverse Element: *For any $a \in \mathcal{G}$ there exists an inverse element $b \in \mathcal{G}$ such that $a \diamond b = b \diamond a = e$.*

A group is called abelian *or* commutative *if, in addition, the following property holds:*

Commutativity: $a \diamond b = b \diamond a$ *for all $a, b \in \mathcal{G}$.*

Observe that the identity element is simultaneously left identity $(e \diamond a = a)$ and right identity $(a \diamond e = a)$, and that b is at the same time left inverse $(b \diamond a = e)$ and right inverse $(a \diamond b = e)$ to a. It can be shown that the corresponding statement for one side already implies the one for the other side (Exercise 10.1).

The additive and multiplicative groups over $\mathbb{Z}_m$. The set of residues $\mathbb{Z}_m = \{0, 1, 2, \ldots, m-1\}$ together with addition "+" forms a commutative group, where we define addition of elements $a, b \in \mathbb{Z}_m$ as

$$a + b = c \bmod m \iff \text{there is } i \in \mathbb{Z} \text{ such that } a + b = c + i \cdot m.$$

In other words, one adds the elements a, b over the integers and subtracts a multiple of m to map the value to an element c between 0 and $m-1$. In particular, for any $a \in \mathbb{Z}_m$ and any integer i one has $a + im = a \bmod m$. We also use the common notation $a = b = c = \cdots = y = z \bmod m$ if $a = b \bmod m$, $b = c \bmod m$, ..., and $y = z \bmod m$.

It is easy to verify that $\mathbb{Z}_m$ with addition forms a commutative group with identity element 0 (Exercise 10.2). The inverse of an element a for such an additive group is usually denoted as $-a$.

Example 10.2. *Consider $m = 6$ and $\mathbb{Z}_6 = \{0, 1, 2, 3, 4, 5\}$ with addition. Then $3 + 4 = 1 \bmod 6$ and $-3 = 3 \bmod 6$ since $3 + (-3) = 3 + 3 = 0 \bmod 6$, i.e., 3 is self-inverse.*

For the discrete-logarithm problem one uses the group defined by multiplication "$\cdot$" over the residues $\mathbb{Z}_m$, where multiplication is specified analogously to addition as

$$a \cdot b = c \bmod m \iff \text{there is } i \in \mathbb{Z} \text{ such that } a \cdot b = c + i \cdot m.$$

Here, the identity element is 1 and commutativity and associativity hold, but not every element $a \in \mathbb{Z}_m$ has a multiplicative inverse a^{-1} with $a \cdot a^{-1} = 1 \bmod m$. Consider for example the element 2 in $\mathbb{Z}_6$ where the multiplication with any element from $\mathbb{Z}_6$ yields a value different from the identity element 1:

$$2 \cdot 0 = 0 \bmod 6 \qquad 2 \cdot 2 = 4 \bmod 6 \qquad 2 \cdot 4 = 2 \bmod 6$$
$$2 \cdot 1 = 2 \bmod 6 \qquad 2 \cdot 3 = 0 \bmod 6 \qquad 2 \cdot 5 = 4 \bmod 6$$

When restricting the set $\mathbb{Z}_m$ to the set of elements which have a multiplicative inverse, denoted as

$$\mathbb{Z}_m^* := \{a \in \mathbb{Z}_m \mid \text{there is } b \in \mathbb{Z}_m \text{ such that } a \cdot b = 1 \bmod m\},$$

one obtains a commutative group. Commutativity and associativity of the superset $\mathbb{Z}_m$ (with multiplication) are inherited, and 1 is also the identity element for $\mathbb{Z}_m^*$. Each element in $\mathbb{Z}_m^*$ has a multiplicative inverse by definition. The final point is to note that $a \cdot b$ for $a, b \in \mathbb{Z}_m^*$ is again an element in $\mathbb{Z}_m^*$. To see this note that both elements a, b have inverses a^{-1}, b^{-1} in $\mathbb{Z}_m^*$ such that $b^{-1} \cdot a^{-1}$ is the inverse to $a \cdot b$ according to the group laws:

$$(b^{-1} \cdot a^{-1}) \cdot (a \cdot b) = b^{-1} \cdot (a^{-1} \cdot (a \cdot b)) = b^{-1} \cdot ((a^{-1} \cdot a) \cdot b) = b^{-1} \cdot (1 \cdot b) = b^{-1} \cdot b = 1.$$

Computing multiplicative inverses in $\mathbb{Z}_m^*$. An alternative way to characterize $\mathbb{Z}_m^*$ is to use the notion of *relative primality* (also called *coprimality*). Two integers a, b are called relative prime (alias coprime) if the greatest common divisor $\gcd(a, b)$—the largest integer that divides both a and b without remainder—of both values is 1. In other words, the integers are relatively prime if they do not have a prime factor in common. Then,

$$\mathbb{Z}_m^* = \{a \in \mathbb{Z}_m \mid \gcd(a, m) = 1\}.$$

To see this we use Bézout's lemma, which says that, for any positive integers a, b, there exist integers $x, y \in \mathbb{Z}$ such that

$$ax + by = \gcd(a, b).$$

If we now use $b = m$ and $a \in \mathbb{Z}_m$ with $\gcd(a, m) = 1$ in this lemma, then we obtain x, y with

$$1 = \gcd(a, m) = ax + my = ax \bmod m,$$

such that x is the multiplicative inverse a^{-1} to a in $\mathbb{Z}_m$. Vice versa, if for $a \in \mathbb{Z}_m$ there exists a^{-1} with $a \cdot a^{-1} = 1 \bmod m$, then this means that there exists $i \in \mathbb{Z}$ such that $a \cdot a^{-1} - i \cdot m = 1$ over the integers, implying that $\gcd(a, m) = 1$. Otherwise, if a and m had a common divisor $d \geq 2$, then $d \cdot \left(\frac{a}{d} \cdot a^{-1} - i \cdot \frac{m}{d}\right) = 1$, where the term in parentheses would be an integer, such that $d \geq 2$ would divide 1 over the integers.

Example 10.3. *For $m = 6$ the multiplicative group $\mathbb{Z}_6^*$ consists of the elements $\mathbb{Z}_6^* = \{1, 5\}$ since only these two integers are relative prime to $m = 6$ with prime factors 2 and 3. Indeed, $5^{-1} = 5$ because $5 \cdot 5 = 25 = 1 \bmod 6$.*

Euler's totient function $\phi(m)$ is defined by the number of positive integers up to m that are relatively prime to m, in other words, as the number of elements in $\mathbb{Z}_m^*$. For a prime $m = p$, all elements of $\mathbb{Z}_m$ except for 0 are relatively prime to p such that

$$\phi(p) = p - 1 \quad \text{for } p \text{ prime}.$$

Similarly, for a prime power $m = p^k$ only the $(p^k - p)$ many multiples $i \cdot p$ (for $i = 0, 1, \ldots, (p^k - p) - 1$) share a non-trivial factor p with p^k; all other elements are coprime to p^k such that we have altogether

$$\phi(p^k) = p^k - (p^k - p) = p^{k-1}(p - 1) = p^k \left(1 - \frac{1}{p}\right)$$

relatively prime elements in $\mathbb{Z}_{p^k}$. For composite numbers N with prime factorization $N = \prod_{i=1}^n p_i^{k_i}$, Euler's function is given by

gcd(a, b)

   // Input: Integers a, b with $a \geq b > 0$

1 : **if** $a \bmod b = 0$ **do**

2 :   **return** a

3 : **return** gcd$(b, a \bmod b)$

egcd(a, b)

   // Input: Integers a, b with $a \geq b > 0$

   // Output: (d, x, y) such that $d = \gcd(a, b)$

   //   and $ax + by = \gcd(a, b)$

1 : **if** $b = 0$ **then return** $(a, 1, 0)$

2 : $(d, x', y') \leftarrow$ egcd$(b, a \bmod b)$

3 : $q \leftarrow a$ div b // integer division

4 : **return** $(d, y', x' - q \cdot y')$

Fig. 10.1: The Euclidean algorithm for computing the greatest common divisor on the left and the extended Euclidean algorithm on the right, which in addition to the gcd outputs values x and y such that $ax + by = gcd(a, b)$.

$$\phi(N) = \prod_{i=1}^{n} \phi(p_i^{k_i}) = \prod_{i=1}^{n} p_i^{k_i - 1}(p_i - 1).$$

The Euclidean algorithm computes the greatest common divisor of two numbers. The extended Euclidean algorithm, given a, b as in Bézout's lemma, also allows to compute gcd(a, b) and, in addition and without significant overhead, also integers x and y such that $ax + by = $ gcd(a, b). In particular, for $b = m$ one obtains the multiplicative inverse $a^{-1} \in \mathbb{Z}_m^*$ to a by adding or subtracting the right multiple of m to resp. from x. The runtime of the algorithm is polynomial in the length of the numbers a and b. We give the pseudocode of the extended Euclidean algorithm in Figure 10.1.

The structure of the group $\mathbb{Z}_m$. From now on we consider finite groups in multiplicative form. We use the common notation that ab is short for $a \cdot b$ and $a^i = a \cdot \ldots \cdot a$ is the product of multiplying i times element a. The *order* ord$(\mathcal{G})$ of a (finite) group $\mathcal{G}$ is the number of elements. We can also speak of the *order* ord$_{\mathcal{G}}(a)$ of an element $a \in \mathcal{G}$, which is the smallest positive integer $i \in \mathbb{N}$ such that $a^i = e$ in the group. Here e denotes the identity, which in a multiplicative group would be 1 and in additive groups would be 0. Also see the following example:

Example 10.4. *The multiplicative group $(\mathbb{Z}_6^*, \cdot)$ has order 2 since it consists of $\{1, 5\}$. The order of the element 1 is 1, because $1^1 = 1 \bmod 6$. The order of 5 is 2, since $5^1 \neq 1 \bmod 6$ and $5^2 = 1 \bmod 6$.*

For the additive group $(\mathbb{Z}_6, +)$ the powers a^i correspond to the i-fold sum of the element a, usually written as $i \cdot a$. The group $(\mathbb{Z}_6, +)$ consists of the elements $\{0, 1, 2, 3, 4, 5\}$ and thus has order 6. The order of the element 0 in this group is 1, because $1 \cdot 0 = 0 \bmod 6$. The order of 2 is 3, because $3 \cdot 2 = 2 + 2 + 2 = 0 \bmod 6$ while $1 \cdot 2$ and $2 \cdot 2$ are non-zero. Similarly, the order of 1 is 6 since all other sums $1 + \cdots + 1$ with fewer elements are non-zero.

A (finite) group $\mathcal{G}$ is *cyclic* if there is an element $g \in \mathcal{G}$ such that $\mathcal{G} = \{g^i \mid i \in \{0, 1, 2, \ldots, \mathrm{ord}(\mathcal{G}) - 1\}\}$. This means that the whole group is generated by the powers of g, and in this case one writes $\mathcal{G} = \langle g \rangle$. In particular, a cyclic group is always commutative because any $a, b \in \mathcal{G}$ can be written as $a = g^i$ and $b = g^j$ and hence

$$a \cdot b = g^i \cdot g^j = g^{i+j} = g^{j+i} = g^j \cdot g^i = b \cdot a.$$

Element g is also called *generator* of group $\mathcal{G}$.

Example 10.5. *The groups* $(\mathbb{Z}_6, +)$ *and* $(\mathbb{Z}_6^*, \cdot)$ *from the above example are cyclic and have generator 1 and 5, respectively.*

An important result is that for any prime p the groups $(\mathbb{Z}_p, +)$ and $(\mathbb{Z}_p^*, \cdot)$ are cyclic.

Subgroups

A subgroup $\mathcal{H} \subseteq \mathcal{G}$ to a group is a (non-empty) subset of elements which is closed under the group operation and inverses. That is, if $a, b \in \mathcal{H}$, then so are $a \diamond b$ and the inverse element b^{-1} to b. This can be expressed equivalently by demanding that for each $a, b \in \mathcal{H}$ one also has $a \diamond b^{-1} \in \mathcal{H}$.

Example 10.6. *The elements* $\{0, 2, 4\}$ *with addition form a subgroup of* $(\mathbb{Z}_6, +)$, *since any sum of two elements is again in the set and each element has its additive inverse in the set.*

For a finite cyclic group $\mathcal{G} = \langle g \rangle$ any subgroup can be described by the powers $\langle g^i \rangle$ for some $i \in \mathbb{N}$. In particular, if one considers the group $\mathbb{Z}_p^*$ generated by some element g, then the order of the group is $p - 1$ and the group is given by the elements $g^0, g^1, \ldots, g^{p-2}$. Since we also have that $g^{p-1} = g^0 = 1$, we obtain *Fermat's little theorem*:

$$a^{p-1} = 1 \bmod p \quad \text{for any } a \in \mathbb{Z}_p^*.$$

The reason is that we can write a as $a = g^i$ in the cyclic group, and then have

$$a^{p-1} = (g^i)^{p-1} = g^{i \cdot (p-1)} = (g^{p-1})^i = 1^i = 1 \bmod p.$$

Fermat's little theorem also enables us to pick subgroups of special forms: Suppose that $p - 1 = wq$ for another prime q and some integer w. Such primes are often beneficial in cryptographic settings. Note that while p has only the trivial factors 1 and p, the value $p - 1$ has more prime factors for $p \geq 5$. Which order has the cyclic subgroup $\langle g^w \rangle$? Clearly, all powers $(g^w)^i$ for $i = 0, 1, 2, \ldots, q - 1$ are distinct elements in $\mathbb{Z}_p^*$, and $g^{wq} = g^{p-1} = 1 \bmod p$. Furthermore for $i > q$ the powers repeat. For instance,

$$(g^w)^{q+1} = g^{wq} \cdot g^w = g^{p-1} \cdot g^w = 1 \cdot g^w = g^w \bmod p.$$

Hence, the order of g^w is q. This gives us a method to pick subgroups of a certain order for $\mathbb{Z}_p^* = \langle g \rangle$ if we know g and the prime factorization of $p - 1$.

Generating a subgroup. Assume that our goal is to pick a subgroup of $\mathbb{Z}_p^*$ of prime order q for some prime p. Usually, the stipulation is that p and q are of certain bit sizes λ_p and λ_q. For this, we can first generate a prime q of bit size λ_q. The *prime number theorem* says that there are approximately $n/\ln(n)$ primes smaller than n. In other words, a random number of bit length λ_q is prime with probability $1/\ln(2^{\lambda_q})$, such that we can find a prime number of the right length by choosing sufficiently many random numbers. With an efficient primality test one can verify for each randomly picked number if it is prime or not. This testing may have a small error, but the error can usually be made too small to matter.

Once we have a prime q we repeatedly multiply q with (even) integers w of $\frac{\lambda_p}{\lambda_q}$ bits to obtain a prime $p = wq + 1$ of λ_p bits. This again requires to test for primality and it also relies on the property that a sufficient number of primes of this special form lies in the integers of λ_p bits.

Next we pick a generator g for the subgroup. We start by choosing a random group element h from $\mathbb{Z}_p^*$. Then we compute $h^w \bmod p$ and check that this element is distinct from 1. If so, then we have found a generator g for our subgroup. If the element is 1 then we repeat the procedure. Suppose that the integer w does not have too many small prime factors, then a generator will be found quite fast.

10.1.2 The Discrete-Logarithm Assumption

With cyclic groups we now have the basis for discussing the discrete-logarithm assumption. Let $\mathcal{G}$ be a finite cyclic group (with multiplication) and g a generator. Since the group could for instance be a subgroup of $\mathbb{Z}_p^*$ or an elliptic curve, we prefer to treat it in an abstract way here. Given an element $y \in \mathcal{G}$ the discrete logarithm asks to find the smallest integer x such that $g^x = y$. Value x is called the *discrete logarithm* of y. In certain settings it is assumed that it is difficult to compute the discrete logarithm which, in the following, we will use as the basis for constructing a one-way function.

The one-way function based on the discrete-logarithm problem consists of a parameter generation algorithm DL.KGen and the evaluation algorithm DL.Eval. The former algorithm determines a group $\mathcal{G}$, such as $\mathbb{Z}_p^*$, and outputs the group's representation (where we usually simply identify the group with the representation and write $\mathcal{G}$ for both). The algorithm also outputs a generator g of a subgroup of $\mathcal{G}$ of order q, where q and $\mathcal{G}$ are chosen in dependence of the security parameter λ:

$$(\mathcal{G}, q, g) \leftarrow\!\!\$ \ \mathsf{DL.KGen}(1^\lambda).$$

The evaluation algorithm $\mathsf{DL.Eval}((\mathcal{G}, q, g), x)$ for $x \in \mathbb{Z}_q$ returns g^x in $\mathcal{G}$.

Computing $y = g^x$ from $\mathcal{G}, g, q, x$

// let $x_1 \ldots x_n$ be the binary representation of $x = \sum_{i=1}^{n} x[i]2^{i-1}$

1 : $y \leftarrow 1$

2 : **for** $i = n$ **downto** 1 **do**

3 : $y \leftarrow y^2$

4 : $y \leftarrow y \cdot g^{x[i]}$

5 : **return** y

Fig. 10.2: Square-and-multiply method for exponentiations.

For the function to be practical, generating the parameters $\mathcal{G}, q, g$ as well as computing g^x in group $\mathcal{G}$ needs to be done efficiently. The latter is possible if multiplication in the group $\mathcal{G}$ can be done efficiently. In this case we can use the *square-and-multiply* method from Figure 10.2. Starting from the most significant bit $x[n]$ of x and with $y = 1$, this procedure multiplies $g^{x[i]}$ by the current value y for each bit $x[i]$ of x and "shifts" the bit to the right position by squaring y then $i - 1$ times in the subsequent executions of the **for**-loop. Overall, the procedure makes at most n multiplications and n squarings in the group $\mathcal{G}$ and can be carried out efficiently if multiplication in $\mathcal{G}$ is efficient. For example, for $\mathcal{G} = \mathbb{Z}_p^*$ one can, in principle, apply textbook methods to multiply over the integers and then perform division with remainder for the $\bmod p$ reduction, although faster methods such as Montgomery multiplication exist for such structures.

The final step is to assume that recovering a preimage from g^x is infeasible, which yields the discrete-logarithm assumption.

Definition 10.7 (Discrete-Logarithm Assumption).
The discrete-logarithm assumption *holds for* DL = (DL.KGen, DL.Eval) *if advantage* $\mathsf{Adv}_{\mathsf{DL},\mathcal{A}}^{\mathrm{dl}}(\lambda)$ *defined as*

$$\mathsf{Adv}_{\mathsf{DL},\mathcal{A}}^{\mathrm{dl}}(\lambda) := \Pr\left[\mathit{Exp}_{\mathsf{DL},\mathcal{A}}^{\mathrm{dl}}(\lambda)\right]$$

is negligible for any PPT *algorithm* $\mathcal{A}$. *Here experiment* $\mathit{Exp}_{\mathsf{DL},\mathcal{A}}^{\mathrm{dl}}(\lambda)$ *is defined as*

Experiment $\mathit{Exp}_{\mathsf{DL},\mathcal{A}}^{\mathrm{dl}}(\lambda)$

1 : $(\mathcal{G}, q, g) \leftarrow\!\!{}_\$ \; \mathsf{DL.KGen}(1^\lambda)$

2 : $x \leftarrow\!\!{}_\$ \; \mathbb{Z}_q$

3 : $y \leftarrow \mathsf{DL.Eval}((\mathcal{G}, q, g), x)$ // $y \leftarrow g^x$

4 : $x' \leftarrow\!\!{}_\$ \; \mathcal{A}(1^\lambda, \mathcal{G}, q, g, y)$

5 : **return** $y = \mathsf{DL.Eval}((\mathcal{G}, q, g), x')$ // $y = g^{x'}$

There may be restrictions on the choice of groups such that the discrete logarithm is not trivial in practice.

10.1.3 The RSA Assumption

The well-known one-way function proposed by Rivest, Shamir, and Adleman (RSA) works over groups $\mathbb{Z}_N^*$ over composite integers $N = pq$ for distinct primes p and q. The underlying assumption is that it is hard to compute eth roots of random group elements from $\mathbb{Z}_N^*$, for e being relatively prime to Euler's totient function $\phi(N) = \phi(p) \cdot \phi(q) = (p-1)(q-1)$.

The interesting aspect of the RSA function is that it is one-to-one over $\mathbb{Z}_N^*$, i.e., for N and e relatively prime to $\phi(N)$ each element $y \in \mathbb{Z}_N^*$ has a unique preimage x with $x^e = y \bmod N$. Moreover, the function allows for a trapdoor d with which one can efficiently compute preimages: Given this value d with $d \cdot e = 1 \bmod \phi(N)$ one can efficiently compute eth roots for any value $y \in \mathbb{Z}_N^*$. More precisely, for any $x \in \mathbb{Z}_N^*$ we have

$$(x^e)^d = (x^d)^e = x \bmod N.$$

Of course, it must be also hard to compute d from N and e, as otherwise it cannot be infeasible to derive eth roots for random y.

To formally capture the RSA assumption we again consider a parameter generation algorithm RSA.KGen and corresponding evaluation algorithm RSA.Eval. The key generator picks RSA parameters N, e, d. The size of the modulus N is chosen to match the security parameter λ, and we require that the exponent e is relatively prime to $\phi(N)$. The trapdoor d satisfies $e \cdot d = 1 \bmod \phi(N)$:

$$(N, e, d) \leftarrow_\$ \mathsf{RSA.KGen}(1^\lambda).$$

The evaluation algorithm RSA.Eval$((N, e), x)$ for $x \in \mathbb{Z}_N^*$ returns $x^e \bmod N$ in $\mathbb{Z}_N^*$. The inversion algorithm RSA.Inv$((N, d), y)$ for $y \in \mathbb{Z}_N^*$ returns $y^d \bmod N$ in $\mathbb{Z}_N^*$, such that $(x^e)^d = x \bmod N$ for any $x \in N^*$.

As in the case of discrete logarithms we require key generation and evaluation to be efficient for the function to be useful in practice. For this note that the exponentiation $x^e \bmod N$ can be computed efficiently with the same square-and-multiply method (see Figure 10.2) that we used for the discrete-log-based function (but over the composite modulus N). Similarly, the generation of the primes p, q, and e for the RSA parameters can be done efficiently as discussed earlier, and computing the inverse d to e modulo $\phi(N)$ can be done as before with the extended Euclidean algorithm. We note that it may be advantageous to store the prime factorization p and q of N as part of the trapdoor information, enabling faster computations via the Chinese Remainder Theorem. We do not discuss this speed-up here, though.

Definition 10.8 (RSA Assumption). *The RSA assumption holds for* RSA = (RSA.KGen, RSA.Eval) *if advantage* $\mathsf{Adv}^{\mathrm{rsa}}_{\mathsf{RSA},\mathcal{A}}(\lambda)$ *defined as*

$$\mathsf{Adv}^{\mathrm{rsa}}_{\mathsf{RSA},\mathcal{A}}(\lambda) := \Pr\left[\mathit{Exp}^{\mathrm{rsa}}_{\mathsf{RSA},\mathcal{A}}(\lambda)\right]$$

is negligible for any PPT *algorithm* $\mathcal{A}$. *Here experiment* $\mathit{Exp}^{\mathrm{rsa}}_{\mathsf{RSA},\mathcal{A}}(\lambda)$ *is defined as*

Experiment $\mathit{Exp}^{rsa}_{\mathsf{RSA},\mathcal{A}}(\lambda)$
1 : $(N, e, d) \leftarrow\!\!\$\ \mathsf{RSA.KGen}(1^\lambda)$
2 : $x \leftarrow\!\!\$\ \mathbb{Z}_N^*$
3 : $y \leftarrow \mathsf{RSA.Eval}((N, e), x)$ $/\!/\ y \leftarrow x^e \bmod N$
4 : $x' \leftarrow\!\!\$\ \mathcal{A}(N, e, y)$
5 :   **return** $y = \mathsf{RSA.Eval}(N, e, x')$ $/\!/\ y = (x')^e \bmod N$

We note that in practice some restrictions concerning the choices of the RSA parameters apply in order to prevent known attacks.

10.2 Fiat–Shamir Signatures

We now have the necessary number-theoretic background for our discussion of practical random oracle schemes. We begin our discussion with the Fiat–Shamir transformation, which is a general technique to turn interactive identification schemes into (non-interactive) signature schemes. The Fiat–Shamir transformation (dating back to 1986) has also been the source of the random oracle model by assuming that a hash function is modeled as a random function. We discuss the general transformation here concretely for the case of Schnorr signatures in the discrete logarithm case.

10.2.1 Schnorr Identification and Signature Scheme

We first develop the Schnorr signature scheme out of the interactive identification protocol.

Interactive Identification Protocol

Our starting point is the interactive Schnorr identification scheme, an interactive scheme between a prover and a verifier. Both parties know the public information $\mathcal{G}, g, q$, where q is prime. They both also know $X = g^x$, but only the prover knows the secret x. Here, and in the remainder of this section we denote scalars from $\mathbb{Z}_q$ by small letters and group elements by capital letters. The goal of the prover P is to convince the verifier V that it knows the discrete logarithm without revealing it in the clear, thus identifying as the authorized communication partner.

In the protocol the prover sends a "randomly blurred" version of the secret x to the verifier, where the prover commits to the randomness r in the first step by sending $R \leftarrow g^r$ to the verifier. The verifier then gets to choose the "contribution" of x to the blurred value by returning a scalar c, and the prover responds with $y \leftarrow r + cx \bmod q$. The verifier then checks that y is correctly formed:

Schnorr identification protocol

$\mathsf{P}(x)$	$\mathcal{G}, g, q, X$	$\mathsf{V}()$
$r \leftarrow_\$ \mathbb{Z}_q$		
$R \leftarrow g^r$	$\xrightarrow{\quad R \quad}$	$c \leftarrow_\$ \mathbb{Z}_q$
	$\xleftarrow{\quad c \quad}$	
$y \leftarrow r + cx \bmod q$	$\xrightarrow{\quad y \quad}$	$g^y \stackrel{?}{=} RX^c$

More abstractly, the three messages of the protocol, R, c, and y, are also often called commitment, challenge, and response.

The security of the protocol is argued by showing that a prover who is able to pass the verification in the protocol with sufficiently high probability must already know the discrete logarithm x to X and thus must be the legit communication partner. Here, "knowledge of x" is captured by showing that one can actually compute x when given access to such a prover with high success probability. A protocol having this property is also called a *proof of knowledge*.

As a toy case assume that the verifier in the protocol only uses $c = 0$ or $c = 1$ as challenge, the choice made at random, and that the (possibly malicious) prover is able to answer both challenge values correctly after having sent some value R. If the prover would form $y \leftarrow r + cx \bmod q$ according to the protocol description, we can imagine—in a thought experiment—to let it complete the protocol execution for the same value R and both values of $c = 0$ and $c = 1$, and then recover x as $y' - y = (r + x) - r \bmod q$ from the answers y' for $c = 1$ and y for $c = 0$. Note that this approach assumes that we have the algorithm of the prover available, or at least resettable access to the prover in order to run it twice for the same value R. But this assumption is valid since we aim to describe that the prover itself must know x if it passes the test sufficiently often.

There are two shortcomings to the approach above. One is that a malicious prover may actually pass verification with probability $1/2$ for binary challenges without knowing x, as we will show later. One therefore uses a larger challenge space, requiring us to check how to compute discrete logarithms for distinct non-binary challenges as above. The other problem is that we cannot presume that a malicious prover actually forms the reply y according to the protocol description. Instead, we can only rely on the verification test $g^y = RX^c$ of the verifier, without assuming how the responses are derived. We consider this general setting next.

Assume once more that the (possibly malicious) prover in the Schnorr protocol is able to correctly answer two challenges $c \neq c'$ after having sent R. This time we do not make any assumptions about the challenge space or how the responses are formed. Let the two responses of the prover for the challenges c and c' be y and y'. These responses both satisfy the verification equation for the same value R:

$$g^y = RX^c \quad \text{and} \quad g^{y'} = RX^{c'}.$$

We can rewrite this as

$$g^y X^{-c} = R \quad \text{and} \quad g^{y'} X^{-c'} = R$$

and thus

$$g^y X^{-c} = R = g^{y'} X^{-c'}.$$

Rearranging the equations once more we obtain

$$g^y g^{-y'} = g^{y-y'} = X^c X^{-c'} = X^{c-c'}.$$

If we are able to compute the inverse $(c - c')^{-1}$ of $c - c'$ over the group order q then we can actually compute the discrete logarithm x of X from the two challenges c, c' and responses y, y' as

$$x = (y - y') \cdot (c - c')^{-1} \bmod q,$$

because

$$g^x = g^{(y-y') \cdot (c-c')^{-1}} = \left(g^{y-y'}\right)^{(c-c')^{-1}} = \left(X^{c-c'}\right)^{(c-c')^{-1}} = X.$$

Fortunately, the inverse of $c - c'$ over $\mathbb{Z}_q$ exists since $c - c' \neq 0 \bmod q$ and all elements except for 0 are invertible modulo the prime q (because $\gcd(q, c-c') = 1$ for prime q and such non-trivial differences $c-c'$). Computing this inverse can be done efficiently with the extended Euclidean algorithm. Hence, any prover being able to answer two challenges after having sent the commitment R allows to compute the discrete logarithm of X. Put differently, the prover in this case must already know x.

In the above protocol it is critical that the challenge c is sent only after R has been chosen. Suppose for the moment that the verifier sent the challenge c as the first protocol message and the prover chose R only afterwards. Then a malicious prover could pick $r \leftarrow\!\!\$\ \mathbb{Z}_q$, compute $R \leftarrow g^r X^{-c}$, and then complete the protocol by sending $y \leftarrow r$. As

$$g^y = g^r = g^r(X^{-c}X^c) = (g^r X^{-c})X^c = RX^c$$

would satisfy the verification equation, the verifier would assume that the prover knows x. However, our malicious prover does not use x in the computations, but only the public information X. Our security argument above breaks down in this case because $R = g^r X^{-c}$ now changes with the challenge value, whereas before we exploited that R is fixed.

Remarkably, the sketched strategy for a malicious prover also gives rise to the argument that the honest prover does not reveal any fundamental information about x when executing the protocol. That is, assume that the verifier internally has already chosen $c \leftarrow\!\!\$\ \mathbb{Z}_q$. Then it could itself create the same distribution on (R, y) as the honest prover would, by picking $r \leftarrow\!\!\$\ \mathbb{Z}_q$ and setting $R \leftarrow g^r X^{-c}$, with the response being $y \leftarrow r$. In both cases, R either generated by the honest prover or by the verifier itself, the value R is a random group element, and y is then fully determined by R, X, and c for both cases. Hence, the verifier could generate a perfectly indistinguishable execution transcript itself given only the public key X. Put differently, the verifier cannot learn more information from an execution than what is already computable from X alone. This is known as the *zero-knowledge* property of the protocol (or, rather, as honest-verifier zero-knowledge since our argument assumed that the verifier chooses c faithfully according to the protocol description).

Removing Interaction with Random Oracles

The inevitable order of protocol messages is where the unpredictability of the random oracle is helpful. Assume that the prover does not receive the challenge c from the verifier, but instead applies the random oracle RO to the commitment message R to compute $c \leftarrow \mathsf{RO}(R)$. This "preserves" the order in the sense that the prover gets to learn the challenge only when calling the random oracle about R. But now the protocol has become non-interactive:

Schnorr identification protocol in the random oracle model

$\mathsf{P}^{\mathsf{RO}}(x)$	$\mathcal{G}, g, q, X$	$\mathsf{V}^{\mathsf{RO}}()$
$r \leftarrow\!\!\$\ \mathbb{Z}_q$		
$R \leftarrow g^r$		
$c \leftarrow \mathsf{RO}(R)$		
$y \leftarrow r + cx \bmod q$	$\xrightarrow{\quad R, y \quad}$	$c \leftarrow \mathsf{RO}(R)$
		$g^y \stackrel{?}{=} RX^c$

We note that the random oracle actually maps to bit strings of size $\mathsf{RO.ol}(\lambda)$ which we can embed into $\mathbb{Z}_q$ in the straightforward way, as long as the bit length is appropriately bounded. To ensure that challenges are still unpredictable we require that the bit size is super-logarithmic in the security parameter.

The formal security argument now requires the programmability property of random oracles (Section 9.3; page 382) because we seek two valid responses y, y' for different challenges $c \neq c'$ such that we need to be able to reprogram the random oracle output $\mathsf{RO}(R)$ for the same commitment R. That is, in the proof one runs the malicious prover twice, with the same randomness, and only reprograms one of the prover's random oracle queries, hoping to hit the value R in both executions and thus getting two valid responses y, y' for different challenges $c \neq c'$. Then one can compute the discrete logarithm of the public key as in the interactive case. We discuss this in more detail in the next part.

One can even derive a secure signature scheme from the above idea by including the message m to be signed in the hash evaluation of R. This is called the Schnorr signature scheme:

Definition 10.9 (Schnorr Signature Scheme). *The Schnorr signature scheme (in the random oracle model) based on the discrete logarithm problem* $\mathsf{DL} = (\mathsf{DL.KGen}, \mathsf{DL.Eval})$ *consists of the following algorithms (where, for brevity, we write* g^x *instead of* $\mathsf{DL.Eval}((\mathcal{G}, q, g), x)$*):*

$\mathsf{Sig.KGen}(1^\lambda)$	$\mathsf{Sig}^{\mathsf{RO}}.\mathsf{Sign}(\mathsf{sk}, m)$	$\mathsf{Sig}^{\mathsf{RO}}.\mathsf{Vf}(\mathsf{pk}, m, \sigma)$
$(\mathcal{G}, q, g) \leftarrow_\$ \mathsf{DL.KGen}(1^\lambda)$	$r \leftarrow_\$ \mathbb{Z}_q$	$(R, y) \leftarrow \sigma$
$x \leftarrow_\$ \mathbb{Z}_q$	$R \leftarrow g^r$	$c \leftarrow \mathsf{RO}(R, m)$
$X \leftarrow g^x$	$c \leftarrow \mathsf{RO}(R, m)$	**return** $(g^y = RX^c)$
$(\mathsf{pk}, \mathsf{sk}) \leftarrow ((X, \mathcal{G}, q, g), (x, \mathcal{G}, q, g))$	$y \leftarrow r + cx \bmod q$	
return $(\mathsf{pk}, \mathsf{sk})$	$\sigma \leftarrow (R, y)$	
	return σ	

Instead of using (R, y) as the signature it actually suffices to output (c, y) and have the verifier check that $\mathsf{RO}(g^r X^{-c}, m) \overset{?}{=} c$. Both versions can be shown to be existential unforgeable under adaptive chosen-message attacks, under the discrete-logarithm assumption, in the random oracle model.

Remark 10.10. Note that in the above scheme we write $\mathsf{RO}(R, m)$ to denote an evaluation of the random oracle on tuple (R, m). This is to be understood as first unambiguously encoding tuple (R, m) as a bit string and then applying the random oracle on the resulting string.

Remark 10.11. Fiat–Shamir originally proposed the transformation of interactive protocols to non-interactive ones via the random oracle model for an identification protocol based on factoring. But the concept applies to other number-theoretic protocols, too, for example for the discrete logarithm-based protocol above.

10.2.2 Security Proof via Forking

In this section we argue security of the Schnorr signature scheme formally (and thus implicitly also of the Fiat–Shamir transformation in general). Assume for the moment that we consider key-only attacks in which the adversary tries to produce a forgery (R, y) for some message m without requesting signatures for different messages before (but the adversary may make polynomially many random oracle queries to find the forgeries). Note that a valid forgery (R, y) for m stipulates $g^y = RX^c$ for $c \leftarrow \mathsf{RO}(R, m)$. To apply the security argument of the interactive identification scheme above, to find another challenge $c' \neq c$ for the same commitment value R in order to be able to extract, we use the programming ability of the random oracle and *fork* into another execution where we answer the adversary's random oracle query about R, m with an independent random value c' instead. Ideally, this gives us two executions with two valid forgeries, (R, y) for m and c, as well as (R, y') for m but for a different value c'. Then we can again compute the discrete logarithm as above. The idea is visualized in the following picture.

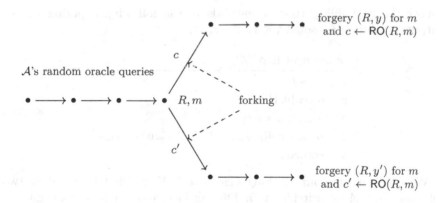

Still, we need to argue carefully that the above forking strategy yields the desired result. The adversary may for example switch to a forgery for a different random oracle query (R', m') in the second execution, such that we obtain two equations for different values R and R'. Such equations, however, are not known to support extraction of the discrete logarithm of X. With the following lemma, called the *general forking lemma*, we show in an abstract way that this cannot happen too often, or viewed the other way, that we roughly have the expected squared success probability of obtaining two valid forgeries, but loose a factor $1/\mathsf{q}$ proportional to the number of random oracle queries $\mathcal{A}$ makes. In the following we omit the security parameter because the forking lemma holds in the concrete setting.

Forking Lemma

The abstract game we consider is an adversary receiving some value p, distributed according to some distribution $\mathcal{P}$, as well as q many random values $h_1, \ldots, h_\mathsf{q}$ sampled uniformly from some domain $\mathcal{H}$. We can view the input p as the public key in our signature scheme and the values h_i to be the random oracle replies. The task of the adversary is now to compute some "solution" s and to indicate via a value k to which hash value this solution belongs. In our case the solution is the signature forgery for the kth random oracle query. We also allow the adversary to output $k = 0$ to indicate failure. Below it is sometimes convenient to make $\mathcal{A}$'s random coins explicit, sampling sufficiently many coins $\alpha \leftarrow\!\!{}_\$ \{0,1\}^{\mathsf{rl}}$ for $\mathcal{A}$ and giving them as input to $\mathcal{A}$. As usual, we then write $\mathcal{A}(p, h_1, \ldots, h_\mathsf{q}; \alpha)$ for the (now deterministic) execution for fixed coins α.

For fixed adversary $\mathcal{A}$ with randomness pool $\{0,1\}^{\mathsf{rl}}$ and distributions $\mathcal{P}$ and $\mathcal{H}$, we let

$$\mathsf{break} := \Pr\left[\mathsf{Exp}^{\mathsf{break}}_{\mathcal{A},\mathcal{P},\mathcal{H},\mathsf{q}} \in [\mathsf{q}]\right]$$

denote the probability that $\mathcal{A}$ succeeds in the following experiment, i.e., outputs a solution for some $k \in \{1, 2 \ldots, \mathsf{q}\}$:

Experiment $\mathsf{Exp}^{\mathsf{break}}_{\mathcal{A},\mathcal{P},\mathcal{H},\mathsf{q}}$
1 : $\quad p \leftarrow\!\!{}_\$ \mathcal{P}$
2 : $\quad \alpha \leftarrow\!\!{}_\$ \{0,1\}^{\mathsf{rl}}$
3 : $\quad h_1, \ldots, h_\mathsf{q} \leftarrow\!\!{}_\$ \mathcal{H}$
4 : $\quad (k, s) \leftarrow\!\!{}_\$ \mathcal{A}(p, h_1, \ldots, h_\mathsf{q}) \quad /\!\!/ \ k = 0$ for failure
5 : $\quad$ **return** k

We consider now our "forking algorithm" $\mathcal{F}$, which tries to elicit two solutions from $\mathcal{A}$ by switching to a different branch of random oracle queries. We let $\mathcal{F}$ output a bit b, indicating success, and two potential solutions s, s' which it got from $\mathcal{A}$. In the signature case the solutions will be the valid forgeries, and the bit b will indicate if the forgeries are for the same random oracle query (and whether the random oracle answers are distinct). The input to $\mathcal{F}$ will be $p \leftarrow\!\!{}_\$ \mathcal{P}$, representing the given value for which $\mathcal{F}$ tries to compute the discrete logarithm in our signature scheme, such that we can compute $\mathcal{F}$'s success probability for the given value in experiment $\mathsf{Exp}^{\mathsf{fork}}_{\mathcal{F},\mathcal{P},\mathcal{H},\{0,1\}^{\mathsf{rl}},\mathsf{q}}$ as specified in Figure 10.3.

Experiment $\mathsf{Exp}^{\text{fork}}_{\mathcal{F},\mathcal{A},\mathcal{P},\mathcal{H},\mathsf{q}}$	Forking Algorithm $\mathcal{F}(p)$
1 : $\quad p \leftarrow\!\!\$\ \mathcal{P}$	1 : $\quad \alpha \leftarrow\!\!\$\ \{0,1\}^{\mathsf{rl}}$
2 : $\quad (b,s,s') \leftarrow\!\!\$\ \mathcal{F}(p)$	2 : $\quad h_1,\ldots,h_{\mathsf{q}} \leftarrow\!\!\$\ \mathcal{H}$
3 : $\quad \mathbf{return}\ b$	3 : $\quad (k,s) \leftarrow \mathcal{A}(p,h_1,\ldots,h_{\mathsf{q}};\alpha)$
	4 : $\quad h'_k,\ldots,h'_{\mathsf{q}} \leftarrow\!\!\$\ \mathcal{H}$
	5 : $\quad (k',s') \leftarrow \mathcal{A}(p,h_1,\ldots,h_{k-1},h'_k,\ldots,h'_{\mathsf{q}};\alpha)$
	6 : $\quad \mathbf{if}\ k = k' \wedge k \in [\mathsf{q}] \wedge h_k \neq h'_k\ \mathbf{then}$
	7 : $\qquad \mathbf{return}\ (1,s,s')$
	8 : $\quad \mathbf{else}$
	9 : $\qquad \mathbf{return}\ (0,\perp,\perp)$

Fig. 10.3: Experiment $\mathsf{Exp}^{\text{fork}}_{\mathcal{F},\mathcal{A},\mathcal{P},\mathcal{H},\{0,1\}^{\mathsf{rl}},\mathsf{q}}$ together with the "forking algorithm" $\mathcal{F}$ that executes adversary $\mathcal{A}$ twice on the same random coins α but with different random oracle answers.

For fixed $\mathcal{F},\mathcal{A},\mathcal{P},\mathcal{H},\mathsf{q}$ let

$$\mathsf{fork} := \Pr\left[\mathsf{Exp}^{\text{fork}}_{\mathcal{F},\mathcal{A},\mathcal{P},\mathcal{H},\mathsf{q}} = 1\right]$$

be the probability that $\mathcal{F}$ in the above experiment succeeds and outputs a tuple with a 1-bit. The reader may think of this as the probability of being able to compute the discrete logarithm of the values in the parameter p. We can now state the general forking lemma:

Lemma 10.12 (General Forking Lemma). *Let $\mathcal{P}$ be an arbitrary distribution and let $\mathcal{H}$ be the uniform distribution on some finite set H. Let $\mathcal{A}$ be an algorithm (consuming coins from the set $\{0,1\}^{\mathsf{rl}}$). Then for*

$$\mathsf{break} := \Pr\left[\mathsf{Exp}^{\text{break}}_{\mathcal{A},\mathcal{P},\mathcal{H},\mathsf{q}} \in [\mathsf{q}]\right]$$

and

$$\mathsf{fork} := \Pr\left[\mathsf{Exp}^{\text{fork}}_{\mathcal{F},\mathcal{A},\mathcal{P},\mathcal{H},\mathsf{q}} = 1\right]$$

it holds that

$$\mathsf{fork} \geq \frac{1}{\mathsf{q}} \cdot \mathsf{break}^2 - \frac{1}{|H|}.$$

Unlike other results where the advantages are usually related by polynomial factors, the statement here says that fork is quadratic related to break. Note that break is usually a small probability less than 1, such that squaring it yields even smaller results. For instance, if break is on the order of 2^{-20} and thus significant from a cryptographic point of view, then fork would be guaranteed to be at least on the order of 2^{-40} times $1/\mathsf{q}$.

In the proof below we make use of Jensen's inequality, stating that for any convex function f over the reals and non-negative values $\rho_1, \ldots, \rho_n$ with $\sum_{i=1}^n \rho_i = 1$ it holds that

$$\sum_{i=1}^n \rho_i \cdot f(x_i) \geq f\left(\sum_{i=1}^n \rho_i x_i\right).$$

In the proof we will apply this bound multiple times for the convex squaring function $f(x) = x^2$.

Proof. We will relate the probability of the two runs of $\mathcal{A}$ in the execution of $\mathcal{F}$ by writing out the winning condition for algorithm $\mathcal{F}$:

$$\mathsf{fork} = \Pr[k = k' \wedge k \in [\mathsf{q}] \wedge h_k \neq h'_k]$$

and using $\Pr[A \wedge B \wedge C] = 1 - \Pr[\neg(A \wedge B \wedge C)] = 1 - \Pr[\neg(A \wedge B) \vee \neg C] \geq \Pr[A \wedge B] - \Pr[\neg C]$ for events A, B, C,

$$\geq \Pr[k = k' \wedge k \in [\mathsf{q}]] - \Pr[h_k = h'_k]$$

$$= \Pr[k = k' \wedge k \in [\mathsf{q}]] - \frac{1}{|H|}.$$

It remains to bound the probability of $k = k'$ and k being in the admissible range. For this it is convenient to marginalize the probability as

$$\Pr[k = k' \wedge k \in [\mathsf{q}]] = \sum_{k_0 = 1}^{\mathsf{q}} \Pr[k = k_0 \wedge k' = k_0].$$

For such a fixed value $k_0 \in [\mathsf{q}]$ let $\mathsf{break}_{k_0}(p_0, \alpha_0, h_{1,0}, \ldots, h_{k_0-1,0})$ be the conditional probability that $\mathcal{A}$ picks $k = k_0$ for its solution s, given that the values $p, \alpha, h_1, \ldots, h_{k-1}$ hit the fixed values:

$$\mathsf{break}_{k_0}(p_0, \alpha_0, h_{1,0}, \ldots, h_{k_0-1,0})$$

$$= \Pr\left[\mathsf{Exp}_{\mathcal{A}, \mathcal{P}, \mathcal{H}, \mathsf{q}}^{\mathsf{break}} = k_0 \,\middle|\, p = p_0, \alpha = \alpha_0, h_1 = h_{1,0}, \ldots, h_{k_0-1} = h_{k_0-1,0}\right].$$

The probability is then over the random choice of the remaining values $h_{k_0}, \ldots, h_{\mathsf{q}}$. Noteworthily, if one considers a run of the forking algorithm $\mathcal{F}$ for fixed $p_0, \alpha_0, h_{1,0}, \ldots, h_{k_0-1,0}$ in which $\mathcal{A}$ has picked k_0 in the first execution, and then $\mathcal{F}$ runs $\mathcal{A}$ for the second time with fresh values $h'_{k_0}, \ldots, h'_{\mathsf{q}}$, then the conditional probability of $\mathcal{A}$ picking $k' = k_0$ is again given by $\mathsf{break}_{k_0}(p_0, \alpha_0, h_{1,0}, \ldots, h_{k_0-1,0})$. Furthermore, both (conditional) probabilities multiply, since the remaining values $h_{k_0}, \ldots, h_{\mathsf{q}}$ and $h'_{k_0}, \ldots, h'_{\mathsf{q}}$ are chosen independently.

Letting fix_0 be the event that $p = p_0 \wedge \alpha = \alpha_0 \wedge h_1 = h_{1,0} \wedge \cdots \wedge h_{k_0-1} = h_{k_0-1,0}$, we get

$\Pr[k = k' \wedge k \in [\mathsf{q}]]$

$$= \sum_{k_0=1}^{\mathsf{q}} \Pr[k = k_0 \wedge k' = k_0]$$

$$= \sum_{k_0=1}^{\mathsf{q}} \sum_{p_0,\alpha_0,h_{1,0},\ldots,h_{k_0-1,0}} \Pr[k = k_0 \wedge k' = k_0 \wedge \mathsf{fix}_0]$$

$$= \sum_{k_0=1}^{\mathsf{q}} \sum_{p_0,\alpha_0,h_{1,0},\ldots,h_{k_0-1,0}} \Pr[\mathsf{fix}_0] \cdot \Pr[k = k_0 \wedge k' = k_0 \mid \mathsf{fix}_0]$$

$$= \sum_{k_0=1}^{\mathsf{q}} \sum_{p_0,\alpha_0,h_{1,0},\ldots,h_{k_0-1,0}} \Pr[\mathsf{fix}_0] \cdot \Pr[k = k_0 \mid \mathsf{fix}_0] \cdot \Pr[k' = k_0 \mid \mathsf{fix}_0]$$

$$= \sum_{k_0=1}^{\mathsf{q}} \sum_{p_0,\alpha_0,h_{1,0},\ldots,h_{k_0-1,0}} \Pr[\mathsf{fix}_0] \cdot (\mathsf{break}_{k_0}(p_0,\alpha_0,h_{1,0},\ldots,h_{k_0-1,0}))^2$$

and applying Jensen's inequality to the inner sum,

$$\geq \sum_{k_0=1}^{\mathsf{q}} \left(\sum_{p_0,\alpha_0,h_{1,0},\ldots,h_{k_0-1,0}} \Pr[\mathsf{fix}_0] \cdot \mathsf{break}_{k_0}(p_0,\alpha_0,h_{1,0},\ldots,h_{k_0-1,0}) \right)^2.$$

Let $\mathsf{break}_{k_0} := \sum_{p_0,\alpha_0,h_{1,0},\ldots,h_{k_0-1,0}} \Pr[\mathsf{fix}_0] \cdot \mathsf{break}_{k_0}(p_0,\alpha_0,h_{1,0},\ldots,h_{k_0-1,0})$ be the probability that $\mathcal{A}$ outputs $k = k_0$ in its attack, such that we can rewrite the last term further as

$$= \sum_{k_0=1}^{\mathsf{q}} (\mathsf{break}_{k_0})^2.$$

Applying Jensen's inequality once more in the form $\sum x_i^2 = \mathsf{q} \cdot \sum \frac{1}{\mathsf{q}} \cdot x_i^2 \geq \mathsf{q} \cdot (\sum \frac{1}{\mathsf{q}} \cdot x_i)^2 = \frac{1}{\mathsf{q}} \cdot (\sum x_i)^2$ we derive the lower bound

$$\geq \frac{1}{\mathsf{q}} \cdot \left(\sum_{k_0=1}^{\mathsf{q}} \mathsf{break}_{k_0} \right)^2 = \frac{1}{\mathsf{q}} \cdot \mathsf{break}^2.$$

This proves the forking lemma. □

Security of Schnorr Signatures

The forking lemma allows us almost immediately to conclude that Fiat–Shamir signatures are secure if finding two valid executions for the same commitment breaks some hardness assumption. We discuss this for Schnorr signatures again, but first deal with key-only attacks in which the adversary tries to forge a signature given the public key only (and not being allowed to request other signatures before). More formally, for an adversary $\mathcal{B}$ against signature scheme Sig let $\mathsf{Adv}^{\text{euf-ko}}_{\text{Sig},\mathcal{B}}(\lambda)$ be $\mathsf{Adv}^{\text{euf-cma}}_{\text{Sig},\mathcal{B}}(\lambda)$ if $\mathcal{B}$ does not make any signature queries. In the following proposition we assume that the random oracle RO in the Schnorr signature scheme outputs values from $\{0,1\}^{\text{RO.ol}(\lambda)}$ and that these bit strings can be embedded into $\mathbb{Z}_q$ (where the prime q is also chosen in dependence on the security parameter λ, of course).

> **Proposition 10.13.** *If the discrete logarithm assumption (Definition 10.7) holds then the Schnorr signature scheme (Definition 10.9) is existentially unforgeable under key-only attacks. More specifically, for any PPT adversary $\mathcal{B}$ against the Schnorr signature scheme Sig, making at most $\mathsf{q}_{\text{RO}}(\lambda)$ random oracle queries to random oracle RO : $\{0,1\}^* \to \{0,1\}^{\text{RO.ol}(\lambda)}$, there is a PPT algorithm $\mathcal{D}$ against the discrete logarithm problem such that*
>
> $$\mathsf{Adv}^{\text{euf-ko}}_{\text{Sig},\mathcal{B}}(\lambda) \leq \sqrt{(\mathsf{q}_{\text{RO}}(\lambda)+1) \cdot (\mathsf{Adv}^{\text{dl}}_{\text{DL},\mathcal{D}}(\lambda) + 2^{-\text{RO.ol}(\lambda)})}.$$

Proof. Assume that we have an adversary $\mathcal{B}$ against key-only unforgeability of the Schnorr scheme. This adversary receives (only) the public key $\mathsf{pk} = (X,\mathcal{G},q,g)$ as input, then makes (at most) $\mathsf{q}_{\text{RO}} := \mathsf{q}_{\text{RO}}(\lambda)$ queries to the random oracle, before outputting a forgery attempt (R,y) for a message m. We can assume that $\mathcal{B}$ has queried the random oracle about (R,m) before terminating, otherwise we can make this extra query, increasing the number of oracle calls by one. We can also assume that $\mathcal{B}$ never queries the random oracle about the same value twice; such queries can be eliminated by common table look-up techniques.

We can now view the adversary $\mathcal{B}$ against the signature scheme as a special case of adversary $\mathcal{A}$ in the Forking Lemma 10.12 (for fixed parameter λ), by taking the distribution $\mathcal{P}$ to be the one generating the public key, letting each sample h_i be the reply to the (distinct) random oracle queries, letting $s = (R,y,m)$ be the forgery attempt, and having k denote the (unique) index of the query of (R,m) to the random oracle for s. We can also let $\mathcal{A}$ check the verification equation and output $(0,\perp)$ instead of (k,s) if it does not hold, such that an output (k,s) with $k \neq 0$ means that $\mathcal{B}$ succeeded with the forgery attempt. It follows that $\mathcal{B}$'s success probability in creating a forgery is identical to probability break in the forking lemma.

We can therefore build algorithm $\mathcal{F}$ which computes two solutions (R,y,m) and (R',y',m') for the same index k and different $h_k \neq h'_k$, both satisfying the corresponding verification equation:

$$g^y = RX^{h_k} \quad \text{and} \quad g^{y'} = R'X^{h'_k}.$$

The success probability of $\mathcal{F}$ is given by fork as in the forking lemma. An important observation here is that, up to the kth random oracle query, all inputs to adversary $\mathcal{A}$ resp. $\mathcal{B}$ in the two executions are identical, including the public key as well as the previous random oracle answers. Both executions even use the same randomness. It follows that $\mathcal{A}$ resp. $\mathcal{B}$ in both executions outputs the same value $R = R'$ when making the kth query. Only the replies h_k and h'_k are then chosen independently, and for a successful run of $\mathcal{F}$ are distinct. But then we can extract the discrete logarithm of X once more as $(y - y') \cdot (h_k - h'_k)^{-1} \bmod q$.

The overall running time of this discrete-log finder (using $\mathcal{F}$) is polynomial, and the success probability of computing the discrete logarithm is the one of $\mathcal{F}$ and thus equal to fork. Rearranging the equation for fork and break from the forking lemma yields the claimed bound for our proposition.   □

It remains to extend the above argument from key-only to chosen-message attacks, i.e., we need to argue that seeing other signatures does not facilitate the task of forging significantly. Abstractly, this follows from the zero-knowledge property of the interactive protocol, stating that one can simulate protocol executions (and thus signatures) with knowledge of the public key X only. In the random oracle model we exploit this property by carefully programming the random oracle, showing that we can turn any chosen-message attacker $\mathcal{C}$ against the Schnorr signature scheme into a key-only attacker $\mathcal{B}$ as above.

> **Lemma 10.14.** *For any* PPT *adversary* $\mathcal{C}$ *mounting an adaptive chosen-message attack against the Schnorr signature scheme (Definition 10.9), making at most* $\mathsf{q}_{\mathsf{RO}}(\lambda)$ *random oracle queries and* $\mathsf{q}_{\mathsf{Sign}}(\lambda)$ *signature queries, there exists a* PPT *adversary* $\mathcal{B}$ *against the scheme in a key-only attack with at most* $\mathsf{q}_{\mathsf{RO}}(\lambda)$ *random oracle queries, such that*
>
> $$\mathsf{Adv}^{\mathrm{euf\text{-}cma}}_{\mathsf{Sig},\mathcal{C}}(\lambda) \leq \mathsf{Adv}^{\mathrm{euf\text{-}ko}}_{\mathsf{Sig},\mathcal{B}}(\lambda) + \frac{\mathsf{q}_{\mathsf{Sign}}(\lambda) \cdot (\mathsf{q}_{\mathsf{RO}}(\lambda) + \mathsf{q}_{\mathsf{Sign}}(\lambda))}{q},$$
>
> *where q is the prime output by the key generator for security parameter λ.*

Note that since q is usually exponential in λ the loss in the advantage when moving from chosen-message attacks to key-only attacks is negligible.

Proof. We describe how to construct the key-only adversary $\mathcal{B}$ given $\mathcal{C}$. Algorithm $\mathcal{B}$ will simulate a signature query m of $\mathcal{C}$ by preselecting the random oracle value $c \leftarrow_{\$} \{0,1\}^{\mathrm{RO.ol}(\lambda)}$, computing $R \leftarrow g^r X^{-c}$ for random $r \leftarrow_{\$} \mathbb{Z}_q$, programming the random oracle at (R, m) to be c, and returning the signature (R, y) for $y \leftarrow r$. It will also redirect any query of $\mathcal{C}$ to the random oracle about such a value (R, m) to the chosen value c. The only problem which can arise is that the reprogramming of the random oracle may fail because the adversary $\mathcal{C}$ has already queried the random oracle about this input. But since $R \leftarrow g^r X^{-c}$ is a random group element, chosen only during the signing request, this is unlikely.

$\mathcal{B}^{RO}(\text{pk})$	$\text{OSign}(m)$
1: $(X, \mathcal{G}, q, g) \leftarrow \text{pk}$	1: $c \leftarrow\!\!\$\ \{0,1\}^{RO.ol(\lambda)}$
2: $T \leftarrow []$	2: $r \leftarrow\!\!\$\ \mathbb{Z}_q$
3: $(m^*, \sigma^*) \leftarrow\!\!\$\ \mathcal{C}^{ORO, OSign}(\text{pk})$	3: $R \leftarrow g^r X^{-c}$
4: return (m^*, σ^*)	4: $y \leftarrow r$
	5: if $T[(R, m)] \neq \bot$ then abort
$\underline{ORO(x)}$	6: $T[(R, m)] \leftarrow c$
1: if $T[x] = \bot$ then	7: return (R, y)
2: $\quad T[x] \leftarrow RO(x)$	
3: return $T[x]$	

Note that $\mathcal{B}$ only makes random oracle queries for values not chosen by the signature simulation step, such that it also makes at most $q_{RO}(\lambda)$ many random oracle queries on its own.

Suppose now that $\mathcal{B}$ does not abort due to an already selected value for (R, m) in a signature simulation in line 5. Then $\mathcal{B}$ perfectly simulates $\mathcal{C}$'s attack on the actual scheme, when having access to a true random oracle and the genuine signer. The reason is that $\mathcal{B}$ then also returns valid signatures for random R and also sets the random oracle (table) for (R, m) to a random value c. The simulated random oracle thus provides random but consistent answers.

It remains to bound the probability that $\mathcal{B}$ aborts. This can only happen if in any of the $q_{Sign}(\lambda)$ simulated signature queries of $\mathcal{C}$ the value (R, m) has already been set among the (at most) $q_{RO}(\lambda) + q_{Sign}(\lambda)$ previously chosen entries in the table. But since R is a random group element, the probability of any such collision is at most $(q_{RO}(\lambda) + q_{Sign}(\lambda)) \cdot \frac{1}{q}$ for each query. Summing over all $q_{Sign}(\lambda)$ signature requests yields the claimed bound.   □

We can now put the claims together, first turning an adversary against the Schnorr scheme in a chosen-message attack into one running a key-only attack, and then apply the proposition showing security against key-only attacks via forking:

Theorem 10.15. *If the discrete logarithm assumption (Definition 10.7) holds then the Schnorr signature scheme (Definition 10.9) is existentially unforgeable in adaptive chosen-message attacks. More specifically, for any PPT adversary $\mathcal{C}$ against the Schnorr signature scheme* Sig, *making at most* $q_{RO}(\lambda)$ *random oracle queries to random oracle* RO $: \{0,1\}^* \rightarrow \{0,1\}^{RO.ol(\lambda)}$ *and at most* $q_{Sign}(\lambda)$ *signature queries,*

> *there is a* PPT *algorithm* $\mathcal{D}$ *against the discrete logarithm problem such that*
>
> $$\mathsf{Adv}_{\mathsf{Sig},\mathcal{C}}^{\text{euf-cma}}(\lambda) \le \sqrt{(\mathsf{q}_{\mathsf{RO}}(\lambda) + 1) \cdot (\mathsf{Adv}_{\mathsf{DL},\mathcal{D}}^{\text{dl}}(\lambda) + 2^{-\mathsf{RO.ol}(\lambda)})} \\ + \frac{\mathsf{q}_{\mathsf{Sign}}(\lambda) \cdot (\mathsf{q}_{\mathsf{Sign}}(\lambda) + \mathsf{q}_{\mathsf{RO}}(\lambda))}{q},$$
>
> *where q is the prime output by the key generator for security parameter λ.*

We note that a similar proof strategy applies to general Fiat–Shamir protocols. The main ingredients are the ability to break some hardness assumption from two valid executions of a prover, and one needs to be able to simulate signatures to reduce chosen-message attackers to key-only attackers.

10.3 Optimal Asymmetric Encryption Padding—OAEP

The *optimal asymmetric encryption padding* (OAEP) scheme provides a method to encrypt a plaintext with a trapdoor permutation like RSA, trying to make optimal use of the space for the message and minimizing other security-related parts such as redundancy and randomness. The scheme uses two independent random oracles, denoted as G and H, for encryption and decryption. The random oracles can be derived in principle from a single random oracle RO via domain separation (see Section 8.3.2; page 357) as $\mathsf{G}(\cdot) = \mathsf{RO}(0\|\cdot)$ and $\mathsf{H}(\cdot) = \mathsf{RO}(1\|\cdot)$, truncating the outputs to appropriate length. Specifically, here we will use $\mathsf{G} : \{0,1\}^* \to \{0,1\}^{\ell_m + \ell_z}$ and $\mathsf{H} : \{0,1\}^* \to \{0,1\}^{\ell_r}$, where the parameters ℓ_m, ℓ_z, ℓ_r depend on the security parameter λ and denote the message length ℓ_m, the length ℓ_z of the all-zero redundancy, and the bit length ℓ_r of the randomness. We assume that the message, the redundancy, and the randomness together fit tightly into the domain $D_\lambda \subseteq \{0,1\}^\lambda$ of the trapdoor permutation, in particular $\lambda - 1 \le \ell_m + \ell_z + \ell_r \le \lambda$.

Encryption first performs a two-round "unbalanced" Feistel encoding (see Section 3.3.3; page 129) of the message $m \in \{0,1\}^{\ell_m}$, padded with redundancy 0^{ℓ_z}, and a fresh random string $r \in \{0,1\}^{\ell_r}$. The random oracles G and H act as the round functions. This is shown on the left-hand side of Figure 10.4. The derived strings s and t are then put into the trapdoor permutation to derive the ciphertext. Decryption—see the right-hand side of Figure 10.4—computes these steps backwards, applying the inverse trapdoor permutation first and then undoing the Feistel computations again. The decryption algorithm finally checks that the redundancy part z in the padded message equals 0^{ℓ_z}. If so, it outputs the unpadded message, else it returns an error symbol $\bot$. We give the OAEP construction in pseudocode as Construction 10.16 below, and note that it is easy to check from the scheme's description that the scheme is correct: properly encrypted messages can always be decrypted.

Construction 10.16 (Optimal Asymmetric Encryption Padding).
Let G *and* H *be two random oracles and* T := (T.KGen, T.Eval) *a trapdoor function. Then the OAEP construction of a public-key encryption scheme for messages of length* ℓ_m *and with redundancy length* ℓ_z *and randomness length* ℓ_r *is given as*

PKE.KGen(1^λ)	PKE^{G,H}.Enc(pk, m)	PKE^{G,H}.Dec(sk, c)
(pk, tk) ←$ T.KGen(1^λ)	// $m \in \{0,1\}^{\ell_m}$	$s\|t \leftarrow$ T.Inv(tk, c) // sk = tk
return (pk, sk) ← (pk, tk)	$r \leftarrow$$ \{0,1\}^{\ell_r}$	// $s \in \{0,1\}^{\ell_m + \ell_z}$, $t \in \{0,1\}^{\ell_r}$
	$s \leftarrow$ G(r) $\oplus m\|0^{\ell_z}$	$r \leftarrow$ H(s) $\oplus t$
	$t \leftarrow$ H(s) $\oplus r$	$m\|z \leftarrow$ G(r) $\oplus s$
	$c \leftarrow$ T.Eval(pk, $s\|t$)	**if** $z = 0^{\ell_z}$ **then**
	return c	**return** m
		else return $\bot$

The idea of the Feistel construction in the OAEP scheme is to let G(r) for random r mask the padded message, but then this random-looking value G(r) $\oplus m\|0^{\ell_z}$ itself masks r through the other random oracle H. This requires some form of correlation resistance of the random oracles, because one input is used to mask the other one. If it is ensured that s and t are quasi-independent random values, recovering them from the ciphertext $c \leftarrow$ T.Eval(pk, $s\|t$) should be infeasible by the one-wayness of the trapdoor function.

Let us touch upon the role of the randomness parameter ℓ_r and of the 0-padding. As briefly discussed in Section 5.1.3 for symmetric encryption schemes, any IND-CPA-secure scheme must be randomized and the length of the random input must be sufficiently large. This holds for OAEP as well such that the length ℓ_r of the randomness r cannot be too small. Otherwise one could potentially predict value r that was used to create a ciphertext and then check a message guess m' by computing s' and t' for m' and r according to the scheme, eventually verifying whether T.Eval(pk, $s'\|t'$) matches the given ciphertext or not.

The 0-padding of the message is only required when looking at IND-CCA security. In this case it must be ensured, among others, that the adversary cannot maul a ciphertext c into a related one. If, for example, the trapdoor permutation is given by the RSA function $x \mapsto x^e \bmod N$ then the adversary could try to multiply the ciphertext with $2^e \bmod N$ to derive the ciphertext $c^* \leftarrow c \cdot 2^e = (s\|t)^e \cdot 2^e = (2 \cdot (s\|t))^e \bmod N$. Ignoring the wrap-around of the multiplication this transform shifts the strings s and t by one bit position. Denoting the encapsulated values in c^* as s^* and t^*, the decryption of c^* would then yield $m^*\|z^* \leftarrow s^* \oplus$ G(H(s^*) $\oplus t^*$). Because of the random outputs

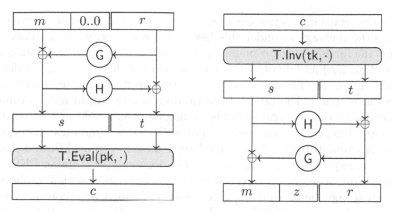

Fig. 10.4: OAEP encryption (left) of message m with randomness r using trapdoor permutation T.Eval (for public key pk) and random oracles G and H, and decryption (right) with inverse T.Inv (for secret key tk). Decryption outputs the message m if and only if $z = 0 \ldots 0$, and an error message $\perp$ otherwise.

of oracles H and G it is likely that the value z^* differs from 0^{ℓ_0} such that decryption returns the error symbol $\perp$.

The formal security argument for OAEP is tricky; see also the Chapter Notes at the end of this chapter. While one can state the scheme for general trapdoor permutations, the only sound security proof today requires *partial-domain one-wayness* of the trapdoor permutation. This property roughly says that even recovering only the s-part from $f(s||t)$ for random s, t is infeasible. We note that the RSA function is known to have this property.

10.4 Fujisaki–Okamoto Hybrid Encryption

Fujisaki and Okamoto presented a construction of a hybrid encryption scheme which combines an asymmetric encryption scheme PKE = (PKE.KGen, PKE.Enc, PKE.Dec) with a symmetric encryption scheme SE = (SE.KGen, SE.Enc, SE.Dec) using two random oracles G and H. The so-called FO transform has the advantage that it lifts a public-key encryption scheme with a weak one-way property to a strong one achieving IND-CCA security. Furthermore, the resulting scheme is efficient as the (potentially long) message is encrypted with the symmetric scheme—note that symmetric encryption schemes are usually much more efficient than public-key encryption schemes— and the public-key encryption scheme is only used to encrypt a relatively short string of a fixed length. To encrypt a message m one picks a random value $\sigma \leftarrow_\$ \{0,1\}^{\ell_\sigma}$ and computes

$$c_{\text{sym}} \leftarrow \text{SE.Enc}(\text{G}(\sigma), m), \quad c_{\text{asym}} \leftarrow \text{PKE.Enc}(\text{pk}, \sigma; \text{H}(\sigma, c_{\text{sym}})).$$

That is, one maps σ to a key $G(\sigma)$ for the symmetric encryption scheme and encrypts the message m under this key to get a ciphertext c_{sym}. Then one encrypts the random string σ under the public key but uses the random oracle output $H(\sigma, c_{sym})$ as randomness. Here we again write $H(\sigma, c_{sym})$ to denote an evaluation of the random oracle where the input tuple is unambiguously encoded as a string. The usage of the random oracle output as randomness is analogous to the encrypt-with-hash scheme we discussed in Section 9.5.2 (page 400). Encryption obviously requires that the symmetric encryption scheme uses uniform keys of the same length as the output of G, and that H outputs the required number of random bits for encryption under PKE.

Decryption works by first recovering σ from the asymmetric ciphertext c_{asym}. Then one checks that c_{asym} is correctly formed by recomputing the encryption of σ under PKE.Enc with randomness $H(\sigma, c_{sym})$. If this check fails then one outputs an error message $\perp$. Else, one decrypts the message m from the symmetric ciphertext c_{sym} under key $G(\sigma)$. It is easy to see that a genuinely encrypted message gets correctly decrypted again. We give the pseudocode of the FO construction as Construction 10.17 below:

Construction 10.17 (Fujisaki–Okamoto Construction).
Let G and H be random oracles, $PKE := (PKE.KGen, PKE.Enc, PKE.Dec)$ a public-key encryption scheme, and $SE := (SE.KGen, SE.Enc, SE.Dec)$ a symmetric encryption scheme. Then the FO hybrid encryption construction PKE^{FO} is given by

$PKE^{FO}.KGen(1^\lambda)$	$PKE^{G,H}.Dec(sk, c)$
1: $(pk, sk) \leftarrow_{\$} PKE.KGen(1^\lambda)$	1: $(c_{asym}, c_{sym}) \leftarrow c$
2: **return** (pk, sk)	2: $\sigma \leftarrow PKE.Dec(sk, c_{asym})$
	3: **if** $\sigma = \perp$ **then**
$PKE^{FO\,G,H}.Enc(pk, m)$	4: **return** $\perp$
1: $\sigma \leftarrow_{\$} \{0,1\}^{\ell_\sigma}$	5: **if** $c_{asym} \neq PKE.Enc(pk, \sigma; H(\sigma, c_{sym}))$ **then**
2: $c_{sym} \leftarrow SE.Enc(G(\sigma), m)$	6: **return** $\perp$
3: $c_{asym} \leftarrow PKE.Enc(pk, \sigma; H(\sigma, c_{sym}))$	7: **return** $m \leftarrow sk.Dec(G(\sigma), c_{sym})$
4: **return** $c \leftarrow (c_{asym}, c_{sym})$	

The FO hybrid encryption scheme achieves IND-CCA security in the random oracle model if symmetric encryption scheme SE is indistinguishable for a single ciphertext (IND, Definition 5.2 on page 213), and public-key encryption scheme PKE is one-way (i.e., if one cannot recover the value σ from a ciphertext), and finally if the public key encryption scheme "distributes well." The latter is captured by a technical condition that the scheme is γ-spread which says that for any key pair $(pk, sk) \leftarrow_{\$} PKE.KGen(\lambda)$ and any $\sigma \in \{0,1\}^{\ell_\sigma}$ we have that

$$H_\infty(PKE.Enc(pk, \sigma)) \geq \gamma(\lambda)$$

for some super-logarithmic function γ. In other words, ciphertexts (over the random coin tosses) hit a certain ciphertext c with negligible probability of at most $2^{-\gamma(\lambda)}$. Note that all stipulations on the underlying schemes are very mild and yet the transformed scheme achieves a very strong security property, thanks to the power of the random oracles.

Let us briefly discuss why the FO transform is IND-CCA secure. Let us start with the simpler IND-CPA case. The one-wayness of the public-key encryption scheme ensures that the adversary cannot recover σ—recall that value σ is chosen uniformly at random—from a given ciphertext $(c_{\mathrm{asym}}, c_{\mathrm{sym}})$. This holds also if we use $H(\sigma, c_{\mathrm{sym}})$ as randomness when encrypting σ to c_{asym}, because until the adversary queries H about σ the hash value is uniformly random to the adversary. But if the adversary cannot recover (the entire string) σ, then $G(\sigma)$ is a fresh random key due to G being a random oracle. The IND property of the symmetric encryption scheme SE therefore suffices to hide the encrypted message m in c_{sym}.

To set the above argument forth to the IND-CCA case one needs to account for decryption queries which the adversary may make. This is where we use that the underlying public-key encryption scheme PKE is γ-spread and that we include c_{sym} in the hash evaluation of H. The latter ensures that if the adversary takes a challenge ciphertext $(c_{\mathrm{asym}}, c_{\mathrm{sym}})$ and only modifies the symmetric-key part to c^*_{sym} then the hash value $H(\sigma, c^*_{\mathrm{sym}})$ would be independently distributed from the original value $H(\sigma, c_{\mathrm{sym}})$. But then the public-key encryption check (line 5 of the decryption algorithm) would most likely fail as it will hit c_{asym} only with negligible probability due to the scheme being γ-spread. With the same line of reasoning one can show that the adversary cannot submit a valid ciphertext $c^* = (c^*_{\mathrm{asym}}, c^*_{\mathrm{sym}})$ to the decryption oracle without having queried H about $(\sigma^*, c^*_{\mathrm{sym}})$ before, for the encapsulated value σ^* in c^*_{asym}. Else the unknown random value $H(\sigma^*, c^*_{\mathrm{sym}})$ would make the encryption scheme return c^*_{asym} with negligible probability only. Hence, the adversary must already know σ^* and thus could decrypt to the message m^* itself. This shows that decryption queries are useless for the adversary.

10.5 Probabilistic Signature Scheme—PSS

The probabilistic signature scheme (PSS) is a variant of the RSA-based full-domain hash signature scheme (Section 9.3.1, page 382) which provides a tighter security bound. The security proof for FDH signatures guesses a hash query to insert a given image under the trapdoor function, losing a factor proportional to the number of hash queries. In contrast to the deterministic FDH scheme, the PSS scheme introduces randomness into the signing process. This enables a security proof which relates the unforgeability of the signature scheme tightly to the one-wayness of RSA. Note that in the FDH security proof we had a loss that is linear in the number of random oracle queries by the adversary.

Construction 10.18 (Probabilistic Signature Scheme RSA-PSS).
Let ℓ_h, ℓ_r, ℓ_p be length parameters denoting the length of hashed messages, the randomness length, and the length of the zero pad. Let $\mathsf{G} : \{0,1\}^{\ell_h} \to \{0,1\}^{\ell_r + \ell_p}$ and $\mathsf{H} : \{0,1\}^* \to \{0,1\}^{\ell_h}$ be random oracles and let $\mathsf{RSA} := (\mathsf{RSA.KGen}, \mathsf{RSA.Eval}, \mathsf{RSA.Inv})$ be the RSA trapdoor function. Then the RSA-PSS construction is given by

$\mathsf{Sig.KGen}(1^\lambda)$

$(N, e, d) \leftarrow_\$ \mathsf{RSA.KGen}(1^\lambda)$

$(\mathsf{pk}, \mathsf{sk}) \leftarrow ((N, e), (N, d))$

return $(\mathsf{pk}, \mathsf{sk})$

$\mathsf{Sig}^{\mathsf{G},\mathsf{H}}.\mathsf{Sign}(\mathsf{sk}, m)$

$r \leftarrow_\$ \{0,1\}^{\ell_r}$

$w \leftarrow \mathsf{H}(m||r)$

$r^*||p \leftarrow \mathsf{G}(w) \oplus r||0^{\ell_p}$

$/\!/ \; r^* \in \{0,1\}^{\ell_r}, \; p \in \{0,1\}^{\ell_p}$

$\sigma \leftarrow \mathsf{RSA.Inv}(\mathsf{sk}, 0||w||r^*||p)$

return σ

$\mathsf{Sig}^{\mathsf{G},\mathsf{H}}.\mathsf{Vf}(\mathsf{pk}, m, \sigma)$

$b||w||r^*||p \leftarrow \mathsf{RSA.Eval}(\mathsf{tk}, c)$

$/\!/ \; b \in \{0,1\}, \; w \in \{0,1\}^{\ell_h}, \; r^* \in \{0,1\}^{\ell_r}, \; p \in \{0,1\}^{\ell_p}$

$r||z \leftarrow \mathsf{G}(w) \oplus r^*||0^{\ell_p}$

if $\mathsf{H}(m||r) = w$ *and* $z = p$ *and* $b = 0$ **then**

    return 1

else

    return 0

As in the OAEP and FO schemes, the PSS scheme makes use of two random oracles $\mathsf{G} : \{0,1\}^{\ell_h} \to \{0,1\}^{\ell_r + \ell_p}$ and $\mathsf{H} : \{0,1\}^* \to \{0,1\}^{\ell_h}$, where the length parameters ℓ_h, ℓ_r, ℓ_p denote the length of the hashed, randomized messages $m||r$, the length of the randomness r, and the length of the remaining ℓ_p bits. The signing process is depicted in Figure 10.5. The scheme first computes the hash value $w = \mathsf{H}(m||r)$ and then masks the 0-padded randomness $r||0^{\ell_p}$ with $\mathsf{G}(w)$ to get $r^*||p$. The scheme puts a 0-bit in the most significant position of the string to ensure that the integer is guaranteed to be smaller than N. It can then safely apply the inverse RSA function to the integer which represents the string $0||w||r^*||p$. The parameters are chosen such that $\ell_h + \ell_r + \ell_p = \lambda - 1$ for the RSA parameter N of λ bits.

Verification of a signature σ undoes the RSA inversion by applying the RSA function in forward direction. It recovers a string $b||w||r^*||p$ and then demasks $r^*||p$ with $\mathsf{G}(w)$ to obtain r. Once randomness r is recovered, together with message m one can check that p and w are correctly formed and that the leading bit is indeed 0.

The RSA-PSS scheme can be shown to be secure under the RSA assumption in the random oracle model. The randomness r plays a crucial role in giving a tight reduction. Recall that in the FDH case we needed to guess in advance

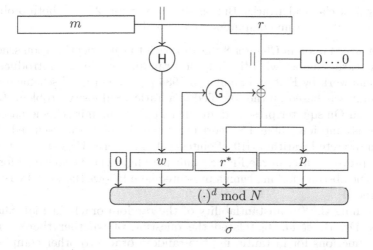

Fig. 10.5: PSS signature generation for message m with randomness r using RSA trapdoor permutation and random oracles G and H.

which H-query m will be used later to create a forgery. In the PSS case, however, we can divide the H-queries $m||r$ of the adversary into those relevant for forgeries and those for simulating signatures, because when we need to sign for a message m we pick a fresh string r which, most likely, has not appeared in an adversarial H-query before. The role of G is to be able to program the other input parts in the proof. The all-zero padding is only used to expand the string to the desired length but does not play any significant role in the proof.

Chapter Notes and References

Diffie and Hellman [5], in their ground-breaking work about public-key cryptography, used the assumed hardness of the discrete logarithm to derive their key exchange protocol. They pointed out that (back then) the best algorithms for this problem, even over $\mathbb{Z}_p^*$, still take time proportional to $q^{1/2}$ and were thus infeasible. But it was not immediately clear how the discrete-logarithm problem could be used to build a public-key encryption scheme, such that Rivest, Shamir, and Adleman [18] based their solution on factoring and introduced what is nowadays known as the RSA trapdoor function. Only later, El Gamal [7] showed that the Diffie–Hellman protocol can also be used to derive a (probabilistic) encryption scheme. Both problems, computing discrete logarithms and inverting the RSA function, are still considered to be secure against classical attacks. But, as shown by Shor [20, 21], both problems become easy if quantum computers are available.

As remarked upon in Chapter 8 the approach to turn identification schemes into signature schemes with the help of a random oracle was introduced in the seminal work by Fiat and Shamir in 1986 [8]. The original scheme of Fiat and Shamir was based on the so-called quadratic residuosity problem. Later, Guillou and Quisquater presented an efficient Fiat–Shamir scheme based on the RSA assumption [13] and Schnorr presented the protocol discussed above based on discrete logarithms [19]. Pointcheval and Stern [17] were the first to formally prove security of the Fiat–Shamir paradigm via the so-called forking lemma. The abstract forking lemma presented here follows the work by Bellare and Neven [1].

Concerning the (un)instantiability of the random oracle in Fiat–Shamir schemes, Dwork *et al.* [6] related the question of whether there can be "magic" functions for instantiating the random oracle to other complexity-theoretic problems such as languages outside of BPP having three-message zero-knowledge protocols. Goldwasser and Tauman Kalai [12] showed that there are identification schemes which are provably secure in the random oracle model but become insecure under any instantiation of the random oracle through an efficient hash function. It is currently unclear if this result also applies to concrete schemes such as the Schnorr protocol. We will discuss what it means for a random oracle to be (un)instantiable in more detail in Chapter 12.

Among the Fiat–Shamir signature schemes the Schnorr version (especially over elliptic curves) prevails over the RSA variants today, mainly because of efficiency reasons and since there are viable alternatives for RSA. Schnorr signatures can be found for instance in ISO 14888-3 [14] and in RFC 8032 [15].

OAEP was introduced in a work by Bellare and Rogaway [2]. In that paper they also claimed IND-CCA security of OAEP. This was shown later by Shoup [22, 23] to not hold in general, identifying a gap in the original proof. Shoup also gave a proof for specific cases of the RSA trapdoor function (with exponent $e = 3$) and for RSA in general for a variation of OAEP. Subsequently Fujisaki *et al.* [11] presented a proof for the original OAEP scheme for the general RSA case.

The Fujisaki–Okamoto transform appears in [10] with slight changes to the conference version [9]. In the conference version the authors formulated the min-entropy requirement differently (but semantically equivalent) and called it γ-uniformity instead. More importantly, in the original conference version the message was used as input to the random oracle, $H(\sigma, m)$, instead of $H(\sigma, c_{\text{sym}})$ as displayed here and in the journal version.

We note that also for the Fujisaki–Okamoto transformation it is unclear whether the random oracles can be instantiated by standard model hash functions such that security guarantees remain valid for any choice of admissible public-key and symmetric encryption scheme. A conditional uninstantiability result was given by Brzuska *et al.* [4], who show that if so-called indistinguishability obfuscators exist—indistinguishability obfuscators are a strong form of cryptographically secure code obfuscators that we will briefly encounter in Section 18.5.1—then the random oracles in the transformation are not instantiable in general.

RSA-PSS was proposed by Bellare and Rogaway [3]. In some standards it appears in slight variations but which do not seem to affect the security claims. PSS and OAEP can be found for instance in RFC 8017 [16].

Exercices

Exercise 10.1. Show that any left identity element in a group is also a right identity element (and vice versa). Show that the analogous statement holds for left and right inverses.

Exercise 10.2. Show that $\mathbb{Z}_m$ with addition forms a commutative group with identity element 0 for any $m \in \mathbb{N}^+$.

Exercise 10.3. Compute the greatest common divisor of 486 and 300 with the extended Euclidean algorithm in Figure 10.1 (page 411).

Exercise 10.4. In the Fiat–Shamir protocol we also allow for challenges $c = 0$, although this means that the response $y \leftarrow r + cx \bmod q$ does not depend on the secret key x. Argue that this does not violate security.

Exercise 10.5. Explain why we cannot use σ directly in the symmetric encryption scheme in the Fujisaki–Okamoto transform if we assume (only) one-wayness of the public-key encryption scheme.

Chapter Bibliography

1. Mihir Bellare and Gregory Neven. Multi-signatures in the plain public-key model and a general forking lemma. In Ari Juels, Rebecca N. Wright, and Sabrina De Capitani di Vimercati, editors, *ACM CCS 2006: 13th Conference on Computer and Communications Security*, pages 390–399, Alexandria, Virginia, USA, October 30 – November 3, 2006. ACM Press.
2. Mihir Bellare and Phillip Rogaway. Optimal asymmetric encryption. In Alfredo De Santis, editor, *Advances in Cryptology – EUROCRYPT'94*, volume 950 of *Lecture Notes in Computer Science*, pages 92–111, Perugia, Italy, May 9–12, 1995. Springer, Heidelberg, Germany.
3. Mihir Bellare and Phillip Rogaway. The exact security of digital signatures: How to sign with RSA and Rabin. In Ueli M. Maurer, editor, *Advances in Cryptology – EUROCRYPT'96*, volume 1070 of *Lecture Notes in Computer Science*, pages 399–416, Saragossa, Spain, May 12–16, 1996. Springer, Heidelberg, Germany.

4. Christina Brzuska, Pooya Farshim, and Arno Mittelbach. Random-oracle uninstantiability from indistinguishability obfuscation. In Yevgeniy Dodis and Jesper Buus Nielsen, editors, *TCC 2015: 12th Theory of Cryptography Conference, Part II*, volume 9015 of *Lecture Notes in Computer Science*, pages 428–455, Warsaw, Poland, March 23–25, 2015. Springer, Heidelberg, Germany.
5. Whitfield Diffie and Martin E. Hellman. New directions in cryptography. *IEEE Transactions on Information Theory*, 22(6):644–654, 1976.
6. Cynthia Dwork, Moni Naor, Omer Reingold, and Larry J. Stockmeyer. Magic functions. In *40th Annual Symposium on Foundations of Computer Science*, pages 523–534, New York, NY, USA, October 17–19, 1999. IEEE Computer Society Press.
7. Taher ElGamal. A public key cryptosystem and a signature scheme based on discrete logarithms. *IEEE Transactions on Information Theory*, 31:469–472, 1985.
8. Amos Fiat and Adi Shamir. How to prove yourself: Practical solutions to identification and signature problems. In Andrew M. Odlyzko, editor, *Advances in Cryptology – CRYPTO'86*, volume 263 of *Lecture Notes in Computer Science*, pages 186–194, Santa Barbara, CA, USA, August 1987. Springer, Heidelberg, Germany.
9. Eiichiro Fujisaki and Tatsuaki Okamoto. Secure integration of asymmetric and symmetric encryption schemes. In Michael J. Wiener, editor, *Advances in Cryptology – CRYPTO'99*, volume 1666 of *Lecture Notes in Computer Science*, pages 537–554, Santa Barbara, CA, USA, August 15–19, 1999. Springer, Heidelberg, Germany.
10. Eiichiro Fujisaki and Tatsuaki Okamoto. Secure integration of asymmetric and symmetric encryption schemes. *Journal of Cryptology*, 26(1):80–101, January 2013.
11. Eiichiro Fujisaki, Tatsuaki Okamoto, David Pointcheval, and Jacques Stern. RSA-OAEP is secure under the RSA assumption. In Joe Kilian, editor, *Advances in Cryptology – CRYPTO 2001*, volume 2139 of *Lecture Notes in Computer Science*, pages 260–274, Santa Barbara, CA, USA, August 19–23, 2001. Springer, Heidelberg, Germany.
12. Shafi Goldwasser and Yael Tauman Kalai. On the (in)security of the Fiat-Shamir paradigm. In *44th Annual Symposium on Foundations of Computer Science*, pages 102–115, Cambridge, MA, USA, October 11–14, 2003. IEEE Computer Society Press.
13. Louis C. Guillou and Jean-Jacques Quisquater. A practical zero-knowledge protocol fitted to security microprocessor minimizing both trasmission and memory. In C. G. Günther, editor, *Advances in Cryptology – EUROCRYPT'88*, volume 330 of *Lecture Notes in Computer Science*, pages 123–128, Davos, Switzerland, May 25–27, 1988. Springer, Heidelberg, Germany.
14. ISO. Information technology. security techniques. digital signatures with appendix. discrete logarithm based mechanisms. Norm ISO/IEC 14888-3:2018, International Organization for Standardization, November 2018.
15. Simon Josefsson and Ilari Liusvaara. Edwards-curve Digital Signature Algorithm (eddsa). RFC 8032, RFC Editor, January 2017.
16. Kathleen Moriarty, Burt Kaliski, Jakob Jonsson, and Andreas Rusch. PKCS #1: RSA Cryptography Specifications Version 2.2. Technical Report 8017, November 2016.
17. David Pointcheval and Jacques Stern. Security arguments for digital signatures and blind signatures. *Journal of Cryptology*, 13(3):361–396, June 2000.
18. Ronald L. Rivest, Adi Shamir, and Leonard M. Adleman. A method for obtaining digital signatures and public-key cryptosystems. *Communications of the Association for Computing Machinery*, 21(2):120–126, 1978.
19. Claus-Peter Schnorr. Efficient signature generation by smart cards. *Journal of Cryptology*, 4(3):161–174, January 1991.
20. Peter W. Shor. Algorithms for quantum computation: Discrete logarithms and factoring. In *35th Annual Symposium on Foundations of Computer Science*, pages 124–134. IEEE Computer Society, 1994.
21. Peter W. Shor. Polynomial-time algorithms for prime factorization and discrete logarithms on a quantum computer. *SIAM J. Comput.*, 26(5):1484–1509, 1997.

22. Victor Shoup. OAEP reconsidered. In Joe Kilian, editor, *Advances in Cryptology – CRYPTO 2001*, volume 2139 of *Lecture Notes in Computer Science*, pages 239–259, Santa Barbara, CA, USA, August 19–23, 2001. Springer, Heidelberg, Germany.

23. Victor Shoup. OAEP reconsidered. *Journal of Cryptology*, 15(4):223–249, September 2002.

Chapter 11
Limitations of Random Oracles

Random oracles are a very powerful tool. As we have seen, they simultaneously give rise to one-way functions, collision-resistant hash functions, pseudorandom generators, symmetric encryption schemes, and more. This brings up the question if there are cryptographic primitives which cannot be built from random oracles. We give strong indications here that this is indeed the case. Namely, we show that secure public-key encryption, and even key exchange protocols, appear to be hard to construct from a random oracle only.

In a key exchange protocol two parties agree on a common secret which the adversary cannot deduce. As we will show, such protocols are easy to derive from specific number-theoretic assumptions, especially from the Diffie–Hellman problem. But we show that the task appears to be out of reach if one merely relies on random oracles. Only a very limited form of key agreement is possible in this case, using so-called Merkle puzzles.

11.1 Key Exchange Protocols

The idea of key exchange protocols[1] is that two parties interact over a public communication channel in order to agree on a cryptographic key. An adversary, observing only the communication between the two parties, on the other hand, should not be able to compute the key. This enables the two parties to use the key to secure the subsequent communication. This approach is fundamental for security of modern communication, and key exchange protocols are clearly among the most widely deployed cryptographic protocols today.

Formally, a key exchange protocol is an interactive protocol between two parties A and B, for Alice and Bob. Both parties receive security parameter 1^λ as input and then exchange messages. In addition, each party holds a random

---

[1] The terms "key exchange" and "key agreement" are usually used synonymously in the literature.

© Springer Nature Switzerland AG 2021

A. Mittelbach, M. Fischlin, *The Theory of Hash Functions and Random Oracles*, Information Security and Cryptography, https://doi.org/10.1007/978-3-030-63287-8_11

string of sufficient length, denoted by r_A (for A) and r_B (for B). By convention we say that A sends the first message m_1, B the second one m_2, A the third one m_3, and so on, and that B sends the last message m_t. This is without loss of generality, since we can assume that A in her first message and B in his last message sends a redundant value to make the protocol fit our format. Since the round complexity is irrelevant for us as long as it is polynomial, this does not obstruct our impossibility result.

Each outgoing message of a party depends on the input, the previously received messages, and the party's randomness. We describe this by running the algorithms $A(1^\lambda, r_A, m_1, m_2, \dots)$ and $B(1^\lambda, r_B, m_1, m_2, \dots)$ on the partial transcripts up to some round, and each algorithm then outputs the next message. At some point both parties stop and output local keys k_A and k_B. We model this by having algorithms A and B return a dedicated symbol output together with the key. We denote by $\mathsf{transc} = (m_1, m_2, \dots, m_t)$ the transcript of the execution, consisting of the sequence of exchanged messages, where t is polynomial but may depend on the parties' inputs. We give a schematic of a key exchange protocol below in Figure 11.1.

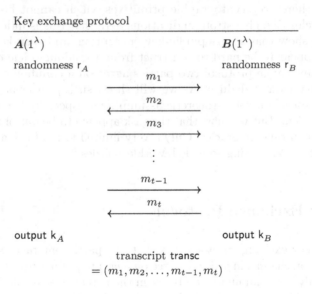

Fig. 11.1: Schematic overview of a key exchange protocol.

We write $\mathsf{KE} = \langle A, B \rangle$ for the key exchange protocol between A and B. Similarly, we let $(\mathsf{k}_A, \mathsf{transc}, \mathsf{k}_B) \leftarrow\!\!\!{}^\$ \langle A(1^\lambda), B(1^\lambda) \rangle$ denote the outcome of a randomized execution of the key exchange protocol, where the probability is over the randomness r_A and r_B of both parties. The outcome comprises the local outputs of both parties as well as the transcript. If we consider the execution for fixed random tapes r_A and r_B we get a deterministic output, $(\mathsf{k}_A, \mathsf{transc}, \mathsf{k}_B) \leftarrow \langle A(1^\lambda; r_A), B(1^\lambda; r_B) \rangle$.

So far we have not made any stipulation on the parties' keys k_A and k_B. Ideally, they should coincide, of course, such that both parties can use the key $k_A = k_B$ to communicate reliably afterwards. If this always holds then we call the scheme *perfectly* correct. In general, however, a negligible error of ending up with different keys may be acceptable. For our impossibility results we consider protocols with perfect correctness to simplify the presentation.

Another property we still need to consider is security. The goal of a key exchange protocol is to make sure that only A and B know the key. In particular, this should hold even if an adversary $\mathcal{E}$ (for Eve) eavesdrops on the communication during the key exchange step. Put differently, the adversary should not be able to deduce, say, A's key k_A from the transcript. Since we assume that the keys are (almost surely) identical, we only consider the case that the adversary tries to predict k_A and can ignore k_B for security. Both properties are subsumed in the following definition:

Definition 11.1 (Weakly Secure Key Exchange Protocol). *A key exchange protocol* $\mathsf{KE} = \langle A, B \rangle$ *between* PPT *algorithms A and B is a weakly secure key exchange protocol if:*

(Perfect) Correctness: *The probability that $k_A \neq k_B$ for*

$$(k_A, \mathsf{transc}, k_B) \leftarrow_{\$} \langle A(1^\lambda), B(1^\lambda) \rangle$$

is negligible, where the probability is over the randomness of A and B. The protocol is perfectly correct *if always $k_A = k_B$.*

Weak Security: *For all* PPT *algorithms $\mathcal{E}$ the probability that*

$$\mathcal{E}(1^\lambda, \mathsf{transc}) = k_A$$

for $\langle k_A, \mathsf{transc}, k_B \rangle \leftarrow_{\$} \langle A(1^\lambda), B(1^\lambda) \rangle$ *is negligible, where the probability is over the random choices of all parties A, B, and $\mathcal{E}$.*

Weak security refers to the fact that $\mathcal{E}$ must recover the entire key in order to win. This, in turn, requires that the key length is super-logarithmic. Stronger requirements for modern key exchange protocols usually ask that $\mathcal{E}$ cannot distinguish the key from an independent random string, and thus cannot even compute individual key bits significantly better than by guessing. Another restriction of the adversary here is that it remains entirely passive during the execution; modern key exchange protocols should also withstand active attacks in which the adversary can modify or inject messages sent over the communication channel. A third simplification is that we do not touch upon the question of authentication of communication partners, another property which is common in today's protocols. The weaker stipulations here only strengthen our negative result in the sense that, if the weak form of key exchange cannot be based on random oracles, then neither can stronger forms.

Key Transport Protocols

Assume that we have a public-key encryption scheme PKE = (PKE.KGen, PKE.Enc, PKE.Dec) which is IND-CPA (Definition 5.27 on page 246). Then we can build a weakly secure key exchange protocol by having one party encrypt the shared key under the public key of the other party:

Key transport protocol
_____

$A(1^\lambda)$ $B(1^\lambda)$

$(\mathsf{pk}, \mathsf{sk}) \leftarrow_\$ \mathsf{PKE.KGen}(1^\lambda)$

$\xrightarrow{\quad \mathsf{pk} \quad}$

$\qquad\qquad\qquad\qquad\qquad\qquad\qquad\quad k_B \leftarrow_\$ \{0,1\}^\lambda$

$\qquad\qquad\qquad\qquad\qquad\qquad\qquad\quad C \leftarrow_\$ \mathsf{PKE.Enc}(\mathsf{pk}, k_B)$

$\xleftarrow{\quad\quad C \quad\quad}$

$k_A \leftarrow \mathsf{PKE.Dec}(\mathsf{sk}, C)$

output k_A output k_B

This method of generating a shared key is called *key transport*. Completeness follows from the completeness of the encryption scheme, saying that A obtains the encrypted key. Secrecy of the key follows from the IND-CPA security of the encryption scheme, because the key exchange adversary $\mathcal{E}$ receives the transcript $\mathsf{transc} = (\mathsf{pk}, C)$ and is supposed to compute the encrypted value k_B. This is infeasible by the IND-CPA security of the encryption scheme because computing the correct message k_B with non-negligible probability allows to distinguish it from some other message (say, the constant 0^λ). In fact, one-wayness of the encryption scheme would suffice here.

We note that the example can be combined with our impossibility result about deriving key exchange protocols using random oracles only. This then shows that one cannot build IND-CPA-secure public-key encryption schemes from random oracles only. Otherwise one would also have such a weakly secure key exchange protocol by the construction in the above example.

11.2 Diffie–Hellman Key Exchange

Diffie and Hellman in their seminal paper about public-key encryption proposed a key exchange protocol based on the discrete-logarithm problem (see Section 10.1.2; page 413). The plain version of the protocol is given in Figure 11.2. Here, both parties A and B already share a description of a group $\mathcal{G}$ with generator g for security parameter λ. Unlike in the original proposal we assume that the order of the group is prime q. Each party now picks a secret exponent, x for A resp. y for B, and sends $X \leftarrow g^x$ resp. $Y \leftarrow g^y$ to

Plain Diffie–Hellman key exchange protocol		
$A(1^\lambda)$	$\mathcal{G}, g, q$	$B(1^\lambda)$
$x \leftarrow\!\!\$\ \mathbb{Z}_q$		$y \leftarrow\!\!\$\ \mathbb{Z}_q$
$X \leftarrow g^x$		$Y \leftarrow g^y$
	$\xrightarrow{\qquad X \qquad}$	
	$\xleftarrow{\qquad Y \qquad}$	
$k_A \leftarrow Y^x$		$k_B \leftarrow Y^x$

Fig. 11.2: Plain version of the Diffie–Hellman key exchange protocol.

the other party. Then A computes the shared secret key as $k_A \leftarrow Y^x$ and B as $k_B \leftarrow X^y$ in the group. Note that for well-formed data we have

$$k_A = Y^x = (g^y)^x = g^{xy} = (g^x)^y = X^y = k_B,$$

which means that both parties agree on the same value.

We note that in practice the Diffie–Hellman value $k_A = k_B$ would be run through a key derivation function to derive a smoothly distributed bit string as key. We omit this step from the description here but note that we have already encountered such steps briefly in Section 7.2 about (non-cryptographic) extractors, and will look at such key derivation functions more comprehensively in Section 16.6 when discussing the HMAC-based key derivation function HKDF.

When saying that the protocol is based on the discrete-logarithm problem we refer to the fact that the intractability of the discrete-logarithm problem is necessary for the protocol's security. That is, if an adversary could compute the discrete logarithm of either X or Y then it can also compute the shared key of both parties. However, it is unknown if the discrete-logarithm assumption is also sufficient to show security. While there are no known general attacks on the Diffie–Hellman protocol, currently we cannot give any security reduction to the discrete-logarithm assumption. Based on the longstanding intractability of the protocol it is nonetheless reasonable to assume the security directly, namely that it is infeasible to compute g^{xy} from g^x and g^y. The latter is called the *Diffie–Hellman assumption*.

The Diffie–Hellman protocol relies on the properties of the underlying number-theoretic structure. When A and B raise the received group element to their secret exponent, they end up with the same value by the commutativity of the cyclic group $\mathcal{G}$. This gives little guidance on how to build secure key exchange protocols based on random oracles where such features are missing. In the next section we show that weaker forms of protocols are possible, though.

11.3 Merkle Puzzles

We begin by describing a simple protocol by Merkle to agree on a key using a random oracle only. The caveat of the solution is that it only gives a quadratic runtime advantage for the honest parties over the eavesdropping adversary and, thus, does not match the required negligible security risk according to Definition 11.1, where $\mathcal{E}$ may indeed have a quadratic overhead in comparison with A and B. We also note that the protocol is not perfectly correct but has a negligible error that A and B actually do not agree on the same key.

Merkle's idea is based on so-called *puzzles*. These are small problems which can be solved with some small yet noticeable effort. Concretely, for the random oracle-based solution the puzzle will be to find a preimage for a hash value $P_i = \mathrm{RO}(x)$, where x is short but not too short. If RO acts as a random oracle then finding a preimage should require roughly $2^{|x|}$ steps. Now suppose that A sends a puzzle to B, where the puzzle contains a puzzle key puzk of κ bits, where $\kappa \ll \lambda$ cannot be too large. This puzzle key is used to encrypt the actual key $\mathsf{k} \in \{0,1\}^{\lambda}$ under some symmetric encryption scheme:

$$P = (\mathrm{RO}(\mathsf{puzk}), \mathrm{Enc}(\mathsf{puzk}, \mathsf{k})).$$

Obtaining this puzzle P from A, party B can search through all possible puzzle keys puzk in time roughly 2^{κ} to eventually recover the shared key k. There are, however, two issues: First, since the adversary $\mathcal{E}$ can also perform the search, A and B would not obtain any advantage over $\mathcal{E}$. Second, we have to ensure that B actually picks the right puzzle key and does not coincidentally derive a different key $\mathsf{k}_B \neq \mathsf{k}$, at least not too often.

To give A and B some performance advantage over $\mathcal{E}$, party A not only creates a single puzzle, but 2^{κ} independent puzzles $P_1, P_2, \ldots, P_{2^{\kappa}}$ instead. She sends all puzzles to B. Party B only solves one of these puzzles, P_j, the choice made at random. Then B informs A about his choice j, but this is done in such a way that $\mathcal{E}$ does not learn j. For this A also encrypts a hidden unique identifier $\mathsf{id}_i \in \{0,1\}^{\kappa}$ with the key k_i in the ith puzzle, and B returns id_j to A after having decrypted the jth puzzle. A can then identify the puzzle which B has solved and output the corresponding key. The attacker $\mathcal{E}$, on the other hand, cannot deduce the choice j from the identifier id_j and needs to solve approximately half of the transmitted puzzles before finding the right identifier, yielding a runtime advantage for A and B. We argue this more formally below.

To take care of the correctness property in the protocol, $\mathsf{k}_A = \mathsf{k}_B$, we add redundancy 0^{λ} to the encryption of id_i and k_i, computing $\mathrm{Enc}(\mathsf{puzk}_i, 0^{\lambda}||\mathsf{id}_i||\mathsf{k}_k)$. Then a wrong puzzle key puzk'_i most likely does not yield a valid decryption with leading 0's. In fact, since we work in the random oracle model, we combine the hashing of the puzzle key and the encryption into a single hash operation and set

$$P_i = \mathrm{RO}(i||\mathsf{puzk}_i) \oplus 0^{\lambda}||\mathsf{id}_i||\mathsf{k}_i.$$

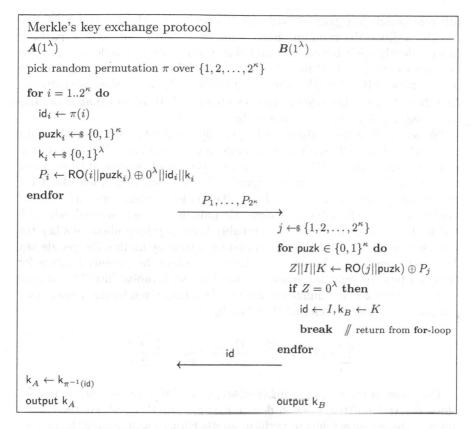

Fig. 11.3: Merkle's key exchange protocol based on a random oracle

Here we assume that the integer $i \in \{1, 2, \ldots, 2^\kappa\}$ is encoded with κ bits and that the output of the random oracle is $2\lambda + \kappa$ bits. The latter can be achieved in the random oracle model by iterating the hash function for different prefixes and concatenating the outputs.

The protocol is depicted in Figure 11.3. The identifiers id_i are generated as $\pi(i)$ for a random permutation π over $\{1, 2, \ldots, 2^\kappa\}$, known only to A.[2] We again assume that such integers between 1 and 2^κ are encoded with κ bits. The protocol also assumes that both parties know the complexity parameter κ. This parameter can be set arbitrarily except that we require $2\kappa \leq \lambda$ for overwhelming correctness.

Analysis. We first discuss correctness. Since the identifiers $\mathsf{id}_i = \pi(i)$ are unique, B's answer id unambiguously yields the number $j = \pi^{-1}(\mathsf{id})$ of the puzzle which B has solved. Hence, the only mismatch can origin from a

---

[2] An alternative to random permutation π is for A to keep a lookup table where she stores 2^κ random (but distinct) identifiers.

different puzzle key $\mathsf{puzk} \neq \mathsf{puzk}_j$ in B's search which also yields leading zero bits. Since the random oracle value $\mathsf{RO}(j\|\mathsf{puzk})$ for $\mathsf{puzk} \neq \mathsf{puzk}_j$ is independently distributed, the probability for a fixed puzzle key puzk to obtain zero bits in Z is at most $2^{-\lambda}$. The probability that there exists any key $\mathsf{puzk} \neq \mathsf{puzk}_j$ with $Z = 0^\lambda$ is thus at most $(2^\kappa - 1) \cdot 2^{-\lambda}$. Since we assumed that $2\kappa \leq \lambda$ this is bounded from above by $2^{-\lambda/2}$. It follows that B obtains the wrong key k_B with negligible probability only.

We next look at the runtimes and especially the number of hash evaluations. A and B both need 2^κ hash computations in the worst case. The adversary $\mathcal{E}$ receives a transcript $((P_1, \ldots, P_{2^\kappa}), \mathsf{id})$ as input and is supposed to compute A's key k_A. We note that unless $\mathcal{E}$ queries the hash function oracle about the right input $i\|\mathsf{puzk}_i$ of the ith puzzle P_i, all other hash values yield independent random answers which leak no information about the encapsulated values id_i and k_i. In other words, in order to reliably learn anything about A's key the adversary needs to solve the corresponding puzzle by finding the puzzle key. This corresponds to a linear search where $\mathcal{E}$ orders the potential values for puzk and hits the right key (chosen at random) with probability $2^{-\kappa}$ for each iteration. The expected number of hash trials is thus given by the average-case runtime of a linear search and therefore by

$$\sum_{i=1}^{2^\kappa} i \cdot 2^{-\kappa} = \frac{(2^\kappa + 1) \cdot 2^\kappa}{2} \cdot \frac{1}{2^\kappa} = \frac{2^\kappa + 1}{2}.$$

The above is the average number of steps for $\mathcal{E}$ to solve *one* of the puzzles. Since B's transmitted value id does not reveal anything about the chosen index j, the adversary has to perform another linear search over the puzzles $P_1, \ldots, P_{2^\kappa}$ to find the one which holds $\mathsf{id} = \pi(j)$ for the random j. It follows that $\mathcal{E}$ thus needs to solve at least an expected number of $\frac{2^\kappa+1}{2}$ puzzles, each requiring $\frac{2^\kappa+1}{2}$ hash evaluations on average. In total, $\mathcal{E}$ needs to perform an expected number of

$$\frac{2^\kappa + 1}{2} \cdot \frac{2^\kappa + 1}{2} \geq \frac{2^{2\kappa}}{4}$$

hash evaluations to recover the shared key. This number is quadratic in the number of hash evaluations of A and B (up to a constant).

11.4 Key Exchange and Complexity Theory

Merkle's key exchange protocol only gives a slight advantage for the honest parties over the adversary. We next show our main result that one cannot build weakly secure key exchange protocols based on random oracles only, with the usual super-polynomial advantage. For this we need to make sure that the key exchange protocol does not ignore the random oracle and uses some other cryptographic mechanism instead, such as a public-key encryption scheme to transport the key securely. This is accomplished by ensuring that all other cryptographic primitives except for the random oracle are broken. One way to do so is by assuming that there are no hard problems at all. In the language of complexity theory, we assume that $\mathsf{P} = \mathsf{NP}$ (see Section 1.4 on page 36 for the definition of these classes). We first show that in such a world any attempt to build a secure protocol, without relying on the random oracle model, is hopeless. The reader is advised to inspect the proof in this simpler case, because we will later use a similar approach when extending the impossibility result to protocols using the random oracle.

Recall that $\mathsf{P} = \mathsf{NP}$ not only allows to decide NP-languages $\mathscr{L}$ efficiently, but also allows to find a witness efficiently (see Theorem 1.21). More formally, there is a polynomial-time algorithm W which on input $x \in \mathscr{L}$ outputs a witness w such that $(x, w) \in \mathscr{R}$ for the relation associated to the language. We use this property to break any key exchange protocol. For this we specify a suitable NP-relation $\mathscr{R}_A$ which captures all possible runs of A which match the given transcript transc. The randomness r_A of A will serve as a witness, such that we can use W to recover a matching randomness and from there compute A's key k_A. One of the problems we have to overcome is that algorithm W may not output the same witness r_A which A has actually used. The algorithm only guarantees that some witness is found, but we show below that this is sufficient.

> **Theorem 11.2.** *Suppose* $\mathsf{P} = \mathsf{NP}$. *Then there is no weakly secure key exchange protocol with perfect correctness.*

Proof. Assume towards contradiction that there exists a weakly secure key exchange protocol $\mathsf{KE} = \langle A, B \rangle$. Let transc $= (m_1, m_2, \ldots, m_t)$ be the transcript of an execution between A and B, where A used secret randomness r_A and B used secret randomness r_B. The task of our adversary is to compute A's key k_A from $(1^\lambda, \mathsf{transc})$.

We first specify the NP-relation $\mathscr{R}_A$. Let $\mathrm{TCons}(1^\lambda, \mathsf{transc}, r'_A)$ be a "transcript consistency" predicate which takes the security parameter, the transcript transc $= (m_1, m_2, \ldots, m_t)$, and a random input r'_A for A, possibly different from the actual randomness r_A used to produce transc. The predicate outputs 1 if and only if for all $i = 1, 3, \ldots, t - 1$ we have $A(1^\lambda, r'_A, m_1, m_2, \ldots, m_{i-1}) = m_i$, that is, if A for randomness r'_A in each round generates the same outgoing messages as in transc when receiving B's messages as in transc. Note that the output key is then completely determined from r'_A and the transcript. Set

$$\mathscr{R}_A = \left\{ ((1^\lambda, \mathsf{transc}), r'_A) \mid \mathrm{TCons}(1^\lambda, \mathsf{transc}, r'_A) \right\}$$

to be the NP-relation which consists of public data $(1^\lambda, \mathsf{transc})$ and consistent random strings r'_A as witnesses.

Our adversary $\mathcal{E}$ now simply runs the guaranteed witness finder W for this relation to recover a consistent randomness r_A^* for the computation of A. Once found, it completes the computation of A on r_A^* to produce a candidate key k_A^*:

$$\mathcal{E}(1^\lambda, \mathsf{transc})$$

$\quad 1: \quad r_A^* \leftarrow \mathsf{W}(1^\lambda, \mathsf{transc})$

$\quad 2: \quad (\mathsf{output}, \mathsf{k}_A^*) \leftarrow A(1^\lambda, r_A^*, \mathsf{transc})$

$\quad 3: \quad \textbf{return } \mathsf{k}_A^*$

Obviously, $\mathcal{E}$ runs in polynomial time because the witness finder runs in polynomial time for $\mathsf{P} = \mathsf{NP}$. It remains to argue that $\mathcal{E}$ recovers the right key, that is, $\mathsf{k}_A^* = \mathsf{k}_A$. For this note that we must have $\mathsf{k}_A = \mathsf{k}_B$ for the actual keys computed by A (with randomness r_A) and B (with randomness r_B) according to perfect correctness. Consider now that, potentially, B had communicated with our A instance using randomness r_A^* instead. Then it would have seen the same incoming messages $m_1, m_3, \ldots$ and would have sent the same messages $m_2, m_4, \ldots$ This would then have been a valid execution between A with "randomness" r_A^* and B with randomness r_B. While r_A^* is not random at all, but generated by the deterministic algorithm W, it is a valid and consistent content for the random tape of A. Perfect correctness then implies that also these two instances must derive the same key $\mathsf{k}_B = \mathsf{k}_A^*$, from which it follows that $\mathsf{k}_A^* = \mathsf{k}_A$, as required. $\qquad\square$

Remark 11.3. The theorem can also be proved with negligible correctness error. For this one needs to use a probabilistic algorithm W which generates a uniformly distributed witness for the given NP relation (or outputs an error with some probability). This is possible with a more involved strategy for W and can then be used above to generate a uniformly distributed string r_A^*, such that correctness ensures that $\mathsf{k}_A^* = \mathsf{k}_A$ with sufficiently high probability.

Does the theorem above mean that, trivially, $\mathsf{P} = \mathsf{NP}$ also implies the impossibility of basing secure key exchange on random oracles? Unfortunately, this does not follow immediately, because in this case A and B would be algorithms with access to the random oracle RO. Designing an algorithm W which verifies or even finds a witness relative to relation $\mathscr{R}_A$ would then need oracle access to RO, too. The relation and the language would reside in the class $\mathsf{NP}^{\mathsf{RO}}$. But for a random oracle RO we have $\mathsf{P}^{\mathsf{RO}} \neq \mathsf{NP}^{\mathsf{RO}}$ with probability 1. This means that a random oracle actually separates easy-to-decide and easy-to-verify problems, whereas in Theorem 9.16 (page 395) we have shown that a random oracle allows to derandomize probabilistic algorithms and that $\mathsf{P}^{\mathsf{RO}} = \mathsf{BPP}^{\mathsf{RO}}$. Hence, since $\mathsf{P}^{\mathsf{RO}} \neq \mathsf{NP}^{\mathsf{RO}}$ it would be unclear how to implement the witness finder in polynomial time. In the next section we nonetheless show that the idea of using a witness finder still works, but requires a more sophisticated argument.

11.5 Impossibility of Key Exchange from Random Oracles

In this section we show that deriving a secure key exchange protocol using only a random oracle is infeasible. The approach is similar to Simon's separation result of collision resistance from one-wayness (Section 4.4.2, page 181). Here, we show that relative to an NP-oracle (such that P = NP) one can break any key exchange protocol which relies solely on a random oracle RO. In other words, no reduction relativizes (holds relative to any oracle), thus ruling out a large class of black-box reductions (also see our discussion on black-box separations on page 181).

In order to show the result, let us first present the definition of a weakly secure key exchange protocol in the presence of a random oracle RO.

Definition 11.4 (Weakly Secure Key Exchange Protocol). *A key exchange protocol* $\mathsf{KE} = \langle A, B \rangle$ *between* PPT *oracle algorithms A and B is a weakly secure key exchange protocol in the random oracle model if:*

(Perfect) Correctness: *The probability that* $k_A \neq k_B$ *for*

$$(k_A, \mathsf{transc}, k_B) \leftarrow_\$ \left\langle A^{\mathsf{RO}}(1^\lambda), B^{\mathsf{RO}}(1^\lambda) \right\rangle$$

is negligible. Here, the probability is over the randomness of A and B but holds for any choice of RO. *The protocol is perfectly correct if always* $k_A = k_B$.

Weak Security: *For all* PPT *oracle algorithms $\mathcal{E}$ the probability that*

$$\mathcal{E}^{\mathsf{RO}}(1^\lambda, \mathsf{transc}) = k_A$$

for $\langle k_A, \mathsf{transc}, k_B \rangle \leftarrow_\$ \left\langle A^{\mathsf{RO}}(1^\lambda), B^{\mathsf{RO}}(1^\lambda) \right\rangle$ *is negligible, where the probability is over the random choices of all parties and the choice of random oracle* RO.

The central idea of the impossibility result is to assume again that P = NP, even though we work in the presence of the random oracle RO. Confining NP in P breaks any cryptographic primitive which does not take advantage of the random oracle. In particular any secure key exchange protocol must therefore rely on RO in this setting. We therefore consider the queries $\mathcal{Q}_A$ and $\mathcal{Q}_B$ of A and B to the random oracle RO during the execution. We are mainly interested in queries which both parties make and which thus lie in the intersection $\mathcal{Q}_A \cap \mathcal{Q}_B$. These are the gray areas in Figure 11.4. Other queries which only one of the parties makes yield a random answer y which only the asking party can use. One could think of this party simply picking a random value y instead, such that this random oracle query would not help to agree on the shared key. There are now two cases to consider, both depicted in Figure 11.4:

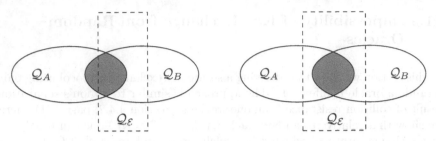

Fig. 11.4: Queries of A,B, and $\mathcal{E}$ to random oracle RO during execution resp. attack. The left-hand side shows a situation where A and B have made a query which $\mathcal{E}$ has not made (gray area outside of the dashed box). The right-hand side shows the situation in which $\mathcal{E}$ knows all these queries and is able to break the key exchange protocol.

1. In the left scenario, A and B have a joint query $x \in \mathcal{Q}_A \cap \mathcal{Q}_B$ which $\mathcal{E}$ has not made, i.e., $x \notin \mathcal{Q}_{\mathcal{E}}$ for the dashed set of $\mathcal{E}$'s queries. This gives A and B some advantage over $\mathcal{E}$ in terms of shared secret information between them, potentially allowing to agree on a joint key which $\mathcal{E}$ cannot compute.
2. In the right scenario, $\mathcal{E}$ knows all queries in the intersection. Hence, A and B have not established any shared information $\mathcal{E}$ is oblivious about. In this case the honest parties do not have any advantage over $\mathcal{E}$ and should not be able to derive a joint secret key.

In the impossibility proof below we will show that adversary $\mathcal{E}$ can always enforce the right situation. To cover all joint queries as well as to eventually break the key exchange protocol, $\mathcal{E}$ will again use the witness finder for an NP relation describing A's computation for some randomness. However, we still have to overcome the problem of A and B making RO queries. This is accomplished by encoding queries and answers as bit strings which are consistent with $\mathcal{E}$'s knowledge about the random oracle RO. Details are given in the poof.

> **Theorem 11.5.** *Assume* P = NP. *Then there is no weakly secure key exchange protocol in the random oracle model with perfect correctness.*

As remarked above the theorem does not unconditionally rule out the possibility of building such a protocol; it uses the assumption P = NP to break any potential protocol. To get a better feeling for the meaning we can also turn the statement of the theorem upside down. If one was able to design a weakly secure protocol using only a random oracle and confirm its security, then this must implicitly contain a proof that P ≠ NP. While the latter is widely believed to be true, a proof for this belief has been missing for decades now. It thus seems also hard to devise such a key exchange protocol.

Proof. Assume that we have an arbitrary key exchange protocol KE = $\langle A, B \rangle$ relative to a random oracle RO which achieves perfect correctness. Consider an execution

$$(k_A, \text{transc}, k_B) \leftarrow_\$ \left\langle A^{\text{RO}}(1^\lambda; r_A), B^{\text{RO}}(1^\lambda; r_B) \right\rangle$$

between the two parties for randomness r_A and r_B. Let $\mathcal{Q}_A$ and $\mathcal{Q}_B$ be the sets of random oracle queries the corresponding party has made in this execution. Let $\mathcal{P}_A$ and $\mathcal{P}_B$ be the sets which contain the pairs of query and answer of the random oracle:

$$\mathcal{P}_A = \{(x, \text{RO}(x)) \mid x \in \mathcal{Q}_A\}, \qquad \mathcal{P}_B = \{(x, \text{RO}(x)) \mid x \in \mathcal{Q}_B\}.$$

We can assume that A and B always make the same number a and b of queries to the random oracle, independently of the actual execution. This can always be achieved because the numbers are upper bounded by the runtime and one can let the party repeat previous queries if necessary.

We design an efficient attacker $\mathcal{E}$ which receives as input 1^λ and transcript $\text{transc} = (m_1, m_2, \ldots, m_t)$ and which will output $k_A = k_B$ with probability 1, using $P = NP$. During its computation $\mathcal{E}$ will continuously add elements to an initially empty set $\mathcal{Q}_\mathcal{E}$ of queries to the random oracle. Analogously to the query sets of A and B let $\mathcal{P}_\mathcal{E} = \{(x, \text{RO}(x)) \mid x \in \mathcal{Q}_\mathcal{E}\}$ be the pairs of queries and answers. Note that we can easily compute $\mathcal{Q}_\mathcal{E}$ from $\mathcal{P}_\mathcal{E}$.

For defining our NP-relation for which $\mathcal{E}$ applies the witness finder we need to replace random oracle queries and answers by strings. For an oracle algorithm $M^O(z)$ making q queries to its oracle let $M^{[(x_1, y_1), \ldots, (x_q, y_q)]}(z)$ be the oracle-free algorithm which performs exactly the same steps as $M^O(z)$ but where the query x_i to O uses the list entry y_i as the answer instead; any query x not appearing in the list, or inconsistencies in the list, makes the Turing machine abort with some distinct error message $\perp$ (which is not a protocol message). Note that we could view $[(x_1, y_1), \ldots, (x_q, y_q)]$ as input to M, written $M(z, x_1, y_1, \ldots, x_q, y_q)$, such that we obviously then have a Turing machine operating on bit strings. We prefer to make the special meaning of the x_i's and y_i's more explicit by writing them in the form above.

Analogously to the result of Theorem 11.2 we define a predicate

$$\text{TCons}(1^\lambda, \text{transc}, r'_A, x'_1, y'_1, \ldots, x'_a, y'_a)$$

which outputs 1 if and only for all $i = 1, 3, \ldots, t-1$ we have

$$A^{[(x'_1, y'_1), \ldots, (x'_a, y'_a)]}(1^\lambda, r'_A, m_1, m_2, \ldots, m_{i-1}) = m_i,$$

and also

$$A^{[(x'_1, y'_1), \ldots, (x'_a, y'_a)]}(1^\lambda, r'_A, \text{transc}) = (\text{output}, k'),$$

for some string k'. The latter requirement needs to be included because A may make random oracle queries in the final derivation step. Observe that in case of inconsistencies in the list $[(x'_1, y'_1), \ldots, (x'_a, y'_a)]$, or if A made a query which is not included in the list, then A aborts with $\perp$, which we defined not to be a protocol message. Hence, the predicate ensures that the list is sound in this regard and only contains all (unique) answers to oracle queries.

We will now define our relation $\mathcal{R}_A$ by allowing the witness finder to also choose the query-answer values as part of the witness $(r'_A, x'_1, y'_1, \ldots, x'_a, y'_a)$. We are then, however, faced with the following dilemma:

- Without any stipulation about the values y'_i the witness finder could choose arbitrary values which have no relation to the actual random oracle values, potentially leading to a useless witness.
- We cannot necessarily enforce that all values y'_i comply with the correct random oracle replies $\mathsf{RO}(x'_i)$ for the corresponding queries, since we cannot encode the entire random oracle into a string.

The expedient is to only enforce compliance with the random oracle queries and answers which $\mathcal{E}$ already holds at this point. Let

$$ \mathsf{QCons}(\mathcal{P}_\mathcal{E}, x'_1, y'_1, \ldots, x'_a, y'_a) $$

be the predicate which evaluates to 1 if and only if there is no $i \in \{1, 2, \ldots, a\}$ such that $x'_i \in \mathcal{Q}_\mathcal{E}$ and $(x'_i, y'_i) \notin \mathcal{P}_\mathcal{E}$. In other words, if the answer y'_i in the witness to the query x'_i, already made by $\mathcal{E}$, did not match the expected answer $\mathsf{RO}(x'_i)$ already captured in $\mathcal{P}_\mathcal{E}$, then we would have an inconsistency. Set

$$ \mathcal{R}_A = \Big\{ \ ((1^\lambda, \mathsf{transc}, \mathcal{P}_\mathcal{E}), (r'_A, x'_1, y'_1, \ldots, x'_a, y'_a)) \ \Big| $$
$$ \mathsf{TCons}(1^\lambda, \mathsf{transc}, r'_A, x'_1, y'_1, \ldots, x'_a, y'_a) $$
$$ \land \ \mathsf{QCons}(\mathcal{P}_\mathcal{E}, x'_1, y'_1, \ldots, x'_a, y'_a) \ \Big\}. $$

Our adversary $\mathcal{E}$ runs the witness finder W for this relation iteratively in $2b+1$ rounds for the maximal number b of B's queries to the random oracle. In each round it will ask the witness finder for a consistent witness and compute and store the derived key k^*_A. Then, for all previously unobserved queries x^*_i which the witness finder outputs, $\mathcal{E}$ queries the random oracle about x^*_i to learn the value and adds the query (with the random oracle's answer) to its set $\mathcal{P}_\mathcal{E}$ of such pairs. Since we may obtain the same key k^*_A multiple times during these iterations we assume that we store these keys in a multiset $\mathcal{K}$ which stores pairs (k, i) where i counts the multiplicity of k in the set $\mathcal{K}$. We let $\max \mathcal{K}$ be an element (k, i) where i is maximal among all elements in $\mathcal{K}$; ties are broken arbitrarily. We give the pseudocode of adversary $\mathcal{E}$ in Figure 11.5.

Analysis. First, note that $\mathcal{E}$ runs in polynomial time. The number of iterations is bounded by the polynomial number $2b+1$ of queries the polynomial-time algorithm B makes in protocol executions.[3] In each iteration $\mathcal{E}$ runs the

---

[3] The maximum number b of random oracle queries by B is bounded by a polynomial in the security parameter.

$\mathcal{E}^{\mathsf{RO}}(1^\lambda, \mathsf{transc})$

---

1 : $\quad \mathcal{K} \leftarrow \{\}, \mathcal{P}_\mathcal{E} \leftarrow \{\}$

2 : $\quad \textbf{for } i = 1..(2b+1) \textbf{ do}$

3 : $\quad\quad (r_A^*, x_1^*, y_1^*, \ldots, x_a^*, y_a^*) \leftarrow \mathsf{W}(1^\lambda, \mathsf{transc}, \mathcal{P}_\mathcal{E})$

4 : $\quad\quad (\mathsf{output}, k_A^*) \leftarrow A^{[(x_1^*, y_1^*), \ldots, (x_a^*, y_a^*)]}(1^\lambda, r_A^*, \mathsf{transc})$

5 : $\quad\quad \mathcal{P}_\mathcal{E} \leftarrow \mathcal{P}_\mathcal{E} \cup \{(x_i^*, \mathsf{RO}(x_i^*)) \mid i = 1, 2, \ldots, a\}$

6 : $\quad\quad \mathcal{K} \leftarrow \mathcal{K} \cup \{k_A^*\}$

7 : $\quad (k_A^*, i) \leftarrow \max \mathcal{K}$

8 : $\quad \textbf{return } k_A^*$

Fig. 11.5: Adversary $\mathcal{E}$ runs witness finder W for $2b+1$ times. In each run it derives one potential key k_A^* which it adds to a multiset $\mathcal{K}$. In addition, it updates its oracle query–answer set $\mathcal{P}_\mathcal{E}$ to include all queries x_i^* that were part of the found witness. Finally, adversary $\mathcal{E}$ selects the key k_A^* as its guess which it encountered most often (line 7).

witness finder (which runs in polynomial time as $\mathsf{P} = \mathsf{NP}$) and then recomputes the key of A. Finally, it needs to make at most polynomially many random oracle queries. Hence each iteration itself only requires polynomial time. Also, the set $\mathcal{P}_\mathcal{E}$ only contains at most $2ab + a$ elements at each point in time. For the success analysis we first argue that in each iteration of the **for**-loop we either add a new query $x \in \mathcal{Q}_B$ of B in the actual execution together with the answer $\mathsf{RO}(x)$ to $\mathcal{P}_\mathcal{E}$, or we at least compute the correct key $k_A^* = k_A$ in this iteration. For this let $\mathcal{Q}_A^* = \{x_1^*, \ldots, x_a^*\}$ be the queries computed in line 3, and $\mathcal{P}_A^* = \{(x_1^*, y_1^*), \ldots, (x_a^*, y_a^*)\}$. Assume that we have just completed line 4 to get the witness and the candidate for the key, but before adding the new queries to $\mathcal{P}_\mathcal{E}$ in line 5, such that $\mathcal{P}_\mathcal{E}$ still refers to the set which has been used to compute the witness. Then we distinguish the following cases:

CASE $\mathcal{Q}_A^* \cap \mathcal{Q}_B \not\subseteq \mathcal{Q}_\mathcal{E}$. This corresponds to the left-hand side in Figure 11.4 (with $\mathcal{Q}_A^*$ instead of $\mathcal{Q}_A$). Since there exists at least one query $x_i^* \in \mathcal{Q}_A^*$ which is not in $\mathcal{Q}_\mathcal{E}$ at this point, but this query also belongs to $\mathcal{Q}_B$, we add this previously undiscovered query and its random oracle value to $\mathcal{P}_\mathcal{E}$ in line 5. This brings us one step closer to capturing all the joint queries in $\mathcal{Q}_\mathcal{E}$.

CASE $\mathcal{Q}_A^* \cap \mathcal{Q}_B \subseteq \mathcal{Q}_\mathcal{E}$. This corresponds to the right-hand side in Figure 11.4 (again, with $\mathcal{Q}_A^*$ instead of $\mathcal{Q}_A$). We define now a modified oracle RO^* which the parties could have used and would still have obtained the same key. We remark that RO^* will not actually give random answers but the perfect completeness demands that both parties still compute the same key for *any* oracle. Let

$$\mathsf{RO}^*(x) = \begin{cases} y & \text{if } (x, y) \in \mathcal{P}_\mathcal{E} \cup \mathcal{P}_B \\ y^* & \text{if } (x, y^*) \in \mathcal{P}_A^* \\ 0 & \text{else} \end{cases}.$$

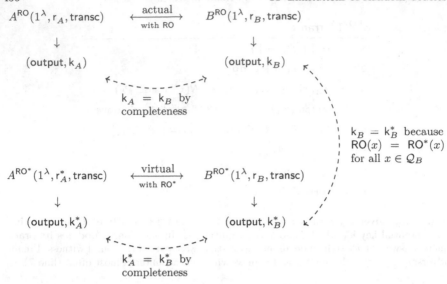

$A^{\mathsf{RO}}(1^\lambda, r_A, \mathsf{transc})$ $\xleftarrow[\text{with RO}]{\text{actual}}$ $B^{\mathsf{RO}}(1^\lambda, r_B, \mathsf{transc})$

$\downarrow$ $\downarrow$

(output, k_A) (output, k_B)

$k_A = k_B$ by
completeness

$k_B = k_B^*$ because
$\mathsf{RO}(x) = \mathsf{RO}^*(x)$
for all $x \in \mathcal{Q}_B$

$A^{\mathsf{RO}^*}(1^\lambda, r_A^*, \mathsf{transc})$ $\xleftarrow[\text{with RO}^*]{\text{virtual}}$ $B^{\mathsf{RO}^*}(1^\lambda, r_B, \mathsf{transc})$

$\downarrow$ $\downarrow$

(output, k_A^*) (output, k_B^*)

$k_A^* = k_B^*$ by
completeness

Fig. 11.6: Correctness argument for computed key k_A^* in case $\mathcal{Q}_A^* \cap \mathcal{Q}_B \subseteq \mathcal{Q}_\mathcal{E}$.

Note that $y = \mathsf{RO}(x)$ coincides with the random oracle for all $(x, y) \in \mathcal{P}_\mathcal{E} \cup \mathcal{P}_B$ by construction, because $\mathcal{P}_B$ contains the random oracle values which B actually computed in the execution with RO, and our algorithm only adds pairs $(x, \mathsf{RO}(x))$ to $\mathcal{P}_\mathcal{E}$. Furthermore, any query $x \in \mathcal{P}_A^* \cap \mathcal{P}_B$ in the intersection of queries of A and B is covered by $\mathcal{E}$'s query set $\mathcal{Q}_\mathcal{E}$ at this point, according to our assumption $\mathcal{Q}_A^* \cap \mathcal{Q}_B \subseteq \mathcal{Q}_\mathcal{E}$. Hence, the consistency requirement QCons for the NP-relation $\mathscr{R}_A$ requires that for any $(x_i^*, y_i^*) \in \mathcal{P}_A^* \cap \mathcal{P}_B$ the value y_i^* must be consistent with the value in $\mathcal{P}_\mathcal{E}$—which is exactly the value $\mathsf{RO}(x_i^*)$.

We argue next that the computed key k_A^* coincides with the actual key k_A. The line of reasoning is shown in Figure 11.6. In a thought experiment, displayed in the lower right corner of the figure, assume now that we would have executed B on the correct randomness r_B and feeding B with the correct A-messages $m_1, m_3, \ldots, m_{t-1}$ from transc, but giving B oracle access to RO^* instead of RO. Let k_B^* be the key output by B when having access to RO^*. Querying the virtual RO^* instead of the actual RO does not change B's perspective on the protocol execution, since the first query x of B^{RO^*} is identical to the one of B^{RO} and belongs to $\mathcal{Q}_B$ as well. The reply is then $\mathsf{RO}^*(x) = \mathsf{RO}(x)$ by assumption. This is then also true for all further queries, such that

$$B^{\mathsf{RO}^*}(1^\lambda, r_B, \mathsf{transc}) = (\mathsf{output}, k_B^*) = (\mathsf{output}, k_B) = B^{\mathsf{RO}}(1^\lambda, r_B, \mathsf{transc}).$$

In addition, $k_B = k_A$ are the identical keys computed in the actual execution between A and B for oracle RO (upper part of Figure 11.6). Perfect completeness now also demands that the protocol execution between $A^{\mathsf{RO}^*}(1^\lambda; r_A^*)$ and $B^{\mathsf{RO}^*}(1^\lambda; r_B)$ yields the same key $\mathsf{k}_A^* = \mathsf{k}_B^*$, which is identical to k_A by the argument above. This is shown in the lower part of Figure 11.6. It follows that we indeed obtain the correct key $\mathsf{k}_A^* = \mathsf{k}_A$.

The final step in the proof is to note that B has made at most b queries in the actual execution. Hence, latest after the first b iterations of the **for**-loop we cannot add new elements of $\mathcal{Q}_B$ to $\mathcal{Q}_{\mathcal{E}}$, and therefore must have at least $b+1$ times the correct key k_A in $\mathcal{K}$. As there cannot exist any other key appearing more often, our algorithm $\mathcal{E}$ therefore finds the correct key eventually and thus breaks the key exchange protocol. □

We note that the above argument also works for protocols with negligible error. See the Chapter Notes for more information.

Remark 11.6. As opposed to the separation of collision-resistant hash functions from one-way functions in Section 4.4.2 we do not apply the Borel–Cantelli lemma (Lemma 4.28; page 202) here to find a random oracle which works against all possible protocols. The reason is that cryptographic protocols in the random oracle model are fully specified before the random oracle is initialized, and are thus independent of the concrete random oracle instance. For excluding key exchange protocols in the random oracle model it therefore suffices to show—as we did—that any such protocol, which receives a fresh random function oracle at the beginning of the attack, can be broken (if P = NP). We stress, however, that we could also apply the Borel–Cantelli technique to derive the stronger result that there exists a random oracle such that no secure key exchange protocol exists relative to this oracle. One can even go a step further and show that one of these random oracles must give a deterministic one-way function oracle relative to which no secure key exchange protocol can exist, when P = NP. Indeed, proving that key exchange cannot be derived from one-wayness was the original motivation of the result we presented here.

Let us state explicitly that the impossibility result also means that it is unlikely that one can build secure public-key encryption schemes from random oracles only. The line of reasoning is that an IND-CPA-secure public-key encryption scheme allows to build weakly secure key exchange protocols via key transport. Hence, if we could build such an encryption scheme from a random oracle, this would contradict Theorem 11.5, assuming P = NP:

Corollary 11.7. *Suppose* P = NP. *Then there is no IND-CPA-secure public key encryption in the random oracle model.*

Chapter Notes and References

Diffie and Hellman proposed their key exchange protocol in 1976 [4]. This work is sometimes seen as the starting point of modern cryptography.

Merkle himself reports that he came up with his idea for key exchange in 1974 in a Computer Security course. He submitted his idea about the puzzles to communicate securely to the *Communications of the ACM* (CACM) in 1975. The proposal was initially rejected but eventually got published in 1978 in CACM, two years after the seminal work of Diffie and Hellman. Complementing the positive result about a quadratic advantage for the honest parties in Merkle's protocol, Barak and Mahmoody-Ghidary [1] showed later that any protocol in the random oracle model where the honest parties make n oracle queries can be broken with $O(n^2)$ queries by the adversary.

The impossibility result for key exchange protocols in the random oracle model was shown by Impagliazzo and Rudich [6, 5]. They show the result for protocols with negligible correctness error, requiring additional results about the uniform generation of NP witnesses. In addition, they prove the more general separation that there exists a one-way permutation oracle but no weakly secure key exchange protocol based on this oracle, hence showing that it is infeasible to build secure key exchange from one-way permutations. Our presentation here for the easier case of perfect correctness follows the work of Brakerski *et al.* [3].

Rudich's Ph.D. thesis [9] contains another separation result, showing that one-way permutations cannot be constructed from random (and thus one-way) function oracles. The proof also assumes P = NP but at the time of writing was based on a combinatorial conjecture. This conjecture was later shown to hold by Kahn et al. [8].

The possibility of uniform generation of NP witnesses when P = NP was first discussed by Jerrum *et al.* [7]. This generation algorithm was subsequently improved by Bellare *et al.* [2].

Exercices

Exercise 11.1. Argue that any key exchange protocol with varying numbers of rounds (e.g., if the number of message exchanges depends on sampled values) can be turned into a protocol with a fixed (polynomial) number of rounds.

Exercise 11.2. Suppose that A and B in the Diffie–Hellman key agreement protocol would compute the shared key as $g^x \cdot g^y$. Argue that this protocol version is not secure.

Exercise 11.3. Identify in the proof of Theorem 11.5 (page 452) where we used perfect completeness and where additional steps would be necessary for protocols with negligible correctness error.

Chapter Bibliography

1. Boaz Barak and Mohammad Mahmoody-Ghidary. Merkle's key agreement protocol is optimal: An $O(n^2)$ attack on any key agreement from random oracles. *Journal of Cryptology*, 30(3):699–734, July 2017.
2. Mihir Bellare, Oded Goldreich, and Erez Petrank. Uniform generation of NP-witnesses using an NP-oracle. *Information and Computation*, 163(2):510–526, 2000.
3. Zvika Brakerski, Jonathan Katz, Gil Segev, and Arkady Yerukhimovich. Limits on the power of zero-knowledge proofs in cryptographic constructions. In Yuval Ishai, editor, *TCC 2011: 8th Theory of Cryptography Conference*, volume 6597 of *Lecture Notes in Computer Science*, pages 559–578, Providence, RI, USA, March 28–30, 2011. Springer, Heidelberg, Germany.
4. Whitfield Diffie and Martin E. Hellman. New directions in cryptography. *IEEE Trans. Inf. Theory*, 22(6):644–654, 1976.
5. Russell Impagliazzo and Steven Rudich. Limits on the provable consequences of one-way permutations. In *21st Annual ACM Symposium on Theory of Computing*, pages 44–61, Seattle, WA, USA, May 15–17, 1989. ACM Press.
6. Russell Impagliazzo and Steven Rudich. Limits on the provable consequences of one-way permutations. In Shafi Goldwasser, editor, *Advances in Cryptology – CRYPTO'88*, volume 403 of *Lecture Notes in Computer Science*, pages 8–26, Santa Barbara, CA, USA, August 21–25, 1990. Springer, Heidelberg, Germany.
7. Mark R. Jerrum, Leslie G Valiant, and Vijay V Vazirani. Random generation of combinatorial structures from a uniform distribution. *Theoretical Computer Science*, 43:169–188, 1986.
8. Jeff Kahn, Michael E. Saks, and Clifford D. Smyth. A dual version of reimer's inequality and a proof of rudich's conjecture. In *Proceedings of the 15th Annual IEEE Conference on Computational Complexity, Florence, Italy, July 4-7, 2000*, pages 98–103. IEEE Computer Society, 2000.
9. Steven Rudich. *Limits on the Provable Consequences of One-way Functions*. PhD thesis, EECS Department, University of California, Berkeley, Dec 1988.

Chapter 12
The Random Oracle Controversy

Over the course of the previous chapters we have seen how random oracles allow for the creation of elegant and efficient schemes which can furthermore be proven secure in the random oracle model. In this chapter we have a closer look at what it means to have a security proof in the random oracle model rather than in the standard model. Recall the random oracle methodology in which we build cryptographic schemes in two steps:

i) We first construct a cryptographic scheme and prove its security in the random oracle model.

ii) Then, we instantiate the random oracle with a good hash function H that *behaves like a random oracle* in order to obtain a construction that can be implemented and used in practice.

Let us use a concrete example and consider the case that we have devised a signature scheme Sig. In a first step we prove that $\mathsf{Sig}^{\mathsf{RO}}$ is existentially unforgeable under chosen-message attacks given that RO is a random oracle and that possibly some additional assumptions hold. For deploying the scheme in practice (aka the real world) we need to now specify a concrete and efficient hash function H to *instantiate* the random oracle. That is, in practice we deploy signature scheme $\mathsf{Sig}^{\mathsf{H}}$. Since we have shown that $\mathsf{Sig}^{\mathsf{RO}}$ is secure if RO is a random oracle, the assumption for the security of the instantiated scheme is:

Hash function H behaves like a random oracle.

But what exactly does this mean? Do we have such functions that behave like a random oracle? Can we prove that a function behaves like a random oracle, or at least show that a given function does not behave like a random oracle. And if we cannot show that a function behaves like a random oracle then what does this mean for the security of our scheme $\mathsf{Sig}^{\mathsf{H}}$?

In this chapter we will answer a few of these questions, although not necessarily to the satisfaction of the cryptographer. Indeed, we will show that

© Springer Nature Switzerland AG 2021
A. Mittelbach, M. Fischlin, *The Theory of Hash Functions and Random Oracles*,
Information Security and Cryptography, https://doi.org/10.1007/978-3-030-63287-8_12

no efficient function behaves sufficiently much like a random oracle such that it can securely instantiate all random oracles. More concretely, we will show how to construct an (artificial) signature scheme which is secure in the random oracle model but which becomes insecure for any efficient hash function. This then leaves open the question of what to make of random oracle proofs. After all, if a scheme that is proven secure in the random oracle model may be completely insecure when used in practice, then why bother giving a random oracle proof in the first place?

There is no easy answer to this question and, indeed, random oracles have led to various, sometimes emotional, discussions in the cryptographic community. We try to give these justice by presenting a discussion on the "meaning of random oracle proofs" from various angles. But first, let us present one of the negative results which ignited the debate.

12.1 Random Oracle Uninstantiability

Our goal in the following section is to create a signature scheme[1] which is provably secure in the random oracle model, but which fails to be secure when the random oracle is replaced by any efficient hash function. The underlying idea for the construction of such a signature scheme is to insert a backdoor into the signing mechanism of the scheme which allows an attacker to extract the secret signing key in case the scheme is used relative to an efficient hash function and not relative to a random oracle.

This idea deserves some dwelling upon. Recall the setup of the signature experiment for proving existential unforgeability (see Definition 6.2 on page 264). Here an adversary is given access to a signing oracle $\mathsf{Sign}^O(\mathsf{sk}, \cdot)$ which implements the signature scheme for a randomly chosen signing key. The task of the adversary is to come up with a valid signature for a fresh message, i.e., a message that the adversary did not send to its signature oracle. Note that in the random oracle setting, the signing oracle is relative to the random oracle, that is, we consider $\mathsf{Sign}^{RO}(\mathsf{sk}, \cdot)$. If, on the other hand, we were proving security for the instantiated scheme where a particular hash function H replaces the random oracle, then we consider the setup $\mathsf{Sign}^{\mathsf{H}}(\mathsf{sk}, \cdot)$.

Let us suppose that the adversary can somehow "prove" to the signing oracle that it was not given access to a random oracle RO but instead to some concrete hash function H. Then, we could implement a backdoor in the signature scheme that checks for such a proof and if it is given a valid proof outputs the secret signing key as part of the signature. Otherwise, it would create a genuine signature. The following pseudocode of a signature generation

---

[1] There is nothing special about signature schemes for this example. In fact, the presented technique can be easily adapted to generate uninstantiable variants for most cryptographic primitives.

algorithm exemplifies the idea. Here we consider the signing algorithm of a scheme $\mathsf{Sig}_{\mathsf{bad}}$ which is based upon a secure signature scheme Sig.

$\mathsf{Sig}^{\mathsf{O}}_{\mathsf{bad}}.\mathsf{Sign}(\mathsf{sk}, m)$

---

1 : **if** m contains proof that O is not a random oracle **then**

2 : $\sigma \leftarrow \mathsf{sk}$

3 : **else**

4 : $\sigma \leftarrow \mathsf{Sig}^{\mathsf{O}}.\mathsf{Sign}(\mathsf{sk}, m)$

5 : **return** σ

If we had a way to prove that an oracle O is not a random oracle that could not be spoofed (i.e., no algorithm can create a convincing proof in case oracle O is a random oracle), then clearly, signature scheme $\mathsf{Sig}_{\mathsf{bad}}$ is secure in the random oracle model if and only if scheme Sig is secure in the random oracle model. In this case the security of $\mathsf{Sig}_{\mathsf{bad}}$ directly reduces to the security of the underlying scheme Sig. However, in the real world when we instantiate the scheme with a concrete hash function, then the scheme would be insecure as any adversary would simply need to send a proof to the signing oracle that oracle O is not a random oracle but, in fact, some efficiently implementable hash function H.

Proving That Oracle O Is Not a Random Oracle

So how can we prove to an algorithm that only has black-box access to an oracle O, that its oracle O is implementing an efficient hash function H rather than a random oracle RO? For this we need to look at the differences between random oracles and efficient functions.

One of the main distinguishing features between a random oracle and an efficient function is that the latter has a compact representation. That is, for an efficient PPT hash function H we can write down its "code," for example, as pseudocode or a Turing machine or circuit. Indeed, by definition we have that an efficient algorithm must have a Turing machine representation that is of polynomial size in the security parameter. Random oracles, on the other hand, do not have such a compact description. On the contrary, as discussed, we cannot do much better than to write down the entire function table if we wanted to fully specify a random oracle. Already for a small fixed-input-sized random oracle mapping λ bit inputs to 1-bit outputs we would end up with a description of roughly 2^{λ} many bits which is, of course, exponential in the security parameter.

The proof idea. The idea for proving to an algorithm that its oracle does not implement a random oracle is to provide the algorithm with the code of its oracle. Given access to the code, it can then test the code against its oracle

by generating random inputs and testing whether or not evaluating the code
on these inputs matches the corresponding results from the oracle. Given that
the output of the oracle is sufficiently long already a few or even a single test
is sufficient to be relatively certain of the fact that the oracle is not random.

For this, consider a random oracle RO with output length λ. We are
interested in the probability of an efficient adversary $\mathcal{A}^{\mathsf{RO}}$ with access to
the random oracle of generating a program that with noticeable probability
predicts the random oracle output on a random value. We formalize the
advantage of adversary $\mathcal{A}$ in this setting by the probability of it winning in
the random oracle prediction game ROPred which we define as follows:

$$\begin{array}{l}
\underline{\mathrm{ROPred}_{\mathcal{A}}^{\mathsf{RO}}(\lambda)} \\[4pt]
1: \quad (\langle \mathsf{M} \rangle, 1^t) \leftarrow\!\!{\$}\; \mathcal{A}^{\mathsf{RO}}(1^\lambda) \\[2pt]
2: \quad x \leftarrow\!\!{\$}\; \{0,1\}^\lambda \\[2pt]
3: \quad y \leftarrow \mathsf{RO}(x) \\[2pt]
4: \quad y' \leftarrow\!\!{\$}\; \mathsf{UM}_t(\langle \mathsf{M} \rangle, x) \\[2pt]
5: \quad \textbf{return } y = y'
\end{array}$$

In line 1, adversary $\mathcal{A}$ generates a Turing machine program M for some
fixed encoding, as well as an integer t (in unary encoding) denoting the number
of steps the program runs on inputs of length λ. The challenger then picks
a random value x and computes $y \leftarrow \mathsf{RO}(x)$ before it evaluates the created
program on input x by running it through the universal Turing machine for t
steps. We here extend our notation of universal Turing machines to denote by
UM_t the universal Turing machine that evaluates programs for a maximum
of t steps and which outputs $\bot$ in case the program does not stop within the
allotted amount of computation steps (also see Section 1.3.1 on page 19).

First note that game ROPred is efficient if adversary $\mathcal{A}$ is efficient. For this
note that if $\mathcal{A}$ is efficient then t (decoded as unary) must be polynomial in the
security parameter. As evaluating a Turing machine via the universal Turing
machine only adds polynomial overhead, evaluating the generated program
$\langle \mathsf{M} \rangle$ for t steps must thus also be efficient.

Next, we analyze the advantage of adversary $\mathcal{A}$ in winning game ROPred
in the random oracle model. For this, let q be an upper bound on the number
of random oracle queries by the adversary. As $\mathcal{A}$ is by assumption efficient
we have that q is polynomial in the security parameter. Thus we can upper
bound the probability that the adversary has already queried the subsequently
sampled value x by $(1 - \frac{\mathsf{q}(\lambda)}{2^\lambda})$. But if the adversary did not query the random
oracle on x then program $\langle M \rangle$ cannot contain any information on value $\mathsf{RO}(x)$
and the probability that $M(x) = \mathsf{RO}(x)$ is at most $2^{-\lambda}$. This yields an overall
bound on the advantage of the adversary as

$$\Pr\left[\mathrm{ROPred}_{\mathcal{A}}^{\mathsf{RO}}(\lambda) = 1\right] \leq \frac{\mathsf{q}(\lambda)}{2^\lambda} + \frac{1}{2^\lambda}.$$

Here the first summand covers the probability of the adversary querying value x while the second caters for the probability that program $\langle M \rangle$ "guesses" value $\mathsf{RO}(x)$.

We have seen that an adversary wins game ROPred only with negligible probability in the random oracle model. When replacing RO with a standard model hash function H this changes dramatically. All the adversary needs to do now is to output an encoding of the code of hash function H that is used to instantiate the random oracle together with a large enough value t to win with a probability of 1. A formal analysis of this case will be given in the next section.

12.2 An Uninstantiable Signature Scheme

Let us use the above idea in the creation of our (artificial) signature scheme $\mathsf{Sig}_{\mathsf{bad}}$, a scheme that is secure in the random oracle model but insecure with any concrete and efficient hash function H. This allows us to show the following *uninstantiability result*:

> **Theorem 12.1.** *There exists a signature scheme* $\mathsf{Sig}_{\mathsf{bad}}$ *such that* $\mathsf{Sig}_{\mathsf{bad}}^{\mathsf{RO}}$ *is existentially unforgeable under chosen-message attacks in the random oracle model. Furthermore, for all* PPT *functions* H, *the instantiated signature scheme* $\mathsf{Sig}_{\mathsf{bad}}^{\mathsf{H}}$ *is insecure.*

Remark 12.2. Note that the result holds without any additional assumptions such as the existence of one-way functions. This is because random oracles alone are sufficient for the generation of secure signature schemes (see Section 6.6; page 296).

Proof of Theorem 12.1. Let $\mathsf{Sig}^{\mathsf{RO}} := (\mathsf{Sig}^{\mathsf{RO}}.\mathsf{KGen}, \mathsf{Sig}^{\mathsf{RO}}.\mathsf{Sign}, \mathsf{Sig}^{\mathsf{RO}}.\mathsf{Vf})$ be a signature scheme that is existentially unforgeable under chosen-message attacks relative to random oracle RO. We will construct an adapted signature scheme $\mathsf{Sig}_{\mathsf{bad}}$ based on scheme Sig that is still secure relative to random oracle RO but not when random oracle RO is replaced by any standard model hash function H. Scheme $\mathsf{Sig}_{\mathsf{bad}}$ inherits its key generation and signature verification from the secure scheme Sig but uses an adapted signature generation algorithm as follows (the pseudocode is given below in Construction 12.3): In a first step, our signing algorithm parses message m into two parts, an encoding of a Turing machine $\langle M \rangle$ and an integer t encoded in unary. For this, the parse algorithm simply searches for a 0-bit in message m such that all subsequent bits are 1. It then splits the message at this point, returning the bits up to the 0 as $\langle M \rangle$ and returning the number of 1 bits at the end of message m as integer t in unary. In case message m consists solely of 1-bits then parse returns $(\varepsilon, 0)$.

Construction 12.3. *Let* $\mathsf{Sig}^{\mathsf{RO}} := (\mathsf{Sig}^{\mathsf{RO}}.\mathsf{KGen}, \mathsf{Sig}^{\mathsf{RO}}.\mathsf{Sign}, \mathsf{Sig}^{\mathsf{RO}}.\mathsf{Vf})$ *be a signature scheme in the random oracle model. We construct signature scheme* $\mathsf{Sig}_{\mathsf{bad}}$ *which inherits key generation and signature verification from* Sig *but adapts signature generation as*

$\mathsf{Sig}_{\mathsf{bad}}^{\mathsf{RO}}.\mathsf{Sign}(\mathsf{sk}, m)$	$\mathsf{parse}(m)$
$1:\ \ (\langle \mathsf{M}\rangle, 1^t) \leftarrow \mathsf{parse}(m)$	$1:\ \ \textit{let } i \in \{0, \ldots, \|m\|\} \textit{ be}$
$2:\ \ x \leftarrow\!\!{\scriptstyle\$}\ \{0,1\}^\lambda$	$\qquad \textit{minimal s.t. } \forall j > i : m[j] = 1$
$3:\ \ y \leftarrow \mathsf{RO}(x)$	$2:\ \ \textbf{return } (m[1..(i-1)], 1^{|m|-i})$
$4:\ \ y' \leftarrow\!\!{\scriptstyle\$}\ \mathsf{UM}_t(\langle \mathsf{M}\rangle, x)$	
$5:\ \ \textbf{if } y = y' \textbf{ do}$	
$6:\ \ \quad \sigma \leftarrow \mathsf{sk}$	
$7:\ \ \textbf{else}$	
$8:\ \ \quad \sigma \leftarrow\!\!{\scriptstyle\$}\ \mathsf{Sig}^{\mathsf{RO}}.\mathsf{Sign}(\mathsf{sk}, m)$	
$9:\ \ \textbf{return } \sigma$	

Recall from our discussion of Turing machines (Section 1.3) that we can fix an encoding for Turing machines such that every bit string is mapped to a valid Turing machine. Thus, we can assume that $\langle \mathsf{M}\rangle$ is always a valid Turing machine encoding even in case we set it to the empty string ε in line 2 of parse.

In a next step, a random value x is sampled and $y \leftarrow \mathsf{RO}(x)$ is computed. In line 4 the extracted Turing machine $\langle TM \rangle$ is run on input x for t steps to produce output y'. Finally, if $y = y'$ then signature value σ is set to be the secret key sk. Otherwise, a *genuine* signature is generated as $\mathsf{Sig}^{\mathsf{RO}}.\mathsf{Sign}(\mathsf{sk}, m)$ (line 8).

After having parsed message m into an encoding of a Turing machine and an integer t, signature scheme $\mathsf{Sig}_{\mathsf{bad}}$ executes the "random oracle verification proof" from the previous section. As t is encoded in unary and simulating the execution of a Turing machine via a universal Turing machine for a polynomial number of steps is efficient, we have that also the signing operation of $\mathsf{Sig}_{\mathsf{bad}}$ is efficient. Furthermore, as discussed above in Section 12.1, in the random oracle model the probability of an algorithm (even an unbounded one) of producing a message m such that the condition $y = y'$ in line 5 evaluates to true is negligible. It follows that in the random oracle model the security of $\mathsf{Sig}_{\mathsf{bad}}$ reduces to the security of the underlying scheme Sig, which by assumption is secure.

What remains to show in order to complete the proof is that for any efficient function H the scheme $\mathsf{Sig}_{\mathsf{bad}}^{\mathsf{H}}$ is insecure. For this we construct an adversary against the existential unforgeability (see Definition 6.2 on page 264) of the scheme as follows. Since, by assumption, hash function H is efficient there must be a polynomial upper bound on the number of computation steps for inputs of length λ. Let p be that upper bound. On input the security parameter 1^λ and the public verification key pk adversary $\mathcal{A}$ generates a message as

$$m \leftarrow \langle H \rangle \| 0 \| 1^{p(\lambda)}.$$

That is, message m consists of an encoding of the Turing machine that implements hash function H followed by a single 0 and $p(\lambda)$ many 1 bits. It then asks its signature oracle for a signature for m. By design, the signature will always be set to sk as the branch for line 6 will always be triggered for an m of this form. To see that this is indeed the case, consider the following pseudocode of an execution of $Sig_{bad}^{RO}.Sign$ for such a message m.

$Sig_{bad}^{H}.Sign(sk, \langle H \rangle \| 0 \| 1^{p(\lambda)})$

---

1 : $(\langle H \rangle, t) \leftarrow parse(\langle H \rangle \| 0 \| 1^{p(\lambda)})$

2 : $x \leftarrow\!\!\$ \{0,1\}^\lambda$

3 : $y \leftarrow H.Eval(x)$

4 : $y' \leftarrow\!\!\$ UM_t(\langle H \rangle, x)$

5 : **if** $y = y'$ **do**

6 : $\quad \sigma \leftarrow sk$

7 : **else**

8 : $\quad \sigma \leftarrow\!\!\$ Sig^{RO}.Sign(sk, m)$

9 : **return** σ

Note that for our carefully constructed message m we thus always have that

$$UM_t(\langle H \rangle, x) = H.Eval(x).$$

It follows that y and y' will always match, and the resulting signature value σ is set to secret key sk. Having extracted the secret key, all that remains for adversary $\mathcal{A}$ is to generate a signature for a new message m' to win with probability 1.

As the above adversary and analysis was independent of the choice of hash function H and only relied on H being efficient, this concludes the proof. $\square$

Remark 12.4. If you carefully read the definition of our above signature scheme you may have noticed that it is not *correct* in the sense that there is the (negligible) probability that for a message m it holds that

$$Sig_{bad}^{RO}.Vf(pk, m, \sigma) = false$$

for a key pair generated as $(pk, sk) \leftarrow\!\!\$ Sig_{bad}.KGen(1^\lambda)$ and a signature generated as $\sigma \leftarrow\!\!\$ Sig.Sign(sk, m)$. While it is not noticeable for any efficient algorithm that Sig_{bad} is not always correct, it is also not difficult to adapt the scheme to be in fact always correct. We leave showing the existence of a fully correct uninstantiable scheme as Exercise 12.1.

12.3 The Random Oracle Methodology—A Controversy

The random oracle uninstantiability result may come as a bit of a surprise and immediately raises the question:

> *What does the result mean for random oracle-based schemes in theory, and in practice?*

The random oracle methodology was first implicitly proposed in 1986 and made explicit in 1993. The first uninstantiability results of which we have seen one above appeared in 1998. Now, more than 25 years after the introduction of the random oracle methodology and more than 20 years after the first uninstantiability result the cryptographic community is still divided as to how to take random oracles and how to interpret uninstantiability results.

Ex Falso Quodlibet

Cryptographers are usually a cautious bunch. For example, we tend to give more power to the adversary than might seem reasonable since we rather want to err on the side of caution. If we can prove that a powerful adversary cannot break a scheme then this also holds for all weaker adversaries, while the inverse, naturally, does not hold. Our security proofs follow rigorous mathematical reasoning. Since there is some uncertainty about various results (such as whether $P = NP$ after all, in which case one-way functions would not exist) we state our assumptions clearly.

> *If the discrete-logarithm problem in certain groups is hard then one-way functions exist, then we can construct pseudorandom functions and hence IND-CPA-secure symmetric encryption schemes.*

And in case the assumption is wrong and the discrete-logarithm problem can be solved in polynomial time, then the interpretation is clear

> *ex falso quodlibet: from falsehood, anything follows.*

If the assumption is wrong then the conclusion may, or may not hold.

Now, since we have shown that there exists a scheme that is secure relative to random oracles but insecure relative to any efficient function we have, in fact, shown the following corollary:

> **Corollary 12.5** (informal). *No* PPT *algorithm* behaves like a random oracle.

This, of course, invalidates the underlying assumption of the random oracle methodology, namely that there exist functions that behave like a random oracle. Consequently, a security proof in the random oracle model for some scheme V^{RO} does not allow to conclude that the scheme instantiated with efficient hash function H is secure. It may well be that H is good enough and the resulting scheme V^{H} is secure. But it may also be the case that the resulting scheme is not secure and, thus, the security of any instantiated scheme is, in fact, based on an ad hoc assumption:

Relative to hash function H *the scheme is secure.*

Random Oracle Proof Techniques

Added to the fact that the assumption that there exist functions that behave like a random oracle does not hold, we can also question certain proof techniques often employed in the random oracle setting.

When we follow the random oracle methodology then we construct cryptographic schemes in two steps. First we build a cryptographic scheme and prove its security in the random oracle model. Then, for obtaining a scheme that can be used in practice, we instantiate the random oracle with a good hash function H that "behaves like a random oracle." On first sight this approach is identical to the provable security approach introduced in Part I. In Section 5.1.3 (page 221), for example, we showed how to construct an IND-CPA-secure symmetric encryption scheme based on pseudorandom functions. Let us state this construction in the language of the random oracle methodology:

- First we create a cryptographic scheme relative to a pseudorandom function and prove it secure assuming that the pseudorandom function is secure.
- Then, to use the scheme in practice we instantiate the pseudorandom function by choosing a concrete instance.

There is, however, a big difference. By modeling hash functions as random oracles we are externalizing the hash function and forcing adversaries to publicly announce any hash function call they make. This we have seen allows for so-called *observing reductions* (Section 9.2, page 376) in which the reduction exploits the knowledge gained by observing the oracle calls of the adversary. *Programmable reductions* (Section 9.3, page 382) go one step further and allow the reduction not only to observe the adversary's interaction with the hash function, but to even *program* the hash function to return specific values. This programming does not even need to be done upfront but can be done on the fly.

Yet, why should an adversary that we otherwise treat as a black box be so kind as to announce its hash function computation? The whole idea of black-box reductions is to not argue about the internal workings of the adversary. Do we even know that an adversary computes hash values by executing the hash function step by step in order to complete its attack? So how can we expect to turn an adversary against the instantiated scheme V^H into an adversary against the corresponding random oracle scheme V^{RO}. The "black box" that is the adversary might be given in a way that we cannot understand. Its code may be obfuscated or otherwise protected. In any case, there is certainly no guarantee that its hash function calls (if it makes hash function calls) will be as exposed as they need to be for the random oracle-based reduction.

While the proof techniques seem to be dodgy in light of the above discussion one can also argue that they appear to stand on solid ground with our current understanding of practical hash functions. Observability can be interpreted as saying that the only way for the adversary to derive a useful hash value is by evaluating the hash function for some input, thus actually "knowing" the input.[2] But if the adversary knows the hash function input it seems to be fair that a reduction should also get to learn it. Observability captures this forwarding of knowledge from the adversary to the reduction. Having access to internal information of the adversary somehow turns the reduction into a non-black-box one. Yet we note that the notion of black-box reductions merely indicates a certain proof technique. From a security point of view a non-black-box-reduction is equally adequate to argue security.

Arguing that programmability is still reasonable is harder, at least for the form we have used, for example, in the proof of full domain hash signatures (Section 9.3.1 on page 382). There, the reduction has replaced a hash value by some image of the RSA function. One could claim that programmability in a sense models the fact that a hash value is only discovered at the point in time when the function is evaluated on some preimage, and then takes an arbitrary value as long as it is random. In the proof for full domain hash signatures we went, nonetheless, even a step further and correlated random oracle values with values of the trapdoor function. Weaker forms of programming, e.g., if the reduction can choose from a set of truly random and independent candidate values, may better reflect our idea of practical hash functions which are designed independently of specific trapdoor functions.

The Random Oracle Heuristic

We have questioned the soundness of the random oracle methodology by stating that its assumption is wrong and also raised questions as to the

---

[2] Of course, the adversary could "create" a hash value by simply picking a string from $\{0,1\}^{RO.ol(\lambda)}$. But without having the slightest idea about the preimage such hash values seem to be of limited use for attacks.

validity of random oracle-based proof techniques. So why do we even have this debate instead of simply dismissing random oracles and moving on?

Things are, of course, not that simple and as it turns out the random oracle methodology has divided the cryptographic community in the sense that there is no clear and accepted interpretation as to how we should view and deal with random oracles. On the one hand, a large body of work has been devoted to adapting schemes proven in the random oracle model to assumptions that do not require the use of random oracles but instead rely on "standard model assumptions."[3] Yet, random oracles are also still used extensively today, both in theory and practice, and there are several good reasons for this.

From a theoretical standpoint, random oracles provide a very good indication of whether a cryptographic construction is plausible. If we cannot prove it secure with random oracles, then why even attempt a proof without? Furthermore, for most constructions that rely on random oracles, it has been shown that we can provide adapted (yet usually more complex) constructions that no longer need random oracles. In that sense, random oracles can be regarded as a design pattern. First design your scheme relative to a random oracle and make sure everything works. Then see how to alleviate the random oracle.

From a practical standpoint there are also many good reasons for the use of random oracles. The most compelling reason is probably that practical random oracle schemes simply seem to work. They are not only often much more elegant and efficient than their counterparts that do not need random oracles, but they also seem to be secure. Until today there has not been a single attack on a practical random oracle scheme that can be traced back to the use of random oracles. Instead when trying to circumvent the use of random oracles, schemes often become more complex and chances are that the workarounds introduced to alleviate the random oracle assumption introduce weaknesses (e.g., side-channel attacks) in the resulting scheme.

Also if we consider the hash functions that we use in practice, it is hard to argue against the random oracle methodology. Hash functions such as SHA-2 or SHA-3—we will discuss practical hash function constructions in general in Part III and SHA-2 and SHA-3 in Chapter 15—are themselves not based on clearly specified assumptions and computationally hard problems but instead on ad hoc assumptions. Here, we sacrifice the end-to-end security proof for performance and pragmatism and rely instead on heuristics, best practices, and empirical evidence. So if it is good enough for hash functions to rely on empirical evidence, why is it a problem if we do the same for cryptographic schemes?

Another argument often brought forward is that uninstantiability results are usually very artificial. This is certainly true for our signature scheme Sig_{bad}, and it is also the case for most known uninstantiability results. Why

---

[3] To understand the amount of effort, conduct a web search for a phrase such as "without random oracles". At the time of writing Google scholar lists more than 8000 articles, many of which are high-profile cryptographic papers.

should any practical scheme have such a backdoor? So could it be the case that hash functions exist that behave like random oracles for all practical purposes?

In that sense, the random oracle methodology could be regarded as a best practice or heuristic for the design of secure and practical cryptographic schemes.

The Random Oracle Assumption

In the previous paragraphs we presented some of the arguments in favor and against the use of random oracles for practical cryptographic schemes. We here want to argue for a middle ground. All practical evidence points to the fact that schemes proven secure in the random oracle model are, in fact, secure unless specifically designed not to be. This, however, does not mean that we should stop at a random oracle proof. Instead we should understand it as a good first step, but first step only. From there it should be the goal to base the security of the (ideally unchanged[4]) scheme on strong yet specific assumptions.

This brings us to a point that was missing so far in the discussion. Maybe the biggest flaw of the random oracle methodology is the lack of a rigorous definition of what it means to "behave like a random oracle." Consider any of the definitions of cryptographic primitives that we have presented. What they all have in common is that they are precise and, in particular, allow to prove positive results. We can prove that a function is a pseudorandom function or that it is collision resistant under certain assumptions. Instead, "behaving like a random oracle" is vague and does not allow for a positive result. It is more wishful thinking than a definition. What does it mean for a function to behave like a random oracle? How can we prove it?

Thus, one critical avenue is to better understand random oracles and their properties and to come up with rigorous definitions for these. Consider for a moment that we had a definitional framework that allows for fine-tuning definitions from weak to strong. If on one end of the spectrum of assumptions that can be stated in this framework we have our classical properties such as one-wayness or pseudorandomness and on the other end we have "behaves like a random oracle" then we can try to find the exact point at which properties become unachievable. If a scheme cannot be based on any of the achievable properties but only on those that are provably unachievable then this should ring alarm bells.

---

[4] In many cases, in order to alleviate the random oracle from a scheme, the scheme needs to be adapted. If that is the case and in particular in case the resulting scheme is much more complex it should be weighed carefully whether or not the added complexity really yields additional security or whether it is needed only because we are missing proof techniques.

For now, we leave the world of random oracles and instead look at how to construct cryptographic hash functions. We will, however, return to the topic of random oracles in Chapters 17 and 18, where we discuss two attempts at closing the gap between practical hash function constructions and random oracles. In Chapter 17 we discuss the so-called indifferentiability framework which allows to break up random oracles into smaller and simpler (yet still ideal) primitives that can be arranged in ways similarly to how practical cryptographic hash functions are usually built. Finally, in Chapter 18 we introduce the UCE framework, a recent attempt at providing a definitional framework for stating hash function properties. The UCE framework starts with the question of how a definition of "behaving like a random oracle" can look like to then define various flavors of definitions on a scale from weak to strong. While many of the UCE definitions are very strong and it is not yet clear how to construct these (without random oracles) they provide several advantages over random oracles. On the one hand, as we will see, security proofs using UCEs can often be simpler than direct proofs in the random oracle model. But most importantly, the precise assumptions provide us further insights into the properties the underlying scheme requires from its hash function, and ultimately UCEs may allow to alleviate random oracles all together.

Chapter Notes and References

The random oracle controversy started in 1998 with a paper by Canetti, Goldreich, and Halevi [4] which proved the existence of cryptographic schemes secure in the random oracle model but insecure with any standard model instantiation of the random oracle. Our presentation here (Section 12.2) follows the presentation of Maurer, Renner, and Holenstein [14]. If you read the result carefully, then you may have noticed that we required the signature scheme to allow for signing long messages: after all, the "bad message" as constructed by the adversary contains an encoding of a hash function. This, however, is only an artifact of the proof and uninstantiability results can also be shown for signatures schemes that do only allow for signing a priori bounded messages [5]. Since the work of Canetti *et al.* various uninstantiability results for different cryptographic schemes have been shown [15, 8, 1, 6, 10, 13, 2, 3, 9].

For a glimpse into the "random oracle controversy" we suggest to start with the final section of [4], which contains the original conclusions by Canetti, Goldreich, and Halevi. Further noteworthy articles include [12, 7, 11].

Exercices

Exercise 12.1. Show how to adapt the uninstantiable signature scheme Sig_{bad} from Theorem 12.1 (page 465) to be fully correct while remaining secure in the random oracle model but insecure for any efficient hash function H.

Chapter Bibliography

1. Mihir Bellare, Alexandra Boldyreva, and Adriana Palacio. An uninstantiable random-oracle-model scheme for a hybrid-encryption problem. In Christian Cachin and Jan Camenisch, editors, *Advances in Cryptology – EUROCRYPT 2004*, volume 3027 of *Lecture Notes in Computer Science*, pages 171–188, Interlaken, Switzerland, May 2–6, 2004. Springer, Heidelberg, Germany.
2. Christina Brzuska, Pooya Farshim, and Arno Mittelbach. Indistinguishability obfuscation and UCEs: The case of computationally unpredictable sources. In Juan A. Garay and Rosario Gennaro, editors, *Advances in Cryptology – CRYPTO 2014, Part I*, volume 8616 of *Lecture Notes in Computer Science*, pages 188–205, Santa Barbara, CA, USA, August 17–21, 2014. Springer, Heidelberg, Germany.
3. Christina Brzuska, Pooya Farshim, and Arno Mittelbach. Random-oracle uninstantiability from indistinguishability obfuscation. In Yevgeniy Dodis and Jesper Buus Nielsen, editors, *TCC 2015: 12th Theory of Cryptography Conference, Part II*, volume 9015 of *Lecture Notes in Computer Science*, pages 428–455, Warsaw, Poland, March 23–25, 2015. Springer, Heidelberg, Germany.
4. Ran Canetti, Oded Goldreich, and Shai Halevi. The random oracle methodology, revisited (preliminary version). In *30th Annual ACM Symposium on Theory of Computing*, pages 209–218, Dallas, TX, USA, May 23–26, 1998. ACM Press.
5. Ran Canetti, Oded Goldreich, and Shai Halevi. On the random-oracle methodology as applied to length-restricted signature schemes. In Moni Naor, editor, *TCC 2004: 1st Theory of Cryptography Conference*, volume 2951 of *Lecture Notes in Computer Science*, pages 40–57, Cambridge, MA, USA, February 19–21, 2004. Springer, Heidelberg, Germany.
6. Yevgeniy Dodis, Roberto Oliveira, and Krzysztof Pietrzak. On the generic insecurity of the full domain hash. In Victor Shoup, editor, *Advances in Cryptology – CRYPTO 2005*, volume 3621 of *Lecture Notes in Computer Science*, pages 449–466, Santa Barbara, CA, USA, August 14–18, 2005. Springer, Heidelberg, Germany.
7. Oded Goldreich. On post-modern cryptography. Cryptology ePrint Archive, Report 2006/461, 2006. http://eprint.iacr.org/2006/461.
8. Shafi Goldwasser and Yael Tauman Kalai. On the (in)security of the Fiat-Shamir paradigm. In *44th Annual Symposium on Foundations of Computer Science*, pages 102–115, Cambridge, MA, USA, October 11–14, 2003. IEEE Computer Society Press.
9. Matthew D. Green, Jonathan Katz, Alex J. Malozemoff, and Hong-Sheng Zhou. A unified approach to idealized model separations via indistinguishability obfuscation. In Vassilis Zikas and Roberto De Prisco, editors, *SCN 16: 10th International Conference on Security in Communication Networks*, volume 9841 of *Lecture Notes in Computer Science*, pages 587–603, Amalfi, Italy, August 31 – September 2, 2016. Springer, Heidelberg, Germany.
10. Eike Kiltz and Krzysztof Pietrzak. On the security of padding-based encryption schemes - or - why we cannot prove OAEP secure in the standard model. In Antoine Joux, editor, *Advances in Cryptology – EUROCRYPT 2009*, volume 5479 of *Lecture Notes in Computer Science*, pages 389–406, Cologne, Germany, April 26–30, 2009. Springer, Heidelberg, Germany.

11. Neal Koblitz and Alfred Menezes. The random oracle model: A twenty-year retro-spective. Cryptology ePrint Archive, Report 2015/140, 2015. http://eprint.iacr.org/2015/140.

12. Neal Koblitz and Alfred J. Menezes. Another look at "provable security". *Journal of Cryptology*, 20(1):3–37, January 2007.

13. Gaëtan Leurent and Phong Q. Nguyen. How risky is the random-oracle model? In Shai Halevi, editor, *Advances in Cryptology – CRYPTO 2009*, volume 5677 of *Lecture Notes in Computer Science*, pages 445–464, Santa Barbara, CA, USA, August 16–20, 2009. Springer, Heidelberg, Germany.

14. Ueli M. Maurer, Renato Renner, and Clemens Holenstein. Indifferentiability, impos-sibility results on reductions, and applications to the random oracle methodology. In Moni Naor, editor, *TCC 2004: 1st Theory of Cryptography Conference*, volume 2951 of *Lecture Notes in Computer Science*, pages 21–39, Cambridge, MA, USA, February 19–21, 2004. Springer, Heidelberg, Germany.

15. Jesper Buus Nielsen. Separating random oracle proofs from complexity theoretic proofs: The non-committing encryption case. In Moti Yung, editor, *Advances in Cryptology – CRYPTO 2002*, volume 2442 of *Lecture Notes in Computer Science*, pages 111–126, Santa Barbara, CA, USA, August 18–22, 2002. Springer, Heidelberg, Germany.

Part III
Hash Function Constructions

Chapter 13
Iterated Hash Functions

So far we have studied various hash function properties as well as use cases of hash functions. When unkeyed or used with a public key, hash functions can be collision resistant, second-preimage resistant, or one-way. On the other hand, when keeping the key hidden and considering the private-key setting, hash functions may be pseudorandom or act as message authentication codes. Hash functions with their various properties are basic building blocks used in almost all more complex cryptographic schemes. They are used as part of signature schemes or as a primitive in the construction of public-key encryption schemes. With the random oracle methodology we even have a recipe for how to construct provable cryptographic schemes—based on hash functions. What is missing from our discussion is the question of how we actually construct hash functions. This is the topic of Part III.

One of the main challenges when constructing hash functions is dealing with arbitrarily long messages. While hash functions are usually defined with a fixed output length—although we will see also constructions with variable output length such as the sponge construction underlying SHA-3—hash functions need to be able to consume messages of any length. A natural decomposition of hash function design is to first consider primitives that can deal with only a fixed amount of input and show that this fixed-input-length primitive enjoys the desired property, say, collision resistance. Then, in order to obtain a collision-resistant function that can process arbitrarily long messages we need in addition a scheme that uses the fixed-input-length primitive multiple times in order to process large messages. Such a scheme is usually referred to as an *iteration scheme* or *domain extension scheme*. If we can now prove for the iteration scheme that it preserves certain properties, say, that if the iterated fixed-input-length function is collision resistant that then the resulting scheme for arbitrarily long messages is collision resistant, then we have built ourselves a hash function.

What is intriguing about this decomposition is that we can study the construction of hash functions in two separate (and hopefully simpler) parts. We can study iteration schemes and their properties, and we can study fixed-

© Springer Nature Switzerland AG 2021
A. Mittelbach, M. Fischlin, *The Theory of Hash Functions and Random Oracles*,
Information Security and Cryptography, https://doi.org/10.1007/978-3-030-63287-8_13

input-length primitives. Furthermore, in case we find a weakness with a construction we can replace just the failing part and do not need to start from scratch.

In this chapter we will start our investigation of hash function constructions by looking at *iteration schemes* for the unkeyed and publicly keyed setting in order to construct collision-resistant hash functions. We will look at constructions of the iterated fixed-input-length primitives in Chapter 14 and study the private-key setting in Chapter 16, where we discuss constructions of message authentication codes and pseudorandom functions and, in particular, have a close look at the popular HMAC construction. In Chapter 15 we look at prominent hash function constructions that are widely used in practice and discuss MD5 as well as SHA-1, SHA-2, and SHA-3. Finally, we will look again at the idealized setting and consider how to build random oracles (or at least get as close as possible) in Chapters 17 and 18.

Domain Extension via Iteration

Let $h : \{0,1\}^{h.il(\lambda)} \to \{0,1\}^{h.ol(\lambda)}$ be a function where the input size $h.il(\lambda)$ is fixed for each security parameter $\lambda \in \mathbb{N}$. The idea is to use fixed-input-length function h in an iteration scheme H to build a function H^h that uses h and which is of the form $H^h : \{0,1\}^* \to \{0,1\}^{H.ol(\lambda)}$. That is, H^h can process input messages of arbitrary length and produces outputs of a fixed length. Note that we write H^h to emphasize the fact that iteration scheme H uses core function h only in a black-box way, that is, it does not depend in any way on the implementation details of function h.

In many cases, the core function will be compressing, that is, $h.il(\lambda) > h.ol(\lambda)$. Of course, there are exceptions, such as the SHA-3 construction in which the iterated function is a permutation. Iteration schemes are easier to understand when highlighting the computation as a diagram, and we will often use graphic representations to accompany definitions. When a core function h is a compressing function and takes an input x to produce output y we will visualize this as

$$x \longrightarrow \boxed{h} \longrightarrow y$$

Usually, we will treat the input to h not as a single value but instead consider functions $h : \{0,1\}^{bl(\lambda)} \times \{0,1\}^{cl(\lambda)} \to \{0,1\}^{ol(\lambda)}$ that take two values as input—often referred to as *message block* and *chaining value*. Here the polynomials in the definition stand for block length (bl) and chaining value length (cl). As the idea is to use multiple calls to the core function in order to process a large message $m = m_1 \| \dots \| m_\ell$ consisting of ℓ blocks we need to somehow utilize the output of an earlier computation in later computations.

Usually we have that one input to h corresponds to a message block m_i while the second input y_i is the output of a previous computation (the chaining value). Thus, we will often see functions where $\mathsf{h.ol}(\lambda) = \mathsf{h.cl}(\lambda)$ and that take the following form:

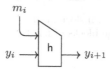

With that we have the basic building blocks to present one of the most fundamental methodologies in hash function design, the so-called Merkle–Damgård transformation, which will be the topic of the following section. As iteration schemes such as Merkle–Damgård are generic in the sense that they are independent of the underlying function h, attacks on the iteration scheme are powerful attacks that may immediately apply to a large number of functions: Any hash function based on the attacked iteration scheme will be vulnerable. We will look at generic attacks in Section 13.2. In Section 13.3 we will have a look at a close relative of the Merkle–Damgård transformation: *cryptographic sponges*. The cryptographic sponge (or simply sponge) is an iteration scheme that not only allows to process arbitrarily long messages but also allows to produce output values of arbitrary lengths.

13.1 The Merkle–Damgård Transformation

The Merkle–Damgård transformation was the first generic domain extension scheme for hash functions. It was proposed independently by Ivan Damgård and Ralph Merkle and hence the name Merkle–Damgård transformation, often abbreviated as MD. Today, the Merkle–Damgård transformation provides the core of, for example, the widely used MD5 hash function as well as the SHA-1 and SHA-2 hash functions, which we will discuss in Chapter 15.[1]

The Merkle–Damgård transformation allows to construct a hash function $\mathsf{H}_{\mathsf{MD}}^{\mathsf{h}}$ that is able to process arbitrarily long inputs from a compression function h of the form $\mathsf{h} : \{0,1\}^{\mathsf{h.bl}(\lambda)} \times \{0,1\}^{\mathsf{h.cl}(\lambda)} \to \{0,1\}^{\mathsf{h.cl}(\lambda)}$. Recall that bl is short for *block length* and cl is short for *chaining value length*. Furthermore, note that here the output length of the compression function is identical to the length of the chaining value, that is, $\mathsf{h.ol}(\lambda) = \mathsf{h.cl}(\lambda)$. As input, MD considers messages m that can be broken up into blocks of equal size: $m = m_1 \| \ldots \| m_\ell$ for some $\ell \in \mathbb{N}$ and where $|m_i| = \mathsf{bl}(\lambda)$ for all $i \in [\ell]$. The output of an MD hash function $\mathsf{H}_{\mathsf{MD}}^{\mathsf{h}}$ for compression function h is of length $\mathsf{h.ol}(\lambda)$ and thus of the length of a chaining value $\mathsf{h.cl}(\lambda)$.

---

[1] Note that MD in MD5 stands for *message digest* and not for Merkle–Damgård.

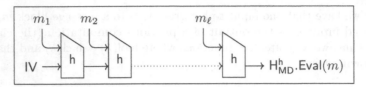

Fig. 13.1: The Merkle–Damgård transformation. A hash value for some message $m = m_1 \| \ldots \| m_\ell$ consisting of ℓ message blocks of length $\mathsf{h.bl}(\lambda)$ each is computed iteratively using compression function h.

Following our syntax for hash functions, we denote by $\mathsf{H}_{\mathsf{MD}}^{\mathsf{h}}.\mathsf{Eval}(1^\lambda, m)$ the computation of a hash value for message m via the Merkle–Damgård transformation with compression function h. For simplicity we drop the use of the security parameter 1^λ when denoting the evaluation of a hash function and write $\mathsf{H}^{\mathsf{h}}.\mathsf{Eval}(m)$ instead of $\mathsf{H}^{\mathsf{h}}.\mathsf{Eval}(1^\lambda, m)$ from here onwards. Often, we also drop the Eval part and simply write $\mathsf{H}^{\mathsf{h}}(m)$. Similarly, we may omit the security parameter when speaking about individual length functions and, for example, write bl instead of $\mathsf{bl}(\lambda)$ to denote the block length of function h.

To compute the hash value $\mathsf{H}_{\mathsf{MD}}^{\mathsf{h}}(m)$ for some message m, the individual message blocks are processed iteratively, one after the other, using compression function h. To process the ith message block the result y_i from the previous computation together with message block m_i is passed to the fixed-input-length compression function h to compute the next chaining value $y_{i+1} = \mathsf{h}(m_i, y_i)$. The result of the final h call, that is, value $y_{\ell+1}$ (given that the message consisted of ℓ blocks), yields the resulting hash value for message m. It remains to specify how the very first message block is processed as here no intermediate result y_1 is available. For this, we simply fix value $y_1 := \mathsf{IV}$ to some arbitrary value called the *initialization vector* (or initialization value). We can thus fully define a Merkle–Damgård hash function by defining initialization vector IV and core function h. Hash values for messages $m = m_1 \| \ldots \| m_\ell$ are then computed as

$$\mathsf{H}_{\mathsf{MD}}^{\mathsf{h}}.\mathsf{Eval}(m) := y_{\ell+1}, \qquad y_1 := \mathsf{IV}, \qquad y_{i+1} := \mathsf{h}(m_i, y_i).$$

Construction 13.1. *We refer to the Merkle–Damgård transformation* $\mathsf{H}_{\mathsf{MD}}^{\mathsf{h}}$ *for a compression function* h *as defined above as Construction 13.1.*

A graphical representation of the Merkle–Damgård transformation is given in Figure 13.1.

13.1.1 Message Padding

Our definition of the Merkle–Damgård transformation considers only messages that are a multiple of the block length bl. This form of the Merkle–Damgård transformation is also sometimes called the *plain* Merkle–Damgård transformation as it does not allow to process messages of arbitrary length. To extend the scheme to allow for arbitrary messages we need to specify an encoding that transforms a message m into a new message that has a length that is a multiple of the block length. As our goal is to achieve collision resistance it is easily seen that the encoding needs to be injective since collisions on the encoding yield collisions on the resulting hash function. Furthermore, the encoding should be efficient, not only in the sense of polynomial time but for practical purposes, and should not expand the message too much. In other words, the encoding scheme should be injective, fast, and produce outputs that are as short possible.

Usually we employ a simple *padding* as encoding, which adds bits to the end of the message to extend it to a multiple of the block size. A standard padding scheme for Merkle–Damgård with a block length bl is

$$\mathsf{pad}(m) := m \| 10^{\mathsf{bl}-(|m| \bmod \mathsf{bl})-1} \| \langle |m| \rangle_{\mathsf{bl}},$$

that is, a 1-bit is appended to the message followed by as many zeros as needed to fill the current block. Then an additional block is appended that contains the length of the message encoded in binary. Note that in order to not be ambiguous all messages are padded even if the original message m happens to be a multiple of the block size. This form of encoding is often also referred to as *Merkle–Damgård strengthening* or *length padding*.

While Merkle–Damgård strengthening is the predominant padding scheme used in practice it is usually slightly tuned so as to not always add an extra message block. For example, MD5, SHA-1, and SHA-2 do not reserve an entire block for storing the length, but only 64 bits of the last message block. Besides the Merkle–Damgård strengthening other padding schemes are plausible. Under certain additional assumptions about compression function h we may even drop the encoding of the length of the message altogether. SHA-3, for example, simply adds a 1-bit, zero or more 0-bits, and a final 1-bit to the message in order to obtain a message that is a multiple of the block length. This simpler form of padding is also known as the 10*1 *padding* or *multirate padding*. We will discuss this in greater detail in Section 13.3.2.

Remark 13.2. Merkle and Damgård independently proposed the iterative construction of hash functions from compression functions (where both set $\mathsf{IV} = 0^{\mathsf{h.cl}(\lambda)}$). Both also discussed the issue of non-aligned messages and how to pad them. Merkle proposed a solution which resembles what is used by practical hash functions like SHA-1 and SHA-2. He suggested to pad the message with sufficiently many 0-bits (but without a leading 1-bit) and to then append the original message length $|m|$ with a fixed number ℓ of bits. The latter may potentially add extra blocks to the padded messages, namely if the ℓ bits cannot be placed in the final message block.

Damgård proposed to append 0's to fill the message to a multiple of the block size, and then to append the number of padded 0's in binary, encoded in a full block. In addition, Damgård reserved one bit of each block in each iteration, effectively reducing the block size by one, and encoded the bit 0 in the first iteration, $y_2 = h(0||m_1, \text{IV})$, and 1 in all other iterations, $y_{i+1} = h(1||m_i, y_i)$. In the security argument this extra bit is used to deal with collisions of different block lengths but where the number d of padded bits are identical. Strictly speaking, this construction therefore violates the prefix condition in our abstract requirements below. Yet, modern constructions do not use this extra bit but rather follow the idea of Merkle and our MD strengthening above.

Let us next formally capture common properties of padding functions.

Definition 13.3. *Let* pad *be a deterministic function. We call* pad *a padding function if the following properties are observed:*

- *function* pad *is injective,*
- *for all messages m it holds that m is a prefix of* pad(m)*, and*
- *for all messages m and m' such that $|m| = |m'|$ we have that*

$$|\text{pad}(m)| = |\text{pad}(m')|.$$

Remark 13.4. While we claimed that the (strengthened) Merkle–Damgård transformation H^h_{MD} can process messages of arbitrary length this is only true in theory. In practice we may run into (mostly theoretical) problems with length padding if messages get very, very long. As Merkle–Damgård strengthening encodes the message length into the last message block the maximum length that can be encoded is 2^{bl} if we consider a block size of length bl. In many cases the theoretical maximum length is even shorter when the padding is optimized to not use a full block for encoding the message length. In case the length of the message is encoded in the last 64 bits (as, e.g., in SHA-1 and SHA-2) the maximum message length for these functions is restricted to $2^{64} - 1$ bits. Note that the padding of SHA-3 does not have this restriction as it is independent of the message length.

Remark 13.5. For easier notation we write H^h_{MD} to denote the (strengthened) Merkle–Damgård transformation and do not explicitly identify the padding function. It is either assumed to be the above padding or clear from context.

Remark 13.6. While padding is necessary in practice and, in fact, necessary for the security of hash functions, padding also often complicates the presentation (and hence the understanding) of proofs. Luckily, proof strategies are in many cases identical (or at least very similar) independent of whether or not padding is considered, and we will thus often first omit padding in analyses. If this is the case we will, however, always mention it explicitly and discuss how proofs would need to be adapted in order to incorporate padding.

13.1.2 Merkle–Damgård Preserves Collision Resistance

We said above that the standard padding function for the Merkle–Damgård transformation is usually referred to as *Merkle–Damgård strengthening*. This is for a good reason as padding is crucial to prove the security of the transformation as we will see in the following analysis. Note, however, that Merkle–Damgård strengthening is just one of many possible padding functions (or encodings in general) that allow to argue security.

In the following we will show that the strengthened Merkle–Damgård transformation H_{MD}^h is a *collision-resistance-preserving* transformation, meaning that the resulting hash function is collision resistant if compression function h is collision resistant. Besides collision resistance we will later also study other properties that are (or are not) preserved by Merkle–Damgård. Formally, we can capture *P-preserving* for some property P as follows.

Definition 13.7. *Let* H^O *be an oracle Turing machine relative to some oracle* O. *We say that* H *is* P-preserving *for a security property P (for example, collision resistance) if for any Turing machine* h *that has property P as well as the same domain and range as* O *the interactive Turing machine* H^h *also has property P. That is, for any efficient adversary* $\mathcal{A}$ *against property P of* H^h *there exists an adversary* $\mathcal{B}$ *against property P of* h *and a polynomial* p *such that*

$$\mathsf{Adv}_{H^h,\mathcal{A}}^p(\lambda) \leq p(\lambda) \cdot \mathsf{Adv}_{h,\mathcal{B}}^p(\lambda).$$

When arguing that Merkle–Damgård preserves collision resistance, we immediately run into a syntactical problem. Recall Definition 4.2 (page 162), which defines collision resistance for hash functions. A crucial ingredient was that the hash function is keyed as otherwise it is difficult to even define what it means for a function that is compressing to be collision resistant: Since collisions necessarily exist for a compressing function (due to the pigeon hole principle) there also exists the (non-uniform) adversary that simply has a collision hardcoded for each security parameter λ. Although we may not know how to construct this adversary it is clear that we cannot prove its non-existence: The adversary exists even if we are not able to write it down.

The Merkle–Damgård transformation, on the other hand, is unkeyed. While we could introduce an artificial key, for example, consider the compression function h to be keyed or to consider the initialization vector IV as some form of key, we here choose a different approach.[2]

Tracing oracle calls. Let us define the *execution trace* of a hash function as the sequence of all the internal executions of the underlying compression function h on an evaluation of $H^h(m)$ for some message m.

---

[2] We will come back to keyed variants shortly.

Definition 13.8. *Let* H^{O} *be a deterministic oracle Turing machine relative to oracle* O. *On input* m *we denote by* $\mathsf{trace}_{\mathsf{H}^{\mathsf{O}}}(m)$ *the sequence of oracle calls of* H *to* O *when computing* $\mathsf{H}^{\mathsf{O}}(m)$, *that is,*

$$\mathsf{trace}_{\mathsf{H}^{\mathsf{O}}}(m) := (x_1, x_2, \ldots),$$

where x_i *for* $i \in \mathbb{N}$ *denotes the input to the* i*th call to* O *during the evaluation of* $\mathsf{H}^{\mathsf{O}}(m)$.

If we consider our Merkle–Damgård hash function $\mathsf{H}_{\mathsf{MD}}^{\mathsf{h}}$ relative to compression function h then $\mathsf{trace}_{\mathsf{H}_{\mathsf{MD}}^{\mathsf{h}}}(m)[1]$ would correspond to the first h call, that is,

$$\mathsf{trace}_{\mathsf{H}_{\mathsf{MD}}^{\mathsf{h}}}(m)[1] = (m_1, \mathsf{IV}),$$

where m_1 is the first message block and IV the initialization vector. Note that entries in $\mathsf{trace}_{\mathsf{H}_{\mathsf{MD}}^{\mathsf{h}}}$ are thus always pairs consisting of a message block and a chaining value. Below we sometimes use the notation $(x, y) \in \mathsf{trace}_{\mathsf{H}_{\mathsf{MD}}^{\mathsf{h}}}(m)$ to denote the fact that the input pair (x, y) is an entry in the vector $\mathsf{trace}_{\mathsf{H}_{\mathsf{MD}}^{\mathsf{h}}}(m)$.

In the following we will show that any collision on hash function $\mathsf{H}_{\mathsf{MD}}^{\mathsf{h}}$ also yields a collision on the underlying compression function h. That is, if message pair (m, m') with $m \neq m'$ is a collision on $\mathsf{H}_{\mathsf{MD}}^{\mathsf{h}}$ then there exists a pair $((x, y), (x', y'))$ such that

$$(x, y) \in \mathsf{trace}_{\mathsf{H}_{\mathsf{MD}}^{\mathsf{h}}}(m) \qquad \text{and} \qquad (x', y') \in \mathsf{trace}_{\mathsf{H}_{\mathsf{MD}}^{\mathsf{h}}}(m')$$

for which

$$\mathsf{h}(x, y) = \mathsf{h}(x', y') \qquad \text{and} \qquad (x, y) \neq (x', y').$$

In other words, given a collision on hash function $\mathsf{H}_{\mathsf{MD}}^{\mathsf{h}}$ we show how to extract a collision also for compression function h. "Extracting" the underlying collision will be straightforward and requires only to look at the calls to h that occur during the computation of $\mathsf{H}_{\mathsf{MD}}^{\mathsf{h}}$ on the colliding messages m and m', respectively.

Suffix-free functions. Before we can prove the above claim we need one more ingredient: a special property of the padding function pad. Recall that Merkle–Damgård strengthening pads a message by appending a single 1-bit, filling up the current message block with 0-bits to then add an extra block that encodes the length of the message. While the first part of the padding allows us to hash messages of arbitrary length, the second part (encoding the message length) is relevant for the security of the resulting hash function.[3]

---

[3] We note that the property is not *necessary* in the mathematical sense of word. We can also obtain secure hash functions under different properties. See, for example, Exercise 13.2.

Encoding the message length in the final block ensures that the padding function is *suffix free*, which means that for any two messages $m \neq m'$ with $|m| < |m'|$ we have that pad(m) is not a suffix of pad(m').

> **Definition 13.9.** *A function* f *with domain* $\{0,1\}^*$ *is called* suffix free *if for all* $m, m', x \in \{0,1\}^*$ *with* $m \neq m'$ *we have that*
>
> $$f(m') \neq x\|f(m).$$

It is easily seen that pad as we have defined it for Merkle–Damgård is suffix free. For any pair of messages (m, m') that are of equal length the padding function appends the same bit string so either $m = m'$ or the prefix (to the padding) differs. If, on the other hand, $|m| \neq |m'|$ then the final blocks of pad(m) and pad(m') are different as they encode the length and $|m| \neq |m'|$.

Merkle–Damgård Preserves Collision Resistance

Suffix-free paddings were the last ingredient needed for proving that Merkle–Damgård preserves collision resistance.

> **Theorem 13.10.** *Let* h $: \{0,1\}^{\mathsf{h.bl}(\lambda)} \times \{0,1\}^{\mathsf{h.cl}(\lambda)} \to \{0,1\}^{\mathsf{h.cl}(\lambda)}$ *be a compression function and let* pad *be a suffix-free padding that maps inputs to a multiple of block length* h.bl(λ). *Let* $m, m' \in \{0,1\}^*$ *be two colliding messages under hash function* $\mathsf{H}^{\mathsf{h}}_{\mathsf{MD}}$, *that is,*
>
> $$m \neq m' \qquad and \qquad \mathsf{H}^{\mathsf{h}}_{\mathsf{MD}}(m) = \mathsf{H}^{\mathsf{h}}_{\mathsf{MD}}(m').$$
>
> *Then there exists* $(x, y) \in \mathsf{trace}_{\mathsf{H}^{\mathsf{h}}_{\mathsf{MD}}}(m)$ *and* $(x', y') \in \mathsf{trace}_{\mathsf{H}^{\mathsf{h}}_{\mathsf{MD}}}(m')$ *such that*
>
> $$\mathsf{h}(x, y) = \mathsf{h}(x', y') \qquad and \qquad (x, y) \neq (x', y').$$

Let us discuss how Theorem 13.10 captures the security of the Merkle–Damgård transformation (with appropriate padding function). After all, it is rather different in style from what we have seen so far in terms of security statements. As hash functions are compressing, collisions necessarily do exist and thus we need a way to deal with the (artificial and non-uniform) adversary that simply has a colliding message pair hardcoded (see Section 4.1.1 on page 163 for further details). The way we usually deal with that is to consider hash functions that are *keyed*, which then allows us to define a meaningful notion of what it means for a function to be collision resistant in spite of this adversary (see Definition 4.2 on page 162). Hash functions in practice, however, are often not keyed and also the Merkle–Damgård transformation does not require the use of a key.

Luckily, we can use a trick to prove the security of the transformation. Instead of relating the security to the capabilities of an efficient algorithm we base the security of the transformation on the security of the underlying core functionality: We base the security of H_{MD}^h on the security of compression function h and show that if h is secure so is H_{MD}^h. There is a caveat. As long as we do not consider keyed core functions we cannot formally prove the security of the underlying compression function h and thus the combined security of H_{MD}^h. However, if for some reason or other we believe that it is extremely difficult to find colliding inputs for some (unkeyed) compression function h then Theorem 13.10 tells us that it is as difficult to find a colliding message pair for the resulting Merkle–Damgård hash function H_{MD}^h. This viewpoint, in essence, is the *human ignorance approach* (Section 4.1.1; page 164) in which we demand an *actual instance* of an adversary: If you can provide an adversary that finds collisions for H_{MD}^h then Theorem 13.10 provides a concrete recipe to find collisions also for compression function h. Finally, let us note that the proof also extends to the keyed setting when we consider keyed compression functions underlying the MD transformation.

Proof of Theorem 13.10. Let $m, m' \in \{0,1\}^*$ be two messages with $m \neq m'$ that form a collision under hash function H_{MD}^h, that is, $H_{MD}^h(m) = H_{MD}^h(m')$. We will show that then there exist pairs

$$(x, y) \in \text{trace}_{H_{MD}^h}(m) \qquad \text{and} \qquad (x', y') \in \text{trace}_{H_{MD}^h}(m')$$

such that

$$h(x, y) = h(x', y') \qquad \text{and} \qquad (x, y) \neq (x', y').$$

We distinguish two cases:

1. Messages of equal length. First let us consider the case that, after padding, the two colliding messages are of the same length. That is, we have that

$$|\text{pad}(m)| = |\text{pad}(m')|.$$

Let $\ell = |\text{pad}(m)|/h.\text{bl}(\lambda)$ denote the number of message blocks for either message. By design of the Merkle–Damgård transformation we have that the resulting hash value is computed as

$$H_{MD}^h(m) := h(m_\ell, y_\ell),$$

where m_ℓ is the last message block corresponding to message m and y_ℓ is the last chaining value as computed by the second to last evaluation of compression function h (see also Figure 13.1). At the same time, since $H_{MD}^h(m) = H_{MD}^h(m')$ we know that also

$$H_{MD}^h(m) = h(m'_\ell, y'_\ell),$$

where m'_ℓ is the last message block corresponding to message m' and y'_ℓ is the last chaining value occurring in the evaluation of $H_{MD}^h(m')$.

Now we can again distinguish between two cases: either $(m_\ell, y_\ell) \neq (m'_\ell, y'_\ell)$ and we have found a collision for h or $(m_\ell, y_\ell) = (m'_\ell, y'_\ell)$. In the first case we are done. In the second case we can repeat the above analysis but now without the last message block. We know that $y_\ell = y'_\ell$ and by construction we have that

$$y_\ell = h(m_{\ell-1}, y_{\ell-1}) = h(m'_{\ell-1}, y'_{\ell-1}).$$

If it turns out that also $(m_{\ell-1}, y_{\ell-1}) = (m'_{\ell-1}, y'_{\ell-1})$ then we can "work our way backwards" up to the first message blocks (m_1, IV) and (m'_1, IV). As by assumption $m \neq m'$, there must exist index $i \in [\ell]$ such that $(m_i, y_i) \neq (m'_i, y'_i)$, which yields the desired h collision.

2. Messages of unequal length. If, on the other hand, the two messages are not of equal length, that is, if

$$|\mathsf{pad}(m)| \neq |\mathsf{pad}(m')|$$

then the above analysis fails, as at some point we might "run out of message blocks" to consider.

For the specific case of the MD strengthening the argument becomes straightforward as in this case, by construction, the last message blocks are different as they encode the message lengths. For the more general case, we need the suffix-free property of the padding function.

Without loss of generality let $|m| < |m'|$. By the suffix-freeness of pad it follows from $m \neq m'$ that there is no value $x \in \{0,1\}^*$ such that

$$x \| \mathsf{pad}(m) = \mathsf{pad}(m').$$

Let again $\ell = |\mathsf{pad}(m)| / \mathsf{h.bl}(\lambda)$ denote the number of message blocks for message m and $\ell' = |\mathsf{pad}(m')| / \mathsf{h.bl}(\lambda)$ the number of message blocks for message m'. If we now deploy our above analysis once more and first consider the last h evaluation (that is, (m_ℓ, y_ℓ) and $(m'_{\ell'}, y'_{\ell'})$), then the second to last h evaluation $((m_{\ell-1}, y_{\ell-1})$ and $(m'_{\ell'-1}, y'_{\ell'-1}))$ and so forth it must be the case that there exists index $i \in [\ell]$ such that

$$m_i \neq m_{\ell'-\ell+i}$$

as otherwise m would be a suffix of m'. (Note that $\ell' - \ell + i$ denotes the ith block of message m' starting from offset $\ell' - \ell$, the number of blocks message m' has in addition to message m.) Thus, the analysis must necessarily find a pair

$$(m_i, y_i) \neq (m_{\ell'-\ell+i}, y_{\ell'-\ell+i})$$

for which

$$h(m_i, y_i) = h(m_{\ell'-\ell+i}, y_{\ell'-\ell+i}),$$

which concludes the proof. $\qquad\square$

Remark 13.11. For the proof of Theorem 13.10 we required the padding function pad to be suffix free. An alternative to the suffix-freeness requirement is to require that no PPT adversary can compute a preimage from the initialization vector IV under compression function h. That is, no PPT algorithm on input the security parameter 1^λ and initialization value IV, can find values (x, y) such that $h(x, y) = $ IV. (Note that for this notion to be meaningful we either need to consider keyed compression functions or choose the initialization value uniformly at random.) In this case the first part of the proof (messages of equal length) remains identical. For the second part where we argue that we can also extract an h collision for messages of unequal length we now need to argue that either we can extract a collision for compression function h or we can extract a preimage for the initialization value. Exercise 13.2 asks to formalize this intuition.

13.1.3 Keyed Merkle–Damgård

While for collision resistance we were able to provide an analysis also for an unkeyed version of Merkle–Damgård, this is not possible for other security properties. In particular, for privately keyed primitives such as pseudorandom functions and message authentication codes that we will briefly discuss in Section 13.1.6 and in depth in Chapter 16, we require a mechanism to introduce keys into the MD transformation. But also for properties closely related to collision resistance such as second-preimage resistance or target-collision resistance, switching to explicitly modeling a public key in the transformation becomes a necessity.

While there are countless possibilities of introducing keys into the MD transformation, the two predominant ones are considering keyed compression functions or treating the initialization value IV as the function's key.[4] From the two, using keyed compression functions can lead to a more secure scheme as the key goes into every compression function evaluation instead of just into the first. On the other hand, the latter choice has the advantage that it does not need any change in the implementation of the hash function and can be "added on top" of any unkeyed function such as SHA-1. We will discuss the various ways of introducing keys and their security implications in detail in Chapter 16. For now let us simply define the two above versions.

Let us first consider the keyed Merkle–Damgård transformation where the compression function h is itself a keyed function family. In this scenario we extend the compression function in the natural way and consider compression function h $=$ (h.KGen, h.Eval) to be a tuple of two efficient algorithms, a probabilistic key generation algorithm and a deterministic

---

[4] A variant of the latter is to treat the first message block as the function's key, which we also discuss in greater detail in Chapter 16.

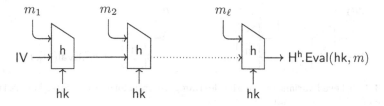

Fig. 13.2: A keyed variant of the Merkle–Damgård transformation with a keyed compression function h.

evaluation algorithm. In order to be able to digest the key we now need to extend the compression function's evaluation algorithm and consider $h.\mathsf{Eval} : \{0,1\}^{h.\mathsf{kl}(\lambda)} \times \{0,1\}^{h.\mathsf{bl}(\lambda)} \times \{0,1\}^{h.\mathsf{cl}(\lambda)} \rightarrow \{0,1\}^{h.\mathsf{cl}(\lambda)}$ to now take three inputs where the first input corresponds to a key $\mathsf{hk} \in \{0,1\}^{h.\mathsf{kl}(\lambda)}$. As usual, function $h.\mathsf{kl}(\lambda)$ denotes the key length for security parameter 1^λ.

To incorporate a keyed compression function we also extend the Merkle–Damgård transformation and add a key generation algorithm. The resulting hash function $\mathsf{H}^h = (\mathsf{H}^h.\mathsf{KGen}, \mathsf{H}^h.\mathsf{Eval})$ is now a tuple of two efficient algorithms where we set the key generation algorithm to be the key generation algorithm of the underlying compression function: $\mathsf{H}^h.\mathsf{KGen}(1^\lambda) := h.\mathsf{KGen}(1^\lambda)$. During the evaluation of $\mathsf{H}^h.\mathsf{Eval}(\mathsf{hk}, m)$ on a message m and with key hk the key is simply passed to every evaluation of compression function h. Figure 13.2 contains a graphical representation of this variant of a keyed MD transformation.

The second variant is a lot simpler to define. Here we simply replace the initialization value with the key. The schematic is given in Figure 13.3.

Remark 13.12. We refer to the standard unkeyed variant of the Merkle–Damgård transformation as $\mathsf{H}^h_{\mathsf{MD}}$. We do not provide special syntax to differentiate different keyed variants and simply refer to these generically as H^h. The variant we refer to should always be clear from context.

Collision Resistance for Keyed Merkle–Damgård

We showed that the unkeyed Merkle–Damgård transformation preserves collision resistance. The same is true for both keyed variants defined above. Given that we are now in the keyed setting we can give a standard reductionist argument. From an adversary $\mathcal{A}$ against the keyed variable-length hash function we can construct an adversary $\mathcal{B}$ against the compression function. The strategy of adversary $\mathcal{B}$ is to simply extract the collision as in the proof above for Theorem 13.10. The fact that we have introduced a key does not change the argument that a collision for h must exist in the trace.

Fig. 13.3: A keyed variant of the Merkle–Damgård transformation where key hk is used in place of initialization value IV.

> **Proposition 13.13.** *Let* H^h *be one of the keyed variants of the Merkle–Damgård transformation as defined above with a suffix-free padding scheme. Then we have that* H^h *is collision-resistance preserving. Furthermore, for any efficient adversary* $\mathcal{A}$ *against the collision resistance of* H^h *there exists an efficient adversary* $\mathcal{B}$ *against the collision resistance of* h *such that*
> $$\mathsf{Adv}^{\mathrm{cr}}_{H^h,\mathcal{A}}(\lambda) = \mathsf{Adv}^{\mathrm{cr}}_{h,\mathcal{B}}(\lambda).$$

Remark 13.14. Note that our two keyed variants of Merkle–Damgård differ substantially with regards to the compression function. In one case we consider keyed compression functions (Figure 13.2), while in the other we consider unkeyed functions (Figure 13.3). For the latter note that the above Proposition 13.13 on its own is somewhat meaningless as, naturally, an adversary against an unkeyed compression function exists that can break collision-resistance: the non-uniform adversary that has collisions hardcoded (also see Section 4.1.1 on page 163). In the unkeyed compression function setting the proposition is thus best understood in the same way as Theorem 13.10 above. Part of the proof of Proposition 13.13 (which, as discussed, is analogous to the proof of Theorem 13.10) is to give an *actual construction* of an adversary that finds collisions instead of only arguing the existence of such an adversary.

13.1.4 MD Does Not Preserve SPR and TCR

We have seen that the Merkle–Damgård transformation preserves collision resistance. Perhaps surprisingly, we will see that the same is not true for the related properties second-preimage resistance and target-collision resistance (Definitions 4.6 and 4.8; pages 173ff.).

Similarly to collision resistance both weaker notions, i.e., second-preimage resistance (SPR) and target-collision resistance (TCR), are defined relative to keyed hash functions. While the notion of second-preimage resistance is certainly meaningful in the unkeyed setting (consider, for example, forging a signature for a given message for a hash-and-sign scheme using an unkeyed hash function such as SHA-1), the notion of target-collision resistance is inherently keyed. Recall that here an adversary should fix a target message before the function's key is chosen. When removing the key in this scenario the notion basically reduces to collision resistance (for an unkeyed hash function).

For our negative result here we thus consider both cases: For SPR and TCR we show that the keyed variant of the Merkle–Damgård transformation iterating a keyed compression function does not preserve the underlying property and for second-preimage resistance we argue, in addition, that it is not preserved by the unkeyed Merkle–Damgård transformation.

Proposition 13.15. *The keyed Merkle–Damgård variant* H^h *iterating a keyed compression function* h *as specified in Figure 13.2 does not preserve target-collision resistance nor second-preimage resistance.*

Furthermore, the unkeyed Merkle–Damgård transformation H^h_{MD} *does not preserve second-preimage resistance.*

In order to show a negative result it suffices to present a concrete counterexample. In this case we need to come up with a compression function h that is second-preimage resistant (resp. target-collision resistant) and then show that when used in the Merkle–Damgård transformation the resulting hash function is not second-preimage resistant (resp. target-collision resistant).

A common approach to construct such counterexamples is to start with a compression function that is secure and then adapt it to inject a weakness that does not directly compromise the security of the function but which will affect the security when using the function within the transformation. Here, the idea is to embed specific collisions into the compression function. While known collisions would immediately render a function insecure with respect to collision resistance, having known collisions does not necessarily affect the security with regards to second-preimage or target-collision resistance as one part of the collision is fixed during the beginning of the security game and independently of the function's key. Thus if, with overwhelming probability, the collision target in the security game does not hit one of the embedded collisions then the security of the function is not affected by the introduced changes.

In summary, we start with a second-preimage-resistant (resp. target-collision-resistant) compression function h. We then adapt function h and introduce artificial collisions to obtain our target compression function h*. The injected collisions will be such that

1. they do not compromise the security of the compression function, but
2. allow to break the security of the resulting Merkle–Damgård hash function.

Remark 13.16. Admittedly, such a *constructed* counterexample is artificial and would probably not occur in practice. But remember, the concept of *preserving a property under transformation* requires the property to be preserved for *every* compression function as long as it fulfills the security requirements. In particular this needs to hold also for "somewhat artificial functions."

The key observation in preparing compression function h^* is that in both security games for second-preimage and target-collision resistance one part of the collision is fixed prior to choosing the hash function's key. This means that when crafting the adapted compression function it is safe to embed collisions that contain the key as part of the message. Before we get to the actual construction, let us give a simple example. Let h be a second-preimage-resistant compression function. Now define h^* to behave exactly as h with one exception: In case the input corresponding to the message block is equal to hash key hk then function h^* outputs $1^{h.ol(\lambda)}$:

$$h^*(hk, m, y) := \begin{cases} 1^{h.ol(\lambda)} & \text{if } m = hk \\ h(hk, m, y) & \text{otherwise} \end{cases}$$

Naturally, h^* is not collision resistant even in case h is, since we have embedded a large number of collisions. For example, the following constitutes a collision under h^* for key hk:

$$h^*(hk, hk, 0^{h.cl(\lambda)}) = 1^{h.ol(\lambda)} = h^*(hk, hk, 1^{h.cl(\lambda)}).$$

However, it is not hard to argue that h^* is second-preimage resistant given that h is. To see that this is indeed the case note that the adversary in the second-preimage resistance game is given a random target message (m, y) for which it has to find a second preimage, i.e., a message $(m', y') \neq (m, y)$ such that the pair $((m, y), (m', y'))$ forms a collision under function h^* with key hk. Figure 13.4 presents once more the security experiments underlying the definitions of second-preimage resistance and target-collision resistance. Note that, in particular, it is the case that target message (m, y) is chosen independently of the key. In both definitions the key is, indeed, chosen only after the target was fixed. In the case of second-preimage resistance we have that the target is chosen uniformly at random and thus with overwhelming probability will not contain the (independently chosen) key. In case of target-collision resistance we cannot make this assumption as here the message is adversarially chosen. However, assuming that key hk as generated by key generation algorithm h.KGen can only be guessed with negligible probability[5] we can also argue for TCR that with overwhelming probability target message (m, y) is such that $m \neq hk$ and thus our inserted collisions are of no help to the adversary.

So far we have seen how we can introduce artificial collisions in a compression function without compromising its security with regards to second-preimage and target-collision resistance. But how does this help in order to break the security of the resulting Merkle–Damgård hash function? For this, we need to exploit the iterative style of Merkle–Damgård. Consider a

---

[5] While it is reasonable to assume that keys cannot be guessed it is not required by the definition of second-preimage- or target-collision-resistant functions. We will see below how we can ensure that this is, indeed, the case.

Experiment $\mathsf{Exp}^{\mathrm{spr}}_{\mathsf{h},\mathcal{A}}(\lambda)$	Experiment $\mathsf{Exp}^{\mathrm{tcr}}_{\mathsf{h},\mathcal{A}_1,\mathcal{A}_2}(\lambda)$
1: $(m,y) \leftarrow\!\!\$ \ \{0,1\}^{\mathsf{h.bl}(\lambda)\times\mathsf{h.cl}(\lambda)}$	1: $(m,y,\mathsf{state}) \leftarrow\!\!\$ \ \mathcal{A}_1(1^\lambda)$
2: $\mathsf{hk} \leftarrow\!\!\$ \ \mathsf{h.KGen}(1^\lambda)$	2: $\mathsf{hk} \leftarrow\!\!\$ \ \mathsf{h.KGen}(1^\lambda)$
3: $(m',y') \leftarrow\!\!\$ \ \mathcal{A}(1^\lambda,\mathsf{hk},m,y)$	3: $(m',y') \leftarrow\!\!\$ \ \mathcal{A}_2(1^\lambda,\mathsf{hk},m,y,\mathsf{state})$
4: **return** $\mathsf{h}(\mathsf{hk},m,y) = \mathsf{h}(\mathsf{hk},m',y')$	4: **return** $\mathsf{h}(\mathsf{hk},m,y) = \mathsf{h}(\mathsf{hk},m',y')$
$\wedge\ (m,y) \neq (m',y')$	$\wedge\ (m,y) \neq (m',y')$

Fig. 13.4: The security definition of second-preimage resistance (Definition 4.6; page 173) on the left and of target-collision resistance (Definition 4.8; page 175) on the right. Both experiments are adapted to our compression function scenario.

Merkle–Damgård hash function iterating compression function h for an input consisting of only two message blocks (and let us ignore padding for now). Then the resulting hash value would be computed as

$$\mathsf{H}^{\mathsf{h}}(\mathsf{hk}, m_1 \| m_2) = \mathsf{h}(\mathsf{hk}, m_2, \mathsf{h}(\mathsf{hk}, m_1, \mathsf{IV}))$$

or given in graphical form as

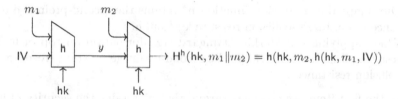

The idea now is to adapt h and to include key hk as part of its output. In that way key hk goes into the second invocation of h during the computation of the Merkle–Damgård hash function and we can use our technique of embedded collisions to break the security. In the following we make this intuition formal for the case of keyed compression functions. We leave the proof that unkeyed Merkle–Damgård does not preserve second-preimage resistance as Exercise 13.3 (also see Remark 13.17 following the proof).

Proof of Proposition 13.15. Let h be a second-preimage-resistant (resp. target-collision-resistant) compression function with $\mathsf{h.ol}(\lambda) = \mathsf{h.cl}(\lambda)$ (the output length corresponds to the length of the chaining value) and $\mathsf{h.bl}(\lambda) > \mathsf{h.kl}(\lambda)+\lambda$ (the block length is greater than the key length plus the security parameter). We will shortly see why this restriction is without loss of generality. We construct an adapted compression function h^* based on h as follows. Key generation is similar to that of h except that we append a uniformly random string of length λ to the key:

$$\underline{h^*.\mathsf{KGen}(1^\lambda)}$$

1 : $r \leftarrow\!\!\$ \{0,1\}^\lambda$

2 : $k \leftarrow\!\!\$ h.\mathsf{KGen}(1^\lambda)$

3 : **return** $k\|r$

The additional randomness ensures that keys are hard to guess, even if this was not the case for keys generated by h.KGen. Evaluation of h^* is adapted as follows: If the first $h^*.kl(\lambda) = h.kl(\lambda) + \lambda$ bits of y are equal to key hk, then the function outputs a string of 1-bits prefixed by key hk. Otherwise it outputs whatever h outputs but also prepends the hash key hk. That is, we define function h^* as

$$h^*(\mathsf{hk}, m, y) := \begin{cases} \mathsf{hk}\|1^{h.\mathsf{ol}(\lambda)} & \text{if } y[1..h^*.kl(\lambda)] = \mathsf{hk} \\ \mathsf{hk}\|h(\mathsf{hk}, m, y) & \text{otherwise} \end{cases}$$

Note that, as h^* as defined now has an output length of $h.\mathsf{ol}(\lambda) + h.kl(\lambda) + \lambda$ we needed the requirement that $h.\mathsf{bl}(\lambda) > h.kl(\lambda) + \lambda$ to ensure that our resulting compression function h^* is, indeed, compressing.

To complete the proof we need to show the following:

1. Our adapted compression function h^* retains the second-preimage resistance (resp. target-collision resistance) from h.
2. When applying the Merkle–Damgård transformation on top of h^* the resulting hash function will not be second-preimage resistant (resp. target-collision resistance).

For the first item, we can again argue that h^* retains the security of h by the fact that the target for the collision (both in the second-preimage and in the target-collision resistance security game) are chosen independently of key hk and thus the introduced collisions do not affect the security. For this note that all introduced collisions begin with key hk which, by design, can only be guessed with negligible probability.

It thus remains to show the existence of an adversary against the second-preimage resistance (resp. target-collision resistance) of the Merkle–Damgård hash function H^{h^*} for our compression function h^*. For this, consider the evaluation of H^{h^*} for two message blocks:

$$\begin{aligned} H^{h^*}(\mathsf{hk}, m_1\|m_2) &= h^*(\mathsf{hk}, m_2, h^*(\mathsf{hk}, m_1, \mathsf{IV})) \\ &= h^*(\mathsf{hk}, m_2, \mathsf{hk}\|h(\mathsf{hk}, m_1, \mathsf{IV})) \\ &= \mathsf{hk}\|1^{h.\mathsf{ol}(\lambda)}. \end{aligned}$$

The last equality is due to the construction of h^*. When the chaining value starts with key hk then h^* is defined as $\mathsf{hk}\|1^{h.\mathsf{ol}(\lambda)}$. Note that the above evaluation is independent of the values of m_1 and m_2. Furthermore, consider the case that we evaluate not two rounds of h^* but three:

$$\mathsf{H}^{\mathsf{h}^*}(\mathsf{hk}, m_1 \| m_2 \| m_3) = \mathsf{h}^*(\mathsf{hk}, m_3, \mathsf{h}^*(\mathsf{hk}, m_2, \mathsf{h}^*(\mathsf{hk}, m_1, \mathsf{IV})))$$
$$= \mathsf{h}^*(\mathsf{hk}, m_3, \mathsf{h}^*(\mathsf{hk}, m_2, \mathsf{hk} \| \mathsf{h}(\mathsf{hk}, m_1, \mathsf{IV})))$$
$$= \mathsf{h}^*(\mathsf{hk}, m_3, \mathsf{hk} \| 1^{\mathsf{h.ol}(\lambda)})$$
$$= \mathsf{hk} \| 1^{\mathsf{h.ol}(\lambda)}.$$

It is easy to see that the same holds for any message of block length bigger than one and that, indeed, any message consisting of two or more blocks will be mapped to $\mathsf{hk} \| 1^{\mathsf{h.ol}(\lambda)}$ under $\mathsf{H}^{\mathsf{h}^*}$. Note that this, in particular, also holds for arbitrary padding schemes as the observation above is independent of the actual content of the message. Consequently, adversaries for both second-preimage resistance and target-collision resistance can trivially find valid collisions.

To finalize the proof we need to argue that the length restriction—recall that we demanded that $\mathsf{h.bl}(\lambda) > \mathsf{h.kl}(\lambda) + \lambda$—is without loss of generality. For this consider the case that such secure compression functions do not exist but that, instead, the Merkle–Damgård transformation is a good domain extender for functions with $\mathsf{h.bl}(\lambda) \leq \mathsf{h.kl}(\lambda) + \lambda$. But then we could use the Merkle–Damgård transformation to construct a second-preimage-resistant (resp. target-collision-resistant) function satisfying $\mathsf{h.bl}(\lambda) > \mathsf{h.kl}(\lambda) + \lambda$ by iterating the compression function sufficiently often, but at most a polynomial number of times, and viewing this as a compression function with sufficiently large block length. This yields a contradiction to the assumption of such compression functions not existing, and concludes the proof. □

Remark 13.17. We leave as Exercise 13.3 the case to argue that the (unkeyed) Merkle–Damgård transformation does not preserve second-preimage resistance. For this note that in the second-preimage resistance experiment (see also Figure 13.4) the target message is not just chosen independently from the key but uniformly at random. When adapting a second-preimage-resistant compression function h we can thus safely inject collisions at fixed points and, for example, define derived function h^* as

$$\mathsf{h}^*(m, y) := \begin{cases} 1^{\mathsf{h.ol}(\lambda)} & \text{if } m = 0^{\mathsf{h.bl}(\lambda)} \\ \mathsf{h}(\mathsf{hk}, m, y) & \text{otherwise} \end{cases}$$

Now, as long as $\mathsf{h.bl}$ grows super-logarithmically in the security parameter the adapted function remains second-preimage resistant given that h is second-preimage resistant.

13.1.5 Domain Extension for SPR and TCR

We saw that, in general, Merkle–Damgård is not a good domain extender for second-preimage and target-collision resistance as there are compression functions for which the transformation does not retain the security. In the following we show that we can adapt the MD transformation to obtain a secure domain extender also for second-preimage-resistant (or target-collision-resistant) functions. A key difference of the presented scheme is that the key size depends on the size of the message: longer messages also need longer keys. This is in stark contrast to the keyed MD transformations considered above where we used a *fixed* size key for arbitrarily long messages. Regrettably, for domain extension of second-preimage and target-collision resistance it seems to be a necessity that keys grow at least logarithmically with the message length.

XOR Linear Hash (XLH)

The following construction doubles the input domain of a second-preimage-resistant function at the cost of also increasing the size of the key. We start with a keyed compression function

$$h : \{0,1\}^{h.kl(\lambda)} \times \{0,1\}^{h.bl(\lambda)} \times \{0,1\}^{h.cl(\lambda)} \to \{0,1\}^{h.cl(\lambda)}$$

such that $\{0,1\}^{h.bl(\lambda)} > \{0,1\}^{h.cl(\lambda)}$, that is the block length is greater than the chaining value length (and thus the output length) of the function. From this we construct a function

$$H^h : \{0,1\}^{h.kl(\lambda)+2 \cdot h.cl(\lambda)} \times \{0,1\}^{2 \cdot h.bl(\lambda)} \times \{0,1\}^{h.cl(\lambda)} \to \{0,1\}^{h.cl(\lambda)}.$$

That is, we double the message block length but also increase the key size. The construction itself is, essentially, the Merkle–Damgård transformation with two executions of the underlying function, which uses two additional keys k_1 and k_2 that are XORed on top of the intermediate chaining values. Following is the pseudocode for the construction, and Figure 13.5 provides a graphical representation:

$H^h.\mathsf{KGen}(1^\lambda)$	$H.\mathsf{Eval}((hk, k_1, k_2), m)$
1 : $hk \leftarrow\!\!\$\ h.\mathsf{KGen}(1^\lambda)$	1 : $m_1 \leftarrow m[1..h.bl(\lambda)]$
2 : $k_1 \leftarrow\!\!\$\ \{0,1\}^{h.cl(\lambda)}$	2 : $m_2 \leftarrow m[(h.bl(\lambda)+1)..(2 \cdot h.bl(\lambda))]$
3 : $k_2 \leftarrow\!\!\$\ \{0,1\}^{h.cl(\lambda)}$	3 : **return** $h(hk, m_2, k_2 \oplus h(hk, m_1, k_1))$
4 : **return** (hk, k_1, k_2)	

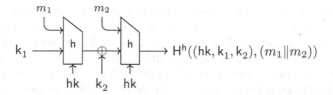

Fig. 13.5: The XLH construction (for two input blocks) for extending second-preimage- and target-collision-resistant hash functions.

Generalized to arbitrarily many blocks (instead of just two), the construction is also known as the *XLH construction*, which is short for *XOR linear hash*. Note that in this case the key is expanded by $n \cdot \mathsf{h.cl}(\lambda)$ bits when considering n-block inputs.

> **Proposition 13.18.** *Let h be a second-preimage-resistant (resp. target-collision-resistant) function. Then the XOR linear hash construction H^h, as defined above, is also second-preimage resistant (resp. target-collision resistant).*

The statement follows by a security reduction. The basic idea is that the additional keys k_1 and k_2 allow a reduction to embed a challenge for an adversary against H^h. We here discuss the security reduction for second-preimage resistance. The reduction for target-collision resistance works analogously. Note, however, that both settings need to be proved independently. While target-collision resistance implies second-preimage resistance (see Proposition 4.10 on page 175), when considering preservation of second-preimage resistance we start with a weaker assumption: here the iterated function is only second-preimage resistant.

Consider now an adversary $\mathcal{A}$ against the second-preimage resistance of function H^h. From $\mathcal{A}$, we construct an adversary $\mathcal{B}^\mathcal{A}$ against the second-preimage resistance of the underlying compression function h. In the second-preimage resistance security game, reduction $\mathcal{B}^\mathcal{A}$ gets as input a target message m and a hash key hk. Its task is to produce a collision $(m, y) \neq (m', y')$ such that $\mathsf{h}(\mathsf{hk}, m, y) = \mathsf{h}(\mathsf{hk}, m', y)$. To compute this collision, adversary $\mathcal{B}^\mathcal{A}$ flips a bit deciding where to embed its challenge when simulating the second-preimage resistance game for adversary $\mathcal{A}$: either in the first iteration or the second iteration of h. Note that in case $\mathcal{A}$ finds a collision then, necessarily, there must be a collision on one of the compression function calls (also see Theorem 13.10). In order to embed the challenge, reduction $\mathcal{B}^\mathcal{A}$ will use keys k_1 and k_2. The reduction receives hk and a random input (m, y) and first picks a random bit b. For $b = 0$ it sets $\mathsf{k}_1 \leftarrow y$ and $m_1 \leftarrow m$ and chooses k_2 and m_2 randomly. For $b = 1$ it picks k_1 and m_1 randomly and sets $\mathsf{k}_2 \leftarrow \mathsf{h}(\mathsf{hk}, m_1, \mathsf{k}_1) \oplus y$ and $m_2 \leftarrow m$. It runs $\mathcal{A}$ on input $(\mathsf{hk}, \mathsf{k}_1, \mathsf{k}_2, m_1 \| m_2)$.

First note that the input given to $\mathcal{A}$ is distributed as expected by the adversary. The target message $m_1 \| m_2$ is uniformly distributed and so are keys k_1 and k_2. Consequently adversary $\mathcal{A}$ must find a collision with the same probability as in the original experiment. If adversary $\mathcal{A}$ is successful, then, however, in 50% of the cases, reduction $\mathcal{B}^{\mathcal{A}}$ will be able to extract a second preimage for its own target message for its choice of b. In case we consider larger extensions for n message blocks then the success probability of $\mathcal{B}^{\mathcal{A}}$ drops correspondingly to $1/n$ times the success probability of adversary $\mathcal{A}$. We leave the formalization as Exercise 13.4.

Remark 13.19. The domain extension for second-preimage and target-collision resistance that we have seen above is quite different from that for collision resistance as the latter allows to process arbitrarily long messages while the construction above merely extends the input domain by a given factor. While we can expand on this idea to get an arbitrarily long expansion we have the problem that with a further increase of the message length we also need to increase the key space. The reason for this increased key length is that in our security reduction we need to give the reduction the necessary freedom to embed its challenge and for that it needs to have further control, which it gets by being able to choose the keys for the underlying adversary. While there are constructions that only require a logarithmic increase of the key length—we provide references in the notes section of this chapter—there is no known construction that provides domain extension without an increase of the key length as we have with Merkle–Damgård for collision resistance.

Remark 13.20. In Proposition 13.18 above we considered the XLH construction for fixed-length messages consisting of two blocks. As the key length grows with the message length we cannot hope to construct a function for arbitrary inputs. We can, however, fix a maximum message length, say n message blocks, and then use the construction for messages shorter than n blocks. In this case the messages need to be padded appropriately, for example, using Merkle–Damgård strengthening.

13.1.6 Length-Extension Attacks on Merkle–Damgård

In the previous sections we looked at keyed versions of Merkle–Damgård and studied the publicly keyed properties second-preimage and target-collision resistance. In particular, we saw that for these the Merkle–Damgård transformation is not a good domain extender. Let us next take a brief detour to the world of privately keyed properties and show that similarly for pseudorandom functions and message authentication codes the plain Merkle–Damgård transformation may not yield a secure domain extender. We will have a lot more to say about the private-key case in Chapter 16 but for now focus on one of the main attack vectors against Merkle–Damgård: so-called *length extension attacks*.

Recall that the setting of pseudorandom functions and message authentication codes is different from collision-resistance-based properties in the sense that the key is kept hidden from the adversary (see Definition 3.21 on page 126). Whether or not the key is public or private does, of course, not change how we can introduce a key into the Merkle–Damgård transformation, and as we will see in Chapters 16 and 17 it can make quite a difference how we choose to introduce it. Maybe the most commonly chosen approach, due to its simplicity, is to replace the initialization vector with the key. This yields a candidate PRF as shown in the following diagram:

Note that we denote the compression function here as f instead of h to indicate it to be a (privately) keyed function such as a pseudorandom function. While usually we consider pseudorandom functions of the form $f(k, m)$ that take the key as first input, when chaining we mostly consider the key to be used as chaining value and thus write $f(m, k)$. Note that in the above pictures we added a little black triangle at the input of the chaining value for function f to denote that this is the input of the function that takes the key. Usually, we will omit from graphical representations where the key should go, as this is not a property of the iteration but a requirement of security statements. The iteration scheme does not care whether function f takes a key as its first or second input. It only cares about f taking two inputs of a specific length.

Length-Extension Attacks on Merkle–Damgård

For both pseudorandom functions and message authentication codes, it holds that if an adversary learns the function value for a message m it does not allow the adversary to infer anything about the function's values for related messages (assuming, of course, that the key remains hidden). For example, knowing that for some message m the authentication tag is τ should not allow an adversary to deduce tags for messages $m\|x$ that have m as a prefix. In case of Merkle–Damgård this is, however, possible.

For simplicity let us assume that we do not use a padding scheme and that m is of a single block. In this case we would have that $\mathsf{PRF}^f(k, m)$ is exactly

$$\mathsf{PRF}^f(k, m) = f(m, k).$$

If we now consider a longer message $m' = m\|x$ that is of length two message blocks where the first block is exactly m then due to the construction of Merkle–Damgård we have that

$$\mathsf{PRF}^{\mathsf{f}}(\mathsf{k}, m') = \mathsf{PRF}^{\mathsf{f}}(\mathsf{k}, m\|x) = \mathsf{f}(x, \mathsf{f}(m, \mathsf{k})).$$

But then, given $y = \mathsf{f}(m, \mathsf{k})$ we can compute $\mathsf{PRF}^{\mathsf{f}}(\mathsf{k}, m')$ simply as

$$\mathsf{PRF}^{\mathsf{f}}(\mathsf{k}, m') = \mathsf{f}(x, y).$$

The important thing to note is that for the computation of $\mathsf{f}(x, y)$ knowing key k is not necessary, thus violating the security guarantees of both pseudorandom functions and message authentication codes. Or in other words, Merkle–Damgård where the key plays the role of initialization value cannot be a secure pseudorandom function or message authentication code.

The above attack is called a *length-extension attack*, and it is important to note that it works independently from the choice of compression function, i.e., it is a *generic* attack on the Merkle–Damgård transformation. We simply exploit the iterative construction where the result of a compression function evaluation is used either as the final hash value (in case it was the computation for the final message block) or as intermediate state in the next compression function evaluation. Thus, knowing a hash value is the same as knowing an intermediate state value. Also note that this property still holds even if we consider message padding (see Exercise 13.5). In this case knowing the value for a message m simply allows to compute any function value for messages that have the prefix $\mathsf{pad}(m)$ (instead of the prefix m as in our above example).

Remark 13.21. We presented the length-extension attack above for privately keyed primitives on top of Merkle–Damgård such as pseudorandom functions. The attack itself, however, is of course valid also in the public-key setting. While for properties such as collision resistance the length-extension attack is not technically an attack (as it does not help to find collisions) it shows that iterated hash functions are very different from monolithic objects such as random oracles where length-extension attacks are not possible. We will have more to say on generic attacks on iterated schemes such as Merkle–Damgård in Section 13.2 but first present a brief discussion on countermeasures that can prevent the length-extension attack.

Remark 13.22. There is a lot more to say about constructions of privately keyed primitives on top of Merkle–Damgård. For example, the variant that uses a keyed compression function to introduce the key is, indeed, secure (yet the result should be taken with some caution). We will discuss constructions of pseudorandom functions and message authentication codes based on Merkle–Damgård in detail in Chapter 16.

13.1.7 Wide-Pipe Constructions and Chopped MD

The length-extension attack exploits the fact that the results of compression function evaluations serve a double role. They can be either an intermediate state in the computation of a hash value, which is the case if not all message blocks have been processed yet, or they can serve as the actual hash value for the message if the result is the final compression function call. Consequently, when an adversary learns a hash value for some message m it learns not only the hash value but at the same time the complete internal state of any hash function evaluation for messages that start with m.

There are several approaches to strengthen iterative hash function constructions to not fall prey to such extension attacks. The straightforward solution is to decouple the role of compression function results, that is, to not output a complete internal state as result of a hash function computation. This can be achieved by implementing a small modification to the Merkle–Damgård transformation. For this we consider a transformation function $g : \{0,1\}^{\mathsf{H.cl}(\lambda)} \to \{0,1\}^{\mathsf{H.ol}(\lambda)}$ which is applied to the final state to generate the actual hash function output. The resulting function then looks as given below in Figure 13.6.

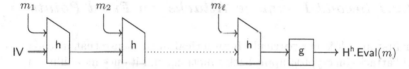

Fig. 13.6: The Merkle–Damgård construction with a final transformation function g.

When function g is the identity we recover the original Merkle–Damgård transformation. However, if we choose g to also be compressing we can decouple the size of the internal state $\mathsf{H.cl}(\lambda)$ from the size of the final hash function $\mathsf{H.ol}(\lambda)$, which allows us to protect against length-extension attacks. Consider a transformation g that outputs the first half of its input. In this case we have $\mathsf{H.ol}(\lambda) = \frac{1}{2} \cdot \mathsf{H.cl}(\lambda)$ and thus an adversary that learns the hash value for a message m does not learn a complete internal state but only the first half of an internal state. Given that the chaining value is long enough, this prevents an adversary from mounting length-extension attacks since in order to continue the Merkle–Damgård computation for some message m' with prefix m the attacker would need to predict the remaining bits of the state.

Hash functions that have the property that the internal state $\mathsf{H.cl}(\lambda)$ is larger than the size of hash values $\mathsf{H.ol}(\lambda)$ are called *wide-pipe* hash functions, in contrast to *narrow-pipe* hash functions. The simple variant of a wide-pipe function where the iteration is according to Merkle–Damgård and a final transformation g simply drops part of the state is also referred to as *chopped Merkle–Damgård* or *chopped MD* for short.

13.2 Generic Attacks on Iterated Hash Functions

While we could show that the Merkle–Damgård construction preserves collision resistance we have also seen that it is subject to a generic length-extension attack: An adversary who learns a hash value $H(m)$ for some message m can easily compute hash values for extensions of $pad(m)$ without having to actually know message m, which for an ideal hash function should certainly not be possible.

The length extension attack is a so-called *structural attack* on the iteration scheme of the hash function but not an attack on the underlying compression function. This makes it generic in the sense that it can be applied independently of the chosen compression function. We have seen that we can protect against length-extension attacks by adapting the iteration scheme, for example, by adding a final transformation to the hash function construction (see Section 13.1.7). Regrettably, the length-extension attack is not the only structural attack on iterated hash functions, and in the following we will look at several different attacks that exploit the underlying iterated structure of cryptographic hash functions.

13.2.1 Second-Preimage Attacks via Fixed Points

Our first attack is not particularly practical in the sense that it leads to real-world attacks on cryptographic hash functions, but it once more illustrates that the iterated construction of hash functions needs to be carefully scrutinized. Consider a hash function H that produces hash values of length $H.ol(\lambda) = \lambda$ and consider the second-preimage scenario where an adversary is given a random target message m and has to find a different message $m' \neq m$ such that $H(m) = H(m')$.[6] Now the best security we can hope for is a security level of λ bits, meaning that an adversary on average would need $\mathcal{O}(2^\lambda)$ operations to find a matching message m'. If the hash function has no weaknesses and distributes well, and the best an adversary can do is to try each possible input in turn, then we can estimate the success probability of the adversary by noting that for any message m' the probability that $H(m') = H(m)$ is $2^{-\lambda}$. As in this case the underlying probability distribution can be modeled by a geometric distribution[7] we have that on average after 2^λ many trials the adversary should have found a matching second preimage.

---

[6] We here consider the unkeyed scenario. The observations remain, however, valid also with the keyed variants that we discussed.

[7] The *geometric distribution* describes the number of independent Bernoulli trials—random experiments with exactly two outcomes, "success" or "failure"—needed until the first success. If p denotes the probability that a trial is successful then the expected number of trials is given by $1/p$.

Let us assume that our hash function is a Merkle–Damgård construction and for the moment let us neglect padding, that is, we only consider messages that are a multiple of the block length. In case the target message m is very large, say, it consists of 2^n message blocks for some $n \in \mathbb{N}$ then an adversary can find a second preimage for m in time $\mathcal{O}(2^{\lambda-n})$ (and thus faster than the expected 2^λ steps) by exploiting the underlying structure as follows. Instead of testing random messages m' on the full hash function H it searches for a collision on the compression function for any of the intermediate values y_i (for $i \in [2^n]$), that is, it searches for a message block m' such that the computation of $\mathsf{H}(m') = \mathsf{h}(m, \mathsf{IV})$ hits one of the chaining values y_i. With Definition 13.8 (the trace of a Merkle–Damgård evaluation) we can formalize this as follows: The adversary searches for some message block m' such that

$$\exists i \in [2^n] : \mathsf{h}(\mathsf{trace}_{\mathsf{H}^\mathsf{h}}(m)[i]) = \mathsf{h}(m', \mathsf{IV}),$$

which can be done in time $\mathcal{O}(2^{\lambda-n})$ as it succeeds in case we hit any one of the 2^n many intermediate chaining values occurring during the computation of $\mathsf{H}(m)$.

Given such a message block m' it is now trivial to construct a collision for message m. As $\mathsf{h}(m', \mathsf{IV})$ is a collision for $\mathsf{h}(m_i, y_i)$, all that is left to do is to append message blocks m_{i+1} to m_{2^n} to m' as visualized in the following schematic:

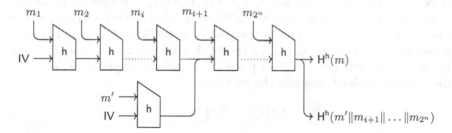

Remark 13.23. The attack is also known as the *long-message attack*.

Length encoding. For the above attack strategy to be useful it is important that the colliding compression function value can be at any point $i \in [2^n]$ in the evaluation chain of the computation of $\mathsf{H}(m)$. Consequently we have that with high probability the two colliding messages are not of the same length (also compare the above diagram). Consequently, the attack becomes void once we deploy the Merkle–Damgård strengthening (i.e., padding strategy) where the length of the messages is encoded in the extra padding block (see Section 13.1.1). Note that if the inner collision on the compression function is for the ith message block, then the constructed message consists of $2^n - i + 1$ message blocks while our target message by assumption was 2^n message blocks. Thus, when using the above strategy we have that, while parts of the computation will match, the very last compression function calls will be

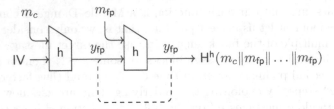

Fig. 13.7: An expandable message consisting of a fixed point (m_{fp}, y_{fp}) and a message block that "connects" the initialization value IV to the fixed point.

different due to the different lengths of the two messages, thus producing distinct hash values with overwhelming probability.

Fixed Points

One idea of fixing the attack is to adapt the strategy to only search for a collision for the first compression function call. While in this case the two resulting messages are of the same length and thus collide, we have that the complexity of the attack is exactly the complexity of finding a collision for $h(m_1, IV)$. If h is an ideal compression function this will take on average $\mathcal{O}(2^\lambda)$ steps and thus not gain any advantage over searching collisions for H directly.

In case the underlying compression function h has a certain structure then there is, however, a way to make the attack work. For this we require that h allows to easily find so-called *fixed points*. A fixed point for a function f is a point x such that $f(x) = x$. This property allows us to repeatedly evaluate the function without changing the result since

$$f(f(x)) = f(x) = x.$$

When considering a compression function, such a fixed point can, of course, not exist as the output is smaller than the input. Here instead, we consider fixed points of the form $h(m, y) = y$, that is, an input such that the chaining value is recovered. A fixed point for the compression function in a Merkle–Damgård hash construction thus allows us to increase the length of a message without changing the hash value. To see that this is the case let us consider that we have a fixed point (m_{fp}, y_{fp}) for h such that

$$h(m_{fp}, y_{fp}) = y_{fp}.$$

If, in addition, we have a colliding message block m_c such that $h(m_c, IV) = y_{fp}$ then we can construct arbitrarily long messages that have hash value y_{fp} by repeatedly adding message block m_{fp} as outlined in Figure 13.7. We call such a message an *expandable message*.

Using Fixed Points to Attack MD Strengthening

We can use fixed points and expandable messages to extend our earlier second-preimage attack for long messages so that it is also applicable in case padding and Merkle–Damgård strengthening is used. The idea is to run the attack in two steps:

1. First we search for an expandable message as given in Figure 13.7 that contains a fixed point $(m_{\mathsf{fp}}, y_{\mathsf{fp}})$ which is reachable from the initialization vector IV.
2. Once we have the expandable message we run our original attack with one modification. Instead of searching for a collision on the compression function with the initialization value IV we search for a collision containing the fixed point y_{fp} from our expandable message.

Given these two ingredients we can use the expandable message to control the overall length of our colliding message and ensure that it has the same length as the original message. The following diagram outlines the idea:

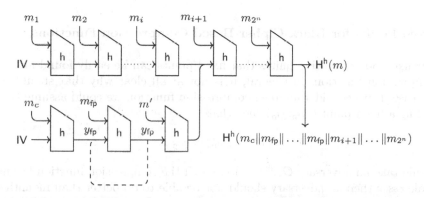

What remains is to analyze the complexity of this attack. At the beginning of the section we already estimated the runtime of an adversary that tries to find second preimages for long messages assuming no padding is used. Assuming a message consists of 2^n many message blocks we argued that an adversary needs time $\mathcal{O}(2^{\lambda-n})$ for the attack. Here we now additionally need to estimate the time necessary to find an expandable message. One strategy of doing that is the following:

findExpandableMessage(1^λ)

---

1 : **for** $i = 1..2^{\lambda/2}$ **do** // Generate $2^{\lambda/2}$ random fixed points

2 : $m_{\mathsf{fp}}^i \leftarrow_\$ \{0,1\}^{\mathsf{h.bl}(\lambda)}$

3 :   find matching fixed point $(m_{\mathsf{fp}}^i, y_{\mathsf{fp}}^i)$ such that $\mathsf{h}(m_{\mathsf{fp}}^i, y_{\mathsf{fp}}^i) = y_{\mathsf{fp}}^i$

   // Connect one fixed point to IV

4 : find collision point m_c such that $\mathsf{h}(m_c, \mathsf{IV}) = y_{\mathsf{fp}}^i$ for some $i \in [2^{\lambda/2}]$

To find an expandable message via the above algorithm, an adversary first needs to generate $2^{\lambda/2}$ fixed points. Assuming for the moment fixed points can be generated in constant time, generating $2^{\lambda/2}$ many fixed points takes $\mathcal{O}\big(2^{\lambda/2}\big)$ steps. Then a connection between IV and one of the fixed points is searched. Here we can reuse the analysis for long messages. As there are $2^{\lambda/2}$ potential target blocks an adversary should find a valid connection message m_c after approximately $2^{\lambda-\lambda/2}$ steps. Combined, we have that the average runtime of an adversary trying to find an expandable message via the above algorithm is $\mathcal{O}\big(2^{\lambda/2+1}\big)$.

If we combine the runtime of the two steps of the fixed point attack (i.e., finding an expandable message and then running the original attack) we get an overall average runtime of $\mathcal{O}\big(2^{\lambda/2+1} + 2^{\lambda-n}\big)$ for messages consisting of 2^n message blocks. Note that depending on the size of n this is only slightly larger than the original attack and much better than what we would expect from an ideal hash function. Furthermore, this generic attack now applies to any iterated hash function, given that we can efficiently construct fixed points for the underlying compression function. We discuss the latter point next.

Fixed Points for Block-Cipher-Based Compression Functions

Our fixed point attack requires that fixed points can be easily found for the compression function. In general, it is not at all clear why that should be the case. If we consider an ideal compression function we could assume that finding a fixed point $(m_{\mathsf{fp}}, y_{\mathsf{fp}})$ such that

$$\mathsf{h}(m_{\mathsf{fp}}, y_{\mathsf{fp}}) = y_{\mathsf{fp}}$$

should take an adversary $\mathcal{O}\big(2^{\mathsf{h.cl}(\lambda)}\big)$ steps. If the compression function has no weaknesses then an adversary should not be able to do better than mounting a brute-force search for a fixed point, in which case each "test message" would have a probability of roughly $2^{-\mathsf{h.cl}(\lambda)}$ of hitting the target value y_{fp}. Recall that $\mathsf{h.cl}(\lambda)$ denotes the length of the chaining value, that is, $|y_{\mathsf{fp}}| = \mathsf{h.cl}(\lambda)$.

In practice, compression functions are often constructed from block ciphers[8]. We will have a closer look at block-cipher-based compression functions in Chapter 14 and here only give a brief introduction. A block cipher E is an efficient keyed permutation (we usually assume it to be a strong pseudorandom permutation). This means, given a key k and message x, we can efficiently compute $c \leftarrow \mathsf{E}(\mathsf{k}, x)$ as well as its inverse $x \leftarrow \mathsf{E}^{-1}(\mathsf{k}, c)$. As E is a permutation it holds that

$$\mathsf{E}^{-1}(\mathsf{k}, \mathsf{E}(\mathsf{k}, x)) = x.$$

---

[8] As the name suggests, block ciphers are usually used as building blocks in encryption schemes. Practical block ciphers are, for example, AES or DES.

While being able to efficiently invert is essential for building encryption schemes it may be used to compute fixed points for block-cipher-based compression functions. A popular example is the so-called Davies–Meyer construction (which is used, amongst others, in MD5, SHA-1, and SHA-2), which defines a compression function h based on a block cipher E as

$$h_{DM}^{E}(m, y) := E(m, y) \oplus y.$$

Now, for a given target message m_{fp} we could get a fixed point in case we can find a chaining value y_{fp} such that $E(m_{fp}, y_{fp}) = 0^{|y_{fp}|}$. For this note that in this case

$$h_{DM}^{E}(m_{fp}, y_{fp}) := E(m_{fp}, y_{fp}) \oplus y_{fp} = 0^{|y_{fp}|} \oplus y_{fp} = y_{fp}.$$

As it turns out, finding such a fixed point is trivial. For a given message m_{fp} which in the Davies–Meyer construction is used as key for the block cipher we can find the corresponding value y_{fp} by simply inverting the block cipher on value $0^{|y_{fp}|}$. That is we compute

$$y_{fp} \leftarrow E^{-1}(m_{fp}, 0^{|y_{fp}|}),$$

which yields the fixed point (m_{fp}, y_{fp}) such that $h_{DM}^{E}(m_{fp}, y_{fp}) = y_{fp}$. Thus, finding fixed points for compression functions based on the Davies–Meyer construction can be, indeed, achieved in constant time.

13.2.2 Multicollisions

While, so far, we have looked at generic attacks to find second preimages, we now turn our attention to generic attacks to find plain collisions. Finding a collision for hash function H with hash values of length λ takes on average $2^{\lambda/2}$ steps due to the generic birthday attack (see Section 4.1.2 on page 165). For an ideal hash function finding n collisions should thus take time $\mathcal{O}(n \cdot 2^{\lambda/2})$ and finding 2^n collisions should take time $\mathcal{O}(2^n \cdot 2^{\lambda/2})$. For iterated hash functions that are of the narrow pipe type, that is, for which the internal chaining value is as long as the final hash value (see Section 13.1.7; page 503), this is generally not the case.

Consider a Merkle–Damgård construction H_{MD}^{h}.[9] In order to find a collision for H_{MD}^{h} it is sufficient to find a collision for compression function h on chaining value $y_1 = IV$ as a collision $((m_1, IV), (m_1', IV))$ with $m_1 \neq m_1'$ induces the collision (m_1, m_1') on hash function H_{MD}^{h}. Once more as a schematic:

---

[9] The attack works similarly on the keyed variants discussed above.

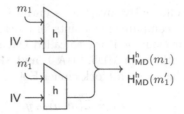

Note that as the messages are of the same length (in this case of a single block length) the messages collide also in case we deploy padding such as Merkle–Damgård strengthening.

The idea in a multicollision attack is now to build a chain of compression function collisions. That is, first a collision is searched for the initialization value IV. Once colliding blocks m_1 and m_1' are found, we search for a collision for chaining value $y_2 = h(m_1, IV)$. Once also colliding blocks (m_2, y_2) and (m_2', y_2) are found we continue with the next chaining value $y_3 = h(m_2, y_2)$, and so forth. The following diagram visualizes the resulting structure of collisions:

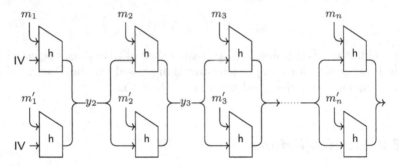

Once we have constructed a structure consisting of n collisions for compression function h it is easy to see that, in fact, we have constructed 2^n collisions for hash function H_{MD}^h. For this consider that any path from one of the two starting message blocks m_1 and m_1' to the final output yields a message with hash value $H_{MD}^h(m_1 \| m_2 \| \ldots \| m_n)$.[10] The following pseudocode implements the entire attack:

FindMultiCollisions($1^\lambda, n$)
_____

1 : $y_1 \leftarrow IV$

2 : **for** $i = 1..n$ **do**

3 :   search for (m_i, m_i') such that $h(m_i, y_i) = h(m_i', y_i)$ and $m_i \neq m_i'$

4 : $y_{i+1} = h(m_i, y_i)$

5 : **return** $\big\{(m_1^*, \ldots, m_n^*) : i \in [n], m_i^* \in \{m_i, m_i'\}\big\}$

_____

[10] Note that we have, in fact, created even more colliding messages: we have two colliding 1-block messages ($H_{MD}^h(m_1) = H_{MD}^h(m_2)$), 2^2 colliding 2-block messages ($H_{MD}^h(m_1 \| m_2) = H_{MD}^h(m_1 \| m_2') = H_{MD}^h(m_1' \| m_2) = H_{MD}^h(m_1' \| m_2')$), and so forth.

It remains to analyze the time complexity of the multicollision attack. In order to construct the 2^n collisions for function H_{MD}^h an adversary needs to find n collisions for the underlying compression function h. Assuming that h has an output length of λ the birthday attack tells us that finding a collision takes on average $\mathcal{O}(2^{\lambda/2})$ steps. Thus, an adversary can find 2^n multicollisions in time $\mathcal{O}(n \cdot 2^{\lambda/2})$ (instead of the expected $\mathcal{O}(2^n \cdot 2^{\lambda/2})$).

Multicollisions as Expandable Messages

We have seen how to construct expandable messages via fixed points which, in turn, can be used to attack the second-preimage resistance of iterated hash functions. In the following we show how we can construct expandable messages via multicollisions and thus remove the necessity of being able to find fixed points for the underlying compression function.

In our basic multicollision attack above we searched for n collisions on the compression function. The resulting structure allowed to extract 2^n collisions by choosing either message block m_i or message block m_i' at each step. To construct an expandable message we will as before construct n collisions. However, while before the multicollision structure allowed to choose one of two message blocks in each step, here for the ith step we allow to choose between a single message block m_i or a longer message M_i consisting of $2^{n-i} + 1$ blocks. Figure 13.8 highlights the idea. Thus, depending on which "route" you take while constructing the message, you end up with collisions of different lengths. The shortest possible message is of length n and is constructed by always choosing the single message block in the top path of Figure 13.8. To obtain the longest possible message we need to always choose the multiple-block part in the lower part at each step, which sums up to a message consisting of

$$2^{n-1} + 1 + 2^{n-2} + 1 + \ldots + 2^0 + 1 = 2^n - 1 + n$$

many message blocks.

While it is not too difficult to see how this structure allows to create colliding messages of length n message blocks and $2^n - 1 + n$ blocks it is also possible to construct messages for any length in between. To build a collision of $N + n$ blocks one writes $N = \sum_{i=0}^{n-1} N_i 2^i$ in its binary form. Then one takes the long path of length $2^i + 1$ for each bit $N_i = 1$ and the short path of length 1 for each i with $N_i = 0$. The overall number of blocks then adds up to $N + n$.

Constructing multicollisions of differing block length. In the above construction of an expandable message we constructed collisions between a message consisting of a single block and a structure of many blocks, for example $2^{n-1} + 1$ message blocks. Constructing such a collision is, in fact, no more difficult than constructing a simple collision on h for a chaining value y. Let us say that, starting from chaining value y, we want to construct a

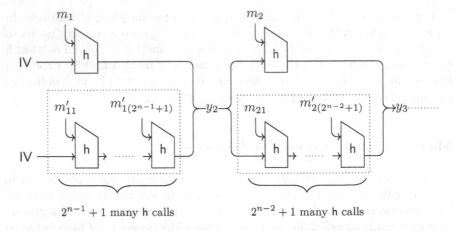

Fig. 13.8: Constructing an expandable message via multicollisions. The structure consists of n colliding pairs where the ith pair consists of message block m_i (displayed on top) and a longer message consisting of $2^{n-i} + 1$ message blocks (displayed on the bottom).

collision which on one path takes a single h invocation and on the other takes two h invocations. The following picture exemplifies the situation:

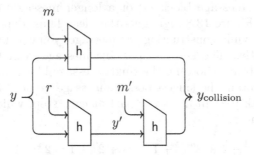

To construct the collision starting from chaining value y we choose a random message block r and compute $y' \leftarrow h(r, y)$. To finalize the collision we now search for message blocks m and m' such that (m, y) and (m', y') collide, that is, such that

$$h(m, y) = h(m', y').$$

As the chaining value for the brute-force search is not identical (i.e., $y \neq y'$) we need to assume that we lose roughly a factor of 2 in the birthday attack. For this note that if we choose $\frac{1}{2} \cdot 2^{\lambda/2}$ potential target values for m as well as for m' then the birthday bound tells us that we should have a collision over the combined values of both lists with good probability. With probability $\frac{1}{2}$ the collision is not confined to one of the two lists, in which case we have found pairs (m, y) and (m', y') such that $h(m, y) = h(m', y')$.

In case the path should not be of length 2 but of length ℓ we can simply choose $\ell - 1$ random message blocks or repeat the same block $\ell - 1$ times as shown in the picture below:

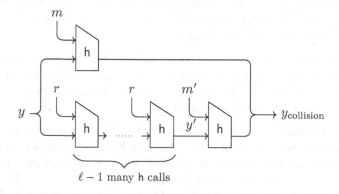

13.2.3 Second-Preimage Attacks via Multicollisions

In the following we describe an attack on the second-preimage resistance of an iterated hash function for long target messages that, instead of using fixed points, uses expandable messages from multicollisions. As before in Section 13.2.1 we consider an adversary that tries to find a collision to a given target message m_{target} consisting of 2^n message blocks. The attacker now proceeds by the following steps:

1. Generate an expandable message consisting of n multi-message multicollisions where the ith multicollision is a collision of a single message block and $2^{n-i} + 1$ message blocks (see Figure 13.8). Call the final chaining value of the expandable message y_{link}.
2. Search for a collision that connects y_{link} from the expandable message with any of the intermediate chaining values in target message m_{target}. In more detail, the adversary searches for a message block m_{con} such that

$$\exists i \in \{n+2, n+3, \dots, 2^n\} : h(\text{trace}_{H^h}(m_{target})[i]) = h(m_{con}, y_{link}).$$

Note that for the next step we require that the collision is not within the first $n + 1$ blocks of the message as our expandable message only allows to generate messages of arbitrary block length between n and $2^n - 1 + n$. If the collision is within the first $n + 1$ blocks the resulting message will be longer than the target message m_{target}. For this note that the resulting number of blocks of the colliding message is given by the length $i - 1$ of the expandable message, plus one for the connecting block, plus $2^n - i$ for the remaining iterations for index i.

3. The adversary can now output a collision for message m_{target}. The final collision consists of the expandable message, expanded to length $i - 1$ where i is the index from the previous step. The next message block is m_{con}, which "connects" the expandable message with the target message m_{target}. Finally, the remaining message blocks are message blocks $m_i, \ldots, m_{2^n}$ taken from target message m_{target}.

By construction, the resulting second preimage has the same length as the target message m_{target}, which ensures that padding will be identical for both messages even in case Merkle–Damgård strengthening is used. The entire attack scheme is visualized in Figure 13.9.

The time complexity of the complete attack is the time complexity of generating n multi-message multicollisions plus searching for a collision of chaining value y_{link} with one of the intermediate chaining values in target message m_{target}. Summing it all up, we get a time complexity of $\mathcal{O}\!\left(n \cdot 2^{\lambda/2+1} + 2^n + 2^{\lambda-n}\right)$ where the first summand corresponds to the n collisions that need to be found for the multicollisions, the second summand to the number of compression function evaluations (recall that m_{target} is of length 2^n), and finally the last summand corresponds to finding the collision between y_{link} and the target message. Note that in most setups we would find that $n < \frac{\lambda}{2}$ in which case the dominating part would be the last summand $2^{\lambda-n}$.

13.2.4 Predicting the Future with Herding Attacks

As we have seen, hash functions are used in various different schemes and contexts. For example, the hash-and-sign scheme simplifies signature schemes by first hashing a message to then only sign the resulting hash value (see Section 6.3 on page 272). If the signature scheme is secure for fixed-length messages and the hash function is collision resistant then we can show that the resulting signature scheme for variable-length messages is also secure (Theorem 6.8). Or consider commitment schemes which we have built in the random oracle model in Section 8.4.1 (page 360). Here we publish hash value $\mathsf{H}(m)$ for some document m to *commit* to the content of m. When we later reveal message m the fact that the hash function is collision resistant should convince any party that we did not change document m from when we published its hash value.

Now consider Alice who claims that she can predict the closing prices of all stocks of the S&P 500 as of the last business day of the year. To this end she publishes a commitment $c_{\mathsf{S\&P}} \leftarrow \mathsf{H}(m_{\mathsf{S\&P}})$ to a document $m_{\mathsf{S\&P}}$ that supposedly contains the closing prices. When New Year's Day comes Alice publishes a document that first lists all the correct stock prices and then continues with some rambling about how she is the greatest seer of all times. The document hashes to $\mathsf{H}(m_{\mathsf{S\&P}})$.

Target Message $m_{\text{target}} = m_1^{\text{target}} \| \ldots \| m_{2^n}^{\text{target}} \| \text{pad}(|m_{\text{target}}|)$

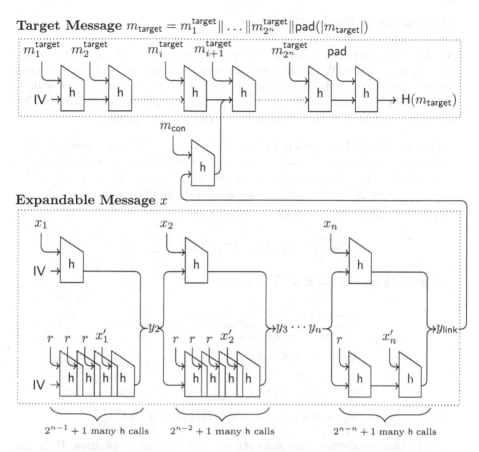

Fig. 13.9: The second-preimage attack on long messages using variable-block-length multicollisions. On the top we have the target message m_{target} for which an adversary tries to find a collision (i.e., a second preimage). For this the adversary first constructs an expandable message x (bottom part of diagram). Then a collision between y_{link}, the "hash value" of the expandable message, and an intermediate block m_i^{target} in m_{target} is searched (for some index $n + 1 < i < 2^n$). Let m_{con} denote the connecting message block. Then, finally the adversary can extract a collision for m_{target} by choosing a path through the expandable message x such that the colliding message is exactly as long as target message m_{target}. In that way it is guaranteed that the final padding block is identical, even in case length padding such as Merkle–Damgård strengthening is used.

Assuming that Alice is no seer, Alice must have found a second-preimage collision for a document $m_{\text{S\&P}}$ but, contrary to the attacks presented so far, the document is highly structured. It starts with a list of the closing prices of the S&P index.

In the following we discuss an attack known as *herding* or *Nostradamus* that Alice could have used (with sufficient computational effort) to pull off this trick.

Chosen-Target Forced Prefix

Neither of our collision resistance properties properly captures the scenario Alice finds herself in. While she has full control over the suffix of the document (except for that it probably should not be too long) she only has very little control over the prefix, which needs to contain the precise stock prices. This scenario is captured by the *chosen-target forced-prefix* property.

Definition 13.24 (Chosen-Target Forced-Prefix Preimage Resistance). *An efficient keyed hash function* $\mathsf{H} = (\mathsf{H.KGen}, \mathsf{H.Eval})$ *is called* chosen-target forced-prefix preimage resistant *(CTFP) for a set of prefixes* $\mathcal{P}$ *if advantage* $\mathsf{Adv}^{\mathsf{ctfp}}_{\mathsf{H},\mathcal{A}_1,\mathcal{A}_2}(\lambda)$ *is negligible for all* PPT *algorithms* $\mathcal{A} := (\mathcal{A}_1, \mathcal{A}_2)$. *Here, the advantage is defined as*

$$\mathsf{Adv}^{\mathsf{ctfp}}_{\mathsf{H},\mathcal{P},\mathcal{A}_1,\mathcal{A}_2}(\lambda) := \Pr\left[\mathsf{Exp}^{\mathsf{ctfp}}_{\mathsf{H},\mathcal{P},\mathcal{A}_1,\mathcal{A}_2}(\lambda)\right]$$

relative to experiment $\mathsf{Exp}^{\mathsf{ctfp}}_{\mathsf{H},\mathcal{A}_1,\mathcal{A}_2}(\lambda)$:

Experiment $\mathsf{Exp}^{\mathsf{ctfp}}_{\mathsf{H},\mathcal{P},\mathcal{A}_1,\mathcal{A}_2}(\lambda)$
1: $(m, \mathsf{state}) \leftarrow\!\!\$\ \mathcal{A}_1(1^\lambda)$
2: $\mathsf{hk} \leftarrow\!\!\$\ \mathsf{H.KGen}(1^\lambda)$
3: $p \leftarrow\!\!\$\ \mathcal{P}$
4: $m' \leftarrow\!\!\$\ \mathcal{A}_2(1^\lambda, \mathsf{hk}, p, \mathsf{state})$
5: $\mathbf{return}\ \mathsf{H.Eval}(\mathsf{hk}, m) = \mathsf{H.Eval}(\mathsf{hk}, p\|m')$

Note that we defined the property relative to a set of prefixes $\mathcal{P}$. In the extreme this can be the set of all strings $\{0,1\}^*$. In the above Alice example it would be the set of all possible stock price combinations.

Herding Attack: A Long-Message Attack using Tree Structures

In Sections 13.2.1 and 13.2.3 we considered attacks on the second-preimage resistance of hash functions. While in theory Alice could use such an attack scheme there is a serious downside to it. First, let us convince ourself that the attack works in principle. In case Alice wants to execute a long message attack her target message $m_{\mathsf{S\&P}}$ must be long. Once she knows prefix p she then "simply" needs to find a connecting message block m_{con} connecting prefix p to some intermediate value in her target message.

The problem with the approach is that the message needs to be very, very long. Recall that the runtime for finding a collision depends on the length of the message. If the message has 2^n blocks, then the expected runtime for finding a matching collision is $2^{\lambda-n}$ assuming $\mathsf{h.ol}(\lambda) = \lambda$. The maximum message length of SHA-1 is $2^{64} - 1$ bits or roughly $2^n = 2^{55}$ message blocks whereas the output length is $\mathsf{h.ol}(\lambda) = 160$ bits. To achieve a decent value for the runtime of $2^{\mathsf{h.ol}(\lambda)-n} = 2^{160-n}$ a message would therefore need to be close to the maximum length of 55 blocks (ideally longer). But such a message would be on the order of exabytes (or 1 million terabyte). That is rather large for a document that should just contain the closing prices of 500 stocks.

The tree structure. In order for the attack to be plausible, Alice needs a strategy such that the resulting message remains reasonable in size. That is, the suffix that she can append to the message needs to be small. For this we will use an adapted version of the multicollision attack. Recall that the multicollision structure that we used so far was simply a chain where at each index i we could choose between one of two messages. This simple chain structure is, however, not necessary and we can consider different types of structures. For example, we could consider a chain but at each level not consider only two colliding messages but four.

In case of a herding attack the idea is to not use a chain structure but a tree. We have already used trees in the construction of signatures (Chapter 6) and here use the same terminology (see page 284). We will construct an inverse binary tree. Usually in a tree, edges are directed from the root towards the leaves but in our case the direction is reversed and we will consider paths from the leaves to the root. The tree will be of height n and thus contain $2^{n+1} - 1$ nodes with 2^n leaves. The tree will contain partial evaluations of hash function H^{h}. That is, edges in the tree are labeled with chaining values while nodes are labeled with message–chaining value pairs. There are three restrictions. All ingoing edges to a node must be labeled with the same chaining value. Furthermore, the node's chaining value must be the same as that from the ingoing edges. The chaining value on an outgoing edge of node (m, y) is computed as $\mathsf{h}(m, y)$. Note that this means that any two child nodes that have the same parent must form a collision for compression function h. The following picture shows a tree of height 3 with a partial legend on the right:

We index nodes by level and position in the level. Thus, the node with label (m_{43}, y_{43}) is the third node of the fourth level and, consequently, the root node is labeled (m_{11}, y_{11}). In the picture we have added an outgoing edge to the root node labeled c which would be computed as $c \leftarrow \mathsf{h}(m_{11}, y_{11})$. In a herding attack on a commitment scheme, c is the value used as commitment.

As mentioned above, the tree captures partial hash function computations; to be precise, suffixes of hash computations. Independent from which leaf we start from, all computations end up with hash value c. For example, by construction we have that $\mathsf{h}(m_{33}, y_{33}) = y_{22}$ and $\mathsf{h}(m_{22}, y_{22}) = y_{11}$ and thus

$$\mathsf{h}(m_{11}, \mathsf{h}(m_{22}, \mathsf{h}(m_{33}, y_{33}))) = c.$$

Let us ignore padding for the moment (we will later discuss how padding affects the attack) and assume that we have a tree structure such as the above for a tree of height n and are now given a prefix p. Then, in order to find a message $m_{\mathsf{forge}} = p\|?$ that starts with p and that is such that $\mathsf{H}^{\mathsf{h}}(m_{\mathsf{forge}}) = c$ we need to find one message block m_{con} that connects p to any of our leaf nodes. In more detail, if we compute hash function $\mathsf{H}^{\mathsf{h}}(p)$ then the last h evaluation yields a chaining value y_{con}. In order to connect y_{con} to one of the 2^n leaves in our tree structure we need to find a message block m_{con} such that there exists index $i \in [2^n]$ for which

$$y_{n,i} = \mathsf{h}(m_{\mathsf{con}}, y_{\mathsf{con}}).$$

Let $\mathsf{path}(n, i)$ denote the message blocks on the path from node $(m_{n,i}, y_{n,i})$ to the root. That is, in our above tree

$$\mathsf{path}(3, 3) = m_{33}\|m_{22}\|m_{11}.$$

Then, by construction we have that message $p\|m_{\mathsf{con}}\|\mathsf{path}(n, i)$ hashes to value c:

$$\mathsf{H}^{\mathsf{h}}(p\|m_{\mathsf{con}}\|\mathsf{path}(n, i)) = c.$$

The above attack is called a *herding attack*: we "herd" a given prefix to the desired hash value c. When used as an attack against a commitment scheme it is also referred to as a *Nostradamus attack*. We give a visual representation of the attack in Figure 13.10.

Remark 13.25 (Diamonds). The tree structure used in the herding attack is often also referred to as a *diamond structure* and the creation of the structure as the *diamond construction*. The diamond shape emerges once the connecting message is added to the tree (see Figure 13.10).

Runtime analysis of online phase. Let us analyze the runtime of the attack assuming that the adversary already has access to the search tree. This corresponds to the online phase of the herding attack. We will tackle the creation of the search tree later in this section.

Once the adversary gets access to the prefix it needs to find a message block m_{con} that connects the prefix to one of the leaf values of the search tree. Depending on the structure of the hash and the padding used (we will look at padding shortly) it might also suffice to connect to any intermediate node in the search tree, but for this analysis we consider only leaves. As we consider a

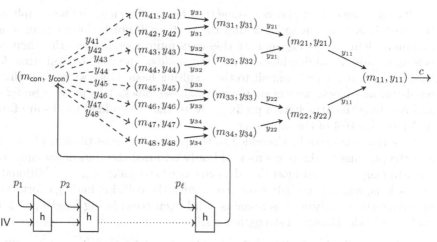

Fig. 13.10: The herding attack. In an offline phase we prepare a binary search tree of height n (in the picture $n = 4$). Any two child nodes of a parent form a collision on h. That is, for example, $h(m_{45}, y_{45}) = h(m_{46}, y_{46}) = y_{33}$. Once the tree is computed we have a target value $c \leftarrow h(m_{11}, y_{11})$ that we can herd prefixes to and use, for example, as commitment in a Nostradamus attack. When we learn prefix $p = p_1 \| p_2 \| \ldots \| p_\ell$ we can now search for a connecting message block m_{con} to herd the prefix to hash value c. Note that in the picture and this description we ignored the additional complications caused by padding.

tree of height n there are 2^n possible target values. By assumption compression function h produces outputs of $h.ol(\lambda) = \lambda$, and thus with each attempt the adversary has a probability of at least $2^{-\lambda+n}$ to hit one of the target values. We can thus expect to hit one of the leaves after roughly $2^{\lambda-n}$ tries.

Padding. So far we neglected padding in the description of the herding attack. There are multiple ways to deal with padding. Depending on the scenario of the attack the length of the prefix might be known. Consider the opening example of Alice. The S&P 500 lists 500, stocks and we can assume that while Alice does not know the content of the prefix, she knows its length. Let ℓ be the length of the prefix. Then the final message will consist of $\ell + n + 1$ many blocks as the tree has a height of n and we need one block to connect the prefix to the tree. Thus instead of committing to value $h(m_{11}, y_{11})$ we add the relevant padding block(s) and commit to the resulting value. This is shown in the following graphic:

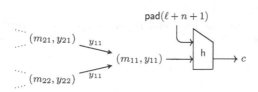

Of course, we cannot always assume that the prefix length is known upfront. However, it is sufficient to know that the prefix will not be longer than some maximum length. Let ℓ_{max} denote this maximum message length. Then, as before, we add a padding block to the root node of the tree, but this time for length $\ell_{\mathsf{max}} + n + 1$ and commit to the resulting hash. Once we get a prefix p consisting of ℓ blocks we can simply add $\ell_{\mathsf{max}} - \ell$ blocks to p to get a prefix p' and continue the attack with prefix p'. Note that the added blocks are fully under the control of the adversary.

Note that the extra blocks added to the prefix as well as the extra block to add the padding to the tree's root add only minimal computational effort on the adversary's side. At most the adversary needs to make $\ell_{\mathsf{max}} + 1$ additional h evaluations, which is negligible compared with the collision finding effort. The above runtime analysis thus remains valid even considering length padding such as Merkle–Damgård strengthening.

Runtime analysis of offline phase. What remains is to discuss the offline phase in which the search tree is generated. In the worst case the adversary needs to brute force the entire tree. Yet, specific collision-finding attacks for the hash function in question can, of course, speed up this process.

In the following we give a generic (but not optimal) recipe for generating the tree via a brute-force attempt. The tree is constructed from the leaves up via the following steps:

1. First we choose 2^n random chaining values in $\{0,1\}^{\mathsf{h.ol}(\lambda)}$ that will be used to construct the leaf nodes. We label the ith value as $y_{n,i}$. In Figure 13.10 these would correspond to values $y_{41}, \ldots, y_{48}$ on the left-hand side of the diagram.
2. We next search for collisions between pairs of values, that is, between the first and second, the third and fourth, and so on. Note that since we have the chaining value fixed (step 1 above), we are looking for corresponding message blocks such that the pair collides. For example, if we consider the first pair $y_{n,1}, y_{n,2}$ we are looking for two message blocks $m_{n,1}$ and $m_{n,2}$ such that $\mathsf{h}(m_{n,1}, y_{n,1}) = \mathsf{h}(m_{n,2}, y_{n,2})$. By the birthday bound we have that we should find colliding message blocks with good probability after trying roughly $2^{\lambda/2}$ message blocks per chaining value.
   Restricting the search for collisions to neighboring pairs is of course not optimal. For example, in case we find a collision between $y_{n,1}$ and $y_{n,5}$ we could simply exchange $y_{n,2}$ and $y_{n,5}$. But more on that below.
3. Once we have found collisions for all $2^n/2$ pairs and all leaf nodes are constructed, we can compute the outgoing edges as $y_{n-1,i} \leftarrow \mathsf{h}(m_{n,2i-1})$ for $i \in \{1, 2, \ldots, \frac{n}{2}\}$.
4. We move forward one level and repeat steps 2 to 4 until we have reached the root node.

Fig. 13.11: A degenerate herding structure where all nodes of the leaf level collide.

As the tree consists of $2^{n+1} - 1$ nodes we can estimate the effort of constructing the tree as twice the effort of constructing the leaf layer. This yields an expected runtime of $\mathcal{O}\left(2^{n+\lambda/2+1}\right)$.

In the above algorithm we constructed collisions one after the other. With sufficient storage space we can do better. Consider that for every chaining value we generate $2^{\lambda/2-n/2+1/2}$ many messages and compute the resulting hash value. We can think of the result as having 2^n buckets—each chaining value makes up one bucket—with each containing $2^{\lambda/2-n/2+1/2}$ random hash values. We are now interested in the probability that two randomly chosen buckets collide, that is, that two randomly chosen buckets share a common hash value. Note that two hash values collide with probability at least $2^{-\lambda}$ and furthermore that we have $(2^{\lambda/2-n/2+1/2})^2$ pairs of hash values between two buckets. We can thus expect about

$$\frac{(2^{\lambda/2-n/2+1/2})^2}{2^\lambda} = \frac{2^{\lambda-n+1}}{2^\lambda} = 2^{-n+1}$$

many collisions between any two buckets. As we have 2^n buckets we can expect that each bucket should be in at least one collision.

While from the above analysis we are not guaranteed that we end up with pairs of collisions and thus not with a binary tree—in the extreme we could find that one bucket contains a collision with every other bucket, even though this is rather unlikely. However, such a case would only speed up the process as this means that for the next level fewer collisions need to be searched. In the above extreme case we would not need any additional collision and for each remaining level only a single h computation suffices to complete the tree structure. This case is visualized in Figure 13.11.

In the worst case for the adversary the collisions are evenly spread in each level, in which case we can approximate the expected runtime as twice the runtime for the leaf level and thus as $\mathcal{O}\left(2 \cdot 2^n \cdot 2^{\lambda/2-n/2+1/2}\right) \approx \mathcal{O}\left(2^{\lambda/2+n/2+2}\right)$.

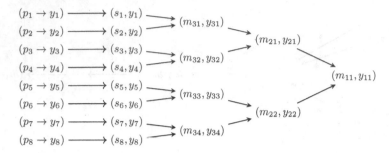

Fig. 13.12: A herding tree constructed via chosen-prefix attacks. Here the p_i denote the eight prefixes and $(p_i \rightarrow y_i)$ indicates that the final chaining value of $\mathsf{H}^h(p_i)$ is y_i. In a first step colliding suffixes are searched for neighboring prefixes via a chosen-prefix attack. This yields suffixes s_i such that, for example, $\mathsf{H}^h(p_1\|s_1) = \mathsf{H}^h(p_2\|s_2) = y_{31}$. The attack is repeated until the root node is reached.

13.2.5 On the Practicality of Generic Attacks

Over the previous sections we discussed a number of generic attacks on iterated hash functions. While we presented the attacks for the standard Merkle–Damgård iteration scheme, it is not hard to see that they will also work for various variants of iteration schemes. Yet it is not at all clear how far these attacks can be mounted in practice. This is, of course, with the exception of the length-extension attack (Section 13.1.6), which does not pose any computational strain on the adversary.

For the multicollision attack, the attacks on second-preimage resistance, and the herding attack it is crucial for the attacker to be able to break collision resistance. Thus as long as the function in question is secure with respect to collision finding an attacker will have a hard time mounting any of these attacks, especially if the output of the underlying compression function is long enough. (Recall that due to the birthday bound, collisions on the compression function can be brute-forced in time $2^{h.\mathsf{ol}(\lambda)/2}$.) Collision resistance, however, is usually the first property of a hash function to be attacked, and any advance in collision-finding techniques immediately simplifies the above attack schemes.

When hash functions are attacked, a common pattern is that first techniques for generating random collisions are found, which are then refined to allow finding collisions with a certain structure. One such attack is a *chosen-prefix attack* in which for a pair of chosen prefixes p and p' two suffixes s and s' are searched such that messages $p\|s$ and $p'\|s'$ collide. This immediately allows a simpler form of herding attacks. Consider the Nostradamus attack where the number of prefixes is small, say 8. Then using a chosen-prefix attack we can construct for each of the 8 prefixes p_1 to p_8 suffixes s_1 to s_8 as visualized in Figure 13.12.

In the picture we have the prefixes on the left-hand side and assume that for prefix p_i the final chaining value in a computation of $H^h(p_i)$ is y_i: We write $(p_i \rightarrow y_i)$. In a first step we mount four chosen-prefix attacks for each two neighboring prefixes. For example, for prefix p_1 and p_2 this yields suffixes s_1 and s_2 such that the messages $p_1 \| s_1$ and $p_2 \| s_2$ collide. In the picture the colliding chaining value is y_{31}. Once we have the collisions for the eight original prefixes, this yields four new messages: $p_1 \| s_1$, $p_3 \| s_3$, $p_5 \| s_5$, $p_7 \| s_7$.[11] We can now once again use chosen-prefix attacks to further combine the four messages. We this time use two chosen prefix attacks on the messages $p_1 \| s_1$ and $p_3 \| s_3$ as well as on $p_5 \| s_5$ and $p_7 \| s_7$. For the first pair this yields suffixes m_{31} and m_{32} in the picture with resulting hash value y_{21} and suffixes m_{33} and m_{34} with hash value y_{22}. We repeat this strategy one final time to complete the construction of the tree. By construction we have created eight suffixes for our eight original prefixes such that the resulting messages all hash to the same value. All it took were seven chosen-prefix attacks.

In 2007 such an attack was, indeed, presented on MD5, where researchers from Eindhoven and Lausanne "predicted" the outcome of the 2008 US presidential elections. For this, they prepared 12 PDF documents, one for each of the candidates, which all hashed to the same value:

$$\texttt{0x3D515DEAD7AA16560ABA3E9DF05CBC80}$$

By this they showed that Nostradamus-type attacks are feasible in practice once chosen-prefix attacks on the underlying hash function are plausible. We discuss MD5 in more detail in Chapter 15.

13.3 Cryptographic Sponges

With Merkle–Damgård we have seen an example of how we can construct a domain extender for hash functions, in particular, for collision resistance. In this section we discuss an alternative construction that gained a lot of popularity in the past years as it forms the basis for the SHA-3 hash function: *cryptographic sponges* (or simply sponges).

Domain extension considers the question of constructing from a fixed-input-length primitive, say a collision-resistant compression function, a variable-length function that can process inputs of arbitrary length. The output size of a hash function is, however, usually of a fixed length. That is, the hash functions we considered so far were of the form $H : \{0,1\}^* \rightarrow \{0,1\}^{H.ol(\lambda)}$, where H.ol is a polynomial and thus for each security parameter specifies a fixed output length. Sponges bring a new dimension to the picture. They not

---

[11] We could have similarly chosen $p_2 \| s_2$, $p_4 \| s_4$, $p_6 \| s_6$, $p_8 \| s_8$. For this note that, by construction, for odd i messages $p_i \| s_i$ and $p_{i+1} \| s_{i+1}$ hash to the same value.

only consider arbitrarily long inputs but also, potentially, infinite outputs. That is, a sponge is of the form $H_{Sp} : \{0,1\}^* \to \{0,1\}^\infty$, where $\{0,1\}^*$ denotes the set of all finite bit strings while $\{0,1\}^\infty$ is the set of all infinite bit strings. We use subscript Sp to indicate that function H_{Sp} is a sponge-type function (in contrast to, for example, a Merkle–Damgård-type hash function H_{MD}).

Naturally, infinitely long images are problematic for practical use cases. An efficient algorithm would run forever to create a single output. Thus, we consider finite substrings of outputs that can be obtained by truncating an output to the first L bits. That is, a sponge takes two inputs: the message m and the length L of the output, and we set $H_{Sp}(m, L) := H_{Sp}(m)[1..L]$.

13.3.1 Defining Cryptographic Sponges

In the following we will introduce the particulars of sponge functions. For this it may be helpful to consider Figure 13.14 on page 527, which provides a schematic of the sponge construction similar to the schematics we have used for the Merkle–Damgård-type hash functions.

Like Merkle–Damgård, sponges are built from a core function that is iterated to process messages block by block. While Merkle–Damgård iterates a fixed-input-length compression function, a sponge iterates a length-preserving function, that is, a function with a fixed input length and an identical output-length. This is usually a permutation but can also be an arbitrary transformation. As in Merkle–Damgård, in order to preprocess messages to be of a multiple of the block length, a padding function pad is used. To complete the definition of a sponge function we require an additional parameter, the *bitrate r*. While bitrate is a new term it is not a new concept. In Merkle–Damgård terminology the bitrate would be called the *block length*, and indeed bitrate and block length may be used interchangeably in the context of sponges. The bitrate does, however, play a bigger role than simply specifying how inputs are chunked into fixed-length blocks as we will see shortly.

The core function h in a sponge construction operates on a fixed number of bits which is usually referred to as the *width* of the sponge function (often denoted by b). We denote the width for security parameter λ by $H_{Sp}.\text{width}(\lambda)$. Note that for all $\lambda \in \mathbb{N}$ we have that $h.il(\lambda) = h.ol(\lambda) = H_{Sp}.\text{width}(\lambda)$. We define $c(\lambda) = H_{Sp}.\text{width}(\lambda) - H_{Sp}.bl(\lambda)$ to be the *capacity*. In other words for a sponge we have that width $H_{Sp}.\text{width}$ equals capacity c plus bitrate r.

Capacity and bitrate make up the state a sponge operates on and which is updated in every iteration. The state is usually initialized to zero—think of this as the initialization value in Merkle–Damgård. Then in each step, one message block is incorporated into the current state and the result is transformed by a call to core function h to produce the new state. Figure 13.13 shows the first two iterations of a sponge function on a message $m := m_1 \| m_2 \| \ldots$ split up

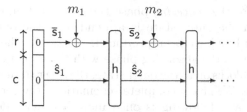

Fig. 13.13: The first two iterations of a sponge function showcasing how a message is *absorbed* by XORing it onto the outer part of the state $\bar{s}$ in between applications of core function h.

into multiple blocks of length r where on the left we have the initial state, the all-zero string.

The state is split into two parts, the outer state consisting of r many bits and the inner state consisting of c bits. The idea is that the inner state always remains hidden to an outside observer.[12] We denote the inner state by $\hat{s}$ and the outer state by $\bar{s}$. We start with an initial state $s_1 := \bar{s}_1 \| \hat{s}_1 = 0^{r(\lambda)+c(\lambda)}$ which, as mentioned before, is usually set to the all-zero string. Then, to process the first message block m_1 the block is XORed onto the outer state $\bar{s}_1$ and the resulting value $(\bar{s}_1 \oplus m_1)\|\hat{s}_1$ is subsequently run through core function h to produce the next state $s_2 := \bar{s}_2\|\hat{s}_2 \leftarrow h((\bar{s}_1 \oplus m_1)\|\hat{s}_1)$. To simplify notation we often write $(\bar{s}_{i+1}, \hat{s}_{i+1}) \leftarrow h(\bar{s}_i \oplus m_i, \hat{s}_i)$ instead of $s_{i+1} \leftarrow h(s_i)$, that is, we treat core function h as if it takes two inputs. This is also how we draw core function h in the sponge schematics (see, for example, Figure 13.13).

The process outlined above is repeated for each message block until padded message $\mathsf{pad}(m)$ has been processed completely. This part of the processing is also called the *absorbing phase* in sponge lingo. Once the entire message was absorbed into the state, the *squeezing* phase starts in which the variable-length output is generated. Let s be the final state after the absorbing phase. Then the output of the squeezing phase is computed in multiple steps where in each step state s is transformed and part of the state is appended to the output. Following is a pseudocode specification of the squeezing phase to produce L output bits:

$\underline{\mathsf{squeeze}(s, L)}$

1 : $z \leftarrow \bar{s}$ // i.e., $s[1..r]$

2 : **while** $|z| < L$ **do**

3 : $s \leftarrow h(s)$

4 : $z \leftarrow z\|\bar{s}$

5 : **return** $z[1..L]$

---

[12] Recall that in standard Merkle–Damgård hash functions a hash value is equivalent to a full internal state, which makes Merkle–Damgård constructions vulnerable to length-extension attacks (see Section 13.1.6; page 500). Keeping parts of the state hidden protects sponges from these types of attacks.

That is, also for the *squeezing* phase the core function is iterated, where at each iteration the outer state is appended to the output string until sufficiently many bits have been produced. In essence, the squeezing phase works analogously to the absorbing phase with the exception that instead of XORing message blocks on to the outer state, the outer state is appended to the function's output. We give a complete schematic of the sponge construction in Figure 13.14, and following is once more a concise description of the construction in pseudocode:

Construction 13.26 (Sponge). *Let* r *and* c *be polynomials denoting* bitrate *and* capacity. *Let* $h : \{0,1\}^{r(\lambda)+c(\lambda)} \to \{0,1\}^{r(\lambda)+c(\lambda)}$ *be a permutation (or transformation) and let* pad *be a padding function that pads inputs to a multiple of bitrate (aka block length)* $r(\lambda)$. *Then the sponge construction* $H_{Sp}^h[r, pad]$ *is defined as*

$H_{Sp}^h[r, pad](m, L)$	squeeze(s, L)
$1:$ $(m_1, \ldots, m_\ell) \leftarrow pad(m)$	$1:$ $z \leftarrow \bar{s}$ $/\!/$ $i.e.,$ $s[1..r]$
$2:$ $s \leftarrow 0^{r(\lambda)+c(\lambda)}$	$2:$ **while** $|z| < L$ **do**
$3:$ **for** $i = 1..\ell$ **do**	$3:$ $s \leftarrow h(s)$
$4:$ $s \leftarrow h(s \oplus (m_i \| 0^{c(\lambda)}))$	$4:$ $z \leftarrow z \| \bar{s}$
$5:$ $z \leftarrow$ squeeze(s, L)	$5:$ **return** $z[1..L]$
$6:$ **return** z	

We usually drop the extra parameters $[r, pad]$ *when clear from context and write* H_{Sp}^h *instead of* $H_{Sp}^h[r, pad]$.

Extendable Output Functions (XOFs)

The sponge construction allows to construct arbitrarily long outputs. Hash functions, on the other hand, are usually considered to have a fixed output length. To distinguish the two the term *extendable output function* (or XOF, pronounced zoff) is used to denote constructions such as sponges that allow to provide the expected output length as a parameter. Thus, the sponge construction, by default, is a XOF. Of course, we can also recover a "standard hash function" with a fixed output length by simply fixing the length parameter L. Usually for this the output length is fixed to bitrate r, that is, $L := r$. In this case, the squeezing phase becomes void and the final hash value is simply the outer state after the final h iteration of the absorbing phase.

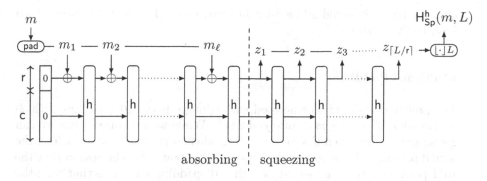

Fig. 13.14: The sponge construction. To process a message, the message is padded and then processed iteratively in blocks. In the absorbing phase each block is XORed onto the outer part of the state before the state is transformed with core function h. After the absorbing phase the output is generated in the squeezing phase by again iterating function h on the state but now after each iteration outputting the outer part of the state.

13.3.2 Message Padding

The standard padding used in Merkle–Damgård-style functions is Merkle–Damgård strengthening: a length padding that adds a 1-bit, sufficiently many 0-bits, and finally an encoding of the message's length (see Section 13.1.1). We have seen that this form of padding is suffix free (Definition 13.9), which allowed us to prove that the MD transformation preserves collision resistance (Theorem 13.10).

While Merkle–Damgård strengthening is essential for arguing security for Merkle–Damgård schemes, security for sponges, as we will see, is argued quite differently. Here, stronger requirements are placed onto the core function h, which in turn allows to work with simpler padding schemes that, in particular, do not need to be suffix free. With sponges we thus usually use one of two simpler padding schemes: the 10*-padding or the 10*1 padding, with the latter being the preferred mode, for reasons that will become apparent later.

10*-padding: Appends a single 1-bit and zero or more 0-bits to fill up the current block such that the resulting message is a multiple of the block length r.

10*1-padding: Appends a single 1-bit followed by as many 0-bits as needed and a final 1-bit such that the message is a multiple of the block length r.

Note that both padding schemes may add an extra block to the message as the 10*-padding appends at least a single bit and the 10*1-padding appends at least two bits to the message. Consequently, in case a message is already of a multiple of the block length both schemes add an extra block. In addition, if the last message block has r − 1 bits then the 10*1-padding would also add an extra block: it would add a 1-bit followed by $r - 1$ many 0-bits and a final 1-bit to the message.

Multirate Padding

The preferred padding scheme used with sponges is the 10^*1-padding, which is also referred to as a *multirate padding*.[13] While we said above that we can get secure sponges even if we use padding schemes that are not suffix free, the actual padding scheme used still plays an important role. The reason that the 10^*1-padding is to be preferred over the 10^*-padding scheme is that with the latter we can simulate the former. Before we discuss the security implications of this simulatability property let us look at the simulation itself in more detail.

Let us denote by $\text{SPONGE}[h, \text{pad}10^*1, r]$ a sponge construction using core function h, 10^*1-padding and bitrate r. We next show that for any bitrate $r_{max} \geq r$ we have that function $\text{SPONGE}[h, \text{pad}10^*, r_{max}]$ can be used to compute also function $\text{SPONGE}[h, \text{pad}10^*1, r]$. Note that since both functions use the same core function h we have that the width of both functions is identical, that is, bitrate and capacity sum up to the same value for both functions. Formally, we show the following statement:

> **Proposition 13.27.** *Let* $\text{SPONGE}[h, \text{pad}10^*, r_{max}]$ *be a sponge construction with bitrate* r_{max} *and using* 10^**-padding. Then for any bitrate* $0 < r \leq r_{max}$ *there exist bitrate-dependent functions* $I[r, r_{max}]$ *and* $O[r, r_{max}]$ *such that*
>
> $$\text{SPONGE}[h, \text{pad}10^*1, r] = O[r, r_{max}] \circ \text{SPONGE}[h, \text{pad}10^*, r_{max}] \circ I[r, r_{max}].$$
>
> *Here* $f \circ g$ *denotes function composition of functions* f *and* g*, that is,* $(f \circ g)(x) := f(g(x))$*.*

Proof. We define input preprocessing function $I[r, r_{max}]$ via three steps. The preprocessing is visualized in Figure 13.15, and we give the pseudocode in Figure 13.16. To preprocess a message m we execute the following steps in order:

1. We define q as the multirate padding of m for bitrate r: $q \leftarrow \text{pad}10^*1(m, r)$.
2. We construct q' by splitting-up q into r-bit blocks, appending to each block $(r_{max} - r)$ many 0-bits, and concatenating the result.
3. We construct message m' by unpadding q' according to the 10^*-padding rule. Message m' is the final result of the preprocessing.

First note that the padding applied in step 1 produces the exact message that would be processed by $\text{SPONGE}[h, \text{pad}10^*1, r]$ after padding. By filling

---

[13] The SHA-3 function, for example, uses 10^*1 padding.

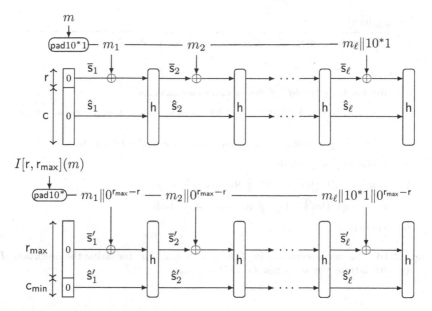

Fig. 13.15: On the top we consider the absorbing phase of SPONGE[h, pad10*1, r] for some message m consisting of ℓ-bit blocks. (Note that in the picture we assume that the padding did not add an extra message block.) In the diagram below we show the absorbing phase of SPONGE[h, pad10*, r_{max}] for the same message m. Here the message blocks are preprocessed and "filled-up" with 0-bits. Note that, by construction, we have that at every step the state of both functions matches, that is, we have $\bar{s}_i \| \hat{s}_i = \bar{s}'_i \| \hat{s}'_i$ for $i \in \{1, 2, \ldots, \ell + 1\}$.

up the individual message blocks with 0-bits (step 2) we ensure that at every step the internal computation states s of SPONGE[h, pad10*1, r](m) and s' of SPONGE[h, pad10*, r_{max}](m') match, that is, we have $s_i = \bar{s}_i \| \hat{s}_i = \bar{s}'_i \| \hat{s}'_i = s'_i$ for $i \in \{1, 2, \ldots, \ell + 1\}$ (see also Figure 13.15). For this note that even though the bitrate in SPONGE[h, pad10*, r_{max}](m') is larger the additional bits in the message block are set to 0 and thus do not affect the state when being XORed onto the outer part. Finally, step 3 ensures that the padding operation pad10* that is applied by function SPONGE[h, pad10*, r_{max}](m') yields as result q' (the output of the second step). For this, note that after step 2 we have that $|q'|$ is a multiple of r_{max}. Thus, by performing the inverse padding operation (with respect to pad10*) we get that pad10*$(m') = q'$.

By the above reasoning we have that at the end of the final h call in the absorbing phase the state of both executions match. During the squeezing phase, however, function SPONGE[h, pad10*1, r] outputs only the first r bits of the current state at every step while function SPONGE[h, pad10*, r_{max}] outputs the first r_{max} bits. We can thus recover the original output by setting the output postprocessing function $O[r, r_{max}]$ to work as follows: On input value

$$I[r, r_{\max}](m)$$

---

1 : $q \leftarrow \text{pad}10^*1(m, r)$ // 1) Construct multirate padding for bitrate r

2 : $q' \leftarrow \varepsilon$ // 2)

3 : **for** $i = 1..(|q|/r)$ **do**   // Split q into r-bit blocks and

4 : $q' \leftarrow q' \| q[i..(i + r)] \| 0^{r_{\max} - r}$ // fill-up each block with $(r_{\max} - r)$ many 0-bits

5 : $m' \leftarrow q'$ // 3) Define m' as q' unpadded according to 10^*-padding

6 : **while** $m'[|m'|] = 0$ **do**

7 : $m' \leftarrow m[1..(|m'| - 1)]$ // Remove trailing 0-bit

8 : $m' \leftarrow m[1..(|m'| - 1)]$ // Remove trailing 1-bit

9 : **return** m'

Fig. 13.16: The input preprocessing function $I[r, r_{\max}]$ for simulating the execution of a sponge with bitrate r by a sponge with bitrate $r_{\max}$.

z', function $O[r, r_{\max}]$ splits up z' into blocks of length $r_{\max}$. Each block is then truncated to the first r bits, and the resulting bits are concatenated.

$$O[r, r_{\max}](z')$$

---

1 : $z \leftarrow \varepsilon$

2 : **for** $i = 1..\lceil |z'|/r_{\max} \rceil$ **do**

3 : $z \leftarrow z \| z'[i..\min(i + r, |z'|)]$

4 : **return** z

It follows that we recover the exact same output bits and that for the input preprocessing and output postprocessing functions as defined above we have, indeed, that

$$\text{SPONGE}[h, \text{pad}10^*1, r] = O[r, r_{\max}] \circ \text{SPONGE}[h, \text{pad}10^*, r_{\max}] \circ I[r, r_{\max}]. \quad \square$$

Remark 13.28. Note that the construction crucially depends on function $\text{SPONGE}[h, \text{pad}10^*, r_{\max}]$ using as padding $\text{pad}10^*$. For $\text{pad}10^*1$ the construction would fail as now the last message block would be set to $m_\ell \| 10^*1 \| 0^{r_{\max} - r - 1)} \| 1$ and thus the input to the final h invocation would differ on one bit (also see Figure 13.15).

Security Considerations

So why should we prefer the 10^*1-padding over the simpler 10^*-padding? The answer is twofold. Consider that you fix a core function h and thus a width for your sponge. You are still free to choose your bitrate r or even define multiple bitrates for different applications. Let r_{max} denote the maximum bitrate that we want to support with function h and let r for $0 < r \leq r_{max}$ denote a smaller bitrate. When using the 10*1-padding we have that all functions SPONGE[h, pad10*1, r] for $0 < r \leq r_{max}$ are *independent* in the sense that they have a unique suffix. For this note that with pad10*1 the last bit of a padded message is 1 and that this bit is at position r. We thus have that the input to the final h evaluation of the absorbing phase for a message m consisting of ℓ blocks after padding is given by

$$(\bar{s}_\ell \oplus m_\ell) \| \hat{s}_\ell = s_\ell \oplus (m_\ell \| 0^c) = s_\ell \oplus (m_\ell[1..(r-1)] \| 1 \| 0^{width-r}).$$

(Note that value $width - r$ is exactly the capacity of the sponge, which depends on the bitrate for a fixed width.) It follows that for two distinct bitrates $0 < r < r' \leq r_{max}$ and any two messages m and m' consisting of ℓ (resp. ℓ') many blocks after padding, we have that after padding

$$m_\ell[1..(r-1)] \| 1 \| 0^{width-r} \neq m'_{\ell'}[1..(r'-1)] \| 1 \| 0^{width-r'}.$$

For two distinct bitrates the resulting sponge functions SPONGE[h, pad10*1, r] and SPONGE[h, pad10*1, r'] are, thus, independent in the sense that if we assume the functions "behave like a random oracle" that we then have effectively implemented *domain separation* (see also Section 8.3.2 on page 357).

This, of course, still does not explain the simulatability property. For this we need to look more closely at how security is argued for sponges, which we will do next.

13.3.3 Security of Cryptographic Sponges

So far we have not yet discussed the rational behind the sponge construction with regards to security. This we do in the following. Interestingly, the security of sponges is argued quite differently from that of Merkle–Damgård. Recall that for MD, we considered security in the sense of *property preservation* and showed that, for example, if the underlying compression function is collision resistant, then so is the hash function built via the Merkle–Damgård transformation (Theorem 13.10; page 487). For sponges, as we will see such a notion is difficult to argue. For this, let us try to cast the sponge construction as a special case of Merkle–Damgård.

Sponges as Chopped MD

Both the Merkle–Damgård transformation and cryptographic sponges construct hash functions iteratively using a core function h; a compression function in the case of Merkle–Damgård and a permutation (or length-preserving transformation) in case of sponges. One interpretation of sponges when restricted to a single round of squeezing (i.e., sponges as classical hash functions but not as XOFs) is as a special case of Merkle–Damgård, namely as chopped MD (Section 13.1.7; page 503). The idea is to consider the combination of the XOR operation to absorb a message block together with the application of the sponge transformation as a compression function. Let f denote the sponge permutation (or transformation). Then when combining it with the XOR operation we yield a compression function $h_{\mathsf{Sp}}^{\mathsf{f}}$ as

$$h_{\mathsf{Sp}}^{\mathsf{f}}(m_i, \bar{s}_i \| \hat{s}_i) := f((m_i \oplus \bar{s}_i) \| \hat{s}_i).$$

This is most easily understood graphically. The following picture shows the processing of a single message block. On the left we use our standard sponge visualization, and on the right we overlayed compression function $h_{\mathsf{Sp}}^{\mathsf{f}}$:

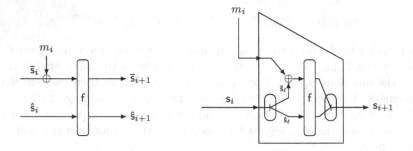

As usual in MD-style pictures we consider a single chaining value (state s), which on the right we "split up" into inner and outer state. In Figure 13.17 we show the final part of the sponge construction as chopped MD including the chopping operation.

MD-style security. Now that we know that it is possible to view the sponge construction as a special form of chopped MD we might want to analyze security in a similar way as we have done for Merkle–Damgård. There we showed that, if the compression function is collision resistant, then so is the resulting construction. That is, Merkle–Damgård (as well as chopped MD) *preserves* collision resistance.

As shown above, the compression function extracted from the sponge construction is

$$h_{\mathsf{Sp}}^{\mathsf{f}}(m, \bar{s} \| \hat{s}) := f((m_i \oplus \bar{s}_i) \| \hat{s}_i)$$

for some permutation (or transformation) f. The problem now is that $h_{\mathsf{Sp}}^{\mathsf{f}}$ cannot possibly be collision resistant, whatever the properties of f. The culprit is the XOR operation on the input, which makes finding collisions trivial. Consider, for example,

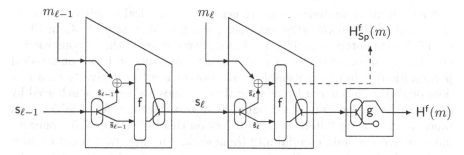

Fig. 13.17: The sponge construction interpreted as chopped MD. In the picture we overlayed compression functions on top of the sponge construction. The sponge permutation (or transformation) in the picture is given as f. The compression function takes as input message block m_i and chaining value s_i. It first splits the chaining value into outer state $\bar{s}_i$ and inner state $\hat{s}_i$. It then calls the sponge's core function f on input $\bar{s}_i \oplus m_i$ and $\hat{s}_i$. The output of f is then joined (concatenated) to produce the output s_{i+1} of the compression function. Recall that in sponge (when used as classical hash function and not as XOF) the final output is the rate part of the last f call. Note that this is nothing but a chop operation, which in the above picture we have overlayed with function box g.

$$h_{Sp}^f(0^r, 1^{r+c}) = h_{Sp}^f(1^r, 0^r \| 1^c) = f(1^{r+c}).$$

Thus, while we can interpret a sponge function as a special case of Merkle–Damgård, this interpretation does not help much to argue security. Instead, sponge security is usually argued by turning to an idealized model.

Ideal Permutations

The idea underlying the Merkle–Damgård transformation is to modularize hash function design into the design of a compression function and an iteration scheme. The iteration scheme should be such that when used with a good compression function that then the resulting function would be secure, thus allowing practitioners to focus on the design of compression functions. The security validation for the iteration scheme is given in the standard model.

Sponges aim at a similar scenario in that they modularize the design of hash functions into an iteration scheme (the sponge construction) and the design of a permutation. Security for the sponge construction is, however, not given in the standard model but an idealized model similar to the random oracle model (see Part II). The security of a sponge is usually analyzed assuming that the underlying permutation (or transformation) h is ideal. Here ideal means that h is assumed to be sampled uniformly at random from the space of all permutations (or transformations) of the form $h : \{0,1\}^{r+c} \to \{0,1\}^{r+c}$. Under this assumption we can then show that the sponge construction is, for example, collision resistant.

Such a security analysis of a construction from an ideal primitive is usually given in the *indifferentiability framework*, which we discuss in detail in Chapter 17. In simple terms, indifferentiability allows to argue that a construction out of an idealized primitive (e.g., the sponge construction based on an ideal permutation) is indistinguishable from another ideal primitive (e.g., a random oracle). In other words, showing that sponges are secure is achieved by arguing that sponges are indistinguishable (or rather indifferentiable) from random oracles. We will have more to say on this in Section 17.5.3 once we have covered the indifferentiability framework. An important point to note, however, is that the security of sponges is tightly bound to the size of the capacity c. Recall that the capacity specifies the size of the inner state; the state that remains hidden from an adversary. Assuming that the underlying permutation is ideal one can show that attacks on sponges necessarily need to find collisions for the inner state. We can thus estimate the bit security of a sponge by $c/2$ as we can expect to find collisions on the inner state in approximately $2^{c/2}$ steps due to the birthday bound.

Multirate Padding Revisited

We can now come back to the multirate padding and simulatability property discussed above in Proposition 13.27 (page 528) and argue why we should prefer the 10*1-padding over the simpler 10*-padding. Consider a fixed permutation h and a set of derived sponges SPONGE[h, pad10*1, r] with different bitrates $0 < r \le r_{max}$. As the security of sponges is tied to the capacity we have that, intuitively, the weakest sponge of the set is SPONGE[h, pad10*1, r_{max}] as here the bitrate is maximal and thus the capacity smallest. The simulatability property now allows to argue that it is, indeed, at least as hard to distinguish SPONGE[h, pad10*, r_{max}] (note the change in padding function) from a random oracle as it is to distinguish the set of sponge functions SPONGE[h, pad10*1, r] for $0 < r \le r_{max}$ from a set of r_{max} many independent random oracles. We will have more to say on this in Section 17.5.3 but will here already give the formal statement. In the lingua of indifferentiability we can formalize the above as:

Proposition 13.29. *Let* h *be a random permutation (or transformation). Then differentiating the list of sponge functions* SPONGE[h, pad10*1, r] *for* $0 < r \le r_{max}$ *from a list of independent random oracles* $(RO_i)_{i \in [r_{max}]}$ *has the same advantage as differentiating* SPONGE[h, pad10*, r_{max}] *from a single random oracle. That is, if for any function* ϵ *and for any* PPT *distinguisher* $\mathcal{D}$ *such that for any* PPT *simulator* Sim *and sufficiently large* λ *we have that*

$$\mathsf{Adv}^{\mathrm{indiff}}_{(\mathrm{SPONGE}[h,\mathrm{pad}10^*1,r])_{r \in [r_{max}]},(RO_i)_{i \in [r_{max}]},\mathcal{D},\mathsf{Sim}}(\lambda) > \epsilon(\lambda),$$

then there exists a PPT *distinguisher* $\mathcal{D}'$ *such that for all* PPT *simulators* Sim *and sufficiently large* λ *we have that also*

$$\mathsf{Adv}^{\mathrm{indiff}}_{\mathrm{SPONGE[h,pad10^*,r_{max}],RO,}\mathcal{D}',\mathrm{Sim}}(\lambda) > \epsilon(\lambda).$$

The idea behind the proof is that by the simulatability property (Proposition 13.27) we can use function SPONGE[h, pad10*, r_{max}] to also evaluate SPONGE[h, pad10*1, r] for any bitrate $r \leq r_{max}$. We can thus adapt a distinguisher $\mathcal{D}$ that distinguishes SPONGE[h, pad10*, r_{max}] from a random oracle to also distinguish the set of sponge functions SPONGE[h, pad10*1, r] from a set of independent random oracles. We leave the proof as Exercise 13.7 but note that you should first read Chapter 17, where we cover the indifferentiability framework.

Chapter Notes and References

The construction today known as Merkle–Damgård was proposed independently by Ralph Merkle [16] and Ivan Damgård [9] in the late 1980s. Yuval [23] states that the idea of using iterated schemes for the construction of hash functions can, however, be traced back to a work of Rabin [19], published already in 1978. The work by Yuval also describes a birthday attack on Rabin's hash function. The analysis of MD-style functions for weaker forms of collision resistance such as second-preimage resistance and target-collision resistance is due to Bellare and Rogaway [3] as is the XOR linear hash construction XLH presented in Section 13.1.5. Further studies of domain extenders for various properties as well as for keyed compression functions are given by Andreeva et al. [1] and Bellare and Ristenpart [2].

Length-extension attacks on Merkle–Damgård hash functions were observed by Tsudik [21]. Multicollisions were first introduced by Joux [11] in 2004. The generic second-preimage attack using expandable messages is due to Kelsey and Schneier [13]. Kelsey and Schneier also show how to construct expandable messages via multicollisions. How to construct expandable messages from fixed points was first shown by Dean [10].

The compression function construction from a block cipher usually referred to as the Davies–Meyer construction was attributed to Meyer and Davies by Winternitz [22]. Interestingly, Davies never actually proposed the function as he confirmed to Preneel et al., who studied the construction along a number of different constructions [18]. Preneel et al. also point out the vulnerability to fixed-point attacks of the Davies–Meyer construction.

Herding attacks and the Nostradamus attack were introduced by Kelsey and Kohno [12] in 2006. That the Nostradamus attack is, in fact, practical was demonstrated in 2007 by Stevens *et al.* [20]. We present more details in Section 15.1.2 (page 589).

As a hardening against Joux's multicollisions, Lucks proposed wide-pipe constructions in 2004 [14, 15]. Chopped MD was proposed by Coron *et al.* [8] as a version of Merkle–Damgård that is not susceptible to length-extension attacks and that can be shown indifferentiable from a random oracle (see Chapter 17).

The sponge construction was introduced by Bertoni *et al.* at the Dagstuhl seminar on Symmetric Cryptography in January 2007 and finalized for the Ecrypt Hash Workshop [5]. It forms the basis of the KECCAK hash function [7], which was chosen by NIST in 2012 as the winner of the SHA-3 competition [4] and which was subsequently standardized as FIPS PUB 202 [17]. We will discuss KECCAK in greater detail in Chapter 15. An in-depth discussion of sponges is given by Bertoni *et al.* in [6].

Exercices

Exercise 13.1. Let $h : \{0,1\}^{bl} \times \{0,1\}^{cl} \to \{0,1\}^{cl}$ be a compression function and consider the padding function $\mathsf{pad}(m) := x\|0^{[|m| \bmod h.bl]}$ that appends zero or more 0-bits to fill up the last block. Show that the resulting Merkle–Damgård function H^h_{MD} is not collision resistant.

Exercise 13.2. Prove Theorem 13.10 without requiring that padding function pad is suffix free but instead assuming that no PPT adversary can compute a preimage of initialization vector IV under compression function h (see the paragraph following the proof of Theorem 13.10 on page 489).

Exercise 13.3. Finish the proof of Proposition 13.15 (page 493) and show that the (unkeyed) Merkle–Damgård transformation does not preserve second-preimage resistance.

Exercise 13.4. Prove Proposition 13.18 and show that the XLH (XOR linear hash) construction from Section 13.1.5 (page 498) is a secure domain extender for target-collision resistance and second-preimage resistance.

Exercise 13.5. Show how to mount length-extension attacks on strengthened Merkle–Damgård and discuss how padding affects the attack. See also Section 13.1.6 on page 500.

Exercise 13.6. Assume collision-resistant hash functions exist. Give a construction of a compression function h that is not collision resistant, but which becomes collision resistant when used in the Merkle–Damgård transformation H^h_{MD}.

Exercise 13.7. Prove Proposition 13.29 (page 534). Note that you should work through the material covered in Chapter 17 before you attempt the proof.

Chapter Bibliography

1. Elena Andreeva, Gregory Neven, Bart Preneel, and Thomas Shrimpton. Seven-property-preserving iterated hashing: ROX. In Kaoru Kurosawa, editor, *Advances in Cryptology – ASIACRYPT 2007*, volume 4833 of *Lecture Notes in Computer Science*, pages 130–146, Kuching, Malaysia, December 2–6, 2007. Springer, Heidelberg, Germany.
2. Mihir Bellare and Thomas Ristenpart. Hash functions in the dedicated-key setting: Design choices and MPP transforms. In Lars Arge, Christian Cachin, Tomasz Jurdzinski, and Andrzej Tarlecki, editors, *ICALP 2007: 34th International Colloquium on Automata, Languages and Programming*, volume 4596 of *Lecture Notes in Computer Science*, pages 399–410, Wroclaw, Poland, July 9–13, 2007. Springer, Heidelberg, Germany.
3. Mihir Bellare and Phillip Rogaway. Collision-resistant hashing: Towards making UOWHFs practical. In Burton S. Kaliski Jr., editor, *Advances in Cryptology – CRYPTO'97*, volume 1294 of *Lecture Notes in Computer Science*, pages 470–484, Santa Barbara, CA, USA, August 17–21, 1997. Springer, Heidelberg, Germany.
4. Guido Bertoni, Joan Daemen, Michaël Peeters, and Gilles Van Assche. Keccak. In Thomas Johansson and Phong Q. Nguyen, editors, *Advances in Cryptology – EUROCRYPT 2013*, volume 7881 of *Lecture Notes in Computer Science*, pages 313–314, Athens, Greece, May 26–30, 2013. Springer, Heidelberg, Germany.
5. Guido Bertoni, Joan Daemen, Michaël Peeters, and Gilles Van Assche. Sponge functions. *ECRYPT hash workshop*, 2007(9), 2007.
6. Guido Bertoni, Joan Daemen, Michaël Peeters, and Gilles Van Assche. Cryptographic sponge functions. http://sponge.noekeon.org/, 2011.
7. Guido Bertoni, Joan Daemen, Michaël Peeters, and Gilles Van Assche. The Keccak SHA-3 submission. *Submission to NIST (Round 3)*, 3, 2011.
8. Jean-Sébastien Coron, Yevgeniy Dodis, Cécile Malinaud, and Prashant Puniya. Merkle-Damgård revisited: How to construct a hash function. In Victor Shoup, editor, *Advances in Cryptology – CRYPTO 2005*, volume 3621 of *Lecture Notes in Computer Science*, pages 430–448, Santa Barbara, CA, USA, August 14–18, 2005. Springer, Heidelberg, Germany.
9. Ivan Damgård. A design principle for hash functions. In Gilles Brassard, editor, *Advances in Cryptology – CRYPTO'89*, volume 435 of *Lecture Notes in Computer Science*, pages 416–427, Santa Barbara, CA, USA, August 20–24, 1990. Springer, Heidelberg, Germany.
10. Richard Drews Dean and Andrew Appel. *Formal aspects of mobile code security*. Princeton University Princeton, 1999.
11. Antoine Joux. Multicollisions in iterated hash functions. Application to cascaded constructions. In Matthew Franklin, editor, *Advances in Cryptology – CRYPTO 2004*, volume 3152 of *Lecture Notes in Computer Science*, pages 306–316, Santa Barbara, CA, USA, August 15–19, 2004. Springer, Heidelberg, Germany.
12. John Kelsey and Tadayoshi Kohno. Herding hash functions and the Nostradamus attack. In Serge Vaudenay, editor, *Advances in Cryptology – EUROCRYPT 2006*, volume 4004 of *Lecture Notes in Computer Science*, pages 183–200, St. Petersburg, Russia, May 28 – June 1, 2006. Springer, Heidelberg, Germany.

13. John Kelsey and Bruce Schneier. Second preimages on n-bit hash functions for much less than 2n work. In Ronald Cramer, editor, *Advances in Cryptology – EUROCRYPT 2005*, volume 3494 of *Lecture Notes in Computer Science*, pages 474–490, Aarhus, Denmark, May 22–26, 2005. Springer, Heidelberg, Germany.

14. Stefan Lucks. Design principles for iterated hash functions. Cryptology ePrint Archive, Report 2004/253, 2004. http://eprint.iacr.org/2004/253.

15. Stefan Lucks. A failure-friendly design principle for hash functions. In Bimal K. Roy, editor, *Advances in Cryptology – ASIACRYPT 2005*, volume 3788 of *Lecture Notes in Computer Science*, pages 474–494, Chennai, India, December 4–8, 2005. Springer, Heidelberg, Germany.

16. Ralph C. Merkle. One way hash functions and DES. In Gilles Brassard, editor, *Advances in Cryptology – CRYPTO'89*, volume 435 of *Lecture Notes in Computer Science*, pages 428–446, Santa Barbara, CA, USA, August 20–24, 1990. Springer, Heidelberg, Germany.

17. National Institute of Standards and Technology (NIST). FIPS PUB 202: SHA-3 standard: Permutation-based hash and extendable-output functions. https://csrc.nist.gov/publications/detail/fips/202/final, 8 2015.

18. Bart Preneel, René Govaerts, and Joos Vandewalle. Hash functions based on block ciphers: A synthetic approach. In Douglas R. Stinson, editor, *Advances in Cryptology – CRYPTO'93*, volume 773 of *Lecture Notes in Computer Science*, pages 368–378, Santa Barbara, CA, USA, August 22–26, 1994. Springer, Heidelberg, Germany.

19. Michael O Rabin. Digitalized signatures. *Foundations of Secure Computation*, pages 155–168, 1978.

20. Marc Stevens, Arjen K. Lenstra, and Benne De Weger. Chosen-prefix collisions for MD5 and applications. *Int. J. Appl. Cryptol.*, 2(4):322–359, July 2012.

21. Gene Tsudik. Message authentication with one-way hash functions. *ACM SIGCOMM Computer Communication Review*, 22(5):29–38, 1992.

22. Robert S. Winternitz. Producing a one-way hash function from DES. In David Chaum, editor, *Advances in Cryptology – CRYPTO'83*, pages 203–207, Santa Barbara, CA, USA, 1983. Plenum Press, New York, USA.

23. Gideon Yuval. How to swindle Rabin. *Cryptologia*, 3(3):187–191, 1979.

Chapter 14
Constructing Compression Functions

We have seen that cryptographic hash functions that can process arbitrarily long inputs can be built from fixed-input-length compression functions via the Merkle–Damgård transformation (Chapter 13). In the following chapter we discuss constructions of such fixed-input-length compression functions. Most constructions of compression functions can be divided into four classes: constructions from block ciphers, constructions based on permutations, dedicated constructions, and constructions based on number-theoretic or combinatorial problems. We will discuss these in turn.

Block-cipher-based constructions. Basing new cryptographic constructions on established primitives such as block ciphers has a number of advantages. To begin with, designing efficient and secure cryptographic primitives is hard and the number of failed attempts by far exceed the number of good designs. Also implementation effort may be reduced as existing implementations in hardware or software may be reusable for the new primitive. Reusing existing building blocks may thus significantly speed up the design and implementation as well as increase the chance of the design being a decent one. A modularized design also facilitates analysis of the result as it can be analyzed from both sides: We can analyze the construction and try to prove that it achieves certain properties (e.g., collision resistance) given that the underlying primitive has certain properties. And we can analyze the underlying primitive in isolation, which is usually a much easier task (though far from easy). This is the same argument as we have put forward as one of the main advantages of iteration schemes such as Merkle–Damgård; we simply work "one level below" now.

Another argument for such an approach is that the result can leverage trust in the underlying primitive. Consider the block cipher AES, which has been scrutinized for years and ask yourself: which design would you trust more: a relatively simple construction which uses AES as a building block, or an ad hoc construction that needs to be evaluated from scratch?

© Springer Nature Switzerland AG 2021
A. Mittelbach, M. Fischlin, *The Theory of Hash Functions and Random Oracles*,
Information Security and Cryptography, https://doi.org/10.1007/978-3-030-63287-8_14

We will discuss block-cipher-based constructions of compression functions in Section 14.1.

Permutation-based constructions. An important component of a real-world block cipher is its key schedule, which from the key computes various sub-keys, for example, distinct round keys. Often the key schedule is rather computationally expensive. When using a block cipher as an encryption box, this is usually not a big problem as the key schedule is evaluated only once as keys are reused many times. However, when used as a building block for compression functions, in many cases a new key is used for every compression function call and thus the key schedule may become a significant part of the computational cost. A second feature that can make block ciphers problematic in the design of compression functions is that many real-world block ciphers have a block length of 128 or 256 bits. The expected strength with regards to collision resistance is thus only 64 or 128 bits. While the latter security may be acceptable it is today regarded to be at the lower end of the spectrum. One option around these drawbacks is to consider unkeyed primitives such as permutations which are ideally wider than 256 bits.

A major difference between block ciphers and permutations is that the former are already compressing if one views the key as part of the input. A permutation, on the other hand, is not. Assume that we want to build a compression function $h : \{0,1\}^{2\lambda} \to \{0,1\}^{\lambda}$ from a permutation $\pi : \{0,1\}^{\lambda} \to \{0,1\}^{\lambda}$ and for efficiency reasons π should be evaluated only once during the computation of h. There are $2^{2\lambda}$ different inputs to compression function h but only 2^{λ} inputs to π. Thus, each input in π must on average correspond to 2^{λ} inputs of h. An unbounded adversary can then after only two queries to π evaluate h on roughly $2 \cdot 2^{\lambda}$ inputs without further π-queries. As this is already more than the number of outputs, the adversary must necessarily find a collision with probability 1. This, of course, does not mean that we cannot build compression functions from permutations. But it means that constructions need to be more complicated than making only a single call to the underlying permutation.

Another approach became popular with the emergence of the sponge construction (Section 13.3; page 523). As we have seen we can cast sponge constructions as a form of chopped Merkle–Damgård. However, the resulting compression function which is built from just a single call to the permutation is not collision resistant. Still, we can prove that if the permutation is ideal (that is, it behaves like a random permutation) then the sponge construction using the permutation is collision resistant. This approach is taken by KECCAK, aka SHA-3. We will have a closer look at its underlying permutation in Chapter 15.

Dedicated designs. We call compression functions that are not based on other cryptographic primitives *dedicated designs*. Dedicated designs break with the modular design approach, and the result usually needs to be analyzed en bloc. The biggest advantage of dedicated designs is that they can be tuned towards efficiency. After all, block ciphers are designed first and foremost for encryption, not for hashing. A second advantage may be that hash functions based on dedicated designs may not fall under export regulations for strong cryptography.

Dedicated designs have been and still are popular, especially in practice. Examples of widely used hash functions that can be regarded as falling into the dedicated design class are MD4 and MD5 as well as SHA-1 and SHA-2. Interestingly though, in many cases dedicated designs do follow block-cipher-based constructions. For example, we can extract block ciphers from SHA-1 and SHA-2, which have subsequently been named SHACAL-1 and SHACAL-2. Similarly, we can extract a block cipher from MD5, which as SHA-1 and SHA-2 follows the so-called Davies–Meyer approach which we will discuss shortly. We will have a closer look at the compression functions of MD5, SHA-1, and SHA-2 in Chapter 15.

Constructions based on number-theoretic problems. Number-theoretic constructions play an important role in cryptography, especially in public-key cryptography. Consider the RSA problem based on factoring and which was used to construct widely used public-key encryption and signature schemes. Similarly, the discrete logarithm problem is at the basis of many real-world constructions, for example, for securely exchanging keys over insecure channels. When it comes to hash functions, number-theoretic approaches play a mostly theoretic role as the resulting schemes are usually not efficient enough for real-world scenarios. They do, however, allow us to study hash functions and, in particular, to verify our definitions. If it is not possible to construct collision-resistant functions down to well-studied assumptions then it might be a bad idea to consider dedicated "ad hoc" designs. As it stands, we can construct collision-resistant functions based on various number-theoretic problems, and in Section 14.2 we will present two such constructions: the first will be based on the discrete-logarithm problem while the second one will utilize the RSA assumption.

While number-theoretic constructions are significantly slower than the above-mentioned alternatives and thus rarely used in practice they may allow to exploit interesting additional properties. In Section 14.2.3 we discuss one such example: *Chameleon hashes* introduce a trapdoor concept which allows anybody who knows the trapdoor to efficiently generate collisions while without knowledge of the trapdoor the function remains collision resistant.

14.1 Compression Functions from Block Ciphers

Block ciphers are not a new concept. In fact, we have already encountered them in Chapter 3 under the name *strong pseudorandom permutation* and for the remainder of this section you can simply mentally replace any occurrence of the term block cipher with strong pseudorandom permutation. In the following section we will present a brief introduction to block ciphers and their uses outside of compression function designs. The material covered is purely informational and will not be needed for our discussion of block-cipher-based constructions. It is thus safe to skip the section and directly proceed with Section 14.1.2.

14.1.1 Block Ciphers

Recall that a pseudorandom permutation is nothing but a pseudorandom function which happens to be a permutation (see Section 3.3.2; page 127). While a pseudorandom permutation remains indistinguishable from a random permutation for an adversary that gets oracle access to evaluate the permutation (or a randomly chosen permutation) in *forward* direction, a strong pseudorandom permutation remains indistinguishable even if the adversary gets oracle access both to evaluate the permutation in forward direction as well as to invert the permutation (see Definition 3.24; page 128). This property allows us to base encryption schemes on strong pseudorandom permutations.

Let $\mathsf{E} : \{0,1\}^{\mathsf{kl}(\lambda)} \times \{0,1\}^{\mathsf{bl}(\lambda)} \to \{0,1\}^{\mathsf{bl}(\lambda)}$ be a block cipher with key length $\mathsf{kl}(\lambda)$ and block length $\mathsf{bl}(\lambda)$. Note that a block cipher implements a permutation for each key and thus its output length is also $\mathsf{bl}(\lambda)$. We write $\mathsf{E.Eval}(k,m)$ to denote "forward" evaluation (or encryption of message m under key k) and $\mathsf{E.Inv}(k,c)$ to denote inversion or "backwards" evaluation (or decryption of ciphertext c under key k). We may also simply write $\mathsf{E}(k,m)$ and $\mathsf{E}^{-1}(k,c)$ to denote encryption and decryption, respectively.

While block ciphers can be used as building blocks in encryption schemes they should not be regarded as encryption schemes themselves. Since block cipher E is deterministic, an encryption scheme (for fixed-length messages in $\{0,1\}^{\mathsf{E.bl}(\lambda)}$) defined as

$\mathsf{KGen}(1^\lambda)$	$\mathsf{Enc}(k,m)$	$\mathsf{Dec}(k,c)$
$k \leftarrow\!\!\$\ \mathsf{E.KGen}(1^\lambda)$	$c \leftarrow \mathsf{E.Eval}(k,m)$	$m \leftarrow \mathsf{E.Inv}(k,c)$
return k	**return** c	**return** m

is not IND-CPA secure. We can, however, easily construct a secure scheme by introducing randomness:

$\mathsf{KGen}(1^\lambda)$	$\mathsf{Enc}(k,m)$	$\mathsf{Dec}(k,(r,c))$
$k \leftarrow\!\!\$\ \mathsf{E.KGen}(1^\lambda)$	$r \leftarrow\!\!\$\ \{0,1\}^{\mathsf{E.bl}(\lambda)}$	$m \leftarrow \mathsf{E.Eval}(k,r) \oplus c$
return k	$c \leftarrow \mathsf{E.Eval}(k,r) \oplus m$	**return** m
	return (r,c)	

Note that here we did not even need to invert the block cipher. In fact, we have seen this construction before when constructing IND-CPA-secure schemes from pseudorandom functions (see Section 5.1.3 on 221).

Modes of Operation

Similarly to the case of hash functions, in practice we are usually not satisfied with fixed-input-length constructions but require constructions that can process (in this case encrypt or decrypt) arbitrarily long messages. The ideas behind such full-fledged encryption schemes are similar to those of iteration schemes for hash functions. Starting from a primitive (a block cipher) we consider an iteration scheme that defines how to process arbitrarily long messages. In the case of block ciphers iteration schemes are usually referred to as *modes of operation*.

In Figure 14.1 we present five classical modes of operation which have also been standardized by the National Institute of Standards and Technology (NIST). Each mode of operation defines how a message m is to be processed iteratively by splitting the message into blocks of length $bl(\lambda)$. For example, the electronic code book (ECB) mode (the first mode in Figure 14.1) processes each block independently of all other blocks and the resulting ciphertext for a message $m = m_1 \| m_2 \| m_3$ consisting of three message blocks of length $bl(\lambda)$ would be

$$c \leftarrow \mathsf{E.Eval}(k, m_1) \| \mathsf{E.Eval}(k, m_2) \| \mathsf{E.Eval}(k, m_3).$$

It should be noted that the ECB mode does not yield a secure cipher and should thus usually not be used (also see Exercise 14.1). In contrast, the four remaining modes presented in Figure 14.1 can all be shown to achieve IND-CPA security (see Exercise 14.2).

Besides the presented modes, several additional modes have been proposed and standardized. Many of these go beyond constructions of encryption schemes and consider the construction of *authenticated* encryption schemes. We provide references in the notes section of this chapter.

Padding. As with hash functions we need to define how to preprocess messages such that their size is a multiple of the block length. Again, we can choose between various padding schemes and a common scheme employed with block ciphers is the 10*-padding which appends a single 1-bit and then as many 0-bits as needed to fill up the block. Note that in order to be unambiguous this will add an extra padding block in case the original message was already of length a multiple of the block length.

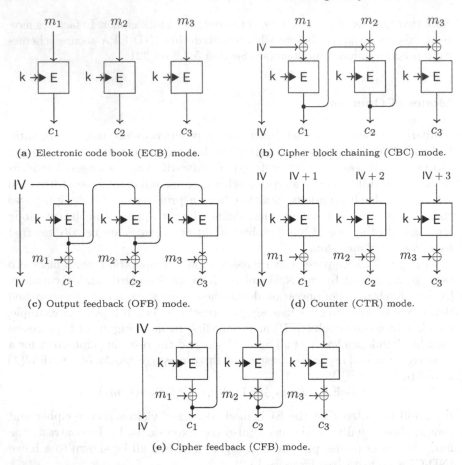

(a) Electronic code book (ECB) mode.

(b) Cipher block chaining (CBC) mode.

(c) Output feedback (OFB) mode.

(d) Counter (CTR) mode.

(e) Cipher feedback (CFB) mode.

Fig. 14.1: Various (classical) modes of operation for building encryption schemes from block ciphers. ECB mode (Figure 14.1a) is not IND-CPA or even IND secure (also see Exercise 14.1). All modes except for ECB require an initialization vector IV which is part of the ciphertext and which should be chosen uniformly at random for each new encryption. All diagrams are to be understood as encrypting a longer message m split into multiple blocks m_i of length $\mathsf{bl}(\lambda)$ each. In the diagrams we consider the encryption of a message consisting of three blocks (after padding). The black triangle ▶ in the block cipher box E denotes the key input of the block cipher.

Message Authentication Codes from Block Ciphers

Block ciphers are a versatile building block. We cannot only build encryption schemes or compression functions, but a common practice is also to construct message authentication codes from block ciphers. Following is an example of a prominent construction in practice: the *cipher block chaining message authentication code* (CBC-MAC) which is closely related to the CBC mode of operation (see Figure 14.1). There are a few very important differences.

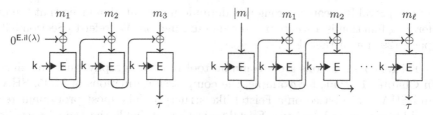

(a) CBC-MAC for fixed-length messages.   (b) CBC-MAC for variable-length messages.

Fig. 14.2: The cipher block chaining message authentication code (CBC-MAC) construction of a secure message authentication code from a block cipher. Note that while security for CBC encryption depends on using a random IV, using a random IV with CBC-MAC makes the construction insecure, which is why usually the IV is fixed to zero (construction on the left). Note, however, that in this mode CBC-MAC is only secure for fixed-length messages and each key should only ever be used for messages of a known and fixed length. On the right we give a construction that is secure also for variable-length messages. Also see Exercise 14.3.

To begin with, the tag is the output of the last block-cipher call. All other intermediate values are not part of the output. The crucial difference is, however, the treatment of the initialization vector. While for encryption it is crucial that the IV is chosen fresh and uniformly at random for each new message, this would make CBC-MAC insecure. Instead, what is usually done is to use a fixed all-zero IV. While this produces a secure message authentication code, it is only secure for fixed-length messages. The standard construction for variable-length messages is to prepend the message length to the message before applying CBC-MAC (see Figure 14.2).

CBC-MAC, similarly to modes of operation, is not a requirement for studying block-cipher-based compression functions. It does, however, provide additional insights into block-cipher-based constructions, and Exercise 14.3 asks to prove basic properties about CBC-MAC.

Practical Constructions of Block Ciphers

A full discussion of practical constructions is beyond the scope of this book, but we nevertheless briefly mention the two most common designs found in practice. One of these we have actually already seen when discussing pseudorandom functions: *Feistel networks* (Section 3.3.3; page 129).

Feistel networks. A Feistel network allows to create pseudorandom permutations of length $2n$ from any length-preserving pseudorandom function of length n bits via repeated execution of the pseudorandom function: To compute the ith round the input is split in half $L_i\|R_i$ and the round result is computed as $L_{i+1}\|R_{i+1} \leftarrow R_i\|(L_i \oplus \mathsf{PRF}(\mathsf{k}_i, R_i))$. Here PRF is a pseudorandom function and k_i is the ith round key. Feistel networks of at least four rounds provably create a strong pseudorandom permutation given that the underlying function is a secure pseudorandom function. We refer to Section 3.3.3 (page 129) for further details.

Feistel constructions are a common tool in cryptography, and we will see in Chapter 15 that, for example, the compression functions of MD5, SHA-1 and SHA-2, are based on a Feistel-like structure. The most prominent real-world block cipher based on a Feistel network is probably the *Data Encryption Standard* (DES), which was developed by IBM in the early 1970s. DES consists of a 16-round Feistel network. It has a key size of 56 bits (eight bytes with one parity bit per byte) and a block size of 64 bits. The best known practical attack on DES reduces the security to about 40 bits, such that a brute-force attack is feasible on commodity hardware today, and DES should thus be regarded as broken. A version of DES that is still considered adequate and which has a theoretical security of 112 bits (but an assumed security of about 80 bits) is *Triple DES*, which chains three executions of DES with three different keys and computes a ciphertext for a message m as

$$c \leftarrow \mathsf{DES}(k_3, \mathsf{DES}^{-1}(k_2, \mathsf{DES}(k_1, m))).$$

Here, DES^{-1} denotes decryption.[1]

Confusion–diffusion paradigm. Feistel networks provide a provably secure construction of pseudorandom permutations out of pseudorandom functions. They do not, however, answer the question of how to introduce pseudorandomness in the first place. The second common design pattern that we discuss here considers the task of introducing pseudorandomness while constructing a permutation from scratch via the so-called *confusion–diffusion paradigm*, usually implemented via *substitution–permutation networks* (see below).

Assume for the moment that for each key k the block cipher behaves ideally and provides a random permutation, similar to a random oracle which idealizes a hash function. As discussed in our introduction to random oracles (Section 8.1.1; page 341) storing random functions becomes infeasible very quickly. A function mapping n-bit inputs to n-bit outputs would require roughly $n \cdot 2^n$ bits of space, which already for small choices of n is impractical if not outright infeasible. The subset of random permutations among such functions is not significantly smaller such that the description size of a random permutation becomes very large even for moderate values of n. Block ciphers today usually use block sizes of 128 bits or 256 bits, and it is thus impossible

---

[1] While with three keys, each of length 56 bits, security might be assumed to be 168 bits this is not the case as the triple execution can be attacked via a *meet-in-the-middle attack* which reduces the security to 112 bits. This is also why in many implementations keys 1 and 3 are set to the same key, in which case the actual key length equals the theoretical strength of the cipher. The assumed bit strength of Triple DES today is about 80 bits.

to store just one random permutation of that size, much less 2^{kl} many, one for each key of length kl.

Already in 1945, Shannon proposed the *confusion–diffusion* principle as basis for constructing (pseudo)random permutations. The basic idea is similar to that of Merkle–Damgård: provide a domain-extending construction that constructs a larger permutation out of smaller building blocks: We construct a permutation PRP : $\{0,1\}^n \to \{0,1\}^n$ of length n bits by a number of ℓ smaller permutations as

$$\mathsf{PRP}(m) := \pi_1(m_1)\| \ldots \|\pi_\ell(m_\ell).$$

Here m_i denotes the ith chunk of length $\frac{n}{\ell}$ bits of message m, that is, $m_i = m[((i-1) \cdot \frac{n}{\ell} + 1)..i \cdot \frac{n}{\ell}]$, and we here assume that ℓ exactly divides n. Each of the ℓ small permutations is thus of the form $\pi_i : \{0,1\}^{n/\ell} \to \{0,1\}^{n/\ell}$. In practice it is not uncommon that functions π_i operate on 8 bits or less such that if we consider $n = 128$ we end up with 16 different functions π_i. Implementing them as lookup tables thus requires $16 \cdot 8 \cdot 2^8$ bits or roughly four kilobytes.

The above process is said to *introduce confusion* into the output, but of course it does not yet yield a pseudorandom permutation as small changes in the input only affect small parts of the output. For example, a flip of the first bit in the input only affects the first block of the output. Ideally though, a single bit flip should affect roughly half of the output bits; this is also called an *avalanche effect*. To obtain a pseudorandom permutation we need two additional ingredients. The first is a *diffusion* or *mixing* step, which is usually a reordering of bits. The second ingredient is to repeat the two steps *confusion* and *diffusion* multiple times each time with a different key. A single repetition is usually referred to as a *round*. Permutations and mixing functions can, of course, be different in every round.

Since permutations and mixing functions are invertible the result is an invertible function. However, this does not need to be the case and, for example, the confusion step could also be many-to-one. The result would then be a pseudorandom function rather than a pseudorandom permutation.

Remark 14.1. Above we wrote that the result is a pseudorandom function or permutation. We note that the construction here is a purely heuristic construction that is not based on any hardness assumption and is thus not a "provable construction" in the sense of provable security. Yet, modern designs are usually based on years of experience, providing confidence in their security.

Substitution–permutation networks. Substitution–permutation networks can be regarded as an implementation of the confusion–diffusion paradigm. They usually work with a small number of fixed small permutations called S-boxes (for substitution boxes) and a single mixing function. Since now S-boxes and mixing function do not depend on the key any longer, the key needs to be added in a different way. For this, individual round keys are computed from

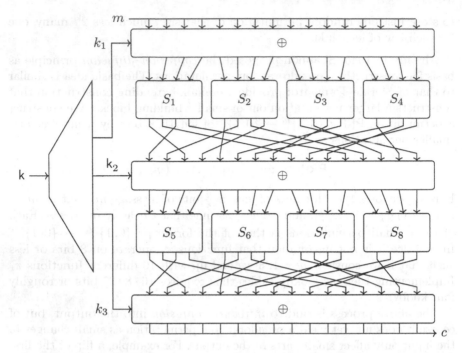

Fig. 14.3: A substitution–permutation network working on 16-bit messages and with eight 4-bit S-boxes and a single mixing function. On the left a schematic of the key schedule is shown which computes from the master key k the three round keys k_1, k_2, and k_3.

a single master key—this process is also referred to as a key schedule—and the round key is then usually XORed onto the current intermediate result at the beginning of each round. We give a simple schematic of a two-round substitution–permutation network in Figure 14.3.

The most prominent real-world block cipher based on a substitution–permutation network is *Rijndael*, better known as AES, the *Advanced Encryption Standard*. AES works on message blocks of size 128 bits. It comes in three forms with 128-, 192-, or 256-bit keys and with 10, 12, or 14 rounds, respectively. Interestingly, AES uses only a single 8-bit S-box which is applied to each of the 16 bytes of the intermediate state values. At present, there are no practical attacks known on AES, given that it is properly implemented.

14.1.2 The Ideal Cipher Model

Before we can start looking at constructions of compression functions from block ciphers we need to answer the question of how we analyze such constructions: What do we expect from a secure construction? If you think back to hash function iteration schemes such as Merkle–Damgård then there we defined iteration schemes as *property preserving* if for a certain property, for example, collision resistance, the iteration scheme has the property if the underlying compression function has the property (see Definition 13.7 on page 485). In the case of block-cipher-based compression functions we cannot use property preservation as a security target as the underlying primitive (a block cipher) is very different from the result: a compression function. While we would like the resulting compression function to be, for example, collision resistant, collision resistance is not a helpful notion for a block cipher. For each key a block cipher is a permutation, and a permutation is trivially collision resistant as collisions simply do not exist. Thus a security notion of the form

> "*a construction is good if it is collision resistant given that the underlying block cipher is collision resistant*"

is futile. Instead of collision resistance we thus need to base the security of the resulting construction on a different property of the block cipher.

As it turns out, finding the right property is difficult. Properties that come to mind would be that the block cipher is a (strong) pseudorandom permutation. After all, this is what a block cipher should be and we have seen that for encryption schemes and message authentication codes this is a sufficient assumption. For example, we can build IND-CPA- or even IND-CCA-secure symmetric encryption schemes based on strong pseudorandom permutations and thus ultimately on one-way functions. For the latter, recall that we can construct pseudorandom functions from one-way functions and strong pseudorandom permutations (e.g., via a Feistel construction) from pseudorandom functions. Regrettably, it can be shown that one-way functions as well as one-way permutations[2] are most likely not sufficient to construct collision-resistant compression functions as we have seen in Section 4.4.2 (Theorem 4.16 on page 184). There we showed that no construction that only uses black-box access to a one-way function (or permutation) can be collision resistant without using any other assumption. Since we can construct pseudorandom permutations from one-way functions it follows that neither can we construct a collision-resistant compression function from a pseudorandom function (or permutation) via black-box techniques. One reason as to why we should expect it to be difficult to base collision resistance on pseudorandom functions is that the respective security games are quite different. A hash function (or compression function) should be collision resistant given its key which, once chosen, is public knowledge. Pseudorandom functions, on the other hand, are solely defined under the assumption that the key remains private. Once the key is known, all bets are off and it is not at all clear what type of security, if any, the function still provides.

---

[2] Maybe surprisingly, it can be shown that one-way permutations cannot be constructed in a black-box manner from one-way functions. See also the chapter notes of Chapter 11.

The ideal cipher model. Above we said that we cannot hope to verify black-box constructions on the assumption that our block cipher is one-way or even a strong pseudorandom permutation. A black-box construction is, however, exactly what we would like to build as it is the most simple and general type of construction and it would work for any block cipher. The way cryptographers usually take to resolve this dilemma is to perform the security analysis in an idealized model, the so-called *ideal cipher model*.[3] The ideal cipher model is very similar to the random oracle model which we studied in detail in Part II of this book. In particular, it comes with the same gap: No real-world block cipher can behave like an ideal cipher. Thus, a construction proven secure in the ideal cipher model may not be secure once the ideal cipher is replaced by (aka instantiated with) an actual construction of a block cipher. As with the random oracle model, a security proof does, however, provide a strong argument for the security of a construction given that it is instantiated with a good block cipher. After all, in order to break the construction an adversary would need to exploit some weakness in the used cipher.

But what is an ideal cipher in the first place? The idea of the ideal cipher model goes back, as so often, to Shannon, who considered an ideal cipher to be a block cipher which for every key implements a uniformly random permutation. That is, if we consider a block cipher of the form $\mathsf{E} : \{0,1\}^{\mathsf{kl}(\lambda)} \times \{0,1\}^{\mathsf{bl}(\lambda)} \to \{0,1\}^{\mathsf{bl}(\lambda)}$, that is, a block cipher that takes keys of length $\mathsf{kl}(\lambda)$ and which processes message blocks of length $\mathsf{bl}(\lambda)$ then an ideal cipher of that form would assign to every of the $2^{\mathsf{kl}(\lambda)}$ possible keys a randomly chosen permutation. As with random oracles, it is clear that even for small choices of λ we cannot possibly implement such a function, let alone, efficiently. Instead, in the ideal cipher model, we give each party oracle access to the ideal cipher E in both forwards and backwards direction. We write $\mathsf{E}.\mathsf{Eval}(\cdot,\cdot)$ for evaluating the cipher in forwards direction and $\mathsf{E}.\mathsf{Inv}(\cdot,\cdot)$ to denote inversion. We may also write the same more compactly as $\mathsf{E}(\cdot,\cdot)$ and $\mathsf{E}^{-1}(\cdot,\cdot)$. Note that the oracle does not fix the key, but instead, parties can evaluate the cipher on any key.

Since in the ideal cipher model all parties including adversaries only have oracle access to the block cipher, the standard model for adversaries is an information-theoretic model rather than a computational one. That is, the adversary is not restricted in terms of runtime nor space but the only restriction put on the adversary is that the number of oracle queries it poses is bounded by a polynomial. Of course a proof in this model also holds for efficient, that is, probabilistic polynomial-time adversaries.

In summary we can say that the ideal cipher model is identical to the random oracle model with the exception that the oracle is not a random oracle, that is, a function of the form $\mathsf{RO} : \{0,1\}^* \to \{0,1\}^{\mathsf{ol}(\lambda)}$ chosen uniformly at random. Instead, the oracle is of the form $\mathsf{E} : \{0,1\}^{\mathsf{kl}(\lambda)} \times \{0,1\}^{\mathsf{bl}(\lambda)} \to$

---

[3] The ideal cipher model is also known under the name *Shannon model*. The term ideal cipher model is, however, the standard term in the field of cryptography today.

$\{0,1\}^{\mathsf{bl}(\lambda)}$, where for each key $\mathsf{k} \in \{0,1\}^{\mathsf{kl}(\lambda)}$ oracle $\mathsf{E}(\mathsf{k},\cdot)$ implements a random permutation over $\mathsf{bl}(\lambda)$ many bits. Furthermore, for each key the oracle exposes both evaluation in forward direction as well as computing the inverse of the permutation.

A word of caution. Not every hash function behaves sufficiently like a random oracle, and thus a scheme proven secure in the random oracle model may be insecure depending on the hash function chosen in practice. We have a lot more to say about this in Chapters 17 and 18. The same is true for the ideal cipher model. Even if we prove that a construction from an ideal cipher is collision resistant the result may be trivially broken depending on which block cipher is chosen in practice. This is especially the case for block ciphers which are usually designed as the basis for encryption schemes first.

When used in encryption schemes, keys remain hidden from the adversary. Thus, analyses for weak keys usually concentrate on finding large classes of weak keys such that there is a reasonable probability of such a key being actually chosen. If weak keys exist, but the probability that one is chosen is negligible, this does not have a significant impact on the security of the block cipher in encryption schemes. When block ciphers are instead used in the construction of compression functions, keys are not secret. Thus, to break a compression function cryptanalysts search for the weakest possible key to then construct messages that ensure that the key is hit.

An example of a real-world block cipher that has weak keys which opens up the possibility for attacks when used in various compression function constructions is the International Data Encryption Algorithm (IDEA). A second example of a block cipher with weak keys is TEA, the *Tiny Encryption Algorithm*. In case of TEA this weakness was indeed exploited by an attack on Microsoft's first Xbox. In their first design of their Xbox gaming console Microsoft needed a hash function that has a compact description and the choice ultimately fell on a construction from TEA. The TEA block cipher, however, is known to have equivalent keys, that is, for each key three others exist that all produce identical ciphertexts for all plaintexts. While not problematic in encryption mode, when used as the basis for a hash function, such a weakness can be catastrophic and in the Xbox case led to a break of the hash function. We provide further references in the notes and references section of this chapter.

14.1.3 Rate-1 Constructions

As before we consider compression functions to be of the form

$$\mathsf{h}^\mathsf{E} : \{0,1\}^{\mathsf{h}\cdot\mathsf{bl}(\lambda)} \times \{0,1\}^{\mathsf{h}\cdot\mathsf{cl}(\lambda)} \to \{0,1\}^{\mathsf{h}\cdot\mathsf{cl}(\lambda)},$$

where we call the first input the message input (or message block) and the second input the chaining value or state value. We always consider messages to be of length bl and leave it to a possible iteration scheme (e.g., Merkle–Damgård) to ensure that compression functions are called appropriately.

Let h^E be a compression function which makes black-box use of a block cipher E. One way to capture the efficiency of the construction is by looking at the number of block cipher evaluations needed to process a message. Let s denote the maximum number of block cipher calls by h^E for any input, then we can define rate r as

$$r := \frac{h.bl(\lambda)}{s \cdot E.bl(\lambda)}.$$

If we consider a compression function processing 128-bit message blocks and which makes two calls to a block cipher with block length 128 bits, then the function has a rate of $\frac{1}{2}$. If, instead the underlying block cipher has a block length of 64 bits, then the compression function would be rate 1 even though the compression function makes two cipher calls per compression function evaluation. Usually, however, a rate $\frac{1}{t}$ compression function makes t block cipher calls.

The PGV Constructions

In the following we study the most efficient and simplest type of constructions, that is, rate-1 compression functions that make a single call to the underlying block cipher per compression function invocation. The first systematic study of rate-1 compression functions, and indeed of block-cipher-based compression functions, was conducted in 1993 by Preneel, Govaerts, and Vandewalle. They studied a total of 64 rate-1 compression functions which are today often referred to as PGV constructions.

We can capture any rate-1 block-cipher based compression function by

$$h^E(m_i, y_i) := f_2(m_i, y_i, E(f_1(m_i, y_i))), \tag{14.1}$$

where f_1 on input message block and chaining value outputs a key and a message block for block cipher E, and function f_2 gets as input the result as well as inputs m_i and y_i; the ith message block and ith chaining value. We provide a visualization of the above generic construction of a rate-1 compression function based on functions f_1 and f_2 in Figure 14.4. Note that since we consider only deterministic functions we do not need to provide the output of f_1 to f_2 as this could simply be recomputed.

While in theory functions f_1 and f_2 could be arbitrarily complex, we are usually interested in as simple a scheme as possible. The rate-1 functions studied by PGV were of the form $E : \{0,1\}^\lambda \times \{0,1\}^\lambda \to \{0,1\}^\lambda$ and thus mapped inputs of length 2λ to outputs of length λ. Furthermore, functions

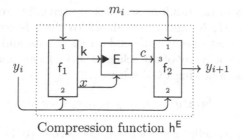

Compression function h^E

Fig. 14.4: A generic representation of a rate-1 compression function decomposed into two deterministic functions f_1 and f_2. The small numbers in the above diagram for function boxes f_1 and f_2 denote the order of parameters. That is, we consider $f_1(m_i, y_i)$ and $f_2(m_i, y_i, c)$. The latter is important for Exercise 14.4. The black triangle ▶ in the block cipher box E denotes the key input of the block cipher.

f_1 and f_2 as used by PGV consisted of at most an exclusive-or operation. In more detail, a PGV compression function is of the form

$$h^E(m, y) := E(K, M) \oplus F,$$

where the inputs K, M, and F are each chosen from the following set: $\{m, y, m \oplus y, V\}$. Here m and y are the inputs to the compression function and V is a fixed constant set to the all-zero vector. In total we thus have $4^3 = 64$ different possible PGV compression functions. In Figure 14.5 below we give a schematic representation of the PGV compression function with the possible inputs on the left.

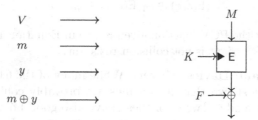

Fig. 14.5: The PGV compression function on the right with considered choices for inputs on the left. Here m and y are the message and chaining value inputs to the compression function and V is the all-zero vector. To get a specific instance, fix values M, K, and F as either V, m, y, or $m \oplus y$. We thus have a total of $4^3 = 64$ different PGV functions.

Remark 14.2. The PGV compression functions are also said to be *single block-length compression functions* as the output length of the compression function matches the block length of the underlying block cipher. This is in contrast to, for example, double block-length compression functions which have an output twice the size of the block length of the underlying block cipher. We will discuss double block-length constructions in Section 14.1.5.

Naturally, many of the resulting schemes are trivially broken. For example, the scheme where M, K, and F are all set to the all-zero constant V is a constant function that does not depend on its inputs and is, of course, not collision resistant. For many of the schemes, attacks are more subtle though. Let us consider the following PGV scheme:

$$\mathsf{h}^{\mathsf{E}}(m, y) := \mathsf{E}(m \oplus y, m \oplus y) \oplus m. \qquad (14.2)$$

Here we can construct collisions as follows. Let $y_0, c \in \{0,1\}^\lambda$ be two randomly chosen values. We next compute y_1 as

$$
\begin{aligned}
y_1 &= \mathsf{h}^{\mathsf{E}}(y_0 \oplus c, y_0) \\
&= \mathsf{E}(y_0 \oplus c \oplus y_0, y_0 \oplus c \oplus y_0) \oplus y_0 \oplus c \\
&= \mathsf{E}(c, c) \oplus y_0 \oplus c.
\end{aligned}
$$

Using value y_1 as chaining value and as message block the result of $\mathsf{E}(c, c) \oplus y_0$ we now get

$$\mathsf{h}^{\mathsf{E}}(\mathsf{E}(c, c) \oplus y_0, y_1) = \mathsf{E}(\mathsf{E}(c, c) \oplus y_0 \oplus y_1, \mathsf{E}(c, c) \oplus y_0 \oplus y_1) \oplus \mathsf{E}(c, c) \oplus y_0.$$

Replacing y_1 with $\mathsf{E}(c, c) \oplus y_0 \oplus c$ as computed above we get

$$
\begin{aligned}
&= \mathsf{E}(c, c) \oplus \mathsf{E}(c, c) \oplus y_0 \\
&= y_0.
\end{aligned}
$$

It follows that for all $c \in \{0,1\}^\lambda$ and all $y_0 \in \{0,1\}^\lambda$ all inputs of the form

$$(\mathsf{E}(c, c) \oplus y_0, \mathsf{E}(c, c) \oplus y_0 \oplus c)$$

map to y_0 under the PGV function given above in Equation 14.2. It, of course, follows that this variant is not collision resistant.

Fixed points and Davies–Meyer. While many of the 64 schemes are not secure it can be shown that 20 schemes are provably collision resistant in the ideal cipher model. Twelve of these have also good bounds for preimage resistance and are thus regarded as the twelve secure PGV schemes. We present all twelve schemes together with schematics in Figure 14.7 (page 556). Interestingly, eight of the twelve schemes (schemes 5 to 12 in Figure 14.7) are known to be vulnerable to fixed-point attacks. Recall that a fixed point for a compression function h is an input (m, y) such that

$$\mathsf{h}(m, y) = y.$$

In Section 13.2.1 on page 504 we have seen how fixed points can be used in a second-preimage attack against Merkle–Damgård-style schemes as, within the iteration scheme, a fixed point allows to generate *expandable messages*.

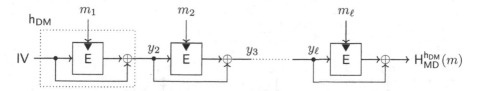

Fig. 14.6: The Merkle–Damgård transformation with a Davies–Meyer compression function based on block cipher E.

Consider now scheme 5 given in Figure 14.7e, a construction also known as the *Davies–Meyer compression function*

$$h_5^E(m, y) := E(m, y) \oplus y.$$

We give a schematic of the resulting Merkle–Damgård hash function using the Davies–Meyer compression function in Figure 14.6. Here, block cipher E is called with message block m taking the role of the key. For the Davies–Meyer construction we get fixed points if we can find an input (m, y) such that $E(m, y) = 0^\lambda$ as in this case

$$h_{DM}^E(m, y) := E(m, y) \oplus y = 0^\lambda \oplus y = y.$$

By construction, for every value $m \in \{0, 1\}^\lambda$ there must exist a value $y \in \{0, 1\}^\lambda$ such that $E(m, y) = 0^\lambda$ as for a fixed key a block cipher implements a permutation. As it turns out, finding such a fixed point is trivial. For a given message m_{fp} we can find the corresponding value y_{fp} by simply inverting the block cipher on value $0^{|y_{fp}|}$. That is we compute

$$y_{fp} \leftarrow E^{-1}(m_{fp}, 0^{|y_{fp}|}),$$

which yields the fixed point (m_{fp}, y_{fp}) such that $h_{DM}^E(m_{fp}, y_{fp}) = y_{fp}$.

Collision-Resistant PGV Schemes

While allowing to easily compute fixed points is certainly a weakness in a compression function that, for example, allows distinguishing the compression function from a *uniformly random* compression function, it does not yield direct attacks on a resulting Merkle–Damgård-type hash function. This is why all schemes from Figure 14.7 are usually considered secure even though schemes 5 to 12 allow for the computation of fixed points. While no weaknesses are known for the first four schemes from Figure 14.7—the first construction is also known as the *Matyas–Meyer–Oseas compression function* and the second construction as the *Miyaguchi–Preneel compression function*—the scheme that is found most often in practice is the Davies–Meyer construction

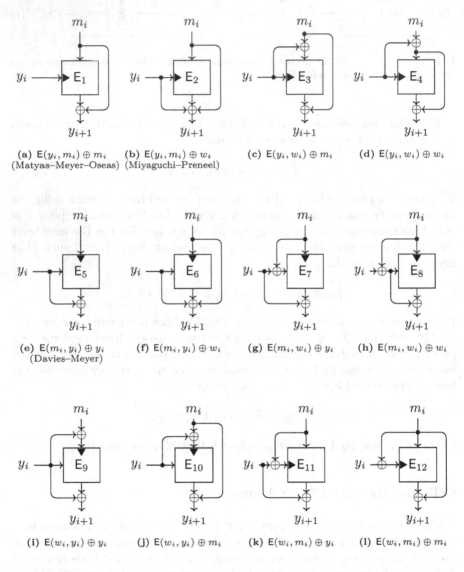

(a) $\mathsf{E}(y_i, m_i) \oplus m_i$ **(b)** $\mathsf{E}(y_i, m_i) \oplus w_i$ **(c)** $\mathsf{E}(y_i, w_i) \oplus m_i$ **(d)** $\mathsf{E}(y_i, w_i) \oplus w_i$
(Matyas–Meyer–Oseas) (Miyaguchi–Preneel)

(e) $\mathsf{E}(m_i, y_i) \oplus y_i$ **(f)** $\mathsf{E}(m_i, y_i) \oplus w_i$ **(g)** $\mathsf{E}(m_i, w_i) \oplus y_i$ **(h)** $\mathsf{E}(m_i, w_i) \oplus w_i$
(Davies–Meyer)

(i) $\mathsf{E}(w_i, y_i) \oplus y_i$ **(j)** $\mathsf{E}(w_i, y_i) \oplus m_i$ **(k)** $\mathsf{E}(w_i, m_i) \oplus y_i$ **(l)** $\mathsf{E}(w_i, m_i) \oplus m_i$

Fig. 14.7: The twelve secure PGV schemes. Here, value w_i denotes the exclusive-or of message block m_i and chaining value y_i, that is, $w_i = m_i \oplus y_i$. The black triangle ▶ inside the cipher box E_i denotes the key input. We here consider block ciphers of the form $\mathsf{E} : \{0,1\}^\lambda \times \{0,1\}^\lambda \to \{0,1\}^\lambda$ where, as usual, the first input takes the key.

(Construction 5). Real-world schemes that are based on the Davies–Meyer construction include MD5, SHA-1, and SHA-2 as we will see in Chapter 15.

In the following we examine the collision resistance of the twelve secure schemes and show the following result:

> **Theorem 14.3.** *Let h^E be one of the compression function constructions from a block cipher E given in Figure 14.7. When block cipher E is modeled as an ideal cipher the advantage of any (possibly unbounded) adversary $\mathcal{A}$ in finding a collision for h^E is upper bounded by*
>
> $$\mathsf{Adv}^{cr}_{h^E,\mathcal{A}}(\lambda) \leq \frac{(q(\lambda)+2)(q(\lambda)+3)}{2^\lambda}.$$
>
> *Here $q(\lambda)$ denotes the total number of queries to block cipher E and inverse E^{-1} by adversary $\mathcal{A}$.*

Remark 14.4. Note that we stated the theorem in the concrete setting and gave a bound on the adversary's advantage as a function of the number of queries the adversary poses. When restricting the number of queries to be polynomial in the security parameter then the bound becomes a negligible function.

We will here prove Theorem 14.3 only for the Davies–Meyer construction and leave the full proof as Exercise 14.4. While throughout this book most of our proofs are given in the form of a security reduction we here give a direct proof based on the idealization assumption of the block cipher. The reason is that assuming the block cipher is ideal is already sufficient such that we can directly estimate the success probability of an (unbounded) adversary finding a collision and bound its success solely by its number of oracle queries. Note that this is similar to many of our random oracle proofs (see, for example, Proposition 8.6 on page 348, where we show that the random oracle is one-way).

Proof of Theorem 14.3. Let h^E denote the Davies–Meyer construction (Construction 5 in Figure 14.7), that is,

$$h^E(m,y) := E(m,y) \oplus y.$$

Further let $\mathcal{A}$ be a collision-finding adversary asking no more than $q := q(\lambda)$ oracle queries to E and E^{-1} altogether. We assume that $\mathcal{A}$ never repeats a query to either E or E^{-1}, and neither asks an oracle about a result from the other oracle in inverse direction. This can be ensured by simple table-lookup techniques for the otherwise unbounded adversary.

To prove the statement we will keep a set T of triples (m,y,z) of the form $z = h^E(m,y)$ that can be computed by the adversary. Note that the adversary found a collision if there are two entries $(m,y,z) \in T$ and $(m',y',z') \in T$ such that $(m,y) \neq (m',y')$ but $z = z'$. At the beginning set T is empty and we will show that with every oracle query to either E or E^{-1} the set T grows by exactly one entry with value z being beyond the control of the adversary.

For any input $(m, y) \in \{0, 1\}^\lambda \times \{0, 1\}^\lambda$ we can model the value $h^E(m, y)$ by a random variable Z which will manifest once the result of oracle query $E(m, y)$ is known. As block cipher E is an ideal cipher we can model the result of an oracle query to E by a random variable C that is close to uniformly distributed in $\{0, 1\}^\lambda$. For this consider an adversary making t distinct queries of the form $E(m, \cdot)$, that is, with the same message. As $E(m, \cdot)$ is a permutation over 2^λ bits we have that for the tth query there are exactly $2^\lambda - t - 1$ many possible outcomes, all equally likely. We thus get that

$$h^E(m, y) = E(m, y) \oplus y = C \oplus y = Z$$

with Z being distributed similarly to C: on the tth query there are at least $2^\lambda - t - 1$ many possible outcomes, all equally likely. It follows that with each new forward query (m, y) to oracle E, the set T of computable values grows by exactly one entry (m, y, z).

We can similarly analyze inverse oracle queries, that is, queries to oracle E^{-1}. Here, we can model the results to an oracle query to $E^{-1}(m, c)$ by a random variable Y that is close to uniformly distributed. Recall that m takes the role of key and thus for value $y \leftarrow E^{-1}(m, c)$ it holds tht $E(m, y) = c$. It follows that for any pair $(m, c) \in \{0, 1\}^\lambda \times \{0, 1\}^\lambda$ we can model the compression function value that is uniquely induced by $E^{-1}(m, c)$ as a random variable Z' since

$$h^E(m, Y) = E(m, Y) \oplus Y = c \oplus Y = Z'.$$

Again, we can conclude that with every oracle query to E^{-1} set T grows by at most one entry (m, y, z).

Above we have argued that with each distinct oracle query, set T grows by a single entry. Thus after $i - 1$ many queries set T contains $i - 1$ entries. The ith query will add a new entry with z chosen uniformly at random from at least $2^\lambda - (i - 1)$ many values. It follows that the probability that the ith query will collide with any of the $i - 1$ many z values in T is at most

$$\frac{i - 1}{2^\lambda - (i - 1)}.$$

Note that in case adversary $\mathcal{A}$ does not find a collision within its q queries, it can take a final guess for a collision. To capture also this final guess, we thus allow the adversary "two additional queries." Using the above analysis, the probability of a collision on h^E after q + 2 queries can then be upper bounded by a union bound as

$$\Pr[\text{z-collision}] \leq \sum_{i=1}^{q+2} \frac{i-1}{2^\lambda - (i-1)} \leq \frac{1}{2} \cdot \frac{(q+2)(q+3)}{2^\lambda - q}. \tag{14.3}$$

Here we use that

$$\sum_{i=1}^{n}(i-1) \leq \sum_{i=1}^{n} i = \frac{1}{2}n(n+1).$$

Note that the theorem's bound becomes useless for $q \geq 2^{\lambda-1}$, as the stated term exceeds 1. We can thus set $q < 2^{\lambda-1}$ and simplify Equation (14.3) to

$$\frac{1}{2} \cdot \frac{(q+2)(q+3)}{2^\lambda - q} \leq \frac{1}{2} \cdot \frac{(q+2)(q+3)}{2^\lambda - 2^{\lambda-1}} \leq \frac{(q+2)(q+3)}{2^\lambda}.$$

This yields our final advantage and concludes the proof

$$\mathsf{Adv}^{\mathsf{cr}}_{\mathsf{hE},\mathcal{A}}(\lambda) \leq \frac{(q(\lambda)+2)(q(\lambda)+3)}{2^\lambda}. \qquad \square$$

Preimage Resistance of PGV Schemes

We have seen that Davies–Meyer is collision resistant, and Exercise 14.4 asks to prove the same for the other eleven PGV constructions from Figure 14.7. Since all PGV functions are compressing we can conclude with Theorem 4.10 (page 175) that all the functions are also target-collision resistant, second-preimage resistant, and one-way.

Optimal security. While the above approach allows to argue security, it does not provide optimal bounds. As an example, let us consider preimage resistance (aka one-wayness). Here an adversary is tasked to find a preimage for an image chosen uniformly at random (see Definition 2.15 on page 84). What is the best security bound we can expect from a compression function? For this, let us consider an ideal compression function h_{ideal} (i.e., a fixed-input-length random oracle) which similar to the PGV functions maps 2λ bits to λ bits. Let $\mathcal{A}$ be an adversary that gets as input a target value y generated as $y \leftarrow h_{\mathsf{ideal}}(x)$ for x chosen uniformly at random in $\{0,1\}^{2\lambda}$.[4] The adversary's task is to find some value x' such that $h_{\mathsf{ideal}}(x') = y$. Note that the adversary does not necessarily need to find the original x.

As h_{ideal} is a fixed-input-length random oracle with inputs of length 2λ and outputs of length λ we can reuse our analysis of preimage resistance for random oracles (see Proposition 8.6 and the following remark on page 348) and upper bound the success probability of an adversary making at most $q := q(\lambda)$ many queries by

---

[4] Note that for simpler presentation we here consider compression function h_{ideal} to take only a single input of length 2λ.

$$\mathsf{Adv}^{\mathrm{owf}}_{\mathsf{h}_{\mathrm{ideal}},\mathcal{A}}(\lambda) \leq \frac{\mathsf{q}+1}{2^{\lambda}} + \frac{\mathsf{q}+1}{2^{2\lambda}} \leq 2 \cdot \frac{\mathsf{q}+1}{2^{\lambda}} = \frac{\mathsf{q}+1}{2^{\lambda-1}}. \tag{14.4}$$

If we instead reduce the security of preimage resistance to the security of collision resistance, the best bound that we can get is that an adversary needs at least $2^{\lambda/2}$ many trials. This is due to the birthday bound for collision resistance (see also Section 4.1.2; page 165). For the PGV functions this means that the best bound we can get for preimage resistance when going via collision resistance and Theorem 4.10 is the bound obtained in the above Theorem 14.3:

$$\mathsf{Adv}^{\mathrm{owf}}_{\mathsf{h}_{\mathrm{ideal}},\mathcal{A}}(\lambda) \leq \frac{(\mathsf{q}+2)(\mathsf{q}+3)}{2^{\lambda}}.$$

Here, however, the adversary's advantage grows quadratically in the number of queries while in the bound we obtained above as Equation (14.4) the advantage only grows linearly. The bound derived for preimage resistance by a reduction via collision resistance is thus far from optimal.

Preimage security of PGV constructions. Instead of using Theorem 4.10, in the following we give a direct analysis of the preimage resistance of PGV constructions in the ideal cipher model. This yields the following result:

> **Theorem 14.5.** *Let h^{E} be one of the compression function constructions from a block cipher E given in Figure 14.7. Then, when block cipher E is modeled as an ideal cipher the advantage of any (possibly unbounded) adversary $\mathcal{A}$ in breaking preimage resistance for h^{E} is upper bounded by*
>
> $$\mathsf{Adv}^{\mathrm{owf}}_{\mathsf{h}^{\mathsf{E}},\mathcal{A}}(\lambda) \leq \frac{\mathsf{q}(\lambda)+1}{2^{\lambda-1}}.$$
>
> *Here $\mathsf{q}(\lambda)$ denotes the number of queries to block cipher E by adversary $\mathcal{A}$.*

As before we here only provide a formal proof for the Davies–Meyer construction and leave the full proof as Exercise 14.5.

Proof. Let $\mathcal{A}$ be an adversary against the preimage resistance (aka onewayness) of the Davies–Meyer construction h^{E} given by

$$\mathsf{h}^{\mathsf{E}}(m,y) := \mathsf{E}(m,y) \oplus y.$$

Adversary $\mathcal{A}$ gets as input a target value τ chosen by applying h^{E} to a uniformly random input. Its task is to find a pair (m,y) such that $\mathsf{h}^{\mathsf{E}}(m,y) = \tau$ (see also Definition 2.15 on page 84).

Recall the analysis from the proof of Theorem 14.3. After i distinct queries to oracle E or its inverse E^{-1}, set T of computable h^{E} values contains exactly i many entries. Furthermore, the entry of the form (m,y,z) that is added on the ith query is such that z is chosen uniformly at random from a set of at least $2^\lambda - t - i$ many possible values. The adversary is successful on the ith query (given that all previous attempts were unsuccessful) if the z value of the resulting entry in T matches the target value τ. The probability of this event is at most

$$\frac{1}{2^\lambda - (i - 1)}.$$

The success probability of adversary $\mathcal{A}$ after making $\mathsf{q} := \mathsf{q}(\lambda)$ many queries can thus be upper bounded by the probability that in any of the q queries $\mathcal{A}$ is successful. But, in case the adversary is successful, there must also be a first query where it finds the preimage. This allows us to bound the adversary's advantage as

$$\Pr[\mathcal{A} \text{ is successful after } \mathsf{q} \text{ queries}]$$
$$= \Pr[\exists i \in [\mathsf{q}] : \mathcal{A} \text{ successful on } i\text{th query}]$$
$$= \Pr[\exists i \in [\mathsf{q}] : \mathcal{A} \text{ successful on } i\text{th query} \wedge \mathcal{A} \text{ unsuccessful before } i\text{th query}]$$
$$\leq \sum_{i=1}^{\mathsf{q}} \Pr[\mathcal{A} \text{ successful on } i\text{th query} \mid \mathcal{A} \text{ unsuccessful before } i\text{th query}]$$
$$\leq \sum_{i=1}^{\mathsf{q}} \frac{1}{2^\lambda - (i - 1)}$$
$$\leq \frac{\mathsf{q}}{2^\lambda - (\mathsf{q} - 1)}.$$

In case the adversary was not successful after q queries, it can take a final guess which we can simply treat as "one more query." We thus get the following upper bound for the success probability of adversary $\mathcal{A}$:

$$\mathsf{Adv}_{h^\mathsf{E}, \mathcal{A}}^{\mathsf{owf}}(\lambda) \leq \sum_{i=1}^{\mathsf{q}+1} \frac{1}{2^\lambda - (i - 1)} \leq \frac{\mathsf{q} + 1}{2^\lambda - \mathsf{q}}.$$

Again, the bound only makes sense for values $\mathsf{q} < 2^{\lambda-1}$. If we consider only $\mathsf{q} < 2^{\lambda-1}$ and set the advantage to 1 otherwise we can simplify the above and obtain as final bound

$$\mathsf{Adv}_{h^\mathsf{E}, \mathcal{A}}^{\mathsf{owf}}(\lambda) \leq \frac{\mathsf{q}(\lambda) + 1}{2^{\lambda-1}}. \qquad \square$$

14.1.4 Impossibility of Highly Efficient Constructions

Since block ciphers are usually designed for encrypting many message blocks using the same key, the key schedule is often not tuned for maximum performance as it is evaluated only infrequently. When used in any of the secure PGV constructions this is quite different. Here, the key is always either the current message block, the current chaining value, or the exclusive-or of the two. This, however, means that the block cipher is evaluated on a different key for every message block and thus with every evaluation also the key schedule needs to be computed. Ideally, we would consider a rate-1 construction where the key, as in encryption mode of operations, changes only infrequently such that the key schedule needs to be recomputed rarely. We call such constructions *highly efficient* but, as it turns out, such highly efficient constructions are trivially broken (in the ideal cipher model against unbounded adversaries).

Proving the impossibility result is rather technical and will be omitted here (see the chapter notes for further references). As an intuition for why this is the case, let us revisit an example from the introduction and consider that we want to build a highly efficient compression function $h^E : \{0,1\}^\lambda \times \{0,1\}^\lambda \to \{0,1\}^\lambda$ from a block cipher $E : \{0,1\}^\lambda \times \{0,1\}^\lambda \to \{0,1\}^\lambda$. In the extreme case we would fix the key to a single value in which case the block cipher can be regarded as a permutation $E_k : \{0,1\}^\lambda \to \{0,1\}^\lambda$ for some fixed key k and since the compression function should be highly efficient each call to compression function h^E should induce at most a single call to E_k. Now, there are $2^{2\lambda}$ different inputs to compression function h^E but only 2^λ inputs to E_k. Thus, each input to E_k on average corresponds to 2^λ inputs of h^E or, in other words, for any value $x \in \{0,1\}^\lambda$ there are roughly 2^λ inputs $(m,y) \in \{0,1\}^\lambda \times \{0,1\}^\lambda$ such that during the evaluation of $h^E(m,y)$ a call to $E_k(x)$ is made.

For our attack, note that the decision on which value E_k will be called depends only on the input to h^E. An unbounded adversary can thus find values $x \in \{0,1\}^\lambda$ that maximize the cardinality of the following set:

$$Q(x) := \{(m,y) : E_k(x) \text{ is called during evaluation of } h^E(m,y)\}.$$

If the evaluations of E_k are evenly spread then each value $x \in \{0,1\}^\lambda$ corresponds to exactly 2^λ inputs (m,y) to h^E. If the evaluations are not evenly spread there are some values x which correspond to even more than 2^λ many h^E inputs.

Assume now that as a first step the adversary searches for two values x and x' in $\{0,1\}^\lambda$ such that $|Q(x)| \geq |Q(x')| \geq 2^\lambda$. Note that by the above reasoning these values must exist and, furthermore, for finding them the adversary does not need to make even a single call to its E oracle. Once it has values x and x' it calls its oracle to get values $E_k(x)$ and $E_k(x')$. By construction we now have that the adversary can evaluate h^E on at least $2 \cdot 2^\lambda$ inputs. As this is already more than the number of outputs the (unbounded) adversary must necessarily find a collision with probability 1 with only two calls to E.

Impossibility of Efficient Permutation-Based Constructions

In the above example we considered a block cipher with a fixed key. This is, of course, equivalent to a permutation $\pi : \{0,1\}^\lambda \to \{0,1\}^\lambda$, and the above impossibility result thus carries over to highly efficient constructions from permutations. These are constructions of only a few permutations where per invocation of the compression function only a single permutation is evaluated.

Remark 14.6. The impossibility result rules out highly efficient constructions mapping 2λ-bit inputs to λ-bit outputs from permutations of the form $\pi : \{0,1\}^\lambda \to \{0,1\}^\lambda$. It does, however, not rule out constructions that make multiple permutation calls per compression function call (constructions with rate $r < 1$) nor constructions from wide permutations, that is, permutations on 2λ bits or more. Note that in this case the counting argument used above no longer applies.

14.1.5 Double Block-Length Compression Functions

The PGV compression functions we have studied above are so-called *single block-length* compression functions, meaning that the function's output length matches the block length of the underlying block cipher. Given a block cipher with a block length of λ bits we thus obtain a compression function with λ-bit output. The best possible collision security we can expect in this case is given by the birthday bound (Section 4.1.2; page 165), which states that an adversary will find collisions with good probability after roughly $2^{\lambda/2}$ steps. For the PGV functions the bound that we obtained in Theorem 14.3 is slightly worse, and after $2^{\lambda/2}$ we should expect the adversary to have found a collision with probability close to 1.

Somewhat regrettably, most real-world block ciphers work with relatively small block lengths which usually do not exceed 128 bits. For example, AES, RC5, RC6, and Twofish use 128-bit blocks, while DES, IDEA, or Blowfish use block lengths of only 64 bits. While short block lengths are in most cases not a problem for encryption schemes, short block lengths are a no-go as the basis of single block-length compression functions: A single block-length compression function instantiated with a block cipher using 128-bit blocks is trivially broken as the best case security against collision attacks is less than 64 bits.

As a result, existing block ciphers are rarely used in real-world hash function constructions. This, however, does not mean that real-world constructions do not use block ciphers in their design. On the contrary, as we will see in Chapter 15, the functions MD5, SHA-1, and SHA-2 can be regarded as Davies–Meyer constructions. Also, many of the SHA-3 candidates used block-cipher-based designs. The finalist *Skein*, for example, is based on the block cipher Threefish, a block cipher that was designed as part of Skein and which in Skein is turned into a compression function using a variant of the Matyas–Meyer–Oseas construction (Construction 1 in Figure 14.7).

An alternative to using dedicated designs is to consider more complex compression function constructions with longer output lengths, which we discuss in the following.

Double Block-Length Compression Functions

In contrast to single block-length (SBL) compression functions a double block-length (DBL) function has output length 2λ when instantiated with a block cipher using λ-bit blocks. Thus, the optimal security bounds we can expect would be 2^λ for collision resistance and $2^{2\lambda}$ for preimage resistance. Consequently, when based on AES we could, in theory, obtain security against collision-finding attacks of up to 128 bits.

Regrettably, as with single block-length functions we cannot hope to construct highly efficient schemes for DBL constructions. For SBL compression functions highly efficient meant that only a small number of distinct keys are used for block cipher evaluations (see page 561). For DBL functions it can be shown that most rate-1 constructions will not provide better security than optimal single block-length schemes.[5] It is thus not surprising that most double block-length constructions have a rate of $\frac{1}{2}$ or lower.

Most double block-length compression functions map 3λ inputs to 2λ outputs, and this is also the form that we will focus on in the following. When iterating a compression function the output of one call becomes the chaining value for the next call and thus a DBL compression function is of the form $h : \{0,1\}^\lambda \times \{0,1\}^{2\lambda} \to \{0,1\}^{2\lambda}$: they process message blocks of length λ and have a state size (chaining value size) of 2λ.

We can categorize DBL constructions broadly into two categories based on the type of block cipher they require:

DBL_λ Double block-length constructions of the DBL_λ type are based on the same type of block ciphers as the PGV functions. That is, the underlying block cipher $\mathsf{E} : \{0,1\}^\lambda \times \{0,1\}^\lambda \to \{0,1\}^\lambda$ processes messages of length λ bits while using keys of λ bits.

$\mathrm{DBL}_{2\lambda}$ Double block-length constructions of the $\mathrm{DBL}_{2\lambda}$ type are based on block ciphers with key size 2λ. That is, the underlying block cipher E is of the form $\mathsf{E} : \{0,1\}^{2\lambda} \times \{0,1\}^\lambda \to \{0,1\}^\lambda$.

---

[5] Note that rate-1 double block-length constructions still make at least two block cipher calls per compression function invocation. To achieve rate 1 the compression function needs to work on message blocks twice the length of the block length of the underlying block cipher.

MDC-2(m_i, y_i)

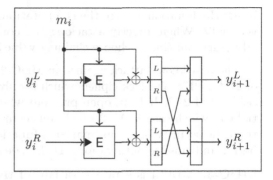

// split state in left and right half
1 : $y_i^L = y_i[1..\lambda]$
2 : $y_i^R = y_i[\lambda + 1..2\lambda]$
    // Compute Matyas–Meyer–Oseas
3 : $v_L = \mathsf{E}(y_i^L, m_i) \oplus m_i$
4 : $v_R = \mathsf{E}(y_i^R, m_i) \oplus m_i$
    // Reorder the outputs
5 : $y_{i+1}^L = v_L[1..\lambda/2] \| v_R[\lambda/2 + 1..\lambda]$
6 : $y_{i+1}^R = v_R[1..\lambda/2] \| v_L[\lambda/2 + 1..\lambda]$
7 :   **return** $y_{i+1}^L \| y_{i+1}^E$

Fig. 14.8: The MDC-2 compression function as pseudocode and schematic. MDC-2 maps 3λ bits to 2λ bits using a block cipher E with block size λ and key size λ. MDC-2 splits the chaining value into two λ-bit halves. As a first step the Matyas–Meyer–Oseas function is computed independently for both halves of the chaining value with the same message block. The final result is then constructed by reordering these intermediate results.

While a large body of research exists on double block-length constructions we will here content ourself with giving a few examples. The reason is that DBL constructions become very complex—consider, for example, Figures 14.8 and 14.9—and formal analyses are long, technical, and difficult to obtain in the first place. The interested reader will find further reading materials in the notes and reference section of this chapter.

MDC-2. Figure 14.8 contains the pseudocode and a schematic of the MDC-2 compression function. MDC-2—short for *Modification Detection Code 2* and also known as the *Meyer–Schilling compression function* (after the first authors to describe them in a paper)—is a DBL$_\lambda$-type function, meaning that the underlying block cipher takes keys of length λ bits. As most DBL-type functions, MDC-2 splits the chaining value into two halves. Each half is then processed in parallel by a Matyas–Meyer–Oseas compression function (see Figure 14.7a) to produce two intermediate results which are then mixed to compute the final output of the MDC-2 function.

Due to the parallel nature of MDC-2, we can find collisions for the MDC-2 compression function in time $2^{\lambda/2}$ and thus in time comparable to optimal SBL constructions such as Matyas–Meyer–Oseas. To see that this is the case, note that any collision (m, y) and (m', y') for the Matyas–Meyer–Oseas compression function induces a collision on MDC-2. For this we simply need to duplicate the chaining value. That is, if (m, y) and (m', y') collide for Matyas–Meyer–Oseas then $(m, y\|y)$ and $(m', y'\|y')$ form a collision for MDC-2.

Interestingly, when used in an iteration scheme such as Merkle–Damgård it can be shown that the resulting hash function has a collision security of at least $2^{3\lambda/5}$. The reason that the function is more secure when used in the iteration scheme is that an adversary has much less control over the chaining values inside the iteration as here the computation starts with a fixed initialization vector IV. When directly attacking the compression function, however, an adversary can simply choose chaining values.

The best known attack against an MDC-2 hash function takes in the order of 2^{124} for 128-bit block ciphers which is only slightly better than the optimal security of 2^{128}. It is an open problem whether the lower bound of $2^{3\lambda/5}$ is tight in which case MDC-2's collision security would only be slightly better than the security of an optimal SBL function, or whether it is in fact a lot better and close to optimal for a DBL-type compression function.

MDC-4. MDC-4 is a rate $\frac{1}{4}$ variant of the MDC-2 compression function that makes four calls to the underlying block cipher. MDC-4 can be regarded as a sequential execution of two MDC-2 functions where the original chaining values are used as message inputs for the second MDC-2. Similar observations on the collision resistance of MDC-4 apply. When used in an iteration scheme the resulting hash function has a collision security of at least $2^{5\lambda/8}$, which slightly improves upon the bound for MDC-2. Again, it is not known whether the bound is tight.

DBL$_{2\lambda}$-type functions. Figure 14.9 contains three examples of rate $\frac{1}{2}$ DBL$_{2\lambda}$-type functions that are based on block ciphers with λ-bit message blocks and 2λ-bit keys. Similarly to MDC-2 and MDC-4, all three are constructed based on well-known SBL compression functions. The Hirose function is based on Matyas–Meyer–Oseas, while both Tandem-DM and Abreast-DM, as the names suggest, are based on Davies–Meyer. All three functions also split the chaining values into two halves, but in contrast to MDC-2 both chaining value halves are used in each of the block cipher calls. All three functions have been shown to yield nearly optimal security for collision resistance and preimage resistance in the ideal cipher model.

14.2 Number-Theoretic Constructions

Number-theoretic constructions play an important practical role for various cryptographic primitives. As an example, think of RSA-based encryption or signature schemes or Diffie–Hellman-based key exchange. When it comes to practical hash functions, on the other hand, number-theoretic constructions only play a minor role. They are mostly used as validation of concepts to, for example, verify that we can construct collision-resistant (compression) functions from reasonable and well-studied assumptions. Where number-theoretic constructions can provide an edge over other designs is when we exploit additional properties present in the underlying structure in order to "enhance" hash functions. Towards the end of this chapter we will present so-called *chameleon hashes* that do exactly this and which can be constructed from number-theoretic assumptions.

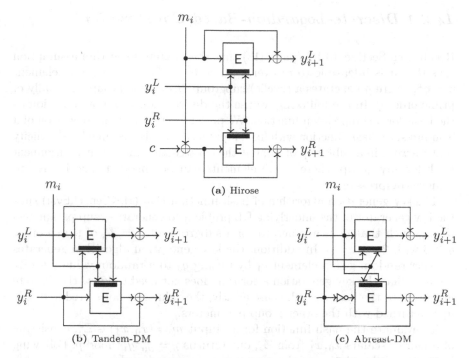

Fig. 14.9: Three double block-length compression functions $h^E : \{0,1\}^\lambda \times \{0,1\}^{2\lambda} \to \{0,1\}^{2\lambda}$ based on block ciphers of the form $E : \{0,1\}^{2\lambda} \times \{0,1\}^\lambda \to \{0,1\}^\lambda$. That is, the compression functions map 3λ bits to 2λ bits using a block cipher with block length λ and key size 2λ. All functions treat the chaining value as being split into two halves above denoted by y^L and y^R. All wires in the above schematics hold λ-bit values. In the schematics the 2λ-bit keys for block ciphers E are denoted by the black rectangle; the two inputs are concatenated (left to right) to form the key. All three functions are proven optimally secure for collision resistance and preimage resistance in the ideal cipher model. The $\bowtie$ symbol used in Abreast-DM denotes the bitwise complement. Value c in the Hirose construction denotes a fixed constant.

In this section we present two constructions of fixed-input-length hash functions, aka compression functions, and show that the functions are provably collision resistant down to a number-theoretic assumption. Our first construction is based on the *discrete-logarithm problem* which, basically, states that it is hard to compute the logarithm $x = \log_g y$ of $y = g^x$ to some base g. While this problem is easy over the reals it is believed to be infeasible for certain discrete structures, such as the residue classes of the ring of integers. Our second construction will be based on the well-known RSA problem. While RSA is usually associated with encryption or signature schemes we can utilize the underlying structure also for constructing a provably secure hash function. In essence, the RSA problem states that in certain structures finding the eth root of an element is hard. For additional background see Section 10.1 (page 408).

14.2.1 Discrete-Logarithm-Based Construction

Recall from Section 10.1.2 (page 413) that the discrete-logarithm assumption says that it is infeasible to recover a random $x \in \mathbb{Z}_q$ from a group element $y = g^x$, where g generates a (cyclic) subgroup $\mathcal{H}$ of some group $\mathcal{G}$, usually of prime order q. In the following we use the discrete-logarithm assumption as the basis for a compression function. We present here the simplest version of a (compressing) hash function with fixed input size. We also assume for simplicity that we work in a subgroup of $\mathbb{Z}_p^*$, but the construction and security argument work for any group where group elements can be encoded "succinctly" to achieve compression.

The key generation algorithm of hash function $\mathsf{H} = (\mathsf{H.KGen}, \mathsf{H.Eval})$ runs the key generator of the underlying DL problem to generate group parameters $\mathcal{G}, q, g_0$ such that g_0 is a generator of a subgroup of $\mathcal{G} = \mathbb{Z}_p^*$ of prime order $q \geq 3$ with $2q + 1 = p$. In addition, the key generation algorithm generates another random group element g_1 by raising g_0 to a random value $z \leftarrow\!\!\$ \, \mathbb{Z}_q$. We note that the key generation algorithm does not need to know the discrete logarithm to the base g_0 and, consequently, the value z is not stored and only g_1 is returned with the other group parameters.

To evaluate the hash function for an input $m = (x_0, x_1) \in \mathbb{Z}_q^2$, consisting of a pair of scalars x_0, x_1 from $\mathbb{Z}_q$, one returns $y = g_0^{x_0} g_1^{x_1} \bmod p$. Following is a detailed description of the construction as pseudocode:

Construction 14.7 (Discrete-Logarithm-Based Hash Function).
Let $\mathsf{DL} = (\mathsf{DL.KGen}, \mathsf{DL.Eval})$ *be an instance of the discrete-logarithm problem (Definition 10.7 on page 414). Then we define hash function* $\mathsf{H} := (\mathsf{H.KGen}, \mathsf{H.Eval})$ *as*

$\mathsf{H.KGen}(1^\lambda)$	$\mathsf{H.Eval}(hk, m)$
1: $(\mathbb{Z}_p^*, q, g_0) \leftarrow\!\!\$ \, \mathsf{DL.KGen}(1^\lambda)$	*1:* $(\mathbb{Z}_p^*, q, g_0, g_1) \leftarrow parse \; hk$
2: $z \leftarrow\!\!\$ \, \mathbb{Z}_q$	*2:* $(x_0, x_1) \leftarrow parse \; m \quad /\!\!/ \; (x_0, x_1) \in \mathbb{Z}_q^2$
3: $g_1 \leftarrow g_0^z \bmod p \quad /\!\!/ \; via \; Eval$	*3:* $y \leftarrow g_0^{x_0} g_1^{x_1} \bmod p$
4: $hk \leftarrow\!\!\$ \, (\mathbb{Z}_p^*, q, g_0, g_1)$	*4:* **return** y
5: **return** hk	

Compressing. Recall that the input space is of size q^2 which, by assumption is larger than p (as $q \geq 3$ and $2q + 1 = p$). Hence, the function is compressing, as required for a hash function. If we use the standard string encoding for integers and noting that values from $\mathbb{Z}_q$ have between $|q|$ and $|q| - 1$ bits, then our function maps at least $2(|q| - 1)$ input bits to at most $|p| \leq |q| + 1$ outputs bits, and therefore also compresses in terms of string representations.

Security. In the following we show that our above construction is collision resistant given that the underlying discrete-logarithm problem is hard:

> **Proposition 14.8.** *Assume that the discrete-logarithm assumption (Definition 10.7) for* $\mathsf{DL} = (\mathsf{DL.KGen}, \mathsf{DL.Eval})$ *holds. Then hash function* H *as defined in Construction 14.7 is compressing and collision resistant.*

To prove Proposition 14.8 we present a reduction from an alleged collision finder to a solver for the discrete-logarithm problem

Proof. Assume that there exists an adversary $\mathcal{C}$ against the hash function. In particular, with non-negligible probability, adversary $\mathcal{C}$ is able to find distinct inputs $(x_0, x_1), (x_0', x_1') \in \mathbb{Z}_q$ which map to the same hash value under H. We show how to use $\mathcal{C}$ to build a discrete-log finder $\mathcal{D}^{\mathcal{C}}$.

Algorithm $\mathcal{D}^{\mathcal{C}}$ gets as input the group information $(\mathbb{Z}_p^*, q, g)$ as well as a target value $y \in \mathbb{Z}_q$. Its task is to find the discrete logarithm of y to g, that is, value z^* such that $g^{z^*} = y \bmod p$. To this end it sets $g_0 \leftarrow g$ and $g_1 \leftarrow y$ and constructs a hash key as $\mathsf{hk} \leftarrow (\mathbb{Z}_p^*, q, g_0, g_1)$. It then calls collision finder $\mathcal{C}$ on input the constructed hash key hk. First note that target value y constructed by the challenger by evaluating g^z for z chosen uniformly at random in $\mathbb{Z}_q$. It thus follows that the simulation of $\mathcal{C}$ is perfect in the sense that key hk as created by algorithm $\mathcal{D}^{\mathcal{C}}$ is distributed identically to an honestly generated key.

If collision finder $\mathcal{C}$ is successful and produces a collision

$$(x_0, x_1) \neq (x_0', x_1') \leftarrow\!\!\$\ \mathcal{C}(\mathsf{hk})$$

then algorithm $\mathcal{D}^{\mathcal{C}}$ can exploit the fact that an admissible collision satisfies

$$g_0^{x_0} g_1^{x_1} = g_0^{x_0'} g_1^{x_1'} \bmod p.$$

Here note that hash key hk was constructed as $(\mathbb{Z}_p^*, q, g_0, g_1)$ with $g_0 = g$ (the generator of the underlying discrete-logarithm problem) and $g_1 = y$ (the target value). The above can be expressed equivalently as

$$g_0^{x_0 - x_0'} = g_1^{x_1' - x_1} \bmod p. \tag{14.5}$$

If the multiplicative inverse of $x_1' - x_1$ in $\mathbb{Z}_q$ exists—which is the case if the difference is not 0 since q is prime—then the computed value $z^* = (x_0 - x_0') \cdot (x_1' - x_1)^{-1} \bmod q$ yields the discrete logarithm of y to g:

$$g^{z^*} = g_0^{z^*} = g_0^{(x_0 - x_0') \cdot (x_1' - x_1)^{-1} \bmod q}$$
$$\overset{(14.5)}{=} g_1^{(x_1' - x_1) \cdot (x_1' - x_1)^{-1} \bmod q} = g_1^1 = y \bmod p.$$

The final step in the proof is to note that an admissible collision $(x_0, x_1) \neq (x_0', x_1')$ cannot be equal in the second component (and the inverse therefore exists if the collision is valid). The reason is that equality $x_1 = x_1' \bmod q$ would necessitate $x_0 \neq x_0' \bmod q$ for a valid collision. But then multiplying the distinct values

$$g_0^{x_0} \neq g_0^{x_0'} \bmod p$$

with $g_1^{x_1} = g_1^{x_1'} \bmod p$ on both sides would result in different hash values:

$$g_0^{x_0} g_1^{x_1} \neq g_0^{x_0'} g_1^{x_1'} \bmod p.$$

In summary, whenever $\mathcal{C}$ succeeds in finding an admissible collision, algorithm $\mathcal{D}$ succeeds in computing the discrete logarithm. In particular, $\mathcal{D}$'s success probability is at least as large as the one of $\mathcal{C}$ and therefore non-negligible, in contradiction to the assumed hardness of the discrete-log problem.   □

14.2.2 Construction Based on the RSA Problem

As a second construction of a compression function from a number-theoretic assumption we present a construction based on the well-known RSA assumption. Recall from Section 10.1.3 (page 415) that the assumption says that it is infeasible to recover $x \in \mathbb{Z}_N^*$ from $y = x^e \bmod N$, even when knowing the public information N and e.

We next describe the RSA-based hash function and give the pseudocode below as Construction 14.9. The key generation algorithm of the hash function $\mathsf{H} = (\mathsf{H.KGen}, \mathsf{H.Eval})$ invokes the key generator of the underlying RSA problem to generate parameters N, e. It also picks a random element $g \leftarrow_\$ \mathbb{Z}_N^*$. The key is then given by the tuple (N, e, g). To compute the hash value for $m = (x, r) \in \mathbb{Z}_e \times \mathbb{Z}_N^*$, one returns $y = g^x r^e \bmod N$ from $\mathbb{Z}_N^*$. Since the input space is by a factor of e larger than the output space, we derive a compressing function.

Construction 14.9 (RSA-Based Hash Function).
Let $\mathsf{RSA} = (\mathsf{RSA.KGen}, \mathsf{RSA.Eval})$ *be an instance of the RSA problem (Definition 10.8; page 416). Then we define hash function* $\mathsf{H} :=$ $(\mathsf{H.KGen}, \mathsf{H.Eval})$ *as*

$\mathsf{H.KGen}(1^\lambda)$	$\mathsf{H.Eval}(\mathsf{hk}, m)$
1: $(N, e) \leftarrow_\$ \mathsf{RSA.KGen}(1^\lambda)$	*1:* $(N, e, g) \leftarrow$ parse hk
2: $g \leftarrow_\$ \mathbb{Z}_N^*$	*2:* $(x, r) \leftarrow$ parse m $/\!/ (x, r) \in \mathbb{Z}_e \times \mathbb{Z}_N^*$
3: $\mathsf{hk} \leftarrow_\$ (N, e, g)$	*3:* $y \leftarrow g^x r^e \bmod N$
4: **return** hk	*4:* **return** y

Security. The proof of security is very similar to the one for the discrete logarithm case.

> **Proposition 14.10.** *Assume that the RSA assumption (Definition 10.8) for* RSA = (RSA.KGen, RSA.Eval) *holds. Then hash function* H *as defined above in Construction 14.9 is compressing and collision resistant.*

Analogously to the case of discrete logarithms for the proof of Proposition 14.10 we again turn a collision finder $\mathcal{C}$ into an adversary $\mathcal{R}$ against the RSA problem.

Proof. Let adversary $\mathcal{C}$ be a collision finder for hash function H. We construct algorithm $\mathcal{R}^{\mathcal{C}}$ to solve the RSA problem as follows. Algorithm $\mathcal{R}^{\mathcal{C}}$ receives as input RSA parameters N, e as well as a value $y \in \mathbb{Z}_N^*$ and its task is to compute the eth root of y. To this end, algorithm $\mathcal{R}^{\mathcal{C}}$ sets $g \leftarrow y$ and uses its challenge value together with the public RSA parameters to construct a hash key hk $\leftarrow (N, e, g)$. It then calls collision finder $\mathcal{C}$ on input the generated hash key. Note that, as in the discrete-logarithm case, the keys generated by the reduction are identically distributed to honestly generated keys. For this note that target value y is constructed by the challenger as $x^e \bmod N$ for value x chosen uniformly at random in $\mathbb{Z}_N^*$. But since the RSA function is one-to-one we have that y is distributed identically to a uniformly random value.

If now collision finder $\mathcal{C}$ produces a valid collision

$$(x, r), (x', r') \leftarrow_{\$} \mathcal{C}(\text{hk})$$

then we can rewrite the collision equation (noting that hk $= (N, e, g)$ where g was set to target value y)

$$g^x r^e = g^{x'} (r')^e \bmod N$$

as

$$g^{x-x'} = (r^{-1} r')^e \bmod N. \tag{14.6}$$

Let us assume $x = x' \bmod e$. This is equivalent to $x = x'$ over the integers for the values x, x' from $\mathbb{Z}_e$ and, consequently, we must have $(r^{-1} r')^e = 1 \bmod N$. Because exponentiation with the prime e is one-to-one over $\mathbb{Z}_N^*$ this can only happen if also $r^{-1} r' = 1 \bmod N$ and thus $r = r' \bmod N$. In this case, however, the whole collision would be trivial (that is, $(x, r) = (x', r')$).

If, on the other hand $x \neq x' \bmod e$, then the difference $x - x'$ (over the integers) lies in the interval $-e + 1, -e + 2, \ldots, e - 1$. It is thus relatively prime to the prime number e and via the extended Euclidean algorithm we can compute $i, j \in \mathbb{Z}$ such that $(x - x') \cdot i + e \cdot j = 1$. Our RSA finder sets

$$x^* \leftarrow (r^{-1} r')^i \cdot g^j \bmod N$$

for the output.

It remains to argue that x^* is, indeed, the eth root of y. For this note that we can rewrite $(x^*)^e$ as follows where the third equality is due to Equation (14.6):

$$(x^*)^e = \left((r^{-1}r')^i \cdot g^j\right)^e$$

$$= \left((r^{-1}r')^e\right)^i \cdot g^{e \cdot j} \stackrel{(14.6)}{=} g^{(x-x') \cdot i} \cdot g^{e \cdot j} = g^{(x-x') \cdot i + e \cdot j} = g^1 = g \bmod N.$$

Because the RSA finder has set $g \leftarrow y$ for its input, it follows that x^* is indeed an eth root of y.

Overall, if $\mathcal{C}$ finds a non-trivial collision, algorithm $\mathcal{R}$ breaks the RSA property. Since the input provided by $\mathcal{R}$ has the same distribution as a genuine input to the collision finder, it follows that the probability of solving the RSA problem is at least as large as the probability to find collisions in the RSA-based hash function.   □

Remark 14.11 (Public/Secret Coins). An interesting difference between the two presented number-theoretic constructions of hash functions can be found in their key generation algorithms. In the discrete-logarithm-based hash function from Section 14.2.1 we generate g_1 as g_0^z and finding collisions means to recover z. In some groups, however, it is possible to generate g_1 without knowing the discrete logarithm with respect to g_0. In this case it would be safe to make the random coins of the key generator public (for example, to publish them alongside the generated key). In the RSA-based case this would render the hash function trivially broken. This is due to the fact that when generating the RSA parameters value N is generated as $N \leftarrow p \cdot q$ for primes p and q, and it is essential for security that factors p and q remain hidden. Given the random coins that were used during key generation it is, of course, trivial to extract the two factors.

This allows us to classify hash function constructions into two groups called *public coin hash functions* (such as the discrete-logarithm-based construction) and *secret coin hash functions*. While any public coin hash function is trivially also a secret coin hash function, a secret coin hash function may not be secure as a public coin hash function, as is the case with the above RSA-based construction. We note that the distinction is meaningful in the sense that the existence of secret coin hash functions does not necessarily imply the existence of public coin hash functions.

14.2.3 Chameleon Hash Functions

The number-theoretic constructions of compression functions in the previous sections are significantly slower than compression functions based on block ciphers, and are therefore seldomly used in practice. Only if one aims to exploit additional properties of the number-theoretic solutions may they be advantageous. For instance, the discrete-logarithm-based compression function displays homomorphic properties when multiplying hash values in the group:

$$H.\text{Eval}(hk, (x_0, x_1)) \cdot H.\text{Eval}(hk, (y_0, y_1))$$
$$= g_0^{x_0} g_1^{x_1} \cdot g_0^{y_0} g_1^{y_1}$$
$$= g_0^{x_0+y_0} g_1^{x_1+y_1}$$
$$= H.\text{Eval}(hk, x_0 + y_0 \bmod q, x_1 + y_1 \bmod q).$$

We discuss here that such homomorphic properties can be used to build so-called *chameleon* hash functions for which one can find collisions easily if given some trapdoor information, and discuss that these chameleon hashes are useful to lift non-adaptively secure signature schemes to adaptively secure ones. For sake of concreteness we only discuss the case of discrete logarithms, RSA-based solutions can be derived analogously.

Chameleon Hash Functions

A chameleon hash function is a probabilistic hash function which takes an input $m \in \{0,1\}^*$, picks some randomness r from some space $\mathcal{R}_{hk}$, and computes the hash value $y = \text{CH.Eval}(hk, m, r)$. The key generation algorithm $\text{CH.KGen}(1^\lambda)$ in addition to the public key hk generates a secret trapdoor key tk. The idea is that, if one knows trapdoor key tk, then one can compute collisions in the sense that, given m, r, and m', one can derive $r' \leftarrow \text{CH.Adapt}(tk, m, r, m')$ such that

$$H.\text{Eval}(hk, m, r) - H.\text{Eval}(hk, m', r').$$

Furthermore, if r is uniform, so is r'. We note that without the trapdoor key the hash function is still collision resistant in the first argument.

Definition 14.12 (Collision-Resistant Chameleon Hash Function). *An efficient chameleon hash function* $\text{CH} = (\text{CH.KGen}, \text{CH.Eval}, \text{CH.Adapt})$ *is called* collision resistant *(CR) if advantage* $\text{Adv}_{\text{CH},\mathcal{A}}^{\text{cr}}(\lambda)$ *is negligible for all* PPT *algorithms* $\mathcal{A}$. *Here, the advantage is defined as*

$$\text{Adv}_{\text{CH},\mathcal{A}}^{\text{cr}}(\lambda) := \Pr\left[\text{Exp}_{\text{CH},\mathcal{A}}^{\text{cr}}(\lambda)\right]$$

relative to experiment $\text{Exp}_{\text{CH},\mathcal{A}}^{\text{cr}}(\lambda)$:

Experiment $\text{Exp}_{\text{CH},\mathcal{A}}^{\text{cr}}(\lambda)$

1: $(hk, tk) \leftarrow_{\$} \text{CH.KGen}(1^\lambda)$

2: $(m_1, r_1, m_2, r_2) \leftarrow_{\$} \mathcal{A}(1^\lambda, hk)$

3: **return** $\text{CH.Eval}(hk, m_1, r_1) = \text{CH.Eval}(hk, m_2, r_2) \wedge m_1 \neq m_2$

We next show how to construct a chameleon hash function under the discrete-logarithm assumption. We present our construction for simplicity for fixed-length inputs $m \in \mathbb{Z}_q$ only; if one uses an upstream (ordinary) collision-resistant hash function to map longer messages to $\mathbb{Z}_q$ first, then the construction below works, too.

Our construction of a chameleon hash function is similar to our earlier discrete-logarithm-based construction with the exception that we now need to generate a trapdoor key. For this we output value z which was used to generate g_1 as $g_1 \leftarrow g_0^z \bmod p$. We give the pseudocode as Construction 14.13 below:

Construction 14.13 (Chameleon Hash Function Based on Discrete Log). *Let* DL $=$ (DL.KGen, DL.Eval) *be an instance of the discrete-logarithm problem (Definition 10.7 on page 414). Then we define chameleon hash function* CH $:=$ (CH.KGen, CH.Eval, CH.Adapt) *as*

CH.KGen(1^λ)

1 : $(\mathbb{Z}_p^*, q, g_0) \leftarrow\!\!\$ \text{ DL.KGen}(1^\lambda)$

2 : $z \leftarrow\!\!\$\ \mathbb{Z}_q^*$

3 : $g_1 \leftarrow g_0^z \bmod p$

4 : $\text{hk} \leftarrow (\mathbb{Z}_p^*, q, g_0, g_1)$

5 : $\text{tk} \leftarrow (\text{hk}, z)$

6 : **return** (hk, tk)

CH.Eval(hk, m, r)

1 : $(\mathbb{Z}_p^*, q, g_0, g_1) \leftarrow parse\ \text{hk}$

2 : $y \leftarrow g_0^m g_1^r \bmod p$ //$\ m, r \in \mathbb{Z}_q$

3 : **return** y

CH.Adapt(tk, m, r, m')

1 : $(\text{hk}, z) \leftarrow parse\ \text{tk}$

2 : $r' \leftarrow z^{-1} \cdot (m - m') + r \bmod q$

3 : **return** r'

Analysis. We first check that the Adapt algorithm satisfies the required properties. For this we have to show that the output r' yields a valid collision and that it is uniform if r is. The latter follows since r' adds the random r to the output. The former holds because

$$g_0^{m'} g_1^{r'} = g_0^{m'} (g_0^z)^{r'} = g_0^{m' + z \cdot r'} = g_0^{m + (m' - m) + z \cdot r} = g_0^{m + z \cdot r} = g_0^m g_1^r \bmod p.$$

Collision resistance follows as for the regular discrete-log-based hash function.

From Non-adaptively to Adaptively Secure Signatures

Let us briefly discuss the most prominent application of chameleon hash functions: upgrading the security of signature schemes from non-adaptive attacks to adaptive attacks. In an adaptive attack (see Definition 6.2 on page 264) the adversary determines the next message m_i after having obtained the signature for the previous message. In a non-adaptive attack we consider a less powerful adversary in the sense that the adversary needs to specify all messages upfront and the adversary only learns all signatures, before trying to create its forgery. Following is a formal definition of non-adaptive security for signature schemes:

Definition 14.14 (Existential Unforgeability under Non-adaptive Chosen-Message Attacks). *A* signature scheme Sig = (Sig.KGen, Sig.Sign, Sig.Vf) *is called* existentially unforgeable under non-adaptive chosen-message attacks *if for any* PPT *algorithm* $\mathcal{A} = (\mathcal{A}_1, \mathcal{A}_2)$ *we have that the advantage* $\mathsf{Adv}_{\mathsf{Sig},\mathcal{A}}^{\text{euf-nacma}}(\lambda)$ *defined as*

$$\mathsf{Adv}_{\mathsf{Sig},\mathcal{A}}^{\text{euf-nacma}}(\lambda) := \Pr\left[\mathit{Exp}_{\mathsf{Sig},\mathcal{A}}^{\text{euf-nacma}}(\lambda)\right]$$

is negligible, and where experiment $\mathit{Exp}_{\mathsf{Sig},\mathcal{A}}^{\text{euf-nacma}}(\lambda)$ *is defined as*

Experiment $\mathit{Exp}_{\mathsf{Sig},\mathcal{A}}^{\text{euf-nacma}}(\lambda)$
---

1 : $(\mathsf{pk},\mathsf{sk}) \leftarrow\!\!\$\ \mathsf{Sig.KGen}(1^\lambda)$

2 : $(m_1,\ldots,m_{\mathsf{q}},\mathsf{state}) \leftarrow\!\!\$\ \mathcal{A}_1(1^\lambda,\mathsf{pk})$

3 : **for** $i = 1..\mathsf{q}$ **do**

4 : $\quad \sigma_i \leftarrow\!\!\$\ \mathsf{Sign}(\mathsf{sk},m_i)$

5 : $(m^*,\sigma^*) \leftarrow\!\!\$\ \mathcal{A}_2(1^\lambda,\mathsf{state},\sigma_1,\ldots,\sigma_{\mathsf{q}})$

6 : **return** $\mathsf{Sig.Vf}(\mathsf{pk},m^*,\sigma^*) = \mathsf{true} \wedge m^* \notin \{m_1,\ldots,m_{\mathsf{q}}\}$

We next discuss that the hash-and-sign approach, where we use a chameleon hash function, suffices to build an adaptively secure signature scheme from a non-adaptive one. Following is the chameleon hash-and-sign construction:

Construction 14.15. *Let* Sig := (Sig.KGen, Sig.Sign, Sig.Vf) *be a signature scheme and* CH := (CH.KGen, CH.Eval, CH.Adapt) *be a chameleon hash function such that* $\mathsf{Sig.il}(\lambda) = \mathsf{H.ol}(\lambda)$, *that is, such that the signature scheme can process messages of the length of hash values. Then the* Chameleon hash-and-sign *scheme is constructed as*

$\mathsf{CHSig.KGen}(1^\lambda)$
---

1 : $(\mathsf{pk},\mathsf{sk}) \leftarrow\!\!\$\ \mathsf{Sig.KGen}(1^\lambda)$

2 : $(\mathsf{hk},\mathsf{tk}) \leftarrow\!\!\$\ \mathsf{CH.KGen}(1^\lambda)$

3 : $\mathsf{chpk} \leftarrow (\mathsf{hk},\mathsf{pk}); \mathsf{chsk} \leftarrow (\mathsf{hk},\mathsf{sk})$

4 : **return** $(\mathsf{chpk},\mathsf{chsk})$

$\mathsf{CHSig.Sign}(\mathsf{chsk},m)$ | $\mathsf{CHSig.Vf}(\mathsf{chpk},m,(r,\sigma_{ch}))$
---

1 : $(\mathsf{hk},\mathsf{sk}) \leftarrow \mathsf{chsk}$ $\qquad$ 1 : $(\mathsf{hk},\mathsf{pk}) \leftarrow \mathsf{chpk}$

2 : $r \leftarrow\!\!\$\ \mathcal{R}_{\mathsf{hk}}$ $\qquad\qquad$ 2 : $y \leftarrow \mathsf{CH.Eval}(\mathsf{hk},m,r)$

3 : $y \leftarrow \mathsf{CH.Eval}(\mathsf{hk},m,r)$ $\quad$ 3 : **return** $\mathsf{Sig.Vf}(\mathsf{pk},y,\sigma_{ch})$

4 : $\sigma_{ch} \leftarrow\!\!\$\ \mathsf{Sig.Sign}(\mathsf{sk},y)$

5 : **return** (r,σ_{ch})

Formally, Construction 14.15 yields the following security guarantee:

> **Proposition 14.16.** *Let* Sig *be a signature scheme that is existentially unforgeable under* non-adaptive *chosen-message attacks and let* CH *be a collision-resistant chameleon hash function. Then Construction 14.15 yields a signature scheme that is existentially unforgeable under* adaptive *chosen-message attacks.*

We only sketch the security of the construction here, since the proof is close to the one for the (non-chameleon) hash-and-sign construction given in Section 6.3 on page 272. The proof is done in two steps. The first step is almost identical to the other case, i.e., one bounds the probability that the adaptive adversary against the scheme in its forgery finds a hash collision for its forgery message m^* (with random input r^*) with some previously queried message m_i (with random input r). Because $m^* \neq m_i$ for a successful forgery, this would yield a collision finder $\mathcal{A}_{\mathsf{CH}}$ against the chameleon hash.

The second step is analogous to the other proof but uses the trapdoor property of the chameleon hash function. In the original proof the adversary has now asked to sign the hash values y_i of the messages. We act accordingly here, but we can create the hash values y_i already at the outset by hashing a fixed message, each time with fresh randomness r_i. When we later learn the adversary's message m_i to be signed, we will adapt the randomness to r_i' such that the message together with this randomness is mapped to the preselected hash value. This is possible since we will now hold the trapdoor key tk of the chameleon hash function.

More formally, we build a reduction $\mathcal{A}_{\mathsf{Sig}} = (\mathcal{A}_{\mathsf{Sig},1}, \mathcal{A}_{\mathsf{Sig},2})$ against the non-adaptive unforgeability of the signature scheme. In the first-stage algorithm $\mathcal{A}_{\mathsf{Sig}_1}$ receives 1^λ and the public key pk of the signer, creates a key pair $(\mathsf{hk}, \mathsf{tk}) \leftarrow\!\!\$\ \mathsf{CH.KGen}(1^\lambda)$, and now hashes $\mathsf{q} := \mathsf{q}(\lambda)$ times a fixed message m_0 to get hash values $y_i \leftarrow \mathsf{CH.Eval}(\mathsf{hk}, m_0, r_i)$ for $r_i \leftarrow\!\!\$\ \mathcal{R}_{\mathsf{hk}}$. Here, q is an upper bound of the number of queries of the adaptive adversary $\mathcal{A}$. The non-adaptive adversary outputs the "messages" $y_1, \dots, y_{\mathsf{q}}$ and $\mathsf{state} = (\mathsf{pk}, \mathsf{hk}, \mathsf{tk}, r_1, \dots, r_{\mathsf{q}})$ in the first stage.

Then $\mathcal{A}_{\mathsf{Sig},2}$ in the second stage receives $\sigma_{ch1}, \dots, \sigma_{ch\mathsf{q}}$ as signatures for the q hash values. The adversary invokes the adaptive adversary $\mathcal{A}$ against the combined scheme for public key $(\mathsf{hk}, \mathsf{pk})$. Every time that adversary makes a signature query about message m_i, our adversary $\mathcal{A}_{\mathsf{Sig},2}$ first looks up in the state the data tk and r_i, then computes $r_i' \leftarrow \mathsf{CH.Adapt}(\mathsf{tk}, m_0, r_i, m_i)$, and returns (r_i', σ_{chi}) to the adversary. When $\mathcal{A}$ finally outputs m^* and (r^*, σ_{ch}^*) as its forgery, $\mathcal{A}_{\mathsf{Sig},2}$ outputs $y^* \leftarrow \mathsf{CH.Eval}(\mathsf{hk}, m^*, r^*)$ and σ_{ch}^* as its own forgery.

By the trapdoor property of the hash function we can conclude that each adapted value r_i' has the same distribution as r in the signature scheme. It follows that, from $\mathcal{A}$'s point of view, the reduction's simulation is perfectly indistinguishable from the actual attack. Finally, we note that the hash value

y^* computed by $\mathcal{A}_{\mathsf{Sig},2}$ does not collide with any of the other hash values $y_1, \ldots, y_{\mathsf{q}}$ and thus constitutes a valid forgery against the signature scheme. But $\mathcal{A}_{\mathsf{Sig}}$ outputs all "messages" to be signed at the beginning and is thus a valid non-adaptive adversary.

Chapter Notes and References

Block ciphers are one of the most basic primitives in modern cryptography. The confusion–diffusion paradigm was introduced by Shannon in his 1945 work "A mathematical theory of cryptography" [39]. Feistel networks are due to Horst Feistel [8], whose work at IBM was the foundation for the Data Encryption Standard (DES). DES was developed at IBM together with the National Security Agency (NSA). It was standardized in 1977 by the National Institute of Standards and Technology (NIST) as FIPS PUB 46 [27]. The standard was revised three times, last in 1999 [30], and finally withdrawn on May 19, 2005. The development of the Advanced Encryption Standard (AES) was initiated by NIST in January 1997 [29]. To find a replacement for DES, NIST decided to hold an open competition which lasted three years [26]. Finalist candidates of the AES competition were MARS, RC6, Rijndael, Serpent, and Twofish, with Rijndael being finally selected as AES on October 2, 2000. AES was standardized by NIST in 2001 as FIPS PUB 197 [31].

The block cipher modes ECB, CBC, CFB, and OFB for the construction of symmetric encryption schemes were first standardized by NIST for use with DES in 1980 [28]. The standard was withdrawn in 2005. Today, standardized modes of operations by NIST are specified in SP 800-38 [32], which includes the modes ECB, CBC, CFB, OFB, and CTR.

As reported for example in [36], block-cipher-based hashing was first proposed by Rabin [37] who suggested to construct a hash function from the DES block cipher as

$$\mathsf{H}(m) := \mathrm{DES}(m_\ell, \mathrm{DES}(\ldots, \mathrm{DES}(m_2, \mathrm{DES}(m_1, \mathsf{IV})))).$$

That is, the message is split into 64-bit blocks and message blocks are used as key in the DES calls. The above can thus be considered as a Merkle–Damgård hash function with DES as compression function.

The first systematic study of block-cipher-based compression functions is due to Preneel, Govaerts, and Vandewalle [36], who in 1993 studied a large class of single block-length compression functions which became known as PGV functions (see Section 14.1.3). Among the considered constructions were the Miyaguchi–Preneel construction—suggested independently by Miyaguchi and Preneel [25, 34], as reported in [34]—the Davies–Meyer construction [46], and the Matyas–Meyer–Oseas construction [20]. The study conducted by

Preneel *et al.* was attack based, that is, they did not prove the security of schemes but instead discussed possible attack vectors. A proof-based analysis of the 64 PGV functions was conducted in 2002 by Black, Rogaway, and Shrimpton [4]. Black *et al.* similar to our treatment in Theorem 14.3 presented their result by presenting proofs for example functions. Stam [41] identified a set of easily verifiable properties that allow to proof collision and preimage resistance (see also Exercise 14.4). A combined paper was published by Black, Rogaway, Shrimpton, and Stam in 2010 [5]. The ideal cipher model that was used by Black *et al.* as the basis for their analysis dates back to Shannon [38]. The impossibility of basing collision resistance on one-wayness was shown by Simon in 1999 [40] (see also Section 4.4.2).

The (im)possibility of highly efficient single block-length compression functions was studied by Black, Cochran, and Shrimpton [2, 3]. The analysis of efficient double block-length compression functions is due to Knudsen, Lai, and Preneel [13, 14]. A generic study of double block-length compression function constructions is given by Özen and Stam [33].

The double block-length constructions Tandem-DM and Abreast-DM were proposed by Lai and Massey in 1992 [17], and Hirose's construction was presented by Hirose in 2007 [11]. Hirose's construction was the first double block-length construction which was accompanied by a proof of collision resistance in the ideal cipher model. The collision resistance of Tandem-DM and Abreast-DM was studied in [18, 10, 19, 9]. A preimage analysis of the schemes was conducted by Armknecht *et al.* [1].

According to Preneel [35], the double block-length constructions MDC-2 and MDC-4 were developed already in the 1980s [24], and MDC-2 has been standardized as ISO/IEC10118-2 [12]. Both MDC-2 and MDC-4 were originally patented by IBM [6]. Collision resistance of MDC-2 was studied by Steinberger [43]. The best known attack on MDC-2 is due to Knudsen *et al.* [15]. The security of MDC-4 was studied by Fleischmann *et al.* [9] and Mennink [22]. The first optimal compression function of type DBL_λ was published by Mennink in 2012 [21, 23].

The tiny encryption algorithm (TEA) was developed by Wheeler and Needham [45]. An article describing attacks on the first version of Microsoft's Xbox including the design and attacks on the TEA-based hash function is given by Steil in [42]. The unsuitability of the IDEA cipher as primitive in block-cipher-based compression function was shown by Wei *et al.* in 2012 [44].

Chameleon hashes were investigated by Rabin and Krawczyk [16]. They are based on the ideas of chameleon blobs [7], which are commitment schemes with the chameleon property.

Exercices

Exercise 14.1. Show that the ECB mode of operation (see Figure 14.1; page 544) for block ciphers does not yield an IND-secure scheme (see Definition 5.2 on page 213).

Exercise 14.2. Formalize encryption and decryption operations for the modes of operations given in Figure 14.1 (page 544). Show that CBC, OFB, CTR, and CFB modes yield IND-CPA-secure schemes (see Definition 5.5; page 219).

Exercise 14.3. Let E be a block cipher that is a pseudorandom permutation (but not necessarily a strong pseudorandom permutation). Show the following statements about CBC-MAC as given in Figure 14.2 (page 545):

- Show that the version given in Figure 14.2 on the left with a fixed initialization vector IV = 0 is a secure message authentication code (see Definition 3.39 on page 151) for fixed-length messages.
- Show that it is not secure when for each new message a random initialization vector IV is chosen that is XORed onto the first message.
- Show that the version given in Figure 14.2 on the right where initialization vector IV is chosen as IV $\leftarrow$ E(k, $|m|$) is a secure message authentication code also for variable-length messages.

Exercise 14.4. Show that all twelve secure PGV compression functions (Figure 14.7; page 556) are collision resistant, that is, prove Theorem 14.3. Instead of giving a proof for each of the compression functions consider the generic decomposition of a rate-1 compression function given in Figure 14.4 (page 553) and show that any such compression function fulfilling the following three properties is collision resistant:

P1 Function f_1 is a bijection.
P2 For any fixed pair $(m, y) \in \{0, 1\}^\lambda \times \{0, 1\}^\lambda$ function $f_2(m, y, \cdot)$ is a bijection.
P3 As with property **P1** function f_1 is bijective we can define f^* as

$$f^*(k, x, c) := f_2(m, y, c)$$

for $(m, y) = f_1^{-1}(k, x)$. Property **P3** holds if for any fixed pair $(k, c) \in \{0, 1\}^\lambda \times \{0, 1\}^\lambda$ function $f^*(k, \cdot, c)$ is a bijection.

Additionally show that all twelve secure PGV functions fulfill the above properties.

Exercise 14.5. Show that all twelve secure PGV compression functions (Figure 14.7; page 556) are preimage resistant, that is, prove Theorem 14.5 (page 560).

Exercise 14.6. Show that there are signature schemes which are existentially unforgeable under non-adaptive chosen-message attacks, but can be broken easily in adaptive attacks.

Exercise 14.7. Define a hash function analogously to the discrete-logarithm-based one (Construction 14.7; page 568), but this time let $\mathsf{H.Eval}(\mathsf{hk}, x_0, x_1, x_2) = g_0^{x_0} g_1^{x_1} g_2^{x_2} \bmod p$ for another generator $g_2 \leftarrow g_0^{z'}$. Show that this hash function, too, is collision resistant.

Chapter Bibliography

1. Frederik Armknecht, Ewan Fleischmann, Matthias Krause, Jooyoung Lee, Martijn Stam, and John P. Steinberger. The preimage security of double-block-length compression functions. In Dong Hoon Lee and Xiaoyun Wang, editors, *Advances in Cryptology – ASIACRYPT 2011*, volume 7073 of *Lecture Notes in Computer Science*, pages 233–251, Seoul, South Korea, December 4–8, 2011. Springer, Heidelberg, Germany.
2. John Black, Martin Cochran, and Thomas Shrimpton. On the impossibility of highly-efficient blockcipher-based hash functions. In Ronald Cramer, editor, *Advances in Cryptology – EUROCRYPT 2005*, volume 3494 of *Lecture Notes in Computer Science*, pages 526–541, Aarhus, Denmark, May 22–26, 2005. Springer, Heidelberg, Germany.
3. John Black, Martin Cochran, and Thomas Shrimpton. On the impossibility of highly-efficient blockcipher-based hash functions. *Journal of Cryptology*, 22(3):311–329, July 2009.
4. John Black, Phillip Rogaway, and Thomas Shrimpton. Black-box analysis of the block-cipher-based hash-function constructions from PGV. In Moti Yung, editor, *Advances in Cryptology – CRYPTO 2002*, volume 2442 of *Lecture Notes in Computer Science*, pages 320–335, Santa Barbara, CA, USA, August 18–22, 2002. Springer, Heidelberg, Germany.
5. John Black, Phillip Rogaway, Thomas Shrimpton, and Martijn Stam. An analysis of the blockcipher-based hash functions from PGV. *Journal of Cryptology*, 23(4):519–545, October 2010.
6. Bruno O Brachtl, Don Coppersmith, Myrna M Hyden, Stephen M Matyas Jr, Carl HW Meyer, Jonathan Oseas, Shaiy Pilpel, and Michael Schilling. Data authentication using modification detection codes based on a public one way encryption function, 1987. US Patent 4,908,861. Awarded March 13, 1990 (filed August 28, 1987).
7. Gilles Brassard, David Chaum, and Claude Crépeau. Minimum disclosure proofs of knowledge. *J. Comput. Syst. Sci.*, 37(2):156–189, 1988.
8. Horst Feistel. Cryptography and computer privacy. *Scientific American*, 228(5):15–23, 1973.
9. Ewan Fleischmann, Christian Forler, and Stefan Lucks. The collision security of MDC-4. In Aikaterini Mitrokotsa and Serge Vaudenay, editors, *AFRICACRYPT 12: 5th International Conference on Cryptology in Africa*, volume 7374 of *Lecture Notes in Computer Science*, pages 252–269, Ifrance, Morocco, July 10–12, 2012. Springer, Heidelberg, Germany.
10. Ewan Fleischmann, Michael Gorski, and Stefan Lucks. Security of cyclic double block length hash functions. In Matthew G. Parker, editor, *12th IMA International Conference on Cryptography and Coding*, volume 5921 of *Lecture Notes in Computer Science*, pages 153–175, Cirencester, UK, December 15–17, 2009. Springer, Heidelberg, Germany.

11. Shoichi Hirose. Some plausible constructions of double-block-length hash functions. In Matthew J. B. Robshaw, editor, *Fast Software Encryption – FSE 2006*, volume 4047 of *Lecture Notes in Computer Science*, pages 210–225, Graz, Austria, March 15–17, 2006. Springer, Heidelberg, Germany.

12. ISO/IEC. 10118-2:1994: Information technology — Security techniques — Hash-functions — part 2: Hash-functions using an n-bit block cipher, 1994. Last revised 2010.

13. Lars R. Knudsen and Xuejia Lai. New attacks on all double block length hash functions of hash rate 1, including the parallel-DM (rump session). In Alfredo De Santis, editor, *Advances in Cryptology – EUROCRYPT'94*, volume 950 of *Lecture Notes in Computer Science*, pages 410–418, Perugia, Italy, May 9–12, 1995. Springer, Heidelberg, Germany.

14. Lars R. Knudsen, Xuejia Lai, and Bart Preneel. Attacks on fast double block length hash functions. *Journal of Cryptology*, 11(1):59–72, January 1998.

15. Lars R. Knudsen, Florian Mendel, Christian Rechberger, and Søren S. Thomsen. Cryptanalysis of MDC-2. In Antoine Joux, editor, *Advances in Cryptology – EURO-CRYPT 2009*, volume 5479 of *Lecture Notes in Computer Science*, pages 106–120, Cologne, Germany, April 26–30, 2009. Springer, Heidelberg, Germany.

16. Hugo Krawczyk and Tal Rabin. Chameleon signatures. In *ISOC Network and Distributed System Security Symposium – NDSS 2000*, San Diego, CA, USA, February 2–4, 2000. The Internet Society.

17. Xuejia Lai and James L. Massey. Hash function based on block ciphers. In Rainer A. Rueppel, editor, *Advances in Cryptology – EUROCRYPT'92*, volume 658 of *Lecture Notes in Computer Science*, pages 55–70, Balatonfüred, Hungary, May 24–28, 1993. Springer, Heidelberg, Germany.

18. Jooyoung Lee and Daesung Kwon. The security of Abreast-DM in the ideal cipher model. Cryptology ePrint Archive, Report 2009/225, 2009. http://eprint.iacr.org/2009/225.

19. Jooyoung Lee, Martijn Stam, and John P. Steinberger. The collision security of tandem-DM in the ideal cipher model. In Phillip Rogaway, editor, *Advances in Cryptology – CRYPTO 2011*, volume 6841 of *Lecture Notes in Computer Science*, pages 561–577, Santa Barbara, CA, USA, August 14–18, 2011. Springer, Heidelberg, Germany.

20. Stephen M Matyas. Generating strong one-way functions with cryptographic algorithm. *IBM Technical Disclosure Bulletin*, 27:5658–5659, 1985.

21. Bart Mennink. Optimal collision security in double block length hashing with single length key. In Xiaoyun Wang and Kazue Sako, editors, *Advances in Cryptology – ASIACRYPT 2012*, volume 7658 of *Lecture Notes in Computer Science*, pages 526–543, Beijing, China, December 2–6, 2012. Springer, Heidelberg, Germany.

22. Bart Mennink. On the collision and preimage security of MDC-4 in the ideal cipher model. *Designs, codes and cryptography*, 73(1):121–150, 2014.

23. Bart Mennink. Optimal collision security in double block length hashing with single length key. *Designs, Codes and Cryptography*, 83(2):357–406, 2017.

24. Carl H Meyer and Michael Schilling. Secure program load with manipulation detection code. In *Proc. Securicom*, volume 88, pages 111–130, 1988.

25. Shoji Miyaguchi, Masahiko Iwata, and Kazuo Ohta. New 128-bit hash function. In *Proc. 4th International Joint Workshop on Computer Communications, Tokyo, Japan*, pages 279–288, 1989.

26. National Institute of Standards and Technology (NIST). Cryptographic standards and guidelines. https://csrc.nist.gov/projects/cryptographic-standards-and-guidelines/archived-crypto-projects/aes-development.

27. National Institute of Standards and Technology (NIST). FIPS PUB 46: Data Encryption Standard (DES). https://csrc.nist.gov/publications/detail/fips/46/archive/1977-01-31, 1 1977.

28. National Institute of Standards and Technology (NIST). FIPS PUB 81: DES modes of operation. https://csrc.nist.gov/publications/detail/fips/81/archive/ 1980-12-02, 12 1980.

29. National Institute of Standards and Technology (NIST). Announcing development of a Federal Information Processing Standard for Advanced Encryption Standard. https://csrc.nist.gov/news/1997/ announcing-development-of-fips-for-advanced-encryp, 01 1997.

30. National Institute of Standards and Technology (NIST). FIPS PUB 46-3: Data Encryption Standard (DES). https://csrc.nist.gov/publications/detail/fips/ 46/3/archive/1999-10-25, 10 1999.

31. National Institute of Standards and Technology (NIST). FIPS PUB 197: Advanced Encryption Standard (AES). https://csrc.nist.gov/publications/ detail/fips/197/final, 11 2001.

32. National Institute of Standards and Technology (NIST). SP 800-38A: Recommendation for block cipher modes of operation: Methods and techniques. https: //csrc.nist.gov/publications/detail/sp/800-38a/final, 11 2001.

33. Onur Özen and Martijn Stam. Another glance at double-length hashing. In Matthew G. Parker, editor, *12th IMA International Conference on Cryptography and Coding*, volume 5921 of *Lecture Notes in Computer Science*, pages 176–201, Cirencester, UK, December 15–17, 2009. Springer, Heidelberg, Germany.

34. Bart Preneel. Analysis and design of cryptographic hash functions. *Ph. D. thesis, Katholieke Universiteit Leuven*, 1993.

35. Bart Preneel. MDC-2 and MDC-4. In Henk C. A. van Tilborg and Sushil Jajodia, editors, *Encyclopedia of Cryptography and Security*, pages 771–772, Boston, MA, 2011. Springer US.

36. Bart Preneel, René Govaerts, and Joos Vandewalle. Hash functions based on block ciphers: A synthetic approach. In Douglas R. Stinson, editor, *Advances in Cryptology – CRYPTO'93*, volume 773 of *Lecture Notes in Computer Science*, pages 368–378, Santa Barbara, CA, USA, August 22–26, 1994. Springer, Heidelberg, Germany.

37. Michael O Rabin. Digitalized signatures. *Foundations of Secure Computation*, pages 155–168, 1978.

38. Claude E Shannon. Communication theory of secrecy systems. *Bell System Technical Journal*, 28(4):656–715, 1949.

39. Claude Elwood Shannon. A mathematical theory of cryptography. *Bell System Technical Memo MM 45-110-02*, 9 1945.

40. Daniel R. Simon. Finding collisions on a one-way street: Can secure hash functions be based on general assumptions? In Kaisa Nyberg, editor, *Advances in Cryptology – EUROCRYPT'98*, volume 1403 of *Lecture Notes in Computer Science*, pages 334–345, Espoo, Finland, May 31 – June 4, 1998. Springer, Heidelberg, Germany.

41. Martijn Stam. Blockcipher-based hashing revisited. In Orr Dunkelman, editor, *Fast Software Encryption – FSE 2009*, volume 5665 of *Lecture Notes in Computer Science*, pages 67–83, Leuven, Belgium, February 22–25, 2009. Springer, Heidelberg, Germany.

42. Michael Steil. 17 mistakes Microsoft made in the Xbox security system. In *22nd Chaos Communication Congress*, 2005.

43. John P. Steinberger. The collision intractability of MDC-2 in the ideal-cipher model. In Moni Naor, editor, *Advances in Cryptology – EUROCRYPT 2007*, volume 4515 of *Lecture Notes in Computer Science*, pages 34–51, Barcelona, Spain, May 20–24, 2007. Springer, Heidelberg, Germany.

44. Lei Wei, Thomas Peyrin, Przemyslaw Sokolowski, San Ling, Josef Pieprzyk, and Huaxiong Wang. On the (in)security of IDEA in various hashing modes. In Anne Canteaut, editor, *Fast Software Encryption – FSE 2012*, volume 7549 of *Lecture Notes in Computer Science*, pages 163–179, Washington, DC, USA, March 19–21, 2012. Springer, Heidelberg, Germany.

45. David J. Wheeler and Roger M. Needham. TEA, a tiny encryption algorithm. In Bart Preneel, editor, *Fast Software Encryption – FSE'94*, volume 1008 of *Lecture Notes in Computer Science*, pages 363–366, Leuven, Belgium, December 14–16, 1995. Springer, Heidelberg, Germany.

46. Robert S. Winternitz. Producing a one-way hash function from DES. In David Chaum, editor, *Advances in Cryptology – CRYPTO'83*, pages 203–207, Santa Barbara, CA, USA, 1983. Plenum Press, New York, USA.

Chapter 15
Iterated Hash Functions in Practice

In the previous chapters we discussed how hash functions can be constructed by iterating fixed-input-length primitives such as compression functions. We now take a brief detour away from the theory of hash functions and instead discuss a few of the most important hash functions used in practice. We note that the material covered here is not relevant for the understanding of the following chapters and could thus be skipped safely. The chapter is also structured somewhat differently: As a big part of this chapter is explaining the history of each presented function we have references inlined throughout the chapter instead of a final notes and references section.

The Era of Hash Functions

In the search for a one-way hash function that was "easy to implement, use, and understand; resistant to cryptographic attack, and ... fast" Ralph Merkle in 1990 proposed Snefru [64], which was broken shortly after by Eli Biham and Adi Shamir [16] using the newly introduced technique of differential cryptanalysis [14, 15]. Around the same time Ronald Rivest published MD4 and MD5 [93, 95] which seemed immune to differential cryptanalysis, which were made available without any license, and which were quickly adopted in a wide variety of applications. Shortly after MD5 was published, the National Institute of Standards and Technology (NIST) published in 1993 the first version of their Secure Hash Algorithm (SHA) as part of the Secure Hash Standard (SHS) [67]. While not explicitly mentioned it looks very much inspired by Rivest's design. In 2002 and again in 2003 NIST extended the standard and added a family of four additional functions which are today usually referred to as SHA-2. Once again in 2012 the standard was updated to add two additional functions to the SHA-2 family.

After practical collision attacks for MD5 [114] and theoretical attacks on SHA-1 [113] were presented in 2005, NIST announced the *SHA-3 Cryptographic Hash Algorithm Competition* [75]. Cryptographic competitions for the design

© Springer Nature Switzerland AG 2021

A. Mittelbach, M. Fischlin, *The Theory of Hash Functions and Random Oracles*,
Information Security and Cryptography, https://doi.org/10.1007/978-3-030-63287-8_15

of new primitives had already yielded good results in the past and produced, for example, the block cipher AES [69]. As part of the SHA-3 competition various new hash functions were proposed before in 2012 KECCAK was selected as SHA-3 [83, 85].

In the following we take a closer look at MD5 and the SHA family of functions.

Remark 15.1. We will consider all indexes in this chapter to be 0-based as this allows easier notation for the "real-world" algorithms presented below. Thus, for example, we break up messages m into $\ell + 1$ blocks as $(m_0, m_1, \ldots, m_\ell) \leftarrow m$ and would address the first bit of the first block as $m_0[0]$.

15.1 MD5

The MD5 hash function—here, MD is short for message digest, not for Merkle–Damgård—was designed by Ronald Rivest at MIT and published as RFC 1321 in 1992 [95]. It is an extension to Rivest's MD4 [93, 94] which was published two years earlier but which was designed for speed and for which security concerns had been raised. Indeed, a collision-finding attack was later presented for MD4 in 1996 [27, 30].

MD5 was made available without a license and (in terms of runtime performance) outperformed block ciphers such as DES. Being "a mere hash function" it was also not subject to export regulations and, thus, MD5 quickly attracted interest from the cryptographic community, in particular, for usage as a building block in other primitives such as message authentication codes [110] (also see Chapter 16). MD5 has been used in numerous applications, and even though it should be considered broken nowadays (see below) it is still widely in use today.

MD2. As the names suggest there have been also functions MD, MD2, and MD3 out of which only MD2, which was optimized for 8-bit machines, was ever published [60, 50, 111]. The design of MD2 is very different from that of MD4 and MD5 and is, in particular, not based on the Merkle–Damgård transformation but instead processes messages byte by byte.

MD6. With MD6 a team led by Rivest published in 2008 a successor to MD5 which was also entered into the SHA-3 competition (see below) [96]. It was designed to allow for highly parallelized computations of hash values in which case the internal computation follows a tree structure. Parallelization can be controlled via a parameter and at the extreme when parallelization is disabled computation follows a Merkle–Damgård-like sequential structure. While no attacks on MD6 were known, a proof for a more performant version with reduced round functions was missing and consequently MD6 did not advance to the second round of the SHA-3 competition. A proof for a reduced round version was subsequently given in 2011 [45].

In the following we take a more detailed look at MD5.

15.1.1 The MD5 Function

MD5 is a Merkle–Damgård hash function using as padding a variant of Merkle–Damgård strengthening where the message length is encoded in the last 64 bits of the last block. Consequently, MD5 supports messages of length at most $2^{64} - 1$ bits.[1] MD5 uses a block size of 512 bits and produces hash values of size 128 bits. Being a standard Merkle–Damgård hash function the size of the internal state is also 128 bits.

The MD5 Compression Function

The compression function is of a dedicated design, meaning that it is not constructed from other cryptographic primitives such as a block cipher. To process a single message block the ingoing state (chaining value) is split up into four words A, B, C, D of 32 bits each and the message block is divided into 16 words of 32 bits. Over the course of 64 iterations grouped into four rounds the message is mixed into the state. Each round uses its own set of constants and non-linear round function. The resulting value consists of again four words A', B', C', D' which are then added (modulo 2^{32}) to the original state A, B, C, D to produce the function's output. A sketch of the compression function is given in Figure 15.2. We give the pseudocode in Figure 15.1.

While the compression function was not built from cryptographic primitives, we can, nevertheless, interpret the function as a block-cipher-based construction. Here, the 64 iterations form a permutation where we can interpret the message block as the block cipher's key. The result is a Davies–Meyer-type compression function (see Section 14.1.3; page 554). Instead of using an XOR operation as in the original Davies–Meyer formulation, MD5 uses an addition modulo 2^{32}.

Remark 15.2. MD4, MD5, as well as SHA-1 and SHA-2 use a so-called ARX design (short for addition, rotation, and exclusive-or (XOR)), meaning that they are built mostly upon addition, rotation, and exclusive-or operations. The use of modular addition has the nice property that it adds extra diffusion through the propagation of carry bits, which is not the case for XOR operations.

---

[1] The RFC [95], indeed, allows input messages of arbitrary length. In the (unlikely) case that a message is longer than $2^{64} - 1$ bits only the low-order 64 bits of the message length should be used as part of the padding operation.

MD5(m)

---

1 : $(K_0, \dots, K_{63}) \leftarrow \dots$ // Initialize 64 32-bit word constants for each iteration
2 : $(s_0, \dots, s_{63}) \leftarrow \dots$ // Initialize shift constants for each iteration
     // Initialization vector IV
3 : $A_0 \leftarrow$ 0x67452301; $B_0 \leftarrow$ 0xefcdab89; $C_0 \leftarrow$ 0x98badcfe; $D_0 \leftarrow$ 0x10325476
     // Pad message and split into 512 bit chunks.
4 : $(m_0, \dots, m_\ell) \leftarrow \mathsf{pad}(m)$
5 :   **for** $i = 0..\ell$ **do**   // Process each message block
6 : $A \leftarrow A_0$; $B \leftarrow B_0$; $C \leftarrow C_0$; $D \leftarrow D_0$
7 : $(m_{i0}, \dots, m_{i15}) \leftarrow m_i$ // Split message block into 16 32-bit chunks
8 :   **for** $j = 0..63$ **do**   // Ingest each message block in 64 iterations into the state
9 :   **if** $0 \le j \le 15$ **then**
10 : $F \leftarrow (B \wedge C) \vee (\neg B \wedge D)$
11 : $g \leftarrow j$
12 :   **elseif** $16 \le j \le 31$ **then**
13 : $F \leftarrow (D \wedge B) \vee (\neg D \wedge C)$
14 : $g \leftarrow (5j + 1) \bmod 16$
15 :   **elseif** $32 \le j \le 47$ **then**
16 : $F \leftarrow B \oplus C \oplus D$
17 : $g \leftarrow (3j + 5) \bmod 16$
18 :   **elseif** $48 \le j \le 63$ **then**
19 : $F \leftarrow C \oplus (B \vee \neg D)$
20 : $g \leftarrow 7j \bmod 16$
21 : $F \leftarrow F \boxplus A \boxplus K_j \boxplus m_{i_g}$
22 : $A \leftarrow D$; $D \leftarrow C$; $C \leftarrow B$; $B \leftarrow B \boxplus (F \lll s_i)$
23 : $A_0 \leftarrow A_0 \boxplus A$; $B_0 \leftarrow B_0 \boxplus B$; $C_0 \leftarrow C_0 \boxplus C$; $D_0 \leftarrow D_0 \boxplus D$
24 :   **return** $A_0 \| B_0 \| C_0 \| D_0$

Fig. 15.1: The MD5 compression function. MD5 depends on 64 32-bit constants K_i and 64 shift amounts s_i set up in lines 1 and 2. The specific values are omitted from this description. Both are used in line 22. The Davies–Meyer structure can nicely be seen in lines 6 and 23 wrapping a permutation in between. That is, indeed, a permutation is more easily seen from the schematic (Figure 15.2) which exhibits the Feistel-like structure. $\boxplus$ denotes addition modulo 2^{32} and $(x \lll s)$ denotes a left rotate of x by s bits. Note that the index for this pseudocode block is 0 based. As a side note, note that the constants when written as low-order bytes first read $A = $ 01234567, $B = $ 89abcdef, $C = $ fedcba98, $D = $ 76543210.

Furthermore, modular addition is not linear and not associative with rotation, bit shifts, or XOR as can be seen by the following equivalence:

$$a \boxplus b = (a \oplus b) \boxplus ((a \wedge b) \ll 1). \tag{15.1}$$

Here, $\boxplus$ denotes modular addition and $\ll s$ a left shift by s bits (i.e., $\ll 1$ denotes a multiplication by 2 modulo 2^n). Basically, the equation decomposes addition into the computation of carry bits $((a \wedge b) \ll 1)$ and the computation of addition of places without overflow $(a \oplus b)$. To see the non-associativity it is easiest to consider an example such as $a = 100$ and $b = 101$ with $\boxplus$

denoting addition modulo 2^3. For the non-linearity note that a function $f(x)$ is linear if it can be written as $f(x) = g(x) + c$ where $+$ denotes addition in the underlying field, c is a scalar, and function g has the property that $g(x + y) = g(x) + g(y)$ and $g(t \cdot x) = t \cdot g(x)$ with t also being a scalar.[2] A function $f(x, y)$ of two arguments is linear (or bilinear) in case both $f(x, t)$ and $f(s, y)$ are linear for any scalars s and t. Now for field $\mathbb{GF}(2^n)$ we have that addition and multiplication are bitwise exclusive-or and bitwise AND. Noting that the right-hand side of Equation (15.1) contains a multiplication of the two arguments (bitwise AND) it follows that function $a \boxplus b$ cannot be linear in $\mathbb{GF}(2^n)$.

Since addition is relatively efficient in software, modular addition is a popular building block in many practical cryptographic schemes. There is, however, also a cost to addition. Adders in hardware are either compact (small in size) or fast but not both. Bitwise Boolean operations such as AND, OR, NOT, or XOR do not have this tradeoff. A second, and maybe more pressing downside is that addition makes cryptanalysis more difficult due to the treatment of carry bits.[3] Bitwise operations are simpler to grasp and formalize. While addition and the ARX design remain a valid and popular tool also in modern designs (for example, the SHA-3 finalists BLAKE [3] and Skein [35] are based on ARX) some modern schemes explicitly bypass the use of addition: Examples are NORX [4] (one of the finalists of the CAESAR competition for authenticated encryption [5]) and KECCAK, the winner of the SHA-3 competition (see Section 15.4).

15.1.2 Attacks on MD5

Being a standard Merkle–Damgård hash function, MD5 is vulnerable to length-extension attacks (see Section 13.1.6).

First weaknesses in the compression function were reported in 1993 [24], and a first collision for the compression function was given by Dobbertin in 1996 [28, 29]. A first full collision for MD5 was published by Wang et al. in 2004 [112], and an attack that reduced the complexity of finding collisions from 2^{64} (trivial birthday bound) to roughly 2^{40} was given in 2005 by Wang and Yu [114]. In follow-up works the complexity for finding random MD5 collisions has been brought down significantly, and today collisions can be found within 2^{16} compression function calls [52, 53, 102, 101, 115, 109, 116].

---

[2] In a strict mathematical sense only g would be linear and f would be affine.

[3] Of course, a scheme that is difficult to analyze also makes it harder for genuine attackers. Such difficulties should, however, never be the source of security of a scheme. On the other hand, if researchers are less inclined to study a scheme due to inherent complexity then, in the worst case, this could lead to an insecure scheme going undetected.

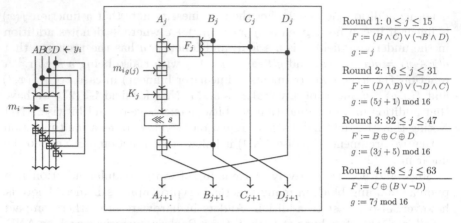

Fig. 15.2: The MD5 compression function. Index i denotes the message block being currently processed, and index j denotes the current iteration. Note that contrary to our usual notation and to be consistent with the notation in RFC 1321 indexes are 0-based. On the left is the Davies–Meyer construction which provides a high-level view onto the MD5 compression function. The extracted MD5 block cipher E takes as key message block m_i and as message chaining value y_i. It consists of 64 iterations grouped into 4 rounds. The iteration function is shown in the middle and is initialized with values $A_0\|B_0\|C_0\|D_0 \leftarrow y_i$. It is of a Feistel type, making the iteration function reversible. The output of block cipher E is $A_{64}\|B_{64}\|C_{64}\|D_{64}$. Non-linear round function F is given on the right. Value K_j for $0 \le j \le 63$ denotes a 32-bit constant. Value m_{i_k} for $0 \le k \le 15$ denotes the kth 32-bit word in message block m_i. $\boxplus$ denotes addition modulo 2^{32}, and $\lll s$ denotes a left bit rotation by s bits.

That collisions for random messages can be used to generate meaningful collisions was shown by Lenstra and de Weger [55], who presented attack scenarios using random collisions as generated by the method of Wang and Yu. In 2006 Gebhardt *et al.* showed how from random collision one can derive meaningful documents in various file formats such as PDF or PostScript that hash to the same value [36]. Chosen-prefix attacks on MD5 were given in 2007 by Stevens *et al.* [107], who also showed how to use their attack to generate pairs of colliding X.509 certificates for different identities.[4] While early chosen-prefix attacks were still taking 2^{50} compression function calls, also this complexity was brought down significantly [109, 108].

In 2007 Stevens *et al.* showed how to use chosen-prefix collisions to mount a Nostradamus-style attack [108]. They prepared 12 documents each of which "predicted" a different candidate as the winner of the 2008 US presidential elections. All 12 documents hash to the same value.

The most notable (known) real-world attack was probably the *Flame malware*, which was discovered in 2012 but which could have been active as early as 2010 [37]. For distribution the malware registered itself as a Microsoft

---

[4] X.509 certificates use a hash-and-sign scheme (see Section 6.3) and are thus vulnerable to second-preimage attacks on the used hash function.

update server, which was possible due to a forged Microsoft code signing certificate that still used MD5 [65].

While collision resistance of MD5 is effectively broken, there are no known practical attacks on preimage resistance. The best known attacks still have a complexity in the range of 2^{123} [99].

15.2 SHA-1

The Secure Hash Algorithms (SHA) are a series of cryptographic hash functions standardized by the National Institute of Standards and Technology (NIST). The first version of SHA—later renamed SHA-0—was published by NIST in 1993 as FIPS PUB 180 [67]. Two years later, NIST discovered weaknesses in SHA-0 (details remain unpublished) which prompted an update under the name SHA-1 [68]. The difference in the function description is minute: a single left rotate by one bit was added to the message schedule; see line 8 in Figure 15.3. That this small change indeed strengthened the function became evident by later attacks on SHA-0 [18] which did not work for SHA-1. While also SHA-1 today is regarded broken, it took a lot longer for researchers before a full collision for SHA-1 was published. A first full collision for SHA-0 was found already in 2004 [12, 13], while for SHA-1 it took another ten years before the first collision was published in 2017 [105]. In 2011 SHA-1 was deprecated by NIST in favor of SHA-2 [78] (and later also of SHA-3 [86]) for applications where collision resistance is a requirement, such as signature generation. As of today, NIST still allows the usage of SHA-1 in protocols such as HMAC (see Chapter 16) whose security is based on other properties [88].

15.2.1 The SHA-1 Function

The design of SHA-1 seems heavily inspired by MD5, which becomes evident especially in the design of the compression function which follows a similar structure and which reuses parts of the round functions and even the constants for the initialization vector from MD5. Similarly to MD5, SHA-1 is a Merkle–Damgård hash function working with a block size of 512 bits but producing slightly larger hash values of 160 bits. As padding function SHA-1 uses the Merkle–Damgård strengthening with the last 64 bits encoding the message length. Following the standard Merkle–Damgård design, the size of the internal state is the same as the size of the final digest and thus 160 bits.

The compression function used in SHA-1 is of a dedicated design but similarly to MD5 can be interpreted as a Davies–Meyer-type construction (with modular addition instead of an exclusive-or) out of a block cipher.[5] To process a single message block the current state (i.e., chaining value) is split into five words of 32 bits each, named A, B, C, D, and E. The message block is then mixed into the state in 80 iterations grouped into four rounds each with a different mixing function and mixing constant. Note that MD5 used a different constant per iteration while SHA-1 only uses a different constant per round.

To ingest a message block, a message schedule picks a different 32-bit word from the message block for each of the 80 iterations.[6] In each iteration the message block is then combined with the current state using one of four mixing constants and one of four non-linear mixing functions. The output after the last iteration yields the final hash value. We present the pseudocode of SHA-1 in Figure 15.3 and a schematic of the compression function (i.e., the iteration function) in Figure 15.4.

15.2.2 Attacks on SHA-1

First cryptanalytical results for SHA-1 were given in 2005 by Biham *et al.* [13], who gave collisions for a round-reduced version of SHA-1 with up to 40 rounds. In the same year Wang *et al.* [113] gave a theoretical attack on full SHA-1 which would take 2^{69} hash operations and which was thus significantly faster than a brute-force attack: With the birthday bound for SHA-1 we should expect collisions via a brute-force attack after roughly 2^{80} hash operations.

While 2^{69} computational steps were practically infeasible, cryptanalytic research focused on round-reduced versions in the following years. De Cannière and Rechberger presented a collision on a 64-round variant of SHA-1 in 2006 [23]. In 2007 De Cannière *et al.* [22] published an attack on 70-round SHA-1 taking roughly 2^{44} hash operations. In 2010 Grechnikov [38] showed how the method by De Cannière *et al.* can be extended to reach 73-round SHA-1 and shortly after, in 2011, Grechnikov and Adinetz presented a collision for a 75-round version of SHA-1 [39] which was computed on a GPU cluster.

In 2013 a new attack on full SHA-1 was published by Stevens *et al.* [103], bringing the computational effort for a full collision down to 2^{61} calls to the compression function and thus into the realm of practical attacks. In 2016 a first full attack on the SHA-1 compression function was presented by Stevens *et al.* [106], and finally in 2017 Stevens *et al.* published the first collision for full SHA-1 [105, 104].

---

[5] The block cipher embedded in the SHA-1 compression function named SHACAL-1 was submitted as a candidate for the NESSIE project but was not amongst the selected finalists [43, 44, 90].

[6] It is this message schedule which is different in SHA-0, which did not contain the additional left-rotate operation (see line 8 in Figure 15.3).

SHA-1(m)

// Initialization vector IV

1 : $A_0 \leftarrow$ 0x67452301; $B_0 \leftarrow$ 0xefcdab89; $C_0 \leftarrow$ 0x98badcfe; $D_0 \leftarrow$ 0x10325476; $E_0 \leftarrow$ 0xc3d2e1f0

// Pad message and split into 512 bit chunks.

2 : $(m_0, \ldots, m_\ell) \leftarrow \mathsf{pad}(m)$

3 : **for** $i = 0..\ell$ **do** // Process each message block

4 : $A \leftarrow A_0$; $B \leftarrow B_0$; $C \leftarrow C_0$; $D \leftarrow D_0$; $E \leftarrow E_0$

  // Set up message schedule and pick one 32 bit word for each iteration.

6 : $(m_{i0}, \ldots, m_{i\,15}) \leftarrow m_i$

7 :   **for** $j = 16..79$ **do**

8 : $m_{ij} \leftarrow (m_{ij-3} \oplus m_{ij-8} \oplus m_{ij-14} \oplus m_{ij-16}) \lll 1$ // SHA-1 added $\lll$ 1 here

9 :   **for** $j = 0..79$ **do** // Ingest each message block in 80 iterations into the state

10 :   **if** $0 \leq j \leq 19$ **then**

11 : $F \leftarrow (B \wedge C) \vee (\neg B \wedge D)$

12 : $K \leftarrow$ 0x5a827999

13 :   **elseif** $20 \leq j \leq 39$ **then**

14 : $F \leftarrow B \oplus C \oplus D$

15 : $K \leftarrow$ 0x6ed9eba1

16 :   **elseif** $40 \leq j \leq 59$ **then**

17 : $F \leftarrow (B \wedge C) \vee (B \wedge D) \vee (C \wedge D)$

18 : $K \leftarrow$ 0x8f1bbcdc

19 :   **elseif** $60 \leq j \leq 79$ **then**

20 : $F \leftarrow B \oplus C \oplus D$

21 : $K \leftarrow$ 0xca62c1d6

22 : $F \leftarrow E \boxplus F \boxplus (A \lll 5) \boxplus m_{ij} \boxplus K$

23 : $E \leftarrow D$; $D \leftarrow C$; $C \leftarrow B \lll 30$; $B \leftarrow A$; $A \leftarrow F$

24 : $A_0 \leftarrow A_0 \boxplus A$; $B_0 \leftarrow B_0 \boxplus B$; $C_0 \leftarrow C_0 \boxplus C$; $D_0 \leftarrow D_0 \boxplus D$; $E_0 \leftarrow E_0 \boxplus E$

25 : **return** $A_0 \| B_0 \| C_0 \| D_0 \| E_0$

Fig. 15.3: The SHA-1 compression function. SHA-1 is very similar to MD5. For example, the first 4 words of the initialization value are identical and so are some of the round functions F. In contrast to MD5 (see Figure 15.1), SHA-1 only uses a single constant K per round rather than per iteration. The single change between SHA-0 and SHA-1 is the left rotate by one bit in line 8. $\boxplus$ denotes addition modulo 2^{32}, and $(x \lll s)$ denotes a left rotate of x by s bits. Note that the index for this pseudocode block is 0 based.

After the first collision had been published for MD5 it only took a few years until practical attacks were shown to be reasonable (see Section 15.1.2). We can thus expect real-world attacks on SHA-1 in the upcoming years. With chosen-prefix collisions computable with a complexity of between $2^{66.9}$ and $2^{69.4}$, Leurent and Peyrin recently took the first step [56].

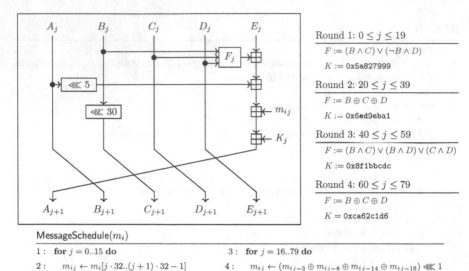

Round 1: $0 \leq j \leq 19$
$F := (B \wedge C) \vee (\neg B \wedge D)$
$K := \text{0x5a827999}$

Round 2: $20 \leq j \leq 39$
$F := B \oplus C \oplus D$
$K := \text{0x6ed9eba1}$

Round 3: $40 \leq j \leq 59$
$F := (B \wedge C) \vee (B \wedge D) \vee (C \wedge D)$
$K := \text{0x8f1bbcdc}$

Round 4: $60 \leq j \leq 79$
$F := B \oplus C \oplus D$
$K = \text{0xca62c1d6}$

MessageSchedule(m_i)

1 : **for** $j = 0..15$ **do**   3 : **for** $j = 16..79$ **do**

2 : $m_{ij} \leftarrow m_i[j \cdot 32..(j+1) \cdot 32 - 1]$ 4 : $m_{ij} \leftarrow (m_{ij-3} \oplus m_{ij-8} \oplus m_{ij-14} \oplus m_{ij-16}) \lll 1$

Fig. 15.4: The SHA-1 iteration function. The SHA-1 compression function, similarly to MD5, can be regarded as a Davies–Meyer compression function (see Figure 15.2 on the left). The iteration function works on a 160-bit state split into five 32-bit words and is of a Feistel type, making the iteration reversible. The difference between SHA-0 and SHA-1 is in the message schedule. SHA-0 does not have the left rotate in line 4. ⊞ denotes addition modulo 2^{32}, and $\lll$ s denotes a left bit rotation by s bits.

15.3 SHA-2

In 2002 NIST extended its *Secure Hash Standard* and published three new hash functions that are commonly referred to as SHA-2: SHA-256, SHA-384, and SHA-512 [70], where the suffix describes the output length of the corresponding function. Two years later SHA-224 was added in a change notice [71], which is a truncated version of SHA-256 but which uses a different initialization vector. The third revision of the standard was published in 2008, which now officially included also SHA-224 [76]. Finally, in 2012 two additional functions were added to the family [81]: SHA-512/256 and SHA-512/224, where the value 512 indicates that these versions use a 512-bit internal state.[7] The latest revision was published in 2015 [84], referencing the newly created SHA-3 standard which was published separately as FIPS 202 [85]. Note that both standards FIPS 202 and FIPS 180 coexist and that, in particular, SHA-3 is not seen as a replacement for SHA-2. NIST currently approves all SHA-2 versions as well as SHA-3. For guidelines on the usage of SHA-2 in practice see [82].

---

[7] The standard especially mentions and approves the two version SHA-512/224 and SHA-512/256 but actually specifies a generic method of generating functions SHA-512/t for $t < 512$ and $t \neq 384$. For the case of $t = 384$ SHA-384 should be used instead.

Algorithm	Message size	Block size	Word size	State size	Output size
SHA-1	$< 2^{64}$	512	32	160	160
SHA-224	$< 2^{64}$	512	32	256	224
SHA-256	$< 2^{64}$	512	32	256	256
SHA-384	$< 2^{128}$	1024	64	512	384
SHA-512	$< 2^{128}$	1024	64	512	512
SHA-512/224	$< 2^{128}$	1024	64	512	224
SHA-512/256	$< 2^{128}$	1024	64	512	256

Table 15.1: An overview of the hash functions standardized by NIST in FIPS 180 [84]. All sizes are in bits.

15.3.1 The SHA-2 Functions

The SHA-2 functions, like SHA-1 and MD5, are Merkle–Damgård functions using a dedicated compression function design which, however, can be regarded as a variant of the Davies–Meyer compression function using modulo addition rather than an exclusive-or.[8] Table 15.1 provides an overview over the parameters of the six SHA-2 functions.

The six SHA-2 functions can be grouped into two larger groups: one with SHA-256 as basis and one with basis SHA-512. The first group contains SHA-256 and SHA-224 and is based, as SHA-1, on 32-bit word operations using a message block size of 512 bits and an internal state of 256 bits. As padding, Merkle–Damgård strengthening is used with a reserved width of 64 bits for the message length. SHA-256 and SHA-224 thus support a theoretical maximum message length of $2^{64} - 1$ bits.

The second group of functions contains SHA-384, SHA-512, SHA-512/256, and SHA-512/224. The functions are based on 64-bit word operations and use a message block length of 1024 bits and an internal state of 512 bits. They, similarly, use Merkle–Damgård strengthening yet encode the message length in 128 bits. The theoretical maximum message length is thus $2^{128} - 1$ bits.

SHA-224 is based on SHA-256 and is simply a truncated version of SHA-256 where the output length is reduced to the first 224 bits. Similarly, functions SHA-384, SHA-512/256, and SHA-512/224 are truncated versions of SHA-512 with the outputs reduced to 384, 256, and 224 bits, respectively. While functions SHA-512/256 and SHA-512/224 were added primarily for performance reasons [80]—using 64-bit operations may be more efficient on modern 64-bit architectures—they also break with the plain Merkle–Damgård iteration scheme and instead implement the chopped MD variant (see Section 13.1.7). Besides protecting the functions from length-extension attacks this also allows

---

[8] The block cipher that can be extracted from SHA-2 is also referred to as SHACAL-2.

proving that the functions are indifferentiable from a random oracle, as we will see in Chapter 17.

The SHA-2 Compression Function

The compression function of the SHA-2 functions is similar to that of SHA-1 in structure. We give a schematic in Figure 15.5. The SHA-2 iteration function (i.e., the block cipher within the Davies–Meyer construction) works on 256 bits of state for SHA-256-based functions and on 512-bit states for SHA-512-based functions. The state is split into eight 32-bit (resp. 64-bit) words labeled $A, \ldots, H$. SHA-256-based functions use 64 iterations, while the SHA-512 functions use 80 iterations. In contrast to MD5 and SHA-1 the iteration function is not grouped into rounds but instead the same mixing functions are used for all iterations. In addition to the mixing functions, each iteration uses a different mixing constant K_j. Each of the six SHA-2 functions uses different mixing constants K_j as well as different initialization vectors IV.

15.3.2 Security of SHA-2

The choice of a larger internal state (256 bits or 512 bits) so far seems to have prevented full collision-finding attacks. Furthermore, the choice of chopped Merkle–Damgård for SHA-512/256, SHA-512/224, and SHA-384 protects the functions against trivial length-extension attacks. While also SHA-224 has a slightly larger internal state it only hides 32 bits, which may slow down adversaries but does not prevent adversaries from using length-extension attacks. Consequently, the SHA-2 functions and in particular SHA-512/256 and SHA-512/244 are a good choice for practical applications.

While SHA-2 has been studied extensively by the cryptographic community, so far no attacks on the full variants of any of the SHA-2 functions are known. Instead, research and attacks currently focus on reduced versions with fewer iterations [63, 89, 98, 97, 47, 2, 54, 51, 57, 62, 33, 31].

An investigation on the possibility of quantum attacks against the preimage resistance of SHA-256 was recently given by Amy et al. [1], concluding that attacks would require approximately 2^{166} basic operations and are thus, so far, beyond practical reach even with access to a quantum computer.

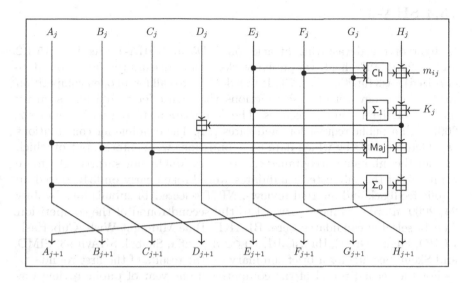

Ch(E, F, G)
___
return $(E \wedge F) \oplus (\neg E \wedge G)$

Maj(A, B, C)
___
return $(A \wedge B) \oplus (A \wedge C) \oplus (B \wedge C)$

$\Sigma_0(A)$ // for SHA-256
___
return $(A \ggg 2) \oplus (A \ggg 13) \oplus (A \ggg 22)$

$\Sigma_0(A)$ // for SHA-512
___
return $(A \ggg 28) \oplus (A \ggg 34) \oplus (A \ggg 39)$

$\Sigma_1(E)$ // for SHA-256
___
return $(E \ggg 6) \oplus (E \ggg 11) \oplus (E \ggg 25)$

$\Sigma_1(E)$ // for SHA-512
___
return $(E \ggg 14) \oplus (E \ggg 18) \oplus (E \ggg 41)$

MessageSchedule(m_i) // for SHA-256
___
for $j = 0..15$ **do**
$\quad m_{ij} \leftarrow m_i[j \cdot 32..(j+1) \cdot 32 - 1]$
for $j = 16..63$ **do**
$\quad \sigma_0 \leftarrow (m_{ij-15} \ggg 7) \oplus (m_{ij-15} \ggg 18) \oplus (m_{ij-15} \gg 3)$
$\quad \sigma_1 \leftarrow (m_{ij-2} \ggg 17) \oplus (m_{ij-2} \ggg 19) \oplus (m_{ij-2} \gg 10)$
$\quad m_{ij} \leftarrow \sigma_1 \boxplus m_{ij-7} \boxplus \sigma_0 \boxplus m_{ij-16}$

MessageSchedule(m_i) // for SHA-512
___
for $j = 0..15$ **do**
$\quad m_{ij} \leftarrow m_i[j \cdot 64..(j+1) \cdot 64 - 1]$
for $j = 16..79$ **do**
$\quad \sigma_0 \leftarrow (m_{ij-15} \ggg 1) \oplus (m_{ij-15} \ggg 8) \oplus (m_{ij-15} \gg 7)$
$\quad \sigma_1 \leftarrow (m_{ij-2} \ggg 19) \oplus (m_{ij-2} \ggg 61) \oplus (m_{ij-2} \gg 6)$
$\quad m_{ij} \leftarrow \sigma_1 \boxplus m_{ij-7} \boxplus \sigma_0 \boxplus m_{ij-16}$

Fig. 15.5: The SHA-2 iteration function. The SHA-2 compression function, similarly to MD5 and SHA-1, can be regarded as a Davies–Meyer compression function (see Figure 15.2 on the left). In contrast to MD5 and SHA-1 the iterations are not grouped into rounds and, consequently, the mixing functions are valid for all iterations. Initialization value $(A_0, \ldots, H_0) \leftarrow$ IV and mixing constants K_j are different for each of the different SHA-2 functions. The SHA-2 functions can be grouped into two groups: 64-bit functions based on SHA-512 and 32-bit functions based on SHA-256 (see Table 15.1). Functions based on SHA-512 use 80 iterations, 64-bit words, and a message block size of 1024 bits. Functions based on SHA-256 use 64 iterations, 32-bit words, and message blocks of 512 bits. Mixing functions Ch and maj are common to all functions. Mixing functions Σ_0 and Σ_1 are slightly different for 32- and 64-bit versions. Similarly, the message schedule is slightly different. $\boxplus$ means addition modulo 2^{32} for SHA-256 and 2^{64} for SHA-512. $\lll s$ (resp. $\ggg s$) denotes a left rotate (resp. right rotate) by s bits. $\gg s$ denotes a right shift by s bits.

15.4 SHA-3

In light of the devastating attacks on MD5 and SHA-1 (Sections 15.1.2 and 15.2.2), NIST held two public workshops to discuss the future of (standardized) hash functions [72, 73]. It was decided to call for an open competition to develop a new set of hash functions that can offer a sufficient security margin for the upcoming decades. The competition started on November 2, 2007 with a public request for candidates [74]. The deadline for contributions was October 2008 by which date 64 submissions were entered, out of which 51 met the minimum acceptance criteria [77]. Maybe not surprisingly, more than half of the submitted candidates were broken early on [34]. Based on public feedback and internal reviews, NIST selected 14 submissions by July 24, 2009 in order to move forward to the second round of the competition. The 14 selected candidates were: BLAKE, Blue Midnight Wish, CubeHash, ECHO, Fugue, Grøstl, Hamsi, JH, KECCAK, Luffa, Shabal, SHAvite-3, SIMD, and Skein. See [91] for a brief summary on the results of the first round.

For the second round of the competition one year of public review was allocated before NIST announced on December 9, 2010 the five SHA-3 finalists: BLAKE, Grøstl, JH, Keccak, and Skein [79]. After another 18 months of public review NIST announced the winner on October 2, 2012: KECCAK [83]. The final algorithm package and further information on the history of the competition are available on the SHA-3 project website [75].

The SHA-3 Standard

In 2015 NIST standardized KECCAK as part of FIPS 202 under the name SHA-3 [85]. In total, NIST standardized four cryptographic hash functions with a fixed output length (SHA3-224, SHA3-256, SHA3-384, and SHA3-512) as well as two extendable-output functions (XOFs; see Section 13.3 on 523) called SHAKE128 and SHAKE256. The output sizes of the SHA-3 functions correspond with those standardized as SHA-2, allowing to use SHA-3 as an alternative to SHA-2, or vice versa. Note that SHA-3 is not meant as a replacement for SHA-2 but as a supplement and alternative. We give an overview of the functions in Table 15.2.

In December 2016, NIST published four additional functions that can be derived from SHAKE128 and SHAK256: cSHAKE, KMAC, TupleHash, and ParallelHash [87]. cShake is a customizable variant of SHAKE, KMAC a variable-length message authentication code, TupleHash a variable-length hash function designed for hashing tuples of strings, and ParallelHash a SHAKE variant that supports parallel hashing of very long messages.

While this concludes the functions in the KECCAK family that have been standardized by NIST, the team behind KECCAK has in the past years published additional schemes based on KECCAK-p, the permutation underlying

Algorithm	Rate r (block size)	Capacity c (inner state)	Message suffix	Output size
SHA3-224	1152	448	01	224
SHA3-256	1088	512	01	256
SHA3-384	832	768	01	384
SHA3-512	576	1024	01	512
SHAKE128	1344	256	1111	Variable
SHAKE256	1088	512	1111	Variable

Table 15.2: An overview of the functions standardized by NIST in FIPS 202 [85]. Note that the optimal security level of a sponge function is $c/2$ (where c denotes the capacity). The algorithm's suffix thus specifies both output length and security level (resp. the security level for the variable-length functions SHAKE128 and SHAKE256). All sizes are in bits.

KECCAK. Amongst these are the authenticated encryption schemes KEYAK and KETJE as well as speed-optimized versions of KECCAK called KANGA-ROOTWELVE and MARSUPILAMIFOURTEEN [10, 11, 8]. Both KEYAK and KETJE were submitted to the CAESAR competition for authenticated encryption [5] and proceeded to the final round (round 3) but were not selected as part of the final portfolio.

15.4.1 KECCAK and Its Permutation KECCAK-p

In FIPS 202 [85], NIST standardized the sponge construction using 10*1-padding (see Section 13.3 on page 523) as well as the parameterizable permutation KECCAK-p, the permutation underlying KECCAK. NIST specifies four parameter sets for fixed-output-length cryptographic hash functions (SHA3-224, SHA3-256, SHA3-384, and SHA3-512) as well as two parameter sets for expandable-output functions (XOFs): SHAKE128 and SHAKE256. The number suffix denotes the (theoretical) bit strength of the function, which is given by $c/2$, i.e., half the size of the capacity. In case of the fixed-output-length functions the suffix also specifies the output length of the function. An overview of the chosen parameters for the sponge construction for the various functions is given in Table 15.2. Note that for the SHA-3 functions no additional permutation evaluations are needed for the squeezing phase as the rate is chosen sufficiently large in all four cases such that the result from the final absorbing call yields sufficiently many bits as part of the outer state. In addition to the sponge-related parameters, Table 15.2 specifies a message suffix. This suffix is appended to the message before being padded and is intended as domain separation between the different function types. For the

SHA-3 hash functions the suffix is 01, while for the two XOFs the suffix is 1111. We can, thus, define the four SHA-3 hash functions as

$$\text{SHA3-224}(m) = \text{KECCAK}[448](m\|01, 224)$$
$$\text{SHA3-256}(m) = \text{KECCAK}[512](m\|01, 256)$$
$$\text{SHA3-384}(m) = \text{KECCAK}[768](m\|01, 384)$$
$$\text{SHA3-512}(m) = \text{KECCAK}[1024](m\|01, 512)$$

Here, $\text{KECCAK}[c]$ denotes a sponge construction using 10^*1-padding with a capacity of c and rate $r := 1600-c$ and using as permutation $\text{KECCAK-}p[1600, 24]$. We discuss permutation $\text{KECCAK-}p[b, n_r]$ shortly. Similarly, we can define the two extendable-output functions SHAKE128 and SHAKE256 as

$$\text{SHAKE128}(m, L) = \text{KECCAK}[256](m\|1111, L)$$
$$\text{SHAKE256}(m, L) = \text{KECCAK}[512](m\|1111, L)$$

The KECCAK-p Permutations

In the following we want to take a closer look at the permutation underlying the KECCAK family of functions: KECCAK-p. As with all SHA-3 candidates also KECCAK comes with a detailed analysis and design rational and we refer to the KECCAK reference [9] and FIPS 202 [85] for further information going far beyond our discussion here.

Permutation $\text{KECCAK-}p[b, n_r]$ is parameterized by two values: the width b denoting the input and output size of the permutation, as well as the number n_r of rounds. While KECCAK allows various combinations of these parameters, for SHA-3 the parameters are fixed to $b = 1600$ and $n_r = 24$.

State s in $\text{KECCAK-}p[b, n_r]$ comprises b bits that can be interpreted as being organized in a three-dimensional structure of $5 \times 5 \times w$ bits. Possible values for w are powers of 2 with quantity $\log(b/25)$ often being denoted by ℓ. The seven settings considered for KECCAK-p are given in Table 15.3 below:

$b := 25 \cdot w$	25	50	100	200	400	800	1600
$w := 2^\ell$	1	2	4	8	16	32	64
ℓ	0	1	2	3	4	5	6

Table 15.3: KECCAK-p width b and related quantities.

Remark 15.3. While we usually consider indexes as 1-based throughout this book, recall that in this chapter we use 0-based indices.

By s we consider the b-bit state string and by a its representation as a three-dimensional array of elements in $\mathbb{GF}(2)$. We identify the bit position

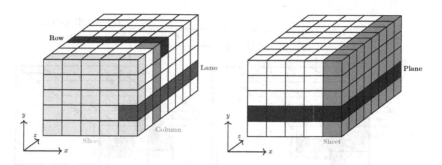

Fig. 15.6: The KECCAK-p state as a three-dimensional array $\mathfrak{a}[5, 5, w]$ with $w = 8$ and $\ell = 3$ and $b = 200$ and various lower-dimensional sub-arrays. The cube structure allows us to specify subsets by easily understood terms. We denote by *slice* a set of 25 bits with constant z coordinate. A *lane* is a set of w bits with constant x and y coordinates. A *column* is a set of 5 bits with constant x and z coordinates, and a *row* is a set of 5 bits with constant y and z coordinates. A *sheet* is a set of $5w$ bits with constant x coordinate and, likewise, a *plane* is a set of $5w$ bits but with constant y coordinate.

(x, y, z) by $\mathfrak{a}[x, y, z]$ with $x, y \in \mathbb{Z}_5$ and $z \in \mathbb{Z}_w$ (where $\mathbb{Z}_p$ denotes the set of integers modulo p). The mapping to bit string s is given by

$$\mathsf{s}[w(5y + x) + z] = \mathfrak{a}[x, y, z].$$

The three-dimensional representation $\mathfrak{a}$ of state s can be visualized as a cube, which allows us to define various subsets as easily identifiable parts of the cube such as *slices* or *planes*. We visualize a state for KECCAK-$p[200, n_r]$ in Figure 15.6.

The evaluation of KECCAK-$p[b, n_r]$ consists of n_r rounds R indexed by i_r from 0 to $n_r - 1$.[9] A round R consists of the composition of five step functions called θ, ρ, π, χ, and ι:

$$R := \iota \circ \chi \circ \pi \circ \rho \circ \theta.$$

All step functions take as input the current state, and output an updated state. In addition to the current state, function ι takes as additional input the current round number i_r. All other step functions are independent of the round number.

In the following we briefly discuss each of the step functions. With the exception of ι, which simply adds a round constant to the $(0, 0)$-lane, each step function has a graphical representation in the cube structure shown in Figure 15.6.

---

[9] For the standardization of SHA-3 the number of rounds was made explicit (and fixed to 24), while in the original KECCAK specification the number of rounds was set to $12 + 2\ell$ and thus depended on the size of the state.

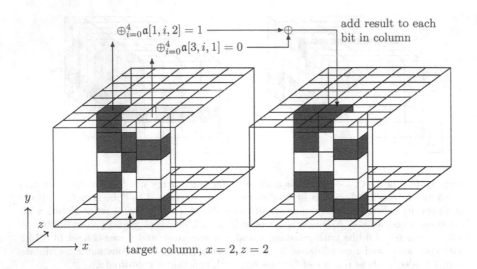

$\bigoplus_{i=0}^{4}\mathfrak{a}[1,i,2]=1$ ———————————————→ $\oplus$

$\bigoplus_{i=0}^{4}\mathfrak{a}[3,i,1]=0$ ——————————→

add result to each
bit in column

target column, $x=2,z=2$

Fig. 15.7: The θ step function. Each bit is updated as follows: compute the parity of the column to the left ($x-1 \bmod 5$) as well as the parity of the column to the front right ($x+1 \bmod 5$ and $z-1 \bmod 5$). Add the two values modulo 2 and add the result (modulo 2) to each bit in the target column. In the above picture the target column is the center column with $x=2,z=2$. Dark boxes represent 1-bits, while light boxes represent 0-bits. The result of the computation is given in the picture on the right.

Remark 15.4. We note that all step functions are efficiently invertible and, thus, also KECCAK-p is efficiently invertible: KECCAK-p is a permutation. While it is easy to see for some of the step functions that they can be inverted, this is not obvious, in particular, for step function θ. We here only discuss the "forward" mapping and refer to [9] for a detailed treatment also on the inverse mappings.

Step function θ. The first step function θ mixes the inner and outer parts of the state. Recall that the state in sponge constructions is given as $\mathsf{s}=\bar{\mathsf{s}}\|\hat{\mathsf{s}}$ and that before the application of the permutation the current message block is XORed onto the outer state $\bar{\mathsf{s}}$ (see Figure 13.13 on page 525). Function θ can be interpreted in the following way: each bit of the state is mixed with bits from the column to the left and the column to the front right. To update a bit, the parity of the two columns is computed and the result is added to the bit in $\mathbb{GF}(2)$. A schematic of the computation is given in Figure 15.7. In pseudocode we can capture the computation of step θ as

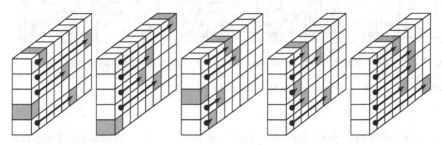

Fig. 15.8: The ρ step function applied to the lanes of state $\mathfrak{a}$ here depicted for $\ell = 3$ and $w = 8$. Note that $x = y = 0$ is depicted in the center of the slice. The leftmost sheet is the $x = 3$ sheet, while the sheet in the center is the $x = 0$ sheet. The offsets are given in Table 15.4. As an example consider the top lane on the leftmost sheet ($x = 3, y = 2$), which is rotated by $153 \bmod 8 = 1$ bits. The center lane at $x = y = 0$ is not rotated.

Function $\theta(\mathfrak{a})$

---

1 : **for** $x = 0..4$, $z = 0..w - 1$ **do**   // compute parity of each column

2 : $C[x, z] \leftarrow \mathfrak{a}[x, 0, z] \oplus \mathfrak{a}[x, 1, z] \oplus \mathfrak{a}[x, 2, z] \oplus \mathfrak{a}[x, 3, z] \oplus \mathfrak{a}[x, 4, z]$

3 : **for** $x = 0..4$, $z = 0..w - 1$ **do**   // added parity of left and front right column

4 : $D[x, z] \leftarrow C[(x - 1) \bmod 5, z] \oplus C[(x + 1) \bmod 5, (z - 1) \bmod w]$

5 : **for** $x = 0..4$, $y = 0..4$, $z = 0..w - 1$ **do**   // update each bit

6 : $\mathfrak{a}'[x, y, z] = \mathfrak{a}[x, y, z] \oplus D[x, z]$

7 : **return** $\mathfrak{a}'$

Step function ρ. The effect of function ρ is to rotate the bits within each lane. The offset, i.e., the amount by which the lane is rotated, depends only on the x and y coordinates of the row. Note that this is independent of the choice of ℓ and thus the offsets are identical for different parameterizations of KECCAK-p. The rotation is captured in pseudocode as:

Function $\rho(\mathfrak{a})$

---

1 : **for** $z = 0..w - 1$ **do**

2 : $\mathfrak{a}'[0, 0, z] = \mathfrak{a}[0, 0, z]$

3 : $(x, y) \leftarrow (1, 0)$

4 : **for** $t = 0..23$ **do**

5 :   **for** $z = 0..w - 1$ **do**

6 : $\mathfrak{a}'[x, y, z] \leftarrow \mathfrak{a}[x, y, (z - (t + 1)(t + 2)/2) \bmod w]$

7 : $(x, y) = (y, (2x + 3y) \bmod 5)$

8 : **return** $\mathfrak{a}'$

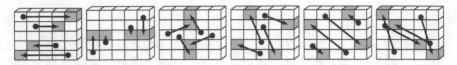

Fig. 15.9: The π step function rearranges the lanes except for the center lane $x = y = 0$. Note that $x = y = 0$ is depicted in the center of the slice. Thus the topmost and leftmost bit is $x = 3, y = 2$ and is moved to the top right ($x = 2, y = 2$).

The 25 offsets are given by $i(i + 1)/2$ for $0 \le i \le 24$. When checking the resulting constants for lanes of length 64 and 32 it can be seen that each constant is unique. For a choice of $\ell = 4$ and a lane length of 16, nine of the constants appear twice and for lane lengths 8, 4, and 2 all translation constants except the zero constant appear equally often. Table 15.4 gives the raw constants, and a graphical representation of function ρ is given in Figure 15.8.

	$x = 3$	$x = 4$	$x = 0$	$x = 1$	$x = 2$
$y = 2$	153	231	3	10	171
$y = 1$	55	276	36	300	6
$y = 0$	28	91	0	1	190
$y = 4$	120	78	210	66	253
$y = 3$	21	136	105	45	15

Table 15.4: Offsets for the ρ step function which are to be used modulo the lane length w.

Step function π. The effect of step function π is to rearrange the individual lanes in state array $\mathfrak{a}$. The lane with coordinates (x, y) is moved to $(x + 3y \bmod 5, x)$. This means that the only lane that remains untouched is the lane at $(0, 0)$. Following is a pseudocode specification of step function π. Figure 15.9 visualizes how the different lanes are rearranged within the cube.

Function $\pi(\mathfrak{a})$

1 :   **for** $x = 0..4$, $y = 0..4$, $z = 0..w - 1$ **do**

2 : $\mathfrak{a}'[x, y, z] = \mathfrak{a}[(x + 3y) \bmod 5, x, z]$

3 :   **return** $\mathfrak{a}'$

Step function χ. Step function χ is the only non-linear mapping in KECCAK-p and can be understood as a simple mapping that is applied to each row in state $\mathfrak{a}$. Each bit will be combined with the two bits to its right

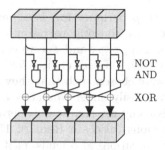

Fig. 15.10: The χ step function is the only non-linear function within the KECCAK-p permutation and is applied to every row in state $\mathfrak{a}$.

within the same row. Function χ is defined by the following pseudocode and visualized as a circuit diagram in Figure 15.10:

Function $\chi(\mathfrak{a})$

1 : **for** $x = 0..4,\ y = 0..4,\ z = 0..w - 1$ **do**

2 : $\quad \mathfrak{a}'[x, y, z] \leftarrow \mathfrak{a}[x, y, z] \oplus (\neg \mathfrak{a}[(x + 1) \bmod 5, y, z] \wedge \mathfrak{a}[(x + 2) \bmod 5, y, z])$

3 : **return** $\mathfrak{a}'$

Step function ι. The final step function ι adds a round constant to the $(0, 0)$ lane. We can capture the computation for each $x, y \in \mathbb{Z}_5$ and $z \in \mathbb{Z}_w$ as

$$\mathfrak{a}[x, y, z] \leftarrow \mathfrak{a} \oplus \mathrm{RC}[i_r][x, y, z],$$

where i_r from 0 to $n_r - 1$ denotes the current round. The round constants outside the $(0, 0)$ lane are set to zero, that is, $\mathrm{RC}[i_r][x, y, z] = 0$ for all $x \neq 0$ or $y \neq 0$. For the remaining lane the constant is set to 0 for all but $(\ell + 1)$ many bits, which are computed via a linear feedback shift register (LFSR) as:

RoundConstant RC	$\mathrm{rc}(t)$ // returns a bit
// initialize round constant to 0	1 : **if** $t \bmod 255 = 0$ **then return** 1
1 : **for** $x = 0..4, y = 0..4, z = 0..w - 1$ **do**	2 : $R \leftarrow 10000000$
2 : $\quad \mathrm{RC}[i_r][x, y, z] \leftarrow 0$	3 : **for** $i = 1..(t \bmod 255)$ **do**
	4 : $\quad R \leftarrow 0 \| R$
// compute round constant for lane $(0, 0)$	5 : $\quad R[0] = R[0] \oplus R[8]$
3 : **for** $j = 0..\ell$ **do**	6 : $\quad R[4] = R[4] \oplus R[8]$
4 : $\quad \mathrm{RC}[i_r][0, 0, 2^j - 1] \leftarrow \mathrm{rc}(j + 7i_r)$	7 : $\quad R[5] = R[5] \oplus R[8]$
	8 : $\quad R[6] = R[6] \oplus R[8]$
	9 : $\quad R \leftarrow R[0..7]$
	10 : **return** $R[0]$

Discussion. The KECCAK-p permutation is a flexible permutation that comes in seven different sizes allowing to permute between 25 and 1600 bits. The round functions θ, ρ, π, χ, and ι were carefully chosen such that they can operate similarly with different choices for the size of the state. Furthermore, the functions were chosen such that they have a simple graphical representation and are thus easily understandable (and analyzable). For this, note that all functions also only use simple bit operations and, in particular, do not use modular additions (also see Remark 15.2 on ARX designs on page 587). Using only bit operations also lends itself well to implementations in hardware, where KECCAK was faster than all other SHA-3 candidates [42]. On the other hand, in software and on CPUs that do not come with optimized instruction sets for computing KECCAK, KECCAK can be significantly slower than SHA-2 or SHA-1 [7]. Since SHA-3 comes in various forms, one option is to switch to SHAKE128 or SHAKE256, which use a larger rate than SHA3-512 or SHA3-384 and thus per invocation of KECCAK-p can process more bits from the ingoing message. When input messages are very large, one can also use the ParallelHash variant (see below) which was standardized by NIST in 2016 [87]. Recently, the designers of KECCAK also published KANGAROOTWELVE, which uses a round-reduced version of KECCAK-p together with a tree-based scheme on top of sponge for optimal speeds [8]. We note that the latter two functions have not undergone the same level of scrutiny as did KECCAK.

15.4.2 SHA-3 Function Specifications

In the following we briefly outline the different variants of KECCAK that were standardized by NIST in FIPS 202 [85] and in SP 800-185 [87]. The base standard FIPS 202 specifies four fixed-output-length hash functions and two expandable-output functions. SP 800-185 adds to this four additional functions: a salted XOF, a message authentication code, a function aimed at hashing tuples of strings, and a version for fast parallel hashing of long strings. An overview of the base functions is given in Table 15.2 (page 599), and the additional derived functions are given in Table 15.5.

All functions are ultimately based on KECCAK-$p[1600, 24]$, that is, permutation KECCAK-p with a width (rate plus capacity) of 1600 bits and using 24 rounds. We let KECCAK[c] denote KECCAK, i.e., a sponge construction using 10*1 padding and KECCAK-$p[1600, 24]$ as permutation and with capacity c and rate r := 1600 − c.

SHA-3 Cryptographic Hash Functions

Standard FIPS 202 [85] specifies four fixed-output-length cryptographic hash functions defined as

Algorithm	Function Name	Rate r (block size)	Capacity c (inner state)	Message suffix	Output size
cSHAKE128	-	1344	256	00	Variable
cSHAKE256	-	1088	512	00	Variable
KMAC128	KMAC	1344	256	-	Variable
KMAC256	KMAC	1088	512	-	Variable
TupleHash128	TupleHash	1344	256	-	Variable
TupleHash256	TupleHash	1088	512	-	Variable
ParallelHash128	ParallelHash	1344	256	-	Variable
ParallelHash256	ParallelHash	1088	512	-	Variable

Table 15.5: The SHA-3 derived functions as specified in SP 800-185 [87]. cSHAKE can be regarded as a salted version of SHAKE. All other functions depend on cSHAKE, and the function name specifies parameter N for the cSHAKE invocation. A message suffix is only needed for the cSHAKE function as it depends directly on KECCAK. Base functions SHA-3 and SHAKE are given in Table 15.2 on page 599.

$$\text{SHA3-224}(m) = \text{KECCAK}[448](m\|01, 224)$$
$$\text{SHA3-256}(m) = \text{KECCAK}[512](m\|01, 256)$$
$$\text{SHA3-384}(m) = \text{KECCAK}[768](m\|01, 384)$$
$$\text{SHA3-512}(m) = \text{KECCAK}[1024](m\|01, 512)$$

The fixed output-length cryptographic hash functions are assigned message suffix 01, which is appended to the input message to obtain domain separation between the various SHA-3 function types.

SHAKE

Standard FIPS 202 [85] specifies two extendable-output functions defined as

$$\text{SHAKE128}(m, L) = \text{KECCAK}[256](m\|1111, L)$$
$$\text{SHAKE256}(m, L) = \text{KECCAK}[512](m\|1111, L)$$

The SHAKE functions are assigned message suffix 1111.

cSHAKE

The cSHAKE functions can be regarded as salted versions of the SHAKE functions. In addition to the input message and the required output length they take two additional parameters:

N Parameter N is used by NIST in the definition of functions based on cSHAKE such as, for example, KMAC (see below). For direct use of cSHAKE the parameter should be set to the empty string and, instead, parameter S should be used for additional customization.

S A customization bit string (aka a salt) to achieve domain separation between different usage scenarios.

The two cSHAKE functions are then defined as

cSHAKE128(m, L, N, S)
1 : **if** $N = \varepsilon$ and $S = \varepsilon$ **do**
2 :   **return** SHAKE128(m, L)
3 : $m' \leftarrow \mathsf{pad}(\mathsf{enc}(N)\|\mathsf{enc}(S), 1344)\|m$
4 : **return** KECCAK$[256](m'\|00, L)$

cSHAKE256(m, L, N, S)
1 : **if** $N = \varepsilon$ and $S = \varepsilon$ **do**
2 :   **return** SHAKE256(m, L)
3 : $m' \leftarrow \mathsf{pad}(\mathsf{enc}(N)\|\mathsf{enc}(S), 1088)\|m$
4 : **return** KECCAK$[512](m'\|00, L)$

Here, the enc function encodes a string by prepending an encoding of its length. Function pad pads the result with zero bits to a multiple of the block size which is provided as the second parameter. Note that pad in this context is different from the 10*1 padding used inside KECCAK.

KMAC

KMAC is a variable-output-length message authentication code based on cSHAKE. It incorporates a secret key using the secret-suffix method that we will discuss in greater detail in Section 16.1.3. KMAC takes the following parameters:

k The function's secret key which can be of any length, including zero.
m The message to be authenticated.
L The desired output length in bits.
S An optional salt to obtain domain separation between different usage scenarios.

The KMAC functions are then defined by

KMAC128(k, m, L, S)
1 : $N \leftarrow$ "KMAC"
2 : $m' \leftarrow \mathsf{pad}(\mathsf{enc}(\mathsf{k}), 1344)\|m\|\mathsf{rEnc}(L)$
3 : **return** cSHAKE128(m', L, N, S)

KMAC256(k, m, L, S)
1 : $N \leftarrow$ "KMAC"
2 : $m' \leftarrow \mathsf{pad}(\mathsf{enc}(\mathsf{k}), 1088)\|m\|\mathsf{rEnc}(L)$
3 : **return** cSHAKE256(m', L, N, S)

Functions enc and pad are as before and prepend the length of the string and pad to a multiple of the block length using zero bits. Function rEnc is an encoding of integer L that can be parsed unambiguously from the right. This is achieved by using a standard binary encoding of L and adding as an extra byte the number of bytes used for the encoding.

NIST specifies two additional variants of KMAC called KMACXOF128 and KMACXOF256. These can be used as an extendable-output function and do not need to specify length L upfront. Instead of adding an encoding of length L to the message here an encoding of zero is appended (line 2).

TupleHash

TupleHash is a variant of cSHAKE for hashing tuples of strings. In particular, TupleHash ensures that the tuples ("a", "bcd") and ("ab", "cd") hash to different values. In the following pseudocode **m** denotes a list of strings. As always in this chapter, we consider the list to be indexed 0-based.

TupleHash128($\mathbf{m}, L, S$)	TupleHash256($\mathbf{m}, L, S$)
1 : $N \leftarrow$ "TupleHash"	1 : $N \leftarrow$ "TupleHash"
2 : $m' \leftarrow \varepsilon$	2 : $m' \leftarrow \varepsilon$
3 : **for** $i = 0..\lvert\mathbf{m}\rvert - 1$ **do**	3 : **for** $i = 0..\lvert\mathbf{m}\rvert - 1$ **do**
4 : $m' \leftarrow m' \lVert \mathsf{enc}(\mathbf{m}[i])$	4 : $m' \leftarrow m' \lVert \mathsf{enc}(\mathbf{m}[i])$
5 : $m' \leftarrow m' \lVert \mathsf{rEnc}(L)$	5 : $m' \leftarrow m' \lVert \mathsf{rEnc}(L)$
6 : **return** cSHAKE128(m', L, N, S)	6 : **return** cSHAKE256(m', L, N, S)

Functions enc and rEnc, as before, encode strings by prepending their lengths and integers by appending their length in order to be parseable unambiguously from the left, or right respectively. As in the case of KMAC two additional variants called TupleHashXOF128 and TupleHashXOF256 are specified that can be used to dynamically generate arbitrarily many output bits. Again, in this case the added length encoding in line 5 is replaced by an encoding of zero.

ParallelHash

ParallelHash is the final function in the SHA-3 family defined in SP 800-185. It is a variant of cSHAKE that allows parallel hashing of very long messages. To achieve this, evaluation of cSHAKE is done in two levels. First input string m is split into n blocks of length B. Each of these blocks are then processed by cSHAKE. All results are concatenated to form the final string m', which is run through cSHAKE once more. Parameter B is specified in bytes.

ParallelHash128(m, B, L, S)	ParallelHash256(m, B, L, S)
1 : $N \leftarrow$ "ParallelHash"	$N \leftarrow$ "ParallelHash"
2 : $n \leftarrow \lceil |m|/8B \rceil$	$n \leftarrow \lceil |m|/8B \rceil$
3 : $m' \leftarrow \mathsf{IEnc}(B)$	$m' \leftarrow \mathsf{IEnc}(B)$
4 : **for** $i = 0..n - 1$ **do**	**for** $i = 0..n - 1$ **do**
5 : $s \leftarrow m[i \cdot B \cdot 8..(i+1) \cdot B \cdot 8 - 1]$	$s \leftarrow m[i \cdot B \cdot 8..(i+1) \cdot B \cdot 8 - 1]$
6 : $m' \leftarrow m' \| cSHAKE128(s, 256, \varepsilon, \varepsilon)$	$m' \leftarrow m' \| cSHAKE128(s, 512, \varepsilon, \varepsilon)$
7 : $m' \leftarrow m' \| \mathsf{rEnc}(n) \| \mathsf{rEnc}(L)$	$m' \leftarrow m' \| \mathsf{rEnc}(n) \| \mathsf{rEnc}(L)$
8 : **return** cSHAKE128(m', L, N, S)	**return** cSHAKE256(m', L, N, S)

Function IEnc, similarly to rEnc, encodes integers but instead of appending the length information it is prepended such that it can be unambiguously parsed from the left. As with TupleHash and KMAC two additional variants called ParallelHashXOF128 and ParallelHashXOF256 are specified that can be used to dynamically generate arbitrarily many output bits. As before, in this case the added length encoding in line 7 is replaced by an encoding of zero.

15.4.3 Security of SHA-3

Both during the SHA-3 competition and after, KECCAK and its permutation KECCAK-p have been studied extensively by the cryptographic community. However, as with SHA-2 no attacks on the full version of KECCAK are known, and research thus currently focuses on cryptanalyzing round-reduced versions of KECCAK [17, 21, 32, 25, 66, 26, 49, 41, 92, 100, 46, 61, 59, 58, 40]. Practical attacks, so far, are restricted to reduced versions with at most six rounds [40]. An up-to-date overview of available cryptanalytical research is provided by the team behind KECCAK at [6].

Investigations of sponge constructions in the presence of quantum computers have been conducted in [19, 20].

Acknowledgement

The diagrams presented in this chapter are based on diagrams provided by the TikZ for Cryptographers project [48].

Chapter Bibliography

1. Matthew Amy, Olivia Di Matteo, Vlad Gheorghiu, Michele Mosca, Alex Parent, and John M. Schanck. Estimating the cost of generic quantum pre-image attacks on SHA-2 and SHA-3. In Roberto Avanzi and Howard M. Heys, editors, *SAC 2016: 23rd Annual International Workshop on Selected Areas in Cryptography*, volume 10532 of *Lecture Notes in Computer Science*, pages 317–337, St. John's, NL, Canada, August 10–12, 2016. Springer, Heidelberg, Germany.
2. Kazumaro Aoki, Jian Guo, Krystian Matusiewicz, Yu Sasaki, and Lei Wang. Preimages for step-reduced SHA-2. In Mitsuru Matsui, editor, *Advances in Cryptology - ASIACRYPT 2009*, volume 5912 of *Lecture Notes in Computer Science*, pages 578–597, Tokyo, Japan, December 6–10, 2009. Springer, Heidelberg, Germany.
3. Jean-Philippe Aumasson, Luca Henzen, Willi Meier, and Raphael C-W Phan. SHA-3 proposal BLAKE. *Submission to NIST*, 2008.
4. Jean-Philippe Aumasson, Philipp Jovanovic, and Samuel Neves. NORX: Parallel and scalable AEAD. In Miroslaw Kutylowski and Jaideep Vaidya, editors, *ESORICS 2014: 19th European Symposium on Research in Computer Security, Part II*, volume 8713 of *Lecture Notes in Computer Science*, pages 19–36, Wroclaw, Poland, September 7–11, 2014. Springer, Heidelberg, Germany.
5. Daniel J. Bernstein. CAESAR: Competition for authenticated encryption: Security, applicability, and robustness. https://competitions.cr.yp.to/caesar.html.
6. Guido Bertoni, Joan Daemen, Seth Hoffert, Michaël Peeters, and Gilles Van Assche. Team Keccak: Software performance figures. https://keccak.team/sw_performance.html.
7. Guido Bertoni, Joan Daemen, Seth Hoffert, Michaël Peeters, and Gilles Van Assche. Team Keccak: Third-party cryptanalysis. https://keccak.team/third_party.html.
8. Guido Bertoni, Joan Daemen, Michaël Peeters, Gilles Van Assche, Ronny Van Keer, and Benoît Viguier. KangarooTwelve: Fast hashing based on keccak-p. In Bart Preneel and Frederik Vercauteren, editors, *ACNS 18: 16th International Conference on Applied Cryptography and Network Security*, volume 10892 of *Lecture Notes in Computer Science*, pages 400–418, Leuven, Belgium, July 2–4, 2018. Springer, Heidelberg, Germany.
9. Guido Bertoni, Joan Daemen, Michaël Peeters, and Gilles Van Assche. The Keccak reference. *Submission to NIST (Round 3)*, 2011.
10. Guido Bertoni, Joan Daemen, Michaël Peeters, Gilles Van Assche, and Ronny Van Keer. The Ketje authenticated encryption scheme. http://ketje.noekeon.org/, 3 2014.
11. Guido Bertoni, Joan Daemen, Michaël Peeters, Gilles Van Assche, and Ronny Van Keer. The Keyak authenticated encryption scheme. http://keyak.noekeon.org/, 3 2014.
12. Eli Biham and Rafi Chen. Near-collisions of SHA-0. In Matthew Franklin, editor, *Advances in Cryptology - CRYPTO 2004*, volume 3152 of *Lecture Notes in Computer Science*, pages 290–305, Santa Barbara, CA, USA, August 15–19, 2004. Springer, Heidelberg, Germany.
13. Eli Biham, Rafi Chen, Antoine Joux, Patrick Carribault, Christophe Lemuet, and William Jalby. Collisions of SHA-0 and reduced SHA-1. In Ronald Cramer, editor, *Advances in Cryptology - EUROCRYPT 2005*, volume 3494 of *Lecture Notes in Computer Science*, pages 36–57, Aarhus, Denmark, May 22–26, 2005. Springer, Heidelberg, Germany.
14. Eli Biham and Adi Shamir. Differential cryptanalysis of DES-like cryptosystems. In Alfred J. Menezes and Scott A. Vanstone, editors, *Advances in Cryptology - CRYPTO'90*, volume 537 of *Lecture Notes in Computer Science*, pages 2–21, Santa Barbara, CA, USA, August 11–15, 1991. Springer, Heidelberg, Germany.

15. Eli Biham and Adi Shamir. Differential cryptanalysis of DES-like cryptosystems. *Journal of Cryptology*, 4(1):3–72, January 1991.

16. Eli Biham and Adi Shamir. Differential cryptanalysis of Snefru, Khafre, REDOC-II, LOKI and Lucifer. In Joan Feigenbaum, editor, *Advances in Cryptology – CRYPTO'91*, volume 576 of *Lecture Notes in Computer Science*, pages 156–171, Santa Barbara, CA, USA, August 11–15, 1992. Springer, Heidelberg, Germany.

17. Christina Boura, Anne Canteaut, and Christophe De Cannière. Higher-order differential properties of Keccak and Luffa. In Antoine Joux, editor, *Fast Software Encryption – FSE 2011*, volume 6733 of *Lecture Notes in Computer Science*, pages 252–269, Lyngby, Denmark, February 13–16, 2011. Springer, Heidelberg, Germany.

18. Florent Chabaud and Antoine Joux. Differential collisions in SHA-0. In Hugo Krawczyk, editor, *Advances in Cryptology – CRYPTO'98*, volume 1462 of *Lecture Notes in Computer Science*, pages 56–71, Santa Barbara, CA, USA, August 23–27, 1998. Springer, Heidelberg, Germany.

19. Jan Czajkowski, Leon Groot Bruinderink, Andreas Hülsing, Christian Schaffner, and Dominique Unruh. Post-quantum security of the sponge construction. In Tanja Lange and Rainer Steinwandt, editors, *Post-Quantum Cryptography - 9th International Conference, PQCrypto 2018*, pages 185–204, Fort Lauderdale, Florida, United States, April 9–11 2018. Springer, Heidelberg, Germany.

20. Jan Czajkowski, Andreas Hülsing, and Christian Schaffner. Quantum indistinguishability of random sponges. In Alexandra Boldyreva and Daniele Micciancio, editors, *Advances in Cryptology – CRYPTO 2019, Part II*, volume 11693 of *Lecture Notes in Computer Science*, pages 296–325, Santa Barbara, CA, USA, August 18–22, 2019. Springer, Heidelberg, Germany.

21. Joan Daemen and Gilles Van Assche. Differential propagation analysis of Keccak. In Anne Canteaut, editor, *Fast Software Encryption – FSE 2012*, volume 7549 of *Lecture Notes in Computer Science*, pages 422–441, Washington, DC, USA, March 19–21, 2012. Springer, Heidelberg, Germany.

22. Christophe De Cannière, Florian Mendel, and Christian Rechberger. Collisions for 70-step SHA-1: On the full cost of collision search. In Carlisle M. Adams, Ali Miri, and Michael J. Wiener, editors, *SAC 2007: 14th Annual International Workshop on Selected Areas in Cryptography*, volume 4876 of *Lecture Notes in Computer Science*, pages 56–73, Ottawa, Canada, August 16–17, 2007. Springer, Heidelberg, Germany.

23. Christophe De Cannière and Christian Rechberger. Finding SHA-1 characteristics: General results and applications. In Xuejia Lai and Kefei Chen, editors, *Advances in Cryptology – ASIACRYPT 2006*, volume 4284 of *Lecture Notes in Computer Science*, pages 1–20, Shanghai, China, December 3–7, 2006. Springer, Heidelberg, Germany.

24. Bert den Boer and Antoon Bosselaers. Collisions for the compression function of MD5. In Tor Helleseth, editor, *Advances in Cryptology — EUROCRYPT '93*, pages 293–304, Berlin, Heidelberg, 1994. Springer Berlin Heidelberg.

25. Itai Dinur, Orr Dunkelman, and Adi Shamir. Collision attacks on up to 5 rounds of SHA-3 using generalized internal differentials. In Shiho Moriai, editor, *Fast Software Encryption – FSE 2013*, volume 8424 of *Lecture Notes in Computer Science*, pages 219–240, Singapore, March 11–13, 2014. Springer, Heidelberg, Germany.

26. Itai Dinur, Orr Dunkelman, and Adi Shamir. Improved practical attacks on round-reduced Keccak. *Journal of Cryptology*, 27(2):183–209, April 2014.

27. Hans Dobbertin. Cryptanalysis of MD4. In Dieter Gollmann, editor, *Fast Software Encryption – FSE'96*, volume 1039 of *Lecture Notes in Computer Science*, pages 53–69, Cambridge, UK, February 21–23, 1996. Springer, Heidelberg, Germany.

28. Hans Dobbertin. Cryptanalysis of MD5 compress. *Rump session of Eurocrypt*, 96:71–82, 1996.

29. Hans Dobbertin. The status of MD5 after a recent attack. *Crypto-Bytes The technical newsletter of RSA Laboratories, a division of RSA Data Security, Inc.*, 2(2), 1996.

30. Hans Dobbertin. Cryptanalysis of MD4. *Journal of Cryptology*, 11(4):253–271, September 1998.

31. Christoph Dobraunig, Maria Eichlseder, and Florian Mendel. Analysis of SHA-512/224 and SHA-512/256. In Tetsu Iwata and Jung Hee Cheon, editors, *Advances in Cryptology – ASIACRYPT 2015, Part II*, volume 9453 of *Lecture Notes in Computer Science*, pages 612–630, Auckland, New Zealand, November 30 – December 3, 2015. Springer, Heidelberg, Germany.

32. Alexandre Duc, Jian Guo, Thomas Peyrin, and Lei Wei. Unaligned rebound attack: Application to Keccak. In Anne Canteaut, editor, *Fast Software Encryption – FSE 2012*, volume 7549 of *Lecture Notes in Computer Science*, pages 402–421, Washington, DC, USA, March 19–21, 2012. Springer, Heidelberg, Germany.

33. Maria Eichlseder, Florian Mendel, and Martin Schläffer. Branching heuristics in differential collision search with applications to SHA-512. In Carlos Cid and Christian Rechberger, editors, *Fast Software Encryption – FSE 2014*, volume 8540 of *Lecture Notes in Computer Science*, pages 473–488, London, UK, March 3–5, 2015. Springer, Heidelberg, Germany.

34. ECRYPT II European Network of Excellence for Cryptology II. The SHA-3 zoo. https://ehash.iaik.tugraz.at/wiki/The_SHA_3_Zoo.

35. Niels Ferguson, Stefan Lucks, Bruce Schneier, Doug Whiting, Mihir Bellare, Tadayoshi Kohno, Jon Callas, and Jesse Walker. The Skein hash function family. *Submission to NIST (round 3)*, 2010.

36. Max Gebhardt, Georg Illies, and Werner Schindler. A note on the practical value of single hash collisions for special file formats. *Sicherheit 2006, Sicherheit – Schutz und Zuverlässigkeit*, pages 333–344, 2006.

37. Alexander Gostev. The Flame: Questions and answers. https://securelist.com/the-flame-questions-and-answers/34344/, 6 2012.

38. E.A. Grechnikov. Collisions for 72-step and 73-step SIIA-1: Improvements in the method of characteristics. Cryptology ePrint Archive, Report 2010/413, 2010. http://eprint.iacr.org/2010/413.

39. E.A. Grechnikov and A.V. Adinetz. Collision for 75-step SHA-1: Intensive parallelization with GPU. Cryptology ePrint Archive, Report 2011/641, 2011. http://eprint.iacr.org/2011/641.

40. Jian Guo, Guohong Liao, Guozhen Liu, Meicheng Liu, Kexin Qiao, and Ling Song. Practical collision attacks against round-reduced SHA-3. *Journal of Cryptology*, Feb 2019.

41. Jian Guo, Meicheng Liu, and Ling Song. Linear structures: Applications to cryptanalysis of round-reduced Keccak. In Jung Hee Cheon and Tsuyoshi Takagi, editors, *Advances in Cryptology – ASIACRYPT 2016, Part I*, volume 10031 of *Lecture Notes in Computer Science*, pages 249–274, Hanoi, Vietnam, December 4–8, 2016. Springer, Heidelberg, Germany.

42. Xu Guo, Sinan Huang, Leyla Nazhandali, and Patrick Schaumont. Fair and comprehensive performance evaluation of 14 second round SHA-3 ASIC implementations. In *The Second SHA-3 Candidate Conference*. Citeseer, 2010.

43. Helena Handschuh, Lars R. Knudsen, and Matthew J. B. Robshaw. Analysis of SHA-1 in encryption mode. In David Naccache, editor, *Topics in Cryptology – CT-RSA 2001*, volume 2020 of *Lecture Notes in Computer Science*, pages 70–83, San Francisco, CA, USA, April 8–12, 2001. Springer, Heidelberg, Germany.

44. Helena Handschuh and David Naccache. SHACAL. *Preproceedings of NESSIE First Workshop*, 11 2000.

45. Ethan Heilman. Restoring the differential resistance of MD6. Cryptology ePrint Archive, Report 2011/374, 2011. http://eprint.iacr.org/2011/374.

46. Senyang Huang, Xiaoyun Wang, Guangwu Xu, Meiqin Wang, and Jingyuan Zhao. Conditional cube attack on reduced-round keccak sponge function. In Jean-Sébastien Coron and Jesper Buus Nielsen, editors, *Advances in Cryptology – EURO-*

CRYPT 2017, Part II, volume 10211 of *Lecture Notes in Computer Science*, pages 259–288, Paris, France, April 30 – May 4, 2017. Springer, Heidelberg, Germany.

47. Takanori Isobe and Kyoji Shibutani. Preimage attacks on reduced Tiger and SHA-2. In Orr Dunkelman, editor, *Fast Software Encryption – FSE 2009*, volume 5665 of *Lecture Notes in Computer Science*, pages 139–155, Leuven, Belgium, February 22–25, 2009. Springer, Heidelberg, Germany.

48. Jérémy Jean. TikZ for cryptographers. https://www.iacr.org/authors/tikz/, 2016.

49. Jérémy Jean and Ivica Nikolic. Internal differential boomerangs: Practical analysis of the round-reduced keccak- f f permutation. In Gregor Leander, editor, *Fast Software Encryption – FSE 2015*, volume 9054 of *Lecture Notes in Computer Science*, pages 537–556, Istanbul, Turkey, March 8–11, 2015. Springer, Heidelberg, Germany.

50. Burton S. Kaliski Jr. The MD2 message-digest algorithm. RFC 1319, RFC Editor, April 1992. http://www.rfc-editor.org/rfc/rfc1319.txt.

51. Dmitry Khovratovich, Christian Rechberger, and Alexandra Savelieva. Bicliques for preimages: Attacks on Skein-512 and the SHA-2 family. In Anne Canteaut, editor, *Fast Software Encryption – FSE 2012*, volume 7549 of *Lecture Notes in Computer Science*, pages 244–263, Washington, DC, USA, March 19–21, 2012. Springer, Heidelberg, Germany.

52. Vlastimil Klima. Finding MD5 collisions – a toy for a notebook. Cryptology ePrint Archive, Report 2005/075, 2005. http://eprint.iacr.org/2005/075.

53. Vlastimil Klima. Tunnels in hash functions: MD5 collisions within a minute. Cryptology ePrint Archive, Report 2006/105, 2006. http://eprint.iacr.org/2006/105.

54. Mario Lamberger and Florian Mendel. Higher-order differential attack on reduced SHA-256. Cryptology ePrint Archive, Report 2011/037, 2011. http://eprint.iacr.org/2011/037.

55. Arjen K. Lenstra and Benne de Weger. On the possibility of constructing meaningful hash collisions for public keys. In Colin Boyd and Juan Manuel González Nieto, editors, *ACISP 05: 10th Australasian Conference on Information Security and Privacy*, volume 3574 of *Lecture Notes in Computer Science*, pages 267–279, Brisbane, Queensland, Australia, July 4–6, 2005. Springer, Heidelberg, Germany.

56. Gaëtan Leurent and Thomas Peyrin. From collisions to chosen-prefix collisions application to full SHA-1. In Yuval Ishai and Vincent Rijmen, editors, *Advances in Cryptology – EUROCRYPT 2019, Part III*, volume 11478 of *Lecture Notes in Computer Science*, pages 527–555, Darmstadt, Germany, May 19–23, 2019. Springer, Heidelberg, Germany.

57. Ji Li, Takanori Isobe, and Kyoji Shibutani. Converting meet-in-the-middle preimage attack into pseudo collision attack: Application to SHA-2. In Anne Canteaut, editor, *Fast Software Encryption – FSE 2012*, volume 7549 of *Lecture Notes in Computer Science*, pages 264–286, Washington, DC, USA, March 19–21, 2012. Springer, Heidelberg, Germany.

58. Ting Li and Yao Sun. Preimage attacks on round-reduced keccak-224/256 via an allocating approach. In Yuval Ishai and Vincent Rijmen, editors, *Advances in Cryptology – EUROCRYPT 2019, Part III*, volume 11478 of *Lecture Notes in Computer Science*, pages 556–584, Darmstadt, Germany, May 19–23, 2019. Springer, Heidelberg, Germany.

59. Zheng Li, Xiaoyang Dong, Wenquan Bi, Keting Jia, Xiaoyun Wang, and Willi Meier. New conditional cube attack on Keccak keyed modes. *IACR Transactions on Symmetric Cryptology*, 2019(2):94–124, 2019.

60. J. Linn. Privacy enhancement for internet electronic mail: Part III: algorithms, modes, and identifiers. RFC 1115, RFC Editor, August 1989.

61. Silvia Mella, Joan Daemen, and Gilles Van Assche. New techniques for trail bounds and application to differential trails in Keccak. *IACR Transactions on Symmetric Cryptology*, 2017(1):329–357, 2017.

62. Florian Mendel, Tomislav Nad, and Martin Schläffer. Improving local collisions: New attacks on reduced SHA-256. In Thomas Johansson and Phong Q. Nguyen, editors, *Advances in Cryptology – EUROCRYPT 2013*, volume 7881 of *Lecture Notes in Computer Science*, pages 262–278, Athens, Greece, May 26–30, 2013. Springer, Heidelberg, Germany.

63. Florian Mendel, Norbert Pramstaller, Christian Rechberger, and Vincent Rijmen. Analysis of step-reduced SHA-256. In Matthew J. B. Robshaw, editor, *Fast Software Encryption – FSE 2006*, volume 4047 of *Lecture Notes in Computer Science*, pages 126–143, Graz, Austria, March 15–17, 2006. Springer, Heidelberg, Germany.

64. Ralph C. Merkle. A fast software one-way hash function. *Journal of Cryptology*, 3(1):43–58, January 1990.

65. Microsoft Security Response Center. Flame malware collision attack explained. https://msrc-blog.microsoft.com/2012/06/06/flame-malware-collision-attack-explained, 5 2012.

66. Pawel Morawiecki, Josef Pieprzyk, and Marian Srebrny. Rotational cryptanalysis of round-reduced Keccak. In Shiho Moriai, editor, *Fast Software Encryption – FSE 2013*, volume 8424 of *Lecture Notes in Computer Science*, pages 241–262, Singapore, March 11–13, 2014. Springer, Heidelberg, Germany.

67. National Institute of Standards and Technology (NIST). FIPS PUB 180: Secure Hash Standard. https://csrc.nist.gov/publications/detail/fips/180/archive/1993-05-11, 5 1993.

68. National Institute of Standards and Technology (NIST). FIPS PUB 180-1: Secure Hash Standard. https://csrc.nist.gov/publications/detail/fips/180/1/archive/1995-04-17, 4 1995.

69. National Institute of Standards and Technology (NIST). FIPS PUB 197: Advanced Encryption Standard (AES). https://csrc.nist.gov/publications/detail/fips/197/final, 11 2001.

70. National Institute of Standards and Technology (NIST). FIPS PUB 180-2: Secure Hash Standard. https://csrc.nist.gov/publications/detail/fips/180/2/archive/2002-08-01, 8 2002.

71. National Institute of Standards and Technology (NIST). FIPS PUB 180-2: Secure Hash Standard. https://csrc.nist.gov/publications/detail/fips/180/2/archive/2004-02-25, 2 2004.

72. National Institute of Standards and Technology (NIST). First cryptographic hash workshop. https://csrc.nist.gov/events/2005/first-cryptographic-hash-workshop, 10 2005.

73. National Institute of Standards and Technology (NIST). Second cryptographic hash workshop. https://csrc.nist.gov/events/2006/second-cryptographic-hash-workshop, 8 2006.

74. National Institute of Standards and Technology (NIST). Announcing request for candidate algorithm nominations for a new cryptographic hash algorithm (SHA-3) family. https://www.federalregister.gov/d/E7-21581, 11 2007.

75. National Institute of Standards and Technology (NIST). SHA-3 project. https://csrc.nist.gov/projects/hash-functions/sha-3-project, 11 2007.

76. National Institute of Standards and Technology (NIST). FIPS PUB 180-3: Secure Hash Standard. https://csrc.nist.gov/publications/detail/fips/180/3/archive/2008-10-31, 10 2008.

77. National Institute of Standards and Technology (NIST). Status report on the first round of the SHA-3 cryptographic hash algorithm competition. https://csrc.nist.gov/publications/detail/nistir/7620/final, 9 2009.

78. National Institute of Standards and Technology (NIST). SP 800-131A: Transitions: Recommendation for transitioning the use of cryptographic algorithms and key lengths. https://csrc.nist.gov/publications/detail/sp/800-131a/archive/2011-01-13, 2011.

79. National Institute of Standards and Technology (NIST). Status report on the second round of the SHA-3 cryptographic hash algorithm competition. `https://csrc.nist.gov/publications/detail/nistir/7764/final`, 2 2011.

80. National Institute of Standards and Technology (NIST). Announcing approval of Federal Information Processing Standard (FIPS) publication 180-4, Secure Hash Standard (SHS); a revision of FIPS 180-3. `https://www.federalregister.gov/d/2012-5400`, 2012.

81. National Institute of Standards and Technology (NIST). FIPS PUB 180-4: Secure Hash Standard. `https://csrc.nist.gov/publications/detail/fips/180/4/archive/2012-03-06`, 3 2012.

82. National Institute of Standards and Technology (NIST). SP 800-107: Recommendation for applications using approved hash algorithms. `https://csrc.nist.gov/publications/detail/sp/800-107/rev-1/final`, 2012.

83. National Institute of Standards and Technology (NIST). Third-round report of the SHA-3 cryptographic hash algorithm competition. `https://csrc.nist.gov/publications/detail/nistir/7896/final`, 11 2012.

84. National Institute of Standards and Technology (NIST). FIPS PUB 180-4: Secure Hash Standard. `https://csrc.nist.gov/publications/detail/fips/180/4/final`, 8 2015.

85. National Institute of Standards and Technology (NIST). FIPS PUB 202: SHA-3 standard: Permutation-based hash and extendable-output functions. `https://csrc.nist.gov/publications/detail/fips/202/final`, 8 2015.

86. National Institute of Standards and Technology (NIST). SP 800-131A Rev.1: Transitions: Recommendation for transitioning the use of cryptographic algorithms and key lengths. `https://csrc.nist.gov/publications/detail/sp/800-131a/rev-1/archive/2015-11-06`, 2015.

87. National Institute of Standards and Technology (NIST). SP 800-185: SHA-3 derived functions: cSHAKE, KMAC, TupleHash, and ParallelHash. `https://csrc.nist.gov/publications/detail/sp/800-185/final`, 12 2016.

88. National Institute of Standards and Technology (NIST). SP 800-131A Rev.2: Transitions: Recommendation for transitioning the use of cryptographic algorithms and key lengths. `https://csrc.nist.gov/publications/detail/sp/800-131a/rev-2/final`, 2019.

89. Ivica Nikolic and Alex Biryukov. Collisions for step-reduced SHA-256. In Kaisa Nyberg, editor, *Fast Software Encryption – FSE 2008*, volume 5086 of *Lecture Notes in Computer Science*, pages 1–15, Lausanne, Switzerland, February 10–13, 2008. Springer, Heidelberg, Germany.

90. Bart Preneel. The NESSIE project: towards new cryptographic algorithms. In *3rd International Workshop on Information Security Applications, WISA*, pages 16–33, 2002.

91. Bart Preneel. The first 30 years of cryptographic hash functions and the NIST SHA-3 competition (invited talk). In Josef Pieprzyk, editor, *Topics in Cryptology – CT-RSA 2010*, volume 5985 of *Lecture Notes in Computer Science*, pages 1–14, San Francisco, CA, USA, March 1–5, 2010. Springer, Heidelberg, Germany.

92. Kexin Qiao, Ling Song, Meicheng Liu, and Jian Guo. New collision attacks on round-reduced keccak. In Jean-Sébastien Coron and Jesper Buus Nielsen, editors, *Advances in Cryptology – EUROCRYPT 2017, Part III*, volume 10212 of *Lecture Notes in Computer Science*, pages 216–243, Paris, France, April 30 – May 4, 2017. Springer, Heidelberg, Germany.

93. Ronald L. Rivest. The MD4 message digest algorithm. In Alfred J. Menezes and Scott A. Vanstone, editors, *Advances in Cryptology – CRYPTO'90*, volume 537 of *Lecture Notes in Computer Science*, pages 303–311, Santa Barbara, CA, USA, August 11–15, 1991. Springer, Heidelberg, Germany.

94. Ronald L. Rivest. The MD4 message-digest algorithm. RFC 1320, RFC Editor, April 1992. `http://www.rfc-editor.org/rfc/rfc1320.txt`.

95. Ronald L. Rivest. *RFC 1321: The MD5 Message-Digest Algorithm.* Internet Activities Board, April 1992.

96. Ronald L Rivest, Benjamin Agre, Daniel V Bailey, Christopher Crutchfield, Yevgeniy Dodis, Kermin Elliott Fleming, Asif Khan, Jayant Krishnamurthy, Yuncheng Lin, Leo Reyzin, et al. The MD6 hash function–a proposal to NIST for SHA-3. *Submission to NIST,* 2(3):1–234, 2008.

97. Somitra Kumar Sanadhya and Palash Sarkar. Deterministic constructions of 21-step collisions for the SHA-2 hash family. In Tzong-Chen Wu, Chin-Laung Lei, Vincent Rijmen, and Der-Tsai Lee, editors, *ISC 2008: 11th International Conference on Information Security,* volume 5222 of *Lecture Notes in Computer Science,* pages 244–259, Taipei, Taiwan, September 15–18, 2008. Springer, Heidelberg, Germany.

98. Somitra Kumar Sanadhya and Palash Sarkar. New collision attacks against up to 24-step SHA-2. In Dipanwita Roy Chowdhury, Vincent Rijmen, and Abhijit Das, editors, *Progress in Cryptology - INDOCRYPT 2008: 9th International Conference in Cryptology in India,* volume 5365 of *Lecture Notes in Computer Science,* pages 91–103, Kharagpur, India, December 14–17, 2008. Springer, Heidelberg, Germany.

99. Yu Sasaki and Kazumaro Aoki. Finding preimages in full MD5 faster than exhaustive search. In Antoine Joux, editor, *Advances in Cryptology – EUROCRYPT 2009,* volume 5479 of *Lecture Notes in Computer Science,* pages 134–152, Cologne, Germany, April 26–30, 2009. Springer, Heidelberg, Germany.

100. Ling Song, Guohong Liao, and Jian Guo. Non-full sbox linearization: Applications to collision attacks on round-reduced keccak. In Jonathan Katz and Hovav Shacham, editors, *Advances in Cryptology – CRYPTO 2017, Part II,* volume 10402 of *Lecture Notes in Computer Science,* pages 428–451, Santa Barbara, CA, USA, August 20–24, 2017. Springer, Heidelberg, Germany.

101. Marc Stevens. Fast collision attack on MD5. Cryptology ePrint Archive, Report 2006/104, 2006. http://eprint.iacr.org/2006/104.

102. Marc Stevens. On collisions for MD5, 8 2007. Student thesis: Master.

103. Marc Stevens. New collision attacks on SHA-1 based on optimal joint local-collision analysis. In Thomas Johansson and Phong Q. Nguyen, editors, *Advances in Cryptology – EUROCRYPT 2013,* volume 7881 of *Lecture Notes in Computer Science,* pages 245–261, Athens, Greece, May 26–30, 2013. Springer, Heidelberg, Germany.

104. Marc Stevens, Elie Bursztein, Pierre Karpman, Ange Albertini, and Yarik Markov. SHATTERED. https://shattered.io/.

105. Marc Stevens, Elie Bursztein, Pierre Karpman, Ange Albertini, and Yarik Markov. The first collision for full SHA-1. In Jonathan Katz and Hovav Shacham, editors, *Advances in Cryptology – CRYPTO 2017, Part I,* volume 10401 of *Lecture Notes in Computer Science,* pages 570–596, Santa Barbara, CA, USA, August 20–24, 2017. Springer, Heidelberg, Germany.

106. Marc Stevens, Pierre Karpman, and Thomas Peyrin. Freestart collision for full SHA-1. In Marc Fischlin and Jean-Sébastien Coron, editors, *Advances in Cryptology – EUROCRYPT 2016, Part I,* volume 9665 of *Lecture Notes in Computer Science,* pages 459–483, Vienna, Austria, May 8–12, 2016. Springer, Heidelberg, Germany.

107. Marc Stevens, Arjen K. Lenstra, and Benne de Weger. Chosen-prefix collisions for MD5 and colliding X.509 certificates for different identities. In Moni Naor, editor, *Advances in Cryptology – EUROCRYPT 2007,* volume 4515 of *Lecture Notes in Computer Science,* pages 1–22, Barcelona, Spain, May 20–24, 2007. Springer, Heidelberg, Germany.

108. Marc Stevens, Arjen K. Lenstra, and Benne De Weger. Chosen-prefix collisions for MD5 and applications. *Int. J. Appl. Cryptol.,* 2(4):322–359, July 2012.

109. Marc Stevens, Alexander Sotirov, Jacob Appelbaum, Arjen K. Lenstra, David Molnar, Dag Arne Osvik, and Benne de Weger. Short chosen-prefix collisions for MD5 and the creation of a rogue CA certificate. In Shai Halevi, editor, *Advances in*

Cryptology – CRYPTO 2009, volume 5677 of *Lecture Notes in Computer Science*, pages 55–69, Santa Barbara, CA, USA, August 16–20, 2009. Springer, Heidelberg, Germany.

110. Gene Tsudik. Message authentication with one-way hash functions. *ACM SIG-COMM Computer Communication Review*, 22(5):29–38, 1992.

111. S. Turner and L. Chen. MD2 to historic status. RFC 6149, RFC Editor, March 2011. http://www.rfc-editor.org/rfc/rfc6149.txt.

112. Xiaoyun Wang, Dengguo Feng, Xuejia Lai, and Hongbo Yu. Collisions for hash functions MD4, MD5, HAVAL-128 and RIPEMD. Cryptology ePrint Archive, Report 2004/199, 2004. http://eprint.iacr.org/2004/199.

113. Xiaoyun Wang, Yiqun Lisa Yin, and Hongbo Yu. Finding collisions in the full SHA-1. In Victor Shoup, editor, *Advances in Cryptology – CRYPTO 2005*, volume 3621 of *Lecture Notes in Computer Science*, pages 17–36, Santa Barbara, CA, USA, August 14–18, 2005. Springer, Heidelberg, Germany.

114. Xiaoyun Wang and Hongbo Yu. How to break MD5 and other hash functions. In Ronald Cramer, editor, *Advances in Cryptology – EUROCRYPT 2005*, volume 3494 of *Lecture Notes in Computer Science*, pages 19–35, Aarhus, Denmark, May 22–26, 2005. Springer, Heidelberg, Germany.

115. Tao Xie, Fanbao Liu, and Dengguo Feng. Could the 1-MSB input difference be the fastest collision attack for MD5? Cryptology ePrint Archive, Report 2008/391, 2008. http://eprint.iacr.org/2008/391.

116. Tao Xie, Fanbao Liu, and Dengguo Feng. Fast collision attack on MD5. Cryptology ePrint Archive, Report 2013/170, 2013. http://eprint.iacr.org/2013/170.

Chapter 16
Constructions of Keyed Hash Functions

In the previous chapters we studied constructions of hash functions in the unkeyed (resp. publicly keyed) setting for security properties such as collision resistance or second-preimage resistance. In this chapter we will extend the discussion to the private-key setting and show how to construct efficient privately keyed cryptographic primitives which can process arbitrarily long inputs. In particular, we will study pseudorandom functions (see Section 3.3.1 on page 124) and message authentication codes (see Section 3.5 on page 150).

We start our investigation with a good old acquaintance: the Merkle–Damgård transformation (see Section 13.1 on page 481). When constructing collision-resistant hash functions we use Merkle–Damgård to iterate a collision-resistant compression function. When targeting a pseudorandom function instead, the natural assumption would be to consider the compression function to be pseudorandom as well. However, as we have seen already in Section 13.1.6 (page 500) this approach is susceptible to length-extension attacks where an adversary exploits the fact that knowledge of a hash value $H(m)$ is equivalent to knowledge of an intermediate result in the computation of a hash value for message $m\|x$ for any value of x. Equipped with such an intermediate value an adversary is then capable of computing hash values for messages of the form $m\|x$ for arbitrary choices of x, thus clearly breaking the security of a pseudorandom function. The same applies to message authentication codes.

Interestingly, in case we consider only restricted settings where length-extension attacks are no longer possible (e.g., in case we enforce a prefix-free encoding or accept only messages of a certain fixed length) then, indeed, it can be shown that Merkle–Damgård yields a secure MAC or PRF based on the compression function being a secure MAC or PRF, respectively. We will discuss such Merkle–Damgård-based PRFs in Section 16.2.

Of course, in many cases we cannot assume such a restricted scenario and, thus, need to consider also different approaches. For this, we will turn to *HMAC*, the predominant construction in use today for message authentication and as a pseudorandom function. HMAC is short for *hash-based message authentication code*, and it is the pragmatic counterpart to a construction called NMAC

© Springer Nature Switzerland AG 2021

A. Mittelbach, M. Fischlin, *The Theory of Hash Functions and Random Oracles*,
Information Security and Cryptography, https://doi.org/10.1007/978-3-030-63287-8_16

(short for *nested message authentication code*). HMAC is optimized for easy implementations in practice that are based on existing unkeyed hash functions.

NMAC (and by extension HMAC) is based on the Merkle–Damgård transformation but with a twist. In order to obtain a *keyed variant* from a standard iterative hash function NMAC deploys two keys k_1 and k_2. Key k_1 is used instead of the initialization vector IV, yielding a keyed variant of the Merkle–Damgård function. Then, in order to avoid length-extension attacks NMAC employs an additional evaluation of the hash function in the last step with an additional hidden key k_2 and with the output of the previous evaluation as message. If $\mathsf{H}^h(\mathsf{k}, m)$ denotes a hash function where the initialization vector is set to IV := k then we obtain NMAC as

$$\mathrm{NMAC}((\mathsf{k}_1, \mathsf{k}_2), m) := \mathsf{H}^h(\mathsf{k}_2, \mathsf{H}^h(\mathsf{k}_1, m)).$$

When considering practical hash functions, the outer hash evaluation usually boils down to only a single application of the compression function. This is the case if the output of the inner hash evaluation is short enough such that the padding operation does not add an extra message block, a property that holds for most hash functions including, in particular, all those considered in Chapter 15. For example, for SHA-1[1] we have hash values of length 160 bits and a block size of 512 bits, and use as padding a length padding which adds a 1-bit, sufficiently many 0-bits, and then an encoding of the message length using the last 64 bits of a block. Thus, in this case the input message for the outer hash evaluation is given as

$$\mathrm{SHA\text{-}1}(\mathsf{k}_1, m) \| 1 \| 0^{287} \| \langle 160 \rangle_{64}.$$

The resulting construction can then be depicted as follows:

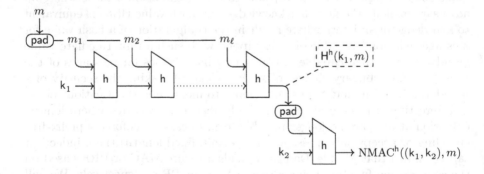

Given an implementation (possibly in hardware) of an unkeyed hash function, say again SHA-1, it is often infeasible to adapt the initialization vector at runtime for performance reasons and consequently it is impossible to run

---

[1] Recall from Chapter 15 that SHA-1 may still be used for HMAC according to NIST, despite the weaknesses in collision resistance.

NMAC on top of such an implementation without changing it. The idea of HMAC is to add a small modification to the NMAC construction such that the result can be executed on top of the implementation of any unkeyed hash function, even if the implementation does not expose the initialization vector. The idea is to use the key as the first input block instead. We will discuss both NMAC and HMAC in Section 16.3.

Finally, we will look at a particular use case of HMAC for the generation of keys (Section 16.6.1). For this we will formalize the notion of a *key derivation function* and discuss the HKDF construction, a popular key derivation function based on HMAC.

Notation. In this chapter we use H^h to denote *publicly keyed* iterated hash functions built from publicly keyed compression function h. If considering a public hash function key we denote it by hk. In order to emphasize the fact that we are in the *private-key* setting, we will use k instead of hk as function keys and denote by F^f the privately keyed iterated hash function F that is based on a privately keyed compression function f. Instead of F^f we may also write PRF^f or MAC^f when considering a pseudorandom function (resp. a message authentication code).

Unless otherwise stated, we consider compression functions $f : \{0,1\}^{f.bl(\lambda)} \times \{0,1\}^{f.cl(\lambda)} \mapsto \{0,1\}^{f.cl(\lambda)}$ that are secure message authentication codes or pseudorandom functions when the key is provided as second input (i.e., the key is provided as chaining value):

We thus also write $f(m, k)$ yet, $F^f(k, m)$.

16.1 Keying Merkle–Damgård

Message authentication codes as well as pseudorandom functions are privately keyed primitives (see Chapter 3). When considering (variants of) Merkle–Damgård as domain extenders for such privately keyed primitives we thus first need to specify how we treat keys within the Merkle–Damgård construction. There are various possibilities for how to introduce a key into the transformation, and over the following pages we present commonly used constructions.

Let us first recall the basic Merkle–Damgård construction H^h_{MD} (Construction 13.1; page 482) which processes a message m by first padding it to a multiple of the block length and then iteratively processing it message block

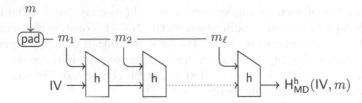

Fig. 16.1: The Merkle–Damgård construction $H^h_{MD}(IV, m)$ with padding function pad, initialization vector IV and compression function h.

by message block. In Figure 16.1 we present once more a schematic where $H^h_{MD}(IV, m)$ denotes the Merkle–Damgård construction with the initialization vector fixed to value IV.

16.1.1 The Secret-IV Method

Arguably the most common construction of a keyed Merkle–Damgård function is to consider the basic unkeyed Merkle–Damgård construction and use the function's key k as the initialization vector IV. In other words, when computing the hash value for a message m and key k the initialization vector is set to IV $:=$ k and then the hash value for m is computed as usual. Formally, we capture this *secret*-IV variant (SecIV) as Construction 16.1.

Construction 16.1 (SecIV-Construction).
Let $f : \{0,1\}^{f.bl(\lambda)} \times \{0,1\}^{f.cl(\lambda)} \to \{0,1\}^{f.cl(\lambda)}$ *be a compression function and let* pad *be some appropriate padding function. Then we define the* SecIV *construction* $F^f := (F.KGen, F.Eval)$ *of an iterated hash function as*

$F^f.KGen(1^\lambda)$	$F^f.Eval(k, m)$
$1:$ k $\leftarrow\!\!\$ \{0,1\}^{f.cl(\lambda)}$	$1:$ $y \leftarrow H^f_{MD}(k, m)$
$2:$ **return** k	$2:$ **return** y

Here $H^f_{MD}(k, m)$ *denotes an evaluation of the standard Merkle–Damgård construction with initialization vector* k, *compression function* f, *and padding function* pad.

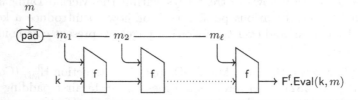

16.1.2 The Secret-Prefix Method

Instead of treating the initialization vector as the key for the resulting function we can also prepend the key to the message and use a fixed initialization vector IV. In this case the (possibly padded) key should have the length of a single block and we have that $F^f(k, m) := H^f_{MD}(k\|m)$, where again H^f_{MD} is the standard unkeyed Merkle–Damgård construction. We refer to this *secret-prefix* variant (SecPre) with the key being prepended to the message as Construction 16.2.

Construction 16.2 (SecPre-Construction).
Let $f : \{0,1\}^{f.bl(\lambda)} \times \{0,1\}^{f.cl(\lambda)} \to \{0,1\}^{f.cl(\lambda)}$ *be a compression function, let* $IV \in \{0,1\}^{f.cl(\lambda)}$ *be a fixed initialization vector, and let* pad *be some appropriate padding function. Then we define the* SecPre *construction* $F^f := (F.KGen, F.Eval)$ *of an iterated hash function as*

$F^f.KGen(1^\lambda)$	$F^f.Eval(k, m)$
1 : $k \leftarrow_\$ \{0,1\}^{f.bl(\lambda)}$	*1 :* $y \leftarrow H^f_{MD}(IV, k\|m)$
2 : **return** k	*2 :* **return** y

Here $H^f_{MD}(IV, m)$ *denotes an evaluation of the standard Merkle–Damgård construction with initialization vector* IV, *compression function* f, *and padding function* pad.

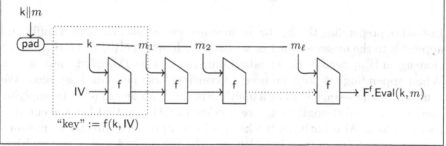

As hinted at in the above diagram we can also consider the entire first block $f(k, IV)$ to be the function's key. For this note that the result of the compression function call only depends on key k and is thus identical for all messages m. This then, however, is exactly the secret-IV setting (Construction 16.1) with the exception that now the initialization value is set to $IV := f(k, IV')$ instead of to a uniformly random value.

Which of the two constructions should be preferred? From a security point of view the secret-prefix construction, where the first message is used as keying material, is inferior. For this, consider that if the IV is used directly as key, then we can assume that it is chosen uniformly at random. If, however, we "construct" the initialization value (aka key) indirectly via $IV := f(k, IV')$ then the distribution of the resulting values depends heavily on the properties of function f. For this note that, while we assume f to be a pseudorandom function when keyed via the chaining value (i.e., the second input), this does not imply that it is also a pseudorandom function when the key is provided as message input (i.e., first input).

While possibly inferior in security (depending on the properties of f), the secret-prefix method (Construction 16.2) may in many cases be the more pragmatic construction in practice. Consider that you have an implementation of an unkeyed version of some hash function $H_{MD}^f(\cdot)$. In many cases, the implementation may not expose setting an initialization vector but instead comes with a fixed initialization vector. For example, consider that you have access to an implementation of SHA-1, possibly even in hardware. SHA-1 has a standardized and thus fixed IV of (in hexadecimal):

$$IV := 0x67452301EFCDAB8998BADCFE10325476C3D2E1F0$$

Chances are high that the provided API does not allow for setting the IV which, in particular for hardware implementations, may be for performance considerations. In this case, the secret-prefix construction allows to turn the unkeyed Merkle–Damgård transformation which does not expose the IV into a keyed version without having to change the implementation.

16.1.3 The Secret-Suffix Method

Instead of prepending the key to the message we can also use it as a suffix and append it to the message. That is, we consider function $F^f(k, m) := H_{MD}^f(m\|k)$. Here again H_{MD}^f denotes the standard unkeyed Merkle–Damgård construction. When appending the key, we need to consider how padding is applied. We could first pad message m to be a multiple of the block length (e.g., by applying Merkle–Damgård strengthening; see Section 13.1.1) such that key k is entering its own block. Alternatively, the key could be appended directly to message m without padding m first, in which case the key might be split over multiple message blocks. Indeed, it makes a difference for the security whether or not padding is applied to message m, as we will see in Section 16.2.5. Following is a pictorial representation of the construction including Merkle–Damgård strengthening and where $\nu = f.bl(\lambda) - |m_\ell| - 1$ denotes the number of bits required to fill the last block:

We refer to the secret-suffix variant (SecSuf) as Construction 16.3.

Construction 16.3 (SecSuf-Construction).
Let $f : \{0,1\}^{f.bl(\lambda)} \times \{0,1\}^{f.cl(\lambda)} \to \{0,1\}^{f.cl(\lambda)}$ *be a compression function,
let* $IV \in \{0,1\}^{f.cl(\lambda)}$ *be a fixed initialization vector, and let* pad *be some
appropriate padding function. Then we define the* SecSuf *construction*
$F^f := (F.KGen, F.Eval)$ *of an iterated hash function as*

$F^f.KGen(1^\lambda)$	$F^f.Eval(k, m)$
1: $k \leftarrow\!\!{}^\$ \{0,1\}^{f.bl(\lambda)}$	*1:* $y \leftarrow H^f_{MD}(IV, m)$
2: **return** k	*2:* $y' \leftarrow f(k, y)$
	3: **return** y'

Here $H^f_{MD}(IV, m)$ *denotes an evaluation of the standard Merkle–Damgård
construction with initialization vector* IV, *compression function* f, *and
padding function* pad.

16.1.4 Keyed Compression Function

The last alternative for keying Merkle–Damgård that we discuss is to consider
a keyed compression function of the form

$$f.Eval : \{0,1\}^{f.kl(\lambda)} \times \{0,1\}^{f.bl(\lambda)} \times \{0,1\}^{f.cl(\lambda)} \to \{0,1\}^{f.cl(\lambda)}.$$

Here kl denotes the key length, bl the message-block length, and cl the length
of the chaining value. This keyed compression function is then used in the
standard Merkle–Damgård transformation where we provide key k to every
call of compression function f. The following diagram shows the resulting
construction:

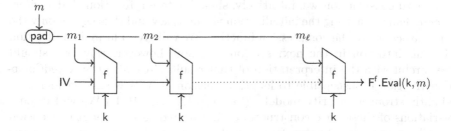

We refer to the keyed compression-function variant (KeyedComp) as Construction 16.4.

Construction 16.4 (KeyedComp-Construction).
Let $f : \{0,1\}^{f.kl(\lambda)} \times \{0,1\}^{f.bl(\lambda)} \times \{0,1\}^{f.cl(\lambda)} \rightarrow \{0,1\}^{f.cl(\lambda)}$ be a keyed compression function, let $IV \in \{0,1\}^{f.cl(\lambda)}$ be a fixed initialization vector, and let pad be some appropriate padding function. Then we define the KeyedComp construction $F^f := (F.KGen, F.Eval)$ of an iterated hash function as

$F^f.KGen(1^\lambda)$	$F^f.Eval(k, m)$
$1:\quad k \leftarrow\!\!\$\ \{0,1\}^{f.kl(\lambda)}$	$1:\quad y \leftarrow H_{MD}^{f(k,\cdot,\cdot)}(IV, m)$
$2:\quad$ **return** k	$2:\quad$ **return** y

Here $H_{MD}^{f(k,\cdot,\cdot)}(IV, m)$ denotes an evaluation of the standard Merkle–Damgård construction with initialization vector IV, padding function pad, and with compression function f keyed with key k.

We can construct such a keyed variant of Merkle–Damgård also from existing unkeyed Merkle–Damgård functions such as SHA-1 by simply pre-processing the ingoing message. SHA-1 has a block length of 512 bits. If we consider a key for the compression function to be of 160 bits, we could split the message blocks into two parts where the first 160 bits take the key and the remaining 352 bits take the actual message. This variant is visualized in the following diagram. Note that this is an ad hoc construction and security would need to be evaluated based on the compression function in question. Also note that the function is less performant as we need about one-third more compression function calls for the computation of a hash value.

Security. When keying each compression function call within the Merkle–Damgård construction we, intuitively, should obtain a function that is *more secure* than when using the initialization vector as key and thus keying only the first invocation of the compression function. We will give a formal justification for this intuition in the next section. We note however, that one should be careful with the interpretation of that result, since also the KeyedComp-construction is susceptible to length-extension attacks when considering a slightly stronger security model.[2] (See also Exercise 16.1.) We will discuss variations of these base constructions that overcome such length-extension attacks later in this chapter. However, if we sufficiently restrict the use of the

---

[2] For length-extension attacks on Construction 16.4 the adversary needs to get (black-box) access also to the keyed compression function. This attack model is usually referred to as the indifferentiability model, which we will discuss in detail in Chapter 17.

hash function to, for example, fixed-length invocations, we can indeed show that the result is secure.

16.2 Iterating PRFs with Merkle–Damgård

In the following we formally study our four keyed Merkle–Damgård constructions SecIV, SecPre, SecSuf, and KeyedComp when iterating a pseudorandom function in a restricted setting that excludes length-extension attacks. In Section 13.1.2 (page 485) we have seen that the Merkle–Damgård transformation preserves collision resistance. That is, if the iterated compression function h is collision resistant, then so is the resulting Merkle–Damgård function H_{MD}^h. The question now is, does the same hold for our four constructions above, when assuming that the iterated function f is a pseudorandom function?

We begin our discussion with the simplest case, which is Construction 16.4 where a *keyed* compression function is iterated. But in order to make the analysis formal, we first need to introduce a variant of collision resistance.

16.2.1 Weak Collision Resistance

For a function H to be collision resistant it must be infeasible for an adversary to find two messages m_1 and m_2 such that $m_1 \neq m_2$ and $H(m_1) = H(m_2)$. If the function is keyed, then collision resistance means that the above holds even if the adversary gets access to the function's key: Given a randomly chosen key hk the adversary must find messages m_1 and m_2 such that $H(hk, m_1) = H(hk, m_2)$.

When considering privately keyed primitives such as pseudorandom functions, full collision resistance may not be required for arguing security. This is the case, in particular, in scenarios where the adversary does not learn the function key. In these cases a weaker form of collision resistance, often simply referred to as *weak collision resistance* or *black-box collision resistance*, may be sufficient. In order to break this weaker form of collision resistance an adversary must still find two distinct messages m_1 and m_2 that collide, but contrary to before, the adversary only gets black-box (i.e., oracle) access to the function and thus in particular not access to the function's key; the scenario is identical to the PRF experiment (see also Definition 3.22; page 126). In the following we formalize this property:

Definition 16.5 (Weakly Collision-Resistant Hash Function).
An efficient keyed hash function $H = (H.KGen, H.Eval)$ *is called* weakly collision resistant *(WCR) if advantage* $\mathsf{Adv}_{H,\mathcal{A}}^{wcr}(\lambda)$ *is negligible for all PPT*

algorithms $\mathcal{A}$. The advantage is defined as

$$\mathsf{Adv}^{\mathrm{wcr}}_{\mathsf{H},\mathcal{A}}(\lambda) := \Pr\left[\mathit{Exp}^{\mathrm{wcr}}_{\mathsf{H},\mathcal{A}}(\lambda)\right]$$

relative to experiment $\mathit{Exp}^{\mathrm{wcr}}_{\mathsf{H},\mathcal{A}}(\lambda)$:

Experiment $\mathit{Exp}^{\mathrm{wcr}}_{\mathsf{H},\mathcal{A}}(\lambda)$

1 : $\mathsf{hk} \leftarrow\!\!{}_\$ \mathsf{H.KGen}(1^\lambda)$

2 : $(m_1, m_2) \leftarrow\!\!{}_\$ \mathcal{A}^{\mathsf{H.Eval}(\mathsf{hk},\cdot)}(1^\lambda)$

3 :   **return** $\mathsf{H.Eval}(\mathsf{hk}, m_1) = \mathsf{H.Eval}(\mathsf{hk}, m_2) \wedge m_1 \neq m_2$

Here the adversary gets oracle access to the hash function's evaluation algorithm with generated key hk.

Note that we can view a compression function f as a special form of a fixed-input-length hash function where the key is the chaining/initialization value. In this sense we can also speak of the weak collision resistance of a compression function f.

To prove the security of Constructions 16.1 to 16.4 we need the following result on the relationship between pseudorandom functions (and message authentication codes) with weak collision resistance:

> **Proposition 16.6.** Let $\mathsf{F} := (\mathsf{F.KGen}, \mathsf{F.Eval})$ be a tuple of efficient algorithms. Then the following hold:
>
> - If F is a secure (deterministic) message authentication code then F is also weakly collision resistant.
> - If F is a pseudorandom function and $\mathsf{F.ol}(\lambda) \in \omega(\log(\lambda))$ (i.e, the output length of F grows at least super-logarithmically in the security parameter) then F is also weakly collision resistant.

We will not formally prove Proposition 16.6 but instead discuss the intuition behind the statement and leave a formal proof as Exercise 16.2.

Proof outline. An adversary or forger against a message authentication code gets access to a MAC oracle and needs to output a valid tag for some message m that has not been queried to the oracle. To show the first statement we need to show how we can turn an adversary that breaks weak collision resistance into an adversary forging message authentication tokens. In case messages m and m' form a collision then a tag τ for m would also be valid for m' as the message authentication code is deterministic (see Definition 3.39 on page 151). Thus, in order to turn a collision finder into a forger, the adversary needs to simulate the function oracle for the collision finder, ensuring that not both messages m and m' are queried to its MAC oracle as otherwise the forgery would not be valid. This can be accomplished by guessing the right query number for the second colliding input m', and outputting the requested message m' together with the first tag for m as the forgery before making the query for m'.

When considering pseudorandom functions we need to assume that the function's output length grows sufficiently with the security parameter. For MACs this is also the case but here it is a necessary condition already for the security of a MAC, as short tokens can be guessed. Pseudorandom functions on the other hand have no such restriction, and if there exist pseudorandom functions, then there exists a pseudorandom function with output length only a single bit. To see that the requirement on the function's output is indeed necessary, consider a pseudorandom function that outputs only a single bit. As the function only has two possible output values (0 and 1) any two randomly chosen messages will collide with probability at least $\frac{1}{2}$. On the other hand, if the output length is sufficiently long, then random messages should form collisions only with negligible probability. Indeed, for a random function with sufficiently long output the best strategy a collision finder has is to query its oracle $q(\lambda)$ many times in the hope of finding a collision. It will thus succeed with probability at most $\frac{q(\lambda) \cdot (q(\lambda) - 1)}{2} \cdot 2^{-\text{F.ol}(\lambda)}$ which is negligible, given that $\text{F.ol}(\lambda)$ is super-logarithmic (also see the proof of Proposition 8.7 on page 353 showing that random oracles are collision resistant). Consequently, if a collision finder is significantly better for the pseudorandom function, this algorithm can be turned into a PRF distinguisher. Alternatively, we can use Proposition 3.41 (page 153) which states that a pseudorandom function with super-logarithmic output length is a secure (deterministic) message authentication code. The statement then follows from our above argument that MACs are weakly collision resistant.

Weak Collision Resistance and Merkle–Damgård

One might be tempted to think that, since Merkle–Damgård preserves collision resistance and since weak collision resistance is "weaker" than collision resistance, Merkle–Damgård must thus also preserve weak collision resistance. This is, however, not the case in general but depends on the way we introduce the key.

> **Proposition 16.7.** *Assume that there are compression functions which are weakly collision resistant but not collision resistant. Then, for Merkle–Damgård and weak collision resistance the following statements hold:*
>
> - *Constructions 16.1 (SecIV), 16.2 (SecPre), and 16.3 (SecSuf) do not preserve weak collision resistance.*
> - *Construction 16.4 (KeyedComp) does preserve weak collision resistance.*

We will prove the negative statements for Constructions 16.1, 16.2, and 16.3. For the positive result about Construction 16.4 the proof is essentially identical to that of Theorem 13.10 on page 487 about Merkle–Damgård preserving collision resistance, and we leave the proof as Exercise 16.3. Note that since every compression function call in Construction 16.4 (KeyedComp) is keyed, the attack strategy displayed below for the other three constructions does not work.

Proof of Proposition 16.7. Let f be a compression function that is weakly collision resistant but not collision resistant. To be consistent with compression function notation we write $f(m, k)$, that is, the message goes in the first slot and the key into the second. Recall that the key is used as the chaining value. As f is weakly collision resistant we have that no adversary can find collisions for $f(\cdot, k)$ for a random key k that is not given to the adversary. But since f is not collision resistant there exists a collision finder $\mathcal{C}$ that given a randomly chosen key k finds collisions with non-negligible probability. The following argument first considers both Constructions 16.1 (SecIV) and 16.2 (SecPre) simultaneously.

We construct an adversary $\mathcal{A}$ that uses the collision finder $\mathcal{C}$ to find weak collisions. Adversary $\mathcal{A}$ gets oracle access to $F^f(k, \cdot)$ and as input the security parameter 1^λ. It picks a random message x and computes $y \leftarrow F^f(k, x)$ by calling its oracle. It then runs collision finder $\mathcal{C}$, providing it value y as the key on which to find a collision. In case $\mathcal{C}$ succeeds and outputs $m \neq m'$ such that $f(m, y) = f(m', y)$, adversary $\mathcal{A}$ stops and outputs as a weak collision the messages

$$x \| \mathsf{pad}(x) \| m \qquad \text{and} \qquad x \| \mathsf{pad}(x) \| m'.$$

For the padding note that when calling the oracle to compute $F^f(k, x)$ message x will be padded according to the padding chosen for F (e.g., Merkle–Damgård strengthening). Note that, by construction, the two messages collide with probability one in case collision finder $\mathcal{C}$ is successful as the result after digesting the padding block yields the chaining value y and we have that $f(m, y) = f(m', y)$. This concludes the proof for these two constructions.

For Construction 16.3 (SecSuf) note that we can let the collision finder for input IV determine two values $m \neq m'$ such that they collide in the first iteration of the compression function, $f(m, \mathsf{IV}) = f(m', \mathsf{IV})$. Then these two messages also collide under Construction 16.3 as padding and appending of the secret key k only affect subsequent blocks and, in particular, the added blocks are identical for both messages.   □

From the above proof we can extract a minimum requirement for Constructions 16.1, 16.2, and 16.3 to be weakly collision resistant. At the very least, the underlying compression function must be collision resistant.

Corollary 16.8. *Collision resistance of the underlying compression function is a necessary (and sufficient) requirement for Constructions 16.1, 16.2, and 16.3 to be weakly collision resistant.*

Let us take a step back and rephrase the implication of Corollary 16.8. In case of domain extension via Merkle–Damgård weak collision resistance of the iterated function is *not sufficient* to guarantee weak collision resistance of the resulting hash function. Instead, to achieve weak collision resistance of the resulting function the iterated function needs to be *collision resistant*. Since collision resistance implies weak collision resistance for the iterated hash function we have established that collision resistance of the compression function is not just necessary but also sufficient for the resulting hash function to be weakly collision resistant.

16.2.2 Security of Iterating Keyed Compression Functions

With the definition of weak collision resistance we now have the necessary tools to discuss the security of Construction 16.4 (KeyedComp)—Merkle–Damgård iterating a keyed compression function—as a domain extender for pseudorandom functions and message authentication codes. We start by stating positive results for both pseudorandom functions as well as for message authentication codes. Note, however, that these results should be taken with a bit of skepticism, as we discuss towards the end of this section (also see Exercise 16.1): Under a slightly stronger (yet reasonable) security model length-extension attacks are, in fact, possible.

PRF Security

We start by showing that Merkle–Damgård iterating a pseudorandom function where the key is provided on each iteration is a secure domain extender for pseudorandom functions.

> **Proposition 16.9.** *The Merkle–Damgård variant* KeyedComp *specified in Construction 16.4 preserves pseudorandomness for compression functions* f *with super-logarithmic output length (i.e.,* $f.cl(\lambda) \in \omega(\log(\lambda))$*).*

Proof. Let f be a compression function as in the proposition, that is, f is a pseudorandom function with an output length that grows at least super-logarithmically in the security parameter.

Let $\mathcal{D}_F$ be a PRF distinguisher for function F^f (aka Construction 16.4, KeyedComp). We will construct a distinguisher $\mathcal{D}_f$ against the underlying function f as follows: Distinguisher $\mathcal{D}_f$ runs $\mathcal{D}_F$ and simulates the Merkle–Damgård construction using its oracle as compression function, and returns whatever $\mathcal{D}_F$ returns as output. That is, distinguisher $\mathcal{D}_f$ gets as input security parameter 1^λ and oracle access to an oracle O which is either function $f(k, \cdot, \cdot)$

initialized with a random key $k \leftarrow\!\!\$\; f.KGen(1^\lambda)$ or to a random function R_f of the same form as f.[3] It runs distinguisher $\mathcal{D}_F$ answering all its oracle queries m by evaluating the Merkle–Damgård iteration scheme for message m and using its oracle O as compression function, that is, it computes $y \leftarrow H_{MD}^O(m)$, which it returns to distinguisher $\mathcal{D}_F$. When distinguisher $\mathcal{D}_F$ finishes and outputs 0 or 1, distinguisher $\mathcal{D}_f$ also stops forwarding the verdict.

Analysis. When oracle O is function f then the simulation for distinguisher $\mathcal{D}_F$ is perfect and we have

$$\Pr\left[\mathcal{D}_F^{F^{f(k,\cdot)}}(1^\lambda) = 1\right] = \Pr\left[\mathcal{D}_f^{f(k,\cdot,\cdot)}(1^\lambda) = 1\right]. \qquad (16.1)$$

In both cases the probability is over the choice of key k and the random coins of distinguisher $\mathcal{D}_F$.

In case oracle O is a random function R_f we need to argue that the simulation as done by $\mathcal{D}_f$ perfectly simulates a random function R_F of the form of F^f. For this, we will use weak collision resistance. By Proposition 16.6, pseudorandomness of the compression function f (plus a super-logarithmic output length) implies its weak collision resistance. Similarly, a random function with the same input and output lengths as f is weakly collision resistant. Now, using Proposition 16.7 yields that F^O (for both choices of oracle O) is also weakly collision resistant.

The above argument allows us to upper bound the distinguishing probability of distinguisher $\mathcal{D}_F$ as we can now consider two possibilities in case oracle O implements random function R_f. Let $\mathcal{Q}$ denote the set of queries that distinguisher $\mathcal{D}_f$ sends to its oracle O (implementing R_f) when running distinguisher $\mathcal{D}_F$. Let collision denote the event that there are two queries in $\mathcal{Q}$ that form a collision on R_f, that is,

$$collision := [\exists q, q' \in \mathcal{Q} : q \neq q' \wedge R_f(q) = R_f(q')].$$

As R_f is a random function, we can quantify the probability of event collision as a function of its output length

$$\Pr[collision] \leq \binom{|\mathcal{Q}|}{2} \cdot 2^{-f.cl(\lambda)} \leq \frac{|\mathcal{Q}|^2}{2^{f.cl(\lambda)-1}}.$$

Note that $|\mathcal{Q}|$ is polynomial because the number of queries of $\mathcal{D}_F$ is polynomial and each query consists of at most a polynomial number of blocks.

On the other hand, in case no collision occurs we have that the output distribution generated by distinguisher $\mathcal{D}_f$ towards distinguisher $\mathcal{D}_F$ when computing $F^{R_f}(\cdot)$ is uniformly random in $\{0,1\}^{f.cl(\lambda)}$. The reason is that all evaluations are for different inputs, resulting in independent outputs. Similarly, a random function R_F of the form of F has an output distribution that is

---

[3] We write $f(k, \cdot, \cdot)$ to denote the keyed compression function of arity 3 (with slots for key, message, and chaining value).

uniformly random in $\{0,1\}^{\mathsf{f}.\mathsf{cl}(\lambda)}$ and thus the two are indistinguishable. It follows that

$$\Pr\left[\mathcal{D}_{\mathsf{f}}^{\mathsf{R}_{\mathsf{f}}(\cdot)}(1^{\lambda}) = 1\right] \leq \Pr[\mathsf{collision}] + \Pr\left[\mathcal{D}_{\mathsf{F}}^{\mathsf{R}_{\mathsf{F}}(\cdot)}(1^{\lambda}) = 1\right]. \qquad (16.2)$$

The result follows by combining Equations (16.1) and (16.2).   □

MAC Security

As seen above, Merkle–Damgård preserves PRF security in case the compression function is a fixed-input-length PRF and the key is used in every iteration of the underlying compression function. In the following we will discuss Construction 16.4 (KeyedComp) as a domain extender for message authentication codes. Similar to the PRF case, we can show that in this scenario Merkle–Damgård yields a secure message authentication code, given that the iterated function is a secure MAC.

> **Proposition 16.10.** *The Merkle–Damgård variant* KeyedComp *specified in Construction 16.4 preserves security of message authentication codes.*

In contrast to the PRF version of the result, in the MAC version we do not need the explicit requirement on the output length of the compression function. This is, however, not because we do not require weak collision resistance in the proof of the statement but simply because MAC security on its own already requires the function output to be sufficiently long (otherwise it would be easy to just guess a valid tag).

To prove Proposition 16.10 the idea is to, similarly to the PRF case, use weak collision resistance to argue that either:

- we can turn a MAC forger for function F^{f} into a (weak) collision finder for function f, or
- we can turn a MAC forger for function F^{f} into a MAC forger for the iterated fixed-input-length message authentication code f.

The result then follows with the fact that MACs are weakly collision resistant (Proposition 16.6) and that Merkle–Damgård as in Construction 16.4 preserves weak collision resistance (Proposition 16.7).

We do not formally prove the statement here, but instead leave a formal proof as Exercise 16.4.

On Length-Extension Attacks

In Chapter 13 we saw that Merkle–Damgård is susceptible to length-extension attacks. Given the hash value $\mathsf{F}^{\mathsf{f}}(m)$ for some message m, an attacker can

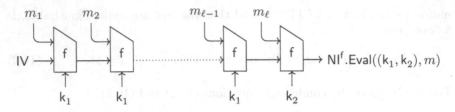

Fig. 16.2: The *nested iterate* scheme NI is almost identical to our Construction 16.4 (see page 626) but with a twist. Instead of a single key k, the nested iterate takes a key that is twice as long and split into two components $k = (k_1, k_2)$. During an evaluation, all compression function calls except for the last one take key k_1. Key k_2 is used only in the very last call to f.

compute hash values for extensions of m, e.g., for message $\mathsf{pad}(m)\|x$, without knowing m.[4] Clearly a MAC or a PRF that is vulnerable to such attacks cannot be secure. Construction 16.4 gets around the problem by providing the key to every call to the compression function. Thus, an adversary cannot compute extensions as it cannot evaluate the compression function on the correct key directly. For this note that the adversary only gets oracle access to function $\mathsf{F}^{f(k,\cdot,\cdot)}$ but no direct oracle access to $f(k,\cdot,\cdot)$. And since key k remains hidden from the adversary, the adversary can also not evaluate the function locally.

If we assume, on the other hand, that the adversary not only has access to oracle $\mathsf{F}^{f(k,\cdot,\cdot)}$, but also to the underlying function, that is, it has oracle access to $f(k,\cdot,\cdot)$, then it can also mount length-extension attacks and the proofs presented above are void. The question thus is, how likely is it that an attacker can somehow utilize the underlying function?

Taking the conservative approach we should assume that the attacker has at its disposal too many rather than too few capabilities and thus not use the above constructions in practice. A security model where the attacker gets access to the underlying primitive instead of just to the final construction is called *indifferentiability*, and we dedicate Chapter 17 to it.

One way to protect against length-extension attacks is to introduce a second key which is used in the final iteration. This scheme is known as the *nested iterate* NI, and we depict it in Figure 16.2. While we will not formally analyze the nested iterate scheme, as intuition, consider an adversary with access to oracles for $f(k_1,\cdot,\cdot)$ and possibly also for $f(k_2,\cdot,\cdot)$ that tries to mount a length-extension attack. Since the final compression function evaluation when computing $\mathsf{NI}^f((k_1, k_2), m)$ for some message m is not done with key k_1 but with key k_2, the resulting hash value is only with negligible probability an intermediate result when computing the hash value for an extension of m such as $m\|\mathsf{pad}(m)\|x$.

---

[4] Note that we made use of a length-extension attack in the proof of Proposition 16.7.

The predominant construction used in practice to avoid length-extension attacks is, however, not the nested iterate but HMAC. An important feature of HMAC is that it can be constructed on top of existing unkeyed hash functions such as SHA-1, which is not possible with the nested iterate. We will discuss HMAC in detail later in this chapter in Section 16.3.

16.2.3 Security of the Secret-IV Method

While Construction 16.4 (KeyedComp) is a secure domain extender for pseudorandom functions and message authentication codes, the simpler Construction 16.1 (SecIV) from page 622 where the compression function is unkeyed and a key is introduced by simply interpreting the IV as key is not a secure domain extender. For this, recall that the standard (unkeyed) Merkle–Damgård hash function is susceptible to length-extension attacks and, thus, so is Construction 16.1.

In order to better understand the security of Merkle–Damgård and in particular the security of Construction 16.1, in the following we investigate the question of whether length-extension attacks are the only weakness of the construction. What if we restricted the class of adversaries such that length-extension attacks are no longer possible, for example, by considering only a single fixed message length? Would in this case Construction 16.1 yield a secure domain extender for pseudorandom functions?

Prefix-freeness. Instead of restricting Construction 16.1 to a fixed input length we consider a broader scope: We restrict the class of adversaries to only those adversaries that make prefix-free queries to their oracle. That is, if $\mathcal{A}^O$ is an adversary relative to oracle O then we call adversary $\mathcal{A}$ *prefix free* if with probability 1 over the coins of adversary $\mathcal{A}$ it holds that for all queries $\mathcal{Q}$ to oracle O the following holds:

$$\{q, q' \in \mathcal{Q} : q \neq q' \land q \text{ is prefix of } q'\} = \{\,\}.$$

We say that a string q is a prefix of string q' if the first $|q|$ bits of q' are identical to q, that is, if $q'[1..|q|] = q$. Thus a prefix-free adversary is an adversary that does not make any two oracle queries such that one query is the prefix of another.

Padding. When considering prefix-freeness and hash function constructions such as Merkle–Damgård we would need to consider padding. For example, instead of the above definition of a prefix-free adversary we would need to require that for any two queries q and q' the string $\mathsf{pad}(q)$ is not a prefix of $\mathsf{pad}(q')$. As padding does not add to the deeper understanding but instead complicates the syntax we will ignore it in the following discussion. Note that we thus here also assume that the adversary only makes queries to the hash functions which are a multiple of the block length.

Notation. As before, we write $f(m, k)$ and add the key to the fixed-input-length pseudorandom function f as second parameter. This is to keep notation consistent with compression functions within standard Merkle–Damgård, where the second input denotes the chaining value while the first denotes the message block.

PRF Security

In the following we show that the secret-IV Merkle–Damgård construction (i.e., Construction 16.1) is a secure PRF domain extender against prefix-free adversaries as formalized in the following proposition:

> **Proposition 16.11.** *Let* $f = (f.KGen, f.Eval)$ *be a tuple of efficient algorithms. If* f *is a secure fixed-input-length and compressing pseudorandom function with super-logarithmic output length (i.e., $f.cl(\lambda) \in \omega(\log(\lambda))$), then the Merkle–Damgård variant* F^f *as specified in Construction 16.1 with compression function* f *is a secure variable-input-length pseudorandom function against prefix-free adversaries.*
>
> *Concretely, we have that for any* PPT *adversary* $\mathcal{A}$ *against* F^f *that makes at most* $q(\lambda)$ *prefix-free queries of length at most* $\ell(\lambda)$ *blocks (after padding), there exists a* PPT *adversary* $\mathcal{B}$ *against the pseudorandomness of* f *such that*
>
> $$\mathsf{Adv}^{prf}_{F^f,\mathcal{A}}(\lambda) \leq q(\lambda) \cdot \ell(\lambda) \cdot \mathsf{Adv}^{prf}_{f,\mathcal{B}}(\lambda).$$

Remark 16.12. In the secret-IV method the key is passed in as a chaining value and thus the function's output length is identical to the key length. The requirement of super-logarithmic output length is thus a necessary condition for function f being a secure pseudorandom function.

Remark 16.13. We note that the following proof is a bit on the long side and involves two nested hybrid arguments. While we will make use of Proposition 16.11 for an important result on the security of NMAC (Theorem 16.20), working through the proof is not required for the understanding of later parts of this chapter. It is thus safe to continue with Section 16.2.5 on page 647.

Let us consider for a moment an adversary $\mathcal{A}$ that makes only queries that are at most of three message blocks. To include padding in the discussion we demand that the adversary only makes queries that are at most three blocks after padding. In this case, we need to consider the following function:

Now, in order to prove that F^f is pseudorandom, we need to show that no adversary $\mathcal{A}$ can distinguish the above function from a random function R_F that has the same input and output specification as F^f: In the above simplified version R_F takes as input, messages of at most three blocks and generates hash values in $\{0,1\}^{f.cl(\lambda)}$.

One attempt to show the statement would be to start with a game where adversary $\mathcal{A}$ interacts with hash function F^f to then iteratively replace calls to pseudorandom function f with calls to a random function R_f of the same form as f. Once all functions are replaced we could look into a final hop to replace iterative function F^{R_f} with monolithic random function R_F. If we can show that each step only provides negligible gain to the adversary, then the statement follows.[5] In Figure 16.3 we exemplify this approach and give the first three games as pseudocode. Here $Game_1$ implements the scenario in which adversary $\mathcal{A}$ gets as oracle the real function F^f and thus would win if it outputs as guess $b = 0$ (see game-based Definition 3.22 of a pseudorandom function on page 126). While the first game hop seems straightforward down to the security of function f as a pseudorandom function we get stuck already in the next step. In $Game_2$ the evaluation of function f in line 4 (of procedure HASH) is no longer with a fixed randomly chosen key, but instead with a "fresh key" upon every call with a different first message block m_1. For this note that the "key" in line 4 is chaining value y which is computed as $y \leftarrow f(m_1, k)$ in $Game_1$ and now as $y \leftarrow\$ R_f(m_1, k)$ in $Game_2$: it changes with the first message block m_1. The security experiment for PRFs on the other hand considers a single fixed key that is chosen uniformly at random and only once (see Definition 3.21 on page 126).

Intuitively, a secure pseudorandom function should remain secure also in the scenario where an adversary can query the function on different (hidden) keys. As an ingredient for the proof of Proposition 16.11 we thus first need to consider a different characterization of pseudorandom functions that captures the above scenario where an adversary sees images under various keys. This we formalize next as Lemma 16.14. The idea is to consider an extended *multi-key* security experiment in which an adversary does not get access to only a single function but $q(\lambda)$ many functions for some polynomial q. These are all independent random functions of the same form as the pseudorandom function or all instances of the pseudorandom function with independently sampled keys. This scenario is captured by providing the distinguisher with a real-or-random oracle ROR which takes an index $i \in [q(\lambda)]$ and a value x and either evaluates $PRF(k[i], x)$ (where $k[i]$ denotes the ith key) or $R_i(x)$ where R_i for all $i \in [q(\lambda)]$ denotes an independent random function. We capture the latter via lazy sampling. The lemma then states that the distinguisher in the

---

[5] Note that this is not necessarily true for an adversary asking queries of polynomial length $\ell(\lambda)$. Here we would transform the starting game in $\ell(\lambda) + 2$ many steps and thus need to be careful when arguing that the sum of all negligible losses remains negligible. For this note that if the number of negligible summands depends on the security parameter that then the sum may not be negligible (also see Example 2.5 on page 78).

$$\text{Game}_1^{\mathcal{A}}(\lambda)\xrightarrow{\quad\text{PRF}\quad}\text{Game}_2^{\mathcal{A}}(\lambda)\xrightarrow{\quad?\quad}\text{Game}_3^{\mathcal{A}}(\lambda)$$

$\text{Game}_1^{\mathcal{A}}(\lambda)$	$\text{Game}_2^{\mathcal{A}}(\lambda)$	$\text{Game}_3^{\mathcal{A}}(\lambda)$
1:	$T \leftarrow []$	$T \leftarrow []$
2: $\quad k \leftarrow\!\!\$ \, \{0,1\}^{\text{f.cl}(\lambda)}$	$k \leftarrow\!\!\$ \, \{0,1\}^{\text{f.cl}(\lambda)}$	$k \leftarrow\!\!\$ \, \{0,1\}^{\text{f.cl}(\lambda)}$
3: $\quad b \leftarrow\!\!\$ \, \mathcal{A}^{\text{HASH}}(1^\lambda)$	$b \leftarrow\!\!\$ \, \mathcal{A}^{\text{HASH}}(1^\lambda)$	$b \leftarrow\!\!\$ \, \mathcal{A}^{\text{HASH}}(1^\lambda)$
4: $\quad$ **return** $b = 0$	**return** $b = 0$	**return** $b = 0$

$\text{HASH}(m)$	$\text{HASH}(m)$	$\text{HASH}(m)$
1: $\quad m_1, m_2, m_3 \leftarrow \mathsf{pad}(m)$	$m_1, m_2, m_3 \leftarrow \mathsf{pad}(m)$	$m_1, m_2, m_3 \leftarrow \mathsf{pad}(m)$
2: $\quad y \leftarrow \mathsf{f}(m_1, k)$	$y \leftarrow\!\!\$ \, \mathsf{R_f}(m_1, k)$	$y \leftarrow\!\!\$ \, \mathsf{R_f}(m_1, k)$
3: $\quad$ **if** $m_2 \neq \varepsilon$ **do**	**if** $m_2 \neq \varepsilon$ **do**	**if** $m_2 \neq \varepsilon$ **do**
4: $\qquad y \leftarrow \mathsf{f}(m_2, y)$	$y \leftarrow \mathsf{f}(m_2, y)$	what to do?
5: $\quad$ **if** $m_3 \neq \varepsilon$ **do**	**if** $m_3 \neq \varepsilon$ **do**	**if** $m_3 \neq \varepsilon$ **do**
6: $\qquad y \leftarrow \mathsf{f}(m_3, y)$	$y \leftarrow \mathsf{f}(m_3, y)$	$y \leftarrow \mathsf{f}(m_3, y)$
7: $\quad$ **return** y	**return** y	**return** y

	$\mathsf{R_f}(m, y)$	$\mathsf{R_f}(m, y)$
	if $T[m, y] = \bot$ **do**	**if** $T[m, y] = \bot$ **do**
	$\quad T[m, y] \leftarrow \{0,1\}^{\text{f.cl}(\lambda)}$	$\quad T[m, y] \leftarrow \{0,1\}^{\text{f.cl}(\lambda)}$
	return $T[m, y]$	**return** $T[m, y]$

Fig. 16.3: The first two game hops for the proof attempt of Proposition 16.11. Game_1 is the original security game with adversary $\mathcal{A}$ getting access to the actual hash function. Padding function $\mathsf{pad}(m)$ applies padding and splits up the message m into its individual message blocks. If message m is shorter than the maximum number of blocks, then the remaining blocks are set to the empty string ε. The first game hop reduces to the security of the pseudorandomness of f, and in Game_2 the first call to f is replaced with a call to a random function $\mathsf{R_f}$. The next game hop, however, is not clear as from here on onwards the iteration function f is not called on a static single key.

multi-key experiment is at most $\mathsf{q}(\lambda)$ times more successful than an adversary in the standard PRF security game.

Lemma 16.14. *Let function* $\mathsf{q} : \mathbb{N} \to \mathbb{N}$ *be a polynomial and let* $\text{PRF} = (\text{PRF.KGen}, \text{PRF.Eval})$ *be a tuple of efficient algorithms. Then for all* PPT *algorithms* $\mathcal{D}$ *there exists* PPT *algorithm* $\mathcal{D}_{\text{PRF}}$ *such that advantage* $\text{Adv}_{\text{PRF},\mathcal{D}}^{\text{multi-key-prf}}(\lambda)$ *defined as*

$$\text{Adv}_{\text{PRF},\mathcal{D}}^{\text{multi-key-prf}}(\lambda) := 2 \cdot \left| \Pr\left[\textit{Exp}_{\text{PRF},\mathcal{D}}^{\text{multi-key-prf}}(\lambda) \right] - \frac{1}{2} \right|$$

is upper bound by

$$\mathsf{Adv}_{\mathsf{PRF},\mathcal{D}}^{\text{multi-key-prf}}(\lambda) \le \mathsf{q}(\lambda) \cdot \mathsf{Adv}_{\mathsf{PRF},\mathcal{D}_{\mathsf{PRF}}}^{\text{prf}}(\lambda).$$

Here advantage $\mathsf{Adv}_{\mathsf{PRF},\mathcal{D}_{\mathsf{PRF}}}^{\text{prf}}(\lambda)$ *is as defined in Definition 3.22 (page 126) and experiment* $\mathsf{Exp}_{\mathsf{PRF},\mathcal{D}}^{\text{multi-key-prf}}(\lambda)$ *is defined as*

$\mathsf{Exp}_{\mathsf{PRF},\mathcal{D}}^{\text{multi-key-prf}}(\lambda)$	$\mathrm{RoR}(i,x)$
1 : $T \leftarrow []; \ b \leftarrow\!\!\$ \ \{0,1\}$	1 : **if** $b = 0 \wedge T[i,x] = \bot \wedge i \in [\mathsf{q}(\lambda)]$ **then**
2 : **for** $i = 1..\mathsf{q}(\lambda)$ **do**	2 : $\quad T[i,x] \leftarrow \mathsf{PRF.Eval}(\mathsf{k}[i], x)$
3 : $\quad \mathsf{k}[i] \leftarrow\!\!\$ \ \mathsf{PRF.KGen}(1^\lambda)$	3 : **elseif** $T[i,x] = \bot$ **then**
4 : $b' \leftarrow\!\!\$ \ \mathcal{D}^{\mathrm{RoR}}(1^\lambda)$	4 : $\quad T[i,x] \leftarrow\!\!\$ \ \{0,1\}^{\mathsf{PRF.ol}(\lambda)}$
5 : **return** $b = b'$	5 : **return** $T[i,x]$

Proof. Lemma 16.14 is a variant of the question of whether from the indistinguishability of two random variables X and Y we can conclude that also the q-fold repetition $X_{\times\mathsf{q}}$ of X is indistinguishable from $Y_{\times\mathsf{q}}$. Such statements are usually proven via a hybrid argument. In Section 3.2.2 (page 111) we have studied the hybrid argument proof strategy and, in particular, the question of the indistinguishability of the q-fold repetition of a random variable.

The statement can be shown with Theorem 3.17 (page 120), and we will here make use of item 2 of the statement (in the oracle version, see Remark 3.19 after the theorem statement). As hybrids we consider a sequence of $\mathsf{q}(\lambda) + 1$ many intermediate distributions: For the jth hybrid (for $0 \le j \le \mathsf{q}(\lambda)$) we fix $b = 0$ in experiment $\mathsf{Exp}_{\mathsf{PRF},\mathcal{D}}^{\text{multi-key-prf}}(\lambda)$ and replace line 1 of the real-or-random oracle RoR with

$$\textbf{if } T[i,x] = \bot \wedge i > j \textbf{ then} \ .$$

This yields the following definition of hybrid H^j:[6]

$H^j(1^\lambda)$	$\mathrm{RoR}(i,x)$
1 : $T \leftarrow []$	1 : **if** $T[i,x] = \bot \wedge i > j$ **then**
2 : **for** $i = 1..\mathsf{q}(\lambda)$ **do**	2 : $\quad T[i,x] \leftarrow \mathsf{PRF.Eval}(\mathsf{k}[i], x)$
3 : $\quad \mathsf{k}[i] \leftarrow\!\!\$ \ \mathsf{PRF.KGen}(1^\lambda)$	3 : **elseif** $T[i,x] = \bot$ **then**
4 : $b' \leftarrow\!\!\$ \ \mathcal{D}^{\mathrm{RoR}}(1^\lambda)$	4 : $\quad T[i,x] \leftarrow\!\!\$ \ \{0,1\}^{\mathsf{PRF.ol}(\lambda)}$
5 : **return** $b' = 0$	5 : **return** $T[i,x]$

It follows that hybrid H^0 is identical to $\mathsf{Exp}_{\mathsf{PRF},\mathcal{D}}^{\text{multi-key-prf}}(\lambda)$ with hidden bit $b = 0$, that is, for any index i pseudorandom function $\mathsf{PRF}(\mathsf{k}[i], \cdot)$ is used

---

[6] We note that we assume that the adversary never queries oracle RoR on an index i outside of the specified range of $0 < i \le \mathsf{q}(\lambda)$. While this can be easily enforced in code it only complicates the presentation.

to answer queries to real-or-random oracle RoR. For the jth hybrid H^j we have replaced the first j many functions with random functions, that is, for index $1 \le i \le j$ random function R_i is used while for indices $i > j$ calls are still answered with pseudorandom function PRF and key $k[i]$.[7] At the other end of the hybrid spectrum we have that hybrid $H^{q(\lambda)}$ is identical to experiment $\mathsf{Exp}_{\mathsf{PRF},\mathcal{D}}^{\text{multi-key-prf}}(\lambda)$ with hidden bit $b = 1$, as for all $i \in [q(\lambda)]$ we have that $i \le j = q(\lambda)$. Now, Theorem 3.17, item 2, tells us that the distinguishing advantage against the extreme hybrids H^0 and $H^{q(\lambda)}$ can be upper bounded by the distinguishing advantage of telling apart two uniformly random (neighboring) hybrids $H^{U(\lambda)}$ and $H^{U(\lambda)+1}$ as

$$\mathsf{Adv}_{H^0,H^{q(\lambda)},\mathcal{D}}^{\text{indist}}(\lambda) \le q(\lambda) \cdot \mathsf{Adv}_{H^{U(\lambda)},H^{U(\lambda)+1},\mathcal{D}}^{\text{indist}}(\lambda).$$

Here $U(\lambda)$ denotes the random variable that is distributed uniformly in $\{0, 1, \ldots, q(\lambda) - 1\}$.

Let $\mathcal{D}$ be a distinguisher against hybrids $H^{U(\lambda)}$ and $H^{U(\lambda)+1}$ then we can construct a distinguisher $\mathcal{D}_{\mathsf{PRF}}$ against the security of pseudorandom function PRF as follows. Distinguisher $\mathcal{D}_{\mathsf{PRF}}$ gets oracle access to an oracle O that implements either function $\mathsf{PRF}(k, \cdot)$ with a uniformly random key k or a uniformly random function R. It picks an index $j \leftarrow\!\!\$ [q(\lambda)]$ uniformly at random and then simulates hybrid H^j for distinguisher $\mathcal{D}$ but with a twist. When $\mathcal{D}$ asks its real-or-random oracle RoR on index $i = j$ then instead of answering it with pseudorandom function PRF and key $k[i]$ it uses its own oracle O to answer the query. Following is the pseudocode for distinguisher $\mathcal{D}_{\mathsf{PRF}}$.

$\mathcal{D}_{\mathsf{PRF}}^{\mathsf{O}}(1^\lambda)$	$\mathrm{RoR}(i, x)$
1: $j \leftarrow\!\!\$ [q(\lambda)]$	1: **if** $T[i, x] = \perp \wedge i = j$ **then**
2: $T \leftarrow []$	2: $\quad T[i, x] \leftarrow \mathsf{O}(x)$
3: **for** $i = 1..q(\lambda)$ **do**	3: **elseif** $T[i, x] = \perp \wedge i > j$ **then**
4: $\quad k[i] \leftarrow\!\!\$ \mathsf{PRF.KGen}(1^\lambda)$	4: $\quad T[i, x] \leftarrow \mathsf{PRF.Eval}(k[i], x)$
5: $b' \leftarrow\!\!\$ \mathcal{D}^{\mathrm{RoR}[k,b]}(1^\lambda)$	5: **elseif** $T[i, x] = \perp$ **then**
6: **return** $b' = 0$	6: $\quad T[i, x] \leftarrow\!\!\$ \{0, 1\}^{\mathsf{PRF.ol}(\lambda)}$
	7: **return** $T[i, x]$

By design we have that distinguisher $\mathcal{D}_{\mathsf{PRF}}$ simulates hybrid H^{j-1} if its oracle O implements pseudorandom function $\mathsf{PRF}(k, \cdot)$ with a random key and it simulates hybrid H^j in case its oracle implements a random function. As j is chosen uniformly at random we have that

$$\mathsf{Adv}_{H^{U(\lambda)},H^{U(\lambda)+1},\mathcal{D}}^{\text{indist}}(\lambda) \le \mathsf{Adv}_{\mathsf{PRF},\mathcal{D}_{\mathsf{PRF}}}^{\text{prf}}(\lambda).$$

The statement now follows with Theorem 3.17.   □

---

[7] In the pseudocode we capture random functions R_i implicitly via lazy sampling.

With the multi-key security experiment in our tool belt we can now attempt to prove Proposition 16.11. Instead of trying to apply a game-hopping proof as in our introductory example and replace, step by step, function calls to f with function calls to a random function, we will make use of another hybrid argument. At the outset of this argument is the scenario in which the adversary gets access to iterated function F^f. Over the course of the argument we will then "pull" more and more message blocks into the evaluation of a monolithic random function R such that at the end of the spectrum we end up with a game in which queries $m = m_1\|\dots\|m_{\ell(\lambda)}$ by adversary $\mathcal{A}$ will be answered simply with $R(m)$. Note that this is exactly what we are after as now the adversary is given access to a single monolithic random function. Thus, if we can show that the loss due to the hybrids is not too large—we will use the above multi-key security experiment for this—then we have, in fact, shown that the secret-IV Merkle–Damgård variant F^f as specified in Construction 16.1 is preserving pseudorandomness against prefix-free adversaries: If iterated function f is pseudorandom then so is F^f against adversaries making only prefix-free queries.

Proof of Proposition 16.11. Let $\mathcal{A}$ be an adversary against the pseudorandomness of iterated function F^f that makes at most $q(\lambda)$ many oracle queries of at most $\ell(\lambda)$ many message blocks, after padding. That is, any oracle query m is such that $|\mathsf{pad}(m)| \leq \ell(\lambda) \cdot \mathsf{f.bl}(\lambda)$. Furthermore, we assume that adversary $\mathcal{A}$ is prefix free, that is, we have that for all its oracle queries $\mathcal{Q}$ it holds that

$$\{q, q' \in \mathcal{Q} : q \neq q' \wedge q \text{ is prefix of } q'\} = \{\}.$$

We consider a sequence of $\ell(\lambda) + 1$ many hybrids H^i (for $0 < i \leq \ell(\lambda)$) and give the pseudocode of hybrid H^i in Figure 16.4. Hybrid H^i implements the PRF security experiment for adversary $\mathcal{A}$ as follows. Adversary $\mathcal{A}$ expects an oracle—we call the oracle HASH—that either implements iterated function $F^f(\mathsf{k}, \cdot)$ with a uniformly random key or a random function of the same form. To simulate oracle HASH as expected by $\mathcal{A}$, hybrid H^i implements an adapted iteration scheme. Here the first i message blocks are not run through the iteration but instead are concatenated and evaluated as $R(m_1\|\dots\|m_i)$ for some random function $R : \{0,1\}^{\leq \ell(\lambda)\cdot\mathsf{f.bl}(\lambda)} \to \{0,1\}^{\mathsf{f.cl}(\lambda)}$. The result $y \leftarrow R(m_1\|\dots\|m_i)$ is then used as starting point for the iteration scheme together with the remaining message blocks. The simulation of oracle HASH as performed by the ith hybrid H^i can thus be visualized as

Note that for hybrid H^0 we have that $m_1\|\dots\|m_i$ is the empty string ε. Since $R(\varepsilon)$ is simply a uniformly random value in $\{0,1\}^{\mathsf{f.cl}(\lambda)}$ it thus follows

$H^i(1^\lambda)$	$\text{HASH}(m)$	$R(m)$
1 : $T \leftarrow [\,]$	1 : $m_1, m_2, \ldots, m_\ell \leftarrow \mathsf{pad}(m)$	1 : **if** $T[m] = \bot$ **do**
2 : $b \leftarrow\!\!{}_\$ \mathcal{A}^{\text{HASH}}(1^\lambda)$	2 : $y \leftarrow R(m_1 \| \ldots \| m_i)$	2 : $\quad T[m] \leftarrow \{0,1\}^{\mathsf{f.cl}(\lambda)}$
3 : **return** $b = 0$	3 : **for** $j = (i+1)..\ell$ **do**	3 : **return** $T[m]$
	4 : $\quad$ **if** $m_j \neq \varepsilon$ **do**	
	5 : $\qquad y \leftarrow \mathsf{f}(m_j, y)$	
	6 : **return** y	

Fig. 16.4: Definition of the ith hybrid (for $0 \leq i \leq \ell(\lambda)$) in the proof of Proposition 16.11. Padding function $\mathsf{pad}(m)$ applies padding and splits up the message m into its individual message blocks. Note that by assumption the adversary never queries for messages that after padding are longer than $\ell(\lambda)$ blocks. If message m is shorter than the maximum number of blocks, then the remaining blocks are set to the empty string ε.

that H^0, in fact, simulates an honest evaluation of F^f with a uniformly random key. The following diagram highlights the simulation as given by the first hybrid H^0:

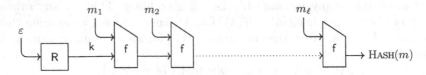

Finally, the last hybrid $H^{\ell(\lambda)}$ is such that all message blocks are concatenated and handled, en bloc, by random function R and no call to function f takes place. The picture thus simply degrades to

$$m_1 \| \ldots \| m_\ell$$
$$\boxed{R} \longrightarrow \text{HASH}(m)$$

It follows that hybrid $H^{\ell(\lambda)}$ implements the scenario in which adversary $\mathcal{A}$ gets access to a function R chosen uniformly at random. Note that this holds even though we are still padding message m (see line 1 in function HASH of Figure 16.4). The reason is that padding function pad, by assumption, is an injective function and thus the resulting distribution of $H^{\ell(\lambda)}$ is identical whether or not messages are padded first.

Applying the hybrid argument (Theorem 3.17, item 2) now allows us to bound the distinguishing advantage of adversary $\mathcal{A}$ as

$$\mathsf{Adv}^{\mathsf{prf}}_{\mathsf{F}^\mathsf{f},\mathcal{A}}(\lambda) = \mathsf{Adv}^{\mathsf{indist}}_{H^0, H^{\ell(\lambda)},\mathcal{A}}(\lambda) \leq \ell(\lambda) \cdot \mathsf{Adv}^{\mathsf{indist}}_{H^{U(\lambda)}, H^{U(\lambda)+1},\mathcal{A}}(\lambda). \qquad (16.3)$$

Here $U(\lambda)$ denotes the random variable that is distributed uniformly in $\{0, 1, \ldots, \ell(\lambda) - 1\}$.

It remains to upper bound Equation (16.3), which we will do down to the multi-key security of the underlying pseudorandom function f. To this end, we will construct a distinguisher $\mathcal{D}$ that uses adversary $\mathcal{A}$ to break the security of f in the multi-key security experiment from Lemma 16.14. Distinguisher $\mathcal{D}$ gets as input security parameter 1^λ as well as access to a real-or-random oracle RoR that either implements $q(\lambda)$ many instances of function f, each with a randomly chosen key, or $q(\lambda)$ many independently sampled random functions of the same form as f. Distinguisher $\mathcal{D}$ chooses $i \leftarrow\!\!{\tiny\$}\ [\ell(\lambda)]$ uniformly at random to then simulate hybrid H^i towards adversary $\mathcal{A}$ but with a twist. Recall that in hybrid H^i adversarial calls to (simulated) oracle HASH are answered by first computing the starting chaining value $y \leftarrow \mathsf{R}(m_1\|\ldots\|m_i)$ to then process the remaining message blocks with the standard Merkle–Damgård iteration. In case message m consists of fewer than i many blocks, distinguisher $\mathcal{D}$ chooses the response uniformly at random. In order to stay consistent it keeps track of messages in a table T. In case the message is at least i many blocks long, then distinguisher $\mathcal{D}$ does not simulate a random function R but instead uses its oracle RoR to compute the starting point as $y \leftarrow \mathrm{RoR}(\mathsf{index}, m_i)$. Here index defines the index of which key (resp. random function) should be used within oracle RoR and distinguisher $\mathcal{D}$ will pick the index such that for each prefix $m_1\|\ldots\|m_{i-1}$ a different key is chosen. To this end it keeps a counter t (initialized to 1) and a (prefix) table P. On each new prefix it sets $P[m_1\|\ldots\|m_{i-1}] \leftarrow t$ to then increment the counter $t \leftarrow t + 1$. We give the pseudocode of distinguisher $\mathcal{D}$ in Figure 16.5.

We now claim that, when distinguisher $\mathcal{D}$ samples value $i \in [\ell(\lambda)]$, it simulates hybrid H^{i-1} in case its oracle implements real functions f (with independently sampled keys) and it simulates hybrid H^i in case its oracle implements $q(\lambda)$ many independent random functions. Before we argue that this is, indeed, the case, let us note that this allows us to bound adversary $\mathcal{A}$'s advantage in Equation (16.3). Lemma 16.14 tells us that the advantage of distinguisher $\mathcal{D}$ is upper bound by $q(\lambda)$ times the advantage of a distinguisher $\mathcal{D}_\mathsf{f}$ against pseudorandom function f. Putting it all together we thus get

$$
\begin{aligned}
\mathsf{Adv}^{\mathrm{prf}}_{\mathsf{Ff},\mathcal{A}}(\lambda) &= \mathsf{Adv}^{\mathrm{indist}}_{H^0, H^{\ell(\lambda)}, \mathcal{A}}(\lambda) \\
&\leq \ell(\lambda) \cdot \mathsf{Adv}^{\mathrm{indist}}_{H^{U(\lambda)}, H^{U(\lambda)+1}, \mathcal{A}}(\lambda) \\
&= \ell(\lambda) \cdot \mathsf{Adv}^{\mathrm{multi\text{-}key\text{-}prf}}_{\mathsf{f}, \mathcal{D}}(\lambda) \\
&\leq \ell(\lambda) \cdot \mathsf{q}(\lambda) \cdot \mathsf{Adv}^{\mathrm{prf}}_{\mathsf{f}, \mathcal{D}_\mathsf{f}}(\lambda).
\end{aligned}
$$

It remains to argue that the simulation of distinguisher $\mathcal{D}$ of hybrids H^{i-1} (resp. H^i) for adversary $\mathcal{A}$ is as claimed, thereby establishing the third equality above, that is, that

$$
\mathsf{Adv}^{\mathrm{indist}}_{H^{U(\lambda)}, H^{U(\lambda)+1}, \mathcal{A}}(\lambda) = \mathsf{Adv}^{\mathrm{multi\text{-}key\text{-}prf}}_{\mathsf{f}, \mathcal{D}}(\lambda).
$$

$\mathcal{D}^{\text{RoR}}(1^\lambda)$	$\text{HASH}(m)$	$R(m)$
1 : $\;\; i \leftarrow_\$ [\ell(\lambda)]$	1 : $\;\; m_1, m_2, \ldots, m_\ell \leftarrow \text{pad}(m)$	1 : $\;\;$ **if** $T[m] = \perp$ **do**
2 : $\;\; P \leftarrow []; T \leftarrow []$	2 : $\;\;$ **if** $|m| \leq (i-1) \cdot \text{f.bl}(\lambda)$ **do**	2 : $\;\;\;\;\; T[m] \leftarrow \{0,1\}^{\text{f.cl}(\lambda)}$
3 : $\;\; t \leftarrow 1$	3 : $\;\;\;\;\; y \leftarrow R(m)$	3 : $\;\;$ **return** $T[m]$
4 : $\;\; b \leftarrow_\$ \mathcal{A}^{\text{HASH}}(1^\lambda)$	4 : $\;\;$ **else**	
5 : $\;\;$ **return** $b = 0$	5 : $\;\;\;\;\;$ **if** $P[m_1\|\ldots\|m_{i-1}] = \perp$ **do**	
	6 : $\;\;\;\;\;\;\;\; P[m_1\|\ldots\|m_{i-1}] = t$	
	7 : $\;\;\;\;\;\;\;\; t \leftarrow t+1$	
	8 : $\;\;\;\;\;$ index $\leftarrow P[m_1\|\ldots\|m_{i-1}]$	
	9 : $\;\;\;\;\;$ $y \leftarrow \text{RoR}(\text{index}, m_i)$	
	10 : $\;\;\;\;\;$ **for** $j = (i+1)..\ell$ **do**	
	11 : $\;\;\;\;\;\;\;\;$ **if** $m_j \neq \varepsilon$ **do**	
	12 : $\;\;\;\;\;\;\;\;\;\;$ $y \leftarrow \text{f}(m_j, y)$	
	13 : $\;\;$ **return** y	

Fig. 16.5: Distinguisher $\mathcal{D}$ in the proof of Proposition 16.11. Distinguisher $\mathcal{D}$ picks a random $i \in [\ell(\lambda)]$ to then simulate hybrid H^{i-1} or hybrid H^i (depending on its own oracle RoR) towards adversary $\mathcal{A}$. As before, padding function $\text{pad}(m)$ applies padding and splits up the message m into its individual message blocks, filling up unused blocks with empty strings. Note that the check in line 2 tests whether the input message is of fewer than i blocks, in which case the response is chosen uniformly at random.

First, consider the case that oracle RoR implements functions f with randomly chosen keys. Hybrid H^{i-1} computes a hash value for message m by computing $y \leftarrow R(m_1\|\ldots\|m_{i-1})$ to then compute the iteration for the remaining blocks. In case messages are of length less than i blocks, then, clearly, distinguisher $\mathcal{D}$ produces the same output distribution as in this case it similarly chooses answers as $y \leftarrow R(m_1\|\ldots\|m_{i-1})$. In case message m has at least i blocks, distinguisher $\mathcal{D}$, on the other hand, first checks whether it has already seen prefix $m_1\|\ldots\|m_{i-1}$, and if this is not the case it sets $P[m_1\|\ldots\|m_{i-1}] \leftarrow t$ and increments counter t. It then sets index $\leftarrow P[m_1\|\ldots\|m_{i-1}]$, calls its oracle to obtain $y \leftarrow \text{RoR}(\text{index}, m_i)$, and similarly finishes the computation via the iteration scheme for the remaining blocks. Following are once more the relevant parts from the simulation of oracle HASH for hybrid H^{i-1} on the left and distinguisher $\mathcal{D}$ on the right:

1 : $\;\; y \leftarrow R(m_1\|\ldots\|m_{i-1})$	1 : $\;\;$ **if** $P[m_1\|\ldots\|m_{i-1}] = \perp$ **do**
2 : $\;\; y \leftarrow \text{f}(m_i, y)$ $\;\;$ // compute "y_{i+1}"	2 : $\;\;\;\;\; P[m_1\|\ldots\|m_{i-1}] = t$
3 : $\;\;$ Compute iteration for remainder	3 : $\;\;\;\;\; t \leftarrow t+1$
	4 : $\;\;$ index $\leftarrow P[m_1\|\ldots\|m_{i-1}]$
	5 : $\;\;$ $y \leftarrow \text{RoR}(\text{index}, m_i)$ $\;\;$ // compute "y_{i+1}"
	6 : $\;\;$ Compute iteration for remainder

Here we now use the *prefix-freeness* of adversary $\mathcal{A}$. In case the adversary asks a query with prefix $m_1 \| \ldots \| m_{i-1}$ it will never also call $\text{HASH}(m_1 \| \ldots \| m_{i-1})$. It follows that starting value y in hybrid H^{i-1} (line 1) remains hidden from the adversary and is simply a uniformly random value which then goes into the computation of $f(m_i, y)$. In case of distinguisher $\mathcal{D}$ the real-or-random oracle, by assumption, implements function f. Since now prefix $m_1 \| \ldots \| m_{i-1}$ is mapped to a unique index we have that here value y in line 5 is, in fact, computed as

$$y \leftarrow f(m_i, k[\text{index}]).^8$$

Let us stress that the same prefix $m_1 \| \ldots \| m_{i-1}$ is consistently mapped to the same key $k[\text{index}]$ which is distributed uniformly at random in $\{0,1\}^{f.cl(\lambda)}$. As key $k[\text{index}]$ is used as chaining value we have that y_{i+1} in line 5 of distinguisher $\mathcal{D}$ is distributed identically to y_{i+1} in hybrid H^{i-1} (line 1). Furthermore, since adversary $\mathcal{A}$ is prefix free it never queries its oracle on input $m_1 \| \ldots \| m_{i-1}$. Note that if it were to query its oracle on input $m_1 \| \ldots \| m_{i-1}$, then distinguisher $\mathcal{D}$ would answer the query as $R(m_1 \| \ldots \| m_{i-1})$ (see line 3 in function HASH of Figure 16.5). As value $R(m_1 \| \ldots \| m_{i-1})$ would be different from key $k[\text{index}]$ with overwhelming probability the adversary could then easily detect the simulation. However, as adversary $\mathcal{A}$ is prefix free it never makes this query and can thus not notice the "discrepancy" that the $(i+1)$st chaining value is computed as

$$y \leftarrow f(m_i, k[\text{index}])$$

rather than as

$$y \leftarrow f(m_i, R(m_1 \| \ldots \| m_{i-1}))$$

as is the case in hybrid H^{i-1}. We conclude that

$$\mathcal{D}^{\text{RoR}}(1^\lambda) \stackrel{\text{p}}{\equiv} H^{i-1}(1^\lambda)$$

in case oracle RoR implements functions f with uniformly random keys. For this also note that adversary $\mathcal{A}$ asks at most $q(\lambda)$ many queries and thus distinguisher $\mathcal{D}$ records at most $q(\lambda)$ many different prefixes. As we considered the multi-key PRF setup with $q(\lambda)$ many keys (resp. random functions) the simulation is thus perfect.

In case oracle RoR implements $q(\lambda)$ many random functions we can argue that distinguisher $\mathcal{D}$ implements hybrid H^i. For this note that hybrid H^i computes the starting point of the iteration as

$$y \leftarrow R(m_1 \| \ldots \| m_i),$$

---

[8] Note that we here apply the key as second input to pseudorandom function f, in order to stay consistent with our Merkle–Damgård notation: the chaining value is used as key.

a uniformly random value. In case of distinguisher $\mathcal{D}$ we have that line 5 now reads

$$y \leftarrow \mathsf{R}_{\mathsf{index}}(m_i),$$

that is, the unique random function for prefix $m_1 \| \dots \| m_{i-1}$ is called on input m_i to produce value y. It follows that also here value y is uniformly distributed. Similarly to before we use the prefix-freeness of adversary $\mathcal{A}$ to then argue that in this case we have

$$\mathcal{D}^{\mathrm{RoR}}(1^\lambda) \overset{\mathrm{p}}{=} H^i(1^\lambda).$$

This concludes the proof.   □

Enforcing Prefix-freeness

We saw that Construction 16.1 is a secure PRF domain extender against prefix-free adversaries. Restricting the class of adversaries to prefix-free adversaries is, however, quite a significant limitation. In the following we briefly discuss two extensions to Construction 16.1 which enforce prefix-freeness.

A first idea is to run a deterministic transformation on every query that ensures the message given to Construction 16.1 is prefix free. One such option is to prepend the message with an encoding of the message length. The downside of this construction is that we now need to know the message length in advance which, in practice, means that we need to "parse the message twice." Consequently, the resulting construction would not allow computation in a pure streaming fashion and is thus not suitable for long messages.

A second option is to use a randomized transformation. Consider the following randomized hash function:

$$
\begin{array}{l}
\underline{\mathsf{RF}^f(\mathsf{k}, m)} \\[4pt]
1: \quad r \leftarrow\!\!\$ \; \{0,1\}^{f.\mathsf{bl}(\lambda)} \\[2pt]
2: \quad y \leftarrow \mathsf{F}^f(\mathsf{k}, r \| m) \\[2pt]
3: \quad \mathbf{return} \;\; (r, y)
\end{array}
$$

Here we generate a random message block that we prepend to the message before evaluating F^f. The final hash value is then the combination of the random block plus the result of the F^f evaluation. While in this case prefix-freeness is guaranteed only with overwhelming probability for adversaries making at most polynomially many queries, our previous proof carries over also to this randomized variant.

16.2.4 Security of the Secret-Prefix Method

Let us recall Construction 16.2, the secret-prefix method. Here, key k is prepended to the message (and possibly padded to ensure that it is of length of a single block). The first compression function call irrespective of the choice of message is thus always $f(k, IV)$. If we set $k' \leftarrow f(k, IV)$ we thus have that Construction 16.2 for key k is exactly Construction 16.1 (SecIV) for key $k' = f(k, IV)$. This is once more exemplified in the following diagram:

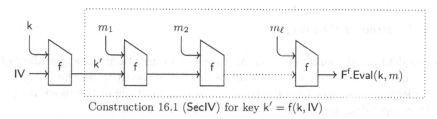

Construction 16.1 (SecIV) for key $k' = f(k, IV)$

Exercise 16.5 asks you to show that we can reduce the security of Construction 16.2 to the security of Construction 16.1 assuming that compression function f is a pseudorandom function keyed through its message input. Note that this is an additional assumption on the compression function than it being simply pseudorandom. So far we assumed that for compression functions the key is provided as the second input (the input for the chaining value). Here, however, the key is now provided through the message input for the first compression function call. We thus require for the security of the key generation step (first compression function call) that the compression function is a pseudorandom function when using the first input as key and for the remainder of the security (Proposition 16.11) that it is a pseudorandom function that is keyed via the chaining value.

16.2.5 Security of the Secret-Suffix Method

We have seen that, when prepending the key or using the initialization vector IV as key, the resulting hash function is vulnerable to length-extension attacks but that it is secure against prefix-free adversaries. The suffix method where we append the key to the message fares better on that account as appending the key successfully thwarts off such attacks. For this consider that as long as the key remains hidden an adversary cannot extend a full query $m\|k$ as this would mean constructing a query $m\|k\|y$ which contains the key k. In that sense, the suffix method is thus clearly better than the prefix method. It does, however, also have a big weakness as the following generic attack shows.

Let H^f be an iterated (unkeyed) hash function and let $m \neq m'$ be two messages of the same length that collide under H^f. Since we now have that

$H^f(m) = H^f(m')$ it necessarily is also the case that $H^f(m\|y) = H^f(m'\|y)$ for any value y and thus, in particular, also $H^f(m\|y\|k) = H^f(m'\|y\|k)$. As usual we here glossed over padding, but the argument similarly works when considering padding. As for the starting collision the key is irrelevant, this collision can be searched via an offline search and independent of the key. What we have thus shown is that any collision on the unkeyed function H^f induces collisions on the keyed variant of H^f when using the secret-suffix method.

On the Role of Padding

When defining the suffix method on page 625 we mentioned that padding of message m before appending the key is crucial for security. In the following we briefly discuss how forgoing padding m to a multiple of the block length before appending key k allows for a key recovery attack.

Let us assume that we have access to an oracle implementing $F^f(k, \cdot)$; Construction 16.3 with a randomly chosen key k. With the suffix method and Merkle–Damgård strengthening applied after the key was appended, message m is preprocessed as

$$m\|k\|10^\nu\|\langle|m\|k|\rangle_{f.bl(\lambda)}.$$

First comes the message m, then key k, before the current block is filled up by appending a single 1-bit and sufficiently many 0-bits. The last block contains the combined length of message and key encoded in binary.

Let $L := f.bl(\lambda)$ denote the block length. We start with a brute-force search for collisions of single-block messages that are 32 bits shorter than the block length. Suppose we find such a colliding pair (m, m') with $|m| = |m'| = L - 32$. By the design of the Merkle–Damgård iteration we know that the collision induces a collision on the underlying compression function f, and chances are that the collision appears already after the first block in which case we can continue.

By construction we have that the last 32 bits of the first message block are the first 32 bits of key k and thus the first message block for our collision is $m\|k[1..32]$ and $m'\|k[1..32]$, respectively. It follows that the f-collision on the first block is

$$f(m\|k[1..32], IV) = f(m'\|k[1..32], IV).$$

It remains to extract the 32 bits from the key. For this we can use the hash function oracle and simply enumerate all 2^{32} possibilities. That is, we ask oracle $F^f(k, \cdot)$ on message pairs $(m\|i, m'\|i)$ for $i = 0..(2^{32} - 1)$ encoded as 32 bits. When we hit the correct key bits, that is, if $i = k[1..32]$, then the two hash values will match. Furthermore, for all other values of i the probability of a collision is minute. If we model f as a fixed-length random oracle then the probability for two values to collide is $2^{-\mathsf{f.cl}(\lambda)}$. Thus, finding a collision for which $i \neq \mathsf{k}[1..32]$ should happen with probability at most $2^{32-\mathsf{f.cl}(\lambda)}$.

Once the key bits have been determined the attack can be repeated to find the next slice of the key. Naturally, one can also extract more than 32 bits (e.g., 64) in one go. This allows fine-tuning the attack to trade-off collision finding and the subsequent exhaustive search step.

We have presented two attacks which are both based on the assumption that it is feasible to find collisions on the hash function or compression function, respectively. While collision resistance is one of the main design goals for hash functions the attacks should not be taken lightly. In particular, the first attack allows for an offline search for a collision. Furthermore, collision resistance is usually among the first security properties to break for hash functions over time.[9]

Remark 16.15. When assuming that a hash function does not have any design flaws, the vulnerability of collision attacks is mostly influenced by the size of available intermediate state (i.e., the size of chaining values $\mathsf{f.cl}(\lambda)$) as well as the size of the resulting hash values. Modern hash functions such as SHA-3 have significantly larger internal state as well as output values. While MD5 has an internal state and output size of 128 bits and SHA-1 produces 160-bit outputs with also a 160-bit internal state, the standardized versions of SHA-3 have an internal state of between 448 and 1024 bits with output sizes ranging between 224 and 512 bits.

16.3 Hash-Based Message Authentication Codes

We have laid the foundations for our discussion on HMAC, which is short for *hash-based message authentication code* and which is one of the most widely deployed cryptographic primitives in practice. Although its name suggests it is a message authentication code it is not only used for message authentication. Indeed, the maybe predominant use case for HMAC is as a pseudorandom function. As such, it is, for example, used in the key derivation steps of TLS and IPSec. Another important application of HMAC is in user authentication schemes, where it is often deployed as a one-way function to *hash* passwords. And, of course, HMAC is also used for message authentication, for example, in SSH or with JSON web tokens (JWT).

Whether HMAC satisfies the security guarantees of a pseudorandom function or only those of a message authentication code depends on the security

---

[9] Collisions have been presented, for example, for MD5 and SHA-1. Indeed, for MD5 collisions can be produced in a matter of seconds on regular off-the-shelf hardware. Similarly, collision attacks on SHA-1 are becoming more and more practical with latest numbers quoting collision-finding attacks to be in the five-digit dollar range. Also first collision attacks on round-reduced SHA-3 have been published.

of the underlying compression function. As we will see, HMAC is a variant of Merkle–Damgård (to be more precise, a variant of the secret-prefix Construction 16.2), and thus its security is intimately tied to the security of the underlying compression function.

In the following sections we will take a closer look at the security guarantees offered by HMAC and start by discussing its "theoretical counterpart" *NMAC*, which is short for *nested MAC*. The security of HMAC then follows from the security of NMAC similarly to how the security of Construction 16.2 (SecPre) follows from the security of Construction 16.1 (SecIV) together with reasonable assumptions about the security of the underlying compression function. We will discuss the relationship in detail in Section 16.3.2.

16.3.1 Nested Message Authentication Code (NMAC)

NMAC, short for *nested message authentication code*, can be regarded as a variant of Construction 16.1 (page 622), the keyed Merkle–Damgård variant which treats the initialization value IV as the function's key. As we have seen, Construction 16.1 alone is not a secure pseudorandom function (nor a secure message authentication code) since it is vulnerable to length-extension attacks. In order to avoid such attacks, NMAC introduces an additional hash function evaluation step at the very end of the iteration scheme but with a twist. After computing hash value y for message m as in Construction 16.1, value y (after being padded appropriately) is used as the *message* in a second hash function call which uses a second (and independently sampled) key k_2. If we let $F^f(k, m)$ denote the evaluation of the standard unkeyed Merkle–Damgård transformation with compression function f, message m, and key k as initialization vector, then we can define NMAC for key $k = (k_1, k_2)$ as

$$\text{NMAC}^f((k_1, k_2), m) = F^f(k_2, F^f(k_1, m)).$$

Note that $F^f(k_1, m)$ for a key k_1 is exactly Construction 16.1 (SecIV). We depict a schematic version of NMAC in Figure 16.6.

Padding. The NMAC function inherits the padding scheme from the underlying function F^f and thus, in particular, padding is applied twice, once on the inner invocation of F^f and once on the outer invocation (see also Figure 16.6). For most functions it is the case that a hash value fits into a single message block together with padding. This is, in particular, the case for all functions discussed in Chapter 15. Consider, for example, SHA-1 with 160-bit hash values, a block size of 512 bits, and length padding that adds a 1-bit and sufficiently many 0-bits, and which appends the message length in the last 64 bits of a block. In such cases the outer hash function evaluation then degrades to an application of a single compression function.

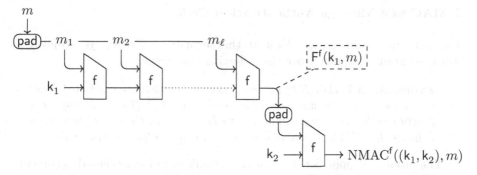

Fig. 16.6: A schematic of the NMAC construction. If F^f is a standard Merkle–Damgård hash function that allows setting initialization vector IV (i.e., Construction 16.1), then we can describe the construction via $\mathrm{NMAC}((\mathsf{k}_1, \mathsf{k}_2), m) = \mathsf{F}^\mathsf{f}(\mathsf{k}_2, \mathsf{F}^\mathsf{f}(\mathsf{k}_1, m))$. Here $\mathsf{F}^\mathsf{f}(\mathsf{IV}, m)$ denotes the evaluation of the Merkle–Damgård transformation with compression function f, message m, and IV as initialization vector.

To simplify the presentation for our analysis and discussion of NMAC we will ignore padding for the moment and thus consider NMAC as visualized below:

Notation. Given the above simplification, the outer application of F^f in NMAC consists of only a compression function call. We can, thus, alternatively write

$$\mathrm{NMAC}^\mathsf{f}((\mathsf{k}_1, \mathsf{k}_2), m) = \mathsf{F}^\mathsf{f}(\mathsf{k}_2, \mathsf{F}^\mathsf{f}(\mathsf{k}_1, m)) = \mathsf{f}(\mathsf{F}^\mathsf{f}(\mathsf{k}_1, m), \mathsf{k}_2).$$

We write NMAC^f to highlight that NMAC is constructed based on compression function f. Note that NMAC only accesses F^f (resp. f) in a black-box manner but replaces the IV by key values. When clear from context, we drop the superscript and simply write NMAC.

As before, to stay consistent with compression function terminology (but break with standard pseudorandom function terminology) we keep that compression function f takes the key as its second input. This means we write $\mathsf{F}^\mathsf{f}(\mathsf{k}_1, \cdot)$ but $\mathsf{f}(\cdot, \mathsf{k}_2)$.

NMAC as a Message Authentication Code

For our first result we will look at the security of NMAC as a message authentication code and prove the following statement:

> **Proposition 16.16.** *If keyed compression function* $f = (f.\mathsf{KGen}, f.\mathsf{Eval})$ *is a secure message authentication code and if* F^f *(Construction 16.1 (SecIV) with compression function* f *) is weakly collision resistant then it holds that* NMAC^f *is also a secure message authentication code.*

The proof of Proposition 16.16 uses a standard reduction-based argument, but instead of a single reduction target we need to deal with two targets: weak collision resistance for F^f and unforgeability under chosen-message attacks for f. In other words, we show that if an adversary is successful against NMAC then we can use this adversary to construct a new adversary that either breaks the weak collision resistance of F^f or forges authentication tags for f. As by assumption f is a secure message authentication code and F^f is weakly collision resistant such an adversary cannot exist and hence NMAC must also be a secure message authentication code and the statement follows.

The approach to argue security based on the two underlying assumptions is to assume that the outer compression function $f(\cdot, k_2)$ acts as a secure MAC. Then any forgery means to break the unforgeability of this function unless one finds a collision in the inner computation $F^f(k_1, \cdot)$. The latter is unlikely assuming weak collision resistance of f.

Proof of Proposition 16.16. Let $\mathcal{A}$ be an adversary against NMAC^f as a message authentication code. From this we construct two adversaries: $\mathcal{B}_{\mathsf{mac}}$ against compression function f as a message authentication code, and $\mathcal{B}_{\mathsf{col}}$ against the weak collision resistance of F^f. At least one of them will be successful if $\mathcal{A}$ breaks NMAC.

The formal proof is via game-hopping, where we first argue that collisions in the inner evaluations are unlikely and declare the adversary to lose if it finds a collision in the inner evaluations for a query and the forgery attempt. We account for this by the advantage of $\mathcal{B}_{\mathsf{col}}$. The next step is to argue that, if no collision for the forgery exists, then adversary $\mathcal{A}$ must break the MAC security. This is captured by $\mathcal{B}_{\mathsf{mac}}$'s advantage. We leave filling in the details for the game hopping to the reader and focus on the construction and analyses of adversaries $\mathcal{B}_{\mathsf{col}}$ and $\mathcal{B}_{\mathsf{mac}}$.

First, we describe an adversary $\mathcal{B}_{\mathsf{col}}$ against the weak collision resistance of function F^f, derived from $\mathcal{A}$. Adversary $\mathcal{B}_{\mathsf{col}}$ gets oracle access to $F^f(k_1, \cdot)$ initialized with a random key k_1. It simulates NMAC for $\mathcal{A}$ but uses its oracle to compute the nested part of NMAC, while locally computing the final compression function call for a chosen key k_2. Following is the pseudocode for collision finder $\mathcal{B}_{\mathsf{col}}$:

$\mathcal{B}_{col}^{F^f(k_1, \cdot)}(1^\lambda)$	$\mathrm{NMAC}(m)$
1 : $i \leftarrow 1; \mathcal{Q} \leftarrow []$	1 : $\mathcal{Q}[i] \leftarrow m$
2 : $k_2 \leftarrow\!\!\$ \ f.\mathsf{KGen}(1^\lambda)$	2 : $i \leftarrow i + 1$
3 : $(m, \tau) \leftarrow\!\!\$ \ \mathcal{A}^{\mathrm{NMAC}}(1^\lambda)$	3 : $y' \leftarrow F^f(k_1, m)$ // oracle call to F^f
4 : if $\exists j : \mathcal{Q}[j] \neq m \ \wedge$	4 : $y \leftarrow f(y', k_2)$
5 : $F^f(k_1, \mathcal{Q}[j]) = F^f(k_1, m)$ then	5 : return y
6 : return $(m, \mathcal{Q}[j])$	
7 : return $\bot$	

The second adversary $\mathcal{B}_{mac}$ gets oracle access to function f initialized with a uniformly random key k_2. Note that we name the key k_2 to be consistent with naming of keys in NMAC, indicating how it is used later in a simulation. Adversary $\mathcal{B}_{mac}$ first chooses an additional key $k_1 \leftarrow\!\!\$ \ f.\mathsf{KGen}(1^\lambda)$ to then call adversary $\mathcal{A}$, for which it simulates the expected NMAC oracle. Whenever $\mathcal{A}$ makes an oracle query m, adversary $\mathcal{B}_{mac}$ computes $y \leftarrow f(F^f(k_1, m), k_2)$. Note that for this it first computes $y' \leftarrow F^f(k_1, m)$ locally to then query its f-oracle on y' to receive $y \leftarrow f(F^f(k_1, m), k_2)$. Finally, when adversary $\mathcal{A}$ returns a forgery attempt (m, τ), adversary $\mathcal{B}_{mac}$ outputs as its own forgery $(F^f(k_1, m), \tau)$. Following is the code of adversary $\mathcal{B}_{mac}$ once more as pseudocode:

$\mathcal{B}_{mac}^{f(\cdot, k_2)}(1^\lambda)$	$\mathrm{NMAC}(m)$
1 : $k_1 \leftarrow\!\!\$ \ f.\mathsf{KGen}(1^\lambda)$	1 : $y' \leftarrow F^f(k_1, m)$
2 : $(m, \tau) \leftarrow\!\!\$ \ \mathcal{A}^{\mathrm{NMAC}}(1^\lambda)$	2 : $y \leftarrow f(y', k_2)$ // oracle call to f
3 : $m' \leftarrow F^f(k_1, m)$	3 : return y
4 : return (m', τ)	

Analysis. Let us analyze the success probabilities of our $\mathcal{B}$-adversaries. First note that $\mathcal{B}_{mac}$ perfectly simulates $\mathrm{NMAC}^f((k_1, k_2), \cdot)$ towards $\mathcal{A}$. It uses its own sampled key k_1 in the inner cascade of NMAC and uses its oracle which implements $f(\cdot, k_2)$ for the final compression function call. Similarly, adversary $\mathcal{B}_{col}$ perfectly simulates $\mathrm{NMAC}^f((k_1, k_2), \cdot)$, this time using the oracle for computing the inner cascade of NMAC and locally computing the final compression function call. Indeed, the distribution up to and including adversary $\mathcal{A}$ outputting its forgery is identical for both variants of $\mathcal{B}$. It follows that if adversary $\mathcal{A}$ successfully breaks NMAC^f with probability $\epsilon(\lambda)$ then it outputs correct forgeries in both simulations also with probability $\epsilon(\lambda)$.

Let us assume that adversary $\mathcal{A}$ is successful and outputs a valid message–tag pair (m, τ) when interacting with $\mathcal{B}_{mac}$. Recall that $\mathcal{B}_{mac}$ computes $m' \leftarrow F^f(k_1, m)$ and outputs (m', τ) as its forgery. By construction the forgery attempt (m', τ) output by $\mathcal{B}_{mac}$ is correct in the sense that $f(m', k_2) = \tau$. There are now two possibilities. Either the forgery attempt is also valid, or message m' has been queried to the f-oracle, in which case the forgery attempt is not valid. However, since forgery (m, τ) by $\mathcal{A}$ is valid, message m was not queried by $\mathcal{A}$ to its simulated NMAC oracle. If we denote by $\mathcal{Q}$ the sequence of queries by $\mathcal{A}$ then this means that there must be an index i such that for the ith query $\mathcal{Q}[i]$ by $\mathcal{A}$ it holds that $m' = F^f(k_1, m) = F^f(k_1, \mathcal{Q}[i])$ as well as $m \neq \mathcal{Q}[i]$. In other words, m and $\mathcal{Q}[i]$ form a collision on $F^f(k_1, \cdot)$.

We can now apply the game-hopping technique, arguing that the first hop disallows collisions in the inner computation, and then we bound the probability of finding a valid forgery in the outer evaluation in the new game:

$$\mathsf{Adv}_{\mathrm{NMAC}^f, \mathcal{A}}^{\mathrm{uf\text{-}cma}}(\lambda) \leq \mathsf{Adv}_{F^f, \mathcal{B}_{\mathrm{col}}}^{\mathrm{wcr}}(\lambda) + \mathsf{Adv}_{f, \mathcal{B}_{\mathrm{mac}}}^{\mathrm{uf\text{-}cma}}(\lambda).$$

Since by assumption F^f is weakly collision resistant and f is a secure message authentication code we have that the two summands on the right-hand side are negligible and thus also adversary $\mathcal{A}$ cannot win in the message authentication code experiment against NMAC^f with more than negligible probability. □

Remark 16.17. In the above Proposition 16.16 we assumed that function F^f is weakly collision resistant. Lemma 16.8 (page 630) now tells us that a sufficient condition for this is that underlying function f is *collision resistant*. In particular, note that the weak collision resistance of f (which is guaranteed by Proposition 16.6 (page 628) and the fact that f is a secure pseudorandom function) is not sufficient for F^f to also be weakly collision resistant as Construction 16.1 (SecIV) does not preserve weak collision resistance (Proposition 16.7; page 629).

Remark 16.18. While in the above proof we did not consider padding, this can be easily added. When incorporating padding, the reductions need to be slightly adapted to properly simulate NMAC with padding. This is, however, only a minor syntactical change. The proof structure, on the other hand, remains as is.

NMAC as a Pseudorandom Function

Earlier we mentioned that NMAC (resp. HMAC) is often used as a pseudorandom function. So far, however, we have only given a security proof for the weaker MAC security property. In the following we extend this to also cover the security of NMAC as a pseudorandom function.

To start with, recall the proof strategy for Proposition 16.16 where we showed that NMAC is a secure message authentication code given that the iterated function f is a secure message authentication code and that F^f is weakly collision resistant. A natural way to show that NMAC is a pseudorandom function would be to adapt Proposition 16.16 for this scenario. For this we now assume that compression function f is a secure pseudorandom function while keeping the requirement that F^f is weakly collision resistant. In the following proposition we make this statement formal:

> **Proposition 16.19.** *If keyed compression function* $f = (f.\mathsf{KGen}, f.\mathsf{Eval})$ *is a secure pseudorandom function and if* F^f *(Construction 16.1 (SecIV) with compression function* f *) is weakly collision resistant then it holds that* NMAC^f *is also a secure pseudorandom function.*

We can prove Proposition 16.19 following the same strategy as in the proof of the MAC case (Proposition 16.16). That is, we start with a distinguisher $\mathcal{D}_{\mathrm{NMAC}}$ that can break the security of NMAC as a pseudorandom function, i.e., given oracle access only, it can distinguish between NMAC^f initialized with a random key and a uniformly random function of the same form. Assuming that such a distinguisher exists we give a reduction and show how to build adversaries against the weak collision resistance of F^f and the pseudorandomness of f, respectively. The constructed adversary against the weak collision resistance of F^f is identical to that in the proof of Proposition 16.16. For the second adversary we need to adapt the MAC adversary to a PRF adversary. The strategy, however, remains the same, and we leave a formal proof as Exercise 16.6.

Dropping weak collision resistance. For our previous results we required that function F^f that underlies NMAC is weakly collision resistant. Regrettably, this is not as straightforward an assumption as one might think. For this just look at hash functions widely deployed in practice today, such as MD5 or SHA-1. In 2004 it was shown that MD5 is not collision resistant, and only a year later it was shown that also SHA-1 is susceptible to collision-finding attacks (although it took until 2017 for the first collision to be published). In case F^f is not collision resistant for a fixed initialization vector it follows that also the underlying compression function f is not collision resistant (see Theorem 13.10 on preserving collision resistance for Merkle–Damgård on page 487). This, however, means that F^f with a dynamic (and secret) IV (i.e., as Construction 16.1) is also not weakly collision resistant (see Lemma 16.8 on page 630). Consequently Propositions 16.16 and 16.19 do not apply for NMAC based on MD5 or SHA-1.[10]

In the following we thus drop the requirement that F^f is weakly collision resistant and prove that NMAC is a secure pseudorandom function under the sole assumption that compression function f is a secure PRF. That is, we prove the following theorem:

> **Theorem 16.20.** *Let* $f = (f.\mathsf{KGen}, f.\mathsf{Eval})$ *be a compression function with super-logarithmic output length (i.e.,* $f.\mathsf{cl}(\lambda) \in \omega(\log(\lambda))$ *). If function* f *is a secure pseudorandom function then so is* NMAC^f *.*

For proving Theorem 16.20 we will show how to reduce an adversary against NMAC to a prefix-free adversary against F^f. The result then follows with Proposition 16.11. In order to capture the proof steps concisely we need to

---

[10] That is, a variant of MD5 or SHA-1 that allows specifying the initialization value IV.

introduce some additional notation. We note that, as before, we will present the proof without considering padding.

Notation. Recall that NMAC is nothing but the serial composition of F^{f} (Construction 16.1) with compression function f. To compute NMAC for some message m and key $\mathsf{k} = (\mathsf{k}_1, \mathsf{k}_2)$ we first compute $y' \leftarrow \mathsf{F}^{\mathsf{f}}(\mathsf{k}_1, m)$ to then use the result in our computation of $\mathsf{f}(y', \mathsf{k}_2)$. To capture this composition succinctly we write

$$\mathsf{F}^{\mathsf{f}}_{\mathsf{k}_1} \triangleright \mathsf{f}_{\mathsf{k}_2} := \mathsf{f}(\mathsf{F}^{\mathsf{f}}(\mathsf{k}_1, \cdot), \mathsf{k}_2),$$

noting the function keys in subscript. If no key has been fixed yet we drop the subscript.

Besides function composition the upcoming proof requires us to work a lot with distinguishing advantages of adversaries. Definition 3.21 (page 126), which captures the security of pseudorandom functions, specifies for a distinguisher $\mathcal{D}$ against the pseudorandomness of some function PRF advantage $\mathsf{Adv}^{\mathrm{prf}}_{\mathsf{PRF},\mathcal{D}}(\lambda)$ as

$$\mathsf{Adv}^{\mathrm{prf}}_{\mathsf{PRF},\mathcal{D}}(\lambda) = \left| \Pr\left[\mathcal{D}^{\mathsf{PRF}(\mathsf{k},\cdot)}(1^\lambda) = 1 \right] - \Pr\left[\mathcal{D}^{\mathsf{R}(\cdot)}(1^\lambda) = 1 \right] \right|.$$

Advantage $\mathsf{Adv}^{\mathrm{prf}}_{\mathsf{PRF},\mathcal{D}}(\lambda)$ quantifies how well distinguisher $\mathcal{D}$ can distinguish between getting oracle access to function PRF from getting oracle access to a random function $\mathsf{R} : \{0,1\}^{\mathsf{PRF}.\mathsf{il}(\lambda)} \rightarrow \{0,1\}^{\mathsf{PRF}.\mathsf{ol}(\lambda)}$ of the same form as PRF. Note that random function R is implicit in $\mathsf{Adv}^{\mathrm{prf}}_{\mathsf{PRF},\mathcal{D}}(\lambda)$. In the following we need to make this explicit and write

$$\Delta^{\mathcal{D}}(\mathsf{PRF}, \mathsf{R}) := \left| \Pr\left[\mathcal{D}^{\mathsf{PRF}(\mathsf{k},\cdot)}(1^\lambda) = 1 \right] - \Pr\left[\mathcal{D}^{\mathsf{R}(\cdot)}(1^\lambda) = 1 \right] \right|$$

to capture the advantage of adversary $\mathcal{D}$ when distinguishing between functions PRF and R. Here the probability is over the coins of distinguisher $\mathcal{D}$, as well as the choice of key in case the function is keyed or the choice of function if we consider a random function. Note that we treat the security parameter implicit in our definition of Δ. Further note that now $\mathsf{Adv}^{\mathrm{prf}}_{\mathsf{PRF},\mathcal{D}}(\lambda) = \Delta^{\mathcal{D}}(\mathsf{PRF}, \mathsf{R})$.

Combining the two introduced notations allows us to, for example, capture the distinguishing advantage of an adversary $\mathcal{D}$ between $\mathsf{NMAC}^{\mathsf{f}}$ and NMAC where the final compression function is replaced by some random function $\mathsf{r} : \{0,1\}^{\mathsf{f}.\mathsf{bl}(\lambda)} \times \{0,1\}^{\mathsf{f}.\mathsf{cl}(\lambda)} \rightarrow \{0,1\}^{\mathsf{f}.\mathsf{cl}(\lambda)}$. This then simply becomes

$$\Delta^{\mathcal{D}}(\mathsf{F}^{\mathsf{f}} \triangleright \mathsf{f}, \mathsf{F}^{\mathsf{f}} \triangleright \mathsf{r}).$$

And with this we have all the ingredients necessary to prove Theorem 16.20.

Proof of Theorem 16.20. Let $\mathsf{R} : \{0,1\}^* \rightarrow \{0,1\}^{\mathsf{F}^{\mathsf{f}}.\mathsf{ol}(\lambda)}$ be a random function with variable-length inputs and the same output size as compression function f. Furthermore, let $\mathsf{r} : \{0,1\}^{\mathsf{f}.\mathsf{bl}(\lambda)} \times \{0,1\}^{\mathsf{f}.\mathsf{cl}(\lambda)} \rightarrow \{0,1\}^{\mathsf{f}.\mathsf{cl}(\lambda)}$ be a fixed-input-length random function with the same input and output size as compression function f. Finally, let $\mathcal{D}$ be a distinguisher against the pseudorandomness of $\mathsf{NMAC}^{\mathsf{f}}$. Then we have that

$$\mathsf{Adv}^{\mathrm{prf}}_{\mathrm{NMAC}^f,\mathcal{D}}(\lambda) = \varDelta^{\mathcal{D}}(\mathsf{F}^f \triangleright f, \mathsf{R}), \qquad (16.4)$$

and in the following our goal will be to upper bound this quantity by the advantage of an adversary against the pseudorandomness of compression function f.

We begin by constructing an adversary $\mathcal{D}_f$ against the pseudorandomness of compression function f. Adversary $\mathcal{D}_f$ gets oracle access either to compression function f initialized with a uniformly random key or to a uniformly random function r of the same form as f. As the description of $\mathcal{D}_f$ is more easily understood relative to function f, assume for now that $\mathcal{D}_f$ gets oracle access to compression function f initialized with some uniformly random key k_2. It chooses an additional key $k_1 \leftarrow\!\!\$\ f.\mathsf{KGen}(1^\lambda)$ to then call distinguisher $\mathcal{D}$ for which it simulates the expected NMAC^f oracle as follows. Whenever $\mathcal{D}$ makes an oracle query m, adversary $\mathcal{D}_f$ computes $y \leftarrow f(k_2, \mathsf{F}^f(k_1, m))$. Note that for this it first computes $y' \leftarrow \mathsf{F}^f(k_1, m)$ locally and then queries its f-oracle on y' to receive $y \leftarrow f(k_2, \mathsf{F}^f(k_1, m))$. Finally, when distinguisher $\mathcal{D}$ returns a bit b, adversary $\mathcal{D}_f$ simply forwards the verdict. Following is adversary $\mathcal{D}_f$ once more as pseudocode:

$\mathcal{D}_f^{f(k_2,\cdot)}(1^\lambda)$	$\mathrm{NMAC}(m)$
1 : $k_1 \leftarrow\!\!\$\ f.\mathsf{KGen}(1^\lambda)$	1 : $y' \leftarrow \mathsf{F}^f(k_1, m)$
2 : $b \leftarrow\!\!\$\ \mathcal{D}^{\mathrm{NMAC}}(1^\lambda)$	2 : $y \leftarrow f(k_2, y')$ // oracle call to f
3 : **return** b	3 : **return** y

If distinguisher $\mathcal{D}_f$ gets oracle access to compression function f then it simulates $\mathsf{F}^f \triangleright f$ (aka NMAC^f) for distinguisher $\mathcal{D}$. If, instead, $\mathcal{D}_f$ gets access to a (fixed-input-length) random oracle r, then it computes the same output as $\mathcal{D}$ relative to function $\mathsf{F}^f \triangleright r$. Hence, with the simulation of NMAC for distinguisher $\mathcal{D}$ we have that for adversary $\mathcal{D}_f$ it holds that

$$\mathsf{Adv}^{\mathrm{prf}}_{f,\mathcal{D}_f}(\lambda) = \varDelta^{\mathcal{D}}(\mathsf{F}^f \triangleright f, \mathsf{F}^f \triangleright r). \qquad (16.5)$$

This allows us to rewrite Equation (16.4) as follows:

$$\begin{aligned}
\mathsf{Adv}^{\mathrm{prf}}_{\mathrm{NMAC}^f,\mathcal{D}}(\lambda) &= \left| \Pr\!\left[\mathcal{D}^{\mathsf{F}^f\triangleright f}(1^\lambda) = 1\right] - \Pr\!\left[\mathcal{D}^{\mathsf{R}}(1^\lambda) = 1\right] \right| \\
&= \left| \Pr\!\left[\mathcal{D}^{\mathsf{F}^f\triangleright f}(1^\lambda) = 1\right] - \Pr\!\left[\mathcal{D}^{\mathsf{F}^f\triangleright r}(1^\lambda) = 1\right] + \right. \\
&\qquad \left. \Pr\!\left[\mathcal{D}^{\mathsf{F}^f\triangleright r}(1^\lambda) = 1\right] - \Pr\!\left[\mathcal{D}^{\mathsf{R}}(1^\lambda) = 1\right] \right| \\
&\le \varDelta^{\mathcal{D}}(\mathsf{F}^f \triangleright f, \mathsf{F}^f \triangleright r) + \varDelta^{\mathcal{D}}(\mathsf{F}^f \triangleright r, \mathsf{R}) \\
&= \mathsf{Adv}^{\mathrm{prf}}_{f,\mathcal{D}_f}(\lambda) + \varDelta^{\mathcal{D}}(\mathsf{F}^f \triangleright r, \mathsf{R}). \qquad (16.6)
\end{aligned}$$

The second equality comes from adding "zero," the inequality from the triangle inequality. All other equalities are simply "by definition." Since by assumption advantage $\mathsf{Adv}^{\mathrm{prf}}_{f,\mathcal{D}_f}(\lambda)$ is negligible it thus remains to upper bound quantity $\Delta^{\mathcal{D}}(\mathsf{F}^f \triangleright r, \mathsf{R})$.

Upper bounding $\Delta^{\mathcal{D}}(\mathsf{F}^f \triangleright r, \mathsf{R})$. Quantity $\Delta^{\mathcal{D}}(\mathsf{F}^f \triangleright r, \mathsf{R})$ captures the distinguishing advantage of adversary $\mathcal{D}$ against NMAC^f where the final compression function call was replaced by a call to random function r from a variable-input-length random function R. Since r and R have the same output length it follows immediately that distinguishing $\mathsf{F}^f \triangleright r$ from R must be at least as hard as finding collisions on F^f. To see that this is the case consider for a moment an execution of $\mathcal{D}^{\mathsf{F}^f_k \triangleright r}(1^\lambda)$ and let $\mathcal{Q}$ denote the set of oracle queries. If now for all $m \in \mathcal{Q}$ we have that values $\mathsf{F}^f(k, m)$ are distinct it follows that r is called on $|\mathcal{Q}|$ distinct values. Since r is a uniformly random function the result are $|\mathcal{Q}|$ values uniformly distributed in $\{0, 1\}^{f.\mathrm{cl}(\lambda)}$. But then this is identical to $|\mathcal{Q}|$ distinct queries to random function R, and it follows that in order to distinguish $\mathsf{F}^f \triangleright r$ from R distinguisher $\mathcal{D}$ must find collisions on F^f.

Let event collision$^{\mathcal{D}}$ denote the event that during an execution of $\mathcal{D}^{\mathsf{F}^f_k \triangleright r}(1^\lambda)$ a collision occurs on function F^f. That is, there exist queries $m, m' \in \mathcal{Q}$ such that $m \neq m'$ and $\mathsf{F}^f(k, m) = \mathsf{F}^f(k, m')$. Here again $\mathcal{Q}$ denotes the set of oracle queries by adversary $\mathcal{D}$. Then we have that

$$\Pr\left[\mathcal{D}^{\mathsf{F}^f \triangleright r}(1^\lambda) = 1 \,\middle|\, \overline{\mathsf{collision}}^{\mathcal{D}}\right] = \Pr\left[\mathcal{D}^{\mathsf{R}}(1^\lambda) = 1\right]$$

and, in particular, that

$$\Delta^{\mathcal{D}}(\mathsf{F}^f \triangleright r, \mathsf{R}) \leq \Pr\left[\mathsf{collision}^{\mathcal{D}}\right]. \tag{16.7}$$

In the following we will proceed with constructing from distinguisher $\mathcal{D}$ less powerful adversaries that are more and more restricted but for which the probability of a collision occurring remains unchanged. The first of these adversaries is a *non-adaptive* adversary $\mathcal{D}_{\mathsf{na}}$ which asks all its oracle queries en bloc. Adversary $\mathcal{D}_{\mathsf{na}}$ runs distinguisher $\mathcal{D}$ answering all its queries with uniformly random responses (using bookkeeping in order to answer duplicate queries consistently). We denote the oracle in the following by HASH as we are interested in finding collisions. Once $\mathcal{D}$ stops, adversary $\mathcal{D}_{\mathsf{na}}$ queries its oracle on all the queries that $\mathcal{D}$ asked during the simulation. Following is the pseudocode of adversary $\mathcal{D}_{\mathsf{na}}$:

$\mathcal{D}_{\mathsf{na}}^{\mathsf{F}^f_k \triangleright r}(1^\lambda)$	$\mathrm{HASH}(m)$
1: $T \leftarrow []; \mathcal{Q} \leftarrow \{\}$	1: **if** $T[m] = \bot$ **do**
2: $\mathcal{D}^{\mathrm{HASH}}(1^\lambda)$	2: $\quad \mathcal{Q} \leftarrow \mathcal{Q} \cup \{m\}$
$\quad$ // Ask oracle on all queries	3: $\quad T[m] \leftarrow\!\!\$\ \{0,1\}^{f.\mathrm{cl}(\lambda)}$
3: **for** $m \in \mathcal{Q}$ **do**	4: **return** $T[m]$
4: $\quad \mathsf{F}^f_k \triangleright r(m)$ $\quad$ // oracle call	
5: **return** 0	

There are two things to note. First, we defined adversary $\mathcal{D}_{na}$ relative to oracle $F_k^f \rhd r$. Furthermore, it always returns 0. The reason for both is that we do not try to build a distinguisher in the PRF sense but only try to bound the probability of event $\text{collision}^{\mathcal{D}}$, that is, the probability that during an execution of $\mathcal{D}^{F_k^f \rhd r}(1^\lambda)$ a collision occurs on function F^f. We now claim that

$$\Pr\left[\text{collision}^{\mathcal{D}}\right] = \Pr\left[\text{collision}^{\mathcal{D}_{na}}\right]. \tag{16.8}$$

To see that this is the case note that, unless $\mathcal{D}$ actually makes two colliding queries, the simulation as performed by our non-adaptive adversary is perfect. Similarly, in case $\mathcal{D}$ makes a colliding query the simulation up to this query was perfect, and we can thus deduce that the probability of a collision occurring during an execution of $\mathcal{D}^{F_k^f \rhd r}(1^\lambda)$ is exactly the same as during an execution of $\mathcal{D}_{na}^{F_k^f \rhd r}(1^\lambda)$, thereby establishing Equation (16.8).

In a next step we will construct from adversary $\mathcal{D}_{na}$ an adversary $\mathcal{D}_{pf}$ that is not only non-adaptive but also *prefix free*. To this end we let adversary $\mathcal{D}_{pf}$ run non-adaptive adversary $\mathcal{D}_{na}$, simulating the expected oracle by again producing random answers, and recording all of $\mathcal{D}_{na}$'s queries. Once $\mathcal{D}_{na}$ stops, adversary $\mathcal{D}_{pf}$ selects a message block m^* that does not appear in any of the recorded queries. This value can be found efficiently, e.g., by iterating through all possible block values in lexicographic order and checking each time if it is not in the polynomially sized list of queried blocks. Algorithm $\mathcal{D}_{na}$ appends block m^* to each recorded query, sending the result to its own oracle. Following is the pseudocode for prefix-free adversary $\mathcal{D}_{pf}$:

$\mathcal{D}_{pf}^{F_k^f \rhd r}(1^\lambda)$	$\text{HASH}(m)$
1: $T \leftarrow []; \mathcal{Q} \leftarrow \{\}; B \leftarrow \{\}$	1: if $T[m] = \bot$ do
2: $\mathcal{D}_{na}^{\text{HASH}}(1^\lambda)$	2: $\quad \mathcal{Q} \leftarrow \mathcal{Q} \cup \{m\}$
3: choose $m^* \in \{0,1\}^{f.bl(\lambda)}$ s.t. $m^* \notin B$	3: $\quad T[m] \leftarrow\!\!\$\ \{0,1\}^{f.cl(\lambda)}$
$\quad$ // Ask oracle on all queries	$\quad$ // Split message into blocks
4: for $m \in \mathcal{Q}$ do	4: $m_1, \ldots, m_\ell \leftarrow \text{parse}(m)$
5: $\quad F_k^f \rhd r(m \| m^*)$ // oracle call	5: for $i = 1..\ell(\lambda)$ do
6: return 0	6: $\quad B \leftarrow B \cup \{m_i\}$
	7: return $T[m]$

Fix a key k and assume that $m \neq m'$ are two colliding messages under F_k^f, that is, $F^f(k, m) = F^f(k, m')$. Then it holds for any message block m^* that also $m \| m^*$ and $m' \| m^*$ are colliding since

$$F^f(k, m \| m^*) = f(m^*, F^f(k, m)) = f(m^*, F^f(k, m')) = F^f(k, m' \| m^*).$$

Once more in diagram form:

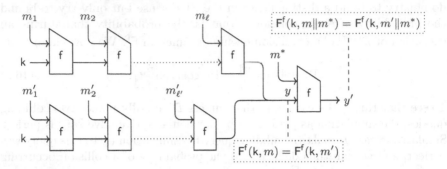

It follows that the probability of a collision occurring during an execution of adversary $\mathcal{D}_{pf}$ is at least as high as in an execution of non-adaptive adversary $\mathcal{D}_{na}$

$$\Pr\left[\text{collision}^{\mathcal{D}_{na}}\right] \leq \Pr\left[\text{collision}^{\mathcal{D}_{pf}}\right]. \tag{16.9}$$

Furthermore, note that, by construction, adversary $\mathcal{D}_{pf}$ is prefix free since all its queries end on block m^*, which was chosen such that it does not occur anywhere else in any of the queries.

We can now use Proposition 16.11 (page 636) to bound the probability of event $\text{collision}^{\mathcal{D}_{pf}}$ occurring. Recall that Proposition 16.11 tells us that, for a prefix-free adversary, function F^f is indistinguishable from a random function given that compression function f is a secure pseudorandom function. Consider now an adversary $\mathcal{D}_{pf}^*$ that simply runs $\mathcal{D}_{pf}$ and outputs 1 if a collision occurs, that is, if event $\text{collision}^{\mathcal{D}_{pf}}$ happens. As for a uniformly random function R (with output length $R.ol(\lambda) = f.cl(\lambda)$) collisions will be found only with a probability of at most $q(\lambda)^2/2^{f.cl(\lambda)}$ (due to the birthday bound), we have that

$$\Delta^{\mathcal{D}_{pf}^*}(F^f, R) = \left|\Pr\left[\text{collision}^{\mathcal{D}_{pf}}\right] - \frac{q(\lambda)^2}{2^{f.cl(\lambda)}}\right|$$
$$\leq (\ell(\lambda) + 1) \cdot q(\lambda) \cdot \mathrm{Adv}_{f,\mathcal{B}}^{prf}(\lambda). \tag{16.10}$$

Here the inequality is due to Proposition 16.11, and $\mathcal{B}$ denotes the adversary against compression function f guaranteed by the proposition. Note that the plus 1 in the term $(\ell(\lambda)+1)$ is due to the fact that adversary $\mathcal{D}_{pf}$ adds an extra block to queries from $\mathcal{D}$ and thus makes queries of length at most $\ell(\lambda) + 1$. Rearranging Equation (16.10) and noting that $|a - b| \leq c$ implies $a \leq b + c$ for non-negative a, b, c, yields

$$\Pr\left[\text{collision}^{\mathcal{D}_{pf}}\right] \leq (\ell(\lambda) + 1) \cdot q(\lambda) \cdot \mathrm{Adv}_{f,\mathcal{B}}^{prf}(\lambda) + \frac{q(\lambda)^2}{2^{f.cl(\lambda)}},$$

which allows us to upper bound the event of a collision for adversary $\mathcal{D}$:

$$\Pr\left[\text{collision}^{\mathcal{D}}\right] \leq \Pr\left[\text{collision}^{\mathcal{D}_{\text{pf}}}\right]$$

$$\leq (\ell(\lambda) + 1) \cdot \mathsf{q}(\lambda) \cdot \mathsf{Adv}_{\mathsf{f},\mathcal{B}}^{\text{prf}}(\lambda) + \frac{\mathsf{q}(\lambda)^2}{2^{\mathsf{f}.\mathsf{cl}(\lambda)}}. \qquad (16.11)$$

All that remains now is to put the pieces together:

$$\mathsf{Adv}_{\mathsf{NMAC}^{\mathsf{f}},\mathcal{D}}^{\text{prf}}(\lambda)$$

$$\overset{(16.6)}{\leq} \mathsf{Adv}_{\mathsf{f},\mathcal{D}_{\mathsf{f}}}^{\text{prf}}(\lambda) + \Delta^{\mathcal{D}}(\mathsf{F}^{\mathsf{f}} \triangleright \mathsf{r}, \mathsf{R})$$

$$\overset{(16.7)}{\leq} \mathsf{Adv}_{\mathsf{f},\mathcal{D}_{\mathsf{f}}}^{\text{prf}}(\lambda) + \Pr\left[\text{collision}^{\mathcal{D}}\right]$$

$$\overset{(16.11)}{\leq} \mathsf{Adv}_{\mathsf{f},\mathcal{D}_{\mathsf{f}}}^{\text{prf}}(\lambda) + \frac{\mathsf{q}(\lambda)^2}{2^{\mathsf{f}.\mathsf{cl}(\lambda)}} + (\ell(\lambda) + 1) \cdot \mathsf{q}(\lambda) \cdot \mathsf{Adv}_{\mathsf{f},\mathcal{B}}^{\text{prf}}(\lambda). \qquad (16.12)$$

By assumption f is a secure pseudorandom function with super-logarithmic output length and q and ℓ are polynomials, such that the above expression is negligible. This concludes the proof. $\qquad \square$

On the output length. In the above proof we assumed that the underlying function is a Merkle–Damgård function and thus that $\mathsf{F}^{\mathsf{f}}.\mathsf{ol}(\lambda) = \mathsf{f}.\mathsf{cl}(\lambda)$. In case of a chopped MD function such as SHA-512/256 this is not the case as the final transformation truncates the state value before output. However, as long as the output length is sufficiently long (super-logarithmic in an asymptotic setting) the above proof remains valid. Here the bound in Equation (16.12) then uses $\mathsf{F}^{\mathsf{f}}.\mathsf{ol}(\lambda)$ rather than $\mathsf{f}.\mathsf{cl}(\lambda)$.

Padding. To incorporate padding into the proof of Theorem 16.20 we need to consider padding both on the inner function evaluation as well as on the outer evaluation. For the latter, note that as long as the function's structure with padding is such that the outer function evaluation degrades to a single compression function computation then our proof still applies. For the inner function evaluation, however, padding does affect the proof. For this recall that Equation (16.7) on page 658 upper bounds the distinguishing advantage of a distinguisher $\mathcal{D}$ for functions $\mathsf{F}^{\mathsf{f}} \triangleright \mathsf{r}$ and R as

$$\Delta^{\mathcal{D}}(\mathsf{F}^{\mathsf{f}} \triangleright \mathsf{r}, \mathsf{R}) \leq \Pr\left[\text{collision}^{\mathcal{D}}\right].$$

Here $\text{collision}^{\mathcal{D}}$ denotes the event that a collision occurs during the execution of distinguisher $\mathcal{D}$ when relative to an oracle implementing $\mathsf{F}^{\mathsf{f}} \triangleright \mathsf{r}$. In the proof we upper bound the probability of event $\text{collision}^{\mathcal{D}}$ by constructing a prefix-free adversary from distinguisher $\mathcal{D}$ which in its interaction with oracle $\mathsf{F}^{\mathsf{f}} \triangleright \mathsf{r}$ has at least the same probability as $\mathcal{D}$ of finding a collision. If we now consider function $\mathsf{F}_{\mathsf{pad}}^{\mathsf{f}}$ to be Construction 16.1 (SecIV) *with padding* then the step from distinguisher $\mathcal{D}_{\mathsf{na}}$ to $\mathcal{D}_{\mathsf{pf}}$ (page 659) no longer works. For this note that, if messages $m \neq m'$ collide under $\mathsf{F}_{\mathsf{pad}}^{\mathsf{f}}$ and some key k, then this does not necessarily imply that also

$$F^f_{pad}(k, m\|m^*) = F^f_{pad}(k, m'\|m^*)$$

nor that

$$F^f_{pad}(k, pad(m)\|m^*) = F^f_{pad}(k, pad(m')\|m^*)$$

for some message block m^*. The reason is that the padding for $m\|m^*$ and $m'\|m^*$ is now shifted to the end of the augmented messages. In particular, note that in case $|m| \neq |m'|$ that the final padding block will be different.

The trick instead is to have one additional hop in between the adversaries. If $\mathcal{D}_{na}$ finds collisions on F^f_{pad} with probability $\epsilon(\lambda)$ then we can construct an adversary $\mathcal{D}^*_{na}$ that finds collisions on F^f with identical probability $\epsilon(\lambda)$. Here F^f is the SecIV construction as assumed in the proof that does not use padding and is only defined on inputs that are a multiple of the block length. Adversary $\mathcal{D}^*_{na}$ simply runs $\mathcal{D}_{na}$ and on any query first applies padding before forwarding it to its own oracle. From adversary $\mathcal{D}^*_{na}$ we can then continue as in the above proof and construct prefix-free adversary $\mathcal{D}_{pf}$. Note that $\mathcal{D}_{pf}$ is now relative to F^f and we have that

$$\Pr\left[\text{collision}^{\mathcal{D}}_{F^f_{pad}}\right] = \Pr\left[\text{collision}^{\mathcal{D}_{na}}_{F^f_{pad}}\right] = \Pr\left[\text{collision}^{\mathcal{D}^*_{na}}_{F^f}\right] \leq \Pr\left[\text{collision}^{\mathcal{D}_{pf}}_{F^f}\right].$$

Here we have added in subscript the function relative to which the event is defined.

Tightness of the bound. As part of Theorem 16.20 we have not only shown that NMAC is a secure domain extender for fixed-input-length pseudorandom functions but in Equation 16.12 we provide a concrete bound on the resulting security. The security loss with respect to the security of the underlying compression function f is amplified by a factor linear in the product of $q(\lambda)$ and $\ell(\lambda)$. In order to give recommendations on key sizes in practice it is important to understand whether this loss is an artifact of the proof strategy or whether it is inherent in the construction. In the case of NMAC it can be shown that the reduction is essentially tight: one can show that there exists a pseudorandom function f with security $\epsilon(\lambda)$ as well as an attack on the resulting $NMAC^f$ achieving advantage of roughly $\ell(\lambda) \cdot q(\lambda) \cdot \epsilon(\lambda)$.

16.3.2 Hash-Based Message Authentication Code (HMAC)

In the following we have a closer look at HMAC, the pragmatic counterpart to NMAC which is usually encountered in practice. While NMAC is a construction that builds on an existing hash function it requires that the implementation allows setting the initialization value IV. However, as discussed earlier in this chapter, in many cases implementations do not provide this flexibility and thus an implementation of NMAC would require a reimplementation of the underlying hash function. To overcome this inflexibility and have a construction with similar characteristics as NMAC but which allows it to be constructed on top of existing unkeyed implementations of hash functions that have a hardcoded IV, HMAC was proposed. HMAC is short for *hash-based message authentication code* and is to NMAC as Construction 16.2 (the secret-prefix method) is to Construction 16.1 (the secret-IV method). In order to allow working with a fixed initialization value an additional compression function call is added to the outset of the computation which takes as message the key. As NMAC takes two keys, this requires two additional compression function calls. In contrast, HMAC only takes a single key, which is then masked (XORed) with two fixed values ipad and opad in order to obtain the two keys needed for the construction.

If F^f is Construction 16.2, standard Merkle–Damgård that is keyed by prepending the key to the message, then we can define HMAC as

$$\mathrm{HMAC}^{\mathsf{F}^f}(\mathsf{k}, m) := \mathsf{F}^f(\mathsf{k} \oplus \mathsf{opad}, \mathsf{F}^f(\mathsf{k} \oplus \mathsf{ipad}, m)).$$

Key k should be of length of a single message block, that is, HMAC.kl(λ) = f.bl(λ). We discuss below how to deal with the other cases. Values ipad and opad are simple 1-byte bit masks that are repeated as many times as needed to obtain a bit mask of the length of a single message block. They are defined as

$$\mathsf{ipad} = \mathsf{0x5c} = \mathsf{0b01011100}$$
$$\mathsf{opad} = \mathsf{0x36} = \mathsf{0b00110110}$$

The names are simple mnemonics for the "i"nner and "o"uter pad. The pads were chosen to be both simple and to have a relatively high Hamming distance (they have a Hamming distance of 4) while selecting half of the available bits.

We can easily define HMAC based on an unkeyed hash function, for example, SHA-1. If H^f is an unkeyed hash function then the corresponding function HMAC would be

$$\mathrm{HMAC}^{\mathsf{H}^f}(\mathsf{k}, m) := \mathsf{H}^f(\mathsf{k} \oplus \mathsf{opad} \| \mathsf{H}^f(\mathsf{k} \oplus \mathsf{ipad} \| m)).$$

Note that, as is the case for NMAC, the padding scheme is inherited from the underlying function H^f and thus, in particular, applied twice, once on the inner invocation of H^f and once on the outer invocation. We provide a schematic view of HMAC in Figure 16.7.

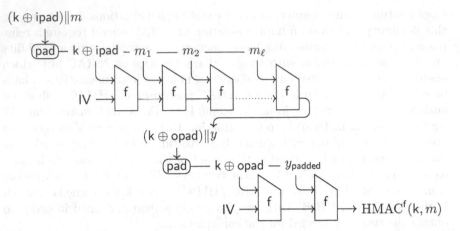

Fig. 16.7: A schematic of the HMAC construction including padding. If H^f is a standard (unkeyed) Merkle–Damgård hash function, then we can describe the construction via $\mathsf{HMAC}^\mathsf{f}(\mathsf{k}, m) := \mathsf{H}^\mathsf{f}((\mathsf{k} \oplus \mathsf{opad}) \| \mathsf{H}^\mathsf{f}((\mathsf{k} \oplus \mathsf{ipad}) \| m))$ where key k is assumed to be of length of a single message block, i.e., $|\mathsf{k}| = \mathsf{f.bl}(\lambda)$ and ipad and opad are fixed constants. Note that we assume that value y as output by the inner hash evaluation is short enough to fit into a single message block together with the message padding (the resulting message block is denoted above by y_{padded}). This is the case with most practical hash functions including those covered in Chapter 15. For example, for SHA-1 we have $y_{\mathsf{padded}} = y\|1\|0^{287}\|\langle 672 \rangle_{64}$.

Security of HMAC

For NMAC we require that keys k_1 and k_2 are chosen uniformly at random and, in particular, independent of one another. In order to transfer the security proof over to HMAC we thus require that the keys derived using compression function f cannot be distinguished by a PPT adversary from truly random keys. Similarly to the case of reducing security of the secret-prefix Construction 16.2 to the secret-IV Construction 16.1 (Section 16.2.4; page 647), we require an additional assumption on the security of compression function f in order to reduce the security of HMAC to NMAC. This assumption we can formalize by requiring that the compression functions that generate the keys behave like a pseudorandom generator. That is, we require that function PRG, defined as

$$\mathsf{PRG}(\mathsf{k}) := \mathsf{f}(\mathsf{k} \oplus \mathsf{opad}, \mathsf{IV}) \| \mathsf{f}(\mathsf{k} \oplus \mathsf{ipad}, \mathsf{IV}),$$

is a secure pseudorandom generator (i.e., that the result is indistinguishable from a truly random string of the same length).[11] We can thus capture the security of HMAC via Theorem 16.21 below. The formal proof is left as Exercise 16.7.

---

[11] Note that if f is significantly compressing then the function PRG might not actually be stretching. The important point is that the result is pseudorandom.

Theorem 16.21. *Let* $f = (f.\mathsf{KGen}, f.\mathsf{Eval})$ *be a compression function with super-logarithmic output length (i.e.,* $f.\mathsf{cl}(\lambda) \in \omega(\log(\lambda))$*). If function* f *is a secure pseudorandom function and function* PRG *defined as*

$$\mathsf{PRG}(k) := f(k \oplus \mathsf{opad}, \mathsf{IV}) \| f(k \oplus \mathsf{ipad}, \mathsf{IV})$$

is a secure pseudorandom generator, then HMAC^f *is a secure pseudorandom function.*

On the length of keys. So far we have considered key k in the construction of HMAC to be of length $f.\mathsf{bl}(\lambda)$, that is, of the length of a single block. This is also the recommended setting. The version of HMAC standardized by NIST does, however, allow for keys of arbitrary length. In case the key is longer than a block length then the key is first hashed using the underlying hash function H^f to obtain a new key of length $\mathsf{H.ol}(\lambda)$. As usually $\mathsf{H.ol}(\lambda) \leq f.\mathsf{bl}(\lambda)$ the resulting key needs to be padded with zeros to end up with a key of block length $f.\mathsf{bl}(\lambda)$. Also, in case the ingoing key is shorter than a single block length, then it is padded with zeros to obtain a key of block length $f.\mathsf{bl}(\lambda)$.

While the standard does not specify a minimal key length it is clear that keys of only a few bits are easily guessed. But what is a sufficiently long key length? In the following we present an (artificial) attack on HMAC in the presence of short keys. Even though this attack is hardly feasible in practice, it still makes a good case for how small details may lead to unexpected decreases in security and, thus, if possible one should stick to a key length of a single block length.

In the following attack we generate an artificial compression function that will lead to trivially insecure instantiations of HMAC on short keys while remaining secure when keys of length $f.\mathsf{bl}(\lambda)$ are chosen. Let f be some compression function and let $\hat{f}$ be an adapted compression function working as follows:

$$\hat{f}(m, y) := \begin{cases} 0^{f.\mathsf{cl}(\lambda)} & \text{if } y = \mathsf{IV} \text{ and the last } f.\mathsf{bl}(\lambda)/2 \text{ bits of } m \\ & \text{match either padding vector } \mathsf{opad} \text{ or } \mathsf{ipad} \\ f(m, y) & \text{otherwise} \end{cases}$$

Note that when using a key of length less than or equal to half a block length then our contrived function $\hat{f}$ will output $0^{f.\mathsf{cl}(\lambda)}$ on the first iteration call of both the inner and outer hash evaluation. Consequently, no secret goes into the computation, thus making it trivial to distinguish the function from random.

16.4 The Sandwich Construction

While HMAC is the predominant construction used in practice today, there are other ways of creating secure domain extenders for pseudorandom functions based on the Merkle–Damgård transformation. In the following we will discuss a method known as the *envelope* or *sandwich* method. It has been suggested mostly for the creation of secure message authentication codes, but we will see that its proof also yields security as a pseudorandom function.

The sandwich scheme is a combination of the secret-prefix and secret-suffix schemes (Constructions 16.2 and 16.3) in that the key is prepended as well as appended to the message. Similarly to the suffix scheme it is crucial for security that the message is appropriately padded. Let f be a compression function and let pad be a padding function such as Merkle–Damgård strengthening (see Section 13.1.1) and let $k = (k_1, k_2)$ be a composite key consisting of two keys each of the length of a single message block, i.e., $|k_1| = |k_2| = f.bl(\lambda)$. Then we can define the sandwich hash scheme on top of iterated hash function H^f as

$$SW^{H^f}((k_1, k_2), m) = H^f(k_1 \| m \| pad(|m|) \| k_2).$$

As before we denote by SW^f the version of sandwich which is only based on compression function f and which is given in the following schematic overview:

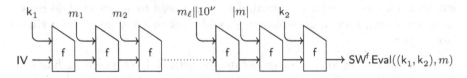

Note that when basing the sandwich construction on a standard unkeyed hash function then an additional padding operation will be added which we did not depict above. For the security this additional padding step is, however, not necessary. In contrast the padding step before the application of the second key is crucial. If this padding is omitted then a key-recovery attack similar to the attack we presented on the suffix method (Section 16.2.5; page 647) can be mounted.

When padding is properly applied one can prove that the sandwich scheme is a secure domain extender for pseudorandom functions given that the compression function is a secure pseudorandom function both when keyed via the message input as well as when being keyed via the chaining value input. In that sense, the security requirements for the underlying function are identical to those for HMAC.

> **Proposition 16.22.** *Let* f = (f.KGen, f.Eval) *be a compression function with super-logarithmic output length (i.e.,* $f.cl(\lambda) \in \omega(\log(\lambda))$*). If function* f *is a secure pseudorandom function when keyed via the*

message input as well as when keyed via the chaining value input, then SW^f *is also a secure pseudorandom function.*

The proof of Proposition 16.22 is similar to the proofs of Theorems 16.20 and 16.21, the proofs that NMAC and HMAC are secure domain extenders for pseudorandom functions. For this consider that SW is somewhat of a hybrid of NMAC and HMAC. We can identify k_1 in SW with the inner key of HMAC and k_2 of SW with the outer key of NMAC. The difference from how NMAC applies its outer key is that in the last compression function call NMAC takes the key as chaining value while in SW the key is provided as the message input. We leave the proof of Proposition 16.22 as Exercise 16.8.

A single key suffices. While we defined the sandwich construction with two independent keys k_1 and k_2, it can be shown that the function remains secure in case we set $k_1 = k_2$, that is, when we use only a single key.

Performance. While from security aspects SW and HMAC are similar, the sandwich construction can be more efficient. For this consider that, similarly to NMAC, it requires only two extra compression function evaluations to introduce the two keys while HMAC requires three. Furthermore, when constructed on top of an unkeyed hash function H^f it requires only a single H^f evaluation. However, in the naïve implementation using function H^f one needs to ensure the padding operation before the second key application. In particular this would induce two padding operations, thus potentially adding an extra compression function evaluation. For hash functions such as SHA-2 that use length padding but reserve only the last 64 bits for the message's length this can be avoided by choosing k_2 slightly shorter than a single block length such that it fits into one message block together with padding.

16.5 Sponge-Based MACs

So far we have presented results for message authentication codes and pseudorandom functions based on Merkle–Damgård-style hash functions. For sponge constructions (see Section 13.3 on page 523) we can use similar techniques of introducing keys. After all, as we saw in Section 13.3.3 we can characterize a sponge function as a chopped MD construction with compression function

$$h_{\mathsf{Sp}}^f(m_i, \overline{\mathsf{s}}_i \| \hat{\mathsf{s}}_i) := f((m_i \oplus \overline{\mathsf{s}}_i) \| \hat{\mathsf{s}}_i),$$

where f is the permutation (or length-preserving transformation) underlying the sponge construction. Thus, if compression function h_{Sp}^f is a pseudorandom function in the sense of Theorem 16.21 and Proposition 16.22 then the function can be used within HMAC or the sandwich construction to obtain a pseudorandom function.

The suggested construction of message authentication codes for sponges (standardized as part of SHA-3; Section 15.4.2 on page 608) is, however, the secret-prefix method (Section 16.1.2; page 623). With regards to sponges the secret-prefix method is usually referred to as *KMAC* for KECCAK message authentication code. While we saw that for plain Merkle–Damgård the secret-prefix method is problematic as it is susceptible to length-extension attacks it can be shown secure for chopped MD and sponge constructions. The security of the construction is argued in an idealized model using the so-called indifferentiability framework. We will discuss indifferentiability in detail in Chapter 17 and show that, assuming that the compression function is ideal, that then chopped MD with the secret-prefix method is indistinguishable from a random oracle. A similar proof can be given for sponge constructions assuming that the underlying permutation (or transformation) is ideal thus giving formal arguments for the security of the KMAC scheme (in an idealized model).

16.6 Key Derivation

In the final part of this chapter we present an important application of HMAC for the derivation of keys from sources of randomness that may not be truly uniform.

In most of our proofs we assume that keys are chosen from the uniform distribution. But how do we generate such keys to be used in cryptographic applications in practice? Usually, we do not have access to a proper source of randomness but instead have to rely on imperfect sources. Following are two examples of sources for *keying material* in practice:

Unix-like operating systems offer a special file called /dev/random to obtain "random numbers." However, computers are by nature very reliable, and thus in order to generate such random numbers the system relies on "environmental noise" such as inter-keyboard, inter-interrupt timings or other events that are ideally non-deterministic and hard for an outside observer to guess or measure. While such noise has some inherent uncertainty, it is not clear how random the output is.[12]

As a second example of imperfect randomness consider the case of a key exchange protocol where two parties agree on a shared secret. For example, in the Diffie–Hellman protocol based on the discrete-logarithm problem (see Section 11.2 on page 444 for an introduction to the protocol) parties share values g^x and g^y over a potentially insecure channel to obtain a shared secret of g^{xy}. However, since values g^x and g^y are "public" the resulting value g^{xy}

---

[12] Unix' /dev/random does indeed not provide access to the collected noise directly but outputs only a hash value of the noise. Which hash function is used depends on the specific distribution.

has zero statistical entropy. Furthermore, the element g^{xy} lives in a group structure and the format may be far from a uniform bit string.

The topic of *key derivation* deals with the question of how to generate cryptographically secure keys in situations such as the above where the *source keying material* (SKM) is imperfect. HKDF is a key derivation function based on HMAC which follows the two-step *extract-then-expand* approach. It has been standardized by the IETF as RFC 5869 and is one of NIST's approved *extract-then-expand* algorithms.

In the following we will first present the HKDF construction to then briefly discuss individual aspects of the design.

16.6.1 HKDF: HMAC-Based Key Derivation

HKDF produces a stream of pseudorandom output bits, referred to as *output keying material* (OKM), which are safe to use as cryptographic keys. Depending on the output length of the underlying HMAC variant a single call to HKDF can produce outputs of up to $255 \cdot$ HMAC.ol bits.[13] In case of HMAC-SHA-1, which produces outputs of 160 bits we can thus produce roughly 5000 bytes of keying material.

As input, HKDF takes source keying material SKM of appropriate computational min-entropy (see below), an optional salt (non-cryptographic randomness), optional context- and application-specific information info, as well as a length parameter L denoting the required number of output bits.

Construction 16.23 (HKDF). *Fix a variant of* HMAC *(e.g.,* HMAC-SHA-1*). Key derivation function* HKDF *based on* HMAC *takes as input a bit string referred to as source keying material* SKM, *an optional* salt, *optional context information* info, *as well as a length parameter* $1 \leq L \leq 255 \cdot$ HMAC.ol. *It is computed as*

HKDF(SKM, salt, info, L)	extract(SKM, salt)
1 : prk $\leftarrow$ extract(SKM, salt)	*1 :* if salt $= \varepsilon$ then
2 : $t \leftarrow \varepsilon$; OKM $\leftarrow \varepsilon$	*2 :* salt $\leftarrow 0^{\text{HMAC.ol}}$
3 : for $i = 1..\lceil L/\text{HMAC.ol} \rceil$ do	*3 :* return HMAC(salt, SKM)
4 : $t \leftarrow$ HMAC(prk, $t\|\text{info}\|\langle i \rangle_8$)	
5 : OKM $\leftarrow$ OKM$\|t$	
6 : return OKM$[1..L]$	

---

[13] We note that for a practical scheme it usually does not make sense to consider an asymptotic setting. We thus consider a specific HMAC variant and let HMAC.ol denote its output length.

Remark 16.24. RFC 5869 and most implementations specify the output length L in bytes rather than in bits. For our presentation here we choose to specify L in bits as this simplifies pseudocode.

As an example consider that we need an AES key (128 bits) as well as an HMAC-SHA-1 key (160 bits). We thus require in total 288 bits of output from HKDF, and we consequently set $L = 288$. When using HKDF based on HMAC-SHA-256 we have that HMAC.ol $= 256$ and thus execute the loop in line 3 of HKDF twice. As key for the HMAC computation in line 4 we use value prk (short for pseudorandom key) which was computed by the extract procedure executed on the salt and source keying material SKM. Each call during the *expand* phase to HMAC takes as input the last HMAC output concatenated with info and a counter counting from 1 up to 255 (provided as a single byte).

Extract-then-expand. The execution of HKDF distinguishes between the *extract* phase in which an internal pseudorandom key prk is generated from the source keying material and the *expand* phase in which key prk is used to generate the output keying material. The reason for this explicit separation between the two phases is to support the analysis of the scheme as the security of each phase can be considered separately. As a nice side-effect the resulting scheme may be also more efficient. Consider, for example, a traditional key derivation function which in this (or similar form) has been standardized by multiple standardization bodies:

$$\mathsf{OKM} = \mathsf{H}\,(\mathsf{SKM}\|\langle 1\rangle_8\|\mathsf{info})\ \|\ \mathsf{H}\,(\mathsf{SKM}\|\langle 2\rangle_8\|\mathsf{info})\ \|\ \ldots$$

Here the extract and expand phases are combined in a single step, making it difficult to formally analyze the resulting construction. On top, the source keying material is input to every invocation, which requires additional cycles.

As a sanity check for a key derivation function it makes sense to consider the case in which the source keying material is already a strong cryptographic key. In case of HKDF the scheme reduces to applications of HMAC. The above ad hoc scheme, on the other hand, reduces to the prefix method (Section 16.1.2) which we have seen can be problematic as it is vulnerable to length-extension attacks.

To salt or not to salt. HKDF supports both modes of operation, with and without a salt value. A salt is a non-cryptographic random value that, in particular, is not secret and which can be reused. Salts can, however, add greatly to the security of the derived keys as they ensure independence between different uses of the key derivation function. If we model HMAC as a random oracle then a salt effectively implements domain separation (see Section 8.3.2 on page 357). Salts also make it a lot harder to use precomputed tables of hash values for an attack as for each salt a different table would be needed.

An ideal salt would be randomly chosen (per use-case; as mentioned it can be reused) and should be of length of a single message block. When feasible and salts can be kept secret this can further increase the security of the derived keys.

16.6.2 Key Derivation Security Model

With HKDF we have described a specific instance of a key derivation function (KDF), but we have yet to formalize what a KDF should be and what type of security it should provide. Let us begin with a formal definition of a key derivation function.

> **Definition 16.25** (KDF). *We call a deterministic* PPT *algorithm* KDF *a key derivation function if it accepts four inputs: a value* SKM *sampled from some source of keying material (see Definition below), a length value* $L \geq 1$, *as well as two additional optional values (which can be the empty strings): a* salt *defined over a set of possible salt values and a context value* info. *Function* KDF(SKM, salt, info, L) *produces outputs of L bits.*

Next, we want to define the *source of keying material*, that is, the source of randomness for the key derivation function. We require that the source Σ is a sampleable distribution (see Section 2.3.2 on page 83) that can be sampled efficiently by some PPT sampler Sam$_\Sigma$. Besides generating the value SKM on which the key derivation function will be called, the source will generate a second value aux that can contain algorithm-specific auxiliary information. This information is assumed to be known by the adversary and will thus be given to the adversary in the below security experiment. For example, in a Diffie–Hellman protocol (see introduction to this section) the auxiliary information could include the group description $(\mathcal{G}, q, g)$ as well as the publicly transmitted elements g^a and g^b.

> **Definition 16.26** (Source of keying material). *A source of keying material (or simply source)* $\Sigma = (\Sigma_\lambda)_{\lambda \in \mathbb{N}}$ *is an efficiently sampleable probability distribution with* PPT *sampler* Sam$_\Sigma$. *A sample from Σ always consists of a tuple of two values* (SKM, aux).

We can now define what it means for a key derivation function to be secure. We will give both an asymptotic as well as a concrete security version which would be needed in practice to estimate the security of a specific instance of a KDF. The definition itself is similar in style to many of the definitions seen so far. Depending on a hidden bit b the adversary is presented with either genuine keys generated using function KDF or keys that were sampled uniformly at random. If no adversary can distinguish the two cases with better than guessing probability we say that the key derivation function is secure. We present the definition for a uniformly chosen salt for sake of simplicity:

Definition 16.27 (KDF security). *A key derivation function* KDF *is called* secure *with respect to source* Σ *with sampler* Sam_Σ *if for all adversaries* $\mathcal{A}$ *we have that advantage* $\mathsf{Adv}^{\mathrm{kdf}}_{\mathrm{KDF},\Sigma,\mathcal{A}}(\lambda)$ *is negligible. Here, the advantage is defined as*

$$\mathsf{Adv}^{\mathrm{kdf}}_{\mathrm{KDF},\Sigma,\mathcal{A}}(\lambda) := 2 \cdot \Pr\left[\mathit{Exp}^{\mathrm{kdf}}_{\mathrm{KDF},\Sigma,\mathcal{A}}(\lambda)\right] - 1,$$

where experiment $\mathit{Exp}^{\mathrm{kdf}}_{\mathrm{KDF},\Sigma,\mathcal{A}}(\lambda)$ *is defined as*

Experiment $\mathit{Exp}^{\mathrm{kdf}}_{\mathrm{KDF},\Sigma,\mathcal{A}}(\lambda)$	$\mathrm{RoR}(b, \mathsf{SKM}, \mathsf{salt}, \mathsf{info}, L)$
$1:\quad T \leftarrow [\,]; b \leftarrow_{\$} \{0,1\}$	$1:\quad$ **if** $T[\mathsf{salt}, \mathsf{SKM}] = \bot \wedge b = 0$ **then**
$2:\quad (\mathsf{SKM}, \mathsf{aux}) \leftarrow_{\$} \mathrm{Sam}_\Sigma(1^\lambda)$	$2:\quad\quad T[\mathsf{salt}, \mathsf{SKM}] \leftarrow \mathrm{KDF}(\mathsf{SKM}, \mathsf{salt}, \mathsf{info}, L)$
$3:\quad \mathsf{salt} \leftarrow_{\$} \{0,1\}^\lambda$	$3:\quad$ **elseif** $T[\mathsf{salt}, \mathsf{SKM}] = \bot$ **then**
$4:\quad b' \leftarrow_{\$} \mathcal{A}^{\mathrm{RoR}(b, \mathsf{SKM}, \mathsf{salt}, \cdot, \cdot)}(1^\lambda, \mathsf{salt}, \mathsf{aux})$	$4:\quad\quad T[\mathsf{salt}, \mathsf{SKM}] \leftarrow_{\$} \{0,1\}^L$
$5:\quad$ **return** $(b = b')$	$5:\quad$ **return** $T[\mathsf{salt}, \mathsf{SKM}]$

We say that function KDF *is* $(\mathsf{t}, \mathsf{q}, \epsilon)$ secure *if for all adversaries* $\mathcal{A}$ *running in time* $\mathsf{t}(\lambda)$ *and making at most* $\mathsf{q}(\lambda)$ *queries we have that for large enough security parameter* λ *advantage* $\mathsf{Adv}^{\mathrm{kdf}}_{\mathrm{KDF},\Sigma,\mathcal{A}}(\lambda)$ *is at most* $\frac{1}{2} + \epsilon(\lambda)$.

Remark 16.28. As most of our definitions, we have stated Definition 16.27 first in the asymptotic setting. For a concrete choice of, for example, HKDF based on HMAC-SHA-1 an asymptotic security statement has, however, only limited value. In the concrete setting, we thus consider a specific bound on the capabilities of adversaries. Note that t, q, and ϵ are functions in the security parameter λ and we call function KDF secure if the bound on the advantage holds for large enough λ. Specifying t, q, and ϵ does, however, also allow us to consider the bounds for a specific instance, say HKDF-SHA-1, by fixing the security parameter to obtain concrete length parameters as well as a concrete bound on the success probabilities of adversaries.

Unpredictability of Source Σ

It is clear that a key derivation function can only be secure in the sense of Definition 16.27 when outputs of source Σ cannot be guessed. In case adversary $\mathcal{A}$ can guess value SKM with non-negligible probability it can simply recompute the KDF output and compare it with the result of its oracle. To better understand the definition we will next look at characterizations of "probability distributions that cannot be guessed."

In the statistical setting (against unbounded adversaries) we can capture the hardness of guessing the output of distribution Σ via the notion of *min-entropy* (see Definition 1.45 on page 55). If a distribution has min-entropy m

bits then even an unbounded adversary cannot do better than guessing and will guess correctly with probability at most 2^{-m}. A sufficient requirement for Σ could thus be that it has super-logarithmic min-entropy. If with an increase in the security parameter the min-entropy increases super-logarithmically then the guessing probability will be negligible (see also Exercise 2.2 on page 91).

An algorithmic way of saying that a probability distribution has a certain amount of min-entropy is via *unpredictability*, which we can define as follows:

Definition 16.29. *Let Σ be a source of keying material. We call Σ statistically unpredictable if for all (possibly unbounded) algorithms* P, *called predictor, we have that advantage* $\mathsf{Adv}^{\mathrm{pred}}_{\Sigma,\mathsf{P}}(\lambda)$ *is negligible. Here, the advantage is defined as*

$$\mathsf{Adv}^{\mathrm{pred}}_{\Sigma,\mathsf{P}}(\lambda) := \Pr\left[\mathsf{Exp}^{\mathrm{pred}}_{\Sigma,\mathsf{P}}(\lambda)\right],$$

where experiment $\mathsf{Exp}^{\mathrm{pred}}_{\Sigma,\mathsf{P}}(\lambda)$ *is defined as*

$$\text{Experiment } \mathsf{Exp}^{\mathrm{pred}}_{\Sigma,\mathsf{P}}(\lambda)$$

1 : $(\mathsf{SKM},\mathsf{aux}) \leftarrow\!\!\$\ \mathsf{Sam}_\Sigma(1^\lambda)$
2 : $\tau \leftarrow \mathsf{P}(1^\lambda,\mathsf{aux})$
3 : **return** $\mathsf{SKM} = \tau$

We say that Σ is a statistical ϵ-source *if for all algorithms* P *and large enough security parameter λ it holds that* $\mathsf{Adv}^{\mathrm{pred}}_{\Sigma,\mathsf{P}}(\lambda)$ *is less than $\epsilon(\lambda)$.*

Note that we provide the predictor with the auxiliary information aux and require that SKM remains unpredictable given aux. The relationship between min-entropy and unpredictability is captured by the following lemma. We leave its proof as Exercise 16.9.

Lemma 16.30. *Let Σ be a source of keying material and* k *be a function. Then we have that for all (possibly unbounded) algorithms* P *and sufficiently large λ it holds that*

$$\mathsf{Adv}^{\mathrm{pred}}_{\Sigma,\mathsf{P}}(\lambda) \leq 2^{-\mathsf{k}(\lambda)} \iff \mathrm{H}_\infty(\mathsf{SKM} \mid \mathsf{aux}) \geq \mathsf{k}(\lambda).$$

Here, on the right, values are sampled as $(\mathsf{SKM},\mathsf{aux}) \leftarrow\!\!\$\ \mathsf{Sam}_\Sigma(1^\lambda)$.

Requiring that Σ is statistically unpredictable may, however, be too demanding for many practical scenarios. For this consider, once more, the Diffie–Hellman protocol example where given a group description and some generator g two parties locally choose random values x and y, respectively, to then share values g^x and g^y over a potentially insecure channel. Knowing x and receiving g^y allows the first party to compute $(g^x)^y = g^{xy}$, and similarly the second party can compute the joint secret as $(g^y)^x = g^{xy}$. In this case auxiliary information aux should contain at least values (g, g^x, g^y) and thus the corresponding source keying material $\mathsf{SKM} = g^{xy}$ would have zero min-entropy: $H_\infty(g^{xy} \mid g, g^x, g^y) = 0$.

As usual, the answer is to consider only adversaries that are computationally bound as these are the ones we will encounter in practice. Luckily, Definition 16.29 can be extended easily to capture also the computational case. We simply need to restrict predictors to be computationally bounded.

Definition 16.31. *Let Σ be a source of keying material. We call Σ* computationally unpredictable *if for all* PPT *algorithms* P *we have that advantage* $\mathsf{Adv}^{\mathrm{pred}}_{\Sigma,\mathsf{P}}(\lambda)$ *is negligible. Here, the advantage is defined as*

$$\mathsf{Adv}^{\mathrm{pred}}_{\Sigma,\mathsf{P}}(\lambda) := \Pr\left[\mathit{Exp}^{\mathrm{pred}}_{\Sigma,\mathsf{P}}(\lambda)\right],$$

where experiment $\mathit{Exp}^{\mathrm{pred}}_{\Sigma,\mathsf{P}}(\lambda)$ *is defined as in Definition 16.29.*

We say that Σ is a computational (t, ϵ)-source *(or simply a* (t, ϵ)-source*) if for all algorithms* P *running in time* $\mathsf{t}(\lambda)$ *and large enough security parameter λ we have that*

$$\mathsf{Adv}^{\mathrm{pred}}_{\Sigma,\mathsf{P}}(\lambda) \leq \epsilon(\lambda).$$

There is also a computational variant of min-entropy capturing computational unpredictability of probability distributions.

Definition 16.32. *We say that a sequence of random variables $X = (X_\lambda)_{\lambda \in \mathbb{N}}$ has* computational min-entropy k *if there exists a sequence of random variables $Y = (Y_\lambda)_{\lambda \in \mathbb{N}}$ such that*

- *Y has min-entropy of at least $\mathsf{k}(\lambda)$ bits (i.e., $H_\infty(Y_\lambda) \geq \mathsf{k}(\lambda)$),*
- *X and Y are computationally indistinguishable (i.e., $X \stackrel{c}{\approx} Y$).*

We say that $X = (X_\lambda)_{\lambda \in \mathbb{N}}$ has (t, ϵ)-computational min-entropy k if there exists $Y = (Y_\lambda)_{\lambda \in \mathbb{N}}$ with $H_\infty(Y_\lambda) \geq \mathsf{k}$ and for all distinguishers $\mathcal{D}$ running in time t and large enough security parameter λ it holds that

$$\mathsf{Adv}^{\mathrm{indist}}_{X,Y,\mathcal{D}}(\lambda) \leq \epsilon(\lambda).$$

Remark 16.33. The above notion of computational min-entropy is also known as HILL entropy, named after the initials of the authors who introduced the concept (see the chapter notes).

With this we have a sufficient requirement for sources of key derivation functions. They need to be *computationally unpredictable*, and with that we can now look at the security of HKDF.

16.6.3 Security of HKDF

We will prove the security of HKDF in two steps. We will first look at a generic construction based on the *extract-then-expand* paradigm and argue its security. The security of HKDF will then follow by it being a concrete instantiation of the extract-then-expand scheme.

Construction 16.34 (Extract-then-Expand KDF).
Let PRF *be a deterministic function that takes as input a key* prk, *an optional string* info, *and a length parameter* L *and which produces an* L-*bit output. Let* Ext *be a deterministic function that takes as input a value* salt *from some space of salt values and a value* SKM *from some source* Σ *and which produces a key* prk *for* PRF. *Then the extract-then-expand construction is given by*

---
extract-then-expand(SKM, salt, info, L)

---
1 : prk ← Ext(salt, SKM)

2 : OKM ← PRF(prk, info, L)

3 : **return** OKM

In order for the extract-then-expand construction to be secure we require two things: first we require that function PRF is, as the name already suggests, a secure pseudorandom function. In order for function PRF to produce a pseudorandom output we require its key prk to be indistinguishable from a key chosen uniformly at random. This yields the requirement on function Ext, which needs to be a secure *computational randomness extractor*. We have already encountered randomness extractors in the statistical setting when looking at non-cryptographic hash functions in Chapter 7. There we defined statistical randomness extractors in Definition 7.8 (page 313), which on input a sample from a distribution with a certain min-entropy are required to output a string that is statistically close to a sample from the uniform distribution. In the following we define a computational version of randomness extraction.

While we defined statistical extractors for only fixed length parameters, it makes sense to model computational extractors in the asymptotic setting where length parameters and bounds are given by polynomials.

Definition 16.35 (Computational Randomness Extractor). *Let* n, s, m *be polynomials and let* U_n *over* $\{0,1\}^{n(\lambda)}$ *denote the uniform random variable over* $n(\lambda)$ *bits and let* S *denote a uniform random variable over* $\{0,1\}^{s(\lambda)}$ *bits modeling salts.*

A deterministic function Ext $: \{0,1\}^{s(\lambda)} \times \{0,1\}^{m(\lambda)} \to \{0,1\}^{n(\lambda)}$ *is a secure computational randomness extractor if for all* PPT *distinguishers* $\mathcal{D}$ *and all computationally unpredictable random variables* X *over* $\{0,1\}^{m(\lambda)}$

we have that advantage $\mathsf{Adv}^{\mathsf{ext}}_{\mathsf{Ext},X,\mathcal{D}}(\lambda)$ *defined as*

$$\mathsf{Adv}^{\mathsf{ext}}_{\mathsf{Ext},X,\mathcal{D}}(\lambda) := \mathsf{Adv}^{\mathsf{indist}}_{\mathsf{Ext}(S,X),U_n,\mathcal{D}}(\lambda)$$

is negligible. It is called a strong *computational extractor if advantage* $\mathsf{Adv}^{\mathsf{strong\text{-}ext}}_{\mathsf{Ext},X,\mathcal{D}}(\lambda)$ *defined as*

$$\mathsf{Adv}^{\mathsf{strong\text{-}ext}}_{\mathsf{Ext},X,\mathcal{D}}(\lambda) := \mathsf{Adv}^{\mathsf{indist}}_{(S,\mathsf{Ext}(S,X)),U_{n+s},\mathcal{D}}(\lambda)$$

is negligible, where U_{n+s} *denotes the uniform random variable over* $\mathsf{n}(\lambda) + \mathsf{s}(\lambda)$ *bits and where* S *denotes the same sample in both occurrences in* $(S, \mathsf{Ext}(S,X))$.

We call function Ext *a* $(\mathsf{t}, \mathsf{k}, \epsilon)$-*computational randomness extractor if for all distinguishers* $\mathcal{D}$ *running in time* $\mathsf{t}(\lambda)$ *and all random variables* X *over* $\{0,1\}^{\mathsf{m}(\lambda)}$ *with computational min-entropy at least* $\mathsf{k}(\lambda)$ *bits we have that*

$$\mathsf{Adv}^{\mathsf{indist}}_{\mathsf{Ext}(S,X),U_n,\mathcal{D}}(\lambda) \le \epsilon(\lambda),$$

and it is called a strong *computational extractor if*

$$\mathsf{Adv}^{\mathsf{indist}}_{(S,\mathsf{Ext}(S,X)),U_{n+s},\mathcal{D}}(\lambda) \le \epsilon(\lambda).$$

We can now formalize a security theorem for the generic extract-then-expand construction. While we have usually defined pseudorandom functions to have a fixed-length output, we here require a function with variable-length outputs that is given a length parameter L as input to denote how many output bits are expected.

Theorem 16.36. *Let* Ext *be a secure strong computational randomness extractor with respect to source* Σ *and let* PRF *be a variable-length-output pseudorandom function. Then the* extract-then-expand *construction (Construction 16.34) instantiated with* Ext *and* PRF *is a secure key derivation function.*

Furthermore, for any adversary $\mathcal{A}$ *against the* extract-then-expand *construction there exist adversaries* $\mathcal{A}_{\mathsf{PRF}}$ *against the pseudorandomness of* PRF *and* $\mathcal{A}_{\mathsf{Ext}}$ *against the extractor* Ext *such that*

$$\mathsf{Adv}^{\mathsf{kdf}}_{\mathsf{extract\text{-}then\text{-}expand},\Sigma,\mathcal{A}}(\lambda) \le \mathsf{Adv}^{\mathsf{prf}}_{\mathsf{PRF},\mathcal{A}_{\mathsf{PRF}}}(\lambda) + \mathsf{Adv}^{\mathsf{strong\text{-}ext}}_{\mathsf{Ext},\Sigma,\mathcal{A}_{\mathsf{Ext}}}(\lambda).$$

Having gone through the expenditure of defining all relevant security notions in the concrete setting, we can similarly state a version of the theorem in the concrete setting:

Theorem 16.37. *Let* Ext *be a* $(\mathsf{t}_{\mathsf{Ext}}, \epsilon_{\mathsf{Ext}})$-*computational strong randomness extractor with respect to source* Σ. *Let further* PRF *be a*

> *variable-length-output* $(t_{PRF}, q_{PRF}, \epsilon_{PRF})$-*pseudorandom function. Then the* extract-then-expand *construction (Construction 16.34) instantiated with* Ext *and* PRF *is a* $(\min(t_{Ext}, t_{PRF}), q_{PRF}, \epsilon_{Ext} + \epsilon_{PRF})$-*secure key derivation function.*

While the concrete security bounds in the statement look complex, the proofs are identical except for that we need to carry around the individual parameters throughout the individual steps. The proof itself is a straightforward reduction from an adversary against the key derivation function to adversaries against the PRF and extractor. We leave a formal proof as Exercise 16.10.

Security of HKDF

Finally, we can state the security of the HKDF construction. For this note that HKDF is nothing but a concrete instance of extract-then-expand where HMAC takes the role of extractor as well as the role of the pseudorandom function.

> **Lemma 16.38.** *Fix a version of* HMAC *(e.g.,* HMAC-SHA-256*). If* HMAC *is a computational strong randomness extractor and if* HMAC *is a secure pseudorandom function, then* HKDF *is a secure key derivation function.*

Remark 16.39. Note that the HKDF construction during the extract phase iterates HMAC in counter-like mode in order to obtain variable output length. It is straightforward to show that if HMAC is a secure pseudorandom function that then the version used in HKDF is a variable-output-length pseudorandom function.

16.6.4 Key Derivation from Low-Entropy Sources

We saw that the security of key derivation functions formalized according to Definition 16.27 (page 672) requires sources to be computationally unpredictable. Otherwise, an adversary can simply guess the output of the source and thus has all the information it needs in order to recompute the actual key.

In many settings in practice sources are, however, not unpredictable. At least not in the strong sense of our definition of unpredictability (Definition 16.31; page 674). A common use case is, for example, to base keys on user-generated passwords, which in many cases consist of only a handful of characters and thus brute-force attacks are very much practical. For this, consider that a user chooses a password consisting of upper- and lowercase letters as well as numbers. Then we have in total a symbol pool of $(26 + 26 + 10) = 62$ different symbols. A common practice is to measure the strength of a password by the number of bits of information it conveys, that is, by considering its entropy (see Section 1.5.4 on page 49). Assuming that a user chooses each symbol with equal probability then each symbol has an entropy of $\log(62) \approx 5.954$ bits. If a user chooses a password of length 8 then this is equivalent to roughly 48 bits of information. Or in other words, an adversary would need to guess the equivalent of a 48-bit random string for which there are roughly 281 trillion possibilities. To put this into proportion, as of 2019 the Bitcoin hash rate which measures the estimated number of hash computations in the Bitcoin network (which uses SHA-256) was around 100 million tera hashes (or 100 million trillion hashes) per second. While you usually do not have the computing power of the entire Bitcoin network at your disposal, even on commodity hardware brute-force attacks are feasible. On a modern laptop with a decent GPU you can easily do upwards of 100 million SHA-256 computations per second. At this rate trying all the 281 trillion passwords takes about 32 days.

When the entropy of the incoming source material is low, functions such as HKDF are far from optimal and there is only little that we can do to prove security from a theoretical standpoint. However, in practice we can still do a lot to make it as hard as possible for adversaries. This is where *password-based key derivation functions* are usually used which, in contrast to most other applications in computer science, do not try to achieve optimal runtime performance but, instead, try to make it infeasible to come up with an efficient implementation. The idea is to provide a key derivation mechanism which makes it as cumbersome as possible to break using a brute-force approach. To this end, each "guess" should take as much computational resources from an adversary as feasible. (Note that we cannot make it too hard, as the function still needs to be usable in normal situations to derive keys.) If in addition, the function is theoretically sound and the best an adversary can do is to use a brute-force attack then at least due to the inefficiency of the function the cost is increased and attacks are slowed down.

PBKDF2

An example of a widely used password-based key derivation function is PBKDF2 which, like HKDF, is a scheme based on a hash function and which often is used together with HMAC. The PBKDF2 scheme has been around since 2000, and its name is short for *Password-Based Key Derivation Function 2*.[14] It was standardized originally by the IETF as RFC 2898 and as of 2017 is part of RFC 8018 and the IETF recommended schemes for password-based key derivation. The main idea behind PBKDF1 and PBKDF2 is to not only hash the source material (i.e., the password) once but many times, for example, 100,000 times. Applied to our example calculation above, this

---

[14] It supersedes PBKDF1, which was only able to produce fixed-length keys of 160 bits.

would slow down an attacker by a factor of 10^5, and the time to try out all passwords on a laptop would increase from 32 days to more than 8000 years.

PBKDF2 takes as input a password pw, a salt, an iteration count c, and a length parameter L to specify the required number of output bits. Let PRF be some concrete pseudorandom function, for example, HMAC-SHA-256. Then PBKDF2 is computed as follows:

PBKDF2(pw, salt, c, L)	F(pw, salt, c, i)
1 : OKM $\leftarrow \varepsilon$	1 : $U[1] \leftarrow$ PRF(pw, salt$\|\langle i \rangle_{32}$)
2 : **for** $i = 1 .. \lceil L/\text{PRF.ol} \rceil$ **do**	2 : **for** $i = 2..c$ **do**
3 : $t \leftarrow F$(pw, salt, c, i)	3 : $U[i] \leftarrow F$(pw, $U[i-1]$)
4 : OKM $\leftarrow$ OKM$\|t$	4 : **return** $U[1] \oplus U[2] \oplus \cdots \oplus U[c]$
5 : **return** OKM$[1..L]$	

For each application of function F a chain of c hash values is computed sequentially in order to make it difficult to parallelize attacks.

While PBKDF2 increases the computation cost for generating a single hash value its main weakness is that it can be implemented with very little memory, which allows for implementations on specialized hardware (such as GPUs, ASICs, or FPGAs) and which may render the increase in complexity introduced via the iteration count ineffective. Alternatives such as *scrypt* or *Argon2* were designed explicitly to make it hard to find an implementation on such specialized hardware. They exploit the fact that specialized chips usually are memory restricted and thus have tunable parameters for how much memory a hash computation should take.

Chapter Notes and References

In the early 1990s Ron Rivest introduced the iterated hash functions MD4 and MD5 [28, 29], which allowed to process arbitrarily long messages and which were significantly faster than existing message authentication codes such as CBC-MAC based on DES as standardized by NIST in [22]. Besides the better performance, hash algorithms, unlike encryption schemes, were not subject to export regulations, which triggered the interest in using iterated hash functions as the basis for message authentication. Hash-based authentication schemes were subsequently proposed, for example, for Kerberos [21], IPSec [15], or SNMP, for which the Internet Security and Privacy Working Group (SPWG) suggested the secret-prefix method, according to Tsudik [30]. Tsudik also gave a first analysis of the secret-prefix and secret-suffix method in 1992 and also suggested the sandwich method (without additional padding) to counteract the weaknesses of the prefix- and suffix methods (being prone to length-extension and collision attacks, respectively). In 1995 Preneel and van

Oorschot published a key recovery attack (we present an adapted version for the suffix method in Section 16.2.5) on the sandwich method without additional padding [26, 27]. The first formal analysis of the sandwich method with padding was given in 2007 by Yasuda [34], who showed that the method is, in fact, secure even when using only a single key.

The formal study of hash-function-based message authentication in the provable security sense was initiated by Bellare, Canetti, and Krawczyk, who introduced NMAC and HMAC in 1996 [4, 5, 20]. HMAC was standardized by the American National Standards Institution as ANSI X9.71-2000 in 2000 [13] and the National Institute of Standards and Technology (NIST) in 2002 as FIPS 198 [23]. The latest revision of the standard is FIPS 198-1 from 2008 [24].

The original security proof of HMAC by Bellare *et al.* [4] assumed weak collision resistance of the underlying hash function (see Proposition 16.16). When in 2005 collision attacks were published on MD5 [32] and SHA-1 [31] collision resistance (and thus weak collision resistance) could no longer be assumed for the two most widely used base functions for HMAC and thus the question of HMAC's security was again open. In 2006, Bellare published a new proof showing that HMAC is a secure pseudorandom function under the sole assumption that the underlying compression function is also a pseudorandom function [2, 3]. The practical implications of Bellare's new proof were critiqued by Koblitz and Menezes [16, 17], who, in particular, discuss that the proof was given in the non-uniform model of complexity. The attack on short keys presented in Section 16.3.2 is from the same paper by Koblitz and Menezes. The proof in the uniform setting that NMAC (and subsequently HMAC) is a secure domain extender for pseudorandom functions assuming that the compression function is pseudorandom (presented as Theorem 16.20) is due to Gaži, Pietrzak, and Rybár and was published in 2014 [10, 11].

Bellare, Canetti, and Krawczyk also considered the case of pseudorandom functions [6] and showed that Merkle–Damgård when replacing the initialization vector with a key yields a secure domain extender for pseudorandom functions against prefix-free adversaries (Proposition 16.11 in Section 16.2.3). The nested iterate construction NI is due to An and Bellare [1].

The secret-suffix method as a basis for message authentication codes and pseudorandom functions for sponge-based constructions was proposed by Bertoni *et al.* [7]. A discussion of keyed sponges is given in [8].

HKDF was proposed by Krawczyk in 2010 [19], who also provides a formal model for analyzing the security of key derivation functions. HKDF was standardized by the Internet Engineering Task Force (IETF) as RFC 5869 [18]. The notion of computational entropy was introduced earlier in a work of Håstad, Impagliazzo, Levin, and Luby [12] and is also referred to as HILL entropy in recognition of the authors' contribution. A first formal treatment of password-based key exchange was given by Yao and Yin [33]. The password-based key derivation function PBKDF2 was first published by

RSA Laboratories and subsequently published by IETF as RFC 2898 [14]. Argon2 [9] was the winner of the 2013 *Password Hashing Competition* [25], a competition organized by the cryptographic community.

Exercices

Exercise 16.1. Show that Constructions 16.1, 16.2, and 16.4 are susceptible to length-extension attacks (pages 622ff.). For Construction 16.4 assume that the adversary gets additionally oracle access to keyed compression function $f(k, \cdot, \cdot)$. See also the final paragraph in Section 16.2.2 (page 633).

Exercise 16.2. Formally prove Proposition 16.6 (page 628), that is, show that both MACs and PRFs are weakly collision resistant. Are the reductions tight?

Exercise 16.3. Prove the remainder of Proposition 16.7 (page 629). That is, show that Construction 16.4 preserves weak collision resistance.

Exercise 16.4. Formally prove Proposition 16.10 (page 633) and show that Merkle–Damgård preserves MAC security if the MAC key is used in every iteration of the underlying compression function (Construction 16.4).

Exercise 16.5. Show that the following statement holds: Let f be a secure pseudorandom function when being keyed via the message input, as well as when being keyed via the chaining value input (also see Section 16.2.4 on page 647). Then, Construction 16.2 is a secure pseudorandom function (resp. message authentication code) given that Construction 16.1 is a secure pseudorandom function (resp. message authentication code).

Exercise 16.6. Prove Proposition 16.19 (page 655) and show that NMAC^f is a secure pseudorandom function given that f is a secure PRF and that F^f is weakly collision resistant.

Exercise 16.7. Prove Theorem 16.21 (page 665) and show how to reduce the security of HMAC to NMAC.

Exercise 16.8. Prove that the sandwich construction with two independently sampled keys is secure. That is, prove Proposition 16.22 (page 666).

Exercise 16.9. Prove Lemma 16.30 from page 673.

Exercise 16.10. Prove Theorem 16.37 (page 676).

Chapter Bibliography

1. Jee Hea An and Mihir Bellare. Constructing VIL-MACs from FIL-MACs: Message authentication under weakened assumptions. In Michael J. Wiener, editor, *Advances*

in *Cryptology – CRYPTO'99*, volume 1666 of *Lecture Notes in Computer Science*, pages 252–269, Santa Barbara, CA, USA, August 15–19, 1999. Springer, Heidelberg, Germany.

2. Mihir Bellare. New proofs for NMAC and HMAC: Security without collision-resistance. In Cynthia Dwork, editor, *Advances in Cryptology – CRYPTO 2006*, volume 4117 of *Lecture Notes in Computer Science*, pages 602–619, Santa Barbara, CA, USA, August 20–24, 2006. Springer, Heidelberg, Germany.

3. Mihir Bellare. New proofs for NMAC and HMAC: Security without collision resistance. *Journal of Cryptology*, 28(4):844–878, October 2015.

4. Mihir Bellare, Ran Canetti, and Hugo Krawczyk. Keying hash functions for message authentication. In Neal Koblitz, editor, *Advances in Cryptology – CRYPTO'96*, volume 1109 of *Lecture Notes in Computer Science*, pages 1–15, Santa Barbara, CA, USA, August 18–22, 1996. Springer, Heidelberg, Germany.

5. Mihir Bellare, Ran Canetti, and Hugo Krawczyk. Message authentication using hash functions: The HMAC construction. *RSA Laboratories' CryptoBytes*, 2(1):12–15, 1996.

6. Mihir Bellare, Ran Canetti, and Hugo Krawczyk. Pseudorandom functions revisited: The cascade construction and its concrete security. In *37th Annual Symposium on Foundations of Computer Science*, pages 514–523, Burlington, Vermont, October 14–16, 1996. IEEE Computer Society Press.

7. Guido Bertoni, Joan Daemen, Michaël Peeters, and Gilles Van Assche. On the indifferentiability of the sponge construction. In Nigel P. Smart, editor, *Advances in Cryptology – EUROCRYPT 2008*, volume 4965 of *Lecture Notes in Computer Science*, pages 181–197, Istanbul, Turkey, April 13–17, 2008. Springer, Heidelberg, Germany.

8. Guido Bertoni, Joan Daemen, Michaël Peeters, and Gilles Van Assche. Cryptographic sponge functions. http://sponge.noekeon.org/, 2011.

9. Alex Biryukov, Daniel Dinu, and Dmitry Khovratovich. Argon2: new generation of memory-hard functions for password hashing and other applications. *2016 IEEE European Symposium on Security and Privacy (EuroS&P)*, pages 292–302, 2016.

10. Peter Gaži, Krzysztof Pietrzak, and Michal Rybár. The exact PRF-security of NMAC and HMAC. In Juan A. Garay and Rosario Gennaro, editors, *Advances in Cryptology – CRYPTO 2014, Part I*, volume 8616 of *Lecture Notes in Computer Science*, pages 113–130, Santa Barbara, CA, USA, August 17–21, 2014. Springer, Heidelberg, Germany.

11. Peter Gaži, Krzysztof Pietrzak, and Michal Rybár. The exact PRF-security of NMAC and HMAC. Cryptology ePrint Archive, Report 2014/578, 2014. http://eprint.iacr.org/2014/578.

12. Johan Håstad, Russell Impagliazzo, Leonid A. Levin, and Michael Luby. A pseudorandom generator from any one-way function. *SIAM Journal on Computing*, 28(4):1364–1396, 1999.

13. American National Standards Institute. ANSI X9.71-2000: Keyed hash message authentication code (MAC), 2000.

14. B. Kaliski. PKCS #5: Password-based cryptography specification version 2.0. RFC 2898, RFC Editor, September 2000. http://www.rfc-editor.org/rfc/rfc2898.txt.

15. B Kaliski and M Robshaw. Message authentication with MD5. *CryptoBytes (RSA Labs Technical Newsletter)*, 1(1), 1995.

16. Neal Koblitz and Alfred Menezes. Another look at HMAC. Cryptology ePrint Archive, Report 2012/074, 2012. http://eprint.iacr.org/2012/074.

17. Neal Koblitz and Alfred Menezes. Another look at HMAC. *Journal of Mathematical Cryptology*, 7(3):225–251, 2013.

18. H. Krawczyk and P. Eronen. HMAC-based extract-and-expand key derivation function (HKDF). RFC 5869, RFC Editor, May 2010. http://www.rfc-editor.org/rfc/rfc5869.txt.

19. Hugo Krawczyk. Cryptographic extraction and key derivation: The HKDF scheme. Cryptology ePrint Archive, Report 2010/264, 2010. http://eprint.iacr.org/2010/264.

20. Hugo Krawczyk, Mihir Bellare, and Ran Canetti. HMAC: Keyed-hashing for message authentication. RFC 2104, RFC Editor, February 1997. http://www.rfc-editor.org/rfc/rfc2104.txt.

21. J. Linn. The Kerberos version 5 GSS-API mechanism. RFC 1964, RFC Editor, June 1996.

22. National Institute of Standards and Technology (NIST). FIPS PUB 113: Standard for computer data authentication. http://www.itl.nist.gov/fipspubs/fip113.htm, May 1985.

23. National Institute of Standards and Technology (NIST). FIPS PUB 198: The keyed-hash message authentication code (HMAC), march 2002.

24. National Institute of Standards and Technology (NIST). FIPS PUB 198-1: The keyed-hash message authentication code (HMAC), july 2008.

25. PHC. Cryptographic competition: Password hashing competition, 2013. https://password-hashing.net/.

26. Bart Preneel and Paul C. van Oorschot. MDx-MAC and building fast MACs from hash functions. In Don Coppersmith, editor, *Advances in Cryptology – CRYPTO'95*, volume 963 of *Lecture Notes in Computer Science*, pages 1–14, Santa Barbara, CA, USA, August 27–31, 1995. Springer, Heidelberg, Germany.

27. Bart Preneel and Paul C. van Oorschot. On the security of two MAC algorithms. In Ueli M. Maurer, editor, *Advances in Cryptology – EUROCRYPT'96*, volume 1070 of *Lecture Notes in Computer Science*, pages 19–32, Saragossa, Spain, May 12–16, 1996. Springer, Heidelberg, Germany.

28. Ronald L. Rivest. The MD4 message digest algorithm. In Alfred J. Menezes and Scott A. Vanstone, editors, *Advances in Cryptology – CRYPTO'90*, volume 537 of *Lecture Notes in Computer Science*, pages 303–311, Santa Barbara, CA, USA, August 11–15, 1991. Springer, Heidelberg, Germany.

29. Ronald L. Rivest. The MD5 message-digest algorithm. RFC 1321, RFC Editor, April 1992. http://www.rfc-editor.org/rfc/rfc1321.txt.

30. Gene Tsudik. Message authentication with one-way hash functions. *ACM SIGCOMM Computer Communication Review*, 22(5):29–38, 1992.

31. Xiaoyun Wang, Yiqun Lisa Yin, and Hongbo Yu. Finding collisions in the full SHA-1. In Victor Shoup, editor, *Advances in Cryptology – CRYPTO 2005*, volume 3621 of *Lecture Notes in Computer Science*, pages 17–36, Santa Barbara, CA, USA, August 14–18, 2005. Springer, Heidelberg, Germany.

32. Xiaoyun Wang and Hongbo Yu. How to break MD5 and other hash functions. In Ronald Cramer, editor, *Advances in Cryptology – EUROCRYPT 2005*, volume 3494 of *Lecture Notes in Computer Science*, pages 19–35, Aarhus, Denmark, May 22–26, 2005. Springer, Heidelberg, Germany.

33. Frances F. Yao and Yiqun Lisa Yin. Design and analysis of password-based key derivation functions. In Alfred Menezes, editor, *Topics in Cryptology – CT-RSA 2005*, volume 3376 of *Lecture Notes in Computer Science*, pages 245–261, San Francisco, CA, USA, February 14–18, 2005. Springer, Heidelberg, Germany.

34. Kan Yasuda. "sandwich" is indeed secure: How to authenticate a message with just one hashing. In Josef Pieprzyk, Hossein Ghodosi, and Ed Dawson, editors, *ACISP 07: 12th Australasian Conference on Information Security and Privacy*, volume 4586 of *Lecture Notes in Computer Science*, pages 355–369, Townsville, Australia, July 2–4, 2007. Springer, Heidelberg, Germany.

Chapter 17
Constructing Random Oracles— Indifferentiability

The holy grail of hash function design is to construct a hash function which *behaves like a random oracle*. This is, of course, impossible (see Chapter 12). Nevertheless, while we know that we cannot construct an actual random oracle the goal should still be to come as close as possible.

In this and the following chapter we are going to discuss two approaches: *indifferentiability* and *universal computational extractors*. A random oracle is a single monolithic object. However, when we design hash functions, for example, via the Merkle–Damgård transformation, we construct a hash function iteratively out of small building blocks. The result is thus nothing like a single monolithic object, and this fact might be exploited by adversaries that know the building blocks of the function. This is where *indifferentiability* comes into play. The indifferentiability framework provides us with a formal model to prove that a construction out of idealized primitives (i.e., idealized small building blocks) is as good as a single monolithic primitive. Translated to the case of iterative hash functions, indifferentiability provides us with a proof model to show that an iterative construction is as a good as a random oracle assuming that the building blocks of the construction are ideal, for example, assuming that the compression function used in the construction is itself a fixed-input-length random oracle. In that sense, indifferentiability allows us to validate the iterative design used in the construction of hash functions and to prove that, as long as the iterated function does not have any weaknesses, then the resulting hash function can replace a random oracle. Note that indifferentiability stays fully in the idealized setting and does not make a jump into the standard model. It provides a framework to construct monolithic ideal objects (e.g., random oracles) out of other ideal objects (e.g., ideal compression functions).

Universal computational extractors (UCEs for short) take a very different route. UCE is a standard model security definition, albeit a very strong one. One of the main criticism of random oracles is that the notion "to behave like a random function" is not well defined. Consequently it is not possible to verify that a function indeed behaves like a random function. The best we can

685

A. Mittelbach, M. Fischlin, *The Theory of Hash Functions and Random Oracles*,
Information Security and Cryptography, https://doi.org/10.1007/978-3-030-63287-8_17

do is to rule out functions by showing that a random function has a certain property that the function in question does not possess. Without a clear definition there is, however, no way of proving a positive result based on well-defined assumptions, for example, that a function is one-way or pseudorandom. UCEs mitigate that situation by providing a rigorous definition of what it could mean to behave like a random function. Even more, UCEs provide a framework of definitions which allow to fine-tune the assumption needed for an application. As we will see, UCEs can be used as the basis, for example, for standard model constructions of deterministic public-key encryption (see Section 9.5.1). Regrettably, there is a catch. So far, for UCEs we do not have any standard model constructions but only constructions in idealized models. But more on that in Chapter 18.

17.1 Indifferentiability

A random oracle is an idealized monolithic object that we use in the random oracle methodology to simplify security proofs. Monolithic in this context means that we think of a random oracle as an unstructured box of which we can only observe its input and output behavior. In particular, the random oracle box accepts inputs of arbitrary length.

If we look at how hash functions are constructed in practice then it becomes obvious that a monolithic object is far from the truth. Iterative hash functions such as the MD or SHA family operate by iterating a function with a fixed input length. The following diagram recalls the basic Merkle–Damgård construction which underlies many real-world hash functions:

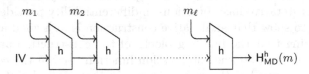

Of course, we can always lift one abstraction and go one layer further down. Fixed-input-length compression functions are, as we have seen, often constructed from block ciphers, for example, via the Davies–Meyer construction as displayed below (also see Chapter 14).

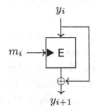

Now, the case with adversaries is that they seldom play by the rules. In particular, if they know that a hash function is constructed from smaller building blocks they might try to attack the function by finding weaknesses in the smaller building blocks or in the way these are assembled. Suppose, for example, that an adversary learns hash value $y = H(m)$ for some message m while message m remains hidden. Let us further assume that for some reason the adversary is actually interested in the hash value for message $m\|x$ for some string x. If H was a random oracle then given only $y = H(m)$ the best the adversary could do is to guess the hash value of $H(m\|x)$. It could not even validate its guess since for that it would need to know message m. When the hash function is of the Merkle–Damgård type then things are very different. Here the adversary only needs to compute $h(x, y)$. If we ignore padding and assume that message m is of a multiple of the block length and that x has the length of a single block then the adversary successfully computed $H(m\|x)$.

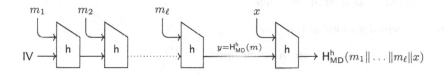

Let us stress that for this computation the adversary did not need to know a single bit of message m. In contrast, in a security proof in the random oracle model the above length-extension attack would not be feasible as there the adversary does not have access to the underlying function h as there is no underlying function h. This then raises the question:

Are there iteration schemes where an adversary cannot exploit the iteration scheme down to some reasonable assumption on the function being iterated?

Constructions vs. Monolithic Objects

In the following we will answer this question by providing a structured way of analyzing idealized constructions. In the most abstract terms, our goal is to find a security notion for a construction G that allows us to state that whenever primitive g has a certain property that then the combination of G and g (i.e., G^g) is as secure as some monolithic object Π. Let us get a bit more specific. Ideally we would like to argue that an iterative hash function H^h (for example, a variant of Merkle–Damgård) is as secure as a random oracle. As running example, let us assume that the iterated object h is a fixed-input-length compression function. Now we know that we cannot construct a random oracle in the standard model so the next best thing would be to show that H^h is a secure construction of a random oracle assuming that compression function h is a fixed-input-length random oracle, which is the same as saying h is an *ideal compression function*.

This brings us to the so-called *indifferentiability framework*, which provides the means to analyze compound constructions (such as a hash function constructed out of a compression function). Though not limited to constructions of idealized primitives, the indifferentiability framework is especially helpful when analyzing constructions of idealized objects such as random oracles.

At the core of the indifferentiability framework is a composition theorem which informally states that if H^h is *indifferentiable* from a random oracle—we will shortly formally define the term—and if h is an ideal compression function, then we can safely replace a random oracle RO for H^h.[1] In other words, in any cryptosystem that uses a random oracle RO we can now safely plug in H^h without any implications as to the security. In fact, we minimized the security assumptions for the cryptosystem from the assumption that

function H is a random oracle

to the "simpler assumption" that

h *is a fixed-input-length random oracle.*

And, of course, we do not need to stop here but could go further. In case we use a compression function h built from a block cipher E we could try to minimize the assumption to

E *is an ideal cipher.*[2]

For this, we would need to show that h^E—where now the superscript indicates that h internally uses ideal block cipher E—is indifferentiable from a fixed-input-length random oracle, or we do the full analysis in one step and show that H^{h^E} is indifferentiable from a variable-input-length random oracle.

17.2 Defining Indifferentiability

Indifferentiability takes a leaf out of the semantic security book; it is based on simulation. Let RO be a random oracle and H^h an iterative hash function for a compression function h which we assume is ideal. When we construct H^h then we aim at building something that behaves like a random oracle out of an ideal compression function h and iteration scheme H. This is essentially

---

[1] We note that there are exceptions, as we will see in Section 17.7. But for now let us go with that indifferentiability shows that H^h is as secure as a random oracle.

[2] The ideal cipher model treats block ciphers (i.e., permutations) as ideal, similarly as the random oracle model treats hash functions as ideal. An ideal cipher $E : \{0,1\}^{128} \to \{0,1\}^{128}$ is thus a permutation chosen uniformly at random from all permutations of the form $\{0,1\}^{128} \to \{0,1\}^{128}$. Also see Section 14.1.2 (page 548).

what indifferentiability demands, that $\mathsf{H^h}$ looks like RO to any distinguisher $\mathcal{D}$. But the distinguisher $\mathcal{D}$ may also have access to the underlying compression function h and may thus interact both with $\mathsf{H^h}$ and with h. The left-hand side of Figure 17.1 visualizes this setting.

Now that $\mathcal{D}$ interacts with two objects, this raises the question of what we compare the simultaneous availability of h with, if we require $\mathsf{H^h}$ to behave like RO. The idea of simulation-based security is to bound the information available to $\mathcal{D}$ by the additional oracle h. We demand that there is a simulator Sim that when given access to a random oracle RO could simulate something that behaves like an ideal compression function h. This is depicted on the right-hand side of Figure 17.1. The existence of the simulator can be interpreted as saying that the distinguisher in the RO setting cannot learn more from the second oracle than what is available through the interaction with RO anyway. If the simulation is truly good then it should be infeasible for an attacker to distinguish whether it interacts with $\mathsf{H^h}$ and h, or with a real monolithic random oracle RO and simulator Sim.

Indifferentiability formalizes the above idea. We call a hash function iteration scheme H for an ideal compression function h indifferentiable from a random oracle if a simulator Sim as above exists. The two scenarios in Figure 17.1 are also often called the *real world* and the *ideal world*.[3] In the real world the distinguisher interacts with hash function construction $\mathsf{H^h}$ and ideal compression function h, while in the ideal world the distinguisher interacts with a monolithic random oracle RO and a simulator Sim. All communication is executed in a black-box manner, which means that distinguisher $\mathcal{D}$ has oracle access to either $\mathsf{H^h}$ and h or to RO and $\mathsf{Sim^{RO}}$. In the ideal world, the simulator for its simulation has oracle access to the random oracle but does not see the queries made by distinguisher $\mathcal{D}$ to the random oracle.

We can now formally define indifferentiability via the distinguishing advantage of an efficient distinguisher figuring out whether it is placed into the real or the ideal world.

Definition 17.1. *A construction* H *from ideal primitive* h *is called (weakly)* indifferentiable *from ideal primitive* G *if for all efficient distinguishers* $\mathcal{D}$ *there exists an efficient simulator* Sim *such that advantage*

$$\mathsf{Adv}^{\mathrm{indiff}}_{\mathsf{H^h},\mathsf{G},\mathcal{D},\mathsf{Sim}}(\lambda) := \left| \Pr\left[\mathcal{D}^{\mathsf{H^h},\mathsf{h}}(1^\lambda) = 1 \right] - \Pr\left[\mathcal{D}^{\mathsf{G},\mathsf{Sim^G}}(1^\lambda) = 1 \right] \right|$$

is negligible. Here, on the left, the probability is over the choice of h *and the coins of distinguisher* $\mathcal{D}$, *while on the right the probability is over the choice of* G *and the coins of simulator* Sim *and distinguisher* $\mathcal{D}$.

Remark 17.2. Note that the definition does not speak of hash functions and random oracles but of ideal primitives h and G. In the case of an iterated hash

---

[3] The term "real world" is not quite fitting as we still assume that h is an ideal primitive. However, we analyze the *real-world construction* H, hence the term.

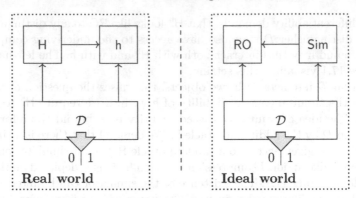

Fig. 17.1: The indifferentiability setting. In the real world a distinguisher interacts with hash function construction H and ideal compression function h, while in the ideal world the distinguisher interacts with a monolithic random oracle RO and simulator Sim. The arrows indicate the direction of communication requests. In both settings, the distinguisher can query the function boxes (H^h and h in the real world and RO and Sim^{RO} in the ideal world). As construction H needs h it can query h and in the ideal world the simulator Sim is given access to random oracle RO. All communication is in a black-box manner. Also note that the simulator does not see the distinguisher's queries to random oracle RO, nor does the adversary see the simulator's queries.

function construction replace H by the construction, h by the idealized iterated primitive (e.g., ideal compression function), and G by a random oracle.

Remark 17.3. In the definition we speak of *weak indifferentiability*. We obtain a stronger form of indifferentiability, usually referred to as *strong indifferentiability*, when interchanging the order of quantifiers. That is, we demand the existence of a single simulator that is good for all distinguishers instead of allowing a different distinguisher for each simulator. Weak indifferentiability is usually sufficient for security arguments, and from here on we identify indifferentiability with weak indifferentiability.

Remark 17.4. In the definition above we did not specify how we model parties and how they interact. The reader may for now think of interactive and oracle Turing machines, although the framework can be cast with other computational models. The modeling with Turing machines where parties are locally connected also agrees with the stipulation that queries of $\mathcal{D}$ to RO are not visible to Sim.

17.3 The Indifferentiability Composition Theorem

Now that we have a formal notion of indifferentiability, let us make some use of it. As explained in the introduction, the idea is to argue that a construction H^h, if indifferentiable from monolithic object RO, is just as secure as RO in the sense that in any cryptographic system we can securely replace any usage of RO with H^h. In order to prove such a result we would first need a precise definition of what it means to be "just as good."

Being at Least as Secure

Intuitively, the concept of being "at least as secure" is pretty clear. If a cryptographic system V is secure when using object A, and some object B is at least as secure as A, then system V should be secure when we replace A with B. To capture this formally we take the perspective of a judge that can interact with an adversary $\mathcal{A}$ and a cryptosystem V using object A or B and whose task it is to determine how good the adversary is doing. For its experiments, we allow the judge to freely interact with adversary $\mathcal{A}$ and system V in a black-box manner, meaning it can call the adversary and system on their predefined interfaces but cannot look into the boxes. For example, if the system is a signature scheme the judge could simulate the challenger from the security definition to see whether the adversary is able to produce forgeries. If now, for any adversary $\mathcal{A}$ there exists an adversary $\mathcal{B}$ such that no judge can distinguish the settings when it is interacting with $\mathcal{A}$ and V^A or with $\mathcal{B}$ and V^B, then we say that B is at least as secure as A.

This idea for a definition sounds complicated and certainly is. The reason for this is that the definition needs to exclude edge cases and that it is targeted towards its use within the composition theorem that we will see shortly. To better understand the complexities, consider the simpler definition where a judge needs to tell apart the settings when it is interacting with $\mathcal{A}$ and V^A, or with $\mathcal{A}$ and V^B? If an adversary is able to break system V^B but not able to break V^A then clearly B cannot be at least as secure as A, or can it? The problem is that A and B may not be exposing the same interfaces towards the adversary and so an adversary could potentially easily tell apart setups with A from setups with B. Consider iterative hash functions. The hash function H^h provides the interface of the ideal (fixed-input-length) compression function h towards the adversary which can on its own compute the iteration scheme. A random oracle RO, on the other hand, provides as an interface an unbounded input-length interface. So an adversary that breaks V^{H^h} will not work without changes against V^{RO}. Hence, in the definition, we allow for such cases where the adversary needs to be adapted for the other setting. And, if an adversary exists for one setting but cannot be adapted for the other, then we say that an object B is *not at least as secure as* A.

Let us now formally state the definition. As in the indifferentiability literature the role of judge is usually called *environment* $\mathcal{E}$, we obtain the following definition.

Definition 17.5. *A cryptographic scheme V^{F} with black-box access to functionality F is called* at least as secure as V^{G} *with black-box access to G, if for all efficient environments $\mathcal{E}$ the following holds: for any PPT adversary $\mathcal{A}$ there exists a PPT adversary $\mathcal{B}$ such that*

$$\left| \Pr\left[\mathcal{E}^{V^{\mathsf{F}}, \mathcal{A}^{V^{\mathsf{F}}, \mathsf{F}}}(1^{\lambda}) = 1 \right] - \Pr\left[\mathcal{E}^{V^{\mathsf{G}}, \mathcal{B}^{V^{\mathsf{G}}, \mathsf{G}}}(1^{\lambda}) = 1 \right] \right|$$

is negligible.

Remark 17.6. One way to understand Definition 17.5 is the following: if A is at least as secure as B then if there exists an adversary against V^A then there exists an adversary with roughly the same advantage against V^B. When used in a reduction this allows us to argue that if a system V is secure relative to B then it must be secure relative to A. We note that there are exceptions to this interpretation, as briefly discussed below and in more detail in Section 17.7.

Remark 17.7. In Definition 17.5 we defined the notion of *at least as secure as* for two not further specified functionalities F and G. When plugging in the specific functionalities of our running example, then these would be iterative hash function H^{h} with ideal compression function h and a monolithic random oracle RO. We visualize this setup in Figure 17.2. As noted above, the interfaces exposed by these are very different from one another. In the case of H^{h} we need to assume that the adversary knows how the iteration scheme works and thus we provide direct (black-box) access to h. In the case of a random oracle, there is no iteration scheme, so there the adversary only has (black-box) access to random oracle RO. Thus the advantage definition for environment $\mathcal{E}$ becomes

$$\left| \Pr\left[\mathcal{E}^{V^{\mathsf{H}^{\mathsf{h}}}, \mathcal{A}^{V^{\mathsf{H}^{\mathsf{h}}}, \mathsf{h}}}(1^{\lambda}) = 1 \right] - \Pr\left[\mathcal{E}^{V^{\mathsf{RO}}, \mathcal{B}^{V^{\mathsf{RO}}, \mathsf{RO}}}(1^{\lambda}) = 1 \right] \right|.$$

Remark 17.8. Note that Definition 17.5 speaks only of *efficient* adversaries and an *efficient* environment. As usual, in the idealized setting we could also state this definition for inefficient parties and only restrict the number of oracle queries of each party to be polynomial.

Definition 17.5 now provides us with the formal means to argue that, if a construction F^{f} out of some primitive f (for example, an iterative hash function out of a fixed-input-length random oracle) is indifferentiable from some monolithic primitive G (for example, a variable-input-length random oracle), then any cryptosystem $V^{\mathsf{F}^{\mathsf{f}}}$ relative to F^{f} is at least as secure as V^{G} relative to G. In other words, if F^{f} is indifferentiable from G and there exists an adversary $\mathcal{A}$ that breaks the security of $V^{\mathsf{F}^{\mathsf{f}}}$ then there exists an adversary $\mathcal{B}$—we will construct adversary $\mathcal{B}$ in the proof of the upcoming

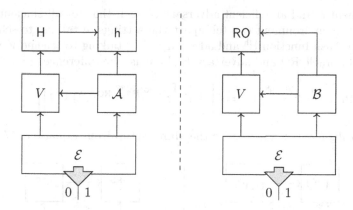

Fig. 17.2: Visualizing the setup of what it means for a system V to be as secure with a hash function construction H^h as with a random oracle RO. If V^{H^h} is as secure as V^{RO} (compare Definition 17.5) then for any adversary $\mathcal{A}$ there must exist an adversary $\mathcal{B}$ such that no environment $\mathcal{E}$ can detect a different behavior.

theorem that breaks the security of V^G. We emphasize that adversary $\mathcal{B}$ against system V^G may be an arbitrary stateful algorithm with no further restrictions on the number of direct oracle queries to G, except for that $\mathcal{B}$ is efficient if $\mathcal{A}$ is. Or, in case $\mathcal{A}$ is unbounded but makes at most polynomially many oracle queries to f, then also the number of oracle queries by $\mathcal{B}$ to G will be polynomially bounded. The reason of this emphasis is that being "at least as secure" can be less of a guarantee than one might expect at first, and one needs to be a bit careful when using it to argue security of a scheme. We will get back to this in Section 17.7 but for now continue with the indifferentiability composition theorem.

> **Theorem 17.9** (The Indifferentiability Composition Theorem). *Let construction F^f from ideal primitive f be indifferentiable from ideal primitive G. Let furthermore V be a cryptosystem. Then it follows that V^{F^f} is at least as secure as V^G.*

For simplicity of presentation we will in the following proof identify F^f with a hash function H with ideal compression function h and G with a random oracle RO. In this setup, the theorem reads as: Let hash function construction H^h from ideal compression function h be indifferentiable from random oracle RO and let furthermore V be a cryptosystem. Then it follows that V^{H^h} is at least as secure as V^{RO}.

Proof of Theorem 17.9. Let us assume that the statement is not true and that V^{H^h} is not at least as secure as V^{RO}. Hence there must be an efficient environment $\mathcal{E}$ and an efficient adversary $\mathcal{A}$ such that for all efficient adversaries $\mathcal{B}$ the environment can tell apart the settings of talking to scheme V relative to hash function H^h and adversary $\mathcal{A}$ or talking to scheme V relative to random oracle RO and adversary $\mathcal{B}$. That is, the difference

$$\left| \Pr\left[\mathcal{E}^{V^{H^h}, \mathcal{A}^{V^{H^h}, H^h}}(1^\lambda) = 1 \right] - \Pr\left[\mathcal{E}^{V^{RO}, \mathcal{B}^{V^{RO}}, RO}(1^\lambda) = 1 \right] \right| \qquad (17.1)$$

is *non-negligible*. Let us visualize the above setup from Equation (17.1):

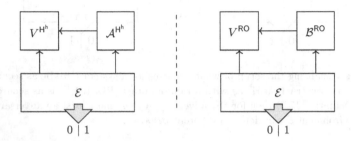

On the left we have the environment which can make oracle calls to either system V^{H^h} (which is set up to interact with hash function construction H^h) as well as to adversary $\mathcal{A}^{H^h}$, which itself can make oracle calls to system V^{H^h} but can also directly interact (via oracle calls) with construction H^h. On the right-hand side, the system is set up to use a monolithic random oracle RO instead. Arrows in the visualization indicate who is the requesting party in the communication. As environment $\mathcal{E}$ may call V^{H^h} the arrow goes from $\mathcal{E}$ to V^{H^h}.

As we have explained earlier, we cannot assume that an adversary plays by the rules. Instead we need to assume that, in the left setup, adversary $\mathcal{A}$ is aware that H^h is a construction out of primitive h. Note that in the right setup this does not apply as random oracle RO is a monolithic object and not constructed from another primitive. A more accurate picture thus also visualizes the "interfaces" that system V and the adversary use in order to compute hash values. This was exactly the situation as shown in Figure 17.2.

We now make the interfaces explicit for both setups. On the left, adversary $\mathcal{A}$ can be aware of the underlying primitive h and we thus allow oracle calls to it directly. (In case $\mathcal{A}$ wants to compute H^h for some message m it can always locally perform the computation of the iteration scheme H.) On the right-hand side adversary $\mathcal{B}$ does not have any knowledge about an underlying primitive as the random oracle is monolithic. Thus here, both system V and adversary $\mathcal{B}$ make oracle calls to random oracle RO.

Our goal now is to find a contradiction. For this we will make use of the fact that hash function construction H^h is, by assumption, indifferentiable from random oracle RO. With the indifferentiability definition (Definition 17.1) it follows that for any efficient distinguisher $\mathcal{D}$ there exists an efficient simulator

Sim such that the distinguishing advantage

$$\text{Adv}^{\text{indiff}}_{\text{H}^h, \text{G}, \mathcal{D}, \text{Sim}}(\lambda) := \left| \Pr\left[\mathcal{D}^{\text{H}^h, h}(1^\lambda) = 1 \right] - \Pr\left[\mathcal{D}^{\text{RO}, \text{Sim}^{\text{RO}}}(1^\lambda) = 1 \right] \right|$$

is negligible. Recall our earlier visualization of the indifferentiability setup with distinguisher $\mathcal{D}$ being connected to hash function H^h and ideal compression function h in the "real world" and with random oracle RO and simulator Sim^{RO} in the "ideal world":

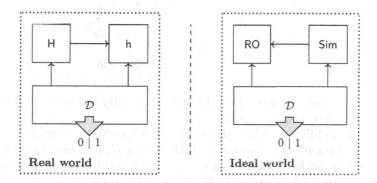

The setups look quite similar. Consider the left-hand side. The difference between the indifferentiability setup and the setup in Figure 17.2 is that in the latter there is an additional layer between blocks H and h and the bottom block. The right-hand side is similar, except that here in the indifferentiability setup we have an additional simulator.

The idea for the remainder of the proof is to bring the indifferentiability setup and the "as least as good setup" together and transform the latter into the former. For this we will construct an indifferentiability distinguisher $\mathcal{D}$ out of environment $\mathcal{E}$ together with system V and adversary $\mathcal{A}$.

The distinguisher in the indifferentiability setting expects two oracles: construction H and primitive h in the real world, and random oracle RO and simulator Sim in the ideal world. We will thus set our distinguisher $\mathcal{D}$ to be

$$\mathcal{D}^{L,R}(1^\lambda) := \mathcal{E}^{V^L, \mathcal{A}^{V^L, R}}(1^\lambda).$$

Here L and R denote the oracles of the distinguisher, which depending on the world the distinguisher is placed in are

$$(L, R) := (\text{H}^h, h) \qquad \text{or} \qquad (L, R) := (\text{RO}, \text{Sim}^{\text{RO}}).$$

Note that as environment $\mathcal{E}$, adversary $\mathcal{A}$, and scheme V are all efficient (i.e., PPT), the resulting distinguisher $\mathcal{D}$ is also efficient. If we start from the left-hand side of the "at least as good setup" then we can visualize the above construction of distinguisher $\mathcal{D}$ (on the right) as

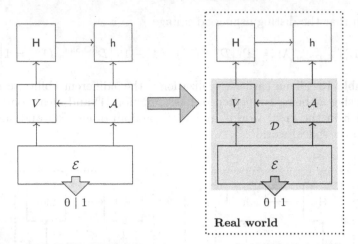

Observe here that the setting on the right is exactly the real-world setting from the indifferentiability setup.

Now, the indifferentiability property of construction H^h guarantees the existence of a simulator Sim such that distinguisher $\mathcal{D}$ as we have just defined it cannot distinguish between the real and the ideal world. That is, distinguisher $\mathcal{D}$ cannot distinguish between the following two setups:

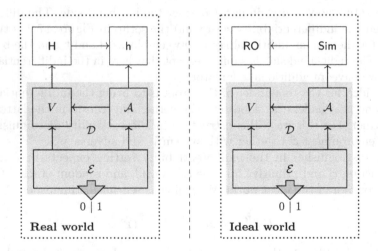

Note that, by assumption, Sim must work properly even if it does not see V's internal calls to H^h resp. RO. Compare now the ideal-world setup with the right-hand side of Figure 17.2. The setups are identical except for the simulator that is in-between the adversary and the random oracle. To solve this we can simply identify the composition of adversary $\mathcal{A}$ with simulator Sim as adversary $\mathcal{B}$ and set

$$\mathcal{B}^{\mathsf{RO}}(1^\lambda) := \mathcal{A}^{\mathsf{Sim}^{\mathsf{RO}}}(1^\lambda).$$

Observe that we allow $\mathcal{B}$ to be an arbitrary stateful algorithm with an unlimited (polynomial) number of oracle calls to RO, such that $\mathcal{B}$ certainly constitutes an admissible adversary against V^{RO}, independently of how (efficient) simulator Sim works and how many oracle queries it performs. Hence, we have found our contradiction that we were looking for. Starting from the ideal world above we can visualize the construction of $\mathcal{B}$ as

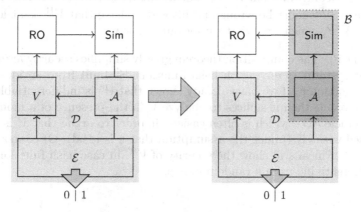

We are now in a position to put it all together. This is, again, done best via a visualization:

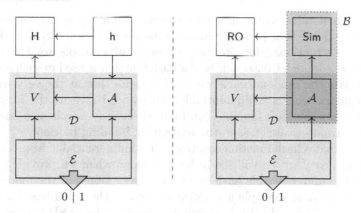

If we ignore distinguisher $\mathcal{D}$ on both sides and identify the combination of $\mathcal{A}$ with simulator Sim as $\mathcal{B}$ then this yields exactly the setup of the "at least as secure property." By assumption, environment $\mathcal{E}$ and adversary $\mathcal{A}$ were chosen such that

$$\left| \Pr\left[\mathcal{E}^{V^{H^h}, \mathcal{A}^{V^{H^h}, H^h}}(1^\lambda) = 1 \right] - \Pr\left[\mathcal{E}^{V^{RO}, \mathcal{B}^{V^{RO}}, RO}(1^\lambda) = 1 \right] \right| \qquad (17.2)$$

is non-negligible. On the other hand, if we consider the combination of environment $\mathcal{E}$ together with scheme V and adversary $\mathcal{A}$ as distinguisher $\mathcal{D}$ then we have exactly the indifferentiability setup for H^h and RO. As H^h by assumption is indifferentiable from random oracle RO it follows that

$$\left| \Pr\left[\mathcal{D}^{\mathsf{H}^h,h}(1^\lambda) = 1\right] - \Pr\left[\mathcal{D}^{\mathsf{RO},\mathsf{Sim}^{\mathsf{RO}}}(1^\lambda) = 1\right] \right| \qquad (17.3)$$

is negligible. As, by construction, Equations (17.2) and (17.3) are identical this yields a contradiction. Hence, our assumption that V^{H^h} is not at least as secure as V^{RO} must be wrong and instead we have that V^{H^h} is at least as secure as V^{RO}, which was what we set out to show.   □

Remark 17.10. The composition theorem greatly simplifies security arguments for cryptosystems V relying on hash functions H^h built from an ideal compression function h. If we have already shown that H^h is indifferentiable from a random oracle then it suffices to analyze V in the presence of a monolithic random oracle RO—which is often easier—in order to argue that V is secure when used with H^h (under the assumption that h is ideal). Of course, there may be other means to show the security of V^{H^h} in case hash function H^h is *not* indifferentiable from a random oracle.

17.4 Merkle–Damgård Is Not Indifferentiable

The concept of indifferentiability allows us to examine constructions of idealized objects and is thus perfectly suited to better understand real-world hash function constructions. Here in many cases security proofs are given in the random oracle model. Consequently, if a hash function is used in such a scheme to instantiate the random oracle we should ensure that at the very least the chosen construction is indifferentiable. This would give us the immediate guarantee that the hash function can be used securely in schemes (assuming that there are no weaknesses in the underlying building blocks).

Showing that a hash function construction is indifferentiable from a random oracle is not easy, as we will see in later sections when we provide positive examples of indifferentiable hash function constructions. In the following we first give a negative example and examine Merkle–Damgård-based constructions such as MD-5 and SHA-1, as well as various modes of SHA-2. As we will see, the underlying Merkle–Damgård iteration scheme is not indifferentiable and consequently MD-5, SHA-1, and SHA-2 cannot be used indiscriminately to instantiate random oracles. The lack of indifferentiability should not come as a surprise as Merkle–Damgård-based constructions are prone to length-extension attacks (see page 501). If we consider a message $m = m_1 \| m_2$ where m_1 and m_2 are of the size of a single message block, then given $\mathsf{H}^h_{\mathsf{MD}}(m)$ an adversary can compute hash values for any message with prefix m.[4] The

---

[4] In this example we ignore padding for simpler presentation. A similar attack is possible also if padding is used.

following figure exemplifies the length-extension attack (as so often we gloss over padding here):

The reason the attack is possible is that the final hash value $H_{MD}^h(m)$ is essentially an intermediate value in any hash computation for messages that have m as prefix. A random oracle, of course, does not expose such a structural weakness. Knowing a random oracle value $RO(m)$ for some message m does not yield any information on the random oracle's values for *any* message $m' \neq m$. This holds, in particular, also in case messages m' and m are related via some property. In the following we show that such a discrepancy between a random oracle and a hash function construction allows us to formally show that the construction cannot be indifferentiable.

Proposition 17.11. *The Merkle–Damgård hash function construction* H_{MD}^h *from a compression function* $h : \{0,1\}^{h.bl(\lambda)} \times \{0,1\}^{h.cl(\lambda)} \to \{0,1\}^{h.cl(\lambda)}$ *is not indifferentiable from a random oracle* RO.

In order to formally show that Merkle–Damgård is not indifferentiable we will build a distinguisher that executes the length-extension attack. The remainder of the proof will then be an analysis of the distinguisher in both the real and ideal world and a formal argument that the distinguisher behaves differently in the two worlds for any simulator Sim. For simpler presentation we ignore padding and assume that hash function H_{MD}^h (and random oracle RO) can only be called on multiples of block length $h.bl(\lambda)$.

Proof of Proposition 17.11. We consider the following distinguisher $\mathcal{D}$ that gets access to two oracles L and R (for left and right). Depending on the world in which the distinguisher is placed, the oracles are either Merkle–Damgård hash function H_{MD}^h with ideal compression function h (real world) or random oracle RO and simulator Sim^{RO} (ideal world). The distinguisher attempts a length-extension attack as defined by the following pseudocode:

Distinguisher $\mathcal{D}^{L,R}(1^\lambda)$

1: $m_1 \leftarrow\!\!{}_\$ \{0,1\}^{h.bl(\lambda)}$

2: $m_2 \leftarrow\!\!{}_\$ \{0,1\}^{h.bl(\lambda)}$

3: $y_1 \leftarrow L(m_1)$

4: $y_2 \leftarrow L(m_1 \| m_2)$

5: $y_2' \leftarrow R(m_2, y_1)$

6: **return** $(y_2 = y_2')$

Distinguisher $\mathcal{D}$ chooses two message blocks m_1 and m_2 at random. It then computes hash value $y_2 \leftarrow L(m_1\|m_2)$ using its left oracle (which is either hash function $\mathsf{H}^h_{\mathsf{MD}}$ or random oracle RO). It then recomputes the same hash value by computing the intermediate value $y_1 \leftarrow L(m_1)$ by using its left oracle to then continue the computation with its right oracle $y'_2 \leftarrow R(y_1, m_2)$. If the two computations yield identical values it outputs one and otherwise it outputs zero. Note that distinguisher $\mathcal{D}$ is efficient and makes only three oracle calls.

Analysis. Let us now analyze distinguisher $\mathcal{D}$ in both the real and the ideal world. In the following we present the two scenarios as pseudocode with the real world on the left hand-side and the ideal world with some, not further specified, simulator Sim on the right-hand side.

Real world: $\mathcal{D}^{\mathsf{H}^h_{\mathsf{MD}}, h}(1^\lambda)$	Ideal world: $\mathcal{D}^{\mathsf{RO}, \mathsf{Sim}^{\mathsf{RO}}}(1^\lambda)$
1 : $m_1 \leftarrow\!\!{}_\$ \{0,1\}^{h.\mathsf{bl}(\lambda)}$	1 : $m_1 \leftarrow\!\!{}_\$ \{0,1\}^{h.\mathsf{bl}(\lambda)}$
2 : $m_2 \leftarrow\!\!{}_\$ \{0,1\}^{h.\mathsf{bl}(\lambda)}$	2 : $m_2 \leftarrow\!\!{}_\$ \{0,1\}^{h.\mathsf{bl}(\lambda)}$
3 : $y_1 \leftarrow \mathsf{H}^h_{\mathsf{MD}}(m_1)$	3 : $y_1 \leftarrow \mathsf{RO}(m_1)$
4 : $y_2 \leftarrow \mathsf{H}^h_{\mathsf{MD}}(m_1\|m_2)$	4 : $y_2 \leftarrow \mathsf{RO}(m_1\|m_2)$
5 : $y'_2 \leftarrow h(m_2, y_1)$	5 : $y'_2 \leftarrow \mathsf{Sim}^{\mathsf{RO}}(m_2, y_1)$
6 : **return** $(y_2 = y'_2)$	6 : **return** $(y_2 = y'_2)$

In the real world the length-extension attack will always succeed due to the construction of hash function H_{MD} as

$$\mathsf{H}^h_{\mathsf{MD}}(m_1\|m_2) = h(m_2, h(m_1, \mathsf{IV})) = h(m_2, \mathsf{H}^h_{\mathsf{MD}}(m_1)).$$

Here the first equality is simply the definition of the Merkle–Damgård transformation. It follows that the distinguisher in the real world will always output 1, no matter the choice of ideal compression function h or initialization vector IV.

Let us next analyze the ideal world. In order for H_{MD} to be indifferentiable from a random oracle there must be a simulator that can also make distinguisher $\mathcal{D}$ output 1 except with negligible probability. We will argue that no such simulator (not even an inefficient one) can exist. For this consider the single simulator call in line 5. Simulator Sim gets as input message block m_2 as well as value y_1 which was computed as $y_1 \leftarrow \mathsf{RO}(m_1)$. In order for simulator Sim to make distinguisher $\mathcal{D}$ output 1 it would need to output value $\mathsf{RO}(m_1\|m_2)$. However, both its inputs are independent of message block m_1 so that m_1 remains effectively hidden from simulator Sim. For this note that m_2 was chosen uniformly at random and a random oracle value $\mathsf{RO}(m_1)$ does not yield any information on input m_1 nor on random oracle values for any message $m' \neq m_1$.[5]

If we discard the possibility of simulator Sim querying random oracle RO on message m_1 in a game hop (down to the security of the random oracle as a one-way function) then it follows that the simulator Sim must guess the random oracle output in the resulting scenario. But simply guessing value $\mathsf{RO}(m_1\|m_2)$ is upper bounded by $2^{-\min(\mathsf{h.bl}(\lambda),\mathsf{h.cl}(\lambda))}$. Here the minimum is due to the fact that the simulator can choose to either guess m_1 or to guess $\mathsf{RO}(m_1\|m_2)$. This concludes the proof. □

Remark 17.12. We have simplified the proof by ignoring the padding operation pad (see Section 13.1.1; page 482). Exercise 17.1 asks you to provide a length-extension attack that takes an arbitrary padding function into account. Given the attack, we can use the above blueprint to show that padding does not save the plain Merkle–Damgård construction. Thus also with padding Merkle–Damgård is not indifferentiable from a random oracle.

17.5 Indifferentiable Hash Function Constructions

Showing that a hash function is indifferentiable from a random oracle is a difficult endeavor, and as we have seen, many hash functions used in practice are, in fact, not indifferentiable. Of course, when the SHA-1 and SHA-2 families of hash functions were designed the notion of indifferentiability was not yet devised. However, length-extension attacks against Merkle–Damgård-based constructions were known. For the SHA-3 competition indifferentiability played a major role, and indeed all five finalists have been shown to be indifferentiable from a random oracle.

In the following we show that a simple extension to Merkle–Damgård that thwarts off length-extension attacks is also sufficient to prove indifferentiability. Chopped Merkle–Damgård (see Section 13.1.7 on page 503), which adds a transformation to the end of the function that truncates the final intermediate state before outputting it, is indifferentiable from a random oracle. Interestingly, some variants of SHA-2, namely SHA-512/256 and SHA-512/224, have exactly that characteristic and are thus indifferentiable. Others, such as SHA-512 that omit the final truncation, are not, as we have seen in the previous section.

Proving indifferentiability of constructions is difficult, and formal proofs are usually rather long. The proof that we exhibit here is no exception. Indeed,

---

[5] We note that with access to RO the simulator may try to find m_1 by guessing and validating its guesses by calling the random oracle. With only polynomially many oracle calls this strategy has, however, only negligible chances of success. Also see Section 8.2.2 on page 347 about the one-wayness of random oracles.

we will show the statement only for the case when the underlying compression function is modeled as a fixed-input-length random oracle. We could have gone one step further and assumed instead that the compression function was itself a construction from an ideal cipher, for example, via the Davies–Meyer construction (see Section 14.1.3; page 554). However, the additional complexity added by this intermediate construction does not significantly change the proof structure but only adds to complexity and additional edge cases to be considered. We thus opt for the simpler statement in the hope that it is easier to follow.

17.5.1 Chopped Merkle–Damgård Is Indifferentiable

Before we go on to proving indifferentiability of chopped Merkle–Damgård (chopped MD) let us formally define it. For a constant fraction $0 < c < 1$ we define function g_c as

$$g_c(x) := x[1 .. \lceil (1 - c) \cdot |x| \rceil],$$

that is, the function g_c on input x outputs the first $\lceil (1 - c) \cdot |x| \rceil$ bits of x. Or in other terms, g_c chops off the last $\lfloor c \cdot |x| \rfloor$ bits from its input. We obtain chopped MD with chop factor $0 < c < 1$ when composing a standard Merkle–Damgård construction with function g_c (see also Figure 17.3). Consequently, we obtain hash values of length $\mathsf{H.ol}(\lambda) = \lceil (1 - c) \cdot \mathsf{h.cl}(\lambda) \rceil$.

Chopped MD is a special case of so-called wide-pipe constructions (see Section 13.1.7; page 503) in which the inner state kept by the hash function is larger than what is output as final hash value. For chopped MD with chop factor c the difference between the inner state length and hash value length is exactly $\mathsf{h.cl}(\lambda) - \mathsf{H.ol}(\lambda) = \lfloor c \cdot \mathsf{h.cl}(\lambda) \rfloor$. It is this property which protects chopped MD from length-extension attacks, and ultimately it will allow us to show that chopped MD is not only immune to length-extension attacks but that it is, in fact, indifferentiable from a random oracle if we model the underlying compression function h as a fixed-input-length random oracle. Note that for this the chop factor c of final truncation function g_c is irrelevant when we consider hash functions in an asymptotic setting where the output size of the hash function grows with the security parameter. For the concrete setting the chop factor is, of course, crucial as it determines the difficulty for an adversary in the indifferentiability setting, as we will see next.

Theorem 17.13. *Let* $\mathsf{H^h}$ *be a chopped MD function with constant chop factor* $0 < c < 1$. *If compression function* $\mathsf{h} : \{0,1\}^{\mathsf{h.bl}(\lambda)} \times \{0,1\}^{\mathsf{h.cl}(\lambda)} \to \{0,1\}^{\mathsf{h.cl}(\lambda)}$ *is modeled as a fixed-input-length random oracle with super-logarithmic output length (i.e.,* $\mathsf{h.cl}(\lambda) \in \omega(\log(\lambda))$*), then* $\mathsf{H^h}$ *is indifferentiable from a random oracle.*

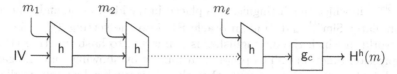

Fig. 17.3: The Merkle–Damgård construction with a final transformation function g_c. We obtain chopped MD when transformation g_c is a projection on a fixed fraction of the input bits, for example, a projection on the first half of the input bits.

Remark 17.14. In Theorem 17.13 we consider compression function h to be a fixed-input-length random oracle. As we have seen, compression functions are usually constructed from primitives such as block ciphers. A stronger statement can thus be obtained by showing that chopped MD is indifferentiable assuming that the underlying block cipher is an ideal cipher and considering the combined construction of the iteration scheme together with the construction of the compression function, for example, via Davies–Meyer. Depending on the compression function construction this proof may not necessarily hold. For the Davies–Meyer construction, however, it can be shown that chopped MD is indifferentiable.

In order to prove Theorem 17.13 we need to show that for any efficient distinguisher $\mathcal{D}$ there exists an efficient simulator Sim such that the indifferentiability advantage

$$\mathsf{Adv}^{\mathsf{indiff}}_{\mathsf{H}^{\mathsf{h}},\mathsf{RO},\mathcal{D},\mathsf{Sim}}(\lambda) := \left| \Pr\left[\mathcal{D}^{\mathsf{H}^{\mathsf{h}},\mathsf{h}}(1^\lambda) = 1 \right] - \Pr\left[\mathcal{D}^{\mathsf{RO},\mathsf{Sim}^{\mathsf{RO}}}(1^\lambda) = 1 \right] \right|$$

is negligible. We will show an even stronger statement. Namely that there exists a universal (and efficient) simulator Sim such that for all distinguishers $\mathcal{D}$ (even unbounded ones) that make at most polynomially many oracle queries advantage $\mathsf{Adv}^{\mathsf{indiff}}_{\mathsf{H}^{\mathsf{h}},\mathsf{RO},\mathcal{D},\mathsf{Sim}}(\lambda)$ is negligible.[6]

In order to simplify the presentation of the proof we will prove Theorem 17.13 without taking padding into account. For this we assume that hash function H^{h} (and random oracle RO) is only defined on inputs with a length that is a multiple of the block size $\mathsf{h.bl}(\lambda)$. Note that, as before, this simplification is purely for the benefit of the proof's presentation and Exercise 17.2 asks you to discuss those parts of the proof that would need to be adapted for the general proof that includes padding functions.

Proof of Theorem 17.13. The proof consists of two parts. First we present the universal simulator Sim. We will then show that this simulator is indeed good for any distinguisher $\mathcal{D}$ that makes at most polynomially many queries to its oracles by presenting a sequence of games that transform the setting

---

[6] This corresponds to the *strong* indifferentiability setting (see Definition 17.1 on page 689 and the following remark).

$\mathcal{D}^{\mathsf{RO},\mathsf{Sim}^{\mathsf{RO}}}$ in which the distinguisher is placed in the ideal world and connected to simulator $\mathsf{Sim}^{\mathsf{RO}}$ and random oracle RO into the setting $\mathcal{D}^{\mathsf{H}^{\mathsf{h}},\mathsf{h}}$, i.e., the real world in which the distinguisher is connected to hash function H^{h} and compression function h. The proof then follows by showing that the games are negligibly close, thus showing that the distinguisher has only negligible chances of distinguishing the two settings.

The simulator. The goal of simulator Sim is to present a view towards distinguisher $\mathcal{D}$ that is consistent with the answers of random oracle RO. For example, $\mathcal{D}$ may first query its left oracle (either H^{h} or RO) about some input, to then locally iterate H^{h} by making all the corresponding queries to the right oracle (either h or Sim). Then the simulator would need to give consistent answers for the right oracle to ensure that they match the response of RO with respect to iterations of H.

To this end, the simulator keeps a directed graph $\mathcal{G}$ as its state. Both nodes and edges will be labeled. Consider a query (m, y) to simulator Sim. Here m corresponds to a part of a message and y is a chaining value, i.e., an intermediate state value of a hash computation. Nodes in graph $\mathcal{G}$ will be used to keep track of all seen state values (e.g., chaining value y), while edges correspond to message parts (e.g., message block m).

At the beginning of the computation, graph $\mathcal{G}$ contains only a single node labeled with the initialization value IV used by the chopped MD construction:

To answer a query (m, y) the simulator will perform the following steps. It first attempts to add the query into graph $\mathcal{G}$ unless it is already present. The latter is the case if there exists a node labeled y with an outgoing edge labeled m. In this case the simulator returns the label of the node that the m-edge is pointing to. On the other hand, if the query is not yet part of graph $\mathcal{G}$, then the simulator adds the query as follows. In case there is not yet a node labeled y, a new node is added with label y. Then an outgoing edge with label m is added to node y. Next, the simulator creates a new node as the target of the new m-edge. The label y' of this new node is then chosen either uniformly at random or by a random oracle query (we will define the specifics shortly). Finally, label y' is returned to distinguisher $\mathcal{D}$.

What is left to define is how labels of new nodes are chosen by the simulator. In the previous paragraph we specified that these are either chosen uniformly at random or via a random oracle query. Which alternative is chosen depends on whether there exists a path from node IV to the new node. If there exists no such path, then simulator Sim simply chooses the new label uniformly at random. If there exists a path then the label of the node is chosen by querying random oracle RO on message $m = m_1 \| \ldots \| m_\ell$ where message blocks m_1 to m_ℓ are the labels of the edges on the path starting from node IV. As we are considering chopped MD the output size of RO is shorter than the output size of h due to the application of the final truncation function g_c. In order to produce a label of size $h.cl(\lambda)$ the missing bits are chosen uniformly at random and appended to the random oracle output.

The workings of the simulator are best understood with a few example queries. Consider a simulator with its starting state of a graph $\mathcal{G}$ that only contains the single node IV. On a query (m_1, IV) the simulator updates its graph as follows:

As there exists a path from node IV to the newly inserted node, value y_1 is chosen by first computing $RO(m_1)$ and then adding as many random bits as are necessary to produce a label of size $h.cl(\lambda)$.

Now, suppose distinguisher $\mathcal{D}$ issues another query (m_2, IV). Then graph $\mathcal{G}$ will change into

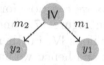

Label y_2 is chosen similarly to y_1 but with random oracle query $RO(m_2)$. Next, let us suppose distinguisher $\mathcal{D}$ makes a query (m_3, y_1). In this case, the graph is updated into the following state:

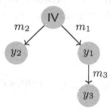

In this case, as the path from IV to y_3 is via edges m_1 and m_3, label y_3 is chosen by first computing $RO(m_1 \| m_3)$ and again by filling up the result with random bits to get a label of length $h.cl(\lambda)$.

What we have not yet covered is the case that the distinguisher makes a query (m_4, y_4) for a state value y_4 which is not yet in the graph. In this case, the node for y_4 is simply added to the graph without any connection to an existing node:

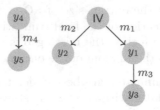

Consequently, in this case there is no direct path from IV to y_5 and thus simulator Sim chooses label y_5 simply as a random bit string of length h.cl(λ).

We formally describe simulator Sim via pseudocode where $\mathcal{G}$.nodes denotes the set of nodes of graph $\mathcal{G}$ and where a node is identified by its label. We let $\mathcal{G}$.edges denote the set of edges. An edge is modeled as a tuple (n_1, n_2, label) where the first two elements denote the start and end nodes of the edge and the third element denotes the edge's label. Furthermore, $\mathcal{G}$.path(n_1, n_2) is a function that returns the shortest path from node n_1 to node n_2. In case multiple paths exist, a random path is picked from the candidates. A path is returned in the form of a string $m_1 \| \ldots \| m_\ell$ where m_i is the label of the ith edge in the path. Note that there always exists a path from a node to itself, that is, $\mathcal{G}$.path(n_1, n_1) = ε where ε is the empty string. In case no path exists between nodes n_1 and n_2 function $\mathcal{G}$.path(n_1, n_2) returns $\perp$.

With this additional syntax we can now formally capture simulator Sim. We provide the pseudocode in Figure 17.4 and note that at the beginning graph $\mathcal{G}$ consists of the single node IV. Further note that all the individual graph operations are efficient and hence we have that also the simulator is efficient as long as it is queried at most polynomially many times. With this we can go on to the second step of the proof.

Proving indifferentiability. In order to complete the proof we need to show that for any distinguisher $\mathcal{D}$ that makes at most polynomially many queries we have that the indifferentiability advantage $\text{Adv}^{\text{indiff}}_{\text{H}^\text{h},\text{RO},\mathcal{D},\text{Sim}}(\lambda)$ is negligible. That is, we must show that there exists some negligible function negl such that

$$\text{Adv}^{\text{indiff}}_{\text{H}^\text{h},\text{RO},\mathcal{D},\text{Sim}}(\lambda)$$
$$:= \left| \Pr\left[\mathcal{D}^{\text{H}^\text{h},\text{h}}(1^\lambda) = 1 \right] - \Pr\left[\mathcal{D}^{\text{RO},\text{Sim}^{\text{RO}}}(1^\lambda) = 1 \right] \right| \leq \text{negl}(\lambda).$$

To this end we give a game-based proof where the first game Game$_1$ puts distinguisher $\mathcal{D}$ into the ideal world where it is connected to random oracle RO and simulator Sim^{RO} and the final game will be the real world with distinguisher $\mathcal{D}$ connected to hash function H^h and compression function h. We will present each game in turn and show that two neighboring games are negligibly close.

Game$_1$ The first game is the ideal-world setting $\mathcal{D}^{\text{RO},\text{Sim}^{\text{RO}}}$ where distinguisher $\mathcal{D}$ is connected to random oracle RO and simulator Sim^{RO}. Hence, we

Simulator $\mathsf{Sim}^{\mathsf{RO}}(m, y)$

---

1 :   **if** $\exists y'$ such that $(y, y', m) \in \mathcal{G}.\mathsf{edges}$ **then**

2 :   **return** y'

3 :   **else**

4 : $\mathsf{path} \leftarrow \mathcal{G}.\mathsf{path}(\mathsf{IV}, y)$ // note that $\mathcal{G}.\mathsf{path}(\mathsf{IV}, \mathsf{IV}) = \varepsilon$

5 :   **if** $\mathsf{path} = \bot$ **then**

6 : $y' \leftarrow\!\!\$\ \{0,1\}^{\mathsf{h.cl}(\lambda)}$

7 :   **else**

8 : $z \leftarrow\!\!\$\ \{0,1\}^{\mathsf{h.cl}(\lambda) - \mathsf{H.ol}(\lambda)}$

9 : $y' \leftarrow \mathsf{RO}(\mathsf{path}\|m)\|z$

        // we will later show the quasi uniqueness of y'

        // and let the simulator fail if already $y' \in \mathcal{G}.\mathsf{nodes}$

10 :   add (y, y', m) to $\mathcal{G}.\mathsf{edges}$

11 :   **return** y'

Fig. 17.4: Pseudocode of simulator Sim in the proof of Theorem 17.13. Note that at the beginning graph $\mathcal{G}$ is initialized with the single node IV.

have that
$$\Pr[\mathsf{Game}_1(\lambda) = 1] = \Pr\left[\mathcal{D}^{\mathsf{RO},\mathsf{Sim}^{\mathsf{RO}}}(1^\lambda) = 1\right].$$

Game$_2$ In the second game we introduce a relay algorithm R in-between the distinguisher and random oracle RO. This means that the distinguisher is now placed into the following setting $\mathcal{D}^{R^{\mathsf{RO}},\mathsf{Sim}^{\mathsf{RO}}}$. For now the role of the relay algorithm is simply to forward any queries to the random oracle and return the results without any change. As this is merely a syntactical change we thus have that
$$\Pr[\mathsf{Game}_2(\lambda) = 1] = \Pr[\mathsf{Game}_1(\lambda) = 1].$$

Game$_3$ In Game$_3$ we adapt simulator Sim to fail explicitly in certain situations. After generating a new label y' and before adding it to graph $\mathcal{G}$ (line 10 in Figure 17.4) the simulator checks if a node with label y' exists already. If this is the case, the simulator fails explicitly and we count the game as a win for the distinguisher.

By the Fundamental Lemma of Game Playing (Lemma 5.13 on page 224) we have that games Game$_2$ and Game$_3$ are identical unless distinguisher $\mathcal{D}$ makes the simulator fail in Game$_3$. The probability of this happening is the probability that a newly generated label y' collides with one that is already in graph $\mathcal{G}$.

Labels are generated in one of two forms: either uniformly at random (line 6) or via a random oracle query and subsequent filling with random bits (line 9). In the first case the simulator chooses $\mathsf{h.cl}(\lambda)$ many random

708 17 Constructing Random Oracles—Indifferentiability

bits, while in the latter case it chooses $\lfloor c \cdot \mathsf{h.cl}(\lambda) \rfloor$ many random bits (for constant chop factor $0 < c < 1$).[7] Thus, the probability of a collision of a newly generated label y' with any existing label is upper bounded by the probability of having a collision on values of length (at least) $\lfloor c \cdot \mathsf{h.cl}(\lambda) \rfloor$ chosen uniformly at random.

By assumption distinguisher $\mathcal{D}$ is efficient, and we can thus upper bound its number of queries $q_{\mathsf{Sim}} := q_{\mathsf{Sim}}(\lambda)$ to simulator Sim by a polynomial. As each simulator query adds at most a single node to graph $\mathcal{G}$, polynomial q_{Sim} (plus one) is also an upper bound for the number of nodes in the graph. In particular, as graph $\mathcal{G}$ on the outset contains only the single node IV we have that at the time of the ith query the graph contains at most i many nodes: the ith query adds node number $i + 1$ (unless it collides or the query is a duplicate of an earlier query in which case in line 2 the earlier response is repeated). By the above argument we can upper bound the probability of a collision of a newly generated label y' on the ith query as

$$\Pr[\text{Simulator } \mathsf{Sim} \text{ fails on } i\text{th query}] = \Pr[y' \in \mathcal{G}.\mathsf{nodes}] \leq \frac{i}{2^{\lfloor c \cdot \mathsf{h.cl}(\lambda) \rfloor}}.$$

Here $\mathcal{G}.\mathsf{nodes}$ denotes the set of all nodes in graph $\mathcal{G}$. As distinguisher $\mathcal{D}$ makes at most q_{Sim} many queries we can bound the probability that simulator Sim fails in any of the queries as

$$\Pr[\text{Simulator } \mathsf{Sim} \text{ fails}] = \Pr[\exists i : \text{Simulator } \mathsf{Sim} \text{ fails on } i\text{th query}]$$
$$\leq \sum_{i=1}^{q_{\mathsf{Sim}}} \frac{i}{2^{\lfloor c \cdot \mathsf{h.cl}(\lambda) \rfloor}}$$
$$\leq \frac{q_{\mathsf{Sim}}^2}{2^{c \cdot \mathsf{h.cl}(\lambda)}}.$$

It follows that the difference between games Game_2 and Game_3 can be upper bound by

$$|\Pr[\mathsf{Game}_3(\lambda) = 1] - \Pr[\mathsf{Game}_2(\lambda) = 1]| \leq \Pr[\text{Simulator } \mathsf{Sim} \text{ fails}]$$
$$= \frac{q_{\mathsf{Sim}}^2}{2^{c \cdot \mathsf{h.cl}(\lambda)}}.$$

Note that as c is a constant fraction, $\mathsf{h.cl}(\lambda)$ is super-logarithmic in the security parameter, and q_{Sim} is a polynomial, the difference is negligible. In case we consider a fixed real-world hash function, say SHA-512/256, then here is where the chop factor enters. In case of SHA-512/256 the chop factor is 0.5 and the probability of an adversary distinguishing games Game_2 and Game_3 for SHA-512/256 would be $q_{\mathsf{Sim}}^2 \cdot 2^{-256}$ where q_{Sim} denotes the number of oracle queries by the adversary.

---

[7] The simulator needs to fill up the remaining $\mathsf{h.cl}(\lambda) - \mathsf{H.ol}(\lambda)$ bits, which it chooses uniformly at random.

Also note that in case we had a chop factor of 0, i.e., no chopping, then the argument above would not work (as in standard Merkle–Damgård). In this case the denominator would be 1 and the bound meaningless.

Let us point out how collision freeness of the labels helps the simulator. If there are no collisions among labels it follows that, if there is a path from IV to some label y, then this path is unique. It follows that the simulator always picks the correct path if it exists. Moreover, the absence of collisions also means that the distinguisher is not able to (deliberately or accidentally) connect two "loose" paths, say from IV to y and from y' to y'', with a query to the simulator. In this case the simulator would have already picked y'' randomly in line 6 instead of calling RO. But by connecting the paths the distinguisher could now iterate the hash function and check consistency with the reply from RO. Yet, such a bridge to an existing label would violate the collision freeness.

Game$_4$ In Game$_4$ we consider an adapted distinguisher $\mathcal{D}_*$. Distinguisher $\mathcal{D}_*$ runs distinguisher $\mathcal{D}$, relaying all its oracle queries while recording all its queries to the left oracle (i.e., the random oracle in the ideal world). Once distinguisher $\mathcal{D}$ finishes, distinguisher $\mathcal{D}_*$ evaluates the chopped MD construction on all recorded queries using its right oracle as compression function (i.e., the simulator in the ideal world). It then outputs whatever $\mathcal{D}$ had output before. As Game$_4$ is still in the real-world scenario but with the left oracle being relayed through a relay algorithm R, distinguisher $\mathcal{D}_*$ in Game$_4$ finds itself relative to oracles $(R^{\text{RO}}, \text{Sim}^{\text{RO}})$. Once more as pseudocode:

$\mathcal{D}_*^{R^{\text{RO}}, \text{Sim}^{\text{RO}}}(1^\lambda)$	$\text{HASH}(m)$
1 : $\mathcal{Q} \leftarrow \{\}$	1 : $\mathcal{Q} \leftarrow \mathcal{Q} \cup \{m\}$
2 : $b \leftarrow_\$ \mathcal{D}^{\text{HASH}, \text{Sim}^{\text{RO}}}(1^\lambda)$	2 : $y \leftarrow R^{\text{RO}}(m)$ // Forward query to left oracle
3 : **for** $m \in \mathcal{Q}$ **do**	3 : **return** y
4 : $\quad H^{\text{Sim}^{\text{RO}}}(m)$	
5 : **return** b	

First note that distinguisher $\mathcal{D}_*$ always returns the same value as original distinguisher $\mathcal{D}$, as it does not further process the responses from its additional queries. As it does make additional queries to the simulator it may, however, be the case that during these final queries simulator Sim fails. To quantify the resulting loss, let $q_{\text{RO}} := q_{\text{RO}}(\lambda)$ denote an upper bound on the number of queries by distinguisher $\mathcal{D}$ to its left oracle, i.e., to the random oracle (or rather the relay algorithm R^{RO}). Let furthermore $q_{\text{RO}}^{\text{len}} := q_{\text{RO}}^{\text{len}}(\lambda)$ denote the maximum length of a query to the random oracle measured in message blocks. Consequently, distinguisher $\mathcal{D}_*$ makes $q_{\text{Sim}} + (q_{\text{RO}} \cdot q_{\text{RO}}^{\text{len}})$ many queries to its right oracle (the simulator): the q_{Sim} queries from distinguisher $\mathcal{D}$ plus the additional queries stemming from recorded random oracle queries (lines 3 and 4). By the same analysis as in the previous game hop we get that

$$|\Pr[\mathsf{Game}_4(\lambda) = 1] - \Pr[\mathsf{Game}_3(\lambda) = 1]| \leq \Pr[\text{Simulator Sim fails}]$$

$$\leq \frac{(q_{\mathsf{Sim}} + (q_{\mathsf{RO}} \cdot q_{\mathsf{RO}}^{\mathsf{len}}))^2}{2^{c \cdot h \cdot \mathsf{cl}(\lambda)}}.$$

Again, we simply count the maximum number of nodes in graph $\mathcal{G}$, which is upper bounded by the total number of simulator queries. As for each query the probability is at most $(q_{\mathsf{Sim}} + (q_{\mathsf{RO}} \cdot q_{\mathsf{RO}}^{\mathsf{len}})) \cdot (2^{-c \cdot h \cdot \mathsf{cl}(\lambda)})$ we obtain the claimed bound via a union bound.

In the following we implicitly condition on aborts not occurring (also see our discussion on handled events in game-hopping proofs in Section 5.1.4 on page 226).

Game$_5$ In Game$_5$ we leave both simulator and distinguisher as is, but instead change the relay algorithm. Instead of merely relaying queries to the random oracle, the relay algorithm is chosen as $R := \mathsf{H}^{\mathsf{Sim}^{\mathsf{RO}}}$, that is, the relay algorithm implements chopped MD with simulator $\mathsf{Sim}^{\mathsf{RO}}$ as the compression function. Note that this change does not affect the output of the relay algorithm. For this observe that $\mathsf{RO}(m)$ and $\mathsf{H}^{\mathsf{Sim}^{\mathsf{RO}}}(m)$ are, by construction of the simulator, always identical: During the computation of $\mathsf{H}^{\mathsf{Sim}^{\mathsf{RO}}}(m)$ the simulator will build up a chain which at the end results in a value $y \leftarrow \mathsf{RO}(m)\|z$, which will be returned to H, which in turn removes suffix z before returning the value. We give a more detailed example below. We now claim that the distributions of Game$_4$ and Game$_5$ are identical, that is, we claim that

$$\Pr[\mathsf{Game}_5(\lambda) = 1] = \Pr[\mathsf{Game}_4(\lambda) = 1].$$

To see that this is the case, first note that the additional queries to the simulator introduced by changing the relay algorithm are exactly those queries that distinguisher $\mathcal{D}_*$ makes at the end (lines 3 and 4). Distinguisher $\mathcal{D}_*$ recorded all random oracle queries and as its final step runs them through simulator $\mathsf{Sim}^{\mathsf{RO}}$ by executing the chopped MD construction with oracle $\mathsf{Sim}^{\mathsf{RO}}$ as the compression function. With the changed relay algorithm these queries are now merely made earlier. In particular, this means that the number of *distinct* queries to simulator $\mathsf{Sim}^{\mathsf{RO}}$ does not change and that thus the probability of the simulator aborting remains the same. Here note that duplicate queries are answered already in line 2 of the simulator (Figure 17.4).

Similarly, the changed order of queries does not have an effect on the game's distribution. Consider a query $m = m_1\|\ldots\|m_\ell$ by the distinguisher to its left oracle (i.e., the relay algorithm). For this query, the relay algorithm will now make the following chain of simulator queries: $y_1 \leftarrow\!\!\$\ \mathsf{Sim}^{\mathsf{RO}}(m_1, \mathsf{IV})$, $y_2 \leftarrow\!\!\$\ \mathsf{Sim}^{\mathsf{RO}}(m_2, y_1)$, $\ldots$, and finally $y_\ell \leftarrow\!\!\$\ \mathsf{Sim}^{\mathsf{RO}}(m_\ell, y_{\ell-1})$. Consequently, the following chain will be built up as part of the simulator's graph $\mathcal{G}$ (noting that we have already dealt with the probability of aborts and can thus here assume that an abort does not occur):

Here, label y_i will be generated by the simulator as $\mathsf{RO}(m_1\|\dots\|m_i)\|z$ for z chosen uniformly at random in $\{0,1\}^{\mathsf{h.cl}(\lambda)-\mathsf{H.ol}(\lambda)}$ (line 9 of the simulator). Furthermore, the result of relay algorithm R will be $\mathsf{RO}(m_1\|\dots\|m_\ell)$ as it chops off the last $\lfloor c\cdot\mathsf{h.cl}(\lambda)\rfloor$ bits from value y_ℓ before returning it as part of its simulation of chopped MD.

As we have already dealt with aborts due to label collisions in the previous game hops, the only way the additional simulator state can affect its observable behavior is if a query (m^*,y^*) made by the distinguisher to simulator $\mathsf{Sim}^{\mathsf{RO}}$ would have been answered with a uniformly random response (line 6 of the simulator) in Game_4 but is now answered via a random oracle query (line 9) in Game_5. Let us assume that this situation occurs in Game_4. Then, at the time of query (m^*,y^*) we necessarily have that $\mathcal{G}.\mathsf{path}(\mathsf{IV},y^*)=\bot$ (line 4) such that the query is answered with a uniformly random response (line 6). On the other hand, we have that query (m^*,y^*), by assumption, is part of a random oracle query as otherwise it would not be part of a relay algorithm query in Game_5. Then, however, it will be part of distinguisher $\mathcal{D}_*$'s additional simulator queries of recorded random oracle queries (lines 3 and 4 of distinguisher $\mathcal{D}_*$). As distinguisher $\mathcal{D}_*$ makes query (m^*,y^*) in the context of an honest chopped MD evaluation it follows that the query directly preceding query (m^*,y^*) must have been answered with value y^*. But since this is an honest evaluation of chopped MD there must exist now a path in the simulator's graph $\mathcal{G}$ from initialization value IV to node y^*. This can, however, only be the case if some query to the simulator "connected" the previously unconnected node y^*, in which case the simulator would have aborted. As we have already discarded the possibility of aborts this cannot be the case and we can conclude that, indeed,
$$\Pr[\mathsf{Game}_5(\lambda)=1]=\Pr[\mathsf{Game}_4(\lambda)=1].$$

Game$_6$ By now we consider the following setup:
$$\mathcal{D}^{\mathsf{H}^{\mathsf{Sim}^{\mathsf{RO}}},\mathsf{Sim}^{\mathsf{RO}}}.$$

Note that here the random oracle is no longer directly accessible from the adversary. Thus, towards the adversary it makes no difference whether or not the simulator chooses labels y' in line 9 as $y'\leftarrow\mathsf{RO}(\mathsf{path}\|m)\|z$ for a uniformly random z or whether it simply chooses $y'\leftarrow\!\!{}_\$\{0,1\}^{\mathsf{h.cl}(\lambda)}$ completely at random. In one case the randomness stems from the random oracle and in the other from the simulator. Towards distinguisher $\mathcal{D}$ there is no observable difference between the two as the observed values are distributed identically.

In Game_6 we can now consider the following simplified simulator Sim' which no longer uses a random oracle and where we have replaced lines 8 and 9. Also note the grayed out line 10 which considers the event in which the simulator aborts due to a label collision, an event which we have already dealt with in earlier game hops and which we here implicitly condition on not occurring (also see our discussion on handled events in game-hopping proofs on page 226).

Simulator $\mathsf{Sim}'(m, y)$

---

1 : **if** $\exists y'$ such that $(y, y', m) \in \mathcal{G}$.edges **then**

2 :   **return** y'

3 : **else**

4 :   path $\leftarrow \mathcal{G}$.path(IV, y)

5 :   **if** $\bot = $ path **then**

6 : $y' \leftarrow\!\!{\$}\ \{0, 1\}^{\mathsf{h.cl}(\lambda)}$

7 :   **else**

8 :

9 : $y' \leftarrow\!\!{\$}\ \{0, 1\}^{\mathsf{h.cl}(\lambda)}$

10 :   **if** $y' \in \mathcal{G}$.nodes **then abort**

11 :   add (y, y', m) to $\mathcal{G}$.edges

12 :   **return** y'

Now, however, the entire graph structure is no longer used to determine the simulator's output except for keeping track of queries and their corresponding return value. This allows us to further simplify the simulator to yield

---

Simulator $\mathsf{Sim}'(m, y)$

---

1 : **if** $\exists y'$ such that $(y, y', m) \in \mathcal{G}$.edges **then**

2 :   **return** y'

3 : **else**

4 : $y' \leftarrow\!\!{\$}\ \{0, 1\}^{\mathsf{h.cl}(\lambda)}$

5 :   **if** $y' \in \mathcal{G}$.nodes **then abort**

6 :   add (y, y', m) to $\mathcal{G}$.edges

7 :   **return** y'

In the above pseudocode of simulator Sim' it becomes evident that the graph structure is only used as a lookup table to find repeated queries. This, however, is nothing but a lazily sampled (fixed-input-length) random oracle. If we name that lazily sampled fixed-input-length random oracle h, then we get

$$\Pr[\mathsf{Game}_6(\lambda) = 1] = \Pr\left[\mathcal{D}^{\mathsf{H}^{\mathsf{h}},\mathsf{h}}(1^{\lambda}) = 1\right].$$

Furthermore, note that the change again is only a syntactical change and in particular does not come with any loss. We thus have that games Game_5 and Game_6 are identical:

$$\Pr[\mathsf{Game}_6(\lambda) = 1] = \Pr[\mathsf{Game}_5(\lambda) = 1].$$

Summing it all up we have that

$$
\begin{aligned}
\mathsf{Adv}^{\mathsf{indiff}}_{\mathsf{H}^h,\mathsf{RO},\mathcal{D},\mathsf{Sim}}(\lambda) &= \left| \Pr\left[\mathcal{D}^{\mathsf{H}^h,h}(1^\lambda) = 1 \right] - \Pr\left[\mathcal{D}^{\mathsf{RO},\mathsf{Sim}^{\mathsf{RO}}}(1^\lambda) = 1 \right] \right| \\
&= \left| \Pr[\mathsf{Game}_6(\lambda) = 1] - \Pr[\mathsf{Game}_1(\lambda) = 1] \right| \\
&\leq \frac{q^2_{\mathsf{Sim}}}{2^{c \cdot \mathsf{h.cl}(\lambda)}} + \frac{(q_{\mathsf{Sim}} + (q_{\mathsf{RO}} \cdot q^{\mathsf{len}}_{\mathsf{RO}}))^2}{2^{c \cdot \mathsf{h.cl}(\lambda)}},
\end{aligned}
\tag{17.4}
$$

which concludes the proof. □

Remark 17.15. One way to interpret the bound given in Equation (17.4) is that the security is directly tied to the size of the state, which remains hidden. The more bits that are chopped off (and thus the bigger c is) the bigger the amount of state that is kept from the distinguisher and the more leeway the simulator has in its simulation.

17.5.2 Other Indifferentiable Hash Constructions

In the previous section we have shown that chopped MD is indifferentiable from a random oracle assuming that the underlying compression function h is a fixed-input-length random oracle. Chopped MD is, however, by no means the only practical hash function construction that has been shown indifferentiable from random oracles. Indeed, indifferentiability has become an accepted design criterion for new hash functions: If a function cannot be shown indifferentiable from a random oracle, most likely this will mean that there are practical attacks. Indifferentiable constructions include the popular HMAC and NMAC constructions (see Chapter 16) as well as all the finalists of the SHA-3 competition, including the winner KECCAK. On the other hand, many practical hash functions that are based on the plain Merkle–Damgård transformation are not indifferentiable. Most notable, this includes MD5, SHA-1, and many functions in the SHA-2 family. There are however also functions within the SHA-2 family that are indifferentiable: the chopped MD functions SHA-512/256 and SHA-512/224.

17.5.3 Security of Sponges Revisited

Recall the sponge construction from Section 13.3 (page 523) that forms the basis of the SHA-3 hash function. While we can try to interpret sponges as a special form of chopped MD (see Section 13.3.3) this does not allow to argue security. Instead, the security of sponges mostly hinges upon a proof of indifferentiability from a random oracle down to the assumption that the underlying permutation (or transformation) is ideal. Following is an asymptotic version of the indifferentiability statement for sponges:

> **Theorem 17.16.** *Let* $\mathsf{H}^h_{\mathsf{Sp}}$ *be a sponge function with bitrate* r *and capacity* c. *If capacity* c *is super-logarithmic in the security parameter and if permutation (resp. transformation)* $h : \{0,1\}^{\mathsf{r}+\mathsf{c}(\lambda)} \to \{0,1\}^{\mathsf{r}+\mathsf{c}(\lambda)}$ *is modeled as an ideal permutation (resp. length-preserving random oracle with a fixed input length), then* $\mathsf{H}^h_{\mathsf{Sp}}$ *is indifferentiable from a random oracle.*

The proof itself is similar to that of chopped MD, which should not be surprising given that sponges are special forms of chopped MD. Note, however, that for proving the statement for h being a permutation, the simulator needs to simulate not only the forward direction of the permutation but also the inverse direction.

For chopped MD the distinguishing advantage of an adversary was roughly $(\mathsf{l}_{max} \cdot \mathsf{q})^2 \cdot 2^{-c \cdot h.cl}$, where q denotes the number of queries and l_{max} the maximum length of queries (see Equation (17.4)). Similar, for sponges the distinguishing advantage can be shown to grow quadratically in the number of queries. While in chopped MD the size of the state that remains hidden is given by $\lfloor c \cdot h.cl \rfloor$ (where $0 < c < 1$ denotes the chop factor) the size of the hidden state in sponge constructions is given by capacity c. The distinguishing advantage of sponges is thus roughly $\frac{\mathsf{q}^2}{2^{\mathsf{c}}}$.

Bounds on the various specific properties, such as collision resistance or preimage resistance, can be derived in similar analyses assuming that the underlying permutation (or transformation) is ideal. For example, for finding a collision on outputs of length ℓ bits, an adversary either uses a brute-force approach taking roughly $2^{\ell/2}$ steps or can search for a collision on the inner state $\hat{\mathsf{s}}$ of a sponge of size c (where c is the sponge's capacity). Thus the expected workload would be $\min(2^{\ell/2}, 2^{c/2})$.

Multirate Padding Revisited

In Section 13.3.2 (page 527) we discussed padding schemes for sponges and, in particular, the multirate padding scheme $\mathsf{pad}10^*1$ which appends a 1-bit, sufficiently many 0-bits, and a final 1-bit such that the message is a multiple of block length r. In Proposition 13.27 we have seen that a single sponge function $\mathrm{SPONGE}[h, \mathsf{pad}10^*, \mathsf{r}_{max}]$ with bitrate r_{max} can be used to evaluate also any sponge function of the form $\mathrm{SPONGE}[h, \mathsf{pad}10^*1, \mathsf{r}]$, i.e., sponges for the same core function h but with 10^*1-padding and for bitrates $\mathsf{r} \leq \mathsf{r}_{max}$. This allows to extend the above indifferentiability result for sponges (Theorem 17.16) to also cover the indifferentiability of a set of sponge functions $\mathrm{SPONGE}[h, \mathsf{pad}10^*1, \mathsf{r}]$ from a set of independently sampled random oracles. We gave the corresponding statement already as Proposition 13.29 (page 534). This result is important, in particular, if we consider practical sponge constructions such as KECCAK (i.e., SHA-3). Here a single permutation KECCAK-p was formalized, on top of which various sponges with different bitrates can be constructed. Proposition 13.29 now yields that it is not easier to differentiate the list of KECCAK variants from a list of independent random oracles than it is to differentiate the weakest of the specified functions (i.e., the function with the largest bitrate and consequently the smallest capacity) from a single random oracle when using 10* padding. In case of SHA-3 this is variant SHA3-224 with a capacity of 448 bits. In other words, the differentiating advantage for an array of sponge functions is not larger than the differentiating advantage for the weakest of the functions.

17.6 Indifferentiability of Compression Functions

Indifferentiability cannot only be applied to hash function iteration schemes but to constructions in general. For hash functions, the construction we are most interested in besides the iteration scheme is the construction of the underlying functionality, a compression function in the case of Merkle–Damgård.

Regrettably, most block-cipher-based compression functions are not indifferentiable. For example, all PGV compression functions (see Section 14.1.3; page 552) including the popular Davies–Meyer construction are shown not to be indifferentiable. Exercises 17.4 and 17.5 ask to show this for the Davies–Meyer compression function as well as for the compression function that can be extracted from the sponge construction (see Section 13.3.3).

While a positive result on a compression function construction would allow for a modular analysis—an indifferentiable construction of a compression function can be used in an iteration scheme that is shown indifferentiable from a random oracle—a negative result does not mean that we cannot show the hash function indifferentiable based on the primitive underlying the compression function. As an example consider chopped MD. In Section 17.5.1 we showed that chopped MD was indifferentiable from a random oracle assuming that the compression function is a fixed-input-length random oracle. It is, however, possible to also prove the following stronger statement:

Proposition 17.17. *Let $\mathsf{H}^{\mathsf{h}^\mathsf{E}}$ be a chopped MD function with constant chop factor $0 < c < 1$ and super-logarithmic output length $\mathsf{h.cl}(\lambda)$. If compression function h is constructed via the Davies–Meyer construction from block cipher E, and E is an ideal block cipher, then $\mathsf{H}^{\mathsf{h}^\mathsf{E}}$ is indifferentiable from a random oracle.*

Remark 17.18. The proposition similarly holds, for example, for HMAC.

If we cannot show that the Davies–Meyer construction is indifferentiable from an ideal compression function why can then the above be true? The reason is that the distinguisher in the indifferentiability game when using its left oracle (which implements either the actual hash construction or a random oracle) cannot fully control how the compression function is called, as it is called indirectly via the hash construction. When considering the chopped MD construction, the distinguisher, for example, cannot control the chaining value as it is set to the initialization vector IV for the first call and then always to the result of the last call. Let us assume that the compression function construction exhibits a weakness when the chaining value y is the all-zero string. Then in order to make use of that, a distinguisher would need to find an input such that the output of the compression function is the all-zero string as this will then become the chaining value y for the next iteration. However, in the indifferentiability game for the compression function construction (rather than for the full hash function), the distinguisher could simply call its left oracle (the compression function or a fixed-input-length random oracle) on some value $(m, 0^{h \cdot cl(\lambda)})$ as, here, it has direct access to the compression function.

Interestingly, we have negative indifferentiability results for most popular compression function constructions, and hence indifferentiability results for hash functions are usually not modular but immediately consider the entire construction down to, for example, the underlying block cipher. While there are also compression function constructions that can be shown indifferentiable they all make multiple calls to the underlying block cipher and are thus less efficient than the simpler constructions such as Davies–Meyer.

17.7 Multi-stage Security Definitions

While indifferentiability certainly should be a necessary requirement for cryptographic hash functions used in practice (in particular if they are used in schemes that have only been proven secure in the random oracle model), indifferentiability alone may not be sufficient. This may be surprising as an indifferentiable hash function should be *at least as secure as* a random oracle (at least according to our Definition 17.5 and Theorem 17.9). However, as we will see next, the wording of Definition 17.5 may be misleading and *at least as secure* may not be *at least as secure* in all circumstances.

We explain by a simple example. While in the past, data was usually stored locally, the trend goes more and more towards storing data in the cloud. Now suppose you are storing your backups with a cloud vendor. A backup is usually only used as a last resort, and in most cases it is not touched for years. But how can we be sure that the cloud vendor is, indeed, storing our data? We might simply download the data from time to time and compare it with a local copy. But, of course, this would require us to keep a local copy of the entire backup. Using hash functions, there are better alternatives.

Consider the following cryptographic scheme that would allow us to test the cloud vendor from time to time. Before uploading the data m to the cloud vendor we compute for a few challenge values $c_1, \ldots, c_\ell$ chosen uniformly at random in $\{0,1\}^\lambda$ (for a large enough $\lambda \in \mathbb{N}$) hash values $z_1, \ldots, z_\ell$ as

$$z_i \leftarrow \mathsf{H}(m \| c_i).$$

Storing the challenge values together with the corresponding hash value requires only a small fraction of the entire data. But now, say, every half a year we could present one of the challenge values c_i to the cloud vendor and request them to compute the hash value $\mathsf{H}(m \| c_i)$. In case the response matches our stored value z_i we can be relatively assured that the cloud vendor still stores our entire dataset. Or so we might think.

17.7.1 The Challenge-Response Protocol

The following *challenge-response protocol* CRP formalizes the above proof of storage idea. In the CRP game the adversary is split into two stages, somewhat similar to the IND-CPA security game for encryption. However, unlike in the IND-CPA game the two adversarial stages may not share arbitrary state. Instead, the first-stage adversary $\mathcal{A}_1$ in the CRP game outputs some state that needs to be shorter than some polynomial $\mathsf{n}(\lambda)$, the idea being that the adversary tries to store significantly less than the entire message and is still able to pass our test. Formally, we demand that $\mathsf{n}(\lambda) \ll \mathsf{p}(\lambda)$ where $\mathsf{p}(\lambda)$ is the length of message m. The task of the second-stage adversary is to compute hash value $\mathsf{H}(m \| C)$ for a randomly chosen value $C \in \{0,1\}^{\mathsf{s}(\lambda)}$. As additional information adversary $\mathcal{A}_2$ is given the state as output by $\mathcal{A}_1$. In the definition we give both adversaries access to a hash oracle H which we will model as a random oracle.

$$\underline{\mathrm{CRP}_{\mathsf{p},\mathsf{n},\mathsf{s}}^{\mathsf{H},\mathcal{A}_1,\mathcal{A}_2}(\lambda)}$$

1 : $m \leftarrow\!\!{\scriptstyle\$}\ \{0,1\}^{\mathsf{p}(\lambda)}$

2 : $\mathsf{state} \leftarrow\!\!{\scriptstyle\$}\ \mathcal{A}_1^{\mathsf{H}}(m, 1^\lambda)$

3 : **if** $|\mathsf{state}| \geq \mathsf{n}(\lambda)$ **do**

4 :   **return** false

5 : $C \leftarrow\!\!{\scriptstyle\$}\ \{0,1\}^{\mathsf{s}(\lambda)}$

6 : $z \leftarrow\!\!{\scriptstyle\$}\ \mathcal{A}_2^{\mathsf{H}}(\mathsf{state}, C)$

7 : **return** $(z = \mathsf{H}(m \| C))$

Now, in case $n(\lambda) \geq p(\lambda)$ it is easy for an adversary to win as in this case adversary $\mathcal{A}_1$ can simply set $\text{state} = m$. In case $n(\lambda) \ll p(\lambda)$ this is no longer possible and, indeed, we can show that in this case no adversary (even no unbounded adversary) can win the CRP game with better than negligible probability when we model the hash function H as a random oracle.

> **Proposition 17.19.** *Let* p, n, s *be polynomials with* $s \in \omega(\log(\lambda))$ *and* $(p - n) \in \omega(\log(\lambda))$. *Let* RO *be a random oracle. Then for all (possibly unbounded) adversaries* $\mathcal{A} = (\mathcal{A}_1, \mathcal{A}_2)$ *there exists a negligible function* negl *such that*
>
> $$\Pr\left[\mathrm{CRP}_{p,n,s}^{H,\mathcal{A}_1,\mathcal{A}_2}(\lambda) = 1\right] \leq \mathsf{negl}(\lambda).$$

The proof of Proposition 17.19 should by now be straightforward, and we leave it as Exercise 17.6. The underlying idea is, as with many random oracle proofs, that if the precise query to the random oracle cannot be guessed, then the result looks utterly random. Since message m is chosen uniformly at random and since $n(\lambda) \ll p(\lambda)$—we demand that the difference $(p(\lambda) - n(\lambda))$ grows super-logarithmically in the security parameter—we have that at least some parts of message m must be omitted from the state. Furthermore, the length restriction on s ensures that challenges cannot be guessed, which allows to establish the claim.

17.7.2 The Challenge-Response Protocol Is Not Secure

Proposition 17.19 states that the CRP protocol is secure if the hash function is a random oracle. Combined with the indifferentiability composition theorem (Theorem 17.9 from page 693) we should thus expect that the protocol is also secure for any hash function that is indifferentiable. For example, it should be secure for chopped MD.

Astonishingly, this is not the case as the following attack shows. Consider the pair of adversaries $\mathcal{A}_1$ and $\mathcal{A}_2$. On input message m the first-stage adversary $\mathcal{A}_1$ computes the plain Merkle–Damgård hash value and stores it as $\text{state} \leftarrow H_{MD}^h(m)$. Although we are considering chopped MD the adversary has access to the underlying compression function h and can thus easily compute the hash value without the final chop operation. Now, on input challenge C, all that is left for adversary $\mathcal{A}_2$ is to complete the hash computation by setting

$$z \leftarrow g(h(C, \text{state})).$$

Here we assumed for simpler presentation that the challenge is exactly one message block long and that no padding takes place. If we consider m to consist of ℓ blocks as $m = m_1, \ldots, m_\ell$ then Figure 17.5 exemplifies the successful attack.

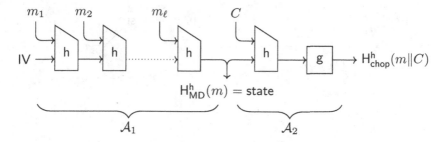

Fig. 17.5: Showcasing an attack against the CRP protocol when implemented with chopped MD. The first-stage adversary computes an intermediate hash state value; the second-stage adversary finalizes the hash computation given access to the intermediate state value and the challenge value C.

So where did we go wrong? Did we not prove that chopped MD is indifferentiable and thus that it is *just as secure* as a random oracle? The answer is that the security guarantees of indifferentiability and, in particular, the phrasing of Definition 17.5 can be misleading. Indifferentiability only guarantees that we can securely replace a random oracle by an indifferentiable hash construction in case of *single-stage games*.

17.7.3 Single-Stage vs. Multi-stage Games

Recall the underlying idea behind indifferentiability. In case an adversary is good against an indifferentiable hash function the composition theorem provides us with a means to turn the adversary into one that is also good against the random oracle. For this, indifferentiability simulator Sim takes the role of compression function h. In case of the CRP game, the resulting picture looks as follows:

$$\underline{\mathrm{CRP}^{\mathrm{RO},\mathcal{A}_1,\mathcal{A}_2}_{\mathrm{p,n,s}}(\lambda)}$$

1 : $m \leftarrow_\$ \{0,1\}^{\mathsf{p}(\lambda)}$

2 : state $\leftarrow_\$ \mathcal{A}_1^{\mathrm{RO},\mathrm{Sim}^{\mathrm{RO}}}(m, 1^\lambda)$

3 : **if** $|\text{state}| \geq \mathsf{n}(\lambda)$ **do**

4 :   **return** false

5 : $C \leftarrow_\$ \{0,1\}^{\mathsf{s}(\lambda)}$

6 : $z \leftarrow_\$ \mathcal{A}_2^{\mathrm{RO},\mathrm{Sim}^{\mathrm{RO}}}(\text{state}, C)$

7 : **return** $(z = \mathrm{RO}(m\|C))$

In line 2 the first-stage adversary has oracle access to random oracle RO and simulator Sim (which in turn has oracle access to random oracle RO).

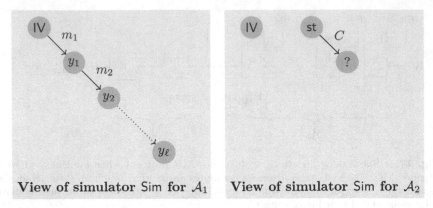

View of simulator Sim for $\mathcal{A}_1$ **View of simulator Sim for $\mathcal{A}_2$**

Fig. 17.6: The state of the two simulators in the CRP game. On the left we have the simulator for the first-stage adversary $\mathcal{A}_1$ which sees all the queries while the second-stage simulator only sees the final query.

Similarly, in line 6 the second-stage adversary has access to random oracle RO and simulator Sim. The crucial observation is that the two simulators are *independent* as they do not share state. To see this observe that, when combining adversary $\mathcal{A}$ with Sim to obtain adversary $\mathcal{B}$ against the cryptographic scheme in the proof of the composition Theorem 17.9 (page 693), this derived adversary $\mathcal{B}$ also needs to obey the restrictions which apply to $\mathcal{A}$ in the CRP game. Here this is that $\mathcal{B}$ cannot pass arbitrarily large state between the two stages.

The restriction on $\mathcal{B}$ and thus on Sim, however, is deadly for the simulating capabilities of the second-stage simulator. Recall that our simulator for chopped MD constructed an internal graph structure based on the queries it had seen so far. This graph structure is crucial for the simulator in order to decide when to use the random oracle to answer queries. Now in the attack scenario the only query the second-stage simulator sees is compressed in (C, state). In Figure 17.6 we showcase the internal structure of the two simulator instances.

Given the incomplete state of the second simulator, it becomes evident that it cannot possibly simulate the answer for the adversary correctly and thus the adversary's attack that works against chopped MD becomes void when playing against an actual random oracle. Note that this does not infringe the validity of the general composition Theorem 17.9 because there we have proven security under the assumption that the combined adversary $\mathcal{B}$ out of $\mathcal{A}$ and Sim can be arbitrary, with no restrictions on how it operates. Put differently, we have proven the composition theorem for a certain class of schemes.

This brings us to an important characterization of cryptographic security definitions (aka cryptographic games). We need to distinguish *single-stage* games from *multi-stage* games. We consider a game to be *single-stage* if all adversarial stages share arbitrary state. Note that this means that single-stage does not necessarily require that there is only a single adversarial stage. If there is, then the game is definitely single stage. However, even in case multiple adversarial stages exist, we consider the game to be single-stage in case they share arbitrary state. This, for example, is the case with the IND-CPA security game for public-key encryption schemes. Following is, once more, the security game taken from Definition 5.27 (see page 246).

$$\underline{\text{Experiment } \mathsf{Exp}_{\mathsf{PKE},\mathcal{A}}^{\mathsf{ind\text{-}cpa}}(\lambda)}$$

1 : $(\mathsf{pk}, \mathsf{sk}) \leftarrow\!\!\$\ \mathsf{PKE}.\mathsf{KGen}(1^{\lambda})$

2 : $(m_0, m_1, \mathsf{state}) \leftarrow\!\!\$\ \mathcal{A}_1(1^{\lambda}, \mathsf{pk})$

3 : if $|m_0| \neq |m_1|$ then return false

4 : $b \leftarrow\!\!\$\ \{0, 1\}$

5 : $c \leftarrow\!\!\$\ \mathsf{PKE}.\mathsf{Enc}(\mathsf{pk}, m_b)$

6 : $b' \leftarrow\!\!\$\ \mathcal{A}_2(1^{\lambda}, c, \mathsf{state})$

7 : return $(b = b')$

Here we considered two adversarial stages $\mathcal{A}_1$ and $\mathcal{A}_2$ but via the (unrestricted) state variable they can communicate an arbitrary amount of information. Translated to the indifferentiability setting this means that we can make composition work as we can leverage the state to also pass on the internal state for the simulator.

The main difference between the above IND-CPA and the CRP game are lines 3 and 4 of the CRP game which restrict the communication between the adversarial stages. The CRP game is thus a *multi-stage* game.

> **Informal Definition 17.20.** *A security game is called* single-stage *if all adversarial stages share arbitrary state. Otherwise it is called* multi-stage.

While many of the standard cryptographic definitions, for example, for encryption or signature schemes, are single-stage definitions, multi-stage security games are quite common, especially when the properties in question become more complex. Besides the above CRP game, we have also already seen a few security definitions which are, in fact, multi-stage. Examples are *correlated-input security* (Section 9.4.1 on page 391) or *deterministic public-key encryption* (Section 9.5.1 on page 396).

Salvaging Indifferentiability in Multi-stage Settings

The main application of indifferentiability is the indifferentiability composition theorem, which allows us to prove security in the random oracle model and then argue security also for indifferentiable hash functions. As we have just seen, this works only for security games that are single-stage. In case of multi-stage definitions a proof in the random oracle model together with a proof of indifferentiability is not sufficient to argue security. For the CRP game, a small change is already sufficient to allow secure instantiation with, for example, chopped MD. All we need to change is the final check (line 7) and prepend the challenge to the message, rather than append it.

$$\underline{\mathrm{CRP2}_{\mathsf{p,n,s}}^{\mathsf{RO},\mathcal{A}_1,\mathcal{A}_2}(\lambda)}$$

1 : $m \leftarrow\!\!\$\ \{0,1\}^{\mathsf{p}(\lambda)}$

2 : state $\leftarrow\!\!\$\ \mathcal{A}_1^{\mathsf{H}^h,h}(m,1^\lambda)$

3 : **if** $|\mathsf{state}| \geq \mathsf{n}(\lambda)$ **do**

4 :   **return** false

5 : $C \leftarrow\!\!\$\ \{0,1\}^{\mathsf{s}(\lambda)}$

6 : $z \leftarrow\!\!\$\ \mathcal{A}_2^{\mathsf{H}^h,h}(\mathsf{state},C)$

7 : **return** $\big(z = \mathsf{H}^h(C\|m)\big)$

Note that we here check for $\mathsf{H}^h(C\|m)$ instead of $\mathsf{H}^h(m\|C)$. Thus, instead of using the secret-suffix method (see Section 16.1.3; page 624) we are now using the secret-prefix method (see Section 16.1.2; page 623).

While the above change works, the corresponding security proof for CRP2 would be a direct proof and indifferentiability (say when proving the result for chopped MD) would not help. This then raises the question of whether we can somehow make use of indifferentiability also in multi-stage settings. The short answer is: not really. While we can try to formulate additional properties of games and hash functions or try to create stronger variants of indifferentiability, such attempts become complicated very quickly. Luckily, there is a way out via so-called *universal computational extractors*, which we will study in the next chapter.

Chapter Notes and References

The concept of indifferentiability was introduced in 2003 by Maurer, Renner, and Holenstein [18, 19]. It was first applied to popular Merkle–Damgård-style hash functions by Coron, Dodis, Malinaud, and Puniya [10], who showed that chopped MD and HMAC are indifferentiable from random oracles and who established indifferentiability as an important criterion for hash function design. The indifferentiability proof for chopped MD presented here is based on the proof given by Coron *et al.* Hash function constructions since then have usually been accompanied by an indifferentiability analysis, and for example all SHA-3 finalists have been shown to be indifferentiable [2, 3, 6, 8, 13, 14].

The indifferentiability of sponges was analyzed by Bertoni *et al.* [6]. An overview of the sponge construction including the indifferentiability proof and bounds and discussions on various standard properties is given in [7].

Indifferentiability of various compression function constructions from block ciphers was studied in [16, 23, 21]. The negative result for the Davies–Meyer construction is due to Kuwakado and Morii [16]. Positive results for the MDC-4 compression function [22] and Mennink's compression function [20] were given by Mennink [21].

Indifferentiability is not only used to verify hash function constructions. It has also been applied to the design of block ciphers, for example, by Chang *et al.* [9] and Andreeva *et al.* [1], or to better understand the relationship between the random oracle model and the ideal cipher model [11, 15, 4].

In 2011, Ristenpart, Shacham, and Shrimpton [24] pointed out that indifferentiability is not sufficient to argue security in multi-stage settings. They introduce a stronger notion of *reset indifferentiability* which allows composition in multi-stage settings but at the same time show that this notion cannot be met by practical constructions. Notions that fall in between indifferentiability and reset indifferentiability are discussed, for example, in [17, 12, 4].

Universal computational extractors (UCEs) were proposed by Bellare, Hoang, and Keelveedhi [5] in 2013 and are the topic of the upcoming chapter.

Exercices

Exercise 17.1. Give a length-extension attack for Merkle–Damgård hash functions that works for arbitrary padding functions pad and use it to show that Merkle–Damgård hash functions are not indifferentiable from random oracles.

Exercise 17.2. Discuss which parts of the proof for Theorem 17.13 (page 702) need to be adapted when considering chopped MD with padding function pad implementing, for example, Merkle–Damgård strengthening (see also Section 13.1.1 on page 482).

Exercise 17.3. Let RO be a fixed-input-length and length-preserving random oracle with $RO.il(\lambda) = RO.ol(\lambda) = \lambda$. Let furthermore H be a collision-resistant hash function which for security parameter 1^λ maps messages of arbitrary length to hash values of length λ. Is construction

$$G^{RO}(m) := RO(H(m))$$

indifferentiable from a (variable-input-length) random oracle?

Exercise 17.4. Show that the Davies–Meyer compression function (see Section 14.1 and Figure 14.7e on page 556) from an ideal block cipher E is not indifferentiable from an ideal compression function. Note that the simulator in this case would need to simulate both the encryption and decryption functionality of the block cipher.

Exercise 17.5. Show that the compression function (based on an ideal permutation) that can be extracted from the sponge construction (see Section 13.3.3 on page 531) is not indifferentiable from an ideal compression function. Note that the simulator in this case would need to simulate both the forward and inverse operations of the permutation.

Exercise 17.6. Formally prove that the CRP game is secure in the random oracle model. That is, prove Proposition 17.19 (page 718).

Chapter Bibliography

1. Elena Andreeva, Andrey Bogdanov, Yevgeniy Dodis, Bart Mennink, and John P. Steinberger. On the indifferentiability of key-alternating ciphers. In Ran Canetti and Juan A. Garay, editors, *Advances in Cryptology – CRYPTO 2013, Part I*, volume 8042 of *Lecture Notes in Computer Science*, pages 531–550, Santa Barbara, CA, USA, August 18–22, 2013. Springer, Heidelberg, Germany.
2. Elena Andreeva, Atul Luykx, and Bart Mennink. Provable security of BLAKE with non-ideal compression function. In Lars R. Knudsen and Huapeng Wu, editors, *SAC 2012: 19th Annual International Workshop on Selected Areas in Cryptography*, volume 7707 of *Lecture Notes in Computer Science*, pages 321–338, Windsor, Ontario, Canada, August 15–16, 2013. Springer, Heidelberg, Germany.
3. Elena Andreeva, Bart Mennink, and Bart Preneel. On the indifferentiability of the Grøstl hash function. In Juan A. Garay and Roberto De Prisco, editors, *SCN 10: 7th International Conference on Security in Communication Networks*, volume 6280 of *Lecture Notes in Computer Science*, pages 88–105, Amalfi, Italy, September 13–15, 2010. Springer, Heidelberg, Germany.
4. Paul Baecher, Christina Brzuska, and Arno Mittelbach. Reset indifferentiability and its consequences. In Kazue Sako and Palash Sarkar, editors, *Advances in Cryptology – ASIACRYPT 2013, Part I*, volume 8269 of *Lecture Notes in Computer Science*, pages 154–173, Bengalore, India, December 1–5, 2013. Springer, Heidelberg, Germany.
5. Mihir Bellare, Viet Tung Hoang, and Sriram Keelveedhi. Instantiating random oracles via UCEs. In Ran Canetti and Juan A. Garay, editors, *Advances in Cryptology – CRYPTO 2013, Part II*, volume 8043 of *Lecture Notes in Computer Science*, pages 398–415, Santa Barbara, CA, USA, August 18–22, 2013. Springer, Heidelberg, Germany.
6. Guido Bertoni, Joan Daemen, Michaël Peeters, and Gilles Van Assche. On the indifferentiability of the sponge construction. In Nigel P. Smart, editor, *Advances in Cryptology – EUROCRYPT 2008*, volume 4965 of *Lecture Notes in Computer Science*, pages 181–197, Istanbul, Turkey, April 13–17, 2008. Springer, Heidelberg, Germany.
7. Guido Bertoni, Joan Daemen, Michaël Peeters, and Gilles Van Assche. Cryptographic sponge functions. http://sponge.noekeon.org/, 2011.
8. Rishiraj Bhattacharyya, Avradip Mandal, and Mridul Nandi. Security analysis of the mode of JH hash function. In Seokhie Hong and Tetsu Iwata, editors, *Fast Software*

Encryption – FSE 2010, volume 6147 of *Lecture Notes in Computer Science*, pages 168–191, Seoul, Korea, February 7–10, 2010. Springer, Heidelberg, Germany.

9. Donghoon Chang, Sangjin Lee, Mridul Nandi, and Moti Yung. Indifferentiable security analysis of popular hash functions with prefix-free padding. In Xuejia Lai and Kefei Chen, editors, *Advances in Cryptology – ASIACRYPT 2006*, volume 4284 of *Lecture Notes in Computer Science*, pages 283–298, Shanghai, China, December 3–7, 2006. Springer, Heidelberg, Germany.

10. Jean-Sébastien Coron, Yevgeniy Dodis, Cécile Malinaud, and Prashant Puniya. Merkle-Damgård revisited: How to construct a hash function. In Victor Shoup, editor, *Advances in Cryptology – CRYPTO 2005*, volume 3621 of *Lecture Notes in Computer Science*, pages 430–448, Santa Barbara, CA, USA, August 14–18, 2005. Springer, Heidelberg, Germany.

11. Jean-Sébastien Coron, Jacques Patarin, and Yannick Seurin. The random oracle model and the ideal cipher model are equivalent. In David Wagner, editor, *Advances in Cryptology – CRYPTO 2008*, volume 5157 of *Lecture Notes in Computer Science*, pages 1–20, Santa Barbara, CA, USA, August 17–21, 2008. Springer, Heidelberg, Germany.

12. Gregory Demay, Peter Gaži, Martin Hirt, and Ueli Maurer. Resource-restricted indifferentiability. In Thomas Johansson and Phong Q. Nguyen, editors, *Advances in Cryptology – EUROCRYPT 2013*, volume 7881 of *Lecture Notes in Computer Science*, pages 664–683, Athens, Greece, May 26–30, 2013. Springer, Heidelberg, Germany.

13. Yevgeniy Dodis, Leonid Reyzin, Ronald L. Rivest, and Emily Shen. Indifferentiability of permutation-based compression functions and tree-based modes of operation, with applications to MD6. In Orr Dunkelman, editor, *Fast Software Encryption – FSE 2009*, volume 5665 of *Lecture Notes in Computer Science*, pages 104–121, Leuven, Belgium, February 22–25, 2009. Springer, Heidelberg, Germany.

14. Niels Ferguson, Stefan Lucks, Bruce Schneier, Doug Whiting, Mihir Bellare, Tadayoshi Kohno, Jon Callas, and Jesse Walker. The Skein hash function family. *Submission to NIST (round 3)*, 2010.

15. Thomas Holenstein, Robin Künzler, and Stefano Tessaro. The equivalence of the random oracle model and the ideal cipher model, revisited. In Lance Fortnow and Salil P. Vadhan, editors, *43rd Annual ACM Symposium on Theory of Computing*, pages 89–98, San Jose, CA, USA, June 6–8, 2011. ACM Press.

16. Hidenori Kuwakado and Masakatu Morii. Indifferentiability of single-block-length and rate-1 compression functions. *IEICE Transactions on Fundamentals of Electronics, Communications and Computer Sciences*, 90(10):2301–2308, 2007.

17. Atul Luykx, Elena Andreeva, Bart Mennink, and Bart Preneel. Impossibility results for indifferentiability with resets. Cryptology ePrint Archive, Report 2012/644, 2012. http://eprint.iacr.org/2012/644.

18. Ueli Maurer, Renato Renner, and Clemens Holenstein. Indifferentiability, impossibility results on reductions, and applications to the random oracle methodology. Cryptology ePrint Archive, Report 2003/161, 2003. http://eprint.iacr.org/2003/161.

19. Ueli M. Maurer, Renato Renner, and Clemens Holenstein. Indifferentiability, impossibility results on reductions, and applications to the random oracle methodology. In Moni Naor, editor, *TCC 2004: 1st Theory of Cryptography Conference*, volume 2951 of *Lecture Notes in Computer Science*, pages 21–39, Cambridge, MA, USA, February 19–21, 2004. Springer, Heidelberg, Germany.

20. Bart Mennink. Optimal collision security in double block length hashing with single length key. In Xiaoyun Wang and Kazue Sako, editors, *Advances in Cryptology – ASIACRYPT 2012*, volume 7658 of *Lecture Notes in Computer Science*, pages 526–543, Beijing, China, December 2–6, 2012. Springer, Heidelberg, Germany.

21. Bart Mennink. Indifferentiability of double length compression functions. In Martijn Stam, editor, *14th IMA International Conference on Cryptography and Coding*,

volume 8308 of *Lecture Notes in Computer Science*, pages 232–251, Oxford, UK, December 17–19, 2013. Springer, Heidelberg, Germany.

22. Carl H Meyer and Michael Schilling. Secure program load with manipulation detection code. In *Proc. Securicom*, volume 88, pages 111–130, 1988.

23. Yusuke Naito. Blockcipher-based double-length hash functions for pseudorandom oracles. In Ali Miri and Serge Vaudenay, editors, *SAC 2011: 18th Annual International Workshop on Selected Areas in Cryptography*, volume 7118 of *Lecture Notes in Computer Science*, pages 338–355, Toronto, Ontario, Canada, August 11–12, 2012. Springer, Heidelberg, Germany.

24. Thomas Ristenpart, Hovav Shacham, and Thomas Shrimpton. Careful with composition: Limitations of the indifferentiability framework. In Kenneth G. Paterson, editor, *Advances in Cryptology – EUROCRYPT 2011*, volume 6632 of *Lecture Notes in Computer Science*, pages 487–506, Tallinn, Estonia, May 15–19, 2011. Springer, Heidelberg, Germany.

Chapter 18
Constructing Random Oracles—UCEs

Indifferentiability provides us with a framework to analyze and sanity-check hash function constructions that are based on a simpler primitive such as a compression function or a block cipher. As all real-world hash functions today are constructed in such a way, indifferentiability has become the de facto standard security goal for modern hash functions. If a hash function is *not indifferentiable* from a random oracle this directly points to possible attack vectors. For example, the classical Merkle–Damgård construction which is susceptible to length-extension attacks is, not surprisingly, not indifferentiable. A proof of indifferentiability excludes such structural attacks and thus provides a baseline security standard for modern hash functions.

On the other hand, we should be careful with the interpretation of a positive proof of indifferentiability as we have seen towards the end of the last chapter. In essence, indifferentiability from a random oracle means that the indifferentiable hash function in question can securely replace a random oracle in a large number of security games (i.e., single-stage security games) assuming that the primitive that the hash function is built upon, for example, a compression function, is ideal. We thus need to be aware of the following limitations to indifferentiability results:

1. Indifferentiability is not applicable in every situation. If a security notion cannot be defined via a single-stage game then it is not clear whether indifferentiability is sufficient to argue security. As we have seen in Section 17.7, replacing a random oracle with an indifferentiable hash function can lead to an insecure setting. While many classical security notions are single-stage, multi-stage security definitions are becoming more and more ubiquitous as we tend to build more and more complex cryptographic primitives.

2. Indifferentiability embraces the idealized setting. While it allows us to bring analyses closer to the real-world setting by, for example, taking into account the iteration schemes of hash functions, the resulting security

A. Mittelbach, M. Fischlin, *The Theory of Hash Functions and Random Oracles*,
Information Security and Cryptography, https://doi.org/10.1007/978-3-030-63287-8_18

guarantees remain in the idealized "random oracle" setting with all its controversy (see Chapter 12).

Over the following sections we present an attempt to mitigate these limitations, which requires us to study the question of *what it means for a family of functions to behave like a random oracle*. Recall the *random oracle methodology* (Section 8.4; page 360), a recipe for constructing practical (and hopefully secure) cryptographic schemes in two steps:

1. Build a cryptographic scheme and prove its security in the random oracle model.
2. Instantiate the random oracle with a *good hash function* H *that behaves like a random oracle* in order to obtain a construction that can be implemented and used in practice.

As we have seen, a proof of security of a scheme in the random oracle model does not provide a proof of security for the instantiated scheme where the random oracle has been replaced by a *standard model hash function*. This, of course, remains the case even if we instantiate the scheme with an indifferentiable hash construction as there we would need to also instantiate the underlying primitive by, for example, an actual compression function. When working with the random oracle model the key question thus is: what is a *good* hash function, and what exactly does it mean for a hash function to *behave like a random oracle*?

While modern cryptography builds upon the provable security approach where security is based upon well-defined assumptions, when it comes to random oracles we lack such a well-defined assumption. Instead, every instantiated random oracle scheme relies upon the ad hoc assumption that the hash function that was used to instantiate the random oracle makes the resulting scheme secure.

Seen in this light, it is evident that what we are lacking is a precise definition as to what it means to *behave like a random oracle*. The problem with such a definition is that if it truly captures all the properties of a random oracle then it will not be achievable by any real-world hash function. As we have seen in Chapter 12 building random oracles is beyond our reach. On the other hand, even though we are not able to build fully fledged random oracles, there are many properties of a random oracle that we can achieve. For example, random oracles are pseudorandom and collision resistant, two classical properties that we can achieve in the standard model.

If we consider our classical security properties of hash functions to be on one end of the spectrum and *behaving like a random oracle* on the other end of the spectrum then it is plausible that there are a bundle of additional properties that are lying somewhere in-between. Some of these may, like random oracles, belong to the world of idealized cryptographic primitives while others fall into the standard model. In either case, we are better off using more specific definitions for security proofs as they concretize the security assumptions. And, ideally, we are able to remove idealized assumptions altogether eventually.

Universal Computation Extractors

This chapter is devoted to the universal computational extractor (UCE) framework, a framework that at its core provides a structure for hash function security definitions which can be parameterized to obtain weak, or very strong security definitions. As we will see, the strongest ones will live in the world of idealized assumptions and can only be achieved with the help of random oracles or other idealized primitives. Yet even in this case, we gain a lot as with more concrete definitions we better understand the requirements of cryptographic schemes that are built upon them. But this is not the only advantage. As we will see, using UCEs may significantly simplify security proofs over proofs that directly use random oracles. This may be counterintuitive as random oracles are the stronger assumption. However, UCEs provide structure and a set of helper lemmas that assist proofs in the UCE setting. And there is still a third advantage to using UCEs over random oracles even when staying in the ideal-world setting. As we have seen, indifferentiability breaks down when security definitions span multiple stages. An example of such a definition is the security definition for deterministic public-key encryption. UCEs, on the other hand, are themselves built upon a two-stage definition, and as it turns out we can show that several hash functions such as HMAC or chopped MD can securely replace a large number of UCEs in the indifferentiability setting; that is, assuming the underlying compression function or block cipher is ideal. A security proof with UCEs thus immediately provides additional guarantees for several real-world hash functions, which would need to be proved separately for each hash function when proving security directly on the basis of random oracles.

But, of course, ultimately UCEs aim higher. Besides the advantages that they offer in the idealized setting, they may have the potential to provide us with strong hash function security definitions that can still be achieved in the standard model, thus alleviating the necessity of idealized assumptions for at least some constructions altogether.

18.1 Behaving Like a Random Oracle

For the remainder of this chapter we will exclusively work in the keyed hash function setting.

Let us begin with trying to formalize what it means for a function to "behave like a random oracle." In the private-key setting we have had tremendous success with the definition of pseudorandom functions. There we consider a distinguisher $\mathcal{D}$ which is placed in one of two worlds, the *real world* where it gets oracle access to the pseudorandom function F initialized with a randomly chosen key k, or the *ideal world* where it gets oracle access to a function R chosen uniformly at random. The distinguisher has to guess in which world it

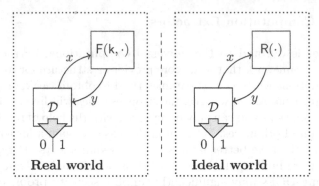

Fig. 18.1: A schematic showing the two worlds a distinguisher against a pseudorandom function can be placed in.

is in by outputting either 0 or 1. Figure 18.1 gives a schematic to exemplify the setup. If no polynomial-time distinguisher can tell the two worlds apart, we call function F a pseudorandom function (see Section 3.3.1; page 124).

In contrast to the pseudorandom setting where key k remains hidden from the adversary, the standard hash function setting considers a public key hk which is known to the adversary. Thus, if we directly translated the above to the public-key setting, we would end up with a picture such as the following:

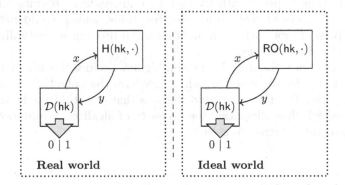

As before, the distinguisher gets oracle access to either the real function H initialized with a random key hk or a random oracle RO. However, as we are in the public-key setting the distinguisher is given the hash key hk as input. In the ideal world, we consider a keyed random oracle and similarly return the randomly chosen key to the adversary.

At first glance, one might say that if a function H would be such that no polynomial-time distinguisher $\mathcal{D}$ could distinguish the two worlds in the above experiment, then function H would truly behave like a random oracle: no distinguisher could distinguish between whether H or a real random oracle was used. Yet, as it turns out, what we have defined is so strong that no standard model function H can fulfill it.

Consider a distinguisher that implements the following strategy: It chooses a random value x, queries its oracle O to obtain the corresponding value y to then check whether the obtained value y is equal to hash value $H(hk, x)$, which it can compute locally. In pseudocode:

$$\text{Distinguisher } \mathcal{D}^O(1^\lambda, hk)$$

1 : $x \leftarrow\!\!\$ \ \{0, 1\}^{H.il(\lambda)}$

2 : $y \leftarrow O(x)$

3 : $y' \leftarrow H(hk, x)$

4 : **return** $(y = y')$

In the real world, oracle O implements hash function H with key hk hardcoded and hence the distinguisher will always output 1. On the other hand, in the ideal world the distinguisher will only output 1 in case the random oracle on input x returns $H(hk, x)$, which occurs only with probability $2^{-H.ol(\lambda)}$. Thus even if we consider a hash function with just a single output bit the advantage of our distinguisher for any hash function H is still $\frac{1}{2}$. It always correctly identifies the real world, and in half of the cases it correctly identifies the ideal world. And, the longer the output of the hash function, the higher the distinguisher's advantage.

As it turns out, even a random oracle could not fulfill this security definition. In the random oracle model, the picture would change to look as follows:

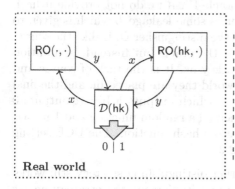 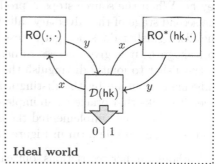

Real world   Ideal world

Note the subtle difference in the top right oracle. In the random oracle model, the distinguisher gets access to the random oracle, here named RO. Now, in the real world, the random oracle implements the function, so the top right oracle is also RO but now fixed to a specific key. In the ideal world, however, we consider a uniformly random function which is *chosen independently from the random oracle* and here indicated as RO*. It follows that our distinguisher's strategy still works. While it cannot locally recompute result y, it can use the random oracle (its left oracle) to do the recomputation as it was given hash key hk as input. In the ideal world, this recomputation will with overwhelming probability yield a different result as the oracles RO and RO* were chosen independently of each other.

Limiting the Distinguisher's Capabilities

As we have seen our first attempt at a definition was too strong as it allowed the distinguisher to easily recompute the oracle's answer in the real world. On the other hand, the setup looked promising. So if we could just restrict the distinguisher and somehow disallow the *trivial* recomputation attack, we might just make it work.

Of course, we cannot restrict the internals of the distinguisher beyond restricting it to polynomial time. Why should a real-world adversary adhere to such restrictions? However, in many interesting cryptographic schemes, an adversary would not be able to mount a recomputation attack because it is not able to fully observe a query–answer pair (x, y).

The idea underlying UCEs is to restrict the capabilities of our single distinguisher by splitting it up into two stages. As we need to prohibit the trivial recomputation attack, at the very least, we need to ensure that neither stage has access to both the oracle and the hash key, as both are needed in order to mount the attack. The idea is thus to give the first stage, called the source S, access to the oracle (referred to as HASH) which, as before, either implements the hash function for a randomly chosen key hk or a random function. As the source has access to oracle HASH we do not provide it hash key hk. When the source stops it produces some leakage L which is given to the second stage of the adversary called the distinguisher D. Unlike the source, the distinguisher does not get access to the oracle but instead, in addition to leakage L, it is given access to hash key hk. It is the task of source and distinguisher to jointly distinguish the world they are placed in, and the final judgement is made by the distinguisher which outputs a bit: It outputs 0 when it thinks that oracle HASH implemented a random function and 1 in case it thinks the oracle implemented the actual hash function. The UCE setting is given in schematic form in Figure 18.2.

Without further restrictions, our earlier distinguishing strategy still works. The only difference is that, now, we must implement the strategy across source S and distinguisher D. Consider a source that chooses a random x, calls its HASH oracle on x to obtain y, and then sets leakage L to (x, y). Given $L = (x, y)$ together with hash key hk, distinguisher D can easily complete the recomputation attack by computing $y' \leftarrow H(hk, x)$ and checking whether or not $y = y'$.

In order to get achievable security assumptions additional restrictions are thus necessary, which are usually placed on leakage L. One possibility could be to restrict the length of L to less than $|x| + |y|$ as this would intuitively mean that source S could no longer communicate a full pair (x, y). As we will

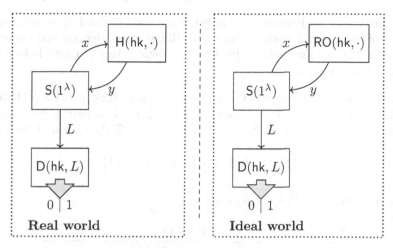

Fig. 18.2: The UCE setting. In the real world the source S interacts with the hash function initialized with a randomly chosen hash key hk (which remains hidden from the source). In the ideal world the source interacts with a randomly chosen function. The distinguisher D gets as input leakage L from the source as well as the genuine hash key in the real world, or a uniformly random key in the ideal world. It is the joint task of source and distinguisher to tell apart the setup they are placed in.

see this restriction is not a good one. Instead, common UCE restrictions are usually a bit more complex, but before we get to these let us first formally define the UCE setting.

18.2 Defining Universal Computational Extractors

Universal computational extractors (UCEs) are defined via the two-stage UCE game. First, the source S is run with oracle access to an oracle called HASH which is initialized with a hidden bit b. Depending on b, oracle HASH either implements the real hash function H (for a randomly chosen key hk) or a random oracle. When source S finishes, it outputs some leakage L. Subsequently, distinguisher D is run on the leakage L and hash key hk as input, but without access to oracle HASH. In case $b = 1$ and HASH implements the actual hash function H, hash key hk given to distinguisher D is the real hash key used by oracle HASH. In case $b = 0$, distinguisher D is given a uniformly random hash key hk. Distinguisher D outputs a single bit b' indicating whether it thinks that oracle HASH implements a random oracle or hash function H(hk, ·). In case $b = b'$ we say that adversary (S, D), that is the combination of source and distinguisher, wins the UCE game.

Note that in the following definition we do not yet require that the success probability of adversaries is negligible but only specify what the advantage of an adversary is. Precise UCE notions are then defined by considering a subset of sources and distinguishers with different restrictions and expecting that no adversary that adheres to these restrictions can win with better than negligible advantage.

Definition 18.1 (Universal Computational Extractor). *Let* $\mathsf{H} = (\mathsf{H.KGen},$ $\mathsf{H.Eval})$ *be a hash function family and let* (S, D) *be a pair of* PPT *algorithms. We define the UCE advantage of a pair* (S, D) *against* H *through*

$$\mathsf{Adv}^{\mathrm{uce}}_{\mathsf{H},\mathsf{S},\mathsf{D}}(\lambda) := 2 \cdot \Pr\left[\mathrm{UCE}^{\mathsf{S},\mathsf{D}}_{\mathsf{H}}(\lambda) = 1\right] - 1,$$

where game $\mathrm{UCE}^{\mathsf{S},\mathsf{D}}_{\mathsf{H}}(\lambda)$ *is defined as*

$\mathrm{UCE}^{\mathsf{S},\mathsf{D}}_{\mathsf{H}}(\lambda)$	$\mathrm{HASH}(x)$
$1:\quad b \leftarrow\!\!{\scriptstyle\$}\ \{0,1\}$	$1:\quad$ **if** $T[x] = \bot$ **then**
$2:\quad \mathsf{hk} \leftarrow\!\!{\scriptstyle\$}\ \mathsf{H.KGen}(1^\lambda)$	$2:\qquad$ **if** $b = 1$ **then**
$3:\quad L \leftarrow\!\!{\scriptstyle\$}\ \mathsf{S}^{\mathrm{HASH}}(1^\lambda)$	$3:\qquad\quad T[x] \leftarrow \mathsf{H.Eval}(\mathsf{hk}, x)$
$4:\quad b' \leftarrow\!\!{\scriptstyle\$}\ \mathsf{D}(1^\lambda, \mathsf{hk}, L)$	$4:\qquad$ **else** $T[x] \leftarrow\!\!{\scriptstyle\$}\ \{0,1\}^{\mathsf{H.ol}(\lambda)}$
$5:\quad$ **return** $(b = b')$	$5:\quad$ **return** $T[x]$

Restricting Sources to Obtain Concrete UCE Assumptions

As we have seen in the introduction, without any additional restrictions on source and distinguisher the UCE game models a form of "indistinguishability from a random oracle" that is not achievable. In order to get a meaningful UCE notion it is thus necessary to define such a restriction. Given this flexibility, a key issue is to come up with *good UCE notions* that strike the right balance between applicability and achievability. It has been shown useful to only restrict sources rather than distinguishers, although the framework allows for both. Here we will only consider source restrictions and always consider distinguishers to be unrestricted PPT algorithms.

In order to capture restrictions for sources we define UCE security relative to a class $\mathcal{S}$ that captures a set of sources adhering to a certain restriction. For example, we could consider the set of sources that output leakage of at most length $\mathsf{H.ol}(\lambda)$ and denote these by class $\mathcal{S}^{\mathrm{len}(\mathsf{H.ol}(\lambda))}$. This would then define a concrete UCE assumption, namely UCE security relative to source class $\mathcal{S}^{\mathrm{len}(\mathsf{H.ol}(\lambda))}$, the class of all sources which output leakage of length at most $\mathsf{H.ol}(\lambda)$.

Definition 18.2. *We say that a hash function* H *is UCE secure relative to source class* $\mathcal{S}$ *denoted by* $\mathsf{H} \in \mathrm{UCE}[\mathcal{S}]$, *if for all* PPT *sources* $\mathsf{S} \in \mathcal{S}$ *and all* PPT *distinguishers* D *the advantage* $\mathsf{Adv}^{\mathrm{uce}}_{\mathsf{H},\mathsf{S},\mathsf{D}}(\lambda)$ *is negligible.*

Is a length restriction any good? We have used a length restriction on the output of the source as an example of a possible restriction that can be used in the UCE framework. But is this restriction actually appropriate? Maybe surprisingly, it turns out that a restriction on the length of the source's output is, at least by itself, not a good restriction. While it prohibits the simple recomputation attack, it still allows for a variant of said attack scheme. Let us consider the most drastic length restriction and restrict sources to output only a single bit: source class $\mathcal{S}^{\text{len}(1)}$. We can show that no hash function H can be in $\text{UCE}[\mathcal{S}^{\text{len}(1)}]$, that is, no hash function can be UCE secure relative to sources that are restricted to output only a single bit. To formally prove this claim, we need to provide a pair (S, D) that has better than negligible advantage in the UCE game and, furthermore, source S needs to adhere to the restrictions of class $\mathcal{S}^{\text{len}(1)}$.

Consider the following attack. Source S queries oracle HASH on value 0 to receive $y \leftarrow \text{HASH}(0)$. It then sets leakage L to the first bit of y, that is, $L \leftarrow y[1]$. Clearly, we have that $S \in \mathcal{S}^{\text{len}(1)}$. Distinguisher D gets as input leakage L together with hash key hk. It computes $y' \leftarrow \text{H}(\text{hk}, 0)$ and then outputs 1 if the first bit of y' equals leakage L, that is, it outputs $y'[1] = L$.

In case oracle HASH implements hash function H, the adversary pair (S, D) will always win in the UCE game. On the other hand, in case HASH implements a random function, then the first bit of $\text{HASH}(0)$ will only match the first bit of $\text{H}(\text{hk}, 0)$ with probability $\frac{1}{2}$ and hence in this case the success probability will be 50%. It follows that the advantage is constant and thus far from negligible:

$$\text{Adv}^{\text{uce}}_{\text{H,S,D}}(\lambda) = 2 \cdot \Pr\left[\text{UCE}^{\text{S,D}}_{\text{H}}(\lambda) = 1\right] - 1$$

$$= \Pr\left[\text{UCE}^{\text{S,D}}_{\text{H}}(\lambda) = 1 \mid b = 0\right] + \Pr\left[\text{UCE}^{\text{S,D}}_{\text{H}}(\lambda) = 1 \mid b = 1\right] - 1$$

$$= \frac{1}{2} + 1 - 1 = \frac{1}{2}.$$

Predictable queries. What source and distinguisher exploited in the above attack is that the source made a predictable query. It always queries oracle HASH on $x = 0$, and hence it does not need to actually communicate x to distinguisher D. Furthermore, we have seen that a single bit from a known query is sufficient to win the UCE game with high probability.

In order to get achievable UCE definitions we thus need to put stronger restrictions upon the source, and the above analysis will guide our way. The main attack vector in the above example and the original recomputation attack is that the distinguisher knows a (partial) result to a full query x from source S to oracle HASH. What if we somehow restricted it to not know such a full x? This leads to so-called *unpredictable sources*, which, as we will see, have many interesting properties and are one of the main UCE restrictions in use today. How we can place such a restriction onto sources (and distinguishers) will be discussed in the next section.

18.2.1 Unpredictable Sources

In the following we want to formalize the notion that

> *a distinguisher should not be able to guess any* HASH-*oracle query made by the source,*

and the idea is to model this property in yet another cryptographic game, this time between a source S and a predictor P. This will even allow us to formulate different types of unpredictability depending on the strength of the predictor. For example, we can consider predictors that need to run in polynomial time, which will yield a *computational variant* of unpredictability. On the other hand, if we consider stronger predictors we will get a stronger variant of unpredictability as this will leave the source S with less "wriggle room." One option is to consider unbounded predictors. We call the resulting notion *statistical unpredictability*. Let us make these ideas formal.

Definition 18.3. *We denote by $\mathcal{S}^{\mathrm{cup}}$ the class of all* computationally unpredictable sources *and by $\mathcal{S}^{\mathrm{sup}}$ the class of all* statistically unpredictable sources. *A source* S *is computationally unpredictable (resp. statistically unpredictable) if the advantage of any* PPT *(resp. unbounded) predictor* P, *defined by*

$$\mathsf{Adv}^{\mathrm{pred}}_{\mathsf{S},\mathsf{P}}(\lambda) := \Pr\left[\mathrm{Pred}^{\mathsf{P}}_{\mathsf{S}}(\lambda) = 1\right],$$

is negligible, where game $\mathrm{Pred}^{\mathsf{P}}_{\mathsf{S}}(\lambda)$ *is defined as*

$\mathrm{Pred}^{\mathsf{P}}_{\mathsf{S}}(\lambda)$	HASH(x)
$1: \quad \mathcal{Q} \leftarrow \{\}$	$1: \quad \mathcal{Q} \leftarrow \mathcal{Q} \cup \{x\}$
$2: \quad L \leftarrow\!\!\$\ \mathsf{S}^{\mathrm{HASH}}(1^{\lambda})$	$2: \quad$ **if** $T[x] = \bot$ **then**
$3: \quad x \leftarrow\!\!\$\ \mathsf{P}(1^{\lambda}, L)$	$3: \qquad T[x] \leftarrow\!\!\$\ \{0,1\}^{\mathsf{H.ol}(\lambda)}$
$4: \quad$ **return** $(x \in \mathcal{Q})$	$4: \quad$ **return** $T[x]$

We call the resulting UCE notions UCE secure with respect to computationally (resp. statistically) unpredictable sources, denoted by UCE[$\mathcal{S}^{\mathrm{cup}}$] *and* UCE[$\mathcal{S}^{\mathrm{sup}}$].

Remark 18.4. Note that the HASH oracle given to the source in the definition of unpredictability game Pred is the random oracle variant of the HASH oracle of the UCE game. In particular, this means that there is no particular hash function involved in the definition of an unpredictable source. It is purely a property of a source S.

In order for the unpredictability restriction to be meaningful, we need to place the predictor into a situation that is similar to that of a distinguisher D in the UCE game. Hence, the predictor needs to see leakage L as output by the source S. If, on the other hand, we want to put the predictor into the same position as the distinguisher, why then the two flavors of unpredictability (computational and statistical)? After all, the distinguisher is PPT. Would it then not suffice to only consider computational unpredictability where the predictor is also restricted to be PPT?

Before we continue, let us point out that $\text{UCE}[\mathcal{S}^{\text{cup}}]$ is a strictly stronger requirement than $\text{UCE}[\mathcal{S}^{\text{sup}}]$, meaning that any hash function that is UCE secure with respect to *computationally* unpredictable sources is also UCE secure with respect to *statistically* unpredictable sources. The reason is that statistical unpredictability requires security to hold against a broader class of predictors, such that the set of valid sources is smaller.

Proposition 18.5 $(\text{UCE}[\mathcal{S}^{\text{cup}}] \subseteq \text{UCE}[\mathcal{S}^{\text{sup}}])$. *Let* H *be a family of hash functions. If* $H \in \text{UCE}[\mathcal{S}^{\text{cup}}]$, *then also* $H \in \text{UCE}[\mathcal{S}^{\text{sup}}]$.

Proof. Proving this statement is straightforward. From the definition of the source classes $\mathcal{S}^{\text{cup}}$ and $\mathcal{S}^{\text{sup}}$ it follows that $\mathcal{S}^{\text{sup}} \subseteq \mathcal{S}^{\text{cup}}$. Consequently, any legitimate and successful pair (S, D) against the $\text{UCE}[\mathcal{S}^{\text{sup}}]$ security of H would also be successful against $\text{UCE}[\mathcal{S}^{\text{cup}}]$. $\square$

Remark 18.6. Note that the proof of Proposition 18.5 is in fact much more general than the statement itself. What we argue is that whenever we have a subset of legitimate UCE adversaries such as $\mathcal{S}^{\text{sup}} \subseteq \mathcal{S}^{\text{cup}}$ then we also have a strict hierarchy as to the strength of the resulting UCE notions: $\mathcal{S}_1 \subseteq \mathcal{S}_2 \implies \text{UCE}[\mathcal{S}_2] \subseteq \text{UCE}[\mathcal{S}_1]$.

What we still have not answered is why we need the two flavors of unpredictability and whether or not they make a difference. Interestingly, there seems to be a huge difference between the two resulting UCE notions. As far as we suspect today, the computational variant $\text{UCE}[\mathcal{S}^{\text{cup}}]$ can only be achieved in idealized models while we hope that the more restrictive statistical variant $\text{UCE}[\mathcal{S}^{\text{sup}}]$ can be achieved by standard model hash functions. Note that there is a lot of uncertainty as to the power and limitations of UCEs. We will get back to this topic in later parts of this chapter.

Remark 18.7. What we have not yet commented on is the name: "universal computational extractors". According to the inventors of the UCE notion, the name was chosen in reference to computational unpredictability, which was the first and, originally, one of the two main notions of UCEs.[1] (The statistical variant of unpredictability was only added later when it was found that there is ample evidence that $\text{UCE}[\mathcal{S}^{\text{cup}}]$ may not be achievable in the standard model.)

In cryptographic literature, the term *computational extractor* has been associated with primitives that extract (pseudo)randomness from distributions

---

[1] UCE with respect to computationally unpredictable sources $\text{UCE}[\mathcal{S}^{\text{cup}}]$ was originally simply named UCE1.

that have (computational) min-entropy. UCEs, similarly extract randomness but from distributions that are restricted otherwise; restricted to be, for example, computationally unpredictable in case of UCE[$\mathcal{S}^{\mathrm{cup}}$]. The term *universal* refers to the fact that UCEs should be able to extract pseudorandomness from *all* such restricted distributions.

Unpredictability and the recomputation attack. We have seen that, in case of the simple length restriction, a variant of the recomputation attack could still be implemented. If so, could there not also be a variant that can be used with unpredictable sources? Our current assumption is that this is not the case when considering statistical unpredictability, but that it might be possible when restricting sources to be only computationally unpredictable. As we will see, random oracles are sufficient to achieve both variants of UCEs. Yet under certain, strong but plausible, assumptions on the existence of certain code obfuscation mechanisms we can show that no standard model hash function can achieve UCE[$\mathcal{S}^{\mathrm{cup}}$] security. These attacks, however, become void once we move to the more restrictive *statistical unpredictability* setting, which is why this setting should be the preferred one for security proofs. We will discuss the construction and attacks in Section 18.4 but first dwell a bit on better understanding the resulting UCE notions and how they can be used in security proofs.

18.2.2 UCEs vs. Classical Hash Function Properties

In order to get a better understanding of UCE notions let us compare them with our classical hash function security notions such as collision resistance and pseudorandomness. Since with UCEs we are targeting very strong security notions that might allow us to replace random oracles it would make sense to suspect that UCEs are strictly stronger than both collision resistance and pseudorandomness. Yet, this is not the case. Instead the UCE notions are incomparable, meaning that a collision-resistant function may or may not be UCE secure and similarly a UCE secure function may or may not be collision resistant. The same is true for pseudorandom functions.

Proposition 18.8. *Let* PRF *denote the class of all hash function families that are pseudorandom functions. Let* CR *denote the class of all hash function families that are collision resistant. Then the following properties hold:*

(1) UCE[$\mathcal{S}^{\mathrm{cup}}$] $\not\subseteq$ PRF
(2) PRF $\not\subseteq$ UCE[$\mathcal{S}^{\mathrm{sup}}$]
(3) UCE[$\mathcal{S}^{\mathrm{cup}}$] $\not\subseteq$ CR
(4) CR $\not\subseteq$ UCE[$\mathcal{S}^{\mathrm{sup}}$]

Remark 18.9. Note that we used $\mathrm{UCE}[\mathcal{S}^{\mathrm{cup}}]$ when on the left-hand side and $\mathrm{UCE}[\mathcal{S}^{\mathrm{sup}}]$ when on the right-hand side. For this note that $\mathrm{UCE}[\mathcal{S}^{\mathrm{cup}}] \subseteq \mathrm{UCE}[\mathcal{S}^{\mathrm{sup}}]$, and the resulting statement is thus stronger.

Let us discuss the intuition behind each of the statements. For (1) consider a hash function H that is $\mathrm{UCE}[\mathcal{S}^{\mathrm{cup}}]$. Now if we slightly change H such that one fixed input, say 0^λ, is always mapped to 0^λ under all keys then this should not affect its UCE security. The reason for this is that a source could not simply query 0^λ with more than negligible probability because then it would become predictable. On the other hand, our adapted H is clearly not a pseudorandom function since any pseudorandomness distinguisher would simply query its oracle on input 0^λ (note that it is not restricted as to which queries it may pose) and check whether the result is 0^λ or not. A similar strategy can be used to show (3). Instead of just adapting a single value we could adapt two values and *hardcode* a collision into the function. While UCE security is not affected due to the source not being allowed to query for that hardcoded collision, the resulting function is, of course, not collision resistant.

For (2) note that if there exists a pseudorandom function F then there also exists a pseudorandom permutation (Theorem 3.25; page 129). Now consider that F is a pseudorandom permutation. Then, by the definition of a pseudorandom permutation, given the key, it is possible to invert the permutation. Now consider the following UCE adversary (S, D). The source picks a random input x with the only constraint that it starts with a 0-bit. It queries $y \leftarrow \mathrm{HASH}(x)$ and sends y to distinguisher D. The distinguisher gets as additional input the function's key and can thus invert y to retrieve x. All that is left to do is to check the first bit of x. If it matches 0 the distinguisher outputs 1 (guessing that HASH implements the pseudorandom permutation), and otherwise it outputs 0. If oracle HASH indeed implements the pseudorandom permutation, distinguisher D will always output 1. In case HASH implements a random function, D will output 1 only with probability $\frac{1}{2}$. It follows that the pair (S, D) has constant (and thus non-negligible) advantage. Furthermore, note that source S is statistically unpredictable as its sole query x is selected (almost) uniformly at random and it only leaks $\mathrm{HASH}(x)$ and a random oracle is one-way even against unbounded adversaries (given that the number of oracle queries is polynomially bounded; Section 8.2.2). For this note that the prediction game Pred (Definiton 18.3) is always in the random oracle setting and predictor P does not get access to the oracle.

Finally, for claim (4) consider that from a collision-resistant hash function H we can create a new collision-resistant hash function H′ which has some structure in its output. For example, we can define $\mathsf{H}'(x) := 1\|\mathsf{H}(x)$. Clearly, H′ is still collision resistant but showing that H′ is not UCE secure is straightforward. For this, consider the pair (S, D) where S makes a random query x to H and outputs the first bit of the response as leakage. Distinguisher D simply echoes the bit. In case HASH implements H′ the first bit will always be 1. On the other hand, a random function outputs 1 as the first bit only with probability $\frac{1}{2}$.

Formal proofs (especially for claims (1) and (3)) are a bit technical but a good exercise in order to get more comfortable working with UCEs. We leave them as Exercise 18.1.

18.3 Applying UCEs

Now that we have a basic understanding of UCEs, we present a number of examples to showcase how UCEs facilitate security proofs.

Challenge response. We start with the proof of the storage challenge-response protocol (see Section 17.7.1 on page 717), the counterexample to the applicability of indifferentiability in two-stage games. Since UCEs are themselves two-stage we have no problem showing the security of the protocol for a statistically unpredictable UCE-secure function.

Universal hardcore functions. Next, we will take a look at universal hardcore functions. We have come across hardcore functions already in the context of public-key encryption schemes (see Section 5.3.2 on page 250) where we combined hardcore functions with trapdoor functions to build a PKE scheme (Construction 5.38; page 255). While we have several candidates for hardcore functions for specific trapdoor functions we have no candidate construction of a universal hardcore function that is hardcore for any one-way function *and* that has long output. Recall that the Goldreich–Levin construction (Section 5.3.3; page 252) allows us to construct from a one-way function f a slightly adapted function g together with a hardcore function HC for g. There are two things to note. First is that hardcore function HC is not necessarily hardcore for the original function f. The second, and more crucial observation is that the Goldreich–Levin construction yields a *hardcore bit*, that is, a hardcore function that outputs a single bit. While this construction can be adapted to output slightly longer values, the output size is, nonetheless, significantly restricted: It can only yield logarithmically many output bits in the security parameter. As the output length of the hardcore function can have a direct influence on the efficiency of constructions, being thus restricted can cause severe limitations for practical schemes. As an example where this is the case, have a look at our Construction 5.38 (page 255) of a PKE scheme.

The hardcore functions we are going to construct here based on UCEs have no such restriction.[2] Indeed, they not only provide standard model constructions of universal hardcore functions (functions that are hardcore for all keyed one-way functions) but are also very efficient (given that the

---

[2] While we here usually consider functions with a fixed output length, it can be shown that given a UCE-secure function with a fixed output length we can construct another UCE-secure function with arbitrarily long (polynomially bounded) output.

employed UCE function is efficient) when used in constructions such as the above-mentioned construction of a public-key encryption scheme.

Deterministic public-key encryption. In Section 9.5.1 (page 396) we introduced the notion of deterministic public-key encryption and claimed (Theorem 9.20) that in the random oracle model we can construct deterministic public-key encryption schemes, for example, via the encrypt-with-hash construction. We have so far not yet proven this claim, and indeed proving it directly in the random oracle model is far from trivial. Luckily, it becomes simpler when using UCEs, which also highlights that UCEs are not only a means towards getting closer to the standard model but also a tool to make security proofs easier in the random oracle setting.

18.3.1 Proofs of Storage from UCEs

Recall the challenge-response protocol CRP from Section 17.7.1 (page 717).

$$\underline{\mathrm{CRP}^{\mathsf{H},\mathcal{A}_1,\mathcal{A}_2}_{\mathsf{p},\mathsf{n},\mathsf{s}}(\lambda)}$$

1 : $m \leftarrow_\$ \{0,1\}^{\mathsf{p}(\lambda)}$

2 : $\mathsf{state} \leftarrow_\$ \mathcal{A}_1(m,1^\lambda)$

3 : **if** $|\mathsf{state}| \geq \mathsf{n}(\lambda)$ **do**

4 :   **return** false

5 : $C \leftarrow_\$ \{0,1\}^{\mathsf{s}(\lambda)}$

6 : $z \leftarrow_\$ \mathcal{A}_2(\mathsf{state}, C)$

7 : **return** $(z = \mathsf{H}(m\|C))$

We consider a scenario where a storage provider $\mathcal{A} = (\mathcal{A}_1, \mathcal{A}_2)$ is given access to a large message m and we want to periodically check that it still can reproduce the entire message. Instead of asking it to send the entire message, we instead send a random challenge value C to then check that the return value matches $\mathsf{H}(m\|C)$ for some hash function H. We have seen that in the random oracle model the adversary (aka the malicious storage provider) cannot cheat (i.e., win without actually storing message m) but that in the indifferentiability setting it might.

In the following we show that UCEs are sufficient to argue security of the CRP protocol. As UCEs consider *keyed* hash functions, the protocol, however, needs to be slightly adapted to match the UCE setting. Instead of considering a challenge value C that is appended to the message we simply use hash key hk as challenge. We formalize the adapted protocol as CRP3 below. Formally, we want to show the following claim:

Proposition 18.10. *Let* p, n *be polynomials with* $(\mathsf{p}-\mathsf{n}) \in \omega(\log(\lambda))$. *If* $\mathsf{H} \in \mathrm{UCE}[\mathcal{S}^{\mathrm{sup}}]$, *then there exists no* PPT *adversary* $\mathcal{A} = (\mathcal{A}_1, \mathcal{A}_2)$ *that can win the* $\mathrm{CRP3}_{\mathsf{p},\mathsf{n},\mathsf{s}}^{\mathsf{H},\mathcal{A}_1,\mathcal{A}_2}$ *game with better than negligible probability. Here, game* $\mathrm{CRP3}_{\mathsf{p},\mathsf{n},\mathsf{s}}^{\mathsf{H},\mathcal{A}_1,\mathcal{A}_2}$ *is defined as*

$$\underline{\mathrm{CRP3}_{\mathsf{p},\mathsf{n}}^{\mathsf{H},\mathcal{A}_1,\mathcal{A}_2}(\lambda)}$$

1: $\quad m \leftarrow\!\!{\scriptstyle\$}\ \{0,1\}^{\mathsf{p}(\lambda)}$

2: $\quad \mathsf{state} \leftarrow\!\!{\scriptstyle\$}\ \mathcal{A}_1(m, 1^\lambda)$

3: $\quad \mathbf{if}\ |\mathsf{state}| \geq \mathsf{n}(\lambda)\ \mathbf{do}$

4: $\quad\quad \mathbf{return}\ \mathsf{false}$

5: $\quad \mathsf{hk} \leftarrow\!\!{\scriptstyle\$}\ \mathsf{H.KGen}(1^\lambda)$

6: $\quad z \leftarrow\!\!{\scriptstyle\$}\ \mathcal{A}_2(\mathsf{state}, \mathsf{hk})$

7: $\quad \mathbf{return}\ (z = \mathsf{H}(\mathsf{hk}, m))$

How do we prove security via UCEs? The answer is the same as with any other underlying security property: we provide a reduction. Given an adversary against the proof of storage protocol we turn it into an adversary against the UCE security of hash function H.

Proof of Proposition 18.10. From an adversary $\mathcal{A} = (\mathcal{A}_1, \mathcal{A}_2)$ against the proof of storage protocol we will show how to construct an adversary (S, D) against the $\mathrm{UCE}[\mathcal{S}^{\mathrm{sup}}]$ security of hash function H such that

$$\mathsf{Adv}_{\mathsf{f},\mathsf{H},\mathcal{A}}^{\mathrm{crp}}(\lambda) \leq \mathsf{Adv}_{\mathsf{H},\mathsf{S},\mathsf{D}}^{\mathrm{uce}}(\lambda) + \mathsf{negl}(\lambda)$$

for some negligible function negl. As by assumption $\mathsf{Adv}_{\mathsf{H},\mathsf{S},\mathsf{D}}^{\mathrm{uce}}(\lambda)$ is negligible this proves the claim.

For the construction of the UCE adversary (S, D), consider a definition of source and distinguisher as follows:[3]

$\underline{\mathsf{S}^{\mathrm{HASH}}(1^\lambda)}$	$\underline{\mathsf{D}(\mathsf{hk}, L)}$
1: $\quad m \leftarrow\!\!{\scriptstyle\$}\ \{0,1\}^{\mathsf{p}(\lambda)}$	1: $\quad (\mathsf{state}, z) \leftarrow L$
2: $\quad \mathsf{state} \leftarrow\!\!{\scriptstyle\$}\ \mathcal{A}_1(m, 1^\lambda)$	2: $\quad z' \leftarrow\!\!{\scriptstyle\$}\ \mathcal{A}_2(\mathsf{state}, \mathsf{hk})$
3: $\quad z \leftarrow \mathrm{HASH}(m)$	3: $\quad \mathbf{return}\ (z = z')$
4: $\quad L \leftarrow (\mathsf{state}, z)$	
5: $\quad \mathbf{return}\ L$	

We now need to show two things: (1) source and distinguisher as defined above win in the UCE game with non-negligible advantage if $(\mathcal{A}_1, \mathcal{A}_2)$ wins

---

[3] We here assume that adversary $\mathcal{A}_1$ does not violate the length restriction on state. The length check could, however, be easily integrated into source S.

the CRP game with non-negligible advantage, and (2) source S is statistically unpredictable.

Let us begin with the latter and easier claim. Source S makes only a single query to oracle HASH for message m which is chosen uniformly at random. While leakage L contains value HASH(m) as well as state we can argue that it still hides sufficiently many bits of m. For this note that the prediction game is relative to a random oracle, that is, in game Pred oracle HASH always implements a random function. As such HASH(m) is simply a uniformly random value that by itself does not convey any information about message m. Also note that the predictor in prediction game Pred does not have oracle access to HASH and thus the only information it has about m is whatever is given as part of state (also see Proposition 8.6 on page 348 and the following discussion about the one-wayness of random oracles). As, by assumption, we have that the length difference between message m and state is super-logarithmic in the security parameter it follows that a significant portion of m cannot be guessed with better than negligible probability. We conclude that the single HASH query remains hidden, which concludes the claim.

For claim (1) note that together source S and distinguisher D perfectly simulate the steps of the CRP game for adversaries $\mathcal{A}_1$ and $\mathcal{A}_2$. In case oracle HASH implements a random oracle (hidden bit $b = 0$) then z is a uniformly random value of length $\mathsf{H.ol}(\lambda)$ which can be guessed by adversary $\mathcal{A}_2$ with probability $2^{-\mathsf{H.ol}(\lambda)}$. Consequently, adversary (S, D) wins the UCE game with hidden bit $b = 0$ with probability

$$\Pr\left[\mathrm{UCE}_{\mathsf{H}}^{\mathsf{S},\mathsf{D}}(\lambda) = 1 \mid b = 0\right] = 1 - 2^{-\mathsf{H.ol}(\lambda)}.$$

On the other hand, if $b = 1$ and HASH implements hash function H we have that, by design, the UCE game and game CRP3 are identical and hence

$$\Pr\left[\mathrm{UCE}_{\mathsf{H}}^{\mathsf{S},\mathsf{D}}(\lambda) = 1 \mid b = 1\right] = \Pr\left[\mathrm{CRP}_{\mathsf{p},\mathsf{n},\mathsf{s}}^{\mathsf{H},\mathcal{A}_1,\mathcal{A}_2}(\lambda) = 1\right].$$

Summing up the two equations[4] and reordering yields the desired result

$$\Pr\left[\mathrm{CRP}_{\mathsf{p},\mathsf{n},\mathsf{s}}^{\mathsf{H},\mathcal{A}_1,\mathcal{A}_2}(\lambda) = 1\right] \leq \mathsf{Adv}_{\mathsf{H},\mathsf{S},\mathsf{D}}^{\mathsf{uce}}(\lambda) + 2^{-\mathsf{H.ol}(\lambda)}. \qquad \square$$

---

[4] Note that we can rewrite the UCE advantage as

$$\mathsf{Adv}_{\mathsf{H},\mathsf{S},\mathsf{D}}^{\mathsf{uce}}(\lambda) := \Pr\left[\mathrm{UCE}_{\mathsf{H}}^{\mathsf{S},\mathsf{D}}(\lambda) = 1 \mid b = 0\right] + \Pr\left[\mathrm{UCE}_{\mathsf{H}}^{\mathsf{S},\mathsf{D}}(\lambda) = 1 \mid b = 1\right] - 1.$$

18.3.2 Universal Hardcore Functions from UCEs

Let us recall the notion of a hardcore function. A function H is hardcore for one-way function F if no PPT adversary $\mathcal{A}$ can win in the following experiment with better than negligible probability beyond $\frac{1}{2}$ (see also Definition 5.33 on page 251):

$$\underline{\text{Experiment } \mathsf{Exp}_{\mathsf{F},\mathsf{H},\mathcal{A}}^{\text{hardcore}}(\lambda)}$$

1 : $b \leftarrow\!\!\$\ \{0,1\}$

2 : $\mathsf{fk} \leftarrow\!\!\$\ \mathsf{F.KGen}(1^\lambda)$

3 : $x \leftarrow\!\!\$\ \{0,1\}^\lambda$

4 : $y \leftarrow \mathsf{F.Eval}(\mathsf{fk}, x)$

5 : $\mathsf{hk} \leftarrow\!\!\$\ \mathsf{H.KGen}(1^\lambda)$

6 : $z_0 \leftarrow \mathsf{H.Eval}(\mathsf{hk}, x)$

7 : $z_1 \leftarrow\!\!\$\ \{0,1\}^{\mathsf{H.ol}(\lambda)}$

8 : $b' \leftarrow\!\!\$\ \mathcal{A}(1^\lambda, \mathsf{fk}, \mathsf{hk}, y, z_b)$

9 : **return** $b = b'$

Adversary $\mathcal{A}$ is given the keys of both functions H and F as well as an image $y = F(\mathsf{fk}, x)$ for a randomly chosen preimage x under one-way function F. Depending on a hidden bit b it is additionally given either a uniformly random value (in case $b = 1$) or $H(\mathsf{hk}, x)$ and needs to distinguish the two cases.

In the previous example we showed that UCEs with respect to *statistically* unpredictable sources are sufficient for the proof of the storage challenge-response game. For our proof of hardcore functions no such proof is known and we instead need to use the stronger assumption of UCE security with respect to *computationally* unpredictable sources.

> **Proposition 18.11.** *If* $H \in \mathsf{UCE}[\mathcal{S}^{\mathrm{cup}}]$ *then* H *is a universal hardcore function.*

Proof. The proof strategy will be similar to before. Let F be a one-way function. We will show that, for any adversary $\mathcal{A}$ against the hardcore property of H for F, there exists a PPT source S and PPT distinguisher D such that

$$\mathsf{Adv}_{\mathsf{F},\mathsf{H},\mathcal{A}}^{\mathrm{hc}}(\lambda) \leq \mathsf{Adv}_{\mathsf{H},\mathsf{S},\mathsf{D}}^{\mathrm{uce}}(\lambda). \tag{18.1}$$

As before the proof follows by assuming that $\mathsf{Adv}_{\mathsf{H},\mathsf{S},\mathsf{D}}^{\mathrm{uce}}(\lambda)$ is negligible. This time, however, instead of imitating the proof of storage game we construct the pair (S, D) to imitate the hardcore function game. Source S runs the setup of the hardcore game, that is, it samples the function's key fk, chooses random value x, and computes $y \leftarrow \mathsf{f.Eval}(\mathsf{fk}, x)$. It then queries its HASH oracle on x to obtain z. Note that if HASH is a random oracle, then z is a uniformly random value (i.e., z_1 in the hardcore game), while if HASH is the actual hash function then it represents z_0 in the hardcore game. Key fk as well as values y and z are passed on as leakage to distinguisher D, which completes the hardcore game simulation. Following is the pseudocode for both source S and distinguisher D.

$S^{\text{HASH}}(1^\lambda)$	$D(1^\lambda, \text{hk}, L)$
1: fk $\leftarrow$$ f.KGen(1^λ)	1: $(\text{fk}, y, z) \leftarrow L$
2: $x \leftarrow$$ $\{0,1\}^{\text{f.il}(\lambda)}$	2: $b' \leftarrow$$ \mathcal{A}(1^\lambda, \text{fk}, \text{hk}, y, z)$
3: $y \leftarrow$ f.Eval(fk, x)	3: return b'
4: $z \leftarrow$$ HASH(x)	
5: $L \leftarrow (\text{fk}, y, z)$	
6: return L	

Let b denote the hidden bit in the UCE game. If $b = 1$ then oracle HASH implements function H with a uniformly random key. Otherwise, in case $b = 0$ then oracle HASH implements a random oracle and value z is set to a uniformly random string. It follows that the pair (S, D) within the UCE game perfectly simulate the hardcore game for adversary $\mathcal{A}$, which establishes the equivalence in Equation (18.1). What remains to show is that source S is also computationally unpredictable.

Let P be a predictor. It is predictor P's task to output a query which the source has made when running relative to a random oracle. But the source only makes a single query, namely about the one-way function's preimage x. Then we construct an inverter $\mathcal{B}$ against the one-way function F as follows. On input an image y and a one-way function key fk, inverter $\mathcal{B}$ samples a uniformly random string $z \leftarrow$$ \{0,1\}^{\text{H.ol}(\lambda)}$. It then runs predictor P on "leakage" (fk, y, z) to obtain a query x, which it returns.

We observe that $\mathcal{B}$ perfectly simulates the prediction game Pred_S^P for predictor P and thus $\mathcal{B}$ is successful with the same probability as predictor P. For this note that game Pred is always in the random oracle setting and the predictor expects z to be a random string. We, thus, have that

$$\text{Adv}_{S,\text{Pred}}^{\text{pred}}(\lambda) = \text{Adv}_{F,\mathcal{B}}^{\text{owf}}(\lambda).$$

Note that, by design, we have that inverter $\mathcal{B}$ is PPT: As we consider *computational* unpredictability we have that predictor P is efficient. Furthermore, the runtime of $\mathcal{B}$ is mostly governed by its single call to P. As by assumption F is one-way, the right-hand side of the equation is negligible, thus showing that $S \in \mathcal{S}^{\text{cup}}$, i.e., source S is computationally unpredictable. This concludes the proof. $\square$

Remark 18.12. The above proof would not work in the statistical unpredictability setting. To see this, note that if predictor P is unbounded, then inverter

$\mathcal{B}$, which internally runs predictor P, also needs to be unbounded. But then we could not argue that the advantage of $\mathcal{B}$ against one-way function F must be negligible since an unbounded algorithm can clearly invert a function F.

18.3.3 Deterministic Public-Key Encryption from UCEs

We introduced deterministic public-key encryption in Section 9.5.1 (page 396). A deterministic public-key encryption scheme is similar to a regular public-key encryption scheme with the exception that the encryption algorithm is not randomized but deterministic. If we encrypt the same message twice with the same key, we will in both cases get the exact same ciphertext. Deterministic public-key encryption schemes have various interesting properties, but for a long time no standard model construction was known that achieved the strongest form of security. As we will see, UCEs that are secure with respect to computationally unpredictable sources are sufficiently strong to construct deterministic public-key encryption schemes. Furthermore, it can be shown that UCEs with respect to *statistically* unpredictable sources are sufficient when in addition a primitive known as a lossy trapdoor function[5] is used.

Here, we will show only the first statement, namely that UCE-secure functions with respect to *computationally* unpredictable sources are sufficient to instantiate the random oracle in the encrypt-with-hash construction. This not only shows that we can obtain deterministic public-key encryption from UCEs, but together with a construction of UCEs from random oracles which we will present in the upcoming section, this also proves Theorem 9.20 (page 400), which states that random oracles are sufficient for obtaining deterministic public-key encryption. Interestingly, attempting a direct proof in the random oracle model is far from trivial and requires quite a bit of careful reasoning. Instead, when using UCEs the proof is rather straightforward, as we will see shortly.

Let us recall the encrypt-with-hash construction and the IND security notion of deterministic public-key encryption schemes. The encrypt-with-hash (short EwH) construction builds a deterministic public-key encryption scheme from a regular (randomized) public-key encryption scheme PKE and a hash function H. The idea is that the randomness needed for the encryption scheme is generated deterministically by hashing both the message to be encrypted and the public encryption key. In Figure 18.3 we give the pseudocode for EwH[PKE, H], encrypt-with-hash from public-key encryption scheme PKE and hash function H. To obtain the standard random oracle formulation simply

---

[5] Lossy trapdoor functions are trapdoor functions (see Section 5.3.1) but with a twist. Key generation allows to generate evaluation keys k and k* that are indistinguishable when not given the corresponding inversion key but such that k* maps only to a small part of the image of the function such that values cannot be inverted even by unbounded algorithms.

EwH[PKE, H].KGen(1^λ)	EwH[PKE, H].Enc((pk, hk), m)	EwH[PKE, H].Dec(sk, c)
1 : hk $\leftarrow\!\!\$$ H.KGen(1^λ)	$r \leftarrow$ H(hk, pk$\|m$)	$m \leftarrow$ PKE.Dec(sk, c)
2 : (pk, sk) $\leftarrow\!\!\$$ PKE.KGen(1^λ)	$c \leftarrow$ PKE.Enc(pk, $m; r$)	**return** m
3 : **return** ((pk, hk), sk)	**return** c	

Fig. 18.3: The encrypt-with-hash construction of a deterministic public-key encryption scheme from a randomized public-key encryption scheme PKE and a hash function H.

replace H by a random oracle and remove the generation of the hash function key.

The strongest form of security for deterministic public-key encryption schemes is IND security (see Definition 9.17 on page 398), which considers a two-stage adversary $\mathcal{A} = (\mathcal{A}_1, \mathcal{A}_2)$. First $\mathcal{A}_1$ outputs two unpredictable message vectors of the same length.[6] Then, depending on a hidden bit b one of the vectors is encrypted and given to the second-stage adversary $\mathcal{A}_2$. It is adversary $\mathcal{A}_2$'s task to guess which of the two vectors was encrypted. Following is the pseudocode of the security experiment for a deterministic public-key encryption scheme DPKE:

$$\underline{\text{IND}^{\mathcal{A}}_{\text{DPKE}}(\lambda)}$$

1 : $b \leftarrow\!\!\$ \{0, 1\}$

2 : $(\mathbf{m}_0, \mathbf{m}_1) \leftarrow\!\!\$ \mathcal{A}_1(1^\lambda)$

3 : $(\mathsf{pk}, \mathsf{sk}) \leftarrow\!\!\$ \text{DPKE.KGen}(1^\lambda)$

4 : **for** $i = 1..|\mathbf{m}_0|$ **do**

5 : $\quad \mathbf{c}[i] \leftarrow \text{DPKE.Enc}(\mathsf{pk}, \mathbf{m}_b[i])$

6 : $b' \leftarrow\!\!\$ \mathcal{A}_2(\mathsf{pk}, \mathbf{c})$

7 : **return** $(b = b')$

Our goal is to show that any UCE[$\mathcal{S}^{\text{cup}}$]-secure function is sufficiently strong to build an IND-secure deterministic public-key encryption scheme from a randomized one. Formally we will show the following statement:

> **Proposition 18.13.** *If* H $\in$ UCE[$\mathcal{S}^{\text{cup}}$] *and* PKE *is IND-CPA secure then* EwH[PKE, H] *is an IND-secure deterministic public-key encryption scheme.*

Proof. Our proof strategy will again be reduction based. We will give a reduction from an adversary against the DPKE scheme to an adversary against either the UCE security of H or the IND-CPA security of PKE.

---

[6] There are some additional requirements (see Definition 9.17; page 398) which we can, however, ignore for the upcoming discussion.

Let $(\mathcal{A}_1, \mathcal{A}_2)$ be an adversary against the IND security of $\mathsf{EwH[PKE, H]}$. We construct an adversary (S, D) against the UCE security of H as well as an adversary $\mathcal{B}$ against the IND-CPA security of PKE. For both adversaries the idea is to simulate the DPKE environment for adversary $(\mathcal{A}_1, \mathcal{A}_2)$ such that we are successful if $(\mathcal{A}_1, \mathcal{A}_2)$ is. Let us start with the adversary against UCE. We define source S and distinguisher D as

$\mathsf{S}^{\text{HASH}}(1^\lambda)$	$\mathsf{D}(\mathsf{hk}, L)$
$1:\quad d \leftarrow\!\!\$\ \{0,1\}$	$1:\quad (\mathsf{pk}, d, \mathbf{c}) \leftarrow L$
$2:\quad (\mathbf{m}_0, \mathbf{m}_1) \leftarrow\!\!\$\ \mathcal{A}_1(1^\lambda)$	$2:\quad d' \leftarrow\!\!\$\ \mathcal{A}_2((\mathsf{pk}, \mathsf{hk}), \mathbf{c})$
$3:\quad (\mathsf{pk}, \mathsf{sk}) \leftarrow\!\!\$\ \mathsf{PKE.KGen}(1^\lambda)$	$3:\quad \mathbf{return}\ (d = d')$
$4:\quad \mathbf{for}\ i = 1..|\mathbf{m}_0|\ \mathbf{do}$	
$5:\qquad r \leftarrow \text{HASH}(\mathsf{pk}\|\mathbf{m}[i])$	
$6:\qquad \mathbf{c}[i] \leftarrow \mathsf{PKE.Enc}(\mathsf{pk}, \mathbf{m}_d[i]; r)$	
$7:\quad L \leftarrow (\mathsf{pk}, d, \mathbf{c})$	
$8:\quad \mathbf{return}\ L$	

The source simulates the environment for $\mathcal{A}_1$. It samples a random bit d, runs $\mathcal{A}_1$ to obtain the two message vectors, and then according to the sampled bit d encrypts one of the two message vectors using the encrypt-with-hash construction. For this it generates a fresh key pair $(\mathsf{pk}, \mathsf{sk}) \leftarrow\!\!\$\ \mathsf{PKE.KGen}(1^\lambda)$ for encryption scheme PKE. For the hash function, however, it does not sample its own key but instead uses its access to oracle HASH. Finally it sets leakage L to contain encryption key pk, sampled bit d, as well as ciphertext vector $\mathbf{c}$.

Distinguisher D simulates the remainder of the IND game for adversary $\mathcal{A}_2$ to obtain a guess d'. If $d = d'$ it returns 1 (guessing that oracle HASH implements the actual hash function H), and if $d \neq d'$ it returns 0.

Assume that the hidden bit in the UCE game is $b = 1$, meaning that oracle HASH implements hash function H. In this case, source S and distinguisher D perfectly simulate the IND game for adversary $\mathcal{A} = (\mathcal{A}_1, \mathcal{A}_2)$ and thus we have that

$$\Pr\left[\mathsf{UCE}_{\mathsf{H}}^{\mathsf{S},\mathsf{D}}(\lambda) = 1 \,\middle|\, b = 1\right] = \Pr\left[\mathsf{IND}_{\mathsf{EwH[PKE,H]}}^{\mathcal{A}}(\lambda) = 1\right]$$

$$= \frac{1}{2} + \frac{1}{2} \cdot \mathsf{Adv}_{\mathsf{EwH[PKE,H]},\mathcal{A}}^{\mathrm{ind}}(\lambda). \qquad (18.2)$$

For the last equality recall that the advantage definition for DPKE is

$$\mathsf{Adv}_{\mathsf{EwH[PKE,H]},\mathcal{A}}^{\mathrm{ind}}(\lambda) := 2 \cdot \Pr\left[\mathsf{IND}_{\mathsf{EwH[PKE,H]}}^{\mathcal{A}}(\lambda) = 1\right] - 1.$$

On the other hand, if the hidden bit in the UCE game is $b = 0$ and oracle HASH implements a random oracle then the encryptions generated by source S are, in fact, genuine randomized encryptions. In other words, the simulation that source and distinguisher provide for adversary $(\mathcal{A}_1, \mathcal{A}_2)$ is a simulation of the IND-CPA security game for randomized public-key encryption schemes (see also Definition 5.27 on page 220). To make this more explicit, let us introduce an adversary $\mathcal{B}$ against the IND-CPA security of PKE that captures the simulation performed by (S, D).

$$\underline{\mathcal{B}^{\mathrm{LoR}}(1^\lambda, \mathsf{pk})}$$

1 : $(\mathbf{m}_0, \mathbf{m}_1) \leftarrow\!\!\$\ \mathcal{A}_1(1^\lambda)$

2 : **for** $i = 1 .. |\mathbf{m}_0|$ **do**

3 : $\mathbf{c}[i] \leftarrow\!\!\$\ \mathrm{LoR}(\mathsf{pk}, \mathbf{m}_0[i], \mathbf{m}_1[i])$

4 : $\mathsf{hk} \leftarrow\!\!\$\ \mathsf{H.KGen}(\lambda)$

5 : $b' \leftarrow\!\!\$\ \mathcal{A}_2((\mathsf{pk}, \mathsf{hk}), \mathbf{c})$

6 : **return** b'

Let us rephrase what we just did. When the hidden bit in the UCE game is $b = 0$ and thus oracle HASH implements a random oracle then the perspective of adversary $\mathcal{A} = (\mathcal{A}_1, \mathcal{A}_2)$ is exactly the same as that of adversary $\mathcal{B}$ in a reduction to the IND-CPA game. In the latter case the public key is generated by the IND-CPA challenger and given to $\mathcal{B}$, which uses it in its simulation. In the former case source S generates the key "taking on the role" of the IND-CPA challenger. What this means is that we can upper bound the success probability of (S, D) in the UCE game by the success probability of $\mathcal{B}$ in the IND-CPA game:

$$\Pr\left[\mathrm{UCE}_\mathsf{H}^{\mathsf{S},\mathsf{D}}(\lambda) = 1 \,\middle|\, b = 0\right] = \Pr\left[\mathrm{IND\text{-}CPA}_{\mathsf{PKE}}^{\mathcal{B}}(\lambda) = 1\right]$$
$$= \frac{1}{2} + \frac{1}{2} \cdot \mathsf{Adv}_{\mathsf{PKE},\mathcal{A}}^{\mathrm{ind\text{-}cpa}}(\lambda). \qquad (18.3)$$

Summing up Equations (18.2) and (18.3) and rearranging the terms yields our desired bound for the advantage of an IND adversary:

$$\mathsf{Adv}_{\mathsf{EwH[PKE,H]},\mathcal{A}}^{\mathrm{ind}}(\lambda) \leq 2 \cdot \mathsf{Adv}_{\mathsf{H},\mathsf{S},\mathsf{D}}^{\mathrm{uce}}(\lambda) + \mathsf{Adv}_{\mathsf{PKE},\mathcal{A}}^{\mathrm{ind\text{-}cpa}}(\lambda).$$

Unpredictability of source S. We have shown that we can construct a successful adversary (S, D) against the UCE security of H from a successful adversary $(\mathcal{A}_1, \mathcal{A}_2)$ against the DPKE scheme $\mathsf{EwH[PKE, H]}$. In order for this adversary to be meaningful, we need to argue that it is a valid $\mathrm{UCE}[\mathcal{S}^{\mathrm{cup}}]$ adversary, that is, we need to show that source S is *computationally unpredictable*.

Recall the workings of source S. It first runs adversary $\mathcal{A}_1$ to receive two message vectors and then encrypts one of them using as randomness for the encryption, random coins computed as $r \leftarrow \mathrm{HASH}(\mathsf{pk} \| m)$. The leakage L of source S then consists of a public encryption key pk, a bit d indicating which plaintext message vector was encrypted, as well as a vector of ciphertexts $\mathbf{c}$.

By assumption we have that adversary $\mathcal{A}_1$ is statistically unpredictable (see Definition 9.17 on page 398), and thus the probability of simply guessing queries to oracle HASH is negligible. On the other hand, ciphertexts $\mathbf{c}$ contain all necessary information: Information theoretically, given that the encryption scheme is correct, a ciphertext contains the exact same information as the underlying plaintext. Consider an adversary that could decrypt a ciphertext. This would yield corresponding message m and thus the query $\mathsf{pk}\|m$ to oracle HASH since the leakage L also contains public key pk. We must thus argue that no PPT predictor can decrypt any of the ciphertexts.

For this we will, once more, make use of the IND-CPA security of encryption scheme PKE. As argued before, if oracle HASH implements a random oracle, then the random coins used in the encryption operation are distributed identically to uniformly random coins. As we only need to show unpredictability in this case (that is, with HASH implementing a random oracle) this allows us to provide a reduction down to IND-CPA.

Let us assume the existence of a predictor P and define an adversary $\mathcal{B}_2$ against the IND-CPA security of PKE. We note that it is easier to work with a left-or-right formulation of IND-CPA where the adversary gets access to an oracle LoR that encrypts either the left or right message (with public key pk) depending on a hidden bit b. Also see Definition 5.27 (page 246) and the subsequent discussion. We give the pseudocode of adversary $\mathcal{B}_2$ next:

$$\underline{\mathcal{B}_2^{\mathrm{LoR}}(1^\lambda, \mathsf{pk})}$$

1 : $d \leftarrow\!\!\$ \{0,1\}$

2 : $(\mathbf{m}_0, \mathbf{m}_1) \leftarrow\!\!\$ \mathcal{A}_1(1^\lambda)$

3 : **for** $i = 1..|\mathbf{m}_0|$ **do**

4 : $\mathbf{m}^*[i] \leftarrow\!\!\$ \{0,1\}^{|\mathbf{m}_0[i]|}$

5 : $\mathbf{c}[i] \leftarrow\!\!\$ \mathrm{LoR}(\mathbf{m}_d[i], \mathbf{m}^*[i])$

6 : $L \leftarrow (\mathsf{pk}, d, \mathbf{c})$

7 : $x \leftarrow\!\!\$ \mathsf{P}(1^\lambda, L)$

8 : **if** $x \in \{\mathsf{pk}\|\mathbf{m}_d[i] : i \in [|\mathbf{m}_0|]\}$ **do**

9 :   **return** 1

10 : **return** 0

Adversary $\mathcal{B}_2$ first samples a random bit d and then runs $\mathcal{A}_1$ to obtain two message vectors $\mathbf{m}_0$ and $\mathbf{m}_1$. It then generates a ciphertext vector by calling its left-or-right oracle LoR, which encrypts either each message of vector $\mathbf{m}_d$ or each message of vector $\mathbf{m}^*$ (containing uniformly random strings) with public key pk. Adversary $\mathcal{B}_2$ then constructs leakage $L \leftarrow (\mathsf{pk}, d, \mathbf{c})$ as would source S and runs predictor P on leakage L to receive a guess x. Finally, if guess x corresponds to any value $\mathsf{pk}\|m$ for some message m from vector $\mathbf{m}_d$ it outputs 1, and otherwise it outputs 0.

Let b denote the hidden bit in the IND-CPA game and consider the case that it is $b = 0$. In this case the left value is encrypted, which in the case of our adversary $\mathcal{B}_2$ would correspond to an encryption of $\mathbf{m}_d[i]$. In this case the game is exactly the unpredictability game and we have that

$$\Pr\left[\text{IND-CPA}_{\text{PKE}}^{\mathcal{B}_2}(\lambda) = 1 \mid b = 0\right] = \Pr\left[\text{Pred}_{\text{S}}^{\text{P}}(\lambda) = 1\right]. \tag{18.4}$$

On the other hand, in case hidden bit $b = 1$ in the IND-CPA game and the right value is encrypted, we get that predictor P receives a vector of encryptions for uniformly random messages. In this case its probability to guess any of the values m as output by $\mathcal{A}_1$ is upper bounded by the min-entropy requirement on $\mathcal{A}_1$. (Recall that adversary $\mathcal{A}_1$ as a valid DPKE adversary must output messages that cannot be guessed.) If we let $\Pr[\text{Guess}_{\mathcal{A}_1}(\lambda)]$ denote the probability that an unbounded adversary guesses an entry m in one of the two vectors as output by $\mathcal{A}_1$ then we can specify the following bound for the case that $b = 1$:

$$\Pr\left[\text{IND-CPA}_{\text{PKE}}^{\mathcal{B}_2}(\lambda) = 1 \mid b = 1\right] \leq \Pr[\text{Guess}_{\mathcal{A}_1}(\lambda)]. \tag{18.5}$$

Subtracting Equations (18.4) and (18.5) and rearranging[7] yields our final bound on the unpredictability of source S

$$\Pr\left[\text{Pred}_{\text{S}}^{\text{P}}(\lambda) = 1\right] \leq \Pr[\text{Guess}_{\mathcal{A}_1}(\lambda)] + \text{Adv}_{\text{PKE},\mathcal{B}_2}^{\text{ind-cpa}}(\lambda).$$

This concludes the overall proof. □

18.4 Constructing UCEs in Idealized Models

In the previous section we have seen multiple examples of how to use UCEs in security proofs. When working with UCEs, the proof strategy is usually as follows: Give a reduction from an adversary against the security of your scheme to the UCE security of the hash function. Especially in the case of two-stage security games UCEs may make proving security much easier, even compared with direct proofs in the random oracle model. However, for our proofs to be meaningful we need to show that we can actually build UCEs.

In the following we will show how we can construct UCEs in the idealized random oracle model.

---

[7] Note that

$$\Pr\left[\text{IND-CPA}_{\text{PKE}}^{\mathcal{B}_2}(\lambda) = 1 \mid b = 1\right] = 1 - \Pr\left[\text{IND-CPA}_{\text{PKE}}^{\mathcal{B}_2}(\lambda) = 0 \mid b = 1\right],$$

and thus subtracting the left sides of Equations (18.4) and (18.5) yields $\text{Adv}_{\text{PKE},\mathcal{B}_2}^{\text{ind-cpa}}(\lambda)$.

18.4.1 Layered Cryptography

Before we get into how we can construct UCEs in idealized models let us briefly discuss a possible interpretation and the value of such a result. After all, a valid question is: If we can only validate a UCE assumption in the random oracle model, why not stick to the idealized model in the first place instead of introducing an intermediate abstraction? It is, however, exactly that intermediate abstraction that makes UCEs valuable as the UCE assumption forms a layer between the random oracle model and the final constructions, for example, of a deterministic public-key encryption scheme. This layered approach is visualized in Figure 18.4.

A layered approach offers various advantages over directly proving schemes secure in the random oracle model. On the one hand, UCEs have a clear definition, which makes them a better cryptanalytic target. In contrast, "behaving like a random oracle" is vague and not clearly graspable. Furthermore, having a layer in-between gives rise to better understanding, what properties of the random oracle a particular scheme needs, as these properties are clearly defined. Finally, as we have seen in the case of the encrypt-with-hash construction, UCEs can be seen as a tool for facilitating cryptographic proofs as they give structure to how to attempt a proof. As we will see, UCEs also provide a means to analyze two-stage games in the indifferentiability setting, which is not covered directly by the indifferentiability composition theorem. The most striking advantage of UCEs over direct proofs in the random oracle model, however, is that UCE assumptions may be validated: We might be able to show that certain forms of UCEs cannot exist, which provides additional insights into unachievable properties of random oracles. But we might also end up finding constructions of UCEs without the need to resort to idealized models, which would provide a much better security validation for the constructions based on these UCEs than a proof in the random oracle model could ever do.

Summing up, it can be said that proofs via UCEs should thus always be preferred to direct proofs in the random oracle model.

18.4.2 UCEs from Random Oracles

Let us now get to actually constructing a UCE-secure function. While it may not be surprising that we can use random oracles to construct both UCE[$\mathcal{S}^{\text{sup}}$]- and UCE[$\mathcal{S}^{\text{cup}}$]-secure functions, showing this formally requires a bit of technical work. The underlying idea is to argue that, clearly, the source on its own cannot distinguish a random oracle from a random function as these are distributed identically. Furthermore, even with the help of the distinguisher that will see the hash key, the two should not be able to correctly distinguish as the distinguisher cannot predict any of the source's queries to oracle HASH due to the unpredictability property of source S.

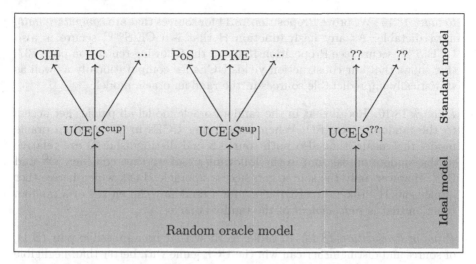

Fig. 18.4: The layered cryptography approach. Here, *base primitives* with standard-model security definitions (such as UCE notions) are validated in idealized models. *End goals* are then built on top of the base primitives and are, thus, reached solely in the standard model. For the layer of assumptions in between it is, however, not clear if these assumptions can be met in the standard model or not.

The formal proof will follow a game-based proof strategy where we start with a UCE game in the $b = 1$ setting where oracle HASH implements the UCE construction. Over the course of a few game hops this is then transformed into the UCE game in the $b = 0$ setting where oracle HASH implements a random function.

It remains to specify how we construct our UCE function from a random oracle. As UCEs are keyed hash functions we could simply switch to the keyed random oracle model (see Section 8.3.5 on page 359) and construct the function as $\mathsf{H}^{\mathsf{RO}}(\mathsf{hk}, m) := \mathsf{RO}(\mathsf{hk}, m)$. Instead, and in preparation for our later discussion of UCEs in the indifferentiability framework (Section 18.4.3), we opt for a construction of a keyed UCE hash function from an unkeyed random oracle that incorporates the key into the message via the secret-prefix method (see Section 16.1.2 on page 623). For this let RO be an (unkeyed) random oracle. We define a keyed variant as

$$\mathsf{H}^{\mathsf{RO}}(\mathsf{hk}, m) := \mathsf{RO}(\mathsf{hk}\|m),$$

where key generation $\mathsf{H}^{\mathsf{RO}}.\mathsf{KGen}(1^\lambda)$ is defined as sampling a key hk uniformly at random from $\{0,1\}^\lambda$. We can now formulate the proposition.

Proposition 18.14. *Let* RO *be a random oracle and let* H^{RO} *be the above-defined idealized hash function family. Then it holds that* $\mathsf{H} \in \mathrm{UCE}[\mathcal{S}^{\mathrm{cup}}]$.

Remark 18.15. We prove Proposition 18.14 for sources that are *computationally* unpredictable. As any hash function H that is UCE[$\mathcal{S}^{\text{cup}}$] secure is also UCE[$\mathcal{S}^{\text{sup}}$] secure (see Proposition 18.5 and the following remark on page 737) this shows that our construction yields UCEs for computationally as well as statistically unpredictable sources in the random oracle model.

Remark 18.16. Recall that in the random oracle model all parties get access to the random oracle RO. When considering UCEs in the random oracle model this means that also both source S and distinguisher D are relative to the random oracle, and in the following proof we thus consider S^{RO} and D^{RO}. However, only the source gets access to oracle HASH, which here either implements $H^{\text{RO}}(\text{hk}, m) := \text{RO}(\text{hk}\|m)$ for a randomly chosen key or a random function that is *independent* of the random oracle.

Proof of Proposition 18.14. In order to show that no admissible pair (S, D) of source and distinguisher can win the UCE game with better than negligible advantage, we transform the UCE game with hidden bit $b = 1$ (oracle HASH implements the UCE function) step by step into the UCE game with hidden bit $b = 0$ (oracle HASH implements a random oracle). The proof follows by arguing that any two neighboring games are negligibly close. The six individual game steps are provided as pseudocode in Figures 18.5 and 18.6 (pages 756f.).

Let b denote the hidden bit in the UCE game. We will discuss the pseudocode of the individual games shortly, but for now we simply claim that by design we have that

$$\Pr\left[\text{Game}_1^{\text{S,D}}(\lambda) = 1\right] = \Pr\left[\text{UCE}_\text{H}^{\text{S,D}}(\lambda) = 1 \mid b = 1\right]$$

as well as

$$\Pr\left[\text{Game}_6^{\text{S,D}}(\lambda) = 1\right] = 1 - \Pr\left[\text{UCE}_\text{H}^{\text{S,D}}(\lambda) = 1 \mid b = 0\right].$$

With the definition of UCE advantage (cp. Definition 18.1) we can thus rewrite the UCE advantage as the difference between our individual game steps.

$$
\begin{aligned}
\text{Adv}_{\text{H,S,D}}^{\text{uce}}(\lambda) &= 2 \cdot \Pr\left[\text{UCE}_\text{H}^{\text{S,D}}(\lambda) = 1\right] - 1 \\
&= \Pr\left[\text{UCE}_\text{H}^{\text{S,D}}(\lambda) = 1 \mid b = 0\right] + \Pr\left[\text{UCE}_\text{H}^{\text{S,D}}(\lambda) = 1 \mid b = 1\right] - 1 \\
&= \Pr\left[\text{Game}_1^{\text{S,D}}(\lambda) = 1\right] - \Pr\left[\text{Game}_6^{\text{S,D}}(\lambda) = 1\right] \\
&= \sum_{i=1}^{i=5} \left(\Pr\left[\text{Game}_i^{\text{S,D}}(\lambda) = 1\right] - \Pr\left[\text{Game}_{i+1}^{\text{S,D}}(\lambda) = 1\right]\right).
\end{aligned}
$$

The last equality is due to our usual game-hopping strategy. In order to complete the proof it remains to show that each two neighboring steps are negligibly close. As the sum of a constant number of negligible functions is negligible, too, it then follows that $\mathsf{Adv}^{\mathsf{uce}}_{\mathsf{H},\mathsf{S},\mathsf{D}}(\lambda)$ is negligible.

In the following we first present the six individual games to then discuss the loss introduced with each introduced change.

Game$_1$ As discussed, Game$_1$ is the UCE game with hidden bit $b = 1$ where the HASH oracle is implemented by our UCE function H^{RO}. When you look at Game$_1$ (Figure 18.5 below) you see that source S as well as distinguisher D and hash function H have access to their own random oracle procedure: RO$_\mathsf{S}$, RO$_\mathsf{D}$, and RO$_\mathsf{H}$. This split of the single random oracle is purely for syntactical reasons: In later parts of the proof we need to adapt the implementation of the individual procedures. The implementation of these random oracle procedures in Game$_1$ is identical, that is, we have RO$_\mathsf{S}$ = RO$_\mathsf{D}$ = RO$_\mathsf{H}$, and all three procedures are backed by a single table T_{RO} which is used to lazily sample a consistent random oracle for all parties: source S, distinguisher D, and oracle HASH.

Game$_2$ In Game$_2$ we introduce sets $\mathcal{Q}_\mathsf{H}, \mathcal{Q}_\mathsf{S}, \mathcal{Q}_\mathsf{D}$ which are used to track queries made to the random oracle by each of the parties. That is, $\mathcal{Q}_\mathsf{S}$ will keep track of all direct queries of source S to its random oracle, $\mathcal{Q}_\mathsf{H}$ stores the queries when evaluating H^{RO}, and $\mathcal{Q}_\mathsf{D}$ keeps track of the queries by distinguisher D (line 1 in each of the random oracle procedures). Besides keeping track of the random oracle queries, we introduce an abort condition (line 5). Here we abort the game in case any of the source's random oracle queries coincide with a random oracle query by oracle HASH (which implements function $\mathsf{H}^{\mathsf{RO}}(\mathsf{hk}, \cdot)$ for a randomly chosen key hk). The intuition for why the abort occurs only with negligible probability is that the source does not know hash key hk, which is part of every random oracle query by oracle HASH.

Game$_3$ In Game$_3$ we introduce a second abort condition (line 7) which aborts in case the distinguisher makes a random oracle query that coincides with an earlier random oracle query by oracle HASH. Intuitively, if distinguisher D finds a query to RO$_\mathsf{H}$ that was also made by oracle HASH, then this violates the unpredictability condition of source S, and thus also this second abort should only occur with negligible probability.

Game$_4$ In Game$_4$ we adapt the implementation of RO$_\mathsf{H}$ to make it independent from the other two random oracle procedures by letting it use its own table T_H rather than the common table T_{RO} for lazily sampling a random oracle. As by the aborts introduced in Game$_2$ and Game$_3$ neither source nor distinguisher share a random oracle query with oracle HASH, this change is not noticeable to either of them.

$\mathsf{Game}_1^{S,D}(\lambda)$	$\mathsf{Game}_2^{S,D}(\lambda)$	$\mathsf{Game}_3^{S,D}(\lambda)$
1 : $\quad T_{RO} \leftarrow []$	$T_{RO} \leftarrow []$	$T_{RO} \leftarrow []$
2 :	$\mathcal{Q}_H \leftarrow \{\}; \mathcal{Q}_S \leftarrow \{\}; \mathcal{Q}_D \leftarrow \{\}$	$\mathcal{Q}_H \leftarrow \{\}; \mathcal{Q}_S \leftarrow \{\}; \mathcal{Q}_D \leftarrow \{\}$
3 : $\quad \mathsf{hk} \leftarrow\!\!\$ \{0,1\}^\lambda$	$\mathsf{hk} \leftarrow\!\!\$ \{0,1\}^\lambda$	$\mathsf{hk} \leftarrow\!\!\$ \{0,1\}^\lambda$
4 : $\quad L \leftarrow\!\!\$ S^{RO_S, \text{HASH}(\mathsf{hk},\cdot)}(1^\lambda)$	$L \leftarrow\!\!\$ S^{RO_S, \text{HASH}(\mathsf{hk},\cdot)}(1^\lambda)$	$L \leftarrow\!\!\$ S^{RO_S, \text{HASH}(\mathsf{hk},\cdot)}(1^\lambda)$
5 :	**if** $\mathcal{Q}_S \cap \mathcal{Q}_H \neq \{\}$ **then abort**	if $\mathcal{Q}_S \cap \mathcal{Q}_H \neq \{\}$ then abort
6 : $\quad b' \leftarrow\!\!\$ D^{RO_D}(\mathsf{hk}, L)$	$b' \leftarrow\!\!\$ D^{RO_D}(\mathsf{hk}, L)$	$b' \leftarrow\!\!\$ D^{RO_D}(\mathsf{hk}, L)$
7 :		**if** $\mathcal{Q}_D \cap \mathcal{Q}_H \neq \{\}$ **then abort**
8 : $\quad$ **return** $(1 = b')$	**return** $(1 = b')$	**return** $(1 = b')$

$\text{HASH}(x) = H^{RO_H}(\mathsf{hk}, x)$	$\text{HASH}(x) = H^{RO_H}(\mathsf{hk}, x)$	$\text{HASH}(x) = H^{RO_H}(\mathsf{hk}, x)$
1 : $\quad$ **return** $RO_H(\mathsf{hk}\|x)$	**return** $RO_H(\mathsf{hk}\|x)$	**return** $RO_H(\mathsf{hk}\|x)$

$RO_H(x)$	$RO_H(x)$	$RO_H(x)$
1 :	$\mathcal{Q}_H \leftarrow \mathcal{Q}_H \cup \{x\}$	$\mathcal{Q}_H \leftarrow \mathcal{Q}_H \cup \{x\}$
2 : $\quad$ **if** $T_{RO}[x] = \bot$ **then**	**if** $T_{RO}[x] = \bot$ **then**	**if** $T_{RO}[x] = \bot$ **then**
3 : $\quad\quad T_{RO}[x] \leftarrow\!\!\$ \{0,1\}^{RO.ol(\lambda)}$	$T_{RO}[x] \leftarrow\!\!\$ \{0,1\}^{RO.ol(\lambda)}$	$T_{RO}[x] \leftarrow\!\!\$ \{0,1\}^{RO.ol(\lambda)}$
4 : $\quad$ **return** $T_{RO}[x]$	**return** $T_{RO}[x]$	**return** $T_{RO}[x]$

$RO_S(x)$	$RO_S(x)$	$RO_S(x)$
1 :	$\mathcal{Q}_S \leftarrow \mathcal{Q}_S \cup \{x\}$	$\mathcal{Q}_S \leftarrow \mathcal{Q}_S \cup \{x\}$
2 : $\quad$ **if** $T_{RO}[x] = \bot$ **then**	**if** $T_{RO}[x] = \bot$ **then**	**if** $T_{RO}[x] = \bot$ **then**
3 : $\quad\quad T_{RO}[x] \leftarrow\!\!\$ \{0,1\}^{RO.ol(\lambda)}$	$T_{RO}[x] \leftarrow\!\!\$ \{0,1\}^{RO.ol(\lambda)}$	$T_{RO}[x] \leftarrow\!\!\$ \{0,1\}^{RO.ol(\lambda)}$
4 : $\quad$ **return** $T_{RO}[x]$	**return** $T_{RO}[x]$	**return** $T_{RO}[x]$

$RO_D(x)$	$RO_D(x)$	$RO_D(x)$
1 :	$\mathcal{Q}_D \leftarrow \mathcal{Q}_D \cup \{x\}$	$\mathcal{Q}_D \leftarrow \mathcal{Q}_D \cup \{x\}$
2 : $\quad$ **if** $T_{RO}[x] = \bot$ **then**	**if** $T_{RO}[x] = \bot$ **then**	**if** $T_{RO}[x] = \bot$ **then**
3 : $\quad\quad T_{RO}[x] \leftarrow\!\!\$ \{0,1\}^{RO.ol(\lambda)}$	$T_{RO}[x] \leftarrow\!\!\$ \{0,1\}^{RO.ol(\lambda)}$	$T_{RO}[x] \leftarrow\!\!\$ \{0,1\}^{RO.ol(\lambda)}$
4 : $\quad$ **return** $T_{RO}[x]$	**return** $T_{RO}[x]$	**return** $T_{RO}[x]$

Fig. 18.5: The first set of games for the proof of Proposition 18.14. Game_1 is identical to the UCE game with hidden bit $b = 1$ where the HASH oracle is implemented by our UCE function H^{RO}. Recall that the faded-out line (line 5 of Game_3) indicates that this event has already been dealt with in an earlier game hop. Also see the discussion on the Fundamental Lemma of Game Playing (Section 5.1.4 on page 223).

$\text{Game}_4^{S,D}(\lambda)$

1:	$T_{RO} \leftarrow [\,]; T_H \leftarrow [\,]$
2:	$Q_H \leftarrow \{\,\}; Q_S \leftarrow \{\,\}; Q_D \leftarrow \{\,\}$
3:	$hk \leftarrow\!\!\$\ \{0,1\}^\lambda$
4:	$L \leftarrow\!\!\$\ S^{RO_S,\text{Hash}(hk,\cdot)}(1^\lambda)$
5:	if $Q_S \cap Q_H \neq \{\,\}$ then abort
6:	$b' \leftarrow\!\!\$\ D^{RO_D}(hk, L)$
7:	if $Q_D \cap Q_H \neq \{\,\}$ then abort
8:	return $(1 = b')$

$\text{Hash}(x) = H^{RO_H}(hk, x)$

1:	return $RO_H(hk\|x)$

$RO_H(x)$

1:	$Q_H \leftarrow Q_H \cup \{x\}$
2:	if $T_H[x] = \bot$ then
3:	$\quad T_H[x] \leftarrow\!\!\$\ \{0,1\}^{RO.ol(\lambda)}$
4:	return $T_H[x]$

$RO_S(x)$

1:	$Q_S \leftarrow Q_S \cup \{x\}$
2:	if $T_{RO}[x] = \bot$ then
3:	$\quad T_{RO}[x] \leftarrow\!\!\$\ \{0,1\}^{RO.ol(\lambda)}$
4:	return $T_{RO}[x]$

$RO_D(x)$

1:	$Q_D \leftarrow Q_D \cup \{x\}$
2:	if $T_{RO}[x] = \bot$ then
3:	$\quad T_{RO}[x] \leftarrow\!\!\$\ \{0,1\}^{RO.ol(\lambda)}$
4:	return $T_{RO}[x]$

$\text{Game}_5^{S,D}(\lambda)$

	$T_{RO} \leftarrow [\,]; T_H \leftarrow [\,]$
	$Q_H \leftarrow \{\,\}; Q_S \leftarrow \{\,\}; Q_D \leftarrow \{\,\}$
	$hk \leftarrow\!\!\$\ \{0,1\}^\lambda$
	$L \leftarrow\!\!\$\ S^{RO_S,\text{Hash}}(1^\lambda)$
	if $Q_S \cap Q_H \neq \{\,\}$ then abort
	$b' \leftarrow\!\!\$\ D^{RO_D}(hk, L)$
	if $Q_D \cap Q_H \neq \{\,\}$ then abort
	return $(1 = b')$

$\text{Hash}(x) = RO_H(x)$

return $RO_H(x)$

$RO_H(x)$

$Q_H \leftarrow Q_H \cup \{hk\|x\}$
if $T_H[x] = \bot$ then
$\quad T_H[x] \leftarrow\!\!\$\ \{0,1\}^{RO.ol(\lambda)}$
return $T_H[x]$

$RO_S(x)$

$Q_S \leftarrow Q_S \cup \{x\}$
if $T_{RO}[x] = \bot$ then
$\quad T_{RO}[x] \leftarrow\!\!\$\ \{0,1\}^{RO.ol(\lambda)}$
return $T_{RO}[x]$

$RO_D(x)$

1:	$Q_D \leftarrow Q_D \cup \{x\}$
2:	if $T_{RO}[x] = \bot$ then
3:	$\quad T_{RO}[x] \leftarrow\!\!\$\ \{0,1\}^{RO.ol(\lambda)}$
4:	return $T_{RO}[x]$

$\text{Game}_6^{S,D}(\lambda)$

	$T_{RO} \leftarrow [\,]; T_H \leftarrow [\,]$
	$Q_H \leftarrow \{\,\}; Q_S \leftarrow \{\,\}; Q_D \leftarrow \{\,\}$
	$hk \leftarrow\!\!\$\ \{0,1\}^\lambda$
	$L \leftarrow\!\!\$\ S^{RO_S,\text{Hash}}(1^\lambda)$
	$b' \leftarrow\!\!\$\ D^{RO_D}(hk, L)$
	return $(1 = b')$

$\text{Hash}(x) = RO_H(x)$

return $RO_H(x)$

$RO_H(x)$

if $T_H[x] = \bot$ then
$\quad T_H[x] \leftarrow\!\!\$\ \{0,1\}^{RO.ol(\lambda)}$
return $T_H[x]$

$RO_S(x)$

if $T_{RO}[x] = \bot$ then
$\quad T_{RO}[x] \leftarrow\!\!\$\ \{0,1\}^{RO.ol(\lambda)}$
return $T_{RO}[x]$

$RO_D(x)$

if $T_{RO}[x] = \bot$ then
$\quad T_{RO}[x] \leftarrow\!\!\$\ \{0,1\}^{RO.ol(\lambda)}$
return $T_{RO}[x]$

Fig. 18.6: The remaining games for the proof of Proposition 18.14. By Game_5 we have adapted the game such that it represents the UCE game with hidden bit $b = 0$ where the Hash oracle is implemented by the random oracle. Game_6 is then simply cleaning up the introduced bookkeeping sets.

Game₅ In Game₅ we make the switch in UCE games from hidden bit $b = 1$ to $b = 0$. For this we change oracle HASH to no longer prepend key hk on its queries to RO_H, that is, on input x oracle HASH directly evaluates $\text{RO}_\text{H}(x)$ instead of $\text{RO}_\text{H}(\text{hk}\|x)$. In order to stay consistent, we also need to adapt the way we compute $\mathcal{Q}_\text{H}$. Since we adapted HASH to return $\text{RO}_\text{H}(x)$ instead of $\text{RO}_\text{H}(\text{hk}\|x)$, we also adapt line 1 in RO_H to $\mathcal{Q}_\text{H} \leftarrow \mathcal{Q}_\text{H} \cup \{\text{hk}\|x\}$.

Note that in the previous game, we made RO_H independent—it is now backed by its own table T_H—and, consequently, oracle HASH now has access to its own dedicated random function. It follows that the introduced change does not change the distribution of HASH towards source S.

Game₆ Finally, in Game₆, we simply remove the sets $\mathcal{Q}_\text{H}, \mathcal{Q}_\text{S}, \mathcal{Q}_\text{D}$ and the abort branches again to arrive at the UCE game with hidden bit $b = 0$ where the HASH oracle is implemented by a random function. Note that the return statement of Game₆ (line 8) returns true if $b' = 1$. Thus, when Game₆ returns true, this is identical to an adversary making the wrong guess in the $\text{UCE}_\text{H}^{\text{S,D}}$ with hidden bit $b = 0$ (oracle HASH implementing a random oracle). It follows that

$$\Pr\Big[\text{Game}_6^{\text{S,D}}(\lambda) = 1\Big] = 1 - \Pr\Big[\text{UCE}_\text{H}^{\text{S,D}}(\lambda) = 1 \mid b = 0\Big].$$

Game₁ to Game₂. It remains to analyze the individual game hops. From Game₁ to Game₂ we introduce bookkeeping sets in all RO procedures. These are then used in line 5 to exclude the event that a collision occurs on the queries by oracle HASH (implementing hash function $\text{H}^{\text{RO}_\text{H}}(\text{hk}, \cdot)$) to the random oracle with direct queries from source S to the random oracle. Let $\text{Collision}_\text{S}$ denote the event that a collision occurs with one of the source's queries. If such a collision occurs we abort the game and declare the adversary to win.

As the outcomes of games Game₁ and Game₂ differ only in case event $\text{Collision}_\text{S}$ occurs we can bound the difference between the two games using the Fundamental Lemma of Game Playing (Lemma 5.13 on page 224) as

$$|\Pr[\text{Game}_1(\lambda) = 1] - \Pr[\text{Game}_2(\lambda) = 1]| \leq \Pr[\text{Collision}_\text{S}].$$

Note that all queries in set $\mathcal{Q}_\text{H}$ (queries to the random oracle made during the computation of hash function $\text{H}^{\text{RO}_\text{H}}$) are of the form $\text{hk}\|x$. That is, they have the hash key prepended. As key hk is kept hidden from source S this directly implies that for event $\text{Collision}_\text{S}$ to occur source S must "guess" the uniformly distributed key. As, by assumption, key hk is of length λ bits and, consequently, each guess of source S is correct with probability $2^{-\lambda}$ we can upper bound the probability of a collision via a union bound as

$$\Pr[\text{Collision}_\text{S}] \leq \frac{q_\text{S}(\lambda)}{2^\lambda}.$$

Here q_S denotes an upper bound on the number of random oracle queries of source S to its random oracle RO_S. As source S is restricted to be PPT we have that q_S is polynomially bounded and the above probability is negligible.

Game$_2$ to Game$_3$. In Game$_3$ we introduce the second abort condition, which triggers in case a random oracle query by distinguisher D collides with a query stored in $\mathcal{Q}_H$ (line 7). Let us denote this event by Collision$_D$.

For event Collision$_D$ we cannot make a similar argument as in the previous game hop as distinguisher D gets hash key hk as part of its input. However, in case event Collision$_D$ occurs then distinguisher D has made a query hk$\|x$ to its random oracle RO$_D$ for some value x that source S must have queried to oracle HASH (as otherwise hk$\|x$ would not be in $\mathcal{Q}_H$). Since we assume that source S is unpredictable this should not happen, and the idea is thus to prove that Collision$_D$ occurs only with negligible probability down to the computational unpredictability of source S.

Consider prediction game $\mathrm{Pred}_S^P(\lambda)$ (see Definition 18.3 on page 736). In contrast to Game$_3$, oracle HASH in the prediction game implements a random function and not the hash function in question. In our case (i.e., in Game$_3$) hash function H^{RO} is built using a random oracle, and we have seen in the previous game step that source S guesses the key used in H^{RO} only with negligible probability. We thus have that unless event Collision$_S$ occurs the output distribution of source S is identical whether it is run relative to oracle HASH implementing function H^{RO} or oracle HASH implementing an independently sampled random function as in the setup of the prediction game $\mathrm{Pred}_S^P(\lambda)$. We formalize this intuition next.

In the previous game hop we have already eliminated the possibility of event Collision$_S$. But then towards source S it makes no difference whether it runs relative to a randomly chosen function as in the prediction game or relative to our hash function H^{RO}. We can thus upper bound the probability of event collision$_D$ via the unpredictability of source S.

For this consider the following predictor P which simulates Game$_3$ for distinguisher D and then tries to extract a collision. Predictor P simulates the random oracle for D and records its queries as shown in the following pseudocode. Note that we are in the random oracle setting and thus predictor P has oracle access to random oracle RO (but not to HASH; see Definition 18.3).

Predictor $\mathsf{P}^{RO}(L)$	$\mathsf{RO}_P(x)$
1 : $\mathcal{Q} \leftarrow \{\}$	1 : $\mathcal{Q} \leftarrow \mathcal{Q} \cup \{x[\lambda+1..|x|]\}$
2 : hk $\leftarrow\!\!{\scriptstyle\$}\ \{0,1\}^\lambda$	2 : **if** $T[x] = \bot$ **then**
3 : $b \leftarrow\!\!{\scriptstyle\$}\ \mathsf{D}^{RO_P}(\mathsf{hk}, L)$	3 : $\quad T[x] \leftarrow\!\!{\scriptstyle\$}\ \{0,1\}^{RO.ol(\lambda)}$
4 : $x \leftarrow\!\!{\scriptstyle\$}\ \mathcal{Q}$	4 : **return** $T[x]$
5 : **return** x	

Predictor P gets as input leakage L. It samples a random hash key hk and then runs distinguisher D on input (hk, L). Distinguisher D expects a random oracle which predictor P simulates for D. Predictor P records any query x by D (removing the first λ bits which would correspond to a hash key in a query of the form hk$\|x$) in a set $\mathcal{Q}$ (line 1). Predictor P then ignores the single bit b

as output by distinguisher D and instead chooses a random value x from the set $\mathcal{Q}$ of recorded queries as its output.

Let $q_D(\lambda)$ be an upper bound on the number of random oracle queries by distinguisher D. Then when considering game Pred_S^P we have that predictor P is successful with probability $1/q_D(\lambda)$ given that event $\mathsf{Collision}_D$ occurred: If there was at least one collision within the queries of distinguisher D with the indirect queries of source S to HASH, then predictor P will guess the right query with probability $\frac{1}{q_D(\lambda)}$. It follows that

$$\Pr\left[\mathrm{Pred}_S^P(\lambda) = 1\right] = \frac{1}{q_D(\lambda)} \cdot \Pr[\mathsf{Collision}_D],$$

which yields a bound on the occurrence of event $\mathsf{Collision}_D$ as

$$\Pr[\mathsf{Collision}_D] \le q_D(\lambda) \cdot \mathsf{Adv}_{S,P}^{\mathrm{pred}}(\lambda).$$

Finally, the Fundamental Lemma of Game Playing allows us to use this bound to upper bound the difference between games Game_2 and Game_3 as

$$|\Pr[\mathsf{Game}_2(\lambda) = 1] - \Pr[\mathsf{Game}_3(\lambda) = 1]| \le \Pr[\mathsf{Collision}_D]$$
$$\le q_D(\lambda) \cdot \mathsf{Adv}_{S,P}^{\mathrm{pred}}(\lambda).$$

As, by assumption, source S is computationally unpredictable and $q_D(\lambda)$ is a polynomial, the distance between the two games must be negligible.

Game_3 to Game_4. From Game_3 to Game_4 we change the table underlying the random oracle procedure for RO_H and make it independent from the table used in RO_S and RO_D. In other words, we now simulate an independent random oracle for hash function H^{RO_H}. Since we have already excluded any collisions in queries to RO_H with queries to RO_S and RO_D this introduced change does not have any effect on the outcome of the game and we have that

$$\Pr[\mathsf{Game}_3(\lambda) = 1] = \Pr[\mathsf{Game}_4(\lambda) = 1].$$

Game_4 to Game_5. In Game_5 we make the switch from letting oracle HASH implement the actual hash function to letting it implement a random function. With the work we have done in the previous game hops this is merely a syntactical change and thus

$$\Pr[\mathsf{Game}_4(\lambda) = 1] = \Pr[\mathsf{Game}_5(\lambda) = 1].$$

Game_5 to Game_6. The final game hop is, again, merely a syntactical change which removes the abort conditions and bookkeeping sets to make the game immediately stand out as the UCE game with hidden bit $b = 0$. As the triggering of the abort conditions has been dealt with in earlier stages—also see the discussion on the Fundamental Lemma of Game Playing (Section 5.1.4; page 223)—this does not change the outcome of the game:

$$\Pr[\mathsf{Game}_5(\lambda) = 1] = \Pr[\mathsf{Game}_6(\lambda) = 1].$$

Summary. Summing up the losses in the individual game hops yields as advantage of adversary (S, D)

$$\mathsf{Adv}^{\mathsf{uce}}_{\mathsf{H},\mathsf{S},\mathsf{D}}(\lambda) \leq \frac{q_{\mathsf{S}}(\lambda)}{2^\lambda} + q_{\mathsf{D}}(\lambda) \cdot \mathsf{Adv}^{\mathsf{pred}}_{\mathsf{S},\mathsf{P}}(\lambda).$$

This concludes the proof. $\qquad\qquad\qquad\qquad\qquad\qquad\qquad\qquad\qquad\square$

18.4.3 UCEs in the Indifferentiability Framework

With the result from the previous section we have established that random oracles are sufficient for the construction of UCEs. This, however, was not really surprising as after all, UCEs target to provide achievable (and thus weaker) security definitions for hash functions than "behaving like random oracles."

As UCEs model keyed hash functions a natural candidate for a UCE-secure function in practice is HMAC. Yet, as we have seen, HMAC is highly structured as it is based on an iteration scheme and thus very different from a single monolithic random oracle. In the previous chapter we introduced the *indifferentiability framework*, which allows to analyze hash function constructions in the ideal setting. There we saw that HMAC is indifferentiable from a random oracle, and together with the indifferentiability composition theorem (Theorem 17.9 on page 693) we get that HMAC can securely replace random oracles in single-stage games given that the underlying compression function is assumed to be ideal. The critical point in this discussion is the *single-stage* aspect: the UCE game is not a single-stage game as source and distinguisher cannot share arbitrary state (see Definition 17.20 on page 721). Thus the question remains:

Is HMAC, like our random-oracle-based construction, $\mathrm{UCE}[\mathcal{S}^{\mathrm{cup}}]$ secure given that the underlying compression function is ideal?

As it turns out, it can be shown that HMAC, as well as, for example, a keyed variant of chopped MD, are indeed $\mathrm{UCE}[\mathcal{S}^{\mathrm{cup}}]$ secure given that the underlying compression functions are modeled as ideal compression functions. While indifferentiability cannot be used directly to show this result, we will see that we can "make it work" with a bit of additional effort. As a consequence, UCEs provide a means to analyze multi-stage games while providing similar guarantees to those given by the indifferentiability framework for single-stage games. If security of a cryptographic scheme relies on UCEs, we can securely replace the hash function with, for example, HMAC assuming only that the underlying compression function is ideal. In contrast to the indifferentiability setting, this result is independent of whether the security is proven via a single-stage or a multi-stage game. For example, a direct proof of Theorem 9.20 (page 400) that the encrypt-with-hash construction is secure in the random oracle model would not allow arguing that we can safely use HMAC instead of the random oracle.

Our result in Proposition 18.13 (page 747) via UCEs, on the other hand, directly yields also the stronger result that HMAC down to an ideal compression function can instantiate the hash function in the encrypt-with-hash construction. In the following we explain the intuition behind this result. For this we will again use chopped MD as the running example as it has a slightly simpler iteration scheme than HMAC. However, as chopped MD is not keyed, we first need to introduce a keyed variant of chopped MD.

Recall the chopped MD construction from Section 17.5.1. It is a standard Merkle–Damgård construction with a twist. The final h evaluation does not directly yield the output value but instead an additional transformation g is applied that chops off a fixed fraction of the output bits. In order to get a keyed variant, we now simply consider the initialization vector as the key (also see Section 16.1.1 for this form of keying Merkle–Damgård). The following visualization defines the computation of $H_{cMD}(hk, m_1 \| \ldots \| m_\ell)$, where m_1 to m_ℓ are of the block length of the hash function:

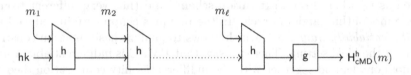

We can now formally state the result that HMAC and chopped MD are UCE secure assuming that the underlying compression function is ideal.

> **Theorem 18.17.** *Assuming that the underlying compression function* $h : \{0,1\}^{h.bl(\lambda)} \times \{0,1\}^{h.cl(\lambda)} \to \{0,1\}^{h.cl(\lambda)}$ *is a fixed-input-length random oracle with super-logarithmic output length (i.e., $h.cl(\lambda) \in \omega(\log(\lambda))$), then we have that* $HMAC^h \in UCE[\mathcal{S}^{cup}]$. *Furthermore, for the above-defined variant of chopped MD it holds that* $H_{cMD}^h \in UCE[\mathcal{S}^{cup}]$.

In the following we provide a proof outline for the case of chopped Merkle–Damgård. For this let us recall the intuition behind indifferentiability. If a hash function H^h is indifferentiable from a random oracle RO, then for any distinguisher $\mathcal{D}$ there exists simulator Sim such that

$$\mathsf{Adv}^{indiff}_{H^h, G, \mathcal{D}, Sim}(\lambda) := \left| \Pr\left[\mathcal{D}^{H^h, h}(1^\lambda) = 1\right] - \Pr\left[\mathcal{D}^{RO, Sim^{RO}}(1^\lambda) = 1\right] \right|$$

is negligible.[8] The indifferentiability result can then be used to argue for cryptographic single-stage games that a security proof in the random oracle setting implies security also in case the random oracle is replaced by hash function H^h and assuming that compression function h is ideal. The intuition for this is that for any adversary $\mathcal{A}^h$ that can break the security of the scheme relative to hash function H^h we can construct an adversary $\mathcal{B} := \mathcal{A}^{\mathrm{Sim}^{\mathrm{RO}}}$ which uses the simulator to simulate the compression function for adversary $\mathcal{A}$. If the hash function is indifferentiable then the adversary cannot detect the difference between h and the simulated compression function $\mathrm{Sim}^{\mathrm{RO}}$ and thus it will break the security of the scheme relative to random oracle RO. Of course, if we have a security proof in the random oracle model, this cannot be the case and thus adversary $\mathcal{B}$ and hence also adversary $\mathcal{A}$ cannot exist.

In case of multi-stage games this approach no longer works. For this, let us consider the UCE game relative to hash function H^h on the left and relative to indifferentiability simulator Sim and random oracle RO on the right.

$\mathrm{UCE}^{S,D}_{H^h}(\lambda)$	$\mathrm{UCE}^{S,D}_{\mathrm{RO}}(\lambda)$
1 : $b \leftarrow\!\!{\$}\ \{0,1\}$	1 : $b \leftarrow\!\!{\$}\ \{0,1\}$
2 : $hk \leftarrow\!\!{\$}\ \mathrm{H.KGen}(1^\lambda)$	2 : $hk \leftarrow\!\!{\$}\ \mathrm{H.KGen}(1^\lambda)$
3 : $L \leftarrow\!\!{\$}\ S^{h,\mathrm{HASH}}(1^\lambda)$	3 : $L \leftarrow\!\!{\$}\ S^{\mathrm{Sim}_S^{\mathrm{RO}},\mathrm{HASH}}(1^\lambda)$
4 : $b' \leftarrow\!\!{\$}\ D^h(1^\lambda, hk, L)$	4 : $b' \leftarrow\!\!{\$}\ D^{\mathrm{Sim}_D^{\mathrm{RO}}}(1^\lambda, hk, L)$
5 : **return** $(b = b')$	5 : **return** $(b = b')$

In the real-world setting both source and distinguisher get oracle access to the ideal compression function h. But now when we want to use the simulator to simulate the ideal compression function relative to the random oracle both source and distinguisher get "their own instance" of simulator Sim (here denoted as Sim_S and Sim_D). The problem is that in order to properly simulate the compression function the simulator instance must keep track of all posed queries. But since the communication between source and distinguisher is restricted the UCE distinguisher's simulator Sim_D might not get the entire state of the source's simulator and thus it may fail to properly simulate the compression function. (For a detailed example see Section 17.7 on page 716.)

For the following discussion we assume that you have a working knowledge of how the simulator in the proof of indifferentiability for chopped MD works (Theorem 17.13 page 702). In short, it builds up an internal representation of all queries in order to recognize queries that correspond to valid evaluations of chopped MD. For any such query it extracts the corresponding message

---

[8] When we talk about distinguisher in the following paragraph we need to be careful to understand which distinguisher we refer to. There exists the UCE distinguisher D and the indifferentiability distinguisher $\mathcal{D}$. We hope that from context, and by the difference in font, it should always be clear which distinguisher is meant.

$m_1 \| \ldots \| m_\ell$ and then uses its access to the random oracle to obtain value $\mathsf{RO}(m_1 \| \ldots \| m_\ell)$. Finally, since the compression function is not "chopped" it fills up the remaining bits with random bits.

A query to the simulator "belongs" to a chopped MD query in case it lies on a path within the simulator's state graph $\mathcal{G}$ starting from node IV which represents the initialization value. For example, in case the graph before the query is

$$\boxed{\text{IV}} \xrightarrow{\;m_1\;} \boxed{y_1}$$

and the distinguisher queries (m_2, y_1) then this corresponds to a valid chopped MD execution and the simulator would update its internal state to

$$\boxed{\text{IV}} \xrightarrow{\;m_1\;} \boxed{y_1} \xrightarrow{\;m_2\;} \boxed{y_2}$$

Furthermore, simulator Sim would choose value y_2 by evaluating the random oracle on $m_1 \| m_2$ and adding sufficiently many random bits to the result to obtain a value of $\mathsf{h.cl}(\lambda)$ bits.

We now have the essentials to discuss the proof strategy, which relies on three observations.

Source S does not learn key hk. For our keyed variant of chopped MD the simulator needs to know the used hash key hk as otherwise it cannot properly simulate queries. This poses a problem to the source's simulator since the source itself does not know the key. We can, however, make this work to our advantage. For this recall the first game hop in the proof of Proposition 18.14 (proving that the random oracle construction is UCE secure; page 753). Here we argue that with overwhelming probability the source will not make any query to its random oracle that collides with a query to the random oracle during the evaluation of a query by the source to oracle HASH (implementing the construction $\mathsf{H}^{\mathsf{RO}}(\mathsf{hk}, \cdot) := \mathsf{RO}(\mathsf{hk} \| \cdot)$) as the latter queries are prefixed by hash key hk.

We can make the same argument also in the case of chopped MD and show that with overwhelming probability none of the source's queries to its h oracle collide with any query to h that occur during a query by source S to oracle HASH implementing $\mathsf{H}^{\mathsf{h}}_{\mathsf{cMD}}(\mathsf{hk}, \cdot)$ for a random hash key hk. For this consider a computation of chopped MD for message $m_1 \| \ldots \| m_\ell$. The first query to h in that computation would be $y_1 \leftarrow \mathsf{h}(m_1, \mathsf{hk})$. Since hk is hidden from the source and h is assumed to be a fixed-input-length random oracle, the result is distributed uniformly at random and has no relation to hash key hk. But then this random value y_1 goes into the computation of the next message block as $y_2 \leftarrow \mathsf{h}(m_2, y_1)$ and so forth up to the last message block. From this computation the source only learns a partial value of the last chaining value y_ℓ as chopped MD truncates the value before returning it. Thus, as the source does not learn the full first input into the compute chain (i.e., it

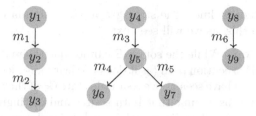

Fig. 18.7: A possible state graph $\mathcal{G}_S$ of simulator $\mathrm{Sim}_S^{\mathrm{RO}}$ after the execution of source S. Note that node hk is not part of the graph.

does not learn hk), with overwhelming probability it does not learn any of the intermediate full inputs. If, as in the proof of Proposition 18.14, we let $\mathcal{Q}_S$ and $\mathcal{Q}_H$ denote bookkeeping sets that, this time, record h queries by source S and indirect h queries occurring during the evaluation of HASH queries then it follows that in a first game hop we can make the jump to

$\mathrm{UCE}_H^{S,D}(\lambda)$	$\mathrm{HASH}(x)$
1: $b \leftarrow\!\!\$ \{0,1\}$	1: **if** $T[x] = \perp$ **then**
2: $\mathrm{hk} \leftarrow\!\!\$ \mathrm{H.KGen}(1^\lambda)$	2: **if** $b = 1$ **then**
3: $L \leftarrow\!\!\$ S^{h,\mathrm{HASH}}(1^\lambda)$	3: $T[x] \leftarrow H_{\mathrm{cMD}}^h \, \mathrm{Eval}(\mathrm{hk}, x)$
4: **if** $\mathcal{Q}_S \cap \mathcal{Q}_H \neq \{\,\}$ **then abort**	4: **else** $T[x] \leftarrow\!\!\$ \{0,1\}^{\mathrm{H.ol}(\lambda)}$
5: $b' \leftarrow\!\!\$ D^h(1^\lambda, \mathrm{hk}, L)$	5: **return** $T[x]$
6: **return** $(b = b')$	

This has an important consequence for our simulator, because if the source does not learn key hk and consequently cannot pose a query containing hk to its compression function oracle, then the simulator does not even need to check whether or not a query by the source corresponds to a correctly chained chopped MD execution starting with "initialization value" hk. Instead, it is sufficient for simulator Sim_S to always choose random values for its output without involving the random oracle (this corresponds to line 6 in the simulator code on page 707). If we consider an execution of source S relative to simulator $\mathrm{Sim}_S^{\mathrm{RO}}$ then the state graph $\mathcal{G}_S$ of $\mathrm{Sim}_S^{\mathrm{RO}}$ after the execution may look like in Figure 18.7. The important observation is that node hk is not part of the graph.

The distinguisher knows the key. In contrast to the source, UCE distinguisher D is given the key as input. We can thus assume that the key is also known by the distinguisher's instance of the simulator Sim_D. It follows that simulator Sim_D can perfectly simulate the compression function for UCE distinguisher D as by the above argument the source S will not make any queries that correspond to partial paths and hence it is unproblematic for simulator $\mathsf{Sim_D}$ not to know the state graph $\mathcal{G}_S$ of simulator $\mathsf{Sim_S}$. There is one exception to this, as we will see next.

Derandomization. While the source S cannot query simulator $\mathsf{Sim_S}$ on any valid chopped MD execution path (as it does not learn key hk) it can query it on arbitrary values. We have seen above a sample state $\mathcal{G}_S$ of the source's simulator after execution. Let us assume that both source and distinguisher query their oracle on input (m_1, y_1). Then in case the oracle is ideal compression function h it naturally returns the same values for both cases. On the other hand, if the oracle is implemented as $\mathsf{Sim_S^{RO}}$ and $\mathsf{Sim_D^{RO}}$ the two return values will be different with overwhelming probability since simulator $\mathsf{Sim_D}$ is not aware of the state $\mathcal{G}_S$ of simulator $\mathsf{Sim_S}$ and thus chooses a fresh random value as output.

The idea to overcome this final problem is to make simulators $\mathsf{Sim_S}$ and $\mathsf{Sim_D}$ *deterministic*. For this, we need to explain how the simulators can generate their "random" responses deterministically, without changing the distribution towards their callers (i.e., source S and distinguisher D). Luckily for us, the simulator runs relative to a random oracle and we have already seen in Chapter 9 (Theorem 9.16 on page 395) that random oracles can be used to derandomize algorithms. The idea is that, instead of relying on random coins directly, the algorithm makes queries to the random oracle whenever it needs to make a random choice. As random oracle results are uniformly distributed, the effect is identical with one catch: Not only the simulator has access to the random oracle but also the UCE source S and distinguisher D. Thus, if the simulator makes a query to the random oracle to generate randomness it needs to ensure that this query is such that it can never be queried by either source S or distinguisher D.

Consider once more the indifferentiability definition (Definition 17.1 on page 689). There we had two flavors *weak* and *strong* indifferentiability where, however, already the weak form was sufficient for the composition theorem. For weak indifferentiability we need to show that for any indifferentiability distinguisher $\mathcal{D}$ there exists a simulator Sim. In particular, this means that the simulator can depend on the code of the distinguisher. Translated to our UCE case we have that the simulator instances $\mathsf{Sim_S}$ and $\mathsf{Sim_D}$ can depend on the code of both UCE source S and distinguisher D.

As UCE source S and distinguisher D are, by definition, efficient, there exists a polynomial upper bound p on the runtime of both S and D. This, however, means that if simulator $\mathsf{Sim_S}$ (resp. $\mathsf{Sim_D}$) queries the random oracle on messages of length longer than $\mathsf{p}(\lambda)$ to generate its randomness, then these queries cannot possibly be made by either UCE source S nor distinguisher D.

As an example, consider a query (m_1, y_1) by S to simulator $\mathsf{Sim_S}$. To answer this query it would need to generate a uniformly random value of length $\mathsf{h.cl}(\lambda)$. To generate the necessary random coins, it makes the following queries to the random oracle RO. (Recall that $\langle i \rangle_\ell$ denotes a binary representation of i using ℓ bits.)

$$\mathsf{RO}(\langle 0 \rangle_{\mathsf{p}(\lambda)} \| m_1 \| y_1)$$
$$\mathsf{RO}(\langle 1 \rangle_{\mathsf{p}(\lambda)} \| m_1 \| y_1)$$
$$\mathsf{RO}(\langle 2 \rangle_{\mathsf{p}(\lambda)} \| m_1 \| y_1)$$
$$\vdots$$

As $\mathsf{RO.ol}(\lambda)$ might be shorter than $\mathsf{h.cl}(\lambda)$ the simulator might need to make multiple queries to get the necessary $\mathsf{h.cl}(\lambda)$ number of random bits. Thus, the first query consists of $\mathsf{p}(\lambda)$ many 0 bits followed by $m_1 \| y_1$ and for each subsequent query the simulator counts one up within the p-bit-long prefix.[9]

If we derandomize both Sim_S and Sim_D with the same steps then, by design, we have that if source S and D pose the same query (m, y) to their simulator then they obtain the same result. This provides the final piece in the puzzle.

Summary. Let us summarize the idea behind proving Theorem 18.17. Let us assume that we have a successful adversary (S, D) against the UCE game with the chopped MD hash function relative to an ideal compression function h.

First, we observe that source S does not make any query to its h oracle which is also made during a computation of any HASH query by S. From S we construct an adapted adversary S_* for the random oracle setting as

$$S_*^{\mathsf{RO}}(1^\lambda) := S^{\mathsf{Sim}_\mathsf{h}^{\mathsf{RO}}(\cdot, \cdot)}(1^\lambda).$$

That is, S_* runs S but with the derandomized simulator Sim_S as its oracle. Similarly, we consider an adapted adversary D_* as

$$D_*^{\mathsf{RO}}(L, \mathsf{hk}) := D^{\mathsf{Sim}_\mathsf{D}^{\mathsf{RO}}[\mathsf{hk}](\cdot, \cdot)}(L, \mathsf{hk}).$$

Adapted UCE distinguisher D_*^{RO} initializes the derandomized simulator Sim_D with hash key hk (such that it can detect correct chopped MD queries keyed with key hk). It then runs the original UCE distinguisher D but with the derandomized simulator Sim_D as its oracle. It outputs whatever D outputs.

The proof now follows with the indifferentiability proof of chopped MD (Theorem 17.13; page 702), and by observing that the simulation of chopped MD is consistent across the two stages of the UCE adversary: source and distinguisher. Finally note that adapted source S_* does not change leakage L in any way and, thus, if $S \in \mathcal{S}^{\mathrm{cup}}$ then also $S_* \in \mathcal{S}^{\mathrm{cup}}$. This concludes the proof sketch for Theorem 18.17.

---

[9] Note that this approach is naturally very inefficient in practical terms, but efficient in complexity-theoretic terms as the length of each query is polynomially upper bounded.

18.4.4 Indifferentiability for Multi-stage Games

In the previous section we saw that a keyed variant of chopped MD is UCE[$\mathcal{S}^{\mathrm{cup}}$] secure. The same can be shown, for example, for the popular HMAC construction. We stress that these results provide a strong advantage of proofs using UCEs over proofs directly in the random oracle model, especially for multi-stage games. If a construction for a multi-stage security definition (e.g., deterministic public-key encryption) is proven secure in the random oracle setting, then this does not immediately imply security for HMAC. Instead, when proving the security relative to UCEs then this does not only imply security in the random oracle setting, but similarly for HMAC assuming that the compression function is ideal.

In that sense UCEs complement the indifferentiability framework and provide a toolset to overcome the limitations of the former for multi-stage settings.

18.5 UCEs in the Standard Model

We have seen that UCEs are very useful for proving the security of cryptographic schemes in idealized models. Yet, the holy grail of UCEs would be to have a standard model construction of, for example, UCE[$\mathcal{S}^{\mathrm{cup}}$] down to standard and well-established cryptographic assumptions.

At least for UCEs relative to computationally unpredictable sources (i.e., UCE[$\mathcal{S}^{\mathrm{cup}}$]) the outlook is not too good. We will present a "1-out-of-2" result showing that UCEs relative to computationally unpredictable sources can only exist in case so-called *cryptographic indistinguishability obfuscators* do not exist. Of course, this does not mean that UCE[$\mathcal{S}^{\mathrm{cup}}$] cannot exist in the standard model, especially since indistinguishability obfuscators are also a relatively recent addition to the cryptographic toolset and all known candidate constructions are based on new and not yet well-studied assumptions. Nevertheless, the current bet is more on the existence of indistinguishability obfuscators than on UCE[$\mathcal{S}^{\mathrm{cup}}$].

On the other hand, UCE[$\mathcal{S}^{\mathrm{sup}}$], that is, UCEs relative to statistically unpredictable sources, are in fact sufficient for many use cases, and the existence of indistinguishability obfuscators does not exclude the existence of such UCEs. Indeed, indistinguishability obfuscators can even be used in the construction of restricted forms of UCE[$\mathcal{S}^{\mathrm{sup}}$]-secure functions.

We begin this section with a detour and briefly introduce the topic of cryptographic code obfuscation to then present the 1-out-of-2 result.

18.5.1 A Brief Introduction to Obfuscation

The current knowledge of standard model UCEs is very much tied together with the cryptographic study of *code obfuscation*. The study of code obfuscation asks:

> *Can we write programs in such a way that they hide their secrets (i.e., how they work) even if their code is published?*

The mere existence of programs that hide their secrets is not sufficient for any practical purpose. We instead need an efficient mechanism to turn programs into obfuscated programs, or in other words, a mechanism which given the code of a program (e.g., as a Turing machine or circuit) as input, outputs code which implements the same program but which hides its secrets. We call such a mechanism a *code obfuscator*, a *program obfuscator*, or simply and shorter an *obfuscator*.

Code obfuscators can be very useful. For example, they can be used to protect intellectual property—assume that you want to grant rights to use software but to prevent anyone from decompiling it and reusing parts of the code. Also in the realm of cryptography obfuscators are useful. Consider the idea of using an obfuscator to turn a symmetric encryption scheme into a public-key encryption scheme by simply obfuscating the encryption algorithm with the secret key hardcoded into it. Given a symmetric encryption scheme SE and secret key sk and a "good obfuscation scheme" O one could define the corresponding public key pk as

$$pk(\cdot) := O(SE.Enc(sk, \cdot)).$$

Note that by the above definition public key pk is a function that takes as input a single value (a message m) which it encrypts with the underlying symmetric encryption scheme and with secret key sk. Since, the obfuscation scheme *hides the code's secrets* it should certainly hide secret key sk, and hence anybody can use the program (i.e., the public key) to generate encryptions but only the knowledge of key sk should allow for decrypting ciphertexts.[10]

Defining Obfuscation

While the intuition behind good obfuscation is easy to state—the obfuscated code should hide the program's secrets—it is challenging to grasp this formally, that is, how to define what exactly *hiding the secrets* means. One approach,

---

[10] Note that this reasoning requires some form of asymmetry in the encryption and decryption process since if we could use the same encryption box to also perform the decryption operation then essentially anybody can decrypt. So even with a good obfuscator it would not necessarily be straightforward to create a public-key encryption scheme out of a symmetric one.

often seen in software engineering, is to consider heuristics (e.g., renaming of variables, introducing bogus methods, etc.) which, so the hope goes, should make "reverse engineering" hard. Here, we are instead interested in a precise mathematical definition which allows us to give formal statements about the security of an obfuscator.

Virtual black-box obfuscation. A natural cryptographic-style definition of obfuscation may ask that an obfuscation of a program should only leak what can be learned from the program when interacting with it as an oracle (i.e., via black-box access). This idea of obfuscation, called *virtual black-box (VBB) obfuscation*, has many interesting applications, but regrettably for most programs it cannot exist, as we can show that virtual black-box obfuscation cannot exist in general. To get some intuition for why such an obfuscator cannot exist, consider a virtual black-box obfuscator O for pseudorandom functions. Let PRF be a pseudorandom function and define a hash function based on PRF and O as follows: Key generation runs the key generation of the pseudorandom function to then obfuscate the program $\mathsf{PRF.Eval}(k, \cdot)$, that is, the pseudorandom function's evaluation procedure with key k hardcoded. The resulting obfuscated program is then output as the key of the hash function. Evaluation of the hash function for a key hk now simply consists of running the obfuscated program hk on a given message. Once more in pseudocode:

$\mathsf{H.KGen}(1^\lambda)$	$\mathsf{H.Eval}(hk, m)$
1 : $k \leftarrow\!\!{\scriptstyle\$}\ \mathsf{PRF.KGen}(1^\lambda)$	1 : $y \leftarrow hk(m)$
2 : $hk \leftarrow\!\!{\scriptstyle\$}\ \mathsf{O}(\mathsf{PRF.Eval}(k, \cdot))$	2 : **return** y
3 : **return** hk	

If the obfuscation scheme was a virtual black-box obfuscator, then our hash function would be indistinguishable from a random oracle. For any adversary $\mathcal{A}$ given access to obfuscation $\mathsf{O}(\mathsf{PRF.Eval}(k, \cdot))$ there should be an adversary $\mathcal{B}$ with only black-box access to the functionality such that

$$\left| \Pr\left[\mathcal{A}\left(1^\lambda, \mathsf{O}(\mathsf{PRF.Eval}(k, \cdot))\right) = 1 \right] - \Pr\left[\mathcal{B}^{\mathsf{PRF.Eval}(k, \cdot)}(1^\lambda) = 1 \right] \right|$$

is negligible. In other words, anything adversary $\mathcal{A}$ can do with direct access, adversary $\mathcal{B}$ can do with black-box access. But since black-box access to a pseudorandom function is indistinguishable from black-box access to a random function we get that, conversely, we could replace any random oracle with a black-box obfuscation of a pseudorandom function. As we know that we cannot instantiate random oracles in every situation (see Chapter 12) it follows that such an obfuscator cannot exist.

Indistinguishability Obfuscation

While black-box obfuscators cannot exist in general—although they can exist for certain functionalities such as point functions[11]—we do have definitions of weaker forms of obfuscation that are deemed to exist in the standard model. One prominent definition is the so-called *indistinguishability obfuscator* which, at first glance, gives a rather strange security guarantee: Given two programs P_1 and P_2 that compute the same functionality, that is, for all inputs x we have that $P_1(x) = P_2(x)$, we have that an adversary that gets as input an obfuscation of either one of them cannot tell whether it was given an obfuscation of P_1 or of P_2.

The notion of indistinguishability obfuscation thus says that $iO(P_1)$ and $iO(P_2)$ are computationally indistinguishable for equivalent programs P_1 and P_2. Hence, indistinguishability obfuscation only hides *how* a program computes the answers. In theory the programs should be described by circuits (Section 1.3.3; page 21), taken from a specific set of circuits. Since larger circuits need more space and the obfuscation of such circuits could be easily distinguishable from smaller circuits by inspecting the size of the obfuscations, it is usually assumed that all obfuscatable circuits obey a common size bound, or that one can pad each circuit from the class to the same length. Below we simply state our theorem saying that one can obfuscate any circuit; the proof reveals which circuits we are particularly interested in.

As it turns out, indistinguishability obfuscation is extremely powerful, and in case it exists, it allows us to show that strong forms of UCEs cannot exist.

18.5.2 Uninstantiability of Strong UCEs

While a detailed treatment of indistinguishability obfuscation is beyond the scope of our discussion of UCEs here we present in the following a proof sketch for a 1-out-of-2 result stating that either indistinguishability obfuscators or UCEs relative to computationally unpredictable sources cannot exist. Of course, it might also be the case that neither of the two notions actually exists. The 1-out-of-2 result is captured by the following theorem:

> **Theorem 18.18.** *If indistinguishability obfuscation exists for all circuits, then no standard model hash function can be* $\mathrm{UCE}[\mathcal{S}^{\mathrm{cup}}]$ *secure. This holds even for sources making only a single query given that the hash function's output length is growing super-logarithmically in the security parameter.*

---

[11] A point function is a function that is zero everywhere except for a single point on which it returns 1. As a possible application consider an authentication scheme that only provides access to users that can make the function return 1: only users that know the correct password get access.

We will here show the result for the simpler case where the output length of the hash function is at least twice as long as the key length. That is, we assume $\mathsf{H.ol}(\lambda) \geq 2 \cdot \mathsf{H.kl}(\lambda)$. Furthermore, as we have not formally defined indistinguishability obfuscation, the following proof will not be fully formal when it comes to working with the obfuscator.

Proof sketch. Let iO be an indistinguishability obfuscator and let H be a standard model hash function. We will construct a UCE adversary (S, D) as follows. Source S chooses a random value $x \in \{0,1\}^\lambda$ to then query its oracle HASH to obtain $y \leftarrow \mathrm{HASH}(x)$. It will then construct a circuit $C[x,y](\cdot)$ that has values x and y hardcoded and which computes

$$
\begin{array}{l}
\underline{C[x,y](\mathsf{hk})} \\[4pt]
\quad 1: \quad y' \leftarrow \mathsf{H.Eval}(\mathsf{hk}, x) \\[4pt]
\quad 2: \quad \textbf{return } y = y'
\end{array}
$$

The circuit takes as input a hash function key hk and then evaluates hash function H on input (hk, x). The circuit returns 1 in case this evaluation matches hardcoded value y. Otherwise it returns 0. Source S then obfuscates circuit $C[x,y]$ with indistinguishability obfuscator iO and sets the leakage L to be the resulting program. That is, $L \leftarrow \mathsf{iO}(C[x,y](\cdot))$.

Distinguisher D gets as input leakage L and hash key hk. It extracts the obfuscated program $\mathsf{iO}(C[x,y](\cdot))$ and evaluates it on its input hash key hk to receive a bit b', which it returns. Following is a pseudocode description of source and distinguisher:

Source $\mathsf{S}^{\mathrm{HASH}}(1^\lambda)$	Distinguisher $\mathsf{D}(\mathsf{hk}, L)$
1: $\quad x \leftarrow_\$ \{0,1\}^\lambda$	1: $\quad \overline{C} \leftarrow L$
2: $\quad y \leftarrow \mathrm{HASH}(x)$	2: $\quad b' \leftarrow \overline{C}(\mathsf{hk})$
3: $\quad \overline{C} \leftarrow_\$ \mathsf{iO}(C[x,y](\cdot))$	3: $\quad \textbf{return } b'$
4: $\quad L \leftarrow \overline{C}$	
5: $\quad \textbf{return } L$	

To complete the proof we need to show that our adversary wins with good probability in the UCE game, and that source S is computationally unpredictable, that is, $\mathsf{S} \in \mathcal{S}^{\mathrm{cup}}$. We tackle these in turn.

UCE advantage. Consider the UCE game with hidden bit $b = 1$ where oracle HASH implements hash function H. In this case, value y as queried by source S is computed as $y \leftarrow \mathsf{H}(\mathsf{hk}, x)$. This means that the constructed circuit $C[x,y]$ on input hk outputs 1 as it also computes $y' \leftarrow \mathsf{H}(\mathsf{hk}, x)$ and then compares y' to y. It follows that

$$
\Pr\left[\mathrm{UCE}_{\mathsf{H}}^{\mathsf{S},\mathsf{D}}(\lambda) = 1 \;\middle|\; b = 1\right] = 1.
$$

On the other hand, if hidden bit $b = 0$ and HASH implements a random function, then with overwhelming probability $C[x, y](\mathsf{hk}) = 0$ as y is chosen uniformly at random and independent of value hk. We thus have that

$$\Pr\left[\mathrm{UCE}_{\mathsf{H}}^{\mathsf{S},\mathsf{D}}(\lambda) = 1 \,\Big|\, b = 0\right] = \Pr\left[C[x, y](\mathsf{hk}) = 1 \,\Big|\, b = 0\right] = \frac{1}{2^{\mathsf{H.ol}(\lambda)}}.$$

It follows that UCE adversary (S, D) has a UCE advantage of almost 1.

Unpredictability. It remains to show that our source S is computationally unpredictable. For this note that the unpredictability game $\mathrm{Pred}_{\mathsf{S}}^{\mathsf{P}}(\lambda)$ is relative to oracle HASH implementing a random function and thus y is chosen uniformly at random. Since by assumption $\mathsf{H.ol}(\lambda) \geq 2 \cdot \mathsf{H.kl}(\lambda)$ we have that with high probability the constructed circuit $C[x, y]$ is 0 on every input. For this note that there are only $2^{\mathsf{H.kl}(\lambda)}$ many possible inputs, each mapping value x to some hash value. Since y is chosen uniformly at random from $\{0, 1\}^{\mathsf{H.ol}(\lambda)}$ we have that the probability for any value hk of mapping x to y is $2^{-\mathsf{H.ol}(\lambda)}$. Taking the union bound we thus get

$$\Pr[\exists \mathsf{hk} : C[x, y](\mathsf{hk}) = 1] \leq \frac{2^{\mathsf{H.kl}(\lambda)}}{2^{\mathsf{H.ol}(\lambda)}} < \frac{2^{\mathsf{H.ol}(\lambda)/2}}{2^{\mathsf{H.ol}(\lambda)}} = \frac{1}{2^{\mathsf{H.ol}(\lambda)/2}},$$

which is negligible in the security parameter.

We can conclude that with overwhelming probability the circuit created by source S is the circuit that returns 0 on every input. As source S leaks an indistinguishability obfuscation of circuit $C[x, y]$ we have that no adversary can distinguish $\mathsf{iO}(C[x, y])$ from $\mathsf{iO}(Z_0)$ where Z_0 is the all-zero circuit padded to the same length as $C[x, y]$ but without any embedded values x or y. As by the security of the indifferentiability obfuscator an obfuscation of Z_0 must be indistinguishable from an obfuscation of $C[x, y]$ for efficient adversaries (such as our predictor) we can conclude that $\mathsf{iO}(C[x, y])$ does not leak value x and that source S must be computationally unpredictable.   □

Remark 18.19. Note that the above proof breaks down for statistical unpredictability. The reason is that obfuscation is a purely computational property and that obfuscators that are secure against unbounded algorithms can be shown to not exist. Thus, in case of an unbounded predictor we cannot argue that circuit $\mathsf{iO}(C[x, y])$ hides value x even if it computes the all-zero circuit.

Remark 18.20. In the above proof we assumed that the hash function's output length is at least twice as long as the key length, that is, $\mathsf{H.ol}(\lambda) \geq 2 \cdot \mathsf{H.kl}(\lambda)$. One way around this requirement is to consider a larger circuit that uses not only a single query–answer pair (x, y) but multiple pairs (x_i, y_i) for $i \in [\mathsf{t}]$ for some polynomial $\mathsf{t} := \mathsf{t}(\lambda)$. The obfuscated circuit then becomes

$$\frac{C[x_1, y_1, x_2, y_2, \ldots, x_t, y_t](\mathsf{hk})}{}$$

1 :   **for** $i = 1..t$ **do**

2 : $y_i' \leftarrow \mathsf{H.Eval}(\mathsf{hk}, x_i)$

3 :   **return** $y_1 = y_1' \wedge y_2 = y_2' \wedge \ldots \wedge y_t = y_t'$

This, of course increases the number of HASH queries by source S. An alternative that requires only a single HASH query is to make use of a pseudorandom generator PRG and define circuit C as

$$\frac{C[x, s \leftarrow \mathsf{PRG}(y)](\mathsf{hk})}{}$$

1 : $s' \leftarrow \mathsf{PRG}\,(\mathsf{H.Eval}(\mathsf{hk}, x))$

2 :   **return** $s = s'$

Here, circuit C does not have value $y \leftarrow \text{HASH}(x)$ hardcoded but $\mathsf{PRG}(y)$. It can now be shown that an indistinguishability obfuscation of circuit C does not leak value x (and thus source S remains computationally unpredictable) down to the security of the pseudorandom generator. We leave proving this statement as Exercise 18.5. Note that, as the security of a pseudorandom generator requires inputs to grow at least super-logarithmically, this only applies to hash functions that have a super-logarithmic output length.

18.5.3 UCEs or Indistinguishability Obfuscation

Which is the more likely scenario? That $\mathrm{UCE}[\mathcal{S}^{\mathrm{cup}}]$ or that indistinguishability obfuscation exists? This is not an easy question to answer as both assumptions are relatively recent. Yet given the flurry of candidate constructions for indistinguishability obfuscation our current bets would be on indistinguishability obfuscation. (Of course, it might also turn out that neither property can be achieved in the standard model.)

Where does that leave UCEs? On the one hand, UCEs remain a good technique for showing results in idealized models and any result based on $\mathrm{UCE}[\mathcal{S}^{\mathrm{cup}}]$ remains preferable to a direct security proof based on random oracles. Nevertheless, the result also showcases that we need to be careful with the interpretation of such results in idealized models since they might not be transferable to the standard model after all, which might open attack vectors in practice. Thus, whenever possible, security proofs should aim at using weaker forms of UCEs. In particular $\mathrm{UCE}[\mathcal{S}^{\mathrm{sup}}]$, that is, UCEs with respect to statistically unpredictable sources, seem powerful enough to facilitate many security proofs while at the same time the notion seems achievable also in the standard model. Indeed, it can be shown that restricted forms of $\mathrm{UCE}[\mathcal{S}^{\mathrm{sup}}]$ can be built based on indistinguishability obfuscation. While such constructions today are far from efficient and feasible in terms of practical efficiency these results are promising and might mean that one day practical and efficient standard model UCE[$\mathcal{S}^{\text{sup}}$]-secure functions might be constructed. Thus, if standard hash function properties are insufficient for a security proof of a construction, UCE[$\mathcal{S}^{\text{sup}}$] should be the target. If also that does not work, instead of giving a proof in the random oracle model a proof should be attempted down to UCEs relative to computationally unpredictable sources. And it should be weighed carefully why UCE[$\mathcal{S}^{\text{sup}}$] is not sufficient. Is it because the scheme is secure but we are missing the right proof technique, or might it be an indication that the scheme is not fully secure after all?

Chapter Notes and References

Universal computational extractors were introduced in 2013 by Bellare, Hoang, and Keelvedhi [4]. In their paper, Bellare *et al.* studied various cryptographic primitives and showed how these can be built based on UCEs. The proofs presented here for proof of storage, deterministic public-key encryption, and hardcore functions are due to them. Additional constructions based on UCEs were studied, for example, in [16, 3, 11, 18]. Extensions to the UCE model that allow interaction between source and distinguisher have been studied by Farshim and Mittelbach [12]. The proof that HMAC assuming an ideal compression function is UCE secure with respect to computationally unpredictable sources is due to Mittelbach [17]. Connections between UCE and indifferentiability have been studied in [5, 17, 15]. The "1-out-of-2" result stating that either UCEs with respect to computationally unpredictable sources or indistinguishability obfuscation cannot exist is due to Brzuska, Farshim, and Mittelbach [7]. Further 1-out-of-2 results for additional UCE definitions are given by Bellare, Stepanovs, and Tessaro [6]. Standard model constructions of restricted forms of UCEs from indistinguishability obfuscation were given by Brzuska and Mittelbach [8, 9].

Code obfuscation has a long tradition in cryptography and was already suggested in 1976 by Diffie and Hellman [10] as a potential means to create public-key encryption schemes from symmetric encryption schemes. Virtual black-box obfuscation was formalized by Barak *et al.* [2, 1] in 2001, building upon work by Hada [14]. Barak *et al.* also showed virtual black-box obfuscation to be impossible to achieve in general and suggested indistinguishability obfuscation as a weaker notion that was not affected by their negative result. A first candidate construction of indistinguishability obfuscation was given by Garg *et al.* [13] in 2013.

Exercices

Exercise 18.1. Formally prove Proposition 18.8 (page 738).

Exercise 18.2. Recall the definition of unpredictable sources (Definition 18.3; page 736). Consider a source S that picks q random values, queries HASH on one of them, and adds all q values to leakage L. Clearly, source S is not unpredictable as a predictor can guess a query with probability at least $\frac{1}{q}$.

An alternative formulation of unpredictability is the following security game:

$\text{AltPred}_S^P(\lambda)$	$\text{HASH}(x)$
1 : done $\leftarrow$ false; $\mathcal{Q} \leftarrow \{\}$	1 : **if** ¬**done then**
2 : $L \leftarrow_\$ S^{\text{HASH}}(1^\lambda)$	2 : $\mathcal{Q} \leftarrow \mathcal{Q} \cup \{x\}$
3 : done $\leftarrow$ true	3 : **if** $T[x] = \bot$ **then**
4 : $\mathcal{Q}' \leftarrow_\$ P(1^\lambda, L)$	4 : $T[x] \leftarrow_\$ \{0,1\}^{\text{H.ol}(\lambda)}$
5 : **return** $(\mathcal{Q} \cap \mathcal{Q}' \neq \{\})$	5 : **return** $T[x]$

A predictor for our alternative definition of the prediction game against above source S would clearly win with probability 1 as it would simply output all q values that are part of leakage L as its guess set $\mathcal{Q}'$.

Show that games AltPred and Pred yield identical UCE restrictions, that is, for any source it holds that it is computationally (resp. statistically) unpredictable if and only if it is also computationally (resp. statistically) unpredictable according to AltPred.

Exercise 18.3. Let H be a UCE[$\mathcal{S}^{\text{sup}}$]-secure function with a fixed output length. Give a construction H' that yields a variable-output-length hash function (a XOF; see also Section 13.3.1) that is UCE[$\mathcal{S}^{\text{sup}}$]. Function H' should take as input the hash key, the message, and an integer ℓ denoting the number of output bits to generate.

Exercise 18.4. In Section 18.2.1 we introduced the UCE class of unpredictable sources (page 736). A source S that queries its oracle HASH on a random value x, ignores the result, but adds x to leakage L would be predictable even though x could not possibly help distinguisher D in understanding whether source S was executed relative to a random oracle or the actual hash function.

A stronger UCE notion that would not discard the above source S is that of so-called *reset-secure sources*. We define reset security for sources similarly to unpredictability by specifying an additional security game that first executes source S relative to a random oracle to then run a reset adversary. A source is called computationally (resp. statistically) reset-secure if no PPT (resp. unbounded) algorithm (i.e., the reset adversary) on input leakage L can distinguish between being given oracle access to the same random oracle as S or to an independently sampled random oracle.

Formalize reset security for UCEs and show that it is a strictly stronger form than unpredictable UCEs. The latter means that any computationally (resp. statistically) unpredictable source is also computationally (resp. statistically) reset secure.

Exercise 18.5. In Remark 18.20 (page 773) we discuss how to drop the length requirement used in the proof of Theorem 18.18. In particular, we suggest that the following source S can be used:

Source $S^{\text{HASH}}(1^\lambda)$	$C[x, s](\mathsf{hk})$
1 : $x \leftarrow_\$ \{0,1\}^\lambda$	1 : $s' \leftarrow \mathsf{PRG}\,(\mathsf{H.Eval}(\mathsf{hk}, x))$
2 : $y \leftarrow \text{HASH}(x)$	2 : **return** $s = s'$
3 : $s \leftarrow \mathsf{PRG}(y)$	
4 : $\overline{C} \leftarrow_\$ \mathsf{iO}(C[x, s](\cdot))$	
5 : $L \leftarrow \overline{C}$	
6 : **return** L	

Show that the above source is computationally unpredictable given that iO is a secure indistinguishability obfuscator and PRG is a secure pseudorandom generator.

Chapter Bibliography

1. Boaz Barak, Oded Goldreich, Russell Impagliazzo, Steven Rudich, Amit Sahai, Salil Vadhan, and Ke Yang. On the (im)possibility of obfuscating programs. *J. ACM*, 59(2):6:1–6:48, May 2012. Preliminary version [2].
2. Boaz Barak, Oded Goldreich, Russell Impagliazzo, Steven Rudich, Amit Sahai, Salil P. Vadhan, and Ke Yang. On the (im)possibility of obfuscating programs. In Joe Kilian, editor, *Advances in Cryptology – CRYPTO 2001*, volume 2139 of *Lecture Notes in Computer Science*, pages 1–18, Santa Barbara, CA, USA, August 19–23, 2001. Springer, Heidelberg, Germany.
3. Mihir Bellare and Viet Tung Hoang. Resisting randomness subversion: Fast deterministic and hedged public-key encryption in the standard model. In Elisabeth Oswald and Marc Fischlin, editors, *Advances in Cryptology – EUROCRYPT 2015, Part II*, volume 9057 of *Lecture Notes in Computer Science*, pages 627–656, Sofia, Bulgaria, April 26–30, 2015. Springer, Heidelberg, Germany.
4. Mihir Bellare, Viet Tung Hoang, and Sriram Keelveedhi. Instantiating random oracles via UCEs. In Ran Canetti and Juan A. Garay, editors, *Advances in Cryptology – CRYPTO 2013, Part II*, volume 8043 of *Lecture Notes in Computer Science*, pages 398–415, Santa Barbara, CA, USA, August 18–22, 2013. Springer, Heidelberg, Germany.
5. Mihir Bellare, Viet Tung Hoang, and Sriram Keelveedhi. Cryptography from compression functions: The UCE bridge to the ROM. In Juan A. Garay and Rosario Gennaro, editors, *Advances in Cryptology – CRYPTO 2014, Part I*, volume 8616 of *Lecture Notes in Computer Science*, pages 169–187, Santa Barbara, CA, USA, August 17–21, 2014. Springer, Heidelberg, Germany.

6. Mihir Bellare, Igors Stepanovs, and Stefano Tessaro. Contention in cryptoland: Obfuscation, leakage and UCE. In Eyal Kushilevitz and Tal Malkin, editors, *TCC 2016-A: 13th Theory of Cryptography Conference, Part II*, volume 9563 of *Lecture Notes in Computer Science*, pages 542–564, Tel Aviv, Israel, January 10–13, 2016. Springer, Heidelberg, Germany.

7. Christina Brzuska, Pooya Farshim, and Arno Mittelbach. Indistinguishability obfuscation and UCEs: The case of computationally unpredictable sources. In Juan A. Garay and Rosario Gennaro, editors, *Advances in Cryptology – CRYPTO 2014, Part I*, volume 8616 of *Lecture Notes in Computer Science*, pages 188–205, Santa Barbara, CA, USA, August 17–21, 2014. Springer, Heidelberg, Germany.

8. Christina Brzuska and Arno Mittelbach. Using indistinguishability obfuscation via UCEs. In Palash Sarkar and Tetsu Iwata, editors, *Advances in Cryptology – ASIACRYPT 2014, Part II*, volume 8874 of *Lecture Notes in Computer Science*, pages 122–141, Kaoshiung, Taiwan, R.O.C., December 7–11, 2014. Springer, Heidelberg, Germany.

9. Christina Brzuska and Arno Mittelbach. Universal computational extractors and the superfluous padding assumption for indistinguishability obfuscation. Cryptology ePrint Archive, Report 2015/581, 2015. http://eprint.iacr.org/2015/581.

10. Whitfield Diffie and Martin E. Hellman. New directions in cryptography. *IEEE Transactions on Information Theory*, 22(6):644–654, 1976.

11. Yevgeniy Dodis, Chaya Ganesh, Alexander Golovnev, Ari Juels, and Thomas Ristenpart. A formal treatment of backdoored pseudorandom generators. In Elisabeth Oswald and Marc Fischlin, editors, *Advances in Cryptology – EUROCRYPT 2015, Part I*, volume 9056 of *Lecture Notes in Computer Science*, pages 101–126, Sofia, Bulgaria, April 26–30, 2015. Springer, Heidelberg, Germany.

12. Pooya Farshim and Arno Mittelbach. Modeling random oracles under unpredictable queries. In Thomas Peyrin, editor, *Fast Software Encryption – FSE 2016*, volume 9783 of *Lecture Notes in Computer Science*, pages 453–473, Bochum, Germany, March 20–23, 2016. Springer, Heidelberg, Germany.

13. Sanjam Garg, Craig Gentry, Shai Halevi, Mariana Raykova, Amit Sahai, and Brent Waters. Candidate indistinguishability obfuscation and functional encryption for all circuits. In *54th Annual Symposium on Foundations of Computer Science*, pages 40–49, Berkeley, CA, USA, October 26–29, 2013. IEEE Computer Society Press.

14. Satoshi Hada. Zero-knowledge and code obfuscation. In Tatsuaki Okamoto, editor, *Advances in Cryptology – ASIACRYPT 2000*, volume 1976 of *Lecture Notes in Computer Science*, pages 443–457, Kyoto, Japan, December 3–7, 2000. Springer, Heidelberg, Germany.

15. Daniel Jost and Ueli Maurer. Security definitions for hash functions: Combining UCE and indifferentiability. In Dario Catalano and Roberto De Prisco, editors, *SCN 18: 11th International Conference on Security in Communication Networks*, volume 11035 of *Lecture Notes in Computer Science*, pages 83–101, Amalfi, Italy, September 5–7, 2018. Springer, Heidelberg, Germany.

16. Takahiro Matsuda and Goichiro Hanaoka. Chosen ciphertext security via UCE. In Hugo Krawczyk, editor, *PKC 2014: 17th International Conference on Theory and Practice of Public Key Cryptography*, volume 8383 of *Lecture Notes in Computer Science*, pages 56–76, Buenos Aires, Argentina, March 26–28, 2014. Springer, Heidelberg, Germany.

17. Arno Mittelbach. Salvaging indifferentiability in a multi-stage setting. In Phong Q. Nguyen and Elisabeth Oswald, editors, *Advances in Cryptology – EUROCRYPT 2014*, volume 8441 of *Lecture Notes in Computer Science*, pages 603–621, Copenhagen, Denmark, May 11–15, 2014. Springer, Heidelberg, Germany.

18. Hui-Ge Wang, Ke-Fei Chen, Bao-Dong Qin, and Liang-Liang Wang. Randomized convergent encryption in the standard model via UCEs. *2015 International Conference on Computer Science and Applications (CSA)*, pages 298–302, 2015.

Index

© Springer Nature Switzerland AG 2021

A. Mittelbach, M. Fischlin, *The Theory of Hash Functions and Random Oracles*,

Information Security and Cryptography, https://doi.org/10.1007/978-3-030-63287-8

Printed in the United States
by Baker & Taylor Publisher Services

Printed in the United States
by Baker & Taylor Publisher Services